FOLK MUSIC AND SONG

IN THE WPA EX-SLAVE NARRATIVES

American Made Music Series

ADVISORY BOARD

David Evans, General Editor
Barry Jean Ancelet
Edward A. Berlin
Joyce J. Bolden
Rob Bowman
Curtis Ellison
William Ferris
John Edward Hasse
Kip Lornell
Bill Malone
Eddie S. Meadows
Manuel H. Peña
Wayne D. Shirley
Robert Walser

FOLK MUSIC AND SONG
— IN THE —
WPA EX-SLAVE NARRATIVES

JOHN MINTON

University Press of Mississippi / Jackson

The University Press of Mississippi is the scholarly publishing agency of the Mississippi Institutions of Higher Learning: Alcorn State University, Delta State University, Jackson State University, Mississippi State University, Mississippi University for Women, Mississippi Valley State University, University of Mississippi, and University of Southern Mississippi.

www.upress.state.ms.us

The University Press of Mississippi is a member of the Association of University Presses.

Any discriminatory or derogatory language or hate speech regarding race, ethnicity, religion, sex, gender, class, national origin, age, or disability that has been retained or appears in elided form is in no way an endorsement of the use of such language outside a scholarly context.

Copyright © 2024 by University Press of Mississippi
All rights reserved
Manufactured in the United States of America

Library of Congress Cataloging-in-Publication Data

Names: Minton, John, 1957– author.
Title: Folk music and song in the WPA ex-slave narratives / John Minton.
Other titles: American made music series.
Description: Jackson : University Press of Mississippi, 2025. |
Series: American made music series | Includes bibliographical references and index.
Identifiers: LCCN 2024050012 (print) | LCCN 2024050013 (ebook) |
ISBN 9781496854278 (hardback) | ISBN 9781496854865 (epub) |
ISBN 9781496854872 (epub) | ISBN 9781496854889 (pdf) | ISBN 9781496854896 (pdf)
Subjects: LCSH: Enslaved persons—United States—Songs and music—History
and criticism. | Slavery—United States—Songs and music—History and criticism. |
African Americans—Music—History and criticism. | Spirituals (Songs)—
United States—History and criticism. | Folk music—United States—History and criticism. |
Folk songs, English—United States—History and criticism. | Slave narratives—
United States. | Enslaved persons—United States—Folklore.
Classification: LCC ML3556 .M57 2025 (print) | LCC ML3556 (ebook) |
DDC 780.89/96073—dc23/eng/20241112
LC record available at https://lccn.loc.gov/2024050012
LC ebook record available at https://lccn.loc.gov/2024050013

British Library Cataloging-in-Publication Data available

publication supported by a grant from

The Community Foundation for Greater New Haven

as part of the Urban Haven Project

CONTENTS

Acknowledgments ix
Racist Language in the WPA Ex-Slave
    Narratives xi
Abbreviations xiii

INTRODUCTION

The WPA Ex-Slave Narratives 3
    Appendix A: John Lomax's Instructions to
    Interviewers 26
    Appendix B: Plagiarized Song Texts in the
    Ex-Slave Narratives 28
Africa, Europe, and African Americans 34

SOCIAL MUSIC

Patting: Juba, Jigging, and General Body
    Percussion 53
The Fiddle 71
Appendix: Musical Instruments in the Ex-Slave
    Narratives 87
Banjos and Guitars 95
The 'Fore Day Horn 112
Appendix: Signal Horns in the Ex-Slave
    Narratives 132
Flutes, Fifes, and Quills 137
Pianos, Organs, and Accordions 151
Frolics, Cornshuckings, and Other Occasions
    for Social Music 170
Musicians 194
Appendix: Slave Musicians Identified in the
    Ex-Slave Narratives 210
Old Pharaoh Exactly: Slave Music and
    Racial Terror 217

Appendix: "Run, Nigger, Run" 247
Dealing with the Devil 255
Appendix A: How to Sell Your Soul to the Devil
    for Music, Song, or Dance 272
Appendix B: Other Supernatural Tales with
    Music, Song, or Dance 279

RELIGIOUS SONG

Shout 291
Appendix: Shout 310
Turning the Pot Down 319
Appendix: Turning the Pot Down 331
When I Can Read My Title Clear: Hymns 347
Appendix: Hymns 363
Spirituals 385
Appendix: Spirituals 410

SECULAR SONG

Singing Games 435
Appendix: Lullabyes and Other Nursery Songs . . 443
Reels and Ring Plays 450
Worksongs 463
Minstrelsy 486
Ballads 502
The War 515
Appendix: Songs of Slavery 545

CONCLUSION

Modern Times 553
Notes 567
Narrators Index 645

Ex-Slaves Interviewed by the WPA Index 695

WPA Interviewers, Writers, and Editors Index . . 717

Other Slaves, Ex-Slaves, and Antebellum
Free Blacks Index. 718

Songs and Tunes Index 719

Tale-Types, Motifs, and Tales Index 729

General Index 732

ACKNOWLEDGMENTS

Sometime much earlier in this millennium, I pitched this book to Craig Gill, director of University Press of Mississippi, and David Evans, general editor of the American Made Music Series, both of whom remained unfailingly patient and supportive as the years passed. Craig took the massive manuscript I eventually delivered in stride and somehow got it to press; David read every single word and lent all his long experience and expertise. Kip Lornell also read the manuscript and offered many helpful insights and suggestions, while Richard Graham and Dan Gutstein rendered other much appreciated aid. At Purdue University Fort Wayne (formerly Indiana University–Purdue University Fort Wayne), I am much indebted to the staff of the Walter E. Helmke Library and their document delivery service, in particular Graham Fredrick, Debra Haley, Sara Scritchfield, Christine Smith, and Cheryl Truesdell. I wish also to thank everyone at University Press of Mississippi, and especially Shane Gong Stewart, Corley Longmire, Rae Switzer, and Katie Turner for helping me through the process. Will Rigby provided the superb copyediting. I am as grateful to all these friends and colleagues as I am glad this book is finally finished.

RACIST LANGUAGE IN THE WPA EX-SLAVE NARRATIVES

As some readers already know, the WPA ex-slave narratives and related materials are full of racist and racially insensitive language, epitomized by the constant, casual use of the *n*-word and other slurs, but expressed in innumerable other ways, some similarly inflammatory, others more subtle but just as pernicious. Even under slavery this vocabulary was recognized as beyond the pale of human decency (not everyone used it), but that was its entire point: these were the idioms of a society in which some people were treated like livestock—and ruthlessly required or brutally conditioned to think and speak of themselves that way—while others deliberately sank to that level or lower. In the late 1930s, seven decades after slavery's abolition, many ex-slaves still described themselves, their lives, and their loved ones in this language—hardly surprising, since in the late 1930s many ex-slaves still daily heard whites address them, their families, and neighbors the same way. Today this kind of talk is named for what it is—*hate speech*—and rightly restricted in most civic settings. A scholarly work like this one is, of course, an exception, beholden to historical context and strict rules of evidence, but even here I do not present these original texts without pause or reflection, and I truly hope they give no undue offense, though they do inevitably offend somewhat. The only alternative, however, would be to rewrite history by doctoring the documentary record, something that would be infinitely worse, especially in this instance. Readers who proceed should thus be prepared to hear about a truly awful time in America, in the vile, ugly language then used to discuss it.

All direct quotations from the ex-slave narratives are identified by parenthetical references including the narrators' names and birthdates, the locations, and page numbers. The locations are those described in the quotes, which may or may not be the same as a narrator's birthplace or interview site, so that ex-slaves who relocated may be identified with multiple locations. In other references, ex-slaves are identified by name alone (or occasionally by name, date, location), but full source bibliographies and additional biographical details are all included in the book's Narrators Index. Quotations appear exactly as they do in the transcripts, except that I have made occasional silent corrections to obvious typos or misspellings (such as *bit* for *but*, *but* for *bit*), and to punctuation (especially quotation marks and commas) to avoid confusion and prevent misreading. I have occasionally altered paragraphing for similar reasons, or for space considerations. Otherwise, I have kept brackets and editorial clarifications to a bare minimum, trusting readers to recognize and resolve any anomalies in the manuscripts for themselves.

ABBREVIATIONS

AM	*American Music*
AFS BSS	American Folklore Society, Bibliographical and Special Series
Atlantic	*Atlantic Monthly*
BMRJ	*Black Music Research Journal*
BMRN	*Black Music Research Newsletter*
BPM	*Black Perspective in Music*
Century	*Century Illustrated Monthly Magazine*
Dwight's	*Dwight's Journal of Music*
FFC	Folklore Fellows Communications
Harper's Monthly	*Harper's New Monthly Magazine*
Harper's Weekly	*Harper's Weekly: A Journal of Civilization*
JAF	*Journal of American Folklore*
JEMFQ	*John Edwards Memorial Foundation Quarterly*
JFI	*Journal of the Folklore Institute*
JFR	*Journal of Folklore Research*
JRAI	*Journal of the Royal Anthropological Institute of Great Britain and Ireland*
Knickerbocker	*The Knickerbocker; or New York Monthly Magazine*
Leslie's	*Frank Leslie's Illustrated Newspaper*
Lippincott's	*Lippincott's Magazine of Popular Literature and Science*
London News	*Illustrated London News*
MAFS	Memoirs of the American Folklore Society
MFR	*Mississippi Folklore Record*
NASS	*National Anti-Slavery Standard*
OTM	*Old Time Music*
Putnam's	*Putnam's Monthly Magazine of American Literature, Science, and Art*
PTFS	Publications of the Texas Folklore Society
Scribner's	*Scribner's Magazine*
SF	*Southern Folklore*
SFQ	*Southern Folklore Quarterly*
SLM	*Southern Literary Messenger*
Southern Workman	*Southern Workman and Hampton School Record*
WF	*Western Folklore*

ABBREVIATIONS

Aarne-Thompson	Antti Aarne and Stith Thompson, *The Types of the Folktale: A Classification and Bibliography*, 2nd rev. ed. FFC 184 (Helsinki: Academia Scientiarum Fennica, 1961).
Abbott and Seroff, *Out of Sight*	Lynn Abbott and Doug Seroff, *Out of Sight: The Rise of African American Popular Music 1889–1895* (Jackson: University Press of Mississippi, 2002).
Agricola, "Management"	Agricola, "Management of Negroes," *De Bow's Review* 19 (September 1855): 361.
Albert, *Charlotte Brooks*	Octavia V. Rogers Albert, *House of Bondage: or, Charlotte Brooks and Other Slaves* (1890; rpt. Freeport, NY: Books for Libraries, 1972).
Aleckson, *Before the War*	Sam Aleckson, *Before the War and After the Union: An Autobiography*. 1929; rpt. *I Belong to South Carolina: South Carolina Slave Narratives*, ed. Susanna Ashton (Columbia: University of South Carolina Press, 2010), 228–93.
Allen, "Editors"	James Lane Allen, "To the Editors of the Critic," *The Critic and Good Literature* 1 (January 5, 1884): 9.
Allen, "Uncle Tom"	James Lane Allen, "Mrs. Stowe's 'Uncle Tom' at Home in Kentucky," *Century* 34 (October 1887): 852–67.
Altamont	*Altamont: Black Stringband Music from the Library of Congress*, Rounder CD 0238, 1989.
Anderson, *From Slavery*	Robert Anderson, *From Slavery to Affluence: Memoirs of Robert Anderson, Ex-Slave*, ed. Daisy Anderson Leonard (1927; rpt. Steamboat Springs, CO: Steamboat Pilot, 1967).
Appalachian Fiddle	Drew Beisswenger, Roy Andrade, and Scott Prouty, *Appalachian Fiddle Music* (New York: Mel Bay, 2021).
Arnold, *Alabama*	Byron Arnold, *Folksongs of Alabama* (Birmingham: University of Alabama Press, 1950).
Asbury and Meyer, "Old-Time"	Samuel E. Asbury and Henry E. Meyer, "Old-Time White Camp-Meeting Spirituals," *Tone the Bell Easy*, ed. J. Frank Dobie, PTFS 10 (Austin, 1932), 169–85.
Atwater, *Southern Tour*	Rev. H. Cowles Atwater, *Incidents of a Southern Tour* (Boston: J. P. Magee, 1857).
Avirett, *Plantation*	James Battle Avirett, *The Old Plantation: How We Lived in Great House and Cabin Before the War* (New York: F. Tennyson Neely, 1901).
Baldwin, *Observations*	Ebenezer Baldwin, *Observations on the Physical, Intellectual, and Moral Qualities of Our Colored Population* (New Haven, CT: L. H. Young, 1834).
Baldwin, *School-Teacher*	Lydia Wood Baldwin, *A Yankee School-Teacher in Virginia: A Tale of the Old Dominion in the Transition State* (New York: Funk & Wagnalls, 1884).
Bales, "Negro Folk-Songs"	Mary Virginia Bales, "Some Negro Folk-Songs of Texas," *Follow De Drinkin' Gou'd*, ed. J. Frank Dobie. PTFS 7 (Austin, 1928), 85–112.

Ball, *Slavery*	Charles Ball, *Slavery in the United States: A Narrative of the Life and Adventures of Charles Ball, A Black Man* (1837; rpt. New York: Negro Universities Press, 1969).
Ballanta, *St. Helena*	Nicholas George Julius Ballanta-(Taylor), *Saint Helena Island Spirituals: Recorded and Transcribed at Penn Normal, Industrial and Agricultural School, St. Helena Island* (New York: G. Schirmer, 1925).
Barrow, "Corn-Shucking"	David C. Barrow Jr., "A Georgia Corn-Shucking," *Century* 24 (October 1882), 873–78.
Barton, *Plantation Hymns*	William E. Barton, *Old Plantation Hymns: A Collection of Hitherto Unpublished Melodies of the Slave and the Freedman* (Boston: Lamson, Wolffe, 1899).
Bass, "Negro Songs"	Robert Duncan Bass, "Negro Songs from the Pedee Country," *JAF* 44 (1931): 418–36.
Baughman	Ernest W. Baughman, *Type and Motif-Index of the Folktales of England and North America*. Indiana University Folklore Series, no. 20 (The Hague, 1966).
Bebey, *African Music*	Francis Bebey, *African Music: A People's Art*, trans. Josephine Bennett (Chicago: Lawrence Hill, 1975).
Belden, *Missouri*	H. M. Belden, *Ballads and Songs Collected by the Missouri Folk-Lore Society*. University of Missouri Studies, vol. 15, no. 1 (Columbia: University of Missouri Press, 1940).
Benners, *Slavery*	Alfred H. Benners, *Slavery and Its Results* (Macon, GA: J. W. Burke, 1923).
Bernhard, *Travels*	Bernhard, Duke of Saxe-Weimar Eisenach, *Travels Through North America, During the Years 1825 and 1826*, 2 vols. (Philadelphia: Carey, Lea & Carey, 1828).
Bibb, *Narrative*	Henry Bibb, *Narrative of the Life and Adventures of Henry Bibb, An American Slave* (New York: Author, 1850).
Black Appalachia	*Black Appalachia: String Bands, Songsters, and Hoedowns*, Rounder CD 1823, 1999.
Black Fiddlers	*Black Fiddlers 1929–c. 1970*, Document CD 5631, 1999.
Black Texicans	*Black Texicans: Balladeers and Songsters of the Texas Frontier*, Rounder CD 1821, 1999.
Blassingame, *Testimony*	John W. Blassingame, ed., *Slave Testimony: Two Centuries of Letters, Speeches, Interviews, and Autobiographies* (Baton Rouge: Louisiana State University Press, 1977).
Blue-Backed Speller	Noah Webster, *The American Spelling Book*, 6th ed. (Boston: Isaiah Thomas and Ebenezer T. Andrews, 1793). (First published in 1788 and regularly revised and reprinted thereafter, this standard reference was cited by numerous ex-slaves, but always under its popular name, derived from the blue binding.)
Blues and Gospel Records	Robert M. W. Dixon, John Godrich, and Howard Rye, *Blues and Gospel Records 1890–1943*. 4th ed. (New York: Oxford University Press, 1997).

Blues Lineage	*Mississippi: The Blues Lineage*, Rounder CD 1825, 1999.
Bolick and Austin, *Mississippi Fiddle*	Harry Bolick and Stephen T. Austin, *Mississippi Fiddle Tunes and Songs From the 1930s* (Jackson; University Press of Mississippi, 2015).
Bolick and Russell, *Fiddle Tunes*	Harry Bolick and Tony Russell, *Fiddle Tunes From Mississippi, Commercial and Informal Recordings, 1920–2018* (Jackson: University Press of Mississippi, 2021).
Bondage to Belonging	B. Eugene McCarthy and Thomas L. Doughton, eds., *From Bondage to Belonging: The Worcester Slave Narratives* (Amherst: University of Massachusetts Press, 2007).
Botkin, *Burden*	B. A. Botkin, *Lay My Burden Down: A Folk History of Slavery* (1945; rpt. New York: Delta, 1989).
Botkin, *Play-Party*	B. A. Botkin, *The American Play-Party Song* (1937; rpt. New York: Frederick Ungar, 1963).
Bradley, "Memories"	A. G. Bradley, "Some Plantation Memories," *Blackwood's Edinburgh Magazine* 161 (March 1897): 331–41.
Bradley, "Southern Negro"	Arthur Granville Bradley, "A Peep at the Southern Negro," *Macmillan's Magazine* 39 (November 1878): 61–68.
Bremer, *New World*	Frederika Bremer, *The Homes of the New World; Impressions of America*, trans. Mary Howitt, 2 vols. (New York: Harper & Brothers, 1853).
Brewster, *Indiana*	Paul G. Brewster, *Ballads and Songs of Indiana* (Bloomington: Indiana University Press, 1940).
Brown I	Paul G. Brewster, Archer Taylor, Bartlett Jere Whiting, George P. Wilson, Stith Thompson, eds. *The Frank C. Brown Collection of North Carolina Folklore*, vol. 1: *Games and Rhymes; Beliefs and Customs; Riddles; Proverbs; Speech; Tales and Legends* (Durham: Duke University Press, 1952).
Brown II	Henry M. Belden and Arthur Palmer Hudson, eds. *The Frank C. Brown Collection of North Carolina Folklore*, vol. 2: *Folk Ballads from North Carolina* (Durham: Duke University Press, 1952).
Brown III	Henry M. Belden and Arthur Palmer Hudson, eds. *The Frank C. Brown Collection of North Carolina Folklore*, vol. 3: *Folk Songs from North Carolina* (Durham: Duke University Press, 1952).
Brown VII	Wayland D. Hand, ed., *The Frank C. Brown Collection of North Carolina Folklore*, vol. 7: *Popular Beliefs and Superstitions from North Carolina* (Durham: Duke University Press, 1964).
Brown, *Slave Life*	John Brown, *Slave Life in Georgia* (1855; rpt. Savannah: Beehive, 1991).
Brown, "Songs"	John Mason Brown, "Songs of the Slave," *Lippincott's* 2 (December 1868): 617–23.
Brown and Owens, *Toting*	Virginia Pounds Brown and Laurella Owens, *Toting the Lead Row: Ruby Pickens Tartt, Alabama Folklorist* (Tuscaloosa, AL: University of Alabama Press, 1981).

Browne, *Alabama*	Ray B. Browne, *The Alabama Folk Lyric: A Study in Origins and Media of Dissemination* (Bowling Green, OH: Bowling Green University Popular Press, 1979).
Browne, *Hants*	Ray B. Browne, *"A Night With the Hants": And Other Alabama Folk Experiences* (Bowling Green, OH: Bowling Green University Popular Press, n.d.).
Bruce, *Hallelujah*	Dickson D. Bruce, *And They All Sang Hallelujah: Plain-Folk Camp Meeting Religion, 1800–1845* (Knoxville: University of Tennessee Press, 1974).
Bruce, "Tobacco-Plantation"	Philip A. Bruce, "A Tobacco-Plantation," *Lippincott's* 36 (December 1885): 533–42.
Bryant, "Old South"	William Cullen Bryant, "A Tour in the Old South," *Prose Writings of William Cullen Bryant*, vol. 2: *Travels, Addresses, and Comments*, ed. Parke Godwin (New York: D. Appleton, 1884), 23–50.
Bryce, "Fiddlers"	C. A. Bryce, "Dusky 'Fiddlers' of Olden Days Tenderly Recalled by Writer," *Richmond Times-Dispatch*, May 22, 1921, 5.
Burwell, *Girl's Life*	Letitia M. Burwell, *A Girl's Life in Virginia Before the War* (New York: Frederick A. Stokes, 1895).
Burwell, *White Acre*	J. G., Esq. [William McCreary Burwell], *White Acre Vs. Black Acre: A Case at Law* (Richmond, VA: J. W. Randolph, 1856).
Cabin I	Thomas P. Fenner, *Cabin and Plantation Songs as Sung by the Hampton Students*, in Mrs. M. F. Armstrong and Helen W. Ludlow, *Hampton and Its Students* (New York: G. P. Putnam's Sons, 1874), 171–255.
Cabin III	Thomas P. Fenner, Frederic G. Rathbun, and Miss Bessie Cleaveland, *Cabin and Plantation Songs as Sung by the Hampton Students*, 3rd ed. (New York: G. P. Putnam's Sons, 1901).
Cable, "Place Congo"	George W. Cable, "The Dance in Place Congo," *Century* 31 (February 1886): 517–31.
Cable, "Mr. Harris"	James B. Cable, Untitled note, *The Current* 2 (August 2, 1884): 76; rpt. as "Mr. Harris and the Messrs. Cable," *The Critic* 32 (August 9, 1884): 65.
Cade, "Ex-Slaves"	John B. Cade, "Out of the Mouths of Ex-Slaves," *Journal of Negro History* 20 (1935): 294–337.
Cameron, "Christmas"	Rebecca Cameron, "Christmas On an Old Plantation," *Ladies' Home Journal* 9 (December 1891): 5.
Carlin, *Banjo*	Bob Carlin, *The Birth of the Banjo: Joel Walker Sweeney and Early Minstrelsy* (Jefferson, NC: McFarland, 2007).
"Carmina Africana"	"Carmina Africana. Dialect and Rhythmic Utterances in Which the Southern Negroes Used to Chant," *Galveston Daily News* 7 (May 2, 1886), 10.
Carter, *Louisiana Negro*	Albert E. Carter, *The Louisiana Negro and His Music* (master's thesis, Northwestern University, 1947).

Castelnau, "Florida"	Comte De Castelnau, "Essay on Middle Florida, 1837–1838 (Essai sur la Floride du Milieu)," trans. Arthur R. Seymour, *Florida Historical Quarterly* 26 (1948): 199–255.
Cauthen, *Fiddle*	Joyce H. Cauthen, *With Fiddle and Well-Rosined Bow: Old-Time Fiddling in Alabama* (Tuscaloosa: University of Alabama Press, 1989).
Chambers-Ketchum, "Violin"	Annie Chambers-Ketchum, "Negro Superstition Concerning the Violin," *JAF* 5 (1892): 329–30.
Charters, *Roots*	Samuel Charters, *The Roots of the Blues: An African Search* (New York: Da Capo, 1981).
Chase, *Dear Ones*	Lucy Chase and Sarah Chase, *Dear Ones at Home: Letters from Contraband Camps*, ed. Henry L. Swint (Nashville: Vanderbilt University Press, 1966).
Child	Francis James Child, *The English and Scottish Popular Ballads*, 5 vols. (1882–98; rpt. New York: Dover, 1965).
Christy, *Plantation Melodies*	E. P. Christy, *Christy's Plantation Melodies* (Philadelphia: Fisher & Brother, 1851).
Clinkscales, *Plantation*	J. G. Clinkscales, *On the Old Plantation: Reminiscences of His Childhood* (Spartanburg, SC: Band & White, 1924).
Cohen, *Ozark*	Vance Randolph, *Ozark Folksongs*, ed. Norm Cohen, abridged ed. (Urbana: University of Illinois Press, 1982).
Cohen, *Rail*	Norm Cohen, *Long Steel Rail: The Railroad in American Folksong* (Urbana: University of Illinois Press, 1981).
Colored Harp	J. Jackson, *The Colored Sacred Harp*, rev. ed. (Montgomery, AL: Paragon, 1973).
Coppin, *History*	Bishop L. J. Coppin, *Unwritten History* (1919; rpt. New York: Negro Universities Press, 1968).
"Corn Shuckin' Down South"	"Corn Shuckin' Down South: Young Marster Sighs for the Good Old Times," *The Sun* 63 (November 11, 1895): 4.
Country Music Records	Tony Russell, *Country Music Records: A Discography, 1921–1942* (New York: Oxford University Press, 2004).
Country Music Sources	Guthrie T. Meade, Jr., Dick Spottswood, and Douglas S. Meade, *Country Music Sources: A Biblio-Discography of Commercially Recorded Traditional Music* (Chapel Hill: Southern Folklife Collection, University of North Carolina Libraries, 2002).
Courlander, "Cuba"	Harold Courlander, "Musical Instruments of Cuba," *Musical Quarterly* 28 (1942): 227–40.
Courlander, *Drum and Hoe*	Harold Courlander, *The Drum and the Hoe: Life and Lore of the Haitian People* (Berkeley: University of California Press, 1960).
Courlander, "Haiti"	Harold Courlander, "Musical Instruments of Haiti," *Musical Quarterly* 27 (1941): 371–83.
Courlander, *NFM*	Harold Courlander, *Negro Folk Music, U.S.A.* (1963; rpt. New York: Dover, 1991).

ABBREVIATIONS xix

Cox, *FSS*	John Harrington Cox, *Folk-Songs of the South* (Cambridge, MA: Harvard University Press, 1925).
Creecy, *Scenes*	Col. James R. Creecy, *Scenes in the South, and Other Miscellaneous Pieces* (Washington, DC: Thomas McGill, 1860).
Cresswell, *Journal*	Nicholas Cresswell, *A Man Apart: The Journal of Nicholas Cresswell, 1774–1781*, ed. Harold B. Gill Jr. and George M. Curtis III (Lanham, MD: Lexington Books, 2009).
Dance, *Shuckin'*	Daryl Cumber Dance, *Shuckin' and Jivin': Folklore from Contemporary Black Americans* (Bloomington: Indiana University Press, 1978).
Davis, *Virginia*	Arthur Kyle Davis Jr., *Traditional Ballads of Virginia* (Charlottesville: University Press of Virginia, 1929).
Davis, *Folk-Songs*	Arthur Kyle Davis Jr., *Folk-Songs of Virginia: A Descriptive Index and Classification of Material* (1949; rpt. New York: AMS, 1965).
Davis, "Plantation Party"	Daniel Webster Davis, "Echoes from a Plantation Party," *Southern Workman* 28 (February 1899): 54–59.
Davis, "Folk-Lore"	Henry C. Davis, "Negro Folk-Lore in South Carolina," *JAF* 27 (1914): 241–54.
Definitive Country	Barry McCloud, ed., *Definitive Country: The Ultimate Encyclopedia of Country Music and Its Performers* (New York: Perigee, 1995).
Dennison, *Scandalize*	Sam Dennison, *Scandalize My Name: Black Imagery in American Popular Music* (New York: Garland, 1982).
Dett, *Hampton*	R. Nathaniel Dett, *Religious Folk-Songs of the Negro As Sung at Hampton Institute* (Hampton, VA: Hampton Institute Press, 1927).
De Voe, *Market Book*	Thomas F. De Voe, *The Market Book: Containing a Historical Account of the Public Markets in the Cities of New York, Boston, Philadelphia, and Brooklyn*, 2 vols. (New York: author, 1862).
Dickens, *American Notes*	Charles Dickens, *American Notes for General Circulation*, 2 vols. (London: Chapman and Hall, 1842).
Diton, *South Carolina*	Carl Diton, *Thirty-Six South Carolina Spirituals* (New York: G. Schirmer, 1928).
Dix, *Transatlantic Tracings*	John R. Dix, *Transatlantic Tracings; Or, Sketches of Persons and Scenes in America* (London: W. Tweedie, 1853).
DjeDje, *Fiddling in West Africa*	Jacqueline Cogdell DjeDje, *Fiddling in West Africa: Touching the Spirit in Fulbe, Hausa, and Dagbamba Cultures* (Bloomington: Indiana University Press, 2008).
DNAH	Dictionary of North American Hymnology. Hymn Society in the United States and Canada. www.hymnary.org/dnah.
Dorson, *Folktales*	Richard M. Dorson, *American Negro Folktales* (New York: Fawcett, 1967).
Douglass, *My Bondage*	Frederick Douglass, *My Bondage and My Freedom* (New York: Miller, Orton, 1857).

Drums and Shadows	Savannah Unit, Georgia Writers' Project, WPA, *Drums and Shadows: Survival Studies Among the Georgia Coastal Negroes* (1940; rpt. Westport, CT: Greenwood, 1973).
Dudley and Payne, "Play-Party"	R. E. Dudley and L. W. Payne Jr., "Some Texas Play-Party Songs," *Round the Levee*, ed. Stith Thompson, PTFS 1 (Austin, 1916), 7–34.
Duke, *Reminiscences*	Basil W. Duke, *Reminiscences of General Basil W. Duke, C.S.A.* (Garden City, NY: Doubleday, Page, 1911).
Eastman, *Aunt Phillis*	Mary H. Eastman, *Aunt Phillis's Cabin; Or, Southern Life as It Is* (Philadelphia: Lippincott, Grambo, 1852).
Epstein, *Sinful*	Dena J. Epstein, *Sinful Tunes and Spirituals: Black Folk Music to the Civil War* (Urbana: University of Illinois Press, 1977).
Evans, *Big Road Blues*	David Evans, *Big Road Blues: Tradition and Creativity in the Folk Blues* (Berkeley: University of California Press, 1982).
Evans, "Eli Owens"	David Evans, "The Music of Eli Owens: African Music in Transition in Southern Mississippi," *For Gerhard Kubik*, ed. August Schmidhofer and Dietrich Schüller (Frankfurt am Main: Peter Lang, 1994), 329–59.
Evans, "Fife and Drum"	David Evans, "Black Fife and Drum Music in Mississippi," *MFR* 6 (1972): 94–107.
Evans, "Reinterpretation"	David Evans, "The Reinterpretation of African Musical Instruments in the United States," *The African Diaspora: African Origins and New World Identities*, ed. Isidore Okpewho, Carole Boyce Davies, and Ali A. Mazrui (Bloomington: Indiana University Press, 1999), 379–90.
Falconer, "Sports"	Frank Falconer, "Sports and Pastimes of the South. A Corn-Shucking Frolic," *Turf, Field and Farm* 9 (July 23, 1869), 54.
Fauset, "Folk Tales"	Arthur Huff Fauset, "Negro Folk Tales From the South (Alabama, Mississippi, Louisiana)," *JAF* 40 (1927): 213–303.
Fedric, *Slave Life*	Francis Fedric, *Slave Life in Virginia and Kentucky; or, Fifty Years of Slavery in the Southern States of America* (London: Wertheim, Macintosh, and Hunt, 1863).
Finch, *Travels*	J. Finch, *Travels in the United States of America and Canada* (London: Longman, Rees, Orme, Brown, Green, and Longman, 1833).
Fithian, *Journal*	Philip Vickers Fithian, *Journal and Letters of Philip Vickers Fithian 1773–1774: A Plantation Tutor of the Old Dominion*, ed. Hunter Dickinson Farish (Williamsburg, VA: Colonial Williamsburg, 1943).
Five Narratives	*Five Slave Narratives: A Compendium*, ed. William Loren Katz (New York: Arno, 1968).
Fletcher, *Story*	Tom Fletcher, *The Tom Fletcher Story: 100 Years of the Negro in Show Business* (New York: Burdge, 1954).
Flint, *Recollections*	Timothy Flint, *Recollections of the Last Ten Years, Passed in Occasional Residences and Journeyings in the Valley of the Mississippi* (Boston: Cummings, Hilliard, 1826).
Foote, *Civil War*	Shelby Foote, *The Civil War: A Narrative*, 3 vols. (1958–74; rpt. New York: Vintage, 1986).

Ford, *Traditional Music*	Ira W. Ford, *Traditional Music of America* (1940; rpt. Hatboro, PA: Folklore Associates, 1965).
Forten, "Sea Islands"	Charlotte Forten, "Life On the Sea Islands. Part I," *Atlantic* 13 (May 1864): 587–96; "Part II" (June 1864): 666–76.
Foster, "Philadelphia"	George G. Foster, "Philadelphia in Slices," 1848; rpt. *Pennsylvania Magazine of History and Biography* 93 (1969): 23–72.
Freedom	*Freedom: Golden Gate Quartet, Josh White at the Library of Congress (1940)*, Bridge CD 9114, 2002.
French, *Sketches*	James Strange French, *Sketches and Eccentricities of Col. David Crockett of West Tennessee*, new ed. (New York: J. & J. Harper, 1833).
Gainer, *West Virginia*	Patrick W. Gainer, *Folk Songs from the West Virginia Hills* (Grantsville, WV: Seneca, 1975).
"Games" (*SW*)	"Games," *Southern Workman* 23 (May 1894): 85-86.
Gilman, *Recollections*	Caroline Gilman, *Recollections of a Southern Matron and a New England Bride*, rev. ed. (Philadelphia: Keystone, 1890).
God Struck	Charles S. Johnson, Paul Radin, and A. P. Watson, eds., *God Struck Me Dead: Religious Conversion Experiences and Autobiographies of Negro Ex-Slaves*, Social Science Documents No. 2 (Nashville: Fisk University, 1945; rpt. Rawick, *American Slave*, S1 19).
Gomme, *Games*	Alice Bertha Gomme, *The Traditional Games of England, Scotland, and Ireland*, 2 vols. (1894, 1898; rpt. New York: Dover, 1964).
Good Time Blues	*Good Time Blues*, Columbia/Legacy CD 46780, 1991.
Gordon, *Folk-Songs*	Robert Winslow Gordon, *Folk-Songs of America*, National Service Bureau, Federal Theatre Project, WPA, Publication No. 73-S (Washington, DC, 1938).
Gospel Discography	Robert Laughton, *Gospel Discography* (Digital files, 2022).
Gumbo Ya-Ya	Lyle Saxon, Edward Dreyer, and Robert Tallant, *Gumbo Ya-Ya: A Collection of Louisiana Folk Tales* (1945; rpt. Gretna, LA: Pelican, 1987).
H. L. F., A. A., "Louisiana"	H. L. F., A. A., "One Hundred Years of Sugar-Making in Louisiana," *Harper's Weekly* (August 11, 1894), 758.
Hague, *Blockaded Family*	Parthenia Antoinette Hague, *A Blockaded Family: Life in Southern Alabama During the Civil War* (Boston: Houghton, Mifflin, 1888).
Halliwell, *Nursery Rhymes*	James Orchard Halliwell, *The Nursery Rhymes of England*. 5th ed. (London: Frederick Warne, 1886).
Hallowell, *Calhoun*	Emily Hallowell, *Calhoun Plantation Songs*, 2nd ed. (Boston: C. W. Thompson, 1907).
Halpert, *Pinelands*	Herbert Halpert, *Folk Tales, Tall Tales, Trickster Tales, and Legends of the Supernatural from the Pinelands of New Jersey*, ed. J. D. A. Widdowson (Lewiston, NY: Edwin Mellen, 2010).
Handbook of Texas	*The Handbook of Texas*, rev. ed., 6 vols. (Austin: Texas State Historical Association, 1996).
Handy, *Blues*	W. C. Handy, *Blues: An Anthology* (1926; rpt. New York: Da Capo, 1990).

Handy, *Father*	W. C. Handy, *Father of the Blues: An Autobiography* (1941; rpt. New York: Da Capo, 1991).
Harris, *Friends*	Joel Chandler Harris, *Uncle Remus and His Friends* (Boston: Houghton Mifflin, 1892).
Harris, "Plantation Music"	Joel Chandler Harris, "Plantation Music," *The Critic* 95 (December 15, 1883): 505.
Harris, *Remus*	Joel Chandler Harris, *Uncle Remus: His Songs and His Sayings* (1880, 1895; rpt. New York: Grosset & Dunlap, 1974).
Hearn, *Levee*	Lafcadio Hearn, *Children of the Levee*, ed. O. W. Frost (1874–1876; rpt. Lexington: University of Kentucky Press, 1957).
Henry, *Highlands*	Mellinger Edward Henry, *Folk-Songs from the Southern Highlands* (New York: J. J. Augustin, 1938).
Higginson, "Leaves"	Thomas Wentworth Higginson, "Leaves from an Officer's Journal," *Atlantic* 14 (November 1864): 521–29; "Leaves from an Officer's Journal. II," (December 1864): 740–48.
Higginson, "Spirituals"	Thomas Wentworth Higginson, "Negro Spirituals," *Atlantic* 19 (June 1867): 685–94.
Holcombe, "Sketches"	William H. Holcombe, "Sketches of Plantation-Life," *Knickerbocker* 57 (June 1861): 619–33.
Howard, *Bond and Free*	Jas. H. W. Howard, *Bond and Free: A True Tale of Slave Times* (Harrisburg, PA: Edwin K. Meyers, 1886).
Hudson, *Mississippi*	Arthur Palmer Hudson, *Folksongs of Mississippi and Their Background* (Chapel Hill: University of North Carolina Press, 1936).
Hundley, *Social Relations*	D. R. Hundley, *Social Relations in Our Southern States* (New York: Henry B. Price, 1860).
Hungerford, *Plantation*	James Hungerford, *The Old Plantation, And What I Gathered There in an Autumn Month* (New York: Harper & Brothers, 1859).
Hurston, "Hoodoo"	Zora Hurston, "Hoodoo in America," *JAF* 44 (1931): 317–417.
Hurston, *Mules*	Zora Neale Hurston, *Mules and Men* (1935; rpt. Bloomington: Indiana University Press, 1978).
Hyatt, *Hoodoo*	Harry Middleton Hyatt, *Hoodoo—Conjuration—Witchcraft—Rootwork*, 5 vols. Memoirs of the Alma Egan Hyatt Foundation (Hannibal, MO, and Cambridge, MD, 1970–78).
Ingersoll, "Atlanta"	Ernest Ingersoll, "The City of Atlanta," *Harper's Monthly* 60 (December 1879): 30–44.
Ingleton, "Pine Fork"	Pen Ingleton, "Pine Fork Plantation: A Chronicle of Old Days in the Old Dominion, part 1," *SLM* 18 (June 1852): 357–70.
Ingraham, *Sunny South*	Joseph Holt Ingraham, *The Sunny South; or, The Southerner at Home* (Philadelphia: G. G. Evans, 1860).
Irving, *Knicker-Bocker*	Washington Irving, *Knicker-Bocker's History of New York* (1809; rpt. New York: Frederick Ungar, 1959).
Jackson, *Dead Man*	Bruce Jackson, *Wake Up Dead Man: Hard Labor and Southern Blues* (Athens: University of Georgia Press, 1999).

Jackson, *Down-East*	George Pullen Jackson, *Down-East Spirituals, And Others* (New York: J. J. Augustin, 1939).
Jackson, *Early*	George Pullen Jackson, *Spiritual Folk-Songs of Early America* (1937; rpt. New York: Dover, 1964).
Jackson, *Sheaf*	George Pullen Jackson, *Another Sheaf of White Spirituals* (Gainesville: University Press of Florida, 1952).
Jackson, *Uplands*	George Pullen Jackson, *White Spirituals in the Southern Uplands* (1933; rpt. New York: Dover, 1965).
Jackson, *WNS*	George Pullen Jackson, *White and Negro Spirituals: Their Life Span and Kinship* (Locust Valley, NY: J. J. Augustin, 1943).
Jacobs, *Slave Girl*	Harriett Jacobs, *Incidents in the Life of a Slave Girl: Written by Herself* (Boston: author, 1861).
Jekyll, *Jamaican Song*	Walter Jekyll, *Jamaican Song and Story* (1907; rpt. Mineola, NY: Dover, 1966).
Johnson, *Highways*	Clifton Johnson, *Highways and Byways of the Mississippi Valley* (New York: Macmillan, 1906).
Johnson, *Supernaturals*	F. Roy Johnson, *Supernaturals Among Carolina Folk and Their Neighbors* (Murfreesboro, NC: Johnson Publishing, 1974).
Johnson, *Social History*	Guion Griffis Johnson, *A Social History of the Sea Islands* (Chapel Hill: University of North Carolina Press, 1930).
Johnson, *Utica Spirituals*	J. Rosamond Johnson, *Utica Jubilee Singers Spirituals: As Sung at the Utica Normal and Industrial Institute of Mississippi* (Boston: Oliver Ditson, 1930).
Johnson, *Spirituals* I	James Weldon Johnson, J. Rosamond Johnson, and Lawrence Brown, *The Book of American Negro Spirituals* (New York: Viking, 1925).
Johnson, *Spirituals* II	James Weldon Johnson and J. Rosamond Johnson, *The Second Book of Negro Spirituals* (New York: Viking, 1926).
Jones and Hawes, *Step It Down*	Bessie Jones and Bess Lomax Hawes, *Step It Down: Games, Plays, Songs and Stories from the Afro-American Heritage* (New York: Harper & Row, 1972).
Kearney, *Slaveholder's Daughter*	Belle Kearney, *A Slaveholder's Daughter*, 7th ed. (New York: Abbey, 1900).
Kemble, *Residence*	Frances Anne Kemble, *Journal of a Residence on a Georgia Plantation in 1837–1838*, ed. John A. Scott (New York: Alfred A. Knopf, 1961).
Kennard, "National Poets"	James K. Kennard. Jr., "Who Are Our National Poets?" *Knickerbocker* 26 (October 1845): 331–41.
Kennedy, *Swallow Barn*	J. P. Kennedy, *Swallow Barn: or, A Sojourn in the Old Dominion*, rev. ed. (1832, 1851; rpt. Philadelphia: J. B. Lippincott, 1860).
Kennedy, *Folksongs*	Peter Kennedy, *Folksongs of Britain and Ireland* (New York: Schirmer, 1975).
Kennedy, *Cameos*	R. Emmet Kennedy, *Black Cameos* (New York: Albert & Charles Boni, 1924).
Kennedy, *Mellows*	R. Emmet Kennedy, *Mellows: A Chronicle of Unknown Singers* (New York: Albert & Charles Boni, 1925).

Kennedy, *More Mellows*	R. Emmet Kennedy, *More Mellows* (New York: Dodd, Mead, 1931).
Kilham, "Sketches"	Elizabeth Kilham, "Sketches in Color. First," *Putnam's* 15 (December 1869): 741–46; "Second" (January 1870): 31–38; "Third" (February 1870): 205–11; "Fourth" (March 1870): 304–11.
Killion and Waller, *Georgia*	Ronald G. Killion and Charles T. Waller, *A Treasury of Georgia Folklore* (Atlanta: Cherokee, 1972).
King, *Great South*	Edward King, *The Great South: A Record of Journeys* (Hartford, CT: American Publishing, 1875).
Kirby, *Instruments*	Percival R. Kirby, *Musical Instruments of the Indigenous People of South Africa*, 3rd ed. (Johannesburg: Wits University Press, 2013).
Kirke, *Among the Pines*	Edmund Kirke, *Among the Pines: or, South in Secession-Time* (New York: J. R. Gilmore, 1862). *Edmund Kirke* was a pseudonym of author and publisher James Robert Gilmore (1822–1903), who also wrote prolifically under his own name. For convenience, I have cited these works with their original author credits.
Kirke, *Southern Friends*	Edmund Kirke, *My Southern Friends: "All of Which I Saw, and Part of Which I Was"* (New York: Carleton, 1863).
Kmen, *New Orleans*	Henry A. Kmen, *Music in New Orleans: The Formative Years, 1791–1841* (Baton Rouge: Louisiana State University Press, 1966).
Knapp, *One Potato*	Mary and Herbert Knapp, *One Potato, Two Potato: The Folklore of American Children* (New York: W. W. Norton, 1976).
Krehbiel, *Folksongs*	Henry Edward Krehbiel, *Afro-American Folksongs: A Study in Racial and National Music* (New York: G. Schirmer, 1914).
Kubik, *Africa*	Gerhard Kubik, *Africa and the Blues* (Jackson: University Press of Mississippi, 1999).
Lanman, *Adventures*	Charles Lanman, *Adventures in the Wilds of the United States and British American Provinces*, 2 vols. (Philadelphia: John W. Moore, 1856).
Larison, *Silvia Dubois*	C. W. Larison, *Silvia Dubois (Now 116 Years Old), A Biografy of the Slav Who Whipt Her Mistres and Gand Her Fredom*, ed. and trans. Jared C. Lobdell (1883; rpt. New York: Oxford University Press, 1988).
Latrobe, *Journal*	Benjamin Henry Latrobe, *The Journal of Latrobe* (New York: D. Appleton, 1905).
Laws (A–I)	G. Malcolm Laws Jr., *Native American Balladry: A Descriptive Study and a Bibliographical Syllabus*, rev. ed. AFS BSS, vol. 1 (Philadelphia, 1964).
Laws (J–Q)	G. Malcolm Laws Jr., *American Balladry from British Broadsides: A Guide for Students and Collectors of Traditional Song*. AFS BSS, vol. 8 (Philadelphia, 1957).
Leigh, *Georgia Plantation*	Mrs. Frances B. Leigh, *Ten Years on a Georgia Plantation Since the War* (1883; rpt. New York: Negro University Press, 1969).
Linscott, *New England*	Eloise Hubbard Linscott, *Folk Songs of Old New England* (1939, 1962; rpt. New York: Dover, 1993).

List, *Indiana*	George List, *Singing About It: Folk Song in Southern Indiana* (Indianapolis: Indiana Historical Society, 1991).
Livermore, *Story*	Mary A. Livermore, *The Story of My Life* (Hartford, CT: A. D. Worthington, 1897).
Lomax, *FSNA*	Alan Lomax, *The Folk Songs of North America in the English Language* (1960; rpt. Garden City, NY: Dolphin, 1975).
Lomax, *Ballads*	John A. Lomax and Alan Lomax, *American Ballads and Folk Songs* (New York: Macmillan, 1934).
Lomax, *Country*	John A. Lomax and Alan Lomax, *Our Singing Country: Folk Songs and Ballads* (1941; rpt. Mineola, NY: Dover, 2000).
Lomax, "Instructions"	"Supplementary Instructions #9-E to The American Guide Manual," 1937; Rawick, *Sundown*, 173–76.
Lomax, *Land*	Alan Lomax, *The Land Where the Blues Began* (1993; rpt. New York: Delta, 1995).
Lomax, *Lead Belly*	John A. Lomax and Alan Lomax, *Negro Folk Songs As Sung by Lead Belly* (New York: Macmillan, 1936).
Lomax, *USA*	John A. Lomax and Alan Lomax, *Folksong: U.S.A.* (New York: Duell, Sloan & Pearce, 1947).
Long, *Slavery*	Rev. John Dixon Long, *Pictures of Slavery in Church and State* (Philadelphia: author, 1857).
Lone Star Ballads	Francis D. Allan, *Allan's Lone Star Ballads: A Collection of Southern Patriotic Songs Made During Confederate Times* (Galveston: J. D. Sawyer, 1874).
Lowery, *Life*	Irving E. Lowery, *Life on the Old Plantation in Ante-Bellum Days* (1911; rpt. *I Belong to South Carolina*, 167–227).
Lullabies to Blues	*Alabama: From Lullabies to Blues*, Rounder CD 1829, 2001.
MacDonald, *Virginia*	James J. McDonald, *Life in Old Virginia*, ed. J. A. C. Chandler (Norfolk: Old Virginia, 1907).
Mackay, *Western World*	Alexander Mackay, *The Western World; Or, Travels in the United States in 1846–47*, 3 vols. (London: Richard Bentley, 1849).
Make You Happy	*Georgia: I'm Gonna Make You Happy*, Rounder CD 1828, 2001.
Malet, *Errand*	Rev. William Wyndham Malet, *An Errand to the South in the Summer of 1862* (London: Richard Bentley, 1863).
Mallard, *Plantation Life*	R. Q. Mallard, *Plantation Life Before Emancipation* (Richmond: Whittet & Shepperson, 1892).
Marcuse, *Instruments*	Sibyl Marcuse, *A Survey of Musical Instruments* (New York: Harper & Row, 1975).
Marsh, *Jubilee Singers*	J. B. T. Marsh, *The Story of the Jubilee Singers; With Their Songs*, rev. ed. (1881; rpt. New York: Negro Universities Press, 1969).
McDowell, *Camp Songs*	L. L. McDowell, *Songs of the Old Camp Ground: Genuine Religious Folk Songs of the Tennessee Hill Country* (Ann Arbor, MI: Edwards Brothers, 1937).

McDowell, *Folk Dances*	Lucien L. McDowell and Flora Lassiter McDowell, *Folk Dances of Tennessee: Old Play Party Games of the Caney Fork Valley* (Ann Arbor, MI: Edwards Brothers, 1938).
McIlhenny, *Spirituals*	E. A. McIlhenny, *Befo' De War Spirituals: Words and Melodies* (Boston: Christopher, 1933).
McNeil, *Folksongs*	W. K. WcNeil, *Southern Mountain Folksongs* (Little Rock: August House, 1993).
Mead, *Travels*	Whitman Mead, *Travels in North America* (New York: C. S. Van Winkle, 1820).
Métraux, *Voodoo*	Alfred Métraux, *Voodoo in Haiti*, trans. Hugo Charteris (New York: Oxford University Press, 1959).
Mitchell, *Old Dominion*	Stephen T. Mitchell, *The Spirit of the Old Dominion* (Richmond: author, 1827).
Mississippi Planter, "Management of Negroes"	A Mississippi Planter, "Management of Negroes upon Southern Estates," *De Bow's Review of the Southern and Western States* 10 (June 1851): 621–27.
Montagu, *Instruments*	Jeremy Montagu, *Origins and Development of Musical Instruments* (Lanham, MD: Scarecrow, 2007).
Morris, *Florida*	Alton C. Morris, *Folksongs of Florida* (Gainesville: University Press of Florida, 1950).
Mother Wit	Ronnie W. Clayton, ed., *Mother Wit: The Ex-Slave Narratives of the Louisiana Writers' Project*. University of Kansas Humanistic Studies 57. (New York: Peter Lang, 1990).
Nathan, *Dan Emmett*	Hans Nathan, *Dan Emmett and the Rise of Early Negro Minstrelsy* (Norman: University of Oklahoma Press, 1962).
Nathanson, "Negro Minstrelsy"	Y. A. Nathanson, "Negro Minstrelsy—Ancient and Modern," *Putnam's* 5 (January 1855): 72–79.
"Negro Folk Songs" (*SW*)	"Negro Folk Songs," *Southern Workman* 24 (1895): 31–32.
Nettl, *Folk Music*	Bruno Nettl, *Folk and Traditional Music of the Western Continents*, 3rd ed. (Englewood Cliffs, NJ: Prentice Hall, 1990).
New Harp	M. L. Swan, *The New Harp of Columbia*, ed. Dorothy D. Horn, Ron Peterson, and Candra Phillips (1867; rpt. Knoxville: University of Tennessee Press, 1978).
Newell, *Games*	William Wells Newell, *Games and Songs of American Children* (1883, 1903; rpt. New York: Dover, 1963).
Nketia, *Music of Africa*	J. H. Kwabena Nketia, *The Music of Africa* (New York: W. W. Norton, 1974).
North Carolina Banjo	*The North Carolina Banjo Collection*, Rounder CDs 0439/40, 1998.
Northrup, *Twelve Years*	Solomon Northrup, *Twelve Years a Slave* (New York: Miller, Orton & Mulligan, 1855).
Odum and Johnson, *NHS*	Howard W. Odum and Guy B. Johnson, *The Negro and His Songs: A Study of Typical Negro Songs in the South* (1925; rpt. New York: Negro University Press, 1968).

Odum and Johnson, *Workaday*	Howard W. Odum and Guy B. Johnson, *Negro Workaday Songs* (1926; rpt. New York: Negro University Press, 1969).
Old-Time String Band	John Cohen and Mike Seeger, eds., *Old-Time String Band Songbook* (New York: Oak, 1964).
Oliver, *Savannah*	Paul Oliver, *Savannah Syncopators: African Retentions in the Blues* (New York: Stein and Day, 1970).
Oliver, *Songsters*	Paul Oliver, *Songsters and Saints: Vocal Traditions On Race Records* (New York: Oxford University Press, 1984).
Olmsted, *Back Country*	Frederick Law Olmsted, *A Journey in the Back Country* (1860; rpt. Williamstown, MA: Corner House, 1972).
Olmsted, *Seaboard*	Frederick Law Olmsted, *A Journey in the Seaboard Slave States in the Years 1853–1854*, 2 vols. (1856; rpt. New York: Knickerbocker, 1904).
Opie, *Nursery Rhymes*	Iona Opie and Peter Opie, eds., *The Oxford Dictionary of Nursery Rhymes* (Oxford: Oxford University Press, 1951).
Owens, *Texas*	William A. Owens, *Texas Folk Songs*, rev. ed. PTFS 23 (Dallas: Southern Methodist University Press, 1976).
Page, *Uncle Robin*	J. W. Page, *Uncle Robin, In His Cabin in Virginia, and Tom without One in Boston*, 2nd ed. (Richmond: J. W. Randolph, 1853).
Paine, *Georgia Prison*	Lewis W. Paine, *Six Years in a Georgia Prison* (New York: author, 1851).
Parker, *Recollections*	Allen Parker, *Recollections of Slavery Times* (1895; rpt. *Bondage to Belonging*, 286–320).
Parrish, *Sea Islands*	Lydia Parrish, *Slave Songs of the Georgia Sea Islands* (1942; rpt. Hatboro, PA: Folklore Associates, 1965).
Parsons, "Guilford County"	Elsie Clews Parsons, "Tales from Guilford County, North Carolina," *JAF* 30 (1917): 168–99.
Paulding, *Slavery*	J. K. Paulding, *Slavery in the United States* (New York: Harper & Brothers, 1836).
Pearson, *Letters*	Elizabeth Ware Pearson, *Letters From Port Royal at the Time of the Civil War* (1906; rpt. New York: Arno, 1969).
Pennington, *Woman Planter*	Patience Pennington, *A Woman Rice Planter* (1904–7; rpt. New York: Macmillan, 1913).
Perkins, "Spirituals"	A. E. Perkins, "Negro Spirituals from the Far South," *JAF* 35 (1922): 223–49.
Perrow, "South"	E. C. Perrow, "Songs and Rhymes from the South," *JAF* 25 (1912): 137–55; 26 (1913): 123–73; 28 (1915): 129–90.
Ping, "Musical Activities"	Nancy R. Ping, "Black Musical Activities in Antebellum Wilmington, North Carolina," *BPM* 8 (1980): 139–60.
Piper, "Play-Party"	Edwin F. Piper, "Some Play-Party Games of the Middle West," *JAF* 28 (1915): 262–89.
Porter, "Negro Songs"	Mary W. Porter, "Some Genuine Negro Songs," *Independent* 30 (May 9, 1878), 1.
Puckett, *Folk Beliefs*	Newbell Niles Puckett, *Folk Beliefs of the Southern Negro* (Chapel Hill: University of North Carolina Press, 1926).

Raboteau, *Slave Religion*	Albert J. Raboteau, *Slave Religion: The "Invisible Institution" in the Antebellum South* (Oxford: Oxford University Press, 1978).
Ralph, "Dixie"	Julian Ralph, "The Old Way to Dixie," *Harper's Monthly* 86 (January 1893): 165–85.
Randolph, *Slave Life*	Peter Randolph, *Sketches of Slave Life: or, Illustrations of the "Peculiar Institution,"* 2nd ed. (Boston: author, 1855).
Randolph, *OFS*	Vance Randolph, *Ozark Folksongs*, 4 vols. (Columbia: State Historical Society of Missouri, 1946–50).
Randolph, *Roll Me*	Vance Randolph, *Roll Me in Your Arms: "Unprintable" Ozark Folksongs and Folklore*, vol. 1: *Folksongs and Music*, ed. G. Legman (Fayetteville: University of Arkansas Press, 1992).
Ravenel, "Recollections"	Henry William Ravenel, "Recollections of Southern Plantation Life," ms., February 1876; *Yale Review* 25 (1936): 748–77.
Ravitz, "Slaves' Christmas"	Abe C. Ravitz, "John Pierpont and the Slaves' Christmas," *Phylon* 21 (1960): 383–86.
Rawick, *American Slave*	George P. Rawick, ed., *The American Slave: A Composite Autobiography*, 41 vols. (Westport, CT: Greenwood, 1972–79).
Rawick, *Sundown*	George P. Rawick, *From Sundown to Sunup: The Making of the Black Community*. Rawick, American *Slave*, vol. 1 (Westport, CT: Greenwood, 1972).
Roberts, *Black Music*	John Storm Roberts, *Black Music of Two Worlds* (Tivoli, NY: Original Music, 1972).
Robinson, *Aunt Dice*	Nina Hill Robinson, *Aunt Dice: The Story of a Faithful Slave* (1897; rpt. Freeport, NY: Books for Libraries, 1972).
Robinson, "Coloured People"	T. L. Robinson, "The Coloured People of the United States. In the South," *Leisure Hour* (January 1889), 54–59.
Robinson, *Log Cabin*	William H. Robinson, *From Log Cabin to the Pulpit, or, Fifteen Years in Slavery*, 3rd ed. (Eau Claire, WI: James H. Tifft, 1913).
Rosenberg, *Virginia*	Bruce A. Rosenberg, *The Folksongs of Virginia: A Checklist of the WPA Holdings, Alderman Library, University of Virginia* (Charlottesville: University of Virginia Press, 1969).
Roud	Roud Folksong Index, English Folk Dance and Song Society, Vaughan Williams Memorial Library, vwml.org.
Russell, *Southern Life*	William Howard Russell, *Pictures of Southern Life, Social, Political, and Military* (New York: James G. Gregory, 1861).
Sacred Harp	B. F. White and E. J. King, *The Sacred Harp*, 3rd ed. (1859; rpt. Nashville: Broadman, 1968).
Saints and Sinners	*Mississippi: Saints and Sinners from Before the Blues and Gospel*, Rounder CD 1824, 1999.
Sandburg, *Songbag*	Carl Sandburg, *The American Songbag* (New York: Harcourt, Brace, 1927).
Scarborough, *Song Catcher*	Dorothy Scarborough, *A Song Catcher in the Southern Mountains: American Folk Songs of British Ancestry* (New York: Columbia University Press, 1937).

Scarborough, *TNFS*	Dorothy Scarborough, *On the Trail of Negro Folk-Songs* (Cambridge, MA: Harvard University Press, 1925).
Schoolcraft, *Gauntlet*	Mrs. Henry R. Schoolcraft, *The Black Gauntlet: A Tale of Plantation Life in South Carolina* (Philadelphia: J. B. Lippincott, 1860).
Seawell, "Fiddler"	Molly Elliot Seawell, "Tubal the Fiddler," *Harper's Weekly* 33 (August 10, 1889): 642–43.
Sharp, *EFSSA*	Cecil J. Sharp, *English Folk Songs from the Southern Appalachians*, ed. Maud Karpeles, rev. ed., 2 vols. (London: Oxford University Press, 1932).
Sharp Collection	Maud Karpeles, ed., *Cecil Sharp's Collection of English Folksongs*, 2 vols. (New York: Oxford University Press, 1974).
Showers, "Weddin' and Buryin'"	Susan Showers, "A Weddin' and a Buryin' in the Black Belt," *New England Magazine* 24 (June 1898): 481–82.
Silber, *Civil War*	Irwin Silber, *Songs of the Civil War* (New York: Bonanza, 1960).
Simond, *Old Slack*	Ike "Old Slack" Simond, *Old Slack's Reminiscence and Pocket History of the Colored Profession from 1865 to 1891* (1892; rpt. Bowling Green, OH: Bowling Green State University Popular Press, 1974).
Slave Songs	William Francis Allen, Charles Pickard Ware, and Lucy McKim Garrison, *Slave Songs of the United States* (1867; rpt. Bedford, MA: Applewood, n.d.).
"Slavery in the US"	"Slavery in the United States: By an American," *Knickerbocker* 10 (October 1837): 325.
Will Slayden	*Will Slayden: African-American Banjo Songs from West Tennessee*, Tennessee Folklore Society CD 123, 2001.
Small Farmer, "Management of Negroes"	A Small Farmer, "Management of Negroes," *De Bow's Review of the Southern and Western States* 11 (October 1851): 369–72.
Smalley, "Sugar-Making"	Eugene V. Smalley, "Sugar-Making in Louisiana," *Century* 35 (November 1887): 100–120.
Smiley, "Folk-Lore"	Portia Smiley, "Folk-Lore from Virginia, South Carolina, Georgia, Alabama, and Florida," *JAF* 32 (1919): 357–83.
Smith, *Fifty Years*	Harry Smith, *Fifty Years of Slavery in the United States of America* (1891; rpt. Grand Rapids: Clarke Historical Library, Central Michigan University, 1971).
Smith, "Persimmon Tree"	William B. Smith, "The Persimmon Tree and the Beer Dance," *Farmer's Register* 6 (April 1838): 60.
Social Harp	John G. McCurry, *The Social Harp: A Collection of Tunes, Odes, Anthems, and Set Pieces*, ed. Daniel W. Patterson and John F. Garst (1855; rpt. Athens: University of Georgia Press, 1973).
Solomon, *Daisies*	Jack P. Solomon and Olivia P. Solomon, *Sweet Bunch of Daisies: Folk Songs Collected in Alabama* (Bessemer, AL: Colonial, 1991).
Solomon, *Honey*	Olivia Solomon and Jack Solomon, *"Honey in the Rock": The Ruby Pickens Tartt Collection of Religious Folk Songs from Sumter County, Alabama* (Macon, GA: Mercer University Press, 1991).

Sounds of the South	*Sounds of the South*, 4-CD set, Atlantic CDs 82496, 1993.
Southern, *Music*	Eileen Southern, *The Music of Black Americans*, 2nd ed. (New York: W. W. Norton, 1983).
Southern and Wright, *Traditions*	Eileen Southern and Josephine Wright, *African-American Traditions in Song, Sermon, Tale, and Dance, 1600s–1920: An Annotated Bibliography of Literature, Collections, and Artworks* (New York: Greenwood, 1990).
"Southern Cabins"	B., "Inside Southern Cabins. Georgia—No. 1," *Harper's Weekly* 24 (November 13, 1880): 733–34; "Georgia—II," (November 20, 1880): 749–50; "III—Charleston, South Carolina" (November 27, 1880): 765–66; "IV—Alabama" (December 4, 1880): 781–82.
Southern Harmony	William Walker, *The Southern Harmony, and Musical Companion*, rev. ed. (1854; rpt. Los Angeles: Pro Musicamericana, 1966).
Spaeth, *Read 'Em*	Sigmund Spaeth, *Read 'Em and Weep: The Songs You Forgot to Remember* (Garden City, NY: Doubleday, Page, 1926).
Spaeth, *Weep Some More*	Sigmund Spaeth, *Weep Some More, My Lady* (Garden City, NY: Doubleday, Page, 1927).
Spaulding, "Palmetto"	H. G. Spaulding, "Under the Palmetto," *Continental Monthly* 4 (August 1863): 188–204.
Spurgeon, *Waltz the Hall*	Alan L. Spurgeon, *Waltz the Hall: The American Play Party* (Jackson: University Press of Mississippi, 2005).
Stearns, *Jazz Dance*	Marshall Stearns and Jean Stearns, *Jazz Dance: The Story of American Vernacular Dance* (New York: Macmillan, 1968).
Steward, *Slave*	Austin Steward, *Twenty-Two Years a Slave, and Forty Years a Free Man* (Rochester, NY: William Alling, 1857).
Stowe, *Writings*	Harriet Beecher Stowe, *The Writings of Harriet Beecher Stowe*, 17 vols. (Boston: Houghton, Mifflin, 1896–98).
Stroyer, *Life*	Jacob Stroyer, *My Life in the South*, 4th ed. (1898; rpt. *Five Narratives*, 1–100).
Stuart, "Camp-Meeting"	Dennar Stuart, "A Camp-Meeting in Tennessee," *Harper's Monthly* 26 (December 1862): 97–101.
Stuart, "Apollo Belvedere"	Ruth McEnery Stuart, "Apollo Belvedere: A Christmas Episode on the Plantation," *Harper's Monthly* 96 (December 1897): 155–58.
Tallant, *Voodoo*	Robert Tallant, *Voodoo in New Orleans* (1946; rpt. New York: Collier, 1962).
Talley, *NFR*	Thomas W. Talley, *Negro Folk Rhymes: A New, Expanded Edition with Music*, ed. Charles K. Wolfe (Knoxville: University of Tennessee Press, 1991).
Tate and Panola	*Afro-American Folk Music from Tate and Panola Counties, Mississippi*, Library of Congress LP AFS L67, 1978.
Taylor, *Revival Hymns*	Marshall W. Taylor, *A Collection of Revival Hymns and Plantation Melodies* (Cincinnati: M. W. Taylor and W. C. Echols, 1882).
Thede, *Fiddle*	Marion Thede, *The Fiddle Book* (New York: Oak, 1967).

Thomas, "Work-Songs"	Gates Thomas, "South Texas Negro Work-Songs: Collected and Uncollected," *Rainbow in the Morning*, ed. J. Frank Dobie. PTFS 5 (1926; rpt. Hatboro, PA: Folklore Associates, 1965), 154–80.
Thomas, *Tennessee Slave*	James Thomas, *From Tennessee Slave to St. Louis Entrepreneur: The Autobiography of James Thomas*, ed. Loren Schweninger (Columbia: University of Missouri Press, 1984).
Thomas, *Ballad Makin'*	Jean Thomas, *Ballad Makin' in the Mountains of Kentucky* (1939; rpt. New York: Oak, 1964).
Thomas, *Devil's Ditties*	Jean Thomas, *Devil's Ditties* (1931; rpt. Detroit: Gale Research, 1976).
Thompson, "Plantation Music"	Maurice Thompson, "Plantation Music," *The Critic and Good Literature* 2 (January 12, 1884): 20.
Thompson, *Motif*	Stith Thompson, *Motif-Index of Folk Literature*, rev. ed., 6 vols. (Bloomington: Indiana University Press, 1955–58).
Thorpe, "Christmas"	T. B. Thorpe, "Christmas in the South," *Leslie's* 108 (December 26, 1857): 62.
Thorpe, "Cotton"	T. B. Thorpe, "Cotton and Its Cultivation," *Harper's Monthly* 8 (March 1854): 447–63.
Thorpe, "Mississippi"	T. B. Thorpe, "Remembrances of the Mississippi," *Harper's Monthly* 12 (December 1855): 25–41.
Thorpe, "Sugar"	T. B. Thorpe, "Sugar and the Sugar Region of Louisiana," *Harper's Monthly* 7 (November 1853): 746–67.
Titon, *Fiddle Tunes*	Jeff Todd Titon, *Old-Time Kentucky Fiddle Tunes* (Lexington: University Press of Kentucky, 2001).
Todd, *Methodism*	Robert W. Todd, *Methodism of the Peninsula* (Philadelphia: Methodist Episcopal Book Rooms, 1886).
Toll, *Blacking Up*	Robert C. Toll, *Blacking Up: The Minstrel Show in Nineteenth-Century America* (New York: Oxford University Press, 1974).
Traveling Through the Jungle	*Traveling Through the Jungle: Fife and Drum Band Music from the Deep South*, Testament CD 5017, 1995.
Unwritten History	Ophelia Settle Egypt, J. Masuoka, and Charles S. Johnson, eds., *Unwritten History of Slavery: Autobiographical Account of Negro Ex-Slaves*, Social Science Documents No. 1 (Nashville: Fisk University, 1945; rpt. Rawick, *American Slave*, 18).
Venable, "Down South"	W. H. Venable, "Down South Before the War," *Ohio Archaeological and Historical Publications*, vol. 2 (Columbus: Ohio Archaeological and Historical Society, 1889): 488–513.
Victor, *Maum Guinea*	Mrs. Metta V. Victor, *Maum Guinea, and Her Plantation "Children"; Or, Holiday-Week on a Louisiana Estate* (New York: Beadle and Co., 1861).
Virginia and the Piedmont	*Virginia and the Piedmont: Minstrelsy, Work Songs, and Blues*, Rounder CD 1827, 2000.
Virginia Secular Music	*Virginia Traditions: Non-Blues Secular Black Music*, Global Village CD 1001, 1995.

Virginia Work Songs	*Virginia Traditions: Virginia Work Songs*, Global Village CD 1007, 1998.
Warner, *Folk Songs*	Anne Warner, *Traditional American Folk Songs from the Anne and Frank Warner Collection* (Syracuse, NY: Syracuse University Press, 1984).
Washington, "Funeral"	Ella B. Washington, "A Colored Funeral in the South," *Leslie's* 821 (June 2, 1871): 242.
"Watch Meeting" (*SW*)	"Watch Meeting," *Southern Workman* 28 (1899): 151–54.
Weevils (*WW*)	Charles L. Perdue Jr., Thomas E. Barden, and Robert K. Phillips, eds., *Weevils in the Wheat: Interviews with Virginia Ex-Slaves* (Bloomington: Indiana University Press, 1980).
Wheeler, *Steamboatin'*	Mary Wheeler, *Steamboatin' Days: Folk Songs of the River Packet Era* (Baton Rouge: Louisiana State University Press, 1944).
Whipple, *Diary*	Henry Benjamin Whipple, *Bishop Whipple's Southern Diary 1843–1844*, ed. Lester B. Shippee (Minneapolis: University of Minnesota Press, 1937).
White, *ANFS*	Newman I. White, *American Negro Folk-Songs* (Cambridge, MA: Harvard University Press, 1928).
Whitney and Bullock, *Maryland*	Annie Weston Whitney and Caroline Canfield Bullock, *Folk-Lore from Maryland*. MAFS 18 (New York, 1925).
Isaac Williams	William Ferguson Goldie, *Sunshine and Shadow of Slave Life: Reminiscences As Told by Isaac D. Williams To "Tege"* (1885; rpt. New York: AMS, 1975).
Williams, *Narrative*	James Williams, *Narrative of James Williams. An American Slave* (New York: American Anti-Slavery Society, 1838).
Wilson, "Old Plantation"	Robert Wilson, "At the Old Plantation. Two Papers.—I," *Lippincott's* 17 (January 1876): 118–24; "II" (February 1876): 241–49.
Windley	Lathan A. Windley, comp., *Runaway Slave Advertisements: A Documentary History from the 1730s to 1790*, 4 vols.: *Vol. 1: Virginia*; *Vol. 2: Maryland*; *Vol. 3: South Carolina*; *Vol. 4: Georgia* (Westport, CT: Greenwood, 1983).
Wolfe, *Middle Tennessee*	Charles K. Wolfe, *Folk Songs of Middle Tennessee: The George Boswell Collection* (Knoxville: University of Tennessee Press, 1997).
Wolford, *Play-Party*	Leah Jackson Wolford, *The Play-Party in Indiana*, ed. W. Edson Richmond and William Tillson, rev. ed. (Indianapolis: Indiana Historical Society Publications, vol. 20, no. 2, 1959).
Woods, "Corn-Shucking"	Henry C. Woods, "A Southern Corn-Shucking," *Appleton's* 4 (November 12, 1870): 571.
Work, *ANSS*	John W. Work, *American Negro Songs and Spirituals* (1940; rpt. New York: Dover, 1998).
Wyeth, *Sabre*	John Allan Wyeth, *With Sabre and Scalpel: The Autobiography of a Soldier and Surgeon* (New York: Harper & Brothers, 1914).

INTRODUCTION

THE WPA EX-SLAVE NARRATIVES

Den dey was anudder one:

> Heavenly land,
> Heavenly land,
> Heavenly land,
> I's gwinter beg God
> For dat Heavenly Land
>
> Some come cripplin'
> Some come lame
> Some come walkin'
> In Jesus' name.

You know I saw you all las' night in my sleep. I ain' never see you befo' but I see you last night. Dey was de two of you, a man and a woman, and you come crost that bridge and up yere askin' me iffen I trus' in de Lord. (Liza Jones, b. 1856, TX, 2119–20, to interviewers Fred Dibble and Bernice Grey)[1]

Between 1937 and 1940 fieldworkers in the Works Progress Administration's Federal Writers' Project (WPA, FWP) interviewed around 3,500 former North American slaves, resulting in roughly 20,000 pages of still unedited, inadequately indexed typescript.[2] This is the most substantial collection by far of folklore and oral history gathered directly from American slaves. It is arguably the single greatest body of African American folklore extant—certainly it is in the top rank—and a significant portion of the collection is devoted to this study's topic, folk music and song. Were it not dramatic enough on its own terms, nineteenth-century Black folk music developed against the backdrop of North American slavery, the Civil War, Emancipation, the Federal occupation of the South, and a successful white supremacist paramilitary and political insurgency leading to Federal withdrawal, officially sanctioned racial terror, and Southern apartheid. The WPA ex-slave narratives describe all of that as well.

Actually, this is an account of all of the music and song in the WPA ex-slave narratives, but since virtually all of that material falls squarely within the definition of folk music and song, I should begin by saying precisely what I mean by *folk music*, and by extension *folklore*. Ideally, folk music and song are passed on only by direct human contact, either through word-of-mouth or customary example, without becoming permanently fixed in such media as sound recordings or print. A community's oral traditions may borrow from other cultures and their folk traditions; from other musical domains (pop, classical); or from mass media like songbooks or sound recordings, but most folksongs originate among the people who perform, preserve, and appreciate them. Still, even within its home community, any given folksong's origins are likely unknown. True, some traditional songmakers or musical innovators are recognized and remembered, but overall, folksingers do not share modern notions of individual authorship and ownership, much less the means of enforcing them. Then too, traditional songmakers often create new songs simply by rearranging older material, other singers then being free to introduce their own changes. Drawing in this way on long-established artistic patterns and models, yet always open to personal touches and new ideas, folk music is both remarkably stable and endlessly variable. Circumstantially, folk music occurs as part of people's daily routines or community calendars in situations characterized by especially high degrees of familiarity, intimacy, and reciprocity, with little or no separation between performer and audience. Folk music thus serves as an essential means of reinforcing basic social relationships and expressing and instilling basic cultural values, attitudes, and beliefs, simultaneously serving immediate interpersonal or practical ends: lulling a baby to sleep, coordinating work, bonding believers in worship, accompanying a dance or game.

The greatest portion of the music the ex-slaves described fits this definition perfectly, while the remainder epitomizes the outside forces sometimes interacting with folksong—for instance, the published Protestant hymns by composers like Isaac Watts (1674–1748) that were ubiquitous among whites and Blacks alike in the antebellum South. Hundreds of ex-slaves knew or named dozens of these titles. A few had learned them directly from hymnals or shape-note songbooks—slave literacy was only around 10 percent but did exist—but most had picked them up word-of-mouth, and many songs had been orally recomposed to the point that they barely resembled their source texts. By and large, American slaves inhabited a purely interpersonal milieu where art, knowledge, and belief were transmitted entirely through oral and customary channels. As a result, no area of slave life was untouched by folklore, which to the contrary permeated all behavior, experience, and expression. The WPA ex-slave narratives were not necessarily intended as a folklore collection—the stated purpose was to record the life histories of former slaves—but inevitably folklorists played a major role, and the final results consist primarily of folklore.

Indeed, given the fundamental folk qualities of slave culture, the study of American slaves and the field of American folklore developed in tandem beginning in the colonial era. The world's fascination with North American slaves—and especially their music, song, dance, and other folk traditions—was routinely registered from that period, early observers serving as *accidental folklorists* merely by circumstance.[3] During the Civil War years the slave spiritual emerged as a major focus, and in 1867 *Slave Songs of the United States*, the first serious American folksong collection, appeared.[4] In the years following the war, similar anthologies (mainly religious, some secular) proliferated, now often edited by Black scholars, composers, and educators and published by Black colleges and universities. On a parallel track, books of African American folktales by Joe Chandler Harris (1848–1908) and others became bestsellers. On January 4, 1888, the American Folk-Lore Society was organized in Cambridge, Massachusetts. The inaugural number of its quarterly, the *Journal of American Folk-Lore*, stated first among the society's aims the collection and publication of "Relics of Old English Folk-Lore (ballads, tales, superstitions, dialect, etc.)," and second, the "Lore of the Negroes in the Southern States of the Union," which at that time meant the former slaves and their immediate descendants.[5] In the decades that followed, the journal made good on that pledge, filling its numbers with articles on Black folklore and song (and Anglo-American ballads and traditions), soon enlarged by book-length studies from university and commercial presses. These were the magisterial African American folksong collections of James Weldon Johnson (1871–1938) and J. Rosamond Johnson (1873–1954), Howard W. Odum (1884–1954) and Guy B. Johnson (1901–1991), R. Emmet Kennedy (1877–1941), Lydia Parrish (1871–1953), Dorothy Scarborough (1878–1935), Thomas W. Talley (1870–1952), Newman I. White (1892–1948), John Wesley Work III (1901–1967), and John A. Lomax (1867–1948) and his son, Alan Lomax (1915–2002).

These developments had initially been driven by an interest in the slaves themselves, and from the 1700s slave biographies and autobiographies also appeared.[6] By the antebellum period, the memoirs of fugitive slaves were a distinct genre of American literature. In response, Southern authors produced their own portraits, generally fictional (or highly fictionalized) but some based on real slaves (and not always proslavery). After the war, the former slaves appear to have attracted as much, perhaps even more attention. Numbers more wrote autobiographies, while others were regularly profiled in, or served as sources for, newspaper and magazine articles and popular books. By the 1930s, however, much of this work had taken an academic turn, with Black scholars, colleges, and universities once more in the forefront.

During 1929 John B. Cade (1894–1970), then head of Southern University's Extension Department at Scotlandville, Louisiana, supervised interviews conducted with ex-slaves by student-teachers in St. Joseph, Monroe, Bastrop, Minden, and Ruston. Some of these were excerpted in "Out of the Mouths of Ex-Slaves" (1935), but most of Cade's interviews from this and later collecting projects remain unpublished. During the same period Charles S. Johnson (1893–1956), Paul Radin (1883–1959), and their students at Fisk University in Nashville completed two similar projects resulting in book-length collections of ex-slave narratives.[7]

However, a good deal of the credit for the national ex-slave project goes to Virginia's Hampton College, which had already played a significant role in the development of American folklore studies. The Hampton Singers and their best-selling spiritual collections were part of this contribution.[8] Often overlooked, however, is the *Southern Workman and Hampton School Record*. Established in 1872, the *Workman* was partly a newsletter for Hampton faculty, students, and donors, but from the beginning carried general articles on African American and Native American education and history. The "Folk-Lore and Ethnology" column became a regular feature, along with separate articles on Black (mainly slave) folklore. In 1893 the Hampton Folk-Lore Society was founded, often coordinating its activities with the newly established American Folk-Lore Society.

Early in 1936 the Virginia Writers' Project contacted the national office to protest the lack of Black writers locally, proposing as a corrective a special study of the state's African Americans from the colonial era to the 1930s. The idea was actually suggested by an ex-slave educator, attorney, and activist then employed by the WPA, Thomas Calhoun Walker (1862–1953), but the project was eventually supervised by a member of the Hampton faculty, Roscoe E. Lewis (1904–1961). Lewis hatched the idea to include interviews with ex-slaves, and by the time the national project was established on April 1, 1937, Hampton and the Virginia Writers' Project had already amassed numerous narratives, a few of which were eventually sent to the Library of Congress. There were many similar efforts underway around the country, but the Virginia project may have been the major catalyst in the national effort.[9]

The inception, administration, and operations of that national project have been recounted elsewhere.[10] We are concerned mainly with the end products—the narratives themselves—and the individuals with the greatest influence over their content and final form were two true giants of American folklore, John A. Lomax (1867–1948) and Benjamin A. Botkin (1901–1975).

At the time both were actually on the federal payroll as folklorists, and both had the attention and full confidence of FWP director Henry G. Alsberg (1881–1970). As a result, the collection and publication of folklore became major components of the project's mission. John Lomax may have had more field experience with African Americans (including ex-slaves) than any other scholar of the day. He was then fully immersed in his own fieldwork for the Library of Congress's Archive of Folk Song, and his involvement in the slave narratives was apparently somewhat fleeting. Lomax's celebrity and enthusiasm for the project were crucial to winning over key supporters, especially among fellow white Southerners, but his most important contribution was drafting the standard questionnaire sent to all participating states, most of which adopted his guidelines. Botkin, who succeeded Lomax as the FWP's general folklore editor, brought the narratives to a conclusion of sorts, gathering all of the materials submitted to Washington by state offices into a set of bound volumes deposited in the Reading Room of the Library of Congress (1941). He later published an anthology of excerpts, *Lay My Burden Down: A Folk History of Slavery* (1945). For decades these materials and a few items available in state archives provided the only general access to the ex-slave narratives, known almost exclusively to folklorists.

By the late 1960s, however, studies had mounted and other anthologies had appeared. In 1972 Washington University professor George P. Rawick (1929–1990) published his landmark facsimile editions of the national ex-slave narratives collection, *The American Slave*. Immediately thereafter, Rawick and a team of collaborators set out to gather and publish the remaining manuscripts from state archives. These local materials were long assumed mainly to duplicate the national collection, but many states had sent only a fraction of their interviews to Washington. A few had retained hundreds of additional narratives, in some cases far outnumbering those they had forwarded. Texas alone yielded an additional four thousand pages of material (much of which did not duplicate the national collection), and Alabama, Georgia,

Fig. 1.1. "Washington, DC. Mr. Ben Botkin of the Library of Congress at work on his victory garden which is part of the large plot on Fairlawn Avenue, Southeast." June 1943. Photo by Joseph A. Horne. Farm Security Administration/Office of War Information Photograph Collection, Library of Congress, Prints and Photographs Division. B. A. Botkin not long after he wrapped up the ex-slave narratives and moved on to the war effort.

and Mississippi almost as much. Between 1977 and 1979 Rawick and his coeditors published their gatherings from the state archives, more than doubling the texts from the Library Congress, shortly followed by independent editions for Virginia (*Weevils in the Wheat*) and Louisiana (*Mother Wit*) (both states had coordinated with the national project but remained autonomous). There are reports of stray matter here and there, but together these books give a reasonably thorough accounting of the WPA ex-slave narratives as a whole. They are the basis of this study.[11]

The greater availability of the ex-slave narratives was a boon to the academic community, inspiring a raft of excellent scholarship that continues to the present. The results have not been entirely positive, however, because some researchers have inadvisably chosen to treat the narratives as a historical chronicle, a modern ethnography, a systematic social science survey, or the like, with outcomes ranging from the unconvincing to the utterly disastrous. Particularly unfortunately, the appearance of Rawick's volumes coincided with the greater availability of computers and a fad for computer-aided statistical studies, many apparently intent on reaffirming the old data processing adage *garbage in, garbage out*. Responding to such missteps and mischaracterizations, some critics have misguidedly faulted the narratives themselves, as if they were intended for such purposes (they definitely were not).

In fairness, the ex-slave narratives do include much material similar to what one would expect from a history, ethnography, or social science database, but these details are in no way systematic, consistent, or uniform. In many cases they are to some degree unreliable, and in rare instances demonstrably fraudulent. And whatever other information the narratives contain is surrounded by, imbedded in, or expressed through folklore. Given its diffuse organization and execution, the ex-slave narratives project was no single thing; but if only by default, it became a folklore collection. In addition to the musical folklore covered in this study, the narratives include supernatural and historical legends; trickster tales; fairy tales; cantefables; etiological legends; jests and jokes; tall tales; personal experience stories and local hero anecdotes; folk poems, rhymes, and recitations; riddles, proverbs, and figurative speech; naming and nicknaming practices; toasts, greetings, and leave-takings; blessings, charms, and curses; prayers and sermons. There are reams of material on folk religion and ritual; hoodoo, conjure, and witchcraft; folk medicine and healing; conversion experiences; holy visions; divination; prophecies, signs, and omens, as well as detailed descriptions of folk architecture, housewares, furnishings, decor, and costume; folk arts and crafts; traditional foodways; traditional work, hunting, and fishing practices; occupational lore; birthing and child-rearing customs; weather, plant, and animal lore; non-singing games, gambling, and sports; luck customs, local manners, and household superstitions; seasonal festivities, calendar observances, and rites of passage. The list could be extended.

Ex-slaves were regularly asked about historical figures like Jefferson Davis. Very few could give much

factual information, but some narrators had heard the apocryphal story that Davis was dressed as a woman when the Yankees captured him, and nearly two dozen knew the folksong about hanging him from a sour apple tree. "The only thing I ever hearded bout Jeff Davis was a song the folks sang. The words was 'Going to hang Jeff Davis to a sour apple tree'" (Ruben Fox, b. ca. 1853, MS, 778). "Dey set us free an' dey say dat dey hung Jeff Davis on a ole apple tree" (Georgianna Foster, b. 1861, NC, 317).

> I also remembers something 'bout Jeff Davis, and they had a song about him. It goes something like this:
>
> > Hang Jeff Davis on a sour apple tree,
> > Hang Jeff Davis on a sour apple tree,
> > Hang Jeff Davis on a sour apple tree,
> > As we go marching along. (Cynthia Erwing,
> > b. ca. 1851, VA, 139)

> [Jimmie Green declares] de history books is wrong. 'Twas Abe Lincoln an' Jeff Davis dat met under de ole apple tree. Lincoln stuck a shotgun in Jeff Davis' face an' yelled, "Better surrender, else I shoot you an' hang you." Davis tole him, "Yessir, Marse Lincoln, I surrender." An' de soldiers heard it, an' made up a song 'bout it. Ain't you never heard dat song? "Hang Jeff Davis to a sour apple tree." Dat's de song an' dat's what de soldiers yelled at Lincoln to do, but he was too kind. (Jimmie Green, b. 1845, VA, 127, orig. brackets)

This sort of history, usually found in the narratives, is indisputably crucial to comprehending how the ex-slaves understood Jefferson Davis and the Civil War but differs noticeably from the accounts accepted by most academics. Ex-slaves routinely claimed to have written well-known folksongs, or told widely distributed folktales as personal experiences, not because they were shameless liars or complete idiots who could not distinguish their own lives from stories they had heard; rather, in some settings traditional songs and tales may more powerfully and comprehensibly express shared values and experiences than any idiosyncratic personal anecdote ever could. This is especially characteristic of oral societies, but contemporary cosmopolitan populations tell urban legends as true stories for exactly the same reasons.

Shockingly, numerous books and articles based largely or entirely on the ex-slave narratives do not cite a single work on African American folklore, or folklore *period* (other than the narratives themselves, of course), a lapse that invariably shows in their results.[12] One wonders how many researchers would tackle the ex-slave narratives with no previous knowledge of North American slavery or the American Civil War; however, a reasonable familiarity with African American folklore is every bit as crucial not only to identifying and sorting the material but to comprehending it on any basic level. Some knowledge of African and of European, especially British and Irish, folklore is also helpful. The purpose of this book is to provide readers with exactly that service for the musical sections of the WPA ex-slave narratives—a major portion of the collection as a whole—illuminating these accounts within the full scope of African American folk music and folklore but also evaluating them as folklore documentation, explaining both what the narratives have to say about Black folksong and how they say it. This study is not necessarily intended as an anthology, though I have quoted as much as possible to provide something of the experience of actually reading the narratives. It is not precisely an index, but because I have been unable to quote nearly as much as I would have liked, I have sometimes resorted to that format for complete coverage. There is, of course, no substitute for digesting the narratives in their entirety, but that is a massive undertaking that may not be in all readers' plans or possibilities. Nor will all readers have the backgrounds in African American folklore needed to facilitate that endeavor. For those persons mainly interested in the music and song, hopefully this book will be of some value as a qualified substitute.

Much to the dismay of professional writers and their guilds, Henry Alsberg upheld the official policy that the Writers' Project was intended not to support authorial excellence, literary genius, or established professionals but to provide relief for any and all writers (including aspiring writers) who could meet the WPA means test, being legally classified as paupers. In response to continued criticism, Alsberg produced a survey demonstrating that the majority of program employees were authors, journalists, academics, and educators with some work experience in research, writing, and editing. Others were stenographers, file clerks, government workers, and so forth. Many participants were, Alsberg admitted, merely "writers of promise," while some simply met the means test. The project did involve nationally recognized figures, as well as future luminaries like Ralph Ellison (1913–1994) and Saul Bellow (1915–2005), but its writers were a wild mix (three convicted forgers managed to get on the payroll).[13] For the ex-slaves project, the names of most fieldworkers, writers, and editors are included with their interviews, and there is background information available for a few. Overall, however, we can only assume that most of the women and men who produced the ex-slave narratives fit the project's diverse profile, borne out by the diversity of their work.

Precisely how much training and instruction these workers received is unclear, but anecdotally, it may have been little to none. The primary instrument appears to have been a set of instructions and sample questionnaire drafted by John Lomax and sent to all participating states, almost all of which adopted it (see chapter appendix A). Copies of this item (sometimes revised for local purposes) also survived in state files, but even lacking that corroboration, a large cross-section of interviews from all participating regions indicate that interviewers were following the Lomax questionnaire or another closely based on it. If this was the interviewers' only orientation, it was not altogether bad. Granted, the leading questions bear the unmistakable imprint of Lomax's own fieldwork, knowledge, and opinions, but then at that time no one in the world knew this material better, or had more experience collecting it.

Fig. 1.2. Aunt Harriet McClintock, dancing and singing "Shing, Shing" for John A. Lomax at a crossroads near Sumterville, AL, October 1941. Lomax Collection, Library of Congress, Prints and Photographs Division. "Marse John used to take me on his knee and sing, 'Here is de hammer, Shing, ding. Gimme de Hammer, shing ding'" (Emma Blalock, b. ca. 1850, NC, 104). This photo was taken by Lomax's wife, Ruby T. Lomax, just after the ex-slave narratives project had ended, on one of their own collecting trips. The recording machine is barely visible in the car's trunk, lower right. Some of McClintock's recorded performances (but not this item) are available on *Lullabies to Blues*; and *Field Recordings, Volume 4*, Document CD 5578.

John Avery Lomax was born in Holmes County, Mississippi, on September 23, 1867, barely two years past the close of the Civil War. In 1869 the family traveled by ox cart to Bosque County, Texas, where his father set to raising cattle and cotton. There the young Lomax became interested in the songs of the local cowhands, but also befriended a former slave who sometimes odd-jobbed on their farm, Nat Blythe. Lomax taught Blythe to read and write, and Blythe taught Lomax to sing slave songs, pat juba, and dance. Blythe remained on the plantation as a tenant until he was twenty-one, then collected his wages and disappeared. Lomax shortly heard the rumor that he had been murdered for his savings, but decades later wrote "as I traveled up and down the South, these recent years, I find myself always looking for Nat, the dear friend and companion of long ago. I loved him as I have loved few people."[14]

Lomax's interest in Black music and song was truly a lifelong affair, but his middle years were largely occupied earning a living in university administration and banking. In 1933, however, he began his association with the Library of Congress and its Archive of American Folk Song, and with that launched his epochal field recording trips through the South, focusing on Black folksong. Lomax was particularly intent on recovering any vestiges of slave music and concentrated on the likeliest sources, obviously including ex-slaves and older performers but also Southern prison farms, where he believed slave traditions might still survive.[15] He was in the midst of this work when he assumed his duties with the FWP and the task of designing and directing the ex-slaves narratives project.

Lomax's interview guidelines were self-evidently an outgrowth of his own work and research interests, but that hardly seems too great a defect, and he tempered his personal agenda with some other excellent general advice to fieldworkers:

> The specific questions suggested to be asked of the slaves should be only a basis, a beginning. The talk should run to all subjects, and the interviewer should take care to seize upon the information already given, and stories already told, and from them derive other questions. . . . The interviewer should attempt to weave the following questions naturally into the conversation, in simple language. Many of the interviews show that the workers have simply sprung routine questions out of context, and received routine answers. . . . It will not be necessary, indeed it will probably be a mistake, to ask every person all of the questions. . . . A second visit, a few days after the first one, is important, so that the worker may gather all the worthwhile recollections that the first talk has aroused.

There is no mistaking, however, that Lomax's questionnaire was designed by someone primarily interested in collecting African American *folklore*—and especially African American *folk music* and *song*—nor is there any doubt that his directions to a great extent determined the ex-slave narratives' final form as a folklore collection. A few preliminary questions deal matter-of-factly with the interview subjects' personal information or the material conditions and historical circumstances of their lives, but most of the remainder ask about songs of the period, weddings, spirituals, baptizings and baptizing songs, funerals and funeral songs, weeknight recreations, Saturday afternoons, Saturday nights, Sundays, Christmas morning, New Year's Day, other holidays, cornshucking, cotton picking, dances, observances of slave and slaveholder marriages and deaths, children's games, play songs, and ring games, riddles, charms, stories about "Raw Head and Bloody Bones" or other "hants" or ghosts, stories about animals, lullabyes, work songs, plantation hollers, funny stories, herbal medicine and medicinal charms, voodoo (hoodoo), churches, and religion.

Even questions on topics not necessarily connected to folklore are phrased in a way almost certain to elicit oral traditions. "How and for what causes were the slaves punished? Tell what you saw. Tell some of the stories you heard." "What did you hear about patrollers? How did slaves carry news from one plantation to another? Did you hear of trouble between blacks and whites?" The ex-slave narratives are the greatest source by far on plantation signal horns, which were used to wake slaves, direct them in the fields, and otherwise communicate long-distance, but which were also played musically, a characteristic of signal horns throughout Africa and the Black diaspora. I have no doubt that this wealth of information results mainly from Lomax's suggested question "How and at what time did the overseer wake up the slaves?"

Average interviewers tended to ignore Lomax's advice not to be bound by his recommendations, sticking fairly close to his instructions, but often with positive results, especially where collecting folklore was concerned. Others, however, followed Lomax's suggestions or their own initiatives, repeatedly visiting ex-slaves and allowing them to talk freely; a few narrators were interviewed on three or more occasions by two or more fieldworkers. Frequently, writers had their own interviewing experience, as well as some familiarity with ex-slaves and their traditions, and the better interviewers (and they were numerous)

seem to have been comfortable relying on their own knowledge and judgment or adapting as interactions unfolded. In those instances, fieldworkers typically gathered a great deal of folklore as well; in fact, interviews by fieldworkers who definitely did not follow Lomax's guidelines are full of the same folklore as those who did. So are interviews with ex-slaves conducted by other organizations and individuals, and all corroborating sources, most crucially including nineteenth-century publications.

Moreover, the WPA narratives and all cognate sources all consistently feature material not on Lomax's list. Somewhat surprisingly, Lomax's instructions contain no questions about the slaves' musical instruments and instrumental music. These topics especially fascinated nineteenth-century observers, and WPA informants provided enough information to fill a major portion of this study. John Lomax may have exerted some undue influence over the ex-slave narratives (that would have been his style), but enough interviewers were open-minded and informed, and enough ex-slaves outgoing and forthcoming to counter that, and in the balance I suspect Lomax's instructions were mainly a great aid to inexperienced fieldworkers, realistically preparing them for what they could expect to hear from ex-slaves, which was the African American folklore Lomax had devoted his life to collecting.

Whether WPA workers actually thought of themselves as *folklorists*, or were guided by some deeper theoretical perspective on *folklore*, is uncertain but not wholly irrelevant. At this time, professional, academically trained folklorists did not yet exist, current standards and practices being even further beyond the horizon. Folklore researchers with academic credentials or affiliations held them in other disciplines (English, music, anthropology, sociology, history). Amateur enthusiasts from all walks of life made up much of the field. The term *folklore* was definitely part of the Depression-era American vernacular, thanks largely to promotion by government agencies like the WPA and FWP, and as a whole the ex-slave project's personnel must have known they were collecting folklore if only because they were constantly told so.

Numerous individuals then at the field's forefront were in some way involved or associated with the project, and while most fieldworkers were in remote outposts having no direct contact with such persons, *folklore* usually appeared somewhere in official communications; standardized interview headings typically included the term; fieldworkers used it in their own notes and discussions.[16]

FOLKLORE SUBJECTS: Songs of Pre-War Days

> You may call me Raggedy Pat,
> 'Cause I wear this raggedy hat,
> And you may think I'm workin'
> But I ain't.

> I used to hear my uncle sing that. That's all the words I can remember. (Ira Foster, b. ca. 1862, AR, 335, int. Bernice Bowden)[17]

Admittedly, many transcripts labeled *folklore* contain little or no folklore per se, being instead fairly matter-of-fact biographies or day-to-day accounts. Some informants flatly stated that they knew no songs, stories, ring games, and so on, and some interviewers showed no interest in these areas. Nevertheless, most ex-slaves could not recall their lives without also recalling the oral traditions that had defined their intellectual, personal, and social worlds, and most interviewers were especially open to these materials, which they generally seem to have recognized as folklore. A few fieldworkers were familiar with folklore publications.[18] Whether some sense of the emerging profession and scholarly field of folklore had any influence on how interviewers conducted their fieldwork or what they collected remains somewhat speculative, but this could be another factor explaining the preponderance of folklore in the ex-slave narratives.

If there were official policies, procedures, or recommendations for locating ex-slaves, they do not seem to have survived. State and local offices did sometimes provide interviewers with lists of names, but how they compiled them is unclear. Comments in manuscripts indicate that fieldworkers relied heavily on personal referrals, tips, and word of mouth; former slaves usually knew any other former slaves living nearby, and these networks were especially important. Ex-slaves tended to be well-known in their communities generally, and many would not have been hard to find. Some fieldworkers simply canvassed Black neighborhoods. Fred Dibble encountered Zeno John by chance on the streets of Beaumont; John appeared to be the right age to have been a slave, which he confirmed, so Dibble interviewed him on the spot (Zeno John, b. ca. 1861, LA, 1948–51).

Correspondence and memos in national and state archives contain a few details about how interviews were conducted, transcribed, revised, and edited, but the definitive documents are the texts themselves, many of which remain in various states of rough draft or revision, directly revealing the writing and editing process; moreover, virtually all of the narratives are identified with specific fieldworkers, many also listing writers or editors. A few of these individuals produced only one or two items, but the majority contributed numerous narratives, many of them several dozen. It is thus possible to get to know the individual fieldworkers, writers, and editors, or at least their interviewing and writing styles, their vices and virtues, and relative reliability. (All identifiable fieldworkers, writers, and editors are listed and credited for their interviews in the Narrators Index.)

With only the rarest exceptions, the narratives were set down in writing. We again have only anecdotal information, but some transcripts state that the interviews were reconstructed after the fact from the interviewers' memories. FWP employees often had actual job experience interviewing and transcribing, and there are other reports of writers taking narratives down shorthand. Some fieldworkers worked in teams, another accepted and effective method of producing complete and accurate written transcriptions. A handful of the Virginia interviews were recorded on aluminum discs, then later transcribed.[19] Scattered materials in state files occasionally contain other sorts of notes or outlines, but in truth it is not entirely clear how most narratives were collected and transcribed.

That the ex-slave narratives were transcribed rather than recorded is a definite drawback where music and song and especially musical performances are concerned. True, many ex-slaves were by their own admission well beyond their primes as performers. "Now yous wants me to sing. I's jus' can't does it 'cause I's lost my teeth an' my voice am raspin'. Sho, I's will name some. Dere was sich as: / In de new Jeru-sa-lem. / In de yeah ob de jube-lee" (Lewis Jones, b. 1851, TX, 2111). "All my old favorite songs us slaves use to sing, I can't separate 'em anymore. I try to think of 'em, so I can sing 'em but I jest find myself mixin' 'em up, and can't tell one from the other" (Mintie Gilbert Wood, b. 1847, TN, 377). Many informants refused to do more than name titles, while song texts that interviewers did gather were often recited rather than sung, either because narrators declined to sing, or to aid the transcribers (common with this kind of collecting). The narratives are rife with information about slave instrumental traditions and instrumentalists, but only a handful of ex-slaves still possessed and played musical instruments. "I was a great hand at fiddlin'. Got one in there now that is 107-year old, but I haven't played for years. Since I broke my shoulder bone, I can't handle the bow" (Charles H. Anderson, b. 1845, VA, 3). Still, writers did report that many ex-slaves remained excellent or affecting performers, and it is unfortunate they were not recorded. There are, however, recordings of ex-slaves from other sources, and many times more of younger generations of Blacks giving performances that may provide some idea of how slave music sounded. I have cited these whenever relevant throughout this book.

Probably the majority of interviews are credited only to the fieldworkers, but others also bear the names of writers, editors, supervisors, and others. In some cases these may have been standard letterheads listing perfunctory titles, but persons other than fieldworkers definitely did sometimes rewrite, revise, or otherwise alter transcripts. Even when the final texts were produced by the interviewers alone (and this

Fig. 1.3. Lewis Jones, ex-slave, July 30, 1937, Fort Worth, TX. Portraits of African American ex-slaves from the US Works Progress Adminstration, Federal Writers' Project slave narratives collection, Library of Congress.

appears to have been most common), they usually reshaped their field material to some extent. Some states or state offices had standard formats followed by all writers. In other cases individuals were apparently free to adopt their own plans. Thus some narratives suggest raw interview transcripts presented as they transpired. Other writers framed their interviews with literary vignettes establishing setting, character, backstory, and so forth. Some accounts are written in the third person, perhaps with quotations from the ex-slaves interspersed, perhaps not. Successive interviews with the same subject may be presented individually or combined into a single narrative. Occasionally interviews with different informants were combined or compiled. Besides interviews with ex-slaves, the national collection but especially the state files included personal manuscripts, newspaper clippings, diaries, letters, scrapbook materials, texts copied from secondary sources, and other outside documents.

On transcripts writers constantly insist that they are following official injunctions to preserve the ex-slaves' exact words. "The foregoing is copied verbatim from conversation with Tinie Force, and Elvira Lewis, LaCenter, Ky" (Tinie Force and Elvira Lewis, b. unk., KY, 115–16, int. J. R. Wilkerson). "As far as possible the stories are given in her exact words" (Amanda Styles, b. ca. 1856, GA, 343, int. A. M. Whitley). "Note: In this interview this man used correct English most of the time and the interview is given in his own words. Lapses into dialect will be noticed" (Austin Pen Parnell, b. 1865, MS, child of ex-slaves, 272, int. Samuel S. Taylor). Lomax's instructions and other correspondence always insisted on the point, and writers and editors clearly took the issue seriously and kept it constantly in mind. Having worked for over three decades with these materials, I have personally come to the conclusion that the majority of narratives are as reliable as any newspaper article based on the written notes of a responsible journalist (which many fieldworkers apparently were). As anyone who has been misquoted in the paper can testify, that is not necessarily a categorical endorsement; but allowing for inevitable misquotes and mistakes, I do believe that most of the narratives meet a journalistic standard of accuracy.

I also believe that almost all of the remaining interviews are relatively reliable, but many writers and editors do seem to have taken *exact words* to mean *the gist* rather than *word for word*, and there are signs of rewriting and revision everywhere. Innumerable typescripts bear handwritten changes and corrections of the sort that were presumably incorporated into other typed copies. Some of these are minor corrections or stylistic adjustments, but others are substantial. Many revisions are actually notated on the manuscripts. The narrative of Sylvia Cannon is credited as a "Personal interview by H. Grady Davis and Mrs. Lucile Young, and written up in question and answer form. Rewritten in story form by Annie Ruth Davis" (Sylvia Cannon, b. ca. 1857, SC, 194). The Mississippi state copy of James Singleton's narrative (S1 7 *MS*: 125–27) bears the note "2nd rework—to be reworked again," then later "Note: This autobiography is recopied from Field Copy practically as it was, except for slightly more uniform. No sentences

or phraseology has been changed. B. Y." (James Singleton, b. 1856, MS, 1957, 1960). The identity of "B. Y." is unknown, but these are not the initials of the interviewer, Iris England. The final copy of Singleton's interview in the Library of Congress is virtually identical, however, indicating any further "reworking" was minimal. The transcript of Sylvia Cannon's narrative appears to have undergone significant rearrangements, but maybe not; James Singleton's original interview transcript may have just been retyped, reformatted, or conformed to style, but who knows. There are hundreds of circumstances like these throughout the narratives.

The differences between drafts of the same narratives found both in the Library of Congress and in state archives are often negligible but other times quite significant. Sometimes there are multiple contrasting versions of the same interview just in the state archives. As a general rule, drafts in the state archives are longer (and sometimes substantially longer) than those in the Library of Congress, indicating many narratives were condensed before being sent to Washington.

We sho had some good dances in my young days when I wah spry. We uster cut all kind o' steps. Dey wah de cotillion, de waltz and de shotty (schottische) and all de rest o' de dances of dat time. De shotty sho a pretty dance an' such a good dance. My preacher uster whup me did he hear I go to dances and he would put me out from de church, too. I wah a good dancer—a right smart dancin' gal. I sho dance a might fo' de white folks. I wah little an' sprite and all dem young bucks want to dance wif me.

Cinto don' know how to do no step, but he could sho nuff fiddle. He play fo' all de dancin'. We uster sing all dem ol' songs and I sho wah a good singer. We uster sing "Colorado." I think it wah name after dat ol' ribber which go right off in dat direction. Dat "Colorado" wah one of de ol' songs but I done forgit how it go. Den dey wah a ol' song which come back to me, "High heel shoes an' Cal'co Stockings." It go sometin' like dis:

Fare you well Miss Nancy Hawkins,
High-heel shoes and cal'co stockings.

I forgits de rest of dat song but it sho wah pretty. (Lucy Lewis, b. ca. 1830, TX, 2363–64, Texas state archive version)

We sho had some good dances in my young days, when I was spry. We used to cut all kind of steps, de cotillion and de waltz and de shotty (schottische) and all de rest de dances of dat time. My preacher used to whup me did he hear I go to dances, but I was a right smart dancin' gal. I was little and sprite and all dem young bucks want to dance with me.

Cinto didn't know how to do no step, but he could fiddle. Dere was a old song which come back to me, "High heels and Calico Stockings."

Fare you well, Miss Nancy Hawkins,
High heel shoes and calico stockin's. (Lucy Lewis, b. ca. 1830, TX, 15, Library of Congress version)

The foregoing example is fairly typical: the Library of Congress version does not necessarily misrepresent the state text, but much has obviously been altered or lost.

The written format comes with other baggage. Almost all of the narratives were written in dialect, in many cases highly exaggerated. This is an inescapable fact not just of the WPA ex-slave narratives but of virtually all published African American folklore collections of this and earlier periods, though the language of white Southerners (and of other ethnic and regional groups) was represented the same way. The device was common to authors, journalists, and academics, including African American authors, journalists, and academics. There is some condescension in a few of these cases, but most of this work bears out the authors' contentions that they were merely attempting to convey the sounds and rhythms of African American vernacular speech. All that said, this is one area where the inexperience and amateur standing of many WPA fieldworkers, writers, and editors can be especially glaring. Early submissions were sometimes so outrageous that Lomax, Botkin, and other national and state officials tried to rein in dialect, not by eliminating but by minimizing and standardizing it. They may have had some limited success, since a great many of the narratives are written with little or no dialect. In others it is used unobtrusively or at least not too distractingly, but in a fair number of transcripts the gimmick does become quite annoying or even disruptive. A few writers seem to have conceived Black phonetics as a variety of orthographic gibberish. Readers will have ample opportunities to judge all of these tendencies for themselves.

Other textual issues are more practically pressing. Many writers repeated examples or descriptions in different interviews, it seems because they came across something too good to use just once. Manuscripts confirm that editors also moved passages between narratives. Almost all such material appears to be authentic, and the original sources are sometimes obvious, but many items attributed to two or more ex-slaves can be traced no further. More problematic, a few writers developed boilerplate styles, repeating rote passages in many, most, or all of the narratives they authored. This material may also be rooted in actual interviews, but it is obviously difficult to credit to any great degree. At the far end of the bad behavior scale, the narratives are full of outright plagiarisms. Probably most common—or at least most conspicuous—are song texts that interviewers, writers, or editors incontrovertibly copied from published collections, but there are throughout many sections of text borrowed or paraphrased from secondary sources.[20] More difficult to prove but nonetheless self-evident in some cases, many authors embellished their texts or simply fabricated material. This chapter's appendix B lists nearly fifty plagiarized song texts I have identified in the narratives, and the following chapters are full of other specific illustrations of all the foregoing. Fortunately, there is such a surplus of genuine material that these issues are for the most part only a sideshow, but they must occasionally be confronted and always borne in mind.

Where folklore specifically is concerned, however, the field's basic comparative methodology is singularly effective as a system of checks and balances for authenticating most material, while also identifying the occasionally suspicious and spurious.[21] On that score, a detailed comparison of the folk music materials in the ex-slave narratives with the storehouse of other evidence from the colonial era to World War II—the thrust of the study that follows—confirms that this is a first-rate collection accurately noted from actual tradition bearers. Folklore moreover provides an excellent general litmus: interviews containing plagiarized song texts or other folk forgeries invariably turn out to be problematic in other respects, while narratives in which the folklore checks out are usually fine overall.

I must also stress that the sort of authorial or editorial malpractice described above was a very rare exception, and that these aberrations are fairly easy (if incredibly tedious) to identify, especially since they are associated with a limited number of writers whose names thereby become instant red flags. (I would personally advise treating any narratives produced by Texas fieldworkers Effie Cowan or Ada Davis as outright forgeries unless proven otherwise; checking always confirms that their materials are at least partly bogus.) Even these problematic interviews frequently appear to contain genuine field materials (though they hardly inspire confidence). And these abuses really are the exceptions. On the whole, the final form of the WPA ex-slave narratives testifies only to the hard work, dedication, and sincere interest of those involved. In the Depression-era, Jim Crow South, with a minimum of training and virtually no administrative or logistical support, for starvation wages, without modern communications and transportation, at the very last possible moment, these women and men miraculously assembled the single greatest body of information by far on North American slaves. That they were employed by the FWP at all meant they were officially destitute and dealing with who knows what else in their personal lives, but they alone deserve credit for this amazing achievement. As a group, they are to be greatly admired and respected.

We might also be somewhat forgiving of a few writers' faults and failings when they were conceivably following the best examples available to them, however clumsily. There are in fact no flaws in the ex-slave narratives that do not occur in the work of some leading folklorists of the period. Editorial embellishments, alterations, or additions are common in early publications, though they can usually be identified and mitigated as well. Borrowing without attribution was not always the offense it is today, even in the top echelons. John Lomax in particular has frequently been criticized for his cavalier approach to editing and publishing his field materials. Among other things, Lomax was one of several early folklorists championing *composite texts*, that is, texts created by combining elements taken from different versions of a song, whether from Lomax's own collecting, from other published texts, or in some cases from Lomax's own imagination. These composite texts are usually acknowledged and the borrowings attributed, at least in early editions of Lomax's books, but not always clearly, accurately, or completely, and as items were reprinted the confusions multiplied, requiring constant vigilance from any serious researcher. No one working with African American folk music and song can afford to ignore John Lomax's immeasurable contributions; no one working with Lomax's indispensable materials can afford to ignore these issues.[22] The WPA ex-slave narratives are no different.

Then too, other works central to our enterprise obviously require the same high level of critical caution. Besides the narratives themselves, this study's most important and most numerous references are published nineteenth-century accounts of Black music and song, providing essential context and corroboration, but also firm dates in the 1800s.[23] To say that few nineteenth-century writings about slavery were impartial or objective requires no further argument, and even treatments of music and song reflect partisan agendas. Slavery's defenders, that is, portrayed slave music as proof positive of slaves' contentment and happiness, abolitionists as complete confirmation of their anguish and sorrow—neither being entirely accurate. Missionaries and clergy often denigrated slave music, song, and dance as the absolute embodiments of their moral degradation and spiritual thirst. Somewhat ironically, slave memoirs were frequently written to document their authors' rise above the condition of slavery, typically through the church or education, and these writers often expressed the same disapproval. Virtually all other period observers—and fortunately there were many—reveal similar bias or special pleading to some degree. Yet by closely comparing these sources to one another, and to the narratives and other relevant materials, it is possible to identify and eliminate, or at least to dim these various filters.

Coming to this clearer understanding also requires asking how the ex-slaves understood the WPA, its field operatives, and their purpose. As the discipline of folklore developed in the capitalist, industrialized West, the norm has always been (and remains) that fieldworkers are distinguished from their subjects by class, education, social standing, but likely also by race, ethnicity, language, religion, residence, or other hierarchical hallmarks, folklorists overall representing the dominant or favored groups. Such factors influence any personal interaction, but especially in situations where strangers are demanding personal information. In the present case, the contrast in backgrounds and social standings of interviewers and interviewees was stark to say the least. The program employed only a handful of Black fieldworkers, all others being white, and this circumstance clearly affected what many ex-slaves said and how they said it. Whether Black interviewers achieved substantially different results is difficult to answer partly because so few participated. Some ex-slaves may have been more comfortable discussing certain topics with other Blacks, and African American fieldworkers are responsible for many of the best narratives; during the writing of this book, Samuel S. Taylor, a Black social worker from Little Rock employed by the Arkansas project, has become a personal hero of mine. On the other hand, Black fieldworkers were separated from their subjects by generations but usually also by education, class, social

connections, and other factors sometimes referenced in interviews, and they encountered their share of reticence and suspicion, while many ex-slaves had no reservations about discussing any and all subjects with whites.

In this and other matters the ex-slaves were always individuals, but overall the slave population represented in the narratives is remarkably homogeneous, especially considering the size of the sample and the variety of North American slavery. Fieldworkers did manage to include members of some subgroups (Gulf Coast Creoles, Gullahs, Afro-Cherokees), also locating many unique or unusual individuals (including a handful of enslaved whites and Native Americans). While there are few interviews with industrial slaves (excepting plantation factories), urban slaves from most major Southern cities are represented, and the Louisiana project focused almost entirely on the New Orleans area. Nonetheless, the overwhelming majority of ex-slaves interviewed by the WPA had lived under nearly identical conditions on rural plantations or farms devoted to the South's cash crops: cotton, tobacco, sugar cane, and rice.

Critics have sometimes charged that a high proportion of the ex-slaves had been freed as small children or infants and could not possibly remember slavery. This is not only factually wrong, but misleading on other counts. Actually, the largest group of narrators was born in the 1850s, but almost as many in the 1840s, significant numbers in the 1830s, and a few in the 1820s. Considering that slaves were routinely assigned adult labor as young as eight, became parents in their teens, and died before middle age, it is an established fact that most narrators had lived to some version of adulthood under slavery. Fieldworkers did contact many persons born in the 1860s or even 1870s, but this is hardly a liability; the stories of the last Americans born into slavery, or the first African Americans born after freedom, are of obvious interest. Indisputably, too, many of the stories in the narratives concern the postbellum period, but the project was always intended to document the life histories of former slaves, not the history of slavery, and Lomax and other supervisors repeatedly urged interviewers to gather more material about ex-slaves' lives after freedom.

However, it is also wrong to assume that North American slavery ended with the Emancipation Proclamation (January 1, 1863), or the surrender of the Army of Northern Virginia at Appomattox (April 19, 1865), or the arrival of Federal troops in Galveston (June 19, 1865, known as Juneteenth), or on any other single date. "Sho' we hear dat all Negroes am free in 1863, but dat rumor not affect us. We work on, 'til Sherman come and burn and slash his way through de state in de spring of 1865" (Alfred Sligh, b. 1837, SC, 92). In many places across the South, slavery outlasted these signposts by decades. Scores of ex-slaves had been forcibly held by their former slaveholders for various terms after the war. "Marster Ingram had 350 slaves when de war wuz over but he didn't turn us loose till a year after surrender" (Wash Ingram, b. ca. 1844, VA, 1855). "I did not know I was free until five years after the war" (Reverend Squire Dowd, b. 1855, NC, 266). "That's all I've ever known—work. I never got a penny. My master kept me and my sister Mary twenty-two long years after we were supposed to be free. . . . My master wouldn't let the poor white neighbors—no one—tell us we was free" (Hannah Davidson, b. 1852, KY, 26, 27). "Old Marster never tol' any of us when we was freed. Slaves frum 'joinin' plantation jus' tol' us, an' old Marse Bill jus' kep' us dere wurkin' fur him. One night my mammy an' we chilluns slipped off way in de night an' run away" (Laura Montgomery, b. 1850, MS, 1556).

Hundreds of ex-slaves did recall being liberated by Union troops or the government officials who circulated in the months after surrender, but many also remembered having no choice but to stay on as tenants or sharecroppers. "I warn't but 6 years old when us was made free. Tellin' de slaves dey wuz free didn't make much diff'unce on our place, for most of 'em stayed right on dar and wukked wid Old Marster jus' lak dey allus done" (Benny Dillard, b. ca. 1858, GA, 288). In this predicament, people understandably saw Emancipation as little but empty promises and a backhanded slap. "Master worked them on several months after the

man was there [and 'read a paper to the slaves telling them they was free']. Master said we was going to get 20 acres of land and a mule but we didn't get it" (Susan Merritt, b. 1851, TX, 2643).

Den one day in May 'bout ten o'clock in de mornin' he blow'd his horn er long time, an' de slaves cum frum de fiel' on hosses an' mules; he made all uf us stand right in frunt uf de kitchen door an' den he tole us we wus all freed, an' he wus going ter "contract" wid 'em. I ast mammy "What is freed?" and mammy sed "iffen I give yer a back han' slap, yer brat, I'll teach yer whut 'freed' is." (Ann Drake, b. 1855, MS, 648)

Well into the late 1800s, many former slaves, their children, and grandchildren subsisted under conditions virtually unchanged by the war or so-called freedom. WPA narrator J. F. Boone was born December 8, 1872, in Woodruff County, Arkansas, on the plantation where his parents had been slaves. Boone still called the former slaveholder *master* and referred to himself and his fellow tenants as *slaves*. In all other respects, the operation he described resembled an antebellum plantation (J. F. Boone, b. 1872, child of ex-slaves, AR, 210–13). His case was not atypical.

As of the late 1930s, several narrators insisted that American slavery still existed. "Den der was some others dat kept der slaves in bondage after de war, just like before de war and de slaves, never know till der dying day dat dey was free folks. Far as dat goes, down dere just below Sunflower, Mississippi, and lots of other countryside places in de deep South, dey got slavery right now" (James Wilson, b. 1850, MO, 372).

There is plenty of Niggers in Louisiana that is still slaves. A spell back I made a trip where I was raised to see my ole Mistress 'fore she died, and there was Niggers in twelve or fourteen miles of that place that didn't know they is free. There's plenty Niggers round Marshall that is same as slaves. They is worked for white fo'ks twenty and twenty-five years and ain't drawed 5¢, jest some old clothes and something to eat. That's the way we was in slavery. (Willis Winn, b. 1822, LA, TX, 4256)

De nigger in de South is jest as much a slave as ever. De nigger now is a better slave den when dey owned him, 'cause he has his own expenses to bear. If you works a horse an' doan have him ter feed, you is better off, dan if you had ter feed and care fer him. Dat is de way dat thing is now. (Parker Pool, b. 1851, NC, 190–91)

In reality, the last slave plantations disappeared only with the aging, dispersal, and deaths of slaves, slaveholders, and their immediate descendants, though across the South, sharecropping and prison farms preserved much of the old system well past the Second World War. Throughout this study, I do distinguish between the *antebellum* and *postwar periods, before* and *after freedom,* and so forth, but I have not been too hard and fast about calendar dates. Generally, I have adopted the ex-slaves' view that plantation slavery existed as long as slaves remained on plantations (and some WPA narrators were interviewed on the plantations where they had been born). Purely from common sense, wherever and whenever the conditions of slavery persisted (even decades after the war), I have treated them as slavery.

While most narrators came from similar backgrounds, their experiences under slavery were often radically different, their present circumstances quite disparate, and these variables definitely affected interviews. A goodly number had been house servants who had enjoyed relatively privileged positions and who had remained in those situations or were otherwise still being supported by whites. Such individuals tended to be especially well-known and well-liked by whites generally, one common method of locating interview subjects. As that also suggests, interviewers sometimes came from the local gentry, meaning they were possibly descendants of slaveholders, in some cases even their informants' former slaveholders. Mississippi ex-slave Elsie Posey described the wartime muster of the Covington County Confederate Vol-unteers to interviewer Ruby Huff: "A Mr. Zeb Patrick was placed head as drummer, a Mr. Thomas Huff (old Elsie informed me that Mr. Huff was my husband's father) was placed on a nearby stand to fiddle and a Mr. Bill Cranford was assigned to play the flute" (Elsie Posey, b. ca. 1840, MS, 1737–38, orig. parentheses). Obviously Elsie Posey was well aware that she was talking to a member-by-marriage of a prominent former slaveholding family who had fought to preserve the institution, and that awareness underpins her entire interview. Elsie Posey's was not an unusual case, and such individuals typically had nothing but good (or at least rarely anything bad) to say about slavery and slaveholders.

By contrast, countless ex-slaves were in truly dire circumstances when interviewers found them, pitifully cadging nickels and dimes, anxious to say anything to ingratiate themselves to fieldworkers. Andrew Boone was living in an abandoned tobacco shed on Harris Farm, Wake County, North Carolina, explaining to fieldworker T. Pat Matthews:

I been living in dese backer barns fifteen years. I built this little shelter to cook under. Dey cut me off the WPA cause dey said I wus too ole to work. Dey tole us ole folks we need not put down our walkin' sticks to git work cause dey jes' won't goin' to put us on.

Well, I had some tomatoes cooked widout any grease for my breakfast. I had a loaf of bread yesterday, but I et it. I ain't got any check from the ole age pension an' I have nothin' to eat an' I am hongry. I jes' looks to God. I set down by de road thinkin' bout how to turn an' what to do to git a meal, when you cum along. I thanks you fer dis dime. I guess God made you give it to me. (Andrew Boone, b. 1857, NC, 131)

On the verge of starvation in the late Depression, these heartrending charity cases were understandably nostalgic for slavery's forced dependency; understandably too, this may not be an entirely accurate gauge of their true experiences under, or attitudes toward

Fig. 1.4. "Old Aunt Julia Ann Jackson, age 102 and the corn crib where she lives. She uses the large, battered tin can for her stove and does her cooking on it. Aunt Julia Ann is an ex-slave and was a grown woman when the Civil 'Wah broke out.'" Sims Studio, El Dorado, AR, 1937–38. Portraits of African American ex-slaves from the US Works Progress Administration, Federal Writers' Project slave narratives collection, Library of Congress.

Fig. 1.5. Andrew Goodman, ex-slave, Dallas, TX, December 1, 1937. Portraits of African American ex-slaves from the US Works Progress Administration, Federal Writers' Project slave narratives collection, Library of Congress.

slavery. "Fer a long time de relief gib me a quart ob milk a day, but now all I has ez w'at mah sistah Harriett gibs me. She ain' got much wuk en sum days we don' hab much ter eat. Ef mah Missis wuz livin' I wouldn' go hongry" (Cecelia Chappel, b. ca. 1835, TN, 8). "Slav'ry times wus not so bad fer some of us who had good masters. Some of us old ones would not min' having somebody to look after us dese days" (James Augustus Holmes, b. 1843, GA, 1047). "I had two wives and seven chilluns but all my folks dies on me and it is pretty rough on a old man like me. My white folks is all dead too or I wouldn't be 'lowed to go hungry and cold like I do or have to pay rent" (Andrew Goodman, b. 1840, AL, 1529).

Suddenly confronted by WPA interviewers, some ex-slaves naturally assumed people from the government must be relief workers, spies, or enforcers, creating distrust or misunderstanding. When Georgia fieldworker Sadie Hornsby asked Ed McCree and his wife Nettie how many children they had, "Ed ignored the question . . . and Nettie made no attempt to take further part in the conversation. There is a deep seated idea prevalent among old people of this type that if the 'giver'ment folks' learn that they have able bodied children, their pensions and relief allowances will be discontinued" (Ed McCree, b. 1861, GA, 65). Alec Bostwick abruptly ended his interview when he realized the unidentified interviewer was not a relief worker.

"In conclusion Alec said: 'I don't want to talk no more. I'se disappointed, I thought sho' you wuz one of dem pension ladies what come for to fetch me some money. I sho' wish dey would come. Goodbye Miss.' Then he hobbled into the house" (Alec Bostwick, b. ca. 1861, GA, 112).

In numerous instances, ex-slaves were self-evidently uncomfortable discussing topics like the mistreatment, torture, murder, and rape of slaves. Many interviewers avoided sensitive subjects altogether, and some writers and editors actually censored or suppressed accounts that were collected. In a note to Lula Cottonham Walker's description of slaves being beaten for holding secret prayer meetings, an unidentified editor ordered "omit account of whipping for 'praying and singing'—preposterous!" Nothing from Walker's narrative was sent to the national archives, but the complete text was retained in state files, and the forbidden passage is quoted in full later in this study (Lula Cottonham Walker, b. 1824, AL, 432–33). The flogging of slaves for holding secret religious services, or clandestine meetings for any purpose, is exhaustively documented in scores of credible sources.

Regrettably, this is not the only instance where the racial insensitivities, biases, or stereotypes of field-workers, writers, and editors intruded on the ex-slave narratives. There are occasional dead giveaways like the foregoing, but more often we must ferret out what we can about racial attitudes from the transcripts, especially given the dearth of specific information on project personnel. We do know that employees were not only by and large white, but by and large white Southerners, which obviously raises certain assumptions. Yet as one might also assume from their professional backgrounds and participation in the Writers' Project (constantly slammed by conservative politicians and others for its alleged leftist agenda), a sizable portion appear to have been among the more enlightened, open-minded, and progressive white Southerners of their day, their careful and respectful portraits of ex-slaves ranking with the period's best fieldwork. At the very least, most workers were plainly sympathetic and well-intentioned. Still, they were people of that time and place, with a measure of the limitations and prejudices that implies, traversing unfamiliar terrain under difficult conditions. Many lacked any personal knowledge of their subject, dutifully following Lomax's guidelines or similar prompts. Often they seemed confused or clueless about what the ex-slaves told them. "The writer was somewhat at a loss to know just what Aunt Ellen meant by 'juking,' but thought best to let her talk on and not make a direct inquiry" (Ellen King, b. 1851, MS, 234–35, int. Mary A. Poole). "Dancing was to the tune of banjoes and some home-made instruments she termed 'quills,' evidently some kind of reeds" (Melinda Mitchell, b. 1853, SC, 442, int. Edith Bell Love). Unlike experienced collectors, many fieldworkers did not know or recognize even the most common folklore items, greatly complicating transcription, so that garbled or anomalous song texts may reflect interviewers' inexperience or uncertainty rather than any lapse on the informants' parts.

> Den de would have some love songs, while dancing, as dese flip, jack flip a jas.

Set up again.

Back Cherter old tones love.
Back ole agger sinder loving summer day.

Rule over, rule under, give me a glass of drink wine,
Don't want no more snow water. (Dave Lowry, b. 1857, VA, 198, orig. brackets, int. Isaiah Volley. The text is given exactly as transcribed and published.)[24]

Other interviewers failed to note song lyrics at all.

> We was always compelled to go to church. Boss like for de slaves to sing while workin'. We had a jackleg preacher who'd hist de tunes. Some was spirituals; my wife and me will sing you one now, "Got to Fight de Devil when You Come Up out de Water." (This was well rendered by the old man and his wife). (Andy Marion, b. 1844, SC, 169, orig. parentheses, int. W. W. Dixon)

> When folkses on our plantation died Marster Allen let many of us as wanted to go, lay offen wuk twell atter the buryin' befo' the funeral sermon was preached. Right now I can't recelleck no song we sung at funerals 'cep'n "Hark from the tombs a doleful sound" [Isaac Watts, 1707]. The reedy old voice carried the funeral hymn for a few minutes then trailed off. James was thinking of the past again. (James Bolton, b. 1852, GA, 98–99, int. Sarah H. Hall)

Moreover, not all fieldworkers were entirely sympathetic, and a few displayed attitudes that, if not always racist, were definitely racially insensitive and inappropriate. Obviously some did their best to suppress any unpleasant truths, others to sanitize slavery and romanticize the antebellum South, portraying ex-slaves in the pattern of the period's plantation nostalgia literature.

Benny's rocky little yard is gay with flowers and a flourishing rose vine shades the small porch at the front of his ramshackle two-room cabin. The old negro was busily engaged at washing his clothes. He is of medium size, darker than gingerbread in color, and his clothing on this day consisted of a faded blue shirt, pants adorned with many patches, and brogans. A frayed sun hat covered the gray hair that is "gittin' mighty thin on de top of my haid."

Benny was singing as he worked and his quavering old voice kept tune and rhythm to a remarkable degree as he carefully and distinctly pronounced:

Jesus will fix it for you,
Just let him have his way
He knows just how to do,
Jesus will fix for you.[25]

Almost in the same breath he began another song:

All my sisters gone,
Mammy and Daddy too
Whar would I be if it weren't
For my Lord and Marster.

About this time he looked up and saw his visitor. Off came the old sun hat as he said: "'Scuse me, Missy, I didn't know nobody was listenin' to dem old songs. I loves to sing 'em when I gits lonesome and blue. But won't you come up on my porch and have a cheer in de shade? Dere's a good breeze on dat little porch." Having placed a chair for the visitor and made himself comfortable on a crude bench, Benny began his story: "Missy, de good Lord gives and he takes away, and us old darkies is a-passin' out of dis world. Dat was why I was a-singin'. One of my bestest friends done passed on to Glory dis very mornin'. . . ." (Benny Dillard, b. ca. 1858, GA, 286, int. Grace McCune)

The added quotation ("gittin' mighty thin on de top of my haid") is from the minstrel song "Who's A Gwine To Take Care of Me" (William S. Hays, 1876). Some interviewers, writers, and editors were thus more than a little paternalistic, and occasionally condescending or even demeaning. Dialect does sometimes seem deliberately to portray the ex-slaves as comically childlike, simpleminded, ignorant, or ill-spoken. "I nebber see nigger in chain, but I shum (see them) in stock. I see plenty nigger sell on banjo table. Dey put you on flatform (platform) en dey buy you. I see my uncle sell he brung one hundred dollars" (Sam Polite, b. ca. 1844, SC, 274–75, int. Clothilde R. Martin, orig. parentheses). "Ain't it diff'rent how peoples lives? Us used to travel wid de ox and now dey flies in de sky. Folks sings in New York and us sits right here and hears dem. Shucks! De way things am gwine, I's all fussed up and can't understand whether I's gwine or comin'" (William M. Thomas, b. ca. 1850, MS, 99, int. Sheldon F. Gauthier).

No'm I shore don't sot much store by dese new fangled ways. Mos' ob 'em is ob de species of de genus of de softshell turtle, case dey sets up to habe ebbery kind of meat in dem, from possum an' taters to pursimmons. An' dey shore do fool de folks. Dey jes' ain't good for yore wholesome. I believes to git mah possums whare dey is possums an' mah taters ware dey is taters. In dat way dere is no foolin' your insides. (Bean Walker, b. 1852, TX, 3922–23, int. Mrs. Edgerton Arnold)

Chile, you ain't neber seen sich flingin' ob de arms an' legs in yo' time. Dem pickinninnies dey had de natural born art ob twistin' dey body any way dey wish. Dat dere ting dey calls truckin' now an' use to be chimmy, ain't had no time wid de dancin' dem chilluns do. Dey claps dey hands and keep de time, while dat old brudder ob mine he blows de quills. (Dora Roberts, b. 1849, GA, 207, int. unk.)

Here are nuther job I master for 2 years ontel I get tired of it. I usto love to call figgers for dance.

I cut out the 8 figger all together, simple because no buddy could master it but myself. Everything not nice was cut out. No card playing, no crap shooting, no whiskey drinking eround, No Cursien among the Girls, no spitting own the floor. I put up a Signed Board for to go by. White people come eround for to see Culard joyous theyselfs, in a nice way. So after all that, they put up a nice Dancing Hall for to joy ourselfs in Respectfully Way. But without no spiting on the floor. Thay was spit toons—12 of them—for such purpose. I hanle that job two to 3 year. (Charles Williams, b. unk., MS, 183, int. unk.)

A few depictions do expressly evoke blackface stereotypes.

Greeting his visitors with politeness, James Lucas, an ex-slave living in Natchez, gave his age as 104. With a twinkle in his eyes he added: "Miss you kin count hit up fer yourself. I was born October 11, 1833. My young marster give me my age when he heired de property of his uncle, Mr. Withers. He was goin' through de papers an' a-burnin' some when he found de one 'bout me. Den he said, 'Jim, dissen 'bout you, hit gives yore birthday.'" ... But for his pension he might exemplify the words of that old song:

> My har am white on de top o' my head
> My boddy am thin cause I ain't half fed,
> Marster and Missus bofe am dead,
> Oh, whose gonna take keer o' me? (James Lucas,
> b. 1833, MS, 1330, 1336, int. Edith Wyatt
> Moore)

The "old song" is, again, "Who's A Gwine To Take Care of Me" (New York: J. L. Peters, 1876) by William Shakespeare Hays (1837–1907), a major white hitmaker of blackface minstrelsy. Fortunately, such tendencies were not the rule, but readers will recognize them throughout the book. Ex-slaves would have recognized them too, of course, having dealt with such

attitudes from whites all their lives, and developed various defense mechanisms, none of which involved being completely open and honest. No doubt some ex-slaves clammed up, played dumb, or dissembled simply because they recognized they were dealing with a naïf, blowhard, or bigot of one sort or another.

Yet whether because fieldworkers were capable and sincere and had established rapport, because ex-slaves wanted their stories told, or simply because like legions of old people everywhere they no longer gave a damn, an equal number of narrators felt no inhibitions whatsoever in expressing themselves on slavery or any other topic. "Lord have mercy, it jes' make my flesh crawl to think about it. And de overseer always strip de men, and women naked in de field and whip 'em. For a woman what is pregnant, dey dig a hole in de ground and lay her over de hole and whip her. Dat's de way dey did my mama" (Lydia Jefferson, b. 1851, LA, 1943, int. C. H. Drake).[26] "Wheee! Nobody needs to ask me. I can tell you that a white man laid a nigger gal whenever he wanted her. Seems like some of them had a plumb craving for the other color. Leastways they wanted to start themselves out on the nigger women. ... There was some redheaded neighbors of the Andrews had a whole crop of redheaded nigger slaves" (Rosa Maddox, b. ca. 1848, LA, 2531, int. Heloise M. Foreman). "The young people today ain't worth a shit. These young people going to school don't mean no good to nobody. They dance all night and all the time, and do everything else. That man across the street runs a whiskey house where they dance and do everything they're big enough to do. They ain't worth nothing" (Silas Dothrum, b. 1855 or 1856, AR, 188, int. Samuel S. Taylor). "I ust to say dat when I got to be a man, I was goin' to kill ever'body I saw. Oh, I tell you, I saw enough o' dem slave times!" (John Barker, b. 1853, TX, 166, int. Florence Angermiller). "Lord, Lord, I hate white people and de flood waters gwine drown some mo'" (Minnie Folkes, b. 1860, VA, 93, int. Susan R. C. Byrd).

Harriet Beecher Stowe, the writer of Uncle Tom's Cabin, did that for her own good. She had her own interests at heart and I don't like her, Lincoln, or none of that crowd. The Yankees helped free us, so they say, but they let us be put back in slavery again. When I think of slavery it makes me mad. I do not believe in giving you my story 'cause with all the promises that have been made the negro is still in a bad way in the United States, no matter in what part he lives, it's all the same. . . .

You are going around to get a story of slavery conditions and the persecutions of negroes before the civil war and the economic conditions of them since that war. You should have known before this late day all about that. Are you going to help us? No! you are only helping yourself. You say that my story may be put into a book, that you are from the Federal Writer's Project. Well, the negro will not get anything out of it, no matter where you are from. Harriet Beecher Stowe wrote Uncle Tom's Cabin. I didn't like her book and I hate her. No matter where you are from I don't want you to write my story cause the white folks have always been and are now and always will be against the negro. (Thomas Hall, b. 1861, NC, 361–62, int. T. Pat Matthews)

This is another situation where folklore may have created special circumstances, since many narrators who were reticent, vague, or unresponsive on some topics had no reservations about singing folksongs, telling folktales, or otherwise performing for fieldworkers, often at length. Perhaps not coincidentally, slaves had constantly been called upon to perform for slaveholders, whether for amusement and entertainment or as tokens of their servitude. Turning the tables, Blacks had long learned to use performance for their own ends, to distract whites or to dissemble and dissuade. Many songs, tales, and other traditions were double-sided, communicating one meaning to whites but something completely different to Blacks. Another factor contributing to the sheer amount of folklore in the narratives may be that some ex-slaves instinctively slipped into performance as a familiar and comfortable way of dealing with whites.

Obviously too, fieldworkers did not always play it safe, grilling indigents or pliant old family retainers. San Antonio interviewer Felix Nixon related an episode that will make many experienced fieldworkers wince in recognition and recollection. On or around June 22, 1937, Nixon followed a tip to the Cactus Cafe, where a crowd of local Blacks was celebrating African American heavyweight Joe Louis's title victory over the previous world champion, white boxer James Braddock.

Hearing of Millie Manuel's vow never to speak to a white man, "dis side or de t'other of de Judgement Gate," a research worker felt none too sanguine in calling on her at the Cactus Cafe, a Negro saloon and restaurant. The saloon was crowded with customers celebrating the knockout of Braddock by the new world champion, Joe Lewis [Louis], and the interviewer would have postponed his call had he not secured a glimpse of Millie. She was the embodiment of peace, frail and thin with a kind expression on her wrinkled old face. She sat against the far wall of the room with her hands serenely folded in her lap. A vacant chair was beside her, and the caller slid into it and spoke:

"Millie, I have been told that you had a lovely voice when you were a girl, and I wonder if you will be kind enough to tell . . ."

"Who dun' tol' yo'? I don't believe nobody tol' yo'! You get away from me white man!"

Her voice was angry and very loud. Instantly a whole room full of brown eyes were focused on Millie—Millie, who had broken her vow and was talking to a white man. Then there was a rush forward in Millie's defense, with the barkeep and the colored woman's daughter elbowing their way through a gathering black semicircle. Much explaining was necessary on the part of the interviewer, and it was some little time before Millie, under protest, let fall a few scattering bits of information.

She was born on the Salado Creek "a pace (six miles) out of San Antone"; her masters, "the

Childers," owned three slaves, herself and her mother and father, and she was "whipped all de time."

"What do you mean—spanked?"

"Spanked nothin'! I got beat most to death. I got put up again' a post and layed into with a cowhide the size of dat." She made a two inch circle with her thumb and finger. "Many's the time I drops—I thought I was dead."

"Why did they whip you?"

"Jes 'cose they could, I guess. They're all dead now and I's a-livin' and waitin' for Glory; and when I go I won't be seein' any of them. And the Lord has spared me and he didn't spare them—They is gone where the Good Shepard has sent them to be slaves for the devil . . . No, sir, I don' 'member any songs. But I used to do a right smart bit of singing, but not till I gets free. Then we used to sing. We didn't have no church. We would gather at one anothers' houses and pray and sing. All night, sometimes, we would pray and sing . . ."

Millie was softening, and the interviewer thought that it was a proper time to approach the subject of having her pose for a photograph.

"What!" she called angrily, "me get my picture taken and get arrested? No, I won't have no picture taken . . . No, I don't care what yo' say. I wouldn't trust a white man no more than a rattler. I was given unto suffer. I got betrayed. And I aint goin' to trust yo' to take my picture, or no white man." And so the interview came to an end without a photograph and without a "good bye" and "call again" from Millie Manuel. (Millie Manuel, b. unk., TX, 2568–71, int. Felix Nixon, orig. parentheses)

Joe Louis (1914–1981) was a flamboyant, newsworthy character with a controversial lifestyle that made him constant fodder for the tabloids, but he became a Black folk hero mainly by beating the hell out of Braddock, Max Schmeling, and a series of other vaunted white opponents, inspiring oral legends as well as numerous recorded tributes by blues singers such as Bill Gaither: "I came all the way from Chicago to see Joe Louis and Max Schmeling fight, / Schmeling went down like the *Titanic* when Joe gave him just one hard right."[27] I like to imagine that Millie Manuel got to enjoy some of these records on the jukebox at the Cactus Cafe.

Not all ex-slaves were unfamiliar or uncomfortable with narrating their life stories to strangers, nor were many at all unwilling. Long before he published his 1891 autobiography, former Kentucky slave Harry Smith (1814–?) had learned to retail his experiences to a rapt white public. In October 1872 Smith embarked on a hunting expedition in Michigan. "After the whites became more acquainted with him, many a long evening was passed away by Smith, singing plantation songs and telling [about] some plantation possum and coon hunts. Many of the older settlers can remember the enjoyment and amusement furnished by Smith."[28] By the 1930s ex-slaves were being formally interviewed on a regular basis by various individuals, organizations, institutions, and publications,[29] but they remained the subject of everyday interest as well, especially as their numbers dwindled.

Yes sir, Boss Man, I sho hopes dat I kin see some of dem white folks ergin, en dat some of dese days dey will fine me. Yo know I is de janitor at de church at Walnut Street whar de two hard roads cross, en whar all de cars cum by. De cars, dey cum by dar frum eberywhare, en so ebery Sunday morning atter I gits through er cleanin' up de church, I sets down on de bench dar close ter Mr. Gibson's sto, whar dey sell de gasolene en de cold drinks, en whar de cars come by frum eberywhar, en I sets dar er lookin' at all dem white folks er passin' in dey cars, en sometimes dey stop fer ter git 'em some gasolene er sumpin, en I says ter myself dat mebbe one er my young marsters sometimes gwine ter be in one of dem cars, en gwine ter drive up dar lookin' fer me. Er heap er times when de cars stop dar will be er white gentman in de cars whut git out an see me a settin' dar on de bench, en he say, "Uncle, yo is rail old, ain't yo?" En den he ax me my name en whar I borned at, en er heap er times dey buy me er cigar. (Uncle Henry Green, b. 1848, AL, 100–101)

Interviewer Watt McKinney does not say whether he took the hint and bought Green his cigar.

Several ex-slaves reported still regularly regaling whites in this way, and also having a fairly clear sense of the current market value of their material. Wade Glenn told interviewer Miriam Logan, "maybe I could think up the words of a lot of those ol' tunes but they ought to pay well for them, for they make money out of them" (Wade Glenn, b. ca. 1860, NC, 38). William "Reverend Bill" Green performed a couple verses of an old minstrel song, "De Wild-Goose Nation" (Dan Emmett, ca. 1840), for Felix Nixon, who noted that "at the end of his narrative 'Reverend Bill', diplomatically, brought out that he thought he should be paid for including the song in his reminiscences; 'There ain't nobody,' he explained, 'dat recollects de words but me, and de Lord gives us memory to be recompensed'" (Reverend Bill Green, b. 1851, MS, 1598). George Briggs let fieldworker Caldwell Sims know that he was accustomed to giving interviews, and that he had his own interests and expectations. "God gits in de heads of men to help de aged and de po' also. I never axes fer nothing, but when I sets around de courthouse and informs men as I been doing dis evening, de Lawd has dem drap a nickel or a dime or a quarter in my hand but He never gits dem to a half of a dollar" (George Briggs, b. 1849, SC, 92). Sims does not indicate whether he gave Briggs his fifty cents.

Some ex-slaves may have been shut-ins, recluses, or county wards, timid, suspicious, or hostile, but by my reckoning the majority had remained active community members accustomed to dealing with all manner of people, Black and white. Interviewers constantly describe them as beloved local figures, renowned for their open hearts and interpersonal skills. They frequently lived in (or headed) extended family households, surrounded by children, grandchildren, and great-grandchildren who linked them to present-day life and the modern world. Often they were still working, and even more often still involved

Fig. 1.6. Rev. Bill Green, ex-slave, San Antonio, TX, July 9, 1937. "I was a buckerman.... yes, *buckerman*—I never heard of *buckeroo* until I knocked around quite a bit. By the time I was twelve, I could break horses along side the best of 'em" (Bill Green, b. 1851, TX, 1595, orig. ellipsis and emphasis). Portraits of African American ex-slaves from the US Works Progress Administration, Federal Writers' Project slave narratives collection, Library of Congress.

in church or civic organizations. Many had traveled America and the world during their younger years, held elected office and other positions of authority, established businesses and founded churches, received formal education (including college and graduate education), taught school and written for newspapers. Under slightly different circumstances several might have authored their own autobiographies, but others who had enjoyed no such advantages were every bit as intelligent, articulate, and gifted. These persons were more than happy to talk to interviewers. They understood the project and its significance as well as, and perhaps better than, the fieldworkers themselves. They knew they had important stories to tell, and they were glad someone was there to gather them. Thus as we go forward with the narratives, we may fall back on one additional cause for considerable confidence in their reliability: on the whole, that is, the ex-slaves were willing, cooperative, and perceptive participants who wanted us to know their stories, and their texts teem with the sense that we really are hearing the voices of former slaves recalling their lives. Having passed through Hell and come out the other side, these imposing souls gave the project their blessing.

Prayer

Lord, Lord, have mercy on dem pre moters [promoters?] an' dis lady here Lord, Lord, who has interested dem selves to write dis history 'bout us slaves um, um, um. Lord! have mercy! have um mercy! Lord you done spared a few un us to tell de tale um, um, um, bout how hit was um, um wid us poor folks in dem days um, um, um. We done pray for dis day to come of freedom. Yes, Hevanely Marster Jesus, Jesus, give dis lady strength an' pow'r to write dis gra' history book. Dear Lord um, um, now let dis um, um, be a greates de greates book—next to yo' Bible um, um, um, fer us colored people fer Christ sake Amen an' thanky Jesus! (John Brown, b. 1860, VA, 62, orig. brackets)

Go to writin'! (Mom Ellen Godfrey, b. 1837, SC, 164)

Appendix A: John Lomax's Instructions for Interviewers

These guidelines for fieldworkers ("Supplementary Instructions #9-E to The American Guide Manual") were drafted by John A. Lomax, FWP National Adviser on Folklore and Folkways, in April 1937, then forwarded by National FWP Director Henry G. Alsberg to the State Directors. This file copy, dated July 30, 1937, also includes follow-up suggestions probably distributed around that time. Rawick, *Sundown*, 169–70, 173–76.

The following general suggestions are being sent to all the States where there are ex-slaves still living. They will not apply *in toto* to your State as they represent general conclusions reached after reading the mass of ex-slave material already submitted. However, they will, I hope, prove helpful as an indication, along broad lines, of what we want.

General Suggestions

1. Instead of attempting to interview a large number of ex-slaves the workers should now concentrate on one or two of the more interesting and intelligent people, revisiting them, establishing friendly relations, and drawing them out over a period of time.

2. The specific questions suggested to be asked of the slaves should be only a basis, a beginning. The talk should run to all subjects, and the interviewer should take care to seize upon the information already given, and stories already told, and from them derive other questions.

3. The interviewer should take the greatest care not to influence the point of view of the informant, and not to let his own opinion on the subject of slavery become obvious. Should the ex-slave, however, give only one side of the picture, the interviewer should suggest that there were other circumstances, and ask questions about them.

4. We suggest that each state choose one or two of their most successful ex-slave interviewers and have them take down some stories *word* for *word*. Some Negro informants are marvelous in their ability to participate in this kind of interview. *All stories should be as nearly word-for-word as is possible.*

5. More emphasis should be laid on questions concerning the lives of the individuals since they were freed.

Suggestions to Interviewers

The interviewer should attempt to weave the following questions naturally into the conversation, in simple language. Many of the interviews show that the workers have simply sprung routine questions out of context, and received routine answers.

1. What did the ex-slaves expect from freedom? Forty acres and a mule? A distribution of the land of their masters' plantation?

2. What did the slaves get after freedom? Were any of the plantations actually divided up? Did their masters give them any money? Were they under any compulsion after the war to remain as servants?

3. What did the slaves do after the war? What did they receive generally? What do they think about the reconstruction period?

4. Did secret organizations such as the Ku Klux Klan exert or attempt to exert any influence over the lives of ex-slaves?

5. Did the ex-slaves ever vote? If so under what circumstances? Did any of their friends ever hold political office? What do the ex-slaves think of the present restricted suffrage?

6. What have the ex-slaves been doing in the interim between 1864 and 1937? What jobs had they held (in detail)? How are they supported nowadays?

7. What do the ex-slaves think of the younger generation of Negroes and of present conditions?

8. Were there any instances of slave uprisings?

9. Were any of the ex-slaves in your community living in Virginia at the time of the Nat Turner rebellion? Do they remember anything about it?

10. What songs were there of the period?
The above sent to: Alabama, Arkansas, Florida, Ga., Kentucky, La., Md., Mississippi, Mo., N. Car., Okla., S. Car., Tenn., Texas, Virginia, W. Va., Ohio, Kansas, Indiana

Stories from Ex-Slaves

The main purpose of these detailed and homely questions is to get the Negro interested in talking about the days of slavery. If he will talk freely, he should be encouraged to say what he pleases without reference to the questions. It should be remembered that the Federal Writers' Project is not interested in taking sides on any question. The worker should not censor any material collected, regardless of its nature.

It will not be necessary, indeed it will probably be a mistake, to ask every person all of the questions. Any incidents or facts he can recall should be written down as nearly as possible just as he says them, but do not use dialect spelling so complicated that it may confuse the reader.

A second visit, a few days after the first one, is important, so that the worker may gather all the worthwhile recollections that the first talk has aroused.

Questions

1. Where and when were you born?

2. Give the names of your father and mother. Where did they come from? Give names of your brothers and sisters. Tell about your life with them and describe your home and the "quarters." Describe the beds where you slept. Do you remember anything about your grandparents or any stories told you about them?

3. What work did you do in slavery days? Did you ever earn any money? How? What did you buy with this money?

4. What did you eat and how was it cooked? Any possums? Rabbits? Fish? What food did you like best? Did the slaves have their own gardens?

5. What clothing did you wear in hot weather? Cold weather? On Sundays? Any shoes? Describe your wedding clothes.

6. Tell about your master, mistress, their children, the house they lived in, the overseer or driver, poor white neighbors.

7. How many acres in the plantation? How many slaves on it? How and at what time did the overseer wake up the slaves? Did they work hard and late at night? How and for what causes were the slaves punished? Tell what you saw. Tell some of the stories you heard.

8. Was there a jail for slaves? Did you ever see any slaves sold or auctioned off? How did groups of slaves travel? Did you ever see slaves in chains?

9. Did the white folks help you to learn to read and write?

10. Did the slaves have a church on your plantation? Did they read the Bible? Who was your favorite preacher? Your favorite spirituals? Tell about the baptizing; baptizing songs. Funerals and funeral songs.

11. Did the slaves ever run away to the North? Why? What did you hear about patrollers? How did slaves carry news from one plantation to another? Did you hear of trouble between the blacks and whites?

12. What did the slaves do when they went to their quarters after the day's work was done on the plantation? Did they work on Saturday afternoons? What did they do Saturday nights? Sundays? Christmas morning? New Year's Day? Any other holidays? Cornshucking? Cotton Picking? Dances? When some of the white master's family married or died? A wedding or death among the slaves?

13. What games did you play as a child? Can you give the words or sing any of the play songs or ring games of the children? Riddles? Charms? Stories about "Raw Head and Bloody Bones" or other "hants" or ghosts? Stories about animals? What do you think of voodoo? Can you give the words or sing any lullabies? Work songs? Plantation hollers? Can you tell a funny story you have heard or something funny that happened to you? Tell about the ghosts you have seen.

14. When slaves became sick who looked after them? What medicines did the doctors give them? What medicine (herbs, leaves, or roots) did the slaves use for sickness? What charms did they wear and to keep off what diseases?

15. What do you remember about the war that brought your freedom? What happened on the day news came that you were free? What did your master say and do? When the Yankees came what did they do and say?

16. Tell what work you did and how you lived the first year after the war and what you saw or heard about the Ku Klux Klan and the Nightriders. Any school then for Negroes? Any land?

17. Whom did you marry? Describe the wedding. How many children and grandchildren have you and what are they doing?

18. What do you think of Abraham Lincoln? Jefferson Davis? Booker Washington? Any other prominent white man or Negro you have known or heard of?

19. Now that slavery is ended what do you think of it? Tell why you joined a church and why you think all people should be religious.

20. Was the overseer "poor white trash"? What were some of his rules?

The details of the interview should be reported as accurately as possible in the language of the original statements.

Appendix B: Plagiarized Song Texts in the Ex-Slave Narratives

The term *plagiarism* can be applied to many types of unattributed borrowing (and many types of unattributed borrowing occur in the ex-slave narratives); however, I use *plagiarism* specifically to describe texts (usually song texts) that can only be explained as deliberate, uncredited copies of previously published texts. As one example of the latter, consider the following, printed in 1892 in Joel Chandler Harris's *Uncle Remus and His Friends* (213–14):

Mammy went away—she tol' me ter stay,
   An' take good keer er de baby,
She tol' me ter stay an sing dis away:
   Oh, go ter sleepy, little baby!

    Chorus.
Oh, go ter sleep! Sleepy, little babe,
   Oh, go ter sleepy, little baby,
Kaze when you wake, you'll git some cake,
   An' ride a little white horsey!

Oh, de little Butterfly, he stole some pie—
   Go ter sleepy, little baby!
An' he flew'd so high, twel he put out his eye—
   Oh, go ter sleepy, little baby!
    Chorus.

Oh, shet yo' eye, an don't you cry—
  Go to sleepy, little baby!
Kaze mammy's boun' fer ter cum bimeby,
  Oh, go ter sleep, little baby!
        Chorus.

We'll stop up de cracks and sow [sew] up de
    seams—
  De Booger Man never shill ketch you!
Oh, go ter sleep and dream sweet dreams—
  De Booger Man never shill ketch you!
        Chorus.

You shill hear dem silver bells ring—
  Bye-oh, sweet little baby!
You shill hear sweet angels sing—
  Oh, go ter sleepy, little baby!
        Chorus.

De river run wide, de river run deep—
  Oh, bye-oh, sweet little baby!
De boat rock slow—shill rock you ter sleep—
  Oh, bye-oh, sweet little baby!
        Chorus.

This is an early published version of the well-known African American lullaby "Go to Sleepy, Little Baby (All the Pretty Horses)." As might be expected, Harris evidently made many additions and embellishments, as well as imposing various literary conventions (dialect spellings, punctuation, line and stanza divisions, and so on). His text is, however, generally consistent with this item's oral tradition as subsequently documented. It is not precisely duplicated anywhere within that tradition, of course, because that is not how oral tradition works. Harris's text is, however, duplicated in the ex-slave materials, in the narrative of Annie Little, produced by prolific Texas fieldworker Effie Cowan.

Mammy went away—she tol' me to stay,
  An take good keer of de baby,
She tol' me ter stay an sing dis away,
  O, go ter sleepy, little baby;

        Chorus,
O, go to sleep; Sleepy little babe,
  Oh, go ter sleepy little baby,
Kase when you wake, you'll git some cake,
  An ride a little white horsey;
O, de little butterfly, he stole some pie—
  Go ter sleepy, little baby;
An he flew so high twel he put out his eye—
  O, go to sleepy, little baby.
        Chorus,
Oh, shut your eye, an don you cry—
  Go to sleepy, little baby,
Kase mamays boun' fur to cum bineby,
  Oh, go to sleep, Little baby.
We'll stop up the cracks and sew up the seams—
  De booger man never shill ketch you,
Oh, go to sleep an dream sweet dreams—
  De Booger man never shill ketch you.
        Chorus,
You shall hear dem silver bells ring—
  Bye-oh, sweet little baby,
You shill hear sweet angels sing—
  Oh go ter sleepy little baby.
De ribber run wide, de ribber run deep—
  Oh Bye-oh, sweet little baby,
Dat boat rock slow—she'll rock you to sleep,
  Oh bye-oh sweet little baby. (Annie Little, b. 1857, TX, 2393–95, int. Effie Cowan; a rearranged version of this text appears in the copy of Little's narrative sent to the Library of Congress [S1 5 *TX* 3: 23])

There is simply no sensible explanation for the correspondences between these two texts other than that someone—almost certainly Effie Cowan herself—deliberately copied the text of "Go to Sleepy, Little Baby" published four decades earlier in *Uncle Remus and His Friends* and inserted it in Annie Little's narrative. Little's transcript not only matches Harris's text word for word but reproduces exactly its literary and typographic affectations (dialect spellings, punctuation, line and stanza divisions, and so on). Even the occasional discrepancies cannot disguise these facts.

In itself this internal textual evidence is conclusive, but as usual in these cases, there are external clues as well. That is, writers who plagiarized once usually did so again, and Effie Cowan cribbed by far more song texts than any other interviewer I have identified. Any transcript bearing her name is, in my opinion, instantly suspect. Fortunately, this practice was confined to Cowan and a relative few others, most of whom plagiarized repeatedly, and often repeatedly from the same sources. Cowan sampled more broadly than most—her knowledge of the folklore literature of her day was actually quite impressive—but Joel Chandler Harris's works were her favorites: she took at least a half dozen other texts just from *Uncle Remus and His Friends*.

In sum, there really is no way to comprehend the text of "Go to Sleepy, Little Baby" that Effie Cowan attributed to Annie Little except as a *plagiarism* in the very narrow sense I have stipulated, which further applies to all of the examples listed below. Not all go to the same length, but many do. Others are briefer, however, even quite brief. Many passages were copied verbatim from their sources as here, but in other cases writers excerpted, rearranged, altered, or expanded what they borrowed. Nonetheless, for all of the following examples, one or more internal or external factors (but usually several of both together) indicate that the WPA texts were copied from specific print sources, which I have always identified and cited. There are many other ex-slave examples that I suspect as plagiarisms, but if I have been unable to trace them to specific published sources, I have not included them here. I am fairly sure that some of these suspect cases truly are bogus, but for others their suspicious-seeming literary affectations and print conventions may have been introduced by WPA writers in the same manner that Joel Chandler Harris, John A. Lomax, and others rewrote and reformatted their texts. There are, in fact, numerous instances in the ex-slave narratives where I am certain that this was so.

The ex-slaves themselves contributed numerous items ultimately derived from print sources (such as Protestant hymnals and minstrel songbooks), although most had learned these by word-of-mouth. Such pieces nonetheless tend to exhibit greater uniformity and stability than other types of folksongs, as well as literary affectations, pop culture references, and the like. Of course, usually they also include adaptations and variations characteristic of oral traditions. In any case this kind of borrowing has been an organic part of Western folk music since the invention of print, easily distinguishable from what I am describing as plagiarism.

The following list, then, does not pretend to give a complete accounting of problematic texts in the ex-slave narratives, merely of those song texts that I have to this point positively identified as plagiarisms. It can, however, be taken as another gauge of the textual problems awaiting anyone who tackles the narratives.

"AIN'T NO MORE CANE ON THE NECHIZ (BRAZIS)." PLAGIARISMS: John Love (b. 1861, TX, 2422), int. Effie Cowan. From Lomax, *Ballads*, 58–59, with slight alterations, such as the substitution of *Nechiz* (Neches) for *Brazis* (Brazos).

"THE BALLAD OF THE BOLL WEEVIL" (LAWS I 17). PLAGIARISMS: John Love (b. 1861, TX, 2428–29), int. Effie Cowan. From Lomax, *Ballads*, 112–17. Cowan borrows stanzas two, eight, four, and twenty-one of the Lomax text, which is itself a composite.

"DE BIG BETHEL CHURCH." PLAGIARISMS: Henry Childers (b. 1844, TX, 704), int. Effie Cowan. From Harris, *Remus*, 198–99.

"BIG YAM TATERS IN DE SANDY LAN'." PLAGIARISMS: Alice Wilkins (b. 1855, TX, 4047–78), int. Effie Cowan. From Lomax, *Ballads*, 236–37.

"BLACK GAL SWEET." PLAGIARISMS: Levi Pollard (b. ca. 1850, VA, 232), int. unk. From Harris, *Remus*, 191–92.

"COME ALONG, TRUE BELIEVER, COME ALONG." PLAGIARISMS: Josephine Tippit Compton (b. 1862, TX, 911), int. Effie Cowan; Wayman Williams (b. ca. 1855, TX, 4150), int. Effie Cowan. Both from Harris, *Friends*, 204–5.

"DE DEBBIL AM A LIAR AN' A KUNJURER TOO." PLAGIARISMS: Lou Austin, (b. 1850, TX, 131), int. Ada Davis. From Puckett, *Folk Beliefs*, 553.

"DOSE BLACKEYED PEAS IS LUCKY." PLAGIARISMS: Patsy Moses (b. ca. 1863, TX, 2789), int. Effie Cowan. From Thomas W. Talley, *Negro Folk Rhymes: Wise and Otherwise* (New York: Macmillan, 1922), 200–201 (167, 1991 ed.).

"GO TO SLEEPY LITTLE BABY (ALL THE PRETTY HORSES)." PLAGIARISMS: Annie Little (b. 1857, MS, 2393–5), int. Effie Cowan. From Harris, *Friends*, 213–14.

"(HE) NEVER SAID A MUMBLING WORD." PLAGIARISMS: Lou Austin (b. 1850, TX, 130), int. Ada Davis; Ned Broadus (b. ca. 1810, AL, TX, 440), int. Ada Davis. Both from R. C. Harrison, "The Negro as Interpreter of His Own Folk-Songs," *Rainbow in the Morning*, ed. J. Frank Dobie. PTFS 5 (1926; rpt. Hatboro, PA: Folklore Associates, 1965), 151.

"HEAVE AWAY! HEAVE AWAY!" PLAGIARISMS: William Warfield (b. unk., KY, 102), int. Mamie Hanberry. From Monroe N. Work, "The Spirit of Negro Poetry," *Southern Workman* 37 (February 1908): 73. Work's article draws its examples from earlier publications, this item coming from *Slave Songs*, 61. However, Hanberry obviously took all five of the song texts she attributes to Warfield from the first two pages of Work's article. (Also see "Nobody Knows Da Truble I Sees," "Oh! I'se A-Gwine To Lib Always," "Ole Massa Take Dat New Brown Coat," and "We'll Walk Dem Golden Streets" below.)

"HITS EIGHTEENHUNDRED AN' FORTYNINE." PLAGIARISMS: Sylvester Brooks (b. 1850, AL 451), int. Effie Cowan. From Harris, *Remus*, 196.

"HOP LIGHT LADIES." PLAGIARISMS: Levi Pollard (b. ca. 1850, VA, 232), int. unk. From Harris, *Remus*, 194.

"I HOLLERED AT MY MULE." PLAGIARISMS: Marshal Butler (b. 1849, GA, 162–63), int. Joseph E. Jaffee. From Odum and Johnson, *NHS*, 154.

"I WRASTLED WID SATAN." PLAGIARISMS: Lou Austin (b. 1850, TX, 130), int. Ada Davis. From Harrison, "Negro as Interpreter," 150.

"IF RELIGION WAS TO BUY." PLAGIARISMS: Martha Jones (b. ca. 1860, TX, 1231), int. Effie Cowan. From White, *ANFS*, 101.

"IF YOU WANT TO GO A COURTIN'." PLAGIARISMS: Marshal Butler (b. 1849, GA, 162–64), int. Joseph E. Jaffe. From Odum and Johnson, *NHS*, 192.

"I'M A GOOD OLD REBEL." PLAGIARISMS: Allen Price (b. 1862, TX, 196), int. Effie Cowan; Alice Wilkins (b. 1855, TX, 4047), int. Effie Cowan. From Lomax, *Ballads*, 536–37.

"I'SE GOIN' FROM DE COTTON FIELD." PLAGIARISMS: Ned Broadus (b. ca. 1810, AL, 439), int. Ada Davis. From Bales, "Negro Folk-Songs," 101, who states "a note made by the Negro pupil of the I. M. Terrill High School of Fort Worth, who gave me this song, states that it was sung by an ex-slave." This is actually a post-Reconstruction popular song, however: "I'm Going from the Cottonfields" (Thomas P. Westendorf, 1879). Arnold, *Alabama*, 115; *Country Music Sources*, 467; Davis, *Folk-Songs*, 130.

"JESUS GONNA MAKE UP MY DYING BED." PLAGIARISMS: Lou Austin (b. 1850, TX, 129), int. Ada Davis; Ned Broadus (b. ca. 1810, AL, 438–39), int. Ada Davis. Both from Martha Emmons, "Dyin' Easy," *Tone the Bell Easy*, ed. J. Frank Dobie, PTFS 10 (Austin, 1932), 60–61. Broaddus's narrative reproduces, verbatim, stanzas three to six of the Emmons text. Austin's text matches the first verse of Broaddus's (stanza three from Emmons).

"JOHN HENRY" (Laws I 1) "JOHN HARDY" (Laws I 2). PLAGIARISMS: This example—a traditional subtype combining two well-known African American ballads—appears after an interview with Tennessee ex-slave Jim Sommerville conducted in New York by fieldworker Ellis Williams (Jim Somerville, b. 1842, TN, 360–61). The text is headed "HEARD IN MR. WILTSHIRE'S OFFICE," but there is no indication of who Mr. Wiltshire might be, where and what his office was, or whether and how ex-slave Sommerville was tied to the song. In any case this item reproduces verbatim the opening three stanzas of a text that first appeared in John Harrington Cox, "John Hardy," *JAF* 32 (1919): 514–15, shortly reprinted in Cox's *Folk-Songs of the South* (1925), 178.

"KEEP 'WAY F'OM ME HOODOO AN' WITCH." PLAGIARISMS: Willis Easter (b. 1852, TX, 1257), int. Ada Davis. From Puckett, *Folk Beliefs*, 168.

"LET'S GO DOWN TO JORDAN." PLAGIARISMS: Harrison Cole (b. 1861, TX, 770–71), int. Effie Cowan. From Lomax, *Ballads*, 582–83.

"MIND HOW YOU WALK ON THE CROSS." PLAGIARISMS: Lou Austin (b. 1850, TX, 131), int. Ada Davis. From Harrison, "Negro as Interpreter," 151.

"MIX DE MEAL, FRY DE BATTER." PLAGIARISMS: Vinnie Brunson (b. ca. 1860, TX, 515), int. Effie Cowan. From Harris, *Friends*, 150–51.

"NIGGER MIGHTY HAPPY WHEN HE LAYIN' BY DE CORN." PLAGIARISMS: William Stone (b. ca. 1863, LA, 65), int. Effie Cowan. From Harris, *Remus*, 190, compare also *Friends*, 193.

"NOBODY KNOWS DA TRUBLE I SEES." PLAGIARISMS: William Warfield (b. unk., KY, 102), int. Mamie Hanberry. From Work, "Spirit of Negro Poetry," 74.

"OH! I'SE AGWINE TO LIB ALWAYS." PLAGIARISMS: William Warfield (b. unk., KY, 103), int. Mamie Hanberry. From Work, "Spirit of Negro Poetry," 74.

"OH, MOLLY COTTON TAIL." PLAGIARISMS: Patsy Moses (b. ca. 1863, TX, 2786–87), int. Effie Cowan. From Talley, *Negro Folk Rhymes* (1922), 8–9 (7, 1991 ed.).

"DE OLE BEE MAKE DE HONEYCOMB, DE YOUNG BEE MAKE DE HONEY." PLAGIARISMS: Sylvester Brooks (b. 1850, AL 451), int. Effie Cowan. From Harris, *Remus*, 197.

"OLE MASSA TAKE DAT NEW BROWN COAT." PLAGIARISMS: William Warfield (b. unk., KY, 102), int. Mamie Hanberry. From Work, "Spirit of Negro Poetry," 73. Hanberry gives the verse, omitting the chorus that follows.

"RABBIT FOOT QUICK." PLAGIARISMS: Josephine Tippit Compton (b. 1862, TX, 912), int. Effie Cowan. From Harris, *Friends*, 197–98, with slight changes.

"DE RACOON HE'S A CU'US MAN." PLAGIARISMS: Sylvester Brooks (b. 1850, AL, 451), int. Effie Cowan. From Harris, *Remus*, 197, with the substitution of *Towser* for *Bringer*.

"RATION DAY." PLAGIARISMS: William Stone (b. ca. 1863, LA, 66), int. Effie Cowan. From Talley, *Negro Folk Rhymes* (1922), 38 (34, 1991 ed.).

"RELIGION IS SO SWEET." PLAGIARISMS: Harrison Cole (b. 1861, TX, 770–71), int. Effie Cowan. From Lomax, *Ballads*, 582–83.

"RIDE ON KING JESUS (NO MAN CAN HINDER)." PLAGIARISMS: Ned Broadus (b. ca. 1810, AL, 439–40), int. Ada Davis. From Bales, "Some Negro Folk-Songs," 92.

"ROW, ROW, WHO LAID DAT RAIL?" PLAGIARISMS: Wayman Williams (b. ca. 1855, TX, 4149), int. Effie Cowan. From Harris, *Friends*, 201–2.

"RUN NIGGER RUN." PLAGIARISMS: Henry Freeman (b. ca. 1865, AL, child of ex-slaves, 1433), int. Effie Cowan. From Harris, *Friends*, 200.

"DE SHADDERS, DEY ER CREEPIN' TODE'S DE TOP OF DE HILL." PLAGIARISMS: Josephine Tippit Compton (b. 1862, TX, 911), int. Effie Cowan. From Harris, *Friends*, 194.

"SOMETIMES I FEEL LIKE A MOTHERLESS CHILD." PLAGIARISMS: Lou Austin (b. 1850, TX, 130), int. Ada Davis. From Harrison, "Negro as Interpreter," 151–52.

"DE TIME IS RIGHT NOW, EN DIS YER'S DE PLACE." PLAGIARISMS: Wayman Williams (b. ca. 1855, MS, 4153), int. Effie Cowan. From Harris, *Remus*, 184.

"WEEVILY WHEAT." PLAGIARISMS: Alice Wilkins (b. 1855, TX, 4049–50), int. Effie Cowan. From Lomax, *Ballads*, 290–91.

"WE'LL STICK TO DE HOE, TILL DE SUN GO DOWN." PLAGIARISMS: William Stone (b. ca. 1863, LA, 3740), int. Effie Cowan. From Talley, *Negro Folk Rhymes* (1922), 123 (106, 1991 ed.).

"WE'LL WALK DEM GOLDEN STREETS." PLAGIARISMS: William Warfield (b. unk., KY, 103), int. Mamie Hanberry. From Work, "Spirit of Negro Poetry," 74.

"W'EN DE TYRANTS SWORD DARKENED OUR LAND." PLAGIARISMS: Nelson Taylor Denson (b. 1847, TX, 1192), int. Effie Cowan. From William Barton, "The Texan's Song of Liberty" (1836). See Alan Dienst, "Contemporary Poetry of the Texas Revolution," *Southwestern Historical Quarterly* 21 (1917): 171–72. Cowan inserted a dialect version of the first four lines of Barton's tribute to the Texas revolution in the draft of Denson's narrative retained in the Texas state archives (SS2 4 *TX* 3: 1168–92). This passage does not appear in the version of Denson's narrative sent to the Library of Congress (S1 4 *TX* 1: 305–6), which is only two pages long. The transcript in the Texas state archives—most of which is obviously Cowan's invention—is thirty-three pages long!

AFRICA, EUROPE, AND AFRICAN AMERICANS

My father's name was George and my mother's name was Nellie. My father was born in Africa. Him and two of his brothers and one sister was stole and brought to Savannah, Georgy, and sol'. Dey was de children of a chief of de Kiochi tribe (the name of the tribe was spelled phonetically by the writer from Tom's pronunciation). De way dey was stole, dey was asked to a dance on a ship which some white men had, and my aunt said it was early in de mornin' w'en dey foun' dey was away from de lan', and all dey could see was de stars and de water all 'roun'. (Thomas Johns, b. 1847, AL, 1959, orig. parentheses)

Those who could talk very well would give tokens of well wishing to their master and mistress, and some who were born in Africa, would sing some of their songs, or tell different stories of the customs in Africa. After this they would spend half a day in dancing in some large cotton house or on a scaffold, the master providing fiddlers who came from other plantations if there were none on the place, and who received fifteen to twenty dollars on these occasions. (Jacob Stroyer [1846–?], *My Life in the South*, [1898], 45, describing South Carolina Christmas celebrations in the 1850s)

I got a daughter and two sisters alive in Africa today—in Liberia, I went there after we was freed. I liked it. Just the thoughts of bein' where Christ traveled—that's the good part of it. They furnished us transportation to go to Africa after the war and a lot of the colored folks went. I come back cause I had a lot of kin here, but I sent my daughter and two sisters there and they're alive there today. . . . I have a daughter in Ethiopia, teaching also two sisters. I have been in several wars and I have been in Ethiopia. (Tom Windham, b. 1845, IT, GA, 212, 213)

Africa was a living presence for the ex-slaves, in many instances a living memory. It was not necessarily the clearest of memories, even when there was some foundation in fact. The tale told by Thomas Johns about his father, uncles, and aunt being lured on board a slave ship for a dance party more likely recalls slaves being forced to dance on slave-ship decks for exercise during the Middle Passage. Other stories ex-slaves told about how Africans were captured typically involved similar transpositions. In the most popular example, narrators told how their ancestors were mysteriously led away into slavery by bits of red cloth.

> Dey talks a heap 'bout de niggers stealin'. Well, you know what was de fust stealin' done? Hit was in Afriky, when de white folks stole de niggers jes' like you'd go get a drove o' hosses and sell 'em. Dey'd bring a steamer down dere wid a red flag, 'cause dey knowed dem folks liked red, and when dey see it dey'd follow it till dey got on de steamer. Den when it was all full o' niggers dey'd bring 'em over here and sell 'em. (Shang Harris, b. ca. 1840, GA, 119)

> Both my granny and grandpa came out of Africa. They didn't know better than to love red and the mens come in a ship and showed the red hankies (handkerchiefs) and fooled them onto the ship. Fore they knowed it they was in the chains and don't see the land no more. Davy Cook, my old master was the owner of the ship. Long as I 'member the niggers called them men the Red Hankies. (Lu Lee, b. 1848 or 1849, TX, LA, 2291, orig. parentheses)

> Dey put a piece of red flannel five yards long on a pole, lak a service flag, an' den dey histed hit up an' waved hit an' waved hit in de air an' de africans jus' rallied 'roun' hit an' followed dat flag; ef hit hadn't been for dat man my gran' mammy wouldn't have been in dis country. (Joanna Thompson Isom, b. ca. 1858, MS, 1095)[1]

This is another far-removed memory of actual fact. Textiles were the European trade good most commonly exchanged for slaves along Africa's coasts, but there was no trickery about it: the bolts of cloth and other commodities were given as payment to the Black Africans

Fig. 2.1. "Slaves on Their Way to the Coast." Sarah Tucker, *Abbeokuta; or, Sunrise Within the Tropics* (London: James Nisbet, 1853), fac. 66. Slavery Images: A Visual Record of the African Slave Trade and Slave Life in the Early African Diaspora. slaveryimages.org. Tucker, an English anti-slavery author and missionary to West Africa, reprinted this image from an 1851 abolitionist pamphlet. It portrays Gatumba, a Liberian slave hunter, driving Dey captives from Sierra Leone to the slave ports.

who captured and then sold virtually all of the other Black Africans sent to the New World as slaves.

"The fun was on Saturday night when master 'lowed us to dance. There was lots of banjo pickin' and tin pan beatin' and dancin', and everybody would talk about when they lived in Africa and done what they wanted" (Toby Jones, b. ca. 1848, SC, 250). If the older slaves on Toby Jones's plantation had done what they wanted in Africa, they may have counted themselves lucky. The African societies that provided most slaves to the New World typically had large standing populations of slaves or war captives of their own, a practice greatly exacerbated by outside demand, first from the Mideast and Europe, then the Americas. Toby Jones was born in South Carolina and had never known Africa, but if he had, he might have known a continent devasted by African ethnic and imperial wars; by European contact, conquest, and emerging colonialism; and by the Arab, European, and New World slave trades. That is, after all, how Toby's ancestors wound up in South Carolina as slaves.

Africa's role in the creation of African American culture is a longstanding controversy, academic and otherwise. On the face of it, the matter seems simple, especially for the antebellum South where, allowing for some Native American influences, one can generally assume that any culture trait among slaves—say, an instrumental technique or dance step—derived either from Africa or Europe, or originated with American Blacks, or whites, or with New World Blacks and whites together. Sorting these different lineages is anything but simple, of course, and that struggle has generated both light and heat. It is, however, a question that constantly confronts anyone delving at all deeply into the ex-slave narratives.

In the early years, arguments were often pursued in near total absence of evidence from Africa, and sometimes in disregard of what little was known. Thus observers could adduce any dimly understood (or completely misunderstood) African American practice as proof either that slaves were purely African, or that they completely lacked a coherent culture of their own, clumsily imitating whites instead. Matters came to a head in 1941 with the publication of Melville Herskovits's *Myth of the Negro Past*.[2] By that time, mountains of reliable material on both Africa and African Americans had been accumulated, and armed with these data, including his own extensive fieldwork in West Africa and Haiti, Herskovits demolished the notion that African Americans were without history or culture, revealing African American communities as coherent, functioning wholes whose African basis could no longer be denied. He also demonstrated that this was not a matter of guesswork but a hypothesis subject to rigorous testing and proof. His systematic comparative approach pointed the way forward, and in the hands of successors has revealed these connections in ever deeper detail. Later studies have also revealed, however, that Herskovits was himself prone to selective evidence and shaky generalizations that have too often been uncritically accepted and repeated as fact. His case for the overall African influence in the Americas is unassailable, but he fails adequately to acknowledge that the same or similar culture traits frequently occur in both Africa and Europe; in fact, he generally avoids European and American white evidence altogether. Then too, most of Herskovits's material, and certainly his strongest arguments, come from the Caribbean and Latin America, where slaves encountered very different conditions than they did in the United States.

Simply put, not all African Americans are African in the same way, nor American to the same degree. In Latin America and the Caribbean, slaves were imported directly from Africa. A sizable proportion were isolated immediately after arrival on remote plantations or projects with limited white contacts, and were constantly replenished by new African captives. In Brazil, the last American state to outlaw slavery, slave ships from Africa continued to evade the British antislavery blockade (1815–51) through midcentury. Only in 1888 was African slavery itself abolished in Brazil. Across Latin America and the Caribbean, African influences were further accentuated by the presence of large communities of *maroons* (escaped slaves who banded together in semiautonomous African-style societies). As a result of these and similar factors, throughout the West Indies and Central and South America major African ethnic, linguistic, religious, and regional groups were able to maintain their identities and solidarity and with these numerous African institutions and traditions, all with the community's full awareness and understanding. In such circumstances, Black music, dance, and song may be best viewed, may only be comprehensible, as organic extensions of Africa's cultural repertoire. This is not to say that Blacks in the West Indies and Latin America were not greatly influenced by new experiences and outside contacts, most obviously with Europeans but also Native Americans and in some cases South and East Asians. Granted too, not all of Latin America and the Caribbean fit this description, but as a general rule the regions' African American communities favored practices, beliefs, and behaviors that were recognizably African in origin, and that were recognized as such by insiders and outsiders alike.

Such direct African offshoots were rare in North America outside the Atlantic Sea Islands but especially in and around New Orleans, more properly viewed as an outpost of the French West Indies. Africa's cultural contributions in North America were every bit as profound, but they were utterly transformed by the very different nature of North American slavery. Hundreds of thousands of slaves arrived in the United States directly from Africa, but a like number came through the West Indies, often after two or three generations in captivity. Even after the 1808 ban on importing slaves, thousands of Africans and West Indians were smuggled into the States. However, by the mid-1800s, almost all North American slaves were native-born. This is the demographic represented in the WPA ex-slave narratives. US slaves also numbered in closer proportion to, and lived in closer association with, whites than did most Brazilian, Cuban, or Haitian slaves. Some slaveholders throughout the Western Hemisphere tried to eradicate African practices (others did not), but such measures were more effective (and sometimes unnecessary) in this North America situation. Into the mid-1800s members of African ethnic, linguistic, or religious groups were acknowledged in the US slave population, but their numbers were low, and they were unable to reestablish or maintain large functioning communities as elsewhere. Then too, the Southern Protestant religion was far less welcoming to African polytheism and ritual than Catholicism's pantheons of saints, choirs of angels, pageantry, feast days, and pre-Lenten Carnival.

Under these conditions, then, the African-born relatives and neighbors that ex-slaves constantly recalled were isolates or anomalies rather than members of living communities. "My father's father was a very black, little, full-blooded, African Negro who could speak only broken English" (Mary Gladdy, b. ca. 1853, GA, 18). "My ma was a black African, an' she sho' was wild an' mean. She was so mean to me, I couldn't believe she was my mammy" (Susan Snow, b. 1850, AL, 2004). "My father was a full blood African. His parents come from there and he couldn't talk plain. . . . They couldn't keep him out of the woods. He would spend two or

three days back in there. Then the Patty Rollers would run him out and back home. He was a quill blower and a banjo picker" (Ellis Jefson, b. ca. 1861, VA, 43, 44).

My pappy he was a blacksmith. He shoe all de horses on de plantation. He wo'k so hard he hab no time to go to de fiel'. His name war Stephen Moore. Mars Jim call him Stephen Andrew. He was sold to de Moores and his mammy too. She war brought over from Africa. She never could speak plain. All her life she been a slave. White folks never recognize 'em any more than effen dey was a dog. (Fannie Moore, b. 1849, SC, 131)

None of this diminished the flow of African ideas, behaviors, and practices into North America; it merely shaped their subsequent course. Certainly, too, North American slaves were continually reminded of their connections to Africa. In dwindling numbers, African-born slaves were imported directly into the US through the mid-1800s. Along the Gulf Coasts of Mississippi, Louisiana, and Texas, the illegal slave trade was particularly rife, with regular latter-day reports of native Africans who could only have arrived after the 1808 ban.[3] "I has seen de 'nigger traders' come 'long with a bunch of slaves what they gather up from fust one place an' de other. Some of them would be Africa niggers what couldn' talk like we do, but de 'nigger traders' would sell 'em to who wanted 'em an' get de money.—jes' like tradin' mules" (Cinto Lewis, b. 1826, TX, 2327). Lu Lee's mother belonged to a family that "refugeed into Texas" from Louisiana after "some trouble come up" over their slave dealing. The departure was made in some haste. "They never could tell if I was born in Louisiana or Texas. They was along to the line and they stopped and my mother went into the covered wagon and I was borned" (Lu Lee, b. 1848 or 1849, LA, TX, 2291).

Emma Weeks was born in 1858 on a plantation four miles north of Austin. In the years just after freedom,

mammy would buy me clothes and give me little money. I enjoyed goin' to de Baptist Chu'ch. I'd go about ever other Sunday mawnin'. Sometimes my brothaws and sometimes my sistahs would go wid me, but I'd never go alone. Den sometimes, we'd go to dances, too.

Some of de boys would beg me, "Come on and dance."

Den pappy would say, "Oh, go on out and dance a set wid de boys."

Pappy hired a coal-black nigger dat had been brought from Africa. He was so black, dat we called him Joe Slick. Nobody ever knowed if he had any other name. If he had any other name, I never knowed it. He was putty near middle-aged at dat time, and he was low and chunky. He'd go wid us to dances, and pick his banjo. I don't think dat he ever got money fo' pickin' his banjo. Old Joe learned most of us to dance. . . . We never did know whut happened to Joe Slick, later in life. We never did find out where he went to. (Emma Weeks, b. 1858, TX, 4014)

The presence of an African-born banjo player and dance leader in 1870s Texas speaks volumes about possible African influences in North American Black music. Then again, Weeks offers no clue about exactly where in Africa Joe Slick, his banjo playing, and dancing may have originated. Based on her description, we are merely assuming that Joe played and danced in an African style. If so, he appears to have been that tradition's only living exponent in this milieu.

By the 1930s a number of ex-slaves interviewed by the WPA had even traveled back to Africa. Tom Windham was born a Creek slave in Indian Territory in 1845. He was sold and taken to Atlanta in 1858, where during Sherman's march he was conscripted into the Union army, playing in a brass band. At some point after the war, he visited a daughter and two sisters who had emigrated to Liberia. Chaney Mack's father was eighteen when he was stolen from Africa.

When ships landed in Africa, the black folks would go down to watch them and sometimes they would show them beads and purty things they carried on the ship. One day when my daddy and his brother, Peter, wuz standing round looking de Bossman axed dem if dey wanted to work and handed dem a package to carry on de boat. When dey got in dere dey see so many curious things dey jest wander aroun' looking, and before they know it the boat has pulled off from de landing and dey is way out in de water and kaint hep demselves, so they jest brought 'em over to Georgy and sold 'em. There wuz a boat load of them—all stolen. (Chaney Mack, b. ca. 1861, GA, 1416)

Mack recalled her father playing a homemade fiddle that he eventually exchanged for a violin, performing at plantation frolics. In 1884 he disappeared and was never heard from again. Mack's family blamed Henry Turner (1834–1915), an emancipated slave who rose to be an AME bishop, and a major activist for Black nationalism and African repatriation.[4] (Mack appears to have rearranged events in her memory, since the Charleston earthquake did not occur until August 1886.)

In 1884, he got up one mawning and walked round de house. My boy axed whar he was goin' and he said "I be back directly"—and we ain't never seen him sence. We think he went with Bishop Turner, an A.M.E. bishop of Atlanta, Ga. It wuz after the earthquake in Charleston, S.C. He wuz carryin' dem over dere until the people of Georgy made him quit. Dey wouldn't 'low his boats to land in Georgy. After Bishop Jones come to our church to talk 'bout taking dem back to Africa, my daddy walk off de next day and we ain't seen or heard from him sence. (Chaney Mack, b. ca. 1861, GA, 1418)

Against this background, the ex-slaves definitely perceived ancestral links to Africa, though for a majority these were generations or even centuries in their personal pasts. Some had occasionally been in contact with Africans and African lifeways, but mainly as oddities. They were, on the other hand, entirely unaware of the African culture traits pervading their own thought and behavior. They sometimes characterized these patterns as distinctively Black, as opposed to white, but they regarded them not as African but as their inventions. Instead, the one overwhelming cultural influence that all ex-slaves acknowledged came from whites; many ex-slaves actually were white, or in any case had white ancestry. "Sarah Anne Garey was my Ma and I was one of dem shady babies. Dere was plenty of dat kind in dem days" (Elisha Garey, b. ca. 1862, GA, 2).

> Our great grand mother wuz named granny Flora. Dey stole her frum Africa wid a red pocket handkerchief. Old man John William got my great grandmother. De people in New England got scured of we niggers. Dey were afrid we would rise aginst em and dey pushed us on down South. Lawd, why didn't dey let us stay whur we wuz, dey nebber wouldn't a been so menny half white niggers, but the old marster was to blame for that. (Hannah Crasson, b. 1853, NC, 190)

> Aunt Charlotte had white baby by her young master. Dat's why dey sold her south.

> God don't love ugly,
> Don't care nothing beauty,
> All he want is your soul. (Liza McCoy, b. 1844,
>   VA, 201)

Hundreds of ex-slaves either strongly suspected or knew for certain that they had white parents or grandparents, almost without exception fathers or grandfathers. "He thinks his Master was his father as he is a mullata" (Noah Rogers, b. 1845, MS, 1877). "I don't know who my parents were, but it seems like I heard them say my father was a white man, and I seem to remember that they said my mother was a dark woman" (Silas Dothrum, b. 1855 or 1856, AR, 187). Others were well-acquainted with white relatives, who may or may not have acknowledged them. Waters McIntosh's father was a white man named Sumter

Durant. "My mother was fourteen years old when I was born. I was her second child. Durant was in the Confederate army and was killed during the War the same year I was born" (Waters McIntosh, b. 1863, SC, 17). Henri Necaise was born January 2, 1832, near Pass Christian, Mississippi, the slave of merchant and stock trader Ursan Ladnier. "We was all French. My father was a white man, Notley (Anatole) Necaise. I knowed he was my father, 'cause he used to call me to him and tell me I was his oldes' son" (Henri Necaise, b. 1832, MS, 1622–23, orig. parentheses).

The experiences of mixed-race children varied as much as slaves overall, however. Some were acknowledged and accepted, but many were disavowed, disregarded, or otherwise dispossessed or abused by white relatives.

> My mastah and his family jes' lived in a log house. My mistress was my grandfather's wife and my grandmother, but I coulden claim 'em. Her and her oldes' chile treated me some rough. I never had no good times till that old white woman died, an' talkin' 'bout somebody glad she died, I sho' was. They tuck turns 'bout treatin' me bad. (Lewis Jenkins, b. 1844, AL, 191)

Edd Shirley (b. ca. 1840, KY) was sold three times while still a young child, the first time by, and the last time back to, his white father. George Jackson Simpson was also the slave of his father, Jim Simpson, who bound him out ca. 1866 at age twelve. "I could have been free at the close of the war, but did not know it, I thought I had to stay with my new boss until I was twenty one" (George Jackson Simpson, 1854, MO, 220). Preely Coleman was born on the Souba plantation in Newberry County, South Carolina. "It's a fact one of the Souba boys was my father" (Preely Coleman, SC, b. 1852, 856). To conceal the indiscretion, Preely and her mother were sold off to Cherokee County, Texas.

In many instances, though, white relations did afford some measure of protection and privilege. "My master was my father; he was kind to me but hard on the field hands who worked in the rice fields" (James Calhart James, 1846, SC, 34).

> I was bawn in Alabama, a little place called Buena Vista. My father's name?—Here she smiled in a cryptic manner, turned her head and hesitated. I helped her out. He must have been a white man?—He was, his name was George Nettles. He didn' own my mother, her marster was George Rackard, he was the one that bought her. George Nettles was a young man that lived on the next place to my mother's boss. He allus give me close an' shoes. I lived with his people some atter freedom, they had to kick me away from them. (Adaline Montgomery, 1859, AL, 1513–14, int. Mrs. Charles E. Wells)

Mixed-race or otherwise, in keeping with conventional wisdom, the most acculturated slaves tended to be house slaves, who were in constant contact with whites. Urban slaves too had opportunities and access unknown on remote rural plantations. Mary Anngady was born around 1857 in Chapel Hill, NC, the slave of a retail merchant. "I never lived on a farm or plantation in my life. My mother was a cook. They allowed us a lot of privileges. The Negro and white children played together, and there was little if any difference made in the treatment given a slave child and a white child" (Mary Anngady, b. ca. 1857, NC, 34). After freedom Mary pursued her formal education at Shaw Collegiate Institute with the former slaveholder's support. Over the subsequent course of her life, she married and assisted a Liberian missionary fundraising in the US; toured nationally as a lecturer for colored relief charities; and worked as a stage entertainer singing and playing the piano, guitar, and violin. "I often recited the recitation written by the colored poet, Paul Laurence Dunbar, When Malinda Sings to the delight of our audiences" (Mary Anngady, b. ca. 1857, NC, 38).[5]

During this period, white and Indian slavery also existed throughout the South, and a few ex-slaves interviewed by the WPA were unaware of any African ancestry. "'My father,' said Aunt Harriet, 'was a Cherokee Indian named Green Norris, and mother was a white woman named Betsy Richards. You see, I am mixed. My mother give me to Mr. George Naves [a plantation overseer] when I was three years old" (Harriet Miller, b. ca. 1837, GA, SC, 127). Berry Clay was born in 1847 in Telfair County, Georgia. His biological father was "Fitema Bob Britt, a full blood Indian," and his mother was white. As a child Berry was taken to Macon by Britt and his mother and sold as a slave (Berry Clay. b. 1847, GA, 189).

Many more ex-slaves knew that they had both Native American and African blood, and possibly white as well. "My father was half African and my grandfather was a full blood African. . . . Caroline Samuel, my mother, was a half Creek Indian" (C. G. Samuel, b. ca. 1870, IT, child of ex-slaves, 267). "My pa says in Virginny Injun's marry slaves. His pa' was a Injun and his ma come from Africy and dey marry in Virginny" (Louis Evans, b. 1853, LA, 1309). "My gran'mudder, dat's my mudder's mudder, she was a Africcy woman. Dey brung her freeborn from d' ol' place in Africcy. . . . My uder gran'maw was a pyore (pure) bred Injun Woman. She raise all my mudder's chillen" (Virginia Newman, b. 1827, LA, 2903, orig. parentheses). "My grandmammy was a juksie, because her mammy was a Nigger and her daddy was a choctaw Indian. That's what makes me so mixed up with Indian, African and white blood" (Cato Carter, b. 1836 or 1837, AL, 641).

> My father uster b'long to dem Guinea men. . . . He was sol' out from de ol' country, dat was Mis'sippi. Dey sol' him but dey didn' sol' my mama. . . . My mama' name was Sarah. She come from de Choctaw country, 'roun' in Georgy. I had a gramma Rebecca, a reg'lar ol' Injun woman. She hab two long black braid down longer'n her waist. . . . My ol' Injun gampa was name' Jim, and I hab grampa and grandma w'at come from Mis'sippi. . . . Dey tells me I got uncles and aunts in Africy but I ain't neber 'spectin' to see 'em. (Mary Johnson, b. ca. 1858, MS, 2021–22, 2030)

Fig. 2.2. Cato Carter, ex-slave, Dallas, TX, September 3, 1937. "You goin' take my picture? I lived through plenty and I lived a long time, but this is the first time I ever had my picture took. If I'd knowed you wanted to do that, I'd have tidied up and put on my best" (Cato Carter, b. 1836 or 1837, AL, 211). Portraits of African American ex-slaves from the US Works Progress Administration, Federal Writers' Project slave narratives collection, Library of Congress.

Because of different colonial approaches to native peoples, the relations of Africans and Indians also differed in the US and Latin America. In Central and South America, Indian or mestizo peasants annexed into colonial systems interacted constantly with African slaves, with observable effects in areas like music, dance, and song. In North America, the policy of extermination, removal, and partition produced very different results. American plantation slavery specifically coincided with the genocide and dispossession of southeastern tribes, and many of the Indian ancestors recalled by ex-slaves appear to have been isolated holdouts or survivors. In Florida, Mississippi and Alabama, and Louisiana, ex-slaves did describe contact with remaining bands of, respectively, Seminole, Choctaw, and Houma. A few even recalled musical interactions, but the impact appears minimal. "When I was young, I remembah dat I played wid Indian chillun. I even knowed how de Injuns sang and danced. I never danced with the Injuns, though" (Rebecca Thomas, b. 1825, AR, 3822). "There was an Indian Camp near Boggy branch and sometimes we would go over and listen to them sing and see them dance and jump, which was their form of amusement" (Juda Dantzler, b. ca. 1850, MS, 554).

[Postwar Black] country frolics (dances) were quite often attended by [Seminole] Indians, whose main reason for going was to obtain whiskey, for which they had a very strong fondness. Berry describes an intoxicated Indian as a "tornado mad man" and recalls a hair raising incident that ended in tragedy for the offender.

A group of Indians were attending one of these frolics at Fort Meyers and everything went well until one of the number became intoxicated, terrorizing the Negroes with bullying, and fighting anyone with whom he could "pick" a quarrel. "Big Charlie" an uncle of the narrator was present and when the red man challenged him to a fight made a quick end of him by breaking his neck at one blow.

For two years he was hounded by revengeful Indians, who had an uncanny way of ferreting out his whereabouts no matter where he went. Often he sighted them while working in the fields and would be forced to flee to some other place. This continued with many hairbreadth escapes, until he was forced to move several states away. (Frank Berry, b. 1858, FL, 28–29, orig. parentheses)

My gran' says when she was a chile, her white folks came from North Car'lina an' brought deir niggahs wid dem. Dey all rid in big covered wagons, an' would camp at nights, an' put up tents. One time dey camped right close to a big Injun camp. De Injuns was havin' a frolic, an' deir gals was all a' dancin' wid deir pretty long hair a hangin' down deir backs, an' de cullud mens was plum ca'hied away wid dem pretty Injun gals, an' wanted to git in de frolic to dance wid 'em. But de Injun mens wouldn' let de cullud mens dance wid deir gals.

Dey let white mens dance wid 'em, but dey didn' like no black mens aroun'. Den one of de cullud mens got mad an' throwed a big rock into de Injun's camp. Den de Injun mens come atter him, but he got away. He hid in a tent under a big pile o' bedclothes. De Injuns rambled all through de tents a lookin' for him. Dat was when my gran' was comin' to Mississippi wid her white folks, but oh, honey, I 'members seein' a heap of Injuns myself. (Mandy Jones, b. ca. 1857, MS, 1238–39)

De Choctaws live all round Second Creek. Some ob dem had cabins like settled folks. I kin remembah dare last chief. He wuz a tall, powerful built man named "Big Sam." What he said wuz de law kaize he wuz de boss ob de whole tribe. One rainy night he wuz kilt in a saloon down in "Natchez Under de Hill." De Injuns went wild wid rage en grief. Dey sung, en wailed en did a heap o' low mutterin. De sheriff kep a stiddy watch on 'em kaize he wuz feared dey would do somethin rash. Aftah a long while he kinda let up in his vigilance. Den some ob de Choctaw men slipped in town en stobbed de man what dey 'bleeved kilt Big Sam. I membahs hit well. (Charlie Davenport, b. ca. 1837, MS, 560)

In the former Indian Territory, Oklahoma fieldworkers interviewed numerous Creek and Cherokee ex-slaves, a few of whom had grown up speaking Native languages or otherwise participating in Native culture. Then again, the Cherokee were especially known for their own large-scale acculturation, including (besides the adoption of slavery) conversion to Southern fundamentalism and the creation of a written form of their language. Cherokee translations of Bible passages began appearing in the 1820s, the complete Cherokee New Testament in 1860.[6] Many Cherokee sang exactly the same church songs as their Black and white neighbors, albeit in Cherokee.[7] Ex-slave Chaney Richardson was born in the 1840s at Tahlequah, Indian Territory. "I've been a good churchgoer all my life until I git too feeble, and I still understand and talk Cherokee

language and love to hear songs and parts of the Bible in it because it make me think about the time I was a little girl before my pappy and mammy leave me" (Chaney Richardson, b. ca. 1847, IT, 262).

Lucinda Davis did not know where she was born, but she was raised near Fort Gibson, Indian Territory. "First thing I remember is when I was a little girl, and I belong to old Tuskaya-hiniha. He was a big man in de Upper Creek, and we have a purty good size farm" (Lucinda Davis, b. ca. 1848, IT, 53). Among other folklore, she recalled a pair of popular African American dance lyrics originating around 1900. She could not have learned them before that time anyway.

> What yo' gwine do when de meat give out?
> What yo' gwine do when de meat give out?
> Set in de corner wid my lips pooched out!
> Lawsy!

> What yo' gwine do when de meat come in?
> What yo' gwine do when de meat come in?
> Set in de corner wid a greasy chin!
> Lawsy!

Dat's about de only little nigger song I know, less'n it be de one about:

> Great big nigger, laying 'hind de log—
> Finger on de trigger and eye on the hawg!
> Click go de trigger and bang go de gun!
> Here come de owner and de buck nigger run!

And I think I learn both of dem long after I been grown, 'cause I belong to a full-blooded Creek Indian and I didn't know nothing but Creek talk long after de Civil War. (Lucinda Davis, b. ca. 1848, IT, 53)[8]

The Territory Creek and Cherokee had in fact maintained some indigenous traditions. "Each year, usually in July they would have their annual stomp dances. At these stomp dances they would tie shells around their ankles and beat on a drum made from a cow hide and they would dance and sing" (John Harrison, b. 1857, IT, 158).[9] However, many of the Indians the ex-slaves had known were themselves fairly Anglicized.

> I been belonging to church ever since there was a colored church, and I thinks everybody should obey the Master. He died, and I wants to go where Jesus lives. Like the poor Indian I saw one time waiting to be hung. There he was, setting on his own coffin box, singing over and over the words I just said: "I wants to go where Jesus lives!" (Victoria Taylor Thompson, b. ca. 1858, IT, 323–24)

William Banjo was interviewed in the Thomy Lafon Old Folks' Home in New Orleans but had also once lived in Oklahoma. "Asked for spirituals, his thin face and sightless eyes turned toward the questioner. 'I might know some Indian songs.' 'Indian songs?' 'Songs I learned in Oklahoma'" (William Banjo, b. unk., OK, LA, 13–14, int. Robert McKinney). To illustrate what he meant by *Indian songs*, Banjo performed the Protestant hymn "I Heard the Voice of Jesus Say" (Horatius Bonar, 1846). Overall, in fact, the music and song Creek and Cherokee ex-slaves remembered was just like the music and song described by ex-slaves generally. "In slavery time the Cherokee negroes do like anybody else when they is a death—jest listen to a chapter in the Bible and cry. We had a good song I remember. It was 'Don't Call the Roll, Jesus, Because I'm Going Home'" (Betty Robertson, b. ca. 1844, IT, 269). Robertson does not indicate whether the preacher took his text from the Cherokee or King James Bible. Lucinda Vann was born near present-day Webber Falls, Oklahoma, on the plantation of Jim Vann, a Cherokee with about five hundred slaves. She remembered the slaves, but also Vann and his family, dancing to the same fiddle music played and danced by slaves and slaveholders everywhere. She even referred to Cherokee slaveholders as "white folks" (Lucinda Vann, b. ca. 1840, IT, 346–47). Johnson Thompson's father passed through several Indian slaveholders, including another member of the Vann

family, but was finally taken to Texas by a mixed-blood Cherokee named Thompson.

> Pappy wanted to go back to his mother when the War was over and the slaves was freed. He made a deal with Dave Mounts, a white man, who was moving into the Indian country, to drive for him. A four mule team was hitched to the wagon, and for five weeks he was on the road from Texas, finally getting to grandmaw Brewers at Fort Gibson. Pappy worked around the farms and fiddled for the Cherokee dances. (Johnson Thompson, b. 1853, IT, 311)

That even Native Americans reinforced Anglo-American standards and traditions reveals a situation that could without overstatement be described as somewhat Eurocentric; and, notwithstanding individual differences in opportunity and access, by the mid-1800s the lifeways of North American slaves predictably reflected Anglo-Americans' complete domination of the antebellum South, cultural and otherwise. Probably this was less a result of any deliberate plan than the basic demographics of US slavery (and the effects of US Indian policies). Granted, there is some evidence of the forced acculturation of African slaves by slaveholders, or of the forcible suppression of African practices, but in truth, most Southern whites had only the foggiest notions about Africa and the African backgrounds of slaves. If US slaveholders banned African traditions, it was not necessarily because they were recognized as African, but more likely because they might allow slaves to organize and communicate secretly, because they violated Protestant doctrines, because they were disruptive or disturbing to whites, and so forth. On the other hand, slaveholders were perfectly willing to exploit the African agricultural practices (recognized or otherwise) that effectively built the plantation South. As generations passed, the majority of North American slaves probably acculturated not so much because of direct pressure, but within the daily course of events through constant contact with whites and the obvious advantages of learning their ways—as well as the negative consequences of defying them. "I was up in Virginny wukin' on de railroad a few years ago. De boss man called me aside one day and said: 'Paul, you ain't lak dese other Niggers. I kin tell white folks raised you'" (Paul Smith, b. ca. 1863, VA, 338). "She has been a great deal in the company of white people, and uses very little dialect" (Cicely Cawthon, b. 1859, GA, 177). "I'll tell you why I speaks better English than some of the other cullud folks. I have a right to, because the woman who raised me—my white folks would c'rect me along with their own children" (Adaline Montgomery, 1859, AL, 1519).

In fact, while ex-slaves recalled many native Africans as misfits who never adjusted to the plantation regimen or learned to speak English properly, other Africans mastered white ways as well as any, and sometimes better. A handful of Mississippi ex-slaves actually described native African preachers leading slave congregations. They were highly acculturated Southern Protestants, however, and certainly not officials of functioning African faiths; to the contrary, they preached the same texts and led the same songs as other clergy, white or Black.

> Mr. Anderson wus er fine Christ'in man. He built er church fur his slaves an' named dat church "Rose Hill" an' I reckin dat church is still standin' dar today. A big black African man done de preachin. Dat African wore long rings in his ears, but he culd preach. On Sundays, de slaves jes sot 'round de cabin doors an' talk an' wrap hair, an' sumtimes dey wud sing. Sum times slaves frum udder plantashuns wud cum an' jine de crowd, but dey all toted passes ter keep de patterollers frum ketchin' 'em . . . . When de African wud cum dat is when we all went ter church an' den dey wud sing—

> Old time 'ligion, old time 'ligion,
> It's good 'nouf fur me. (Ann Drake, b. 1855, MS, 645–46)

They didn't have no schools and the niggers couldn't read or write. Leastways, nobody but Uncle Charlie Frasier. He would read the Bible to the niggers and hold prayer-meeting during the week. Uncle Charlie wus a free nigger from Africa and his wife too. His house was separate from the other niggers and he had his own garden. He raised rice 'cause he been use to living on it. They told him it wouldn't grow here but he showed 'em. (Callie Gray, b. 1857, MS, 866)[10]

Frasier was evidently one of the Africans who established rice agriculture in the American South, but he had also done quite well at assimilating white knowledge and behaviors.[11]

Ex-slaves were obviously aware that they and whites differed fundamentally in many things, and that they were responding to different cultural inheritances, worship styles and musical tastes being oft-cited examples. Narrators constantly characterized songs, dances, instruments, or instrumental styles as uniquely Black or typically white. Scores of ex-slaves juxtaposed the staid proceedings in white churches with their own spirit-filled meetings, where they could sing as they pleased, fully expressing African-based religious concepts and musical principles. They no longer thought or spoke of these practices as African, however, but as completely their own (or as divinely revealed and inspired), a sharp contrast to Latin America, where legions of slaves still knowingly worshipped African gods through African traditions of music, song, and dance, sometimes in the original African languages. Given these differing cultural climates, the same African traditions sometimes took root throughout the Americas, yet with quite varied functions and meanings.

> We had corn shuckin's at night, and candy pullin's. Sometimes we had quiltings and dances. One of the slaves, my aint, she wuz a royal slave. She could dance all over de place wid a tumbler of water on her head, widout spilling it. She sho could tote

Fig. 2.3. Hannah Crasson, ex-slave, NC. 1937–38. Portraits of African American ex-slaves from the US Works Progress Administration, Federal Writers' Project slave narratives collection, Library of Congress.

herself. I always luved to see her come to church. She sho could tote herself. (Hannah Crasson, b. 1853, NC, 191)

Hannah Crasson was one of over a dozen WPA narrators who described North American slaves dancing with water vessels balanced on their heads.[12] Unlike their counterparts in Western Nigeria and broad swaths of the West Indies and South America, none of these ex-slaves identified themselves as Yoruba, and none professed thereby to venerate Shàngó.

Shàngó is the Yoruba *orisha* (god) of thunder, whose worship (also Chángó, Sàngó, Xangô) spread from West Africa throughout the Black Atlantic.[13] In the Americas, his religion has been especially powerful in Brazil, Cuba, Jamaica, and Trinidad, but its influences are far-flung. As an organized faith, Shàngó did not take hold among North American slaves, but circumstantial evidence suggests US slaves were acquainted with Shàngó. Many North American Blacks once believed that a person could "split a thunderstorm" (that is, disperse it) by driving a double-headed axe into the ground, a hazy recollection of Shàngó, who creates storms by brandishing his double-headed thunder-axe and hurling his lightning bolts and thunderstones into the earth.[14] In West Africa, Neolithic celts (stone axe-heads) found in plowed fields were said to be Shàngó's thunderstones (hence his identification with axes).[15] In the plantation South, this doctrine was transformed into the Black folk belief that unearthed Native American arrowheads come from lightning strikes.[16]

As a thunder god, Shàngó is volatility personified, described in praise songs as "water by the side of fire at the center of the sky."[17] Like thunderstorms, he can kill and destroy without warning, but he also brings life-giving rain. His wives are the three largest rivers of the Niger Delta, whose annual floods are the region's lifeblood. Their marital relations are fiery and tempestuous to say the least, and serve as subjects of many of the best stories. This fire-and-water symbolism is expressed in other ways, most spectacularly when Shàngó possesses his followers, enabling them to dance with fire and water balanced on their heads.

In Yoruba art Shàngó is depicted holding a lightning bolt in one hand and his thunder-axe in the other; his devotees can be identified by the lightning bolts or axes balanced on their heads, symbolizing divine possession and spiritual harmony. To dance at Shàngó ceremonies with a pot of water or candle balanced on one's head is the ritual expression of this cosmological balance. It is also a balancing act characteristic of the many African and African American dances requiring performers to twin their bodies, in this instance by shuffling, clogging, swaying, or gyrating below the waist while holding the head and torso perfectly steady and upright.

Master had a small platform built, an' on dat, de jiggin' contest am held. Cullud fo'ks f'om 'roun' thar would come, and dey sees who could jig de best. Sometimes, de two persons would put a cup ob wautah on thar head, an' see who could jig da hahdest widout spillin' any. De whites 'tend de contest too. 'Twas lots ob fun. Thar am one cullud fellow on weuns' place, dat am de jigginest fellow dat ever was. All de neighbahs 'roun' tries to git someone to best him. Well Sar, dat fellow could put a glass ob wautah on his head an' make his feet go lak triphammahs an' sound lak a snaredrum. He could whirl 'roun', an' sich, an' all de movement am f'om his hip down. (James W. Smith, b. 1860, TX, 3634–35)

Head-portage is, moreover, a distinctively African culture trait, inescapable even in the most mundane daily activities. As Robert Farris Thompson observes, "to move in perfect confidence with an object balanced on the head is one of the accomplishments of traditional life in Africa."[18] Head-portage was also among the African cultural traits universally practiced by North American slaves; indeed, images of servile Blacks bearing loads on their heads (cotton baskets, water buckets, produce trays, laundry bundles, firewood, and more) are central to the iconography of the Old South.

Fig. 2.4. "Yoruba Women Carrying Goods." "Africa," *Missions-Bilder*, vol. 3 (Calw & Stuttgart: Bereinsbuchhandlung, 1864–80). Slavery Images: A Visual Record of the African Slave Trade and Slave Life in the Early African Diaspora. slaveryimages.org. From a German missionary society publication on the transatlantic slave trade, focusing on Yorubaland and its diaspora.

> We lived around Hanniberry Creek. It was a pretty lake of water. Some folks called it Hanniberry Lake. We fished and waded and washed. We got our water out of two springs further up. I used to tote one bucket on my head and one in each hand. You never see that no more. Mama was a nurse and house woman and field woman if she was needed. I made fires around the pots and 'tended to mama's children. (Molly Finley, b. 1865, child of ex-slaves, AR, 292)

> When I was young, before I was converted, I loved to dance all night. I could dance with a glass full of water on my head and make bows to my lady partner and never let a drop out. White folks used to get me to do it, and they'd give me five dollars; sometimes more. Colored people don't seem to be able to hold anythin' on their heads anymo', not even a basket of clothes. I wonder if they heads is changed? If I was more steady on my feet, I could do it now. We had nice times frolicking. We sang and danced and drank anisette. (Hunton Love, b. ca. 1840, LA, 162–64)[19]

Besides balancing water vessels or fire pots, Shàngó dancers brandished *oshe* (ritual wooden thunder-axes), pretending to belch lightning bolts. In some cases they actually ate fire, extinguishing candles or other lighted objects in their mouths. In Bahia, Brazil,

> in the cycle of festivals for Shàngó in the shrine of São Gonçalo there is an impressive ceremony, only realized there, wherein the daughters of Shàngó, possessed by their orisha, dance with a vessel that contains material in flames, upon their heads. The fire does not harm them, nor does it burn the hands with which they secure the burning vessel. Later, while still moving in the dance, they eat flaming balls of cotton dipped in oil.[20]

The accompaniment for Shàngó dancing is prescribed by African precedent and fairly consistent throughout the cult's distribution, requiring a complement of three

Fig. 2.5. "At the Pump." Charleston, SC, ca. 1879. Kilburn Brothers. Stereograph Cards Collection, Library of Congress, Prints and Photographs Division. One of a series of staged photos showing Black street vendors, water carriers, and cotton warehouse workers bearing loads on their heads.

double-headed drums, still known in much of the New World by their Yoruba name, *bàtá*.[21]

Shàngó was worshipped in this fashion everywhere in the Americas with a large self-identified Yoruba population. Trinidad's government officially prohibited but informally tolerated Shàngó, embraced by its large Yoruba minority. In the 1930s Trinidadian calypsonians recorded an entire series of satiric songs on the subject: "Shango" (The Lion, 1934), "Yaraba [Yoruba] Shango" (The Tiger, 1936), "Ho Syne No Day" ("*Osine o de*" or "Osine will come") (The Lion, 1937), "The Bongo Dance" (The Growler, 1937). In them they described Shàngó worshippers dancing "wit' a Martiniquan goblet on dey head / An' a broom in dey han' to invoke the dead," or "wiping their faces with stinging nettle / And swallowing lighted pieces of candle," while singing hymns to Shàngó, Osine (god of herbalistic medicine), Ogún (god of war and iron), and other Yoruba *orishas*.[22]

There were New World changes in Shàngó, of course. In the established pattern, his character was conflated with various Catholic saints.[23] Elements of Shàngó were also adopted by other African Americans, including *voudon* worshippers in Haiti and subsequently *hoodoo* practitioners in New Orleans. In the Haitian *brulé-zin* (the ceremony of burning pots), initiates balanced firepots on their heads.[24] A New Orleans informant described local celebrity Doctor Jim as "one of the best hoodoo dancers I ever saw in my life. He would dance naked with hot coals on his head and the women would go wild." Marie Brown was the great-granddaughter of a hoodoo priestess, Queen Eliza of the Dance. "She danced at all the Marie Laveau meetin's on St. John's Eve. One thing she could do was to put a glass of water on her head and dance wit'out spillin' a drop. Sometimes she would dance wit' a lighted candle on her head."[25] Marie Laveau was New Orleans's most powerful and famous hoodoo queen. On St. John's Eve (June 23, the Summer Solstice), she convened large dances on the shores of Lake Ponchartrain, where Laveau herself "used to rise out of the lake with a huge communion candle burning on top of her head and one in each hand."[26]

In another rite, the *Fe Chauffe*, dancers stepped around bottles or firepots with glasses of water or lighted candles balanced on their heads.[27] People also danced this way for fun. Louisiana ex-slave Lizzie Chandler remembered performing the bottle trick at antebellum balls.

> "When I was young I went to dances—not wicked dances like they have now, but the kind that made you happy, the 'Virginny Reel' and things like that—I could dance with a glass of water on my head and cross my leg over a bottle at the same time. No ma'm, tain't hard, no more'n balancin' a heavy basket on your head."
>
> Here, a neighbor came in, and, not to be outdone, remarked: "I could tote on my head one bucket of water and one in each hand, and walk miles and never spill a drop." (Lizzie Chandler, b. unk., LA, 41)

Outside New Orleans, in fact, the custom of dancing while balancing a water glass was always practiced

Fig. 2.6. "Winter holidays in the southern states. Plantation frolic on Christmas Eve." *Leslie's* 5 (December 26, 1857): 64. Slaves jigging, accompanied by fiddle, banjo, and two-handed bones. The male dancer is doing the *pigeon wing*; his partner raises the hem of her skirt to reveal her footwork.

Fig. 2.7. "Dancing Between Decks." *Illustrated London News* 17 (July 6, 1850): 21. Irish Traditional Music Archive. itma.ie. Irish families fleeing the famine, jigging on their way to America.

recreationally. It never served any sacred function, instead being most closely associated with competitive step dancing or *jigging*.

The *African jig*, or *Negro jig* as it is distinguished in period sources, definitely resembles the Anglo-Irish step dance or jig from which it borrowed its name. There were obviously deeper connections, but the African jig was indisputably created by North American slaves; by the late 1700s, it was acknowledged as a unique genre even by whites, who danced it themselves.[28] The African jig was thus no more African than Irish, and it definitely was not Irish. British and Irish jigs are defined by their triple-time signatures (6/8 or 9/8). Negro jigs were invariably in 2/4 allegro, resembling a reel. Ideally, they were danced on wooden surfaces like cabin floors, barn lofts, and porches, though some slaveholders actually built wooden platforms for their slaves to jig. When no floor was available, slaves even laid boards over bare ground. Hard-soled shoes were advantageous but not absolutely necessary. Other so-called *jig dances* (the *buck dance*, the *heel and toe*, the *double shuffle*) were identified by the same sort of acrobatics and percussive footwork, sounding, in James Smith's words, "lak triphammahs" or "lak a snaredrum" (James W. Smith, b. 1860, TX, 3634–35). There seems little doubt that this aspect of jigging was borrowed from Anglo-Irish dance traditions, though

some African Americans may have discovered clogging for themselves. Anyway, there was nothing like it in Africa.[29]

This footwork often served as its own accompaniment, substituting for the sacred *bàtá* drums. There was no obligatory accompaniment for jigging, however, and people jigged to fiddles, banjos, quills (panpipes), accordions, tambourines, bones, or any instruments used for dancing. With or without instruments, jigging was often competitive and always demanding, especially when dancers simultaneously balanced water buckets on their heads. "'My mammy wuz de best dancer on de plantashun,' Malinda proudly asserts, 'She could dance so sturdy she could balance a glass of water on her head and never spill a drop'" (Malinda Mitchell, b. 1853, SC, 442). "Dey dance de ol' fashion dance, de promenade, an' de jig. Some times dey have de jiggin' contest, two niggers puts a glass ob wauter on deir heads an' den see who can dance de hardest wid out spillin' any wauter" (Fred Brown, b. 1853, LA, 468). "My mammy cud dance; I seed her lift her dress an' put a pail uf water on her hed an' dance an' niver spill er drop. Folks cant do dat now" (Gabe Butler, b. 1854, MS, 325). Butler's mother raised her skirt to display her footwork, a common move for female jig dancers (see fig. 2.6).

Jigging was also a spectator sport, encouraged and enjoyed by slaveholders and other whites, who often engaged and paid dancers, awarded prizes, or gambled among themselves.

Whenever dere was a contest, a man name Jolly would win all of 'em. Dis darky sure could dance. Boy, when he started twirling his legs and stickin' out his back, old master would holler. Wouldn't let Jolly work hard either 'cause he was de best dat master Landro had. He won plenty of money dancin' for master. (Elizabeth Ross Hite, b. ca. 1850, LA, 106)

Frolics were often given on the Harper plantation. They usually consisted of dancing and banjo playing. Slaves from other plantations sometimes attended, but it was necessary to obtain a pass from their master and mistress in order to do so. A prize was given to the person who could "buck dance" the steadiest with a tumbler of water balanced on the head. A cake or a quilt was often given as the prize. (Emmaline Heard, b. ca. 1860, GA, 151)

My ma was called Queen Eliza (pronounced E-lee-za) of the Dance because she was a fine dancer. She would put a glass of water on her head, and it never spilled no matter how long she kept it up. . . . The firemens always had her at their balls. Once, when she was sick and couldn't come, they called it off. She made lots of money because people said nobody could dance like her. When big people came to the city, she was brought to entertain them. But she didn't always dance like that. She had been christened Catholic, but when she "got religion" and joined the Baptist Church she gave it all up. (Marie Brown, b. unk., LA, 34, orig. parentheses)

While the WPA narratives provide the most examples of this practice by far, there is ample corroboration from ex-slave memoirs and other period sources. "Some slaves were good dancers, especially the young girls, some of whom could dance so steadily that if a glass of water were placed on their heads none of the water would be spilt. I have often seen a girl dance for ten minutes with a glass cup filled with water on her head without any of it being spilt" (Allen Parker, 1804–1906).[30] " 'Now steady in the farmer,' 'Bounce the ball,' 'Do dat agin' and 'Bounce to your partner' were the other refrains to this peculiar dance. Some of the ladies could dance with a waiter on the head holding a glass of water, and so steady was the motion, that not a drop was spilled" (Daniel Webster Davis, 1862–1913).[31] Stage entertainer Tom Fletcher (1873–1954) had heard about this dancing from ex-slave parents and grandparents.[32] After visiting an 1870s Cincinnati dance hall, Lafcadio Hearn (1850–1904) wrote, "the best performer on the floor was a stumpy little roustabout named Jem Scott, who is a marvelous jig-dancer, and can waltz with a tumbler full of water on his head without spilling a drop."[33]

In some areas, memories of the practice persisted nearly to present. Gladys-Marie Fry collected an account in 1964 from a slave's grandchild in Washington, DC.[34] In the 1800s, this dancing was especially popular among Creoles in and around New Orleans. In the 1980s during my fieldwork on zydeco (urban Creole dance music) in the Houston area, I occasionally saw Creole dancers balance serving trays on their heads. I was told more than once that this was an old trick. I suspect none of my informants knew just how old. At the time I had no clue what I was watching.[35]

Jigging while head-balancing was one practice that Blacks and whites alike regarded as characteristically African American; there are only a couple of reports of whites performing the stunt, and always in imitation of Blacks.[36] (Not coincidentally, slaves daily bore loads on their heads during assigned tasks; slaveholders and other whites obviously did not.) I have not found a single suggestion anywhere, however, that North American slaves or slaveholders were aware of any connection to Africa or Shàngó. Instead, the dance that had once served as an African expression of spiritual balance had been completely transformed into an African American exhibition of athletic prowess. Around New Orleans, the sacred function was occasionally transferred to hoodoo, but even there, the dance was performed recreationally and competitively. Given the other hints of Shàngó in North America, his religion probably had some role in these developments, but New Orleans hoodoo may actually have played a greater part in establishing the US tradition. Nonetheless, if most North American slaves assigned the practice any religious significance, it was because they were Southern Protestants who considered all social dancing sinful (with or without head-balancing). Neither did anyone tie this custom to Anglo-Irish step-dancing, but there is unmistakable evidence of that tradition's impact too, as well as New World Black innovations.

Shàngó's fate in the United States perfectly illustrates the nature of African influences in North American slave music, song, and dance, and the special challenges of identifying and analyzing these currents. West and Central Africa were major sources of North American slaves and also many of their musical traditions, but significant numbers came from other regions, and musical correspondences crop up throughout the continent. Some resemblances reveal direct historical connections, others only the basic unity of African music. Despite its diversity, that is, sub-Saharan Africa does constitute a single musical region, the same aesthetic principles, musical forms, instrument types, vocal techniques, performance strategies, and so on recurring across the continent.[37] In Latin America, tradition bearers may be fully aware of African antecedents—even very specific African

antecedents—forming an integral part of their performances. Given the multicultural African backgrounds of early North American slaves, the rapid ascendancy of a native-born slave population, and the absolute domination of whites, US Black music often suggests no specific African links beyond the overarching musical templates that all Africans shared, wholly transformed in New World surroundings by African Americans' own ingenuity and resourcefulness.[38] If these resources sometimes included Africa, European and especially British, Irish, and Anglo-American equivalents could be just as important.

All of this reaffirms the obvious truism that, from an early date, most African American music was African American or, in many cases, simply American. It evolved from an incessant, recursive process of cultural combination, reinvention, and innovation that had actually begun centuries earlier on the other side of the Atlantic through extensive African-European contacts prior to and then during the North American slave trade. As a result, for every musical trait that can definitely be traced to Africa or Europe, there are dozens that suggest one or the other, or both together, but that can be conclusively assigned to neither. Such is the case with *patting*, a combination of handclapping, thigh-slapping, and foot-stamping that served as the rhythmic foundation of all slave social music. Like the African jig, patting embodies the most fundamental principles of African music, but with unmistakable Anglo-Irish touches; ultimately, however, patting is unlike anything in either Africa or Europe, being entirely a creation of North American slaves.

SOCIAL MUSIC

PATTING

Juba, Jigging, and General Body Percussion

We had us a good time dem days! Danced, an' ever'body pat and somebody call sets. Had a fiddle, had banjos, too, but de best was knockin' two bones behind de fiddle, like dis . . . I *show* hankered ter hurry up an' git big enough ter knock bones! Sometimes, didn' fool wid no fiddle or nothin', jes pat an' sing. Sing "Cotton-Eyed Joe."

> Who been here since I been gone?
> Nobody but cotton-eyed Joe!

an' sing

> Ole gray horse come tearin' out de wilderness. (Ned Chaney, b. ca. 1857,
> MS, 374, orig. emphasis and ellipsis)[1]

Dances? Yes sir, I can hear them fiddles and de pattin' now. Dis de way de dance was called: "Balance all; sashay to your partners; swing her 'round and promenade all; forward on de head; ladies change"; and all dat. Then de jigs went on. Believe me, them was times! (Henry D. Jenkins, b. ca. 1850, SC, 25)

The banjo and the fiddle made up the orchestra, and there were accompanists who "patted" with the hands, keeping accurate time with the music. In patting, the position was usually a half-stoop or forward bend, with a slap of one hand on the left knee followed by the same stroke and noise on the right, and then a loud slap of the two palms together. I should add that the left hand made two strokes in halftime to one for the right, something after the double stroke of the left drumstick in beating the kettledrum. (John Allan Wyeth [1845–1922], *With Sabre and Scalpel* [1914], 59, Alabama, ca. 1850)

For American slaves, instrumental music was with few exceptions dance music. Dancing was music in itself—sometimes the only music—the sounds of bodies in motion serving as their own accompaniment. "At night

Fig. 3.1. Green Cumby, ex-slave, Abilene, TX, July 13, 1937. Portraits of African American ex-slaves from the US Works Progress Administration, Federal Writers' Project slave narratives collection, Library of Congress. "Durin' slavery, I had purty rough times. My grandfather, Tater Cumby, wuz de cullud overseer fo' forty slaves. He called us at four o'clock in de mornin' an' we worked from sun to sun" (Green Cumby, b. 1851, TX, 1002).

the slaves gather roun' the cabins in little bunches and talk 'til bed time. Some times we'd dance while some would knock out time for us by snappin' de finger and slappin' de knee. We didn't have nothin' to make music on" (Green Cumby, b. 1851, TX, 1004). "On Christmas and the 4th of July we would get the old fiddle man to play for us to dance. If we danced any other time, the only music we had was the patting of the hands" (Edward Jones, b. 1855, MS, 1206).

The catchall terms for such body percussion were *patting*, *juba*, or *patting juba*, referring broadly to various combinations of handclapping, body slapping, and foot stamping. More fundamentally, patting reflects the overall rhythmic sophistication of Black music that has impressed outsiders from earliest observations to present. Aside from the prevalence of percussion and percussionists, instruments that elsewhere serve primarily for melody (including the human voice) often acquire percussive qualities and rhythmic functions in Africa and the diaspora, reflecting what J. H. Kwabena Nketia has described as "a distinct bias toward percussion and the use of percussive techniques, not only because of the structural functions of such instruments, but also because of a preference for musical textures that embody percussive sounds or sounds that increase the ratio of noise to pitch."[2]

Indeed, this ratio of noise to pitch—or what I will hereafter call the *grit-to-pitch ratio*—offers one of the best clues to the actual sound of slave music. Even without recordings we can be sure that, however else it sounded, slave music was definitely *gritty*, a term American Blacks have traditionally used in just this sense. We can so conclude partly because twentieth-century sound recordings do exhaustively document these qualities in later African American music. However, nineteenth-century descriptions of slaves *sawing* or *scraping* fiddles, *thumping* or *rapping* banjos, or *banging* guitars make clear that earlier generations applied these same instrumental techniques and aesthetic principles. And the most considerable and consistent proof for the grit-to-pitch ratio as a fundamental feature of North American slave music comes from accounts of patting and body percussion as fixtures in any and all performances, the foundational grit upon which all else was pitched.

Handclapping occurs everywhere, but across Africa it is by far the most common form of musical accompaniment.[3] Reflecting this heritage, African Americans also habitually clap along with music and song.[4] Patting too embodies this basic aesthetic, but patting per se is uniquely African American. Later writers have sometimes linked it to just one rhythm, rhythmic routine, or dance rhyme, but in truth patting was highly variable and infinitely adaptable. "Patting is performed by striking the hands on the knees, then striking the hands together, then striking the right shoulder with one hand, the left with the other—all the while keeping time with the feet, and singing" (LA, 1840s).[5] "I had never seen Juber clapped to the banjor before. . . . The clappers rested the right foot on the heel, and its clap on the floor was in perfect unison with the notes of the banjor, and palms of the hands on the corresponding extremities; while the dancers were all jigging it away" (VA, 1830s).[6] "Some one calls for a fiddle—but if one is not to be found, some one 'pats juber.' This is done by placing one foot a little in advance of the other, raising the ball of the foot from the ground, and striking it in regular time, while, in connection, the hands are struck slightly together, and then upon the thighs" (GA, 1840s).[7] "That peculiar act known as 'beating Juba,' or 'Jubilee,' accompanies the singing of hymns. It is simply the act of beating time with the hands on the body, head, and limbs" (VA, 1880s).[8]

The difference between *patting* and *patting juba*—if there is one—depends on the source. From the earliest reports, the cryptic term *juba* was sometimes applied or tied to *patting*, but also employed in various songs associated with particular patting routines. The most popular concerns a dead yellow cat. "We used to dance jigs by ourself, and we danced the 'hack-back,' skipping backwards and forwards facing each other. When one danced a jig he would sing, 'Juber this, Juber that, Juber kills a yellow cat'" (William Pratt, b. 1860, SC, 278).

At night when the hands come in from the field, they didn't have nothin' to do but eat and cut up 'round the quarters. The boss give them Saturday after dinner off to clean up their clothes ca'se they is gwying to have that big ball Saturday night. They had the ball in a big barn there on the place and had sixty and seventy on the floor at once, singing:

Juba this and Juba that
Juba killed a yellow cat
Juba this and Juba that
Hold your partner where you at.

They sho could knock them songs off with them fiddles and things. (Lizzie Hughes, b. 1848, TX, 1816–17)[9]

There were other juba songs, while the basic techniques of patting could be adapted to almost any piece or performance.[10] In any case, the term *juba* is not nearly so common as some sources suggest. Most ex-slaves simply called the practice patting, or described without naming it. "On Saturday evenin's

the Niggers which had sold their goobers and taters and bought fiddles and guitars would come out and play. The others w'ud clap hands and stomp they feet and we young ones would cut a step around" (Mary Reynolds, b. ca. 1835, LA, 3289). "Whoopee, didn' us have good Saddy night frolics and jubilees, some clapp and some play de fiddle and man dey danced mos alnight" (George Rullerford, b. 1854, AL, 358). "De old time fiddlers played fas' music an' us all clapped our hands an' tromped in time. Us sho' made de raftahs ring" (James Lucas, b. 1833, MS, 1345).

While patting sometimes entailed solo or group dances performed to designated juba songs, more often it simply involved bystanders providing impromptu percussion for instrumentalists or dancers. "In ever cab'n thar war fiddles an' on Sunday we could have a good time. . . . We wud all sing an' pat our hans an' feet ta keep time for the dance" (Eliza Overton, b. 1849, MO, 267). "Saturday nights we most always had a dance. The banjo and the pat of the hands was the music we had" (Smith Simmons, b. ca. 1860, MS, 1939). "Dat night dey had dance and blowing cane at grandmother's (Wilson place). Buster cane blower. Dey wuz pattin' and dancing and going on" (Charlie Grant, b. 1852, SC, 171–72, orig. parentheses).

Some instrumental ensembles actually included designated patters. In 1851 a Mississippi slaveholder wrote to an agricultural advice column: "I must not omit to mention that I have a good fiddler, and keep him well supplied with catgut, and I make it his duty to play for the negroes every Saturday night until 12 o'clock. They are exceedingly punctual in their attendance at the ball, while Charley's fiddle is always accompanied with Ihurod on the triangle, and Sam to 'pat.'" Frederick Douglass (1818–1895) reported "that almost every farm has its 'Juba' beater. The performer improvises as he beats, and sings his merry songs, so ordering the words as to have them fall pat with the movement of his hands."[11]

Just singing for interviewers, some ex-slaves instinctively began to pat. Sam Broach, a former banjo player who fondly recalled dancing to fiddles, still regularly patted at home: "Lou she sets up an' sings a little piece of 'em a heap of nights. An' I pats. I still pats" (Sam Broach, b. ca. 1840, GA, 230).

Jordan Waters temporarily forgot his religious convictions.

> After much persuasion, he finally gave us some old fiddler songs by which he danced (patting all the time):
>
> > Put on the skillet, never mind the lid,
> > Mammy's goin' make some shortenin' bread,
> >
> > Old hen cackle, rooster lay the egg,
> > Old mule couldn't get the saddle on.
> >
> > Two little niggers layin' in bed,
> > Feet crack open like shortenin' bread.[12]
>
> I'll remember some more for the next time you come. It ain't holy to keep them old songs in your head, for dancin' is worldly, and worldly is sinful. (Jordan Waters, b. 1861, LA, 208, orig. parentheses)

Aunt Cicely Cawthon (b. 1859, GA, 185–86) and Uncle Shang Harris also patted while singing for interviewers, though Harris too had second thoughts: "Suddenly his smiling face fell serious and the song stopped. . . . 'Dat's de devil's song, dat is. A-dancin' an' a stompin' data-way!'" (Shang Harris, b. ca. 1840, GA, 119–20). As secular dance or dance music, patting was indeed regarded as sinful, anathematized by church members and clergy. John Dixon Long (b. 1817) had ministered in antebellum Maryland and Delaware:

> The banjo is of all instruments the best adapted to the lowest class of slaves. It is the very symbol of their savage degradation. They talk to it, and a skillful performer can excite the most diverse passions among dancers. Generally, however, they have no instruments, but dance to the tunes and words of a leader, keeping time by striking their hands against the thighs, and patting the right foot, to the words of

> > "'Juber,' 'Cesar boy,'
> > Ashcake in de fire
> > 'Possum up de gum tree,
> > Raccoon in de holler." . . .
>
> I have never known, in a single instance, of a colored man of any moral tone who was fond of the banjo or common dance.[13]

Other hand percussion—typically from ready-made castoffs—provided additional grit. "Knock dem bones tegedder en slap en pat dey hands to aw kind uv pretty tune" (Maggie Black, b. ca. 1858, SC, 59). "Pats our feets and knocks tin pans was the music dat us niggers danced to all night long" (Pick Gladdeny, 1856, SC, 127). "The master frequently let them have dances in the yards on Saturday afternoon. To supply the music they beat on tin buckets with sticks" (Emeline Stepney, b. ca. 1840, GA, 341). "Dere use to be dances almos' ebery week an' the older boys an' gals walk twelve miles dis to be dere. Some time there wus a tamborine beater, some time dey use' ole wash tubs an' beat it with wood sticks, an' some time dey jus' clap their han's" (Thomas Goodwater, b. 1855, SC, 169).[14] Their ready availability aside, most of these items were substitutes for percussion instruments fundamental to Black music globally: rattles, struck bells, hand drums (tambourines), percussion sticks (*claves*), clackers, scrapers. The ringing, scratching, clattering, clanging, and banging of such devices would have been other near-constants in slave dance music. Sometimes these would have been the only sounds not produced by human physiology.[15]

Some ex-slaves obviously regarded patting and makeshift percussion as mere alternatives to, or poor substitutes for, "real" musical instruments. "De music fer de merriments wuz fiddles, banjos an' acordins. Some times when dey didnt have no fiddles or nothing dey would jis pat to dance by" (Sylvia Floyd, b. ca. 1852, MS, 744–45). "Folks done er lots o' dancin' den, en dey ud dance ef dey had ter pat en dance; but dey mos' gen'rally used de fiddle" (Anna Marie Coffee, b. ca. 1852, NC, 288). "Dey didn't hab no kind o' musical instruments so dey held bones in each hand an beat 'em together an' some ob 'em would pop deir fingers" (Dicy Windfield, b. ca. 1843, MS, 2384).

> In de evening when we was through wid our work dey would gather at one of de cabins and visit and sing or dance. We'd pop corn, eat walnuts, peanuts, hickory nuts, and tell ghost stories. We didn't have any music instruments so the music we danced by wasn't so very good. Everybody sang and one or two would beat on tin pans or beat bones together. (James Southall, b. 1855, TN, 308)

However, patting was also appreciated for its own sake, and at slave gatherings, dance programs often alternated between jigs (solo step dances) supported only by patting, and choreographed group dances (cotillions, quadrilles, reels, schottisches) with instrumental accompaniment (probably also supported by patting).

Dancers also doubled as percussionists, audibly registering their synchronized movements. "Dey claps dey hands and keep de time, while dat old brudder ob mine he blows de quills" (Dora Roberts, b. 1849, GA, 207). "Dey played a fiddle fur de musick, dose niggers sho could shuffle deir feet" (James W. Washington, b. 1854, MS, 2200). Tellingly, the dances WPA narrators most often remembered—the heel-and-toe, the double-shuffle, the buzzard lope, the pigeon toe, knocking the backstep, cutting the pigeon wing, the buck-and-wing or buck dance, the breakdown and stomp—were all named for their percussive footwork. Often such dances were lumped together as jigging, although to confuse matters, *jig* could also refer to a particular step. The African jig or Negro jig resembles the Anglo-Irish step dancing from which it took its name, and there is a clear connection, but by the late 1700s the African jig was widely recognized as an original African American creation, even adopted by whites. In whatever way the term was used, *jigging* always connoted the ultimate in rhythmic intensity. "Master had a small platform built, an' on dat, de jiggin' contest am held. Thar am one cullud fellow on weuns' place, dat am de jigginest fellow dat ever

was. . . . Well Sar, dat fellow could put a glass ob wautah on his head an' make his feet go lak triphammahs an' sound lak a snaredrum" (James W. Smith, b. 1860, TX, 3634).

Thus, as Kentucky ex-slave Robert Anderson (1843–1930) observed, some slaves "could play a tune with their feet."[16] Obviously dancers throughout the world keep time with their movements (this might even pass as a basic definition of dancing). Yet white observers by the number made clear that the sheer volume and metrical precision of Black footwork was unlike anything in their previous experiences. "At a signal from the old greyheaded banjoman they struck off into a figure in which foot, hand, head and back, kept time to the music with the precision of a metronome" (VA, 1820s).[17] "One thing will be uniformly observed in these assemblages, almost every person on the floor invariably keeps good time with the music, and everything comes out as regularly as a dance or a fight in a well-drilled melodrama" (Philadelphia, 1840s).[18] "We left them executing those unique, fantastic dances so peculiar to their race—keeping perfect time to the enlivening music of violin, banjo, and bones" (South, ca. 1870).[19] Period descriptions are positively crammed with references to "the beat of the flying feet never missing the time by the space of a midge's breath"; "Negroes dancing every one after his or her own fashion, but keeping time to the beat"; "a genuine darkie keeping time, on the light fantastic heel-and-toe tap"; and so forth.[20]

Footwork was a focal point for participants too. "Dey'ud hab fiddle en dey dance wha' dey call de reel dance den. I 'member use'er lub to watch dey feet when dat fiddle 'ud go' to playing. I jes crawl right down on me knees dere whey I'ud see dey feet jes uh going" (Mom Louisa Collier, b. 1859, SC, 222–23). Robert Anderson recalled:

> The Double Shuffle, Heel and Toe, Buck and Wing, Juba, etc. The slaves became proficient in such dances, and could play a tune with their feet. . . . At some of these social gatherings, the individuals would dance those peculiar shuffling dances,

sometimes for hours at a time, or until exhausted, with the others standing around patting the feet and hands and keeping time to the rhythmical beat of the dancers feet.[21]

Dancers chose their footings most carefully. John Allan Wyeth learned to pat, dance, and play the banjo from slaves on his family's Alabama plantation.

> When on these occasions [slave dances] the crowd was very large, they would divide and go to the cabins in smaller parties, or the big floor of the gin-house may have been selected. Strange to say, they did not relish dancing on the ground, in the manner of the American Indians; and I think this can be explained by the negroes' instinctive love of rhythm, which the Indian does not seem to possess. The shuffle of the feet, in many instances unshod—for in warm weather they would pull off their shoes to keep their feet cool—could not be heard as distinctly on the ground as on a plank floor or a tight puncheon. I have often seen them dance on the bottom of a wagon-bed, which made an excellent sounding-board.[22]

Shod or barefoot, on boards or bare ground, slaves found ways to amplify or accentuate their footwork. Whether by choice or necessity they often danced barefoot, and two of the most common dance spaces—in the yard by the big house, or down in the slave quarters—might offer only bare ground. Likely as not, even slave cabins had dirt floors.[23] "Dey dance out on de grass, forty or fifty darkeys. Dem big gals eighteen an' nineteen year old git out dere an' go to dancin' barefoot as a goose. Dat weren't 'cause dey didn't have no shoes it jes' de habit of de times" (Chris Franklin, b. 1855, LA, 1411). "Mos' times wear yo' shoes to de dance an' den take 'em off. Dem ole hard shoes make too much noise, an' hurt yo' feet. Couldn't do no steppin' in dem field shoes" (Fannie Berry, b. 1841, VA, 49). A Louisiana ex-slave recalled: "some would march and dance by the music of a banjo, others by the beating of a tin-pan. . . . Their pantaloons

Fig. 3.2. "Negerhyddor I Louisiana (Negro Huts in Louisiana)." Adolf Carlsson Warberg, *Skizzer fran Nord-Amerikanska Kriget* (Stockholm: O. L. Lamm, 1867), 308. Slavery Images: A Visual Record of the African Slave Trade and Slave Life in the Early African Diaspora. slaveryimages.org. A Black child jigging to fiddling. The man seated to the fiddler's left is patting, stamping his foot and, judging from their positions, clapping his hands and slapping his thighs.

would be rolled up to the knees, and all would dance barefooted."[24]

Yet even barefoot on bare ground, slave dancers made themselves heard. Virginia ex-slave fiddler Isaac D. Williams (b. ca. 1821) recalled how his fellow slaves "would dance with their bare feet on the clay floor of my cabin and you could hear the perfect time they kept by the noise of the double shuffle. The floor was made of clay, originally put down in a damp state, and which after hardening, could be swept as a clean as a board floor."[25] Several Virginia ex-slaves described a dance called "set the floor":

> Set de flo'? Dat was—well de couples would do dat in turn. Dey come up an' bend over toward each other at de waist, an' de woman put her hands on her hips an' de man roll his eyes all roun' an' grin an' dey pat de flo' wid dey feet jus' like dey was puttin' it in place. Used to do dat bes' on dirt flo' so de feet could slap down hard against it. Sometimes dey would set de flo' alone—either a man or a woman. Den dey would set a glass of water on dey haid an' see how many kinds of steps dey could make widout spillin' de water. (Fannie Berry, b. 1841, VA, 50)[26]

Yards too were maintained in this state. "Cake walkin' wuz a lot of fun durin' slavery time. Dey swept de yards real clean and set benches 'round for de party. Banjos wuz used for music makin'" (Estella Jones, b. ca. 1855, GA, 348). "When de night for de party come on our place, de yard am cleaned off and we makes sandwiches" (Penny Thompson, b. ca. 1851, AL, 104). This was not mere party planning but basic plantation hygiene, and the ceaseless task of sweeping yards was often the first work assigned young slaves. "De only work I done wus to sweep yards an' nurse small chilluns" (Annie Stephenson, b. 1857, NC, 313). "I wuz a little gal, 'bout six or eight years old, when they put me ter sweepin' yards" (Elsie Moreland, b. unk., GA, 454). "Us children was put in a row in de yard and sweep de yard. Dat was us job to keep de yard clean" (A. C. Pruitt, b. 1861 or 1862, TX, 3204).

> One of de cabins was allus ha'nted atter some of de slaves got kilt in it whilst dey was fightin'. Nobody never could live in dat cabin no more atter dat widout ha'nts gittin' atter 'em. De wust of 'em was a 'oman ha'nt what you could hear sweepin' up leaves in de yard and all dat time you might be lookin' hard and not see a leaf move. (Callie Elder, b. ca. 1860, GA, 313)

Thus, on most plantations, yards provided ideal dance floors more or less year round.

By most accounts, however, slaves definitely preferred dancing on wooden surfaces, so that even bare ground might be temporarily boarded. "We fiddled and cut up more in dem days dan we do now. Us had times when we'd take planks to de woods at nite and buck dance. If yo' all ain't never seed a bunch ob niggers buck dance yo' sho' hab missed somethin'" (Glascow Norwood, b. ca. 1852, MS, 1657).[27] Sometimes this was purely opportunistic. In September 1863, Lucy Chase (1822–1909) observed a group of young runaways dancing, singing, and patting in a Virginia contraband camp. "The door of a fallen barrack was their springboard, and upon it they performed their jigs and hornpipes, keeping time to a variety of strange accompaniments[:] the rapid and regular falling of the hands upon the knees, the beating of feet, or the pleasing accompaniment of a tenor and base [bass] voice singing opposite strains of music."[28] However, the custom is also widely reported as routine party planning. Just after the war, Frank Falconer attended a Virginia cornshucking where "several darkies were engaged in the usual 'walk-arounds' and 'break-downs' on a grass plot, temporarily boarded for the occasion."[29] Not much later, writer Kirk Munroe (1850–1930) visited a Florida prison farm:

> For our entertainment a number of them [Black convicts] hastily organized a minstrel troupe and gave a wonderfully good performance. Several plank, laid on the ground, formed a platform, upon which clogs, jigs and shuffles were executed in rapid succession with much grace and skill. A sad, but at the same time most musical, accompaniment to the dancing was furnished by the jingle of the chains that each convict wore upon his legs. The regular music for the performance was provided by a quartet of whistlers and a number of "patters," who patted time on their knees and thighs in remarkable unison.[30]

In competitive dancing, planks had the additional advantage of forcing contestants to perform their elaborate footwork, in perfect time, within restricted spaces. Stage entertainer Tom Fletcher (1873–1954) had heard his ex-slave parents and grandparents describe how "boards would be laid down for an impromptu stage before the verandah so the guests could have a good view of the proceedings and a real shindig would take place with singing and dancing.... There was no prancing, just a straight walk on a path made by turns and so forth, along which the dancers made their way with a pail of water on their heads."[31] In the early 1800s Thomas De Voe had closely observed Long Island slaves busking in New York City's Catherine Market. To keep dancers from "'turning around and shying off' from the designated spot" they were "confined to a 'board,' (or shingle, as they called it)," which he describes as "usually about five to six feet long, of large width, with its particular spring in it, and to keep it in its place while dancing on it, it was held down by one on each end. Their music or time was usually given by one of their party, which was done by beating their hands on the sides of their legs and the noise of the heel [patting]."[32]

There are also reports of couples dancing on planks. Around 1853 a Mississippi slaveholder's son told Frederick Olmsted (1822–1903) "we dance cotillions and reels too, and we dance on a plank; that's the kind of dancin' I like best. . . . You stand face to face with your partner on a plank and keep a dancin'. Put the plank up on two barrel heads, so it'll kind o' spring."[33] He stated that both Blacks and whites danced this way. John Allan Wyeth had witnessed the same on puncheon floors:

A puncheon was the flat surface of a split log, smoothed with an ax and pinned to the joists to make the floors of the rude cabins constructed before sawmills were introduced. Sometimes they became loose, and rocked or rattled when trod upon. When the negroes would dance a *pas de deux*, a tight puncheon was selected, and the two danced forward and back on this single slab. Hence the common expression, "Hunt your puncheon," when something fixed or solid or sure was desired.[34]

WPA narrators also recalled these dances. "We used to dance jigs by ourself, and we danced the 'hack-back', skipping backwards and forwards facing each other" (William Pratt, b. 1860, SC, 278). "Some nights we would get out in de yard and dance jigs to see who could do it de funniest and we would catch hands and see how close we could come to each other's toes, without touchin'" (Samuel Smith, b. 1840, TN, 3661).

At other times boundaries were simply drawn on the dance floor. "Dancin' on de spot was de same thing as set de flo'—almos'. Jus' mean you got to stay in de circle. De fiddler would take a charred corncob an' draw a circle on de flo', den call one arter de odder up an' dance in de circle. Effen yo' feet tetch de edge

you is out" (Fannie Berry, b. 1841, VA, 50). "Sometimes dey danced jigs, too, in a circle, jumping up and down" (Isabella Dorroh, b. ca. 1863, SC, 327). "Some of de dances de niggers had was 'Jump Jim Crow'; one nigger would jump up and down while tripping and dancing in de same spot. Sometimes he say, 'Every time I jump, I jump Jim Crow.' We had what was called a 'Juber' game. He would dance a jig and sing, 'Juber this, Juber that, Juber killed a yellow cat'" (John N. Davenport, b. 1848, SC, 242). In New Orleans, hoodoo initiates also danced in charcoal-drawn circles; crossing the line was an evil omen. In another rite, the *Fe Chauffe*, devotees with lighted candles or vessels balanced on their heads stepped through rings of bottles on barges lined with firepots.[35] "I could dance with a glass of water on my head and cross my leg over a bottle at the same time. No ma'm, tain't hard, no more'n balancin' a heavy basket on your head" (Lizzie Chandler, b. unk., LA, 41). Around 1829 John Pendleton Kennedy saw Virginia slaves perform something resembling a British sword dance, "shuffling through the odd contortions of a jig, with two sticks lying crosswise upon the ground, over which they danced, alternately slapping their thighs and throwing up their elbows to the time of the music."[36]

More than just wooden dance floors, though, slaves favored *raised* wooden dance floors providing still greater volume and resonance. Many narrators described wooden platforms built specifically for dancing. "We won't 'lowed to go nowheres a makin' merriment, but Marse built us a big flatform to have I [our] pleasures on" (Tom Floyd, b. ca. 1842, MS, 748). "Lawd I kin 'member dem holidays, what times we had. De men go in de mill an' mak a gra' big platform an' brung it to de house for to dance on. Den come de music, de fiddles an' all dem other things" (Nancy Williams, b. 1847, NC, 318). "Sometimes we dance on a platform; sometimes just on the ground" (Chaney McNair, b. 1852, IT, 219).

All de fiddlers from ev'ywhars come to Sardis and fiddle fer de dances at de barbecues. Dey had a platform built not fer from de barbecue table to dance on. Any darky dat could cut de buck and de pigeon wing was called up to de platform to perform fer ev'ybody. (Wesley Jones, b. 1840, SC, 73)

In winter white folks danced in the parlor of the big house; in summer they danced on a platform under a great big brush arbor. There was seats all around for folks to watch them dance. Sometimes just the white folks danced; sometimes just the black folks. . . . They'd clap their hands and holler. (Lucinda Vann, b. ca. 1840, IT, 346–47)

In his memoirs, South Carolina slave Jacob Stroyer (b. 1846) also recalled "dancing in some large cotton house or on a scaffold."[37] James W. Smith (b. 1860, TX, 3634) compared the sound of jigging feet on a platform to a snare drum or triphammer.

Generally, though, dancers availed themselves of ready-made flooring. Some even danced on large boxes and barrels. "Now the banjo and the fiddle are taken up, and two negroes are placed each upon a drygoods box for the purpose of ascertaining which of the twain can dance the longest time without stopping to breathe; and then the negro children try their skill, and the patting of Juba seems to become universal."[38] More often they favored planked or puncheoned cabin floors; the galleries, parlors, and halls of slaveholders' homes; porches and dog-runs; work buildings; boardwalks; bridges, landings, and docks. "Massa have de big plantation and I 'member de big log house. It have de gallery on both sides and dey's de long hall down de center. De dogs and sometimes a possum used to run through de hall at night. De hall was big 'nough to dance in and I plays de fiddle" (Larnce Holt, b. 1858, TX, 1779).[39] "Ol' marsa was shorely a good man, an' he wu'ld git all de li'l niggers on de big wide porches an' hab dem dance" (Esther Green, b. 1855, MS, 172). "We had fun in dem days. We used to run from de paterollers. We'd be fiddlin' and dancin' on de bridge (dat was de grown folks, but de chaps would come too), an' dey'd say, 'Here come de paterollers!' an' we'd put out" (Berry Smith, b. 1821, MS, 1979, orig. parentheses). "Nearly every farm had a fiddler. Ever so

Fig. 3.3. "Waiting for the Sunday boat." Photo by William Henry Jackson, ca. 1902. Detroit Publishing Co. Collection, Library of Congress, Prints and Photographs Division. Jigging on a dock or boardwalk. Note that most of the participants are looking directly at the dancer's feet, the obvious focus of the performance.

often he [slaveholder] had a big dance in their parlor. I'd try to dance myself. He had his own music by the hands on his place. He let them have dances at the quarters every now and then. Dancing was a piece of his religion" (Ida Rigley, b. 1855, VA, 44).

Slaveholders' homes usually offered ideal spaces for dancing—parlors, hallways, perhaps even a ballroom. "Mawster Wattles liked to play the fiddle. When they had company at the big house, they would call me and my two sistahs, Jane and Susan into the parlor. . . . I'd dance and jig on my toes and heels. My two sistahs would jig all over the place fo' the company" (Sallie Johnson, b. 1855, TX, 2047). "All de niggers culd dance. Dey culd 'back-step' en do de 'pigeon-toe'—en dar wus times when dar wus fine company in de big house dey wuld call de niggers up en hev 'em dance fur fun. Sum of dem women culd do de 'pigeon-toe' wid a bucket uf water on deir heds" (Harriet Miller, b. 1859, MS, 1503). In truth when slaves danced in the big house they were probably just there to entertain or otherwise serve whites. "If dar was any [slaves] who could dance and sing right kindey good, why dey was always taken to de 'big house,' to entertain Marster and Missus' guests" (Marinda Jane Singleton, b. 1840, NC, 267). "When I was jes big 'nough to nuss an' wash leetle chulluns, I was sol' to Marse Hiram Cassady an' dat man give me ter his darter, Miss Mary, to be her maid.... De white folks had big dances in de Big House and de niggers played de fiddle. Dey was fine times. Dey had good things ter eat, an' I allus got some of whut was lef'" (Fanny Smith Hodges, b. unk., MS, 68, 69).[40]

On the other hand, labor sites were by definition slave domains, and Blacks habitually danced in barns, cotton gins, cane mills, tobacco sheds, storerooms, factories, and other work buildings. "De slaves had balls in de sugar house. Dey would start late and was way out in de field where de master could not hear dem" (Elizabeth Ross Hite, b. ca. 1850, LA, 106).[41] Such structures were generally floored, perhaps multistoried with large sounding chambers. More than any of these outbuildings, the barn is associated with American folk dancing and the institution of the *barn dance*. "Saturday nights were always the time for dancing and frolicking. The master sometimes let them use a barn loft for a big square dance" (Uncle Robert Henry, b. 1855, GA, 197). "They had the ball in a big barn there on the place and had sixty and seventy on the floor at once.... They sho could knock them songs off with them fiddles and things" (Lizzie Hughes, b. 1848, TX, 1816).

A few narrators even recalled designated dance houses on antebellum plantations. "White folks danced de twistification up at de big house, but us had reg'lar old breakdowns in a house what Marster let us have to dance in. Wid all dat toddy helpin' 'em 'long, sometimes dey danced all night, and some of 'em fell out and had to be dragged off de dance flo'" (Alice Hutcheson, b. ca. 1860, GA, 284). "Us had a house wid a raised flatform (platform) at one end whar de music-makers sot. Dey had a string band wid a fiddle, a trumpet, and a banjo, but dere warn't no guitars lak dey has in dis day. One man called de sets and us danced de cardrille (quadrille) de virginia reel, and de 16-hand cortillion" (Liza Mention, b. ca. 1865, child of ex-slaves, GA, 124, orig. parentheses). "Dere was a big house to dance in.... I couldn't play no music myself, but I was terrible on de floor" (Jerry Eubanks, b. 1846, MS, 696).[42]

Slaves also danced in their own homes or, secretly, in remote or abandoned houses. "Down in de quar-

Fig. 3.4. "The Old Barn Floor." Lithograph by Currier & Ives, 1868. Library of Congress, Prints and Photographs Division. Jigging on a favorite sounding board, accompanied by a fretless five-string banjo.

ters de slaves wud dance de 'pigeon-toe' to de tune uf 'Arkansaw Traveler'—an' wus jes larnin' to dance when dey sed I wus freed" (Orris Harris, b. ca. 1858, MS, 930). "At night, after their work was over, the slaves would meet out 'in the sticks' and dance in some of the old houses. Forming into a circle they would march around singing, when suddenly an order was given and they would pair off and begin dancing. Banjos and guitars furnished the music" (George Caulton, b. 1844, VA, 170). "We sometimes had a big dance in the cabins. The folks danced reels, Waltzes, and gallopy—we'd call it that 'cause we'd gallop 'round and 'round" (Mary Edwards, 1853, TX, 1283). Texas ex-slave Julia Blanks also recalled the gallopy.

Though slaves sometimes danced barefoot, especially on wooden surfaces, most seem to have favored the acoustic properties and added volume of footwear. "Niggers had lots of dancing and frolics. Dey danced de 'flat-foot'. Dat was when a nigger would slam his foot flat down on de floor. De wooden bottom shoes sho would make a loud noise" (Nellie Boyd, b. ca. 1850, SC, 64). Shoes and boots were highly prized generally—and highly charged symbolically—not least because on most plantations slaves went barefoot in one-piece shifts until early adolescence. On some places they went barefoot throughout their lives, even in winter. "My feet never saw a shoe until

I was fourteen. I went barefooted in ice and snow. They was tough" (Rachel Hankins, b. 1850, AL, 155). "In de winter us wore cotton clothes, but us went barefoots. My uncle Sam and some of de other Niggers went 'bout wid dey foots popped open from de cold" (Easter Brown, b. 1860, GA, 137). "I seen many a trouble hour since I was born in them long gone days way back in March 1851, just at the time of year when old Master Joe Wiley took the shoes off his slaves, sending the slaves to work barefoot and putting the shoes away in the storage waiting for winter to come again before they'd be give out to the feets that fit 'em easiest" (Eliza Bell, b. 1851, MS, 52).

> I 'member once, my missus bought me a pair o' high top red boots. My! I was proud. In dem days, we went barefoot mos' all year roun'. But my missus tried to make us happy on Christmas. I put dem boots on an' I pranced roun' an' roun' jes' to hear dem squeek. I done thot dat was de purtiest noise I ebber heard. . . . In dem days no nigger got boots till he was big an' able to work for em. I was ol missus pet an' she plum' spoilt me to deaf. (Filmore Taylor Hancock, b. 1851, MO, 186–87)

Accordingly, shoes and boots were not just status symbols, but status symbols implicitly tied to dances and dancing. "Every now and den we would have some good frolics and mostly on Saturday nights and dance to the music, some one would play the fiddle, and O, that Xmas I got my first shoes, they was buttened. I hugged them so tight and even slept with them" (Liza White, b. ca. 1855, GA, 444). "When I want to go to a dance, I say to my missis, 'Look at my shoes'" (Mother Duffy, b. unk., LA, 63). "The first shoe I ever wore had a brass toe. I danced all the time when I was a child" (Lucy Key, b. ca. 1865, MS, child of ex-slaves, 199). "Us sometime walk many a mile t' d' dance 'n' carry us shoes on us back. Dey hab fiddle music an' 'corjian. D' boss man like t' see d' niggers 'joy demse'fs. Lots 'r times us hab t' cross ober w'at we call d' big Lunnon bridge 'n' ober d' ferry boat to git dere. Us dance d'

Fig. 3.5. Virginia Newman, Beaumont, TX, June 11, 1937. Portraits of African American ex-slaves from the US Works Progress Administration, Federal Writers' Project slave narratives collection, Library of Congress. "W'en d' stars fall [1833] I's mos' as big as I is now" (Virginia Newman, b. 1827, LA, 2902).

quadrille. I jus' 'bout run t' git dere den" (Virginia Newman, b. 1827, LA, 2905). "Our white folks had big dances too. Dey danced in dem days. Nobody went but what was invited. Dey was guests. Today—anybody goes. Dey wore fine close. Dey was a high too. Mars Albert paid $150 one time for a pair of fine dancin boots. At des parties dey had good fiddling" (Henry Gibbs, b. 1852, MS, 826).

Folktales even played on these connections:

> I 'member one big time we had in slavery. Master was gone and he warn't gone. He left the house pretending to go on a visit. Mistress and her chil'ren was visiting relations, and the Niggers giv' a big ball the night after Master left. The leader of the ball put on Master's boots and they sang a song he made up:

> Ole Masters gone to Philiman York and
> Won't be back till July or August fourth to come
> Fact is I don't know he will be back at all
> Come on all you Niggers and jine this ball.

The night they was giving the ball, Master had "blacked" up and slipped back in the house. While they was singing and dancing, he was sitting by the fireplace all the time. Directly he spit and the Nigger who had on his boots recognized him by his spit and tried to climb up the chimney. (Nancy Jackson, b. 1830, TN, TX, 1913–14)[43]

We could only have dances during holidays, but dances was held on other plantations. One night a traveler visiting me Master and wanted his boots shined. So Master gave de boots to one of de slaves to shine and de slave put de boots on and went to a dance and danced so much dat his feet swelled so dat when he returned he could not pull 'em off. De next morning as de slave did not show up with de boots dey went to look for him and found him lying down trying to pull de boots off. He told his Master dat he had to put de boots on to shine 'em and could not pull 'em off. So Master had to go to town and buy de traveler another pair of boots. Before he could run away de slave was beaten wid 500 lashes. (Ida Henry, b. 1854, TX, 136–37)[44]

Folktales may have understated the toll dancing took on shoe leather:

Two sisters stayed in North Carolina in a two-room house in Wilson County. There was a big drove of us and we all went to town in the evening to get whiskey. There was one man who had a wife with us, but all the rest were single. We cut the pigeon wing, waltzed, and quadrilled. We danced all night until we burned up all the wood. Then we went down into the swamp and brought back each one as long a log as he could carry. We chopped this up and piled it in the room. Then we went on 'cross the swamp to another plantation and danced there.

When we got through dancing, I looked at my feet and the bottom of them was plumb naked. I had just bought new boots, and had danced the bottoms clean out of them. (Robert Farmer, b. 1854, NC, 275)

Ex-slaves do not describe people dancing the backstep (a variation of the shuffle) or pigeon wing: "Dat was flippin' yo' arms an' legs roun' an' holdin' yo' neck stiff like a bird do" (Fannie Berry, b. 1841, VA, 49). Instead, dancers *knocked* the backstep or *cut* the pigeon wing.[45] The *shuffle* was hardly the soft-shoe routine that term might suggest. In "a regular corn-shucking double-shuffle," wrote Frank Falconer, "the extra allowance of heel, peculiar to all sable bipeds, is brought into full play, affording the performer an excellent opportunity of imitating a bass drum."[46] John Matthews remembered "one time I went to old Jacob's cabin an' some one played de fiddle an' de way dem darkies shuffled dem big feet wus a caution, dey nearly knocked de floor down" (John Matthews, b. 1852, MS, 1457).[47] The heel's bass-drum effect was widely remarked. Alexander Mackay observed slave dances in 1840s Virginia: "The banjo, a sort of rude guitar, is their chief instrumental accompaniment; whilst in dancing, proficiency with them seems to consist in making an elaborate use of the heel."[48] A satiric dance rhyme made the same point:

The niggers have the patting parties on Saturday nights. They call them patting parties 'cause the ones don't dance set 'round and pat they hands. We danced the reels and twenty-five or thirty niggers playin' the fiddles. . . .

> Two barrels pickled pork
> Two barrels meal
> Going to tell Jesus
> Got religion in my heel. (John Crawford, b. 1837, MS, 975)[49]

In the breakdown or buck-and-wing, dancers clogged flatfooted, legs crooked, hips loose, upper body leaning slightly forward.[50] At other times people jigged on their toes or jigged heel-and-toe, alternating toe stands and pirouettes with slides, clogs, toe-taps, and heel-thumps, ideally with the head and upper body rigid enough to balance a water glass. In 1843 William Cullen Bryant observed a party of South Carolina slaves who, to the accompaniment of whistling and stick beating, "executed various dances, capering, prancing, and drumming with heel and toe upon the floor."[51]

All sources also agree on the physical demands of such dancing. John Allan Wyeth recalled Alabama slaves "'cutting the pigeon wing,' 'the back step,' 'the double shuffle,' and other steps which required not only a keen sense of keeping time with the music, but agility and muscular power of a high order."[52] Ex-slaves concurred. "Mama never did 'low us to dance. I never did low my chillen to dance either. I 'member gettin' off one time an' tryin' to dance when they wasn't nobody 'round an' stumped my toe. It broke me tho'. I never did try it no mo. I sho like to broke my toe tho'" (Rose Holman, b. ca. 1855, MS, 1038–39). "They made all the chil'ren set in the corner when they was dancing. I seed them knocking off them songs and wished I was big enuff to dance. If any of the chil'ren got up, mama come over and say, 'You tots stay off that floor, they'll mash your feet'" (Lizzie Hughes, b. 1848, TX, 1816–17). "I wish now dat I hadn't danced so much, and maybe my limbs wouldn't be so bad today. I never did let my girls go to dances, though, 'cause I didn't want no man to swing my girls around" (Rebecca Thomas, b. 1825, AR, TX, 3823).

> Did us lub to dance? Jesus help me. Dem country niggers swing us so hard us lan' in de corner wid a wham. My daddy was a strick man. He beat us for gwineter dances but us jes' hide in de smokehouse all day and run froo de woods dat night. Dey's big black bears in dem 'Sippi woods but eben dat couldn' scare us gals 'way from de fiddlin'. (Mary Johnson, b. ca. 1858, MS, 2024).

The effects could be dramatic. "I kin heah de banjers yet. Law me, us had a good time in dem days. Us danced most eb'ry Sattidy night an' us made de rafters shake wid us foots" (Hattie Clayton, b. 1847, AL, 76). When ex-slaves describe a building "jes' a rollin' and rockin'" (Mary Johnson, b. ca. 1858, MS, 2026) or insist "us sho' made de raftahs ring" (James Lucas, b. 1833, MS, 1345), these are not mere figures of speech. Just

before the war William Holcombe witnessed slaves dancing on the gallery of a Louisiana plantation manor "with such vigor that the old flooring bent and the rafters trembled to their merry evolutions. Some of them danced gracefully and beautifully, and all kept admirable time."[53] In an 1870s Cincinnati dance house, wrote Lafcadio Hearn, recently freed slaves "leaped and shouted, swinging each other off the floor, and keeping time with a precision which shook the building in time to the music."[54] Black dancers are even described rocking bare ground. Benjamin Norman reported that in Congo Square in the early 1800s slaves danced the breakdown and double-shuffle with "such a hearty gusto, upon the green sward, that the very ground trembled beneath their feet."[55]

Given the cumulative effects of patting, hand percussion, step dancing, instruments and voices, slave dances were not merely gritty: often they were positively thunderous. "We was let off Sadday at noon and could go to the fiddlin's and dance all night. You could hear the niggers dancin' a mile away. . . . We did the Back Step and Shuffle" (Charles Willis, b. ca. 1845, MS, 399). "Tom an' Gilbert played de fiddle an' we chilluns down in de quarters cud hear dem stampin' deir feet an' shoutin' an' singin'" (Adam Singleton, b. 1858, AL, 1950). "Dey danced, frolicked, and cut de buck in gen'ral. Dey didn't have no sho nuff music, but dey sho' could sing it down. . . . You could hear 'em a mile away a-whoopin' and hollerin'" (Dosia Harris, b. ca. 1860, GA, 110). "We could have dances on Saturday nights. A banjo player would be dere an' he would sing. . . . De niggers would be pattin' dey feet an' dancin' for life. Master an' dem would be settin' on de front porch listenin' to de music, 'cause you could hear it for a half mile. We would be in one of de big barns. We had a time of our life" (Robert Williams, b. 1843, VA, 326).[56]

In the preamplification period this crowd noise obviously posed a problem for performers. Describing emancipated slaves "hammering away at the breakdowns" on a temporarily boarded plot, Frank Falconer flatly stated, "here the voice and the banjo, the heel and the toe were alternately contending in fierce strife for mastery."[57] One solution was for musicians to stomp as loud or louder than patters and dancers. "My grand-pappy wus mighty good at playin' de fiddle an' pattin' his feet. Yo' cud hear dem feet hittin' de floor fur a mile off. He cud play 'Black Eye Susan,' an' 'Polly put de Kettle on, an' we'll all have a drink' and 'De Arkansaw Traveler' an' mo' dan I can thin uf right now" (Hattie Jefferson, b. ca. 1855, MS, 1132). "I niver know'd 'em to have dances in the big house, but in de quarters when old Joe wud play dat fiddle, de men would step lively and pat ter dat tune: old Joe culd play de 'Arkansaw Traveler' and pat his feet at de same time, an' Patsy culd shuffle her feet an' pat her hed wid one han' an' her stomach wid udder han'" (Jim Martin, b. 1857, MS, 1440). An anonymous Tennessee ex-slave (b. ca. 1845) interviewed by Fisk University remembered "dancing was their main things. One fiddler used to pat his foot out of this country."[58] For fiddler Andy Brice, the habit was so ingrained that it evoked phantom feeling in a missing limb:

One day I see Marse Thomas a twistin' de ears on a fiddle and rosinin' de bow. Then he pull dat bow 'cross de belly of dat fiddle. Sumpin' bust loose in me and sing all thru my head and tingle in my fingers. I make up my mind, right then and dere, to save and buy me a fiddle. I got one dat Christmas, bless God! I learn and been playin' de fiddle ever since. I pat one foot while I playin'. I kept on playin' and pattin' dat foot for thirty years. I lose dat foot in a smash up wid a highway accident but I play de old tunes on dat fiddle at night, dat foot seem to be dere at de end of dat leg (indicating) and pats just de same. Sometime I ketch myself lookin' down to see if it have come back and jined itself to dat leg, from de very charm of de music I makin' wid de fiddle and de bow. (Andy Brice, b. ca. 1856, SC, 76, orig. parentheses)

Again, performers throughout the world tap their feet, but observers constantly marveled at foot-stomping African American instrumentalists. In 1841 Charles Dickens (1812–1870) described "a regular breakdown" in a Five Points dance hall, where "the corpulent black

fiddler, and his friend who plays the tambourine, stamp upon the boarding of the small raised orchestra."[59] With accomplished players, foot stomping could be as rhythmically complex as patting or dancing. As a youngster W. C. Handy (1873–1958) worked as a *straw beater* for an ex-slave fiddler, Whit Walker, drumming with knitting needles on the strings while Walker played and sang: "Uncle Whit stomped his feet while singing. A less expert fiddler, I learned, would have stomped both heels simultaneously, but a fancy performer like Uncle Whit could stomp the left heel and the right forefoot and alternate this with the right heel and the left forefoot, making four beats to the bar. That was real stomping."[60]

Frequently fiddlers or banjo players mounted barrels, placing themselves above the crowd where they could be better heard (or seen) but where they also could drum on the barrels with their heels. "At corn shucking all the slaves from other plantations would come to the barn, the fiddler would sit on top of the highest barrel of corn, and play all kinds of songs" (James V. Deane, b. 1850, MD, 8). An 1852 novel describes a fiddler who "had contrived to elevate himself on a pedestal, sufficiently high to enable him to overlook the whole company—bringing an old salt barrel into requisition for that purpose. . . . His frolicking companions danced more to the time beaten by his right foot, than to the cadence by the fiddle. . . . 'No more joggling; steady um now; dance to time, and don't get ahead.'"[61] In another account a banjo player "had turned down a barrel, and was seated on it. . . . He kicked his slippers off keeping time, and his head dodged about with every turn of the quick tune."[62]

Instrumentalists might even take to the floor themselves, dancing as they played. "Folks had heap more pleasure than they do now in slave time. They had parties and dances and they would bow 'round. They had fiddles and danced by them. Folks danced them days. They don't dance now, just mess around. My brother would scrape the fiddle and dance on, all at the same time" (Laura Thornton, b. ca. 1830, AL, 326–27).[63]

Other percussion helped keep dancers together. Struck bells or struck-bell substitutes—tin pans and

Fig. 3.6. "The Festival." Robert Criswell, *"Uncle Tom's Cabin" Contrasted With Buckingham Hall, the Planter's Home* (New York: D. Fanshaw, 1852), fac. 112. Slavery Images: A Visual Record of the African Slave Trade and Slave Life in the Early African Diaspora. slaveryimages.org. A fiddle-banjo-and-two-handed-bones combo, 1850s South Carolina. The fiddler (Jerry) is seated on a barrel with his heels in thumping positions. The four-string banjo (sans thumb string) appears to have a gourd resonator. The man to the immediate right of the musicians is patting, stamping his foot and slapping his thighs. In the background slaveholders observe from a treehouse.

buckets, triangles, cow bells—were especially well-suited. In coastal South Carolina, timekeepers beat sticks, broom handles, or canes against the floor or ground. "I see em when dey have dem hay pullings. Dey tote torch to gather de hay by en after dey pull two or three stacks of hay, dey have a big supper en dance in de road en beat sticks en blow cane" (Sylvia Cannon, b. ca. 1857, SC, 190).[64] Beating straws served the same purpose. "Umm-h and swell music. A fiddle and a tin can and one nigger would beat his hand on the can and another would beat the strings on the fiddle with broom straws. It wuz almos' like a banjo" (Marshal Butler, b. 1849, GA, 163). "Stretch cowhides over cheeseboxes and you had tambourines. Saw bones off a cow, knock them together, and call it a drum. Or use broom-straws, on fiddle-strings, and you had your entire orchestra" (John Cole, b. ca. 1850, GA, 227).

> Atter I growed up, us niggers on Marse Bob's plantation had big times at our corn shuckin's an' dances. Us 'ud all git tergether at one uv de cabins an us 'ud have er big log fire an' er room ter dance in. Den when us had all shucked corn er good while ever nigger would git his gal an' dey would be some niggers over in de corner ter play fer de dance, one wid er fiddle an' one to beat straws, an one wid er banjo, an' one to beat bones, an' when de music 'ud start up (dey gener'ly played "Billy in de Low Grounds" or "Turkey in de Straw") us 'ud git on de flo. Den de nigger whut called de set would say: "All join hands an' circle to de lef, back to de right, swing corners, swing partners, all run away!" An' de way dem niggers feets would fly. (Fanny Randolph, b. ca. 1835, GA, 195–96, orig. parentheses)

David C. Barrow Jr. left an especially detailed description of straw beating by Georgia slaves:

> The performer provides himself with a pair of straws about eighteen inches in length, and stout enough to stand a good smart blow. An experienced straw-beater will be very careful in selecting his straws, which he does from the sedge-broom.... These straws are used after the manner of drumsticks, that portion of the fiddle-strings between the fiddler's bow and his left hand serving as a drum. One of the first sounds which you hear on approaching the dancing party is the *tum te tum* of the straws, and after the dance begins, when the shuffling of feet destroys the other sounds of the fiddle, this noise can still be heard.[65]

Often, however, when crowd noise drowned out the instruments, dancers simply kept time to their own rhythms. "Sometimes they would all get into such glee when dancing! Ben would stop the banjo for a few minutes, but they all went on dancing just the same, for they thought he was playing."[66] In the 1930s Johnny Shines (1915–1992) performed under identical conditions in juke joints with his friend Robert Johnson (1911–1938).

> Robert sang pretty loud, and most of the time he sang in a high-pitched voice, and, naturally, his voice was carrying. We didn't have too much

trouble in having ourselves heard in those places we played in. The people that was dancing, they'd just pick up the beat, and if they got out of earshot, I guess the rhythm just stayed with them and they kept right on dancing. Because the whole house had the same motion.[67]

By the late eighteenth century, slaves, and following them slaveholders, had adopted another approach to the problem, alternating between noisy step dances accompanied by patting and percussion, and group dances with prearranged figures and coordinated movements directed by instrumentalists and callers. "Somebody play de violin and de banjo, and dey dance scotto [schottische], and reels and waltzes and codry (quadrille). Sometime dey have a buck dance. Dat where jist one dance by himself. Sometimes dey call dat jig dances" (Agatha Babino, b. ca. 1850, LA, 140). "I wont ole 'nough to take part in de frolics an' good times de slaves had, but I can recollect how dey done. Mars had a big platform built under de shade trees. Dis wuz fur dancin' an' a general good time. Sometimes dey would be deir all night dancin' de ole square dance by de music ob de fiddles an' guitars or buck dancin' wid a bunch ob dem a clappin' an' a pattin' deir feet" (Dave Walker, b. 1850, MS, 2150).

Dance calling appeared in the late 1700s with the introduction of the cotillion, quadrille, and other fashionable European dances whose rigid demands and group choreographies required either ballroom instruction or formal direction. "One of the dances was the cotillion, but just anybody couldn't dance that one. There was a heap of bowing and scraping to it, and if you were not 'quainted with it you just couldn't use it" (Green Willbanks, b. 1861, GA, 145). "Could they play the fiddle in them days, unh, unh! Lordy, iffen I could take you back and show you that handsome white lady what put me on the floor and learned me to dance the cotillion" (Aunt Mittie Freeman, b. 1851, AR, 352). "I went to dancin' school wid de white folks an' can dance any kin' o' dance sets. My father was a musicianer. He 'longed to John Carthan, in Warrenton, N.C." (Della Harris, b. 1852, NC, 130).

For those without such advantages, the dance caller or prompter was the answer: "My cousin Tom was the songster. He called the plays at the dances. They turned 'cording to what he sung" (Bert Strong, b. 1864, TX, 3758). "Had banjos—pick wid yo' hands. Say, 'Balance right!' I hear 'em hollerin' back an' forth, an' dey understood what ter do. Say 'Right wheel!' Dey'd handle it good. We chillun stand around an' watch 'em" (Simon Hare, b. 1849, NC, 917).

Dey uster promp' 'em at de dance. Dey call it "promp" de figure. Sometime' dey sing,

"Balance all
Jine right han's"

an mo' lak dat. Time us hab a chord [that is, a musical signal] w'at call de "partner to places" or to a stan'. (George Simmons, b. 1854, AL, 3547)

There are grounds for believing that dance calling was an African American innovation.[68] In any case Blacks dominated early dance calling as much as they did fiddling, especially since the roles were often combined. Bernhard, Duke of Saxe-Weimar Eisenach, authored one of the earliest accounts of a fiddling dance prompter, observed at an 1825 South Carolina plantation ball. "The whole music consisted of two violins and a tamborine [played by slaves]. This tamborine was struck with a terrible energy. The two others scraped the violin, in the truest signification of the word; one of them cried out the figures, imitating with his body all the motions of the dance."[69] Prompting may have been expected of dance musicians. "An' dere was callin' de figgers an' dat meant dat de fiddler would call de number an' all de couples got to cut dat number" (Fannie Berry, b. 1841, VA, 50). "I used to be one of the best banjo pickers. I was good. Played for white folks and called figgers for em" (Jim Davis, b. 1840, NC, 109–10).

Other times designated prompters cooperated with, or substituted for, instrumentalists. "The music we had were fiddles and drums and sometimes just singing and calling figgers" (Mary Jane Jones, b. ca. 1849, MS, 1245).[70]

I used to be a fiddler-player in dem early days. I would fiddle and de prompter would call out:

> Women doo-se-doo,
> And de gents de same, yo' know,
> Rally 'round de canebreak
> And shoot de buffalo.

Den:

> Swing yo' partner,
> Swing him if yo' lak
> Cheat him—if yo' don't!

Den he'd say:

> March—sing—left, right—back—den it's turn again! (William Smith, b. 1845, LA, TX, 3692–93)[71]

Accomplished prompters were of a class with musicians generally, calling for both Blacks and whites, and being paid for their services.

> We was let off Sadday at noon and could go to the fiddlin's and dance all night. You could hear the niggers dancin' a mile away. The same man called for us that called fer the white folks. He could sure call 'em too. We did the Back Step and Shuffle. The tunes was Egg Nog, Sugar and Beer and Natcha Under the Hill. I don't recollect none of the words of the tunes. (Charles Willis, b. ca. 1846, MS, 399)

Ole fiddler was a man named Louis Cane. Chile, he sho' could strung dat fiddle. Never did do much work, but Marsa use to keep him, 'cause he use to have him play fo' de balls in de big house. Marse use to pay him too. We never did pay him, 'cause we ain't never had nothin'. But he use to play an' call de figgers 'long as dere was anyone on de floor.

Chile, when I was a girl guess I'd druther dance dan eat. (Sally Ashton, b. ca. 1845, VA, 14)

Jim says he was never a cotton'-pickin' negro. "I was of a higher class. You see I called the figures for all the balls, both white and colored. Oh! the people had good times in those days. I can remember some of the figures now, but I wouldn't care to call figures no more." (James Brooks, b. ca. 1855, MS, 231)

In between the formal dance sets came the jigging: "Dey uster hab lotser dances. Dey hab fiddle player an' 'corjun (accordion) player. Dey sing 'Swing you partner, promenade.' . . . Dey uster dance de fo' (four) double head w'at was done wid two couples. Dey hab a jig dance and holler" (Mary Kindred, b. ca. 1855, TX, 2204–5, orig. parentheses). "We danced by fiddle music an' guitars. De dancing wuz de ole square dance, whar dey swung deir pardners an' called de sets. Den different ones would cut fancy steps by deir selves, an' de ones could cut de mos' steps wuz counted de bes' dancer" (Robert Weathersby, b. ca. 1847, MS, 2241–42). "Us danced plenty. Some of de men clogged an pidgeoned, but when us had dances dey was real cotillions lak de white folks had. Us always had a fiddler" (Isaac Stier, b. ca. 1857, MS, 2057).

> Sometime dey call for a jig dance. Den one person or not over two get out dere an' jig dance. It usually one person done it. An' I mean some of 'em sho' dance dat jig dance too.
>
> When dey dancin' on de floor dey was from four to eight couple. Sometimes dey was two at de head an' two at de foot an' two on each side. Dey all stand 'round dere each with he gal, waiting for de music for to start. Dey have what dey call a "prompter" for to call de figures. He say, "All git ready." Den dey start de music an' he holler out, "All balance," an' dey puts de feet to de front. Den he sing out, "Swing you pardner an'," an' dey grab dere pardner an' swing 'round. Sometimes he say "Fus' man head off to de right," an' dey go

off dat way. When he tell 'em to "All promenade," dey goes 'round in a circle. Iffen he say, "Change pardners," dey do dat an' keep on changin' pardners again. Dere was lots of different members [numbers] what he call. (Chris Franklin, b. 1855, LA, 1411)

The fiddler would start to fiddling and they would ring up in an old-time square dance. Everybody danced off to themselves. Just let your foot go backward (she illustrated) and then let your foot go forward (she slipped her foot forward) and whirl around. Men, too, danced that way, by themselves, and you could hear them darkies laugh! (Aunt Cicely Cawthon, b. 1859, GA, 190, orig. parentheses)

During these jigs instrumentalists simply took a break or receded into the background, while prompting was moot. Henry William Ravenel (1814–1887) had witnessed all of this on his family's South Carolina plantation in the 1830s.

The jig was an African dance and a famous one in old times, before more refined notions began to prevail. . . . For the jig the music would be changed. The fiddle would assume a low monotonous tone, the whole tune running on three or four notes only (when it could be heard). The stick-knocker changed his time, and beat a softer and slower measure. . . . The feet moved about in a grotesque manner stamping, slamming, and banging the floor, not unlike the pattering of hail on the housetop. The conflict between brogans and the sanded floor was terrific.[72]

Obviously, many people were content to dance even when the only music they had was patting hands and stomping feet. All said, however, the fiddle was the sound that more than any other set slaves to dancing. "The same old fiddler played for us that played for the white folks. And could he play! When he got that old fiddle out you couldn't keep your foots still" (Prince Johnson, b. 1847, MS, 1172). "Chile ah had use ter ruther go ter dances than ter eat. Ah'd go ter dances ah git nearly dare and heah dem fiddles. Uh, my! ah jus couldn' make mah foots act right" (Alice Dixon, b. ca. 1856, AR, 155). "Lawdy Miss, evy time I heayd a fiddle, my feets jes' got to dance" (Nancy Settles, b. 1845, SC, 233).

THE FIDDLE

Amongst my numerous visitors this Morning I had a traveling musician attended by three boys—his instrument was a violin strung with horse hair not in single hairs but a bunch of a bout [about] 1/2 an inch round the bow of the same—the body was made of half a gourd or calabash coverd with the skin of the Guana stretched tightly over the top on it—the brige was fixed which consisted of 2 cross pieces of stick—the neck was about 2 feet long ornamented with plates of brass and had a knob of hollow brass at the head—to this instrument was hung a diminutive pair of sandles to denote his wandering occupation . . . said he would take any thing that was given to him—the 3 boys had gourds with small stones or beens [beans] in them with which they kept time by holding them in one hand & beating them against the other—the Musician himself was past the middle age . . . with an expression half the rogue & half a merry one and when he sang look[ed] some times sublime—his mouth & teeth were good & his voice clear & Melodious . . . he accompanied his instrument with his voice the boys joining in chorous—his songs were ex tempory [extemporary] & I wd have taken it down but it was about my self. . . . I gave him 50 cowries and sent him away rejoicing. (Hugh Clapperton [1788–1827], March 24, 1826, on the Niger River in present-day Benin. *Hugh Clapperton into the Interior of Africa: Records of the Second Expedition 1825–1827*, ed. Jamie Bruce Lockhart and Paul E. Lovejoy [Leiden: Brill, 2005], 185)

I used to be a great fiddler. I fust learned how to play on a long gourd with horsehair strings on it. 'Course I couldn't go very high on it, but it done pretty well. That was the fust of my learning to play. After a while I bought me a fiddle for $1.80, and after so long a time I bought me a fiddle sure enough. (Anon. ex-slave, b. unk., TN, *Unwritten History of Slavery*, 131)

He [father] made him self a fiddle outa pine bark and usta play fer us to dance. He taught me to dance when I wuz little like dey did in Africa. Dey dance by derselves or swing each other 'round. Dey didn't know nothing 'bout dese "huggin'" dances. I'd be settin' on my daddy's lap and he'd tell

Fig. 4.1. Jelleman of Soolimana, Jellaman of Kooranko. *Jalis (griots)*, Sierra Leone, early 1820s. Alexander Gordon Laing, *Travels in Timannee, Kooranka, and Soolima Countries in Western Africa* (London: John Murray, 1825), fac. 148. Slavery Images: A Visual Record of the African Slave Trade and Slave Life in the Early African Diaspora. slaveryimages.org. Laing described and depicted several jalis he encountered in Sierra Leone in the early 1820s, including this pair. The minstrel from Kooranko (right) is playing what Laing described as "a sort of fiddle, the body of which was formed of a calabash, in which two small holes were cut to give it a tone; it had only one string, composed of many twisted horse-hairs, and though he could only bring from it four notes, yet he contrived to vary them so as to produce a pleasing harmony" (148). This is the instrument known throughout much of West Africa as a *goge*. Note that the fiddler is stopping the single string with his thumb, still a conventional technique (fingers are also used). The second jali is playing a *kora* harp.

me all 'bout when he lived in Africa. He usta play de fiddle and sing 'bout "Africa—Dat Good Ole Land."—and den he would cry, when he thought of his mother back dere.... My father was stolen from the jungles of Africa and brought on a slave ship to Georgia where he wuz sold on the block to Mr. Joe Holland, who owned a plantation near Dalton, Ga. (Chaney [Channie] Mack, b. ca. 1861, GA, 1417–18, 1428)

By the colonial era African Americans had mastered the European violin, and for the next two centuries Black fiddlers were prominent, even preeminent, in the former colonies and Southern slave states but also the North and Midwest, often preferred by white dancers and audiences over white violinists. This was not, as sometimes stated, an especially dramatic case of overnight acculturation. Indigenous fiddles had been played in Africa for centuries before European contact, being especially common—in fact, fundamental—in areas of West Africa providing a high proportion of North American slaves, as well as a significant portion of the African contributions to North American music, including the banjo. In fact, fiddles arrived in Africa around the same time they entered Europe, and from the same source: the Islamic world.

Then too, European violins were introduced into Africa soon after contact, so that some slaves arrived in America already acquainted with that instrument. Such was the case with Zamba, a Congolese strongman's son assigned "to procure cargoes of living flesh and blood, to be transported to some far land towards the setting sun." One of his father's clients was an American slaver, Captain Winton. "Amongst other toys he brought a large violin for me; but, as we had no instructor, the sounds which my father, myself, or any of his people elicited from it, would by no means have set the stones a-dancing." (Zamba reports greater success with another of Winton's gifts, "a small barrel organ, which could play eight tunes.") Zamba was himself eventually enslaved and transported to South Carolina.[1]

In short, the conventional wisdom that Africans only began fiddling after they arrived in the New World and there adopted the European violin could not be more mistaken. A few slaves had already encountered the violin in Africa, but hundreds of thousands would have been familiar with African fiddles. In America, however, slaves were suddenly surrounded by violins and violin music, most significantly, the Anglo-American dance fiddling that they widely embraced, made their own, then immeasurably extended. The fiddle was in fact the favorite of Anglo- and African Americans alike throughout the eighteenth and nineteenth centuries; it is by an incredibly wide margin the musical instrument most frequently named in the WPA narratives.[2] Blacks learned to fiddle from whites, and whites from Blacks in about equal numbers, both groups being essential to the development of American folk fiddling. While that fact is universally acknowledged, it is not widely recognized that some of the Black contribution—or at least its inspiration—may have ultimately been *African* rather than newly African American. And some of the strongest intimations of those links are provided by the homemade fiddles regularly described in the ex-slave narratives.

Black and white Americans share a long history of making homemade fiddles, typically as a young musician's first step toward a store-bought violin. In the 1830s, English traveler John Finch declared: "every negro is a musician from his birth. A black boy will make an excellent fiddle out of a gourd and some string. . . . The bandjo is another instrument they are fond of, but the supreme ambition of every negro is to procure a real violin."[3] Following that pattern, ex-slave Chaney Mack's African father eventually exchanged his "pine bark" fiddle for the European variety. Her account of his pine-bark instrument is too vague to draw any conclusions, but numerous other descriptions of homemade African American fiddles do hint at African influences, and especially the gourd-and-horsehair fiddles played throughout Africa's Western Sudan and Guinea Coast.[4]

The ex-slave narratives are the single best source on gourd fiddles in North America, as well as African American homemade fiddles generally. Granted, many narrators merely mention such instruments in passing, with little or no information on materials or construction. "We made our music. Music is natur'l wid our color. They most all had a juice (Jew's) harp. They make the fiddle and banjo" (Solomon Lambert, b. 1848, AR, 230, orig. parentheses). "After work was done, the slaves would smoke, sing, tell ghost stories and tales, dances, music, homemade fiddles" (James V. Deane, b. 1850, MD, 8). "On Saturday night you'd hear them fiddles, banjoes and guitars playing and the darkies singing. All the music gadgets was homemade. . . . One of the oldest fiddlers of slavery time taught my brother Flint to play the fiddle" (Simp Campbell, b. 1860, TX, 614).

More particular accounts may not be particular enough. Jack Maddox recalled: "Judge Maddox bought a nigger man who had a three string fiddle. I used to hear him play and sing" (Jack Maddox, b. ca. 1849, TX, 2531–32). This suggests a homemade instrument, or at least something other than a standard vio-

lin, and there are other references to slaves playing three-string fiddles.[5] These are no more specific than Maddox, however, and it is unclear how they all fit together, or whether the cases are related at all. African American musicians have a long history of creating unique, entirely personal instruments, and some of the homemade fiddles mentioned by ex-slaves were probably just that, the singular creations of unusually imaginative and resourceful individuals.

Nevertheless, other accounts do recall African fiddle-types, especially the West African instrument described by Scottish explorer Hugh Clapperton. Most commonly called the *goge* (alternately *goje, gonje, gondze, goonji*), this monochord gourd-and-horsehair fiddle has been played for centuries throughout the Sudan as far east as Ethiopia and more sporadically along the Guinea Coast. The *goge* is a single-string *spike fiddle*, constructed from a bisected gourd skewered (spiked) by a wooden rod whose protruding ends serve as the instrument's neck and tailpiece. The gourd-resonator's open face is covered with reptile skin or animal hide, then strung with a hank of untwisted horsehair stretching between the rod's two ends over a pressure bridge seated on the membrane top. To alter pitch, the performer lightly touches this horsehair strand at different intervals with the fingers and thumb of one hand while stroking it with a bow also of horsehair, usually with the instrument suspended on a neck-strap or cradled in the lap: the string is never pressed against the neck like a violin. Although bowed rather than plucked, the goge's construction thus closely resembles the membrane-topped gourd lutes played throughout these same regions, the ancestors of the American banjo. Scholarly consensus holds that the fiddle concept entered the Western Sudan from Islamic North Africa. In any event, Arab and later European travelers documented goge fiddles long before the American slave trade, as well as their essential roles in bardic traditions, social dancing, possession rites, life cycle ceremonies, and other major customs and occasions.[6]

Circumstances alone might suggest, then, that the gourd fiddles regularly reported among American slaves would preserve features of the goge, and the evidence is not entirely circumstantial. It is characteristically haphazard, however, and does not mirror Africa. Historically, West African gourd fiddles have been relatively fixed in form not only within specific communities but throughout their distribution. In many cases making and playing these instruments was the privilege of a musician class. Their construction was prescribed by tradition and sometimes entailed ritual acts. They were integral to highly visible institutions and events, being employed, among other things, for dynastic propaganda, devotional music, and folk healing. These and similar factors ensured relative stability (though by no means absolute uniformity) in the West African type's physical form.

By contrast, I have found no description of a fiddle precisely matching the goge in North America. The WPA narratives and other sources do document several of its features in homemade American fiddles, albeit with significant transformations—most of all, obvious imitations of the European violin. Like so many African musical traits, the goge appears to have arrived in North America primarily as a mental template that, absent the bounds of established tradition, was adapted or altered as circumstances or tastes dictated, sometimes quite imaginatively or opportunistically. Ironically, most of these adaptations served slaves' ambitions to procure and play violins in place of goges. If nothing else, though, memories of West African fiddles provided one means to that end.

All that said, what is certain is that during the nineteenth century North American Blacks made and played: 1) one-string fiddles; 2) fiddles strung with horsehair; 3) gourd fiddles; and 4) gourd fiddles topped with animal hide or reptile skin. Relevant sources (including the narratives) may register one or two of these traits, but none capture all together. I have found no North American evidence for other distinguishing features of West African fiddles, such as the means of joining neck and body, the placement of sound holes and bridge, or the attachment or insertion of sound modifiers. Of course, there is every chance

that the traits American sources do document were sometimes combined with other features into something more closely resembling a West African fiddle; more often, however, they were practical expedients in imitation violins.

Most references to gourd fiddles mention only the definitive gourd resonator, but usually without specifying the variety. "We made our own instruments, which was gourd fiddles and quill flutes" (Anderson Edwards, b. 1844, TX, 1262). "We had small dances on Saturday night and play ring plays, and have banjo and fiddle playing and knock bones together. There was all kinds of fiddles made from gourds and things" (Litt Young, b. 1850, MS, 4302). "I made my first fiddle out of a gourd. I played for all the dances both white and black and Sunday School" (Harre Quarls, b. 1841, TX, 3216). Charley Williams described "gourd fiddles, and clapping bones made out'n beef ribs" (Charley Williams, b. 1843, LA, 337). West African goges are constructed from spherical gourds or calabashes. Perhaps this was the case with most American gourd fiddles, but there are reports of differently shaped gourds that would have required significant changes to the goge's basic design. For example, an anonymous Tennessee ex-slave interviewed by Fisk recalled "I fust learned how to play on a *long gourd* with horsehair strings on it," shortly progressing to his goal of a real violin.[7] Oblong or longnecked gourds are regularly reported, in fact, possibly because of their resemblances to violins.

Early sources often do not give string-counts for homemade fiddles, but well into the twentieth century African Americans made and played single-string instruments of African origin (the washtub bass, the mouth bow, the jitterbug or diddley bow).[8] In the 1800s and possibly after, one-string fiddles were also known. Sometimes these are only intimated. John Finch, an English visitor of the 1830s, reported "a black boy will make an excellent fiddle out of a gourd and some string."[9] In 1856 South Carolina Governor John Laurence Manning recalled a slave named Robin as one such prodigy: "Upon a shingle strung, with the hairs of the horse and with a bow made from a twig and horse hairs, Robin first gave evidence of his musical capacity."[10] Other references are, however, categorical. On Ruben Laird's Mississippi plantation, "the Christmas dance lasted three days and three nights. The music was provided principally by a 'fiddle' an improvised instrument made by bending a stick in the shape of a bow, holding it in shape with a string and sawing on it with a crude violin bow made of the hair of a horse's mane and tail" (Ruben Laird, b. 1850, MS, 1298–99). Laird does not describe the fiddle string (gut? wire? more horsehair?), or how the instrument was amplified (probably by attaching a receptacle like a gourd), but he could well be remembering a monochord gourd-and-horsehair fiddle.

By most detailed accounts, however, gourd fiddles usually had four strings like violins, as well as violin-style necks, played in the standard fashion by pressing the strings against a flat or slightly rounded fingerboard. By contrast the one-string fiddle Ruben Laird describes could only have been pitched African-style—that is, by stopping rather than fully depressing the string. Other homemade fiddles mentioned merely in passing may have been fingered this way, but based on all the evidence I have seen, this technique was virtually unknown in North America. With the rarest possible exceptions (ex-slave Ruben Laird being the only certain case), homemade African American fiddles were fingered like violins, not West African goges, an absolutely crucial distinction.

The membrane top is a constant feature of African gourd fiddles. In the New World, this hide-top design is best-known from banjos (originally made from gourds as well), but some American gourd fiddles also had animal or reptile skin tops. At a New Orleans hoodoo ceremony in the 1850s, "music was provided by an aged Negro who scraped a fiddle, said to have been covered with snakeskin, and by drums made of gourds and wine casks over which cowhide had been stretched."[11] Sheepskin and cat hide are also reported, while a Tennessee gourd fiddle made around 1804 had a shoe-leather top.[12] Most period descriptions also neglect this detail, but some American gourd fid-

dles definitely had hide tops. Others did not, however, and the violin seems to have been an influence in this as well.[13]

The horsehair string may be the goge's most unusual element. It is also the object of some of the most unusual North American adaptations, once more reflecting the violin's influence. In Africa horsehair-strung fiddles are invariably monochords with lone hanks of loose horsehair, but African American gourd fiddles usually had multiple strings, and almost always four like the violin.

Frolics usually took place on such holidays as 4th of July, Christmas, or "laying-by time," after cultivating the crops was finished and before gathering them. During the day the master provided a big barbecue and at night the singing and dancing started. Music was furnished by slaves who were able to play the banjo or the fiddle. The slaves usually bought these instruments themselves and in some cases the master bought them. "In my case," declared Mr. Wright, "I made a fiddle out of a large sized gourd—a long wooden handle was used as a neck, and the hair from a horse's tail was used for the bow. The strings were made of catgut. After I learned to play this I bought a better violin." (Henry Wright, b. 1838, GA, 200)

Remarkably, there are several American descriptions not merely of horsehair-strung fiddles but of fiddles with *multiple* horsehair strings. Throughout 1778 a slave fiddler entertained the first settlers of Louisville, Kentucky:

There was a negro named Cato at the fort who had a fiddle that had furnished music for the settlement during the summer and fall. But his crazy old instrument was now reduced to one string, and Cato was not Ole Bull enough to saw music from it. He had tried to make strings of the hair of the horse's tail and of the sinews of the deer, but the former only gave a horrid screech when the bow scraped them, and the latter uttered no sound except a kind of hoarse moan like the melancholy hoots of the night owl.[14]

A Tennessee ex-slave stated, "I fust learned how to play on a long gourd with horsehair strings on it."[15] George Strickland also recalled fiddles with multiple horsehair strings: "De wimmen folks had a big time at quiltings and somebody would play old gourds with horsehair strings, called 'Old gourd horsehair dance'" (George Strickland, b. ca. 1856, AL, 398).

This arrangement obviously raised a practical problem, since adopting the goge's loose hank-of-horsehair to the violin's four-string design required somehow separating and affixing the four horsehair strings. In some cases rosin (resin) was used for that purpose. Virginia slave Isaac Williams (b. ca. 1821) explained: "we generally made our own banjos and fiddles, and I had a fiddle that was manufactured out of a gourd, with horse hair strings and a bow made out of the same material. If you put plenty of rosin on the strings, it would compare very favorably with an ordinary violin and make excellent music."[16] There are also reports of homemade five-string banjos with beeswax-coated horsehair strings. I have found nothing similar in Africa.

Thus while North American slaves definitely recalled African fiddles, or at least certain of their traits, these were generally accommodated to the violin's design. Significantly, similar hybrid fiddles were being constructed *in Africa* during this same period. Between 1811 and 1812 William John Burchell (1781–1863) traveled through South Africa in the company of several Hottentots, one of whom brought along "a *fiddle* of his own making. . . . This mirth-inspiring *utensil* was a kind of oblong bowl, carved out of willow-wood, and covered over with sheepskin or parchment. A fingerboard, with screws [tuning pegs], bridge, and tailpiece, together with a bow, were all formed in imitation of a European violin, and nearly in the proper proportion. The strings, twisted in their due thickness, were made from sheep's entrails, and

the horse's tail supplied the hair for the bow." Burchell judged that "it gave, every thing considered, an excellent tone, and proved, during our travels, a most valuable article."[17]

Meanwhile, in North America homemade gourd fiddles were prevalent if not pervasive in the nineteenth-century South, played by whites as well as Blacks. That whites played them is hardly surprising, since Europeans have for centuries created their own imitation violins from naturally available or castoff materials,[18] and in itself a gourd fiddle does not necessarily denote African or even Black influence.[19] Gourds were the nineteenth-century South's ever-ready, multipurpose receptacles, and some whites—no doubt even some Blacks—made fiddles from gourds for the same commonsensible, purely practical reasons they made fiddles from cigar boxes, discarded cans, and so forth. On the other hand, reports of whites playing gourd fiddles with horsehair strings or hide tops would seem to indicate some Black (though not necessarily a direct African) contribution. Among Arkansas Ozark whites ca. 1840, "'hoe-downs' and reels—'none o' yer huggin' dances'—were tripped lightly, and with jollity, to the tune of 'Roarin' River,' etc., which some deft musicians drew from the gourd 'fiddle' with its horsehair strings and bow, and the gourd banjo with its squirrel-skin head and horsehairs."[20] Country music pioneer Eck Robertson (1887–1975) was born in this same section of Arkansas, but shortly moved to West Texas, where "at the age of five, Eck took up musical instruments, working first with a fiddle he made himself from a longnecked gourd and a tanned cat-hide."[21] He eventually acquired a violin, of course, and became one of the twentieth century's most celebrated fiddlers. Memories of West African fiddles may have made ripples in white communities too, but there is no question that the violin was the absolute standard.

Still, having nurtured numerous celebrity fiddlers, sometimes gourd fiddles themselves became celebrities of sorts. The following much-reprinted news feature originally appeared in the 1893 *San Francisco Examiner*:

A Curious Fiddle

One of the queerest musical instruments ever known, and perhaps the only one of its kind, has reached here from Greenville, east Tennessee. The queer instrument is a violin made from a gourd, and it is 89 years old.

The strangest, weirdest music that ever was heard comes from it. The tones are fine and soft and float on the air as from the land of spirits. James Anderson Taylor, governor of Tennessee, and uncle of the famous Taylor boys who fiddled their way through Tennessee during a recent gubernatorial campaign, used to play on it. He made music from the gourd fiddle at the reception to Andrew Johnson by the people of Greenville, his native town, just after he was made president of the United States. He played the "Old Virginia Reel," the "Fishers' Hornpipe" and many other things, and the president "hoed it down" with everybody present and enjoyed it more than he could tell.

The gourd grew at Johnsville in the said state, and it, with the neck, which is of poplar, is 16 inches long. The keys are common violin keys, the strings catgut and the sounding board of leather from a stitch down shoe, while the bridge is of poplar. The bow is of dark wood, and the hairs black, being plucked from a horse's tail. The older the fiddle grows the better it is, so H. C. Atkinson says, who owns it.[22]

The article confuses some facts but gets enough right to warrant consideration. No James Anderson Taylor ever served as governor of Tennessee; the individual intended is most likely James Patton "Jim" Taylor (1844–1924), one of the illustrious Taylor family of East Tennessee, which also included Jim's younger half-brothers, Robert Love "Bob" Taylor (1850–1912) and Alfred Alexander "Alf" Taylor (1848–1931). The Taylors were prominent citizens—and Jim, Alf, and Bob popular fiddlers—around Andrew Johnson's adopted hometown of Greeneville (not Greenville),

not far from Johnson City (not Johnsville). Bob and Alf (but never Jim) did both serve as Tennessee governors, Bob from 1887–91 then again from 1897–99, Alf from 1921–23. In the 1886 election Bob and Alf actually ran against one another (Bob won). Press coverage played up their fiddling, even reporting that they performed together on stage at their debates (probably fabrication).[23] In 1913 Jim, Alf, and another brother, Hugh, published a personal tribute to the recently deceased Bob, including much about fiddling (and Andrew Johnson) but no mention of the curious gourd.[24] In any case, Bob, Jim, and Alf Taylor all pursued lifelong interests in fiddling; at one time Bob Taylor mentored legendary North Georgia fiddler John Carson (1868–1949), even giving Carson his nickname, "Fiddlin' John." The Taylor fiddle was made around 1804, forty years before any of the brothers were born. The maker, possibly white, possibly not, is never identified, but the hide top would seem to indicate some Black influence.[25]

The Taylors counted as some of the era's most visible fiddlers, but anecdotal evidence suggests innumerable gourd fiddles made and played by lesser-knowns went unnoticed. These might have seemed the queerest instruments ever to a national public, but they were well-remembered by southerners, and by century's end even ranked among the minor icons of plantation literature. Grace MacGowan Cooke's 1904 novel *A Gourd Fiddle* tells the story of Orpheus (aka Orphy), the "sole, orphaned remainder of a long line of [slave] fiddlers," whose virtuosity on a gourd fiddle precipitates an extraordinary chain of events, ending in an audience with Queen Victoria and her gift of a Stradivarius.[26] Author and journalist Cooke (1863–1944) was the daughter of John Encill MacGowan (1831–1903), Civil War colonel of the 1st US Colored Heavy Artillery, Reconstruction-era commander of the Chattanooga district, and longtime editor of the *Chattanooga Times* (1872–1903). Cooke was born in her father's native Ohio but raised in Chattanooga. *A Gourd Fiddle* is a plantation melodrama typical of its time but strongly suggests some firsthand familiarity with real gourd fiddles (and with every gourd fiddler's supreme ambition to procure a real violin).

Indeed, however prevalent gourd fiddles may have been, slave fiddlers usually played violins; revealingly, almost all accounts of African American gourd fiddles come from individuals who eventually advanced to store-bought instruments. Whether goges had any more lasting effect on American fiddling is difficult to answer, but there are indications that African American gourd fiddles may have sounded somewhat like West African goges, and that slaves were producing similar sounds on violins by the early 1800s if not before. The goge's lefthand fingering technique—lightly touching a single suspended string to produce different pitches but also overtones—simply does not transfer to the violin, and this was obviously one of the first traits abandoned in North America, where even gourd-and-horsehair fiddles had multiple strings and violin-style necks. By contrast African bowing and righthand techniques may have influenced early African American fiddling, which evidently favored the same percussive textures and special effects characterizing West African fiddling. After a correspondent to the 1845 *Raleigh Register, and North Carolina Gazette* attended a recital featuring "a variety of curiously rude musical instruments" at a "Chinese museum" in Boston, he reported "I have no doubt but his music was good, according to Chinese taste, but the harmony could be much improved by adding a steam whistle, a sawmill, and a waggon without grease. A *gourd* Fiddle would excel in beauty the Guitars of the ladies, and a Banjo would be an ornament, compared with a Chinese Troubadour."[27]

Sarcasm aside, by 1845 a white North Carolina journalist could take for granted that his readers were acquainted with the sounds of gourd fiddles (and banjos), and the sounds he describes are wholly in keeping with West African goges. As John M. Chernoff observes: "the goonji may sound a bit scratchy at first to Westerners used to the sound of bowed instruments like the violin; nonetheless, the seemingly rough texture of the goonji's sound is consistent with West African concepts of sound richness. . . . Goonji music

offers a superb illustration of how one may attribute the notion of percussive attack to a fiddler's bowing technique."[28] David W. Ames similarly describes the Hausa (West African) fiddler's ability "to improvise endless variations on any tune, and at the same time, to produce a variety of unusual tones and percussive effects."[29] Early descriptions of African American fiddles—like the "horrid screech" attributed to Cato's horsehair strings at Louisville—evoke exactly this sound, which might indeed suggest a sawmill, a steam whistle, or an ungreased wagon to some listeners.

That Black fiddlers can produce similar effects on European violins is definitely supported by twentieth-century sound recordings. Even on first hearing there are obvious resemblances between West African fiddling and early recorded blues and jazz violin: hot rhythms; slurs, slides, and wavering pitches or blue notes; subtle shifts in tone and timbre; percussive bowing with voice-like effects (squeaks, squeals, moans, growls). No wonder David Ames likened Hausa goge playing to the hot jazz violin of Eddie South (Black) (1904–1952) and Joe Venuti (white) (1902–1978), or that the music of Malian gourd-fiddle and guitar master Ali Farka Touré (1939–2006) is sometimes described as West African blues, an anachronism that nonetheless registers an audible affinity.[30]

There are, moreover, many firsthand accounts of North American slaves playing violins in exactly this style. Percussive effects were particular cause for outside comment, the most common descriptions of slave fiddling being *sawing* or *scraping*. Thus at a July 1826 Florida barbecue the music consisted of "an old negro scraping the violin, accompanied by two little negroes playing the tambourine and triangle."[31] In 1840s Philadelphia dance houses, wrote another observer, education among Southern runaways in attendance was "confined to a little, or a good deal, of sawing upon the fiddle, and an intense passion for the real old Virginny breakdown."[32] Maurice Thompson (1844–1901) recalled Georgia and Alabama slaves fiddling in what is actually called the *breakdown* style, typified by highly percussive bowing (scraping) and short rhythmic back-and-forth strokes (sawing), usu-

Fig 4.2. George Simmons, ex-slave, Beaumont, TX, June 28, 1937. Portraits of African American ex-slaves from the US Works Progress Administration, Federal Writers' Project slave narratives collection, Library of Congress.

gourd was said to create some of the strangest, weirdest music ever heard, otherworldly tones that "float on the air as from the land of spirits"), but they *talk* in other ways as well, by imitating human speech and animal sounds or telling stories.

In bowing, a skillful [goge] player may vary the speed and length of the strokes to exploit the imitative possibilities of the instrument. Single bow strokes accompanied by rapidly fingered notes in the left hand can be made to resemble melismatic singing, whereas single strokes paired with single notes produce a syllabic effect. Short, light strokes coupled with harmonics simulate the tones of a flute; rapid strokes in *tremolo* depict animals in flight, while interrupted strokes portray a limping straggler. Such techniques may be used to great effect in musical storytelling or in support of the style and text of a vocalist.[36]

ally with liberal use of double stops (bowing two or more strings at once). "Sometimes one would meet with a negro violinist, but the music that he made was wrenched from all four of the strings at once, with little regard for anything but time and noise."[33]

WPA narrators remembered slave fiddling the same way. "Dere am no parties and sich, but old Jack saw on de fiddle an us sing" (William M. Thomas, b. ca. 1850, MS, 96). "My brother would scrape the fiddle and dance on, all at the same time" (Laura Thornton, b. ca. 1830, AL, 327). "I uster play de fiddle at de dance. I 'member one time in '86 I's sawin' 'way on a piece I jus' pick up. A man come by an' say, 'Gawge, you know w'at dat you playin'?' An' I say, 'No,' an' he say, 'Dat 'De Big Woods,' dat w'at dey play at de s'render of Sabine Pass. It w'er a march tune" (George Simmons, b. 1854, TX, 3547).[34]

Grace MacGowan Cooke described the sound of Orphy's gourd fiddle as "queer and 'throaty,'" while one of Orphy's tormentors taunts "dish yer boy got er po' li'l cat fas'n' up in dat ar gode!"[35] Goges channel spirit voices in religious rites (the Taylors' curious

African American instrumentalists famously employ similar effects to make their instruments talk. "I learned to fiddle, and I can make an old fiddle talk" (Henry Clay, b. ca. 1835, LA, TX, IT, 117). "We use to play at night by moonlight and I can recollec' singin wid the fiddle. Oh, Lord, dat fiddle could almos' talk an' I can hear it ringin now" (Millie Evans, b. 1849, NC, 243). "My pappy also useta play de fiddle for de white folks dances in de big house, an' he played it for de colored frolics too. He sho could make dat thing sing" (Charles Hayes, b. ca. 1855, AL, 174). "Old John play for all de dance on de plantation. He fair (really) mek fiddle talk" (Ephraim Lawrence, b. ca. 1856, SC, 97, orig. parentheses).[37]

And just like West African fiddles, talking African American fiddles told stories and imitated people, animals, and the manmade and natural worlds. "I cud take a fiddle an' make it talk. I played 'Arkansas Traveler' an' 'Sally Goodin' an' 'De Cacklin' Hen' an' jes' meny more dat I done fur git" (Henry Lewis McGaffey, b. 1853, LA, TX, 1399). Probably a slave creation, "Cacklin' Hen" (aka "Hen Cackle," "The Old Hen Cackled and the Rooster Crowed," "Cluck, Old

Hen") mimics a chicken's squawks, crows, and cackles with squeaky, scratchy bow-strokes. Instrumental imitations of this sort are another custom shared by Africa and Europe, and American whites also fiddled "Cacklin' Hen."[38] In fact, in the US this piece is second in popularity only to "The Fox Chase" (aka "Fox and Hounds"), based on an Irish bagpipe tune. "Cacklin' Hen" may extend the West African tradition of talking fiddles.[39]

To be sure, such bowing techniques and talking effects are another obvious expression of the *pitch-to-grit principle* and could have developed among North American slaves with no direct African influence, just as African Americans learned to create similar effects on instruments with no African equivalents (harmonicas, saxophones, electric guitars). That Africans had reportedly played fiddles in this manner for centuries might suggest otherwise. In any case, this apparently was the slave fiddling style, or at least one prevalent slave fiddling style—rough, scratchy, full of screeches and squeals, perfectly complementing but also effectively competing with patting, shuffling, and clogging at slave frolics. Toward that end, fiddlers might add more grit by incorporating straw beating, derived from the African practice of playing stringed instruments with beating sticks. Other popular accompaniments for slave fiddles included the clacking bones, sounding nearly identical to the gourd rattles traditionally paired with West African fiddles. African fiddlers also fit their instruments with jingles, rattles, or other objects that vibrate in response to their playing, further increasing the grit-to-pitch ratio (the knob of hollow brass at the head of the gourd fiddle Hugh Clapperton described would have been filled with pebbles, seeds, or similar objects). The practice is widely documented among African- and Anglo-American fiddlers and guitarists after 1900.[40] Ultimately, the precise African contribution to African American fiddling may be impossible to quantify, the European tradition being ever-present and ever-dominant, but the music's African character is often unmistakable, and it seems inconceivable that African fiddles and fiddling were not somehow factors.

Another type of makeshift fiddle provides one of the narratives' more fascinating sidelights: in a small patch of the southwest Georgia–southeast Alabama border, numerous slaves and their offspring played musical saws. "An sech music! Music played on harps, saws, and blowin' quills. Ever'body had a good time; even de 'white folks' turned out for de dance which went 'way into de night" (Easter Jackson, b. ca. 1850, GA, 300). "Atter dey done shucked dat pile er corn, ole marster wud hab two big hogs kilt en cooked up in de big pots en kittles, en den dem niggers wud eat en frolic fer de longes', makin music wid er hand saw er tin pan, en er dancin', en laffin', en cuttin' up, till dey tired out" (Henry Green, b. 1848, AL, 97). "Many 'frolics' were given and everyone danced where banjoes were available; also, these resourceful people secured much of their music from an improvised fiddle fashioned from a hand saw" (Rhodus Walton, b.ca. 1852, GA, 124).

> De wimmen folks had a big time at quiltings and somebody would play old gourds with horsehair strings, called "Old gourd horsehair dance." Cornshucking was de greatest thing er tall, master took a jug er licker 'roun' and got dem tight and when dey got full, dey would histe master up and toat him 'roun' and holler, then the fun started and dey would play de old gourd and horsehair dance, the handsaw and case knife, dey could run dey hand up and down de saw to change de tune. Leader was on top er de pile er corn and sing, den all would follow. (George Strickland, b. ca. 1856, AL, 398)[41]

In the West Indies, handsaws are sometimes used as scrapers,[42] but Walton's "improvised fiddle" suggests a melodic function, and Strickland made absolutely clear that the instrument ex-slaves recalled was a musical saw, sounded by striking or bowing the blade, which was then manipulated with the other hand to alter the pitch.

Two other examples from southwest Georgia corroborate these ex-slave accounts. In 1940, Fort Valley State, a Black teachers' college in Fort Valley, Peach County, initiated an annual folk festival featuring local music. The program was divided between an "evening devoted to secular performers, principally guitarists and banjoists (Note: we have never had a fiddler!) and a Sunday afternoon (reaching to unpredictable hours, also, of the evening) for religious groups. . . . On the secular evenings, we have had guitarists, banjoists, pianists, harmonica players, jug bands and artists with washboards, 'quills,' saws, bones, and improvised one-string instruments."[43] Unfortunately nothing more is said of saws or sawyers, but they are listed with other instruments commonly named in the narratives. That, coupled with the southwest Georgia provenance, strongly argues these were also musical saws.

But that is not quite all. This same region produced a truly unique *white* recording that almost certainly reflects the Black handsaw fiddle tradition. "Mister Johnson, Turn Me A Loose" (OKeh 45166, 1927) was one of a half-dozen sides by the South Georgia Highballers, a white stringband from Bibb County, which borders Peach County to the north, on the eastern edge of the handsaw fiddle's range. Little is known of the Highballers' activities except that they spent time busking the streets of the county seat Macon, where they would inevitably have encountered Black musicians.[44] Their two best-known recordings are a pair of slide guitar solos showing obvious African American influence.[45] "Mr. Johnson," by contrast, features the entire trio on musical saw, fiddle, and guitar. The performance is loosely based on Ben Harney's "Mr. Johnson, Turn Me Loose" (1896), a well-known 1890s "coon song" regularly collected from Blacks.[46] It is difficult to believe the Highballers' record is not somehow related to the local Black handsaw fiddle tradition; in fact, it may provide the only recorded documentation.[47]

Musical saws can be sounded either by striking the blade or by bowing it like a violin. Rhodus Walton called the instrument a fiddle, so he probably recalled bowing; however, the only ex-slave who specified—George Strickland—indicated the saw was struck with a case knife. I cannot tell whether the saw on the Highballers' record is being struck or bowed. Still, ex-slaves and others likened or linked fiddles and musical saws, which do sound somewhat similar, even when the saw

is struck. (Curiously, the handsaw fiddle's geographical distribution coincides with the gourd fiddle's heaviest concentration.) In any event, the Georgia–Alabama handsaw fiddle offers one of the narratives' more unexpected and interesting revelations.

Chances are a few other fiddles ex-slaves mentioned were homemade instruments, possibly even gourd-and-horsehairs (or musical saws). That said, there is no question that for most American Blacks, the fiddle was the European violin. Of course, advancing from a homemade fiddle to the genuine article could pose a serious challenge for slaves, who acquired violins however they could, whether through slaveholders or by their own devices.

> Music was furnished by slaves who were able to play the banjo or the fiddle. The slaves usually bought these instruments themselves and in some cases the master bought them. "In my case," declared Mr. Wright, "I made a fiddle out of a large sized gourd—a long wooden handle was used as a neck, and the hair from a horse's tail was used for the bow. The strings were made of catgut. After I learned to play this I bought a better violin." (Henry Wright, b. 1838, GA, 200)

In 1851 one planter wrote: "I have a fiddle in my [slave] quarters, and though some of my good old brethren in the church would think it hard of me, yet I allow dancing; ay, I buy the fiddle and encourage it, by giving the boys occasionally a big supper."[48] Henry Bland stated "when darkness came they sang and danced and this was what they called a 'frolic.' As a general rule this same thing was permitted after the crops were gathered. Music for these occasions was furnished by violin, banjo and a clapping of hands. Mr. Bland says that he used to help furnish this music as Mr. Coxton had bought him a violin" (Henry Bland, b. 1851, GA, 81). Jerry Boykins went behind his slaveholder's back to his more sympathetic wife.

> I was full of mischief when I a boy, I would turn the mules out of the lot, just to see the stableboy

get a lickin'. One time I wanted a fiddle that a white man named Coconut Harper kept tryin' to sell to me for $7.50. I didn't neber have no money 'cyptin a little the missie gib me. So I kept teasin' the missie to buy dat fiddle for me. She was mighty good to me, always on my side. So she told me to take some of the co'n in the crib, and trade it fo' the fiddle. In the night I slip out and hitch up the mules and fetched that co'n over to old Harper's house and traded fo' that fiddle. Then I hide out and play the fiddle, so's old Marster wouldn't find out. But he did find out and he whip all the daylight out of me. When the old missie try to whip me I jest wrop up in her big skirts and she neber could hurt me much. (Jerry Boykins, b. 1845, GA, 371–72)

Lacking outside assistance, fiddlers found instruments through various means. An anonymous Tennessee ex-slave "learned how to play on a long gourd with horsehair strings on it," but "after a while I bought me a fiddle for $1.80, and after so long a time I bought me a fiddle sure enough."[49] Tennessee ex-slave author James Thomas (1827–1913) began playing on a borrowed fiddle "with a rat hole in or on one side of it" but eventually acquired a better one.[50] Andy Brice got his violin for Christmas, though he bought it himself.

One day I see Marse Thomas a twistin' de ears on a fiddle and rosinin' de bow. Then he pull dat bow 'cross de belly of dat fiddle. Sumpin' bust loose in me and sing all thru my head and tingle in my fingers. I make up my mind, right then and dere, to save and buy me a fiddle. I got one dat Christmas, bless God! I learn and been playin' de fiddle ever since. (Andy Brice, b. ca. 1856, SC, 76)

Many slaves were in fact able to raise cash in various ways. Isaac Williams (1821–?) began on a gourd fiddle but after a few months "had managed to accumulate over a hundred muskrat skins and taking them to Hampstead I sold them for enough to buy myself a fine violin of good manufacture."[51] Mary Reynolds remembered "when they got through with their clothes

on Saturday evenin's the Niggers which had sold their goobers and taters and bought fiddles and guitars would come out and play. The others w'ud clap hands and stomp they feet and we young ones would cut a step around" (Mary Reynolds, b. ca. 1835, LA, 3289). Celestia Avery described slaves buying fiddles on the sly:

"Once a week Mr. Heard allowed his slaves to have a frolic and folks would get broke down from so much dancing," Mrs. Avery remarked. The music was furnished with fiddles. When asked how slaves came to own fiddles she replied, "They bought them with money they earned selling chickens." At night slaves would steal off from the Heard plantation, go to LaGrange, Ga. and sell chickens which they had raised. Of course the masters always required half of every thing raised by each slave and it was not permissible for any slave to sell anything. (Celestia Avery, b. 1862, GA, 23)

Added Avery, "Mr. Heard was a very mean master and was not liked by any one of his slaves. Secretly each one hated him" (Celestia Avery, b. 1862, GA, 24).

While many, perhaps most slaves obtained violins secondhand from slaveholders, family, or other acquaintances, antebellum storekeepers definitely stocked violins (their advertisements fill period newspapers), and some slaves may have been able to purchase new instruments from retailers. A feature in the 1871 *Leslie's*—"An Artist Selecting an Instrument"— characterizes African Americans as experienced and savvy consumers: "There's no cheating this artist—no palming off on him a worthless instrument. The dealer in musical instruments may wink at the prospect of getting rid of an inferior article, but if the strings will not yield a clear, distinct, and agreeable sound, he had better let it remain on his shelves, for if there is anything suggestive, to a negro, of agony, it is a violin, banjo, or guitar that will not submit gracefully to the pranks of his fingers."[52]

Notwithstanding any African influences, or African American innovations, American fiddling was obviously imbued by centuries of European violin music, and African American fiddlers mastered that repertoire as well. The true mark of a star slave fiddler was performing for both Black and white audiences—but especially for better-paying whites—so suiting white musical tastes was an understandable priority. Slaves (and some whites) may have preferred the gritty Black fiddle style, but slave fiddlers excelled at any and every variety of nineteenth-century violin music. Many received formal instruction, sightread music, played exclusive white soirées, and served as dancing masters for slaveholders' children. "Tony was my father, a carriage driver; he wore his tall hat and fine clothes (livery) and he was a musician—played the violin at the Academy on the 'old-Ninety-Six Road'. All the white people educated their children there, and they had parties" (Richard Mack, b. ca. 1833, SC, 151, orig. parentheses). "This is how good my owner was to me. He sent me to Hendersonville, North Carolina (Henderson?) to learn to fiddle. I was so afraid of the old colored teacher I learned in a month about all he could play. I played for parties in eight states in slavery. All up in the North. They trained children to dance then" (William H. Harrison, b. 1832, VA, 186–87, orig. parentheses).

Thus, in the pattern of topflight musicians everywhere, the best slave fiddlers could play various styles or repertoires to suit any audience or occasion. Even at slave dances they might be called on to play cotillions, quadrilles, polkas, schottisches, or Austrian waltzes alongside breakdowns and shuffles:

I used to play at all the drag downs. Anything I heard played once, I could play. Used to play two steps, one of 'em called "Devil's Dream," and three or four good German waltzes, and "Turkey in the Straw"—but we didn't call it that then. It was the same piece, but I forget what we called it. They don't play the same nowadays. Playin' now is just a time-consumer, that's all; they got it all tore to pieces, no top or bottom to it. (Charles H. Anderson, b. 1845, VA, 3)[53]

Still, most slaves learned to play informally from family and friends, or from slaveholders and other whites.

"One of the oldest fiddlers of slavery time teached my brother Flint to play the fiddle" (Simp Campbell, b. 1860, TX, 614). "I learned to fiddle after the fiddler on the place. Uncle Jim was the fiddler" (William Gant, b. 1837, TN, 12). "My mammy's brother been one of de best fiddlers there was; he teach de other niggers how to play" (Margaret Hughes, b. ca. 1855, SC, 329). "Used to be a fiddlah fo' the white girls to dance. Jes' picked it up, it was a natural gif'. Ah could still play if I had a fiddle" (Richard Toler, b. ca. 1835, VA, 100). "Thar am lots ob music on dat place. De Marster am good fiddler, he larnes some ob de niggers hows to play de fiddel and some de banjo" (Guy Stewart, b. 1850, LA, 3733).

Similarly, the pieces most often attributed to slave fiddlers are so-called fiddle tunes, traditional dance melodies passed on by ear and recreated from memory, some from Great Britain or Ireland, some Anglo-American, others slave creations. W. S. Needham (b. 1854, MS), one of the whites interviewed for the ex-slaves project, had learned to fiddle from his father's slaves:

Mance was a good fiddler. He loved to teach me to play, and I picked it up right away. By rights, a nigger by the name of "Friday" gave me my first lesson, when I wasn't but three years old, but dad gave him to my oldest sister when she married. When I was six, Mance taught me to jig and play such pieces as "Turkey in the Straw," "Molly Put de Kittle On," "Run Nigger Run," "Old Dan Tucker," and such pieces, and taught me to go on like they did. I just picked it right up now, and made a many a dollar by playing for dances and such after I got grown. (W. S. Needham Jr., SS2 10 TX 9: 4364–65)

Other frequently named items include "The Arkansas Traveler," "Cacklin' Hen," "Devil's Dream," "Cotton-Eyed Joe," "Hop Light Ladies," and "Sally Goodin."[54] All can be fiddled in various styles but are especially associated with *breakdown fiddling*; some are actually called *breakdowns* or *breakdown tunes*.

In whatever style they were played, fiddles were with rare exceptions dance instruments, and slave fiddlers are overwhelmingly described at slave dances, sawing and scraping fiddle tunes to handclapping, body slapping, and foot stamping. Many ex-slaves insisted that fiddles were the only real musical instruments at their dances. "We had dances all week. We had square dances an' round dances too. Dere was fiddle music. I never seen no kind of music but a fiddle till I was grown" (Harry Johnson, b. ca. 1850, MO, 2001). "We had lots of dances dem days and with jus' one fiddle" (Willie Blackwell, b. 1834, NC, 304). "The chief entertainment of Frank and his friends was dancing. They did not work at night and had dancing 'bees'. There was one slave that played an old fiddle. This was all the music they had" (Frank Ziegler, b. unk., AL, 467). "Dere was a dance on dis same night. De lone fiddler played 'Saddle Old Ball' and 'I'll Tell You' and other old timey songs" (Isiah Norwood, b. 1852, TX, 2949). "Two cullud men played the fiddle. Just two fiddles was all they had" (Austin Grant, b. unk., TX, 1544). "The black people never had no amusement. They would have an old fiddle—something like that. That was all the music I ever seen. Sometimes they would ring up and play 'round in the yard" (Columbus Williams, b. 1841, AR, 155).

Others simply recalled the fiddle as the most popular or lead instrument, as their personal favorite, or as an instrument they had personally mastered.

> On a platform in a convenient corner of the room the band would be located. This usually consisted of one good fiddler and his fiddle. His requirement was to be able to play good hoedowns and to call the sets. Sometimes another person would call the sets. Sometimes a banjo or guitar would be added to the band. But usually the old fiddler would be the band leader and the band itself. (George Morrison, b. unk., KY, 146)

Many who named only the fiddle probably took supporting instruments for granted and assumed others did too. "There were dances with a fiddler and I'd follow the music" (George Washington Miller, b. 1856, SC, 1491). "When they went to a party the most they

did was to play the fiddle and dance" (Abbie Lindsay, b. 1856, LA, 258). "I's too young to 'member jus' whut de songs waz, but dey had a fiddle an' dey danced an' played all night long" (James Jackson, b. 1850, LA, 1897). "Whoo pee! Yesim we danced every Saturday night, and had a time dancin by de fiddle" (Henry Gibbs, b. 1852, MS, 826). Still, the totals are striking: of the three-hundred-plus narrators who mention the fiddle, over two hundred name it alone, and many state outright that fiddles were the only instruments they knew.

Of course, even solo fiddling would be accompanied by handclapping, patting, clogging, and other percussion. At the very least there would be stamping and clapping from performers, dancers, and onlookers. "I can hear them fiddles and de pattin' now" (Henry D. Jenkins, b. ca. 1850, SC, 25). "Frolics included 'dancing, shouting, pattin 'n fiddling'" (John Watts, b. 1854, GA, 635). "White ladies do that 'kalkilating' trick sometime but you take a blue-gum nigger gal, all wool on de top of her head and like to dance and jig wid her foots, to pattin' and fiddle music, her ain't gonna have money in de back of her head when her pick out a man to marry" (Charley Barber, b. 1856, SC, 31–32).

Besides handclapping, West African goges are most often accompanied by gourd rattles, small drums, and struck bells.[55] After patting, the hand percussion ex-slaves most often mention with fiddles are tambourines but even more so the bones, usually a pair of beef or pork short ribs, balanced between the fingers and rattled, producing timbres and textures very similar to gourd rattles. "Had a fiddle, had banjos, too, but de best was knockin' two bones behind de fiddle, like dis . . . I *show* hankered ter hurry up an' git big enough ter knock bones!" (Ned Chaney, b. ca. 1857, MS, 374, orig. ellipsis and emphasis). "Lady you ought to hear me rattle bones, when I was young. I caint do it much now for my wrists are too stiff. When they [fiddlers] played Turkey in the Straw how we all used to dance and cut up. We'ed cut the pigeon wing, and buck the wind [buck and wing], and all" (George Morrison, b. ca. 1860, KY, 146A). Slaves are in fact often described or depicted playing bones in both hands, greatly expanding the sonic and rhythmic possibilities. "Dey had an ole fiddle and some of 'em would take two bones in each hand and rattle 'em. Dey sang songs like 'Diana had a Wooden Leg' and 'A Hand Full of Sugar,' and 'Cotton-eyed Joe.' I dis'member how dey went" (William M. Adams, b. ca. 1846, TX, 10).[56] Wooden clackers were also used. "Everything lively at Christmas time, dances wid fiddles, pattin' and stick rattlin', but when I jined de church, I quit dancin'" (Adeline Jackson, b. ca. 1849, SC, 3).

The bones were obviously a favored accompaniment for African American fiddles, possibly a direct substitute for African gourd rattles. Moreover, bone or wooden clackers of this sort are common in Africa (and among other New World Blacks), suggesting fairly direct lines of descent.[57] Somewhat clouding the issue, they were also known in Britain from Elizabethan times (Shakespeare mentions them).[58] In the mid-1840s clacking bones also became part of the basic blackface minstrel ensemble: fiddle, banjo, bones, tambourine, sometimes winds.[59] However, by then bones were well documented among African Americans, as was the fiddle-banjo-bones-tambourine lineup.[60] This is one instance where minstrels apparently did imitate Black folk tradition, even if thereafter some African American bone players took their cues from the blackface stage.[61]

By the turn of the twentieth century, however, bones were most common in white stringbands. In 1909 Louise Bascom described amateur North Carolina groups featuring fiddle, banjo, and harmonica. "Mention must also be made of 'the fellers that han'l the bones.' These instruments are long, slightly curved sticks of locust-wood, and they excel any castanets which can be bought."[62] Whites probably adopted the bones both from Blacks and minstrel shows, but British or Irish precedents are at least a possibility. Allowing all of these alternatives, Africa still seems the likely source of the North American Black tradition, at least in the main.

Originating in North Africa, the tambourine was widely adopted throughout Europe and Sub-Saharan Africa. In twentieth-century North Amer-

ica, it became closely associated with Black religious music. Slaves accompanied sacred singing with hand clapping, foot stamping, or other body percussion but seldom with tambourines. Instead, tambourines accompanied social dancing, whether played solo, with patting or other percussion, or with melody instruments, especially fiddles. "Some time there wus a tamborine beater, some time dey use' ole wash tubs an' beat it [with] wood sticks, an' some time dey jus' clap their han's" (Thomas Goodwater, b. 1855, SC, 169). In 1841 Charles Dickens (1812–1870) witnessed the fiddle-tambo combo at "'a regular break-down'" in a New York dance house, where "the corpulent black fiddler, and his friend who plays the tambourine, stamp upon the boarding of the small raised orchestra."[63]

This is precisely the role recalled by ex-slaves. "We had big dances and dinners. We celebrated at different houses and places. We danced to fiddle and tambourine music. My uncle was an A. number one fiddler and good dancer" (George Jackson Simpson, b. 1854, MO, 222). "Somebody ud play de fiddle and de tamberine" (Martin Graham, b. 1851, SC, 170). "Dey didn't 'low me to 'tend de nigger parties, but I 'member 'bout de fiddles an' de tamborenes dey had an' played. Dey sho' made fine music" (Sarah Wilson, b. ca. 1850, LA, TX, 4216). "At night there was a big dance. The fiddlers and the tambourine and bone beaters, was the finest to be got out of Kentucky" (Mark Oliver, b. 1856, MS, 1665). Nancy Williams remembered "two fiddles, two tambourines, two bango, an' two sets o' bones" (Nancy Williams, b. 1847, NC, 316).

Most slave tambourines would have been homemade, typically from cheese boxes (the wooden packing for cheese wheels), bushel hoops, or other castoffs, being much larger (and thus lower in range) than modern tambourines. "Stretch cowhides over cheeseboxes and you had tambourines" (John Cole, b. ca. 1850, GA, 227). Ex-slaves also recalled tin pans as makeshift tambourines, with or without fiddles. "De young folks went out Sadday nights and danced to de music what dey made beatin' on tin pans" (Charlie Hudson, b. 1858, GA, 227). "Sometimes us didn't have no music 'cept jus' beatin' time on tin pans and buckets

Fig. 4.3. Soldiers of the 79th New York at Camp. 1861–1865. Gladstone Collection of African American Photographs, Library of Congress, Prints and Photographs Division. A Black fiddle-tambourine combo entertaining officers in a Federal camp. Their dress indicates they were cooks or other service workers. The tambourine's size suggests it was homemade from a cheese box or similar cast-off. To the far right a Black enlisted man in uniform stands sentry with shouldered rifle.

but most times old Elice Hudson played his fiddle for us" (Neal Upson, b. 1857, GA, 64). "Dem niggers wud eat en frolic fer de longes', makin music wid er hand saw er tin pan, en er dancin', en laffin', en cuttin' up" (Henry Green, b. 1848, AL, 97). A memoir of early 1800s Virginia describes slaves "playing on their rude fiddles, thrumming banjos, and rattling on tin pans and calabashes, to the tunes then in vogue."[64]

Like the bones, the tambourine was adopted by early blackface ensembles, where the endmen (the comedians flanking the fiddle and banjo players) were actually known as *Tambo* and *Bones* after their instruments. Subsequently, these minstrel strains do seem to have influenced the African American tradition, but the extent is again uncertain. Fil Hancock (b. 1851), who had followed postwar Black minstrel troupes like the Georgia Minstrels, was one of a handful of ex-slaves still performing publicly in the 1930s. His interviewer, Mabel E. Mueller, noted that "'Uncle' Fil, as he was familiarly known in Rolla, played for the Folk Festival in Rolla and received so much applause,

he had to be forced off the stage. He is exceedingly active. He plays the old tambourine (he owned so many years) under and over his legs, behind his head, bouncing it and catching it, never losing the rhythm an instant" (Filmore Taylor Hancock, b. 1851, MO, 187, orig. parentheses). Hancock was barbering for a living at the time. It is unclear whether he himself had ever been a professional minstrel.

Numerous narrators also described fiddles accompanied by drums. "The music we had were fiddles and drums and sometimes just singing and calling figgers" (Mary Jane Jones, b. ca. 1849, MS, 1245). "After eating they would sometimes gather in front of a cabin and dance to the tunes played on the fiddle and the drum" (Mack Mullen, b. 1857, GA, 236). "They had big dances at night, sometimes. Somebody would play the fiddles and some the banjo and sometimes had a drum. We did the 'buck dance.' A boy and girl would hold hands and jump up and down and swing around keeping time with the music" (Baily Cunningham, b. ca. 1838, VA, 82).[65] Generally these drums were also homemade, but there are occasional references to store-bought varieties. A couple of narrators may actually have been referring to tambourines (hand drums), but most definitely described full-size cylinder drums. "You takes a coon skin an' make a drum out of hit, stretch hit over a keg—a sawed-off one—dat make a fine drum. An' banjos an' fiddlers! Didn' have no mandolines an' *guitars* then" (Charlie Bell, b. 1856, MS, 124, orig. emphasis). "My mama done told me 'bout de dances dey have in de quarters. Dey take a big sugar hogshead and stretch rawhide over de top. Den de man straddle de barrel and beat on de top for de drum. Dat de onlies' music dey have" (A. C. Pruitt, b. ca. 1861, LA, 219). "We use tuh alluz dance tuh duh drums. We dance roun in a succle an we hab goad rattle an we beat tin pan tuhgedder. Some time dey hab sto-bought drum."[66]

Back in slavery time, old marster uster 'low us to hold dances. Yessir, he say, "'Muse yourself wid de neighbors." Dey 'low niggers from de nearby plantations to come an' us have a big time an' lots of fun an' 'joy ourselves. De way dey do to have music dey take a barrel kivered wid a piece of hide. Dey beat on dat an' dance to it. Dey jes' dance an' dance an' turn 'round and kick up. Dey never had nobody to call de dance number. Dey jes' 'joyed it in dey own way. Us sho' had a good time at dem dance. (Joseph James, b. 1845, LA, 1931)

Slaves also used buckets and other receptacles as drum substitutes. "The musical instruments consisted of fiddles; buckets, which were beaten with the hands; and reeds, called 'blowing quills,' which were used in the manner of a flute" (Robert Henry, b. 1855, GA, 197). "At Christmas time, us allus had a BIG frolic wid music an' dancin'. Us danced de cotillion an' beat on buckets and gourds for music" (Robert Heard, b. ca. 1841, GA, 171).[67]

The jew's harp is another instrument frequently mentioned with the fiddle. Introduced into West Africa by eighteenth-century European traders, jew's harps were shortly being manufactured by African blacksmiths, favored for a percussive, buzzing timbre resembling the African musical bow.[68] In 1800s America they were ubiquitous as novelties or children's toys.[69] "As I done tole you, I was Mars Allens' pet nigger boy. . . . I carried water to Mars Bob's store close by and he would allus give me candy by de double handsfull, and as many juice harps as I wanted" (Jim Allen, b. ca. 1850, AL, 55). "Lawd no, I never earned no money for myself, what I earned belonged to old Marster, but he give me a little money sometimes and I'd buy candy and jews harps" (Lewis Williams, b. 1851, TX, 4093). "All de use we had fer money was to buy fish hooks, barlows [case knives], juice harps and marbles. Boys did not use 'bacca den until dey got twenty-one or over" (Richard Jones, b. 1812, SC, 66). More often, however, ex-slaves recalled jew's harps with fiddles at adult dances. "Dey wuz er church on de plantation fer de slaves, en er dance hall where dey had dances. De music wuz de fiddle, banjo, en Jewsharp; but mos'ly dey played de fiddle" (Henry Bedford, b. ca. 1858, TN, 282). "The singing was usually to the accompaniment of a Jew's harp and fiddle, or banjo" (Dennis Simms, b. 1841, MD, 61–62). "Dey sing, as dey promenade an'

dance to de music of de jew's harp" (Alice Wilkins, b. 1855, TX, 4050).

However, the instrument most often associated with the fiddle was the banjo. Based on what we know about nineteenth-century banjo styles, it would not be amiss to characterize the banjo as the *percussion* instrument most often associated with the fiddle.

Appendix: Musical Instruments in the Ex-Slave Narratives

Below are the musical instruments (excepting signal horns) named by ex-slaves, individually or in combination, though the criteria for that division require some qualification. In many cases, that is, ex-slaves unambiguously described instrumental combos. "Sam an' Rufus was fiddle an' banjo playahs. Lots an' lots ob nights, weuns sing an' play de music" (James West, b. 1854, MS, 4018). "I play d 'corjan (accordion) fo' dances sometime'. . . . Dey was a feller right behin' me w'at was alays playin' d' bass fiddle" (Leo Mouton, b. ca. 1860, LA, 2812, orig. parentheses). At other times, though, narrators merely listed different instruments, or named them in proximity without actually stating that they were played together. "The grown folks didn't have much amusement in slavery times. They had banjo, fiddle, melodian [accordion], things like that" (Lewis Brown, b. 1855, MS, 295). Simply for convenience and manageability, I have also treated these cases as ensembles, which informants may or may not have intended. (My parenthetical glosses for these combos should be self-explanatory.) By the same token, ex-slaves sometimes stated unequivocally that instruments were played solo. "We had lots of dances dem days and with jus' one fiddle" (Willie Blackwell, b. 1834, NC, 304). "The only musical instrument we had was the banjo" (Betty Curlett, b. 1872, child of ex-slaves, MS, 76, 81). Then again, many ex-slaves naming instruments individually did not rule out other accompaniments and may have taken as much for granted. "Lawdy! Lawd! Dat fiddlin' went on all night, and we dance awhile den lay down and sleeps, den gits up and dances some mo'e" (Jack Bess, b. 1854, TX, 73). "Chrissmushtime 'n' Fo'th 'r' July dey had a dance. . . . Some 'r' 'em was banjer (banjo) pickers. My father was a banjer picker" (Horace Overstreet, b. 1856, TX, 2998, orig. parentheses). These cases, whether clearcut or ambiguous, are all listed together as well. Finally, on a more practical note, this classification entails some unavoidable redundancy, since a fiddle-banjo-accordion combo is cited under all three categories (FIDDLE, BANJO, ACCORDION) and so forth. As all of this suggests, certain other nuances and complexities in ex-slave descriptions do not easily submit to this sort of categorization, but these are discussed in detail in the foregoing and other chapters, and, with those caveats, the following table can serve as a general guide to instrumental music in the ex-slave narratives.

FIDDLES, FIDDLING, FIDDLERS Victoria Adams; Charles H. Anderson; Mary Anngady; Katie Arbery; George W. Armstrong; Mary Armstrong; Sally Ashton; Celestia Avery; Charley Barber; Robert Barr; Frank Bell (VA); Cyrus Bellus; James Bertrand; Jack Bess; Ellen Betts; Arrie Binns; Willie Blackwell; Jerry Boykins; Gus Bradshaw; Andy Brice; Henry Broaddus; Fannie Brown; Rina Brown; John Cameron; Simp Campbell; Richard Carruthers; Cato Carter; Aunt Cicely Cawthon; Abraham Chambers; Robert J. Cheatham; Mary Childs; Jeptha (Doc) Choice; Ellen Claibourn; Amos Clark; Anna Clark; Henry Clay; Aunt Clussey; Anna Maria Coffee; Mom Louisa Collier; Valmar Cormier; John Crawford; Bill Crump; Henry Dant; Katie Darling; D. Davis; Louisa Davis; Tob Davis; Jake Dawkins; James V. Deane; Hammett Dell; Alice Dixon; Sally Dixon; Douglas Dorsey; Mary Edwards; Louis Evans; Millie Evans; Lorenza Ezell; Louis Fowler; Robert Franklin; Aunt Mittie Freeman; Fannie Fulcher; William Gant; Laurence Gary; Henry Gibbs; Jennie Wormly Gibson; Jim Gillard; Brawley Gilmore; Hector Godbold; Andrew Goodman; Austin Grant; Callie Gray; Wheeler Gresham; Abner Griffin; Peggy Grigsby; Orris Harris; William H.

Harrison; Charles Hayes; Robert Heard; Jim Henry; Nettie Henry; Will Hicks; Fannie Smith Hodges; H. B. Holloway; Larnce Holt; Molly Horn; Aunt Carolina Houston; Easter Huff; Lizzie Hughes; Margaret Hughes; Squire Irvin; James Jackson; Hattie Jefferson; Henry D. Jenkins; Mahala Jewel; Allen Johnson; Harry Johnson; Prince Johnson; Sallie Johnson; Steve Johnson; Charity Jones; Edward Jones; Wesley Jones; Bell Kelley; Richard Kimmons; Henry Gray Klugh; Robert Laird; Ephraim (Mike) Lawrence; Lu Lee; Cinto Lewis; Frances Lewis; George Lewis; Lucy Lewis; Abbie Lindsay; William Little; James Lucas; Chaney Mack; Richard Mack; Richard Macks; Mary (Old Mary); George McAlilley; Henry Lewis McGaffey; Matilda McKinney; Chaney McNair; Harriet Miller (GA, SC); Jim Martin; John Matthews; George Washington Miller; Tom Morris; Hannah Murphy; Lizzie Norfleet; Glascow Norwood; Isaiah Norwood; Eliza Overton; Aaron Pinnacle; Alec Pope; Betty Powers; George Washington Ramsay; Elsie Reece; George Washington Rice; Shade Richards; Ida Rigley; Harriett Robinson; Mariah Robinson; Melinda Ann "Roty" Ruffin; George Rullerford; Susan Dale Sanders; Nancy Settles; George Simmons; Adam Singleton; James Singleton; Berry Smith; Henry Smith; Gus Smith; William Smith; Leithean Spinks; Wright Stapleton; Isaac Stier; James Henry Stith; Yach Stringfellow; Bert Strong; Emma Taylor; Tishey Taylor; Acie Thomas; Bill Thomas; George Thomas; Ike Thomas; William M. Thomas; Ellen Briggs Thompson; John Thompson; Johnson Thompson; Laura Thornton; Richard Toler; Addie Vinson; Adeline Waldon; Harriet Walker; James W. Washington; Jordan Waters; John Watts; Eliza White; Mingo White; Dock Wilborn; Alice Wilkins; Columbus Williams; John Thomas Williams; Mollie Williams; Steve Williams; Charles Willis; Sampson Willis; Jake Wilson; Willis Winn; Anda Woods; Susannah Wyman; Robert Young; Frank Ziegler

FIDDLES WITH OTHER INSTRUMENTS William M. Adams (bones); Sam Anderson (banjo); Agatha Babino (banjo); Henry Bedford (banjo, jew's harp); Charlie Bell (banjo, drum); Aunt Kate Betters (piano); Henry Bland (banjo, hand clapping); Manda Boggan (guitar); Betty Bormer (banjo, piano); Sam Broach (banjo, patting); James Brown (banjo); Lewis Brown (banjo, melodian); Zek Brown (banjo); C. B. Burton (quills); Marshal Butler (tin can, beating straws); Louis Cain (banjo); Lizzie Chandler (accordion); Ned Chaney (banjo, bones); Harriet Chelsey (guitar); Berry Clay (banjo); John Cole (beating straws, tambourines, bones); Pierce Cody (banjo); Josephine Tippit Compton (fiddle and skillet lids; fiddle and banjo); Baily Cunningham (banjo, drum); Campbell Davis (banjo); Nelson Taylor Denson (drum, banjo); Simon Durr (guitar); George Fleming (quills); Sylvia Floyd (accordions, banjos, patting); Sam Forge (guitar, stamping, beating straws); Rachel Gaines (string band); Martin Graham (tambourine); Isaiah Green (banjo); Squire Harris (banjo); Virginia Harris (banjo, bones); Wash Hayes (accordion); Robert Henry (buckets with hands, quills); Albert Hill (banjo); Bill Homer (quill flute); Ben Horry (fife, drum); Alice Hutcheson (banjo); Adeline Jackson (patting, percussion sticks); Mary Johnson (accordion); Harriet Jones (banjo, guitar); Lewis Jones (banjo); Mandy Jones (banjo); Mary Jane Jones (drums); Ellen King (two small fiddles, big fiddle); Walter Leggett (guitar, banjo); Will Long (clevis-and-pin, jew's harp, hoe-and-case-knife); Ed McCree (banjo); Perry Madden (military fife & drum); Jack Maddox (fiddle band); Primous Magee (guitar); Rosa Mangum (guitar); Louise Mathews (banjoes); Liza Mention (trumpet, banjo); Ann Mickey (banjo); Laura Moore (guitar); Richard C. Moring (banjo); George Morrison (banjo, guitar, bones); Claiborne Moss (banjo, quills); Mack Mullen (drum); Louis Napoleon (fife, banjo); Julius Nelson (banjo); Virginia Newman (accordion); Joe Oliver (jew's harp, hoe-and-case-knife); Mark Oliver (tambourines, bones); Elsie Payne (banjo); Matilda Henrietta Perry (banjo, guitar, harmonica); Elsie Posey (military flute, drum); Isaac Potter (guitar); Salem Powell (guitar); Elsie Pryor (horse ribs on chairback, banjo, patting, whistling); Fanny Randolph (banjo, beating straws, bones); James Reeves (banjo); Mary Reynolds (guitar, clapping, stomping); Manus Robinson (guitar); Henry Rogers (banjo); Joe Rollins (banjo); William Rose (banjo); Violet Shaw (banjo); George Jackson Simpson (tambourine); Dennis Simms (banjo, jew's harp); Melvin Smith (banjo); John Sneed (accordion); Elmo Steele (mandolin); Guy Stewart (banjo); Neal Upson (tin pans, buckets); Lucinda Vann (bones, bugle); Dave Walker (guitar, handclapping, foot patting); Allen Ward (guitar); George Weathersby (guitar); Robert Weathersby (guitar); James West (banjo); Adeline White (accordion); Green Willbanks (banjo); Nancy Williams (banjos, tambourines, bones); Isaac Wilson (guitar); Sarah Wilson (tambourines); Teshan Young (banjos)

HOMEMADE FIDDLES Simp Campbell (homemade fiddle, homemade banjo, guitar); James V. Deane (homemade fiddles); Anderson Edwards (gourd fiddles, quill flutes); Aunt Rhody Holsell (gourd); Ruben Laird (one-string bow fiddle); Solomon Lambert (homemade fiddle, homemade banjo, juice harp); Chaney Mack (pine bark fiddle); Jack Maddox (three-string fiddle); Harre Quarls (gourd fiddle); Charley Williams (gourd fiddles, bones); Henry Wright (gourd fiddle, homemade banjo, store-bought fiddle); Litt Young (gourd fiddles, homemade banjos, bones)

HAND SAW FIDDLE (MUSICAL SAW) Henry Green; Easter Jackson (quills, harmonicas); George Strickland; Rhodus Walton (banjo)

SONGS FEATURING THE FIDDLE Annie Bridges, "Jack of Diamonds"; Ann Drake, "Jaybird died with the whooping cough"; Sam Forge, "Cotton-Eyed Joe"; Charley Johnson, "Froggie Went A-Courting"; Lavinia Lewis, "Uncle Ned"

FOLKTALES FEATURING THE FIDDLE Easter Sudie Campbell, "Fiddler Fends Off Wolves." Lucy Donald, Motif G303.6.2.1. *Devil appears at dance.* Jake Green, "Fooled My Master Seven Years (A Conju' What Didn' Wuk)." Josh Hadnot, "Bre'r Rabbit Fiddles for Bre'r Fox." Julius Jones, Motif

*E337.1.3(b). *Sounds of dance in haunted house.* Roy Redfield, "Fooled My Master Seven Years." Nancy Settles, Motif E402.1.3(a). *Ghost plays violin.* Adeline Waldon, "Turned to Possum in the Pot." Sol Walton, Motif *E337.1.3(b). *Sounds of dance in haunted house.* (Wherever appropriate throughout this study I have employed the standard folktale classifications of Antti Aarne, Stith Thompson, and Ernest W. Baughman, and the folksong classifications of Francis James Child, G. Malcolm Laws, and Steve Roud.)

OTHER FIDDLE REFERENCES *The American Slave* also features a handful of fiddle references from secondary sources. Most interesting is the narrative of W. S. Needham Jr. (b. 1854), a white informant interviewed for the Texas project, who described learning to fiddle from one of his father's slaves on a Mississippi plantation ca. 1860 (SS2 10 *TX* 9: 4359–70). The Kentucky volumes include a "very old Negro sermon . . . found in an old scrap book dated 1839" that condemns "fiddlin an dancin . . . loafin, pitchin cents, an dancin Juba!" (S2 16 *KY*: 37–38). The Oregon narratives include an excerpt from *Heroes and Heroic Deeds of the Pacific Northwest*, vol. 1 (1929), concerning slave fiddler Lou Southworth (KY, MO, OR). (SS1 2 *OR*: 273–75)

BANJOS, BANJO PLAYING, BANJO PLAYERS Berle Barnes; Alice Battle; Alice Baugh; Fannie Berry; Susan Bledsoe; Dan Bogie; Thomas Brown; Susan Castle; Walter Chapman; Fleming Clark; Hattie Clayton; Eli Coleman; Jane Cotton; Betty Curlett; James (Jim) Davis; Louis Davis; Hammett Dell; George Dillard; Lorenzo Ezell; Molly Finley; Abner Griffin; Simon Hare; Mollie Hatfield; Tom Hawkins; Emmaline Heard; Charles (Charlie) Hinton; Marriah Hines; Carrie Hudson; Cordelia Anderson Jackson; George Jackson; Ellis Jefson; Estella Jones; Aunt Hannah Jones; Caroline Malloy; Carrie Mason; Horace Overstreet; Wade Owens; Rosa L. Pollard; Edd Shirley; Martha Showvely; Smith Simmons; Marinda Jane Singleton; Tanner Spikes; Amanda Styles; William Sykes; Phil Towns; Emma Weeks; Robert Williams; Mary Wright

BANJOS WITH OTHER INSTRUMENTS Sam Anderson (fiddle); Lizzie Atkins (tin pan); Katie Arbery (quills); Agatha Babino (fiddle); Harriett Barrett (tin pan); Henry Bedford (fiddle, jew's harp); Bettie Massingale Bell (guitar); Charlie Bell (fiddle, drum); Henry Bland (fiddle, hand clapping); Betty Bormer (fiddle, piano); Isabella Boyd (bones); Sam Broach (fiddle, patting); Fred Brown (accordion, jew's harp, beaten piece of steel); James Brown (fiddle); Lewis Brown (fiddle, melodian); Zek Brown (fiddle); David L. Byrd (tin pan); Sarah Byrd (quills, bones); Louis Cain (fiddle, tin pan); George Caulton (guitar); Ned Chaney (fiddle, bones); Berry Clay (fiddle); Pierce Cody (fiddle); Alice Cole (tin pan); Josephine Tippit Compton (fiddle); Charlie Cooper (tin pan); Baily Cunningham (fiddle, drum); Campbell Davis (fiddle); Elige Davison (tin pan); Nelson Taylor Denson (fiddle, drum); Sylvia Floyd (fiddles, accordions, patting); Tinie Force and Elvira Lewis (guitar); Mary Gaffney (tin pan); Elisha Doc Garey (quills); Isaiah Green (fiddle); Shang Harris (tin pans); Squire Harris (fiddle); Virginia Harris (fiddle, bones); Jack Harrison (tin pan); Albert Hill (fiddle); Tom Holland (tin pan); Easter Huff (tin pans); Alice Hutcheson (fiddle); Harriet Jones (fiddle, guitar); Mandy Jones (fiddle); Toby Jones (tin pan); Lucindy Lawrence Jurdon (quills, clapping, pans); Anna Lee (tin pan); Walter Leggett (fiddle, guitar); Lewis Jones (fiddle); Andy McAdams (tin pan); Ed McCree (fiddle); Rosie McGillery (tin pan); Louise Mathews (fiddles); Liza Mention (fiddle, trumpet); Ann Mickey (fiddle); Malinda Mitchell (quills); Richard C. Moring (fiddle); George Morrison (fiddle, guitar, bones); John Mosley (tin pan); Claiborne Moss (fiddle, quills); Louis Napoleon (fife, fiddle); Julius Nelson (fiddle); Austin Pen Parnell (guitar); Elsie Payne (fiddle); Matilda Henrietta Perry (fiddle, guitar, harmonica); Elsie Pryor (fiddle, horse ribs on chairback, patting, whistling); Fanny Randolph (fiddle, beating straws, bones); James Reeves (fiddle); Henry Rogers (fiddle); Joe Rollins (fiddle); William Rose (fiddle); Charlie Sandles (tin pan);

Violet Shaw (fiddle); Polly Shine (tin pan); Dennis Simms (fiddle, jew's harp); Emma Simpson (tin pan); Charlie Tye Smith (quills); Melvin Smith (fiddle); Guy Stewart (fiddle); Rebecca Thomas (accordion); Jack Terriell (tin pan); Tim Thornton (guitar); Lucinda Vann (fiddle); Rhodus Walton (handsaw fiddle); Callie Washington (guitar); James West (fiddle); Green Willbanks (fiddle); Nancy Williams (fiddles, tambourines, bones); Soul Williams (tin pan, harmonica); Wash Wilson (bones, skillet lids); Teshan Young (fiddles)

HOMEMADE BANJOS Simp Campbell (homemade banjo, homemade fiddle, guitar); Lula Coleman (homemade banjos, quills, clapping); Betty Curlett (tin-pan banjo); Molly Finley (gourd banjos); Solomon Lambert (homemade banjo, homemade fiddle, juice harp); Henry Wright (homemade banjo, gourd fiddle, store-bought fiddle); Litt Young (homemade banjos, gourd fiddles, bones)

SONGS FEATURING THE BANJO Louis Davis, "Mean Old Banjo Thomas"; Lorenza Ezell, "Early in de mawnin'"; Henry Freeman, "Oh Susannah"; R. C. Smith, "Old man, old man, / Your hair is getting gray, / I'd follow you ten thousand miles / To hear your banjo play"

FOLKTALES FEATURING THE BANJO Harriett Robinson, "I fooled Ole Mastah 7 years" (song only). Amanda Styles, Motifs D1786. *Magic power at crossroads*; M211.10*(ca.a*). *Person sells soul for skill on banjo.*

QUILLS Georgia Baker; George Washington Browning; Sister Harrison; Annie Huff; Ellis Jefson; Susan McIntosh; Frank Menefee; Dora Roberts; Phil Towns

QUILLS WITH OTHER INSTRUMENTS Katie Arbery (banjo); James Bolton (buckets, tin pans); C. B. Burton (fiddle); Sarah Byrd (banjo, bones); Lula Coleman (homemade banjos, clapping); Hammett Dell (jew's harps); Anderson Edwards (quill flutes, gourd fiddles); George Fleming (fiddle); Elisha Doc Garey (banjo); Robert Henry (buckets with hands, fiddles); Easter Jackson (harmonicas, saws); Lucindy Lawrence Jurdon (banjo, clapping,

pans); Malinda Mitchell (banjo); Claiborne Moss (fiddle, banjo); Lizzie Norfleet (tin pan); Sallie Paul (bones); Ophelia Porter (tin-cup blow harps); Charlie Tye Smith (banjo)

CANES OR REEDS (possibly quills, fifes, or flutes) Sylvia Cannon (blow cane, beat sticks); Charlie Grant (blowing cane); Jake McLeod (canes, tin pans, buckets); Rebecca Thomas (reed)

FIFES AND FLUTES Julia Bunch (military fife and drum); Polly Turner Cancer (military fife); Jeff Davis (homemade fife and two kinds of drums, different brass horns); Ann J. Edwards (military fife and drum); Mary Ann Gibson (toy fifes and drums); Sarah Gudger (military fife and drum); Lee Hobby (sapling flute, jew's harp); Bill Homer (quill flute, fiddle); Ben Horry (fife, fiddle, drum); Charley Hurt (military fife); Mandy Lee (military fifes and drums, bugles); Perry Madden (military fife and drum, fiddle); Bob Maynard (cane flute, jug or big bottle, skillet lid, frying pan hit with stick, bone); Aunt Jane Morgan (military fife); Louis Napoleon (fife, banjo, fiddle); Hattie Anne Nettles (military fife and drum); Elsie Posey (military flute, fiddle, drum); Jack Rabb (military fife and drum); Easter Reed (military fife and drum); Dave White (military fife and drum).

SONGS FEATURING THE FIFE AND DRUM Annie Bridges, "Pretty Little Pink"; Lafayette Price, "The Battle of Shiloh Hill" (Laws A 11)

WHISTLES Anderson Bates (cane whistles); Vinnie Brunson (whistle); Josephine Tippit Compton (whistle, jew's harp); Mandy Hadnot (toy whistle); John Rudd (hand-whittled whistles)

GUITAR Mary Anngady; Elijah Cox; Wade Glenn; Aunt Katherin; Liza Mention; Jane Thompson; Harriet Walker; Foster Weathersby

GUITAR WITH OTHER INSTRUMENTS Manda Boggan (fiddle); Bettie Massingale Bell (banjo); Charlie Bell (mandolin); Simp Campbell (homemade fiddle, homemade banjo); George Caulton (banjo); Harriet Chelsey (fiddle); Simon Durr (fiddle); Tinie Force and Elvira Lewis (banjo); Elizabeth Ross Hite (homemade drum, pots and pans with sticks); Harriet Jones (fiddle, banjo); Walter Leggett (fiddle, banjo); Primous Magee (fiddle); Rosa Mangum (fiddle); Laura Moore (fiddle); George Morrison (fiddle, banjo, bones); Austin Pen Parnell (banjo); Matilda Henrietta Perry (fiddle, banjo, harmonica); Isaac Potter (fiddle); Salem Powell (fiddle); Mary Reynolds (fiddle, clapping, stomping); Manus Robinson (fiddle); Tim Thornton (banjo); Isaac Wilson (fiddle); Dave Walker (fiddle, handclapping, foot patting); Allen Ward (fiddle); Callie Washington (banjo); George Weathersby (fiddle); Robert Weathersby (fiddle)

JEW'S HARP (JAW HARP, JEWS HARP, JUICE HARP) Jim Allen; Henry Bedford (fiddle, banjo); Fred Brown (accordion, banjo, beaten piece of steel); Josephine Tippit Compton; Hammett Dell (quills); Laurence Gary; Lee Hobby (homemade flute); Bud Jones; Richard Jones; Solomon Lambert (homemade fiddle, homemade banjo); Will Long (fiddle, clevis-and-pin, hoe-and-case-knife); Joe Oliver (fiddle, hoe-and-case-knife); Dennis Simms (fiddle, banjo); Alice Wilkins; Lewis Williams

FOLKTALES FEATURING THE JEW'S HARP Toby Jones, Motif E402.1.3. *Invisible ghost plays musical instrument.* Motif E451.8. *Ghost laid when house it haunts is destroyed or changed.*

MOUTH BOW Hammett Dell

JUG Silas Knox (harmonica, jugs, combs); Bob Maynard (jug or big bottle, skillet lid, frying pan hit with stick, bone, cane flute)

COMB Silas Knox (harmonica, jugs)

HARMONICA (HARP, FRENCH HARP, MOUTH HARP, MOUTH ORGAN) C. B. Burton; Hammett Dell; Easter Jackson (quills, saws); Bud Jones; Silas Knox (jugs, combs); Matilda Henrietta Perry (fiddle, banjo, guitar); Hector Smith; Phil Towns; Soul Williams (banjo, tin pan)

ACCORDION William Banjo; Fred Brown (banjo, jew's harp, beaten piece of steel); Lewis Brown (melodian, fiddle, banjo); Lizzie Chandler (fiddle); Hammett Dell; Wash Hayes (fiddle); Sylvia Floyd (fiddles, banjos, patting); Abner Griffin; Jimmie Johnson (melodian); Mary Johnson (fiddle); Ann Mickey; Leo Mouton (bass fiddle); Virginia Newman (fiddle); Felix Grundy Sadler; John Sneed (fiddle); Rebecca Thomas (banjo); Adeline White (fiddle); Mollie Williams

PIANO Mary Anngady; Henry Bedford; Hattie Douglas; Aunt Kate Betters (fiddle); Betty Bormer (banjo, fiddle); John Cameron; Ned Chaney; Ellen Claibourn; Harriet Chelsey; John Crawford; Tempie Herndon Durham; Lula Flannigan; Laurence Gary; Mandy Hadnot; Orris Harris; Adeline Jackson; Cordelia Anderson Jackson; Ella Johnson (SC); Jimmie Johnson; Hagar Lewis; Jim Martin; George McAlilley; Laura Montgomery; Claiborne Moss; Jeff Stanfield; Isom Starnes; Bill and Ellen Thomas; Kate Thomas; James W. Washington; Mollie Watson; Eugenia Weatherall; Sampson Willis; Mollie Williams

FOLKTALES FEATURING THE PIANO Eliza Bell, Motif E402.1.3(ba). *Ghost plays piano*; N. H. Hobley, Motif E402.1.3(ba). *Ghost (Devil) plays piano*; Susan Jones, Motif E402.1.3(ba). *Ghost plays piano.*

OTHER PIANO REFERENCES The Georgia narratives include a profile of slave piano prodigy Blind Tom Bethune (1849–1909), based on interviews with white acquaintances. Thomas Green Bethune (Blind Tom), (b. May 25, 1849, GA) (SS1 3 *GA* 1: 53–61)

ORGAN Bettie Massingale Bell; Queen Elizabeth Bunts; Ned Chaney; John Crawford; Hattie Douglas; Rebecca Fletcher; Rebecca Jane Grant; Abner Griffin; Jimmie Johnson; Ellis Ken Kannon; George McAlilley; Anna Parkes; Aaron Pinnacle; Gertie Ross

CALLIOPE George Taylor Burns (riverboat); Nelson Cameron (circus); Angie Garrett (riverboat); Alfred Jones (riverboat); Al Rosboro (circus)

MANDOLIN Hammett Dell; Elmo Steele (fiddle)

STRING HARP Amanda Eilers Brice

SONGS FEATURING THE STRING HARP Alice Baugh, "Play on yo' Harp Little David"; Maria Bracey, "David got a harp wid a t'ousand string"; Hannah Davidson, "I Want to Be an Angel"; Rebecca Jane Grant, "I Want to Be an Angel";

Emma Grisham, "Harp fum de Tomb dis Mournful Sound"; Red Richardson, "Harp From the Tune the Doleful Sound"; Gussie Shelby, "And they played on the Harp of a Thousand Strings"; Robert Shepherd, "Harps From De Tomb"; Nancy Smith, "Harps From De Tomb"; Georgia Telfair, "I Want to Be an Angel"

BRASS Nancy Anderson (military bugle); Ed Barber (brass band, horns, drums); Alice Battle (military band); Adeline Blakely (military bugle); George Taylor Burns (showboat band); Maria Sutton Clemments (military bugles); Hannah Crasson (military band); Jeff Davis (different brass horns, homemade fife and two kinds of drums); Sally Dixon (showboat band); Francis Doby (military bugle); William L. Dunwoody (military band); Pick Gladdeny (brass band); Neely Gray (military bugle); Isaiah Green (military bugle); Harriett Gresham (military band); Emma Grisham (Army band); Burt Haygood (military bugle); Mack Henderson (military bugle); Mack Henry (military bugle); Rhody Holsell (military bugle); Patsy Hyde, (military band); Mary Jackson (military band); Pauline Johnson and Felice Boudreuax (military band); Mandy Jones (military band); Mandy Lee (military bugles, fifes and drums); Will Long (showboat band); Liza Mention (trumpet, fiddle, banjo); Joe Oliver (brass band); Louis Piernas (brass band); Aaron Pinnacle (cornet); Parker Pool (military band); William Rose (military band); Katie Rowe (military bugle); Warren Taylor (bands, orchestras); Lucinda Vann (bugle, fiddle, bones); Tena White (military band, drums); Catherine Williams (military band); Tom Windham (military band, bugle); Sophia Word (military band); Litt Young (military horn)

SONGS FEATURING THE TRUMPET James Calhart James, "Oh where shall we go when de great day comes"; Sarah Pittman, "Where shall I be when the first trumpet sounds?"; Ella Stinson, "Hand me down de silver trumpet, Gabriel"; Isaac White, "Blow, Gabr'el, Blow De Trumpet of De Lawd!"

DRUMS AND DRUM SUBSTITUTES Joseph Allen (military drum); Ed Barber (military drums, brass band, horns); Charlie Bell (homemade drum, banjo,

fiddle); James Bolton (buckets, tin pans, quills); Marie Brown (homemade drums, jawbone scrapers); Julia Bunch (military drum and fife); Harrison Camille (homemade drums); Baily Cunningham (drum, fiddle, banjo); Uncle D. Davis (drums, parades of Reconstruction-era Black clubs); Jeff Davis (two kinds of drums and homemade fife, different brass horns); Nelson Taylor Denson (drum, fiddle, banjo); Francis Doby (homemade drum, footwork); Martin Dragney (drums, tambourines, jawbone scrapers); Ann J. Edwards (military drum and fife); Martha Everette (military drums); Mary Ann Gibson (toy drums and fifes); Charlie Giles (military drum); Thomas Goodwater (wash tubs with sticks, tambourine, hand clapping); Sarah Gudger (military drum and fife); John Harrison (Native American cowhide drum, stomp dances, shell anklets); Robert Heard (buckets, gourds); Robert Henry (buckets with hands, fiddles, quills); Elizabeth Ross Hite (homemade drum, guitar, pots and pans with sticks); N. H. Hobley (homemade drum); Ben Horry (drum, fiddle, fife); Josephine Howard (pan with stick); Joseph James (homemade drum); Liza Jones (military drum); Mandy Jones (military drums); Mary Jane Jones (drums, fiddles); Frank Larkin (military drums, kettledrums); Mandy Lee (military drums and fifes, bugles); Perry Madden (military drum and fife, fiddle); Jake McLeod (buckets, tin pans, canes); Patsy Moses (drums); Mack Mullen (fiddle, drum); Hattie Anne Nettles (military drum and fife); Elsie Posey (military drum, flute, fiddle); A. C. Pruitt (homemade drum); Celia Robinson (military drum); Elizabeth Russell (military drums); Millie Simpkins (military drums); Emeline Stepney (buckets with sticks); Neal Upson (buckets, fiddle, tin pans); John White (military drummers); Tena White (military drums, band); Ruben Woods (military drum); John Young (military drums)

SONGS FEATURING THE DRUM Donaville Broussard, "La Boulangere."

FOLKTALES FEATURING THE DRUM Nancy Settles, Motif 402.1.3(c) *Ghost beats a drum.*

TAMBOURINE AND TAMBOURINE SUBSTI-TUTES Lizzie Atkins (tin pan, banjo); Harriett Barrett (tin pan, banjo); James Bolton (tin pans, quills, buckets); David L. Byrd (tin pan, banjo); Louis Cain (tin pan, banjo); Alice Cole (tin pan, banjo); John Cole (tambourines, fiddle, beating straws, bones); Charlie Cooper (tin pan, banjo); Elige Davison (tin pan, banjo); Martin Dragney (tambourines, drums, jawbone scrapers); Tinie Force and Elvira Lewis (tambourine, hand clapping); Mary Gaffney (tin pan, banjo); Martin Graham (tambourine, fiddle); Pick Gladdeny (tin pans, patting feet); Thomas Goodwater (tambourine, wash tubs with sticks, hand clapping); Fil Hancock (tambourine); Shang Harris (tin pans, banjo); Jack Harrison (tin pan, banjo); Tom Holland (tin pan, banjo); Charlie Hudson (tin pans); Easter Huff (tin pans, banjo); Toby Jones (tin pan, banjo); Lucindy Lawrence Jurdon (pans, quills, banjo, clapping); Anna Lee (tin pan, banjo); Andy McAdams (tin pan, banjo); Rosie McGillery (tin pan, banjo); Jake McLeod (tin pans, buckets, canes); John Mosley (tin pan, banjo); Lizzie Norfleet (tin pan, quills); Mark Oliver (tambourines, fiddles, bones); Charlie Sandles (tin pan, banjo); Polly Shine (tin pan, banjo); Emma Simpson (tin pan, banjo); George Jackson Simpson (tambourine, fiddle); Emma Stone (tin pan); Jack Terriell (tin pan, banjo); Neal Upson (tin pans, fiddle, buckets); Nancy Williams (tambourines, fiddles, banjo, bones); Soul Williams (tin pan, banjo, harmonica); Sarah Wilson (tambourines, fiddles)

DANCE PLATFORMS Tom Floyd; Wesley Jones; Chaney McNair; Liza Mention; Glascow Norwood (temporary planks); James W. Smith; Lucinda Vann; Dave Walker; Robert Weathersby (temporary planks); Nancy Williams

BONES William M. Adams (fiddle); Maggie Black; Isabella Boyd (banjo); Sarah Byrd (banjo, quills); Ned Chaney (fiddle, banjo); John Cole (fiddle, beating straws, tambourines); Virginia Harris (fiddle, banjo); Adeline Jackson (fiddle, patting); George Morrison (fiddle, banjo, guitar); Mark Oliver (fiddles, tambourines); Sallie Paul (quills); Fanny Randolph (fiddle, banjo, beating straws); James Southall (tin pans); Lucinda Vann (fiddle, bugle); Charley Williams (fiddle); Nancy Williams (fiddle, banjo, tambourines); Wash Wilson (banjo, skillet lids); Dicy Winfield (finger popping); Litt Young (fiddle, banjo)

SCRAPERS Marie Brown (jawbone scrapers, homemade drums); Martin Dragney (jawbone scrapers, drums, tambourines); Will Long (hoe-and-case-knife, fiddle, clevis-and-pin); Joe Oliver (hoe-and-case-knife, fiddle, jew's harp)

CYMBAL AND STRUCK BELL SUBSTITUTES Fred Brown (beaten piece of steel, accordion, banjo, jew's harp); Marshal Butler (tin can struck with hand, fiddle with beating straws); Josephine Tippit Compton (skillet lids hit together); Will Long (clevis-and-pin triangle, fiddle, hoe scraped with case knife); Bob Maynard (skillet lid or frying pan hit with stick or bone, jug or big bottle, cane flute); Wash Wilson (skillet lids, banjo, bones)

BANJOS AND GUITARS

Sunday. Capt Knox went to Bulo in Virginia to see his brother. Here is no church within 14 or 15 Miles of the place. Mr. Bayley and I went to see a Negro Ball, Sundays being the only days these poor Creatures have to themselves, they generally meet together and amuse themselves with Dancing to the Banjor. This Musical instrument (if it may be so called) is made of a Gourd something in immitation of a Guitar with only four strings and play'd with the fingers in the same manner. Some of them sing to it which is very droll musick indeed, In their songs they generally relate the usage they have received from their Masters and Mistresses, in a very Satirical stile and manner. . . .

At Anchor with a Contrary wind. About noon a Pilot Boat came along side to invite the Captn to A Barbicue. I went with him and have been highly diverted. These Barbicues are Hogs, roasted whole, this was under a large Tree. A great number of Young people met together with a Fiddle and Banjor Play'd by Two Negroes with Plenty of Toddy which both Men and Weomen [*sic*] seems to [be] very fond of. I believe they have Danced and drunk till there is Few Sober people amongst them. (Nicholas Cresswell [1750–1804], *Journal*, 36, 42, Nanjemoy, MD, May 29, 1774; Schooner John, St. Marys River, GA, FL, July 26, 1774 [orig. brackets and parentheses])

The banjo was the real musical instrument of the Southern negroes, not the fancy silver- or nickel-rimmed article with frets seen now on the minstrel stage or in the shops, but a very crude device, which I believe to be of native origin. . . . The most primitive instrument was made from a large gourd with a long, straight neck or handle, shaped like those of smaller growth, used commonly then for drinking-dippers. The bowl of the gourd was cut away on a plane level with the surface of the neck, the seed and contents removed, and over this, like a drumhead, a freshly tanned coonskin was stretched, fastened, and allowed to dry. The five strings of homemade materials passing from the apron behind over a small bridge near the middle of the drumhead were attached to the keys in proper position on the neck.

I learned to play upon a banjo which one of our slaves, who was a very good performer, helped me to make, when I was about eleven years old.

The rim was made from the circle of a cheesebox. A calfskin soaked in lime solution, which removed the hair, was tacked while wet over one surface of this, while the stem was carved from a suitable piece of soft poplar. I was extravagant enough to import four catgut strings and a wire bass, which excited no little curiosity, as they were the first ever seen by our negroes. (John Allan Wyeth [1845–1922], *With Sabre and Scalpel* [1914], 61)

I used to be a banjo picker in Civil War times. I could pick a church song just as good as I could a reel. Some of 'em I used to pick was "Amazing Grace," "Old Dan Tucker." Used to pick one went like this

> Farewell, farewell, sweet Mary;
> I'm ruined forever
> By lovin' of you;
> Your parents don't like me,
> That I do know
> I am not worthy to enter your do.

I used to pick

> Dark was the night
> Cold was the ground
> On which the Lord might lay.

I could pick anything.

> Amazing grace
> How sweet it sounds
> To save a wretch like me.
>
> Go preach my Gospel
> Says the Lord,
> Bid this whole earth
> My grace receive;
> Oh trust my word
> Ye shall be saved. (James "Jim" Davis, b. 1840, NC, 109–10, 114)[1]

The American banjo derives from various plucked lutes widespread in the same areas of the Western Sudan and Guinea Coast as gourd-and-horsehair fiddles (goges); their basic construction is, in fact, very similar to these fiddles except that they are plucked or strummed instead of being bowed. From the colonial era observers have recognized the American banjo's African character, but also its second-place standing: North American slaves always played banjos, but from the beginning the fiddle was their unrivaled favorite. This is not the acculturative puzzle some have made it, but in part reflects the paramount importance of fiddling in the same West African communities providing the banjo's prototypes (and a high proportion of American slaves).[2] Whites' attachment to the violin, by far the most popular instrument among Anglo-Americans during this period, was obviously also a factor.

On this point the ex-slave narratives are perfectly representative of the evidence as a whole. After the fiddle, the banjo is the musical instrument most commonly named by ex-slaves, but there is really no competition. The fiddle is mentioned twice as often as the banjo, two-thirds of the time as the only instrument save body percussion. By contrast, two-thirds of the banjo references describe it accompanying other instruments—and almost always the fiddle—at social dances. Otherwise, the banjo accompanied singing, which usually meant dance songs. These roles are consistently described from the first colonial reports through the 1800s—like Nicholas Cresswell, John Allan Wyeth described slaves playing banjos to accompany dance fiddling, or dance songs, or both together—corroborated by scores of WPA narrators. "We useta have a man on de place dat played a banjo, an' we would dance an' play while he sang" (Hannah Jones, b. ca. 1845, VA, 239). "Durin' the week on Wednesday and Thursday night we had dances an' then they was a lot of fiddlin' an' banjo playin'" (Melvin Smith, b. 1841, SC, 292). "After de days work dey would have banjo pickin', singin' and dancin'" (George Jackson, b. 1858, VA, 47).

In these capacities the banjo's function appears to have been primarily rhythmic or percussive rather than melodic; in fact, it would not be wholly inaccurate to say that the pre-1900 Black folk banjo often functioned as a hand-drum with tuned snares, its customary pairing with fiddle or human voice once more exemplifying the grit-to-pitch principle. In itself the banjo is a quintessential expression of that aesthetic, and of the African and African American attraction to musical instruments simultaneously producing pitch and percussion.

All that said, nineteenth-century descriptions of banjos do not all refer to the same instruments, and certainly not to the banjos known today. The evolution of the American banjo was hardly a unilinear or sequential process, nor should anyone expect as much. As sketchy as evidence for precolonial Africa may be, there is no question that an incredible variety of banjo-type instruments were being played in Africa prior to the transatlantic slave trade, mainly in West Africa but in other regions as well. Since that time their diversity has been documented in especially rich detail.[3] Given this background, millions of slaves would have arrived in the New World acquainted with different instances of this basic instrument type, which one would expect to find reformulated in various ways throughout the Western Hemisphere. That is exactly what happened.

Handcrafted African American banjos thus present a case very similar to homemade African American fiddles. In Africa there are well-established ethnic or regional subtypes among instruments of this class, their construction prescribed by local customs, cultural ideologies, and professional prerogatives. Loosed from such provincial and customary constraints but also from familiar surroundings and resources, African American instrument makers were by need more individualistic, adaptive, and opportunistic, even if they were guided by African templates. Complicating matters, by the 1840s white instrument makers were commercially manufacturing banjos, combining traditional African and African American features with European designs and technologies. From a musical standpoint, these various banjos would have sounded very different, each possessing its own distinct capa-

bilities and technical requirements. Most mentions of banjos among nineteenth-century Blacks—and certainly most WPA references—offer no further elaboration, but such differences must always be borne in mind when trying to imagine slave banjo playing. And while we have only glimpses of those formative years, we can say a few things about what kinds of banjos North American slaves played and how they might have sounded.

The African instruments that most obviously inspired the banjo are *spike lutes* built like goge spike fiddles, their necks consisting of rods inserted (hence, spiked) through their hide-topped gourd or calabash resonators, with one or more strings of horsehair, gut, or fiber suspended on a pressure-bridge seated on the membrane. Pitch was typically altered by stopping (lightly touching) the strings rather than pressing them against a fingerboard; movable metal rings encompassing strings and neck serve as tuners. This neck design was apparently one of the first traits widely altered in the New World. Gourd banjos are regularly described but also pictured in North America and the West Indies beginning in the seventeenth century; even in this early period depictions show guitar-style necks with flat fretless fingerboards and wooden tuning pegs. The necks of early banjos were also considerably longer than their modern counterparts. Occasionally, instead of attaching a wooden neck, slaves used longnecked gourds, the handle of the gourd serving as the banjo's neck. John Allan Wyeth knew such instruments on his family's Northern Alabama plantation. James Lane Allen (1849–1925) recalled similar banjos in antebellum Kentucky: "The banjo was played [by slaves], but more commonly the fiddle. A homemade variety of the former consisted of a crook-necked, hardshell gourd and a piece of sheepskin."[4]

West African lutes of the banjo type typically have from one to five strings. The same was true of American banjos in the eighteenth and nineteenth centuries, one- and two-stringed instruments being reported into the mid-1800s. In New Orleans in February 1819, Benjamin Henry Latrobe (1764–1820) observed a two-string gourd banjo "which no doubt was imported from Africa." The body was a "calabash," while the headstock was adorned with a carved human figure seated before the two tuning pegs. Latrobe's drawing has also survived, depicting a fretless guitar-style neck.[5] Visiting Augusta, Georgia, in 1850, Fredrika Bremer (1801–1865) was treated to an exhibition of slave hymn-singing. "After this, another young negro, who was not so evangelical as the rest, came and sang with his banjo. . . . The banjo is an African instrument, made from a half a fruit called the calabash, or gourd, which has a very hard rind. A thin skin or piece of bladder is stretched over the opening, and over this one or two strings are stretched, which are raised on a bridge. The banjo is the negroes' guitar, and certainly it is the firstborn among stringed instruments."[6]

However, the majority of sources describe four-string slave banjos, which in some cases would have meant four long strings stretching from tail to headstock, in others three long strings and a shorter *thumb* or *drone string* attached to a tuning peg midway up the neck, so-called because it is always sounded open with the thumb.[7] By midcentury, the norm was the five-string banjo with four long strings and a drone; by then professionally crafted or commercially mass-manufactured instruments were also the standard. (For whatever reason, three-string banjos were nonexistent or at least unreported in North America.)[8]

There were two basic body types for slave banjos: the oft-mentioned gourd, and the hoop or cheesebox design described by John Wyeth and also by ex-slave author Isaac D. Williams (b. ca. 1821, VA): "When we made a banjo we would first of all catch what we called a ground hog, known in the north as a woodchuck. After tanning his hide, it would be stretched over a piece of timber fashioned like a cheese box."[9] The back of the instrument's body remains open. Besides hand-fashioned wooden hoops, actual cheese boxes—wooden packing cases for cheese wheels—were used, as well as rims from various other containers (bushels, measures, sieves, and so forth).

The other slave banjo type was the gourd banjo, constantly mentioned but most cases with few other details. In 1855, for instance, ex-slave Peter Randolph (ca. 1825–1897) wrote that on Sundays slaves on Virginia plantations "occupy the time in dancing to the music of a banjo, made out of a large gourd."[10] Similarly, Molly Finley's mother had told her that Arkansas slaves received "a big picnic dinner after they lay by crops and at Christmas. They had gourd banjos. Mama said they had good times" (Molly Finley, b. 1865, child of ex-slaves, AR, 294). Some sources are more forthcoming, however, revealing that this was an area where North American slaves were especially resourceful. Unlike Africa, where the gourd species for a particular instrument is likely stipulated by tradition, African American banjo makers appear to have

Fig. 5.1. "African Americans conversing by a mantel, one playing a banjo, the other holding a hoe." February 16, 1861. Miriam and Ira D. Wallach Division of Art, Prints, and Photographs, New York Public Library. A homemade, fretless, tacked-topped, five-string banjo on the eve of the war. (The fifth-string peg is visible below the player's left hand; as is typical for early five-string banjos, it is set into the fingerboard, rather than on the side of the neck and perpendicular to the fingerboard like modern five-string banjos.) The caption imagines the two characters' dialogue: JEREMIAH. "Is dat 'Hail Columbus! happy Lan'!' dat you's playin', 'Sephus?" JOSEPHUS: "Yes; dat's de chewn." JEREMIAH: "Well, Marster say dat chewn done dead." JOSEPHUS: "He *do*? *Well*, ef dat chewn dead, I jes' as well break my Banjo and gib up, 'cause dat's de prettiest chewn I plays. Dat chewn's too pretty to die!" This alludes to the fact that by February 1861 when this cartoon appeared, seven states—South Carolina, Mississippi, Florida, Alabama, Georgia, Louisiana, and Texas—had seceded to form the Confederacy, shortly to be joined by Virginia, North Carolina, Tennessee, and Arkansas.

availed themselves of any suitable variety. Thus there are descriptions of slave banjos created from globular or oblong gourds in the West African manner, but also from longnecked gourds where the gourd's handle served as the instrument's neck. Maurice Thompson (1844–1901), who had lived in antebellum Cherokee County, Georgia, described a gourd that had been modified during growth specifically for use as a banjo, a detail I have found nowhere else:

The banjo was a common instrument in the plantation quarters. Many excellent banjoists, as "banjo-picking" went in those days, were to be found among the common fieldhands. It may be worth stating that I once heard a negro play on a rude banjo of his own making, a very curious instrument, the body of which was a flat gourd. The strings were, if I recollect aright, of horsehair. The gourd had been flattened by confining it, during its growth, between two boards, and its neck or "handle" had been cut off and a wooden one with screws, etc., attached. I cannot say that the tone of this rude lyre was of the best, but its music was sufficiently exhilarating to call forth a "jubah dance" from a lot of surprisingly supple and antic pickanninies.[11]

Each highly adaptable in its own right, these two basic banjo types—the gourd and the hoop—seem to have coexisted everywhere. John Wyeth described them both just on his family's northern Alabama plantation. Less frequently, slaves employed other found or castoff objects as resonators, usually it seems as gourd substitutes. Tin pan or bucket banjos by no means approach the numbers of hoop or gourd varieties but were well-established nonetheless. WPA narrator Betty Curlett was born in 1872 on her parents' former plantation near Houlka, Mississippi. "Then we had three banjos. The musicians was William Word, Uncle Dan Porter, and Miles Porter. Did we dance? Square dance" (Betty Curlett, b. 1872, MS, child of ex-slaves, 76). Curlett refuted conventional wisdom, naming the banjo (not the fiddle) as her community's

unchallenged favorite, and providing the most detailed description of a homemade banjo in the narratives:

The only musical instrument we had was the banjo. Some made their banjos. Take a bucket or pan [and] a long strip of wood. 3 horse hairs twisted made the bass string. 2 horsehairs twisted made the second string. 1 horse hair twisted made the fourth and the fifth string was the fine one, it was not twisted at all but drawn tight. They were all bees waxed. (Betty Curlett, b. 1872, MS, child of ex-slaves, 81, supplement page, "Folklore Subjects: Musical Instrument")

Tin pan or bucket banjos are also reported during this period among Blacks in South Carolina, Georgia, Tennessee, and Indiana; Art Rosenbaum discovered that multi-instrumentalist Jake Staggers (b. 1899, Oconee Co., SC) "learned to play on a homemade instrument made out of a tin pan with a catskin head, though groundhog and even fish-skin heads were also used at the time."[12] The precise counts of horsehairs in Betty Curlett's description need not (and probably should not) be taken too literally, which is no slight: for a non-musician, she conveys a remarkably clear understanding of a five-string banjo's standard string arrangement.[13] It is obviously significant that these were horsehair strings, an unmistakable litmus of African origin, in this case still being employed after 1870. Unlike horsehair-strung monochords, which feature a single strand of untwisted hair, Curlett's description is one of several intriguing accounts of handcrafted African American banjos and fiddles with multiple horsehair strings requiring a fixative (beeswax, resin) to separate and hold them in place.

There are numerous other reports of banjos strung with horsehair, and occasionally thread or twine as well. In the 1880s Jim Allen Vaughan (b. unk., NC) could not afford a banjo, "so he decided to make one. He obtained a large gourd, cut out one side and covered it over with a shorn sheep hide. A white woman gave him a spool of cotton for the strings."[14] However, catgut strings are most frequently mentioned.

"On Saturday night you'd hear them fiddles, banjoes and guitars playing and the darkies singing. All the music gadgets was homemade. The banjoes was made of round pieces of wood [hoops], civered (covered) with sheepskin and strung with catgut strings" (Simp Campbell, b. 1860, TX, 614, orig. parentheses).

West African lutes are topped with goat-, lizard- or snakeskin. In North America sheep- or goatskin, catskin, dog or groundhog hide, even occasionally snake- or fish-skin were all used as banjo heads.[15] These were tacked in place, which inevitably made them looser and thus lower in timbre than the drums of modern manufactured banjos.[16] Evidently, slave banjos (and nineteenth-century banjos generally) were also tuned below the range of modern banjos, which, combined with the looser drumheads, longer necks, and gut- or horsehair-strings, probably gave them timbres closer to guitars than the bright, piercing treble register now associated with banjos. English educator and clergyman Jonathan Boucher (1738–1804) resided in the Chesapeake region from 1759 until 1775, later writing,

I well remember, that in Virginia and Maryland, the favourite and almost only instrument in use among the slaves there was a *bandore*; or, as they pronounced the word, *banjer*. Its body was a large hollow gourd, with a long handle attached to it, strung with catgut, and played on with the fingers. Its sound is a dull, heavy, grumbling murmur; yet it is not without something like melody.[17]

Modern banjos are typically described as *ringing, chiming, clanging*, and so forth; *dull, heavy, grumbling*, and *murmur* certainly are not descriptives ordinarily associated with the banjo, but such traits are consistent with what one might expect from homemade, gourd-bodied, longnecked, gut-strung lutes, and other descriptions argue that, allowing for Boucher's loaded word choices, this really is how many, perhaps most of the banjos played by slaves sounded.

Beginning in the 1830s, the banjo was widely popularized through blackface minstrelsy. Most early white minstrels professed faithfully to represent the folk tradition, and many are known to have had direct contact with Black instrumentalists. Some acquired handcrafted Black banjos; others constructed their own, but soon professional instrument makers became involved. Over the course of the century they transformed the banjo, basically by Europeanizing it. Their most important antebellum innovation was the screw-and-bracket tightened head, often credited to German-born drum maker William Esperance Boucher Jr. (1822–1899), who was marketing banjos from his Baltimore shop by the mid-1840s. Whether or not Boucher alone deserves credit, the screw-and-bracket design was borrowed directly from European drum technology, and from that point to present the heads of manufactured banjos have possessed timbres not unlike military snares, brightening their tones overall. From the outset, hoop bodies were the absolute norm, originally steam-bent wood, later sometimes nickel. So, too, catgut strings were the norm, but in the 1850s banjo makers introduced the *wire bass* that John Wyeth mentions, actually a wire-wrapped-silk guitar string (a recent invention) serving as fourth or lowest string. Around midcentury, painted fret markers began appearing on fingerboards, soon replaced by raised metal frets. By century's end steel strings and screw-tuners were also standard, necks had been dramatically shortened, tunings had been raised, and the banjo had assumed its current form—which is to say that the banjo as we now know it did not exist during much of the nineteenth century, and certainly not during slavery.

Nonetheless, early shop-made banjos were widely available during the prewar period. Many slaveholders bought instruments for their slaves or allowed them to buy their own, and no doubt some slaves played store-bought banjos from the time they appeared. An 1871 *Leslie's Illustrated* article describes the canny postwar Black consumer: "A negro's ear never fails to catch a pure, sweet tone, and when the article which produces it is found, no argument will prevent its purchase. A banjo may not be covered with the finest skin, nor have the most glittering keys, but if it responds agreeably to the touch, these characteristics will be of no account."[18] The circumstance sounds already well-established, and by the turn of the century manufactured banjos were usual for both Blacks and whites. Still, home-made banjos were common throughout the nineteenth century—some of the best descriptions in the narratives and other sources concern Reconstruction or later—and were not uncommon even in the twentieth century, often as a young person's first instrument.

We can also venture some generalizations about exactly how these various banjos were played. From the colonial era the banjo was always a topic of considerable comment, and nineteenth-century descriptions of slave banjo playing are sometimes surprisingly detailed. These corroborate, and are in turn corroborated by, other sources, including the narratives. From the twentieth century there are also sound recordings or even films credibly capturing aspects of early Black banjo playing. Finally, the blackface minstrel banjo style, which is extraordinarily well-documented in songbooks and banjo instruction manuals as well as eyewitness accounts and minstrel memoirs, provides an indirect if somewhat problematic guide to slave banjo playing.

With some inevitable exceptions, Black banjo players always favored a percussive downstroking technique based on African lute playing, scraping down across the strings and striking the drumhead with the fingernails, simultaneously catching the drone with the thumb on the downstroke, possibly with up-picking as well (plucking individual strings with the index or ring fingers on the upstroke). Later variations on this approach are fittingly called rapping, thumping, banging, beating, clawhammer, or frailing.

These basic techniques were taken over by minstrels, but the connection between minstrel banjo players and their slave counterparts is highly debatable at best. Early minstrels may have been inspired by African American folk banjo styles, but in their usual manner they selectively adapted rather than faithfully represented their Black sources, much as they Europeanized the banjo itself. Although they did borrow the basic African and African American downpicking-

with-thumb-drone approach, minstrels played in a melodic single-note style devoid of chording; the bulk of their repertoire derived from the eighteenth-century English stage, or from British and Irish fiddle tunes and dance songs, some of which slaves sang or fiddled but rarely played on banjos unless accompanying fiddling or singing.[19]

There is no question of minstrelsy's enormous impact, and by the turn of the twentieth century the majority of Southern banjo players Black or white employed variations of this style, which by that time had evolved into an authentic folk tradition no longer directly dependent on the professional stage. This process was obviously underway in the 1800s, some Black banjoists of the day being acquainted with the minstrel approach (Black minstrels certainly).[20] They were evidently a minority, however, since at the time the general consensus among all parties—including minstrels—was that slaves and minstrels played banjos completely differently. White banjo virtuoso and minstrel entrepreneur Frank B. Converse (1837–1903) was also the nineteenth century's most important banjo teacher and marketing guru. Of his early exposure to banjos in the 1840s, he later wrote:

> with but few exceptions it can hardly be said that at this time the instrument was played at all; mainly strummed as a characteristic accompaniment for the darkey songs of the day. Occasionally one could be met who aspired to easy jigs, walkarounds, and the like, but generally speaking, the region above the fifth fret was *terra incognito*. . . . Isn't it remarkable that, with its home on the Southern plantation, the inherent beauties of the banjo awaited development at the hands of its white admirers [minstrels] in the North![21]

Other knowledgeable sources corroborate Converse. Minstrels indisputably borrowed downstroking from slaves, but otherwise slaves are usually described playing banjos in the opposite manner as minstrels, strumming heavily down across all of the strings at once while drumming on the heads, emphasizing rhythmic accompaniments over melodic leads. Not only are slaves constantly described *strumming* banjos—"Sometimes, they gathered in the back yard and some one strummed on a banjo while the others danced" (Caroline Malloy, b. ca. 1840, GA, 411)—but also *thumping, thrumping, thrumming, thumbing, tumming*, and so forth, suggesting both percussive downstroking-with-thumb-droning *and* prominent head-drumming. George Washington Cable (1844–1925) wrote that when slaves gathered on Sundays in New Orleans' Congo Square,

> the grand instrument at last, the first violin, as one might say, was the banjo. It had but four strings, not six: beware of the dictionary. It is not the "favorite musical instrument of the negroes of the Southern States of America." Uncle Remus says truly that is the fiddle; but for the true African dance, a dance not so much of the legs and feet as of the upper half of the body, a sensual, devilish thing tolerated only by Latin American masters, there was wanted the dark inspiration of African drums and the banjo's thrump and strum.[22]

In the 1850s Daniel Hundley (1832–1899) observed Alabama slaves at play: "Evenings are devoted almost wholly to dancing, banjo-playing, singing, chitchatting, or to coon-hunting and night-fishing. Many a night have we lain awake until near twelve o'clock, listening to the distant 'thrum, tumpe tum' of the merry banjo, may be accompanied by a flute or violin, or 'patting,' and always more or less by singing and uproarious shouts of laughter."[23] There is no better expression of the basic downstroking-with-drone rhythm than Hundley's *thrum, tumpe tum*. Two decades later, Joel Chandler Harris (1848–1908) described a gang of Georgia street musicianers: "A year or more ago [ca. 1882], a band of negro serenaders made its appearance upon the streets of Atlanta. The leader of this band carried a banjo, upon which he strummed while singing. His voice drowned out the banjo, but a close observer could see that he was thumping the strings aimlessly."[24] These techniques constantly figure

in period accounts—for instance, James Robert Gilmore's 1864 description of slaves "whose skinny fingers, with handy blow, *could* rap the music out of 'de ole banjo.' "[25] Significantly too, descriptions of slaves picking particular songs on the banjo are almost always accompanied by lyrics or at least mention singing, again suggesting that vocals carried the melody, with banjos rapping out rhythm and harmony.

There are, however, intimations that slaves possessed various banjo styles, strumming-and-thumping merely being most common. Although he insisted that most slaves simply strummed, Frank Converse also described a free Black of his early acquaintance who employed something resembling *two-fingered picking* (a common technique in twentieth-century folk banjo styles). Converse also indicated that he had later heard plantation slaves play banjos (including gourd banjos) this same way, and that this definitely was not the minstrel banjo style that Converse himself subsequently mastered.

> The first banjo I ever heard was in the hands of a colored man—a bright mulatto—whose name I have forgotten. He frequently visited Elmira and the neighboring villages, playing and singing and passing his hat for collections. His *repertoire* was not very exhaustive, but, with his comicalities, sufficed to gain him a living. I cannot say that I learned anything from his execution, which, though amusing, was limited to the thumb and first finger,—pulling or "picking" the strings with both. He was quite conceited as to his abilities (pardonable in banjo players, I believe), and to impress his listeners with a due appreciation of them, he would announce that such a trifling circumstance as the banjo being out of tune caused him no inconvenience and so, with a seemingly careless fumbling of the pegs, he would disarrange the tuning—"fro de banjo out a' tune," he said—but merely pitching the second string a semitone higher. . . . This manner of fingering—as I learned in later years when visiting Southern plantations—was characteristic of the early colored player; an

individual of rare occurrence, however, and whose banjo was of the rudest construction,—often a divided gourd with a coon skin stretched over the larger part for the drum. With this accompaniment he would improvise his song as he went along, generally mentioning his massa or missus or some local incident. His fingering was unique,—requiring only the first finger of the left hand for stopping the strings—on the first string at the first fret and the second string at the second fret. With the right hand he used only the first finger and thumb.[26]

Other slave banjo styles may survive in later materials, or lurk in early descriptions. Even in the twentieth century many African American banjoists still followed the approach of West African lute players, dispensing with the central melody and instead performing repetitive ostinato phrases (riffs) as counterpoints to singing or fiddling. (In the minstrel style, the banjo plays the main melody in unison with all other instruments, the organization generally adopted by Southern stringbands.) This quintessentially African trait (riffing) was later fundamental to the development of blues guitar playing (among other things), possibly with some influence from the banjo. Indeed, while often ambiguous or condescending, many early accounts of Black banjo playing—for instance, the preceding passage from Frank Converse, or Jonathan Boucher's pronouncement that the *banjer* "is not without something like melody"—might actually describe riffing.[27] In any case, considering everything known about African and African American music, it seems not only plausible but probable that slave banjo players sometimes riffed.

Other descriptions of slave banjo picking may reflect the direct influence of African playing styles. Innumerable African-born banjo players were still active across the South well into the postwar period, especially in areas where illegal slaving had been endemic. Describing the 1870s, Emma Weeks remembered "a coal-black nigger dat had been brought from Africa. He was so black, dat we called him Joe Slick. . . .

He was putty near middle-aged at dat time, and he was low and chunky. He'd go wid us to dances, and pick his banjo. I don't think dat he ever got money fo' pickin' his banjo. Old Joe learned most of us to dance" (Emma Weeks, b. 1858, TX, 4014). One certainly wonders what kind of banjo Joe played and exactly how he played it (or, for that matter, what kind of dances he knew), but his presence alone is highly suggestive.

In any case, North American slaves and their immediate descendants definitely played a variety of banjo types in a variety of ways that would have produced a variety of sounds and textures, some dramatically distinct from one another. A few of these instruments may have possessed bright, ringing tones resembling contemporary banjos; most probably did not. Downstroking was the most common but apparently not the only playing technique. Certainly the infinite diversity and complexity of twentieth-century banjo styles strongly suggest a similar situation in the 1800s, and there are occasional hints this was so. If later evidence is also any guide, many slave banjo players (and especially the better ones) could play in several different styles depending on the material, audience, or occasion.

However, by far the greatest number of period descriptions of Black banjo playing evoke what I have termed the strumming-and-thumping approach, probably because banjoists are most often described accompanying dancers at public events where this style had obvious advantages, and in some cases may have been absolutely necessary. "At night endurin' Christmas us had parties, and dere was allus some Nigger ready to pick de banjo" (Susan Castle, b. 1860, GA, 181). "Chrissmushtime 'n' Fo'th 'r' July dey had a dance. Jus' a reg'lar ol' breakdown dance. Some was dancin' 'Swing d' corner,' 'n' some was in d' middle 'r' d' flo' 'Cuttin' d' chicken wing.' Some 'r' 'em was banjer (banjo) pickers. My father was a banjer picker" (Horace Overstreet, b. 1856, TX, 2998, orig. parentheses). "Saturday was the only night we took for frolicing. My pa was a mighty fine banjo player. He furnished the music for the folks to dance. He could all but make that box talk" (Louis Davis, b. 1858, AR, 581–82).

Fig. 5.2. Horace Overstreet, ex-slave, Beaumont, TX, June 28, 1937. Portraits of African American ex-slaves from the US Works Progress Administration, Federal Writers' Project slave narratives collection, Library of Congress.

In such rowdy preamplification settings, banjo players might have to make their instruments "talk" simply to cut through the noise, scraping the strings, popping the drone, and thumping the head while singing, hollering, stomping, and generally cavorting. John Allan Wyeth recalled slaves beating straws on banjos as well as fiddles.[28] In the company of Charley Patton (1891–1934), guitarist Hayes McMullen (1902–1986) had played under similar conditions at Delta house parties in the 1930s, later recalling "I've seen Charley Patton just bump on his guitar, 'stead of pickin' it. . . . I bumped on it too. Colored folks dancin' gonna dance all night, and I'd get tired. So I'd get 'em good'n started, you know, I'd be hollerin', and then I'd just be knockin' on the box when the music get going."[29] Nineteenth-century descriptions reveal that in such circumstances slave musicianers bumped their banjos and hollered as well, and that this may have been the sound of banjo playing most frequently heard in slave communities, a drum-like thumping or thrumping distantly audible through the din of a riotous dance.

To compete with crowd noise and keep dancers together, banjo players also stamped their own feet.

A fictionalized but informed 1833 account describes a turn-of-the-century Tennessee dance party led by a slave musicianer: "Soon the whole house was up, knocking it off—while old Ben thrummed his banjo, beat time with his feet, and sung . . . occasionally calling for particular steps."[30] Overall, banjo pickers were especially renowned for clowning—the "comicalities" Frank Converse mentions—dancing while playing or performing various antics or stunts with their instruments as props. Fanny Kemble (1809–1893) was positively effusive concerning Black performers she observed on Butler's Island, Georgia, in January 1839, but "above all, the feats of a certain enthusiastic banjo player, who seemed to me to thump his instrument with every part of his body at once."[31] William McCreary Burwell's 1856 novel *White Acre Vs. Black Acre* describes a slave performing with "his banjo over his head, behind his back, and under his arm! shouting his song with such stentorian voice that the room was crowded with new comers."[32] Twenty years later Philip A. Bruce visited a Virginia tobacco plantation, reporting that the banjo and accordion were the most popular instruments:

> Their best performers play very skillfully on both, and indulge in as much ecstatic byplay as musicians of the most famous schools. They throw themselves into many strange contortions as they touch the strings or keys, swaying from side to side, or rocking their bodies backward and forward till the head almost reaches the floor, or leaning over the instrument and addressing it in caressing terms.[33]

In the 1920s John Allan Wyeth (1845–1922) demonstrated for Dorothy Scarborough (1878–1935) some of the banjo tricks he had learned from his family's slaves. "Dr. Wyeth performed magical tricks with a banjo, as he had been taught by old Uncle Billy in slavery times. He evoked melodies of wistful gaiety by drawing a handkerchief across the banjo strings, and lively tunes by playing it with a whiskbroom."[34] A couple of decades later, Uncle Dave Macon (1870–1952), who also boasted of learning directly from Black musicians, displayed some of these same tricks in the feature film *Grand Ole Opry* (as he always had in his live performances).[35] Today this type of clowning is best known through blues guitarists like Charley Patton (1891–1934) , Tommy Johnson (1896–1956), T-Bone Walker (1910–1975), and perhaps even more so Jimi Hendrix (1942–1970). Slave banjo players may have established the North American tradition.

Banjos are sometimes mentioned by themselves at dances, but even then they would have been supported by patting, clogging, or hand percussion. "Most o' de holidays wus celebrated by eatin' candy, drinkin' wine an' brandy. Dar wus a heap o' dancin' ter de music of banjoes an' han' slappin' " (William Sykes, b. 1859, NC, 328).[36] More often banjos are described in support of singers and other instruments. "Dey beat on d' bones t' mak d' musick wid banjo an' uder t'ings" (Isabella Boyd, b. ca. 1850, TX, 360). "They clapped hands fer us ter dance by an' played homemade banjos an' harps . . . made out of leetle pieces of reeds-like; you blow in 'em" (Lula Coleman, b. 1851, AL, 431). "We had small dances on Saturday night and play ring plays, and have banjo and fiddle playing and knock bones together" (Litt Young, b. 1850, MS, 4302). "Weuns am 'lowed to have de parties an' de dances. Weuns have fo' de music, sich as de banjo, jew's harp, an' de 'cordian, an' fo' de time, dey beat de piece ob steel" (Fred Brown, b. 1853, LA, 468). "Sometime when the fiddle was all we could get for music, some of the boys would get a pair of bones, horse ribs or something of the kind and keep time beating on a chairback with them to make more time. Then sometimes we'd have a banjo, too. Some would pat and some would whistle and we'd dance" (Elsie Pryor, b. ca. 1855, IT, 263).

However, with the exception of the fiddle, the instrument most often played with slave banjos may have been the tin pan tambourine. This pairing is widely mentioned in the WPA narratives and elsewhere, though its incidence in the narratives is exaggerated by some of their most obvious cases of boilerplate prose, provided by Texas interviewer B. E. Davis. Nearly two dozen of Davis's informants ostensibly described the banjo-tin-pan combination, but in suspiciously similar, almost identical terms. "On Saturday night we have tin pan beating, banjo picking and negro dance all night" (Jack Harrison, b. unk., TX, 1654). "On Saturday nights, we all have banjo and tin-pan beating and negro dance" (Jake Terriell, b. ca. 1845, NC, 3775). "On Saturday night we have banjo picking, tin pan beating and negro dance" (Dave L. Byrd, b. 1852, TX, 566). "Every Saturday night we would have negro dance with that bango picking and tin pan beating. We danced all night long and sure did have a good time" (Louis Cain, b. 1849, NC, 592). "No sir, master always give us a holiday on Saturday. On Saturday nights we always had banjo pickin, tin pan beating and negro dance" (Rosie McGillery, b. 1847, SC, 2501–2). "Maser he always give us Saturday at noon for holiday so we could clean up and rest, for on Saturday night the negro he most always had tin-pan beating and bango picking, then a negro dance would last all night long" (Tom Holland, b. 1840, TX, 1764).[37]

Given the natures of vernacular speech and stylized accounts of traditional music, it is hardly surprising to find ex-slaves describing the same musical phenomena in similar terms, as they often do. These examples are, of course, nothing of the sort, but obvious instances of a writer repeating himself. Davis did not invent the detail, however, and I suspect one or more of his narrators did describe the tin-pan-banjo pairing. The combo is quite well documented elsewhere in the narratives, but also in period sources. "On Sattidy nights dey would have dances an' dance all night long. Somebody would clap hands, beat pans and blow quills or pick de banjer strings" (Lucindy Lawrence Jurdon, b. 1858, GA, 243). "Dere was allus somepin' to do on Sadday night—frolics, dances, and sich lak. Dey picked de banjo and knocked on tin pans to dance by" (Easter Huff, b. 1858, GA, 248). "Christmas we frolic and eat cake. We had serenades, too, on banjos and old tin pans and whatever you wanted to make a noise. And a gallon o' liquor—anything you want!" (Shang Harris, b. ca. 1840, GA, 120). Pen Ingleton recalled that at Christmas in Virginia ca. 1800, "the 'whole plantation' approached the mansion playing on their rude fiddles, thrumming banjos, and rattling on tin pans and calabashes."[38] An 1861 novel describes a slave dance on a Louisiana plantation featuring fiddle, two banjos, tambourine, tin-pan, and kettledrum.[39] B. E. Davis's descriptions may not be altogether fraudulent, but neither can they be taken at face value.

Obviously tin pans and banjos were considered well-matched; for some informants they were even interchangeable. Ex-slave Daniel Webster Davis (1862–1913) wrote that, in antebellum Virginia, "the field hands would gather most any night in the 'quarters,' and shuffle around to the sound of a banjo, or if that was not forthcoming, to the beating of a tin pan, that furnished music not so classical, and yet served the purpose admirably well."[40] Another former slave recalled plantation parties where "some would march and dance by the music of a banjo, others by the beating of a tin-pan."[41] The suggestion that slave banjo playing sounded much like someone beating a tin pan or tambourine is certainly consistent with everything known about slave banjo technique. And just like tin pans and tambourines, banjos were favorite accompaniments for fiddles.

In North America fiddle-banjo duos are reported among slaves beginning in the 1770s (Nicholas Cresswell may have authored the first description). Nineteenth-century reports are ubiquitous. Without question this is the instrumental combination most frequently described in the WPA narratives. "Weuns have singin' an' dancin' at de parties. De dancin' am quadrilles an' de music am fiddles an' banjoes" (Louise Mathews, b. 1854, TX, 2606). "Some of dem niggers played fiddles and picked banjoes for de others to dance down 'til dey was worn out" (Ed McCree, b. 1861, GA, 61–63). "At de parties thar am games, dancin' an' singin'. De music am a banjo an' a fiddle. 'Twas some kind of doin's every Saturday night" (Zek Brown, b. 1857, TN, 498–99). "Sometimes they had parties on Saturday night. The couples got on the floor and go to turning round and round to the music of fiddles and banjoes" (Campbell Davis, b. 1852, TX, 1064–65). "Us niggers sho had good times Sadday nights. Dey played de banjo and de fiddle and de white folks didn't pay

us no mind—dey let us dance all night, if we want to. De patterrollers? Whoopee! Dey sho would git you, if you didn't behave" (Elsie Payne, b. ca. 1840, AL, 293).[42]

Narrators also occasionally described the banjo with the instrument that had to a great extent replaced it by the time they were interviewed, the guitar. Overall, however, ex-slaves recalled the guitar as a late arrival.

> Dances in dem days warn't dese here huggin' kind of dances lak dey has now. Dere warn't no Big Apple nor no Little Apple neither. Us had a house wid a raised flatform (platform) at one end whar de music-makers sot. Dey had a string band wid a fiddle, a trumpet, and a banjo, but dere warn't no guitars lak dey has in dis day. One man called de sets and us danced de cardrille (quadrille) de virginia reel, and de 16-hand cortillion. (Liza Mention, b. ca. 1865, GA, child of ex-slaves, 124, orig. parentheses)

The history of the guitar in American music, and especially African American music, has also been much discussed, and in this instance the conventional wisdom is more than wise. Through much of the nineteenth century, the guitar was an upper-crust parlor instrument, considered especially appropriate for wellborn ladies. Only in the late 1800s did it begin to appear in fiddle-and-banjo–based dance ensembles, and much later as the chief instrument in blues, country music, and other folk-derived Southern genres. Crucially, this transition coincided with a shift from small-bodied, handcrafted, gut-strung guitars—rarified commodities intended for genteel domestic settings—to larger, louder, more affordable, mass-produced, steel-strung guitars that could match the volume of fiddles and banjos in noisy crowds.[43]

In the plantation South, nineteenth-century sources often refer to slaveholders, their wives, and daughters politely playing guitars. Some descriptions even come from former slaves, some of whom were obviously acquainted with the instrument.[44] Still, the guitar does not appear to have been widely played by antebellum Blacks. In the 1850s William H. Holcombe

(1825–1893) visited a plantation outside New Orleans, describing how, upon being displayed to slaves, a young white lady's guitar "produced quite an extravagant exhibition of curiosity and wonder. 'What a big fiddle!' said one to another. 'Hush up, you fool-nigger!' was the reply; 'dat's de white man's banjo.'"[45] Charlie Bell was born around this same time in nearby Pearl River County, Mississippi: "De niggers on de plantation danced a heap—seemed ter me like hit was mos' ever' night. You takes a coon skin an' make a drum out of hit, stretch hit over a keg—a sawed-off one—dat make a fine drum. An' banjos an' fiddlers! Didn' have no mandolines an' *guitars* then" (Charlie Bell, b. 1856, MS, 124, orig. emphasis).

Bell is describing the 1860s, but as his comments imply, guitars (and mandolins) did begin appearing in Black communities not long after. By the 1870s guitar-playing Blacks were being sporadically reported across the South. Just over half a century later, when the ex-slaves were interviewed, the guitar was the unrivaled favorite instrument in Black folk music, having supplemented or supplanted the fiddle and banjo. It was easily incorporated into older vocal or fiddle-and-banjo–based styles, but the rise of the blues, stimulated in the early years by self-accompanied singer-guitarists, was also a major factor in this rapid ascendancy.

Thus by the 1930s guitars were as common as fiddles and banjos had been in the 1830s, and former slaves lived in communities where they could not help but notice. Some like Aunt Katherin had direct exposure. "Yas'm Dug and me is parted, I went to de picnic an' a man bote me a sack o' pop corn, and Dug sed 'Man! whut you mean, dis woman is my lawful wedded wife.' So we fust an' I left. Now I am going to live with Morris (son) dat boy show can play dat git-tar" (Aunt Katherin, b. unk., MS, 1265, orig. parentheses). Aunt Katherin does not say whether Morris also lived in Tate County (apparently her life-long home), nor does she elaborate on his playing, but by the 1930s Tate County and surrounding North Mississippi were particularly well known for blues guitarists. Significantly, this was also an area where

Blacks played older instruments like quills, fiddles, banjos, fifes and drums, and homemade monochords well into the twentieth century. By the 1900s guitars were integral to this music as well. Some local guitarists specialized in one style or another; some played any- and everything. We still cannot precisely categorize Aunt Katherin's guitar-playing son Morris, yet his presence in Depression-era Tate County makes perfect sense (unfortunately, the interview does not provide surnames for Aunt Katherin, Morris, or Dug).[46]

On the other hand, the majority of the three dozen ex-slaves who named the guitar were recalling the 1800s. A few even described antebellum Blacks playing guitars. This would also make sense of a sort, though somewhat less so. Guitars were common enough among the slaveholding class, and given that circumstance, coupled with the slaves' customary role as musicianers and their overall musicality, it must be the case that some slaves played guitars at one time or another. Possibly the narratives establish that this occurred more than generally known, but outside corroboration remains absent. Personally, I suspect that some of these elderly ex-slaves did not remember exactly when during their long lifetimes guitars had become supremely popular; they just recognized as much from the present. However, I also believe that, given the opportunity, slaves played guitars just as they did any musical instruments made available to them, and that other of these narrators were remembering perfectly.

That said, by far the greatest number of ex-slaves mentioning guitars describe them during Reconstruction or later, often tied to musical developments that can then be traced into the twentieth century. In fact, almost all of the narrators naming the guitar were born in the 1850s and '60s and could not have known earlier music. Even narrators in this age group often insisted that guitars were a recent phenomenon (see Liza Mention, b. 1865, Charlie Bell, b. 1856, qtd. above, for examples).

There are, however, other reasons why elderly ex-slaves may have misremembered slaves playing guitars before the war. During these years Blacks and whites alike often equated banjos and guitars, describing banjos as "the slave's guitar" or the guitar as "the white man's banjo," and so forth. "The instrument proper to them is the Banjar, which they brought hither from Africa, and which is the original of the guitar, its chords being precisely the four lower chords of the guitar." "One of their favorite instruments is the *banjo*, a kind of crude guitar." "The banjo, a sort of rude guitar, is their chief instrumental accompaniment."[47] Hettie Campbell, born around 1865 in coastal Georgia, actually called the gourd banjo a *guitar*: "They mostly have guitah now . . . an we use tuh use guitah too, but we makes em frum goad an we beats drums too. We makes em frum coon hide stretched ovuh hoops."[48]

Even to casual observers, banjos and guitars bear outward resemblances; however, it is also possible that these individuals were stating that slave banjos and guitars *sounded* alike, and all evidence does indicate that many nineteenth-century banjos had ranges and timbres closer to guitars than to banjos manufactured after 1900. This may partly explain why beginning around that time, more and more Black performers opted to play guitars rather than banjos: compared to modern banjos, that is, guitars may have more closely matched the sound and register, and thus better filled the musical role, of earlier African American folk banjos.

And there is no question that beginning in the late 1800s the guitar assumed and in many ways usurped the banjo's function, most often being used to accompany singing, dance fiddling, or both. "The only fun we ever had wuz when we would have co'n shuckins and guitar playins'. We would all go to some Nigger's house and somebody would play the guitar. We didn't know nothin' 'bout no piano or nothin' but the guitar and fiddle" (Harriet Chelsey, b. ca. 1853, TX, 693). "When the slaves went to the quarters, after the day's work was done, they could do whatsoever they pleased. Sometime they play the guitar or banjo and sing. Saturday night they most generally went to the log house and danced" (Callie Washington, b. ca. 1859, AR, 2190). "We wasn't taught nothin' but to wuk, but we all had some good times too. We had frolics an'

dances wid fiddlin' music an' singin' wid old guitars" (Harriet Walker, b. ca. 1852, MS, 2159). "We could collect up at times in de evenin', even effen we was tired, and have some enjoyment layin' around under de big trees, hummin' and singin' to de tune of some old guitar" (Foster Weathersby, b. 1855, MS, 2228).

Occasionally guitars are tied to private recreation or self-expression, but like banjos they are most often described at dances accompanying vocalists and/or fiddles and other instruments. "My uncle would play his guitar in his cabin at night. At Christmas dey would have a dance on de plantation" (Jane Thompson, b. unk., MS, 353). "De slaves had a good time in deir quarters. Dey played guitar, danced 'fore de light went out. Dey put skin over a barrel for a drum. Dey talked about de master's business in dere quarters too" (Elizabeth Ross Hite, b. ca. 1850, LA, 107). "A fiddle and guitar would accompany singing at night 'outside de far shanty' and they would dance" (Laura Moore, b. ca. 1852, TX, 2745). "Dey would gib us a pass an' we could go visit on uder plantations an' go to frolics. We would meet wid fiddles an' guitars an' play an' sing an' dance" (Simon Durr, b. 1847, MS, 656).[49] "When they got through with their clothes on Saturday evenin's the Niggers which had sold their goobers and taters and bought fiddles and guitars would come out and play. The others w'ud clap hands and stomp they feet and we young ones would cut a step around" (Mary Reynolds, b. ca. 1835, LA, 3289).

Banjos and guitars were also played together. "Sho we had plenty o' banjo pickers! Dey was 'lowed to play banjos and guitars at night if de Patterollers didn't interfere" (Tim Thornton, b. ca. 1835, VA, 613). "At night, after their work was over, the slaves would meet out 'in the sticks' and dance in some of the old houses. . . . Banjos and guitars furnished the music" (George Caulton, b. 1844, VA, 170).[50] In 1879 Ernest Ingersoll (1852–1946) observed a Black guitar-banjo team singing on an Atlanta street. In 1873, en route from New Orleans to Mobile, Edward King's train stopped "at a little pine-built village, completely shrouded in foliage. . . . A party of roystering negro men and women, carrying banjos and guitars on their shoulders, left the

Fig. 5.3. "Stavin' Chain playing guitar and singing the ballad 'Batson,' (fiddler also in shot), Lafayette, La." June 1934. Photo by Alan Lomax. Lomax Collection, Library of Congress, Prints and Photographs Division. Stavin' Chain (Wilson Jones) with fiddler Octave Amos. In the background is Charles Gobert on banjo-guitar. "Batson" (Laws I 10) describes a turn-of-the-century murder in Lake Charles. For texts, see Lomax, *Country*, 338; Gordon, *Folk-Songs*, 45. Stavin' Chain's recorded performance appears on *Field Recordings, Vol. 16*, Document CD 5675.

forward car." (One of King's companions was outraged to spot a white man in the party.) Shortly afterward, King (1848–1896) reported from Palatka, Florida, that "the banjo and guitar, accompanying negro melodies, are heard in the streets."[51]

A few ex-slaves mentioned fiddles, banjos, and guitars together in full-fledged stringbands. "Saturdays' night the boss man gave us a big dance, regular breakdown with nigger banjo, guitar, and fiddle players. And man they gave the niggers plenty of whiskey" (Walter Leggett, b. 1855, NC, 2324).[52] Beginning in the late 1800s, however, the banjo definitely declined in Black ensembles, while fiddle-guitar duets proliferated. Indeed, though received wisdom holds that the fiddle too receded in twentieth-century Black music, some of the most successful and celebrated Black recording artists of the 1920s and '30s employed the fiddle-guitar format: Andrew Baxter (1869–1955) (fiddle) and James Baxter (1898–1950) (guitar); Henry "Son" Sims (Simms) (1890–1958) (fiddle) and Charley Patton (1891–1934) or Muddy Waters (1915–1983) (guitar); Eddie Anthony (1890–1934) (fiddle) and Peg Leg Howell (1888–1966) (guitar); Will Batts (1904–1956) (fiddle) and Frank Stokes (1888–1955), Dan Sing (Sane) (b. ca. 1900), or Jack Kelly (guitar); James Cole (fiddle) and Tommie Bradley (guitar); The Mississippi Sheiks: Lonnie Chatman (Chatmon) (1887–1950) (fiddle) and Walter Vinson (Jacobs) (1901–1975) (guitar); and others. Some of these acts played music rooted in the nineteenth century, while others offered contemporary blues, pop, or country music; but Black fiddle-and-guitar teams were definitely current by the late 1800s, when the majority of these performers were born. In the 1870s Lafcadio Hearn (1850–1904) heard a dance group featuring violin, guitar, and bass viol in a Black Cincinnati dance hall.[53] In the 1890s in the Arkansas Delta, Clifton Johnson (1865–1940) encountered a Black fiddler, Jack Hamilton, and mulatto guitarist, Ed Smith, performing "in one of the river towns" at "a dingy corner saloon frequented wholly by negroes."[54]

In the twentieth century, African American guitar styles would emerge as a world-class musical art. While all of this is meticulously documented for that period (thanks mainly to the miraculous invention of sound recording), I have found virtually no evidence for Black guitar styles before 1900. Many of the older guitarists recorded in the 1920s and '30s downpicked or strummed in a manner reminiscent of banjo rapping, which certainly makes sense and probably characterizes a great deal of early guitar playing, but this interpretation is tentative at best.[55]

What is certain is that since 1900 the self-accompanied singer-guitarist has assumed an absolutely central place in American music, and African African folk music was a major driving force. The blues was definitely at the forefront, but the guitar is suited to most vocal genres, and early blues singers often widened their appeal by alternating blues with other familiar materials: reels and ring plays, spirituals and hymns, ballads and love lyrics, blackface minstrel and Tin Pan alley songs. Beginning in the 1920s, many of these songsters would enjoy successful recording careers.[56] Though he was born twenty-five years before

Fig. 5.4. Elijah Cox, San Angelo, TX, 1937–38. Portraits of African American ex-slaves from the US Works Progress Administration, Federal Writers' Project slave narratives collection, Library of Congress.

the oldest of these recorded songsters, Elijah Cox might have been right at home in this company.

Elijah Cox (Uncle Cox) was freeborn in Michigan in 1843 and consequently was not a slave. Association with the ex-slaves, however, after he came to Fort Concho, Texas, in 1871, furnished him with a broad knowledge of slavery days and he wished to contribute the following song which he learned at Fort Concho, having heard the ex-slaves sing it many times, as it was one of their favorite songs:

SLAVERY DAYS

1

I am thinking today 'bout the times passed away,
When they tied me up in bondage long ago.
In old Virginia state, is where we separate.
And it fills my heart with misery and woe.
They took away my boy who was his mother's joy.
A baby from the cradle him we raised.
Then they put us far apart and it broke the old man's heart,
In those agonizing, cruel slavery days.

(Chorus)
Though they'll never come again let us give our praise to Him.
Who looks down where the little children play.
Every night and morn' we'll pray for them that's gone.
In those agonizing cruel slavery days.

2

My memory will steal o'er the old cabin floor and at night when all is dark.
We hear the watch dog bark and listen to the murmurs of the wind.
It seemed to say to me, you people must be free.
For the happy times are comin' Lord we pray.

(Chorus)

3

Forget now and forgive has always been my guide.
For that's what the Golden Scripture says.
But my memory will turn 'round back to when I was tied down and for them we'll weep and mourn.
For our souls were not our own,
In those agonizing cruel slavery days.

(Chorus)

4

I'm very old and feeble now my hair is turning gray.
I have traveled o'er the roughest kinds of roads.
Through all the toils and sorrows I have reached the end at last.
Now I'm resting by the wayside with my load.

(Chorus)
(Elijah Cox, b. 1843, TX, 952–53)

Uncle Cox accompanied himself on guitar. The file photo shows him forming a D-chord with his left hand, with the right in a position that could indicate fingerpicking but more likely frailing-style strum-

Fig. 5.5. Ed. Harrigan and David Braham, "Slavery Days" (New York: Wm. A. Pond, 1876).

ming. (For whatever reasons, several other early Black guitarists, including Lead Belly and Henry "Ragtime Texas" Thomas, favored playing in D-position.) Cox's selection is more easily identifiable. "Slavery Days" was composed in 1876 by Ed. Harrigan and David Braham and subsequently popularized by the vaudeville team of Harrigan & Hart.[57] Cox indicated that he learned the song from ex-slaves after moving in 1871 from Michigan to Fort Concho (est. 1867), now the city of San Angelo, in far West Texas. Although he also credited San Angelo's ex-slave population with educating him about slavery, most of the information he provided really came from his parents, former slaves who escaped from a Mississippi plantation to Canada and then to Michigan, where Cox was freeborn in 1843 (Elijah Cox, b. 1843, MI, TX, 950–51).

One assumes a song like "Slavery Days" would appeal widely to ex-slaves and their descendants, but excepting Elijah Cox's example there is little sign of the song's impact in Black tradition, or among whites either for that matter.[58] Cox's text does suggest oral transmission or recomposition, so "Slavery Days" may have been better-known to Blacks than this scant evidence suggests, around Fort Concho anyway. (Harrigan and Braham's original score features three verses and a chorus; Cox's version gives the first verse and chorus more or less as printed, but expands the original second and third verses into three stanzas.) Still, however this item's sentiments registered with ex-slaves or their children, whether or not they accepted, sang, and remade it, "Slavery Days" is self-evidently no slave song but rather a product of late nineteenth-century professional songwriters and popular print. It is also of a kind with innumerable items that were still available through sheet music or songbooks or, in even greater numbers, on commercial recordings at the time Cox was interviewed. And Cox's performance was very much of its immediate time and place, no doubt conforming to many notions of slavery and slave music then current. This may explain why Cox selected, or the white fieldworker (Woody Phipps) wholeheartedly accepted, this particular item.[59] Of course, this is also why Uncle Cox's performance seems so out of time and place in the ex-slave narratives, being more musically attuned to the 1930s than to true slavery days.

THE 'FORE DAY HORN

Massa Bob's house faced the quarters where he could hear us holler when he blowed the big horn fer us to git up. . . . I still got the bugle he woke us with at four in the mornin'. When the bugle blowed you'd better go to hollerin', so the overseer could hear you. If he had to call you, it was too bad. (Willis Winn, b. 1822, LA, 201, 203)

The banjo may be the typical instrument of the plantation negroes, but I have never seen a plantation negro play it. I have heard them make sweet music with the quills—Pan's pipes; I have heard them play passably well on the fiddle, the fife, and the flute; and I have heard them blow a tin-trumpet with surprising skill. (Joel Chandler Harris, "Plantation Music" [1883], 505, describing antebellum Putnam, Jasper, Morgan, Greene, Hancock, and Jones Counties, Georgia)

Ain't no mo' blowin' dat fo' day horn,
Will sing, chillun, will sing,
Ain't no mo' crackin' dat whip over John,
Will sing, chillun, will sing. (Georgianna Preston, b. ca. 1835, VA, 233–34)

In the pre-electronic world, wind instruments were major communications technologies, employed globally for signaling as well as musicmaking. The work horn in fact ranks third among the three most frequently named instruments in the ex-slave narratives, well behind the fiddle and banjo but far ahead of such populars as guitars, accordions, quills, or fifes; it is, without question, the most frequently named wind instrument.

Moreover, signal horns were not used solely to signal. Throughout the Black world they were also played musically. In Jamaica messenger horns sometimes served as melody instruments in dance bands. Observed Helen Roberts: "whether the sheep horn which is sometimes blown takes the place of some African animal's horn, I cannot say. Such horns are used in West Africa." In Jamaica, however, they "seem to be used chiefly for the dance-

Fig. 6.1. "Old Negro (former slave) with horn with which slaves were called." Marshall, TX, April 1939. Photo by Russell Lee. Farm Security Administration/Office of War Information Photograph Collection, Library of Congress, Prints and Photographs Division. The subject is Willis Winn, who had been photographed with his horn two years earlier when he was interviewed for the ex-slave narratives (fig. 6.6).

tunes, which are mostly of Scottish origin."[1] In Haiti Harold Courlander also found "cows' horns are played musically in some parts of the southern peninsula, though usually they are used as ritual instruments and signaling devices. . . . Conch-shell trumpets, known as *lambis*, are commonly used as signaling devices by fishermen. They are also to be found among the coumbites, in Rara festivities, and occasionally in rituals, where they are usually identified with sea deities."[2]

In the plantation South, horns were used mainly to regulate the regimen of slave labor, or for other forms of signaling, but the same cow horns and tin trumpets that woke slaves at four each morning may have sometimes been plumbed for musical possibilities. "We boys used to take the horns of a dead cow or bull, cut the end off of it, we could blow it, some having different notes. We could tell who was blowing and from what plantation" (Silas Jackson, b. 1846 or 1847, VA, 33). Visiting Fernandina, Florida, in the 1870s, S. W. G. Benjamin "was often amused by a rustic musical band which used to come to the hotel of an evening to earn a few pennies drumming on boxes and blowing on tin trumpets. If there was not much music in the performance, there was certainly a rhythm in the stroke and a prodigious earnestness in the efforts of the young musicians."[3] Joel Harris had also heard Georgia plantation slaves "blow a tin-trumpet with surprising skill."[4]

It is unclear exactly what Harris means by "surprising skill," or whether these performances were truly musical or mere noisy revelry. In turn-of-the-century New Orleans, however, Blacks definitely made music on signal horns, a formative influence on the greatest horn player of all time, Louis Armstrong (1901–1971). Armstrong was especially impressed by the rags-bottles-and-bones man Lorenzo, who advertised on a tin trumpet, the pie-man Santiago, who blew a "bugle" (possibly also a tin trumpet), and "Buglin' Sam, the Waffle Man" (self-explanatory). Lorenzo, Armstrong recalled, played "an old, tin, long horn, which he used to blow without the mouthpiece and he would actually play a tune on the darn thing. That knocked me out to hear him do that. He had soul, too."[5] Trombonist Edward "Kid" Ory (1886–1973) reported that Lorenzo had previously influenced cornetist Buddy Bolden (1877–1931), reputedly the first man to play jazz. Ferdinand "Jelly Roll" Morton (1890–1941)—who himself claimed to have invented jazz—declared "the rags-bottles-and-bones men would advertise their trade by playing the blues on the wooden mouthpieces of Christmas horns—yes sir, play more lowdown, dirty blues on those Kress horns than the rest of the country ever thought of" (Christmas horns because they were blown by street revelers at Christmas, many being supplied by the local Kress department store).[6] The white New Orleans cornetist Johnny Wiggs (1899–1977) described Kress horns as about three feet long, with a soldered reed in a wooden mouthpiece—roughly the same dimensions as the tin trumpets still owned by WPA narrators Willis Winn and Sylvia Cannon.

I guess only the most talented blues players went into the [bottle-and-bone] business, because the only ones I can remember played the most beautiful blues you could possibly imagine. It wasn't only one—they were all over town. And that sound later on I heard in Negro trumpet players. The same sound. The bending of notes which they are supreme on. No singing with the bottlemen. All of his talking was through his horn.[7]

New Orleans occupies a very special place in the history of horn playing, but such instruments were everywhere in the nineteenth-century South, including plantations. Granted, ex-slaves regarded signal horns as a species apart from fiddles, banjos, or guitars. There is but scant evidence that they ever figured in social dancing, the litmus for "real" music. They were often, perhaps most often blown by slaveholders or white overseers, suggesting that Europe's (and especially Britain's) long history of messenger horns was a primary and perhaps the main inspiration. There are only occasional hints of African connections, and then only hints. Nor does it appear that North American slaves ever played signal horns musically to the extent found elsewhere in the Black world. Yet these instruments were an inescapable part of the slaves' social and musical universe; Blacks did sometimes blow them; and in whatever small way, they obviously contributed something to the postwar crescendo of African American horn playing that transformed world music.

The foremost function of plantation horns was to regulate the workday: 4 a.m. get up; feed, curry, harness; breakfast; field; dinner; back-to-field; quit time; curfew; lights-out. "Ever' mornin' at four clock th' overseer blowed a conchshell an' all us niggers knowed it was time to git up an' go to work. Sometimes he blowed a bugle that'd wake up the nation" (Melvin Smith, b. 1841, SC, 289). "Slaves on the Harper plantation arose when the horn was sounded at four o'clock and hurried to the fields, although they would sometimes have to wait for daylight to dawn to see to work" (Emmaline Heard, b. ca. 1860, GA, 150). "Old

Fig. 6.2. "The Call to Labor." Detail from "Scenes on a Cotton Plantation." Engraving from a sketch by A. R. Waud. *Harper's Weekly* 11 (February 2, 1867): 72–73. A cowhorn trumpet, blown by a tenant on the Buena Vista Plantation, Clarke County, AL, just after the war.

missus would blow a horn, she called it the farm horn, it was made from a cow's horn and could be heard all over the farm. When she sounded that horn the slaves all knew to come to the house" (Katie Rose, b. ca. 1850, KY, 175). "When they returned from the fields they prepared supper for their families and many times had to feed their children in the dark, for a curfew horn was blown and no lights could be lighted after its warning note had sounded" (Matilda McKinney, b. 1855, GA, 89). "We wuz trained to live by signals of a ole cow horn. Us knowed whut each blow meant. All through de day de ole horn wuz blowed, to git up in de mo'nings, to go to de big kitchen out in Mars' back yard ter eat, to go to de fields, an' to come in an' on lak dat all day" (Dave Walker, b. 1850, MS, 2148–49).[8]

Often overseers blew these horns, sometimes slaveholders or the *nigger driver* (the slave straw boss). Frequently they were blown by slaves, however. "Ole Uncle Alex Hunt wuz the bugler an' ev'ry mornin' at 4:00 o'clock he blowed the bugle fer us ter git up" (Henry Rogers, b. 1864, GA, 220). "Ever'body was woke up at fo' o'clock by a bugle blowed mos'ly by a nigger" (Jim Allen, b. ca. 1850, AL, 4). "We'd git up early every day in de year, rain or shine, hot or cold. A slave blowed de horn and dere no danger of you not wakin' up when he blowed long and loud. He climb up on a platform 'bout ten feet tall to blow dat bugle" (Thomas Cole, b. 1845, AL, 227). "In slavery time de slaves wuz waked up every morning by de colored over-driver blowin' a horn. Ole man Jake Chisolm was his name. Jes' at daybreak, he'd put his horn through a crack in de upper part of de wall to his house an' blow it through dat crack" (Isaiah Butler, b. ca. 1855, SC, 158).

> The big niggers have to come out'n that bed 'bout fo' o'clock when the big horn blow. The overseer have one nigger, he wake up early for to blow the horn and when he blow this horn he make sich a holler then all the res' of the niggers better git out'n that bed and 'pear at the barn 'bout daylight. (Abram Sells, b. ca. 1850, TX, 12)

> There was also a slave known as a "caller." He came around to the slave cabins every morning at four o'clock and blew a "cow-horn" which was the signal for the slaves to get up and prepare themselves for work in the fields. . . . About sundown, the "cow-horn" of the caller was blown and all hands stopped work, and made their way back to their cabins. (Mack Mullen, b. 1857, GA, 235, 236)

Neal Upson's father, Harold Upson, lived his whole life on the same Georgia plantation. "Long as he lived he blowed his bugle evvy mornin' to wake up all de folkses on Marse Frank's plantation. He never failed to blow dat bugle at break of day 'cep on Sundays, and evvybody on dat place 'pended on him to wake 'em up" (Neal Upson, b. 1857, GA, 67).

Besides regulating the daily routine, horns responded to the unexpected. "They called us in frum the fields when a storm wuz blowin' up or when it wuz time to eat with a conch. When they blowed it

Fig. 6.3. Charlotte Beverly, ex-slave, Beaumont, TX. April 28, 1937. Portraits of African American ex-slaves from the US Works Progress Administration, Federal Writers' Project slave narratives collection, Library of Congress.

you could hear it fer' a mighty fur' piece too" (Milton Lackey, b. ca. 1860, MS, 1289). "De horn blowed fer em' to go to wuk an' to come in; an' if a fire broke out, or anything onusual. And we knowed what it meant by the signals" (Lucy Donald, b. 1857, MS, 638). "We had de dances down at de quarters and de white folks would come down and look on. Whenever us niggas on one plantation got ostreperous, white folks [had] hawns dey blowed. When de neighbors heard dat hawn here dey come to help make dat ostreperous nigga behave. Day blowed de hawn to call de neighbors if anybody died or were sick" (Richard Bruner, b. 1840, MO, 59).

Horns signaled other occasions and assemblies. "We had to get up at 3 A. M. in the morning, then we carried our breakfast to the field. . . . When we was working far from the house, we carried our dinner too, but if we was close by they blowed the horn" (Abe Kelley, b. ca. 1835, MS, 1269–70). "Each Sunday morning a bugle was blown and the slaves lined up in front of their cabins and each family was issued a week's 'rashing' consisting of 3–1/2# of meat and one peck of meal" (Ruben Laird, b. 1850, MS, 1297). "On

Saturday evening the horn would sound and every slave would come to get his allowance of provisions" (Henry Walker, b. ca. 1856, AR, 34). "Dey allus blow de horn for us mammies to come up and nuss de babies" (Betty Simmons, b. ca. 1837, TX, 23). "I'd blow the horn for the mudders of the little babies to come in from the fields and nurse 'em, in mornin' and afternoon" (Charlotte Beverly, b. ca. 1847, TX, 86).

Various seasonal activities also took place by the horn. "Den jes a lil atter midnight [at hog-killing time], de boss would blow de ol' horn, an' all de mens would git up an' git in dem hog pens" (Joseph Holmes, b. 1856, VA, 194). "Marse Stone had a big sugar camp with 300 trees. We would be waked up at sunup by a big horn and called to get our buckets and go to the sugar camps and bring water from the maple trees" (Bert Mayfield, b. 1852, KY, 14). "At night [during cotton picking] dey blow'd de horn for 'em to bring in de cotton w'ut de women spinned" (Angie Garrett, b. ca. 1845, De Kalb, MS, 134).

> Niggers all laked thrashin' time. Marster, he growed lots of wheat and de thrashin' machine tuk turn about gwine f'um one plantation to another. Dey had big dinners on thrashin' days and plenty of toddy for de thrashin' hands atter dey done de wuk. Dey blowed de bugle to let 'em know when dey done finished up at one place and got ready to go on to de nex' one. (Alice Hutcheson, b. ca. 1860, GA, 285)

At least one plantation used a horn-and-bell as a scarecrow: "We had 100's o' acres o' rice, rye, an' wheat. My job (me an' one more nigger) had to blow de horn an' ring de bell to keep de birds away" (Henry Murray, b. 1840, AL, 1615, orig. parentheses).[9]

Horns also announced religious services. Will Parker reported, "we had meetings in the brush arbor when the preacher blew the bugle" (Will Parker, b. 1842, GA, 3018), while Andrew Moody recalled "when a hand die they all stop work the nex' day after he die and they blow the horn and old Uncle Bob, he pray and sing songs" (Andrew Moody, b. 1855, TX,

117).[10] In Africa, horns and other wind instruments serve as spirit voices in death rites. African Americans sometimes expressed these ideas: "Old Joe's daid an' gone / But his hant blows de hawn, / An' his houn' howls still / From the top er dat hill!"[11] In the 1800s South, however, horn-blowing was simply the accepted way to assemble slaves, so any African link seems tenuous. In towns and cities, European-style church bells were already the norm, so too on many plantations. "The preacher buried the dead with song and prayer. When it was time for the funeral, the big plantation bell rang, and all would come to the graveyard" (Virginia Harris, b. ca. 1855, MS, 941).

Henry Green categorically stated: "dey neber had no farm bells in slabery times fer ter ring en call de hans in en outen de fiel's. Dey hed horns whut dey blowed early en late. De wuk wud go on till hit so dark dat dey can't see. Den de horn wud blow en de niggers all cum in en git dey supper" (Henry Green, b. 1848, AL, 96). Green was constantly contradicted. "We get up when de morning star rises. De overseer he ring a bell, but we'd be 'round befo' dat mos' times. I was little gal wen dey put me in de cotton fiel" (Hanna Fambro, b. 1850, GA, 334). "When I was a little fellow, the first bell was rung on the plantation at three o'clock in the mornin' during summer time. That was a signal for the slaves to rise, get their breakfasts ready to go to the fields when the second bell rang—at four o'clock" (W. B. Allen, b. 1850, AL, 9). "Ev'y mornin' bout fo' 'clock ol' master would ring de bell for us to git up by an yo could hear dat bell ringin all over de plantation. I can hear hit now. Hit would go ting-a-ling, ting-a-ling" (Millie Evans, b. 1849, NC, 240). "Eat out in the yard, at the cabins, in the kitchen. Eat different places owin to what you be workin at when the bell rung. Big bell on a high post" (Maria Sutton Clemments, b. ca. 1850, GA, 18). "Old marse Bill had a big bell hangin' high in his back yard. An' dat bell rung ebery mornin' an' at dinner an' when eber any thing went wrong bout de place" (Alex Montgomery, b. 1857, GA, 1526). "Deir wuz a time fer everything, de big bell wuz rung fer us to git up in de mornings an' rung fer us to go to de big kitchen to eat an' go to w'uk, an' to come in from de fiel's an' on lak dat" (Lawerence Evans, b. 1858, MS, 704). "We was woke by a bell and called to eat by a bell and put to bed by that bell and if that bell ring outta time you'd see the niggers jumpin' rail fences and cotton rows like deers or something, gettin' to that house, 'cause that mean something bad wrong at massa's house" (Nancy Jackson, b. 1830, TX, 194). "De slaves git so's dey sacred to hear de bell ring. Don' know what it mean. Maybe death, maybe fire, maybe nudder sale o some body. Gwine take 'em way. But when de bell ring dey had to come. Let dat ole bell ring and de woods full o negroes. Maybe 500 come from all over dat country" (Mollie Moss, b. ca. 1855, TN, 58).

When there was distressful news master would ring the bell. When the niggers in the fiel' would hear the bell everyone would lis'en an wonder what the trouble was. You'd see 'em stirrin' too. They would always ring the bell at twelve 'clock. Sometime then they would think it was somethin' serious an they would stan up straight but if they could see they shadow right under 'em they would know it was time for dinner. (Millie Evans, b. 1849, NC, 245)

An old negro man rang a bell to wake slaves up and to call them in from the fields, said Aunt Jennie Bowen. After the Surrender, this old negro stayed on the place and one day when he was out in the fields with others working on the farm, and one of the Fishers rang the bell for them to come in to dinner. All came in but the old man and when asked later why he didn't come, he said "No bell ringing fa' me, I'se a free nigger!" (Jennie Bowen, b. ca. 1847, AL, 70)[12]

Some plantations alternated horns and bells or used them in concert. "Overseer, he said [had] a darky to ring bell or blow horn 4 o'clock to get up mornings" (Sam Anderson, b. 1839, MS, 6). "Den when dey ring dem bells en blow dem horns in de mornin, dat mean you better get up en go bout your task for dat day" (John Glover, b. 1860, SC, 139). "The master had bells

and horns to wake up the slaves. They would start their work at daybreak, soon as the bells ring and the horns blow. At noon the bells ring and the horns would blow again. The slaves come in from the fields and go to the long kitchen eating place" (Maggie Pinkard, b. ca. 1855, TN, 257).

Most narrators seem to recall European-style clapper bells, but struck bells are occasionally mentioned: "When Master was gone off to preach the overseer got so mean and would whip de niggers so bad, mistiss run him off, they had 'bout one-hundred slaves and would wake dem up by beating on a big piece of sheet iron with a long piece of steel" (George Strickland, b. ca. 1856, MS, 397–98). "Ol' Marster would have de slaves waked up evey morning by knockin' a big piece of steel wid a hammer. When day come, all de slaves was in de' fiel'. Dey worked 'till dark" (Jeff Nunn, b. 1862, AL, 279).[13]

Horns also announced mail and stagecoaches. "I 'member stagecoach. Had erbout six or eight hosses to 'em. Driver'd blow bugle for stops jus' like trains. Dey didn' have much trains dem days" (Ruben Woods, b. ca. 1853, AL, 212). "Oh! Lord, yes, I remember the stage coach. As many times as I run carry the mail to them when they come by! They blew a horn before they got there and you had to be on time 'cause they could not wait. There wus a stage each way each day, one up and one down" (Sarah Louise Augustus, b. ca. 1855, NC, 52).

The mail was carried in the same kind of vehicle [as planters' carriages] with negro drivers. In each town there was a certain rack at which this mail carriage would stop in each village or wherever the designated stop was made. Upon nearing the rack and coming to a stop, the driver would blow a bugle call which could be heard for miles around, and people hearing this bugle would come and get their mail. The Reverend remembers that several of these drivers froze to death during the cold weather and that in the winter, many times the horses on the mail carriage upon coming to this rack would stop, and the driver would be sitting frozen to death in his seat. Men would take him down, carefully saving the silk beaver-skin hat for some other driver. (Rev. Wamble [Womble], b. 1859, MS, 203–4)[14]

I didn't even have to carry a pass to leave my own place like other Niggers. I had a cap with a sign on it: "Dont bother this Nigger or there will be hell to pay." I went after the mail in the town all the time. The mail came in coaches and they put on fresh horses at Pineapple. The coachman would run the horses into Pineapple with a big-to-do and a blowing the bugle to get the fresh horses ready. I got the mail. (Cato Carter, b. 1836 or 1837, AL, 644)

I does a little bit of everything round de hotel, helps folks off de stage when it druv up, wait on table and sich. When I hears de horn blow—you know, de stage driver blow it when dey top de hill 'bout two miles 'way, to let you know dey comin'—I sho' hustle 'round and git ready to meet it. (William Davis, b. 1845, TN, 291)

In coastal South Carolina and Georgia horns were used as flatboat signals.[15]

Throughout the world horns are also used in hunting to signal others or direct dogs to the kill. "They kept hounds. Colonel Radford's boys and the colored boys all went hunting. We had 'possum and taters all along in winter; 'possum grease won't make you sick. Eat all you want. I'd hear their horn and dogs" (Ida Rigley, b. 1855, VA, 44). In 1860 D. R. Hundley mocked Southern planters' sons aping English Cavaliers by fox hunting. "Preparatory to entering upon the latter rare old English sport, our young gentleman gets some one of the many dusky uncles on his father's plantation, to procure him a deep intoned horn."[16] (The fox hunter's horn was, of course, an established element of British foxhunting tradition, the Black slave presumably procuring a suitable horn of that description.)

In the plantation South, however, dogs and horns were also used to hunt humans. "Pa said the nigger men run off to get a rest. They'd take to the woods and

canebrakes. . . . The master and paddyrolls took after 'em. They'd been down in there long 'nough. . . . They heard the dogs and the horn" (Mag Johnson, b. ca. 1870, AR, child of ex-slaves, 108–9). "I never will forgit de Klu Klux Klan. Never will forgit de way dat horn soun' at night when dey was a-goin' after some mean Nigger" (Dora Franks, b. ca. 1837, MS, 54). Long after freedom, horns remained tied to white vigilantes. "My mother-in-law was from Memphis. One day she went to church and de Ku Klux Klan came in and beat de people over deir heads with pistols. De people went out de doors and windows. Dey could just blow a horn and de Ku Klux Klan would come from all directions" (Dave Harper, b. 1850, MO, 164).

As a *nigger driver* on an Alabama plantation, ex-slave author James Williams (b. 1805, MD) had himself been obliged to track runaways. After an escape was reported, the overseer "blew the 'nigger horn,' as it is called, for the dogs. This horn was only used when we went in pursuit of fugitives. It is a cow's horn, and makes a short, loud sound."[17] WPA narrators definitely recalled the nigger horns and *nigger dogs*. When Lizzie Hawkens's uncle went wife-visiting without permission, his slaveholders set the dogs on him. "The dog's come up around him. He took a pine knot and killed the lead dog, hit him in the head and put him in a rotten knot hole of a hollow tree been burned out and just flew. The dogs scattered and he heard the horns. He heard the dogs howl and the hoofs of the men's horses" (Lizzie Hawkens, b. ca. 1870, AR, child of ex-slaves, 207). Against odds, Lizzie's uncle escaped there and back undetected, dead dog undiscovered.

Guinea Jim, an incorrigible runaway, was less fortunate. "'Twixt daylight and sunup us all standing at de gate and we heared a fine little horn up de road. Us didn't know what it meant coming to de house. And bimeby Mr. Beesley, what live not fur from Marse Ike, he rode up with five dogs, five nigger dogs, what dey call 'em." After a lengthy pursuit, Jim was finally trapped and whipped by Beesley, who, despite Jim's desperate pleas, set the dogs on him. "Dey caught Jim and bit him right smart. You see dey had to let em bite him a little to satisfy de dogs. Jim could have made it, 'cept he was all hot and worn out" (Josh Horn, b. 1853, AL, 206, 209).

By the same token, horns could warn fugitives of pursuers' approach:

> During de war deir wuz a heap o' [Confederate] deserters hid out. De Cavalrymen would ride through a hunting 'em. We could most nigh alwas' hear 'em coming long fo' dey got in sight, de womens would blow a horn sos dey could hide from 'em. I'se carried food to de woods to de deserters. Sometimes we would have to take it a long ways an' agin dey would be near by. (Julia Stubbs, b. 1852, MS, 2070)

Many of these horns belonged to whites, of course; in fact, at some times and places in the antebellum South, slaves were forbidden to play horns (especially signal horns) as well as drums.[18] Even such periodic bans were never universal or universally enforced, however, and plantation slaves constantly blew horns (and banged drums), whether for their own purposes or at slaveholders' behest. Moreover, some of these horns were of the slaves' own making, used to signal one another. "We boys used to take the horns of a dead cow or bull, cut the end off of it, we could blow it, some having different notes. We could tell who was blowing and from what plantation" (Rev. Silas Jackson, b. 1846 or 1847, VA, 33). "When we wanted to meet at night we had an old conk, we blew that. We all would meet on the bank of the Potomac River and sing across the river to the slaves in Virginia, and they would sing back to us" (James V. Deane, b. 1850, MD, 8).

Moreover, while slaves may have taken cues from slaveholders, messenger horns are also known throughout Africa and the Black diaspora, in the same forms and with the same functions found in Europe and elsewhere. In coastal areas of Africa, fishers and boatmen have for centuries signaled with conch trumpets.[19] African hunting horns are also numerous. Among the Basongye the *epudi* (an ocarina) is used to signal while hunting but also to accompany hunting songs.[20] Many horns serve such dual purposes. Traversing central Africa between 1868 and 1871, Georg

Fig. 6.4. "An Ashantee Soldier." Guinea Coast, 1820. Joseph Dupuis, *Journal of a Residence in Ashantee* (London: Henry Colburn, 1824), fac. 193. Slavery Images: A Visual Record of the African Slave Trade and Slave Life in the Early African Diaspora. slaveryimages.org. With his European trade-rifle, the warrior carries a side-blown signal horn with three finger-holes. The trumpeter blows into or across the hole near the horn's tip.

Schweinfurth found "a great number of signal-horns may be seen made from the horns of different antelopes; these are called 'mangoal,' and have three holes like small flutes, and in tone are not unlike fifes. There is one long and narrow pipe cut by the Bongo out of wood which they call a 'mburrah' . . . very similar to the ivory signal-horns which are so frequently to be seen in all the negro countries."[21] Schweinfurth reports that some of these items were also played musically, or used for music by one group and for signaling by another.

Military bugling was also common throughout Africa, though even there more recent examples may suggest European influences.[22] Thomas Winterbottom observed ivory bugles on the Guinea Coast around 1800:

> The tusks of young elephants, called scrivellas, are hollowed and made into a kind of flute with stops, which emit a very shrill sound. Upon the Gold Coast, these are used like bugle horns, to convey the orders of the general in the time of an engagement, and so skillful are they, that if any part of the army appears to give ground, the general, by ordering his trumpeter to blow a particular note,

which is immediately understood, generally succeeds in imparting fresh courage, and in restoring them to order.[23]

There were African work horns as well. The *phalaphala* was the Venda version of an antelope-horn trumpet once played across southern Africa. "A chief has his official signaller or envoy, who is deputed to summon his subjects to work for him, on occasions when cooperative work is necessary, or to call the dancers from various kraals to the chief's kraal to execute the national dance called *tshikona*. In the former days the *phalaphala* sounded the call to arms."[24] African street vendors used horns, too. Fish merchants in Zanzibar traditionally blew conchs to inform customers the fresh catch had arrived, but by 1900 fish vendors in Cape Town were blowing tin horns like those found in New Orleans and the American South. According to Kirby "these 'horns' consist of conical tubes of tin with a mouthpiece, in the form of that regularly used in a trumpet, soldered to the narrow end," his own specimen being "twelve and a half inches over all."[25]

Possibly, then, this African background served some role in the plantation South, and later African American horn playing definitely displays African characteristics (rough tonality, voicelike effects, and so on). However, North American Black musicmakers have always favored European-style brass and wind instruments, and even in the colonial and antebellum eras evidence of African horn types in North America is virtually nonexistent. WPA informants were characteristically vague—many simply named such instruments as *horns* or *bugles*—and interviewers seldom pursued the subject, but there is no question that numerous different horns were used on Southern plantations. Most varieties ex-slaves identified, however, have been employed globally since antiquity—the conch trumpet, for example. "De oberseer would blow dat big 'konk' every mornin' at de break of day an' den de men had ter git ter de lot an' feed de mules an' hosses an' den dey would eat dey own breakfast an' git ter dat fiel'" (Charity Jones, b. ca. 1853, MS, 1194).[26] Conch trumpets are known in Africa,

but there is no reason to assume African influence in southern US examples.

Throughout the world, animal horns are also used as trumpets. "'The overseer on the plantation had a horn', said Aunt Cicely, 'a great big ram's horn. I never did see such a big horn. It was 'bout two feet long. The overseer blowed it about two hours before day. The darkies had to get up and cook their breakfast, and curry their mules and start for the field'" (Aunt Cicely Cawthon, b. 1859, GA, 183). "Everything 'bout dis plantation wuz kept gwine by de blow ob de ole cow horn. Dey had a signal fer everything, when to go to Ole Missus's fer meals, to de fiel's an' when to come in an' out lak dat. Dis ole horn wuz over a foot long, it wuz polished up 'till hit wuz plumb shinnin', a cord wuz fastened through a hole at one end an' kept hangin' on de back piazza" (Laura Ford, b. 1852, MS, 756).[27] Africa teems with such instruments, but in Africa animal-horn trumpets are typically side-blown or transverse (the performer blows into or across a hole in the instrument's side). In Europe and elsewhere they are, of course, end-blown, and this was always so among North American Blacks, at least as far as the record shows (side-blown horns are known in Latin America and the West Indies).

There are rare intimations of true African horn types among North American slaves. In 1895 the New York *Sun* printed a South Carolina slaveholder's recollections of antebellum corn shuckings:

Most plantations had a bugler who owned an old wooden bugle five or six feet long. These bugles were made generally of poplar wood coated with tar, and kept under water for several days. Soaking it kept the instrument from shrinking, and gave it a resonant sound which could be heard for miles on a clear night. The bugles were carried to the corn shuckin's, and the coming darkies would blow and blow, and be answered by the bugler at the corn pile, and as he did so he would say "Dar's the niggers comin' from Byers's plantation." "Dar dey is from Elliott's." As they drew nearer to the pile of corn the bugle blowers would stop and give way to quill or reed blowers.[28]

Fig. 6.5. Tin horn announcing tobacco auction, Lynchburg, VA, 1870s. Edward King, *The Great South* (1875), 560.

Fig. 6.6. Willis Winn, ex-slave, Marshall, TX. September 7, 1937. Portraits of African American ex-slaves from the US Works Progress Administration, Federal Writers' Project slave narratives collection, Library of Congress.

Large wooden trumpets of this sort also occur globally from antiquity, but are especially common in Africa and the diaspora.[29] In Central Africa in the 1860s, Georg Schweinfurth observed the *manyinyee*, "huge wooden tubes which may be styled the trumpets of the Bongo. . . . They vary from four to five feet in length, being closed at the extremity, and ornamented with carved work representing a man's head, which not unfrequently is adorned with a couple of horns."[30] Manyinyee were side-blown, just like the Haitian *piston*, a similar large wooden horn "capable of playing a range of tones."[31] In Jamaica, end-blown wooden trumpets actually called *wooden trumpets* were featured in mento music, a precursor of ska, rocksteady, and reggae. (Equipped with finger holes for producing different pitches, they supplied the bass.)[32] The technique of soaking or wetting wooden horns—causing them to swell and rendering them airtight—is also commonplace in Africa and throughout the Black world.[33] This is, however, the only case I have come across of such instruments in North America.

By the mid-1800s, mass-produced tin trumpets were the new standard, especially in cities. In Lynchburg, Virginia, the Black worker who blew a long tin horn to announce tobacco auctions became a local landmark, repeatedly featured in period travelogues.[34] Moreover, besides signaling, by the turn of the twentieth century Blacks were definitely playing tin trumpets musically in New Orleans, and possibly earlier elsewhere. Tin horns were also well-known on antebellum plantations, several surviving into the twentieth century. Willis Winn (b. 1822, LA) was photographed on two separate occasions with his slaveholder's tin bugle (figs. 6.1 and 6.6), and Sylvia Cannon also still possessed a tin plantation horn.

> I got Miss Hatchel horn bout here now dat been through nearly 100 head of people. If you talk on it, dere be 100 head of automobiles to see what it is. I sold old Massa's sword last week for ten cents, but I ain' gwine do away wid his old horn. (4 ft. long, 15 in. cross big end 1 in. from top end. Mouth piece is gone. Catch about 15 in. from top). Can talk to anybody 15 to 16 miles away en dat how-come I don' want to sell it cause if anything happen, I can call people to come. Dis horn ain' no tin, it silver.

It de old time phone. (Sylvia Cannon, b. ca. 1857, SC, 192, orig. parentheses)

Numerous other bugles and horns named by narrators were probably tin trumpets. On the other hand, there is a distinct possibility that some of the bugles they mentioned actually were European-style brass bugles. Certainly slaves were familiar with these. "I would get up many mornings and hear the [Union] bugler blowin'. Das when dey was callin' the pickets in. You would see de pickets come in just a-flyin' and out went de fresh pickets on duty. I was not scared of dem" (Rhody Holsell, b. 1848, MO, 196).

Yankee soldiers? Oh Lord—seed em by fifties and hundreds. Used to pint the gun at me jest to hear me holler and cry. I was scared of em. They come in and went in Dr. Jenkins' dairy and got what they wanted. And every morning they'd blow that bugle, bugle as long as a broom handle. Heard em blow "Glory, Glory Hallelujah." I liked to hear em blow it. (Neely Gray, b. ca. 1855, AR, 84)

One bunch [of Confederate soldiers] come and stay in de woods across de road from de overseer's house, and dey was all on hosses. Dey lead de hosses down to Bois d' Arc Creek every morning at daylight and late every evening to git water. When we going to de field and when we coming in we allus see dem leading big bunches of hosses. Dey bugle go jest 'bout time our old horn blow in de mornin'. (Katie Rowe, b. ca. 1850, AR, 279)

Quand les Yankee remtre [entre] dans les quarters, me tande le cor, tout moune suivi ye, ye. Di si vous aute oli, vind e'est comme ca. Dans la campagne, ye te tout frere, soeur, cousines. Chacun te gaignain so l'habitation. (When the Yankees entered the quarters, we heard the bugle, we all followed. They said if you all want to follow, come on. It's that way in the country, they were all brothers, sisters and cousins. Each one had his plantation.) (Francis Doby, b. ca. 1838, LA, 61, orig. translation, brackets, and parentheses)[35]

Granted, *bugle* or *trumpet* can refer to any horn, but there were more than a few brass bugles and trumpets around the wartime South, and when Carrie Davis said "I 'members, too, dat de overseer waked us up wid a trumpet" (Carrie Davis, b. ca. 1855, GA, 106), there is at least a possibility that she was recalling a melody played on a brass bugle or valve trumpet. More likely, though, she remembered a tin trumpet, conch, or animal horn.

However signaling was accomplished, on the average plantation these messages sounded constantly all day. "We got up by a bell and went to bed by a horn, you better get up to go when you hear that bell, Watson's overseer come to the door to see" (William H. Watson, b. ca. 1850, TN, 377). "A horn wuz blowed afore day fer de slaves to git up an' feed de stock an' harnes' 'em ready fer de fiel's. When de horn blowed agin hit meant to go to Mars' to eat breakfas'. By de break o' day de slaves wuz in de fiel's ready to wuk" (Edwin Walker, b. 1849, MS, 2153–54). "De oberseer blowed a horn every mornin' and de slaves knowed to git up, an' when dat horn blowed agin, dey knowed dey must go to de fiel'. Dey blowed de horn at dinner an' night. Afte' supper, we set 'bout an' sing an' go places" (Fanny Smith Hodges, b. unk., MS, 1025).[36] "A big [horn] wuz blowed fer signals. We all knowed what each blow meant. We knowed by de blows ob de horn when to go to Marse's big kitchen to eat. . . . De horn blowed fer em to go to wuk an' to come in; an' if a fire broke out, or anything onusual. And we knowed what it meant by the signals" (Lucy Donald, b. 1857, MS, 637–38).

As a result, throughout the plantation South horns and bells were heard incessantly near and far. "You could hear dat bugle de overseer blowed to wake up de slaves for miles and miles" (Ed McCree, b. 1861, GA, 60). "On Saturday evening the horn would sound and every slave would come to get his allowance of provisions. They used a big bell hung up in a tree to call them to meals and to begin work. They could also hear other farm bells and horns" (Henry Walker, b. ca. 1856, AR, 29). "Long 'fore day, dat overseer blowed a bugle to wake up de Niggers. You could hear it far as High

Shoals, and us lived dis side of Watkinsville. Heaps of folks all over dat part of de country got up by dat old bugle" (Addie Vinson, b. 1852, GA, 103–4). "Farm bells could be heard for miles, calling the workers to the midday meal and also to services every Sunday morning" (Queen Elizabeth Bunts, b. ca. 1865, GA, child of ex-slaves, 119). "The master blew on a big conch shell every morning at four o'clock, and when the first long blast was heard the lights 'gin to twinkle in every Nigger cabin.' Charlie, chuckling, recalled that 'ole Master blowed that shell so it could-a-been heard for five miles'" (Charlie King, b. ca. 1850, GA, 17).

> Come de daybreak . . . you can hear a old bell donging 'way on some plantation a mile or two off, and den more bells at other places and maybe a horn, and purty soon yonder go old Master's old ram horn wid a long toot and den some short toots, and here comes de overseer down de row of cabins, hollering right and left. . . . Bells and horns! Bells for dis and horns for dat! All we knowed was go and come by de bells and horns! (Charley Williams, b. 1843, LA, 335)

In Africa signal horns may literally speak by imitating the pitch contours of tonal African languages. Like American fiddlers, African American horn players made their instruments talk by imitating voices or vocal music, but without conveying specific meanings. Plantation horns did send very particular messages, however, and through various means. In some cases they were simply tied to standing orders or verbal instructions. "It just like dis, de overseer didn' have to be right behind you to see dat you work in dem days. Dey have all de fields name en de overseer just had to call on de horn en tell you what field to go work in dat day" (Sylvia Cannon, b. ca. 1857, SC, 191).

> When I was big enough for the field I would have to go down to the quarters in the evening and hear the rules for the next day. The overseer would get the field negroes all together and give out the rules. If he say, "Henry, tomorrow you pick cotton on

> the west side of the north field," or maybe "you cut four or five good ricks of wood on the south woods lot close to the cane patch side," that would be what I do the next day as soon as that old bell ring. We never have to ask in the morning, because we already had our rules and could go to work on the bell. (Henry Clay, b. ca. 1835, NC, 111–12)

Horns and bells were also combined with another pre-electronic communications medium: the holler. "Dey knowed how to git you up alright—de overseer had a horn dat he blowed an' dem dat didn't wake up when de horn wuz blowed wuz called by some of the others in de quarters" (Amanda Jackson, b. unk., GA, 289). "De overseer, Bill Rowell wus good ter us too, he never worked dem very hard, he blowed a horn ever morning and would holler and say 'I can't get you up dis morning', and den cum round ergin and holler 'Get up frum dar, get your shoes, get your hat, you ought ter be gone, I can't get you up dis morning'" (Sol Webb, b. unk., AL, 441).[37]

Some plantations simply dispensed with horns and bells for hollering alone. "Ebery mornin' he [slaveholder] wud put his han's ober his mouf an' holler, an' dem niggers wud git outern dat bed an' git ter wuk. Marse Elbert hed a mity loud voice, an' when he called, ebry body culd hear him. He had no horn an' he had no bell, he jist holler'd" (Sarah Felder, b. 1852, MS, 713). "An old negro called 'Ole Man Ben' called us to eat. We called him the dinner bell because he would say 'Who-e-e, Goddam your blood and guts'" (George Henderson, b. 1860, KY, 6). "When they fed the children, they cook the food and put it in a great big tray concern and called up the children, 'Piggee-e-e-e, piggee-e-e-e.' My cousin was the one had to go out and call the children; and you could see them runnin' up from every which way, little shirt tails flyin' and hair sticking out. Then they would pour the food out in different vessels till the children could get around them with those mussel-shell spoons" (Amanda Ross, b. 1856, AL, 81–82). "Durin' the week days the field hands would work 'till the sun was jes' goin' down, an' then the overseer would holler 'all right', an' that was the signal to quit. All hands knocked off Saturday noon" (Virginia Bell, b. ca. 1850, LA, 245). "On our plantation Marse Tom had a nigger driver. He'd 'hoop and holler and wake us up at break of day. But befo' freedom come 'long, Marse got a bell; den dat nigger driver rung dat bell at break of day. He was a sorry nigger dat never had no quality in him a'tall, no siree" (Gus Feaster, b. ca. 1840, SC, 49).

Jack Maddox remembered the driver singing a "gettin' up song":

That old bald nigger
With shiny eyes
He's too hard for me.
This old way
A gittin' up fore day
It's too hard for me. (Jack Maddox, b. ca. 1849, TX, 2532)

Many ex-slaves were acquainted firsthand with military bugling and bugle calls. "When the Yankees come to Atlanta they just forced us into the army. After I got into the army and got used to it, it was fun—just like meat and bread. Yankees treated me good. I was sorry when it broke up. When the bugle blowed we knowed our business" (Tom Windham, b. 1845, GA, 210). "Papa went to the War. He could blow his bugle and give all the war signals. He got the military training. Him and his friend Charlie Grim used to step around and show us how they had to march to orders. His bugle had four joints. I don't know what went with it. From what they said they didn't like the War and was so glad to get home" (Nancy Anderson, b. ca. 1870, child of ex-slaves, MS, 50).

During the war even the little children were taught to listen for bugle calls and know what they meant. We had to know—and how to act when we heard them. One day, I remember we were to have peas for dinner, with ham hock and corn bread. I was hungry that day and everything smelled so good. But just as the peas were part of them out of the pot and in a dish on the table the signal came "To Arms." Cannon followed almost immediately. We

all ran for the cellar, leaving the food as it was. (Adeline Blakely, b. 1850, TN, 187)

Some plantations may have employed similar calls, assigning specific messages to particular melodies. Simon Hare remembered: "de Mistis always send ter meet de mail, quick as she hear him play dat tune on a bugle like. . . . Driv a surrey wid two horses. Didn' stop, no'm. Th'owed off Marster's mail, come frum Mobile. Sometimes he brung iron same as letters; had ter git it frum Mobile, too" (Simon Hare, b. 1849, AL, 915). Signaling on most plantations seems to have been more rudimentary, however, simply varying the number or duration of notes, for instance. "Irene recalls the practice of blowing a horn whenever a sudden rain came. The overseer had a certain Negro to blow three times and if shelter could be found, the slaves were expected to seek it until the rain ceased" (Irene Coates, b. 1859, GA, 77). "[At war's end] Marster was cryin' and said, 'I do not own you any longer.' He told her [McLean's grandmother] to get the horn and blow it. It was a ram's horn. She blew twice for the hands to come to the house" (James Turner McLean, b. 1858, NC, 85). On one Virginia plantation, recalled ex-slave author Francis Fedric (b. 1805), "the horn gave three or four quick blasts for all hands to return from the fields."[38] Describing Reconstruction Alabama, *Harper's* reported "in the outside churches the congregations are collected by blowing long tin horns, it being understood that at the third horn service begins."[39]

Finally, signal horns may have occasionally been used for musicmaking, but ex-slaves definitely did not class them with other musical instruments. Fiddles, banjos, and guitars evoked memories of the best of times; horns reminded many of the whip. "Our overseer got us up by light and blowed er horn en I seed him whup er slave one day, wid er Bull-Whip" (Sara Benton, b. 1846, AL, 62). "Master Henry didn't low no overseer on the place. One of my uncles was 'Driver.' Master blowed that old conk-shell long 'fore day and if the darkies didn't get going you'd hear the whips cracking" (Campbell Davis, b. 1852, TX, 1064). "The overseer woke us up. Sometimes he had a kin' of horn to blow, and when you heered that horn, you'd better git up. He would give you a good whippin' iffen he had to come wake you up" (Austin Grant, b. unk., MS, 84). "Moster looked after his own place and it was just very seldom he whipped any of them and then it wus because they would not work and he got us up early too, and they had to work till about dark and got us up by blowing a horn" (Emma Jones, b. 1849, GA, 227). "Well, the horn would blow every morning for you to git up and go right to work; when the sun riz' if you were not in the field working, you would be whipped with whips and leather strops" (Clayborn Gantling, b. 1848, GA, 141). "When that horn blows, you better git out of that house, 'cause the overseer is comin' down the line, and he ain't comin' with nothin' in his hand" (Columbus Williams, b. 1841, AR, 156). "I never git whip, 'cause I allus git my 300 pound [quota of cotton]. Us have to go early do dat, when de horn goes early, befo' daylight" (Sarah Ashley, b. 1844, TX, 35). "Our overseer wus Mr. Green Ross and he wus a bad un too, mean, my goodness, whup you in er minute, put you in de buck and tie your feet, whup you er sight. He waked de slaves wid er horn, blowing hit fore day and us worked till dark" (Sara Colquitt, b. ca. 1830, VA, 100).

In this dread capacity, the 'fore day horn regularly figures in slave folktales and songs:

No slav'ry chains to tie me down,
And no mo' driver's ho'n to blow fer me
No mo' stocks to fasten me down
Jesus break slav'ry chain, Lord
Break slav'ry chain Lord,
Break slav'ry chain Lord,
De Heben gwinter be my home. (Harriett Gresham, b. 1838, SC, 161)[40]

Fannie Berry pointedly combined this same piece with "Cold Frosty Morning," an 1840s minstrel composition depicting happy, carefree slaves off to work in the freezing dawn.

Ain't no mor' blowin' of dat four-day ['fore day] horn,
I will sing, brethern, I will sing.

A col' frosty mornin'.
De nigger's mighty good,
Take your ax upon your shoulder,
Nigger talk [take] to de woods.

Ain't no mor' blowin' of dat four-day horn,
I will sing, brethern, I will sing. (Fannie Berry, b. 1841, VA, 38)[41]

The slave's reality was somewhat different, of course. George Taylor Burns's parents were sold away when he was five. "Motherless, hungry, desolate and unloved, he often cried himself to sleep at night while each day he was compelled to carry wood. One morning he failed to come when the horn was sounded to call the slaves to breakfast. 'Old Miss went to the negro quarters to see what was wrong.' and 'She was horrified when she found I was frozen to the bed'" (George Taylor Burns, b. ca. 1835, MO, 37).

Some ex-slaves actually boasted of being exempt from such summons. "Us go to work at daylight, but us wasn't 'bused. Other massas used to blow de horn or ring de bell, but massa, he never use de horn or de whip" (Lorenza Ezell, b. 1850, SC, 26). "My massa ne'er didn't work us hard lak. . . . Ne'er didn't use no horn to wake dey colored peoples up en didn't make em work on de big Christmas day en New Years' neither" (Washington Dozier, b. 1847, SC, 333). "Master Jess didn't work his slaves like other white folks done. Wasn't no four o'clock wake up horns and the field work started at seven o'clock. Quitting time was five o'clock—just about union hours nowadays" (Beauregard Tenneyson, b. 1857, TX, 311).

Even draught animals were conditioned by the work horn's relentless routine. "At twelve o'clock the cooks would blow a horn at de stump in de yard back o' de cook house. Even de hosses an' de mules knowed dat horn an' dey wouldn't go a step further" (Benjamin Johnson, b. unk., VA, 323). That draconian regularity backfired on at least one slaveholder. "One mornin' Old Townslee rode his horse out under a tree to blow up de slaves. Blow de horn you know, to call 'em to work. Somebody shot 'im. Right off his horse. It was so dark, 'fore daylight, and couldnt see and dey never did find out who shot 'im. Heap o white folks had enemies dem days" (Mollie Moss, b. ca. 1855, TN, 58).

In other slave tales, the plantation horn justly signals the slaveholder's undoing. "I 'members when my young master went to go to the War. They blowed the horn and called all the slaves up to tell him good-by. He come home on furlough twice 'fore the war was over. The first time when he come home, he say, 'I'se seeing and smelling the Devil.' Then he left and when he come back the next time he say, 'Last time I was home I told you I was smelling and seeing the Devil, but I'se smelling and seeing Hell now'" (Bert Strong, b. 1864, TX, 3758–59). "When they brought Mr Jimmie home from the War with his knee all busted, they had him on a long canvas with sticks run in it, and they blowed the horn loud and long. All the niggers come in from the fields; you could hear the chains rattling, you'd think twas the army coming" (Callie Gray, b. 1857, MS, 875).

Charley Williams told how, as a ruined slaveholder lay dying in delirium, emancipated slaves humored his delusion that the shattered plantation was still operating by blowing an old horn and beating a wheel rim "like a bell ringing" (Charley Williams, b. 1843, LA, 335).

But the most common of these stories describes the work horn as Emancipation's upstart clarion. "When the fightin' stopped, people was so glad they rung and rung the farm bells and blowed horns—big old cow horns" (Betty Curlett, b. 1872, MS, child of ex-slaves, 75). "At surrender I kin remember de niggers wuz all so happy. Dey jes rung bells, blowed horns and shouted like deys crazy" (Hamp Santee, b. ca. 1859, MS, 1917). "One day Massa Chapman call all us to de front gallery. Us didn't know what gwine to happen, 'cause it not ord'nary to git called from de work. Him ring de bell and dat an sho' 'nough de liberty bell, 'cause him read from de long paper and say, 'You is slaves no more. You is free'" (John James, b. 1859, LA, 199).

One day we was workin' in the fields and hears the conch shell blow, so we all goes to the back gate of the big house. Massa am there. He say "Call the roll for every nigger big 'nough to walk, and I wants them to go to the river and wait there. They's gwine be a show and I wants you to see it." They was a big boat down there, done built up on the sides with boards and holes in the boards and a big gun barrel stickin' through every hole. We ain't never seed nothin' like that. Massa goes up the plank onto the boat and comes out on the boat porch. He say, "This am a Yankee boat." He goes inside and the water wheels starts movin' and that boat goes movin' up the river and they says it goes to Natchez. The boat wasn't more'n out of sight when a big drove of sojers comes into town. They say they's Fed'rals. More'n half the niggers goes off with the sojers, but I goes on back home 'cause of my old mammy. (Mary Reynolds, b. ca. 1835, LA, 245)

When de war wuz over, my mammy said, "Masta John" blow'd de bugle and call all his slaves together, and stood up on de block and says: "Dis block has parted many a mother and chile, husband and wif'—brother and sister—but, *now you is all free as I am.* You can go or you can stay here wid me. I'll pay you fer yer work." Some of dem stay on wid him, but my mother didn't. She married de second year of de surrender and had five more children. (Lucy Galloway, b. 1863, MS, 805, orig. emphasis)

Ironically, on many plantations it was the work horn or bell—the inexorable, remorseless call to and from slave labor—that finally shattered that regimen and signaled its end. In these anecdotes the slaves knew at the very moment this horn blew that something different was in the air: the signal was sounded at the wrong time, in the wrong way, by the wrong person. "On de plantashun where I work dey had a great big horn dey blow every mornin to get de slaves up to go to de fiel. I allus get up soon aftah it blew, most always, but this mornin dey blew de horn a long time an I says what foh dey blow dat horn so long, an den de mastah say, 'You all is free.' Den he says ter me, 'What you all goin to do now,' an I says, 'I'm goin to fine my mothah'" (Julia Williams, b. ca. 1837, VA, 475). "Weuns don't even know w'en de end of de wah comes, 'cept w'en de Marster rings de headquatahs bell to come dere. He ring it hisself, an' ring it a long time to be sure all de niggers am dere. 'Twas nevah done dat way befo'. . . . Well, weuns gang 'round de f'ont po'ch, an' he comes out to de edge of de steps an' says: 'Boys, youse all free as Ise free'" (Willie Blackwell, b. 1834, NC, 317).

> Marster was comin' then, and he had the paper in his hand and was cryin'. He came to the door and called grandma and said, "You are free, free as I am." . . . He told her to get the horn and blow it [instead of him]. It was a ram's horn. She blew twice for the hands to come to the house. They were workin' in the river lowground about a mile or more away. She blew a long blow and then another. Marster told her to keep blowin'. After awhile all the slaves come home; she had called them all in. (James Turner McLean, b. 1858, NC, 85)

> De oberseer would blow dat big "konk" every mornin' at de break of day an' den de men had ter git ter de lot an' feed de mules an' hosses an' den dey would eat dey own breakfast an' git ter dat fiel'. . . . One day de oberseer, he blowed dat "konk" an' called all de niggers ter de house an' Old Marster tol' us how we was free, an' Old Missus cried an' Marster said iffen we would stay wid him an' finish de crop, he'd share it wid all of us. (Charity Jones, b. ca. 1853, MS, 1194, 1198–99)

Nellie Dunne's account inverts the story's usual structure: the plantation bugle fails to blow one last time, preempted by the liberators' approaching drums.

> I sure 'member when they sot the people free. They was just ready to blow the folks out to the field. I 'member old Mose would blow the bugle and he could *blow* that bugle. If you wasn't in, you better

get in. Yes, ma'am! The day freedom come, I know Mose was just ready to blow the bugle when the Yankees begun to beat the drum down the road. They knowed it was all over then. That ain't no joke. (Nellie Dunne, b. ca. 1860, MS, 223, orig. emphasis)[42]

Of course, work horns continued to sound on plantations long after the war, now rousing serfs or sharecroppers rather than slaves. "Uncle Steven blows the cow horn what they use to call to eat and all the niggers come runnin', 'cause that horn mean, 'Come to the big house, quick.' That man reads the paper tellin' us we's free, but massa make us work sev'ral months after that" (Susan Merritt, b. 1851, TX, 78). J. F. Boone was born in the 1870s, but he still had a "master," and still knew work horns: "My old master had a horn he blowed to call the slaves with, and my brother had that too. He kept them things as particular as you would keep victuals" (J. F. Boone, b. 1872, AR, child of ex-slaves, 211).

These conflicting sentiments may explain why plantation horns became keepsakes for Blacks as well as whites. Along with baby clothes and other family heirlooms, Ferebe Rogers's souvenir chest "yielded up old cotton cards, and horns that had been used to call the slaves" (Ferebe Rogers, b. ca. 1836, GA, 211). Sylvia Cannon and Willis Winn regularly displayed slaveholders' tin trumpets for visitors. The 1898 *Charleston Courier* described a similar case:

> There is an old battered tin horn in the possession of an ancient colored man at Dalton, Ga., around which are associated memories of many deeds of violence.
>
> In antebellum days the horn was the property of Colonel Ben Longbridge, a wealthy planter of Murray county. It was originally used to summon his slaves to work and meals, and its welcome note at sunset was the signal for them to rest from the day's labor.

After the war, the instrument was acquired by moonshiners. "The old tin horn would always warn the whiskey rebels of the approach of their enemies, and many a man's death has it presaged. . . . When the gang was finally disposed of the horn passed into the possession of old Uncle Isaac, a typical 'befo' de war' negro, and the old man often brings it out and recounts its history."[43]

The creepiest example I have found comes from an 1879 *Harper's Weekly*: "Mr. John Butler, of Hamburg, South Carolina, has come North with a pack of hounds, with which he proposes to show the manner in which runaway slaves were formerly hunted, and convicts are still pursued in the South. . . . Mr. Butler called his hounds by sounding an old cow-horn, and started them in pursuit with a kind of 'catcall.' "[44]

In truth, by then most horns were souvenirs or museum pieces, replaced by a new communications technology that regulated large sections of the South until fairly recently: the steam whistle, first from riverboats and trains, later from mills, mines, and factories. "They had a railroad to Swanson's Landing on Caddo Lake and the train crew brung news from boats from Shreveport and New Orleans. Soon as the train pull into town it signaled. Three long, mournful whistles meant bad news. Three short, quick whistles meant good news" (Jerry Moore, b. 1848, TX, 122).

> 'Cose dar wa'n't no railroads dem days an' de onlies' way folks had tabbelin' about was de steamboat which passed most ever week, and de stage coach which passed twice a week. Lawsy, man, dem was de days, and many de time atter my dad, whose name was Green Bonner, heard dat steamboat blow below Pickensville he would hitch up de mules to de waggin and foller Massa John on hossback down to de landin' to fetch back de supply of sugar and coffee and plow-tools needed on de plantation. Dey would take me 'long to hold de mules and watch de waggin and it was a reglar picnic to me to see de big shiney boat and watch de goin's on. (Siney Bonner, b. ca. 1850, AL, 39)[45]

Henri Necaise's interview ended abruptly when the evening mill whistle signaled his coffeetime (Henri Necaise, b. 1832, MS, 1635). A noon mill whistle prompted Lizzie Davis (b. ca. 1865, SC, child of ex-slaves, 267) to complain that her lunch had not made itself.

Most steam whistles that ex-slaves recalled were purely functional, but a handful described calliopes or steam pianos. An American invention, calliopes are pipe organs constructed from tuned steamboat whistles, sounded by pressurized steam instead of wind. They can be operated by a keyboard or mechanically with a pinned cylinder in the manner of a music box or barrel organ. Incredibly loud and shrill, they were ideal for attracting attention or drawing crowds. "Speaking of showboats, Honey, you should have seen the BANJO. It sure was a beautiful sight. I was working on the Gray Eagle when the Banjo used to pass up and down the river. The captain would keep the calliope playing and the roustabouts (all of them negroes) would be out on the deck dancing and shouting to the roustabouts on the Gray Eagle" (George Taylor Burns, b. ca. 1836, Missouri, 32, orig. parentheses). "Wish you could of heered dat calliope on de [steamboat] Cremona. Dey dance some time 'mos' all night, but dey didn't act lac' dey do now. 'Twus nice behaviour. Look lac' ev'ything goin' back ter heathenism, and hits on de way now" (Angie Garrett, b. ca. 1845, MS, 134–35).

> Den I 'member when I useter drive ole missus ober to Cunnel Edmund Harrison place. After while cap'n English live dere. He sho was a fine man. He ran dem steamboats on de Alabama Ribber an' 'twan't sich a fur piece ober to de landin' an' we could allus heah 'em when dey pass. He had one name CAP'N SAM an' hit was a dandy. Hit run lak a skeered rabbit an' when it come chuggin' up de ribber wid dat big steam calliope playin' "Dixie" hit was sho hahd to keep yo' feets still. I ricolleck mighty well when dat boat blow up one day atter hit pass Lowndesboro on de way to Montgomery. Lots o' folks git drowned an' 'mongst 'em some ob Cap'n English's own little chilluns. Hit sho was pitiful. (Alfred Jones, b. 1833, AL, 224)

Steam pianos were in fact widely remembered as sources of public entertainment and amusement. Having traveled on an antebellum Alabama River steamboat, J. Milton Mackie (1813–1894) proclaimed:

> the very great advantage of being on board a boat provided, not, indeed, with a band of music, but with a steam piano. This the engineer plays upon whenever he happens to be in the mood musical. Generally, on going from town, he gives a merry waltz; and on returning, if in advance of his rivals, he entertains the expectant crowd on the wharf with a far-sounding march of triumph. Occasionally, too, he will turn off a jig, or negro melody, at the stopping places along the river, just to wake up Sambo, and tickle the heels of the small negroes.[46]

Ex-slave Al Rosboro related several tales of an especially obnoxious slaveholding drunkard, including his comic-tragic end. "I never see or hear tell of dat white man anymore, 'til one day after freedom when I come down here to Robinson's Circus. Him drop dead dat day at de parade, when de steam piano come 'long a tootin'. 'Spect de 'citement, steam, and tootin', was too much for him" (Al Rosboro, b. ca. 1847, SC, 40).[47]

African Americans had played European brass and wind instruments since the colonial era.[48] In the antebellum period Black brass bands, fifers, and drummers were regularly reported in New Orleans and other American cities north and south. Frederick Olmsted (1822–1903) traveled the southeastern slave states from 1853 to 1854. "In all of the Southern cities, there are music bands, composed of negroes, often of great excellence. The military parades are usually accompanied by a negro brass band."[49] There is no question, however, that the Civil War was a watershed, and ex-slaves most often associated brass bands with the war years. "Lindsey's first knowledge of the approach of freedom came when he heard a loud brass band coming down the road toward the plantation playing a strange, lively tune while a number of soldiers in blue uniforms marched behind" (Lindsey Moore, b. 1850, GA, 231).

Fig. 6.7. "Illustrations of Negro Life in Washington, D.C.: The Colored Band." Drawing by Mrs. Rollinson Colburn, 1887. Library of Congress, Prints and Photographs Division.

I knows dis dat I still hears dat band music ringing in my ears. At dat time I was so young dat all I cared about on dat day, was the brass band what let out so much music. Niggers being free never meant nothing to us chaps, cause we never had no mind fer all such as that nohow. Dat de first band dat I ever seed, and to tell you de truf I never seed no more till the World War fotch de soldiers all through here. Bands charms me so much dat dey just plumb tickles the tips of my toes on both feets. (Pick Gladdeny, b. 1856, SC, 124)

Besides accompanying parades and marches, military bands gave concerts and hosted dances for soldiers and civilians. "I member seein' the Rebels ridin' horses, three double, down the road time of the war. I used to run off to the county band—right where the roundhouse is now. Mama used to have to come after me. You know I wasn't no baby when I shed all my teeth durin' slavery days" (Neely Gray, b. ca. 1855, AR, 83). Harriett Gresham (b. 1838, SC, 161–62) met her future husband while dancing to his regiment's brass band in Charleston just after the war. In 1870 Emma Grisham moved from her native Nashville to Memphis and married another Black soldier, George Grisham. "He jinned de army, as ban' leader, went ter San Antonio"

(Emma Grisham b. ca. 1847, TN, 29). George Grisham died in Texas, and Emma returned from Memphis to Nashville as a nursemaid.

During the war, legions of slaves were recruited by both armies as musicians, receiving invaluable training and experience, yet from the beginning they also introduced their own innovations. "When the Yankees come to Atlanta they just forced us into the army. . . . I used to be in a brass band. I like a brass band, don't make no difference where I hear it. There was one song we played when I was in the army. It was: / Rasslin Jacob, don't weep / Weepin' Mary, don't weep" (Tom Windham, b. 1845, GA, 210, 211). Windham's account of wartime Blacks improvising spirituals on brass instruments more than hints at the roots of jazz.

Also during the war, brass bands became associated with riverboats, including special music boats. "I member when the first regiment started out. The music boat come to the landin' and played 'Yankee Doodle.' They carried all us chillun out there" (Charlie Norris, b. 1857, AR, 219).

> The Yankee soldiers came marching by, put us all in wagons, and carried us up to Memphis. They had a place for us to stay and we was fed out of the commissary. Memphis had already been taken by the Yankees. They made my father a soldier, and he stayed in the army in Memphis till the war was over. The day peace was declared, a big music boat came up the Mississippi river. The band was playing, and everybody on it was singing we done hung Jef. Davis to a sour apple tree. Jef Davis was the rebel man who was trying to keep us slaves, and Abraham Lincoln was the one what freed us. We was told when we got freed we was going to get forty acres of land and a mule. Stead of that we didn't get nothing. (Sally Dixon, b. unk., MS, 628–29)

In the following decades luminaries like W. C. Handy and Louis Armstrong would receive indispensable experience playing in riverboat brass bands.[50]

For many ex-slaves, brass bands ranked with their most vivid wartime memories. Jane Pyatt, who had been in Portsmouth, Virginia, at the start of the war, told what may be a migratory tale though it truly conveys the marching band's attraction: "In 1861 the Seaboard Railroad was on High Street, and box cars stayed on three blocks of this street all of the time. The Yankees would get near these box cars and play music, and the slaves would gather around to hear the music. Then the Yankees would fill the box cars with slaves, and take them away" (Jane Pyatt, b. 1848, VA, 235). Late in 1863 a similar story circulated in various abolitionist publications. "The steamer John Tracey (called by some negroes 'Jesus,' because they were thus taken to what they thought would be their Paradise) reached the wharf at Snow Hill [MD], on Saturday, having on board Col. Birney, and a negro brass band, and some negro soldiers. She left on Monday morning with about two hundred slave negroes, who flocked on board from all parts of the country, some owners losing every one they had."[51]

In the postwar period the effects of this sudden influx of brass music were evident everywhere. A decade after surrender, Edward King (1848–1896) traversed the former slave states. "Throughout the South, wherever the negroes have gathered into large communities by themselves, one will generally find a very good brass band; yet probably not one of its members can read music. They play by rote with remarkable accuracy, and they learn a song by hearing it once. The rhythm mastered, they readily catch the tune, and never forget it."[52] These groups were not found only in cities, either: amateur Black brass bands proliferated around small towns, rural hamlets, and sharecropper plantations across the South, playing for family functions, community dances, and local observances as well as mass public events.[53] "Where Mattie [daughter] marry? Right to my do (door)! Mattie marry right to my do! (door) People here like the leaf on de tree. Had a flowers yard. And people dance and beat the flowers down till they wuzn't a flowers been in the yard. Brass band and kittle drum and the bass and dem horn" (Hagar Brown, b. ca. 1860, SC, 82, orig. parentheses). "I'm a musician—played the fife. Played it to a T. Had two kinds of drums. Had different kinds of brass horns too. I 'member one time they was a fellow thought he could beat the drum till I took it" (Jeff Davis, b. 1853, AR, 116). Louis Piernas was born in 1856 in a free Creole community at Bay St. Louis, Mississippi just east of New Orleans:

> My father's name was also Louis Piernas and we lived right there in the north end of Bay St. Louis, near where the Peerless Factory now stands. My grandmother owned all that land at one time. There was a little settlement of free mulattos there, Piernas, La Bat, Barabino, Lassassare—we all spoke French. We kept ourselves separate from the real negroes, and had our own frolics and dances to which the white folks would come sometimes. . . . In my younger days I also used to play and organized the Promot Brass Band. (Louis Piernas, b. 1856, MS, 1702–3)

Louis Piernas may have helped establish a musical dynasty; in the 1950s acclaimed New Orleans pianist James Booker took lessons in Bay St. Louis from a woman named Piernas.[54]

Some of these musicians were trained, others played by ear. Often they belonged to formal groups, performing the standard brass repertoire of marches, polkas, waltzes, and so forth at civic gatherings. In other settings, horn players joined with fifers and drummers, fiddlers, banjo players, guitarists, even full-fledged stringbands, covering the entire range of Black dance music. "Us had a house wid a raised flatform (platform) at one end whar de music-makers sot. Dey had a string band wid a fiddle, a trumpet, and a banjo, but dere warn't no guitars lak dey has in dis day. One man called de sets and us danced de cardrille (quadrille) de virginia reel, and de 16-hand cortillion" (Liza Mention, b. ca. 1865, child of ex-slaves, GA, 124, orig. parentheses). "There was music, fine music. The colored folks did most of the fiddlin'. Someone rattled the bones. There was a bugler and someone called the dances" (Lucinda Vann, b. ca. 1840, IT, 347). Henry W. Ravenel (1814–1887) recalled that at South Carolina slave weddings, the music was provided by the fiddle

Fig. 6.8. "Callender's Minstrels. 'The Past': The Origin of Minstrelsy: The First Rehearsal," ca. 1880. American Minstrel Show Collection, 1823–1947, Houghton Library, Harvard University. Minstrel stereotyping notwithstanding, this ensemble resembles many antebellum groups actually described by ex-slaves. Besides the banjo, two boys in the front row (far right and third from right) are rattling bones in both hands. In the back row, three others play tin-pan tambourines; the two boys on the far left are using only their hands, but the third, far right, is beating his pan with a stick. Meanwhile, in the center another child blows a signal horn.

or, lacking a fiddle, drum, tambourine, and horn.[55] In the 1840s George G. Foster (ca. 1814–1856) observed a Black band consisting of trumpet, fiddle, and bass drum in a Five Points dance house.[56] Three decades later, at a Black peach pickers' party in rural Delaware, the music was provided by "two fiddlers and a portion of a brass band."[57] Around the same time, "down a dark alleyway" in Atlanta, Ernest Ingersoll found "five laborers, each as black as the deuce of spades, sitting upon a circle of battered stools and soap boxes, and forming a 'string' band, despite the inconsistency of the cornet."[58]

These horns may have all been standard brass bugles or trumpets, but there are occasional, tantalizing hints that slaves also played signal horns musically in such ensembles. Formed in Ohio in 1872, Callender's Original Georgia Minstrels were one of the longest-running and most successful Black minstrel troupes, made up mainly of former slaves. They were not the most authentic of these groups, but they did emphasize plantation traditions.[59] A poster from around 1875 conveys their focus. In the background stands a slave cabin; in the right foreground sits an adult male playing a banjo for a group of youngsters jigging and accompanying him on bones and tin-pan tambourines. At the center of the group, one boy plays a signal horn, possibly homemade of wood, bone or animal horn, or possibly a tin trumpet.

If signal horns nurtured no musician other than Louis Armstrong, their contribution to American music was immeasurable. They may, though, have been a stronger presence in early Black music and a broader undercurrent in the development of African American brass traditions. For slaves, much of this was in the future, however. In their day, the wind instruments they most associated with dancing were fifes, flutes, and quills.

Appendix: Signal Horns and Bells in the Ex-Slave Narratives

HORN Sam Anderson (b. 1839, MS), bell or horn 4 a.m.: get up, by slave; Sarah Ashley (b. 1844, TX), horn before daylight: to field; Henry Barnes (b. 1858, AL), horn, first: wake up, second: to field, by overseer; Spencer Barnett (b. 1856, AL), horn: to work; Sara Benton (b. 1846, AL), horn: get up, by overseer; Charlotte Beverly (b. ca, 1847, TX), horn morning and afternoon: call mothers from field to nurse, by narrator; J. F. Boone (b. 1872 AR, child of ex-slaves), horn: call slaves, by slaveholder or slave; Ebenezer Brown (b. 1852, MS), big horn: for freedom, by slaveholder; Callie Bracey (b. unk., MS, child of ex-slave), horn 4 a.m.: to field; Richard Bruner (b. 1840, MO), horn: summon neighbors to put down unruly slaves, for sickness, by whites; George Taylor Burns (b. ca. 1836, IN), horn: breakfast; Isaiah Butler (b. ca. 1855, SC), horn blown through crack in driver's cabin wall: wake up, bedtime, by driver; Jeff Calhoun (b. 1838, AL), horn, 4 a.m.: get up, feed, chores, breakfast, field by 5 a.m.; Cecelia Chappel (b. ca. 1835, TN), hands in field long 'fore daybreak, horn daylight: start work; Irene Coates (b. 1859, GA), horn, three blows: storm warning, take shelter; Martha Colquitt (b. ca. 1850, GA), horn just 'fore day: cook, eat, fields sunrise, by overseer; Sara Colquitt (b. ca. 1830, VA), big horn

'fore day, by overseer; Joe Coney (b. ca. 1857, MS), big horn: for freedom, by slaveholder; Annie Davis (b. ca. 1857, AL), horn sunup: to work, noon: dinner; Carrie Davis (b. ca. 1855, GA), trumpet: wake up, by overseer; Louis Davis (b. 1858, MS), big horn: dinner; Wallace Davis (b. ca. 1849, SC), horn sunup: wake up; Lucy Donald (b. 1857, MS), big horn, slaves knew what each blow meant: mealtime, work, quit time, fire, anything unusual; Washington Dozier (b. 1847, SC), horn: wake up; Lorenza Ezell (b. 1850, SC), horn or bell, daylight; George Fleming (b. 1854, SC), horn: noon dinner; Clayborn Gantling (b. 1848, GA): morning horn, in field by sunrise; Angie Garrett (b. ca. 1845, MS), night horn: bring cotton for spinning; John Glover (b. 1860, SC), morning bells, horns: to work; Martin Graham (b. 1851, AL), horn 'fore day, by overseer; Austin Grant (b. unk., MS), horn: wake up, by overseer; Charlie Grant (b. 1852, SC), horn: wake up, by overseer; Callie Gray (b. 1857, MS), horn: to announce return of war-wounded slaveholder; Henry Green (b. 1848, AL), horns early, late: quit time at dark, supper, also as warning of Union approach; Harriett Gresham (b. 1838, SC), horn: for freedom, by slaveholder; Milton Hammond (b. 1853, GA), horn before sunrise: get up, 9 p.m.: bedtime; Mollie Hatfield (b. 1860, MS), horn early in morning: to field; Emmaline Heard (b. ca. 1860, GA), horn 4 a.m.: get up, field; Fanny Smith Hodges (b. unk., MS), morning horn, first: get up, second: to field, also dinner, quit time, for freedom; Joseph Holmes (b. 1856, VA), horn midnight: assemble for hog killing, by boss; William Hutson (b. 1839, GA), horn for freedom, by slaveholder; Squire Irvin (b. 1849, TN), horn daylight; Amanda Jackson (b. unk., GA), horn: wake up, by overseer; Carter J. Jackson (b. ca. 1850, AL), horn 4 a.m.: fallout, by overseer; Rev. Silas Jackson (b. 1846 or 1847, VA), horn before sunrise: wake up, work; Benjamin Johnson (b. unk., VA), noon dinner horn; Prince Johnson (b. 1847, MS), horn 4 a.m.: get up, field; Emma Jones (b. 1849, GA), horn: get up, by slaveholder; Fannie Jones (b. 1853, Augusta, GA), horn: to field, by overseer; Harriet Jones (b. 1844, TX), horn 4 a.m.: by slaveholder; Abner Jordan (b. 1832, NC), horn, night quit time, by slave blacksmith-foreman (narrator's father); Abe Kelley (b. ca. 1835, MS), horn 3 a.m.: get up, also dinner; Dellie Lewis (b. unk., AL), horn, by overseer; George Lewis (b. 1849, FL), horn, bugle: wake up, also dinner, by overseer; Uncle Gable Locklier (b. ca. 1851, SC), horn: to work after daylight; Louis Love (b. ca. 1845, TX) noon horn: for freedom; James Lucas (b. 1833, MS), horn: end midday rest, return field; Eison Lyles (b. ca. 1865, SC, child of ex-slaves), horn: for freedom; Jim Martin (b. 1857, MS), big horn: mealtime, also for freedom; Bert Mayfield (b. 1852, KY), big horn: wake up, sugar maple camp, by slaveholder; Duncan McCastle (b. 1860, MS), horn: children's and workers' mealtimes, by slave cook; Matilda McKinney (b. 1855, GA), horn: curfew, lights out; Nap McQueen (b. ca. 1855, TX), noon dinner horn; Jake McLeod (b. 1854, SC), horn sunrise: to work, by overseer; Laura Montgomery (b. 1850, MS), morning horn: to work; Andrew Moss (b. 1852, TN), noon dinner horn; Aunt Mollie Moss (b. ca. 1855, TN), horn 'fore day: to work, bell: death, fire, sale of slaves; Julius Nelson (b. 1860, NC): horn before daylight: breakfast; horn daylight: to field, bell: dinner; Lizzie Norfleet (b. 1850, MS), morning horn: wake up, by overseer; Mark Oliver (b. 1856, MS), horn before day: get up, also noon dinner, dark quit time, by overseer; Wade Owens (b. 1863, AL), risin' horn, by overseer; Elsie Payne (b. 1840, AL), horn before day; Phyllis Petite (b. ca. 1855, TX), old horn before daylight: wake up, work; Maggie Pinkard (b. ca. 1855, TN), bells, horns: wake up, start work daybreak, noon: dinner; Dempsey Pitts (b. 1830, NC), horn before day: get up, by slave; Aunt Ferebe Rogers (b. ca. 1836, GA), horns used to call slaves (keepsakes); Katie Rowe (b. ca. 1850, AR), horn: wake up, for freedom, by overseer; Mary Scott (b. ca. 1847, SC), horn: wake up, by overseer; Abram Sells (b. ca. 1850, TX), big horn 4 a.m.: get up, barn by daylight, by slave; George Selman (b. 1852, TX), horn Saturday noon: quit time for week; Robert Shepherd (b. ca. 1845, GA), big old horn: children's mealtime, call children for chores, punishment, by slave (Aunt Vinney); Allen Sims (b. ca. 1860, AL), horn way 'fore day, by overseer; Adam Singleton (b. 1858, AL), horn 'fore day: feed, milk; Charlie Tye Smith (b. 1850, GA), horn 4 a.m.: turn out, by slaveholder; Eli Smith (b. ca. 1840, GA), horn hour 'fore day, by overseer; Millie Ann Smith (b. 1850, TX), horn 'fore light: wake up, work; Elizabeth Sparks (b. 1841, VA), horn: begin and stop work; Bert Strong (b. 1864, TX), horn: assemble slaves for slaveholder's departure to war, for freedom, by slaveholder's son; Julia Stubbs (b. 1852, MS), horn: warn Confederate deserters of search parties; Louise Terrell (b. unk., MS), horn 4 a.m.: to field; Aleck Trimble, see BUGLE; Edwin Walker (b. 1849, MS), horn afore day, first: get up, feed, harness; second: breakfast; Henry Walker (b. ca. 1856, AR), horn Saturday evening: weekly provisions; Rosa Washington (b. ca. 1845, LA), horn-bugle 4 a.m. (except Sundays): wake up, by overseer; Emma Watson (b. 1852 or 1853, TX), noon dinner horn; Sol Webb (b. unk., AL), horn, hollering: get up, by overseer; John White (b. 1816, TX), horn: wake up, work, by overseer; Columbus Williams (b. 1841, AR), horn: get out of house, by overseer; Julia Williams (b. ca. 1837, VA), horn before day: get up, field, for freedom; Willis Winn, see TIN TRUMPET; Ruben Woods (b. ca. 1853, AL), horn: come for weekly provisions; Tom W. Woods (b. 1854, AL), horn 4 a.m.: get up, field by daylight, by overseers; Henry Wright (b. 1838, GA), horn, 3 a.m.: wake up, feed stock, bell: to field.

BUGLE Rachel Adams (b. ca. 1860, GA), bugle long 'fore day: wake up, breakfast, field before sunrise, by overseer; Jim Allen (b. ca. 1850, AL), bugle 4 a.m.: wake up, work, by slave; Henry Bland (b. 1851, GA), bugle: wake up; James Bolton (b. 1852, GA), bugle: wake up, call slaves from field, by overseer or cook, for freedom, by slaveholder; Julia Cole (b. ca. 1860, GA), bugle 4 a.m.: get up, field by daybreak, by slaveholder's son; Thomas Cole (b. 1845, AL), horn-bugle from ten-foot platform: get up, by slave;

Isaiah Green (b. 1856, GA), morning bugle: to field, by overseer; Nellie Dunne (b. ca. 1860, MS), bugle: to field, by slave; Lucy Galloway (b. 1863, MS): bugle, for freedom, by slaveholder; Alice Hutcheson (b. ca. 1860, GA), bugle: finished thrashing, go to next plantation; Ruben Laird (b. 1850, MS), bugle each Sunday morning: rations; Victoria Randle Lawson (b. ca. 1850, MS), bugle every Sunday: go to barn, shuck and shell corn for Confederate government; George Lewis, see HORN; Ed McCree (b. 1861, GA), bugle: wake up, by overseer; Harriet Miller (b. 1859, MS), bugle 'fore daybreak: field by daybreak, noon: to big house kitchen for dinner, by overseer; Will Parker (b. 1842, GA), bugle: prayer meeting, by preacher; Molly Parker (b. ca. 1850, AL), bugle: wake up, by overseer; Henry Rogers (b. 1864, GA), bugle 4 a.m. (later on Sundays): get up, by slave (Uncle Alex Hunt); Robert Shepherd (b. ca. 1845, GA): bugle: dinner, by overseer's wife, bugle: for freedom, by slaveholder; Melvin Smith, see CONCH TRUMPET; Aleck Trimble (b. 1861, TX), bugle, horn: assemble slaves; Neal Upson (b. 1857, GA), bugle daybreak: wake up, by slave; Addie Vinson (b. 1852, GA), bugle long 'fore day: wake up, by overseer; Rosa Washington, see HORN; Willis Winn, see TIN TRUMPET.

COW HORN Betty Curlett (b. 1872, MS, child of ex-slaves), farm bells, big old cow horns: war's end; Charlie Davis (b. ca. 1849, SC), cow horn: to work, by overseer; Manda Edmonson (b. 1842, MS), cow horn: to work, dinner; Laura Ford (b. 1852, MS), cow horn: to field, dinner, signal for everything; Hector Godbold (b. 1850, SC), cow horn before daylight: wake up, work; Margaret Hughes (b. ca. 1855, SC), big cow horn: wake up, dinner, by overseer; Rev. Silas Jackson (b. 1846 or 1847, VA), cow or bull horn: signaling between plantations, by slaves; Susan Merritt (b. 1851, TX), cow horn: for freedom, by slave; Mary Mitchell (b. ca. 1875, TN, child of ex-slaves), whistle made of a cow's horn, or big farm bell; Mack Mullen (b. 1857, GA), cow horn 4 a.m.: get up, field, also sundown quit time, by slave known as *caller*; Louis Napoleon (b. ca. 1857, FL),

cow horn before dawn: wake up, by slave driver; Katie Rose (b. ca. 1850, KY), cow horn: assembly, by slaveholder; Hamp Santee (b. ca. 1859, MS), cow horn: quit time, by slave, horns, bells: surrender, by slaves; Robert Toatley (b. 1855, SC), cow horn: dinner, by slave cook; Dave Walker (b. 1850, MS), cow horn: wake up, breakfast, field, signals all day; Mollie Williams (b. 1857, MS), powder horn (cow horn), morning 'fo day good, get up.

RAM'S HORN Aunt Cicely Cawthon (b. 1859, GA), great big ram's horn two hours before day: get up, breakfast, curry mules, field; James Turner McLean (b. 1858, NC), ram's horn blown twice: bring slaves to house, announce freedom; Charley Williams (b. 1843, LA), ram's horn, one long toot then some short toots, then hollering: wake up, get up, ram's horn again: to field, by overseer.

CONCH TRUMPET Preely Coleman (b. 1852, TX), conk (mussel shell) daylight: to field, 11:30 a.m.: dinner; James Cornelius (b. ca. 1846, MS), big konk: wake up, dinner, by slaveholders or slave; Campbell Davis (b. 1852), old conk-shell long 'fore day: by slaveholder; James V. Deane (b. 1850, MD), old conk: nighttime gatherings, by slaves; Elijah Green (b. 1843, SC), conch shell 6 a.m.: get up, by overseer; Israel Jackson (b. 1860, MS), conch 4 a.m.: get up, field; Charity Jones (b. ca. 1853, MS), big konk daybreak: feed, breakfast, field, for freedom, by overseer; Charlie King (b. ca. 1850, GA), big conch shell every morning 4 a.m.: get up, by slaveholder; Milton Lackey (b. ca. 1860, MS), conch: storm warning, dinner; Waters McIntosh (b. 1863, SC), conk: for freedom; Frank Menefee (b. ca. 1843, AL), cockle shell daylight: get up; A. J. Mitchell (b. ca. 1858, AR), big old conch shell noon: dinner, by slaveholder; Ivory Osborne (b. 1852, TX), conk: for freedom, by slaveholder; Eda Rains (b. 1853, TX), conk: wake up, dinner, if anything happened special; Mary Reynolds (b. ca. 1835, LA), conch shell afore daylight: roll call, for freedom; Melvin Smith (b. 1841, SC), conch shell or bugle 4 a.m.: wake up, by overseer; Edward Taylor (b. ca. 1812, LA), konk horn or bell: quit time, by slave.

TIN TRUMPET Sylvia Cannon (b. ca. 1857, SC), tin trumpet: direct hands different fields, by overseer; Willis Winn (b. 1822, LA), big horn or bugle (tin trumpet) 4 a.m.: wake up, by slaveholder.

OTHER SIGNAL HORNS: HUNTING HORN: Josh Horn (b. 1853, AL), dogs, hunting horn; John Majors (b. ca. 1852, MS), hunting horn; Ida Rigley (b. 1855, VA), dogs, hunting horns, by Colonel Radford's sons, slaves; Uncle John Spencer (b. ca. 1857, VA), dogs, possum hunting horn, by slaves. SLAVEHUNTERS, NIGHT RIDERS HORN: Dora Franks (b. ca. 1837, MS), Klan horn: racial terrorism; Lizzie Hawkens (b. ca. 1870, AR, child of ex-slaves), dogs, slave-hunters' horns, by slaveholders; Josh Horn (b. 1853, AL), dogs, slave-hunters' horn, by slave-hunter; Mag Johnson (b. ca. 1870, AR, child of ex-slaves), dogs, slave hunters' horn. MAIL AND STAGECOACH HORNS: Sarah Louise Augustus (b. ca. 1855, NC), mail-stagecoach horn, by driver; Cato Carter (b. 1836 or 1837, AL), mail coach bugle: ready fresh horses; William Davis (b. 1845, TN), stagecoach horn: driver blows as stage tops hill two miles from hotel, Davis meets stage, assists guests; Simon Hare (b. 1849, AL), mail coach bugle: driver plays tune, throws off mail, merchandise; Rev. Wamble [Womble] (b. 1859, MS), mail coach bugle: driver blows at mail drop; Ruben Woods (b. ca. 1853, AL), stagecoach bugle: driver blows stops. OTHER HORN SIGNALS, FUNCTIONS: Rev. Frank T. Boone (b. 1858, VA), old horns: distress calls, by members of the Union Laborers (Black mutual aid society), 1870s, SC; Charlie Harvey (b. ca. 1855, SC), opossum horn: all-safe signal during flood, by white ship's captain; Uncle Ben Horry (b. ca. 1850, SC), horn: flatboat signal; Henry Murray (b. 1840, AL), horn, bell to scare birds from rice, rye, wheat; Ophelia Porter (b. unk., TX), cow horn: shivaree noisemaker, by blacks.

PLANTATION SIGNAL BELLS: CLAPPER BELLS: Rev. W. B. Allen (b. ca. 1850, AL), first bell 3 a.m.: get up, breakfast, second bell 4 a.m.: to field; Sam Anderson, see HORN; Celestia Avery (b. 1862, GA), big bell: midday lunch; Willie Blackwell (b. 1834, NC), bell: for freedom, by slaveholder; Jennie Bowen (b. ca. 1847, AL), bell: wake up, by slave; Jerry Boykins (b. 1845, GA), bell 4 a.m.: to work; Easter Brown (b. 1860, GA), bell, by overseer, for freedom; Queen Elizabeth Bunts (b. ca. 1865, GA, child of ex-slaves): farm bells: midday meal, Sunday services; Sallie Carder (b. ca. 1855, TN), bell 4 a.m.: get up, get to work, by overseer or Black carriage driver; Fleming Clark (b. ca. 1860, VA), bell 4 a.m.: get up, by overseer; Henry Clay (b. ca. 1835, NC), morning bell: to work; Mariah Sutton Clemments (b. ca. 1850, GA) dinner bell; George Coleman (b. 1830, VA), bells, guns: war's end, by whites; John Crawford (b. 1837, MS), dinner bell 11:30 a.m.; Betty Curlett, see HORN; Mose Davis (b. unk., GA), large bell near the slave quarters: get up, to field, by overseer; Nelson Dickerson (b. unk., MS), big bell: for freedom, by slaveholder; Lawrence Evans (b. 1858, MS), big bell: get up, mealtime, quit time; Millie Evans (b. 1849, NC), bell 4 a.m.: get up, noon: dinner, when there was distressful news; Hanna Fambro (b. 1850, GA), bell at Morning Star-rise, by overseer; Mattie Fannen (b. 1853, AR), farm bell: freedom; Gus Feaster (b. ca. 1840, SC), bell, break of day, by driver; Ruben Fox (b. ca. 1853, MS), big bell before day: get up and out, by slaveholder; John Glover, see HORN; Orris Harris (b. ca. 1858, MS), bell 'fore day: get up, work, also dinner, by slaveholder; Virginia Harris (b. ca. 1855, MS), bell before day: get up, for funeral; Tom Hawkins (b. ca. 1860, GA), bell: Saturday dinner, quit time for week; George Henderson (b. 1860, KY), "a great big bell, called the 'farm bell'" sunrise, by some boy; Nancy Jackson (b. 1830, TX), bell: wake up, dinner, bedtime; John James (b. 1859, TX), big bell, wake up before dawn, for freedom; Lewis Jefferson, plantation bell: for freedom; Bud Jones (b. ca. 1850, VA), bell: for freedom; Steve Jones (b. 1849, SC): 9 p.m. curfew bell, by slaveholder; Mary Ann Kitchens (b. ca. 1850, MS), plantation bell sunup: to work, at dark: quit time; John Matthews (b. 1852, MS), bell way 'fore day, by overseer; Bob Maynard (b. ca. 1855, TX), big bell: dinner; Lucy McCullough (b. 1858,

GA), bell every morning; William McWhorter (b. ca. 1860, GA), noon dinner bell; George Washington Miller, plantation bell daylight, to work; Mary Mitchell, see COW HORN; Alex Montgomery (b. 1857, GA), big bell: morning, dinner, emergencies, by slaveholder; Maggie Pinkard, see HORN; Hamp Santee, see HORN; Charlie Richardson (b. ca. 1850, MO), big bell hanging in the center of all the cabins 4 a.m.: get up; Red Richardson (b. 1862, TX), large bell early in the mornings: wake up; Aaron Russell (b. 1855, TX), bell 'fore daylight: start work; James Singleton (b. 1856, MS), bell 4 a.m.: get up, field; Leithean Spinks (b. 1855, LA), bell morning: to work, also mealtime, for freedom; Liza Strickland (b. 1847, MS), big dinner bell noon; Edward Taylor, see CONCH TRUMPET; Mollie Taylor (b. 1853, TX), bell, half past 4 a.m.: to fields, by overseer; Ike Thomas (b. 1843, GA), bell: young slaves emerge from hiding after Federal troops search plantation, by slaveholder's wife; Johnson Thompson (b. 1853, TX), bell 4 a.m.: wake up, by slaveholder; Henry Walker (b. ca. 1856, AR), big bell: meals, work; Callie Washington (b. ca. 1859, AR), big bell before day: get up, field by sunup; Rev. James W. Washington (b. 1859, AR), big bell: for freedom; William H. Watson (b. ca. 1850, TN), bell: get up, horn: bedtime; Anderson Williams (b. 1849, MS), bell: one hour after sunup, before dark; John Williams (b. 1862, MS), big bell: get up, dinner, quit time; Willis Woodson (b. unk., TX), bell 9 p.m.: quit singing and making noise in quarters, by slaveholder; Litt Young (b. 1850, MS), big bell 4 a.m.: get up; Robert Young (b. 1844, MS), bell 4 a.m.: to work. STRUCK BELL: Louis Cain (b. 1849, NC), big steel piece: Saturday 9 p.m. curfew; Jeff Nunn (b. 1862, AL), big piece of steel struck with hammer, by slaveholder; George Strickland (b. ca. 1856, MS), big piece of sheet iron struck with long piece of steel: wake up; Callie Williams (b. 1861, AL), "sweep" struck with long piece of metal 4 a.m.: wake up, by driver.

FLUTES, FIFES, AND QUILLS

A gentleman in Savannah told me that, in the morning after the performance of an opera in that city, he had heard more than one negro, who could in no way have heard it before, whistling the most difficult airs, with perfect accuracy. I have heard ladies say that, whenever they have obtained any new and choice music, almost as soon as they had learned it themselves, their servants would have caught the air, and they were likely to hear it whistled in the streets, the first night they were out. (Frederick Law Olmsted [1822–1903], *A Journey in the Seaboard Slave States* [1856] 2: 195)[1]

She [mother] wuz seven foot (?) tall. Dey call her "Big Sarah," and nobody fooled wid her. She walk straight and hold her head high. All of de other niggers wuz afraid of her. She usta whistle "Fisher's Horn Pipe." Dat wuz an Indian song dey sung when dey wuz mad. I never could "ketch" it. (Chaney Mack, b. ca. 1864, GA, 1420, orig. parentheses)[2]

When corn haulin time come, every plantation haul corn en put in circle in front of de barn. Have two piles en point two captains. Dey take sides en give corn shuckin like dat. Shuck corn en throw in front of door en sometimes shuck corn all night. After dey get through wid all de shuckin, give big supper en march all round old Massa's kitchen en house. Have tin pans, buckets en canes for music en dance in front of de house in de road. Go to another place en help dem shuck corn de next time en so on dat way. (Jake McLeod, b. 1854, SC, 160)

Beginning in the colonial period, observers constantly marveled at the whistling of American Blacks. Describing Dutch slaves in early New York, Washington Irving (1783–1859) declared "in whistling they almost boast the far-famed powers of Orpheus' lyre, for not a horse or an ox in the place, when at the plough or before the wagon, will budge a foot until he hears the well-known whistle of his black driver and companion."[3] Notable whistlers occasionally surface in eighteenth-century runaway slave ads alongside more numerous fiddlers and fifers. Tom, who escaped a Virginia plantation in 1779,

Fig. 7.1. Pauline Grice, ex-slave, Fort Worth, TX, September 3, 1937. Portraits of African American ex-slaves from the US Works Progress Administration, Federal Writers' Project slave narratives collection, Library of Congress.

is described as "fond of whistling, which he performs in a peculiar manner with his tongue." Penny, who ran away the year before in Maryland, could "whistle much like a fife, in particular a tune called, The Black Joke." More versatile still was Mark, a fugitive from Fauquier County, Virginia ca. 1784: "He can blow the French horn, play the fiddle, whistles many tunes, well to be heard at a surprising distance, is fond of marches and Church music, particularly of that belonging to the Roman Catholic religion, which he professes."[4]

Later observers reported Black whistling everywhere. Describing 1830s Virginia, J. P. Kennedy (1795–1870) wrote, "I never met a negro man—unless he is quite old—that he is not whistling."[5] Whistling may have been as common as singing in the fields. "Aftah breakfas' in de mo'nin', de niggers am gwine heah, dere an' ever'whar, jus' lak 'twas a big factory. Ever' one to his job, some awhistlin', an' some asingin'" (Pauline Grice, b. ca. 1856, GA, 1602).

Les dimanches les negres avaient les dances rondes (faire un rond, les filles et les garcons, et changer). Ils chantaient et dancaient en meme temps—rarement le samedi ils avaient les balles. Ils chantaient et soufaient les champs. . . . Sunday, the negro slaves would spend the afternoons dancing round dances (the boys and girls would form a circle, change partners). They sang and danced at the same time. Very rarely did they have Saturday night parties or dances. The slaves would sing and whistle in the fields. (La San Mire, b. 1852, LA, 2704, 2707, orig. translation and parentheses)[6]

Whistling also accompanied dancing.

Sometime when the fiddle was all we could get for music, some of the boys would get a pair of bones, horse ribs or something of the kind and keep time beating on a chairback with them to make more time. Then sometimes we'd have a banjo, too. Some would pat and some would whistle and we'd dance. (Elsie Pryor, b. ca. 1855, IT, 263)

Ex-slave author Robert Anderson (1843–1930) recalled performing "those peculiar shuffling dances, sometimes for hours at a time, or until exhausted, with the others standing around patting the feet and hands and keeping time to the rhythmical beat of the dancers feet. Some times we sang, sometimes whistled, some times hummed the music for the dances, and occasionally we had a banjo for accompanyment."[7] In 1843 William Cullen Bryant (1794–1878) observed South Carolina slaves frolicking in a kitchen. "One of them took his place as musician, whistling, and beating time with two sticks upon the floor. Several of the men came forward and executed various dances, capering, prancing, and drumming with heel and toe upon the floor."[8] Four decades later, on a Florida prison farm, Kirk Munroe (1850–1930) attended a concert of convicts clogging, jigging, and shuffling on planks. Besides their footwork and the jingling of shackles, "the regular music for the performance was provided by a quartet of whistlers and a number of 'patters.'"[9]

Whistling is yet another universal custom especially well documented in Africa, and especially well developed among African Americans.[10] Whistling an operatic aria or a tune like "Fisher's Hornpipe" is no small feat, but such reports are routine and do not exaggerate. In 1970 in Senatobia, Mississippi, David Evans recorded Compton Jones, whose fifelike whistling and makeshift percussion matched descriptions of slave dances a century earlier.[11] There is no question that African Americans were (and are) able to whistle with the melodic precision of fifing or fiddling, and at a volume suitable for dancing. According to most ex-slaves, however, the wind instruments best-suited to social dancing were the quills.

> My father was a full blood African. His parents come from there and he couldn't talk plain. . . . My father still held a wild animal instinct up in Virginia; they couldn't keep him out of the woods. He would spend two or three days back in there. Then the Patty Rollers would run him out and back home. He was a quill blower and a banjo picker. (Ellis Jefson, b. ca. 1861, VA, 43–44)

> Evening entertainments at which square dancing was the main attraction, were common. Quill music, from a homemade harmonica, was played when banjoes were not available. These instruments were made by binding with cane five or ten reeds of graduated lengths. A hole was cut in the upper end of each and the music obtained by blowing up and down the scale. (Phil Towns, b. 1824, VA, 40)

> I made some music instruments. We had music. Folks danced more than they do now. Most darkies blowed quills and Jew's harps. I took cane, cut four or six, made whistles then I tuned em together and knit em together in a row [a hand-drawn set of six quills is inserted here] blow like a mouth harp you see. Another way get a big long cane, cut out holes long down to the joint, hold your fingers over different holes and blow. (Hammett Dell, b. 1847, TN, 141)

The quills are the African American version of the *pan pipes* or *syrinx*, an ancient instrument with global dis-

Fig. 7.2. "Women with water pots, listening to the music of the marimba, sansa, and pan's pipes." David and Charles Livingstone, *Narrative of an Expedition to the Zambesi and Its Tributaries; and of the Discovery of Lakes Shirwa and Nyassa, 1858–1864* (London: John Murray, 1865), fac. 63. Slavery Images: A Visual Record of the African Slave Trade and Slave Life in the Early African Diaspora. slaveryimages.org. In December 1858 the Livingstones were passing through present-day Kenya when, they write, "a band of native musicians came to our camp one evening . . . and treated us with their wild and not unpleasant music on the Marimba, an instrument formed of bars of hard wood of varying breadth and thickness, laid on different-sized hollow calabashes, and tuned to give the notes; a few pieces of cloth [as payment] pleased them, and they passed on" (63). Unfortunately, they say nothing of the sansa (thumb piano) and pan pipes also depicted in the accompanying illustration, but the sansa player amplifies his instrument in the traditional fashion by holding it in a large bisected gourd. The pan piper appears to be shaking a rattle of some sort with his free hand; he is definitely wearing a string of cowrie shells or similar objects as a rattle around his right ankle, still common practice among African pipers. This is some of the earliest outside documentation of the African pan pipes.

tribution. They are the wind instruments ex-slaves most often identify with dance music, a cohort of the fiddle and banjo. Their origin is little in doubt: panpipes and similar winds occur throughout Sub-Saharan Africa, sharing many features with the African American tradition—not least that African pipes are sometimes also called quills.[12] Some are even constructed from porcupine or bird quills, suggesting the term's origins.[13]

True panpipes consist of two or more stopped tubes of different lengths producing distinct pitches when blown. Southern Blacks typically used bamboo (called *cane*, *brake-cane*, *fishing pole cane*, or *reed*), with the cane's joints (that is, *brakes*) serving as natural stops; this is most common in Africa as well. The quills were only one of the homemade wind instruments recalled by ex-slaves, however. Hammett Dell (b. 1847, TN, 141–42) described another stopped bamboo flute with finger holes, though it is unclear whether it was end-blown or transverse (both forms are also known in Africa). Other cases are even more problematic. Unfortunately, not everyone called panpipes quills, nor were all quills panpipes. Ex-slaves also referred to panpipes as flutes, canes, reeds, harps, and whistles—names all applied to other instruments as well. Some narrators had their own special terms or simply described panpipes without ever naming them. Logically and grammatically, *quill* (singular) refers to a single flute or pipe, *quills* (plural) to several in a set. Some (but not all) tradition bearers observed that rule—Bill Homer, for instance:

> Weuns was 'lowed de Music, de pahties, an' am given de pass fo' to go to pahties. De music am de fiddle an' de quill. W'at am de quill? I's splain, dey am made f'om de willow stick w'en de sap am up. Yous takes de stick an' poun's on de bahk 'til it am loose, den slips de bahk off. Aftah dat, slit de wood in one end, an' down one side. Put holes in de bahk, an' den put de bahk back on de stick. De quill am den ready to play lak de flute. Some ob de niggers larn to be good quill playahs. (Bill Homer, b. 1850, LA, TX, 1788)

Similar instruments appear in Africa and may once have been fairly widespread in America.[14] Pioneering Black bandleader James Reese Europe (1881–1919) encountered an instance around 1904 in New Orleans, in what he regarded as the original jazz band:

> This band was of truly extraordinary composition. It consisted of a barytone horn, a trombone, a cornet, and an instrument made out of the chinaberry-tree. This instrument is something like a clarinet, and is made by the Southern negroes themselves. Strange to say, it can only be used while the sap is in the wood, and after a few weeks' use has to be thrown away. It produces a beautiful sound and is worthy of inclusion in any band or orchestra. I myself intend to employ it soon in my band.[15]

Anderson Edwards may have recalled something similar when he stated "on Saturday nights they made

Fig. 7.3. Bill Homer, ex-slave, July 3, 1937, Fort Worth, TX. Portraits of African American ex-slaves from the US Works Progress Administration, Federal Writers' Project slave narratives collection, Library of Congress.

us sing and dance. We made our own instruments, which was gourd fiddles and quill flutes" (Anderson Edwards, b. 1844, TX, 1262). Within the vocabulary of ex-slaves, however, Edwards could also refer to panpipes, and many other accounts are no clearer. "I see em when dey have dem hay pullings. Dey tote torch to gather de hay by en after dey pull two or three stacks of hay, dey have a big supper en dance in de road en beat sticks en blow cane" (Sylvia Cannon, b. ca. 1857, SC, 190). "I use to go to a lot of dances in my good days. We'd dance the reels. Dere was times when de only music we had was played by a colored man on a reed" (Rebecca Thomas, b. 1825, AR, TX, 3822–23). "The only musical instruments we had was a jug or big bottle, a skillet lid or frying pan that they'd hit with a stick or a bone. We had a flute too, made out of reed cane and it'd make good music" (Bob Maynard, b. ca. 1855, TX, 224).

"An dey blowed cane."
"What kind of cane?"
"Common reed make music and dance by it. Dat the only way Niggers had music. Dat night dey had dance and blowing cane at grandmothers

(Wilson place). Buster cane blower. Dey wuz pattin' and dancing and going on." (Charlie Grant, b. 1852, SC, 171–72, orig. parentheses)

There were many frolics in those days and other slaves would often attend, after getting permission from their masters. Dancing and singing were the main features. Before a frolic would begin the men would go to the swamps and get long quills, which would furnish music by blowing through them. This music reminded one of the music from a flute. "One song we sang went like this," Mr. Browning remarked, "Shake your leg every body Hallelujah, Hallelujah." (George Washington Browning, b. 1852, GA, 115–16)

Most of these narrators probably refer to panpipes or cane fifes—the most common homemade winds—but it is impossible to be certain. Fortunately, two dozen ex-slaves gave reasonably clear descriptions of quills, all wholly consistent with other accounts, and I will hereafter use *quills* exclusively for the African American panpipes. The earliest I have found appeared in the *New-York Spectator* for February 1, 1828:

Every Drummer his own Fifer.—Yesterday afternoon a drummer was escorted down Courtlandt-street by a cavalcade of sweeps and little white boys, who were gathered round him by the singular fact that he did his own fifing, notwithstanding the busy employment of his hands to keep up a perpetual rub-a-dub. For this purpose he had a singularly contrived instrument, composed of short pipes, modelled we presume, after the flute, or *Syrinx* of the great musical father of the Satyrs [Pan].—We cannot affirm that the music was quite as full, clear and exhilarating as that of the real fife; but it did exceedingly well, and the sweeps and boys aforesaid, marched in about as good keeping as the ordinary militia.[16]

Despite some present-day obscurity, this is obviously an early (possibly the first) documented instance of African American quills. There is no question that the author describes panpipes, or that only Blacks created a significant North American panpipe tradition. However, the fact that the writer took pains to distinguish the "little white boys" establishes that the musician and his "sweeps" were definitely Black. One might assume as much anyway, since New York street musicians during this period were typically Black, while virtually all of the city's chimney sweeps were Black children. (The beastly exploitation of Black preadolescents as chimney sweeps prompted one of America's first child labor scandals.)[17] For a melodist to provide his own percussion is also characteristic (though not uniquely) African or African American. In 1858 in present-day Kenya, David Livingstone and Charles Livingstone saw an African pan pipe player accompany himself on rattle (as in fig. 7.2); a century later, at the 1964 Newport Folk Festival, Alabamian Joe Patterson (1895–1970) did likewise, accompanying his quills on tambourine.[18] African pipers sometimes achieve this same effect by attaching rattles to their legs or ankles (again as in fig. 7.2).[19] If we take the *Spectator* literally, the musician was drumming with both hands, suggesting he had the quills in some sort of mounting, possibly a neck rack. This arrangement did turn up later with quills and remains commonplace with their modern equivalent, the harmonica. (Since the 1800s Black musicians have also used neck racks for kazoos, jugs, stovepipes, and various horns.)

From here, the published record lags until the 1880s and a flurry of recollections from Alabama, Georgia, Louisiana, Mississippi, and South Carolina.[20] Even by then the quills were seen as a vanishing vestige of the antebellum South. Typical is an unsigned 1886 *Galveston Daily News* article recounting "Rhythmic Utterances in Which the Southern Negroes Used to Chant."

In the tangled Mississippi woods, accompanied by the quills, a sort of panpipes made of the common brake cane, these were the favorites:

Er had a little dawg, his name wuz Rice,
He chase der devil mos' every night;

He chase him round der fodder stack,
En po' little dawg he never come back.[21]

The quills had not wholly vanished, however, and cases continued to accumulate through the twentieth century, including the two dozen recollections in the ex-slave narratives. In some areas (Georgia, Mississippi, East Texas) quills were not just remembered but actually played up to and after World War II. All together, these sources provide a remarkably full picture, demonstrating that quills were once common from the South Carolina–Georgia border to East Texas. This area's eastern edge in fact stretches straight from Spartanburg, South Carolina, through Augusta, Georgia, to the Atlantic. Eight narrators described quills along this line: Georgia Baker (b. 1850, Taliaferro Co., GA); C. B. Burton (b. 1858, Newberry Co., SC); Sarah Byrd (b. 1842, Augusta, GA); George Fleming (b. 1854, Laurens Co., SC); Uncle Robert Henry (b. 1855, Wilkes Co., GA); Malinda Mitchell (b. 1853, Edgefield Co., SC); Dora Roberts (b. 1849, Liberty Co., GA). Lydia Parrish reported the quills in the Georgia Sea Islands, and there are suggestions they were known elsewhere in South Carolina.[22]

Georgia's midsection may be the best documented of all regions. In 1883 Joel Chandler Harris (1848–1908) stated he had known quills among slaves in Putnam, Jasper, Morgan, Greene, Hancock, and Jones Counties, and WPA narrators filled in the remaining map for central Georgia: Annie Huff (b. ca. 1830, Bibb Co., GA); Lucindy Lawrence Jurdon (b. 1858, Bibb Co., GA); Claiborne Moss (b. 1857, Washington Co., GA); Charlie Tye Smith (b. 1850, Henry Co., GA); Phil Towns (b. 1824, Taylor Co., GA).[23] This region is also home to Fort Valley College (Peach Co.), where in the 1940s the quills appeared at the Fort Valley Folk Festival, with an array of other instruments or instrumental combinations named in the narratives. Unfortunately, no recordings survived, nor is there any information on the players.[24] Just to the west of Fort Valley, Easter Jackson (b. ca. 1850, Troup Co., GA), and Frank Menefee (b. ca. 1843, Lee Co., AL) described quill music on the Georgia-Alabama border

in the vicinities of Columbus, Georgia, and Auburn, Alabama. Quill blower Joe Patterson (1895–1970) was also from this area. (Patterson was born in Henry Co., Alabama, but was living in neighboring Houston Co. when Ralph Rinzler met him in 1964.)

Accounts for North Georgia and Northwest Alabama are equally numerous. In 1884 Maurice Thompson (1844–1901) wrote of quills in antebellum Cherokee County north of Atlanta as well as "the region from Tallulah Falls in North Eastern Georgia to the middle of the Sand Mountain district of Alabama. . . . I recall once seeing a keelboat loaded with corn and manned by happy, stalwart slaves, gliding by moonlight down the beautiful Coosawattee River, while the music of both banjo and reedpipe cheered the dusky crew on their way between shores festooned with the vines of the wild muscadine." (*Reedpipe* was Thompson's name for the slaves' "Panpipe, for in all its essentials it was a syrinx, made of reed joints of graded diameters and lengths, fastened together in a parallel row. The musician blew into the open ends of the reeds, the diameter and depth limiting the note of each.")[25] Several WPA narrators remembered quills just east of Atlanta around Athens: James Bolton (b. 1852, Oglethorpe Co., GA); Elisha Doc Garey (b. ca. 1862, Hart Co., GA); Susan McIntosh (b. 1851, Oconee Co., GA). George Washington Browning (b. 1852, Walton Co., GA), who may describe quills, also came from this section. Quills may have been especially popular there. North Georgian Doc Barnes (b. 1908, Oglethorpe Co., GA) remembered a quill blower named Joe Peelin who in the early 1900s still drew crowds in downtown Athens. "Oooee! Sometimes the cops had to go up there and make the people scatter. Had the sidewalks blocked." According to Barnes, who learned to make and play quills from Peelin, this was during World War I when Peelin was past eighty.[26]

There are further indications quills were known throughout Alabama. In the 1930s Zack Ivey, a former slave from Macon County in the eastern part of the state, recalled: "we had frolics. We had them in the white folks' yard. The white folks made you play and run and jump. . . . We had guitars and blowing quills."[27] One of the first published quill tunes (1881) came from somewhere in Alabama,[28] and Warren Dodds Sr., patriarch of a legendary jazz family, may have learned to play quills around Montgomery sometime before 1880. They were definitely known there. At a recording session in Montgomery ca. 1950, singer-guitarist John Arthur Lee was accompanied by an unidentified quill player.[29] Ex-slave Lula Coleman (b. 1851, AL) also remembered quills at Livingston in far western Alabama.

The records for Mississippi and Louisiana are as rich as for Georgia. North Mississippi was another area where the quills were played well into the twentieth century. Lizzie Norfleet (b. ca. 1850, MS) remembered them in Quitman County in the 1850s, as did Katie Arbery (b. 1857, AR), just to the west in Union County, Arkansas. Silas Knox (b. ca. 1860, MS) named *harps*, which among ex-slaves can refer to either quills or harmonicas. It may be significant that Knox was born in Panola County and spent his whole life there or in neighboring Tate County, the epicenter of North Mississippi's quill and fife-and-drum traditions. In the twentieth century these were documented largely in the person of fiddler, fifer, and quill player Sid Hemphill (1876–1963), the son of a slave fiddler who for half a century led local dance bands serving both Blacks and whites. Alan Lomax recorded Hemphill's quills in 1942 and again in 1959, along with Alec Askew, another quill player in Hemphill's circle. Hemphill and Askew had both acquired some of their knowledge in the 1890s at Como, Panola County, from a man named James Lomax (no relation to Alan).[30] In the 1960s David Evans found that blues singer Big Joe Williams (1903–1982) of Crawford, Mississippi and Lonnie McDonald of Carthage (then in his mid-thirties) both remembered quills from their childhoods.[31]

In the 1880s the Cable brothers, George W. and James B., vouched for quills throughout southeast Louisiana and southwest Mississippi. George W. Cable provided the first account of the hooting technique as well as the first notations of quill tunes.[32] A century later, David Evans met area native Eli Owens (b. 1909) in Marion County, Mississippi, northeast of New Orle-

Fig. 7.4. "Blowing the Quills." Illus. by Edward W. Kemble. George Washington Cable, "The Dance in Place Congo" *Century* 31 (February 1886), 519. The quills as recalled from antebellum Louisiana.

ans. Owens knew the quills from his great-grandfather, Andy Owens (b. ca. 1825, Marion Co.), who also played fiddle, accordion, guitar, beating-straws, jug, mouth bow, jew's harp, and drum. Although Owens no longer actively played quills, he left a wealth of information on construction and playing techniques. He also stated that some of his uncles played, too. Warren Dodds Sr., the father of New Orleans jazz pioneers Johnny Dodds (1892–1940) and Warren "Baby" Dodds Jr. (1898–1959), was another area quill player. Dodds the elder, who also played fiddle and harmonica, was probably born in Alabama, and after 1880 resided both in New Orleans and at Waveland, Hancock County, Mississippi, not far south of Marion County. Whether Dodds Sr. picked up the quills in Alabama, Mississippi, or Louisiana is unclear. (It is known that Johnny began his own musical career playing fife at Waveland.)[33] An 1886 newspaper piece also refers to quills somewhere "in the tangled Mississippi woods."[34]

The earliest recordings of quill music come from East Texas, the tradition's western boundary. Henry Thomas ("Ragtime Texas") (b. ca. 1874) was a Chicago resident at the time he recorded, but he was originally from northeast Texas. On the two dozen titles he cut for Vocalion between 1927 and 1929, Thomas sang to his own guitar accompaniment and on nine selections also played quills, employing the sort of neck-rack now familiar with harmonicas. As recreated by the blues-rock band Canned Heat, the quill melody of Thomas's "Bull-Doze Blues" (Vocalion 1230, 1928) actually became a 1960s hallmark, particularly after being included in the film *Woodstock*. A recently discovered silent film from 1931 shows Thomas playing on Chicago's Maxwell Street, his quills and neck rack clearly visible; from a century earlier, the very first account of African American quills (above) appears to describe a similar neck rack.[35] For East Texas too, Ophelia Porter (b. unk., TX) remembered quill playing in Cherokee County, and several ambiguous cases are from the region: Anderson Edwards (b. 1844, Rusk Co., TX, "quill flute"); Vinnie Brunson (b. ca. 1860, Leon Co., TX, "whistle"); Bob Maynard (b. ca. 1855, Falls Co., TX, "reed cane"); Rebecca Thomas (b. 1825, Caldwell Co., TX, "reed").[36]

Finally, there is some evidence that the quills' distribution extended along the northern edge of this belt, from North Carolina and Virginia through Tennessee. Sallie Paul (b. ca. 1856, NC) described dancing to quills and bones at quiltings somewhere in North Carolina. Sister Harrison (b. 1846, VA) recalled them around Norfolk in Tidewater Virginia, while Ellis Jefson (b. ca. 1861, VA) also remembered his African father playing banjo and quills somewhere in the state. (The father disappeared during the war not long before Jefson was taken to Holly Springs, Mississippi.) One of the best ex-slave descriptions of quills comes from Hammett Dell, born in 1847 at Murfreesboro, Tennessee. Pioneer African American folklorist Thomas W. Talley (1870–1952), who grew up just south of Murfreesboro in Shelbyville, also recollected quills from his childhood.[37]

I would also wager that quills were once played in the northeastern former slave states, especially given the prevalence there of Black fifers and flautists. The earliest mention of quills I have found is in fact from New York City (though by that period runaways from the southeastern states were already flocking to wide-open New York).

The quills usually follow one globally common pattern for panpipes: a single row of reeds arranged longest to shortest—or, pitch-wise, low to high. (A hand-drawn picture of six pipes in this arrangement

is actually inserted in Hammett Dell's narrative.) Again, this is the norm for Africa. (Elsewhere, pipes may be arranged zigzag, or bound in circular bundles or parallel rows.)[38] How many quills in a set varied. Only three narrators specified: "five in a row, just like my fingers" (Katie Arbery, b. 1857, AR, 64–65); "four or six" (Hammett Dell, b. 1847, TN, 141–42); "five or ten reeds of graduated lengths" (Phil Towns, b. 1824, VA, 40). Other early sources stipulate "three quills" (antebellum–1880s LA); "five reeds in the Little Set" and possibly "twice as many" (ten) in a "Big Set" (1880s TN); and "from three to seven reeds of different sizes and lengths" (antebellum SC).[39] Quill-sets with three, four, five, seven, eight, ten, and fourteen pipes were documented or described after 1900.[40]

Usually the tubes are bound together, though there are reports of quill players holding canes loose in their fingers.[41] Ex-slaves typically indicated the pipes were connected with plaited fabric or fibers. "My cousin used to be a quill blower. Brother Jim would cut fishin' canes and plat 'em together—they called 'em a pack—five in a row, just like my fingers. Anybody that knowed how could sure make music on 'em" (Katie Arbery, b. 1857, AR, 65). "I took cane [and] cut four or six [and] made whistles then I tuned em together and knit em together in a row" (Hammett Dell, b. 1847, TN, 141). "Take blow quills made out of joints of cane 'bout size of your finger; dey would plait dese togedder with twine an' blow through dem like dey was a french harp" (Ophelia Porter, b. unk., AL, TX, 3130–31). "These instruments were made by binding with cane five or ten reeds of graduated lengths" (Phil Towns, b. 1824, GA, 40). George Fleming recalled "all de quills was put in a *rack*" (George Fleming, b. 1854, SC, 128, my emphasis). Perhaps this was the sort of wooden frame for quills that Thomas Talley and Lydia Parrish described, perhaps just a variation on the plaited pack Katy Arbery remembered.[42]

With a single exception, all ex-slaves who described construction materials indicated that quills were made from bamboo.

Atter supper we used to gather round and knock tin buckets and pans, we beat 'em like drums. Some used they fingers and some used sticks for to make the drum sounds and somebody allus blowed on quills. Quills was a row of whistles made outen reeds, or sometimes they made 'em outen bark. Every whistle in the row was a different tone and you could play any kind of tune you wants effen you had a good row of quills. They sho' did sound sweet! (James Bolton, b. 1852, GA, 99)

Bolton may have been remembering a set of the bark-and-sapling flutes Bill Homer described, but more likely he is explaining another African method for making pipes or flutes: a bark tube is cut or stripped from its stem, then wrapped in a thinner strip of bark or other material to render it airtight.[43]

It may (or may not) be significant that Bolton, C. B. Burton, and Hammett Dell all called quills *whistles*. Actually, some ex-slaves used whistle as another generic term for winds, but in the 1970s and '80s David Evans in Mississippi and Art Rosenbaum in Georgia independently documented quill-sets created from tuned whistles (pipes with side apertures affecting pitch and timbre). Evans's and Rosenbaum's informants—Eli Owens (b. 1909) and Doc Barnes (b. 1908), respectively—both traced their instruments to ex-slaves, but both called them quills, not whistles.[44] On the other hand, the labels of Henry (Ragtime Texas) Thomas's records identify his quill playing as "whistling," suggesting Thomas also called his quills whistles; whether they were technically whistles is unknown, nor is it clear just what ex-slaves Bolton, Burton, and Dell meant by *whistles*.

There is no question that all quills were tuned (arranged in a sequence of different pitches). "De quills was made frum cane, same as de spindles was but dey was cut longer and was different sizes. All de quills was put in a rack and you could blow any note you wanted to off of dem" (George Fleming, b. 1854, SC, 128). "We danced and had gigs. Some played de fiddle and some made whistles from canes, having different lengths for different notes, and blowed 'em like mouth organs" (C. B. Burton, b. 1858, SC, 152). "Every whistle in the row was a different tone and

you could play any kind of tune you wants effen you had a good row of quills" (James Bolton, b. 1852, GA, 99). "I took cane [and] cut four or six [and] made whistles then I tuned em together" (Hammett Dell, b. 1847, TN, 141–42). This is all rather vague, but at the very least these and other ex-slave accounts indicate that quill tunings were suitable for playing with other instruments (fiddles, banjos, guitars) and for rendering Black and white dance tunes and folksongs, hymns and spirituals, and minstrel compositions.

We can also state with some confidence that playing techniques remained fairly consistent over the quills' history, and that twentieth-century recordings reasonably represent the nineteenth-century tradition. While the number of pipes in a set imposes obvious limitations, an accomplished player can produce two or more pitches from a single pipe by blowing at different angles, over different areas, or with different force. Thus even three-or-four-pipe quills have considerable ranges, and informants insist quills could accommodate any melody. "All de quills was put in a rack and you could blow any note you wanted to off of dem" (George Fleming, b. 1854, SC, 128). "You could play any kind of tune you wants effen you had a good row of quills" (James Bolton, b. 1852, GA, 99). Describing "quill or reed blowers" at antebellum corn-shuckings, one former slaveholder reported "a set of from three to seven reeds of different sizes and lengths were always on hand, and those darkies could play any tune they'd ever heard on them by shifting them across their lips."[45]

To achieve that melodic precision, however, quill players often employed another African technique, alternating piping with singing, humming, or falsetto whooping to provide missing pitches but also timbral contrasts and rhythmic complexity, all in a familiar call-and-response pattern.[46] George Washington Cable first documented this when in 1886 he described a "black lad, sauntering home at sunset behind a few cows that he has found near the edge of the canebrake whence he has also cut his three quills, blowing and hooting, over and over." Cable also included quill tunes from Louisiana and Alabama, notated for instrument and voice.[47] Describing the same period, Tennessean Thomas W. Talley (1870–1952) transcribed from memory another "intricate [quill] tune that could be played only by the performer's putting in the lowest note with his voice."[48]

Recorded quill playing displays the aggressive staccato attack and percussive overblowing associated with African flutes and pipes, creating a shrill, raspy timbre and highly rhythmic texture.[49] Certainly, ex-slaves recalled quills as musical powerhouses, fully able to compete with fiddles, banjos, and noisy crowds. "Boy, I sho could blow you out of dar wid a rack of quills. I was de best quill blower dat ever put one in a man's mouth. I could make a man put his fiddle up; hit you so hard wid Dixieland dat I would knock you off de seat. Gals wouldn't look at nobody else when I start blowing de quills" (George Fleming, b. 1854, SC, 128). "My brother wuz de captain ob de quill band an' dey sure could make you shout an' dance til you uz nigh 'bout exhausted" (Dora Roberts, b. 1849, GA, 206). Claiborne Moss compared quills not to a flute but to a hammering keyboard: "They had fiddles, banjo and quills. They made the quills and blowed 'em to beat the band. Good music. They would make the quills out of reeds. Those reeds would sound just like a piano. They didn't have no piano" (Claiborne Moss, b. 1857, GA, 161).

In North America as in Africa, quills may be played solo, with other quills, or with other instruments, especially percussion. With or without other instruments, at slave dances they were always accompanied by clapping, stamping, and patting from dancers and spectators. "On Sattidy nights dey would have dances an' dance all night long. Somebody would clap hands, beat pans, blow quills or pick de banjer strings" (Lucindy Lawrence Jurdon, b. 1858, GA, 243). "Dat dere ting dey calls truckin' now an' use to be chimmy [shimmy], ain't had no time wid de dancin' dem chilluns do. Dey claps dey hands and keep de time, while dat old brudder ob mine he blows de quills" (Dora Roberts, b. 1849, GA, 207). "We danced outdoors on de groun'. They clapped hands fer us ter dance by an' played homemade banjos an' harps . . . made out of leetle pieces of reeds-like;

you blow in 'em" (Lula Coleman, b. 1851, AL, 431). In antebellum South Carolina, "everyone had as much as he or she wanted in cornshuckin' time. It was served in bowls. They would eat a while then rest then eat again. And while they were resting, some would pat and sing, play the jewsharp or quills, while others pulled ears and danced."[50]

Besides patting, quills were combined with various other percussion. "Atter supper we used to gather round and knock tin buckets and pans, we beat 'em like drums. Some used they fingers and some use' sticks for to make the drum sounds and somebody allus blowed on quills" (James Bolton, b. 1852, GA, 99). "For the music one man would beat on a tin pan and two would blow quills" (Lizzie Norfleet, b. ca. 1850, MS, 1645). "Blow quills en knock bones together dat would make good a music as anybody would want to dance by" (Sallie Paul, b. ca. 1856, NC, 244). "Folks danced more than they do now. Most darkies blowed quills and Jew's harps" (Hammett Dell, b. 1847, TN, 141–42).[51]

Ex-slaves occasionally mention quills with fiddles (C. B. Burton, George Fleming, Robert Henry) but more often with banjos. In fact, the quills' most typical accompaniment seems to have been banjo with clapping or other hand percussion. Among ex-slaves Katie Arbery, Elisha Doc Garey, Malinda Mitchell, and Charlie Tye Smith described quills and banjo; Sarah Byrd, quills, banjo, and bones; Lula Coleman, quills, homemade banjos, and clapping; and Lucindy Lawrence Jurdon, quills, banjo, clapping, and tin pans. Claiborne Moss recalled quills, banjo, and fiddle; Uncle Robert Henry, quills, fiddles, and buckets; C. B. Burton and George Fleming, quills and fiddles.[52]

The narratives also contain at least two descriptions of quill duets. "Some times we held dances on the place Saturday nights. For the music one man would beat on a tin pan and two would blow quills. That was fine to dance by" (Lizzie Norfleet, b. ca. 1850, MS, 1645).

New Years Day wuz always called Hiring Day by the slaves. It was on that day that the specially favored or hired out slaves went to a place called the hiring grounds to hire their labors out for the next year. That's where that sayin' comes from that whut you do on New Years Day you'll be doin' all the rest of the Year. The Hirin' Grounds was always lively. There was always plenty of dancin' an' kickin' an' fun. I had two brothehs who made good music from quills for dancing. They always played at the hirin' grounds. (Sister Harrison, b. 1846, VA, 135)[53]

There is a widespread African custom of flute duets on instruments in different ranges, customarily classed as male (low) and female (high).[54] Perhaps something similar once occurred with quills. Dora Roberts remembered her brother leading a "quill band," though she does not specify its instrumentation. Several ambiguous cases also appear to describe quills or other homemade winds played in groups or duets.[55]

Aside from signaling or personal expression or recreation, African pipes figure mainly in social dancing and possession rites.[56] In the American South, quills were for dancing. "Oh, dem Sadday nights! Dat was when slaves got together and danced. George, he blowed de quills, and he sho could blow grand dance music on 'em" (Georgia Baker, b. 1850, GA, 46). "Oh, my Lord, dey would dance en carry on all kind of fuss. Yes, mam, blow quills en knock bones together dat would make good a music as anybody would want to dance by" (Sallie Paul, b. ca. 1856, NC, 244). Of the twenty-five WPA narrators recalling quills, twenty-four indicated that they were played for dancing. Only Susan McIntosh did not, but neither did she rule it out.

Generally speaking, then, quills shared the fiddle's role and repertoire. Like fiddles, quills were also employed for storytelling. In later years, these narrative or imitative pieces, and the quills' overall role and repertoire were transferred to the harmonica. The harmonica or harmonicon was developed in Germany in the 1820s and by 1830 had saturated America. By the late 1800s German manufacturers were mass-producing models specifically for the American market, often aimed at children. They became stock items at mercantile establishments, selling for as little as a

nickel. In deference to southern consumers, many were actually inscribed *French harp*, the regional term for harmonicons.[57] "Old master taught me to play the Jew's harp and the French harp and the macordion" (Bud Jones, b. ca. 1850, VA, 2090).

I remember the first little store at Rich Fountain. It was little town or village, only about ten houses. A man by the name of Henry Shroeder, a German opened up the first store in a little twelve by fourteen feet log house. He layed in his first supply of goods, one bolt of calico, called Dutch calico; one bolt domestic; one bolt checked goods for shirting; needles; thread; all sizes of wooden shoes; tin ware, such as tin cups and buckets; "juice" harps, French harps; matches and stick candy. (August Smith, b. 1845, MO, 256)[58]

Writing of his Alabama childhood, W. C. Handy (1873–1958) recalled, "sometimes we were fortunate enough to have a French harp on which we played the fox and hounds and imitated the railroad trains—harmonica masterpieces."[59] Hector Smith used another popular term: "De peoples didn' have nothin more den a mouth organ to make music with in dem times" (Hector Smith, b. ca. 1858, SC, 107).

No doubt African Americans encountered harmonicas at different times in different ways, but for many they were direct substitutes for the quills, used to accompany dancing or for instrumental showpieces. In retrospect many ex-slaves actually characterized quills as homemade harmonicas. "Quill music, from a homemade harmonica, was played when banjoes were not available" (Phil Towns, b. 1824, VA, 40). "Blowed 'em like mouth organs" (C. B. Burton, b. 1858, SC, 152). "Blow through dem like dey was a french harp" (Ophelia Porter, b. unk., AL, TX, 3130–31) "Blow like a mouth harp" (Hammett Dell, b. 1847, TN, 141). James B. Cable (1845–1915) described the quills as a "rude mouthorgan of graded canes."[60]

Exactly when, where, how, and why harmonicas came to be called harps is obscure, but it may be significant that ex-slaves sometimes referred to quills as harps. "They clapped hands fer us ter dance by an' played homemade banjos an' harps. No'm, not harps you picks but harps made out of leetle pieces of reeds-like; you blow in 'em" (Lula Coleman, b. 1851, AL, 431). In fact, it is occasionally unclear whether narrators describe quills or harmonicas. "We had parties on Sataday nights and dem whut could would try to dance, and de niggers played on harps and jugs and combs" (Silas Knox, b. ca. 1860, MS, 1288). "My father, he was a fiddler. My mother, she was a dancin' 'oman! Bill—uh, uh, Buck Robertson—listen now, this here's talkin' 'bout Robertson's songs. Bill Robertson was a banjo picker. Buck Robertson was a guitar player, you know, and blew the harp" (Matilda Henrietta Perry, b. 1852, VA, 225). "My master he give us holiday every Saturday night. We have tin pan, banjo and harp and negro dances until day light" (Soul Williams, b. 1841, TX, 4133). "An sech music! Music played on harps, saws, and blowin' quills" (Easter Jackson, b. ca. 1850, GA, 300).

Many performers (Warren Dodds, Andy Owens, Eli Owens) played both quills and French harps, which served the same functions in stringbands and other groups. Playing techniques and musical concepts were also transposed from quills to harmonicas. Black harmonica players adopted the same percussive overblowing as quill players, flapping and buzzing their lips, singing or humming through their instruments, intermittently shouting or singing; the whooping technique was transferred directly from quills to mouth harp. These percussive and voicelike effects culminate in musical narratives such as "The Fox and Hounds" (aka "The Fox Chase," "The Fox Hunt," "The Hounds"). African and European wind players share a long history of musical storytelling, and "The Fox Chase" was actually composed in 1799 by Irish bagpiper Edward Keating Hyland (1780–1845), originally employing the Uilleann pipes to dramatize a frantic pursuit.[61] The piece was eventually adopted by British, Irish, and Anglo-American fiddlers, and by African American quill and harmonica players (and sometimes fiddlers and banjoists), becoming the most popular instrumental showpiece in the South.[62] The

Fig. 7.5. "The Negro reveillee, Charlestown." 1858. Miriam and Ira D. Wallach Division of Art, Prints, and Photographs, New York Public Library. An integrated martial fife and drum team in 1850s Charleston, South Carolina.

harmonica turned out to be particularly well suited to such musical dramas, train imitations especially. Black harp virtuoso DeFord Bailey (1899–1982), the grandson of a slave fiddler, emerged as an early star of the Grand Ole Opry radio program through his versions of "Fox Hunt," "Cacklin' Hen," and an original train piece, "Pan American."[63]

Transverse flutes are known in Africa, but the fife was borrowed from Europe, and Black fife and drum groups were originally outgrowths of the European-American martial tradition. The first African American drummers and fifers served in colonial armies and militias, or attended powerful colonial elites. Caesar escaped from a Maryland plantation in 1784, subsequently being advertised as "a very cunning artful fellow, plays on the fife and fiddle, and once inlisted as a soldier, and may probably endeavor to pass himself for a free man."[64] Most WPA narrators who mentioned fifes and drums associated them with the Civil War. "You'd see people leaving, drums beating and fifes blowing all leaving for de war and wus sad times, my brother wus sold as a substitute for moster's son" (Hattie Anne Nettles, b. ca. 1857, GA, 271). "Recalling

Confederate 'sojers, marchin', marchin'' to the drums, she beat a tempo on the floor with her crutch. . . . 'I thought: Poah helpless critters, jes' goin' away t' git kilt.' De drums wah beatin' an' de fifes aplayin'" (Sarah Gudger, b. 1816, NC, 351, 357–58). "I kin remember hearing dem Yankees comin' down de road yit. Dey hosses sounded like thunder, and de head man, he allus blowed on a fife and de hosses prance and keep time" (Jane Morgan, b. ca. 1830, MS, 1573).

I 'members de day well when Marster told us was free. I was glad and didn't know what I was glad 'bout. Den 'bout 200 Yankee soldiers come and dey played music right dar by de roadside. Dat was de fust drum and fife music I ever heared. Lots of de Niggers followed 'em on off wid just what dey had on. (Julia Bunch, b. 1853, SC, 158–59)

I remember the beginning of the war well. The conditions made a deep impression on my mind, and the atmosphere of Washington was charged with excitement and expectations. . . . The city was one procession of men in blue and the air was full of martial music. The fife and drum could be heard almost all the time, so you may imagine what emotions a colored person of my age would experience, especially as father's church was a center for congregating the Negroes and advising them. (Ann J. Edwards, b. 1856, DC, 10–11)

At some point, however, Black fifing and drumming diverged from white martial music and became a social dance tradition, substituting cane fifes and homemade drums, expanding the repertoire beyond marches, jigs, and polkas, and incorporating African American playing styles and musical principles. In the postbellum period fife and drum music was also played at country picnics and barbecues, funerals, benevolent society functions, political rallies, and for serenading at Christmas and New Years. In some areas of Georgia and the lower Mississippi, this strain of Black fife and drum music flourished up to and after World War II; it is still played in North Mississippi.[65]

Significantly, early reports of Black fifers and drummers are especially numerous in the Mississippi Valley and Georgia. An advertisement for a 1785 Georgia runaway advises readers that he "can play on the fife and affects to be very religious."[66] Ex-slave F. J. Jackson (?–1940) of Grimball's Point, Georgia, told interviewers: "I use tuh go back tuh duh fahm on Satdy night fuh duh big times. Dey hab wut yuh call shouts. . . . We use drum an fife an we made duh drum frum holluh beehive lawg. I tell yuh how we done it. Yuh cut duh lawg an tak a deah hide an stretch obuh duh hole. . . . How yuh make duh fife? Well, yuh jis cut reed cane."[67] In 1883 Joel Chandler Harris stated that in his youth he had heard slaves play fifes throughout Middle Georgia.[68]

There are also numerous antebellum notices of Black fifers and drummers in the lower Mississippi. James Roberts, a Black veteran of the American Revolution and War of 1812, was born a slave in Maryland in 1753. In January 1814 he fought at the Battle of New Orleans, later describing the aftermath:

Having buried our dead, we returned back to the fort. . . . We formed a line, took our arms, and serenaded the battleground. Gabriel Winton, with his two colored boys, conducted the music. One played the fife, and the other the base [bass] drum. One was named Spot, and the other Wot. These boys excelled, in this department of necessary warfare, any that were upon that battleground.[69]

A slave advertised for sale in New Orleans three years earlier (1811) was guaranteed to play "superbly on the tambourine and a little on the fife, beats the drum better than any other in this city."[70] At the New Orleans carnival of 1839 "from two o'clock in the afternoon until sunset of Shrove Tuesday, drum and fife, valve and trumpet, rang in the streets, and hundreds of maskers cut furious antics, and made day hideous."[71] Around the same time Richard Hildreth (1807–1865) described another Black fife-and-drum team not far up river from New Orleans:

In Vicksburgh, one of the principal towns in the state of Mississippi, the most respectable people of the place assembled in the month of July, 1835, and after pulling down several buildings used as gambling houses, proceeded to seize the persons of *five* professional gamblers and to hang them on the spot, without judge or jury. "These unfortunate men," says the *Louisiana Advertiser*, "claimed to the last the privilege of American citizens,—the trial by jury,—and professed themselves willing to submit to any thing their country would legally inflict upon them; but we are sorry to say, their petition was in vain! The black musicians were ordered to strike up, and the voices of the supplicants were drowned by the fife and drum. Mr. Riddell, the cashier of the Planter's Bank, ordered them to play Yankee Doodle, a tune which we believe has never been so prostituted before, and which we hope, and we trust will never be again."[72]

Jeff Davis was born twenty years after the Vicksburg lynching just across the river near Pine Bluff, growing up to play in local fife and drum bands, sometimes with added brass. "I'm a musician—played the fife. Played it to a T. Had two kinds of drums. Had different kinds of brass horns too. I 'member one time there was a fellow thought he could beat the drum till I took it" (Jeff Davis, b. 1853, AR, 116).[73] At community dances Black fifers and drummers often combined with brass and string bands. "The wicked slaves expended their pent up emotions in song and dance. Gathering at one of the cabin doors they would sing and dance to the tunes of a fife, banjo or fiddle that was played by one of their number" (Louis Napoleon, b. ca. 1857, FL, 244). A holiday parade and slave dance in antebellum South Carolina included "banjo, the bones, triangles, castanets, fifes, drums, and all manner of plantation instruments," while a former Louisiana slave stated: "the slaves were allowed to have socials or balls occasionally. . . . An accordion often furnished the music. On rare occasions, there were fiddles, fifes, and sometimes a drum."[74] South Carolina ex-slave Ben Horry recalled his father and two uncles as "great fiddlers, drummers. Each one could play fiddle, beat drum, blow fife." In addition to playing slave frolics the three brothers were the official musicianers of a powerful slaveholder, Colonel Ward (Ben Horry, b. ca. 1850, SC, 309).

Even more than the fiddle and banjo, though, quills, cane fifes, and homemade drums had dwindled if not disappeared by the time the ex-slaves were interviewed. Their influence may linger still in the blues or jazz, but really Black music's future lay with newer, store-bought instruments.

PIANOS, ORGANS, AND ACCORDIONS

I was fifteen years old, a living in Mobile, when Major DeLorne bought me from Col. John Darrington, I wasn't one of dem cheap nigger gals neither. Major paid de price of a piano for me—something near $900.00. (Kate Thomas, b. 1832, AL, 606–7)

My mother, who stayed on the plantation with the rest of the slaves, said that Sherman and his men found so much good stuff to eat on our plantation that they stayed two weeks, and tried to eat up every bit of it. To celebrate their finding so much food, they took their horses in the house and put their front hoofs on the piano. Said they were teaching him how to play the piano. (She laughed out loud.) Just before they left, they took the piano out in the yard and busted it up. (Ella Johnson, b. 1857, SC, 346, orig. parentheses)

In my father's time, and when I was a boy, there were few regular musicians, and at parties, unless it was a very grand affair, a [white] lady played the piano, accompanied by a [white] gentleman on the violin, and monstrous good jigs and reels they played too. But when it got too much like work, almost anybody's carriage driver could be sent for out of the kitchen who could fiddle well enough to dance the Virginia reel by. But when I grew up negro fiddlers were scarce among the plantation hands, except the "professionals," who were free negroes. . . . Among the city negroes the piano is the favorite instrument, as it is so much easier to acquire a certain proficiency on it than on the violin. In the country, though, it is generally thought unbecoming, at least, for a "chu'ch member" to play the violin, if not actually an audacious communication with Satan himself. But it involves neither deadly sin nor any spiritual risk whatever to play the accordeon or the "lap organ," as they call it. The "'cor'jon," consequently, is a very popular instrument. (Annie Chambers-Ketchum, "Negro Superstition Concerning the Violin," [1892]: 329–30, quoting October 1892 correspondence from a former slaveholder's son)

In the twentieth century, the piano (and to a lesser extent, the organ) was central to all of the most globally influential African American musical innovations: ragtime, jazz, blues, gospel, soul, rock and roll. In the rural antebellum South, however, white slaveholders provided Blacks' only access to pianos and organs, which remained somewhat peripheral to their instrumental traditions, only occasionally being played by slaves or used to accompany slave dancing. In the postwar period, the piano and pump organ came increasingly within reach of average persons, unleashing the African American genius for reimagining European keyboards. By contrast, accordions are reported at slave dances beginning not long after they were introduced into America around 1840.

The organ—a system of mechanically blown pipes or reeds operated by a keyboard—dates to around the first century of the common era. Some early examples were basically panpipes with bellows, eventually culminating in Europe's great Renaissance pipe organs, the world's most complex and expensive musical instruments. In the 1840s, however, American manufacturers began mass-producing small, inexpensive reed organs, and these soon became fixtures in homes and small churches throughout North America.

By contrast, the pianoforte is a recent invention, created in 1709 by Italian harpsichord maker Bartolommeo Cristofori. Some ex-slaves remembered when the piano was altogether new—a bit of an upstart, in fact. "Miss Laura [slaveholder's second wife], she was young an' favored havin' company. Miss Becky [first wife] had a norjin (an organ), but Miss Laura she haves ter have a pi-anner. Conscience! Didn' dey sing an' dance den!" (Ned Chaney, b. ca. 1857, MS, 372, orig. parentheses). These first encounters often involved the square or rectangular pianos current in the mid-1800s, before models were standardized. "I 'members when they got a pianny, didn't look like the ones they got now. Look more like a table. All the niggers come up to the house to see it and folks came in admiring it. Some of the niggers say the organ aplenty good for them" (John Crawford, b. 1837, MS 974–75).[1]

Compared to organs, pianos are fairly expensive to purchase and maintain, requiring regular tuning and repairs. They were nonetheless in high demand even in isolated sections of the plantation South. Narrator Jeff Stanfield was a teamster on Bloomfield farm in rural Virginia. "Bloomfield was a piano salesman and musician. He would sell de pianos and den go to de homes and teach de people to play. He also had a big farm and left it to de care of overseers" (Jeff Stanfield, b. 1837, VA, 280).

Stanfield does not specify, but most of Bloomfield's clients were probably fellow slaveholders with social aspirations. Ironically, the piano's high price has always been one of its major selling points, a mark of attainment, a status symbol displayed as much as played. "She [slaveholder's wife] uster let me bump on her pianny 'n' didn' say nuthin'. She couldn' play d' pianny but she kinder hope maybe I could but I neber did learn how. I like music but I ain' got any in me. I uster sing real purty in d' chu'ch" (Maria Hadnot, b. ca. 1850, TX, 1628). In the antebellum South, pianos were favorite ostentations of planters grown newly rich on slave labor (according to Kate Thomas, a piano represented the same considerable financial expenditure as an adult female house slave). Certainly ex-slaves distinguished between white folks with pianos in their parlors and plantations with nothing but fiddles and folksongs. Planters without pianos were likely mean in every sense of the word. "Dar was no pianny in dat house an' I never 'member a dance bein' dere an' old Mistis didn' sing, she culdn' stop fussin' long 'nuff, but sometimes when we was in my mammy's cabin we youngsters would sing, an' mammy would he'p us" (Laura Montgomery, b. 1850, MS, 1553). "We niver had no dances in de quarters, an' I doan remember eny dances at de big house. Dey hed no pianny but Marse Alex wud play de fiddle hisself" (Orris Harris, b. ca. 1858 MS, 930).

Homes with pianos were higher class on that score alone. "When the Walfords settled here they built a log house and lived in it for a few years then built a better house. It was a two story house and all fixed up nice. I remember there was a parlor for the girls, an a piano.

PIANOS, ORGANS, AND ACCORDIONS   153

Marster's folks wasn't just common folks, they had wait-men" (Sampson Willis, b. ca. 1843, KY, 4162). "De big house of Dr. Bedford's wuz real pretty en furnished what you call fine; big high beds, bookcases, tables en cabinets, en dey had er fine pianny" (Henry Bedford, b. ca. 1850, TN, 281). "Doc Gary had a big piano in his house, and most everybody else had a fiddle or Jews harp" (Laurence Gary, b. 1861, SC, 106).

Not just on Laurence Gary's South Carolina plantation but everywhere slaves had only fiddles, jew's harps, banjos, and such in their homes. "The only fun we ever had wuz when we would have co'n shuckins and guitar playins'. We would all go to some Nigger's house and somebody would play the guitar. We didn't know nothin' 'bout no piano or nothin' but the guitar and fiddle. We would have cake cuttings and put money in the cake and pay to cut to see how much we could win" (Harriet Chelsey, b. ca. 1853, TX, 693). "They had fiddles, banjo and quills. . . . They would make the quills out of reeds. Those reeds would sound just like a piano. They didn't have no piano" (Claiborne Moss, b. 1857, GA, 161).

There are, however, occasional accounts of slaves dancing to pianos and organs, whether played by slaves or slaveholders, sometimes with fiddles and banjos.

Fig. 8.1. Betty Bormer, ex-slave, Fort Worth, TX, June 26, 1937. Portraits of African American ex-slaves from the US Works Progress Administration, Federal Writers' Project slave narratives collection, Library of Congress.

> Sich nigger dat wants to larn to read an' write, de Marster's girls an' boys larns 'em. De girls larned my Auntie how to play pianner. Dere am lots ob music on dat place. Fiddle, banjo, an' de pianner fo' de cullud fo'ks. Singin', we'uns had lots ob dat. You know, songs lak Ol' Black Joe, Swanney Ribber, 'ligious songs an' sich. Of'n de Marster hab we'uns come in his house and clears de dinin' room fo' de dance. His daughtahs, dey plays de pianner, an' wid de fiddle an' banjo, we'uns hab fine music. Dat am big time on special 'ccasion. Dey not calls it dance dem days, dey calls it de "ball." (Betty Bormer, 1857, TX, 342)

> Befo' the war, when we was little, we mostly played dolls, and had doll houses, but sometime young marster would come out on the back porch and play the fiddle for us. When he played "Ole Dan Tucker" all the peoples uster skip and dance 'bout and have a good time. My young mistis played on the piano. (Ellen Claibourn, b. 1852, GA, 185)[2]

Pianos and organs were definitely feminine instruments, firmly associated with the parlor of the big house (a female preserve), and the well-bred wives and daughters of elite planters. Otherwise, keyboards were found in churches (another feminine domain), probably played by slaveholding women.[3] "Our mistress had a big fire place en we'en we would kum in cole she would say ain't you all cole. (You all was always used in the plural and not singular as some writers have it.) W'ile we wuz warmin' she often played de organ fer us ter heer" (Ellis Ken Kannon, b. ca. 1850, TN, 37, orig. parentheses). "Mis' Betsy done made me a weddin' veil out of a white net window curtain. When she played de weddin' ma'ch on de piano, me an' Exter ma'ched down de walk an' up on de po'ch to de altar Mis' Betsy done fixed" (Tempie Herndon Durham, b. 1834, NC, 287). "We chaps didnt play in de yard very much 'cause we made too much noise an' old Mistis culdnt stand the noise. Dey had pianny in de big house but we chaps niver wus 'low'd to go in dar ter see it, but we could hear it" (Jim Martin, b. 1857, MS, 1439–40).

Marster Massingale made his slaves go to church ebery time dere wuz services. Us went right wid de fam'ly and de odder white folks, an' us set down at one end together. I 'members one of de hymns dey used tu sing. Yer sees, young marster, Miss Jane Massingale allers played de organ fer de congregation tu sing de hymns by. (Bettie Massingale Bell, b. ca. 1857, AL, 50)

Miss Marzee, she was Marse Spence en Miss Betsey's daughter. She wuz playin' on de pianny when de Yankee sojers come down de road. Two sojers come in de house an ax her fer ter play er tune dat dey liked. I fergits de name er dey tune. Miss Marzee gits up fum de pianny en she low dat she ain't gwine play no tune for' no Yankee mens. Den de sojers takes her out en set her up top er de high gate post in front er de big house, en mek her set dar twel de whole reggyment pass by. She set dar en cry, but she sho' ain' nebber played no tune for dem Yankee mens. (Lula Flannigan, b. ca. 1860, GA, 247)

Then long months after [the slaveholders' daughter Mary had died] all the children was playing in the yard. The mistress and her two girls, Emma and Lucy, was in the yard too, when somebody pointed

to the front-yard gate and called, "Look yonder! Look, Mistress, at the gate!"

Everybody stopped, looking to see who is coming to visit. The mistress said, "It's Mary!" There she was, standing by the gate post, something bright shining around her head, and the folks knewed they was seeing a ghost. Reckon everybody was too scared to say anything and whatever it was that was Miss Mary didn't say nothing either. The form just kinder melted through the gate and run to the house. Then we heard music from the house, just like when Miss Mary was at home, always playing the piano. But the house was empty.

Aunt Betty (the cook) run to call Master Joe and we all followed him into the house, but the music had stopped when we got to the porch and wasn't heard no more. The master and mistress led the way to the parlor, nobody there. Then us all went around to the different rooms but never saw nobody so we went back to the front yard only there was nothing more we could see. I am an old granny woman myself now, but I can still see her now just like when she come back from the dead. (Eliza Bell, b. 1851, MS, 53–54, orig. parentheses)[4]

Almost all WPA references to keyboards concern these slaveholder wives and daughters. Narrators who had learned to play during slavery were usually taught by these women; with rare exceptions these ex-slaves were also female.

I had an aunt named Annice Henry. She was given to one of Dr. Lyles sons when he married. Young Lyles' new wife said she was going to whip Annice. Annice said she wouldn't let her "missus" whip her. So she was told that she would be sold if she didn't submit to being whipped. Annice didn't and so she was sold to the "Nigger Traders," a group of white men who bought and sold slaves. Annice was forced to leave her husband and mother but was allowed to take her little girl, Mariah with her. The "Nigger Traders" took her from Greenville, South Carolina, to New Orleans, and on the way one of the traders saw Annice crying, and whipped her terribly. . . . Little Mariah learned how to speak French as well as she could English, and she also learned to play piano as well as anybody. After the war, Annice and Mariah came back to South Carolina to see their relatives and Mariah just tickled us all to death speaking French. And the Lyles had her to play piano for them all the time. (Ella Johnson, b. 1857, SC, 347–48)

Even with this limited target demographic, there was a booming prewar Southern market for piano sellers, teachers, and techs, even in rural sections.

My paw's name was Tom Vaughn and he was from the north, born a free man and lived and died free to the end of his days. He wasn't no eddicated man, but he was what he calls himself a piano man. He told me once he lived in New York and Chicago and he built the insides of pianos and knew how to make them play in tune. He said some white folks from the south told him if he'd come with them to the south he'd find a lot of work to do with pianos in them parts, and he come off with them.

He saw my maw on the Kilpatrick place [Concordia Parish, LA] and her man was dead. He told Dr. Kilpatrick, my massa, he'd buy my maw and her three chillun with all the money he had, iffen he'd sell her. But Dr. Kilpatrick was never one to sell any but the old niggers who was past workin' in the fields and past their breedin' times. So my paw marries my maw and works the fields, same as any other nigger. They had six gals: Martha and Panela and Josephine and Ellen and Katherine and me. (Mary Reynolds, b. ca. 1835, LA, 236)

Some antebellum pianists may have improvised or played by ear, sharing a repertoire with dance fiddlers and banjo pickers; however, the majority of titles that narrators name with pianos can be traced to mid-nineteenth-century sheet music and songbooks targeted specifically at the home keyboard market. Many are also well represented in later folksong collections,

the ex-slaves describing the exact circumstances in which these items would have passed from print into oral tradition.

My mistress was a good Christian woman, she give a big supper when I was married. Her house, durin' de war, always had some sick or wounded soldier. I 'member her brother, Zed, come home wid a leg gone. Her cousin, Theodore, was dere wid a part of his jaw gone. My mistress could play de piano and sing de old songs. I 'members Marster Theodore had trouble wid de words. Dere was a song called "Juanita," 'bout a fountain. Marster Theodore would try hard, but would say, everytime, "Jawneeta," and de folks would laugh but mistress never would crack a smile but just go on wid another song. (Adeline Jackson, b. ca. 1849, SC, 3)[5]

I never knew much about music but I sho' did like to hear Miss Betty [slaveholder's daughter] play de piano. I never knew what she'd play unless she sung it. I recollect how she played an' sung, "Shoo Fly, Don't You Bother Me," "Granny Will Yo' Dogs Bite," "Dixie," an "Darling Black Mustache." She uster sing good songs too, sech as "Rock of Ages," "De Lord's a Rock," "Swing Low Sweet Chariot," an' lots o' others. (Mollie Watson, b. ca. 1855, TX, 373)[6]

Miss Marguarite had a piany, a'cordian, a flutena, an a fiddle. She could play a fiddle good as a man. Law, I heerd many as three fiddles goin' in dat house many a time. An' I kin' jes see her l'il ol' fair han's now, playin' jes as fast as lightnin' a chune (tune) 'bout

My father he cried, my mother she cried,
I wasn't cut out fer de army,
O, Capt'in Gink, my hoss me think,
But feed his hoss on co'n an' beans
An' s'port de gals by any means!
'Cause I'm a Capt'in in de army.

All us chillun begged her ter play dat an' we all sing an' dance—*great goodness*! (Mollie

Fig. 8.2. Mollie Williams, age 84, 1937–38, Terry, MS. Portraits of African American ex-slaves from the US Works Progress Administration, Federal Writers' Project slave narratives collection, Library of Congress.

Williams, b. 1853, MS, 2345–46, orig. emphasis and parentheses)[7]

In the fundamentalist South, keyboards were the only instruments allowed in many churches. Some denominations excluded even these.

> My marster and mistress was very 'ligious in deir 'suasions. They was Seceders and 'tended New Hope Church. When us went dere, us went up in de gallery. No piano nor organ was 'lowed in de church them days. I set up dere many a Sabbath and see Marse Robin Stinson knock his [tuning] fork on de bench, hold it to his ear, and h'ist de tune. Then all jine in and let me tell you it had to be one of de Bible psalms, by de sweet singer of Israel, and no common glory hallelujah hymn. No sir, they didn't tolerate deir children engagin' in breakin' de Sabbath in dat way! (George McAlilley, b. 1855, SC, 143)

However, several narrators had heard pianos but more often organs in white churches or plantation chapels before the war.

> The most of what I remembers before the war was when I was in Beaufort. They used to take care of the widows then. Take it by turns. There was a lady, Miss Mary Ann Baker, whose husband had been an organist in the church. When he died they would all take turns caring for Miss Mary Ann. I remember I'd meet her on de street and I'd say, "Good mornin' Miss Mary Ann." "Morning Janie." "How you this mornin' Miss Mary Ann?" She'd say, "Death come in and make alterations, and hard living make contrivance." She'd take any old coat, or anything, and make it over to fit her children, and look good, too. She was a great seamstress. (Rebecca Jane Grant, b. ca. 1843, SC, 183)

> All slaves worshipped in the church in "The Quarters." On special occasions the slaves were allowed to stand outside the "whitefolks" church and listen to Mrs. Norris play and sing the organ. . . . Services were conducted every Sunday by a religious slave either on the Norris Plantation or an adjoining plantation. Once a month the services were conducted by Master Norris and Mrs. Norris would play and sing for the slaves. (Queen Elizabeth Bunts, b. ca. 1865, GA, child of ex-slaves, 122)

> Didn't have no colored churches. De drivers and de overseers, de house-servants, de bricklayers and folks like dat'd go to de white folk's church. But not de field hands. Why dey couldn't have all got in de church. My marsa had three or four hundred slaves. . . . They had colored preachers to preach to de field hands down in de quarters. . . .
> Old Parson Lawton used to preach for us after the war until we got our church organized. He had a daughter named Miss Anna Lawton. At the white folk's church at Lawtonville they had a colored man who used to sing for them, by the name of Moses Murray. He'd sit there back of the organ and roll down on them basses. Roll down just like de organ roll! He was Moses Lawton at that time

[during slavery], you know. (Rebecca Jane Grant, b. ca. 1843, SC, 184–86)

Actually, some plantations did have separate church houses for slaves, who might otherwise worship outdoors or in their cabins (and often in secret). Yet whenever, however, and wherever slaves met on their own, there was invariably singing, but no keyboards until after the war.

Us had our own Negro church [before the war]. I b'lieve dey calls it Foundry Street [Athens, GA] whar de ole church wuz. Us had meetin' evvy Sunday. Sometimes white preachers, and sometimes Negro preachers done de preachin'. Us didn't have no orgin or pianny in church den. De preacher hysted de hymns. No ma'am, I cyan' 'member no songs us sung den dat wuz no diffunt f'um de songs now-a-days 'ceppen' dey got orgin music wid de singin' now. (Anna Parkes, b. ca. 1850, GA, 158)

Her chief sorrow is in being away from her church, her church way back in the country where her membership is. She attends one near her but it's entirely too fashionable. The preacher too doesn't preach like old times, and the congregation doesn't have a chance to sing. The choir does that "and it's high-falutin'." They have a fine organ, "a pipe-organ they calls it, and they wear nightgowns." (Rebecca Fletcher, b. 1842, MS, 70)

After freedom pianos and organs proliferated in Black churches but also Black homes. Piano lessons and musical literacy became inextricably linked with literacy generally and the freed slaves' furious drive for the education they were once denied. Obviously, too, pianos conferred an air of gentility and middle-class respectability, and piano lessons were now a necessity for well-bred Black children. "I hev five chilluns. Three in Chicago. I have one daughter who is de best performer on de piany in de world. She belongs to sum orchestra in Chicago" (Rev. James W. Washington, b. 1854, MS, 2204).

Fig. 8.3. "African American man giving piano lesson to young African American woman." Location unk., 1899–1900. Daniel Murray Collection, Library of Congress, Prints and Photographs Division.

I jined de Baptist church when I lived at Chatawa en atter I cum here [McComb, MS] I wurk for Mr Heber Craft. His son taught me how ter read en play de pinany en fiddle. Den I went to school here in dis town. I wanted ter learn to read so I could read de Bible en learn de Holy Writ. When I finished school I founded de Flowery Mount Baptist Church en pastored it fur 20 years. I preached all ober de country. I believe dis is de time fur de Gentiles. Dey are to have de gospel for 2000 years en den de Jew will reign. De Gentiles abuse deir priverlege just like de Jew once did en de Gospel will be tuk frum dem jist like it wus frum de Jews. (Rev. James W. Washington, b. 1854, MS, 2202–3)

Very early in life she evidenced a desire for music and her parents spared nothing in giving her this education. She finished the Western Conservatory of Music and did postgraduate work in New York. She taught music for a while and for twenty years has been organist and musical director of Shorter A. M. E. Church. (Gertie Ross, b. 1879, KS, child of ex-slaves, 83)

We had six chillun an' three of 'em is still livin'. I can' say much for my chillun. I don' lak to feel hard, but I tried to raise my chillun de bes' I could. I educated 'em; even bought 'em a piano an' give 'em music. One of 'em is in Memphis, nother'n in Detroit, an' de other'n in Chicago. I's old and dey is forgot me, I guess. I writes to 'em to he'p me, but don' never hear from 'em. Dat seems to be de way of de worl' now. (John Cameron, b. 1842, MS, 335)

This new demand for piano teachers was satisfied mainly from within the Black community and, between lessons and church work, community-based keyboardists ranked among the most numerous true professionals in late nineteenth-century Black music.

His wife had had some educational advantages and taught Robert to read and write. He was much interested in the welfare of his community, was a successful farmer, and owned a good home. He reared a family of good citizens. He believed in education, owned a piano, and his daughters taught music in his home. (Robert Bryant, b. 1858, MS, 295)

"My masser would say that Jimmie had sense, was a good boy, so Missus would let me practice on her organ or her piano in the house. I got pretty good on these, so when I got to be a young man, I taught lessons on both the reed organ and the melodian, then on the piano. I taught the rudiments of music and piano for about 25 years. . . .

"No, I never married, and I haven't got anybody kin to me now. My brothers all died and I am the only one left. I adopted four children. I taught them music and we got on pretty well after Missus died. I stayed with her until she died. I told Masser I was going to stay with them even if I was free, and I did. When Masser died, I had no one to love but Missus. I taught music and gave piano lessons, but I can't do that now, as I am too old. Lately I tried to cut some wood. I would cut a lick, then rest; cut a lick, then rest, so I gave it up. . . ."

This ninety-year-old ex-slave then sat down at the piano and played for the writer. (Jimmie Johnson, b. ca. 1847, SC, 54–55, int. F. S. DuPre)

In rural areas around this same time, the organ underwent a similar transformation. In the late nineteenth-century, organs became commonplace in Black homes across the rural South through door-to-door sales on installment plans. Booker T. Washington (1856–1915) routinely visited ex-slaves around Tuskegee, Alabama, in the early 1880s. "In these cabin homes I often found sewing-machines which had been bought, or were being bought, on instalments, frequently at a cost of as much as sixty dollars, or showy clocks for which the occupants of the cabins had paid twelve or fourteen dollars." On one occasion he supped with a family of four who all shared the same fork. "In the opposite corner of that same cabin was an organ for which the people told me they were paying sixty dollars in monthly instalments. One fork, and a sixty-dollar organ!" Washington insists that in most cases "the organ, of course, was rarely used for want of a person who could play upon it."[8]

Predatory lending aside, lessons were often included with the purchase price, and these organs were played. "I used to play banjer, violin, accord'yun, last thing I wind up on was de organ but my organ got burnt up. Wisht' I had one now to play" (Abner Griffin, b. 1849, GA, 273). Aaron Pinnacle recalled that his ex-slave father "could play on the violin, cornet and later learned to play the organ. In fact as he expressed it, he could make music on any instrument" (Aaron Pinnacle, b. ca. 1890, SC, child of ex-slaves, 268).

I used to sew—take in sewing, and teach music—piano and organ.

Before my mother died there was an old gentleman—a colored man—lived with us, was a graduate of a conservatory in Michigan. He told my stepfather if he would buy an organ that he would give me lessons. Professor R. W. Wright was his name. All I know about music I learned in six weeks. He said I learned faster than any pupil

PIANOS, ORGANS, AND ACCORDIONS

he ever had. I just went crazy about it—played night and day. I'm the pianist at our church. For twenty-six years now I've been out here at Ward's Chapel A. M. E. Church. I love to play "himes" (hymns). (Hattie Douglas, b. 1867, AR, child of ex-slaves, 62, orig. parentheses)

Even without lessons, country people played these pump organs, and by the early twentieth century, rural Blacks are described improvising on organs in a manner suggestive of ragtime, jazz, or blues. In 1916 Alice Graham wrote of "The Negro Craze for the Reed Organ in the South":

In the black belt lands of the south, where large plantations flourish cultivated by negro labor, and negro life is similar to what it was in antebellum days, the reed organ agent finds a rich field for his sales. He sells the negroes organs on the installment plan, collecting a pittance from them each month, and often taking back the instrument after nearly its first cost has been paid, because the debtor is unable to meet his last payment.

The negroes admire organ music. It seems to appeal to them particularly, and they will make sacrifices—even to denying themselves food—to be able to purchase an organ. It is also an astonishing fact that without any instruction whatever they soon learn to draw melodies from the instrument. These are usually played at a slow tempo, sad and melancholy in style. Occasionally a familiar tune may be recognized which the performer has picked out, but usually their tunes are original. . . . They call this playing "pranking" on the organ, and they are willing to spend hours at it. Coming into their cabins from work in the late afternoon, they begin "pranking" immediately after their evening meal and continue until the midnight hour.[9]

It is possible some of these pranksters were ex-slaves, though more likely their children and grandchildren.

The organ's voicelike qualities and reedy, buzzing tone perfectly suit an African-based musical aesthetic (and jazz and blues music). These same qualities partly explain the accordion's considerable attraction. Accordions, however, have the added advantages of being portable and relatively affordable, and they assumed a far greater role in nineteenth-century North American Black folk music. (They were also widely adopted in Africa and by Latin American and West Indian Blacks.) Nearly twenty ex-slaves mentioned accordions, a tiny figure compared to fiddles or banjos, but not far behind quills or guitars.

Developed in Germany and Austria in the late 1820s, large numbers of accordions were imported to the United States beginning around 1840, rapidly finding favor everywhere. Others arrived already in the hands of various immigrant communities. A novel instrument with unique capabilities, the accordion sometimes spawned completely new genres, but it was also easily incorporated into established forms, folk and popular.[10] Slaves were playing accordions with fiddles and banjos at plantation dances by the late 1840s, just around the time accordions also began appearing in blackface minstrel ensembles. Whether these minstrels imitated slave accordionists (as they sometimes did slave banjo players) is unclear but not inconceivable; minstrels may have in turn influenced Black accordionists, but this is speculative as well.[11]

Many African Americans did subscribe to the belief that while "de devil is a fiddler . . . it involves neither deadly sin nor any spiritual risk whatever to play the accordeon or the 'lap organ,' as they call it."[12] Accordingly, accordions were often played in Black churches or otherwise used to accompany hymns and spirituals.

William Banjo was sitting on the outer porch of the Thomy Lafon Old Folks Home for colored people, playing a tattered accordion. "I can't play much. I ain't got no glue to fix it with," he explained. Louisiana tax tokens, in lieu of screws, held the bellows to the wooden ends of the instrument. Asked for spirituals, his thin face and sightless eyes turned toward the questioner. "I might know some Indian songs." "Indian songs?" "Songs I learned in Oklahoma." In a stately voice, Will began:

I heard the voice of Jesus saying,
"Come unto me and rest;
Lie down, thy weary one, lie down
Thy head upon My breast"

Chorus

"Feed my lamb
Feed my lamb
Feed my lamb
If you love Me,
Feed My lamb."

I come to Jesus,
I was wearied, wounded and sad,
I found in Him a resting place
And He made me glad.

Bill said the chorus was to be repeated three times. "According to Scripture," he explained, "you can make the spirituals as long as you want to, but I don't [want] them too long." He went on: "Singing is like nature, like an appetite. When a man is hungry, he wants to eat, and when he feels like singin', he wants to sing." (William Banjo, b. unk., OK, LA, 13–14)[13]

However, accordions were most often played for dancing, in which case they were instruments of the Devil as much as fiddles, banjos, or guitars.[14] "Dey uster hab big dances, too, reg'lar breakdown dances. Dey play de corjian (accordion) and de fiddle and de vileen [violin?]. Somebody would call de numbers. Dey hab a big house for de dances. Dat was a dif'runt house from de one dey had preachin' in, 'cause it wouldn' be right to serb de Lord and de debbil in de same house" (Adeline White, b. ca. 1857, LA, 4028, orig. parentheses).

I play d 'corjan (accordion) fo' dances sometime'.
Dey uster sing "Kitty Wells" 'n',

Run, nigger, run,
D' patterroles git you.
Run, nigger, run,
It almos' day.

Dey was a feller right behin' me w'at was alays playin' d' bass fiddle. Befo' I jine d' chu'ch I uster play fo' dances all time. Uster play all dem ol' breakdown tunes, but dem pieces done lef' my head. Since I jine d' church I quit all dat. (Leo Mouton, b. ca. 1860, LA, 2812, orig. parentheses)

Moreover, the pieces most often identified with early Black accordionists are not religious songs but fiddle tunes or reels (secular dance songs) like "Kitty Wells" and "Run Nigger Run." Born at Jasper, Texas, near the Louisiana line, Mary Kindred remembered "Dey uster hab lotser dances. Dey hab fiddle player an' 'corjun (accordion) player. Dey sing 'Swing your partner, promenade.' Dey uster hab a l'il song dat start out, / Dinah got a meat skin lay away, / Grease dat wooden leg, Dinah, / Grease dat wooden leg, Dinah" (Mary Kindred, b. ca. 1855, TX, 2204, orig. parentheses). Also known as "Sal's Got a Meatskin," this composition is widespread among both Blacks and whites, whether as an unaccompanied dance song or fiddle tune with words. Huddie "Lead Belly" Ledbetter (1889–1949) was born three decades after Mary Kindred at Caddo Lake, Louisiana, not far north of Jasper. He later recalled "Dinah's Got a Wooden Leg" as one of the first songs he learned to play on the accordion.[15] Perhaps in this region "Dinah" was specifically associated with the instrument. There is no question that accordions were well established in this section of the Texas-Louisiana border. Chris Franklin (b. 1855) was born a slave in Caddo Parish (later Lead Belly's birthplace). Like Lead Belly, Franklin called the accordion a *windjammer*, the regional vernacular. (Having lived in this same area, ex-slave Mary Johnson also stated "us call de 'corjans 'jammers' 'stead of corjans." Mary Johnson, b. ca. 1858, MS, LA, TX, 2027.)

De white folks uster 'low 'em to hold frolics like, an' ball on de plantation. Den dey 'vite other darkies from other places. Dey was usually somebody 'round wid a violin or a banjo or a win'jammer. You dunno what a win'jammer is? Dat's a 'corjin (accordion). Sometime they jes' have one piece. Sometime dey git all together but dat a rare thing. When dey git 'em all together dey say dey got a string band. (Chris Franklin, b. 1855, LA, 1410–11, orig. parentheses)

In fact, while accordions are now especially associated with South Louisiana's Creoles and Cajuns, they were once played by Blacks throughout the state. Lead Belly and Chris Franklin came from the northwestern border with Texas. From St. Joseph in northeastern Louisiana, an ex-slave identified only as Robinson remembered "the slaves were allowed to have social or balls occasionally. . . . An accordion often furnished the music. On rare occasions, there were fiddles, fifes, and sometimes a drum."[16] It is unclear whether these instruments were all played together, but Black fife and drum music was especially popular in the surrounding areas of Louisiana, Mississippi, and Arkansas.

Indeed, allowing that some local traditions may have been particularly strong, Blacks are reported playing accordions everywhere in the South at one time or another. Besides teaching piano and organ for twenty-five years, South Carolinian Jimmie Johnson (b. ca. 1847, SC, 54–55) had played accordion. During roughly this same period, Spartanburg-born singer-guitarist Pink Anderson (1900–1974) was mentored by another older South Carolina accordionist.[17] Like Jimmie Johnson, Georgia ex-slave Abner Griffin (b. 1849, GA, 273) had once played both accordion and organ. Georgia street musician and recording artist Blind Willie McTell (1898–1959) was best known as a virtuoso twelve-string guitarist, but he could also play accordion; his widow, Kate McTell (1911–1991), told David Evans, "he used to play accordion, I think, before he played guitar."[18] Reports of African American

Fig. 8.4. "John Dyson, FSA (Farm Security Administration) borrower, playing the accordion. He was born into slavery over eighty years ago." Saint Mary's County, MD. September 1940. (Among other initiatives, the FSA offered loans to tenant farmers to help them buy their own farms.) Photo by John Vachon. Farm Security Administration/Office of War Information Photograph Collection, Library of Congress, Prints and Photographs Division.

accordion players from North Carolina and Virginia are especially numerous.[19] Bud Jones was raised on a plantation near Lynchburg. "Old master taught me to play the Jew's harp and the French harp and the macordion" (Bud Jones, b. ca. 1850, VA, 2090). An 1887 article on the barbecue as a southeastern institution describes the standard Black dance ensemble at these events as fiddle, accordion, tambourine, and bones.[20] East Virginia accordionist Clarence Waddy (b. 1892) told Kip Lornell that at the turn of the twentieth century, "accordions were the only kind of music we had back then, weren't nothing else."[21] On the other hand, Blind Jesse Harris, one of the best-documented early twentieth-century African American accordionists, was from the Alabama-Mississippi border.[22] Still farther west, ex-slaves John Sneed (b. unk., Travis Co., TX, 3701–2) and Rebecca Thomas (b. 1825, Caldwell Co., TX, 3822) described slaves playing accordions in these two neighboring Central Texas counties, an area where German, Czech-Bohemian, and Mexican

American accordion traditions became especially prominent.

Nevertheless, most of the ex-slaves naming the accordion came from the general vicinity of New Orleans, the antebellum South's busiest port and musical capital. That advantageous location most likely explains how and why, from an early date, accordions became especially well known in Louisiana, southeast Texas, and western Mississippi.[23]

In Mississippi, accordions are remarked among both Blacks and whites almost from the time the instrument debuted in America. "De pleasures de slaves had wuz things lak fishing, hunting, an' frolicing. Dey usually had a picnic once or twice a year. De music fer de merriments wuz fiddles, banjos an' acordins. Some times when dey didn't have no fiddles or nothing dey would jis pat to dance by" (Sylvia Floyd, b. ca. 1852, MS, 744–45). "We had a grand weddin' an' had a big supper an' frolic dat night. We had plenty ob dancin' wid fiddle music an' an accordion playin' an' darkies singin' dem ole songs ob long ago. Dey wuz a few white folks at our weddin' ceremony but ob course dey didn't stay fo' de frolic" (Wash Hayes, b. ca. 1860, MS, 967).

Traversing the piney woods of southern Mississippi in the 1840s, Charles Lanman stayed overnight with a white homesteader whose main business was cutting spar-timbers for the French government. "Our host's family consisted of a wife and *eighteen* children, three of whom were girls, whose average weight we estimated at two hundred pounds, who could, and to our sorrow did, all play on the violin and accordeon, and who were so fond of dancing that whenever two or three spar-cutters happened along to join them they would 'dance all night till broad daylight.'"[24] Mississippi ex-slave Mollie Williams remembered that her owner's wife "Miss Marguarite had a piany, a'cordian, a flutena, an' a fiddle" (Mollie Williams, b. 1853, MS, 2345–46). The *flutina* was an early form of button accordion, but Blacks throughout the New World used *flutina* as a generic term for *accordion*, the same as *melodian* (taken from another early model).[25]

The grown folks didn't have much amusement in slavery times. They had banjo, fiddle, melodian, things like that. There wasn't no baseball in those days. I never seed none. They could dance all they wanted to their way. They danced the cotillions and the waltzes and breakdown steps, all such as that. Pick banjo! U-umph. They would give corn huskins; they would go shuck corn and shuck so much. Get through shucking, they would give you dinner. Sometimes big rich white folks would give dances out in the yard and look at their way of dancing, and doing. Violin players would be colored. (Lewis Brown, b. 1855, MS, 295)

In the 1960s and '70s, several Mississippi blues musicians—Jim Brewer (1920–1988), K. C. Douglas (1913–1975), Eli Owens (1909–?), Big Joe Williams (1903–1982)—recalled older relatives who had played accordions. At least one of these individuals, Eli Owens's great-grandfather Andy Owens (b. ca. 1825, Marion Co., MS), had been a slave.[26]

WPA fieldworkers interviewed a few French Creoles in southwest Mississippi, but all of the Mississippi ex-slaves naming accordions were English speakers who describe them with fiddles, banjos, and body percussion playing the standard plantation repertoire of reels, breakdowns, waltzes, and cotillions. In the twentieth century, however, many Mississippi accordionists gravitated to the blues, the most important secular music to emerge from the state during this period. Charley Patton (1891–1934), the key figure in the early Delta blues, sometimes performed with Homer Lewis, an accordion and mandolin player from Symonds, Mississippi.[27] From nearby Ruleville, accordionist Walter "Pat" Rhodes recorded a pair of blues songs issued by Columbia Records in 1927.[28] Like the organ, the accordion's raspy, voicelike timbre is perfectly suited to blues, and accordionists elsewhere in the South played blues but also African American blues ballads, many of them composed just around the time accordions came into vogue.[29]

The bluesy potential of the accordion would be most fully explored by the Creoles (French-speaking

Blacks) of southwest Louisiana and southeast Texas; however, this took place only after World War II and the emergence of zydeco music, an urban dance genre foregrounding the accordion (but usually the modern amplified chromatic piano accordion), accompanied by electric guitars, bass, drums, horns, and keyboards.[30]

The relation of zydeco to older Creole music is complex, convoluted, and difficult clearly to define, as much as the term *Creole* itself. Historically, several different, sometimes mutually exclusive Gulf Coast populations (Black and white, slave and free) have been identified as Creoles. WPA fieldworkers managed to cover most of these. Mississippi fieldworkers even located a handful of freeborn French-speakers (Edmond Bradley, Henri Necaise, Louis Piernas) from the Creole communities at Bay St. Louis and Pass Christian. However, the majority of Creole narrators had been born in Louisiana. The Louisiana Writers' Project focused its efforts on New Orleans, interviewing a particularly varied assortment of individuals there, including a high percentage of mixed-race freeborns but also numerous Creole ex-slaves of more or less direct African descent; most had lived their entire lives in the city, but a few came from the surrounding countryside.[31] The greatest number of rural Louisiana Creoles were actually interviewed in southeast Texas as part of that state's collection project. One Creole narrator (Ann Mickey) had even been born in Texas, but most had relocated from Louisiana starting in the late 1800s but especially during World War I, or after the 1927 Mississippi flood.[32]

As the foregoing suggests, in the 1800s Creole identity was a fairly fluid phenomenon, particularly among slaves, whose fortunes were generally governed by happenstance. A few narrators categorically regarded themselves, or were regarded by others as *Creoles*, having spent their entire lives in traditional French-speaking milieus. Even these individuals were as diverse a lot as the musical traditions they recalled. La San Mire was born a slave May 12, 1852, on Prosper Broussard's plantation in Abbeville Parish. (Mire spoke only French, the English translation being provided by interviewer Velma Savoy.)

Fig. 8.5. La San Mire, ex-slave, near Beaumont, TX, 1937–38. Portraits of African American ex-slaves from the US Works Progress Administration, Federal Writers' Project slave narratives collection, Library of Congress.

My father was a Spaniard and spoke Spanish and French. My mother spoke French, the old master also, all "Creoles." I, as all the other slaves, spoke French. . . . Sunday, the negro slaves would spend the afternoons dancing round dances (the boys and girls would form a circle, change partners). They sang and danced at the same time. Very rarely did they have Saturday night parties or dances. (La San Mire, b. 1852, LA, 2706, 2707, orig. parentheses)[33]

Louis Piernas, by contrast, was freeborn at Bay St. Louis, Mississippi, March 11, 1856. His father was from Havana, his mother from Santo Domingo (Haiti).

There was a little settlement of free mulattos there, Piernas, La Bat, Barabino, Lassassare—we all spoke French. We kept ourselves separate from the real negroes, and had our own frolics and dances to which the white folks would come sometimes. We went to church with the white folks at Our Lady of the Gulf Church. . . . In my younger days I also used to play and organized the Promot Brass Band. (Louis Piernas, b. 1856, LA, 1702, 1703)

Piernas was formally educated in both French and English, first at a small private school run by Father Le Duc, the priest of Bay St. Louis, later in New Orleans. He does not say what instrument he played.

Anita Fonvergne was freeborn in New Orleans in 1861. Her maternal grandparents were from Cuba and Santo Domingo, her paternal grandparents from France and Switzerland. "We don't know how or where we got negro blood. . . . We don't class ourselves as negroes and we don't class ourselves as white. We never mix with people very much." The anonymous interviewer noted: "Anita speaks English with a strong French accent. She speaks a pure French, not the patois." Fonvergne had spent most of life struggling just to survive, single motherhood and poverty limiting her contacts with the city's legion musical entertainments. "I didn't go out much, but I used to go to soirees, and I would go to dances at the Franc-Ami Hall. I never like goin' out much. . . . My sister had a book with over a hundred French songs in it. I don't know whether she still has it or not. No, the songs are not Creole, they're French" (Anita Fonvergne, b. 1861, LA, 73–75).

For other narrators, however—and especially those born slaves—being Creole was temporary, circumstantial, or situational. Numerous narrators had one or more Creole parents, had passed through Creole slaveholders, had lived among Creoles and so forth, but without absorbing any permanent French influences themselves. "Yes, ma'am, I 'member a few things about slave times. Mr. Lizi, he was a Creole, dat's who us belonged to. We stayed in Opelousas durin' slavery. Dis man sure did have some slaves" (Mary Ann John, b. 1855, LA, 128). "We first belong to Baugilis, a Creole. He sure was a mean man. After he died we was auctioned off. My older brothers and sisters was sold by deyselves, but me, I was too young, I was sold with my ma. We belonged to Guitlot. He was a Creole too" (Julia Woodrich, b. 1851, LA, 217). Interviewed in Madisonville, Texas, narrator Frank Bell had been born nearly nine decades before to a Creole prostitute in the New Orleans whorehouse of her Creole pimp; by September 1937 that memory marked his only connection to French culture. "I was owned by Johnson Bell and born in New Orleans, in Louisiana. 'Cordin' to the bill of sale, I'm eighty-six years old, and my master was a Frenchman and was real mean to me. He run saloon and kept bad women. I don't know nothing 'bout my folks, if I even had any, 'cept mama. They done tell me she was a bad woman and a French Creole" (Frank Bell, b. 1851, LA, 59).

Other ex-slaves had variously accommodated their cross-cultural contacts. Orelia Alexie Franks grew up before the war on Valerian Martin's Lafayette plantation. "My pa' name was Alexis Franks. He was 'Merican an' Creole. My ma' name Fanire Martin. My pa die' w'en I little. I was raise' w'er eb'rybudy talk' French. I talks 'Merican but I talks French goodes'" (Orelia Alexie Franks, b. unk., LA, 1422–23). Born July 8, 1810, at Baton Rouge, Mary Kincheon Edwards was sold young and taken to Texas. "I don' remembah much about dem days, 'xceptin' dat I know I could talk French but I kan't no mo'e" (Mary Kincheon Edwards, b. 1810, LA, 1279). Adeline White was also living in Texas when interviewer Fred Dibble found her, but she had spent her early life speaking "American" in a Louisiana Creole enclave. "I was b'on at Op'lousas. . . . Us talk reg'lar 'Merican, us didn't talk no French but I learnt how to talk it atter freedom come" (Adeline White, b. ca. 1857, LA, 4025). As a youngster around Opelousas Adeline had attended "reg'lar breakdown dances. Dey play de corjian (accordion) and de fiddle and de vileen [violin?]. Somebody would call de numbers" (Adeline White, b. ca. 1857, LA, 4028, orig. parentheses). She does not say whether the dance calls were in American, French, or both.

The mention of accordions at Opelousas in the 1860s is highly significant. This was the heartland of southwest Louisiana's rural Creoles, the descendants of mixed-race planters who arrived from Santo Domingo in the late 1700s, but also their French-speaking African slaves. Over the next century these groups blended with one another but also with Native American, Spanish, Irish, Italian, German, Cajun, and American Black populations. These are the Gulf Coast Creoles who most completely assimilated

Fig. 8.6. Valmar Cormier, ex-slave, Beaumont, TX, July 3, 1937. Portraits of African American ex-slaves from the US Works Progress Administration, Federal Writers' Project slave narratives collection, Library of Congress.

the accordion, the Creoles who after WWII created zydeco, but in urban settings far removed from their rural roots: Lake Charles, Port Arthur, Houston, Los Angeles, Oakland.

Yet zydeco had its own roots in the large repertoire of fiddle-based dance music and French-language dance songs that rural Creoles developed over the nineteenth and early twentieth centuries. In French Louisiana as everywhere, the fiddle was originally the most popular and sometimes the only instrument. "I 'member de day my ol' master go to de war. I kin 'member dat jes' like yestidday. He uster like to play de fiddle an' mek me dance w'en I was l'il. He went to de war an' got kilt. He name' Duplissant Dugat" (Valmar Cormier, b. ca. 1855, LA, 933).

Marster's old brother-in-law let his slaves have dance outdoors on Sunday sometime. Somebody play de violin and de banjo, and dey dance scotto [schottische], and reels and waltzes and codry (quadrille). Sometime dey have a buck dance. Dat where jist one dance by himself. Sometimes dey call dat jig dances. De tune dey play most "Run Nigger run, de patter-rollers ketch you." (Agatha Babino, b. ca. 1850, LA, 140, orig. parentheses)

When de slaves want a dance dey ax de white folks. Dey never make no objection. De dances was always hold on Sunday afternoon, and dey all have to be back to dere quarters by sundown. Dey do de dancing in a slave house. Dey move de chairs and t'ings out of de way so dey have plenty of room. Dere was always somebody what could play de violin for 'em to dance by. De slaves from de other places was ax to come. (Louis Evans, b. 1853, LA, 1310)

Donaville Broussard remembered dancing to a popular French folksong "La boulangère a des écus (The Baker's Wife Has Plenty of Money)," topicalized to the Civil War.

Dey sho' uster like to play marbles in dem times. Eb'rybody play, young folks and ol' folks. De white folks uster git a lot of fun outen comin' 'roun' on Sunday afternoon and watchin' de niggers play marbles. Dey uster like to dance too. Dey had 'roun' dances. Dey uster sing and dance "La Boulangere" in de time of de war. De song go:

> La Boulangere dans ta victoire
> Et nous qui sont en guerre,
> Voice le jour que je dois partir,
> Mon cher ami, tu pars.
> Tu me laisses un enfant dans les bras et prends tes armes.
> Et moi, je vais dans le moment, verser des larmes.
>
> Quand je serai en guerre, toi tu serais de garnison
> Et tu m'oubliri, moi qui sera en haillons.
> J'entends le tombour qui m'appelle a les points du jour.
> Mon cher armande si tu m'aime tu perserais a moi, quand
> Tu serais dans tes plaisirs
> Moi qui serai au bout du fusil.

Fig. 8.7. Donaville Broussard, ex-slave, Beaumont, TX, July 3, 1937. Portraits of African American ex-slaves from the US Works Progress Administration, Federal Writers' Project slave narratives collection, Library of Congress.

A rough translation of the above is:

> The Baker woman is in her victory and we have to go to war.
> This is the day I must depart.
> You leave me with an infant in my arms while you take arms (weapons)
> and I will be shedding tears at the moment.
>
> When you are following the war and you are dressed in your finery you will forget me in rags.
> I hear the drum which calls me at the break of day.
> My dear if you love me you will think of me when you are following pleasure
> And I am following the butt of a gun. (Donaville Broussard, b. 1850, LA, 457–58, orig. parentheses and transl.)[34]

Sylvester Sostan Wickliffe was freeborn in St. Mary's Parish around 1854, the nephew of a free Creole and extensive slaveholder named Romaine Vidrine.

I kin 'member jes' lots of de songs us sung in French, but I kin not give de 'Merican for dem. Dey was a dance song name' "Mam'selle Marie," but I can't give you de spellin' of de words. Dey was annudder call "Loup garou" and I daresay when I bring dem up dey's others I could 'member. One dat de slaves sung I try to translate for you. It go:

> Master of de house
> Gimme meat widout salt
> When de stranger come
> He gimme roas' chicken. (Sylvester Sostan Wickliffe, b. ca. 1855, LA, 4044–45)

The term *zydeco* (also *zodico*, *zottico*, *zarico*, and so on) is said to derive phonetically from the French *les haricots* (green beans)—more specifically, from the line *les haricots sont pas sale* (the green beans are without salt), a metaphor for hard times or mistreatment found in various Creole dance songs.[35] Wickliffe is describing the 1860s, so his example ("Master of de house / Gimme meat widout salt") may be the earliest documented variation on this elemental trope.

Accordions were easily incorporated into these Creole traditions of music and song, typically supporting or substituting for the fiddle. By the twentieth century, these rural strains had evolved into a unique French-language accordion-and-fiddle–based dance style known as *LaLa* or simply *French music*, in many cases indistinguishable from the music of the Creoles' Cajun neighbors.[36] In later years the key exponents of this rural French music were usually the descendants of free Creoles from close-knit, stable, French-language-only communities in close contact with Cajuns.[37]

The turbulent world of Creole slaves was rather different. Following the Louisiana Purchase, the comings and goings of slaves and slaveholders from other areas of the South accelerated. Creoles of various sorts were thrown together on plantations with American slaves, others sold and transported elsewhere. Coastal Louisiana, Mississippi, and Texas were especially rife with the illegal slave trade, bringing captives directly from Africa or through the West Indies right up to the start of the war. Besides offering cosmopolitan musical resources unmatched in North America, New Orleans (and a half dozen other major ports) tied the Gulf Coast to the world and filled it with international visitors even in antebellum years. Thousands came to stay. And then the war turned everything on its head. Homogeneous Creole communities may have thrived in some isolated Gulf Coast enclaves, but throughout the nineteenth century the region as a whole was characterized by extreme cultural diversity and constant flux.

The accordion itself appeared at different times and in different ways at different places. In some areas Creoles adopted the instrument from the Cajuns in the late 1800s; in other sections Creoles and Cajuns were both introduced to accordions by German immigrants arriving after 1880. Ex-slave Ann Mickey was born in the mid-1840s near Beaumont on the sugar cane plantation of Lassee (Lastie) Hillebrandt (Hildebrandt), where she still lived when interviewed in October 1937. She recalled accordions as relatively late additions: "Dem was a big dances at Chris'mas. Dey have all kinds of music. De cullud folks dey make de music. Dey have banjo an' fiddle but dey didn't have no 'cordions in dem times. Dey have different people from different places. Dey 'vite darkies from other farms 'round, an' dey all dance together. Dey have what they call a 'set dance'" (Ann Mickey, b. ca. 1847, TX, 2647–48).

However, some Creoles were playing accordions as early as the 1840s.

I's a purty big gal w'en I go'd (went) up t' d' big house 'n' 'prentice myse'f t' wuk fo' d' Fosters. Dey hab a big plantation at Franklin 'n' hab lots 'r' slaves. Dey call me d' house gal. One time fo' long time Governor Foster was cripple' in he leg 'n' I do nuthin' but nuss him.

I's been so long in d' woods 'n' don' see nobudy much dat I lub it up wid d' w'ite folks. Dey uster to 'low us t' hab dances. W'en dat ol' corjian (accordion) start' t' play, iffen I ain' eben got my hair comb yit it don' neber git comb. I d' fus' one t' git t'

Fig. 8.8. "Negro musicians playing accordion and washboard in front of store, New Iberia, Louisiana." November 1938. Photo by Russell Lee. Farm Security Administration/Office of War Information Photograph Collection, Library of Congress, Prints and Photographs Division.

dat dance 'n' d' las' one t' leabe. Us sometime walk many a mile t' d' dance 'n' carry us shoes on us back. Dey hab fiddle music 'n' 'corjian. D' boss man like t' see d' niggers 'joy demse'fs. Lots 'r' times us hab t' cross ober w'at we call d' big Lunnon bridge 'n' ober d' ferry boat t' git dere. Us dance d' quadrille. I jus' 'bout run t' git dere den. (Virginia Newman, b. 1827, LA, 2904–5, orig. parentheses)

Moreover, much of the accordion music described among Creoles seems to have differed little from the accordion music recalled by ex-slaves everywhere. Leo Mouton was the child of Creoles but did not appear to consider himself in that category. "My daddy was b'on in LaFayette. He was a Creole.... My mudder was a ol' Creole woman." Leo was born on the plantation of an American named Pitt Jones. "Freedom didn' mean much t' me cause I jus' go on libin' on d' place wid my good people's same's my folks befo' me" (Leo Mouton, b. ca. 1860, LA, 2811, 2815, 2810). Before moving to Texas in 1886, Mouton had played accordion at local dances; the two items he named from his repertoire were "Kitty Wells" (Thomas Sloan Jr., 1858), a minstrel piece current mainly with Southern whites, and "Run, Nigger, Run," the most common dance song among slaves across the South.[38] The latter was also the one item named by self-identified Creole ex-slave Agatha Babino, who recalled it with fiddles and banjos, just as it was played everywhere. In fact, after the fiddle, the banjo is the instrument ex-slaves from all regions (including Louisiana) most frequently named with the accordion.[39]

One of the most distinctive features of zydeco music is the washboard or *rubboard* accompaniment, sometimes with triangle or *'tit fer* (little iron). Actually, this was a customary accordion accompaniment across the South, merely surviving longest among Creoles. The washboard itself was a substitute for the jawbone scraper—the mandible of a large draft animal, rubbed and struck with a stick, rod, or key—an African-based instrument found throughout the New World. It is especially well documented in nineteenth-century New Orleans, sometimes described by ex-slaves.[40] In urban zydeco, the washboard was itself eventually replaced by the *frottoir*, a corrugated-metal vest actually worn by the percussionist. In the 1800s, however, the combination of accordion and jawbone scraper (and sometimes triangle) is best documented in Virginia (where accordions were also especially popular).[41] I have found no references for Louisiana. There are a couple of mentions of accordions and triangles, but from English-speakers, outside the Creole heartland. Fred Brown was an American slave from a plantation near Baton Rouge.

> Weuns am 'lowed to have de parties an' de dances. Weuns have fo' de music, sich as de banjo, jew's harp, an' de 'cordian, an' fo' de time, *dey beat de piece ob steel*. Dey have de ol' fashion dance, de promenade, an' de jig. Sometimes dey have de jiggin' contest, two niggers puts a glass ob wauter on deir heads an' den see who can dance de hardest wid out spillin' any wauter. (Fred Brown, b. 1853, LA, 468, my emphasis)[42]

Thus, the accordion music that began surfacing in Gulf Coast cities like Houston, Port Arthur, and Lake Charles after WWII had numerous sources, including French Louisiana folk music but also broader African American trends. The instrument was by then definitely identified with Creoles, most other

Fig. 8.9. Fred Brown, ex-slave, Fort Worth, TX, June 25, 1937. Portraits of African American ex-slaves from the US Works Progress Administration, Federal Writers' Project slave narratives collection, Library of Congress.

African Americans having discarded accordions in favor of pianos and organs (or electric guitars and saxophones). In Houston, Creole migrants settled in an area of the inner city still known as Frenchtown; a 1955 *Houston Post* feature on the neighborhood is the first print source to document the term *zydeco* in its original sense as a house dance. "On Saturday night, somebody holds a 'zottico,' in his house. Out come the accordion, banjo and rub bo'd. The latter is an old-time washing board. The musician plays it with a thimble on his finger. Off they whirl in a folk dance similar to the square dance."[43] Apparently some Creole accordion music was still not much different from the accordion music ex-slaves described across the South a century earlier, even down to the banjo accompaniment. That was all about to change. In the next logical step, many Creoles in Houston and other Gulf Coast cities were already mixing the accordion with electric urban blues. This is the music most people now know as zydeco.

The very year the *Post* feature appeared, accordionist Clifton Chenier (1925–1987) traveled from his home in Port Arthur, Texas, to Los Angeles to record for Specialty Records. Chenier had been born into a musical Creole family near Opelousas but only took up the accordion after moving to Port Arthur in the 1940s. Moreover, his first instrument was not the older diatonic button accordion used with lala music but the chromatic piano model, and his musical inspiration was the R&B then dominating Gulf Coast dance halls and jukeboxes. Soon Chenier was leading his own R&B combo, amplifying his accordion and adding electric guitars, bass, drums, and saxophone to his brother Cleveland's rubboard. Most of the tracks Chenier cut at that first Specialty session were English-language rhythm and blues—what he called rock and roll—but an oddball French-language track, "Ay-Te Te Fee" ("Eh 'Tite Fil," or "Hey Little Girl") (Specialty 552, 1955), became an unexpected hit, earning Chenier brief national celebrity on the R&B circuit. Afterward he returned to the Gulf Coast, and, using Houston as his base, relentlessly toured with his Creole rock and roll, now joined by dozens of other innovators or imitators. Sometime during this period, Chenier started calling his music zydeco, a nod to its rural Creole roots. Most vestiges of that older French tradition were about to disappear, even in rural areas.[44]

FROLICS, CORNSHUCKINGS, AND OTHER OCCASIONS FOR SOCIAL MUSIC

The regular [slave] holydays are two at Easter, two at Whitsuntide, and a week at Christmas. These he enjoys by prescription, and others, such as Saturday evenings, by the indulgence of his master. He passes them in any way he pleases. Generally they are spent visiting from house to house, and in various amusements. His favourite one, if he can raise a violin, is dancing. But this, unfortunately, is going out of fashion, both with whites and blacks, and no good substitute has been found for it. (Virginia slaveholder to J. K. Paulding, *Slavery in the United States* [1836], 209)

De big niggers sho' had good frolics on Sattiday nights. Us little niggers would clap for dem to dance. Everybody had a day off at Christmas and dey would give us little kids a little trash fer Santy Claus. When dey had cornshuckings, dey sho' would have good times. Dey would shout and sing and drink licker and holler, "Whoo-dee-dee! hey! who-dee, hey! whoo-dee!" When us niggers got married, us would jes' hold hands and jump over de broomstick; den live together. (General Jefferson Davis Nunn, b. 1862, AL, 280)

On Saturday nights we just knocked around the place. Christmas? I don't know as I was ever at home on Christmas. I tell you my boss kep' me hired out. Oh, no, the slaves never did get any Christmas presents that I know of. And big dinners, I never was at nary one. They didn't give us nothin', I tell you but a grubbin' hoe and axe and the whip. (Austin Grant, b. unk., TX, 1535)

For American slaves, most opportunities for social music and dance were micromanaged by slaveholders, Southern clergy, vigilante thugs, and other interested persons. Some slaveholders allowed no partying at all, whether from religious scruples, ruthless enterprise, or pure meanness.

"Never had no frolics neither, no ma'm, and didn' go to none. We would have prayer meetings on Saturday nights, and one night in de week us had a chairback preacher, and sometimes a regular preacher would come in" (Nancy Boudry, b. ca. 1837, GA, 114). "Dey wasn' no dancin' much in North Ca'lina, wasn' what you might say, wild, much. Dey work 'em too close" (Simon Hare, b. 1849, NC, 914). "They had dances and parties for the white fo'ks chil'ren, but Mistress said, 'Niggers was made to work for white fo'ks'" (Katie Darling, b. 1849, TX, 1049). "Dey worked, worked, an' wasn't allowed to go to church dem days; not allowed to have no exercise a-tall. Dances nothin'! What did we know about dances in dem times?" (John Barker, b. 1853, TX, 167). "Music? Honey, de only music us knew was de hoe ringin' 'round de cotton plants" (Louis Meadows, b. ca. 1853, AL, 256).

Generally, slaveholders tolerated, supported, even encouraged regular dance parties, whether out of kindness, for their own entertainment, or as standard business practice, duly sanctioned by advice columns on slavery. To keep slaves content, recommended one Mississippi slaveholder, "I have a fiddle in my [slave] quarters, and though some of my good old brethren in the church would think hard of me, yet I allow dancing; ay, I buy the fiddle and encourage it, by giving the boys occasionally a big supper."[1] Agreed another: "I must not omit to mention that I have a good fiddler, and keep him well supplied with catgut, and I make it his duty to play for the negroes every Saturday night until 12 o'clock."[2]

Some slave entertainments were casual off-hours recreations down in the quarters. "At nights the slaves would go from one cabin to the other, talk, dance or play the fiddle and sing. Christmas everybody had holidays, our mistress never gave presents. Saturdays were half-day holidays unless planting and harvest times, then we worked all day" (Richard Macks, b. 1844, MD, 56). "After work was done, the slaves would smoke, sing, tell ghost stories and tales, dances, music, homemade fiddles. Saturday was work day like any other day" (James V. Deane, b. 1850, MD, 8).

Fig. 9.1. John Barker, ex-slave, Abilene, TX, July 13, 1937. Portraits of African American ex-slaves from the US Works Progress Administration, Federal Writers' Project slave narratives collection, Library of Congress.

Other ex-slaves recalled public dances only as rare special occasions or scattered seasonal observances (Christmas, Fourth of July). "Sometimes dey would cook up a heap o' good grub an' dance an' frolic a bit, but if it wuz during de hard wuking parts ob de year, an' dat wuz mos' all de time, den dey jes' went on wid out de frolicing part" (Temple Wilson, b. ca. 1857, MS, 2370). "If someone asks you 'bout de good times weuns have, jus' tell dem dat 'twarnt much. Weuns not 'lowed to go to church, an' once in a while durin' de wintah, de Marster would 'lows de party. Weuns had couple fiddles fo' de music" (Betty Powers, b. ca. 1850, TX, 3139). "Fourth of July come, everybody would lay by. Niggers all be gathered together dancing and the white folks standin' 'round lookin' at them" (Needham Love, b. ca. 1855, AL, 295). "The slaves on 'Marse Jim's' place were allowed about four holidays a year, and a week at Christmas, to frolic. The amusements were dancing ('the breakdown'), banjo playing, and quill blowing" (Charlie Tye Smith, b. 1850, GA, 275, orig. parentheses). "I don't 'member any camp meetin's 'til after de war.

Fig. 9.2. Teshan Young, ex-slave, Fort Worth, TX, June 26, 1937. Portraits of African American ex-slaves from the US Works Progress Administration, Federal Writers' Project slave narratives collection, Library of Congress.

We had a few den and on Christmas times we jes' tears up de country. Lawdy! Lawd! Dat fiddlin' went on all night, and we dance awhile den lay down and sleeps, den gits up and dances some mo'e" (Jack Bess, b. 1854, TX, 73).

> Chrissmushtime 'n' Fo'th 'r' July dey hab a dance. Jus' a reg'lar ol' breakdown dance. Some was dancin' "Swing d' corner," 'n' some was in d' middle 'r' d' flo' "Cuttin' d' chicken wing." Some 'r' 'em was banjer (banjo) pickers. My father was a banjer picker. Sometime dey hab 'em in d' big house. D' w'ite folks hab dem fo' dey own fun. Seem like my folks was happy w'en dey start dancin'. Sometime dey hab 'em in d' yard in front 'r' d' big house 'n' sometime dey hab 'em 'roun'. (Horace Overstreet, b. 1856, TX, 2998–99, orig. parentheses)

I farm all my life. I own a li'l farm of thutty-two acres, an' dey gimme five dollar pension. In slav'ry days hol'days didn' 'mount to much. Dey give us flour to bake a cake on Crissmus day, an' us hatter jump 'roun' lively befo' han' to git to res' on de Fo'th of July, an' den dat was de w'ite folks' hol'day, it war'n' ours. (Jack White, b. 1857, TX, 4035)

When de chores am done on Sunday or Christmas, we'uns can have de music, dance and singin'. We'uns have some good ole times. De songs am de ole timers, sich as Swannee River, Ole Black Joe and dere am de fiddles and banjos dat dey play. We'uns sho' cel'brate on Christmas. De womens all cooks cakes and cookies and sich. De men saves all de bladders from de howgs dey kill, blows 'em full of air and lets 'em dry. De young'uns puts dem on sticks and holds 'em over a fire in de yard. Dat makes 'em bust and dey goes "bang" jus' like a gun. Dat was de fireworks. (Teshan Young, b. ca. 1852, TX, 237)[3]

Weddings were other occasional opportunities for music and dance. "My Aunt married up at old Moster's house and dey giv her a big dance and had de fiddle, dey jus jumped over de broom, den atter slavery wus over she had to remarry" (Jim Gillard, b. ca. 1850, SC, 167). "I married Alice Thompson. . . . Der were bout a dozen at de weddin'. We had a little dancin' and banjo playin'" (Fleming Clark, b. ca. 1860, VA, 24–25). "We had a big time when any of the slaves got married. De massa and de missus let them get married in de big house, and then we had a big dance et one of de slave house. De white folks furnish all kinds of good things to eat, and de colored peoples furnish de music for de dance. My mammy's brother been one of the best fiddlers there was" (Margaret Hughes, b. ca. 1855, SC, 329). "Back in de days when I married, dey had de weddin' at de gal's house and staid deir dat night. De nex' day dey'd go to his Ma's house an dat wuz de enfare [reception]. Both ob 'em hab good things cooked up an' sometimes give a dance. A dance then lasted all through de night" (Allen Ward, b. 1856, MS, 2174).[4]

However, scores of ex-slaves from across the South recalled the institution of the weekly Saturday night dance or *frolic*, often coinciding with a Saturday half-day of field labor. "They never had to work on Sad'day after twelve o'clock. Sad'day nights they would have

Fig. 9.3. "The Broomstick Wedding." Mary A. Livermore, *The Story of My Life* (Hartford, CT: A. D. Worthington, 1897), 257. Illus. by Howard Helmick. The broomstick custom as recalled from 1840s Virginia.

fiddle dances or quilting" (Callie Gray, b. 1857, MS, 865). "Slaves had half a day off on Saturday. Dey had frolics at night, quiltings, dances, corn-shuckings, and played de fiddle" (Harriet Miller, b. ca. 1837, GA, SC, 128). "When dey got behind wid de field wuk, sometimes slaves wuked atter dinner Saddays, but dat warn't often. But, Oh, dem Sadday nights! Dat was when slaves got together and danced" (Georgia Baker, b. 1850, GA, 46). "Spring plowin' and hoein' times we wukked all day Saddays, but mos'en generally we laid off wuk at twelve o'clock Sadday. That was dinnertime. Sadday nights we played and danced. Sometimes in the cabins, sometimes in the yards" (James Bolton, b. 1852, GA, 99). "Saturday at twelve o'clock we was let off from work. The women did their washing, but the men didn't do nothing. Saturday nights we most always had a dance. The banjo and the pat of the hands was the music we had" (Smith Simmons, b. ca. 1860, MS, 1938–39).

Saturday varied a little from the other week days. The field work was suspended in the afternoon to allow the mothers time to wash their clothing. With sunset came the preparations for the weekly frolic. A fiddler furnished music while the dancers danced numerous square dances until a late hour. (Matilda McKinney, b. unk., GA, 89)

Old Miss gave dem dat wanted one a cotton patch and she didn't make her slaves wuk in her fields atter de dinner bell rung on Saddays. De mens wukked in dem patches of deir own on Sadday evenin' whilst de 'omans washed de clothes and cleaned up de cabins for de next week. Sadday nights dey all got together and frolicked; picked de banjo, and drunk whiskey. (Tom Hawkins, b. ca. 1860, GA, 131)

When dey got f'um de fields at night, de 'omans spun, mended, and knit, and de mens wukked in deir gyardens and cotton patches. Winter nights dey plaited baskets and made hoss collars. All de slaves knocked off at twelve o'clock Sadday. Dere was allus somepin' to do on Sadday night—frolics, dances, and sich lak. Dey picked de banjo and knocked on tin pans for music to dance by. (Easter Huff, b. 1858, GA, 248)[5]

On some plantations frolics occurred on other days or nights, whether on the whims of individual slaveholders or by other customs. "We'uns lived in de cabins and have de fiddle and de banjoes. We'uns sing and have music on Sundays" (James Brown, b. 1853, TX, 160). "Durin' the week on Wednesday and Thursday night we had dances an' then they was a lot of fiddlin' an' banjo playin'" (Melvin Smith, b. 1841, SC, 292). "On Sat'day and Sunday nites dey'd dance and sing all nite long. Dey didn't dance like today, dey danced de roun' dance and jig and do de pigeon wing, and some of dem would jump up and see how many time he could kick his feets 'fore dey hit de groun'. Dey had an ole fiddle and some of 'em would take two bones in each hand and rattle 'em" (William M. Adams, b. ca. 1846, TX, 10).

Once a week the slaves could have any night they wanted for a dance or frolic. Mance McQueen was a slave belonging on the Dewberry place that could play a fiddle and his master would give him a pass to come play for us. Master would give us chickens or kill a fresh beef or let us make lasses candy. We could choose any night for the party. 'Cept in the fall of the year we worked awfully hard and didn't have time then. (Andrew Goodman, b. 1840, AL, 1524)

When de slaves want a dance dey ax de white folks. Dey never make no objection. De dances was always hold on Sunday afternoon, and dey all have to be back to dere quarters by sundown. Dey do de dancing in a slave house. Dey move de chairs and t'ings out of de way so dey have plenty of room. Dere was always somebody what could play de violin for 'em to dance by. De slaves from de other places 'round was ax to come. Dey come in dey ordinary clothes 'cause dey didn't have no other kind. Sometimes de white folks come to see de fun. Dey go and stand by de windows outside and look in. Dey seem to enjoy it right smart too. (Louis Evans, b. 1853, LA, 1310)[6]

These were rarities, though. Saturday night was the norm, with or without the half-day. "Saturday was the only night we took for frolicing. . . . As far as I can recollect, the work went on all day Saturday same as on other days" (Louis Davis, b. 1858, AR, 581–82).

Regular locations for frolics included in or around the quarters, in a barn or some other outbuilding, in the yard by the big house, or, rarely, in the big house itself. Slaveholders might provide food and beverages (alcohol was usually reserved for work parties); they might even hire or maintain musicians for such events. "Marse had two of de slaves jus' to be fiddlers. Dey played for us an' kep' things perked up" (John Cameron, b. 1842, MS, 333).

Supervision and surveillance were obsessively maintained at any slave gatherings by slaveholders, overseers, or patrollers. "De patrole riders kept 'em purty well rounded up an' separated only 'cept long enuf fer a little frolicin'. Dey use to sing dis ole song 'bout 'em. / 'Run, nigger, run, de patrole's a commin'"

(Sylvia Floyd, b. ca. 1852, MS, 742–43). "Used to have big parties sometime. No white folks, jus' de overseer come round to see how dey get erlong. I 'member dey have fiddle. I had a cousin who played for frolics, and for de white folks too" (Fannie Fulcher, b. ca. 1860, GA, 251). "Th' quarters bees' off down a hill frum th' big house. On Sadtittys' when we gets to singin' and cuttin' up crazy, we looks up and dars' de White folks sitten up on de hill a' clappin' an callin' out—'Do us a jig dar Abe. Look ole' Abe stomp de groun'.' Whoopee! Dars' plenty keep us busy all th' time" (Abe McKlennan, b. 1847, MS, 1409).

Other whites involved themselves in various ways. "Ef de fiel wuk wuz up, us didn't wuk Saddy ebenin, en we could hab er banjo dance nearly ebery Saddy night. Lots er times, Ole Mistis en her company come ter our dances en looked on, en when er brash nigger boy cut some cu'is steps, de men would trow him dimes, en dey would all laugh fit to kill" (Hattie Clayton, b. 1847, GA, 96). "White ladies didn't go to de frolics, but some of de white men did. De patrollers was allus around to see dat everybody had passes, and if dey didn't have 'em dey was run back home. Sometimes de overseer was dar, too" (George Fleming, b. 1854, SC, 128). "Old master like fiddlin' and dancin' and dat one thing he lowed de niggers on his place to do. We'd have a big time til he'd go and get drunk and tell de overseer to whip everybody" (Jake Dawkins, b. ca. 1845, MS, 595).

Unapproved dances (or unauthorized attendance) were ruthlessly policed by slaveholders and patrollers.

(Ex-slaves say the best times were when they gathered spontaneously in some cabin of the quarters without permission.) Marsa ain't sayed we cain't have no dance an' he ain't sayed we can. But sometimes feel like raisin' a ruckus'—make plenty noise wid de windows wide open, shout clap and sing. 'Course Marsa don't take de trouble to git outen bed an' come down 'cause he know he gonna fin' ev'y slave in bed an' a-snorin'. Might whip us de nex' day, but we done had our dance. Stay as late as we want—don't care ef we is got to be in de field at sunrise. When de dance break up we go out, slam de do' ef we wants, an shout back at de man what had de party:

> Eat yo' meat an' chaw yo' bone,
> Goodbye, nigger I'se gwine home. (Charles
>   Grandy, b. 1842, VA, 119, orig. parentheses)

We wuzn't 'lowed to go around and have pleasure as the folks does today. We had to have passes to go wherever we wanted. When we'd git out there wuz a bunch of white men called "patty rollers." They'd come in and see if all us had passes and if they found any who didn't have a pass he wuz whipped; give fifty or mo' lashes—and they'd count them lashes. If they said a hundred, you got a hundred. They wuz something lak the Klu Klux. We wuz 'fraid to tell our mastahs 'bout the patty rollers 'cause we wuz skeared they'd whip us again, fur we wuz tol' not to tell. They'd sing a little ditty. I wish I could remember the words, but it went somethin' lak this:

> Run, nigger, run, de patty rollers'll git you,
> Run, nigger, run, you'd bettah git away.

We wuz 'fraid to go any place. Slaves wuz treated in most cases lak cattle. (Julia "Sally" Brown, b. ca. 1852, GA, 95–96)

Apparently these brutal tactics did little to deter some slaves from frolicking without permission or passes.

Without question, however, the most lavish entertainments recalled by ex-slaves were work parties, always held with slaveholders' full approval and support because these directly served their economic interests.

Frolics were mostly given at corn shuckings, cane grindings, hog killings, or quiltings. At hog killing time, huge containers of water were heated in the yard. When it reached the desired temperature, the hogs were driven to a certain spot where they were struck a hard blow on the head. When they fell, they were stuck with a very sharp knife, then scalded in the boiling water. The hair and dirt were then scrubbed off and they were a pretty light color as they hung from a rack to be dressed. When the work was completed, the guests cooked chitterlings and made barbecue to be served with the usual gingercake and persimmon beer. They then dressed in their colorful "Sunday" garments, dyed with maple and dogwood bark, to engage in promenades, cotillions, etc., to the time of a quill instrument. (Annie Huff, b. ca. 1830, GA, 234)[7]

At harvest season dere was cornshuckin's, wheat-thrashin's, syrup cookin's, and logrollin's. All dem frolics came in deir own good time. Cornshuckin's was de most fun of 'em all. Evvybody come from miles around to dem frolics. Soon atter de wuk got started, marster got out his little brown jug, and when it started gwine de rounds de wuk would speed up wid sech singin' as you never heared, and dem Niggers was wuking in time wid de music. Evvy red ear of corn meant an extra swig of liquor for de Nigger what found it. When de wuk was done and dey was ready to go to de tables out in de yard to eat dem big barbecue suppers, dey grabbed up deir marster and tuk him to de big house on deir shoulders. When de supper was et, de liquor was passed some more and dancin' started, and sometimes it lasted all night. (Paul Smith, b. ca. 1863, GA, 334)

We didn' have no dancin' dat I 'member, but had plen'y log rollin's. Had fiddlin', an' all would jine in singin' songs, lak, "Run nigger run, pattyrollers ketch you, run nigger run, it's breakin' day." I still fiddle dat chune.(1) Well, you see, dey jes rolled up all de old dead logs an' trees to a pile, and burned it at night. . . . (1) tune. (James Singleton, b. 1856, MS, 1959, orig. note)

Who-OO! Cornshuckins! Yes, dey would go from one plantation to anoder and shuck corn—plenty to eat and whisky to drink. Lawd, ump! Cotton pickins? Moon shine nights—not on dark nights. Feed you jes like dey does at de penitentiary. Pots full of meat. Yes, I seed em dance—Dance myself. Anoder nigger would play de fiddle and de banjo. Dats de way dey do at de penitentiary too. (Joe Rollins, b. 1845, MS, 1898–99)[8]

The common factor in these gatherings was some seasonal excess or exigency intensifying an already grueling slave labor regimen. At cornshuckings, log rollings, cotton pickings, cane cuttings, and sugar makings slaves worked through the night, sometimes for days, stoked by exceptional quantities and qualities of food and alcohol, contests and competitions, instrumental music, and singing and song leaders. The task completed, they were rewarded with more of the same at an all-night frolic. "We had corn-shuckings and cotton-pickings. De niggers would sing: 'Job, Job, farm in a row; Job, Job, farm in a row.' Sometimes on moonlight nights we had pender [*pinder*, the regional term for peanut] pullings and when we got through we had big suppers, always wid good potatoes or pumpkin pies, de best eating ever" (Caroline Farrow, b. ca. 1857, SC, 40). "When dey had cornshuckings, dey sho' would have good times. Dey would shout and sing and drink licker and holler, 'Whoo-dee-dee! hey! who-dee, hey! whoo-dee!'" (General Jefferson Davis Nunn, b. 1862, AL, 280).

> Marse was sho good to dem gals and bucks what work cuttin' de cane. When dey git done makin' sugar, Marse give a drink dey call "Peach n' Honey" to de women folk and whisky and brandy to de men. And of all de dancin' and caperin' you ever did see. My pa was fiddler and we would cut de pigeon wing and cut de buck and every other kind of buck and dance. (Ellen Betts, b. 1853, LA, 271)

Such bonuses were not guaranteed. Confronted with more work demands, some slaveholders just demanded more work. "I heared tell dey had Christmas fixin's and doin's on other plantations, but not on Marse Frank's place. All corn shuckin's, cotton pickin's,

Fig. 9.4. Jeff Nunn, ex-slave, 1937–38, AL. Portraits of African American ex-slaves from the US Works Progress Administration, Federal Writers' Project slave narratives collection, Library of Congress.

log rollin's, and de lak wuz when de boss made 'em do it, an' den dere sho warn't no extra sompin t'eat" (Easter Brown, b. 1860, GA, 138). "Cotton pickin's warn't planned for fun and frolic lak cornshuckin's. If Marse Billy got behind in his crops, he jus' sont us back to the fields at night when de moon was bright and sometimes us picked cotton all night long" (Callie Elder, b. ca. 1860, GA, 312). "Asked about frolics and recreations, Cora remembered only candy pullings and quiltings. 'Marster never did have no bands or nuthin' like dat on his place.' She could not remember any wedding celebrations" (Cora Shepherd, b. 1855, GA, 554). "We shucked our co'n on rainy days mostly, but de marster lets us have one big co'n shuckin' eber' year an de person what fin's a red year [red ear] can kiss who dey pleases" (Julius Nelson, b. 1860, NC, 146). "My master had no public cornshuckings. His slaves shucked his corn" (Parker Pool, b. 1846, NC, 187).

> We had corn shucking, but it wasn't in the form of a party. We done the shucking in the day time. Everybody was sent to the crib together. They

would sing and have good times, but they didn't have no prizes. The song they liked best was

> Once I was so lucky,
> Old Master set me free
> Sent me to Kentucky
> To see, what I could see
> Mean old banjo Thomas
> Mean old banjo Joe
> Going away to Kentucky
> Won't come back no more. (Louis Davis, b. 1858, AR, 582–83)[9]

For obvious reasons, urban slaves also had little experience with cornshuckings and the like. Mollie Hatfield was born on a boat in Mobile Bay where her mother worked as a cook. "Not ever living on a plantation my ma didn't know anything about Corn shuckins and Cotton pickins, but dey give cullerd folks dances on de boat, and dey would dance by a banjo" (Mollie Hatfield, b. ca. 1860, AL, 955).

Across the rural South, however, certain forms of slave labor customarily doubled as dance parties. Despite their true purposes and the backbreaking exertions these entailed, such events ranked among the ex-slaves' fondest memories. Indeed, cornshucking was the plantation slaves' Carnival, a slaveholder dictate refashioned into a West African–style harvest festival, much as other New World Black populations transformed Mardi Gras celebrations or Yuletide mumming.

Ex-slaves recalled a wide range of work parties, some mentioned but a time or two.[10] The most common were cornshuckings, log rollings, cotton pickings, quiltings, and various events tied to harvesting and processing sugar cane. Log rolling was the arduous final step in clearing new land. Lewis Paine (1819–?) had rolled logs in prewar Georgia. "After a farmer has cleared a piece of land, and gathered all but the large logs, he gives an invitation to his neighbors to come and help him roll the remaining logs into large piles, for the purpose of being burnt."[11] Following the general pattern, however, log rolling was converted to sport accompanied by music and song, concluding with a dinner-dance and bonfire. "Den 'twas de log rollin'. Dat am de contest 'tween two teams, 'bout three to de team, dey see which can roll de log de fastest" (Fred Brown, b. 1853, LA, 468). "W'en we wuk in de fiel', one holler was 'Hoe, Ramsey, Hoe!' W'en we'uns roll logs, dey hab long han' sticks and roll, and holler and sing" (Will Rhymes, b. 1853, LA, 3301).[12] "De men and 'omans would roll dem logs and sing and dey give 'em plenty of good eats, and whiskey by de kegs, at logrollin's" (Carrie Hudson, b. ca. 1860, GA, 217). "Log rollings wuz lots ob fun to me as I wuz strong den, an' I could 'show off' befo' de odder niggers. Dey wasn't much rollin' to it, mostly carrying. I mind de time when I lifted de end ob a log, an' four men tried at different times to lift de odder, but dey couldn't do it" (Frederick Shelton, b. 1857, AR, 145).[13] "Atter de logs was all rolled, dey et, and drunk, and danced 'til dey fell out. I'll bet you ain't never seed nothin' lak dem old breakdowns and dragouts us had dem nights atter logrollin's. Dey sho drug heaps of dem Niggers out" (Lina Hunter, b. ca. 1848, GA, 267).

> I did lak ter take in de good times us had. De ole log rollin's wuz good times. Totin' dem logs on sticks an' a stackin' 'em high while us wuz a hollerin' and a singin'. Us would throw dem logs ober to de time ob a tune, all de time us a thinkin' ob de big dinner a waitin' fer us. Hit wuz spread on long tables in de shade o' de trees. Us had dances dat would last all nite long. How dey would swing deir pardners. I tried so hard to learn ter dance, but somehow I'se jis one nigger dat couldn't neber git de kick. (Manus Robinson, b. ca. 1860, NC, 1859)

> Marse had log rollin's, and 'vited evvybody. Dey all come and brung deir Niggers. Marster had big dinners for 'em, and atter dey done rolled dem logs all day dem Niggers evermore did eat. When dey was wukkin' dey sung somethin' lak dis:

> > I'se wukkin' on de buildin'
> > And hits a sho' foundation,

And when I git done
I'se goin' home to Heb'en. (Alice Hutcheson,
b. ca. 1860, GA, 284)[14]

Cotton pickings were the most practically purposed of these occasions. Amenities might consist merely of food and booze to ply slaves while they worked by moonlight harvesting the planter's cash crop, maybe with competitions as added incentives. "Marster give de 'oman what picked de most cotton a day off, and de man what picked de most had de same privilege" (Callie Elder, b. ca. 1860, GA, 312). Many cotton pickings also ended in frolics. "On bright moonshiny nights folkses would invite the neighbors for cotton pickings. After the cotton wuz picked dey would eat barbecue, and dance and have a big time" (Martha Colquitt, b. ca. 1850, GA, 244). "When we had cotton pickings, just like corn shuckings, there was good things to eat and a dance afterwards" (Cicely Cawthon, b. 1859, GA, 190).[15]

In Louisiana especially, sugar cane was a primary cash crop, and its cultivation, harvest, and processing were year-round operations. "All I's ever knowed was to work. Was born on Mr. Gain's plantation was raised in the sugar cane fields" (Annie Flowers, b. ca. 1860, LA, 70). "I worked in the cane juice place. Big boats stopped at our landin', and they'd take on maybe 150 barrels of sugar 400 barrels molasses at a time. Sugar was 'king' in those days" (Hunton Love, b. ca. 1840, LA, 162). Most plantations across the South raised cane for their own consumption, and its various stages of preparation also became social occasions.[16] "Syrup makin' time at Marse Hamp's was a frolic too" (Mahala Jewel, b. ca. 1862, GA, 320).

Marse Stone had a big sugar camp with 300 trees. We would be waked up at sunup by a big horn and called to get our buckets and go to the sugar camps and bring water from the maple trees. These trees had been tapped and elderwood spiles were placed in the taps where the water dripped to the wooden troughs below. We carried this water to the big poplar troughs which were about 10 feet long and 3 feet

high. The water was then dipped out and placed in different kettles to boil until it became the desired thickness for "Tree Molasses." Old Miss Polly would always take out enough water to boil down to make sugar cakes for us boys. We had great fun at these "stirrin' offs" which usually took place at night.

The neighbors would usually come and bring their slaves. We played Sheep-meat and other games. Sheep-meat was a game played with a yarn ball and when one of the players was hit by the ball that counted him out. One song we would always sing was "Who ting-a-long? Who ting-a-long? Who's been here since I been gone? A pretty little girl with a josey on." (Bert Mayfield, b. 1852, KY, 14–15)[17]

Candy pullings were especially common during sugar making but might occur anytime. Technically they were not in all instances work parties, but they were certainly popular. "Den us had lasses candy pullin's dat wuz gran'. De 'lasses a boilin', an' den, de pullin' o' dat candy wid yo' gal" (Manus Robinson, b. ca. 1860, NC, 1858–59). "'Bout de only rec'ration us niggers had in dem days was candy pullin's. We all met at one house an' tol' ghost stories, sung plantation songs, an' danced de clog while de candy was cookin'" (Hamp Kennedy, b. 1857, MS, 1273). "Us had candy pullings an' water mellon cuttings on de plantation; an us had guitar and fiddle music. All de niggers could sing" (Rosa Mangum, b. 1831, MS, 1435). "We had good times. I danced. We had candy pullings bout at the houses. We had something every week. I used to dance in the Courthouse at Clarendon—upstairs. Paul Wiley was head music man. All colored folks—colored fiddlers" (Molly Horn, b. 1860, AR, 320). "My old Master give the chil'ren a candy pullin' every Saturday night and had them wrestling and knocking each other about. The big fo'ks had dances and parties. They had fiddles but they warn't like these things they have now. The fiddles we had then made music" (Bert Strong, b. 1864, TX, 3758).

Dey had a string band wid a fiddle, a trumpet, and a banjo, but dere warn't no guitars lak dey has in dis day. One man called de sets and us danced de cardrille (quadrille), de virginia reel, and de 16-hand cortillion. When us made syrup on de farm dere would always be a candy pullin'. Dat homemade syrup made real good candy. Den us would have a big time at corn shuckin's too. (Liza Mention, b. ca. 1865, GA, child of ex-slaves, 124, orig. parentheses)

To make the candy itself molasses was *stewed* (heated), congealed in cold water, then *pulled* (stretched by hand), causing it further to harden.

De bigges' fun us had wuz at candy pullin's. Ma cooked de candy in de washpot out in de yard. Fust she poured in some homemade sirup, an' put in a heap o' brown sugar from de old sirup barrel an' dan she biled it down to whar if you drapped a little of it in cold water it got hard quick. It wuz ready den to be poured out in greasy plates an' pans. Us greased our han's wid lard to keep de candy from stickin' to 'em, an' soon as it got cool enough de couples would start pullin' candy an' singin'. Dat's mighty happy music, when you is singin' an' pullin' candy wid your bes' feller. When de candy got too stiff an' hard to pull no mo', us started eatin', an' it sho' would evermo git away from dar in a hurry. You ain't nebber seed no dancin', what is dancin', lessen you has watched a crowd dance atter dey et de candy what dey done been pullin'. (Georgia Telfair, b. 1864, GA, 6)[18]

Quiltings were the slaves' own cooperative work parties, private domestic gatherings, usually with dinner-dances attached. "De only fun de young folks had wuz w'en de ole folks had a quiltin'. W'ile de ole folks wuz wukin' on de quilt de young ones would git in 'nuther room, dance en hab a good time" (Millie Simpkins, b. 1831, TN, 67). "Colored people would have quiltings to one of dey own house, up in de quarter, heap of de nights en dey would frolic en play en dance dere till late up in de night" (Sallie Paul, b. ca. 1856, SC, 244). "Evenings after work slaves were allowed to visit each other. Molasses candy pulls, quiltin' and maybe a little dancin' by de tune of an old banjo" (Marinda Jane Singleton, b. 1840, NC, 267). "The old folks had corn-shuckings, pender pullings, and quiltings. They had quiltings on Saturday nights, with eats and frolics. When dey danced, dey always used fiddles to make the music" (Peggy Grigsby, b. ca. 1831, SC, 215).

De Marster's, dey planned de cornshuckin's, and cotton pickin's, and logrollin's and pervided de eats and liquor, but de quiltin' parties b'longed to de slaves. Dey 'ranged 'em deir own selfs and done deir own 'vitin' and fixed up deir own eats, but most of de Marsters would let 'em have a little sumpin' extra lak brown sugar or 'lasses and some liquor. De quiltin's was in de cabins, and dey allus had 'em in winter when dere warn't no field wuk. Dey would quilt a while and stop and eat apple pies, peach pies, and other good things and drink a little liquor. (Carrie Hudson, b. ca. 1860, GA, 217)

One of the favorite socials was a quilting party. After quilting for a while, they would have refreshments of syrup, bread, potato pudding, and honey cakes. The mistress would have the feast prepared and sent to them to enjoy. Then there would be a dance that lasted far into the night. Banjo music was played. (Alice Battle, b. ca. 1850, GA, 41)[19]

Compared to public frolics, candy pullings and quiltings tended to be relatively genteel affairs—but not always.

I 'member one night dey had a quiltin' in de quarters. De quilt was up in de frame, an' dey was all jes' quiltin' an' singin' "All God's Chilluns are a Gatherin' Home," w'en a drunk man wannid to preach, an' he jumped up on de quilt. Hit all fell down on de flo', an' dey all got fightin' mad at 'im. Dey locked 'im in de smokehouse 'til mornin', but dey diden' nobody tell Mistus nuffin' 'bout it. (Georgia Smith, b. ca. 1850, GA, 283)

One time de niggers was off at a candy stew and just as the leader called out "Promenade and Sociate," a pataroller put his head in the window and said "Promenade and Sociate yourselfs." Well, the niggers tore down the chimney and part of the wall getting away—and he didn't catch them. So then they ran around to the road where he had to pass and strung up wild grape vines so they would stumble his horse or rake him off. (Aaron Jones, b. 1845, MS, 1187)

But beyond doubt the slaves' biggest holiday was cornshucking, a true carnival with torchlit parades accompanied by music and song, bonfires, feasting and drinking, sports and competitions, prizes, fiddle dances, mock royalty and rites of reversal—all centered on the essential task of de-husking the annual supply of feed corn. Moreover, of all work parties cornshuckings exhibited the greatest similarity from plantation to plantation, and from region to region, a well-defined ritual structure presumably based on some deeply shared template or common understanding among participants.

Dem old cornshuckin's was sho 'nough big times, 'cause we raised so much corn dat it tuk several days to shuck it all. Us had to have two generals. Dey chose sides and den dey got on de biggest piles of corn and kept de slaves a-singin' fast so dey would wuk fast. De fust crowd what finished got de prize. Dere ain't much I can 'member of words to dem old cornshuckin' songs. One general would start off singin': "Shuck up dis corn, shuck up dis corn, 'cause us is gwine home," and de other general would be a-shoutin': "Make dem shucks fly, make dem shucks fly, us is gwine to go home." Over and over dey kept on singin' dem lines. Come nighttime Marster would have big bonfires built up and set out torches for 'em to see how to wuk, and evvy time he passed 'round dat jug of corn likker shucks would fly some faster. When all de corn was done shucked and de big supper had been et, der was wrastlin' matches and dancin' and

all sorts of frolickin'. (Benny Dillard, b. ca. 1858, GA, 293–94)[20]

Corn was the plantation's essential fuel, sustaining the horses, mules, hogs, and cattle that then fed the population and profited the planter. Accordingly, all plantations devoted substantial acreage to feed corn, which at harvest had to be shucked before storage. The kernels could then be separated from the cobs as necessary (corn shellings were other festive occasions), the husks being retained to feed wintered cattle or stuff mattresses, the cobs eventually going to the outhouses. Raised on a North Carolina plantation, John Battle Avirett (1835–1912) estimated that the annual crop produced a corn pile two-hundred-and-fifty feet long, four-and-a-half feet high, and fourteen-to-sixteen feet wide, requiring about two hours for two-hundred-and-fifty workers to shuck. Avirett's example was not atypical.[21]

To meet this labor-intensive, time-sensitive imperative, many planters shucked cooperatively in rotation, trouping their slaves from one corn pile to another throughout the harvest season. "'Bout the most fun we had was at corn shuckin's whar they put the corn in long piles and called in the folkses from the plantations nigh round to shuck it. Sometimes four or five hunnert head of niggers 'ud be shuckin' corn at one time. . . . Some years we 'ud go to ten or twelve corn shuckin's in one year!" (James Bolton, b. 1852, GA, 99–100). Freelancers were also welcome, the usual draconian controls on slave movements being temporarily suspended. "Sich and sich a man would have 500 bushels of corn to shuck and invite de slaves from neighbor plantations to come. Didn't need no pass den. We'd all go shuck and holler and whopping—den dere would be a big supper. Dere would be gallons of whiskey. De boss would go around wid de jug, so we could holler clear. Cut the phlegm" (Jerry Eubanks, b. 1846, MS, 696). "De best times was when de corn shuckin' was at hand. Den you didn't have to bother with no pass to leave de plantation, and de patter rolls didn't bother you. If de patter rolls cotch you without de pass any other time, you better wish you dead, 'cause you would have yourself some trouble" (Green Cumby, b. 1851, TX, 260). "Dar was also heaps and lots of other big affairs 'sides de frolics. De cornshuckings—Lawd a-mercy, you ain't seen nothing. . . . Had cotton pickings, too. . . . Sometimes dey be on our plantation; den we sometimes go to other places. Didn't need no passes when a bunch of slaves went to other plantations to dem big gatherings" (George Fleming, b. 1854, SC, 128–29). Kentucky ex-slave William Wells Brown (1814–1884) also reported "on these occasions, the servants, on all plantations, were allowed to attend by mere invitation of the blacks where the corn was to be shucked."[22] (Postwar landowners operated along similar lines, turning out their own tenants while attracting enough additional hands merely with the promise of dinner, drinks, and a dance.) The results were some of the largest gatherings of slaves in the plantation South, given extraordinary latitude to enjoy themselves so long as they got the corn shucked.

To maintain the daily work schedule, cornshuckings were usually held at night, ideally at a full moon, but even then there would torches or bonfires, accentuating the carnival atmosphere. The music and festivities began with the dramatic arrival of shuckers from afar amid song and frivolity. Sometimes individuals casually congregated en route to the site. "When starting for the festivity—for the shuckings were so considered—a solitary refrain might be heard a mile or two away, then another would join, and as they approached, more and more, until they arrived, singing, at the corn-pile in a company of fifteen or twenty; sometimes two or three such companies would approach at the same time, making the night-air resonant with melody."[23] "The guests begin to arrive about dark, and in a short time, they can be heard in all directions, singing the plantation songs, as they come to the scene of the action."[24]

Other times shucking crews from different plantations marched as organized companies in torchlit parades:

When the overseer has a quantity of corn to husk, he allows his Negroes to invite those on the neighboring plantations to come and help them in the evening. When all things are ready, they light the torches of pitch pine, (their [sic] being an abundance of it about here) and march while singing one of their corn songs to the spot. Then the captain mounts the heap of corn, and all sing a *call song* for the others to come, which is immediately answered from the other plantations, in a song that "they are coming." You can hear them distinctly more than a mile. They sing as they march all the way, and when they arrive at the spot, they all join in one *grand chorus*—and make the forest ring with their music.[25]

One night Mr. Taylor, a large planter, had a corn shucking, a Bee it is called. The corn pile was 180 yards long. He sent his slaves on horseback with letters to the other planters around to ask them to allow their slaves to come and help. On a Thursday night, about 8 o'clock, the slaves were heard coming, the corn-songs ringing through the plantations. "Oh, they are coming, they are coming!" exclaimed Mr. Taylor, who had been anxiously listening some time for the songs. The slaves marched up in companies, headed by captains, who had in the crowns of their hats a short stick, with feathers tied to it, like a cockade. I myself was in one of the companies.[26]

Various kinds of horns were also traditionally blown at cornshuckings; many corn songs even mention bugles or horns: "Shuck this corn, boys, let's go home. / Blow, horn, blow." "Going up the country, / Bugle, oh!"[27] In antebellum South Carolina, "most plantations had a bugler who owned an old wooden bugle five or six feet long . . . which could be heard for miles on a clear night. The bugles were carried to the corn shuckin's, and the coming darkies would blow and blow, and be answered by the bugler at the corn pile, and as he did so he would say 'Dar's the niggers comin' from Byers's plantation.' 'Dar dey is from Elliott's.' As they drew nearer to the pile of corn the bugle blowers would stop and give way to quill or reed blowers."[28]

With or without horns, the road march was always accompanied by singing, which continued unabated once the companies reached the worksite. Whether selected for the march or elected at the corn pile, the cornshucking captain or general was first and foremost a song leader, but he also filled the customary carnival role of a King of Fools or Lord of Misrule, a mocking caricature of slaveholder, overseer, and plantation authority overall. From sundown to sunup, the general ruled the topsy-turvy time-space of cornshucking, exceeding daily slave-labor productivity by inverting its authoritarian methods. One nineteenth-century Georgia landowner marveled that "an amount of work which would astonish the shuckers themselves, and which, if demanded of them in the daytime would be declared impossible, is accomplished under the excitement of the corn-song."[29]

Besides an extraordinarily loud voice, the general's main qualifications were being willing and able to play the fool. "Dey had big times at cornshuckin's and log rollin's. My pappy, he was a go-gitter; he used to stand up on de corn and whoop and holler, and when he got a drink of whiskey in him he went hog wild" (Alice Green, b. ca. 1862, GA, 43). At antebellum Virginia cornshuckings, wrote Letitia Burwell (1831–1905), slaves filled the captain's slot by "selecting one of their number—usually the most original and amusing, and possessed of the loudest voice."[30] Garnett Andrews (1798–1873) had closely observed Georgia cornshucking generals:

> Sometimes he would, in the enthusiasm of the occasion, fall on his knees and clap his hands above his head, then rise, holding them, clasping a ear of corn, in the same attitude, then with legs in the form of the letter V inverted, and his left arm akimbo—all the while "giving out" [singing]—he would wave his right, in his rhapsody, gracefully— as if monarch of all he surveyed . . . and go through such other extravagant attitudes as the genius of the actor and fervor of the moment might inspire.[31]

It was through this musical buffoonery that the general drove his troops. "When they had shuckings one Negro would sit on the fence and lead the singing, the

Fig. 9.5. "A plantation 'corn-shucking'—social meeting of slaves." Mary A. Livermore, *The Story of My Life* (Hartford, CT: A. D. Worthington, 1897), 337. Illus. by Howard Helmick. A Virginia cornshucking captain leading a corn song ca. 1840. Educator, journalist, activist, and abolitionist Mary Ashton Rice Livermore (1820–1905) had witnessed cornshuckings as a tutor on a Virginia plantation from 1839–42: "They sang without cessation while they worked, until the cribs were heaped and overflowing, and all the corn was husked, and then supper was announced. / Solo.—'Religion's like a bloomin' rose. / Chorus.—We'll shuck dis cawn before we go! / An none but dem dat feels it knows / we'll shuck dis cawn before we go!'" (336–39).

others shuck on each side" (Henry Walker, b. ca. 1856, AR, 34). "Us had sech good times Saddy nights, frolic, dance and corn-shuckings, they wuz a nuther good time, most uv em would be tight and sing and holler, 'Sheep's in cotton patch, got em out Monday. Had er been a white man, got em out Sunday.' Kid Kimbrough wuz our leader, would sing Dixie too" (Carrie Davis, b. ca. 1850, GA, 119). "They would have a fellow there they would call the general. He would walk from one person to another and from one end of the pile to the other and holler and the boys would answer. His idea was to keep them working. If they didn't do something to keep them working, they wouldn't get that corn shucked that night. Them people would be shucking corn!" (Claiborne Moss, b. 1857, GA, 161).

The one with the most powerful voice was selected to stand on top of the corn pile and lead the singing. They would all get in a working mood to the tune of the shucking song.

> Come to shuck that corn tonight,
> Come to shuck with all your might,

Come for to shuck all in sight,
Come to shuck that corn tonight, etc. (John
    Spencer, b. ca. 1857, VA, 279)

Oh-oo-h! Everybody had cornshuckings. The man designated to act as the general would stick a peacock tail feather in his hat and call all the men together and give his orders. He would stand in the center of the corn pile, start the singing, and keep things lively for them. Now and then he would pass around the jug. They sang a great deal during cornshuckings, but I have forgotten the words to those songs. Great excitement was expressed whenever a man found a red ear of corn, for that counted 20 points, and a speckled ear was 10 points and a blue ear 5 points, toward a special extra big swig of liquor whenever a person had as many as 100 points. After the work was finished they had a big feast spread on long tables in the yard, and dram flowed plentiful, then they played ball, tussled, ran races, and did everything they knew to amuse themselves. (John F. Van Hook, b. 1862, NC, 81)

A gen'ral of de cornshuckin' wuz appointed to lead off in de fun. He sot up on top of de big pile of corn an' hysted de song. He would git 'em started off singin' somethin' lak "Sallie is a Good Gal," an evvybody kept time shuckin' an' a singin'. De gen'ral kept singin' faster an' faster, an' shucks wuz jus' flyin'. When pa started passin' de jug 'roun' dem Niggers sho' nuff begun to sing loud an' fas' an' you wuz 'bliged for to 'low Sallie mus' be a Good Gal, de way de shucks wuz comin' off of dat corn so fas'. (Georgia Telfair, b. 1864, GA, 6–7)

De fus' thing to do was to 'lect a gen'ral to stand in de middle of all dem piles of corn and lead de singin' of de reels. No Ma'am, I don't 'member if he had no shuck stuck up on his hat or not, and I can't ricollec' what de words of de reels was, 'cause us chillun was little den, but de gen'ral, he

pulled off de fus' shuck. Den he started singin' an' dey all sung in answer to him, and deir two hands a-shuckin' corn kep' time wid de song. As he sung faster, dey jus' made dem shucks more dan fly. Evvy time de gen'ral would speed up de song, de Niggers would speed up deir corn shuckin's. (Emma Virgel, b. 1865, GA, child of ex-slaves, 119)

There are occasional reports of instrumentalists accompanying shuckers. "To the tune of an old fiddle in the hands of a plantation musician, they would sing and shuck corn until the whole pile was finished" (Wheeler Gresham, b. ca. 1855, GA, 70). "When there was a big barn full of corn to be shucked the neighbors gladly gathered in, shucked the corn for the owner, who had a fiddler and maybe some one to play the banjo. The corn was shucked to gay old tunes and piled high in another barn" (Henry Rogers, b. 1864, GA, 224).

At corn shucking all the slaves from other plantations would come to the barn, the fiddler would sit on top of the highest barrel of corn, and play all kind of songs, a barrel of cider, jug of whiskey, one man to dish out a drink of liquor each hour, cider when wanted. We had supper at twelve, roast pig for everybody, apple sauce, hominy, and corn bread. We went back to shucking. The carts from other farms would be there to haul it to the corn crib, dance would start after the corn was stored, we danced until daybreak. (James V. Deane, b. 1850, MD, 8)

Judge Maddox bought a nigger man who had a three string fiddle. . . . This nigger would play to us as we worked. He played and sang:

Cotton eyed Joe
Hadn't been for cotton eyed Joe
I'd been married seven year ago.

He had a song for everything. . . . His corn shucking song was:

Sheep shear corn
By the rattle of his horn
Never seen the like
Since I been born. . . .

Then we went to some neighbors for a corn shucking and they had some whiskey. The niggers sang:

All don't form a row shan't drink
Come on all you niggers
Stand in a row.
All don't form a row shan't drink.

It sounded right pretty. (Jack Maddox, b. ca. 1849, TX, 2531–33)

Singing and songs were the true engines of cornshucking, however. Jack Maddox quotes two well-known items. The *sheep-shear-corn* stanza has parallels in sixteenth-century England but is common in Black corn songs.[33] "All Don't Form a Row Shan't Drink," probably a slave creation, typifies the many shucking songs demanding refreshment.[34]

Though little remembered today, the corn song was a fundamental genre of nineteenth-century Black folksong.[35] Certainly it is one of the varieties most often mentioned by ex-slaves. Context is the defining feature of corn songs, form and function being one and the same. Some items were specific to this activity, others were adapted from the general repertoire, but as corn songs they were invariably performed in a call-and-response pattern timed to the task (a feature of Black work songs generally), and with considerable improvisation. "Some of them niggers sure could sing and the ones of us what couldn't joined in the chorus just the same. I wish I could remember that old song we sang. It started out, 'Shuck, shuck, round up your corn.' The rest of the words is sure left me now" (Squire Irvin, b. 1849, TN, 1086). "In de evening when de work was done we would sit 'round and play marbles and sing songs. We made our songs up as we went along. Sometimes dere would be a corn shuckin' and dat was when we had a good time, but

Fig. 9.6. "Husking Corn." *Harper's Weekly* 5 (April 13, 1861): 232. A fiddler accompanies shuckers from the top of the corn pile.

we always shucked a lot of dat corn" (William Black, b. ca. 1850, MO, 32).

De co'n would be piled up high an' one man would git on dat pile. Hit usually was one who was kinda niggah for'man dat could sing an' get de wuck out ob de odder niggers. Dis for'man would sing a verse somethin' lack dis.

Polk an' Clay went to War.
An' Polk cum back wid a broken jar [jaw].

Den all de niggers would sing back to him, an' hallo, a kinder shoutin' soun'. Ginerally dis for'man made up his songs by pickin' dem up from whut he heard white folks tell of wars. (Joseph Holmes, b. 1856, VA, 199)[36]

Ev'ey now and den we would have some good frolics, mostly on Sattiday nights. Somebody would play de fiddle and we all danced to de music. De folks sure had some big times at de cornshuckin's, too. De men would work two or three days, haulin' de corn and pilin' it near de crib. Den dey would invite folks from other quarters to come and help wid de shuckin'. While dey shucked dey would holler and sing:

> You jumped and I jumped;
> Swear by God you outjumped me.
> Huh! Huh! Round de corn, Sally. (Eliza White, b. ca. 1855, GA, 412)[37]

On Sadday nights us would frolic an' dance all night long iffen you wanted to, buck-dance, sixteen-hand reel and cake walk. Dey would blow reed quills an' have all the licker dey wanted. Mistiss, dey ain't jes' now drinkin' licker. Oh, dem cornshuckings! Shuck corn, drink an' holler all night long. Sometimes dey'd sing:

> Dark cloud arising like gwine to rain,
>> Nothing but a black gal coming down the lane,
> Nigger stole a pumkin an' started outer town;
>> Nigger heered it thunder, Lord, an' throwed dat pumkin down.

Mistiss, I don't wanter tell you no mo' of dat. (Frank Menefee, b. ca. 1843, AL, 280)[38]

Writing in 1882, Georgia landowner David C. Barrow Jr. confirmed: "the corn-song is almost always a song with a chorus, or, to use the language of corn-shuckers, the 'gin'r'ls give out,' and the shuckers 'drone.' These songs are kept up continuously during the entire time the work is going on. . . . The most common form is for the generals to improvise words, which they half sing, half recite, all joining in the chorus."[39] To illustrate corn songs, some WPA narrators simply quoted refrains. "Us sung all de time us was shuckin' corn. Dere was a lot of dem old corn shuckin' songs. De one us sung most was: 'Whooper John and Calline all night'" (Callie Elder, b. ca. 1860, GA, 311–12). "Dey hab some co'n hollers. One was sump'n like dis 'Rabbit gittin' up in a holler fo' niggers kotch fo' bre'kfas'—Ol' cow Piedy, Ol' cow Piedy'"

(Dennis Grant, b. ca. 1850, TX, 1550). "Whoopee, didn' us have good Saddy night frolics and jubilees, some clapp and some play de fiddle and man dey danced mos alnight, and cornshucking wus nother big frolic, pile corn high as a small house and have er jug er licker at each corner, and didn't dey pull dat pile er corn down and holler, 'Gallanip-er-horsefly and whoop it, whoo-ooo, whoo-ooo,' and couldn't dey holler hit" (George Rullerford, b. 1854, AL, 358).

Corn songs were often self-referential, describing the act of shucking—"Come to shuck that corn tonight, / Come to shuck with all your might" (John Spencer, b. ca. 1857, VA, 279)—or celebrating various cornfed creatures: "And what do you think the cow want? / Ha, Hi, Ho, / The cow want corn and that what the cow want; / Ha, Hi, Ho."[40] Said Georgia Johnson: "Fust thing us done was choose a gen'ral. He just walked 'roun' de big plies of corn and led de singin'. Somehow, I can't 'member how dat song went, but it was all 'bout corn" (Georgia Johnson, b. 1865, GA, child of ex-slaves, 335). Corn songs also incorporated topical or situational satire and social commentary: mocking authority, complaining of work, demanding refreshment, criticizing what was offered, generally breaching plantation etiquette and its rigid taboos. "When all de Niggers got to singin' and shoutin' as dey made de shucks fly. One of dem songs went somepin lak dis 'Oh! my haid, my pore haid, Oh! my pore head is 'fected.' Dere warn't nothing wrong wid our haids— dat was jus' our way of lettin' our overseer know us wanted some likker" (Robert Shepherd, b. ca. 1845, GA, 254–55). "When us had cornshuckin's, dey would pile de corn up, ring 'round it an' shuck, drink likker an' holler: 'Boss man, boss man, please gimme my time; Boss man, boss man, fer I'm most broke down'" (Lucindy Lawrence Jurdon, b. 1858, GA, 243). "Just before they got through [shucking], they would begin to sing. Some of the songs were pitiful and sad. I can't remember any of them, but I can remember that they were sad. One of them began like this: / The speculator bought my wife and child / And carried her clear away" (Eliza Washington, b. ca. 1860, AR, 52). At antebellum Alabama cornshuckings, wrote

John Wyeth, "extraordinary liberties were permissible, and not infrequently, as the white people of the premises were listening, the bold leader would by suggestion open the way for a holiday, or a barbecue, or a dance, or extra Christmas vacation, when they visited relatives and friends on other plantations."[41] In Maryland in 1832, James Hungerford heard slaves improvise a version of "Roun' De Corn, Sally" naming all the whites present. "This song caused much amusement at the expense of each one of us who in turn became the subject of the satire. . . . Several laughing efforts were made by the ladies to interrupt the singing, when the words began to have reference to those who were present; but the old major insisted on 'having it out.'"[42]

Ridicule, protest, and connivance are found everywhere, of course, but this kind of song-making is characteristically African and African American. Haitian *coumbites* are cooperative work parties closely resembling cornshuckings. At the appointed time volunteers march to the worksite accompanied by music and song. "If the group is a small one, the men line up together. . . . If the group is large it will divide into two or three squads, each trying to outdo the other." The work pace is set by a *samba* or singing leader, whose "job is to 'encourage' the men. He may sing old familiar songs or compose new ones, songs with humor and bite in them, ribald songs, and songs of ridicule. They may criticize men who have failed to join the coumbite, or praise the host, or single out various individuals for comment." Whatever the task, the workers keep time with the samba, "syncopating their movements by pauses as they sing their responsive parts."[43]

The chief function of corn songs was likewise to coordinate and accelerate a large, noisy labor force, and the combined effects of leather-lunged leaders and keyed-up choruses ensured that anyone near the pile could hear (and adhere to) the pace of work. An 1881 account of Georgia cornshuckings insists "the song was never silent. One voice, powerful beyond belief, would lead, and the multitude answer in chorus, that was heard two, sometimes three, miles distant."[44] Individual prizes might be added to reward or encourage speedy work. "Then we used to shuck and shell corn in pairs facing each other. Every time you shucked so much then you get to kiss the gal sittin' cross ways from you. Then we had a big supper" (Walter Leggett, b. 1855, NC, 2324). "Sometimes we'd have corn huskings and dere would be a dollar fer de one dat could shuck de mos' corn in a certain time" (James Boyd, b. 1830, IT, 366). On many plantations red ears were randomly scattered through the corn pile as a kind of lottery. "Dey kisses when dey fin' a red year [ear] an atter dat dey pops some popcorn an' dey dances ter de music of de banjo which Uncle Jed, am a-playin'; Dey dances all night de best I can remember" (Tanner Spikes, b. 1860, NC, 310).

A whole big crowd am a-huskin', an' deys sing while deys wo'k. It am all kinds ob songs. I's can't 'membahs much 'bout dem, 'cause I's not much fo' singin'. I's 'membahs de words ob one, an' it goes lak dis:

Pull de husk, break de ear;
Whoa, I's got a red ear deah.

Yous see, w'en yous find de red ear, dat 'titles yous to de prize, lak kissin' a gal, or de drink ob brandy, or somethin' lak dat. 'Twarnt many red ears, not 'nough fo' to suit weuns. (Charley Hurt, b. 1853, TX, 1843)

Them people would be shucking corn! There would be a prize to the one who got the most done or who would be the first to get done. They would sing while they were shucking. They had one song they would sing when they were getting close to the finish. Part of it went like this:

Red shirt, red shirt
Nigger got a red shirt.

After the shucking was over, they would have pies, beef, biscuits, corn bread, whiskey if you wanted it.

I believe that was the most they had. They didn't have ice-cream. They didn't use ice-cream much in those days. (Claiborne Moss, b. 1857, GA, 161–62)[45]

Riotous celebrations like cornshuckings are also occasions when standing grudges and feuds may escalate into public violence and mayhem—sometimes by established custom. At cornshuckings the competition over the corn might simply get out of hand, but at other times, teams of slaves from different plantations, or different factions from the same plantations, emboldened by the relaxation of ordinary regimens (or by the alcohol), took the opportunity to settle scores. The combat could be in deadly earnest. In autumn 1861, Union private James Madison Stone (1840–?) was posted to Maryland.

> While on doing picket duty out on the railroad, I saw a lot of cornfield negroes at a negro husking. There was a long pile of corn heaped up just as it was cut in the field and all around it sat the negroes husking. They sang most of the time a monotonous singsong tune. There were present negroes from different parts of the plantation and there was a feud to be avenged. All at once each man whipped out an axe-handle and at each other they went with a fury thoroughly brutal, pounding each other on the body, head or anywhere. The overseers were soon after them and had them separated and at their husking again. The axe-handles, all that could be got hold of, were taken away from them.[46]

On the Kentucky plantation where ex-slave author Harry Smith (1814–?) once lived, "after the corn was husked out they would choose leaders and form in two parties. . . . Those who lived on Plum Creek were called Plum Creek Tigers and those on Salt River were called Salt River Tigers. Then dancing, boxing and wrestling." Smith was a Salt River Tiger, recalling an occasion when the competition with Plum Creek also escalated into mortal combat. "The darkies tore the fences all down around the cabin [and] hammered

each other with the pickets until the white men came out with guns and threatened to shoot them if they did not stop."[47]

Even with these diversions and distractions, cornshuckings served their purpose with remarkable economy and efficiency: in the course of an evening, maybe even a couple of hours, slaves could shuck an active plantation's annual corn supply. Assuming that the contest did not end in controversy or melee, one team would be declared the winner, but the prize was usually bragging rights only: everyone shared in the feasting and dancing that followed. First, however, came one of cornshucking's most distinctive rituals: the *walkaround*. Having served their masters to the point of exhaustion, slaves made a full-blown farce of that servitude, roughly manhandling slaveholders and overseers, invading their private residences and destroying their personal property, even violating a cardinal taboo by dining at the same tables—all in the pretense of honoring their betters.

> When the last ear of corn was shucked, the owner of the plantation would begin to run from the place and all would run after him. When they caught him, he was placed on the shoulders of two men and carried around and around the house, all singing and laughing and having a good time. Then they would carry the man into his house, pull off his hat and throw it into the fire; place him in a chair; comb his head; cross his knees for him and leave him alone. They would not let him raise a new crop under his old hat—he had to have a new hat for a new crop. Then they would all, colored and white, gather to eat. (George Woods, b. ca. 1842, SC, 249)

Most often slaves simply rode the boss on their shoulders, but he might also be placed on a chair or saddle. "If we could catch the master after the shucking was over, we put him in a chair, we darkies, and toted him around and hollered, carried him into the parlor, set him down, and combed his hair" (Squire Dowd, b. 1855, NC, 267).

All de boys dat belong to ol' master would take him on a packsaddle around de house den dey bring him to de table and sit on hes side den all de boys dat belong to Master Beven from dat odder plantation take him on de packsaddle 'round and 'round de house always singin' an' a dancin', den dey puts him at de udder side and sits down by hes side—and each marster an' all hes boys dat was dere at the shuckin' do de same 'til ebberbody wuz at de table, den we'd hab a feast. (Green Cumby, b. 1851, TX, 1003)

The rite might involve additional competitions between slaves, or between slaves and masters.

After the corn was shucked the crowd divided into two groups. Their object was to see which could reach the owner of the corn first and carry him where he wanted to go. Usually they marched with him on their shoulders to his big house and set him down on his porch, then he would give the word for them to all start eating the good things spread out on tables in the yard. There was a heap of drinking done then, and dancing too—just all kinds of dancing that could be done to fiddle and banjo music. My Pa was one of them fiddlers in his young days. (Green Willbanks, b. 1861, GA, 144–45)

When they got through shucking, they would hunt up the boss. He would run away and hide just before. If they found him, two big men would take him up on their shoulders and carry him all around the grounds while they sang. My mother told me that they used to do it that way in slave time. (Eliza Washington, b. ca. 1860, AR, 52)

Master he uster be 'roun' 'til all de co'n mos' shuck den he dodge 'way and hide, 'cause iffen dey ketch 'im dey "cattle" 'im. W'at I mean by "cattle" 'im? Why dey ketch 'im and put 'im up on dey shoul'ers, and dey march 'roun' wid 'im and dey sings. De cap'n he settin' on de co'n and givin' out de song. Dey uster sing

Shuck man can't let git away,
Oh, hood a laddy oh hooey.
Mule want co'n and cow want shuck,
Oh, hood a laddy oh hooey. (Lafayette Price,
b. ca. 1850, AL, 3173)[48]

Georgia landlord (and later University of Georgia chancellor) David C. Barrow (1852–1929) had himself experienced the walkaround. "This honor, though of questionable comfort, or rather most unquestionable discomfort, must be undergone, for a refusal is considered most churlish, and a retreat gives too much license to the guests."[49]

Following the walkaround came the feasting, music, and dance—and the wrestling. After music, song, and dance, wrestling was one of the recreations ex-slaves most often mentioned, frequently as children's sport. "As a small boy Douglas used to spend his time shooting marbles, playing ball, racing and wrestling with the other boys" (Douglas Parish, b. 1850, FL, 257). "We played cat, jumping, wrestling and marbles" (Squire Dowd, b. 1845, NC, 266). "Most of the time of the slave children was spent in playing ball and wrestling and foraging in the woods for berries and fruits and playing games as other children" (Duncan Gaines, 1853, VA, 134). "Dey 'lowed us some fun lak dancin', wrestlin' matches, swimmin', fishin', huntin' an' games" (Richard C. Moring, b. 1851, NC, 139).[50] Wrestling was also occasionally used by adults to settle grudges or disputes.[51]

However, wrestling was most often recalled as public entertainment. "My old Master give the chil'ren a candy pullin' every Saturday night and had them wrestling and knocking each other about. The big fo'ks had dances and parties" (Bert Strong, b. 1864, TX, 3758). "De grown niggers had good times Sadday nights, wid dances, suppers and wras'lin. De corn-shuckings was de biggest times dey had, 'cause de neighbors come and they laughed and hollered nearly all night" (Allen Sims, b. ca. 1860, AL, 343). "Before the war the negroes had a big celebration on the 4th of July, a big barbecue, ball game, wrestling matches, lots of music and singing" (Ike Thomas, b. 1843, GA, 27). "On the

Fourth of July we always had a big barbeque.... On that day we played all kinds of games an' some of the men would tussle" (Bob Mobley, b. ca. 1856, GA, 448). "The slaves were allowed to get out and have their fun and play and 'musement for so many hours. Outside of those hours, they had to be found in their house. They had to use fiddles. They had dancing just like the boys do now. They had knockin' and rasslin' and all such like now" (Cyrus Bellus, b. 1865, MS, child of ex-slaves, 142).

Mr. Neal was good to his slaves and gave them every Saturday to "play" and go to "wrestling school." At Xmas, they had such a good time, would go from house to house, the boys would fiddle and they'd have a drink of liquor at each house. The liquor was plentiful for they bought it in barrels. The plantations took turn about having "Frolics" when they "fiddled and danced" all night. (Shade Richards, b. 1846, GA, 202)

On Christmas we had all we could eat and drink and after that a big party, and you ought to see them gals swingin' they partners round. Then massa have two niggers wrestle, and our sports and dances was big sport for the white folks. They'd sit on the gallery and watch the niggers put it on brown. (Will Adams, b. 1857, TX, 2)

Frederick Douglass (1818–1895) recalled that, at Christmas, the majority of Maryland slaves "spent the holidays in sports, ball playing, wrestling, boxing, running foot races, dancing, and drinking whiskey."[52] After antebellum Georgia log rollings, reported Lewis Paine, workers "take up their line of march for the house; and, on arriving there, take a drink all round. Then commence their gymnastic exercises. They wrestle, jump, and run footraces." There was also a fiddle dance.[53]

Cornshuckings were the occasions most commonly tied to wrestling. "When all de corn was done shucked and de big supper had been et, der was wrastlin' matches and dancin' and all sorts of frolickin'"

Fig. 9.7. "The Sabbath among Slaves." Henry Bibb, *Narrative of the Life and Adventure of Henry Bibb, An American Slave* (1849), fac. 23. Library of Congress, Prints and Photographs Division. A Kentucky ex-slave's depiction of slave pastimes, including wrestling in the West African grappling style (far right). Elsewhere, in between the banjo player (far left) and the dancing couple, a man is patting, stamping heel-to-toe and slapping his thighs. Immediately behind the dancers, two men are butting heads (another African-based martial art practiced by slaves). Further in the background, one figure is throwing a ball or pitching a horseshoe and another is sprinting, cheered on by his fellows. To the dancers' right a slaveholder fills one man's glass from a liquor jug while another is napping (or sleeping it off). Attentive whites are everywhere.

(Benny Dillard, b. ca. 1858, GA, 294). "I can't 'member, but I'se hyard my mammy tell o' dances, c'on shuckin's, wrestlin' matches, candy pullin's an' sich things dat wus had by de slaves dem days" (Jerry Davis, b. ca. 1865, NC, child of ex-slaves, 238). "Cornshuckin's was a mighty go dem days, and folks for miles and miles around was axed. When de wuk was done dey had a big time eatin', drinkin', wrestlin', dancin', and all sorts of frolickin'" (William McWhorter, b. ca. 1860, GA, 99). "When dey had a cornshuckin' we slaves had a good time, plenty to eat, whiskey for de grown folks and a rastlin' match after de corn wus shucked. A nigger dat shucked a red ear of corn got an extra drink of whiskey. Dat wus de custom in dem days" (Chaney Hews, b. ca. 1857, NC, 406).

Marse David had cornshuckin's what lasted two or three weeks at a time. Dey had a gen'ral to keep dem brash boys straight. De number of gen'rals 'pended on how much corn us had and how many slaves was shuckin' corn. Atter it was all shucked, dere was a big celebration in store for de slaves. Dey cooked up washpots full of lamb, kid, pork, and beef, and had collard greens dat was wu'th lookin' at. Dey had water buckets full of whiskey. When dem Nigger's danced atter all dat eatin' and drinkin', it warn't rightly dancin'; it was wrastlin'. (Charlie Hudson, b. 1858, GA, 228)

De corn shuckin's wus a great time. Marster give good licker to everybody den. When anybody shucked a red ear he got an extra drink of whiskey. We had big suppers den an' a good time at corn shuckin's. Atter de shuckin' at nite dere would be a wrastlin' match to see who was bes' on de plantation. We got a week holliday at Xmas. Den wus de time shoes wus give to de slaves, an' de good times generally lasted a week. At layby time wus another big time. Dat wus 'bout de Fourth of July. Dey give a big dinner an' everybody et all de barbecue an' cake dat dey wanted. (Henry James Trentham, b. 1845, SC, 365–66)

We had corn shuckings, candy pullings, dances, prayer meetings. We went to camp meetin' on Camp Meeting days in August when the crops were laid by. We played games of high jump, jumping over the pole held by two people, wrestling, leap frog, and jumping. We sang the songs, "Go Tell Aunt Patsy." "Some folks says a nigger wont steal, I caught six in my corn field." "Run nigger run, the patteroller ketch you, Run nigger run like you did the other day." (John C. Bectom, b. 1862, NC, 95)

When us got de corn up from de fields, Niggers come from far and nigh to Marster's cornshuckin'. Dat cornshuckin' wuk was easy wid evvybody singin' and havin' a good time together whilst dey made dem shucks fly. De cornshuckin' captain led all de singin' and he set right up on top of de highes' pile of corn. De chillun was kept busy a-passin' de liquor jug 'round. Atter it started gittin' dark, Marster had big bonfires built up and plenty of torches set 'round so as dere would be plenty of light. Atter dey et all dey wanted of dem good things what had done been cooked up for

Fig. 9.8. John C. Bectom, ex-slave, NC. 1937–38. Portraits of African American ex-slaves from the US Works Progress Administration, Federal Writers' Project slave narratives collection, Library of Congress.

de big supper, den de wrastlin' matches started, and Marster allus give prizes to de best wrastlers. Dere warn't no fussin' and fightin' 'lowed on our place, and dem wrastlin' matches was all in good humor and was kept orderly. (Jasper Battle, b. ca. 1857, GA, 71)

Ex-slave author Irving Lowery (1850–?) had seen cornshucking wrestling in South Carolina: "The supper being over, with the moon shining brightly (moonlight nights were invariably selected for corn-shuckings) the boys spend some time in wrestling, foot racing and jumping before going home."[54] Harry Smith (1814–?) had participated many years before in Kentucky: "After the corn was husked out they would form in two parties, and then dancing, wrestling, and various amusements would be in order."[55] A South Carolina slaveholder's son remembered: "everyone had as much as he or she wanted in cornshuckin' time. It was served in bowls. They would eat a while then rest then eat again. And while they were resting, some would pat and sing, play the jewsharp or quills, while others pulled ears and danced. Others would wrestle and box."[56]

These contests were open to all, but many plantations fielded champion wrestlers to represent the crew at cornshuckings and other events. Wrote David C. Barrow, "the fun usually begins by some one who is a famous wrestler (pronounced 'rasler') offering to throw down anybody on the ground, accompanying the boast by throwing aside his coat and swaggering round, sometimes making a ring and inviting 'eny gemman ez warnts to git his picter tuk on de groun', to come in." The challenge accepted, the contest proceeds. Barrow, a Georgia landlord who himself held yearly huskings, even boasted of one "famous cornshucker and wrestler who is a tenant of the writer."[57] Some planters supported star wrestlers much as they did dancers and musicians, pitting them against neighboring champions in honor or money matches. "As soon as my father was large enough to go walkin' about, his old master given him to his son, Master Warren Junell. Warren would carry him about and make him rassle (wrestle). He was a good rassler. As far as work was concerned, he didn't do nothing much of that. He just followed his young master all around rasslin" (Oscar Felix Junell, b. ca. 1880, AR, child of ex-slaves, 173, orig. parentheses).

Throughout the nineteenth-century, wrestling was ubiquitous among North American Blacks and whites alike. Most whites employed the ferocious "gouging" style made famous by frontiersmen like Davy Crockett, derived from English, Scottish, and Irish wrestling traditions. Blacks generally followed a West African approach, characterized by grappling and leg wrapping, the object being decisively to throw one's opponent.[58] This was the wrestling style recalled by ex-slaves. "Me and seven other boys used to play marbles together and we would practice different things—wrastling, running and jumping. I used to out-wrestle any of 'em because I had a side-hook I used" (William Edward Black, b. 1846, NC, 145). According to a compilation of "Folk Remedies and Superstition" collected from Richmond County ex-slaves by Louise Oliphant, a Black fieldworker with the Georgia project, "If a wrestler can get dirt from the head of a fresh grave, sew it up in a sack, and tie it around his waist, no one

can throw him" (S2 13 *GA* 4: 283). (*Graveyard dirt* is among the most common yet efficacious components in hoodoo charms.)

There are other links between African and African American wrestling traditions. As among African Americans, wrestling is common as child's play throughout West Africa, besides being used by adults to settle scores, win honor, or gamble. Its ritual aspects are even more suggestive. In West Africa, that is, wrestling is found almost exclusively in agricultural societies, and, as public entertainment, occurs mainly at agricultural festivals following harvest or just before planting, when star wrestlers parade between villages or village compounds accompanied by musicians, singers, and other admiring revelers to compete for honors in intra-farm tournaments.[59] Most prominent among these observances is the Yam Festival celebrated throughout the region. Among the Ibo of present-day Nigeria, the different towns

have festivals which they keep annually according to custom. In Owerri there is a festival, called Oru Owerri, kept annually about a month before the new yams are eaten. . . . From beginning to end of Oru all the daughters of Owerri now residing in other towns will come with their children to their parents' home, bringing food such as yams, fish, and palm-wine; friends and relations-in-law come from various parts bringing palm-wine, and from morning to night there is feasting, drinking, and merrymaking.

The girls adorn themselves . . . and sing as they pass round the compounds. The boys go to the bush, cut grass and other plants used for making okwo-okwo masks, and run around. . . . Three days before Oru is due to finish, wrestling is begun and carried on till the end of the festival. All compounds and their rivals will beat the wrestling drums; the men wrestle together and the women also. They wrestle from morning till night and the compound which throws more of its opponents than any other rejoices in its victory, sings the wrestling song, and returns home.[60]

The resemblances to the slaves' cornshuckings require little comment, and the impact of these West African harvest traditions are observable in other New World Black communities, for example, in Haitian *Rara* festivities, held immediately following Mardi Gras between Ash Wednesday and Easter. Besides parades with music, song, dance, mock royalty, and masquerade, Rara prominently features African-style wrestling. "Known as *pingé*, this festival wrestling is done with a background of excited drumming and has a striking resemblance to wrestling traditions in West Africa. Local 'champions' will invade a neighboring community, sometimes traveling considerable distances to make a challenge. As in West Africa, some of these wrestlers take their own musicians with them. The musicians often are provided by the village in which the events take place."[61] Following Rara, the agricultural season begins.

We can with fair certainty date the Southern cornshucking's origins. In the form outlined above, plantation cornshuckings are first reported in the opening years of the nineteenth century. In 1794 Eli Whitney patented the cotton gin, enthroning King Cotton as the South's cash crop and wholly revitalizing and redefining North American plantation slavery. The African slave trade, which had been in decline, suddenly exploded. In the period immediately following, the cornshucking carnival appeared on the large cotton plantations that sprang up or expanded as a result, whose needs required these massive corn reserves, and whose legions of slaves could supply them. A high proportion of these slaves were still native Africans, most of whom had been brought to America due to Whitney's invention but also because of their familiarity with agriculture in a subtropical climate; West African slaves were especially prized for their horticultural knowledge and experience.[62] Thus by the early 1800s Southern plantations housed tens of thousands of native-born West African agriculturalists from societies observing the Yam Festival and similar harvest rites. The lines of descent seem fairly clear.

It is also clear, however, that these West African practices were completely transformed, partly by African American innovations, partly by observances adopted from Anglo-Americans. The red ear custom originated among colonial whites, reported by the late eighteenth century,[63] but other parallels can be traced back even further to the *harvest home*, the British and Irish celebrations that accompanied bringing home the last of the corn (grain) harvest. English antiquarian Henry Bourne (1694–1733) gave one of the first descriptions of the custom of feting "the *Harvest-Men*, and the Servants of the Family," after the corn is all stored. "At this the Servant and his Master are alike, and every Thing is done with an equal Freedom. They sit at the same Table, converse freely together, and spend the remaining Part of the Night in dancing, singing, &c. without any Difference or Distinction."[64]

The harvest home tradition has many resemblances to plantation cornshuckings, including processions, contests and competitions, mock royalty, social leveling and rites of reversal, drinking and feasting, and music, song, and dance, all motivated by the urgent necessity of rapidly gathering and storing the annual grain reserve. Under the direction of a *harvest lord* elected or appointed from their ranks, workers race to outdo themselves or one another in anticipation of the last load and their reward. The harvest lord may ride the final cartload into the farmer's yard accompanied by a procession of workers singing the harvest home song, only to be doused with water or pelted with apples.[65] Musicians were sometimes added to the parade; the reapers did not sing while working, however. The harvesting itself might pit teams against one another or reward individual effort and skill, or sheer luck. In one widespread rite, harvesters competed, under various handicaps, to cut the last bit of grain, plaited where it stood. In Ireland "the successful candidate then places it [the plaited grain] round the neck of the master's wife (in this case, there was no master's wife, so it was placed round the master's neck) and triumphantly leads her into the house."[66] Elsewhere "the successful competitor was tossed up in the air with 'three times three' on the arms of his brother harvesters."[67] Quite often the last sheaf was fashioned into a doll or effigy (the *kern baby*, *harvest queen,* or *cailleac*) that was itself paraded to the main house, groomed and dressed, then installed for the year, to be replaced at the next harvest.[68]

By the late eighteenth century, North American colonists had adapted the harvest home tradition to the novel New World task of husking or shucking the autumn "Indian corn." In 1791 former British admiral Bartholomew James (1752–1828), then a merchant marine shipping on Maine's Kennebec River, reported "during our stay at this place we saw and partook of the ceremony of husking corn, a kind of 'harvest home' in England, with the additional amusement of kissing the girls whenever they met with a red corncob, and to which is added dancing, singing, and moderate drinking."[69] Slaves and free blacks regularly participated in these events both as workers and as performers at the concluding dances, and many of the plantation cornshucking's key elements—parades, contests and competitions, captains and generals, the walkaround, the slaveholder's enthroning, grooming, and (de)crowning, and, of course, the red ear custom—have obvious correspondences in the harvest home.

After 1800, though, the Black cornshucking truly came into its own and diverged from its white counterpart along regional lines. By then, in the northern United States the British harvest home had evolved into the Anglo-American *husking bee*, typically recalled as a social mixer for unmarried young people, who provided the labor in exchange for the occasion and a dinner party. In many respects, for northerners husking corn had become a courtship custom, the red ear with a kiss as reward being the husking bee's most celebrated feature. Most husking bees, however, were scrupulously genteel and carefully chaperoned events, frequently held in the farmer's kitchen. The workers did not sing while husking, and alcohol might or might not be served, but there was always a dinner and sometimes (but not necessarily) a dance. Judging from surviving accounts, Blacks no longer participated to any great degree, except perhaps as musicians at afterparties.[70]

In the plantation South, of course, slaves shucked most of the corn, especially after the rapid economic expansion and concomitant influx of new African slaves in the early 1800s; and from this time if not before, southern slaves typically shucked the corn their own way—pacing the labor with African-style call-and-response singing, for instance. True, slaveholders dictated and supported cornshuckings, inevitably with some supervision and surveillance. However, whites are typically described observing from afar or dropping in periodically, largely trusting the slaves to organize and conduct the activities. In these circumstances, borrowings from the British harvest home could easily blend with similar or compatible West African harvest customs, but also—and most essentially—with the slaves' own innovations and reinterpretations. The results were, once again, completely unlike anything in Africa or Europe while nevertheless recalling both. The ex-slaves were exactly right when they insisted that cornshucking was one occasion that was entirely their own.

MUSICIANERS

Put dis down. My mama an' family all belong to Peter Buck as his slaves. We didn' work 'til after de war; den we came to Petersburg. I went to dancin' school wid de white folks an' can dance any kin' o' dance sets. My father was a musicianer. He 'longed to John Carhan, in Warrenton, N. C. (Della Harris, b. 1852, NC, 129–30, orig. emphasis)

When I'se set free my master called me to the front porch and told me I was free on the 19th day of June. He told me I could go or if I wanted to I could stay and he would give me $5.00 per month if I would stay and help him finish his crop. Some payed us and some didnt. I made a musician after I was set free. If I had made musician before I was freed, they could not have bought me for any price. I made my first fiddle out of a gourd. I played for all the dances both white and black and Sunday School. (Harre Quarls, b. 1841, TX, 3216)

I must not omit to mention that I have a good fiddler, and keep him well supplied with catgut, and I make it his duty to play for the negroes every Saturday night until 12 o'clock. They are exceedingly punctual in their attendance at the ball, while Charley's fiddle is always accompanied with Ihurod on the triangle, and Sam to "pat." (A Mississippi Planter, "Management of Negroes upon Southern Estates" [1851], 625)

The myth that African Americans are naturally musical is deeply rooted indeed. John Finch, an English visitor of the 1820s, reported "in Maryland dancing is fashionable; the slaves frequently dance all night. In Virginia musical parties are more frequent; every negro is a musician from his birth. . . . An instrument of music seems necessary to their existence."[1] Recalling antebellum New Orleans, James R. Creecy insisted: "all Africans have melody in their souls; and in all their movements, gyrations and attitudenizing exhibitions, the most perfect time is kept, making the beats with the feet, heads, or hands, or all, as correctly as a well-regulated metronome!"[2] Another correspondent said much the same of 1830s Florida slaves. "They

Fig. 10.1. "Fiddler Jack of Harper's Ferry." Photo by John H. Tarbell. 1903. Library of Congress, Prints and Photographs Division. An ex-slave musicianer at the turn of the twentieth century.

possess full, rich voices; most of the men perform on the violin, and many of them are proficients on that instrument."[3] Traveling the Mississippi Delta in the 1850s, Frederick Olmsted kept company with "Yazoo," a seventeen-year-old planter's son:

> "Sunday nights we let 'em dance and sing if they want. It does 'em good, you know, to enjoy theirselves."
> "They dance to the banjo, I suppose?"
> "Banjos and violins; some of 'em has got violins."
> "I like to hear negroes sing," said I.
> "Niggers is allers good singers nat'rally," said our host. "I reckon they got better lungs than white folks, they hev such powerful voices."[4]

Some or many, certainly. But most, every, or all? Musical talents are not evenly distributed in any community, and American slaves were no different. "Marse had a fiddle dat us laked to hear him play. I never could dance but I could jump up an' down an' pat my hands. I laked music so well 'till my feet jes' wouldn't be still" (Robert Laird, b. 1854, MS, 1293). "I couldn't play no music myself, but I was terrible [meaning great] on de [dance] floor" (Jerry Eubanks, b. 1846, MS, 696). "I never could dance but I was a fiddler an' I play for white folks an' colored folks both. . . . Lawsy I sho could fiddle" (Cinto Lewis, b. 1826, 2328). "When I wus lit'le I uster dance de back step an' shuffle an' O, boy! I cud dance, but I never cud sing; dey sed I had a voice like a bull frog" (Nelson Dickerson, b. unk., MS, 602). "Uncle Berry has never been musical and neither sings nor remembers any old songs" (Berry Smith, b. 1821, MS, 1987).

Many slaves, of course, faced exceptional obstacles. "I neber seed folks dance till I wus a big boy and den I larnt to shuffle my feet but dey sed I wus a pore dancer. Dar neber wus a dance on Marse Newsome's place" (Lewis Jefferson, b. 1853, MS, 1141). As a rule, though, slaveholders allowed, encouraged, even demanded musicmaking, singing, and dancing. And while the stereotype that all Blacks are musically gifted is only that—a caricature—Black music globally is comparatively inclusive and participatory, typically requiring the active involvement of everyone present, and to a much greater degree than other folk music traditions. Thus, at slave gatherings even persons of little or no ability were expected to clap, stamp, pat, shuffle their feet, and join on responses and choruses, supporting more capable performers of various types.

> Some of them niggers sure could sing and the ones of us what couldn't joined in the chorus just the same. I wish I could remember that old song we sang. It started out, "Shuck, shuck, round up your corn." The rest of the words is sure left me now. There was a old fiddler man that came some Saturday nights and played around at different houses for the slaves to dance. I wasn't big enough for nothing like that so I can't give no understanding about them. (Squire Irvin, b. 1849, TN, 1086)

Then, too, relative to other preindustrial societies, African and African American performance traditions have always exhibited exceptional degrees of specialization and professionalism, particularly among instrumentalists, whose differing functions or levels of ability may be variously ranked, regarded, and rewarded along lines more typical of commercial or academic fields. In this the musical world of American slaves definitely resembled the musical organization of traditional African societies, where such musical hierarchies are even institutionalized, reaching their fullest development in the hereditary classes of professional musicians usually identified as *griots*.

The connection between African American musicians and African griots has become conventional wisdom, albeit often based on a rather romanticized view of griots, recast in Western artistic or countercultural terms as bohemian poet-minstrel protest singers, proto-rock rebels, pre-gangsta rappers, or some such. They were none of these things, of course. The term *griot* itself may be a Western coinage and in any case grossly oversimplifies its subject. Historically, there were innumerable professional or semiprofessional performer roles distributed throughout different African societies.[5] Their nomenclatures are much debated and virtually impenetrable to outsiders. I adopt *griot* simply as the most widely recognized designation for individuals of this type. As a generalization, however, the African musicians and singers now lumped together as griots enjoyed high levels of public adoration and acclaim, wealthy and powerful patrons, certain special privileges and perks, some license to speak truth to power or flaunt taboos, and differing degrees of forbearance for their vices and vagabondage. Conversely, they were frequently outsiders or outcasts, bound to their craft, permitted to marry only their own kind, subject to constant scorn and persecution, even murder and execution. Their material rewards, political connections, and public renown also created envy and resentment. Some had sinister reputations as sorcerers, witches, or black magicians, others as clairvoyants, healers, or sages. Many people thought them mentally ill, many more regarded them as mere lowlifes: layabouts, libertines, liars, drunkards, beggars, gamblers, swindlers, and thieves. Some griots were variously seen as all these

together; some variously were. Perhaps the majority survived only as indentured vassals of strongmen and thugs. In fact, many griots were slaves. Even in contemporary African societies, griot families are often assumed to be of slave or captive origin.[6]

Griots, of course, embody a universal phenomenon: the pariah performer. Everywhere and always music is prized, but musicians are habitually held in low esteem, all the more so in preindustrial subsistence societies where resources are strained and the division of labor fairly basic. Especially in these circumstances musicmaking may not be seen as real work, so that when such communities or their elites do demand specialist music-makers—as they always seem to—they often turn to outcasts or outsiders. Throughout European history, one finds pariah performers resembling griots, accorded the same privileges and benefits but charged with the same outrages and subject to the same contempt and abuse. The Gypsies or *Rom* may be Europe's most conspicuous examples, but they were hardly alone.[7] Indeed, enslaved or indentured musicians—including enslaved African musicians—were commonplace in Europe from antiquity up to and after America's colonization. African musicians were present in England by at least the 1300s.[8] By the 1700s slave musicianers numbered among the commodities shipped home to Britain from America. These included a pair sent ca. 1770 to the Marchioness of Rockingham by the colonial governor of New Hampshire with the note: "by the Tama Sloop of War I have this day embarked Two Negro men slaves (named Romulus & Remus) who are good on the French-Horn, and Remus a remarkable good taste to Music. In hopes that they might be some Amusement in the Country."[9]

Accordingly, by the start of the North American slave trade both Africans and Europeans had centuries of experience with enslaved musicians. More particularly, Africans and Europeans *both* had centuries of experience with enslaved *African* musicians, including enslaved African musicians *in Africa*. This obviously has some bearing on the rapidity with which African slaves assumed a central role in American music. It also suggests a much less romantic but far more tangible link between North American slave musicianers and the African griots serving hundreds of local warlords, petty monarchs, and powerful native slave brokers, particularly as a highly practical New World survival guide. African musicians had thrived for centuries as underlings of the ruthless, rich, and powerful. Adopting the same role in America would have only seemed natural.

It is, in fact, wholly in this capacity that we meet many early musicianers (the Black term for instrumentalists), scores of whom appear in eighteenth-century newspaper ads from slaveholders hunting runaways. "RUN away from the subscriber, a Mulatto Boy named PETER, about 15 years old, well known in and about Charleston, being formerly a drummer to the Grenadier company" (1778). "He [DAVY] is a stout fellow, about 5 feet 10 inches high, 35 or 40 years of age, stoops a good deal, wears a long beard, and is well known in Charleston as a fiddler" (1769). "Abraham is a tall mustee fellow, plays upon the fiddle, well known in Charles-Town and at Goose-Creek" (1769).[10]

These and similar postings are just one gauge of how quickly enslaved Africans conquered American music, and not just in and around Charleston. Slave musicians left a trail of scattered notices in period ephemera, though most are still known by first names only, and little known otherwise. Many descriptions do not name them at all. Yet a few slave and free Black musicians achieved true celebrity. Richmond fiddler and banjo player Sy Gilliat (d. 1820) was sufficiently acclaimed by local elites to be included in one of Virginia's first published histories and painted in oils.[11] First mentioned in 1804, slave bugler and fiddler Philip Bazadier (d. 1848) was for decades a much-remarked musical figure in Wilmington, North Carolina.[12] A few other such superstars dot the documentary landscape, but less celebrated figures as well.[13] Several slave memoirs were actually written by fiddlers: Solomon Northrup (1807 or 1808–?), James Thomas (1827–1913), and Isaac D. Williams (1821–?).[14] Slaveholders, their children, and houseguests also published recollections of slave musicians,[15] others of whom were publicized by famous offspring or relations.[16]

The WPA ex-slave narratives identify more than 150 slave musicians by name, providing the best portraits of slave instrumentalists extant, and certainly the most numerous based on actual interviews with the musicians and their audiences (see chap. appendix). Dozens of interview subjects were players themselves. Others intimately knew such performers, sometimes fleshing them out in considerable detail.

Of course, slave communities supported many other categories of performers who overlapped, cooperated, or even competed with instrumentalists. The narratives abound in references to great singers and dancers, who obviously represented the largest categories of slave performers: after all, at most slave gatherings singing and dancing were general to those present. Yet singers and dancers simply did not attract the same individual attention as musicianers, who were definitely considered a separate, elite class. Tellingly, the performers who were most often paid were instrumentalists (fiddlers, actually), though dance callers were almost on a par with fiddlers, often being paid as well, and star dancers or exceptional singers might be compensated, too.

Nonetheless, given their specialization and special gifts, slave musicianers truly were a class apart. More exactly, musicianers were several classes apart, since even their lives and fortunes could differ drastically. Ex-slave William H. Harrison was owned by Anderson Harrison, a relation of President Benjamin Harrison (1833–1901), serving as valet, carriage driver, dancing master, and fiddler. Sent to war, captured, and conscripted into the Union army, he afterwards moved to Madison, Arkansas, where he worked as a freighter.

I was born March 4, 1832 in Richmond, Virginia. Master Anderson Harrison was a cousin to Benjamin Harrison, the twenty-third President of the United States. Master Anderson Harrison was my owner. . . .

This is how good my owners was to me. He sent me to Hendersonville, North Carolina

(Henderson?) to learn to fiddle. I was so afraid of the old colored teacher I learned in a month about all he could play. I played for parties in eight states in slavery. All up in the North. They trained children to dance then. I took Martha Jane, Easter Ann, Jane Daniel, my young mistresses and their mother's sisters, Emma and Laura, to parties and dances all the time. We went to Ashville, North Carolina to a big party. While they was having fine victuals after the dance they sent me out a plate of turnip greens and turnips, fat meat and corn bread. I took it and set it down. When Miss Martha Jane got in sight I took her to our carriage. She said, "Empty it to the dogs," and give me one dollar fifty cents and told me to go to town and buy my supper. I was treated same as kin folks. I et and drunk same as they had to use. . . .

When I heard Benjamin Harrison had been elected President of the United States, I asked Mr. George Lewis to write to him for me. I was working for him then. . . . I got my fiddle and went and visited for two weeks. I et at the same table with the President. I slept in the White House. We et out of skillets together when I was a little boy and drunk out of the same cups. Me and him and Gummel [another Harrison cousin] raised up together. I played for the president and his Cabinet. (William H. Harrison, b. 1832, VA, 185, 186–87, 188, orig. parentheses)

Deprived of these lofty connections, Harrison's postwar fortunes declined precipitously. "I seen better times in slavery than I ever seen since but I don't believe in slave traffic—that being sold" (William H. Harrison, b. 1832, VA, 186). When African griots lose powerful patrons, they sometimes commit suicide rather than face such hardships and indignities.

The experiences of Richard Toler could not have been more different:

Ah never had no good times till ah was free. . . . We was nevah allowed no pa'ties, and when they had goin' ons at the big house, we had to clear out.

Ah had to wo'k hard all the time every day in the week. Had to min' the cows and calves, and when ah got older ah had to hoe in the fields. . . .

After the wah, ah bought a fiddle, and ah was a good fiddlah. Used to be a fiddlah fo' the white girls to dance. Jes' picked it up, it was a natural gif'. Ah could still play if I had a fiddle. Ah used to play at our hoe downs, too. . . .

Befo' the wah we nevah had no good times. They took good care of us, though. As pa'tacu-lah with slaves as with the stock—that was their money, you know. . . . We had very bad eatin'. Bread, meat, water. And they fed it to us in a trough, jes' like the hogs. And ah went in my shirt tail till I was 16, nevah had no clothes. And the flo' in ouah cabin was dirt, and at night we'd jes' take a blanket and lay down on the flo'. The dog was supe'ior to us; they would take him in the house.

Some of the people I belonged to was in the Klu Klux Klan. Tolah [slaveholder] had fo' girls and fo' boys. Some of those boys belonged. And I used to see them turn out. They went aroun' whippin' niggahs. They'd get young girls and strip 'em sta'k naked, and put 'em across barrels, and whip 'em till the blood run out of 'em, and they would put salt in the raw pahts. And ah seen it and it was as bloody aroun' em as if they'd stuck hogs. (Richard Toler, b. ca. 1835, VA, 97, 98, 100–101)

Judging from these examples, a slave musicianer's lot sometimes boiled down to whether or not you were better than the dog, or merely treated like a hog. Like any slave, a slave fiddler's fortunes were at the whim of others. Nonetheless, slave performers were the recognized musical stars of the plantation South, and the best among them were supported by a fairly well-defined system of supply and demand not dissimilar to African customs of musical professionalism.

Again, the resemblances between griots and slave musicianers are easily overstated. Wealthy and powerful patrons are important to artists everywhere. Most musical cultures recognize and reward different levels of talent or accomplishment, just as music always

Fig. 10.2. Richard Toler, ex-slave, June 17, 1937, Cincinnati, OH. Portraits of African American ex-slaves from the US Works Progress Administration, Federal Writers' Project slave narratives collection, Library of Congress.

tends to run in families. Europe's long history of pariah performers certainly contributed to the ready acceptance of American slave musicians. Still, it hardly seems coincidental that the organization of North American slave musicianers so closely paralleled their African counterparts, providing a segmented, highly specialized labor pool able to handle virtually any musical occasion on various terms.[17] Nor could it be wholly accidental that Africa's musical specialists are also found in rigidly stratified societies consisting of slaves, free persons, and nobles, professional performers occupying ambiguous albeit untouchable niches. The North American situation was never as formalized as many African cases, but American slave musicians were similarly graded, with star fiddlers at the top, followed by other instrumentalists, prompters, percussionists, patters, dancers, vocal soloists, choristers, clappers, and so on.

There are occasional accounts of slave instrumentalists playing privately for recreation or self-expression. "I use to go to a lot of dances in my good days. We'd dance the reels. Dere was times when de only music we had was played by a colored man on a reed. I could play a accordion and my first husband, John, could play de banjo, but we never did play at dances" (Rebecca Thomas, b. 1825, AR, TX, 3822–23). "My uncle would play his guitar in his cabin at night. At Christmas dey would have a dance on de plantation" (Jane Thompson, b. unk., MS, 353). "When the slaves went to the quarters, after the day's work was done, they could do whatsoever they pleased. Sometime they play the guitar or banjo and sing. Saturday night they most generally went to the log house and danced" (Callie Washington, b. ca. 1859, AR, 2190).

Instruments were used mainly for dancing, and the ability to accompany dancers, whether at Saturday night frolics or just down in the quarters, was the minimum qualification for true musicianers. "After eating they would sometimes gather in front of a cabin and dance to the tunes played on the fiddle and the drum. The popular dance at that time was known as the 'figure dance'" (Mack Mullen, b. 1857, GA, 236). "We got in groups in front of the cabins and sang and danced to the music of banjoes until the overseer would come along and make us go to bed" (Susan Bledsoe, b. 1845, TN, 7). "Our ole master Dale that raised my Mammy and her family never was hard or mean like that. He would let us go to church, have parties and dances. One of the ole slaves would come to our cabin with his fiddle and we'd dance" (Susan Dale Sanders, b. unk., KY, 45).

It is in these informal, impromptu settings that narrators usually recall homemade or improvised instruments (gourd fiddles and banjos, quills and other reed pipes, fifes, flutes, tin-pan tambourines, bucket drums). "Mama an' me worked in de field. We danced outdoors on de groun'. They clapped hands fer us ter dance by an' played homemade banjos an' harps [quills]" (Lula Coleman, b. 1851, AL, 431). "After work was done, the slaves would smoke, sing, tell ghost stories and tales, dances, music, homemade fiddles" (James V. Deane, b. 1850, MD, 8). "We had a prutty good time, we have all the hands on our place at some house and dance. We made our music. Music is natur'l wid our color. They most all had a juice (Jew's) harp.

They make the fiddle and banjo" (Solomon Lambert, b. 1848, AR, 230, orig. parentheses).

Overall, musicmaking at these off-hours gatherings is described as fairly offhand, perhaps functional at best. "Some of us young bucks . . . start shuffling while de rest of de niggers pat. Some nigger women go back to de quarters and git de gourd fiddles, and clapping bones made out'n beef ribs, and bring dem back so we could have some music" (Charley Williams, b. 1843, LA, 337).

> Sometimes we had music, but most of this would be pattin'. Onct in a while, somebody'd grab up a fiddle, play all kind of little tunes. Er Mussy! Dey done told you dat, too? Yes'm, I uster play a banjo some, an' play 'long wid it:
>
> > Went up ter de river,
> > Told him not ter go;
> > Let her git in trouble
> > By de frost an' snow. . . .
> >
> > De jawbone hung on de kitchen wall,
> > An' de darkies was 'fraid dat it would fall;
> > Ol' Marster come ridin'. (Sam Broach, b. 1848, MS, 229–30)[18]

> Now, talkin' 'bout frolickin', us really used to dance. What I means, is sho 'nough old-time breakdowns. Sometimes us didn't have no music 'cept jus' beatin' time on tin pans and buckets but most times Old Elice Hudson played his fiddle for us, and it had to be tuned again atter evvy set us danced, he never knowed but one tune and he played it over and over. Sometimes dere was 10 or 15 couples on de floor at de same time and us didn't think nothin' of dancin' all night long. Us had plenty of old corn juice for refreshment, and atter Elice had two or three cups of dat juice, he could git "Turkey in de Straw" out of dat fiddle lak nobody's business. (Neal Upson, b. 1857, GA, 64)

Ex-slave author Allen Parker (1840–1906) was raised on a North Carolina plantation: "If some slave could be found who had an old fiddle and could play it at all, he was called on to furnish music; if not, some one would take an old tin pan and use it like a tambourine. Two or three others 'pat Jubo.'"[19]

Whites also called upon slaves, and especially slave children, for private entertainment, even maintaining them for that purpose. "Marse Bennett would call all us little niggers up to de big house to dance for him, and us sho would cut de pigeon wing, den us would sing 'reels' for him" (Hannah Irwin, b. ca. 1853, AL, 206). "Marster used to git my sister to shout for him. I kin just see her now, a-twistin' and jumpin' and hollerin' for all de world lak grownup Niggers done at meetin's and baptizin's, 'til she done fell out. Den Marster, he say, 'Take her to de kitchen and feed her good'" (Georgia Johnson, b. 1865, GA, child of ex-slaves, 330). "Old Man Ratcliff's hobby was to have us little 'Niggers' around him, sing 'Polly Put The Kettle On,' and many other old time songs and watch us dance. He would also have us wrestle, run races and do a lot of other foolish things to amuse the little ones, while the old folks were in the field" (Chaney McNair, b. 1852, IT, 5680).

> I was called "Gingerbread" by the Revells. They reared me until I reached the age of about nine or ten years old. My duty was to put the logs on the fireplaces in the Revells' house and work around the house. I remember well, when I was taken to Annapolis, how I used to dance in the stores for men and women, they would give me pennies and three cent pieces, all of which was given to me by the Revells. They bought me shoes and clothes with the money collected. . . . As a child I was very fond of dancing, especially the jig and buck. (James Wiggins, b. 1850 or 1851, MD, 66, 67)

Bud Jones grew up in the mansion of his slaveholder, doing chores, caring for bloodhounds, and entertaining whites.

Mr. John Jones was my old master. He told me he brung me up on a bottle and brung me to the Kentucky part of this country from South America [another draft states "from Africa or Haiti, but he never said which"]. He said he was six months on the water and I ain't never had no mammy or pappy what I knowed of. He jes' told me they was sold off in 'nother country indifferent to this one. . . . I growed up in the house of old master. . . . When I was a little boy I didn't have no chilluns to play with like they do now-days. I jes' sat 'round studyin' (thinking). Old master would come in at night though, and say, "Bud, come here and cut me a step or two." He liked to see me dance. I had to dance for all the company. I could do the ground shuffle and the pigeon wing and the back step. I can still do them. Then he taught me how to play the Jews harp and the French harp and the macordion. (Bud Jones, b. ca. 1850, KY, VA, 2077, 2080, orig. parentheses)

For the most part, however, dancing and dance music were tied to public festivities, and many plantations had designated musicianers—almost always fiddlers—some of whom slaveholders purchased specifically to play at Saturday night frolics and similar gatherings. This class obviously outranked the casual music-makers who played just around the quarters, usually being expected to entertain at slaveholder balls and parties as well as more formal slave functions authorized, organized, or supervised by whites: Saturday night frolics, cornshuckings, cotton pickings, log rollings, and so forth. "Befo' I forgits, Marster Edward bought a slave in Tennessee just 'cause he could play de fiddle. Named him 'Tennessee Ike' and he played 'long wid Ben Murray, another fiddler" (Adeline Jackson, b. ca. 1849, SC, 4). "Marse had two of de slaves jus' to be fiddlers. Dey played for us an' kep' things perked up. How us could swing, an' step 'bout by dat old fiddle music always a-goin' on" (John Cameron, b. 1842, MS, 333). "Nearly every farm had a fiddler. Ever so often he [slaveholder] had a big dance in their parlor.

I'd try to dance myself. He had his own music by the hands on his place" (Ida Rigley, b. 1855, VA, 44).

Other slaveholders hired such performers from nearby plantations, paying them or the planter. Touring, then, was the next major step for musicianers, with commensurate rises in compensation and standing. "I played a fiddle for all de weddings and parties in de neighborhood. Dey paid me fifteen or twenty cents each time and I had money in my pockets all de time" (Henry Dant, b. ca. 1832, MO, 99). "In times of our holidays, we always had our own musicians. Sometimes we sent ten or twelve miles for a fiddler. He'd stay a week or so in one place and den he would go on to de next farm, maybe four or five miles away, and dey had a good time for a week" (Gus Smith, b. 1845, MO, 323). "In those days there were many Negro musicians who were always ready to furnish music from their banjo and fiddle for the frolics. If a white family was entertaining, and needed a musician but didn't own one, they would hire a slave from another plantation" (Isaiah Green, b. 1856, GA, 53). "Once a week the slaves could have any night they wanted for a dance or frolic. Mance McQueen was a slave belonging on the Dewberry place that could play a fiddle and his master would give him a pass to come play for us" (Andrew Goodman, b. 1840, AL, 1524). "Ben was a very trusty slave. He went to dances in the homes of the white people and called the figures for the square dance and virginia reel. Before the dances started he would brush the clothes and shine shoes, receiving tips as high as fifty cents" (Ben Wall, b. ca. 1852, MS, 2163–64).

In his autobiography, ex-slave Jacob Stroyer (1846–?) wrote that at Christmas, South Carolina slaves "would spend half a day dancing in some large cotton house or on a scaffold, the master providing fiddlers who came from other plantations if there were none to be had on the place, and who received from fifteen to twenty dollars on these occasions."[20]

Working in this way, a network of local slave musicianers could meet the needs of any occasion, Black or white, whether that meant performing separately, teaming up for larger affairs, or bringing in outside assistance. "At night there was a big dance. The fiddlers and the tambourine and bone beaters, was the finest to be got out of Kentucky" (Mark Oliver, b. 1856, MS, 1665). Describing antebellum Virginia, C. A. Bryce wrote:

> For most dances and balls the musicians consisted of a violinist ("fiddler" they called him), who could call the figures, a banjo picker and tambourine player. A trio of this kind accustomed to playing together furnished all the music required at the average dancing parties of long ago. On special big occasions where large crowds were assembled, I have seen colored players from different sections brought in to help out the local talent.
>
> I remember seeing on one occasion at a large old country mansion, a string band of four violins, one fiddle for bass I suppose they called it, two banjos, two tambourines and mandolin. They were stationed in a wide hallway with doors opening into a big room on each side and dancing going on in each room. It required hundreds of candles to furnish lights for all this crowd, and it took three or four adults to go around snuffing and renewing them. . . .
>
> Nearly every section had its colored "good fiddler," and he was the mainstay and chief reliance of the young people when they gave a dancing party, as it was called, in distinction to a ball. The dancing party was a smaller affair and usually a one fiddler performer.[21]

Ex-slaves could readily name these performers decades later. "Tom an' Gilbert played de fiddle an' we chilluns down in de quarters cud hear dem stampin' deir feet an' shoutin' an' singin' / 'Step Light, ladies, cakes all dough / Neber mind de weather, so de wind dont blow'" (Adam Singleton, b. 1858, AL, 1950). "He [slaveholder] 'lowed de young folks to have dances on Saturday nights, and we played 'ring games'—and my Uncle Dan Calahan always picked de banjo. He lived on a nearby plantation" (Thomas Brown, b. ca. 1862, TN, 292). "We had a good time at the dances on Saturday nights. Marster would give us passes to go so that the patter roller wouldn't molest us. Charles Winn was the fiddler" (Sampson Willis, b. ca. 1843, TX, 4164). "Used to go over to de Saunders place fo' dancin'. Musta been a hundred slaves over thar, an' they always had de bes' dances. Mos' times fo' de dance dey had Dennis to play de banjer. Dennis had a twisted arm, an' he couldn't do much work, but he sho' could pick dat banjer" (Fannie Berry, b. 1841, VA, 49).

Two narrators born a quarter century apart in far separated South Carolina counties remembered a fiddler named Buck Manigault or Manigo. "I sho' like to dance when I was younger. De fiddlers was Henry Copley and Buck Manigault; and if anybody 'round here could make a fiddle ring like Buck could, wouldn't surprise me none if my heart wouldn't cry out to my legs, 'Fust lady to de right and cheat or swing as you like, and on to de right'" (Louisa Davis, b. ca. 1832, York Co., SC, 302). "I didn't jine de church in slavery time; lak to dance then. Our fiddler was Buck Manigo, de best fiddler, black or white in de state, so white folks say" (George McAlilley, b. 1855, Horry Co., SC, 144). I think it reasonable to assume that Buck Manigault and Buck Manigo were the same person, but I have found no more about him, or Henry Copley for that matter.[22]

Playing for whites as well as Blacks represented another major benchmark in standing, reputation, and material rewards. "I used to play the fiddle for dances when I was young, but not after I joined the church. I played for the white people. Oh, yes'm, the cullud folks had dances. Oh, yes'm, they sho did dance. I used to make four or five dollars a night playin' the fiddle" (Bill Thomas, b. 1849, TX, 3789).

> De first work I ever done after I was set free was pickin' cotton at $2 a hundred pounds. . . . No suh, I never belonged to no ch'uch; dey thought I done too much of the devil's work—playin' the fiddle. Used to play the fiddle for dances all around the neighborhood. One white man gave me $10 once for playin' a dance. Played lots of the old-time pieces like "Turkey in the Straw," "Dixie," and so on. (William Little, b. 1855, AR, 262)

We use to git back in de end cabin an' sing an' dance by de fiddle till day break. Sho' had one time, swingin' dem one piece dresses back an' foth, an' de boys crackin' dey coattails in de wind. Nobody never bothered us, not even de patterollers, cause Marsa won't gwine let 'em. Ole fiddler was a man named Louis Cane. Chile, he sho' could strung dat fiddle. Never did do much work, but Marsa use to keep him, 'cause he use to have him play fo' de balls in de big house. Marse use to pay him too. We never did pay him, 'cause we ain't never had nothin'. But he use to play an' call de figgers 'long as dere was anyone on de floor. Chile, when I was a girl guess I'd ruther dance dan eat. (Sally Ashton, b. ca. 1845, VA, 14)

I was jes' a li'l thang; tooked away from mammy an' pappy, jes' when I needed 'em mos'. The only caren' that I had or ever knowed anything 'bout was give to me be a frien' of my pappy. His name was John White. My pappy tol' him to take care of me for him. John was a fiddler an' many a night I woke up to find myse'f 'sleep 'twix' his legs whilst he was playin' for a dance for de white folks. My pappy an' mammy was sold from each other too, de same time as I was sold. I use' to wonder if I had any brothers and sisters, as I had always wanted some. A few years later I foun' out I didn't have none. (Mingo White, b. unk., AL, 413–14)

Narrator Bell Kelley was a fiddler's daughter. "She is now eighty years old and states that her father, King Deam, back in the old slave days, was quite a musician. His instrument was the 'fiddle' and he was called into the mansions of white people to fiddle for their balls and dances. These occasions were often apple-peelings, then a title that brought the fashionable together" (Bell Kelley, b. 1857, KY, 106).

Finally, topping the ranks of slave musicianers were those select few with formal training, some of whom played exclusively for whites in upper-crust venues. C. A. Bryce had personally known numerous slave fiddlers in antebellum Virginia:

The well-to-do slave owners throughout Virginia, in town and country encouraged certain of their servants to learn to play the customary dance music of those days.

Of course, most of them played by ear, but as the negro is a natural musician, he easily caught on to the most popular airs of the day when he heard them sung and played. But some of these negro musicians were taught by their white "young mistises" or some music teacher to play by note and do sight reading well enough to pick up a piece of music and play it at once. . . . [Bryce specifically recalled] a noted violinist by the name of Joseph C. Scott, who played for the wealthiest and most aristocratic people of Richmond and at many of the watering places during the summer seasons. . . . He was an educated musician, as far as it went in those days, which meant that he could play a piece "at sight."[23]

Formally trained slave fiddlers might also rise to the august post of dancing master, schooling white (but sometimes also Black) children in the latest ballroom steps. William H. Harrison (b. 1832, VA) had himself served in that capacity. Della Harris (b. 1852, NC) was the daughter of a dancing master; Richard Mack was the son of another.

Tony was my father, a carriage driver; he wore his tall hat and fine clothes (livery) and he was a musician—played the violin at the Academy on the "Old-Ninety-Six Road." All the white people educated their children there, and they had parties. Oh, the beautifulest ladies—they wore long dresses then and had long hair—the beautifulest! My father—Daddy Tony, they call him—he was a musician—always played the violin. (Richard Mack, b. ca. 1833, SC, 151–52, orig. parentheses)

In his memoir, Tennessee ex-slave (and fiddler) James Thomas (1827–1913) remembered "the leading dancing master of Nashville when I was a boy was a colored man by the name of McGowan. He Instructed many of the leading people of the city [in] the polished art of dancing."[24] This was free Black fiddler Jordan McGowan, a true local celebrity who also played slave dances.

> Eve'y two weeks de Marster would sen' fer Jordan McGowan who wuz de leader ob a string music ban'. Dey would git dere Friday nite early en de slaves would dance in de grape house dat nite en all day Saturday up ter midnite. You don't hab now as good dance music en as much fun as de ole time days had. (Rachel Gaines, b. ca. 1840, TN, 17)

In 1850s Alabama, Frederick Olmsted (1822–1903) met a slave carpenter who was also

> a good violinist and dancer, and who, two nights a week, taught a negro dancing-school, from which he received two dollars a night, which, of course, he spent for his own pleasure. During the winter, the negroes, in Montgomery, have their "assemblies," or dress balls, which are got up "regardless of expense," in very grand style. Tickets to these balls are advertised, "admitting one gentleman and two ladies, $1"; and "Ladies are assured that they may rely on the strictest order and propriety being observed."[25]

For aspiring performers, the opportunity to make money was a major consideration, but being a slave musicianer held other potential attractions.

> I marry Ellen Watson, as pretty a ginger cake nigger as ever fried a batter cake or rolled her arms up in a wash tub. How I git her? I never git her; dat fiddle got her. I play for all de white folks dances down at Cedar Shades, up at Blackstock. De money roll in when someone pass 'round de hat and say "De fiddler?" Ellen had more beaux 'round her than her could shake a stick at but de beau she lak best was de bow dat could draw music out of them five strings, and draw money into dat hat, dat jingle in my pocket de nex' day when I go to see her. (Andy Brice, b. ca. 1856, SC, 76–77)

> My great gran'mother was almost pure Injun, dat what make her yaller wid long hair, but her man was an African. Her folks didn want her to marry him, kase he was so dark, an' dey say if she did, den all her chillun would be Africans. Dey had done picked out a free yaller nigger for her, but my great-gran' fell in love wid dis Dave, kase she was allus a great han' to foller de music, an' Dave was a fine fiddler. Dey doan play on de fiddles an' banjos no more like dey used to, since dey has dese new kin's of music. Her name was Tilda, an Dave an' Tilda was my gran's pappy an' mammy. (Mandy Jones, b. ca. 1857, MS, 1236–37)

As another perk, musicianers might be excused from other work entirely or at least given plum positions. "The ability to play a 'good fiddle' or 'pick a banjo' was worth a good deal to its possessor if he was a slave, for he was given all manner of privileges and favors, the lightest work and good clothes, and the young men for whom he played always passed the hat around before he left and gladdened his heart with the liberal returns."[26] During slavery Charles H. Anderson clerked in his slaveholder's grocery in Richmond and moved about the city fairly freely in his spare time:

> He was trusted to go to the cash drawer for spending money, and permitted to help himself to candy and all he wanted to eat. With the help of the mistress, his mother made all his clothes, and he was "about as well dressed as anybody . . . . Saturday was our busy day at the store; but after work, I used to go to the drag downs. Some people say 'hoe down' or 'dig down,' I guess 'cause they'd dig right into it, and give it all they got. I was a great hand at fiddlin'." (Charles H. Anderson, b. 1845, VA, 1, 3)

Musicianers who were assigned other duties were frequently given tasks requiring above-average intelligence, creativity, and initiative, simultaneously conferring some measure of individual responsibility, latitude, and mobility. Thus, many top-rank fiddlers also served as coachmen, carpenters, shoemakers, or mechanics. Fiddlers William H. Harrison (b. 1832, VA), and Daddy Tony (father of Richard Mack, b. ca. 1833, SC) were coachmen as well as dancing masters. Ike Thomas (b. 1843, GA) was a fiddler and house-and-carriage boy, while pianist and music teacher Jimmie Johnson (b. ca. 1847, SC) was a groom and carriage driver. In 1862 William Wyndham Malet visited a coastal South Carolina plantation. "After dark the courtyard in front of the cottages is illuminated with pinewood bonfires, which destroy the mosquitoes, and the children dance round the blaze. . . . Here the coachman, 'Prince,' is a capital fiddler; his favourite tunes are 'Dixie Land' and country dances."[27] Wade Owens's father was a carriage driver and banjo picker (Wade Owens, b. 1863, AL).

Charles Hayes's father could turn his hand to almost anything: "My mammy was a fiel' han' an' my pappy was a mechanic an' he use to be de handy man aroun' de big house, makin' eve'thing f 'um churns an' buckets to wagon wheels. My pappy also useta play de fiddle for de white folks dances in de big house, an' he played it for de colored frolics too. He sho could make dat thing sing" (Charles Hayes, b. ca. 1855, AL).[28] Multi-instrumentalist Hammett Dell (b. 1847, TN) (banjo, fiddle, mandolin, mouth bow, quill) was a bricklayer, Abner Griffin (b. 1849, GA) (banjo, fiddle, accordion, organ) a shoemaker.[29] Richard Toler (b. ca. 1835, VA, OH) moved to Cincinnati after freedom, where he fiddled and worked as a bricklayer, stone-mason, and carpenter, then for thirty-six years as a blacksmith. An exceptional number of slave fiddlers were carpenters, including an unnamed 1777 Virginia runaway identified as "a carpenter by trade, and is a good cooper. He can read print, pretends to a great deal of religion, has been a good fiddler." A similar 1767 South Carolina fugitive notice targets "a short but square set elderly Negro man, named NOKO, who is very handy in the use of carpenters tools, and as a waiting man; . . . plays on the violin, and belonged formerly to Mr. Brownell, dancing-master."[30] Frederick Olmsted was most impressed by an Alabama slave fiddler, "a carpenter, who was remarkable for mathematical capacities," and who "earned consid-erable money besides, for himself, by overwork at his trade, and still more" by running a dancing academy.[31]

On the Madewood Plantation in Napoleonville, Louisiana, musicianers were ranked with skilled tradespeople. "A number of skilled workers—mechanics, carpenters, brickmasons and musicians, to mention but a few of the artisans on the plantation—had been allowed to keep for themselves part of their earnings" (Old Ex-Slave, b. unk., LA, 21).

By contrast, musicianers were also given some leeway to be of no account whatsoever. Within the ruthlessly conformist plantation police state, slave musicians may have been the only Black deviants not just tolerated but somewhat encouraged. W. S. Needham was a Mississippi slaveholder's child who learned to fiddle from a slave named Mance. "There is one thing that I treasure above all other memories of the old plantation; that was the music and dances they had. Dad bought a nigger by the name of Mance. He got him for $350.00 because he was the worst thief in the country. Dad took him, because he felt that he'd never seen the nigger he couldn't make a good one out of without beating him to death" (W. S. Needham Jr., SS2 10 *TX* 9: 4364). Needham's father failed to reform Mance but did not care since he was an excellent fiddler.

Slave fiddlers were also recalled as habitual runaways, periodically going into hiding to avoid work or punishment. Rather than fleeing north, however, many are described remaining near their plantations, their audiences, and their patrons, eventually returning without the punishments meted out to other slaves in similar circumstances.

In my neighborhood, when a youngster, the fiddler that cared for most of the dances for ten or fifteen miles around was an inky black old man, then past middle age, and generally known as "Dabney's Old Harry." He was some fiddler and handled the bow with a gift, while an eternal grin spread over his features.

He was the greatest runaway in the country and spent almost half his time hiding and skulking about until he was caught, carried back to his master, when he would settle down, get permission from Captain Dabney and play here and there until some altercation would arise between him and the overseer, and he would take to the woods again to escape a whipping.[32]

A cantefable told by several ex-slaves concerns one such fugitive:

> Us used to go to barn dances all the time. I never will forget the fellow who played the fiddle for them dances. He had run away from his marster seven years before. He lived in a cave he had dug in the ground. He stayed in this cave all day and would come out at night. This cave was in the swamp. He stole just 'bout everythin' he et. His marster had been tryin' to catch him for a long time. Well they found out he was playin' for these dances and one night us saw some strange lookin' men come in but us didn't pay it much 'tention. Us always made a big oak fire and thats where us got most of our light from. Well these men danced with the girls a good while and after a while they started goin' out one by one. Way after while they all came back in together, they had washed the blackenin' off their faces, and us seen they was white. This man had a song he would always sing. "Fooled my marster seven years—expect to fool him seven more." So when these men came in they went to him and told him maybe he had fooled 'em for seven years, but he wouldn't fool 'em seven more. When they started to grab him he just reached in the fire and got a piece of wood that was burnin' good on one end and waved it all around (in a circle) until he set three of 'em on fire. While they was puttin' this fire out he run out in the swamp and back in his cave. They tried to catch him again. They painted their faces and done just like they did the first time, but this time they carried pistols. When they pulled their pistols on him he did just like he did the first time, and they

never did catch him. He stopped comin' to play for the dances after they was straight after him. Dogs couldn't trail him 'cause he kept his feet rubbed with onions. (Roy Redfield, b. unk., GA, 306–7, orig. parentheses)[33]

Musicianers were often admired or at least envied, but a sizable population saw their material rewards, errancy, and leisure as sure signs of sloth, deceit, thievery, even *conjure* (sorcery). Narrator Doc Choice remembered a musician actually called Conjure. "They was a nigger by the name of Ole Man Tout, the 'Conjoor,' who could play the violin jus' as good as anyone you hear today. . . . If any one would say, 'I think we'll send Ole Man Tout to the fields today,' the old Missus would say, 'No. The day is too warm, and the work too hard for the old man. He'll stay at the house,' and sure 'nuff he would" (Jeptha "Doc" Choice, b. 1835, TX, 708). In point of fact, numerous tricks (conjure spells) were intended to help slaves avoid work or punishment. Alabama ex-slave Jake Green actually titled the tale of the slave fiddler who fools his master for seven years "A Conju' What Didn' Wuk." Besides being a musicianer, schoolteacher, and barber, Choice himself practiced divine healing (hence *Doc* Choice). Supernaturalism and slave music, and the sinister associations of slave musicians, are subjects so prodigious that they require their own chapter.

While musical talents won forbearance in some quarters, musicianers were occasionally singled out for punishment. "Old man John was de fiddler on our place, and when de patterollers cotched him dey beat him up de wust of all, 'cause him and his fiddle was all de time drawin' Niggers out to de dances" (Addie Vinson, b. 1852, GA, 107). Around Sam Bush's plantation Uncle Dave had been the local caller, until one night Kluxers surprised a dance party he was prompting.

> De niggers sez to uncle, "Youse do de talkin' an' weuns stand behind youse." Uncle does de talkin' an' tells de Klux de niggers have de right [to be]

thar. Den Uncle looks 'hind him an' thar am no niggers in sight. Deys am gone, outter de winder, up de chimney an' anywhar deys could hide. De Klux warnt aftah to interfer wid de dance, 'twas some pa'ticular nigger deys want but 'cause uncle talks lak de niggers ask him an' sez deys stay 'hind him de Klux gives uncle Dave a whuppin's. Deys tell Uncle if youse want to be left 'lone by de Klux stay where yous w'ok. Uncle Dave was a good prompter at de dance an' de cullud fo'ks all wants him to come to de dance fo' to prompt dem but aftah dat him tol' dem, "No sar, youse stand too far 'hind me so Ise can' see youse w'en de Klux come." (Sam Bush, b. 1860, TX, 543)

Slave performers also included the usual assortment of unique personalities. Interviewer Bernice Bowden concluded that Sally Nealy "is a very wicked old woman and swears like a sailor, but she has a remarkable memory" (Sally Nealy, b. ca. 1845, AR, 187). Of Mary Gladdy, J. R. Jones wrote "she is a seventh Day Adventist; is not a psychic, but is a rather mysterious personage," receiving "visitations from the spirits" revealed in "strange writings" (Mary Gladdy, b. ca. 1853, GA, 19). Octogenarian Annie Bridges was still actively performing around Farmington, Missouri, but not to unanimous approval. According to the anonymous interviewer, "Annie Bridges is quite a character. When giving her speeches and singing her songs she dramatizes them while walking across the room. She is hard of hearing and can be heard for quite a distance. She receives an old-age pension. She is considered by many, a sort of nuisance around town, since she is always begging for something. Some are afraid of her" (Annie Bridges, b. 1855, MO, 50).

Even in slavery but especially after, there are intimations of the dissipation and sporting life identified with later Black musicians. "I am a minister of the Gospel. I have been preaching for the last thirty years. I am batching here. A man does better to live by himself. Young people got the devil in them now a days.

Your own children don't want you around. . . . The government gives me a pension. The white folks help me all along. Before I preached, I fiddled, danced, shot craps, did anything" (Robert Barr, b. 1864, MS, 122). Ben Horry's family were official musicians on a South Carolina plantation.

That woods you see been Colonel Josh Ward's taters patch. Right to Brookgreen Plantation where I born. My Father Duffine (Divine) Horry and my brother is Richard Horry. Dan'l and Summer two both my uncle. You can put it down they were Colonel Ward's musicianer. Make music for his dater (daughter) and the white folks to dance. Great fiddlers, drummers. Each one could play fiddle, beat drum, blow fife. All three were treat with the same education. You know, when you going to do anything for them big people you got to do it right. Before time (formerly) they danced different. Before strange city people fetched different steps here. But, then, they could use their feet all right! (Ben Horry, b. ca. 1850, SC, 308–9, orig. parentheses)

Ben Horry's father also had quite a taste for whiskey.

It this way. You ain't LOW to eat the whole rice you kin make money outer. Beat dat rice. But my Daddy been a great whiskey man. Liquor. Didn't have 'em less he go to town. Money scase. ('E wuz kind of musicianer for the Ward fambly.) But he break he jug. He break he whiskey jug. En when de oversheer (overseer) git out de ration and gib 'em to mah Ma and us chillun he hand mah Pa a piece o' dem break jug! That keep him in mind o' that whiskey jug. (Ben Horry, b. ca. 1850, SC, 200–201, orig. parentheses)

The gist of the concluding episode is that after Horry's father angrily broke his empty whiskey jug, the overseer doled out a piece of the broken jug instead of the father's next whiskey ration.

The child of ex-slaves, Walter Chapman grew up busking in mining camps around Denver (Central City, Leadville, Cow Creek).

The father, of the never-do-well type and Indian extraction, moved from one mining camp and trading post to another, music and gambling was his chief asset, and as Walter put it—"he was a two-time loser at that." The father would play the banjo and young Chapman would do the dancing, and by this method they managed to "keep the wolf from the door." . . . Central City, Colorado in those stirring mining days was a place where almost anything was permissible. Itinerant Negro musicians, with their questionable women would come to this place on pay days, and the same was true of the whites. Pete Burns, a Negro, had a pet bear whose name was Zero. Zero was trained to dance—collect money and wrestle. . . . Pete banked on Zero's ability as a wrestler and would often bet as much as a hundred dollars that no man could throw him, but one night Zero got too rough and throwed a man so hard that his neck was broken, a free for all fight ensued and this grew to a mob and Pete and Zero were both lynched. (Walter Chapman, b. ca. 1871, CO, child of ex-slaves, 35, 36)

Tom Morris's talents kept him out of the Mississippi cotton fields. "I larnt to dance de back step, an' when I got grown I larnt to play de fiddle too, I cud sing sum, but I niver wurked in de fiel.'" After the war, however, he was repeatedly jailed or fined for alcohol-related crimes, in one instance including drunken gunplay. "When I was drunk I was bad. I uster whip Cynthia, till one day she throwed er pan uf dishwater on me an' laid me out—well she hit me with the pan too" (Tom Morris, b. ca. 1850, MS, 1589, 1587). By the late 1800s, Southern jails and prison farms were full of musicianers, incarcerated for offenses real or manufactured. Joe Rollins met some of these men in the Mississippi pen after he was railroaded under the infamous postwar *hog laws*. "You know I stayed 2 years in de Penitentiary—cause dey said I stole a hog

Fig. 10.3. "The Bear Dance, Georgetown, Colo." Kilburn Brothers, 1890. Library of Congress, Prints and Photographs Division. Georgetown (est. 1859) was another of the mining boom towns around Denver; its closest neighbor was Central City, where Pete and Zero were lynched.

from Mr. Ben Williams whuts dead. Dat hog come up out of de woods atter I gone to de pen. I was in jail five months. . . . Yes, I seed em dance—Dance myself. Anoder nigger would play de fiddle and de banjo. Dats de way dey do at penitentiary too" (Joe Rollins, b. 1845, MS, 1898–99).[34]

Most slave musicians were not conjures, incorrigibles, derelicts, desperados, or convicts, but in the universal pattern even less flamboyant performers were often eccentrics, neurotics, or paranormals, or simply misfits, outsiders, outcasts, or loners.

I don't know who I am nor what my true name is. I wus born December 25, 1860 on a plantation in New Hanover County. The plantation belonged to John Williams, whose wife wus named Isabella and the farm wus on land which is now in the corporate limits of Wilmington, N.C.

The reason I don't know who I am is I don't remember my father and mother or any of my people. When I got so I could remember anything I wus with the Williams family. Marster an' missus, an' their family are the only ones I ever looked upon as my people. They never told me who I wus.

After the war I stayed with them a long time and helped them on the farm. They run a truck farm. I got along all right while I wus with the Williams family, but when I got grown I left them. I loved them but I realized I wus a nigger and knew that I could never be like them, and that I wus one to myself. . . .

I have nothing to say about being partly white, I leave that to your imagination. I have thought about it a lot. I don't know. . . .

I have been blessed with good health, I am breaking now but I am still able to do light jobs.

I am a good fiddler. The white folks have taught me to do lots of different things. I have had very few advantages and I cannot read and write. I have never been in jail in my life. (John Thomas Williams, b. 1860, NC, 392–93)

In a male-dominated profession peopled by bounders and misfits, there was one class of instrumentalists whose respectability was beyond question. Keyboardists were overwhelmingly women, many of whom played in church or gave lessons professionally. Female pianists were also especially likely to be ordained clergy or lay workers, educators, authors, or journalists.

In the 1820s, South Carolina slave Charles Ball (ca. 1781–?) met a fiddler named Peter, who seemed to come and go as he pleased.

He informed me that his master was always ready to let him go to a ball; and would permit him to leave the cotton field at any time for that purpose, and even lend him a horse to ride. I afterwards learned from this man, that his master compelled him to give him half the money that he received as gratuities from the gentlemen for whom he played at dinner parties.[35]

Such management arrangements were actually quite common in the plantation South.

Whenever dere was a contest, a man named Jolly would win all of 'em. Dis darky sure could dance. Boy, when he started twirling his legs and stickin' out his back, old master would holler. Wouldn't let Jolly work hard either 'cause he was de best dat master Landro had. He won plenty of money dancin' for master. (Elizabeth Ross Hite, b. ca. 1850, LA, 106)

I was at home with my folks [in North Carolina] until I was about fifteen years old I reckon, and then I was sold to a man name Cheet, Dyson Cheet, and he move with us to Louisiana close to Texarkana, but he hire me out to a man name Goodman Carter to work on his steamboat for a long, long time, maybe four or five years in all, so I don't know much about Old Master Dyson Cheet. Then he give me or will me to his boy Tom Cheet and he bring me to the Creek Nation because his wife come from Mississippi and she is just part Creek Indian, so they can get a big farm out here if they want it. . . . On the boat I learned to fiddle, and I can make an old fiddle talk. So I done pretty good playing for the white dances for a long time after the War, and they sure had some good ones. Everything from a waltz to a Schottische I played. Sometimes some white people didn't like to have me play, but young Master (I always called him that till he died) would say, "Where I go my boy can go too." (Henry Clay, b. ca. 1835, LA, TX, IT, 208–9, 116, orig. parentheses)

W. C. Handy (1873–1958) wrote that his maternal grandfather "told me that before he got religion he used to play the fiddle for dances. That had been his way of making extra money back in slavery days. His master, the kindly man that I have mentioned, allowed him to keep what he earned from playing."[36] If Handy's grandfather was allowed to keep all of what he earned, he was probably the exception; slave musicians were typically expected to split with slaveholders. In fact, slaves were customarily required to surrender half of any earnings. In 1853 the Richmond firm of Toler & Cook, General Agents advertised another Black fiddler, leaving no doubt exactly who was to be paid for his services.

FOR HIRE, either for the remainder of the year, or by the month, week, or job, the celebrated musician and fiddler, GEORGE WALKER. All persons desiring the services of George, are notified that they must contract for them with us, and in no case pay to him or any other person, the amount of his hire, without a written order from us.—George Walker is admitted, by common consent, to be the best leader of a band in all eastern and middle Virginia.[37]

Even in the antebellum South one may glimpse the future course of American popular music and the legalistic arrangements that would sometimes enrich, sometimes impoverish, but generally indenture African American performers to white managers and booking agents, club and theater owners, radio stations, and record executives. No wonder later Black artists slipped so easily into these roles. For half a century, Louis Armstrong (1901–1971) worked under a handshake contract with a mobbed-up martinet named Joe Glaser (1896–1969), who in exchange for half of Armstrong's earnings made Louis one of the best-known and most-beloved figures on the planet. Late in life Armstrong liked to quote the advice he had received early in his career from the Black manager of a white-owned New Orleans honky tonk. "Always have a *White Man* who likes you and can and will put his Hand on your shoulder and say—'*This is My Nigger*' and, Can't Nobody Harm Ya."[38] We should almost expect that such arrangements dated to slavery. Many African griots had similar deals. And African American musicianers sometimes made even stranger alliances.

Appendix: Slave Musicians Identified in the Ex-Slave Narratives

Below are listed all of the musical performers I have been able to identify in the WPA narratives, and the ex-slaves describing them. In many cases, of course, the two were one and the same, since numerous ex-slaves had themselves been musicians, while others were kith and kin to performers. Thus while some record of the individual's personal name was a major criterion for inclusion, some ex-slaves identified musicians only as daddy, mama, brother, sister, uncle, and so forth, in which cases I have included them under these familiar terms. Although this chapter is concerned mainly with plantation musicians, for convenience I have included a few performers who passed into full-blown professionalism, mainly through minstrelsy. Almost all individuals listed here were instrumentalists, but I have also included a few persons recognized as exceptional singers or dancers, as well as dance callers. There is also a separate section for white musicians identified by ex-slaves.

I. Black Performers Identifiable by Name

Jess Adams: fiddle, SC (Victoria Adams, b. ca. 1835, SC)

Jim Allen: jew's harp, Bob Allen place, Russell Co., AL (Jim Allen, b. ca. 1850, AL)

Charles H. Anderson: fiddle, J. L. Woodson grocery and environs, Richmond, VA (Charles H. Anderson, b. 1845, VA)

Mary Anngady (Princess Quango Hennadonah Perceriah): singer, guitar, violin, piano, nationally touring stage performer (Mary Anngady, b. ca. 1857, NC)

Antoine: homemade drum, DeGruy place, Opelousas, LA (Frances Doby, b. 1838, LA)

*Auntie: piano, M. T. Johnson place, Tarrant Co., TX (Betty Bormer, b. 1857, TX)

William Banjo: accordion, OK, LA (William Banjo, b. unk., OK, LA)

Robert Barr: fiddle, Chickasaw Co., MS (Robert Barr, b. 1864, MS)

John Bayou: drums, percussion, hoodoo band leader, St. John's Eve, Lake Pontchartrain; New Orleans and environs (N. H. Hobley, b. 1858, LA)

Allen Beaver: fiddle, Robert Beaver place, Macon Co., GA (Louis Fowler, b. 1853, GA)

Thomas Green Bethune (Blind Tom) (1849–1909): piano, touring stage performer (white sources, GA)

Charlotte Beverly: plantation horn, Captain Pankey place, Montgomery Co., TX (Charlotte Beverly, b. ca. 1847, TX)

Henry Bland: violin, Coxton plantation, Putnam Co., GA (Henry Bland, b. 1851, GA)

James Bolton: quills, tin buckets and pans, Whitfield Bolton plantation, Oglethorpe Co., GA (James Bolton, b. 1852, GA)

Jerry Boykins: fiddle, John Thomas Boykin place, Troup Co., GA (Jerry Boykins, b. 1845, GA)

Andy Brice: fiddle, Winnsboro, SC, and environs (Andy Brice, b. ca. 1856, SC)

Annie Bridges: singer, beggar, public nuisance, Farmington, MO (Annie Bridges, b. 1855, MO)

Sam Broach: banjo, William P. Broach place, Marion, MS (Sam Broach, b. 1848, MS)

James Brooks: dance caller, Dr. Parker place, Grand Gulf, MS (James Brooks, b. ca. 1855, MS)

*Brother: quills, quill band leader, Joseph Maxwell plantations, Liberty and Early Cos., GA (Dora Roberts, b. 1849, GA)

*Brother: fiddle, Eford place, Barbour Co., AL (Laura Thornton, b. ca. 1830, AL)

*Brothers: quills, Quickmore place and environs, Norfolk County, VA (Sister Harrison, b. 1846, VA)

Lewis Cain: banjo, dance caller, Ben Tinsley place, Powhatan Co., VA (Martha Showvely, b. 1837, VA)

Uncle Dan Calahan: banjo, Matt Anderson plantation and environs, Williamson Co., TN (Thomas Brown, b. ca. 1862, TN)

Caleb: fiddle, Waco, TX (Joe Oliver, b. 1847, TX)

Flint Campbell: homemade fiddle, W. L. Sloan place, Harrison Co., TX (Simp Campbell, b. 1860, TX)

Louis Cane, fiddle, dance caller, Charles Hancock place, VA (Sally Ashton, b. ca. 1845, VA)

Uncle Richard Carruthers, fiddle, Billy Coates place and environs, Bastrop Co., TX (Richard Carruthers, b. ca. 1848, TX)

Ned Chaney: bones, Coleman place, Choctaw Co., AL (Ned Chaney, b. ca. 1857, AL)

Aunt Charity: plantation cow-horn, John McInnis place, Leakesville, MS (Hamp Santee, b. ca. 1859, MS)

Jake Chisholm: overdriver's horn, Bostick place, Hampton Co., SC (Isaiah Butler, b. ca. 1855, SC)

Amos Clark: dance caller, Ed Roseborough place, McLennan Co., TX (Amos Clark, b. 1841, TX)

Anna Clark: street dancer, mine paydays, Central City, CO (Anna Clark, b. 1847, CO)

Dan Clark: fiddle, street performer, Central City, CO (Anna Clark, b. 1847, CO)

Henry Clay: fiddle, LA steamboat; LA, TX, IT (postwar) (Henry Clay, b. ca. 1835, NC)

Henry Copley: fiddle, with Buck Manigault (below), Jim Lemon place, York Co., SC (Louisa Davis, b. ca. 1832, SC)

James Cornelius: conch trumpet (plantation horn), Sandell farm, Magnolia, MS (James Cornelius, b. ca. 1846, MS).

*Cousin: quills, Paul McCall place, Union Co., AR (Katie Arbery, b. 1857, AR)

*Cousin: fiddle, Piney Woods Place, Augusta, GA (Fannie Fulcher, b. ca. 1860, GA)

Elijah Cox (Uncle Cox): guitar, Fort Concho, TX (Elijah Cox, freeborn 1843, MI, TX)

John Crawford: fiddle, Jake Crawford place, Sabine-Grandiose, MS (John Crawford, b. 1837, MS)

Tom Crump: fiddle, Whitman Smith place and environs, Davidson Co., NC (Bill Crump, b. 1855, NC)

*Daddy: homemade fiddle, fiddle, Joe Holland place, Dalton, GA (Chaney Mack, b. ca. 1864, GA)

*Daddy: fiddle, Bill Robertson: banjo, Buck Robertson: guitar, harp, Danville, VA (Matilda Henrietta Perry, b. 1852, VA)

Henry Dant: fiddle, Judge Daniel Kendrick's farm and environs, Ralls Co., MO (Henry Dant, b. ca. 1832, MO)

Dantel: plantation horn, Ben Avent place, Charlotte, NC (Dempsey Pitts, b. 1830, NC)

*Daughter: classical pianist, Chicago (Rev. James W. Washington, b. 1854, MS)

Dave: fiddle, NC, ca. 1820s (Mandy Jones, b. ca. 1857, MS)

Uncle Dave: dance prompter, Ellis Co., TX (Sam Bush, b. 1860, TX)

Anthony Davis: banjo, Leabough plantation, Little Rock, AR (Louis Davis, b. 1858, AR)

Jeff Davis: fife, drum, Pine Bluff, AR (Jeff Davis, b. 1853, AR)

Jim Davis: banjo, dance caller, Peter Davis place, Raleigh, NC (Jim Davis, b. 1840, NC)

King Deam: fiddle, King Deam plantation, Henry Co., KY (Bell Kelley, b. 1857, KY)

James V. Deane: conch trumpet (plantation horn), Thomas Mason plantation, Charles Co., MD (James V. Deane, b. 1850, MD)

Hammett Dell: banjo, fiddle, mandolin, mouth bow, quills, Pleasant White farm and environs, Murfreesboro, TN (Hammett Dell, b. 1847, TN)

Dennis: banjo, Saunders place, Appomattox Co., VA (Fannie Berry, b. 1841, VA)

George Dillard: banjo, Bob Steele plantation, MS (George Dillard, b. 1852, MS)

Hattie Douglas: piano, organ, music teacher, church pianist, Pine Bluff, AR (Hattie Douglas, b. 1867, AR, child of ex-slaves)

Old John Drayton: fiddle, Murray place, Edisto Island, SC (Ephraim Lawrence, b. ca. 1856, SC)

Willis Easter: dance caller, McLennan Co., TX (Willis Easter, b. 1852, TX)

Queen Eliza of the Dance: dancer, antebellum New Orleans (Marie Brown, freeborn unk., LA)

Lorenza Ezell: fiddle, banjo, Lipscomb plantation and environs, Spartanburg Co., SC (Lorenza Ezell, b. ca. 1850, SC)

*Father: banjo, street performer, Central City, CO (Walter Chapman, b. ca. 1871, CO, child of ex-slaves)

*Father: musicianer, John Carthan place, and ballroom dancing school, Warrenton, NC (Della Harris, b. 1852, NC)

*Father: quills, banjo, Erman place, VA (Ellis Jefson, b. ca. 1861, VA)

*Father: violin, cornet, organ, Ladsden, SC, and environs (Rev. Aaron Pinnacle, b. ca. 1890, SC, child of ex-slaves)

George Fleming: quills, Sam Fleming place, Laurens Co., SC (George Fleming, b. 1854, SC)

William Gant: fiddle, dance caller, and Uncle Jim: fiddle, Jim Gant place, Bedford Co., TN (William Gant, b. 1837, TN)

George: quills, Alec Stephens plantation, Taliaferro County, GA (Georgia Baker, b. 1850, GA)

Mary Gladdy: spiritual singer, visionary-medium, spirit writer, Hines Holt plantation, Muscogee Co., GA (Mary Gladdy, b. ca. 1853, GA)

Caesar Glenn: violin, and *Brother: violin, John Beck farm and environs, Winston-Salem, NC (Wade Glenn, b. ca. 1860, NC)

*Grandpappy: fiddle, Hillery Quinn place, Holmesville, MS (Hattie Jefferson, b. ca. 1855, MS)

*Grandson: piano prodigy, School for Blind Children, Lansing, MI (Eugenia Weatherall, b. 1863, MS)

William Green: fiddle, Tolas and William Parsons plantations, St. Mary's Parish, LA (Ellen Betts, b. 1853, LA)

Abner Griffin: banjo, violin, accordion, organ, Felix Griffin place, Gold Mines, GA (Abner Griffin, b. 1849, GA)

George Grisham: Army bandleader, Memphis–San Antonio (Emma Grisham, b. ca. 1847, TN)

William H. Harrison: fiddle, Anderson Harrison place, Richmond, VA, and environs (William H. Harrison, b. 1832, VA)

Filmore Taylor Hancock: tambourine, Hancock place, Greene County, MO; Rolla-Salem, MO area (Filmore Taylor Hancock, b. 1847, MO)

Burt Haygood: dance caller, Elijah Owens plantation, SC; bugler, Confederate army (Burt Haygood, 1840–1924, SC, information communicated by daughter)

Larnce Holt: fiddle, William Holt place, Woodville, TX (Larnce Holt, b. 1858, TX)

Horry brothers (Divine, Daniel, Summer): all played fiddle, drum, fife, Colonel Josh Ward plantation and environs, Murrell's Inlet, SC (Uncle Ben Horry, b. ca. 1850, SC)

Elice Hudson: fiddle, Frank Upson place, Oglethorpe Co., GA (Neal Upson, b. 1857, GA)

Uncle Alex Hunt: plantation bugle, Jenkins Hunt place, Hancock Co., GA (Henry Rogers, b. 1864, GA)

Jack: fiddle, Katherine de Graffenreid place and environs, ballroom dances, Nashville, TN (John Thompson, b. 1857, TN)

Jack: fiddle, Frank Thomas place, Lauderdale Co., MS (William M. Thomas, b. ca. 1850, MS)

Nigger Jack: bass singer, Robert Beaver plantation, Macon Co., GA (Louis Fowler, b. 1853, GA)

Silas Jackson: cow or bull horns (signaling), Tom Ashbie place, Ashbie's Gap, VA (Rev. Silas Jackson, b. 1846 or 1847, VA)

Uncle Jed: banjo, Fab Haywood place, Wake Co., NC (Tanner Spikes, b. 1860, NC)

Old Joe: fiddle, Lea place, Franklin Co., MS (Rina Brown, b. 1853, MS); John Washington Page place, Amite Co., MS (Charity Jones, b. ca. 1853, MS); Gaul Matthews place, Copiah Co., MS (Jim Martin, b. 1857, MS).

Old Man John: fiddle, Ike Vinson's place, Oconee Co., GA (Addie Vinson, b. 1852, GA)

Uncle John: dance prompter, Jack Turnipseed place, TX (Tob Davis, b. 1857, TX)

Charley Johnson: dance caller, Kleavis Johnson properties, Fort Bend–Waco, TX (Charley Johnson, b. 1850, TX)

Jimmie Johnson: organ, piano, melodion (accordion), music teacher, L. C. Kennedy place, Spartanburg, SC (Uncle Jimmie Johnson, b. ca. 1847, SC)

Jolly: contest dancer, Trinity plantation, New Orleans (Elizabeth Ross Hite, b. ca. 1850, LA)

Bud Jones: jaw harp, French harp, accordion, dancer, John Jones place, Lynchburg, VA (Bud Jones, b. ca. 1850, VA)

Moses Lawton (Moses Murray after freedom): bass singer, white folk's church, Lawtonville, SC (Rebecca Jane Grant, b. ca. 1843, SC)

Uncle Cinto Lewis: fiddle, McNeel plantation and environs, Brazoria Co., TX (Uncle Cinto Lewis, b. 1826, TX; Lucy Lewis, b. unk., TX)

Uncle Bill Little: fiddle, TX (William "Uncle Bill" Little, b. 1855, AR)

Jim Long: fiddle, Berry Wright plantation and environs, MS (Aunt Kate Betters, b. 1848, MS)

Will Long: fiddle, Edward W. Long place, Maury Co., TN; Mississippi river showboats, minstrel parades (Will Long, b. ca. 1850, TN)

*Mammy's brother: fiddle, Daniel Finley plantation, Columbia, SC (Margaret Hughes, b. ca. 1855, SC)

Friday and Mance: fiddles, Needham place, Scott Co., MS (W. S. Needham Jr., b. 1854, MS, slaveholder's child, SS2 10 *TX* 9: 4364–65)

Buck Manigault or Manigo: fiddle, Jim Lemon place, York County, SC, and Jno. S. Douglas place, Horry Co., SC, and environs (Louisa Davis, b. ca. 1832, SC; George McAlilley, b. 1853, SC)

Mariah: piano, New Orleans; Lyles place, Greenville, SC (Ella Johnson, b. 1857, SC)

Henry Lewis McGaffey: fiddle, Lake Charles, LA–Beaumont, TX (Henry Lewis McGaffey, b. 1853, LA, TX)

Jordan McGowan, fiddle, stringband leader, dancing master, Nashville, TN (Rachel Gaines, b. ca. 1840, TN, 17)

Mance McQueen: fiddle, Dewberry place and environs, Smith Co., TX (Andrew Goodman, b. 1840, TX)

Morris: guitar (1930s), Tate Co., MS (Aunt Katherin, b. unk., MS)

Tom Morris: fiddle, Reeber place, Rankin Co., MS (Tom Morris, b. unk., MS)

George Morrison: bones, Union Co., KY (George Morrison, b. ca. 1860, KY)

Mose: plantation bugle, Cy Magby place, Silver Creek, MS (Nellie Dunne, b. ca. 1860, MS)

Leo Mouton: accordion, accompanied by unidentified string bass player, Pitt Jones place, Lake Charles, LA (Leo Mouton, b. ca. 1860, LA)

Ben Murray and Tennessee Ike: fiddles, John Mobley plantation, Fairfield Co., SC (Adeline Jackson, b. ca. 1849, SC)

Monroe Orcutt: fiddle, VA (Melinda Ann Ruffin, b. 1839, VA)

Josh Overstreet: banjo, M. J. Hall place, Harrison Co., TX (Horace Overstreet, b. 1856, TX)

Wade Owens Sr.: banjo, Berry Owens place, Loachapoka, AL (Wade Owens Jr., b. 1863, AL)

*Papa: Civil War bugler, MS (Nancy Anderson, b. ca. 1870, MS, child of ex-slaves)

*Papa: figure caller, Elbe, SC (Louise Pettis, b. ca. 1880, SC, child of ex-slaves)

*Pappy: fiddle, Ben Duncan place, Day's Landing, AL (Charles Hayes, b. ca. 1855, AL)

*Pappy: fiddle, Cherokee dances, Fort Gibson, IT, and environs (Johnson Thompson, b. 1853, IT)

Louis Joseph Piernas: organizer Promot Brass Band, Bay St. Louis, MS (Louis Joseph Piernas, freeborn 1856, MS)

Jim Piper: fiddle, Sneed place, Austin, TX (John Sneed, b. unk., TX)

Harre Quarls: gourd fiddle, fiddle, TX (Harre Quarls, b. 1841, TX)

Jack Rabb: fife, Columbus Riflemen (historic military company), Columbus, MS (Jack Rabb, b. unk., MS)

Pete Robinson: fiddle, Bosque Co., TX (Mariah Robinson, b. ca. 1845, TX)

Tom Rollins: banjo, Paul McCall place, Union Co., AR (Katie Arbery, b. 1857, AR)

Jim Roseborough and Tom: fiddles, Ed Roseborough place, McLennan Co., TX (Amos Clark, b. 1841, TX)

Gertie Ross: music teacher and pianist, A.M.E. Church, Shorter, CO (Gertie Ross, b. 1879, CO, child of ex-slaves)

Sam and Rufus: fiddle, banjo, William West place, Tippah Co., MS (James West, b. 1854, MS)

Charlie Sapp and Grant Sutton: fiddles, Mallet place, Brenham, TX (Mary Edwards, b. 1853, TX)

Sam Scott: baritone singer, minstrel promoter, baseball player, property manager Russellville opera house, Pope Co., AR, and environs (Sam Scott, b. 1859, AR)

George Simmons: fiddle, Steve Jaynes place and environs, Jefferson Co., TX (George Simmons, b. 1854, TX)

James Singleton: fiddle, Elbert Bell place, Simpson Co., AR (James Singleton, b. 1856, AR)

Joe Slick: banjo, Travis Co., TX (Emma Weeks, b. 1858, TX)

William Smith: fiddle, Smith place, LA, and La Grange, TX (William Smith, b. 1845, LA)

Uncle Steven: plantation cow-horn, Andrew Watt place, Henderson, TX (Susan Merritt, b. 1851, TX)

Bill Thomas: fiddle, TX (Bill Thomas, b. 1849, TX)

Ike Thomas: fiddle, William Blanton mill and environs, Jasper Co., GA (Ike Thomas, b. 1843, GA)

Rebecca Thomas: accordion, and John Cato: banjo, Jake Saul place, Caldwell Co., TX (Rebecca Thomas, b. 1825, TX)

John Thompson: fiddle, dance caller, dance teacher, singer, Katherine de Graffenreid place and environs, ballroom dances, Nashville, TN (John Thompson, b. 1857, TN)

Richard Toler: fiddle, Cincinnati (Richard Toler, b. ca. 1835, VA)

Tom: contest dancer, Hallman plantation, Palestine, TX (James W. Smith, b. ca. 1860, TX)

Cousin Tom: songster (dance caller), Dave Cavin place, Harrison Co., TX (Bert Strong, b. 1864, TX)

Old Tom: fiddle, banjo, Fred Tate place, La Grange, TX (Lewis Jones, b. 1851, TX)

Tom and Gilbert: fiddles, George Simmons place, Newton, AL (Adam Singleton, b. 1858, AL)

Daddy Tony: violin, Cherry plantation, Charleston, SC (Richard Mack, b. ca. 1833, SC)

Ole Man Tout the Conjure: fiddle, bandleader, Jezra Choice place, Rusk Co., TX (Jeptha Choice, b. 1835, TX)

*Uncle: fiddler, dancer, Crawford Co., MO (George Jackson Simpson, b. 1854, MO)

*Uncle: guitar, Burgess place, MS (Jane Thompson, b. unk., MS)

Harold Upson: plantation bugle, Frank Upson place, Oglethorpe Co., GA (Neal Upson, b. 1857, GA)

Aunt Vinney: children's dinner horn, Joe Echols plantation, Oglethorpe Co., GA (Robert Shepherd, b. ca. 1845, GA)

Vinson: fiddle, TN, KY (Robert J. Cheatham, b. unk., KY, child of ex-slaves)

Ben Wall: dance caller, Benton Co., MS (Ben Wall, b. ca. 1852, MS)

Rev. James W. Washington: fiddle, piano, McComb, MS (Rev. James W. Washington, b. 1854, MS)

James "Gingerbread" Wiggins: dancer, Revell plantation, Anne Arundel Co. and Annapolis, MD (James Wiggins, b. 1850 or 1851, MD)

Paul Wiley: head music man, colored fiddlers, Black ballroom dances, Clarendon, AR (Molly Horn, b. 1860, AR)

Isom Willbanks: fiddle, Solomon Willbanks plantation, Jackson Co., GA (Green Willbanks, b. 1861, GA)

John Thomas Williams: fiddle, John Williams farm, Wilmington, NC (John Thomas Williams, b. 1860, NC)

Lewis Williams: jew's harp, Billy Sourlock place, Milam, TX (Lewis Williams, b. 1851, TX)

Ed Williamson and Tom Nick: principal dancers, minstrel shows, Russellville, AR, and environs (Sam Scott, b. 1859, AR)

Jake Wilson: fiddle, McLennan Co., TX (Jake Wilson, b. 1855, TX)

Tom Windham: brass band member, Union army, GA (Tom Windham, b. 1845, GA)

Charles Winn: fiddle, Billy and Jimmy Walford place and environs, Rusk Co., TX (Sampson Willis, b. ca. 1843, TX)

Willis Winn: fiddle, Bob Winn plantation and environs, Homer, LA (Willis Winn, b. 1822, LA)

William Word, Uncle Dan Porter, Miles Porter: banjos, Daniel Johnson place, Houlka, MS (Betty Curlett, b. 1872, MS, child of ex-slaves)

Bill Worship: fiddle, Lafayette Co., AR (George Washington Rice, b. 1855, AR)

Henry Wright: gourd fiddle, fiddle, House plantation and environs, Buckhead, GA (Henry Wright, b. 1838, GA)

Uriah Wright: fiddle, Fairfield Co., SC (Jim Henry, b. ca. 1860, SC)

John Young: little drum, and Rheuben Turner, bass drum, Union army, Western theatre (John Young, b. ca. 1845, AR)

II. White Performers Identifiable by Name (All individuals are slaveholders unless otherwise noted)

Mr. Adams (overseer): plantation bugle, Mike Cook place, Magnolia, MS (Harriet Miller, b. 1859, MS)

Miss Mary Ann Baker: widow of church organist, community ward, Beaufort, SC (Rebecca Jane Grant, b. ca. 1843, SC)

Mr. Bloomfield: piano salesman and teacher, musician, Bloomfield farm, VA (Jeff Stanfield, b. 1837, VA)

Captain Boone: plantation horn, Captain Boone's farm, Woodruff Co., AR (J. F. Boone, b. 1872, AR, child of ex-slaves)

Young Marster Boyd: fiddle, and Young Mistis Boyd: piano, Hazie Boyd plantation, Columbia Co., GA (Ellen Claibourn, b. 1852, GA)

Major Thomas Brice (freighter, planter): fiddle, Winnsboro, SC (Andy Brice, b. ca. 1856, SC)

Becky Coleman (slaveholder's first wife): organ, and Laura Coleman (second wife): piano, Coleman place, Choctaw Co., AL (Ned Chaney, b. ca. 1857, AL)

Tom Davis: fiddle, Tom Davis place, Oktibbeha Co., MS (D. Davis, b. ca. 1850, MS)

Mr. Digby (overseer): plantation bugle, Dunn place, Salem, AL (Molly Parker, b. ca. 1850, AL)

Duplissant Dugas: fiddle, Dugas farm, Lafayette, LA (Valmar Cormier, b. ca. 1855, LA)

Jess Durden (overseer): plantation horn, Jim DuBose place, Augusta, GA (Fannie Jones, b. 1853, GA)

Marzee Durham: piano, Durham plantation, Watkinsville, GA (Lula Flannigan, b. ca. 1860, GA)

Bryant Folsom: fiddle, Folsom plantation, Jefferson Co., FL (Acie Thomas, b. 1857, FL)

Willie Grant: plantation horn, John Grant plantation, Monroe, GA (Julia Cole, b. ca. 1860, GA)

Coconut Harper (neighbor): fiddle, Troup Co., GA (Jerry Boykins, b. 1845, GA)

Laura Holloway: plantation cow-horn, Holloway place, Henderson Co., KY (Katie Rose, b. ca. 1850, KY)

Alex Hughey: fiddle, Hughey place, Liberty, MS (Orris Harris, b. ca. 1858, MS, 930)

Johnson daughters: piano, banjo, fiddle, M. T. Johnson place, Tarrant Co., TX (Betty Bormer, b. 1857, TX)

Marse Jones: fiddle, Jones plantation, Copiah Co., MS (Robert Laird, b. 1854, MS)

Miss Jane Massingale: church organ, Massingale plantation, Monroe Co., AL (Bettie Massingale Bell, b. ca. 1857, AL)

Paul McCall, fiddle, McCall place, Union Co., AR (Katie Arbery, b. 1857, AR)

Bill McCarty: fiddle, William McCarty place, Harrison Co., TX (Katie Darling, b. 1849, TX)

Doc McCollum (medical doctor, Klansman): fiddle, Union Co., SC (Brawley Gilmore, b. unk., SC, child of ex-slaves)

Katie Mobley: piano, John Mobley plantation, Fairfield Co., SC (Adeline Jackson, b. ca. 1849, SC)

*Moster's brother: fiddle, Steven Wilson place, Rome, GA (Jim Gillard, b. ca. 1850, SC)

W. S. Needham Jr.: fiddle, Needham place, Scott Co., MS (W. S. Needham Jr., b. 1854, MS. SS2 10 TX 9: 4359–70)

Marguarite Newsome: piano, accordion, flutena [accordion], fiddle, Newsome place, Hinds Co., MS (Mollie Williams, b. 1853, MS)

Mr. Norrell (overseer): plantation horn, GA (Eli Smith, b. ca. 1840, GA)

Mrs. Norris: organ, Norris plantation, Baker Co., GA (Queen Elizabeth Bunts, b. ca. 1865, GA, child of ex-slaves)

Zeb Patrick: drum, Thomas Huff: fiddle, and Bill Cranford: flute, military band, Covington Co. Volunteers, MS (Elsie Posey, b. ca. 1840, MS)

Colonel Radford's sons, slaves: hunting horn, Radford plantation, Richmond, VA (Ida Rigley, b. 1855, VA)

Irving Ramsey (Klansman): fiddle, Spartanburg Co., SC (Lorenza Ezell, b. ca. 1850, SC)

Green Ross (overseer): plantation horn, Bill Slaughter place, Richmond, VA (Sara Colquitt, b. ca. 1830, VA)

Bill Rowell (overseer): plantation horn, AL (Sol Webb, b. unk., AL, 441)

Sam Murry Sandell: conch trumpet (plantation horn), Sandell farm, Magnolia, MS (James Cornelius, b. ca. 1846, MS)

Jabe Smith: fiddle, Jabe Smith's plantation, Oglethorpe Co., GA (Easter Huff, b. 1858, GA)

Jim Smith: plantation horn, Jim Smith place, Locust Grove, GA (Charlie Tye Smith, b. 1850, GA)

Smith Stone: sugar camp horn, Smith Stone place, Garrard County, KY (Bert Mayfield, b. 1852, KY)

Betty Stroud: piano, Squire Garner place, Centerville, TX (Mollie Watson, b. ca. 1855, TX)

Jack Taylor: fiddle, Jack Taylor place, Mansfield Parish, LA (Guy Stewart, b. 1850, LA)

William Tucker: banjo, and Nellie Tucker: piano, Musgrove Tract plantation, Union County, SC, (Cordelia Anderson Jackson, b. ca. 1859, SC)

Walford girls: piano, Walford plantation, KY (Sampson Willis, b. ca. 1843, KY)

Frank Wattles: fiddle, Wattles place, Travis Co., TX (Mrs. Sallie Johnson, b. 1855, TX)

John White: fiddle, Burleson, AL (Mingo White, b. unk., AL)

Dan Wilburn: fiddle, Wilburn place, Huntsville, AL (Dock Wilborn, b. 1843, AL)

Mary Wiley: piano, Joe Wiley plantation, Pontotoc Co., MS (Eliza Bell, b. 1851, MS)

Mr. Wimbeish: military bugle, Confederate drills, Lincoln Co., GA (Mariah Sutton Clemments, b. ca. 1850, GA)

Bob Winn: plantation bugle (tin horn), Bob Winn plantation, Homer, LA (Willis Winn, b. 1822, LA)

Major Tom Woodward: fiddle, Tom Woodward place, SC (Jim Henry, b. ca. 1860, SC)

*Young Massa: fiddle, Etowah Co., AL (Aunt Clussey, b. ca. 1845, AL)

OLD PHARAOH EXACTLY

Slave Music and Racial Terror

The patterollers visited our house every Saturday night, generally. We set traps to catch the patterollers. The patterollers were poor white men. We stretched grape vines across the roads, then we would run from them. They would follow, and get knocked off their horses. I knew many of the patterollers. They are mostly dead. Their children, who are living now in Wake County and Raleigh, are my best friends, and I will therefore not tell who they were. I was caught by the patterollers in Raleigh.

I would have been whipped to pieces if it hadn't been for a white boy about my age by the name of Thomas Wilson. He told them I was his nigger, and they let me go. We had brought a load of lightwood splints [pine kindling] in bundles to town on a steer cart. This was near the close of the war. We sold out one load of splints and had been paid for them in Confederate money. We had several bills. We went into a bar and bought a drink, each paying one dollar a drink, or two dollars for two small drinks. The bar was in the house where the Globe Clothing Store is now located on the corner of Wilmington and Exchange Streets. Just as I swallowed my drink a constable grabbed me by the back of the neck, and started with me to the guard house, where they done their whippin'. Down at the guard house Nick Denton, the bar tender, told Thomas Wilson "Go tell the constable that is your nigger." Thomas came running up crying, and told the constable I was his nigger. The constable told him to take me and carry me on home or he would whip both of us. We then hitched our ox to the cart and went home. (Sam T. Stewart, b. 1853, NC, 321–22)

I remember one time dey was a dance at one ob de houses in de quarters. All de niggers was a laughin' an' pattin' dey feet an' a singin', but dey was a few dat didn't. De paddyrollers shove de do' open and sta't grabbin' us. Uncle Joe's son he decide dey was one time to die and he sta't to fight. He say he tired of standin' so many beatin's, he jes can't stan' no mo. De paddyrollers start beatin' him an' he st'at fightin'. Oh, Lawdy it war tubble. Dey whip him wif a cowhide for a long time den one of dem take a stick an' hit him over de head, an' jes' bus his head wide open. De poor boy fell on de flo' jes a moanin' an' a groanin. De paddy-rollers jes whip bout half dozen niggers an' sen' em home and leve us wif de dead boy. (Fannie Moore, b. 1849, SC, 132)

> Run nigger, run,
> De Patteroll git you!
> Run nigger, run,
> De Patteroll come!
>
> Watch nigger, watch—
> De Patteroll trick you!
> Watch nigger, watch,
> He got a big gun!

Dat one of the songs de slaves all knowed, and de children down on de "twenty acres" used to sing it when dey playing in de moonlight 'round de cabins in de quarters. Sometime I wonder iffen de white folks didn't make dat song up so us niggers would keep in line. (Anthony Dawson, b. 1832, NC, 65)

The Ku Klux and the pateroles were the same thing, only the Klan was more up to date. It's all set up with a hellish principle. It's old Pharaoh exactly. (James Reeves, b. 1870, AR, child of ex-slaves, 28)

The right and wrong of American slavery are beyond dispute, yet the indisputable wrong that was American slavery created a world of complete corruption, constant hypocrisy, and moral ambiguity where pat judgments often foundered on uncomfortable facts, even in the cause of the righteous. Most African slaves transported to the Americas were enslaved in Africa and sold to whites by other Black Africans. Suffering does not always ennoble, and North American slavery was able to function as well as it did only because of countless Black spies, snitches, turncoats, and enforcers. The most hated individuals among field slaves were often the *nigger drivers*, Black underbosses notorious for an especially sadistic brand of self-racism. Throughout the South, free Blacks sometimes owned Black slaves; in much of Louisiana this was the status quo.

Fig. 11.1. "Visit of the Ku-Klux." Engraving from a drawing by Fred Bellew. *Harper's Weekly* 16 (February 24, 1872): 160. Library of Congress, Prints and Photographs Division.

On the other hand, most white Southerners did not own slaves, and large numbers who did conscientiously freed them. The abolition movement had roots in the South, and innumerable fugitives escaped to the North with the assistance of Southern whites. Many who remained in bondage (or who were returned by Northern slave hunters) left genuine memories of white friends, protectors, and allies, even among slaveholders. It is obviously difficult to see slaveholders as victims of any sort: many were absolute monsters. However, others had been trapped by birth, marriage, or their own bad decisions in a system that kept them from being the better people they could have and should have been. Those better natures did occasionally shine through, especially when slaves and masters were making music. Yet in a society this sick and twisted, all that could change in an instant, and even music, song, and dance were routinely employed as tools of racial intimidation, humiliation, and terror.

The plantation police state was maintained like any police state, by violence, torture, death, or the threat thereof, underscored by official propaganda and constant psychological warfare. In the antebellum South, however, these misinformation campaigns were conducted not by officially empowered bureaucracies and state controlled media but through folklore,

Fig. 11.2. "The plantation police or home-guard examining Negro passes on the levee road below New Orleans. From a sketch by our special artist, F. B. Schell." Engraving. *Leslie's* 16 (July 11, 1863): 252.

including music and song but also folktales and legends, supernatural beliefs, folk dramas, rituals, and carnivalesque spectacles. Many of these traditions were propagated by slaveholders or other whites to brutalize, cow, and control slaves, while others register the slaves' response; but almost all revolved around the southern gulag's secret police, the night riders.[1]

Night patrols were mounted throughout the antebellum South. While there were widespread patterns and practices, these groups never represented a single organization or institution, and ex-slaves described many different varieties. Besides capturing runaways, patrollers were generally charged with regulating the movements and activities of slaves and especially with preventing unauthorized nocturnal travel or unsupervised gatherings, always dreaded as potential sources of sedition and insurrection (the first patrols were direct responses to a wave of early nineteenth-century slave revolts). Some of these units were formally organized companies maintained by civil authorities or by the slaveholders themselves, who might ride in their ranks. In these cases, powers and activities tended to be defined by law or custom and subject to oversight, limited perhaps to checking slaves for passes—written permission to be abroad—punishing offenders, then returning them to their plantations. "I remember I hear talk dey say, 'Patroller, Patroller, let nigger pass.' Dey would say dat if de nigger had de strip [pass] wid dem en if dey didn' have it, dey say, 'Patroller, Patroller, cut nigger slash'" (Julia Woodberry, b. ca. 1865, SC, child of ex-slaves, 238). Besides maintaining roadblocks and checkpoints, patrollers sought out and violently dispersed unapproved gatherings, as well as interrupting authorized dances and worship services to examine passes or simply to harass those in attendance. They also visited slaves who remained dutifully at home to deter and intimidate them, and to ensure their continued subservience and devotion to labor.

"My father—Daddy Tony, they call him—he was a musician—always played the violin." Here he mentioned the names of the songs of that day, before the war of 1861, and repeated these words with much merriment:

"Would have been married forty year ago,
If it hadn't been for Cotton Eye Joe

"Songs—lots of um—

"Run, nigger, run, de *Patrol ketch* you"

He roared with laughter—"When de patrol come, I had my badge; I show him my paper and my badge! I got it still." (Richard Mack, b. ca. 1833, SC, 151–52, orig. emphasis)

In other instances, however, patrols were mounted by poor whites who resented planters and their slaves, seeking to undermine and restrict their power and privilege, or simply to repay them in kind for their scorn and contempt.

We could have dances on Saturday nights. A banjo player would be dere an' he would sing. One song dey use to sing was:

Run nigger run, run nigger run,
Don't let de paddle rollers catch you,
Run nigger run.

De niggers would be pattin' dey feet an' dancin' for life. Master an' dem would be settin' on de front porch listenin' to de music, 'cause you could hear it for a half mile. We would be in one of de big barns. We had a time of our life. Po' whites would come over to see de dance. De master wouldn't 'low de po' whites on his place an' dey would have to steal in to see de dance. When ever dey would come 'roun to de big house, dey had to come to de back do', an' de white folks would ask dem, "What in de hell do you want?" Po' whites was just like stray goats. (Robert Williams, b. 1843, VA, 326)

When I was a boy we used to sing, "Rather be a nigger than a poor white man." Even in slavery they used to sing that. It was the poor white man who was freed by the War, not the Negroes. (Waters McIntosh, b. 1863, SC, 20)[2]

Some night riders were nothing more than local thugs and ruffians deriving profit and sadistic pleasure from robbing, beating, and killing vulnerable slaves, even coming into violent conflict with slaveholders. "They used to have dances at Mrs. Dickerson's, a neighbor of General Gano (a preacher in the Christian Church). Mrs. Dickerson wouldn't let the 'Padaroes' come to the dances. If they did come, she would get her pistol and make them leave" (Harriet Mason, b. ca. 1837, KY, 31, orig. parentheses). "Atter de surrender we stayed on an' went through de Ku Klux scare. I know dat de Ku Kluxes went ter a nigger dance one night an' whupped all de dancers. Ole Marster Berry wuz mad, case he ain't sont fer 'em at all an' he doan want dem" (Tina Johnson, b. 1852, GA, 22).

De bushwhackers and night riders were here. But de boss got 'round it this way. He had de slaves dig trenches 'cross de road and tie grape vines over it. Den have de darkies go up on de hill and sing corn songs. Den de nightriders come a-rushing and sometimes dey would get four or five whites in these raids. It would kill de men and horses too, when dey fell into de trench. (W. C. Parson Allen, b. 1859, MO, 18–19)

After de war dem Ku Kluxers what wear false faces try to tinker with Marse's niggers. One day Uncle Dave start to town and a Kluxer ask him where am he pass. Dat Kluxer clout him but Uncle Dave outrun him in de cane. Marse grab de hoss and go 'rest dat man and Marse a jedge and he make dat man pay de fine for hittin' Uncle Dave. After dey hears of dat, dem old poky faces sho' scairt of old Marse. (Ellen Betts, b. 1853, LA, 82)

Master Ingram placed signs at different points on his plantation which read thus: "Paterrollers, Fishing and Hunting Prohibited on this Plantation." It soon became known by all that the Ingram slaves were not given passes by their owner to go any place, consequently they were known as "Old Ingram's Free Nigger's."

Master Ingram could not write, but would tell his slaves to inform anyone who wished to know, that they belonged to J. D. Ingram. "Once," said Pattillo, "my brother Willis, who was known for his gambling and drinking, left our plantation and no one knew where he had gone. As we sat around a big open fire cracking walnuts, Willis came up, jumped off his horse and fell to the ground. Directly behind him rode a 'paterroller.' The master jumped up and commanded him to turn around and leave his premises. The 'Paterroller' ignored his warning and advanced still further. The master then took his rifle and shot him. He fell to the ground dead and Master Ingram said to his wife, 'Well, Lucy, I guess the next time I speak to that scoundrel he will take heed.' The master then saddled his horse and rode into town. Very soon a wagon came back and moved the body." (G. W. Pattillo, b. 1852, GA, 167–68)[3]

Bandits and bushwhackers of this sort proliferated after the war, their ranks swollen by Confederate veterans and former guerillas. "After a while, robbers and low down trash got to wearin' robes an 'tendin dey was Ku Kluxes. Folks called dem 'white caps.' Dey was vicious an' us was more scared of dem dan us'd ever been of de Klan. When dey got licquored up, de debbil sho was turnt loose" (Isaac Stier, b. ca. 1837, MS, 2054). "Whar us lived, Ku Kluxers was called 'night thiefs.' Dey stole money and weepons (weapons) f'um de Niggers atter de war. Dey tuk $50 in gold f'um me and $50 dollars in Jeff Davis' shinplasters f'um my brother" (Charlie Hudson, b. 1858, GA, 231, orig. parentheses). "I never seen no Ku Klux. There was Jay Hawkers. They was folks on neither side jess goin' round, robbin' and stealin', money, silver, stock or anything else they wanted" (Solomon Lambert, b. 1848, AR, 230). "I 'members dat de Ku Klux useter go ter de Free Issues houses, strip all de family an' whup de ole folkses. Den dey dances wid de pretty yaller gals an' goes ter bed wid dem. Dat's what de Ku Klux wuz, a bunch of mean mens tryin' ter hab a good time" (Martha Allen, b. 1859, NC, 15).

> I do remember the "night riders" that come through our country after the war. They put the shoes on the horses backwards and wrapped the horses feet in burlap so we couldn't hear them coming. The colored folks were deathly afraid of these men and would all run and hide when they heard they were coming. These "night riders" used to steal everything the colored people had—even their beds and straw ticks. (David A. Hall, b. 1847, NC, 40)[4]

The 1865 formation of the Ku Klux Klan provided a new umbrella for many night riders, but most ex-slaves recognized the Kluxers as a mere rebranding of the patrols, "old Pharaoh exactly." "The pateroles was awful bad at that time. Ku Klux they called them after the War, but they was the same people. I never heard of the Klan part till this thing come up that they have now. They called them Ku Klux back when I was a boy" (James Henry Stith, b. 1865, child of ex-slaves, GA, 241). "I allus pronounced de patterrollers and de Klu Kluxers 'bout de same" (George Owens, b. ca. 1853, TX, 169). "I heard my mamma talk about the pat-a-rollers what would get you if they caught you away from the plantation. They use to sing 'Run, nigger, run, the pat-a-roller 'll get you.' And I heard her talk

about the Ku Kluxers too, but I never seed 'em" (Alice Shaw, b. ca. 1850, MS, 1921).

> The Ku Klux and the Paddyrollers was all around and doing meanness. They were just as onery and mean as the policemen are now. They never did nothing that amounted to nothing in they life so they think they is smart big mens when ten of them jump on a pore nigger and beat the life out of him. Niggers had to lay mighty low. Their life wan't worth a five cent piece. (Lu Lee, b. 1848 or 1849, TX, 2301–2)

Atter freedom come de darkies uster have a song what go like dis:

> Come along
> Come along
> Make no delayin'
> Soon be so Uncle Sam give us all a farm.

> Come from de way
> Come from de nation
> 'Twont be long 'till Uncle Sam give us all a farm.

Atter while de Klu Kluxers git atter de cullud folks. Den dey mek a song: Run nigger run de Klu Klux git you. (Aleck Trimble, b. 1861, TX, 114)

Nor was this a total rebranding. Ex-slaves all agreed that the Ku Klux *Klan* was a postwar development (an incontestable historical fact), but numerous ex-slaves, corroborated by other sources, insisted that the expression *ku klux* was widely employed before the war as a term for night riders. "I know the Ku Klux must have been in use before the War because I remember the business when I was a little bit of a fellow" (William Brown, b. 1861, AR, 318).

> I remember the Ku Klux. They used to come and whip the niggers that didn't have a pass. I think them was pateroles though. There was some people too who used to steal slaves if they found them

way from home, and then they would sell them. I don't know what they called them. I just remember the Ku Klux and the pateroles. The Ku Klux were the ones that whipped the niggers that they caught without a pass. I don't remember any Ku Klux whipping niggers after the war because they were in politics. (Ella Daniels, b. ca. 1858, NC, 93)

Pateroles, jayhawkers, and the Ku Klux came before the war. The Ku Klux in slavery times were men who would catch Negroes out and keep them if they did not collect from their masters. The pateroles would catch Negroes out and return them if they did not have a pass. They whipped them sometimes if they didn't have a pass. The jayhawkers were highway men or robbers who stole slaves among other things. At least, that is the way the people regarded them. The jayhawkers stole and pillaged, while the Ku Klux stole those Negroes they caught out. The word "Klan" was never included in their name. The Ku Klux Klan was an organization which arose after the Civil War. (Joseph Samuel Badgett, b. 1864, AR, 81)

William Brown, Joseph Samuel Badgett, and Ella Daniels were all interviewed by Samuel S. Taylor, an African American social worker from Little Rock who was one of the Arkansas project's most prolific field-workers. Beyond that, Taylor was one of the national project's best interviewers bar none, having had life-long experience with his subject. For example, with Joseph Samuel Badgett's narrative he noted:

Badgett's distinctions between jayhawkers, Ku Klux, patrollers, and Ku Klux Klan are most interesting.

I have been slow to catch it. All my life, I have heard persons with ex-slave background refer to the activities of the Ku Klux among slaves prior to 1865. I always thought they had the [Ku] Klux Klan and the patrollers confused.

Badgett's definite and clearcut memories, however, lead me to believe that many of the Negroes who were slaves used the word Ku Klux to denote a type of person who stole slaves. It was evidently in use before it was applied to the Ku Klux Klan. (Samuel S. Taylor, "Interviewer's Comment," S2 8 *AR* 1: 82)

Similarly, following Ella Daniels's narrative, Taylor observed: "here again, there is a confusion of patrollers with Ku Klux. It seems to point to a use of the word Ku Klux before the War. Of course, it is clear that the Ku Klux Klan operated after the War" (Samuel S. Taylor, "Interviewer's Comment," S2 9 *AR* 2: 94). Taylor also remarked that, as of 1937, accepted definitions of *Ku Klux Klan* failed to register these distinctions. Nor do they today.

There have been many proposed etymologies for Ku Klux Klan, ranging from utterly implausible to only slightly less so. In the most widely accepted scenario, the Klan's postwar founders followed the custom of fraternal orders by affecting a quasi-Greek title, combining the ancient Greek *kúklos* (circle) with the English *clan*, respelled with a *k* for visual effect. Unfortunately for this theory (regularly printed as established fact), the term *ku klux* (which obviously is not *kúklos*) was in circulation long before the 1865 founding of the Ku Klux Klan, and the ex-slaves gave a far simpler, much more credible explanation for the term's origins in the prewar period: by their accounts, the term *ku klux* derived from an unnerving, clucking nonsense song that night riders sang to intimidate and frighten slaves. "You know de Ku Klux went disguised an' when dey got ter your house dey would say in a fine voice, Ku Klux, Ku Klux, Ku Klux, Ku Klux. Some people say dey are in slavery now an' dat de niggers never been in nothin' else" (Kitty Hill, b. 1860, VA, 426). "Does I 'member paddyrollers! Laws yes! Dey go roun' at night in twos an' three's an' you better be in fo' sun down ketch you lessen you got a note f'om yo' owner. . . . Punish you efn dey cetch you off de plantation minus your pass. Dey hiden in de bushes an' make soun' lak dis 'Klu Kluck'" (William Brooks, b. 1860, VA, 56).

This, then, explains why so many ex-slaves named prewar night riders as ku kluxes, or referred to their activities as ku kluxing, clearing up the term's overall etymology as well. It also puts to rest the oft-expressed assumption that the Ku Klux Klan adopted their name as part of a general effort to obfuscate and mystify; in fact, they did exactly the opposite, simply coopting a well-established term for their brand of racist terrorism.

Not surprisingly, many postwar Klansmen had previously served as antebellum kluxers, and most Klan-affiliated groups shared the basic aims and functions of the prewar patrols: keeping Blacks in their places, whether by maintaining them on their plantations, or, now, by preventing them from voting, from holding office, from going to school, from prospering, or just from getting "uppity." The allegation of an assault on a white female was always a good excuse for burning someone alive. "Now, I went to school right here in dat same Methodist Church after the war. You know we had white teachers from de north. My teacher was named Smith. His hair was long and hung around his neck. He was run out of town by the Ku Klux Klan" (Mollie Hatfield, b. ca. 1860, MS, 954). "One night de Klu Kluxers come an' tole us to move on or else we be mighty sorry lookin' niggahs. We don' foun' out later dis man we wuk fer always had de Klux Kluxers chase away de niggahs what wuk fer him after de' wuk out a good crop fer him" (Lucy Thurston, b. ca. 1836, MS, 2114). "Ah only sees de Klu Klux Klan onct'. De wuz parading de streets here in Brookhaven an' dey had a niggah dey wuz gwine tar an' feather. Slavery times! Oh God ah hates, hates 'em. Mean, cruel, hard" (Charlie Moses, b. 1853, MS, 1603). "Master say when we was freed, 'Some of you is going to get lynched.' 'Fore three years was gone I saw a Nigger lynched close to Hainsville [Haynesville, Webster Parish] for 'saulting a white girl. They tied him to a tree, piled rich pine round him, poured on ten gallons of coal oil and set him on fire" (Willis Winn, b. 1822, LA, 4256).

> De Yankees tried to get some of de men to vote, too, but not many did 'cause dey was scared of de Ku Kluxers. Dey wud cum at night all dressed up lak ghosts an scare us all. We didn' lak de Yankees

anyway. Dey warn't good to us; when dey lef' we wud allus sin' dat leetle song what go lak dis:

> Ole Mister Yankee, think he is so gran',
> Wid his blue coat tail a draggin' on de groun'!
> (Clara C. Young, b. ca. 1842, MS, 2404)

The Klan also assumed the task of ensuring that emancipated slaves stayed dutifully laboring on their plantations, whether as tenants or serfs. "I sho 'members the Ku Klux raging and beating folks. That's the reason ma and my step-pa stayed with old Master. He protect them" (Hannah Jameson, b. ca. 1850, AR, 1938). "The Ku Klux come about and drink water. They wanted folks to stay at home and work. That what they said. We done that. We didn't know we was free nohow. We wasn't scared" (John Wesley, b. ca. 1840, KY, 97).

> Lots of Negroes was killed after freedom. The slaves was turned loose in Harrison County right after the war. Negroes in Rusk County heard about it and lots of them run away from slavery in Rusk to freedom in Harrison County. Their owners had them "bushwhacked" . . . shot down while they was trying to get away. You could see lots of Negroes hanging to trees in Sabine bottom right after freedom. They would catch them swimming across Sabine River and shoot them. There sho' is going to be lots of soul cry against them in Judgement. (Susan Merritt, b. 1851, TX, 2643, orig. ellipsis)

Hammett Dell described Kluxers beating a tenant at the direction of his landlord because the tenant's fields were overrun with weeds.

> I heard em say his whole family and him too was out by day light wid their hoes cuttin' the grass out their crop. . . . They say some places the Ku Klux go they make 'em git down an' eat at the grass wid their mouths then they whoop em. Sometimes they make em pull off their clothes and whoop em. . . . The Ku Klux call that whoopin' helpin'

'em git rid of the grass. (Hammett Dell, b. 1847, TN, 145–46)

During this same period, similar white supremacist vigilantes like the Red Shirts and White Caps organized across the South, often on a regional or even local basis. Again, the precise identities of, or distinctions between, these groups are not always clear. Many ex-slaves, for example, used White Cap as a synonym for Ku Klux, but South Carolinian Waters McIntosh stated: "the white caps operated further to the northwest of where I lived. I never came in contact with them. They were not the same thing as the Ku Klux" (Waters McIntosh, b. 1863, SC, 22).

Moreover, despite what many think, these groups were not composed entirely of whites. "After the war the Ku Klux didn't bother us but the Red Shirts come and wanted us to join them. That is they wanted my brother to join them. He wouldn't join though. My brother-in-law joined and wore one of the shirts with them. He wanted Wade Hampton elected as he believed it was best for us" (William Pratt, b. 1860, SC, 278). "I stay on dere [former plantation] 'til '76. Then I come to Winnsboro and git a job as a section hand laborer on de railroad. . . . Out de fust money, I buys me a red shirt and dat November I votes and de fust vote I put in de box was for Governor Wade Hampton" (Charley Barber, b. ca. 1856, SC, 31). "I 'member de Ku Klux and how dey rid around in white sheets, killing all de niggers. De Red Shirts never killed but dey sometimes whipped niggers. My daddy voted de Republican ticket den, but I know'd two niggers dat was Democrats and rode wid de Red Shirts. Dey was old Zeb and old Jeff Bozard" (Solomon Caldwell, b. 1864, SC, 170). That Blacks willingly assisted or even enlisted with night riders is a puzzle, but a widely reported fact nonetheless. "A nigger republican leader got kilt. I hel't de hosses fer de Ku Klux" (Sim Greeley, b. 1855, SC, 193).

Does I 'member paddyrollers! Laws yes! Dey go roun' at night in twos an' three's an' you better be in fo' sun down ketch you lessen you got a note f'om yo' owner. Dey was white an' colored an' dey beat anybody's chillun. Dey wear long pointed caps an' go roun' nights an' days. Punish you efn dey cetch you off de plantation minus your pass. Dey hiden in de bushes an' make soun' lak dis "Klu Kluck." (William Brooks, b. 1860, VA, 56)

There was a bunch of Ku Klux that a colored man led. He was a fellow by the name of Fount Howard. They would come to his house and he would call himself showing them how to catch old people he didn't like. He told them how to catch my old man. I have heard my mother tell about it time and time again. The funny part of it was there was a cornfield right back of the kitchen. Just about dusk dark, he got up and taken a big old horse pistol and shot out of it, and when he fired the last shot out of it, a white man said, "Bring that gun here." Believe me he cut a road through that field right now. They stayed 'round for a little while and tried to bully his people. But the old lady stood up to them, so they finally carried her and her children in the house and told her to tell him to come on back they wouldn't hurt him. And they didn't bother him no more. (Wesley Graves, b. 1867, TN, child of ex-slaves, 74–75)

I never left that place [MS plantation] till my young master, Mr. Jim Johnson, the one that was the Supreme Judge, came for me. He was living then in South Carolina. He took us all home with him. We got there in time to vote for Gov. Wade Hampton. We put him in office too. I have seen a many a patrol in my life time, but they never did have enough nerve to come on uses [our] place. Now the Ku Klux was different. I have ridden with them a many a time. It was the only way in them days to keep order. (Prince Johnson, b. 1847, SC, 1175)

Ruthlessly to maintain that antebellum status quo, night riders relied on standard police state tactics, including torture and execution staged as public spectacles. What are now known as *psyops* (psychological operations) were always a major component. Again, these practices were dictated and directed not by centralized autocracies, but by traditional precedents and folk customs, most rooted in Europe, where ritual violence reached its apogee in the pre-Lenten Carnival, an utterly unhinged revel venting society's basest instincts. The latent violence of Carnival (sometimes symbolic, sometimes none too latent and all too real) provided a perfect model for other forms of purposed public mayhem, and in Europe, and consequently in America, elements of Carnival and celebration have conspicuously figured in riots, rebellions, lynchings, lootings, ethnic cleansings, inquisitions, industrial sabotage, political activism and political repression, even state-sponsored public punishments, maimings, and executions.

Many of the activities of the night riders fall under one particularly prominent European and American genre of celebratory violence, social censure, and forcible intimidation: the *shivaree*, a carnival-style night visit by masked vigilantes complete with drama, music, song, and dance.[5] These night rider dramas were, moreover, directly predicated on a large body of folktales, legends, and supernatural beliefs, most rooted in Great Britain and Ireland, that had been transmitted to Blacks by whites, often with the specific intention of frightening them from venturing out at night. The slaves themselves were well aware of where stories of ghosts, witches, and demons came from. "The white fo'ks told us there was 'ghosts' in the country and if we slip off at night they'd get us" (Katie Darling, b. 1849, TX, 1050). "Marster would tell de children 'bout Raw Head and Bloody Bones an' other things to skeer us" (Issac Johnson, b. 1855, NC, 18). "One night when Ma was out in de woods a prayin' her heared a loud fuss back of her lak somebody was tearin' down de woods, and hit skeered her so her quit prayin' and run to de big house. Marster told her, hit was de debbil atter her" (Georgia Johnson, b. 1865, GA, child of ex-slaves, 333). "Dey's ghosts dere [prewar Virginia]—we seed 'em. Dey's w'ite people wid a sheet on 'em to scare de slaves [who were] offen de plantation" (William Watkins, b. 1850, VA, 141).

"Mr. Edmunds is convinced that the superstitions of the colored people and their belief in ghosts and goblins is due to the fact that their emotions were worked upon by slave drivers to keep them in subjugation. Oftentime the white people dressed as ghosts, frightened the colored people into doing things under protest. The 'ghosts' were feared more than the slave drivers" (Rev. H. H. Edmunds, b. 1859, VA, MS, TN, 65). Some people believed the stories, others scoffed, but everyone understood exactly what was going on when horsemen in ghostly robes appeared at slave cabins, dances, or prayer meetings after dark, carrying orders straight from Hell.

Disguise was fundamental. "Dey was scared of de Ku Kluxers. Dey wud cum at night all dressed up lak ghosts an scare us all" (Clara C. Young, b. ca. 1842, MS, 2404). "The paddyrollers was bad. . . . they wore black caps and put black rags over their faces and was allus skullduggerying 'round" (Cato Carter, b. 1836 or 1837, AL, 207). "The Ku Kluxers come to our house in Woodlawn, and I got scart and crawled under the bed. They told mammy they wasn't gwine hurt her, but jus' wanted water to drink. They didn't call each other by names. When the head man spoke to any of them he'd say Number 1, or Number 2, and like that" (Richard Jackson, b. 1859, TX, 196). Marshal Butler once received thirty lashes from the patrollers. "If we went visiting we had to have a pass. If nigger went out without a pass de 'Paddle-Rollers' would get him. De white folks were the 'Paddle-Rollers' and had masks on their faces. They looked like niggers wid de devil in dere eyes. They used no paddles—nothing but straps—wid de belt buckle fastened on" (Marshal Butler, b. 1849, GA, 165–66).

To imitate ghosts or devils, night riders did indeed wrap themselves in sheets and mask or blacken their faces. Others wore cow tails or horns or animal hides. Some costumes were fitted with false heads that rotated; others represented headless figures. Masqueraders might suddenly spring to superhuman height on stilts, or claim to be angry spirits thirsty from Hell, forcing Blacks to fetch bucket after bucket of water, which they pretended to drink but really

Fig. 11.3. "Mississippi Ku-Kluxes in the disguises in which they were captured." Engraving from a photograph. *Harper's Weekly* 16 (January 27, 1872): 73. Library of Congress, Prints and Photographs Division.

poured into concealed bladders or funneled onto the ground. "They come to the house one night and asked for water. I never see as much water passed out in my life, but they wasn't drinking it, they wus just pouring it on the ground. They had on Injun rubber clothes so they wouldn't get wet" (Lizzie Fant Brown, b. 1861, MS, 255). "I wus very much afraid o' de Ku Klux. Dey wore masks and dey could make you think dey could drink a whole bucket of water and walk widout noise, like a ghost" (Alex Woods, b. 1858, NC, 419). "After freedom came, the boys would try to scare the negroes by playing 'tall Betty,' or walking on tall stilts and dresses in a white gown" (Henry Gray Klugh, b. ca. 1850, SC, 233).

Other vigilantes wore halters around their necks—hanged murderers back from the dead. Postwar night riders would insist they were the ghosts of Confederate soldiers killed in battle, returning to fight for the Cause and the preservation of slavery. A high percentage were in fact veterans who sometimes incorporated old uniforms into their costumes. "They tried to make the impression that they would be old Confederate soldiers that had been killed in the battle of Shiloh, and they used to ride down from the Ridge hollering, 'Oh! Lordy, Lordy, Lordy!' They would have on those old uniforms and call for water" (William Brown, b. 1861, AR, 319).[6]

Eventually, Klan robes were themselves standardized in the manner of military uniforms or religious regalia, but in the antebellum and immediate postwar eras, night rider costumes were an anthropomorphic motley.[7] "Dey dress all kin's of fashions. Most of dem look lik' ghosts" (Lizzie Williams, b. ca. 1847, AL, 400). "Dem Ku Klux was in all kind of shapes, wid horns and things on dere heads" (Alice Duke, b 1865, SC, 336). "In Manchester de Klu Klux Klan wore big high hats, red handkerchiefs on dere faces en red covers on dere hosses. Dey tuk two niggers out ob jail en hung dem ter a chestnut tree" (Ann Matthews, b. unk., TN, 45). "After de war de Ku Klux broke out. Oh, miss dey was mean. In dey long white robes dey scare de niggers to death. Dey have long horns an' big eyes an' mouth" (Fannie Moore, b. 1849, SC, 136). "Dey wore three cornered hats with de eyes way up high" (Jim Allen, b. ca. 1850, AL, 63). "They wore a black rag around their heads with eyes and mouth out" (Callie Gray, b. 1857, MS, 875). "Dey had on doughfaces and long white robes what come down over de hosses dey was a ridin'" (Alice Hutcheson, b. ca. 1860, GA, 288). "The first Ku Klux wore some kind of hat that went over the man's head and shoulders and had great big red eyes in it" (H. B. Holloway, b. 1849, GA, 298). "Dey jus marched sometimes at night, wid long white sheets over dem and all over de horses. Dere heads were covered with small holes for eyes, nose and mouth, and had long white ears like horses ears" (Mary Johnson, b. 1852, SC, 57). "They wore their wives big wide nightgowns and caps and ugliest faces you eber seed. They looked like a gang from hell—ugliest things you ebber *did* see" (Maria Sutton Clemments, b. ca. 1850, GA, 26). "Dey had on white gowns button' up de front wid black buttons an' masks on dey faces" (Willie Miller, b. 1854, MO, 257). "Some wore white sheets and black dresses on white horses" (Charlie Riggers, b. ca. 1850, GA, 41). "They rode at night, some dressed in dark and some white clothes" (Pauline Fakes, b. 1863, AR, 263).

Then the Ku Klux Klan come 'long. They were terrible dangerous. They wear long gowns, touch the ground. They ride horses through town at night and if they find a Negro that tries to get nervy or have a little bit for himself, they lash him nearly to death and gag him and leave him to do the bes' he can. Some time they put sticks in the top of the tall thing [hood] they wear and then put an extra head up there with scary eyes and great big mouth, then they stick it clear up in the air to scare the poor Negroes to death.

They had another one they call the "Donkey Devil" that was jes as bad. They take the skin of a donkey and get inside of it and run after the pore Negroes. Oh, Miss them was bad times, them was bad times. I know folks think books tell the truth but they shore don't. Us pore niggers had to take it all. (W. L. Bost, b. ca. 1850, NC, 144–45)

A paterole come in one night before freedom and asked for a drink of water. He said he was thirsty. He had a rubber thing on and drank two or three buckets of water. His rubber bag swelled up and made his head or the thing that looked like his head grow taller. Instead of gettin' 'fraid, mother threw a shovelful of hot ashes on him and I'll tell you he lit out from there and never did come back no more. (Leonard Franklin, b. 1867, AR, child of ex-slaves, 337)

I come in early contack wid de Klu Klux. Us lef' de plantation in '65 or '66, and by '68 us was habin' sich a awful time wid de Klu Klux. Fus' time dey come to my mudder's house at midnight. Dey claim dey's de sojers done come back from de dead. Dey all dress up in sheets and mek up like sperrit. Dey groan 'roun' and say dey been kill' wrongly, and come back for jestice. One man he look jes' like ordinary man, but he spring up 'bout eighteen feet high all of a suddent. Annudder say, he so thirsty, he ain' hab no water since he been kilt at Manassa' Junction. He ax for water and he jes' kep po'in' it in. Us thought he sho' mus' be a sperrit, to drink dat much water. Co'se he wasn't drinkin' it, he was po'in' it in a bag under he sheet. My mudder nebber did tek up no truck wid sperrit so she knowed it was jes' a man. Dey tell us w'at dey gwine to do iffen we don' go back to our marsters. Us all 'gree and den dey all dis'pear. (Lorenza Ezell, b. ca. 1850, SC, 1326)

The Ku Klux was going strong in that country. I seen niggers hanging on trees and they done cut their ears off. I don't know what for. They didn't do nothing to me. But niggers used to holler at me, "Run nigger run, or the paddyrollers gwine catch you." I thought I'd be skeered of them if I ever seen them but I never did. Some folks said they looked just like whitefolks. (Bud Jones, b. ca. 1850, TX, 2084)

Like most shivarees, night rider visits also featured *rough music* (noisemaking) with boisterous singing and songs, including the alliterative chant that gave Kluxers their name. "I seen the Ku Klux once or twice when they was Ku Klukin' around. Some of 'em would holler 'Kluk, kluk.' I was quite small, but I could remember 'em 'cause I was scared of 'em" (Jim Ricks, b. 1858, AR, 37). Patrollers and Kluxers were particularly associated with horns and bugles, used in pursuit of fugitive slaves but also to announce their arrival at slave cabins, dances, or meetings. "I never will forgit de Ku Klux Klan. Never will forget de way dat horn soun' at night when dey was a-goin' after some mean Nigger" (Dora Franks, b. ca. 1837, MS, 54). They also clanked tin cans and chains, or shook bags full of cow bones as proof that they could remove and rattle their own skeletons. Josephine Coxe recalled, "they would ride through the niggers yards with their horses stamping and try to scare 'em by carrying [scraping] a stick across the fence" (Josephine Coxe, b. ca. 1853, MS, 527). At least one night rider mask examined by US congressional investigators had a kazoo or some similar noisemaker as a mouthpiece.

Night riders are also described whistling, cackling like geese, and hollering as they descended on slave cabins, where they addressed Blacks in exaggerated false voices, partly for effect but also to conceal their identities. "I remember seeing the Ku Klux men because they was dressed so funny with great long caps on top of their heads. And they talked fine like a woman,—didn't talk like men" (John Gilstrap, b. 1857, MS, 849). "Us allus thought it was our old Marster, all dressed up in dem white robes wid his face kivvered up, and a-talkin' in a strange, put-on lak, voice" (Anderson Furr, b. ca, 1850, GA, 351). "I 'member when de Ku Klux Klan started out dey would dress up in white and dey had a noise like 'O-O' 'O-O'" (Mattie Lee, b. 1862, LA, 225). Tennessee ex-slave Hammett Dell described how Kluxers would grunt and moan while interrogating Blacks. The daughter of Virginia ex-slaves, Minnie Bell Fountaine told Gladys-Marie Fry that night riders would

> Make strange noises that would frighten them such as a weird holler, you know. And then another thing that they, that I have heard that they used . . . if someone killed a beef, they would take the cow horn or the bull's horn . . . crooked like that, and they would fix it in such a way that they would blow the horn and it would make a strange weird sound. Now that I know. That was one of their tricks, I've heard people say. I've heard that would be one of their ways of letting you know that they were out.[8]

Besides the ku klux chant, ex-slaves recalled night riders singing songs explicitly expressing threats or warnings. "A Ku Klux song which sometimes de white and niggers sung was: 'Hide out nigger, hide out, Militia come for you'" (Maggie Wright, b. ca. 1855, SC, 317). "Our trouble would have all been over, if it hadn't been for that Ku Klux. Lord have mercy! How they did scare us. They had a song they sang to you that they would be back to see you. I did know the words to that song, but it has skipped my mind since I have gotten so old" (Calline Brown, b. 1832, MS, 237).

Some of these stories may have been exaggerated, and others had probably acquired a life of their own as migratory tales. But overall, these accounts describe actual practices that ex-slaves had personally witnessed, experienced, or heard about from eyewitnesses. Most are documented in multiple sources. The stories ex-slaves told about the tricks that they in turn played on patrollers may for the most part be folktales or mere wishful thinking. A few narrators even told of magically confounding the night riders by *turning the pot down*, a well-established folktale motif (see chap. 14, Turning the Pot Down, below).

> Mother used to tell we chilluns stories of patterollers ketchin' niggers an' whuppin' 'em an' how some of de men outrun de patterollers an' got away. Dere wus a song dey used to sing, it went like dis. Yes sir, ha! ha! I wants ter tell you dat song, here it is: "Some folks say dat a nigger wont steal, I caught two in my corn field, one had a bushel, one had a peck, one had rosenears [roasting ears], strung 'round his neck. Run nigger run, Patteroller ketch you, run nigger run like you did de udder day." . . . Mother said no prayer meetings wus allowed de slaves in Virginia where she stayed. Dey turned pots down ter kill de noise an' held meetings at night. Dey had niggers ter watch an' give de alarm if dey saw de white folks comin'. Dey always looked out for patterollers. Dey were not allowed any edication an' mother could not read and write nuther. (Kitty Hill, b. 1860, VA, 424, 425)[9]

In the two most popular tales of this sort, slaves foil the night riders by pelting them with shovel-loads of live coals from fireplaces or stoves, or by stringing grapevines or ropes across the road where the riders will pass. The episodes may appear separately or together.

> We had fun in dem days. We used to run from de paterollers. We'd be fiddlin' and dancin' on de bridge (dat was de grown folks, but de chaps would come too), an' dey'd say, "Here come de paterollers!" an' we'd put out. If we could git

to our Marsters house, we was all right, 'cause Mr. Bob wouldn't let no pateroller come on his place, nor Mr. Alf neither. Dey said hit was all right if we could git home but we'd have to take our chances. Sometimes we'd tie a rope 'cross de bridge an' paterollers'd hit it an' go in de creek. (Berry Smith, b. 1821, MS, 1979–80, orig. parentheses)

Papa said in slavery times about two nights in a week they would have a dance. He would slip off and go. Sometimes he would get a pass. He was a figger caller till he 'fessed religion. One time the pattyrollers come in. They said, "All got passes tonight." When they had about danced down my daddy got a shovelful of live coals and run about scattering it on the floor. All the niggers run out and he was gone too. It was a dark night. A crowd went up the road and here come the pattyrollers. One run into grapevines across the road and tumbled off his horse. The niggers took to the woods then. Pa tole us how he studied up a way to get himself and several others outer showing their passes that night. Master never found that out on him. (Louise Pettis, b. ca. 1880, SC, child of ex-slaves, 335)

Dem dances was grand. Ev'y body would be enjoyin' dey se'ves den. I can hear 'em yet hollerin', "swing yo' pardner," on over in a co'ner de fiddles a playin'. . .'till de fus' thing us knowed us had done fer-got eve'y thing an' de patrole riders would be commin' fer to git us. Den us would git busy. Iffen us let 'em git too close on us de womens'ud fight 'em off wid fiah by throwin' hot to'ches an' red coals at 'em, an' by settin long sage brooms on fiah an' runnin' into 'em. De women folks sho did save us a heap o' times lak dat. Den some times us boys 'ud slip down de big road when de moon 'ud be shinin' an' stretch grape vine 'cross de road. De patrole riders 'ud come a ridin' mos' as fas' as lightenin' when sudden lak de ho'ses 'ud trip on de vines an throw 'em about ten miles. Us would be hid out close by a watchin', an' how us 'ud laugh. Dey never

could ketch up wid us an hit was a heap o' fun. (Anda Woods, b. ca. 1841, AL, 2389–91)

In his 1891 memoir, Kentucky ex-slave Harry Smith (b. 1814) recalled an occasion when

the darkies got up a plot to destroy the patrollers. A number met together and arranged the following plan: The plan was this, to get in a ravine and stretch wild grape vines across the road where they knew the patrollers were sure to come. Then they would get on an elevation and commence to sing comic songs. When they would discover them they would start on the run. The patrollers coming in contact with the vines it would knock them off injuring many of them.[10]

Many texts thus acknowledge the reality that these booby traps would have resulted in serious injury and death. According to James Henry Stith, this was the entire point, and Blacks would make sure by waiting for the trap to spring, then shooting the unhorsed riders.

The Negroes were naturally afraid of the Ku Klux but they finally got to the place where they were determined to break it up. They didn't have no ropes, but they would take grapevines and tie them across the road about breast high when a man would be on horseback. The Ku Klux would run against these vines and be knocked off their horses into the road and then the bushwhackers would shoot them. When Ku Klux was killed in this manner, it was never admitted; but it was said that they had gone to Texas. There was several of them went to Texas one night. (James Henry Stith, b. 1865, child of ex-slaves, GA, 242)

Inviting as they are, these accounts warrant some caution. Slaves did forcibly resist whites on occasion, the recently freed slaves somewhat more so; but these episodes typically were followed by a wholly disproportionate, retaliatory bloodbath directed at any convenient Black scapegoats. Ex-slaves described several such resistances and their disastrous aftermaths, but in the grapevine and hot-coal tales no one ever faces consequences. This is so even when the Blacks inflict injury or death, though many narrators presented these episodes as slapstick farces more typical of comic slave tales: the night riders are merely dismounted and discomfited, while the slaves run away taunting and laughing. Some texts contain other identifiable folktale elements. The stories were always told as true, often as personal experiences, but the only examples I have found are from oral sources (and all of these from ex-slaves), with no outside corroboration. While many ex-slaves claimed to have participated in these events, others indicated that they had heard the stories secondhand, and most examples probably share more with folktales than factual accounts. Nevertheless, Black resistance, however sporadic and futile, was a fact in the antebellum and postwar South, and there is every possibility that these incidents or something like them took place on one or more occasions. I seriously doubt, though, that they occurred as often as the stories' popularity suggests.

Fittingly, many night rider tales are told as cantefables, prose narratives incorporating singing and songs as structural plot devices. This form is extraordinarily common throughout Africa and the Black diaspora. It is also especially well suited to stories largely concerned with white attempts to regulate or eliminate slaves' musicmaking. In the tales as in everyday life, frolics and meetings are the usual causes of conflicts with night riders, and it is the music and song more than anything that draw the vigilantes' attention and raise their ire.

> Dey use to be paderollers dat kept de slaves from strollin' round o' nights. De marsters gin 'em passes sometimes, but if de paderollers ketched 'em out atter dark widout a pass dey whupped 'em. One night a crowd o' slaves slipped out atter dark and met in a old house to dance. De banjoman was pickin' his banjo, and dey was dancin' and singin':

> Who dat knockin' at de elder,
> Who dat knockin' at de elder—

> De paderoller, named Jimmy Stevens, was standin' at de window watchin' 'em, enjoyin' de music and de dancin'. Every time dey sung,

> Who dat knockin' at de elder,
> Who dat knockin' at de elder

> de paderoller would sing,

> Little Jimmy Stevens,
> Little Jimmy Stevens,

> It skeered de slaves to death mighty nigh. Dey quit and started to git away from dere. (Berle Barnes, b. ca. 1856, NC, 9–10)

> Sho, an' I'se seen sev'al whuppin's whar de blood run down kinda fast. Dat's mos'ly fo' runawayers. Nigger George am a runawayer, an' am pow'ful fast an' sneaky. He am so skeert an' ready to run, dat de paterollers an' all de dawgs in de country can't catch him. Marster 'ranges one time to have a ball. Sho! We'uns have dances, balls, an' lotsa fun. Now, at dis ball, he 'ranges wid de fiddler to git word to George 'bout de fun, den give de word w'en to close in an' catch George. Well, de ball am gwine on merrily, an' in come mistah George. De fiddler starts de new song lak dis:

> Old Marster, heah we are,
> Old Marster, heah we are,
> Old Marster, heah we are
> Have to slip in easy,
> For he's a little bit wild.

> He sung dat jus' so good, an' w'en he's playin', Ise seen dem niggers buck an' wing dis high off'n de flooah, wid de pots an' pans gwine on an' keepin' time right wid de music. 'Twas pow'ful hahd to keep youse feet still, de music am so good. W'en

de Marster heah dem words, why, de patterrollers jus' slips up and catches mistah George so easy. (Willie Blackwell, b. 1834, NC, 310–11)

I 'mem'ers dar wus a man named Taylor who was a patteroller. He had red hair an' we uster call 'im "Red Taylor." One nite when de colored people wus all a sho'tin' an' havin' a good time one of dem saw "Red Taylor" at de do'r, an' he kep' on a sayin':

Red Taylor at de do'r, Red Taylor at de do'r,
Red Taylor at de do'r,
Bright mansions above,
Bright mansions above,
Red Taylor at de do'r,
Red Taylor at de do'r,
Bright mansions above,
Bright mansions above.

He couldn't make dem understan' him so he got a sho'el of hot co'ls of fire an' he jes th'ew dem rite in de ro'm an' 'erbody got ert an' jes flew. (Bacchus White, b. 1852, VA, 303)[11]

Three ex-slaves (Roy Redfield, Jake Green, Harriett Robinson) told the tale of an elusive runaway fiddler who regularly sneaks back to play plantation frolics and sing "fooled my marster seven years—expect to fool him seven more."[12] The infamous "Run, Nigger, Run" was also incorporated into cantefables.

Dere am only one time dat a nigger gits whupped on dat plantation and dat am not given by massa but by dem patterrollers. Massa don't gin'rally 'low dem patterrollers whup on his place, and all de niggers from round dere allus run from de patterrollers onto massa's land and den dey safe. But in dis 'ticlar case, massa make de 'ception. 'Twas nigger Jack what dey chases home and he gits under de cabin and 'fused to come out. Massa say, "In dis case I gwine make 'ception, 'cause dat Jack he am too unreas'able. He allus chasin' after some nigger wench and not satisfied with de pass I give. Give him 25 lashes but don't

draw de blood or leave de marks." Well, sar, it am de great sight to see Jack git dat whuppin'. Him am skeert, but dey ain't hurtin' him bad. Massa make him come out and dey tie him to a post and he starts to bawl and beller befo' a lick am struck. Say! Him beg like a good fellow. It am, "Oh, massa, massa, Oh, massa, have mercy, don't let 'em whup me. Massa, I won't go off any more." De patterrollers gives him a lick and Jack lets out a yell dat sounds like a mule bray and twice as loud. Dere used to be a patterroller song what went like dis:

Up de hill and down de holler
White man cotch nigger by de collar
Dat nigger run and dat nigger flew
Dat nigger tore he shirt in two.

Well, while dey's whuppin' dat nigger, Jack, he couldn't run and he couldn't tear he shirt in two, but he holler till he tear he mouth in two. Jack say he never go off without de pass 'gain and he kept his word, too. (Louis Fowler, b. 1853, GA, 51–52)

Over fifty WPA narrators mentioned "Run, Nigger, Run," two thirds of them giving texts. This actually exceeds the combined evidence from all other sources and by my reckoning makes "Run, Nigger, Run" the most frequently named song in the ex-slave narratives, without question the most frequently named secular song. It was almost always a dance song or fiddle tune, but there is other evidence of a cantefable tradition. In the 1850s, John Allan Wyeth (1845–1922) was mentored by an Alabama slave banjo player, Uncle Billy, who performed "Run, Nigger, Run" as a story-song.

Another popular song referred to the "patrol," which the negroes styled "patter-rollers":

Run, nigger, run; patter-roller catch you;
Run, nigger, run; it's almos' day;
Run, nigger, run; patter-roller catch you;
Run, nigger, run; you'd better git away.
Dis nigger run; he run his best;

Stuck his head in a hornet's nest.
Jump'd de fence and run frew de paster;
White man run, but nigger run faster.

There was an embellishment of this "star" selection that may be of interest. After playing the music of the chorus, Billy would pause, lay the banjo across his knees, and speak about this style, preluding his remark with one of those long-drawn-out grunts or weirdly intonated expressions of surprise which only the African seems to enjoy: "Golly! folks; I went to see Miss Sal last Sat'day night. Sal's a handsome gal, too, no 'ceptions to dat. I ain't more'n had time to 'spress myself on de occasion when Sal say, 'Looky dar, Peet!' 'Looky whar, Sal?' 'Look at dat Patter-roller peepin' frew de crack!'" Then a second long grunt or ejaculation of surprise.

"Golly! chillun; dis yer nigger riz as quick as a nigger could convenient; jumped frew de winder, fell ober de woodpile, knocked de wood into short sticks, an' took down de road fas' as my laigs could go, an' de white man he tuk airter me, an' ebery jump I make de white man say" (then he would sing):

"Run, nigger, run, patter-roller ketch you," etc.[13]

In 1851—the exact period Wyeth describes—a text closely resembling Uncle Billy's rendition appeared in a songbook from minstrel empresario Charles T. White, either preceded or closely followed by an identical broadside, albeit uncredited and undated (see fig. 11.4). The item is titled "Run, nigger, run! or the M.P.'ll catch you," which presents a bit of a puzzle. *M. P.* could stand for mounted patrol or something else (it was not an acronym for military police until WWII). Slaves never referred to patrollers as M.P.s, however, and certainly not in this song. Also unusual is the diddling in the printed text's chorus (*tum a du daddle da*), typical of the British and Irish folksongs minstrels often recycled but otherwise unknown in "Run, Nigger, Run." Many passages (the first, second, and last stanzas) are in the bombastic minstrel style

Fig. 11.4. "Run, nigger, run! or the M.P.'ll catch you." America Singing: Nineteenth-Century Song Sheets, Library of Congress, Prints and Photographs Division.

and occur only in this text. Other elements do occur in oral tradition, but probably originated there. The printed piece is scripted for the prewar minstrel-show format, to be performed by the endmen, Tambo and Bones (the tambourine and bones players). The asides concluding the spoken passages ("What did he holler, Mr. Bones?") indicate that Tambo recited the speeches, with Bones singing (or leading the singing) on the choruses. The text in White's songbook bears the notation "Composed and sung by C. White, of White's Band of Serenaders, at the Melodeon Concert Saloon, 53 Bowery, N.Y." Opened in the late 1840s, the Melodeon was the most famous of White's New York ventures (the theater's name refers to his primary instrument). He only occasionally toured outside the city.[14] Uncharacteristically, White did not reprint this item in subsequent editions or collections.

One simple explanation for the correspondences between these examples would be that either Uncle Billy or John Wyeth appropriated the minstrel text. But Wyeth is generally a reliable source, and there are significant differences between the minstrel version and Uncle Billy's, the latter very much suggesting traditional origins and oral transmission. Possibly, then,

Charles White or one of his Serenaders encountered and copied a relation of Uncle Billy's cantefable, but without additional examples that is mere speculation. In any case, the cantefable form of "Run, Nigger, Run" is a curious digression and little more; without question this piece was best known as an a cappella reel or fiddle-and-banjo song at slave frolics, where it was reportedly inescapable. "Marster's old brother-in-law let his slaves dance outdoors on Sunday sometime. Somebody play de violin and de banjo. . . . De tune dey play most 'Run Nigger run, de patter-rollers ketch you'" (Agatha Babino, b. ca. 1850, LA, 140).

Nineteenth-century corroboration is in this instance especially plentiful, and period sources confirm that "Run, Nigger, Run" was ubiquitous throughout the nineteenth-century South, associated almost entirely with Blacks. The usual melody, possibly an African American creation, belongs to a widespread family of fiddle tunes also including "Fire on the Mountain" and "Granny Will Your Dog Bite." Anthony Dawson may have been correct when he wondered "iffen de white folks didn't make dat song ['Run, Nigger, Run'] up so us niggers would keep in line" (Anthony Dawson, b. 1832, NC, 65). Certainly whites knew the song, and encouraged slaves to sing it. "After supper Master would drag out his old fiddle on the front porch and the Niggers danced and sang while he played 'Run Nigger Run, the Paddyrollers Will Catch You,' and other tunes" (Katie Darling, b. 1849, TX, 1050). "One song dey use to sing was: / Run nigger run, run nigger run, / Don't let de paddle rollers catch you, / Run nigger run. / De niggers would be pattin' dey feet an' dancin' for life. Master an' dem would be settin' on de front porch listenin' to de music, 'cause you could hear it for a half mile" (Robert Williams, b. 1843, VA, 326).

In fact, WPA interviewers may themselves have encouraged ex-slaves to sing "Run, Nigger, Run." John Lomax's guidelines recommended that fieldworkers ask "What did you hear about patrollers?" and some song texts were clearly given in response to this or similar questions. "Pateroles!! Oh, my God!!! I know 'nough 'bout them. Child, I've heard 'em holler, 'Run, nigger, run! The pateroles will catch you'" (Frank Wil-

liams, b. ca. 1835, MS, 159). Even more, some interviewers knew to ask for this song specifically. "I used to hear the people talkin' 'bout patrollers. Yes ma'am, I heared that song / Run nigger run / Paddyrollers will ketch you / Jes' 'fore day" (Ida May Fluker, b. 1854, AL, 323). "On Saturday night they didn' get together, they would jes' sing at their own houses. Oh, yes'm, I 'member 'em singin' 'Run, nigger, run,' but it's too far back for me to 'member those other songs. They would raise up a song when they was pickin' cotton" (Austin Grant, b. unk., TX, 83). "Oh yessum. I seed de Patterolers, but I never heard no song about 'em" (Hannah Murphy, b. ca. 1857, GA, 468).

Actually, it is none too surprising that white interviewers (many of whom appeared to know little else about slave music) would be familiar with this particular item. Whites' latter-day fascination with "Run, Nigger, Run" is curious and probably has several explanations, not least the mythology of the Old South and the Lost Cause; but by the twentieth century, this piece—in the nineteenth century reported almost exclusively among Blacks—was being collected just as often from whites. Indeed, three of the texts in the ex-slave narratives were provided by whites, two by interviewers who had it passed down in their families from the antebellum or Civil War eras (Merton Knowles, SS1 5 *IN*: 69; Beulah Van Meter, SS1 5 *IN*: 227–28) and a third by a former slaveholder who had heard it from his slaves (O. A. Marsh, SS2 10 *TX* 9: 4353–58). Another white WPA informant, W. S. Needham Jr., described learning to fiddle the tune (without words) from one of his father's slaves (SS2 10 *TX* 9: 4364–65). Conceivably, then, this later white interest exaggerated the song's actual importance, but nineteenth-century sources corroborate its currency among slaves, also suggesting that they either composed "Run, Nigger, Run" themselves or very quickly made it their own.

Whether "Run, Nigger, Run" was created by slaves or foisted upon them by whites, it describes the plantation patrol system in a manner more than intimating direct familiarity. The chorus finds an errant slave fleeing home as daybreak exposes him to discovery and punishment by patrollers; restatements of these

Fig. 11.5. Katie Darling, ex-slave, Marshall, TX, August 3, 1937. "You is ta'kin' now to a Nigger what nu'sed seven white chil'ren in them 'bull-whip' days." Portraits of African American ex-slaves from the US Works Progress Administration, Federal Writers' Project slave narratives collection, Library of Congress.

facts account for most of the refrain's variations: "One song dey wus singin' all de time wus—'Run nigger run, de patroller git yo' / Run nigger run, *it is almost day*'" (Barney Alford, b. ca. 1850, MS, 47, my emphasis). "We all use to sing dis / Run nigger run, / Run nigger run, / Don't let the paddlerollers catch you, / Run nigger run, / Run nigger run, / *Keep on runnin' 'till daylight come*" (George White, b. 1847, VA, 310, my emphasis). "Had fiddlin', an' all would jine in singin' songs, lak, 'Run nigger run, pattyrollers ketch you, run nigger run, *it's breakin' day*.' I still fiddle dat chune" (James Singleton, b. 1856, MS, 1959, my emphasis). "The only thing that Stephen can remember about the patrollers was the little chant that his mother used to frighten the children: 'Run nigger run, run nigger run, the pater-rollers will get you *if you dont look out*'" (Stephen Varner, b. 1852, AL, 426, my emphasis).

> There wuz a bunch of white men called the "patty rollers." They'd come in and see if all us had passes and if they found any who didn't have a pass he wuz whipped; give fifty or mo' lashes—and they'd count them lashes. If they said a hundred, you got a hundred. They wuz somethin' lak the Klu Klux. We wuz 'fraid to tell our mastahs 'bout the patty rollers 'cause we wuz skeared they'd whip us again, fur we wuz tol' not to tell. They'd sing a little ditty. I wish I could remember the words, but it went somethin' lak this:
>
> Run, nigger, run, de patty rollers'll git you,
> Run, nigger, run, *you'd bettah git away*.
>
> We wuz 'fraid to go any place. (Julia "Sally" Brown, b. ca. 1852, GA, 96, my emphasis)

The big fo'ks had dances and parties. They had fiddles but they warn't like these things they have now. The fiddles we had then made music. I can only think of two of them ring plays:

> Run, Nigger, Run, the Pattyrollers will get you
> *Its almost day*
> Run, Nigger, Run, the Pattyrollers will get you
> *You ain't got long to stay*
> Run, Nigger, Run, the Pattyrollers will get you.

The other one was:

> Suzy Gal, Half Moon, Susie Gal
> Suzy Gal, Half Moon, Susie Gal. (Bert Strong, b. 1864, TX, 3758, my emphasis)[15]

This chorus was sometimes sung by itself, perhaps interspersed with fiddling, perhaps unaccompanied and over and over until the dancers finished. Fuller texts incorporate a loose assortment of verses, many well-known floaters. That notwithstanding, the stanzas most frequently collected with "Run, Nigger, Run" are all original with, and exclusive to, that piece. By far the most common of these describe the fleeing slave being stripped of his shoes, shirt, and pants by a pursuing patroller. He may suffer additional indignities or torments—being

Fig. 11.6. Penny Thompson, ex-slave, Fort Worth, TX, June 25, 1937. Portraits of African American ex-slaves from the US Works Progress Administration, Federal Writers' Project slave narratives collection, Library of Congress.

bitten by blacksnakes or getting stung by hornets, for instance.

> Sam an' Rufus was fiddle an' banjo playahs. Lots an' lots ob nights, weuns sing an' play de music. . . . Ol' Sam use to sing a song 'bout de Patter Rollers. It's a long song, Ise can' on'y tell yous a little. An Ise 'membahs, 'tis lak dis:
>
> > Run nigger run, Patter Roller catch you,
> > Run nigger run 'case it's almos' day,
> > Dat nigger run, dat nigger flew,
> > Dat nigger los' his Sunday shoe. (James West, b. 1854, MS, 4018, 4023)
>
> Dere am a song 'bout de Patter Rollers. Ise can't 'membahs it as 'twas, but its somethin' lak dis:
>
> > Up the hill and down the holler
> > Patter Rollers caught dat nigger by de collar
> > Dat nigger run and dat nigger flew
> > Dat nigger tore his shirt in two. (Penny Thompson, b. ca. 1851, AL, 3875)

> I went down to Dad's old corn field.
> Black snake bit me on my heel,
> I turn around and run my best,
> Stuck my head in a hornets nest.
>
> Run nigger, run,
> De Patteroll'll git you!
> Run nigger, run,
> De Patteroll'll come!
> Run nigger, run,
> De Patteroll'll git you!
> Run nigger, run,
> You'd better make it home!
>
> We all sung dat song and had lots of fun singing it but it was true jest the same. Dat was one of the things dat the niggers dreaded most, was a patteroller. (Jim Threat, b. 1851, AL, 325)

Semi-comic melees of this sort are common fare in Black folksongs, and the blacksnake and hornet couplets wander in and out of similar items ("You Shall Be Free," "Eph Got the Coon," "Johnny Booker," "Raise a Ruckus"), usually appearing together, sometimes separately. The other stanzas just quoted are all specific to "Run, Nigger, Run." That the slave's lost shoe is usually a Sunday shoe, sometimes a wedding shoe, indicates he was away from his plantation attending a worship service or dance, common causes of patroller conflicts. Texas convict Mose "Clear Rock" Platt (who sang "Sunday shoe") additionally described the slave overstaying his leave ("Nigger run by my gate / Wake up, nigger, you slept too late"); this would suggest a conjugal visit to a neighboring plantation, another habitual cause of patroller problems.

> If the mawster said the man could marry his slave, he had to come to his sweetheart's cabin . . . and there would be a broomstick across the woman's door entrance, and he had to jump over it . . . and that act made 'em man and wife. After that, he was allowed to come to see his bride every Thursday and Saturday night and he was allowed to come

all day on Sunday. A lot ob times he jes' sneaked away and saw his wife at any ole time, if the patrol didn't catch him. The niggers would sing:

Run nigger, run, the patrol'll git yo',
'cause it's almost day.
That nigger run, that nigger flew,
That nigger run his head in a hornet's nest. (Sallie Johnson, b. 1855, TX, 2048, orig. ellipses)[16]

Ferebe Rogers gave another couplet sometimes figuring in the chase:

In eve'y dee-strick dey had 'bout twelve men dey call patterollers. Dey ride up and down and are looking for niggers widout passes. If dey ever caught you off de plantation wid no pass, dey beat you all over. Yes'm, I 'member a song 'bout—

Run, nigger, run, de patteroller git you,
Slip over de fence slick as a eel,
White man ketch you by de heel,
Run, nigger, run!

No amount of coaxing availed to make her sing the whole of the song, or to tell any more of the words. (Ferebe Rogers, b. ca. 1830, GA, 214)

The slave slipping over the fence may allude to one of the patroller's (and slaveholders') favorite tortures: "I seed em take de bottom rail out of de rail fences and stick de nigger's head in de hole den jam de balance of de fence down on his neck, and beat him till he's stiff" (Edward Taylor, b. ca. 1812, LA, 339). "I never seed no slaves bought or sold and I never was sold, but I seen 'em beat—O. Lawd, yes. I seen 'em make a man put his head through the crack of the rail fence and then they beat him till he was bloody" (Carey Davenport, b. 1855, TX, 282). "I'se seen de patrollers whip niggers an dey would allus put his head under de rail fence an whip him from de back. We used to sing a song like dis: 'Run nigger run de Patrollers will catch you 'tis almost day'" (Lizzie Williams, b. 1849, MS, 2338). "Once ole Marsa held up de

fence for me to put my head between de rails so he could whip me but 'stead o' just puttin my head through, I shot through just like a mink. He yelled: 'You little son-of-a-bitch.' I run a quarter of a mile to where my mammy was washin' an' he never did bother me no more" (Riley Moore, b. ca. 1850, MS, 1570). In his 1891 memoir, Kentucky ex-slave Harry Smith (b. 1814) corroborated these accounts:

Dancing was one of the main amusements in the South. Mr. Smith's old massa would give him a pass to prevent his being whipped, but he seldom asked for it, because he was so fleet of foot no one could catch him, not even the blood hounds. . . . Many were caught by these patrollers when the corners of the fence were raised enough to get their heads through, their backs made bare and they received their punishment in this attitude.[17]

To limit this brutality, many jurisdictions limited the number of lashes paterollers could administer, thirty-nine being most commonly cited.[18] "We slipped off when we got a chance to see young folks on some other place. The patterollers cotched me one night and, Lawd have mercy me, they stretches me over a log and hits thirty-nine licks with a rawhide loaded with rock, and every time they hit me the blood and hide done fly" (Tom Holland, b. 1840, TX, 145).

Sir we got one day a week and Christmas day was all de holiday we ever heard of and we could not go anywhere except we had a pass from our master to another, if we slip off the patter roller would get us and the patter roller hit us 39 licks with the raw hide with nine tails and the patter roller would get 50 cents for hitting us 39 licks. I want to sing you a song about the patterroller. Captain here is the words:

Run negro run, negro patter roller catch you,
How can I run, when he already got me in the
woods and thru the pasture
The white man run but the negro run faster.
(Harre Quarls, b. 1841, TX, 3213–14)

When de nigger leaves de plantation without no pass, and de padder rollers kotched him, dey gives him 39 licks with de bullwhip. When we's in de fields and sees de padder roller ride by, we starts murmerin' out loud, "Patter de pat, patter de pat." One after 'nother took it up and purty soon everybody murmerin'. We allus do dat to let everybody know de padder roller 'round. Den we sing songs 'bout dem too. . . .

> Run nigger run, padder-roller catch you,
> Run nigger run, Dey give you thirty-nine,
> Dat nigger run, dat nigger flew,
> Dat nigger lost his Sunday shoe. (Millie Williams, b. 1851, TX, 4114)[19]

An ex-slave text published in the 1895 *Southern Workman* has "Run, nigger run patteroler'll ketch yer, / Hit yer thirty-nine and sware 'e didn' tech yer."[20]

There are other passing references to documented night rider practices. A Kentucky version refers to patrollers' tricks and disguises, in this case an animal hide:

> Run, Nigger, run, run your best,
> Run, Nigger, run the patteroles will ketch ye.
> Don't go away, child, you can't fool me.
> Do, Johnny Booger, won't you do, do, do.
>
> I went off and I come back again,
> The white man scared me in an old sheep skin.[21]

Besides its original verses, there is also an obvious logic to the wandering stanzas the song has attracted. Several texts incorporate one of the South's best-known floaters. "Dere wus a song dey used to sing, it went like dis. Yes sir, ha! ha! I wants ter tell you dat song, here it is: 'Some folks say dat a nigger wont steal, I caught two in my corn field, one had a bushel, one had a peck, one had rosenears [roasting ears], strung 'round his neck. Run nigger run, Patteroller ketch you, run nigger run like you did de udder day'" (Kitty Hill, b. 1860, VA, 424).[22] It is no mystery why

singers would associate a description of slaves looting a cornfield with "Run, Nigger, Run." Food theft by slaves occurred constantly, and commonly pitted them against patrollers charged with preventing same. With or without this verse, much of the song's action takes place in cornfields.[23]

Matilda Shepard's version includes another of the South's better-known floaters: "I went up on the mountain give my horn a blow. I think I her them say yonder comes old Paddy Rollers Run Negro Run" (Matilda Shepard, b. ca. 1832, GA, 126). Arthur Granville Bradbury (1850–1943) recalled the stanza's more typical form from Black tenants in postwar Virginia: "Away up in de mountain / I took my horn and blow; / I tink I hear Miss Scindy callin', / 'Yonder come my beau.'"[24] Shepard's adaptation instead evokes the infamous slave hunters' horns: "Pa said the nigger men run off to get a rest. They'd take to the woods and canebrakes. . . . The master and paddyrolls took after 'em. They'd been down in there long enough. They heard the dogs and the horn" (Mag Johnson, b. ca. 1870, AR, child of ex-slaves, 108–9).

In what might seem a surprising turn, several songmakers combined "Run, Nigger, Run" with spirituals or spiritual parodies. The development is all the more striking since these examples were obviously created independently, all involving different spirituals.

PATEROLL SONG (PATROL SONG)

> Oh, run nigger, run,
> The patteroll'll ketch you,
> Run, nigger run,
> It's almost day.
>
> Run for your soul,
> My Lord some day give in hand,
> Run, run, run.
>
> When I sot out for to seek my Lord,
> I left this world behind,
> All glory, glory, hallelujah;
> Pray, pray, pray, my Lord

> Pray, oh pray, pray, pray, my Lord,
> Oh, glory, glory hallelujah.
>
> Oh, ain't dat a good thing,
> Pray, pray, isn't dat a good thing,
> Pray, childrun, pray, little childrun,
> Oh ain't dat a good time,
> Hallelu, hallelu.[25]

Upon reflection, it makes perfect sense that different singers would independently combine such a profane piece with religious songs. Running is a common trope in spirituals, and there are noted resemblances between "Run, Nigger, Run" and items like "Run, Sinner, Run" or "Run to the City of Refuge."[26] However, a song about patrollers might remind people of spiritual singing for other reasons, since worship services were among the occasions when slaves were most vulnerable to vigilantes. "Yes, we seed the patterollers, we called 'em pore white trash, we also called patterollers poor white pecks. They had ropes around their necks. They came to our house one night when we were singin' and pra-yin'. It wuz jist before de surrender. Dey were hired by de slave owner" (Hannah Crasson, b. 1853, NC, 190). "Ku Klux used to come to the church well and ask for a drink and say, 'I ain't had a bit of water since I fought the battle Shiloh'" (Hardy Miller, b. 1852, AR, 76). "They didn't have the Ku Klux but it was bout like it what they had. They wore caps shine like de coons eye and red caps and red garments. Red symbolize blood reason they wore red. They broke up our preaching. Some folks got killed" (William Henry Rooks, b. 1853, MS, 77). Sena Moore had suffered personally. "One night de big road full of us niggers was comin' from church. Just as us git to de top of de hill us see, comin' up de hill, a long line of hosses, wid riders dressed in pure white, hoods on deir heads, and painted false faces. They busted into a gallop for us" (Sena Moore, b. 1854, SC, 212). The congregation scattered. Sena's brothers Luther and Bill jumped a gully and escaped through the woods, but Sena landed in the gully, injured her leg, then huddled there all night in misery until Luther came and carried her home.

It is also of some moment that slaves most often sang "Run, Nigger, Run" at frolics, another occasion when they were especially exposed to—perhaps even under the watchful eyes of—patrollers. Unless it was an unauthorized dance (and thus completely fair game for night riders), some form of white surveillance and supervision would have been ever-present. "We would have a few dances, the old marster would come to watch us dance, but dey didn't come from eber where like deys do now, maybe there be some that have wives er men on other plantations dat could get a pass ter come over. When we'ns had dances der wuz no cuttin up lak dere is dese days, dey had to behave der selves" (Jeff Calhoun, b. 1838, AL, 608).

There is no question that whites strongly encouraged slaves to sing "Run, Nigger, Run" at their frolics. Saying that it was obligatory at slave dances might not be a complete overstatement. If nothing else, the mere fact of the song's unparalleled currency meant that, whether by slaveholder dictate or unspoken custom, if slaves were going to get together, socialize, and have a good time, then they were probably going to sing "Run, Nigger, Run," and quite possibly in circumstances precisely mirroring the song's content:

> On Sundays, de slaves jes sot 'round de cabin doors an' talk an' wrap hair, an' sumtimes dey wud sing. Sum times slaves frum udder plantashuns wud cum an' jine de crowd, but dey all toted passes ter keep de patterollers frum ketchin' 'em. Yes, dey sung—
>
> > Run, nigger, run, de pat'roller' ketch yo'
> > Run nigger, run, it's almos' day.
> > Dat nigger run, dat nigger flew,
> > Dat nigger tore his shirt in two.
> > Dat nigger, he, sed don't ketch me,
> > But git dat nigger b'hind de tree.
> > Dat nigger cried, dat nigger lied,
> > Dat nigger shook his old fat side,
> > Run, nigger, run, it's almos' day. (Ann Drake, b. 1855, MS, 646)

Rina Brown described Blacks and whites singing "Run, Nigger, Run" together as the last dance at frolics, just as daybreak exposed the departing slaves to real-world patrollers.

> Yassum, de white folks an' de colored folk uster have big dances an' old Joe wud play de fiddle while dey stepped lightly all de fancy steps, an' jes' fore dey wud break up in morning dey wud dance de Old Virginia Reel an den sing
>
>> Run Nigger, Run, de pateroller'll git yo'
>> Run Nigger, run, it's almost day.
>> Dat nigger run, dat nigger flew
>> Dat nigger lost his brogan shoe
>> Run nigger run, Its almost day. (Rina Brown, b. 1853, MS, 279–80)

"Run, Nigger, Run" thus reveals another common pattern in authoritarian rule. In premodern societies, musical performance itself was likely a mark of servile or in any case low status, and throughout history, persons of power and privilege have found that forcing other people to perform can be an especially effective means of exacting tribute, demonstrating obedience and subservience, or simply demeaning and humiliating one's inferiors, as in the Hollywood cliché of the Old West gunfighter making the Eastern dandy dance like a saloon girl with his six-shooter. For most American slaves, this was no moldy joke but a constant prospect in their daily lives, an obligatory expression of their bondage. Aside from using slaves as entertainers generally, slaveholders stoked their own senses of power and prestige by requiring slaves to pay musical tribute; some even derived sadistic pleasure from forcing slaves to perform unsuitable material in unwelcoming or uncomfortable circumstances. "We niver had no dances in de quarters, an' I doan remember eny dances at de big house. Dey hed no pianny but Marse Alex wud play de fiddle hisself. Sumtimes when he played de fiddle, he made Jim and Tony stand out dar an' 'Knock de back-step' " (Orris Harris, b. ca. 1858, MS, 930). "De folks in de big house use com' down to de' quarters on Sattidy nights an' mek us sing. We sho did some cuttin' up. Ah use to be able to do some right smaht jiggin' when Ah wuz a youngster" (Joe Bouy, b. 1858, MS, 181). "Marse Jabe Smith was a good white man. He was a grand fiddler and he used to call us to de big house at night to dance for him. I couldn't do nothin' 'cept jump up and down and I sho' did git tired" (Easter Huff, b. 1858, GA, 247).

> "Uncle Dock" recalls that his master, Dan Wilborn, who was a good-natured man of large stature, derived much pleasure in playing his "fiddle" and that often in the early summer evenings he would walk down to the slave quarters with his violin remarking that he would supply the music and that he wished to see his "niggers" dance, and dance they would for hours and as much to the master's own delight and amusement as theirs. (Dock Wilborn, b. 1843, AL, 145)

Old Tim sometimes make us children dance out in de yard. Dey ain't no drums nor music,—someone jes' take up a old pan an' stick an' keep time dat way. Old Tim comes up to us children an' puts sand on our head an' den makes us dance, an' when de sand drap down an' get under de dress an' get you all scratchy, he jes' sit an' laff an' laff seein' de squirmin' we does, 'cause when de sand get to de skin you sure goin' to squirm. (Josephine Howard, b. ca. 1830, AL, 1808–9)

Whites routinely bullied devout Blacks by forcing them to dance or to sing sinful songs in violation of their religious convictions. "I uster dance. Ol' marster come in sometime' and say, 'Fate, you dance,' so often I hafter pat. Atter w'ile though he call me and want me to dance. Den I would say, 'I seed sumpin' (meaning that he had received spiritual light that he ought not to dance), so I don' dance no mo' " (Lafayette Price, b. ca. 1850, AL, 3177, orig. parentheses). Former South Carolina slave Jacob Stroyer (1846–?) recalled that at Christmas "a great many of the strict members of the church who did not dance would be forced to do it to please their masters."[27] Another South Carolina ex-slave, WPA narrator Madison Griffin, remembered night riders (of whom he was one) employing the tactic:

> I went wid de Red Shirts, belonged to de company and went to meetings wid dem. I voted fer Hampton. Befo' dat, de Ku Klux had bad niggers dodging like birds in de woods. Dey caught some and threw dem on de ground and whipped dem, but de master say he don't know nothing 'bout it as he was asleep. Dey caught a nigger preacher once and made him dance, put him in muddy water and walloped him around in de mud. (Madison Griffin, b. 1853, SC, 213).

"Dixie" may have originated as a Black folksong, but by the war years it had acquired other connotations, and no one missed the point when slaveholders forced slaves to perform "Dixie." "De ole song I members ez 'Dixie Land,' en 'Run Nigger Run, de Pat-a rollers Will Git You'" (Cecelia Chappel, b. ca. 1835, TN, 8). "Of course we sang 'Dixie.' We had to sing that, it was the leading song" (Ann May, b. 1856, AR, 66–67).

> My old master mean to us. We used to watch for him to come in the big gate, then we run and hide. He used to come to the quarters and make us chillun sing. He make us sing Dixie. Sometimes he make us sing half a day. Seems like Dixie his main song. I tell you I don't like it *now*. But have mercy! He make us sing it. Seems like all the white folks like Dixie. I'se glad when he went away to war. (Eda Harper, b. ca. 1845, AR, 164)

Long after the war, whites still compelled blacks to perform "Dixie." W. C. Handy (1873–1958) got his first big show business break playing with Mahara's Minstrel Men in the 1890s, recalling "the way Confederate soldiers [veterans] tossed their own hats whenever we played *Dixie* for them."[28]

For enslaved Africans, such musical abuse was a condition of their captivity from the moment they left the continent. To maintain their physiques they were forced to dance on transatlantic slave ships, then again in New World slave pens. John Brown (ca. 1818–?) had passed through New Orleans slave trader Theophilus Freeman's infamous operation in the 1840s, later writing "after dinner we were compelled to walk, and dance, and kick about in the yard, for exercise; and Bob [Freeman's mixed-race underboss], who had a fiddle, used to play up jigs for us to dance to. If we did not dance to his fiddle, we used to have to do so to his whip, so no wonder we used our legs handsomely, though the music was none of the best."[29]

To display and demonstrate their well-maintained physiques, or just to draw a crowd, slaves were then obliged to dance and sing on auction blocks. "He [speculator] put us up on the slavery block an' bade us twist an' turn an' sho' our teeth. Marster Dickey bid on Mammy, but some other man out bid him an my Mammy was sol away from me. I cried an cried, but twarnt' no use" (Lucy Thurston, b. ca. 1836, LA, 2112–13). "Frank says these auctions were very much like the present day auctions of horses and mules. The slaves were placed on the auction block and gave demonstrations as to strength and sometimes were made to sing and dance. After they had entertained the crowd the bidding would begin and the slave went to the highest bidder" (Frank Ziegler, b. unk., AL, 465).

> I remembers 'bout one gal dat come from Africa. She was a "puor" African an' had long black hair. She would grease dat hair and plait it in two long braids down her back and tie it wid red ribbon-bows. She say when dey put her on de block to sell, dey tole her to dance fer dem. She show wuz a good dancer. She dance the same way she did in Africa and what she had learned dere. She wuz 15 year old when dey bring her over here. (Lucy Galloway, b. 1863, MS, 803)

> I is heared my mother tell many times about the slave dealers. She said they would take the slaves from place to place all chained together. They would make them sing to attract attention. Some of

them would be crying 'bout leaving their children. Ma said my pa was put on a bench and sold just like stock would be. (Maria White, b. 1853, MS, 2278)

My mudder was sold once for a hundud dollahs and once ag'in for thirty-eight hundud dollahs. Perhaps dis was jist before dey left West Virginia and was shipped to North Ca'liny. De master put her upon a box, she said, made her jump up and pop her heels together three times and den turn around and pop her heels again to show how strong she was. (Bob Potter, b. 1873, AR, child of ex-slaves, 365)

This was a standard tool of night riders as well. Slaves were forced to act in night rider dramas if only by pretending to accept their illusions—no great task since most admitted being terrified whether or not they really believed in hants. They might be strong-armed into more active roles, however, like hauling endless buckets of water for the thirsty ghosts. Or they might be compelled to cavort, sing, and dance. "I's been cotched by them Ku Kluxers. They didn't hurt me, but have lots of fun makin' me cut capers. They pulls my clothes off once and make me run 'bout four hunerd yards and stand on my head in the middle of the road" (Willis Winn, b. 1822, LA, 205). "I have seen the Ku Klux quarter mile long and two breasted on horses. They scared me so bad I never had no experience with them. They run my uncle in. He was a big dancer. One time they made him dance. He cut the pigeonwing for them. That was the name of what he danced" (Cat Ross, b. 1862, TN, 86).

The onlies sperience I had myself wid the Ku Klux was one night fo Grandma and auntie lef. Somebody wrap [rap] on our cabin door. They opened it. We got scared when we seed em. They had the horses wrapped up. They had on white long dresses and caps. Every one of em had a horse whoop (whip). They called me out. Grandma and auntie so scared they hid. They tole me to git em water. They poured it some whah it did not spill

on the ground. Kept me totin' water. Then they say "You bin a good boy?" They still drinkin'. One say, "Just from Hell pretty dry." Then they tole me to stand on my head. I turned summer sets a few times. They tickled me round wid the ends of the whoops. I had on a long shirt. They laugh when I stand on my head. Old Mars White laughed. I knowed his laugh. Then I got over my scare. (Hammett Dell, b. 1847, TN, 144–45, orig. parentheses)

I used to get a whipping now and den but nothing like de other slaves got. I used to be scared to death of those old Ku Klux folks with all dem hoods on dere heads and faces. I never will forget, I saw a real old darkey woman slave down on her knees praying to God for his help. She had a Bible in front of her. Course she couldn't read it, but she did know what it was, and she was prayin' out of her very heart, until she drawed the attention of them old Ku Klux and one of 'em just walked in her cabin and lashed her unmerciful. He made her get up off her knees and dance, old as she was. Of course de old soul couldn't dance but he just made her hop around anyhow. (Lula Chambers, b. ca. 1845, KY, 80–81)

Granted, these practices were basic to Europe's carnivals of violence, and whites used them on each other.[30]

The Yankees passed through and caught "ole Marse" Jim and made him pull off his boots and run barefooted through a cane brake with half a bushel of potatoes tied around his neck; then they made him put his boots back on and carried him down to the mill and tied him to the water post. They were getting ready to break his neck when one of Master's slaves, "ole Peter Smith," asked them if they intended to kill Marse Jim, and when they said "Yes," Peter choked up and said, "Well, please, suh, let me die wid ole Marse!" Well, dem Yankees let ole Marse loose and left! Yes, Missy, dat's de truf 'case I heered my daddy tell it many's the time! (Charlie Tye Smith, b. 1850, GA, 277)

It was night when de white folks tried to go away, and still night when de Yankees brung dem back, and a house nigger come down to de quarters wid three-four mens in blue clothes and told us to come up to de Big House. De Yankees didn't seem to be mad wid old Master, but jest laughed and talked wid him, but he didn't take de jokes any too good. Den dey asked him could he dance and he said no, and dey told him to dance or make us dance. Dar he stood inside a big ring of dem mens in blue clothes, wid dey brass buttons shining in de light from de fire dey had in front of de tents, and he jest stood and said nothing, and it look lak he wasn't wanting to tell us to dance. So some of us young bucks jest step up and say we was good dancers, and we start shuffling while de rest of de niggers pat. Some nigger women go back to de quarters and git de gourd fiddles, and de clapping bones made out'n beef ribs, and bring dem back so we could have some music. We git all warmed up and dance lak we never did dance befo'! I speck we invent some new steps dat night! (Charley Williams, b. 1843, LA, 337)

In fact some of the worst examples of this behavior being visited on slaves involved Federal troops, many of whom were as racist as any slaveholders, and just as opposed to the war's aim to end slavery. Some slaves had been conditioned by slaveholder propaganda to hate or fear Yankees, but others had known their northern liberators firsthand as just one among many sets of bad actors. "We were mortally afraid of the Yankees when they appeared here a short time after surrender. We were afraid of the Ku Klux Klan riders too. The Negroes did act so bad; there were lots of killings going on for a long time after the war was supposed to be over" (Minnie Davis, b. ca. 1860, GA, 262).

When de Yankees come, all de young marsters was off in de 'Federate side. I see them now, gallopin' to de house, canteen boxes on their hips and de bayonets rattlin' by deir sides. De fust thing they ask,

was: "You got any wine?" They search de house; make us sing: "Good Old Time 'Ligion"; put us to runnin' after de chickens and a cookin'. When they leave they burnt de gin house and everything in dere. They burn de smokehouse and wind up wid burnin' de big house. (Anne Broome, b. ca. 1850, SC, 105–6)

I wus jist five years ole when de Yankees come, jist a few of dem to our settlement. I doan know de number of de slaves, but I does 'member dat dey herded us tergether an' make us sing a heap of songs an' dance, den dey clap dere han's an dey sez dat we is good. One black boy won't dance, he sez, so dey put him barefooted on a hot piece of tin an' believe me he did dance. (Margaret Thornton, b. ca. 1860, NC, 353)

When de Yanks come, business took place. I remember white folks was running and hiding, gitting everything dey could from de Yanks. Dey hid dey jewelry and fine dishes and such. Dose Yanks had on big boots. Dey'd drive up, feed dey hosses from old Master's corn, catch dey chickens, and tell old Master's cook to cook 'em, and they'd shoot down old Master's hogs and skin 'em. De Yanks used to make my nephew drunk, and have him sing (dis is kind of bad):

I'll be God O'Mighty
God Damned if I don't
Kill a nigger,
Oh Whooey boys! Oh Whooey!
Oh Whooey boys! Oh Whooey! (Annie Young,
    b. 1851, TN, 360–61, orig. parentheses)

If their liberators often behaved no better than their enslavers, some Blacks actually made common cause with white supremacists. In fact, Blacks—and especially Black musicianers—often assisted night riders or even joined their ranks. Some were forced to participate, but many appear to have willingly taken part.[31]

That Black musicianers would know night riders personally, whether casually, cautiously, or cordially, should come as no surprise. Musicianers were, after all, the focal points of frolics, the circumstances that more than any others brought Blacks into conflict with patrollers. Sometimes performers were even singled out for punishment. "Good Lord! Dem patterollers was awful. Folkses what dey cotched widout no paper, dey jus' plum wore out. Old man John was de fiddler on our place, and when de patterollers cotched him dey beat him up de wust of all, 'cause him and his fiddle was all de time drawin' Niggers out to de dances" (Addie Vinson, b. 1852, GA, 107). In many cases, though, musicianers were given safe passage whether they had their papers or not. Morally suspect, socially marginal, constitutionally dubious, necessarily opportunistic, they occupied a social gray area anyway, constantly consorting with shady company or making unholy alliances. Church people regarded them literally as servants of the Devil. Habitual runaways, some musicians even received special protections from slaveholders, or particular forbearance from patterollers.[32]

Performers' predisposition for deviance and antisocial conduct may also account for why so many night riders were musicians, especially fiddlers. Whether this has any bearing on why some African Americans approved or assisted their activities is more difficult to gauge. Such collaborations usually had various apparent causes, including personal ties to whites but also standing grudges and feuds among Blacks. Brawley Gilmore was the child of ex-slaves. "We lived in a log house during the Ku Klux days. Dey would watch you just like a chicken rooster watching fer a worm" (Brawley Gilmore, b. unk., child of ex-slaves, SC, 120). He described in detail the Kluxers' murderous activities around Union, South Carolina, particularly the depredations of Doc McCollum, a fiddling thug who nonetheless had the sympathy and support of some local Blacks. In a final desperate act, another faction of former slaves met McCollum and his troop in pitched battle near a church afterward known as

Burnt Pilgrim. The black militiamen killed several whites, then were forced underground.

> Dey had a hiding place not fer from "Burnt Pilgrim." A darky name Austin Sanders, he was carrying some victuals to his son. De Ku Klux cotch him and dey axed him whar he was a gwine. He lowed dat he was setting some bait fer coons. De Ku Klux took and shot him and left him lying right in de middle of de road wid a biscuit in his dead mouth.
>
> Doctor McCollum was one of dem Ku Klux, and de Yankees sot out fer to ketch him. Doc, he rid a white pony called "Fannie." All de darkies, dey love Doc, so dey would help him fer to git away from de Yankees, even though he was a Ku Klux. . . . Doc, he liked to fiddle. Old Fannie, she would git up on her hind legs when de doc would play his fiddle. (Brawley Gilmore, b. unk., child of ex-slaves, SC, 121–23)

Gilmore's own sympathies seem mixed. He described several neighbors murdered by Kluxers and appeared to side with the Black militia at Burnt Pilgrim, but he also described how he and his sister smuggled provisions to McCollum while he hid from the Federals in a local graveyard. Many narrators had performed these precarious balancing acts.

> I come in early contack wid de Klu Klux. Us lef' de plantation in '65 or '66, and by '68 us was habin' sich a awful time wid de Klu Klux. . . . Den us move to New Prospect on de Pacolet Riber on de Perry Clemmon's place. Dat was in de upper edge of de county. Dat's w'er de secon' swarm come out. Dey claim dey gwine kill eb'rybudy claim Republican. My papa was charge' wid bein' a leader 'mongst de niggers. . . . De Klu Klux come to us house one night, but my daddy done hid. Den I hear dem say dey gwine go kill ol' man Bart. I jump out de winder and cut short cut t'rough dem wood and warn him. He git out he house in time and I sabe (save) he life.

De funny t'ing was dat I knowed all dem boys. 'Spite dey sheets and t'ings I knowed dey voices and dey saddle hosses. Dey was one young w'ite man name' Irving Ramsey. Us play de fiddle togedder lots of time'. W'en de w'hite boys hab a dance dey allus want me to go. Co'se I didn't dance but I play for all dey party. One day I say, "I done knowed you las' night." He say "W'at you mean?" I say, "You one dem Ku Klux." He wanter know how I know. I say, "Member w'en you go under de chestnut tree and say, 'Whoa, Sont, whoa, Sont,' to yo' hoss?" He say, "Yes," and I laugh and say, "Well, I's right up in dat tree." Dey all knowed dat I knowed dem den, but I nebber tol' on dem. W'en dey seed I ain' nebber gwinter tell on dem dey nebber try whip my daddy or kill Uncle Bart no mo'. (Lorenza Ezell, b. ca. 1850, SC, 1326–27, orig. parentheses)

For the best musicians, such entanglements were practically unavoidable, and not entirely undesirable. In various capacities, Black musicianers moved in white company with an ease unimaginable for other slaves. White musicians accepted them on familiar terms, while slaveholders and other elites exploited them for their own purposes. Aspiring southern aristocrats were expected to have slave minstrels in their retinues, as much as were European or African warlords. A plantation fiddler purchased just for that purpose was as much a status symbol as a piano in the parlor. Following the war, nothing could more perfectly symbolize the Old Regime and Blacks' continued servitude than the public spectacle of African American musicians performing for whites, all the more so at events supporting the Cause. But then, how different was hiring Black musicians to play Jim Crow festivities than forcing slaves to haul buckets of water for Confederate ghosts, dance the pigeon wing on dark deserted roads, or sing "Run, Nigger Run"?[33]

Still, for slave musicianers the attractions of white connections were self-evident; at the same time, their status and white associations but also their disreputable vocations frequently estranged them from other slaves, making them all the more dependent on white patrons. Given their predicaments, slave musicianers, like servile minstrels throughout history, often found themselves supporting causes contrary to their communities' best interests, or even their own.[34] Even run-of-the-mill players were likely to serve as police-state mouthpieces at one time or another, if only by fiddling and singing "Run, nigger, run, the pateroller'll catch you" at slaveholder-approved, patroller-regulated frolics. It was not much of a stretch, then, for Black musicianers to mount up and take part in night rider shivarees, none more dramatically than those who rode with the Red Shirts during South Carolina's 1876 election.

Redshirted vigilantes first appeared in Mississippi in 1875 and rapidly spread to other former slave states.[35] Four years earlier, former Union general and current Massachusetts congressman Benjamin Butler (1818–1893) had delivered a speech from the house floor inveighing against the Klan. (Butler was already especially despised throughout the South for his wartime activities, most of all for establishing the practice of freeing slaves in captured areas under the principle that they were contraband of war.) In an apocryphal story, he was alleged to have waved the bloodstained shirt of a carpetbagger whipped by Mississippi Kluxers. Southern white supremacists purportedly adopted the red flannel shirt as a uniform in response. Officially most of these groups named themselves as rifle companies or gun clubs; they were in fact organized paramilitary units of Confederate veterans, heavily armed, ranked, drilled, and battle-hardened in the deadliest war ever fought in the Western Hemisphere. Mounted, fully outfitted, arms at the ready, Red Shirts paraded and rallied at elections and other public occasions with two stated objectives: 1) preventing freed slaves, the new Republican majority, from voting and 2) electing Democratic candidates who supported their Cause.

The Red Shirt movement peaked in South Carolina, where it became closely associated with the political ambitions of former Confederate general Wade Hampton III (1818–1902). Hampton was reputedly the antebellum South's largest slaveholder and wealthiest landowner, financing his own regiment at the start of the war. The loyalty of his former slaves is more of a mystery, but legendary nonetheless. As late as 1885, Charles Dudley Warner encountered a Black street performer singing to his own banjo and guitar accompaniment in Asheville, North Carolina: "Those who could read might decipher this legend on a standard at the back of the stage: HAPPY JOHN. One of the Slaves of Wade Hampton. *COME AND SEE HIM*."[36]

In 1876 Hampton was nominated as the Democratic gubernatorial candidate against South Carolina's sitting Republican governor Daniel Chamberlain (1835–1907), who during the war had served as a lieutenant with a Black Union regiment, the 5th Massachusetts Cavalry. The lines could not have been more clearly drawn, and, in the words of Civil War historian Richard Zuczek, "far from a political canvass, the 1876 gubernatorial campaign in the Palmetto State was really a military operation, complete with armies, commanders, and bloodshed. Indeed, South Carolina might be a classic case of insurgency, with an attempt to overthrow, by terrorism and violence, a standing government."[37] Hampton, his fellow Democratic candidates (also former Confederate officers and slaveholders), and their Red Shirt enforcers added to their ranks by recruiting legions of former slaves, then launched an all-out assault on Chamberlain's administration. While some Red Shirts skirmished with the Black militias established to protect other newly freed slaves, or harassed and intimidated Republican candidates and their supporters, Hampton made a triumphant tour of the state accompanied by his own armed contingent, with local rifle companies and partisans joining in relay at every rally point before handing Hampton's caravan off to the next town. Redshirted Blacks and Black musicianers were present throughout.

Then dere was Ouillah Harrison [a prominent Black Red Shirt], dat own a four-hoss team and a saddle horse, in red shirt days. One time de brass band at Winnsboro, S. C. wanted to go to Camden, S. C. to play at de speakin' of Hampton. He took de whole band from Winnsboro to Camden dat day, free of charge. Ah! De way dat band did play all de way to Ridgeway, down de road to Longtown, cross de Camden Ferry, and right into de town. Dere was horns a blowin', drums a beatin', and people a shoutin': "Hurrah for Hampton!" Some was singin': "Hang Dan Chamberlain on a Sour Apple Tree." (Ed Barber, b. 1860, SC, 37)

On election day, November 8, 1876, Federal troops were on hand at many polls to ensure that Blacks voted freely, but the fix may have already been in for Hampton.

I got very 'ligious 'bout dat time [Reconstruction], but de brand got all rubbed out, when us went to work for Major Woodward. His 'ligion was to play de fiddle, go fox huntin', and ride 'round gittin' Negroes to wear a red shirt and vote de Democratic ticket. I went 'long wid him and done my part. They tell a tale on Marse Tom Woodward and I 'spects it's true. He was runnin' for some kind of office and was goin', nex' day, up in de dark corner of Fairfield [County] to meet people. Him hear dat a old fellow name Uriah Wright, controlled all de votes in dat box and dat he was a fox hunter to beat de band. . . . They say Marse Tom promised befo' he left to pass a bill dat no fence was to be higher than five rails, to suit fox hunters. Then de old man tell Miss Pinky to bring his fiddle, and he played "De Devil's Dream." When he finished, Marse Tom grab de fiddle and played: "Hell Broke Loose In Georgia," wid such power and skill dat de old man, Uriah, hugged Miss Pinky and cut de "Pigeon Wing" all over de floor. Marse Tom, they say, carry every vote at dat dark corner box. (Jim Henry, b. ca. 1860, SC, 267–69, orig. parentheses)

Robinson's Circus come to Union. De circus folks gib everbody a free ticket to de circus dat 'longed to de Democratic Club. Dey let all de scalawag niggers in fer registration tickets dat de Republicans had done give dem to vote fer Chamberlain. Dem niggers wanted to go to de circus wu'se dan dey wanted to do anything else. Dey never dre'mt dat dey was not going to git to vote like de carpetbaggers, and de scalawags had done tole dem to do. Fact is, dey never much cared jes' since dey got in de circus. Dem dat wanted de registration tickets back when de come out, never seed nobody to git 'em from nohows. (Pen Eubanks, b. 1854, SC, 29)[38]

Federal troops were spread too thin anyway, and in many areas the Red Shirts' intimidation of Black voters, or of poll workers and election officials, seriously disrupted the process. Worse still, some polling places degenerated into gunfire and bloodshed. Andy Brice was another ex-slave who had worn the Red Shirt and stooged for Hampton. Brice was born in 1856 in Winnsboro, leaving home just after Emancipation to escape his stepfather. He found work as a teamster with Major Thomas Brice, who taught him to drive a wagon and to fiddle, then put him in a Red Shirt. Accordingly, Andy Brice was front and center on Election Day 1876 in South Carolina.

I never was popular wid my own color. They say behind my back, in '76, dat I's a white folks nigger. I wear a red shirt then, drink red liquor, play de fiddle at de 'lection box, and vote de white folks ticket. . . .

You wants me to tell 'bout dat 'lection day at Woodward, in 1876? You wants to know de beginnin' and de end of it? Yes? Well, you couldn't wet dis old man's whistle wid a swallow of red liquor now? Couldn't you or could you? Dis was de way of it: It was set for Tuesday. Monday I drive de four-hoss wagon down to dis very town [Winnsboro]. Marse John McCrory and Marse Ed Woodward come wid me. They was in a buggy. When us got here, us got twenty, sixteen shooters and put them under de hay us have in de wagon. Bar rooms was here. I had fetched my fiddle 'long and played in Marse Fred Habernick's bar 'til dinner time. Us leave town 'bout four o'clock. Roads was

bad but us got home 'bout dark. Us put de guns in Marse Andy Mobley's store. Marse Ed and me leave Marse John to sleep in de store and to take care of de guns.

De nex' mornin', polls open in de little school house by de brick church. I was dere on time, help to fix de table by de window and set de ballot boxes on it. Voters could come to de window, put deir arms thru and tuck de vote in a slit in de boxes. Dere was two supervisors, Marse Thomas [Brice] for de democrats and Uncle Jordan [a Black] for de radicals. Marse Thomas had a book and a pencil, Uncle Jordan had de same.

Joe Foster, big buckra nigger, want to vote a stranger. Marse Thomas challenge dis vote. In them times colored preachers so 'furiate de women, dat they would put on breeches and vote de 'Publican radical ticket. De stranger look lak a woman. Joe Foster 'spute Marse Thomas' word and Marse Thomas knock him down wid de naked fist. Marse Irish Billy Brice, when him see four or five hundred blacks crowdin' 'round Marse Thomas, he jump thru de window from de inside. When he hit de ground, pistol went off pow! One nigger drop in his tracks. Sixteen men come from nowhere and sixteen, sixteen shooters. Marse Thomas hold up his hand to them and say: "Wait!" Him point to de niggers and say: "Git." They start runnin' 'cross de railroad, over de hillside and never quit runnin' 'til they git half a mile away. De only niggers left on dat ground was me, old Uncle Kantz (you know de old mulatto, clubfoot nigger), well, me and him and Albert Gladney, de hurt nigger dat was shot thru de neck was de only niggers left. Dr. Tom Douglas took de ball out Albert's neck and de white folks put him in a wagon and sent him home. I drive de wagon. When I got back, de white boys was in de graveyard gittin' names off de tombstones to fill out de talley sheets, dere was so many votes in de box for de Hampton ticket, they had to vote de dead. I 'spect dat was one resurrection day all over South Carolina. (Andy Brice, b. ca. 1856, SC, 76–79, orig. parentheses)[39]

Fig. 11.7. "Let Us Have Pieces! Give Me the State: Better Its Dissolution Than My Defeat." Wade Hampton III (left) and Daniel Chamberlain (right) in caricature, 1876. Miriam and Ira D. Wallach Division of Art, Prints, and Photographs, New York Public Library.

Hampton won the election by just over a thousand votes.

> Atter dat, all de Red Shirts met on de facade in front o' de courthouse. Mos' all de mens made a speech. Another darky sung a song like dis: "Marse Hampton was a honest man; Mr. Chamberlain was a rogue"—Den I sung a song like dis: "Marse Hampton et de watermelon, Mr. Chamberlain knawed de rine." Us jest having fun den, kaise us had done 'lected Marse Hampton as de new govenor of South Ca'linia. (Pen Eubanks, b. 1854, SC, 29)

Chamberlain, however, disputed the election's result and refused to step down. In response, Hampton and the Red Shirts blockaded Chamberlain and his government in the state capitol, then formed their own South Carolina government. Outgoing president Ulysses S. Grant (1822–1885) and his successor, Rutherford B. Hayes (1822–1893), could not or would not intervene effectively, and on April 11, 1877, the helpless Chamberlain handed South Carolina over to Hampton and the Red Shirts then fled.

As for Andy Brice, his case is by no means unique.[40] But then, fiddlers were said to serve all kinds of Devils.

Appendix: "Run, Nigger, Run"

No doubt due to its repellent topic, "Run, Nigger, Run" has received relatively little detailed discussion. No matter how presently repulsive, the song's statistical frequency among ex-slaves was exceptional, and its relevance to this study is inescapable.

The following ex-slaves performed or named "Run, Nigger, Run": TEXTS: Aunt Adeline (chorus), Barney Alford (chorus), Father Baker, John C. Bectom, Willie Blackwell, Julia "Sally" Brown (chorus), Rina Brown, Cicely Cawthon (chorus), William Curtis, Ann Drake, Sylvia Floyd, Ida May Fluker (chorus), Louis Fowler, Kitty Hill, Sallie Johnson, Hannah Jones, Chaney Mack, Cresa Mack (chorus), Tom Morris, Leo Mouton (chorus), Austin Pen Parnell, Harre Quarls, Ferebe Rogers, Joe Rollins (chorus), James Singleton (chorus), Bert Strong (chorus), Penny Thompson, Jim Threat, Henry Turner, Stephen Varner (chorus), Alfred Wells (chorus), James West, George White (chorus), Lizzie Williams (MS) (chorus), Millie Williams, Mollie Williams, Robert Williams (chorus). TITLE/FIRST LINE: Agatha Babino, Cecelia Chappel, Katie Darling, Tom Douglas, Jerry Eubanks, Rebecca Fletcher, Dora Franks, George Govan, Austin Grant, Hattie Hill, Bud Jones, Preston Kyles, Richard Mack, George Morrison, Solomon P. Pattillo, Alice Shaw, George Thomas, Aleck Trimble, Frank Williams. Texas interviewer Effie Cowan also inserted a text plagiarized from Joel Chandler Harris, *Uncle Remus and His Friends*, 200–201, in the narrative of Henry Freeman.

For period texts and references, see Henry Baker (b. 1854, AL), Blassingame, *Testimony*, 656–57 (this is the same individual as WPA narrator Father Baker); Barrow, "Corn-Shucking," 878; "Carmina Africana," 10; T. Thomas Fortune, "Melissa's Christmas Surprise," *New York Age* 13 (December 20, 1890), 3; Harris,

Friends, 200–201; Harris, *Remus*, 32, n.; "Negro Folk Songs" (*SW*), 31; "Run, nigger, run! or the M.P.'ll catch you," broadside, n.d. [ca. 1850]; "Slave Marriages," *Southern Workman* 26 (August 1897): 163; *Slave Songs*, 89; Charles White, *White's Serenaders Song-Book* (Philadelphia: T. B. Peterson and Bros., 1851), 66–68; Wyeth, *Sabre*, 63–64. For other examples, see Arnold, *Alabama*, 121; Bolick and Austin, *Mississippi Fiddle*, 68, 139, 186, 201, 271, 363, 394; Botkin, *Play Party*, 299–300; Brown I: 203–4; Brown III: 509–10, 531–33; Brown and Owens, *Toting*, 131; Cohen, *Ozark*, 225–26; *Country Music Sources*, 762–63; Davis, *Folk-Songs*, 318; Fauset, "Folk Tales," 303; Lomax, *Ballads*, 228–31; Morris, *Florida*, 25–28; Perrow, "South" (1915): 138; Randolph, *OFS* II: 338; Roberts, *Sang Branch*, 187–88; Rosenberg, *Virginia*, 110; Scarborough, *TNFS*, 12, 23–25; Sharp, *EFSSA* II: 359; Solomon, *Daisies*, 217; Talley, *NFR*, 29–30; Thede, *Fiddle*, 63; White, *ANFS*, 168–69. The text in Lomax, *Ballads*, 229–31, is taken verbatim from Harris, *Friends*, 200–201, with the incorporation of the text published in White's *Serenader's Song-Book* (1851), 66–68. Lomax's other two examples (229, 231) appear authentic. RECORDINGS: Mose "Clear Rock" Platt, "Run Nigger Run," TX, 1933, *Field Recordings, Vol. 6: Texas, 1933–1958*, Document CD 5580; Murph Gribble, John Lusk, Albert York, "Pateroller Catch You," TN, ca. 1946, *Altamont*; Elizabeth Cotton, "a) Run . . . Run/b) Mama Your Son Done Gone," *Freight Train and Other North Carolina Folk Songs and Tunes*, Smithsonian/Folkways CD 40009, 1989; Fiddlin' John Carson, "Run, Nigger, Run" (OKeh 40230, 1924); Gid Tanner & His Skillet Lickers with Riley Puckett & Clayton McMichen, "Run Nigger Run (Columbia 15158-D, 1927); Dr. Humphrey Bate & His Possum Hunters, "Run, Nigger, Run" (Brunswick 275, 1928); Sid Harkreader, "Run Nigger Run" (Paramount 3054, 1927); Uncle Dave Macon, "Run, Nigger, Run" (Vocalion 15032, 1925); Eck Robertson, "Run, Boy, Run" (Victor V-40205, 1929); Hobart Smith, "Pateroller Song," VA, 1956, *Instrumental Music of the Southern Appalachians*, Tradition CD 1061, 1997; Jim Smoak & the Louisiana Honeydrippers, "Run, Boy, Run," Baton Rouge, 1961, *Bayou Bluegrass*, Arhoolie CD 9032, 2002.

Several ex-slaves described "Run, Nigger, Run" as an unaccompanied dance or game song, or in any case mentioned no instruments. Anthony Dawson recalled it among children at play in the quarters; Tom Morris remembered that "at school we wud sing— / Run Nigger run, de patroller git yo' / Run Nigger run, it's almos' day. / Dat nigger run, dat nigger flew, / Dat nigger lost his big black shoe" (Tom Morris, b. unk., MS, 1589). More often it served as an adult dance song. "You see when I got ligion I asked de Lawd to take all de foolishness out of my head and make room for his word and you know since den its the hardest thing in de world for me to remember dose songs we useter dance by. I do 'member a few tho' lak 'Shoo, Fly,' and 'Old Dan Tucker' and 'Run, Nigger, Run, de Pateroller Catch You'" (Dora Franks, b. ca. 1837, MS, 791). "'There's a song about the patrollers.' Here Aunt Cicely sang in a musical voice, patting one foot all the while: 'Run, nigger, run, the paddy-role will catch you, run, nigger, run, the paddy-role will catch you, run, nigger, run, the paddy-role will catch you, you better get away, you better get away'" (Cicely Cawthon, b. 1859, GA, 185–86). Barney Alford, Aunt Adeline, Anthony Dawson, Julia "Sally" Brown, Cresa Mack, Alice Shaw, George White, and Lizzie Williams also gave vocal versions, and there are numerous similar examples in outside sources.

However, more ex-slaves described this as an instrumental piece, most often as a fiddle tune. Even with instruments the words were still sung, and many narrators who described instrumental versions also gave lyrics, while others may have just omitted this detail. "My father was stolen from the jungles of Africa and brought on a slave ship to Georgia. . . . He learned to play de fiddle and would play for dances. One of his favorite tunes he used to play wuz: 'Run nigger, run, de pat-a-roller'll git you; Dat nigger run, dat nigger flew, dat nigger tore his shirt in two'" (Chaney Mack, b. ca. 1864, GA, 1428). Willie Blackwell, Rina Brown, Katie Darling, Chaney Mack, Richard Mack, George Morrison, W. S. Needham Jr. (white), James Singleton, Bert Strong, George Thomas, and Beulah Van Meter (white) described the song on the fiddle;

Hannah Jones and Robert Williams on banjo; Agatha Babino and James West on fiddle and banjo; and Austin Pen Parnell on banjo and guitar. Leo Mouton had once played the song on accordion accompanied by bass fiddle.

As with most dance songs, there is considerable textual variation, but less so than in some other cases. While the piece sometimes draws from the familiar stockpile of floating stanzas, its selections are fairly limited, and many of its elements are original and appear nowhere else. Allowing, then, for natural variations, and for a handful of unusual versions, the following components, with the chorus, more or less completely account for the majority of texts.

THE FLEW-SHOE and HOLLER-COLLAR COUPLETS WPA: Willie Blackwell (wedding shoe, pants), Rina Brown (brogan shoe), Ann Drake (shirt), Sylvia Floyd (shirt), Louis Fowler (shirt), Chaney Mack (shirt), O. A. Marsh (white) (Sunday shoe), Tom Morris (big black shoe), Austin Pen Parnell (Sunday shoe), Penny Thompson (shirt), Henry Turner (shirt), Beulah Van Meter (white) (boot and shoe), James West (Sunday shoe), Millie Williams (Sunday shoe), Mollie Williams (big ol' shoe). OTHER SOURCES: Arnold, *Alabama*, 121 (shirt); Bolick and Austin, *Mississippi Fiddle*, 68 (Sunday shoe), 201 (wedding shoe), 271 (shoe), 394 (Sunday shoe, shirt); Botkin, *Play Party*, 299–300 (himself, Sunday shoes); Brown I: 203–4 (shirt); Morris, *Florida*, 25–26 (shirt); Roberts, *Sang Branch*, 187–88 (shirttail); Scarborough, *TNFS*, 12 (shirt), 24–25 (Sunday or wedding shoe, shirt); Talley, *NFR*, 29–30 (shirt); White, *ANFS*, 169 (shirt, himself). RECORDINGS: Mose "Clear Rock" Platt (1933) (Sunday shoe); Fiddlin' John Carson (1924) (gaiter shoe [spats], shirt and shoe, shirt); Skillet Lickers (1927) (himself). DISCUSSION: These couplets are found only in "Run, Nigger, Run," assuming various forms. Most often as the slave *flew*, he loses his *shoe*, or tears his *shirt* (sometimes his *pants*) *in two*; elsewhere he tears *himself* in two. Other variations or rearrangements occur: "Run nigger,

run, the patrol'll git yo', / 'cause it's almost day / That nigger run, that nigger flew, / That nigger run his head in a hornet's nest" (Sallie Johnson, b. 1855, TX, 2048). "Doggone, the paderole flew / Why in the Devil can't a nigger run too?" (John Carson, 1924); "Oh, nigger run, nigger flew, / What in the devil can a white man do?" (Skillet Lickers, 1927). The torn shirt or pants are sometimes combined with another couplet: "Up the hill an' down the holler / White man caught dat nigger by de collar / Dat nigger run an' dat nigger flew / Dat nigger tore his shirt in two" (Louis Fowler, b. 1853, GA, 1391). I have found this holler-collar couplet only in the WPA materials, but its form and distribution (as well as its logic) confirm its authenticity. (The other WPA examples are from Willie Blackwell, O. A. Marsh, and Penny Thompson.)

De darkies used to play pranks on de patrole riders by stretchin' grape vines across de road to throw de horses. At other times de slaves 'ud git a little riled up an' jump de traces a little by fightin' back with fire, but dey couldn't do much fer dey never wuz allowed to git together enough to carry out nothin'. De patrole riders kept 'em purty well rounded up an' separated only 'cept long enuf fer a little frolicin'. Dey use to sing dis ole song 'bout 'em.

> Run, nigger, run, de patrole's a commin',
> Run, nigger, run, de patrole's a commin',
> Dat nigger run, dat nigger flew
> Dat nigger tore his shirt in two
> Run, nigger, run! (Sylvia Floyd, b. ca. 1852,
> MS, 742–43)

Patrollers

I remember my father telling tales about the patrollers, but I can't remember them just now. There was an old song about them. Part of it went like this:

> Run, nigger, run
> The pateroles'll get you,

That nigger run
That nigger flew
That nigger bust
His Sunday shoe.

Run, nigger, run
The pateroles'll get you.

That's all I know of that. There is more to it. I used to hear the boys sing it, and I used to hear 'em pick it out on the banjo and the guitar. (Austin Pen Parnell, b. 1865, child of ex-slaves, MS, 268)

We had lots of dances dem days and with jus' one fiddle. Dere's de "Run, Nigger, Run" song, what go like dis:

Run, nigger, run, patteroller cotch you,
Run, nigger, run, 'cause it 'most de day.
Dat nigger run, dat nigger flew,
Dat nigger los' he weddin' shoe.

Over de hill and down de holler,
Patteroller cotch nigger by collar,
Dat nigger run, dat nigger flew,
Dat nigger tear he pants in two! (Willie Black-well, b. 1834, NC, 304)

THE PASTURE-FASTER COUPLET WPA: Harre Quarls. OTHER SOURCES: Cohen, *Ozark*, 225–26; Randolph, *OFS* II: 338; "Run, nigger, run!" broad-side; Scarborough, *TNFS*, 24; Sharp, *EFSSA* II: 359; Talley, *NFR*, 29–30; *White's Serenaders Song-Book*, 67; Wyeth, *Sabre*, 63. DISCUSSION: This verse, in which the slave runs "in the woods and thru the pasture / The white man run fast but the negro run faster" (Harre Quarls, b. 1841, TX, 3213–14), is found only once in the narratives but is popular in the tradition as a whole. Without doubt it is also original to "Run, Nigger, Run."

THE BEHIND THAT TREE COUPLET WPA: Father Baker, William Curtis, Ann Drake. OTHER SOURCES: Henry Baker (b. 1854, AL), Blassingame,

Testimony, 656–57 (this is the same individual as WPA narrator Father Baker); Harris, *Friends*, 200; "Negro Folk Songs" (*SW*), 31; Solomon, *Daisies*, 217. RECORDINGS: Mose "Clear Rock" Platt (1933); Skillet Lickers (1927). DISCUSSION: Most likely this verse is also original to "Run, Nigger, Run" and in any case first appears there. (It was later collected as a children's rhyme addressed to *Teacher* or the *Police*. See Brown I: 195.) WPA narrators Baker, Curtis, and Drake all gave the couplet in its usual form—"Dat nigger, he, sed don't ketch me, / But git dat nigger b'hind de tree" (Ann Drake, b. 1855, MS, 646)—but this element can vary considerably. A Virginia ex-slave text published in the 1895 *Southern Workman* has "I seed a patteroler hin' er tree / Tryin' to ketch po' little me" ("Negro Folk Songs" [*SW*], 31). Joel Chandler Harris's 1882 text gives it a religious twist: "I'll hide no mo' behime dat tree, / W'en de angels flock fer ter wait on me!" (*Friends*, 200–201).

Run Nigger, run
De Patteroll git ye!
Run Nigger, run,
He's almost here!

Please Mr. Patteroll,
Don't Ketch me!
Jest take dat nigger
What's behind dat tree.

Lawsy, I done heard dat song all my life and it warn't no joke neither. De Patrol would git ye too if he caught ye off the plantation without a pass from your Master, and he'd whup ye too. None of us dassn't leave without a pass. (William Curtis, b. ca. 1844, GA, 48)

"Way back yonder in slavery de paderole would git a nigger fer tryin' ter learn ter read."
"Paderole?" I asked, "what was that?"
He burst into laughter as he began to explain. "Chile, de paderole wuz ter keep bad niggers from

gittin' worse, and ter keep dem from running away. Dey wuz unmerciful white folks. Sometimes dey tie [slaves] on a log and whip 'til de blood jes' run down." He laughed again and continued. "We use ter sing a song 'bout dem." He raised a hand as he began, in a quavering treble:

> "Please ol' moster don't whip me!
> Whip dat nigger behin' de tree.
>
> O, run nigger run, paderole ketch-you
> O, run nigger run, jes' 'fore day.
>
> I run, I run, I run my bes'.
> I run right close ter dat hornets' nes'.
>
> Paderole run, dey run dey bes'.
> Dey run right in dat hornets' nes.'"

As I started to leave, Mother Baker said to Father Baker, "Give her some our sugar cane. She got good teeth. Chew it, chile, and thank God the paderole won't getcha." (Father Baker, b. 1854, AL, 33–34)

Baker's WPA interview was conducted by Rhussus L. Perry. In 1938 Baker was also interviewed by Thomas Monroe Campbell, Tuskegee graduate and US Department of Agriculture farm demonstration agent. Another version of the song appears in that interview. Blassingame, *Slave Testimony*, 656–57.

THE SLICK AS AN EEL COUPLET WPA: Ferebe Rogers. OTHER SOURCES: "Run, Nigger, Run," broadside; Thede, *Fiddle*, 63; *White's Serenaders Song-Book*, 67. DISCUSSION: This couplet, somewhat rare, is also specific to "Run, Nigger, Run." It may allude to the practice of pinioning slaves in fences to flog them.

THE BLACKSNAKE AND HORNETS COUPLETS WPA: Father Baker (hornets), Sallie Johnson (hornets), Merton Knowles (white) (hornets), Jim Threat (blacksnake, hornets). OTHER SOURCES:

Henry Baker (b. 1854, AL), Blassingame, *Testimony*, 656–57 (hornets) (this is the same individual as WPA narrator Father Baker); Arnold, *Alabama*, 121 (hornets); Bolick and Austin, *Mississippi Fiddle*, 394 (blacksnake, hornets); Brown III: 531–33 (blacksnake, hornets); Cohen, *Ozark*, 225–26 (hornets); Harris, *Friends*, 200–201 (hornets); Morris, *Florida*, 25–26 (hornets); Perrow, "South" (1915): 138 (blacksnake, hornets); Randolph, *OFS* II: 338 (hornets); Roberts, *Sang Branch*, 187–88 (blacksnake, hornets); Scarborough, *TNFS*, 24 (hornets); White, *ANFS*, 169 (hornets); Wyeth, *Sabre*, 63 (blacksnake, hornets). RECORDINGS: John Carson (1924) (hornets); Skillet Lickers (1927) (hornets, blacksnake). ALONE OR IN OTHER SONGS: Bass, "Negro Songs," 425 (blacksnake, hornets); Brown III: 221 (blacksnake, hornets, with "Banjo Sam"), 224 (blacksnake, hornets, with "Row the Boat Ashore"); Browne, *Alabama*, 318–19 (blacksnake, hornets); Carlin, *Banjo*, 118 (blacksnake, hornets, with "Whar Did You Cum From?"); Perrow, "South" (1913): 158 (blacksnake, with "Eph Got the Coon"); Scarborough, *TNFS*, 100 (blacksnake, hornets, with "Johnny Booker"), 197 (rattlesnake, hornets, with "You Shall Be Free"); Talley, *NFR*, 87–88 (blacksnake, hornets, with "Outrunning the Devil"); White, *ANFS*, 139 (blacksnake, with "You Shall Be Free"), 203 (blacksnake, hornets, with "You Shall Be Free"), 245–46 (blacksnake, hornets, with "Raise a Ruckus"); 449 (blacksnake, hornets, 1854 minstrel songbook). DISCUSSION: These couplets—in which the slave receives a snakebite on the heel, then jams his head in a hornet's nest—may appear alone or together. They most likely originated independently or in another song, later wandering into "Run, Nigger, Run" (and numerous other items).

THE SOME FOLKS SAY STANZA WPA: John C. Bectom, Kitty Hill, Hannah Jones, Merton Knowles (white), John Moore. OTHER SOURCES: Brown III: 509–10; Harris, *Friends*, 200–201; Lomax, *Ballads*, 229–31; Morris, *Florida*, 25–26; *Slave Songs*, 89; Solomon, *Daisies*, 217. RECORDINGS: Skillet Lickers (1927). ALONE OR IN OTHER SONGS:

Bass, "Negro Songs," 425; Botkin, *Play Party*, 322–23, 326–27 (with "Ain't Gonna Rain No More"); Brown III: 116, 508–10, 566 (with "Eph Got the Coon"); Brown and Owens, *Toting*, 26–27 (with "Satisfied"); Carlin, *Banjo*, 118 (with "Whar Did You Cum From?"); "Carmina Africana," 10; Ford, *Traditional*, 373; *Gumbo Ya-Ya*, 483–84; Hearn, *Levee*, 72; Lomax, *FSNA*, 508–10 (with "You Shall Be Free"); Odum and Johnson, *Workaday*, 174 (with "Raise a Ruckus"); Charles Peabody, "Notes on Negro Music," *JAF* 16 (1903): 149; Perrow, "South" (1915): 135–37 (with "You Shall Be Free"); Piper, "Play Party," 276 (with "Skip to My Lou"); Scarborough, *TNFS*, 224–25 (with "You Shall Be Free"); Frank Shay, *My Pious Friends and Drunken Companions* (1927; rpt. New York: Dover, 1961), 31; Solomon, *Daisies*, 164, 215 (with "Satisfied"); Talley, *NFR*, 95; White, *ANFS*, 137–38 (with "You Shall Be Free"), 370–72, 449. DISCUSSION: This description of a Black caught pilfering a cornfield is one of the South's most popular floating verses. It is often attributed to minstrelsy and in any case has strong minstrel connections. It regularly occurs in "Run, Nigger, Run" but is best known from other songs. Most WPA versions are fairly conventional, but Hannah Jones gave a unique text; her inclusion of the *Gatling gun* (patented November 4, 1862) is an obvious anachronism, but the antebellum attribution is otherwise plausible.

We useta have a man on de place dat played a banjo, an' we would dance an' play while he sang. Dis was one of his songs:

> White folks says a nigger won't steal
> But I cotched six in my cawnfiel'
> If you want to see a nigger run.
> Shoot at dat nigger wid a gattlin' gun. (Hannah Jones, b. ca. 1845, VA, 239)

This *some folks say* verse is in turn closely associated with another wandering stanza that also occasionally appears in "Run, Nigger, Run" but more often independently or other songs.

> Yes Sir, Cap'n, I kin tell yo sum er dem old songs whut de niggers used ter sing in de slabery times. Dis is sum of em: . . .

> My old Mistis promised me
> dat when she died, she gwine set me free,
> But she lived so long an got so po
> dat she lef me diggin wid er garden ho. (Abram Harris, b. 1845, SC, 175)

Beginning in the 1840s, this verse regularly appeared in minstrel songbooks, though Joel Chandler Harris and other period sources attribute it to slaves. Tom Windham, who had served in the Union army, recalled it from the war years. Jack White remembered it as a field holler, Jake Desso as a dance song. White interviewer Merton Knowles included the stanza in a text of "Run, Nigger, "Run" that he provided (SS1 5 *IN*: 69). Whether ex-slave John Moore (below) sang the lines as a verse in "Run, Nigger, Run" or as a separate piece is unclear (I would guess the former). For other instances in "Run, Nigger, Run," see Harris, *Friends*, 200–201; "Negro Folk Songs" (*SW*), 31; Solomon, *Daisies*, 217. ALONE OR IN OTHER SONGS: Arnold, *Alabama*, 94; Botkin, *Play Party*, 322, 324 (with "Ain't Gonna Rain No More"); Brown III: 222, 502–3, 542, 555–56; "Carmina Africana," 10; Loraine Darby, "Ring-Games from Georgia," *JAF* 30 (1917): 220; *Gumbo Ya-Ya*, 447; Davis, *Folk-Songs*, 318; Killion and Waller, *Georgia*, 225; Kinnard, "National Poets," 333; Lomax, *FSNA*, 508–10 (with "You Shall Be Free"); Odum and Johnson, *Workday*, 173–75 (with "Raise a Ruckus"), 175 (with "Ring Jing"), 176 (with "Gwine to Git a Home"); *Out of Sight*, 107; Parrish, *Sea Islands*, 118, 121 (with "Bile Them Cabbage Down"), 234; Perrow, "South" (1915): 138 (with "Johnny Booker"); Rosenberg, *Virginia*, 87; Scarborough, *TNFS*, 106 (with "Jim-A-Long Josie"), 164–65, 194 (with "You Shall Be Free"), 223–36; Solomon, *Daisies*, 114, 119, 215 (with "Satisfied"); Talley,

NFR, 21–22; Toll, *Blacking Up*, 260, 268; White, *ANFS*, 134 (with "You Shall Free"), 151–52.

We has dances sometimes and sings

> Run, nigger, run,
> De patteroles git you;
> Run, nigger run,
> It's almos' day.

Or we sings

> My old missus promise me
>   Shoo a la a day,
> When she die she set me free
>   Shoo a la a day.
> She live so long her head git bald,
>   Shoo a la a day.
> She give up de idea of dyin' a-tall,
>   Shoo a la a day. (John Moore, b. 1843,
>   LA, 126)

WHITE VERSIONS OF "RUN, NIGGER, RUN" IN THE EX-SLAVE NARRATIVES. TEXTS Merton Knowles, O. A. Marsh, Beulah Van Meter. TITLE: W. S. Needham. DISCUSSION: W. S. Needham Jr., the child of a Mississippi slaveholder, was one of several whites interviewed for the Texas ex-slave narratives project. He named this item among the pieces he learned to fiddle from one of his father's slaves (SS2 10 *TX* 9: 4364–65). There are also three full texts from whites included in the narratives, two of which actually came from fieldworkers, both from Indiana. Beulah Van Meter, "whose grandfather was a Kentucky slave holder," had learned the song from family members; Merton Knowles had heard it in Fountain County, suggesting Black migrants or returning Union troops as possible sources. The third example comes from another white interviewed by the Texas Writers' Project. O. A. Marsh (b. 1860, Hazelhurst, MS) had at birth inherited 1,040 acres and nineteen slaves. "Most

of the land was in timber, this explaining why we didn't own the usual ratio of one slave to work each ten acres" (SS2 10 *TX* 9: 4353). He attributed his version to those slaves.

Folklore—Songs Merton Knowles
                Fountain County, Indiana
                          8/17/36

Reference: Memory of Writer
Fountain County received immigrants from at least three sources; from New England, Pennsylvania and Ohio and The South. From the latter came negro songs which became a part of our Folklore. Some were also brought from the South by returning Federal soldiers.

Negro Folk Song:
> My ole missus promise me
> When she died she'd set me free
> But she done dead this many years ago
> And here I'm a hoein' the same old row.

> O run, nigger, run, the paterollers* ketch you
> Run, nigger, run, it's almost day.

> Some folks say that a nigger won't steal
> But I caught one in my corn field.
> He run to the east, and he run to the west
> And he run his head in a hornet's nest.

> * patrol (SS1 5 *IN*: 69; orig. note)

I remember several of the songs about these men [Patter Rollers]. There was a large number of them, but I remember only these two verses:

> Run nigger run, Pattyroll catch you.
> Run nigger run, 'case its almost day.
> Dat nigger run, dat nigger flew,
> Dat nigger lost his Sunday shoe.

Now, I never saw a negro that had a Sunday shoe in those days but that's the way the ditty went. They were all barefooted in those days. Another ditty went this way:

> Up the hill and down the holler,
> White man caught dat nigger by the collar;
> Dat nigger run an' dat nigger flew,
> Dat nigger lost his Sunday shoe.

I don't recall any more of them right now, but they will give you an idea of the fear the patrolmen struck into the negroes. (O. A. Marsh, SS2 10 *TX* 9: 4353–58)

The song, "Run Nigger Run," was sung in derision to begin with but the melody was well adopted to the fiddle and became a favorite dance piece throughout Kentucky and southern Indiana. The words and music were handed down through the family of the writer, whose grandfather was a Kentucky slave holder.

> Run, nigger, run,
> Or a (Pattyroll) will catch you,
> Run, nigger, run.
> And we'll all get away.
> Nigger ran and nigger flew
> Nigger lost his boot and shoe.
> Run, nigger, run,
> Or a Pattyroll will catch you,
> Run, nigger, run,
> And we'll all get away. (Beulah Van Meter, SS1 5
> *IN*: 227–28, orig. parentheses)

DEALING WITH THE DEVIL

At the little village of Stanton Drew, in the county of Somerset, east of the road between Bristol and Wells, stands a well-known Druidical monument.... Although the largest stones are much inferior in their dimensions to those at Stonehenge and Abury, they are by no means contemptible; some of them being nine feet in height by twenty-two feet in girth. There is a curious tradition very prevalent amongst the country people, respecting the origin of these remains.... Many hundred years ago (on a Saturday evening), a newly married couple, with their relatives and friends, met on the spot now covered with these ruins, to celebrate their nuptials. Here they feasted and danced right merrily, until the clock tolled the hour of midnight, when the piper (a pious man) refused to play any longer: this was much against the wish of the guests, and so exasperated the bride (who was fond of dancing), that she swore with an oath, she would not be baulked in her enjoyment by a beggarly piper, but would find a substitute, if she went to hell to fetch one. She had scarcely uttered the words, when a venerable old man, with a long beard, made his appearance, and having listened to their request, proffered his services, which were right gladly accepted. The old gentleman (who was no other than the Archfiend himself) having taken the seat vacated by the godly piper, commenced playing a slow and solemn air, which on the guests remonstrating he changed into one more lively and rapid. The company now began to dance, but soon found themselves impelled round the performer so rapidly and mysteriously, that they would all fain have rested. But when they essayed to retire, they found, to their consternation, that they were moving faster and faster round their diabolical musician, who had now resumed his original shape. Their cries for mercy were unheeded, until the first glimmering of day warned the fiend that he must depart. With such rapidity had they moved, that the gay and sportive assembly were now reduced to a ghastly troop of skeletons. "I leave you," said the fiend, "a monument of my power and your wickedness to the end of time": which saying he vanished. The villagers, on rising in the morning, found the meadow strewn with large pieces of stone, and the pious piper lying under a hedge, half dead with fright,

Fig. 12.1. "The new country dance, as danced at C****, July the 30th 1766." London: J. Pridden in Fleet Street, 1776. "Includes 32 lines of verse in 8 stanzas which end with the refrain 'Doodle, doodle, doo.'" The illustration is from a Colonial-era English broadside combining current Court intrigues with British fiddle-and-devil lore. According to the catalog summary, the "print shows a number of prominent figures in a line dancing, above the dancers is John Wilkes riding behind a witch on a broom, he is defecating on Lord Bute; other dancers include the Prince of Wales, William Pitt (the Earl of Chatham), a Native American woman representing America, the devil dancing with Henry Fox (Lord Holland), . . . George III playing the fiddle," and various other nobles and notables. King George and his fiddle (far left) are flanked by two bagpipers in kilts and bonnets. George's caption reads "I'll fiddle dee dee." Meanwhile, the Devil—far right—declares "Ive got my Old Partner," to which Lord Holland replies, "Aye, You and I Have long connived." British Cartoon Prints Collection, Library of Congress, Prints and Photographs Division.

he having been witness to the whole transaction. (David Stevens, "Stanton Drew and Its Tradition," 1851; rpt. *Choice Notes From "Notes and Queries": Folk Lore* [London: Bell and Daldy, 1859], 182–83)[1]

I recollect one night, I wuz little but its almos' lak it happen yesterday, de darkies wuz havin' a frolic in a old vacant house. Dis frolic wuz lak all de res' ob 'em, wid dancin' by fiddle music, a playin' "Turkey In de Straw" an' "Molly Put De Kettle On." Dey would skip an' play games. It got 'round close to midnight when things wuz likely to happened. Well everything wuz gwine purty when all at once a terrible lookin' man wid fiery eyes run fas' as he could plumb through de crowd an' he wuz a shoutin' "dance up hogs, you ain't half a dancin'." He run on out through de back door an' on into de woods. Part ob de crowd nearly broke deir necks a jumpin' out ob windows a gittin away from deir; while others believed dey had to mind dat ghos' an' went to dancin' fo' all dey wuz wuth. And when dey did de house caved in. I has wondered since den which wuz de bes' off, de ones dat run scart to death out in de nite or de ones dat stayed. (Lucy Donald, b. 1857, MS, 639–40)

The Devil often crashed parties in early America, just as he had for centuries in Britain and Europe. He was particularly drawn to dancers and dance musicians, initially bagpipers and fiddlers, later banjo and guitar players. African Americans got to know him especially well. Some like Lucy Donald swore they had actually seen him on the dance floor, betrayed by his cloven hooves or glowing eyes. For others he was an unseen but omnipresent menace dancing indefatigably any- and everywhere. "Aint no t'ing ebber discourage dat bad sperrit. 'E laugh an' 'e dance de debbil dance any time, an' 'e say de path aint wide 'nough for all dem foot, an dem ones is him meat, an' 'e sho do rotten dem" (Ophelia Jemison, b. ca. 1868, SC, child of ex-slaves, 227). And sometimes he was merely a fairy-tale bogey man or figure of speech. Not everyone took the stories seriously, but even in casual conversation the fiddle was the *Devil's box*, fiddling was the *Devil's work*, reels were the *Devil's tunes*, ballads the *Devil's ditties*, and so on.

If the credence given the Devil is not always clear, there is no mistaking the widespread notion that some kinds of music were wicked enough to summon—or at least to suggest—Satan himself. Among the slaves this was, in fact, a major source of real-world conflict within individuals, families, and communities, directly affecting people's lives, relationships, and behaviors. "I was sinful for a long time. I kept on dancing and singin' reels and cotillion songs. But I ain't did that for a long time now. I wanted to do right but I guess I had a lot of devil in me" (Rosa Maddox, b. ca. 1848, LA, 2529). "I ain't never danced a step nor sung a reel in my life. My Ma allus said we shouldn't do them things and we didn't. She say if we went to the devil it wouldn't be 'cause she give us her 'mission!'" (Emma Hurley,

b. ca. 1855, GA, 279). "No suh, I never belonged to no ch'uch; dey thought I done too much of the devil's work—playin' the fiddle. Used to play the fiddle for dances all around the neighborhood" (William Little, b. 1855, AR, 262).

The Devil's longstanding association with music and musicians is common knowledge. In the late twentieth century, his folkloric links to American fiddlers and blues guitarists gained world fame through reinterpretations in popular music, print, and film, the story of the blues musician's crossroads pact with Satan being especially well publicized. Less has been written on the theme's traditional roots, and much of what has appeared is vague or misleading. Many authors appear to have composed their own narrowly purposed versions of deeply rooted folk legends, conveniently ignoring scores of oral sources (this is to be assumed for creative works, of course). Following fashion, others have strained after ill-conceived African origins.[2] Africans may have arrived in North America somewhat predisposed to the notion that certain forms of music are inherently demonic or evil, but such sentiments are foreign to African cultures, and African Americans not only borrowed these beliefs from outsiders, they expressed them largely through European, specifically British and Irish folktales. As of the mid-1800s, Mississippi Blacks like Lucy Donald were telling the same stories as Somerset peasants.

From the beginning, much of this lore revolved around the fiddle, which was actually introduced into Europe and sub-Saharan Africa around the same time (the late Middle Ages) and from the same source (the Islamic world). In all three areas fiddles became associated with the Christian-Muslim concept of the Devil, but for different reasons. Christendom and Islam, that is, share a dualistic view of good and evil (the basis of the Devil they also hold in common), which led them to draw a rigid distinction between the sacred and secular spheres that is unknown in traditional African societies. Historically, fundamentalist Christians and Muslims alike have shunned secular entertainments and recreations, but especially male-female social dancing and its musical accompaniments, regarded as nothing less than instruments of the Devil. The fiddle was preeminently evil simply because of its abundance in Europe and the Islamic world from the late medieval through the modern eras (lesser dance instruments were similarly vilified).

Fiddles may have entered Africa with Islam, but following their adoption they were doubly damned for Muslims, played not only recreationally but for trance dancing in pre-Islamic rites. In fact, the anathemas of early Muslim chroniclers provide the earliest evidence for these developments.[3] It was outsiders like these, Muslim and Christian, who introduced into Africa the idea of music as evil. Following his 1620–21 voyage up the Gambia, Englishman Richard Jobson became the first European to describe West African *jalis* (griots):

> Juddies, or as wee may terme them, Fidlers of the Countrey, neither the musike they make or instruments they play upon, deserving to have a better title: and may sort also reasonable well to the company, because at all especiall meetings their divell *Ho-re* makes on the relation. . . . And this one especiall note, howsoever the people affect musicke, yet so basely doe they esteeme of the player, that when any of them die, they doe not vouchsafe them buriall, as other people have, but set his dead corps upright in a hollow tree, where hee is left to consume: when they have beene demanded a reason for so doing, they will answer, they are a people, who have always a familiar conversation with their divell *Ho-re*: and therefore do they dispose of them.[4]

Jobson was projecting his own beliefs, of course, but he thereby also documented the *jalis*' ties to spirit possession, even if these spirits were in no way counterparts of his Christian "divell." Whether Jobson communicated these views to his Africans hosts is unclear, but other European visitors definitely voiced such sentiments from an early date.[5] Between 1811 and 1812 William John Burchell (1781–1863) traveled through South Africa with a group of Hottentots who enjoyed dancing to a homemade fiddle. "They even considered it a relaxation of strict discipline and a favor, that I permitted such an instrument to be used: this I discovered by Juli's seriously asking me, whether it was really sinful to dance, or to play on the fiddle; for, said he, the missionaries tell us that such things are an abomination to God, and that a *fiddle* is Satan's own instrument!" (Burchell did his best to dispel what he described as an "absurd doctrine.")[6]

Observers have sometimes marveled at how readily African Americans mastered the European violin, even though fiddles have been played in Africa for as long as in Europe. It may be that something in their African backgrounds also predisposed American slaves to the notion that dancing and dance music—and the fiddle especially—were evil. Indigenous African beliefs definitely assume fundamental links between music, magic, and religion, and having adopted the fiddle from Muslims (or the violin from Europeans), Africans intuitively tied it to their own spirit worlds. These are fairly universal associations, however, and there are irreconcilable differences between African concepts of musically induced spirit possession (used for healing or to help individuals through other life crises) and the demonic possessions ascribed to Muslim or European fiddlers and their Anglo- and African American counterparts. On the other hand, by the beginning of the transatlantic slave trade, Muslims had for centuries demonized African music and musicians—none more so than the fiddlers playing for male-female social dancing and pre-Islamic possession rites—and large numbers of slaves would have arrived in the Americas having heard these opinions, perhaps directed at them personally. Significantly too, by this period Africans were encountering similar sentiments from Christian watchdogs no different from those they would meet on the other side of the Atlantic.

Whatever the underlying causes, from their arrival in North America, Blacks embraced this musicmaking-as-a-deal-with-the-Devil concept with a passion. There is, moreover, no question that slaves acquired such notions mainly from Anglo-Americans in the New World. Folk beliefs and cultural mores spread through various means, some less perceptible or easily traceable than others. These particular beliefs are easier to pinpoint than some, because among other means they spread through a complex of well-documented, fully developed English-language folktales elaborating the specific musical conditions under which people encounter the Devil, and the various possible outcomes. Shared by whites and Blacks in America (and especially the American South), virtually all of these stories can be traced directly back to Britain and Ireland.

That notwithstanding, in America these tales came to be associated almost entirely with African Americans: not only were they most often collected from Blacks, but even Anglo-Americans usually told them about Black fiddlers, Black banjo players, Black guitarists. Several causes suggest themselves, not least the prominence if not predominance of African American musicians (especially fiddlers) from the colonial era through the late nineteenth century. Throughout this same period, Blacks generally were tied to the Devil or otherwise demonized, views even they acknowledged or internalized.[7] Then too, musicians around the world have long recognized the publicity value of diabolical reputations—the concert violinists Giuseppe Tartini (1692–1770) and Niccolò Paganini (1782–1840) fostered rumors that they had the Devil's backing—and African American musicians in particular have deliberately cultivated such images or been subject to such stories.[8]

African Americans may have made these tales their own, but there is no question that their villain is the Christian Devil, more precisely the European folk Devil. Across Europe, the Devil assumes various guises: archfiend, stupid ogre, supernatural helper, trickster, master builder, musical virtuoso.[9] Medieval theologians, clerics, and inquisitors identified him with the biblical Satan or Lucifer, definitely doing more than their share to tie him to music and dance.[10] However, the Devil's folk incarnations were often pre-Christian holdovers, and in English-language tradition most of the musical activities alleged to the Devil were previously attributed to fairies. Like the

Devil, fairies are consummate singers, dancers, and musicians who sometimes imparted these abilities to mortals, albeit at a hefty price. Bagpipes, flutes, and fiddles are their inventions, as are specific songs, tunes, and dance steps.[11] They draw mortals into music and dance competitions, carting the losers off to the underworld. Fairy music can compel humans to dance until they turn to stone or crumble to dust; mortal musicians tricked into playing for fairy dances run similar risks.[12]

Following a general historical trend, Satan gradually replaced the fairies in these stories, by which time fiddles had eclipsed pipes and flutes in Britain, the legends registering that in due proportion as well. This was the form in which the tales reached North America, where they gained wide currency in New England but even more so in the southern slave states. I have in fact found no fewer than 124 US English-language texts (chap. appendix A). The majority are from Blacks and have been recreated to varying degrees. Some were absorbed into the lore of conjure or hoodoo, others were combined with ghost stories slaves also learned from whites. Still others acquired distinctly African American or uniquely personal touches. The most common theme is learning instrumental music from the Devil, closely followed by dance, but there are additional subplots. The instruments most commonly mentioned are fiddles, though banjos, guitars, and others (accordions, pianos, organs, harmonicas) were added as they came into fashion. Texts range from lengthy and detailed narrations to brief offhand statements: "To [learn] a guitar . . .—go to the forks of the road at midnight. The devil comes and teaches you to play it."[13] The tale may be told in the third person or as a personal experience. Numerous examples follow the how-to format of conjure tricks and charms, stated as instructions, prescriptions, or prohibitions, perhaps with specific cases as illustrations.

Notwithstanding these transformations, American texts retain dozens of identifiable elements from the British supernatural folktale repertoire, from which they also take their basic plots.[14] Indeed, despite their remarkable variety, all US texts can be grouped into a mere four scenarios governing musical entanglements with the Devil. In the first and most common, someone deliberately summons the Devil to learn to play music or dance; in a second scenario, someone deliberately summons the Devil *with* music or dance but for some other purpose. In a third variation, musicians or dancers inadvertently produce the Devil; or he may entrap people by possessing their musical instruments, which must then be burned, smashed, or otherwise exorcised (the fourth possibility).

Scenario I

I know a Nigger that they sed wuz kin ter the devil. He told me that he could go out hind the house and make some noise and the devil would come and dance with him. He sed the devil learned him to play a banjo and if you wanted to do anything the devil could do, go to a cross road walk backwards and curse God. But don't nebber let the devil touch any of your works or anything that belonged to you or you would lose your power. (Amanda Styles, b. 1856, GA, 345)

Once upon a time there lived a girl. She wanted to know any kind of dance, and sing any kind of song. One day while she was alone, a man stood before her. He said, "You are always thinking about dancing and singing." He said, "If you want to, I will make you so as long as you want to. You must give your soul to my master when your time is up."—"I should like to be with him for twenty-eight years," she said. The time rolled by quickly. When her time was up, she heard a loud noise, saying, "I am coming! I am coming! I am coming after you! According to your word, I am coming after you!" The master had come after her soul. She did not want to give him her real soul. She took up an old shoe-sole and threw it at him. The ugly, manlike thing did not know the difference, and he was contented. (William Herbert, b. unk., Hampton Institute, Elizabeth City Co., VA, ca. 1899)[15]

Scenario II

De Boss said one man was treated mean and they could not do anything with him. The old fellow would play his gourd and de snakes would come 'round. Finally dey sent him down to New Orleans and sold him on the block. (Rhody Holsell, b. 1848, MO, 202)

Ah've heard dat yo' go to de fo'k of de road between midnight an' day an' yo' take with yo' a violin, an' whatevah de person wants tuh do at de fo'k of de road twelve and one o-clock in de night, dey say they will play that violin an' whatevah evil dey wants done, why that evil spirit will come tuh dem. An' dey will have a conversation wit de evil spirit an' dey can *call dat evil spirit to dwell around an' aggravate de person dat dey want dis evil thing done to.* An' will cause dis person, yo' know, to lose his mind like yo' know, an' holler things in de night. (Anon., GA, ca. 1930, orig. emphasis)[16]

Scenario III

We never wah afraid of no spooks, 'cause dey ain't no sich in dis world. When we die an' answer God's call and is put away, we is jus' dust lak in de beginnin' an' dey ain't no spooks or ha'nts. One time I pass a graveyard after dark an' I ain't afraid of no ghosts meetin' me dar. I ain't afraid of nuffin' 'cause when we is all dead we is nuffin' mo' den jus' dust. I hear tell one time of a man goin' into de graveyard to play his fiddle, sayin' he wah not afraid of no ghosts, but he got scared of somethin' and went into spasms, an' he yell and holler and ever after dat day wah crazy lak a loon. (Lucy Lewis, b. ca. 1830, TX, 2366–67)

Dere is lots of evil around Columbus. Dey puts horse shoes over de door but dat don't turn de evil spirits. We went to a dance out at Dr. Brothers' brother's home. We was up stairs and fo God we was sittin there, preachers, too, and a door was pitched down on us. Oh, I done some running. Dat house is dere now, but

Somin brings em out. Looks like de house goin to be tore down every night. Dey jes runs around all over de house. (Jerry Eubanks, b. 1846, MS, 698–99)

Scenario IV

Shortly after I came to Algiers, I met up with Jim Alexander, whom Marie Laveau called in to work in a certain line. . . . I learned all the secrets of hoodooism. I and Alexander broke up evil spirits in Algiers. At the corner of Valette and Evilina lived a man by the name of Hennessy. Had an adopted daughter—a girl of about twelve—who was possessed of a devil. A neighbor by the name of Leander Joseph witnessed the events. That night she was going from one room to another with a lamp in her hand, when all a sudden she went whirling about the room and was set on a table, and then went whirling again.

The next day, when she was in the kitchen at twelve o'clock, every piece of stove wood broke through a window and fell in the yard. This was in 1882, and Algiers was excited. Hennessy moved the girl from his house nine blocks away to Cash Street, to Leander's house. That night the piano suddenly began to play. No one was near it. It played all night and finally moved itself to the middle of the floor. The third night the spirit visited other places on Valette Street.

Then they sent for Alexander. He got me, we went there together. He lit three candles, got a brand new dinner bucket, bought a quart of beer, and sent everybody from room. He then threw the beer all over the room—into the corners, everywhere. We then went to the other house and did the same thing. (N. H. Hobley, b. 1858, LA, 118–19)

When Jim Allen Vaughan of the Menola community of Hertford County, North Carolina, was a boy in the 1880s he wanted himself a banjo but he did not have enough money to buy one. So he decided to make one. He obtained a large gourd, cut out one side and covered it over with a shorn sheep hide. A white woman gave him a spool of cotton for the strings.

"I got so I could pick the thing right good, and I thought a whole heap of it," said Jim Allen, "but as you know the banjo is the Devil's music instrument. My music box got all crossed up."

About midnight one night Jim Allen was awakened by the noise of something picking his banjo. "I could hear it real clear, but I could see no one. I knew the Devil liked to play the banjo; so I got real scared. I wrapped my head under the kiver. Next day I burned that thing up."

The Devil did not return after that. (Jim Allen Vaughan, b. unk. NC)[17]

The foregoing examples only hint at the variety in the assembled texts; yet those texts are also remarkably consistent in playing out the four basic scenarios. Sabbath-breaking is the act that most commonly summons the Devil, whether a fiddler deliberately courts him at a crossroads at midnight Saturday, or dancers carelessly carry on into Sunday. In the latter case, Satan may actually appear on the dance floor. Otherwise, the most common site for an encounter is a four-way crossroads or fork-of-the-road (sometimes understood as a crossroads, sometimes as one road that splits into two), but graveyards are also popular, bridges only slightly less so.[18] Trees (cedar, holly, oak) also figure as landmarks, but more rarely. Anyone asking the Devil's help may first have to withstand a fear test—usually a succession of specters culminating in Satan himself. He most often appears as a Black man, but also as a black dog; a horseman; a fiend with glowing eyes or cloven hooves; a fireball; a rabbit, a blacksnake, or black bull. In the tradition of English witch-lore, various rites and incantations invert scripture or mock Christian ritual: the initiate may be told to go to the crossroads and draw a cross at the center, to kneel and pray to the Devil and curse God, to say the Lord's Prayer in reverse while walking backwards, and so forth.[19] Animal sacrifice is another common summons, most often a rooster or black cat, the latter killed in advance to obtain a *black cat bone* or *witch bone*.[20] The Devil is usually fearsome and menacing, but occasionally recalls the stupid ogre of European folktales, easily duped into deceptive bargains. Thus, mortals who have sold their souls can extend the term or escape altogether by giving the Devil the soles of their shoes instead.[21] Or the Devil may play the trickster himself: any money musicians receive from him as payment or as part of their deals turns to shit in their pockets.[22] Petitioners may acquire the desired skills merely by observing the rites or withstanding the tests, or the Devil may provide personal instruction, sometimes by showing them how to dance or play, sometimes just by retuning their instruments or clipping their fingernails.

These are, incidentally, the same rites one performs to become a witch, so entering a musical pact with Satan also makes one a sorcerer, bestowing the power to recall him for other purposes (Scenario II). However, people can accidentally summon Satan by the same or similar means (Scenario III), as in the stories of dance parties that last into Sunday or violate other taboos. Jerry Eubanks recalled how the presence of preachers at a dance drew evil spirits, but profanity or blasphemy alone may be enough. In other tales a musician or dancer headed home after breaking a vow to stop at midnight Saturday meets the Devil at a crossroads, graveyard, or bridge, usually followed by a music or dance competition, less often by a music or dance lesson.

Finally, in some accounts the forbidden instrument itself binds someone to the Devil (Scenario IV): whether because of an unholy compact, some careless infraction (such as Sabbath-breaking), or simply because some instruments are intrinsically evil, a fiddle, banjo, guitar, or other instrument seems to play by itself (the Devil is really playing it) until exorcised or destroyed, typically presaging its owner's reformation.[23] Like those who knowingly contract with the Devil, persons who unwittingly contact him tend to survive: mortal fiddlers usually win contests, demonically possessed fiddles are easily eliminated. This is not always so, however, and people tricked into dancing with the Devil are prone to bad outcomes, especially women. This may be because, of the two offenses, dancing or playing a fiddle, fundamentalists held dancing the foremost sin, musical instruments being lesser accessories. That women are mainly scapegoated might further suggest the Christian tenet that women are to blame for all the world's sins, including, by logical extension, male-female dancing.

Given the tradition's British origins, it is remarkable that Black texts hold such a wide margin over white; there are even indications that some Anglo-American versions derive not from Britain but from Black tradition.[24] Other divisions are likewise suggestive. Examples of the first and second scenarios—in which performers deliberately court Satan—are almost without exception told by and about Blacks: only two out of the eighty texts are from whites. By contrast, the third and fourth scenarios—in which people inadvertently summon the Devil—are predominantly Anglo-American: thirty-five of the forty-four texts are from whites, only nine from Blacks. The collective judgment seems to be that Blacks are fairly comfortable dealing musically with demons, whereas whites only fall into that trap by accident, then to escape.

But that begs the question of whether everybody believed these stories, or believed them the same way. The most sensible conclusion is that the slaves responded to these stories exactly the same way people would respond to them today. Modern people may look back at the *superstitions* of earlier generations with horror and amusement, but all indications are that religious and supernatural beliefs have remained remarkably constant since our species evolved. A 2008 Harris Poll of 2,126 US adults reported that 59 percent believed in the Devil, 27 percent did not, and 14 percent were unsure. In other findings, 68 percent believed in a material soul (the kind you can sell to the Devil), 62 percent in Hell, 44 percent in ghosts, and 31 percent in witches.[25] The WPA materials and other evidence (including the constancy of human nature) give every reason to believe that these levels were roughly the same for American slaves, meaning that a majority probably took the stories seriously (at least to a degree), but that many did not.

Even then, it was seldom a simple matter of believing or not believing. Avowed skeptics may hedge their opinions. People harbor personal beliefs they would never admit publicly, while in social situations people acquiesce to beliefs they really doubt or reject. Others willingly suspend disbelief for the sake of a good story, and so forth. The ex-slaves suggest all of these complexities and contradictions and more. Lucy Donald had herself seen Satan on the dance floor ("An' he wuz a shoutin' 'dance up hogs, you ain't half a dancin'"). Amanda Styles merely knew a man reputed to have done the crossroads deal ("He sed the devil learned him to play a banjo"). Lucy Lewis scoffed at such stories ("We never wah afraid of no spooks, 'cause dey ain't no sich in dis world"), then told of another skeptic incurably possessed when he tempted the Devil by playing his fiddle in a graveyard ("An' he yell and holler and ever after dat day wah crazy lak a loon"). Daniel William Lewis had experienced something similar himself but did not seem to take it all that seriously.

> Every evening when I drive up the cows for milking, there's a old, old log cabin right on the way that I pass every night—and it's so haunted won't nobody pass it after the darkness covers in the daylight. I didn't always get by 'fore then, and the sounds I hear! Like they was people inside jumping and knocking on the floor, maybe they was dancing, I dunno. But they was a light in the big room. Wasn't the moon a-shining through the windows either, 'cause sometimes I would stop at the gate and say HELLO, then out go the light and the noises would stop quick, like them haunts was a-scairt as me—and then, then I run like the old preacher's Devil is after me with all his forks. (Daniel William Lucas, b. ca. 1845, MS, 201)[26]

Nancy Williams was plainly joking when she compared herself to the folktale heroine who, desperate for a dance partner, selects the Devil himself:

> Whoops! Dem dances was somepin. Dem de days when me'n de devil was runnin roun in de depths of hell. No, don' even wanna talk 'bout it. Woul'n

do it now for nottin. Lawd, Chris' in Heaven. Guess I didn' know no better den. Anyhow we'd go to dese dances; ev'y gal had a beau. An' sech music! You had two fiddles, two tambourines, two bango, and two sets o' bones. Dem deblish boys 'ud go out'n de wood an git de bones whar de cows done died. Yessuh I'se out dere in de middle o' de flo' jes' a-dancin'; me an Jennie, an de devil. Dancin' wid a glass o' water on my head an' three boys a-bettin' on me. I hada grea' big reaf roun' my head an' a big ribbon bow on each side an' didn't wase a drap o' water on neider. Jes' danced ole Jennie down. Me'n de debil won dat night. (Nancy Williams, b. 1847, NC, 316)

Many narrators seemed to regard these stories as mere jokes. Georgia ex-slave Ike Thomas was himself an in-demand fiddler at local dances, sometimes requiring him to pass an abandoned house known to be haunted.

It seems Sid Scott was a "mean nigger," and everyone was afraid of him. He was cut in two by the saw mill. After his funeral anyone who passed his house at night could hear his "hant" going "ratatat-tat-bang, bang, bang" like feet running. One night when Ike was coming home from "fiddlin'" at a white folks party, he had to pass Scott's house. Now they kept the cotton seed in half of the house and the other half was empty. When Ike got close, he made a racket and sure enough the noise started. "The moon was about an hour up" and he saw these funny white things run from under the house and scatter. It scared him at first but he looked and looked and saw they were sheep that having found a hole into the cotton seed would go in at night to eat. (Ike Thomas, b. 1843, GA, 26–27)

Thomas's tale perfectly sets the stage for an encounter with a ghost (or a fiddling Devil), but instead punctures the Sid Scott legend with a perfectly rational explanation for the strange noises and ghostly apparitions. Sometimes called *anti-legends*, anec-

dotes debunking supernatural beliefs in this manner were told alongside real ghost stories and almost as frequently.[27]

Some people, of course, held these tales to be God's own truth, and even doubters had to confront their underlying beliefs, which were taken very seriously indeed throughout the plantation South. These doctrines divided communities and tore individuals apart, often to the point of genuine self-loathing and anguish. Whether as the Prince of Darkness or a joke, the Devil definitely played a large part in how all slaves felt, thought, and talked about music and dance. Any given individual might or might not believe that the Devil physically possessed fiddles or people's feet, but that was the figure of speech. "Yassum, I'ze had de debbil in my foot w'en de fiddle sing. An' I'ze sorry to say, I'ze danced de clock to a turn a-meny a night" (Adeline Waldon, b. 1857, MO, 3917–18).

"Ma, she chop cotton and plow, and I started choppin' cotton when I wuz twelve years old. When I was a gal I sure wuz into plenty devilment."

"What kind of devilment?"

"Lawdy Miss, evy time I heayd a fiddle, my feets jes' got to dance and dancin' is devilment. But I ain't 'lowed to dance nothin' but de six-handed reel." (Nancy Settles, b. 1845, SC, 233, int. Margaret Johnson)

In fact, while Devil legends were by definition otherworldly, they bore a striking resemblance to the everyday world of the people who told them. Even skeptics or nonbelievers could spot the plotlines in their own experiences, maybe as allegory, symbol, or metaphor, maybe as simple observation or plain common sense. After all, in this culture children were taught from birth that on life's journey everyone comes to a crossroads where they must choose between God or the Devil, the church or the world, everlasting salvation or eternal damnation, hymns or fiddle songs. On that level, the crossroads legend simply registered basic cultural knowledge and personal expectation.

Then again, in daily life as in folktales, people who attended frolics—musicians particularly—did constantly traverse pitch-black rural roads in the witching hours. Typically exhausted, often under the influence, possibly horrorstruck at the debauchery and violence they had just witnessed or ashamed of their own recent behavior, individuals in these dark passways really did experience hellfire visions and born-again epiphanies, forswearing dancing or playing the Devil's music forever. Other community members had apparently contracted for life, heedlessly traveling these nether regions until death (or the Devil) claimed them.

Just like folktale characters, fiddlers who reformed might first have to destroy their instruments. Smashing or burning fiddles, banjos, and guitars to exorcise the Devil (or to burn the sinner's musical bridges) was once a widespread practice among both races in the South, the belief being that "the Devil was in the fiddle—that's the saying exactly."[28] "I was allus wild and played for dances. My wife was religious and knelt and prayed three times a day. After I married I quieted down cause she was religious. When I jined the church, I burned my fiddle up" (Willis Winn, b. 1822, LA, 4257). An item in the May 7, 1878, *Georgia Weekly Telegraph* reads: "An old negro fiddler 'got religion' a few days ago, whereupon he shivered his fiddle on the doorstep, saying: 'No man kin hab religion an' be a fiddler.'"[29] Workers demolishing Southern log cabins sometimes find fiddles dropped behind interior walls by born-again musicians who could not bear to sacrifice their instruments.[30] The custom is mentioned in an Anglo-American spiritual: "I prayed for sovereign mercy, / And Jesus filled my cup. / I went home rejoicing, / And I burned my banjo up."[31] In 1845 Sir Charles Lyell visited the Georgia Sea Islands, reporting that "on the Hopeton plantation above twenty violins have been silenced by the Methodist missionaries."[32] Guion Griffis Johnson found that missionaries also convinced slaves on St. Helena Island, South Carolina, to dispose of their fiddles, so that "the last violin on St. Helena Island before the Civil War is said to have been owned by a Negro on Coffin's Point, but he got rid of it before 'big gun shoot,' as the Negroes called

the battle of Port Royal."[33] At its root this was another British custom. By the late nineteenth century, the Isle of Lewis in the Outer Hebrides was reportedly devoid of musicians because the clergy had "made the people break and burn their pipes and fiddles. If there was a foolish man here and there who demurred, the good ministers and the good elders themselves broke and burnt their instruments." Around 1865 a Nova Scotia clergyman gathered all of the fiddles in his parish and smashed and burned them.[34]

In folktales the Devil appears to sinners at the stroke of midnight Saturday. In some jurisdictions, midnight Saturday also happened to be the legal curfew for weekly frolics, after which night riders had free reign. Most slaveholders decreed that dances end by midnight Saturday anyway, ostensibly to avoid breaking the Sabbath, but personal convenience, labor conservation, and crowd control were other clear motives. "Marse Fair let his niggers have dances and frolics on his plantation, and on Saturdays dey danced till 12 o'clock midnight. . . . In dese times de young folks dance way into Sunday mornings, and nobody to stop 'em, but Marse wouldn't let his slaves dance atter 12 o'clock" (Isabella Dorroh, b. ca. 1863, SC, 327). "Marsa never cared how much his slaves danced an' carried on, jus' so long as dey didn't do it on Sundays. Danced mos' times on Sadday nights 'cause dey got Sunday to res'" (Susie Melton, b. 1853, VA, 212). "Chile, we dance till midnight. To finish de ball, we say 'Balancez, Calinda' (Turn around, Calinda), and den twist and turn and say again, 'Balancez, Calinda,' and just turn around. Den de ball was over" (Francis Doby, b. 1838, LA, 52). "Sometimes a banjo or guitar would be added to the band. But usually the old fiddler would be the band leader and the band itself. . . . This would continue until about midnight then all would go home. 'Old Dan Tucker' was usually the piece played for the dance to disperse" (George Morrison, b. ca. 1860, KY, 146).[35]

Slaves themselves commonly expressed the belief that making music and dancing into Sunday might invoke the Devil. Or it might bring out other demons. "De frolic allus had to bust up at midnight caze Marster would git out his horse pistols an' start shootin' ef it didn't" (Robert Heard, b. ca. 1841, GA, 171). "Dey got to break up de dance at twelve o'clock. Iffen dey don't do dat, after twelve o'clock de patter-rollers go huntin' for 'em" (Chris Franklin, b. 1855, LA, 1412). Plainly the midnight deadline served slaveholders' obsession with regulating nighttime movements of slaves, as did devil-and-ghost stories. For their part, Blacks were well aware that whites told them supernatural tales to scare them indoors after dark. "The old colored fo'ks told us ghost stories they got from the white fo'ks, and we believed them too" (Sol Walton, b. 1849, TX, 3955). And they knew for a fact that people who danced past curfew were likely to meet some very evil creatures playing the parts of devils or hants. "If nigger went out without a pass de 'Paddle-Rollers' would get him. De white folks were the 'Paddle-Rollers' and had masks on their faces. They looked like niggers wid de devil in dere eyes" (Marshal Butler, b. 1849, GA, 165). "Show! Ever'body knowed about de Kloo Kluxes! One bunch of 'em come there one night, ridin' mules. Had things over dey eyes. You'd think hit was de devil" (Simon Hare, b. AL, 1849, 919). "Lawd, Lawd, does I know 'bout de Ku-Kluxes? I know aplenty. Dey wuz shore nuff debbils walkin de earth seekin what dey could devour" (Charlie Davenport, b. ca. 1837, MS, 566). "Mistess, I 'clar to goodness, paterollers was de devil's own hosses. If dey cotched a Nigger out and his Marster hadn't fixed him up wid a pass, it was jus' too bad; dey most kilt him" (William McWhorter, b. ca. 1860, GA, 98).

Ex-slaves had seen the Devil or his servants elsewhere in their daily experiences. "I had a good master, but my Mistress was a devil. I don't believe I can tell you how I was treated" (Susan Merritt, b. 1851, TX, 2643). "My marster, old Buck Adams, could out-mean de devil hisself. I say to my daughter dat it was all Buck Adams meanness dat I seen dat make me lose my eye sight" (William Mathews, b. 1848, LA, 2610). At the time they were interviewed many narrators seemed wholly convinced Satan now ruled absolute. "I am a minister of the Gospel. I have been preaching for the last thirty years. I am batching here. A man does

better to live by himself. Young people got the devil in them now a days. Your own children don't want you around" (Robert Barr, b. 1864, MS, 122). "Its de devil makes folkses do bad, and dey all better change and serve God-a-Mighty, so as he kin save 'em before its too late. I b'lieve folkses 'haved better dem days dan dey does now. Marster made 'em be good 'round his place" (Willis Cofer, b. 1860, GA, 209). "Dey had nice party in slav'ry time and right atterwards. Dey have candy pullin' and co'n shuckin's and de like. Dey didn't have all dese ol' witchcraf' things like dey does today. Dey's a big stink of de jailhouse behin' ev'rything now" (Liza Jones, b. 1856, TX, 2120).

In truth, people who opposed dancing were not all just prudes or killjoys, nor can they be blamed for seeing the Devil's hand in some of this. The fact is that dances could turn utterly hellish, even more so once freedom and the dissolution of the plantation police state perversely unleashed a wave of Black-on-Black violence and other self-destructive behaviors. "Folks use to have fights sometimes at de frolics but dey didn't do no killin'. Hit ain't like dat now. Dey stob you now, but dey didn't do dat den. Somebody'd always stop 'em 'fore it got dat fur" (Shang Harris, b. ca. 1840, GA, 120). " 'We had dances', she continued, 'after the corn shuckings. After they got through, the fiddler would start to fiddling and they would ring up in an old-time square dance. . . . They had a good time! Wasn't no killing, in them days, no liquor, no cussing, no saying 'lying fool' to one another, like 'tis now, no rough doings. There wasn't a pistol on that place but what was up to the house. No'm, there wasn't no killings then' " (Cicely Cawthon, b. 1859, GA, 190).

> After I came back from Ft. Smith I married Sam Jackson. Then I sure did have a good time going to dances. We danced everything that was on the fiddle. . . . Then sometimes somebody would get drunk and kill somebody and that would break up the dance. After a few years of that, my husband and I decided that this ole world was wicked and that we'd better jine the church. So we jined up with the Missionary Baptist, and then we went to

the big turnouts and meetin's, with the big dinners.
(Elsie Pryor, b. ca. 1855, IT, 263–64)

The physically charged congregation of the sexes was one obvious cause of conflict, but other vices or addictions tied to dancing—drinking, gambling, and cursing especially—prompted violence, tragedy, and scandal. "At dem dances dere was always one man dat wanted to start trubble. He'd git a woman and say, 'Let's go and git somethin' to drink.' Den de trubble would start" (William Smith, b. 1845, LA, TX, 3693).

Noah is a member of the Baptist church he does not believe in card playing or dancing, and he thinks if women must smoke they should smoke a pipe instead of cigarettes or cigars. When I asked him why dancing was a sin he said "these young folks can't stand being in each others arms half of the night without getting fool notions in their heads." He is against card playing but his reason for this he has seen so many men killed over cards. (Noah Rogers, b. 1845, MS, 1881)

I'se sarbed four years an' ten months of a eight ter twelve stretch, fer killin' a man. Dis man an' a whole gang o' us wus at his house gamblin'. I had done quit drinkin' er mont' er so 'fore dat, but dey 'sists on hit, but I 'fuses. Atter 'while he pours some on me an' I cusses him, den he cusses me, an' he says dat he am gwine ter kill me, an' he follers me down de road. I turns roun' an' shoots him. (Bill Crump, b. 1855, NC, 211, interviewed at NC state prison, Raleigh)

The fiddlers could beat the fiddlers of today. Get your partners, swing them to the left and to the right, hands up four, swing corners, right hands up four promonate all around all the way, git your partners boys. I shoot dice, drink, I got drunk and broke up church one Sunday night. Me and my sister broke up a dinner once because we got drunk. Whiskey been in circulation a long time.

There have been bad people ever since I been in the world. (Will Hicks, b. ca. 1860, LA, 237)

In legends, cursing and blaspheming are other common means of calling forth the Devil, while aspiring gamblers can master their art at the crossroads through the same rites as fiddlers and witches.[36] *Demon alcohol* was always a recipe for conflict, and for fundamentalists all of these activities were in the same forbidden class as fiddling or dancing. "Dem Baptis' at Big Creek was sho' tight wid dere rules too. Turn you out sho' if you drink too much cawn licker, or dance, or cuss" (Siney Bonner, b. ca. 1850, AL, 40). "When I wus a gal I uster to dance an' knock de pigeon wing, an' step de heel and toe. I wus sho' light on my feet an' I cud cuss like a man. Whar did I larn to cuss? I heard Marse Carter cuss ebery day an' I get dem by heart" (July Ann Halfen, b. ca. 1855, MS, 905). "I am a minister of the Gospel. I have been preaching for the last thirty years. . . . Before I preached, I fiddled, danced, shot craps, did anything" (Robert Barr, b. 1864, MS, 122).

Finally, many, perhaps the majority of African Americans inevitably interpreted British tale-types about musical dealings with the Devil as conjure tales. *Conjure* (aka hoodoo, rootwork, goofering, tricking, witchcraft, and so on) is a uniquely African American system of beliefs and practices including both white and black magic but also divination, herbology, folk healing, traditional meteorology and astrology, folk psychology, and more. Predictably, conjure's sources are many and varied. Slaves generally regarded it as an African institution, or anyway as distinctly non-white and non-Christian.[37] There was a major African component, derived in large part from West African *vodun* as preserved in New Orleans *hoodoo*. Conjure, however, was also practiced by Anglo-Americans and drew substantially from Christianity (Catholic and Protestant) and from English, Scottish, and Irish supernatural traditions. In fact, virtually all of the rites and practices described in British Devil tales (the crossroad pact, the black cat bone, the ritual inversion of scripture, and more) were actively incorporated into conjure, where Satan is especially prominent and powerful, along with God, Christ, and the saints.[38] Nevertheless, most church people equated conjure with devil worship. A widespread spiritual commonplace even pronounces "Old satan is a liar and a cunjorer, too; / If you don't mind, he'll cunjor you" (Mary Gladdy, b. ca. 1853, GA, 24).

There was also an intrinsic link between conjure and musicians, whose devilish vocation alone suggested they might be sorcerers or witches, though many reputedly were active practitioners. Missouri ex-slave Rhody Holsell recalled: "de Boss said one man was treated mean and they could not do anything with him. The old fellow would play his gourd and de snakes would come 'round. Finally, dey sent him down to New Orleans and sold him on the block" (Rhody Holsell, b. 1848, MO, 202). As if his fiddling alone were not enough, the old fellow's ability to summon the serpentine Devil instantly identifies him as a conjurer.[39] French Missouri had its own hoodoo traditions, but for any Missouri conjurer, the ordinarily dread sentence of being sold south to New Orleans (America's busiest slave port and also its hoodoo and conjure capital) effectively meant moving from a farm team to the big leagues.

Then again, the old fellow they could not do anything with uses his power only to escape work. Like other systems of folk magic, conjure was often addressed to fairly mundane everyday concerns, and slaves habitually employed it in hopes of avoiding labor, escaping punishment, or otherwise manipulating slaveholders—areas where musicianers excelled. For many slaves, then, the fact that musicians so often received special treatment further marked them as likely hoodoos. Jeptha "Doc" Choice had been a fieldhand and musicianer on an East Texas plantation. After freedom he farmed, railroaded, taught school, barbered, and practiced divine healing (hence "Doc").

> We niggers had our band, too, and I was one of the players. They was a nigger by the name of Ole Man Tout, the "Conjoor," who could play the violin jus' as good as anyone you hear today. I don' know why he was called "Conjoor," except that he never had to do any hard work and was always around the "Big House." If any one would say, "I think we'll send Ole Man Tout to the fields today," the old Missus would say, "No. The day is too warm, and the work too hard for the old man. He'll stay at the house," and sure 'nuff he would. (Jeptha "Doc" Choice, b. 1835, TX, 708)

Choice is being tongue-and-cheek, of course, since his account makes perfectly clear why Tout was called Conjoor and exempted from work; Choice states outright that this was cause and effect.[40] To slave laborers without such recourse, musicianers' machinations might well seem like witchcraft, cementing their sinister reputations. Several ex-slaves told the folktale of a lazy fiddler who shirks work for seven years or more. Jake Green titled his version "A Conju' What Didn' Wuk."[41]

> Mr. Whitehead owned Dirtin Ferry down to Belmont, an' dey had a darkey dere named Dick what claim sick all de time. So de Massa man said, "Dick, dam it, go to de house. I can't get no work outten you." So Dick went on. He was a fiddler so dey jes' tuck his vittuls to him for seven years. Den one day, Old Massa say to de overseer man, "Let's slip up dere an' see what Dick doin'." So dey did, an' dere sot Dick, fat as he could be a-playin' de fiddle an' a-singin',
>
>> Fool my Massa seben years.
>> Gwiner fool him seben mo'.
>> Hey diddle, de diddle, de diddle, de do'.
>
> 'Bout dat time Ole Massa poked his head in de do' said "Dam iffen you will. Come on outten dere, you black rascal, an' go to work." An' I ain't never hyard of Dick complainin' no mo'. (Jake Green, b. ca. 1852, AL, 168)

Admittedly, the idea that social music originates with the Devil did not come from folktales alone, nor was the decision to dance or not to dance always a matter of individual conscience.

> 'Nuther thing you don't hear of on account of the churches and the womens is the good Saturday night nigger breakdowns. Nor corn-shuckins is 'nuther thing you dont hear of. Saturdays' night the boss man gave us a big dance, regular breakdown with nigger banjo, guitar, and fiddle players. And man they gave the niggers plenty of whiskey. . . . The womens and churches stopped it all. Old woman came and hopped on me 'tuther day and called me a hypocrit. I said, "You ain't aimin' at me, I ain't no church nigger and I ain't no smart free nigger. The folks in the graveyard is the only ones worse off than me but I still got a place to stay at night 'cause the white folks re'lizes that I is the best nigger they is ever seen." (Walter Leggett, b. 1855, NC, 2324)

Ex-slaves definitely recalled preachers and church members as some of the most energetic and aggressive campaigners against dancing and dance music. "My preacherman uster whup me did he hear I go to dances and he would put me out from de church, too. I wah a good dancer—a right smart dancin' gal. I wah little an' sprite and all dem young bucks want to dance wif me" (Lucy Lewis, b. ca. 1830, TX, 2363–64). "I niver jine er church, kase I know'd I might dance an' dey wud turn me out. In dem days, de church folks jes lovd ter turn yer out uf de church" (Orris Harris, b. ca. 1858, MS, 934). "We didn't schottische or waltz an' dem kind o' dances—we danced! Reg'lar jig dances. . . . But I found out dey is more better ways in servin' de Lawd den dancin'. Now, I am a 'black Baptist' an' try to persuade all dem dat wants to dance not to dance" (John Barker, b. 1853, KY, 169).

Slaveholders also imposed their personal beliefs on slaves, and many ex-slaves had been forbidden to make music and dance simply because they were owned by self-professed Christians.[42] "Our white folkses wuz all church folkses and didn't 'low no dancin' at weddin's but dey give 'em big suppers" (Willis Cofer, b. 1860, GA, 207). "De ol' mistus she ain' 'low no dancin' or huzzawin' 'roun' de place 'cause she was Christian" (Sally Banks Chambers, b. unk., TX, 683). "I worked in the fiel'. We didn't do no dancin'; we went ter church fer pleasure" (Bessie Williams, b. 1859, AL, 2303). "Never had no frolics neither, no ma'm, and didn' go to none. We would have prayer meetings on Saturday nights, and one night in de week us had a chairback preacher, and sometimes a regular preacher would come in" (Nancy Boudry, b. ca. 1837, GA, 114). "Us 'tended de white folk's church ever Sunday an' sot in de gal'ry. Dey warn't no dancin' or cyard playin' in Gen'l Heard's house. He said: 'If you serve the Lord you have no time to fiddle and dance'" (Robert Heard, b. ca. 1841, GA, 171).

> Dey neber was no dancin' on de place. I neber l'arn how to dance. I neber was on a ballroom flo' in my life, and I neber tek no strong drink. I neber drink nuthin' stronger dan coffee. I neber try to dance. I was spen'in' my time praisin' de Lawd 'cause He been so good to me, eben in slavery time. Ol' man Lyons he had t'ree brudders. Dey let all dey niggers git togedder and have singin' and prayin'. . . . But de niggers dey sings hymns. Dey was all Christians and didn' sing no light songs. (Clara Brim, b. ca. 1837, LA, 431)

On the whole, however, narrators recalled devout parents—especially mothers—as their most important and lasting influences. "Mama never did 'low us to dance. I never did low my chillen to dance either" (Rose Holman, b. ca. 1855, MS, 1038–39). "Yes, the cullud folks had all kind of frolics, dances an corn huskin's, but I was never 'lowed to go to none of 'em. My daddy an' mammy brought us up in the fear of the Lawd, an' they didn' believe in no sich" (Mandy Jones, b. ca. 1857, MS, 1231). "My mother never knew anything about dances and fiddling and such things; she was a Christian. They had churches you know" (Allen Johnson, b. ca. 1855, GA, 65). "There wuz parties and dancin' on Saturday night fer them as wanted them. But there warn't no whiskey drinkin' and fightin'

Fig. 12.2. Clara Brim, ex-slave, Beaumont, TX, September 29, 1937. Portraits of African American ex-slaves from the US Works Progress Administration, Federal Writers' Project slave narratives collection, Library of Congress.

at the parties. Mammy didn't go to them. She wuz religious an' didn't believe in dancin' and sech like" (Andrew Columbus, b. 1859, TX, 898). "I never did do no dancin'. I never did lak it, and never did believe dat it was right. 'Mary, yo' won't come to a dance 'cause yo' cain't dance.' Folks would say. 'I don't want to learn how to dance.' 'Yo'll have a heap of pleasure.' 'I don't want dat kind of pleasure.' I never did see pappy and mammy on a dance floor in my life" (Mary Glover, b. 1854, TX, 1517–18).⁴³

Some people did reform after intensely personal epiphanies or born-again experiences, perhaps on a dark, deserted road, perhaps on the dance floor itself, where instead of summoning the Devil, taboo-breaking might beckon the Lord.

> W'en I wuz in Manchester I promus de Lawd I wouldin' dance. But one nite I wuz on de ball floor, dancin' fum one end ob de room ter de urthur en sump'in sezs go ter de do'er. I didn't go right den en 'gin hit sezs you ez not keepin' yo promus. I went ter de do'er en you could pick a pin off de groun' hit wuz so light. In de sky wuz de prettiest thing you ebber se'ed, so many culors, blue, white, green, red en yellow. (Ann Matthews, b. unk., TN, 45)

> I can't 'membuh nothing 'bout no churches in slavery. I was a sinner and loved to dance. I remembuh I was on the floor one night dancing and I had four daughters on the floor with me and my son was playing de music—that got me! I jest stopped and said I wouldn't cut another step and I haven't. I'm a member of the Baptist Church and been for 25 or 30 years. I jined 'cause I wanted to be good 'cause I was an awful sinner. (Alice Alexander, b. 1849, LA, 6)

In the end, however, there was no way to stamp out dancing, any more than communities could sidestep the issue. Young people especially just would not or could not be persuaded or dissuaded. "My daddy was a strick man. He beat us for gwineter dances but us jes' hide in de smokehouse all day and run froo de woods dat night. Dey's big black bears in dem 'Sippi woods but eben dat couldn' scare us gals 'way from de fiddlin'" (Mary Johnson, b. ca. 1858, MS, 2024). "I asked her if Lou, her granddaughter was a help to her and she said, 'She is a sweet little gal, but she's a sinner. She dances, she's obeying de debbil cause she dances. She ain't obeying Jesus.' I told her it was not wrong to dance. She said, 'Honey, I done heard scripture read from kiver to kiver, and hits in dar. You is gwina burn in hell if you dances'" (Savannah Rice, b. ca. 1850, AL, 321, int. unk.).

It might be an exaggeration to say the belief that fiddling and dancing were mortal sins was observed more in the breach, but many people did find a middle ground on the question. There is still a saying in the South that "it's a thin line between Saturday night and Sunday morning," meaning that in actual practice, midnight Saturday is more revolving door than portal to Hell. In the bleak world of American slaves, Saturday night frolics and Sunday morning meetings were the two most important, maybe their only two public opportunities for recreation, socializing, and self-expression. Some slaves saw no reason to deny themselves either, and the expectation in many quarters was that people could and would have it both ways. "Now us had our frolics long wid church gwine. . . . We danced by fiddle music an' guitars" (Robert Weathersby, b. ca. 1847, MS, 2241–42). "We goes to church when we wants and we has parties with Sam and Rufus to play de music, de fiddle and de banjo" (James West, b. 1854, MS, 150). "The old people say they used to have breakdowns in slave time—breakdown dances with fiddle and banjo music. Far after slavery, they had them. The only other amusement worth speaking about was the churches" (James Reeves, b. 1870, AR, child of ex-slaves, 28).

Not all preachers and church people were intolerant zealots or grim ascetics, not all congregations were wholly inflexible and unforgiving, and not all slaveholders imposed their own beliefs on others. "At mudder's place d' mistus was a Christian lady. Dey wouldn' 'low us t' dance on dey place. Dey gib us pass t' go t' dance on d' nex' plantation, dat were my father lib" (Charlotte Beverly, b. ca. 1847, TX, 283). "Mr. Davy was a powerful religious man though. He used to let us have dancing and singings on Saturday night. Then we had corn-shucking parties. At the dances they used to have men with fiddles and they hollered out 'Get your partners for the ring dance.' . . . Master Davy said it was wrong to dance but he said 'Seek your enjoyment; niggers got to pleasure themselves someway' " (Lu Lee, b. 1848 or 1849, TX, 2297).

After the day's work was done, house servants and field hands forgot cares in merriment and dancing. Asked how her master, a Baptist divine, condoned the latter, Aunt Malinda replied with the simple statement, "He wasn't only a preacher—he was a religious man." The slaves danced, she said, at the house of "de man that tended de stock" set way off in a field away from "de big house." Dancing was to the tune of banjoes and some homemade instruments that she termed "quills," evidently some kind of reeds. It is fairly certain that the sounds must have carried to the house, but no interference was made. "My mammy wuz de best dancer on de plantashun," Malinda proudly asserts. "She could

dance so sturdy she could balance a glass of water on her head and never spill a drop." (Malinda [Melinda] Mitchell, b. 1853, SC, 442)

Some plantations allowed no slave dances, some no church services, some barred both, but on numberless places frolics and meetings went on side by side. "On Saturday night there would be a prayer meeting in one house and a dance in another. On Sunday some of them went to church and some went visiting" (Ellen Payne, b. 1849, TX, 3041). "Church people would have singin' and prayin' and de wicked people would have dancin' and singin' " (Willis Bennefield, b. ca. 1830, GA, 169). "Dey had frolics in dem days but I couldn' go. De Christians had dere 'fairs on one farm an' de sinners had dere frolics on 'nother farm. Mother was a Christian and so was I. Nowadays you can' tell one from t'other. Christians an' sinners all go to de same things" (Cornelius Garner, b. 1846, MD, 103). Recalling Kentucky cornshuckings of the 1820s, ex-slave author Harry Smith reported "after eating, often preaching and prayer meetings by some of the old folks in some of the cabins, and in others fiddles would ring out. It was a scene never to be forgotten, as the old christians sing and pray until four in the morning, while at the other cabins many would be patting, singing and dancing."[44]

Adeline White's Louisiana plantation had a separate church house and dance hall just for slaves. "Dey uster hab big dances, too, reg'lar breakdown dances. Dey play de corjian (accordion) and de fiddle and de vileen. Somebody would call de numbers. Dey hab a big house for de dances. Dat was a dif'runt house from de one dey had preachin' in, 'cause it wouldn' be right to serb de Lord and de debbil in de same house" (Adeline White, b. ca. 1857, LA, 4028, orig. parentheses). Writing in 1851, an experienced slaveholder advised novices to cut costs by using the same structure for both dances and prayers. "I would build a house large enough, and use it for a dance-house for the young, and those who wished to dance, as well as for prayer meetings, and for church on Sunday—making it a rule to be present myself occasionally at both, and my overseer always."[45]

Fig. 12.3. Adeline White, ex-slave, Beaumont, TX, June 14, 1937. Portraits of African American ex-slaves from the US Works Progress Administration, Federal Writers' Project slave narratives collection, Library of Congress.

Many people, moreover, attended both dances and meetings—with or without others' blessing and approval—and were by all appearances completely unconflicted about straddling the church and the world. "Sadday nights dey all got together and frolicked; picked de banjo, and drunk whiskey. Didn't none of 'em git drunk, 'cause dey was used to it. Dar was barrels of it whar dey stilled it on de place. On Sundays us went f'um cabin to cabin holdin' prayer meetin's" (Tom Hawkins, b. ca. 1860, GA, 131–32). "People nowadays dey joins de church one night and goes to a dance and gits drunk de next night and comes to church de next Sunday and prays like a real Disciple of de Lord. Dar is goin to be more church folks in dat lake of fire dan de devil can stir" (Calvin Moye, b. 1842, TX, 2839).

We sho did have church, large meetin'—camp meetin'—with lot of singin' an shoutin' and it was fine! Nevah was no singer, but I was a good dancer in my day, yes-yes Madam I were a good dancer. I went to dances and to church with my folks. My father played a violin. He played well, so did my brother. . . . I liked to go to church and to dances both. (Wade Glenn, b. ca. 1860, NC, 38).

Lastly, repentance was another widely practiced means of moving between the church and the world. Over their lifetimes innumerable ex-slaves quit fiddling or going to dances and joined the church, an established rite of passage in fundamentalist denominations based on narratives of sin and redemption. Some people did so because of dramatic conversions, traumatic episodes, or outside pressures, others simply as they aged and grew ready to settle down. A sizable number sinned and then repented on a regular basis throughout their lives. Many did not seem particularly remorseful. "I use ter go ter lots of dances. I was what you would call a dancin fool. But since de good Lord has saved mah soul I see jest how foolish hit all was. Iffen I'd used mah strength in church work dat I used goin ter dances I would have been better off. But dances was nice ter go to den" (Vina Moore, b. 1845, MS, 2757). "Befo' I jine d' chu'ch I uster play fo' dances all time. Uster play all dem ol' breakdown tunes, but dem pieces done lef' my head. Since I jine d' church I quit all dat" (Leo Mouton, b. ca. 1860, LA, 2812). "I used to play the fiddle for dances when I was young, but not after I joined the church" (Bill Thomas, b. 1849, TX, 3789).

Of course, the constant movement of community members between these two camps also ensured the constant circulation and recirculation of musical ideas. Dance musicians adapted hymns and spirituals; sacred songmakers fiddle tunes, love lyrics, and ballads. Some churches allowed no instruments, or no instruments save keyboards; other congregations welcomed fiddles, banjos, and guitars, and many musicianers played at both dances and church, especially after the rise of the Pentecostal movement in the late 1800s. "If I had made musician before I was freed, they could not have bought me for any price. I made my first fiddle out of a gourd. I played for all the dances both white and black and Sunday School" (Harre Quarls, b. 1841, TX, 3216). "Sometimes we would, unbeknown to our master, assemble in a cabin and sing songs and spirituals. Our favorite spirituals were—*Bringin' in de sheaves*, *De Stars am Shinin' for us all*, *Hear de Angels callin'*, and *The Debil has no place here*. The singing was usually to the accompaniment of a Jew's harp and fiddle, or banjo" (Dennis Simms, b. 1841, MD, 61–62). Nor was it unknown for hymns to be performed on the Devil's instruments. "I used to be a banjo picker in Civil War times. I could pick a church song just as good as I could a reel" (Jim Davis, b. 1840, NC, 114). Describing his repertoire, Davis named "Amazing Grace" (John Newton, 1779), "Dark Was the Night" (Thomas Haweis, 1792), and "Go Preach My Gospel, Saith the Lord" (Isaac Watts, 1709) alongside "Jack of Diamonds (Rye Whiskey)" and "Young Gal, Come Blow the Coal." In some of the old legends, after his dance repertoire fails, the fiddler finally vanquishes the Devil by playing a spiritual. In another "one old slave was taught [banjo] by the devil at home, but was not able to play reels until he had mastered the tune 'Gimme Jesus.'"[46]

Stories of clergy smashing and burning fiddles are verified. But beginning in the antebellum era, fiddling preachers, Black and white, were also well-known American characters. "De nigger named Allen Beaver am de preacherman an' de leadah in de pahties 'cause him can play de fiddle" (Louis Fowler, b. 1853, GA, 1389).

> Weuns cullud fo'ks have a big time at de pahties. Ol' Tom am de preachahman an' de musician. Him play de fiddle an' de banjo. De cullud fo'ks dat come f'om de udder plantations, deys dance an' sings. Sometimes deys would have de jig contest. Dere am one contest dat am a heap ob fun. Dat am w'en deys put a glass ob wautah on de head an' see who can jig de hahdest widout spillin' de wautah. (Lewis Jones, b. 1851, TX, 2111)[47]

The effects of this cross-pollination were self-evident, and even hardliners were forced to acknowledge that slave meetings and frolics could closely resemble one another. Wrote one period observer, "religious negroes will not *dance*, and a violin is an offence to one who

has joined the Church; but in place of those wicked indulgences, when they meet together they 'shout' to their own singing of a spiritual."[48] In this context, *shout* refers not to vocalizing but to African American trance dancing.

> At the setting of the sun, with their day's work all done, they returned to their cabins and prepared their evening's meal. Having finished this, the religious among them would gather at one of the cabin doors and give thanks to God in the form of long supplications and old fashioned songs. Many of them being highly emotional would respond in shouts and hallelujahs sometimes causing the entire group to become "happy" concluding in shouting and praise to God. The wicked slaves expended their pent up emotions in song and dance. Gathering at one of the cabin doors they would sing and dance to the tunes of a fife, banjo or fiddle that was played by one of their number. (Louis Napoleon, b. ca. 1857, FL, 243–44)

The fact is that for American slaves, music, song, and dance were completely inseparable, and the most devout church members danced at services themselves, all the while preserving their vows to shun dancing. Instead, they called it *shouting*.

Appendix A: How to Sell Your Soul to the Devil for Music, Song, or Dance

Below are summaries for 124 US English-language texts describing musical encounters with the Devil, arranged into four subtypes and further subdivided by ethnicity. To recap: in SCENARIO I, the protagonist deliberately summons the Devil to learn to dance or play music; in SCENARIO II, she or he deliberately summons the Devil with music or dance, but for some other reason. In SCENARIO III, musicians or dancers accidentally summon the Devil, who may challenge them to a music or dance contest, or possess or destroy them; or he may possess their instruments, which (SCENARIO IV) must then be destroyed or exorcised. Within each subdivision, texts are arranged alphabetically by source, followed by basic contextual information and a brief synopsis including the protagonist's goal (such as to fiddle well enough to buy freedom, know any kind of dance, join in with the underworld work) or infraction (breaking the taboo against fiddling or dancing on Sunday, disobeying a mother by buying a guitar or making a gourd banjo, and so on); the story's setting (crossroads, fork of road, graveyard, under a holly tree, and more); the prescribed (or proscribed) day and hour (usually Saturday after midnight or Sunday before day); and ritual repetitions or other special conditions (for example, the requirement to visit the crossroads three, seven, or nine consecutive Sundays before dawn). Other common elements include additional rites (such as saying the Lord's prayer backwards); animal sacrifices (like killing a red rooster or procuring a black cat bone); and supernatural ordeals, usually a series of specters culminating in the Devil, who appears in various traditional forms (with glowing eyes, as a black dog, as a rabbit, on horseback, and so on). As part of a compact, the Devil may personally teach subjects to play, or merely retune their instruments, or he may magically possess their fiddles, banjos, or guitars. Some characters cheat the Devil by giving him a shoe sole instead of an immortal soul, others are cheated by him, receiving manure in payment. Many more flee without sealing the pact. (Motif designations for many of these elements are cited in the chapter text. All emphasis, parentheses, and brackets in quotations from Hyatt, *Hoodoo*, are original.)

In the last decades of the twentieth century, adaptations of these legends proliferated in popular sources, in large part because of their association with Mississippi bluesmen Tommy Johnson (1896–1956) and Robert LeRoy Johnson (1911–1938) (no relation). Both Johnsons were famously associated with the legend of the musician's crossroads pact, which both personally encouraged, and many stories that they, their families, and acquaintances told fall squarely within this tradition, duly included below. With their latter-day celebrity, however, Tommy Johnson, Robert Johnson, and their deals with the devil were taken up and refashioned in various ways; each was even featured in a major motion picture: Robert Johnson in *Crossroads,* dir. Walter Hill (Columbia Pictures, 1986); Tommy Johnson in *O Brother, Where Art Thou?* dir. Joel Coen (Touchstone Pictures, 2000). As interesting as they are, these and the many other recent popularizations of such tales fall outside the scope of this study and accordingly do not figure in the following inventory. For Tommy Johnson, see David Evans, *Tommy Johnson* (London: Studio Vista, 1971); the most up-to-date reexamination of Robert Johnson is Bruce Conforth and Gayle Dean Wardlow, *Up Jumped the Devil: The Real Life of Robert Johnson* (London: Rough Trade, 2019).

Subtype I. Summoning the Devil to Learn Music or Dance

A. AFRICAN AMERICAN   A. M. Bacon and E. C. Parsons, "Folk-Lore from Elizabeth City County," *JAF* 35: 282 (VA): girl wants "to know any kind of dance, and sing any kind of song. One day while she was alone, a man stood before her." Twenty-eight-year term, deceptive bargain (sole of shoe). Bruce Bastin, "The Devil's Goin' To Get You," *North Carolina Folklore Journal* 21 (1973): 190 (NC): learn banjo, crossroads, nine Sunday mornings, ordeal: high wind precedes Devil, Devil as fireball, Devil with glowing eyes, fled without sealing pact. J. Mason Brewer, *American Negro Folklore* (Chicago: Quadrangle, 1968), 281–82 (NC): learn guitar, fork of road, three Sunday mornings, deceptive bargain (sole of shoe), rite: draw circle in road, throw in sole, call Devil three times, Devil in cloud of smoke, instructed by Devil, possessed guitar. Grace MacGowan Cooke, *A Gourd Fiddle* (Philadelphia: H. Altemus, 1904), 45: learn to fiddle, practice on Sunday "an' de Ol' Boy whuls in an' he'ps. . . . 'N' ef he don' come de fus' time, er-tryin' ter show 'em de chunes, an' de quirly-gigs, dey crosses dey foots (dat's a *shore* black chawm) an' scrapes de bow er few, an he comes er-floppin'!" (orig. emphasis). David Evans, *Tommy Johnson*, 22–23 (MS): "to play anything you want to play [on guitar] and learn how to make songs yourself," crossroads, midnight, Devil tunes guitar, Devil as Black man. Harry Middleton Hyatt, *Folk-Lore from Adams County Illinois*, 2nd rev. ed., Memoirs of the Alma Egan Hyatt Foundation (1965), 795 (IL): learn to fiddle, fork of road at midnight, ordeal: black snake appears, followed by Black man with fiddle, instructed by Devil. Hyatt, *Hoodoo* 1: 99 (SC): to learn guitar, crossroads, one o'clock in morning, rite: to "put God behin' you an' the devil in front of you," stand at crossroads, turn face to the west, back to east, right to north, left to south "an' you shall call this man who pretend to do anything that you desires," seven-year term, fled without sealing pact. Hyatt, *Hoodoo* 1: 99–100 (VA): "play the guitar, play a banjo," receive "de *world's gifts*," "a *gold-finding hand*," or "all de music you want," four forks of the road (crossroads), nine mornings, instructed by Devil, deceptive bargain (sole of shoe). Hyatt, *Hoodoo* 1: 100–102 (NC): learn guitar, fork of road, nine Sunday mornings, three a.m. or midnight, animal sacrifice (one-eyed rooster), ordeal: sheep, "somepin black," cow, and "lil ole funny boy" precede Devil, Devil as black dog, instructed by Devil, deceptive bargain (sole of shoe), possessed guitar. Hyatt, *Hoodoo* 1: 103 (VA): "get your music," crossroads, nine mornings or nights at same hour, rite and ordeal: "*get on yore knees* and *prays backwards*, but pray not to God but *to the devil*. . . . If you kin stand the test, den you would get graduated." Hyatt, *Hoodoo* 1: 104 (MD): "to know to how play a banjo or a guitar or do magic tricks," graveyard for nine mornings, take graveyard dirt to crossroads for nine additional mornings, Devil as horseman. Hyatt, *Hoodoo* 1: 107 (MD): "whatever you wanted to be or play . . . if you *wanted to be dancer*," under holly tree, nine Sunday mornings, instructed by Devil ("the *devil would come* himself and *strike a step*"), fled without sealing pact. Hyatt, *Hoodoo*

1: 108 (SC): "to do any *trick* . . . tuh be a banjo picker," fork of road under tree, Sunday morning, rite (lay flat on your back), man "made de second trip in order to prove it [to friends], an' his *han' became tied to his banjo*." Hyatt, *Hoodoo* 1: 108 (NC): guitar, fork of road, four a.m., go just once, Devil tunes guitar. Hyatt, *Hoodoo* 1: 108 (VA): learn accordion, fork of road, nine Sunday mornings at four o'clock, instructed by Devil, Devil detected by tail, fled without sealing pact. Hyatt, *Hoodoo* 1: 108 (VA): "become a professional musician or a man to do sleight of hand or anything or walk out of people's sight," fork of road, nine mornings, rite: "instead of praying to de Lord like most de people pray dey sins away, you pray to the devil," ordeal: "it prob'bly *may get a little windy*" and "a *bunch of birds, chickens,* or something" will precede Devil: "Well, if you got guts enough to stay dere and face what he's going to tell you, you'll be all right—you kin do anything you wanta do." Hyatt, *Hoodoo* 1: 108–9 (VA): "to learn to play music or a fiddle," two roads (crossroads or fork of road), before sunup, rite: turn back to sunrise, lay face down, never turn around, never look up, Devil as blacksnake, Devil as black bull, fled without sealing pact. Hyatt, *Hoodoo* 1: 109 (MD): learn to play "The Fisherman's Hornpipe" on violin, crossroads, nine midnights, ordeal: first night lamb appears, second night high wind rises, third night "*a bull come through a-slinging fire*, wid eyes just as red as could be," fourth night six pallbearers arrive with coffin, fled without sealing pact. Hyatt, *Hoodoo* 1: 109 (NC): "tuh be a piano player or guitar player," road forks nine mornings, ordeal: cow, snake, cat, dog, lion, bear, big smoke precede Devil, "yo' stand there an' meet that fo' nine mawnin's an' aftah de nine mawnin's, yo' supposed tuh leave an' go play any kind of music dat chew wants." Hyatt, *Hoodoo* 1: 109–10 (MD): learn to fiddle, "crossroad or three forks of de road," midnight Sunday, instructed by Devil, Devil as horseman, Devil as black dog, fled without sealing pact. Hyatt, *Hoodoo* 1: 110 (MD): "to play a banjah," "*four-corner road*, nine mornings," rite: initiate "sets there playing de banjah until after awhile *a lot of things* would come up. They'll *go around him nine times*. And after awhile the last one behin'll ast him what would he rather do, do what dey doin' or serve de Lord." Hyatt, *Hoodoo* 1: 110 (GA): learn guitar, fork of road, midnight, Devil's trick payment (fifty-cent piece turns to manure), instructed by Devil. Hyatt, *Hoodoo* 1: 110–11 (GA): learn banjo or guitar, rite: take "*two tin plates*, and go in the woods eight mornings straight and *kneel between two tall oak trees*, and rub these tin plates together, to sell himself to the devil, and pray to the devil that his heart be as free of Jesus Christ as these plates are of rust." Hyatt, *Hoodoo* 5: 4005 (SC): "learn music," fork of road. Hyatt, *Hoodoo* 5: 4005 (NC): "to know how tuh pick a banjo," crossroads, Sunday. Hyatt, *Hoodoo* 5: 4005 (FL): "learn tuh do most any devlish act, . . . tuh play a banjo or guitah or anything lak dat," fork of road, Sunday. Hyatt, *Hoodoo* 5: 4005 (SC): "learn how tuh pick a box, or learn how tuh dance," fork of road, late hours at night: "ah don' know anything dey did, jes' go out dere." Hyatt, *Hoodoo* 5: 4005 (SC): learn to dance, fork of road, seven Sundays: "go to de fo'k of de road seven Sunday mawnin' an' start dancin'; any dance yo' wanta dance, yo' kin dance it." Hyatt, *Hoodoo* 5: 4005 (GA): learn guitar, fork of road, after midnight, ordeal: "anything dat come dere, don't git frightened or don't be scared, until day." Hyatt, *Hoodoo* 5: 4005 (GA): learn to play string music or mouth organ, fork of road, midnight, ordeal: "if yo' stayed dere—dey tell me now—wit whut come tuh see yo', well yo'll learn tuh play music." Hyatt, *Hoodoo* 5: 4006 (MS): learn guitar, fork of road, three nights. Hyatt, *Hoodoo* 5: 4006 (SC): learn to play "a gui-tah or ukulele or either a banjo," fork of road, four a.m., ordeal: "If yo' kin stand tuh see all dose things tuh come befo' yo', when yo' come back home yo' kin pick jes as well as if yo' been doin' it fo' ten or twelve yeahs." Hyatt, *Hoodoo* 5: 4006 (GA): learn guitar, fork of road, midnight, ordeal: "all kinda devils an' all kinda thin's will come." Hyatt, *Hoodoo* 5: 4006–7 (VA): learn guitar, fork of road, midnight, instructed by

Devil: "the devil comes and teaches you to play it." Hyatt, *Hoodoo* 5: 4007 (FL): learn "guitah or whut kind of music yo' wanta make," fork of road, midnight, instructed by Devil: "somepin'll come up an' take yore guitar an' play a piece fo' yo'." Hyatt, *Hoodoo* 5: 4007 (TN): "tuh learn music," fork of road, midnight. Hyatt, *Hoodoo* 5: 4007 (GA): learn guitar, fork of road, midnight, any day except Sunday, animal sacrifice (rooster), instructed by Devil, possessed guitar. Hyatt, *Hoodoo* 5: 4007 (AL): fork of road, at night, instructed by Devil: "he'll come an' learn you any tune yo' wanta know." Hyatt, *Hoodoo* 5: 4007 (VA): learn guitar, "four forks of the road," midnight, instructed by Devil: "the devil will come and take it out of your hand and play a piece of it and hand it back to you. And you can play anything you want." Hyatt, *Hoodoo* 5: 4007–8 (NC): "tuh play a piece of music—a mouth organ, a guitar, anythin'," fork of road, midnight, animal sacrifice (black cat bone), instructed by Devil: "sompin will walk up tuh yo' an' take it from yo', an' tell ev'ry kinda music an' ev'ry kinda song dat it is, good songs an' bad ones. But dat is not lak if yo' would take a cat fo' a black cat bone. Dey used tuh do dat too, but den dat's when yo' sold yo'self tuh de devil." Hyatt, *Hoodoo* 5: 4008 (VA): play music, road with three forks, midnight, instructed by Devil: "the devil will come there and learn you how to play." Hyatt, *Hoodoo* 5: 4008 (VA): "to be a musician," sit under a cedar tree and play, instructed by Devil: "the devil appears there and shows them how to play music." Hyatt, *Hoodoo* 5: 4008 (GA): dance or play guitar, fork of road, midnight, instructed by Devil: "dere'll be sompin appear befo' yo' an' jes' as dey do dey fingers, dat's de way yo' do yorn. Dat's in order of selling yo'self tuh de devil for an infidel." Hyatt, *Hoodoo* 5: 4008 (GA): play guitar, fork of road, midnight, Devil tunes guitar. Hyatt, *Hoodoo* 5: 4008–9 (NC): "tuh play a guitar or sompin lak dat," first to graveyard, then to fork of road, one or two a.m., instructed by Devil. Hyatt, *Hoodoo* 5: 4009 (AL): "if yo' wanta be a good dancer . . . if yo' wanta be a good musician," fork of road, nine mornings. Hyatt,

Hoodoo 5: 4009 (VA): play "guitar, banjo, any kind of string music dat you wanta," fork of road, nine nights, "play dere till a certain hour." Hyatt, *Hoodoo* 5: 4009 (NC): play "a banjo, guitar, or anything," fork of road, nine mornings, "de ninth mawnin' yo'll succeed." Hyatt, *Hoodoo* 5: 4009–10 (NC): "tuh learn how tuh play music," fork of road, nine mornings, Devil tunes instrument. Hyatt, *Hoodoo* 5: 4010 (VA): "play music or be a good gambler," fork of road, nine Sunday nights, ordeal: Devil appears on the ninth night, "yo walk wit him an' yo' come back . . . but de average fellah haven't got de guts tuh do dat." Hyatt, *Hoodoo* 5: 4010 (NC): "if a fellah wants tuh dance . . . wanta play de violin or anything," fork of road, nine Sunday mornings, instructed by Devil. Hyatt, *Hoodoo* 5: 4010 (NC): play banjo, nine Sunday mornings, instructed by Devil. Hyatt, *Hoodoo* 5: 4010 (SC): play guitar, crossroads, nine mornings, Devil tunes guitar, "he take dat instrument an' tune it into tune fo' yo' to play, understand. An' yo' kin play it from den on." Hyatt, *Hoodoo* 5: 4010–11 (NC): play banjo, fork of road, nine mornings, Devil tunes banjo, Devil as stranger. Hyatt, *Hoodoo* 5: 4011 (NC): play guitar, fork of road, nine mornings, Devil as Black man. Hyatt, *Hoodoo* 5: 4011 (FL): "to be a natural professional dancer," fork of road, nine nights between midnight and one, instructed by Devil. Hyatt, *Hoodoo* 5: 4011 (FL): play guitar, fork of road, seven mornings before sunrise. Hyatt, *Hoodoo* 5: 4011 (NC): play guitar, fork of road, nine mornings, rite: on the ninth morning turn around three times, look over left shoulder, Devil appears and grants wishes. Hyatt, *Hoodoo* 5: 4011–12 (SC): play guitar, fork of road, nine mornings, rite: "You gotta cuss God an' give solemn warnin' an' tell Him yo' goin' sell yore soul to de devil. Den you kin pick de guitar." Clifton Johnson, *Battleground Adventures* (Boston: Houghton, Mifflin, 1915), 416–22 (VA): "I used to be told that the way to learn to play the fiddle was to go to a graveyard with it and start practisin'." Go at night alone, ordeal: ghostly noises, spirit in cloud of steam, fled without sealing pact. Collins Lee, "Some

Negro Lore from Baltimore," *JAF* 5 (1892): 110 (MD): "To learn to pick a banjo, go to the forks of the road at midnight: you will see a man. That is *Satan*, and *he* will teach you to play" (orig. emphasis). Chapman J. Milling, "Balaam Foster's Fiddle," 1944; rpt. B. A. Botkin, ed., *A Treasury of American Folklore* (New York: Crown, 1944), 727–31 (SC): fiddle well enough to buy freedom, crossroads for nine nights, rite: make cross mark in middle of road each night, ordeal: Devil as rabbit, Devil in cloud of smoke, instructed by Devil, possessed violin, Devil detected by tail, cloven hooves, pitchfork. Jim O'Neal, "A Traveler's Guide to the Cross Roads," *Living Blues* No. 94 (November-December 1990): 21 (MS): "following instructions from his grandfather, [Napoleon Strickland] learned to play music by going to a cemetery and 'straddling a grave' at midnight." O'Neal, "Traveler's Guide," 24 (MS): "a man named Walter Hearns . . . said that [Robert] Johnson told him he had made a deal with the devil at a graveyard in Crenshaw, Mississippi." After spending the night, Johnson emerged from the graveyard singing "Preaching Blues (Up Jumped the Devil)" (a song about making a deal with the Devil). Robert Palmer, *Deep Blues* (New York: Penguin, 1981), 113 (MS): "several of [Robert] Johnson's relatives told blues researcher Mack McCormick that Robert had sold his soul to the Devil and claimed they knew the exact backcountry crossroads where the deal was made. 'The Devil came there,' said one, 'and gave Robert his talent and told him he had eight more years to live on earth.'" Compare Robert Johnson, "Cross Road Blues" (Vocalion 03519, 1936), which reveals direct familiarity with the crossroad rites. Palmer, *Deep Blues*, 113 (MS): Robert Johnson's mentor Ike Zimmerman "claimed to have learned to play by visiting graveyards at midnight." Puckett, *Folk Beliefs*, 553: (MS): "take your banjo to the forks of the road at midnight and Satan will teach you how to play it." Puckett, *Folk Beliefs*, 553: (MS): learn banjo, instructed by Devil, rite: "one old slave was taught by the devil at home, but was not able to play reels until he had mastered the tune 'Gimme Jesus.'" Puckett, *Folk Beliefs*, 554–55 (LA): "to play any piece you desire to on the guitar" and "do anything you want to do in this world," fork of road, midnight, trim fingernails "as close as you possibly can" beforehand, Devil will "trim the nails until they bleed," animal sacrifice (black cat bone), instructed by Devil. Amanda Styles (b. ca. 1856, 345) (GA): man can go behind his house and summon Devil to dance with him; to play banjo or "to do anything the devil could do, go to a cross road walk backwards and curse God." David Lindsey Thomas and Lucy Blayney Thomas, *Kentucky Superstitions* (Princeton, NJ: Princeton University Press, 1920): 291 (KY): pick the banjo, fork of road on dark night.

B. ANGLO-AMERICAN   Vance Randolph, *Who Blowed Up the Church House? and Other Ozark Folktales* (New York: Columbia University Press, 1952), 168–69 (AR): play fiddle, crossroads at midnight, dancers compelled to continue until consumed by flames, Devil as stranger, Devil casts no shadow, leaves no tracks in snow. Whitney and Bullock, *Maryland*, 78 (MD): play fiddle, end of one of the main roads or crossroads, before sunrise for five mornings, instructed by Devil, Devil dances and plays fiddle at crossroads.

Subtype II. Deliberately Summoning Devil with Music or Dance

AFRICAN AMERICAN   Hyatt, *Hoodoo* 1: 78 (VA): graveyard, nine nights, animal sacrifice (*witchcraft bone* from black cat), ordeal: first night "*a little imp* come an' dance up to you," multiplying until on "*the ninth*, the *whole devil family*, his wife an' the son, a whole bunch of 'em" appear. "If you kin stand fer whut you see *you'll be able* to *witchcraft* in anything you want to." Hyatt, *Hoodoo* 1: 103 (MD): receive "the power to accomplish what you want to do," "*dance and sing* and *put on a little program*" at "four-way road" (crossroads), nine mornings, Devil as Black man, fled without sealing pact. Hyatt, *Hoo-*

doo 1: 106–7 (NC): "whenever somebody wants some help" or to "have anything you want," take "some kin'a music piece . . . a banjo box or either some, you know, [phonograph] record" to fork of road for nine mornings. Hyatt, *Hoodoo* 1: 111 (GA): play a violin at fork of road between midnight and one, "an' dey can *call dat evil spirit to dwell around an' aggravate de person dat dey want dis evil thing done to.*" Hyatt, *Hoodoo* 5: 4003–4 (SC): "to join in with the *underworld* work," play guitar at fork of road between midnight and one, rite: "cuss *the Father, the Son, and the Holy Ghost.*" Hyatt, *Hoodoo* 5: 4005–6 (GA): "do most anything yo' want," take a "banjo or guitar or sompin to attract dis ole devil" to three-forked road at midnight or four a.m., ordeal: "if you kin stand whut comes by yo'self [you have it *made* in this world]!" Hyatt, *Hoodoo* 5: 4011 (NC): rite: to "dance and *cuss* God for nine Sunday mornings at fork of a road sells you to the devil."

Scenario III. Accidentally Summoning Devil with Music or Dance

A. AFRICAN AMERICAN   Bruce Bastin, "The Devil's Goin' to Get You," 192 (NC): man plays guitar until nightfall, returning home through woods, sees something about four feet high "just as black as anything you ever seen." Devil as black dog. Devil leaves no tracks in snow. Lucy Donald (b. 1857, MS, 639–40): people dance to fiddling past midnight Saturday, Devil appears, declares, "dance up hogs, you ain't half a dancin'," half the dancers flee, others carry on as house collapses, Devil with glowing eyes. Jerry Eubanks (b. 1846, MS, 698–99): preachers attend dance at house known for evil spirits. "A door was pitched down on us. Oh, I done some running. . . . Looks like de house goin to be tore down every night." Arthur Huff Fauset, "Tales and Riddles Collected in Philadelphia," *JAF* 41 (1928): 547 (PA): girl allows stranger to escort her home from dance, rebuffs request to come in, goes upstairs, family hears unusual footsteps, discovers girl dying. "Some say she had been dancing with the devil." Hyatt, *Hoodoo* 5: 4007 (NC): musician "used to carry de guitar roun' all de time *from 'joint' tuh 'joint'*" returning home one night meets stranger at bridge or fork in road, instructed by Devil. Lucy Lewis (b. ca. 1830, TX, 2366–67): skeptic is unafraid of spirits, fiddles in graveyard, permanently possessed. Hearn, *Levee*, 26–31 (TN): 2 a.m. returning drunk from a dance Banjo Jim drops his instrument in front of abandoned dance hall and curses ("Hell an' d—tion"). With "a burst of unearthly laughter," hall fills with apparitions of dead friends fiddling and dancing, then disappears in a crash of lightning and thunder. "Five minutes afterward two police officers found an apparently dead negro lying in the rain, opposite the old dance-house, together with an overturned ash-barrel and a broken banjo." Parsons, "Guilford County," 180 (NC): fiddler is gone from home too much, Devil appears on road one night, Devil challenges him to fiddle "The Devil's Black Joke" while he dances, Devil's trick payment (fifty-cent piece turns to horse manure), man renounces fiddling, Devil as horseman, Devil has club foot. Charles M. Skinner, *Myths and Legends of Our Own Land*, 2 vols. (Philadelphia: J. P. Lippincott, 1896), I: 133–35 (NY): Black fiddler passing graveyard late Saturday fiddles as clock strikes midnight, Devil appears with fiddle, they play "The Devil's Joy at Sabbath Breaking" and "Go to the Devil and Shake Yourself," at daybreak fiddler banishes Devil by playing hymn.

B. ANGLO-AMERICAN   Halpert, *Pinelands*, 300 (NJ): accordionist coming home from dance after midnight Saturday plays, hears "this dancin' come under his feet," concludes it is Devil, never plays again. Halpert, *Pinelands*, 283–93 (also see 6–7, 23, 376–90) (NJ): twenty-one variants concerning local fiddler Sammy Giberson (composite summary): Sammy Giberson returns from dance, meets Devil on road or bridge, Devil teaches "Air Tune" or "Devil's Dream," fiddling and dancing contest, Devil better dancer but defeated fiddling or vice versa, Giberson dances jig with glass of water on

head, Giberson plays fiddle until Devil dances legs off, Giberson defeats Devil with "Air Tune" or hymn, Devil identified by cloven hoof, Devil as woman. Charles Pryer, *Reminiscences of an Old Westchester Homestead* (New York: G. P. Putnam's Sons, 1897), 28–33 (NY): Irish gardener returning drunk from dance party after midnight meets stranger who offers work, Devil identified by cloven hoof, Devil vanishes on discovery. John Greenleaf Whittier, *The Supernaturalism of New England*, ed. Edward Wagenknecht (1847; rpt. Norman: University of Oklahoma Press, 1969), 50, illustrated chapbook (NJ): from a childhood book John Greenleaf Whittier (1807–1892) recalled a version in which "a wicked dancing party in New Jersey" declared "they would have a fiddler if they had to send to the lower regions for him." The Devil himself appeared and fiddled "until their feet and legs were worn off to the knees."

Subtype IV. Accidentally Summoning Devil with Music and Dance: Possessed Instruments

A. AFRICAN AMERICAN   Bastin, "The Devil's Goin' to Get You," 191 (NC): man buys banjo, mother warns "the devil's goin' to get you about that banjo. He's goin' to tear it all to pieces." One night about ten o'clock something "ripped that thing all to pieces," man renounces banjo. Browne, *Hants*, 206 (AL): guitarist plays after midnight Saturday, goes home, sets guitar in corner, guitar plays by itself, "it's the old devil playing it because I was out playing it after midnight, and it got Sunday.... Directly it stopped." Evans, *Tommy Johnson*, 30 (MS): In 1918 informant "got tired of living the devil's life," wanted to quit blues for God's word, plays blues one last time for dancers Balling the Jack, goes home, hangs guitar on the wall, "and every time I dozed off to sleep, the devil would wake me up playing the same piece I had them folks dancing by," next day sells guitar for five dollars (had paid seventy-five), plays only church songs afterwards. *Fresno Expositor* (April 7, 1875), qtd. Halpert, *Pinelands*, 394 (CA): two Black waiters are playing cards and arguing, banjo on wall plays by itself. N. H. Hobley (b. 1858, LA, 118–19): Algiers, LA, 1882, possessed girl levitates, stove wood flies through window at twelve o'clock, piano plays unaided, exorcism with three candles, new bucket, quart of beer. Johnson, *Supernaturals*, 106 (NC): informant makes gourd banjo, at midnight it plays by itself. "I knew the Devil liked to play the banjo; so I got real scared," burned it next day. Johnson, *Supernaturals*, 106–7 (NC): musician requests guitar playing at funeral, guitar later plays by itself. "It did that because the guitar is an instrument of the Devil, and it is not supposed to be played in church." Johnson, *Supernaturals*, 107–8 (NC): boy buys guitar though mother forbids it, guitar plays by itself because it "has got the Devil in it," mother makes boy burn it. John F. Szwed, "Musical Adaptation Among Afro-Americans," *JAF* 82 (1969): 114: (MS): "the mother of infamous Mississippi bluesman Robert Johnson claimed that on his deathbed her son hung up his guitar and renounced his blues life, thus dying in glory."

B. ANGLO-AMERICAN   Gerald Milnes, "Wilkie Dennison, County Fiddlemaker," *Goldenseal* 14/1 (1988): 25 (WV): man "returned home from a dance about daybreak one Sunday morning after breaking a pledge to always stop fiddling at midnight on Saturday," possessed fiddle silenced by burning. Halpert, *Pinelands*, 295 (NJ): Sammy Giberson claims he will fiddle until he beats Devil, fiddle plays in box after his death. Halpert, *Pinelands*, 393 n35 (NY): Devil hires fiddler for dance, afterwards fiddle plays by itself, continues to play as it burns.

Appendix B: Other Supernatural Tales with Music, Song, or Dance

There are numerous other supernatural legends in the narratives. Below are items mentioning music, song, and dance that have not been quoted in this or other chapters. Almost all derive from British tradition. There are some additional instances of devil lore or conjure, but most are conventional ghost stories dealing with haunted places (especially cemeteries) or the spirits of known individuals.

> I believes in ghos'. Seein' is believin' an' Ise seed haints all my life. I knows folks can be hoodooed, mighty curious things can be done. One nite I wuz gwine to a dance. We had ter go through thick woods. Hit wuz one o' dem nites dat yo' feels lak deir is somethin' somewhars, yo' feels quir lack an' jumpy an' wants ter look ober yo' sholdier but scart to. Deys alwas' a hant 'round when hits lak dat. De fust thing us knowed deir wuz a ghos' right in front ob us what looked lak a cow. Hit jes stood deir, a gittin' bigger an' bigger, den hit disappeared. Us run lak something wild. I went on ter dat dance but sho didn't dance none, I jes' set 'round an' look on, an' from dat nite I ain't neber gone to a frolic an' danced no mo'. Nor I ain eber gwine to. (Manda Boggan, b. 1847, MS, 158–59)

DISCUSSION: Boggan was still dancing, though; immediately before this story she revealed "de government helps ter take care o' me an' de good white folks helps me long too. A heap o' folk gib me nickles an' dimes ter see me dance" (Manda Boggan, b. 1847, MS, 158). Hers is among the accounts implicating various interconnected themes and belief systems. Although Boggan categorically states that the spectral cow was a *hant* or *ghost* (Motif E423.1.8. *Revenant as cow, bull or calf or steer*), the Devil sometimes appears in bovine form, in which case her story would fall squarely under Scenario III in the Devil legends just discussed, some of which do feature demonic cows. Such hallucinations might also be symptoms of hoodoo (conjure), which Boggan mentions as well.

> I've seed plenty of ha'nts here in Athens. Not long atter I had left Crawfordsville and moved to Athens, I had been in bed jus' a little while one night,

and was jus' dozin' off to sleep when I woke up and sot right spang [spank] up in bed. I seed a man, dressed in white, standin' before me. I sho didn't say nothin' to him for I was too skeered. De very last time I went to a dance, somepin got atter me and skeered me so my hair riz up 'til I couldn't git my hat on my haid, and dat cyored [cured] me of gwine to dances. I ain't never been to no more sich doin's. (Georgia Baker, b. 1850, GA, 48–49)

DISCUSSION: Like the foregoing story from Manda Boggan, this tale would fit comfortably with the devil legends covered in the chapter (Scenario III), save that Georgia Baker categorically names these apparitions as *ha'nts* (ghosts).

One day he was driving his automobile out in the country, and it broke down. He found that he could not fix it so as to continue his journey; so he decided to tow it into a church graveyard which was nearby. He thought this would be the safest place to leave his car until he could return to make the necessary repairs. When he had pulled his car into the church yard, a colored woman came up to him and told him that he had better not leave his car there, as it would be stolen in his absence. She said that most any place was safer than the churchyard to leave the car, as some of the headless men that walked around the nearby graveyard had even stolen the bible and hymn books from the church. (Fletcher Floyd, b. unk., SC, 140)

DISCUSSION: Motif E422.1.1(a). *Headless man.* The headless man (or headless horseman) was a popular European folktale character widely adopted by white and Black Americans. (Headless women, horses, cows, and dogs were also commonly reported.) Church graveyards are favorite haunts, where the headless engage in all sort of mischief, but this is the only case of stolen hymnals I have found. Numerous other narrators related encounters with headless apparitions: Henry Barnes, Jerry Boykins, Henry Cheatam, Annie Coley, Jake Dawkins, Lucy Galloway, Octavia

George, Madison Griffin, Peter Hill, Morris Hillyer, Patsy Hyde, Wilkinson Jones, Duncan McCastle, William McWhorter, Elizabeth Russell, Jordon Smith, and Rosa Washington. For another ex-slave example, see Virginia Jo Hurdle and Herbert Halpert, "Folklore of a Negro Couple in Henry County," *Tennessee Folklore Society Bulletin* 19 (1953): 75.

They's a nigger church and cemetery up the road away from my house where the dead folks come out by twos at night and go in the church and hold service. Me and the preacher what preaches there done seed and heared them. (Charley Mitchell, b. 1852, TX, 113)

DISCUSSION: Motif E273. *Churchyard Ghosts.* Motif E492. *Mass (church service) of the dead.* Mitchell does not explicitly state that the dead folks were singing hymns or spirituals, but one assumes this was some of what he and the preacher would have heard from a phantom church service.

Tuther night I was a-singin' dis tune: "Mother how long 'fore I'se Gwine?" A 'oman riz up and said: "You done raised de daid." Den I laughed and 'lowed: "I knows you is a Sperrit. I'se one too." At dat she faded out of sight. I think folks had ought to be 'ligious 'cause dat is God's plan, and so I jined de church atter Christ done presented Hisself to me. I'se fixin' now to demand my Sperrit in de Lawd.

Yes Ma'am, Miss, I knowed you was a-comin'. I had done seed you, writin' wid dat pencil on dat paper, in de Sperrit. (Elisha Doc Garey. b. ca. 1862, 9–10)

DISCUSSION: Usually a hymn or spiritual exorcises rather than raising the dead (or Devil), but Garey appears to have told this anecdote somewhat in jest, or perhaps as a parable.

One time I wuz passin' a graveyard, and some ghos's wuz in dere singin'. I started runnin', and one of 'em run after me, and he ketched up wid me, and he says, "Where you think you are goin', nigger?" An' I says, "Don' know, Mr. Ghos'. I is jes' goin' 'way from here fas' as I can." He says, "Nex' time you come 'roun' we'll run a race." I says, "Yes sir," but I thought dey ain't goin' to be no nex' time. (Richard Johnson, b. 1836, GA, 2044)

DISCUSSION: Although it is indisputably British, this jest was frequently collected from ex-slaves and other Blacks. Richard Johnson's version is, however, the only example I have found with singing ghosts. Narrator Henry Bufford also told the story. For other Black texts, see A. M. Bacon and E. C. Parsons, "Folk-Lore From Elizabeth City County," *JAF* 35 (1922): 479–80 (three texts from Hampton students); Dance, *Shuckin'*, 27–28; "A Negro Ghost Story," *Southern Workman* 28 (1899): 449; Elsie Clews Parsons, "Folk-Tales Collected at Miami, Fla.," *JAF* 30 (1917): 224 (George Washington, b. 1850, FL); Parsons, "Guilford County," 195 (George Marshall, b. ca. 1845, NC); Puckett, *Folk Beliefs*, 131; Smiley, "Folk-Lore," 367–68 (SC). For Anglo-American and British texts, references, and discussion, see, Halpert, *Pinelands*, 147, 259–60.

I was conjured once, and only once, in my life by a man who gave me some whiskey in a black bottle. . . . If you gets conjured the only way for you to get cured or have the spell lifted is to go to some one who knows more bout it than the one who conjured you. Some folks wore different things in their shoes to keep the spells off. I don't believe nothing like that could help none. Spirits don't show their self now like they used to. There was a time you couldn't stay in certain houses they bothered you so. My grandmother sent me to the crib one night for to get some corn. When I got nearly there I could hear fiddling and dancing going on. The crib was the place dances had been held. (Julius Jones, b. ca. 1847, TN, 1219–20)

DISCUSSION: Motif E337.1.3(b). *Sounds of dance in haunted house*. According to A. G. Bradley (1850–1943), among Virginia Blacks ghosts did not "haunt

bedsides or passages, but were to be seen rather in the neighbourhood of corncribs, wheatfields, or tobacco barns" (Bradley, "Memories," 334). Whiskey was a common medium for conjure tricks (for example, see Puckett, *Folk Beliefs*, 248, 252, 292), and people frequently placed protective charms in their shoes (238–39, 288–93).

The old colored fo'ks told us ghost stories they got from the white fo'ks, and we believed them too. I never seed "ghostes" but once. That was after I was married and come to Harrison County [ca. 1873]. Me and some more men was walking down the Shreveport road. We looked down the road and saw a big house that was all lit up and there was fiddling and dancing going on inside. When we got close to the house all the music stopped and it was so quiet you could hear a pin drap, and the lights went out. When we got on passed it a piece it lit up and the fiddling and dancing started again. I warn't scared, but we didn't hang 'round to see what caused it to do that way. (Sol Walton, b. 1849, TX, 3955)

DISCUSSION: Motif E337.1.3(b). *Sounds of dance in haunted house*. This is Walton's version of the ghost-dance theme, yet another popular British import. For Anglo-American texts, see Thomas E. Barden, *Virginia Folk Legends* (Charlottesville: University Press of Virginia, 1991), 129–30; Browne, *Hants*, 229; William Lynwood Montell, *Ghosts Along the Cumberland: Deathlore in the Kentucky Foothills* (Knoxville: University of Tennessee Press), 111–12.

When the war began and my father went to war, my mother left Helena and came here. They whipped her too much, those white folks did. She got tired of all that beating. She took all of us with her. All six of us children were born before the war. I was the fourth.

There is a place down here where the white folks used to whip and hang the niggers. Baskin Lake they call it. Mother got that far. I don't know

Fig. 12.4. Sol Walton, ex-slave, Marshall, TX, December 4, 1937. Portraits of African American ex-slaves from the US Works Progress Administration, Federal Writers' Project slave narratives collection, Library of Congress.

DISCUSSION: Motif E337.1.3(b). *Sounds of dance in haunted house.* Another example of the ghost dance, though more of Johnson's account concerns the brutal murders behind the haunting.

When I first come to Texas I'se cut logs, and builds me a house on this here very place where I'se now live. I was washing clothes for my wife when I would come in at the door something would nearly knock my hat off, but I never paid no attention to it, but when I gets nearly thru washing I starts in at the door and something hit at my hat and knock me plum back on the ground flat on my back. Then I sees what it was. It was one of these here Panters [panthers] just about grown. Boss, I grab the battling stick that we use to punch the clothes with and killed that panter just as dead as a markel [mackerel]. Then that very night I was just about ready to skin that panther and all at once I heard some music, the sweetest I ever heard. I stop plum still and listen then it finally comes right over me, and just keep playing, Nearer My God to Thee—with the sweetest juice harp you ever heard. It just kept playing for 'bout 30 minutes, then finally goes higher and higher until I couldn't hear it at all. I goes on in the house and asked Govie, that is my wife, if she heard it and she said yes, but she thought it was me. Then that music it come ever week on that very night, Boss I could heard that music until I tore that house down and builds [a new] one, then it quit coming. I'se sure was glad 'cause I'se scared of that music. I thought all the time that was that Babe in the Manger that Mistress told me about coming after me. (Toby Jones, b. ca. 1848, TX, 2148–49)

how. I think that she came in a wagon. She stayed there a little while and then she went to Churchill's place. Churchill's place and John Addison's place is close together down there. That is old time. Them folks is dead, dead, dead. Churchill's and Addison's places joined near Horse Shoe Lake. They had hung and burnt people—killed 'em and destroyed 'em at Baskin Lake. We stayed there about four days before we went on to Churchill's place. We couldn't stay there long.

The ha'nts—the spirits—bothered us so we couldn't sleep. All them people that had been killed there used to come back. We could hear them tipping 'round in the house all night long. They would blow out the light. You would kiver up and they would git on top of the kiver. Mama couldn't stand it; so she come down to General Churchill's place and made arrangements to stay there. Then she came back and got us children. She had an old man to stay there with us until she come back and got us. We couldn't stay there with them ha'nts dancing 'round and carryin' us a merry gait. (Ella Johnson, b. 1852, AR, 77–78)

DISCUSSION: Motif E402.1.3. *Invisible ghost plays musical instrument.* Motif E451.8. *Ghost laid when house it haunts is destroyed or changed.* Toby Jones combines another pair of English supernatural motifs with one of the panther tales popular in American frontier tradition. Frequently related by ex-slaves, these animal stories were sometimes tall tales, sometimes semirealistic accounts of a habitual frontier danger (though typically embellished with folktale motifs). Jones's supernatural twist is unique, however, the implication in his version being that killing the panther (the usual outcome) caused a musical haunting. This then raises the question, "Could or would a panther's ghost play a jew's harp?" (Fortunately for Jones the harpist was not a vengeful Christ as he at first feared.)

> One night I was at Notasulga an' I heerd some singing. I stopped an' hit was right at my feet an' would go further off. I took out wid hit an' hit kept stoppin' an' startin' off ag'in 'twell hit giv' out entirely. I looked to see where I was an' I was at de cemetery an' nothin' didn't bother me neither. I eased out an' shut de gate an' never foun' whut carried me dere. (Wade Owens, b. 1863, AL, 308)

DISCUSSION: The siren song is an ancient theme, but the graveyard setting again indicates these were probably singing ghosts.

> Dar wuz two young brudders dat libed out in de country, dey wuz name de Grimes brudders. Well, dey cum to town, gits drunk an' bein' jes a couple ob thoughtless boys, dey fired 'em a few shots, gits on dar hosses an' rides er long er singing de rebel song "De Gal I Lef' Behime Me." Well dem Yankee soljers tuk atter 'em, an' chaset 'em erpiece an' w'en de brudders won't halt, w'en de soljers yell at dem, de soljers shot 'em down. De boys wuz buried in er brick vault togedder in the ole First Street Cemetery. Dar's a lot ob undergrowth, Johnson grass and jus' a sunken place dar now. But I'se heard tell dat fer many an' many a year, effen you goes by dat place, dat you can hear dem moan de rebel song "De Girl I lef' Behind Me." But dat's only on de full ob de moon. (Aaron Ray, b. ca. 1869, TX, child of ex-slaves, 3259)

DISCUSSION: "The Girl I Left Behind Me" (Laws P 1 B) was a British broadside ballad frequently sung by both Confederate and Federal troops. Silber, *Civil War*, 308, 327.

> "Nancy do you know any ghost stories, or did you ever see a ghost?"
> "No, Ma'am, I ain't never see a ghos' but I heayd de drum!"
> "What drum did you hear—war drums?"
> "No, ma'am de drum de little man beats down at Rock Crick. Some say he is a little man whut wears a cap and goes down the crick beating a drum befo' a war. But some say you can hear de drum 'most any spring now. Go down to the Crick and keep quiet and you hear Brrr, Brrr, Bum hum, louder and louder and den it goes away. Some say dey hav' seen de little man, but I never seen him, but I heayd de drum, 'fo de war, and ater dat too. There was a white man kilt hisself near our place. He uster play a fiddle, and some time he come back an play. I has heayd him play his fiddle, but I ain't seen him. Some fokes say dey is seen him in the wood playin' and walkin' 'bout." (Nancy Settles, b. 1845, SC, 235, int. Margaret Johnson)

DISCUSSION: Motifs E334.4. *Ghost of suicide seen at death spot or nearby*; E402.1.3(a). *Ghost plays violin*; E402.1.3(d). *Ghost beats a drum*; G303.5.2.1. *Devil in green clothing with hat*. Settles gives another traditional description of the European Devil, who sometimes appears as a little man in a cap or hat. For Anglo-American examples, see Browne, *Hants*, 36–38. For another ex-slave version of *Ghost plays violin*, see Hurdle and Halpert, "Folklore of a Negro Couple," 76. For Anglo-American versions, see Barden, *Virginia Folk Legends*, 267–68; John A. Burrison, *Storytellers: Folktales and Legends From the South* (Athens: University of Georgia Press, 1989), 91–92; Bertha McKee Dobie, "Mysterious Music in the San Bernard River," *Legends of Texas*, ed. J. Frank Dobie, PTFS 3 (Austin, 1924): 137–41; Montell, *Ghosts*, 95–96, 123–24; Charles M. Skinner, *Myths and Legends of Our Own Land*, 2 vols. (Philadelphia: J. P. Lippincott, 1896), I: 170–73, 237; II: 184–85. For *Ghost beats a drum*, see

Katherine Briggs, *British Folktales* (New York: Pantheon, 1970), 179.

My grandfather's mother had a chair and that was hers only. She was named Senia and was about eighty years old. We burned nothing but pine knots in the hearth. You would put one or two of those on the fire and they would burn for hours. We were all in bed and had been for an hour or two. There were some others sleeping in the same room. There came a peculiar knocking on grandmother's chair. It's hard to describe it. It was something like the distant beating of a drum. Grandmother was dead, of course. The boys got up and ran out and brought in some of the hands. When they came in, a little thing about three and a half feet high with legs about six or eight inches long ran out of the room. (Waters McIntosh, b. 1863, SC, 21)

DISCUSSION: E402.1.3(d). *Ghost beats a drum.* The initial impression is that the drum was beaten by the ghost of McIntosh's grandmother, but the little thing running out of the room might again suggest a demon or sprite.

We had good times fore we lef' de ole place, fore Ole Massa died. We usta git together in de ebenin's. Dey'd say "I's gon'a step to de udder cabin"—en word ud git aroun' an "for" you knowd it dey'd be a crowd. We allus said "jest step over" no matter how far it wuz. Den some er de women ud put in a quilt an' some ud git to cookin' an' bakin Mmm! de lassus cakes we used to have! An' den wen de quilt wuz finished an de eatin done dey'd clean out de room an dance. Dem sho wuz good times. But I 'members de las' dance we had. Ole Massa wuz sick. We's habbin' de dance an' Aunt Mary wuz dar. She wuz a spiritualis' woman—you knows whut a spiritualis is, don' you? Well, everybody wuz dancin' an' habbin' a good time—Aunt Mary say, "Hush! I's gonna ask is Ole Massa gonna git well." Den she say—"If Ole Massa gonna die, rap three times." Den in a minnit comes a loud blam! blam! blam! right across de house. Den we all cry an' go home cause we know Ole Massa's gonna die! (Emily Camster Green, b. unk., MO, 139–40)

DISCUSSION: As a nineteenth-century occult movement, Spiritualism originated in western New York State in the late 1840s and rapidly spread across America, Britain, and the Continent. Spiritualists' main attraction was their purported ability to summon the spirits of dead, who then communicated with them through encoded raps or knocks (hence the practice was also known, sometimes derisively, as *spirit rapping*). Spiritualism was taken quite seriously by multitudes, and sampled as light entertainment by many others, so it would not have been unusual for a Spiritualist to figure in an antebellum quilting also featuring feasting, music, and dance.

My father died and soon my mother was allowed to marry a slave named Joe, but we called him "That Man." When I was a very young girl my step father died and then I saw my first hant, or ghost. My step father was a hunter and owned a pack of big mouthed dogs. Soon after he died the dogs all went away. Then the hant began coming to our cabin. Mother cooked on the open fire in the big chimney and every night the cabin window would fly open and in would come my step father and his dogs. "Mammy, Mammy," I would call out, "That man is here again." He would go lift the lid from the dinner pot and eat; then he would feed the pack of hungry dogs. A horn would blow far away and the hunter and his dogs always left through the window. Next morning I would tell my mother: "We will starve to death; I know because That Man and his dogs will always eat up all our grub." But Old Missus always gave us plenty to eat. "That Man" and his dogs never stopped coming until after the war. They kept it up as long as my mother cooked on the open fire, and left the food on the crane. (Katy Rose, b. ca. 1850, KY, 175–76)

DISCUSSION: Katy Rose's account of the spectral hunter, ghost dogs, and unearthly horn might be her own independent invention (or extrasensory perception), but it strongly recalls *The Wild Hunt* (Motif E501), a Northern European supernatural tale complex especially well-represented in Britain.

> I aint never seen no hants but I've heard em plenty of times. I wuz working in my garden one day and I heard some one walking in de house and I thought it wuz my sister and I called but she didn't answer and jest kept on walking so I went in and looked high and low but there warn't nobody there and when I started out de door it started again and my hair gan to creep off my head and I nearly broke my neck gittint to de white folks' house. We would stay in de house wid the white girls after dey [slaveholder] father died and lots of times we would hear de peanna playing and dey didn't even have no piano but you could hear them keys jest a playing, and folks would walk up and down de stairs. (Susan Jones, b. 1842, MS, 1258–59)

DISCUSSION: Motif E402.1.3(ba). *Ghost plays piano*; E402.1.2. *Footsteps of invisible ghost heard.* Ex-slaves generally associated pianos—even ghostly pianos— with slaveholders' wives and daughters, this obviously being yet another example. (Ex-slave Eliza Bell told of another piano playing ghost identified as the slaveholder's daughter.)

SLAVE AND NEGRO LORE

The wonderful meteoric display known as the "star shower" or "the time when the stars fell," occurred in 1833. It was on the night of the 12th and 13th of November. Many ignorant persons concluded that the Judgement day had come, or that the end of the world was at hand. Negroes especially were very much frightened. A dance was in progress on a Buchanan County farm, attended exclusively by slaves from the neighborhood. When the star shower began the negroes were first made aware of the fact by a messenger who ran frantically into the cabin and shouted, "If you all wants to git to hebin, you'd better 'gin to say yo' pra'rs mighty sudden, case the Lawd is acomin' wi' de fire an' de glory an' de wuld'll be burnt up like cracklin' 'fo mo'nin." The dancers ran out, fell on their knees and cried for mercy. Not for many days did they recover their fright. One old negro declared that if the world and his life were spared he would agree to break eighty pounds of hemp every day instead of fifty, as he had been accustomed to do. (S2 11 *MO*: 70)

DISCUSSION: This item from Missouri interviewer Carl B. Boyer is included in a compilation of *Buchanan County, Folklore* but is not attributed to a specific ex-slave. Visible across the United States, an estimated 50,000 to 150,000 meteors fell per hour during the Leonid Meteor Storm of November 12–13, 1833. This, "the night when the stars fell," was one of the most celebrated topics in slave legendry, mentioned by scores of WPA narrators, some eyewitnesses, others merely having heard about it. The Buchanan County account is unusual for being set at a slave frolic, the implication being that the dancers believed their own sinful behavior had brought about, or left them especially unready for, the Last Judgment. (At least one individual, though, concluded that work quotas were the issue.)

> Mother used to tell a tale 'bout when she was a little girl. Her mother went to frolics but her father went to bed, he was always tired after his day's work. One night my mother saw a woman come to her father's bed and rub her hand over his head. It didn't wake him up. De next day he took sick and soon died. I don't believe in hoodoo doctors but it is like de blood hounds can run and tree a man but if you can't find de goods it don't count. (Dave Harper, b. 1850, MO, 167)

DISCUSSION: Dave Harper's story strongly suggests another case of dancing raising a devil—in this case a succubus of some sort—but Harper seems to have regarded the mysterious woman as human (that is, a hoodoo, not a demon). His closing comment is obscure but may have intended something like: "I ordinarily don't believe in hoodoo doctors but my mother got the goods on this one."

Rita and Retta was de Nigger 'omans what put pizen in some collards what dey give Aunt Vira and her baby to eat. She had been laughin' at a man 'cause his coattail was a-flappin' so funny whilst he was dancin', and dem two Jezebels thought she was makin' fun of dem. At de graveyard, 'fore dey buried her, dey cut her open and found her heart was all decayed. De overseer driv dem 'omans clear off de plantation, and Marster, he was mighty mad. He said he done lost 'bout $2,000. If he had kotched dem 'omans he woulda hung 'em, cause he was de hanger. In 'bout two weeks dat overseer left dar, and Old Marse had to git him anudder man to take his place. (Addie Vinson, b. 1852, GA, 104–5)

DISCUSSION: Although this episode is presented as a simple murder, the autopsy suggests conjure or witchcraft.

I was conjured once an' don' wan' to be conjured no mo'. I was conjured an' de spell brung big bumps under both my arms. Yes sir, brung fo' big bumps under de right arm an' three bumps under de lef'. I declare dem bumps was so big dat de petticoat what I used to tie roun' me up under my arms, I had to fasten by shoulder straps over top of my shoulders. Couldn't figger out who conjured me. Only one 'oman could git to me. She de only 'oman what ever come in my house an' she didn't hab no cause to conjure me.

My husban' sen' me to de root doctor, ole Dr. Andrews. [There follows a lengthy account of how, through the usual process of trial and error, Dr. Andrews discovers the spell and how to undo it.] . . .

I went home an' taken de medicine. Sho' 'nough on de ninth day 'tween three an' fo' 'clock, Carolina

Crip commence a hollerin' an' runnin' all up an' down her neighborhood. A man what seed me later said, "Dey been a seekin' you all day." Fo' days an' days I been dreamin' 'bout things in trees. De trees was whar two path cross each other. It was a Sunday, an' me an' Jake, my husban', went down back o' de house an' crossed de branch. Fus' thing we saw was two paths crossin'. On each side o' de paths was trees wid augur holes bored in 'em. Dese augur holes had conjure things in 'em. We could hear her voice way cross de woods asingin' all day—singin' an' confessin' 'cause she couldn't he'p it:

Oh yes! Oh yes!
I been conjurin',
Oh yes! Oh yes! Oh yes!
I been killin',
No cause, no cause, no cause,
In de worl'.

Her voice kep' a gittin' nearer. Den my ole man gits mad. Purty soon she was comin' through de yard o' de house nex' to ours. Jake say, "I swear 'fo God, Tilda, ef anybody conjure you, I'se goin' to kill 'em." Went an' got his ax. Closer she got, closer Jake hitch de ax 'tween his knees. I jus' begged him, "Hubban', please don' do nuffin." He cryin', "Wife I goin' kill her." I got scared to def, an' set down in his lap an' say, "Jake, darlin', ain' I been a good 'oman fo' you? I done birth you plenty chillun an' never crossed you, has I? Ef you hit dis 'oman, I ain' goin' hab no husba'd; de chillun goin' hab no father, an' dis house won' hab no haid." He give me de ax jus' as she come into our clearin'. Was still so mad he went down towards de spring jus' acryin'. Dat medicine sho' was workin' powerful strong on her. She stumbled on up in de yard asingin' at de top o' her voice:

Oh yes! Oh yes!
I conjured you,
I conjured you,
No cause in de worl',

No cause in de worl',
Give me yo' han',
Give me yo' han'.

I gave her my han' an' I been all right ever since, 'ceptin' de place gits sore an' itches a little ev'y once in a while. (Matilda Henrietta Perry, b. 1852, VA, 221–23)

DISCUSSION: Perry's story, complete with a spell cast at the crossroads, is similar to countless other accounts of conjure tricks, their discovery, and their undoing, except that here the conjurer is compelled to sing a song revealing her guilt, then another reconciling her to her victim, highly unusual details (though songs or rhymes often figure in casting spells).

RELIGIOUS SONG

SHOUT

For thus saith the Lord; Sing with gladness for Jacob, and shout among the chief of the nations: publish ye, praise ye, and say, O Lord, save thy people, the remnant of Israel. (Jeremiah 31:7)

I neber sing nuffin but religious songs. I believes dat it is a sin to sing dese new fangled songs. De Lord wants yo' to sings bout Him. Dont de good Book say fur yo' to shout an' sing bout de Lord. I is gwine to do my duty. (Lewis Jefferson, b. 1853, MS, 1146)

And there came a fire out from before the Lord, and consumed upon the altar the burnt offering and the fat: which when all the people saw, they shouted, and fell on their faces. (Leviticus 9:24)

Oh Lawdie how dey did baptize down at de wha'f! De Baptist people would gather at de wha'f on de fust Sunday in May. Dey would kum fum all de Baptist Churches. Would leave de chuch singin' en shoutin' en keep dat up 'til dey got ter de river. Hab seen dem wid new clothes on git down on de groun en roll en git covered wid dirt. Sum ob dem would almos' luze dere clothes, en dey'd fall down lak dey wuz dying. Dese last few y'ars dey hab got ter stylish ter shout. (Frankie Goole, b. 1853, TN, 23)

O Clap your hands, all ye people; shout unto God with the voice of triumph. (Psalm 47:1)

Once when Master Gilliam took one of his slaves to church at old Tranquil, he told him dat he musn't shout dat day—said he would give him a pair of new boots if he didn't shout. About de middle of services, de old nigger couldn't stand it no longer. He jumped up and hollered: "Boots or no boots. I gwine to shout today." (Emoline Glasgow, b. 1859, SC, 135)

Shouting—dancing before God—was a near-constant in nineteenth-century Black worship and sacred song, and in ex-slave descriptions thereof. Even

291

Fig. 13.1. "Religious dancing of the Blacks, termed 'Shouting.'" Charles Stearns, *The Black Man of the South, And the Rebels* (New York: American News, 1872), 371. Slavery Images: A Visual Record of the African Slave Trade and Slave Life in the Early African Diaspora. slaveryimages.org.

when banned or barred by slaveholders, shouting was notable (and usually thereby noted) in its absence. It is impossible to comprehend Black sacred song—or Black faith—without the shout, which reaffirms the inseparability of music and dance in the Black world, and the spiritual power of both. Shouting arguably provided the most profound musical experiences recalled by ex-slaves: more than that, the shout is the genre of dance or dance-singing—sacred or secular—most often described in the narratives. It has been mentioned many times already; it will be mentioned many, many times more.[1]

Simply put, *shouting* refers to African American trance dancing. There is little improving on Robert Winslow Gordon's observation: "the word has no reference to shouting in the ordinary sense. Technically the Negro 'shout' is a peculiar combination of singing combined with a rhythmic shuffling dance, a 'holy dance' as it is sometimes called. No song, no matter how boisterous is sufficient; the shuffling about in a circle is the prime essential."[2] The *ring shout* was only one variation, however. Gordon again:

> Shouting took many other forms. One might shout acceptably while standing in one place, the feet either shuffling, or rocking backward and forward, tapping alternately with heel and toe, the knees bending, the body swaying, and the hands clapping. Or the singer could alternately advance and retreat. Not infrequently two singers would shout facing one another in a sort of competition of skill or endurance.[3]

Choreographed group shouts like the ring were disappearing by the first decades of the twentieth century, when they were revived mainly for folklorists and folk festivals.[4] The spontaneous shouting by individuals that Gordon describes can still be observed every Sunday in Black churches across America, as well as at gospel music concerts and conventions and other faith-based events.

The African American tradition of shouting is by and large unique. It does have obvious African antecedents, and similar practices occur throughout the Black diaspora. However, African American shouting also has important points of contact with American white tradition that have been almost willfully ignored in the rush to claim African origins. The term *shout* itself has been widely misrepresented. In the 1940s Lorenzo Dow Turner speculated that, as a designation for "a religious dance in which the participants continue to perform until they become exhausted," the African American *shout* derives from the Arabic *saut*, "to move around the Kaaba (the small stone building at Mecca which is the chief object of the pilgrimage of Mohammedans) until exhausted."[5] In this scenario, Muslim slaves introduced the Arabic term into North America, where it was confused with a vaguely similar English word, then universally adopted.

Regrettably, Turner's flawed reconstruction has since been repeated as fact. Linguistically unfounded, it also flies in the face of the obvious (and of common sense) since the term's true etymology could not be clearer. As Black shouters have always insisted, their use of *shout* comes from the King James Bible and the many passages linking shouting to praise singing, spirit possession, trance dancing, and ecstatic worship generally. For instance, Ezra 3:11: "And they sang together by course in praising and giving thanks unto the Lord; because he is good, for his mercy endureth for ever toward Israel. And all the people shouted with a great shout, when they praised the Lord, because the foundation of the house of the Lord was laid."[6]

Nor is there any question that slaves recognized the scriptural basis of shouting. "Dont de good Book say fur yo' to shout an' sing bout de Lord" (Lewis Jefferson, b. 1853, MS, 1146). Reverend Robert W. Todd (1831–1906) had watched holy dancing "on the colored side of the encampment" at integrated camp meetings in antebellum Maryland and Delaware.

> The grand "march 'round de' campment" was inaugurated, accompanied with leaping, shuffling, and dancing, after the order of David before the ark when his wife thought he was crazy; accompanied by a song appropriate to the exciting occasion. Some of my readers will recognize the following couplets:
>
>> We's a marchin' away to Cana-ann's land;
>> I hears de music ob de angel band.
>>
>> Chorus—O come an' jine de army;
>>> An' we'll keep de ark a movin';
>>> As we goes shoutin' home!
>>
>> Come, childering, storm ole Jericho's walls;
>> Yes, blow an' shout, an' down dey falls!
>>> Chorus—O come, etc.[7]

Reverend Todd's chorus does indeed refer to 2 Samuel.

> [13]And it was *so*, that when they that bare the ark of the Lord had gone six paces, he sacrificed oxen and fatlings. [14]And David danced before the Lord with all *his* might; and David *was* girded with a linen ephod. [15]So David and all the house of Israel brought up the ark of the Lord with shouting, and with the sound of the trumpet. [16]And as the ark of the Lord came into the city of David, Michal Saul's daughter looked through a window, and saw King David leaping and dancing before the Lord; and she despised him in her heart. (2 Samuel 6: 13–16)

Slaves were much taken with this passage and King David overall: "David, David is a 'bediant young boy, / He kilt Goliah, and shouted fer joy" (Jane Sutton, b. ca. 1853, MS, 209).[8] The tale of Joshua shouting down Jericho's walls (see Todd's second stanza) was another favorite.

> [5]And it shall come to pass, that when they make a long blast with the ram's horn, and when ye hear the sound of the trumpet, all the people shall shout with a great shout; and the wall of the city shall fall down flat. . . . [15]And it came to pass on the seventh day, that they rose early about the dawning of the day, and compassed the city after the same manner seven times. . . . [16]And it came to pass at the seventh time, when the priests blew the trumpets, Joshua said unto the people, Shout; for the Lord hath given you the city. . . . [20]So the people shouted when the priests blew with trumpets: and it came to pass, when the people heard the sound of the trumpet, and the people shouted with a great shout, that the wall fell down flat. (Joshua 6:5, 15–16, 20)

In 1817 several young Quakers attended a Black camp meeting near West Chester, Pennsylvania, one later writing that "a wild refrain greeted our ears from a portion of the congregation who were marching round the camp, pausing at each corner to blow a tin horn in a blast that rung out in anything but melodious accents upon the summer air; the meaning of which we could not understand, and thought perhaps it might be intended to represent Joshua's chosen men marching around the walls of Jericho, blowing the rams' horns and shouting."[9] There was no "perhaps" about it. The custom of Black shouters imitating the Israelites shouting at Jericho is amply documented into the post–WWII era. The popular fin de siècle spiritual "That Suits Me" is built around the injunction (successively addressed to various persons): "Come on, brother, let's go around the wall, / That suits me." The wall is, of course, the walled city of Jericho. In his headnote to an Alabama version, Newman I. White writes, "I have heard the first line explained as an invitation to begin one of the marches around the room which sometimes occur in Negro worship."[10] Indeed, spirituals like "That Suits Me," "Little David," and "Joshua" expressly link Patriarchs' shouting to holy dancing and spirit possession in Black churches: "When I get to Heaven, I'm goin' a-put on my crown, and shout all over God's Heaven."[11] "Down in de valley, O Lord! / Didn't go t' stay, O Lord! / An' soul got happy, O Lord! / I stayed all day, O Lord!"[12] "Some join the church for to sing and shout; / Before six months they's all turned out."[13]

The term *shout*, then, came from King James, King David, and Captain Joshua, but the African and African American foundations of shouting are numerous and incontrovertible. Complicating the picture, from colonial times American white nonconformists and Evangelicals routinely practiced trance dancing, which also has European precedents, and which they also called *shouting*, based on these same scriptures. White shouting exploded during the Second Great Awakening (ca. 1800), one of whose most popular innovations was the integrated camp meeting, where Black and white believers shouted together.[14] In the South specifically, white fundamentalists have always shouted just as much as their Black neighbors. "I 'members well de Sunday I fust seen a shoutin'. It was two white ladies" (Eliza White, b. ca. 1855, GA, 411).

Durin' slavery days I went wid de white folks to church. I 'members de first person I saw shout was a white woman an' she started shoutin' right by me. Believe me I darted out dat meetin' house. Old miss grabbed at me when I started by her but shucks, I was gone then. When they got home I was there settin' on the steps. (Rube Montgomery, b. 1856, MS, 1561–62)

My w'ite mistus was a Christian. She'd own her God anyw'ere. She uster shout; jus' sit down 'n' clap her han's 'n' say, "Hallelujah." Once I see her shout in d' chu'ch. I didn' know w'at dat was den.

I t'ink sumpthin' ail her, 'n' I run down d' aisle 'n' went t' fannin her. (Charlotte Beverly, b. ca. 1847, TX, 284–85)[15]

Of course none of this establishes that Blacks borrowed the custom of shouting or even the expression from whites, any more than the reverse. It is even plausible (if in this case unlikely) that different sects would independently adopt the term *shout* simply through literal interpretations of scripture. Then too, holy dancing went by other names: rocking, marching, walking, rolling, jumping, even just dancing.[16] "Good people used to dance 'long at funerals. The Holy Bible says there's a time for everythin', 'A time to dance and a time to refrain from dancin'.' When the procession went along followin' the hearse, there was dancin', but it was different from the other" (Marie Brown, free-born unk., LA, 35). Brown, a Creole and lifelong New Orleans resident, quotes Ecclesiastes: "[3]To everything there is a season, and a time to every purpose under heaven: . . . [4]A time to weep, and a time to laugh; a time to mourn, and a time to dance" (Ecclesiastes 3:4). Granted, some ex-slaves remembered whites shouting, or even described Blacks and whites shouting together. The majority, however, characterized holy dancing as a Black refuge, wholly off-limits to slaveholding infidels. "White folks tell stories 'bout 'ligion. Dey tells stories 'bout it kaise dey's 'fraid of it. I stays independent of what white folks tells me when I shouts. De Spirit moves me every day, dat's how I stays in. White folks don't feel sech as I does; so dey stays out" (Cordelia Anderson Jackson, b. ca. 1859, SC, 5).

The basic motivation for shouting is spirit possession, most often called *getting happy*. As a general rule organized group shouts were intended to incite possession, while individuals shouted after they received the spirit through some other medium: singing, preaching, or praying but also personal crises and victories, visions and epiphanies, and born-again experiences. Group shouts might occur during regular church services, usually at their conclusion, or at separate gatherings, perhaps on another day or night, maybe in a special praise house reserved for the activity. Some shouts were performed seasonally, especially on Christmas or Watch Night (New Year's Eve).[17] Shouts and shouting customarily figured in rites of passage, especially baptisms, wakes, and funerals. They dramatized other Bible stories. Lafayette Price (b. ca. 1850, AL, 3174–75) remembered "Adam in the Garden Pinning Leaves," accompanying a shout where people pretended to pick up and pin fig leaves to their bodies.

Anudder w'at dey uster sing was:

> Oh, Ebe, w'er is Adam
> Oh, Ebe, w'er is Adam
> Adam in de gyarden
> Pinnin' leaves.
>
> Adam heerd God's voice,
> Adam heerd God's voice,
> Adam in de gyarden
> Pinnin' leaves.
>
> Adam hide b'hind a tree,
> Adam hide b'hind a tree,
> Adam in de gyarden
> Pinnin' leaves. (Lafayette Price, b. ca. 1850,
>   AL, 3174–75)[18]

Mississippi ex-slave Hamp Kennedy described Walking Egypt, which reenacted the Exodus. Mary Johnson contributed a shout for shooing the devil.

> Dat chu'ch was a remock'ble t'ing. Dey was a deep trench w'at was cut all 'roun' de bottom and clay steps w'at lead all de way up to de top of de mountain. W'en de cullud folks git to shoutin', dat ch'uch was jes' a rollin' and rockin'. One de songs w'at I 'member bes' was:

> Shoo de debil out de corner,
>   Shoo, members, shoo
> Shoo de debil out de corner,
>   Shoo, members, shoo.

Den all de wimmen folks would "shoo" wid dey aprons. (Mary Johnson, b. ca. 1858, MS, 2025–26)

Some shouts were quite localized. The *Easter Rock* was an elaborate all-night ceremony known only in Concordia Parish, Louisiana.[19] Ex-slave Thomas Goodwater recalled "Room Enough," documented only in his native coastal South Carolina; there, however, wrote the editors of *Slave Songs of the United States* (1867), "this 'shout' is very widely spread, and variously sung."[20]

Dey used to sing dis too:

> Room enough, room enough
> Room enough, room enough
> Room enough in de Heaven I know,
> I can't stay away,
> Room enough in de Heaven I know,
> I can't stay away. (Thomas Goodwater, b. 1855,
>   SC, 170)

There were also recreational shouts, hypothetically allowing church members to dance socially without sin (many church people still disapproved, feeling that such shouting did indeed cross the bright-red line into sinful dancing). Ex-slaves and other sources even describe people shouting to fiddles and other forbidden instruments. "Frolics included 'dancing, shouting, pattin 'n fiddling'" (John Watts, b. 1854, GA, 635). "My brother wuz de captain ob de quill band an' dey sure could make you shout and dance til you uz nigh 'bout exhausted" (Dora Roberts, b. 1849, GA, 206–7). Around 1850 John Dix observed a fiddler playing for hymn singing and shouting aboard an excursion boat bound for a Black camp meeting at Flushing, Long Island.[21]

The shout "Rock Daniel" actually resembled a couple dance. Traditionally performed on Watch Night but also at parties and frolics, people "Rocked Daniel" in pairs, facing, with hands on one another's shoulders.

Us didn't go to church none, but I goes now to de New Prophet Church and my favorite song is:

Set down, set down, set down,
Set down, set down,
Set down, chile, set down.
Soul so happy till I kain't set down.

Move de member, move Danu-el,
Move de member, move Danu-el.
Danu-el, member, don' move so slow.
Danu-el, member, don' move so slow.
Got on my rockin' shoes, Danu-el.
Got on my rockin' shoes, Danu-el.

Shoes gwine to rock me home,
Shoes gwine to rock me home, Danu-el,
Shoes gwine to rock me home, Danu-el,
Shoes gwine to rock me home, Danu-el,
Danu-el.

Shoes gwine to rock by faith,
Shoes gwine to rock by faith, Danu-el,
Shoes gwine to rock by faith, Danu-el.

Move de member, move Danu-el.
Move de member, move Danu-el.
Got on my starry crown, Danu-el.
Got on my starry crown, Danu-el. (Emma
    Crockett, b. ca. 1857, AL, 93)[22]

When young people "Rocked Daniel" recreationally, they sometimes called it "Rock Candy," a clever wordplay on "Rock Daniel."

Katie Holloway recalls playing a game called "Rock Candy" when she went to parties among the negro youths and maidens. She said the girls would stand in two lines, facing each other. The gentlemen would stand at the foot of the two lines of maidens. The girls would place their hands on each others' shoulders, while facing each other, they would keep time to the rhythm of the song singing: "A poor man he sold me, and a rich man he bought me and sent me down to New Orleans, to learn how to rock candy. Rock candy, two and

two, Rock candy, two and two. Rock candy, two and two. For it's no harm to rock candy." The song continued until the entire number of young gentleman and had the opportunity to rock candy with the line of girls. The game was popular with both white and negro youths, Aunt Katie declares. "The preachers and churchgoing people hated for us to 'Rock Candy.' They called it dancing, but that only made us more determined to play it." (Katie Rose née Holloway, b. ca. 1850, KY, 177–78)[23]

Across the Black world, trance dancing is almost always accompanied by drums, but only rarely in North America outside of the Sea Islands and South Louisiana.[24] In the Sea Islands, shouters sometimes also struck broom handles, sticks, or canes against floors as drum substitutes, but in most places the clapping, shuffling, and stamping of participants and onlookers sufficed.[25] Gordon describes the universally recognized version of the shout: a percussive shuffling, stamping, or heel-to-toe step, knees bent, hips swaying, body rigidly upright above the waist or leaning slightly forward, hands clinched, arms held to the sides or extended for balance. Other common movements include bowing, spinning, jumping, jerking, hitching, or waving upraised arms with outstretched palms. There are other local or purely personal variations.

In March of 1936, when a party was given in honor of Father Coates' 108th birthday, one of each of the four generations of his family were present. . . . On the occasion he said that the cause for his long life was due to living close to nature, rising early, going to bed early and not dissipating in any way. He can "shout" (jumping about a foot and a half from the floor and knocking his heels together). He does chores about his yard; looks years younger than he really is and enjoys good health. (Father Charles Coates, b. 1828, VA, 71–72)

As shouters get happy, however, their movements become increasingly erratic and unpredictable. Some spasm and twitch or flail about wildly, falling into waiting arms or to the ground, rolling, writhing, convulsing; others might jump up and down in place, or embrace and shake hands with all around them, or rush forward to shout before or around the pulpit or altar. Adding to the terminological confusion, all of this would be accompanied by declamatory call-and-response singing and various other exclamations or vocalizations describable as shouting: "Glory to God!" (Julia Frazier, b. 1854, VA, 99). "Glory Halle-lu-yah!" (Sarah Thomas, b. ca. 1860, LA, 2108). "Glory and Hallelujah and Amen!" (Gus Feaster, b. ca. 1840, SC, 63). " 'I got the glory.' 'I got that old time religion in my heart' " (Mose Hursey, b. ca. 1855, LA, 1833).[26] "W'en dey would sing deze songs hit would almos' mek your ha'r stand up on yo haid, de way dem peoples would jump en shout!" (Frankie Goole, b. 1853, TN, 21). Reaching full possession, people might weep or sob uncontrollably, shriek or scream, bellow and moan, or speak in tongues. Others would be struck deaf, dumb, and blind, dropping and lying silent and insensible as the rest shouted on around them.

The sheer volume of shouting was occasion for comment. "Forty-seven other people was baptized with me—at the same time, and you could have heared the Niggers shoutin and moanin and singin for two miles!" (Mary Carpenter, b. 1851, GA, 145). "At baptising dey'd give de water invitation an' den go in de water. An' didn't dey come out happy, shouting and praying? Ol' man Buck could hear dem two miles off, but hit was a glorious baptising" (Wade Owens, b. 1863, AL, 307). "De white folks was baptized in de pool first, and den dere darkies. When de darkies time come, dey sung and shouted so loud dat de Patter-rollers come from somewhar, but Marster and Missus made dem go away and let us shout and rejoice to de fullest" (Isiah Jefferies, b. 1851, SC, 19). "I heared 'em shoutin' way into the night. They hollers out, 'Holy,' and 'Glory' " (Bud Jones, b. ca. 1850, VA, 2090). In 1867 a white journalist wrote, "when the shout lasts into the middle of the night, the monotonous thud, thud of the feet prevents sleep within half a mile of the praise-house."[27] The footwork employed in shouting is indistinguishable from many social dances, and the volume of shouting feet matched the thunderous level of frolics, cornshuckings, and other secular celebrations. For that matter, the sound would have been comparable to the drum batteries accompanying holy dancing in other Black communities.

Research and writing on shouting have focused disproportionately on the ring shouts of coastal Georgia and South Carolina, first documented by wartime soldier-diarists, journalists, and social workers, then studied nonstop over the next century. Granted, aside from their early celebrity and subsequent familiarity, Atlantic ring shouts call attention to themselves through their obvious connection to counterclockwise circle dances figuring in possession rites across the Black world, especially at funerals and other life cycle ceremonies. Sylvia Cannon described the classic ring shout at coastal South Carolina funerals, where people sang while "shaking hands, marching around grave. White en Colored marched from church to graveyard. Old people in de ox cart en young people walking" (Sylvia Cannon, b. ca. 1857, SC, 196). Ben Sullivan had been a slave on St. Simons Island, Georgia. "Dey go in a long pruhcession tuh duh buryin groun an dey beat duh drums long duh way an dey submit duh body tuh duh groun. Den dey dance roun in a ring an dey motion wid duh hans. Dey sing duh body tuh duh grabe an den dey let it down an den dey succle roun in duh dance."[28] Shouting was customary at slave funerals everywhere, however, but not always in rings. "When a slave died, there was a to do over dat. Hollering and singing. More fuss dan a little. 'Well, sich a one has passed out and we gwine to de grave to tend de funeral we will talk about Sister Sallie.' De niggers would be jumpin as high as a cow or mule" (Jim Allen, b. ca. 1850, AL, 60).[29]

Beyond the Atlantic coast, in fact, ring shouts are only commonly reported in southern Louisiana, especially in New Orleans hoodoo ceremonies; however, hoodoos also danced solo, in couples, in lines, and in other formations.[30] Even in the Sea Islands, the significance of the ring may have been somewhat, perhaps seriously overstated.[31] Everywhere in the South, slaves are more often reported shouting in lines moving up and down chapel aisles, in processions (from church to cemetery or baptismal pool, through and around camp grounds), in narrative sequences or dramatic tableaux or impromptu formations. People shouted as couples or linked hands en masse. For group shouting, lines or processions were probably most common. Hamp Kennedy described Walking Egypt:

> When a nigger died, we had a wake an' dat was diffrunt too frum what 'tis today. Dey neber lef' a dead nigger 'lone in de house, but all de neighbors was dere an' hoped (helped). Dey turned de mirrirs to de wall 'cause dey say once a long time ago, a nigger died an' three days afte'wards his people looked in a mirror an' dere dey see de dead nigger plain as day in de mirror. At de wake we clapped our han's an' kep' time wid our feet—*Walking Egypt*, dey calls hit—an' we chant an' hum all night 'til de nigger was *funeralized*. (Uncle Hamp Kennedy, b. 1857, MS, 1273, orig. emphasis and parentheses)[32]

Imitating the Exodus (in Augusta it was called "Marching Out of Egypt"),[33] the rite evidently originated as a Georgia Watch Night custom.

> This "walking Egypt" is nothing more than the entire congregation forming in line and filing up one aisle and down the other to the measure of chants which work on the emotions and result in all manner of excesses and abandonment. Under the influence of its spell the marchers seem insensible to pain, and will oftentimes spring through the windows. The women are more susceptible to its intoxication than the men. "Walking Egypt" marks the ending then of the season.[34]

There are, however, also accounts of regular Sunday meetings "culminating in the '*holy dance*' or '*walk in Egypt*,' a relic of African barbarism, in which the contortions of the body furnish a safety-valve to the intense mental excitement."[35] Hamp Kennedy

described it at wakes (another customary occasion for shouting).

Several narrators described linking hands or handshaking as major components of shouts. Sometimes this coincided with the general abandon of spirit possession. "All the Niggers would have a big meetin' at the ch'uch house on New Year's and pray for each other. We would pray all night long and shake hands, cry and shout. Fo'ks had more 'ligion than they does now. Fo'ks ain't got no 'ligion now" (Harriet Chelsey, b. ca. 1853, TX, 693). Social worker Lucy Chase (1822–1909) wrote from Norfolk in 1864: "it is usually the women alone who are so unseemly. In their prayer-meetings, one or many grow 'Happy,' jump, and spin, throw their arms into the air, embrace those near them, shake all the hands they can reach, screech words of religious rapture, and give an occasional staccato howl,—horrible and startling."[36]

In other cases, formations of shouters changed partners hand-to-hand in the manner of social dances. Sir Charles Lyell (1797–1875) visited Georgia's Hopeton plantation in 1845. "At the Methodist prayer-meetings, they [slaves] are permitted to move round rapidly in a ring, joining hands in token of brotherly love, presenting first the right hand and then the left, in which maneuver, I am told, they sometimes contrive to take enough exercise to serve as a substitute for the dance."[37] Thirty years later, St. Ann Johnson joined the church on a Plaquemines Parish sugar plantation:

> Yes, ma'am, I'm a Baptist, I was baptized in de river when I was a little girl. De preacher had to carry me out in de water, and all de people was standin' on de bank singin':
>
> > On de rough, rocky road,
> > I's most done trav-lin',
> > On de rough, rocky road,
> > To my Lord.
> >
> > On de rough, rocky road,
> > I's most done trav-lin',
> > Got to carry my soul
> > To my Lord.

Den dey takes each others hands and they step around:

> My sister, in the Lord,
> I's most done trav'lin',
> On de rough, rocky road,
> To my Lord. (St. Ann Johnson, b. 1865, LA, child of ex-slaves, 138)[38]

Other times the handshake served as a separate shout closing a meeting.

> Dey did 'low us to go to church on Sunday about two miles down de public road, and dey hired a white preacher to preach to us. He never did tell us nothing but be good servants, pick up old marse and old misses' things about de place, and don't steal no chickens or pigs and don't lie 'bout nothing. . . . We used to slip off in de woods in de old slave days on Sunday evening way down in de swamps to sing and pray to our own liking. We prayed for dis day of freedom. . . . And we'd sing "Our little meetins 'bout to break, chillun we must part. We got to part in body, but hope not in mind. Our little meetin's bound to break." Den we used to sing "We walk about and shake hands, fare you well my sisters I am going home." (Alice Sewell, b. 1851, AL, 303, 305–6)

Interviewer J. R. Jones described Mary Gladdy as "a rather mysterious personage" who regularly received "visitations from the spirits" (Mary Gladdy, b. ca. 1853, GA, 18–19):

> According to Mary Gladdy, ex-slave, 806½—Sixth Avenue, Columbus, Georgia, it was customary among slaves during the Civil War period to secretly gather in their cabins two or three nights each week and hold prayer and experience meetings. A large, iron pot was always placed against the cabin door—sideways, to keep the sound of their voices from "escaping" or being heard from the outside. Then, the slaves would sing, pray, and relate experiences all night long. . . .

Practically always, every Negro attendant of these meetings felt the spirit of the Lord "touch him (or her) just before day." Then, all would arise, shake hands around, and begin to chant the canticle above quoted. This was also a signal for adjournment, and, after chanting 15 or 20 minutes, all would shake hands again and go home—confidant in their hearts that freedom was in the offing for them. (Mary Gladdy, b. ca. 1853, GA, 26–27, orig. parentheses)[39]

In 1863 Charles Carleton Coffin observed a meeting of newly freed South Carolina slaves. The worshippers got happy and the shouting "went on till nature was exhausted. When the meeting broke up, they all came round in procession, shaking hands with the superintendent and the strangers present, and singing a parting song, 'There's a meeting here tonight!' "[40] Louisiana ex-slave Orelia Alexie Franks recalled a shout song probably also sung with a farewell handshake: "Marster de kind ob man w'at let his niggers hab dey own prayer meetin'. He give 'em a big cabin for dey prayer meetin'. Shout? Yes, Lawd. Uster sing, / Mourner, fare you well / God Almighty, bless you / 'Til we meet ag'in" (Orelia Alexie Franks, b. unk., LA, 1424). Handshaking is also reported at New Orleans hoodoo ring dances and Primitive Baptist foot-wash ceremonies.[41] Sylvia Cannon (b. ca. 1857, SC, 196) described it graveside during funerary ring shouts, Victoria Williams at Mississippi experience meetings. St. Ann Johnson recounted an especially moving example:

> My Great Grandmother Sue, and another old lady named Ann, were sold together right on the Belaire Plantation. Dey was friends all deir lives, and said dey wanted to go to Jesus together. Well, Grandmother was sick to her death bed, and Aunt Ann come to see her. When she was ready to go, she walked to de bed and took Grandmother's hand and started to sing:

> > Shake hands and goodby—e
> > I'm bound to follow my Jesus;

Fig. 13.2. Orelia Alexie Franks, ex-slave, Beaumont, TX, July 3, 1937. Portraits of African American ex-slaves from the US Works Progress Administration, Federal Writers' Project slave narratives collection, Library of Congress.

Shake hands and goodby—e
I am goin' home.

Well, about half past four in de mornin', Grandmother Sue, she die; and at four that evenin' old Aunt Ann died. It was the first time I ever seen two people laid out at the same time. They met their Jesus together. (St. Ann Johnson, b. ca. 1865, LA, child of ex-slaves, 139)

At large public events like camp meetings and revivals, believers might shout together by the score, but most shouting was done by individuals spontaneously moved to express their faith in motion. Granted, the two categories overlapped. As group shouts reached full pitch, individuals broke off to shout on their own. In other cases, members might begin to shout singly then face off as couples or form into lines or rings. At baptizings, congregations shouted in procession from church to river, then shouted in rings or lines on the bank while new converts surfaced shouting their very personal newborn experiences. "Useter go ter de bap'tisin's en dey would start shoutin' en singin' w'en we lef' de church" (Jenny Greer, b. ca. 1854, AL, 27). "The head deacon would carry de person out in the water that they was gwineter baptize and have all de rest stand around in a circle and shout and sing" (Eugenia Weatherall, b. 1863, MS, 2221). "Fum de camp meetin's dey would go ter de wharf en baptise. Dey would tie handkerchiefs 'roun dere haids. W'en dey wuz dipped under de water sum ob dem would kum up shoutin'" (Ann Matthews, b. unk., TN, 46).

W'en I wuz a young girl hund'eds ob people went ter de wharf at de foot ob Broadway on de fust Sunday in May ob eber'y year fer de annual bap-tizin' ob new members inter de Baptist (culored) churches ob de city [Nashville]. Thousands ob white people would crowd both sides ob de Cumberland Riber, Broadway en de Sparkman Street Bridge ter witnus de doin's. On leavin' de churches de pastor would lead de parade ter de wharf. Dey would sing en chant all de way fum de church ter de river en sum ob de members would be ovuh-kum wid 'ligious feelin' en dey would hop up en down, singin' en shoutin' all de time, or may be dey would start ter runnin' down de street en de brethern would hab ter run dem down en bring dem back. (Patsy Hyde, b. ca. 1830, TN, 35, orig. parentheses)

When St. Ann Johnson, great-granddaughter of a New Orleans hoodoo queen, was baptized, the congregation shouted and shook hands on the shore as God parted the water and another believer stepped across its surface.

De preacher had to carry me out in de water, and all de people was standin' on de bank singin'.... Den dey takes each others hands and they step around.... Den when de preacher started to say his prayers, "I baptize you in de name of Jesus," the Lord did like this—look—just cut the water. And when I come up, I was shoutin', "Look at de gold! Look at the gold!" The sky above me was just like gold. One woman got excited and stepped off into de water, but her feet didn't go under. No, she was walkin' right on top a dat water cryin' out and sayin', "Look at Jesus! Look at Jesus!" Yes, ma'am, faith! Dat's what I believe in. (St. Ann Johnson, b. 1865, LA, child of ex-slaves, 138–39)

Simply as a matter of routine, however, most shouting occurred under less spectacular conditions, inspired by singing, praying, and preaching at regular Sunday services or weekly prayer meetings. "At these services the slaves would 'get happy' and shout excitedly" (Mack Mullen, b. 1857, GA, 237). "Didn' no white preacher ever preach ter us. But de ev'nin's b'longed ter de colored—*ever'* Sunday an' other times, too. De sisters had dey skirts draggin' dey feets then. De preacher preach, an' dey rare (rear) like goats" (Simon Hare, b. 1849, NC, 914, orig. emphasis and parentheses).

The religious among them would gather at one of the cabin doors and give thanks to God in the form of long supplications and old fashioned songs. Many of them being highly emotional would respond in shouts and hallelujahs sometimes causing the entire group to become "happy" concluding in shouting and praise to God. (Louis Napoleon, b. ca. 1857, FL, 244)

They'ud preach and pray and sing—shout too. I heard them git up with a powerful force of spirit clapping they hands and walking 'round the place. They shout "I got the glory." "I got that old time religion in my heart." I seen some powerful 'figurations of the spirit in them days. (Mose Hursey, b. ca. 1855, LA, 1833)

Gracious God! Jesus! We had a sermont yestidday! Mudder Day! Mudder Day all over the world! That man preach! He preach Mudder Day! He ring down on Mudder Day. Mudder teach chillun right. Clare (I declare) that man preach Mudder Day till he preach me out my sense! Know I won't be here nother Mudder's Day. Got to move! (shout) Say, Mudder Day, again, I ain't here! Baby in arms.

Fig. 13.3. Mose Hursey, ex-slave, Dallas, TX, December 1, 1937. "I was just a preacher until about thirty years ago and then God starting making a Prophet out of me. Today I am Mose Hursey, Head Prophet to the World. They is lesser Prophets but I is the main one" (Mose Hursey, b. ca. 1855, TX, 1835). Portraits of African American ex-slaves from the US Works Progress Administration, Federal Writers' Project slave narratives collection, Library of Congress.

Rachel own. Got the child. Had to pitch up! Rachel call:

"Git 'um from Grand Ma! Git 'um fore Grand Ma drop!"

Fire take the church. Heart commence to turn over! I say, "Take this child! Take 'um!" Rachel take the baby (Aunt Hagar shouted up and down the aisle). Rose on for Mudder and suit of white. Great Lord! The whole thing been jump! Fire take the house! (Hagar Brown, b. ca. 1860, SC, 84, orig. parentheses)

Besides preaching and praying, singing—especially spiritual singing—was always essential and often the catalyst. "My favorite song was 'De Ol' Time Religion.' I kin sing dat song now, and bring folks up singin' or shoutin'" (Thomas Johns, b. 1847, AL, 1969). "On Sunday us went to church at de white folks meetin' house. At other times us would git together an' have worship amongst our selves. Den us could sing our songs and shout an' sho' 'nuf' enjie a good meetin'" (Jane Louis,

b. 1851, MS, 1325). "Dey didn't 'low us to sing on our plantation 'cause if we did we just sing ourselves happy and git to shouting and dat would settle de work, yes mam" (Alice Sewell, b. 1851, AL, 303).

> A big level field would be filled wid de slaves an' when de overseer wont [wasn't] out deir wid 'em dey would sing and pray. Dats when de niggers done deir shoutin' and worshipping an' when lef' alone would sing, shout and pray to deir hearts content. Sometimes mighty purty songs would be sung. Dey mos' always made 'em up as dey go an' singing 'em lack niggers do. (Julia Cox, b. 1850, MS, 520)

> Yea, we sang spirituals. My favorite one was "Better Mind How You Walk On De Cross." Yea, we shouted all night. Church lasted all night and way into de mornin'. . . . We got happy when dat hymn was sung. De darkies would sing and you ought to er heard dem. De old preacher would stomp his foots, and all de people would pray and shout. (Elizabeth Ross Hite, b. ca. 1850, LA, 103–4)

However, slaves also shouted to formally composed hymns by Watts, Wesley, and their colleagues. "Us slaves went ter de white church en set in de gallery, your white preacher read de Bible and sung dat good ole song 'Jesus lover of my soul,' en den us had baptizing by de white preacher at Hill's Pond and my, didn' dem niggers shout and holler and sing nother good ole song 'Dark wus de night, cold wus de groun,' which de Lord laid his haid'" (Sara Benton, b. 1846, AL, 62).

> When de slaves died dey wuz buried in de cem'tery lak dey do now, sumtimes dey shouted an' hollered, an' onct in a while wum ob dem fainted and had ter be tuk home. One ob de songs dey usta sing at funerals wuz:

> > Hark! frum de tune ob dornful sorrow
> > Mah years a tender cry
> > He livin' man cum an' view dis groun'
> > Whar yo' mus' shortly lie!

Lor' us sho' did hab plenty ob singing ob dem good ol' hymns, an' shout an' pray. (Henry Barnes, b. 1858, AL, 41)

Other ex-slaves recalled singing and shouting "Jesus Lover of My Soul" (Charles Wesley, 1740), "Dark Was the Night" (Thomas Haweis, 1792), "Hark! From the Tomb" (Isaac Watts, 1707), and similar titles. Whatever the source, song was fundamental. Group shouts were typically accompanied by call-and-response vocals and alliterative, repetitive texts—chants, as they were sometimes described. There even existed a large repertoire of designated shout songs rhythmically, thematically, and kinetically calculated to induce trance states, their lyrics scripting specific movements, formations, or dramas.

Solo shouting, by contrast, might respond to any song whose sound or sense instilled the spirit. Just singing for interviewers, some narrators had to stop themselves from shouting.

> Herodias went down to de river one day.
> Wanted to know what John de Baptist had to say,
> John spoke de words at de risk of his life,
> Not lawful, to mai'iy yous brother's wife.

> Now, dat am nuff, if Ise stay heayh longer youse have dis old womenin dancin'. (Philles Thomas, b. 1860, TX, 3818)[42]

> When my old mammy died a-shoutin',
> All de friend I had done died and gone.
> She died a-prayin', she died a-prayin',

> In dat day dat you died, dat you died,
> Gwine to be a star risin' in dat mornin'.
> Didn't you hear 'em say, 'gwine to be a
> Star risin' in de mornin'.

> De Christians all will know in dat day,
> Dat my old mammy died a-shoutin', died
>   a-shoutin',
> 'Cause dat star sho gwine to be dar.

Oh, Lord! Don't leave me now, Oh, Lord!
But guide me all 'long de way, 'long de way.
'Cause I'se in trouble, dat I am.
Lord! Oh, Lord! Don't leave me now.

Honey, I jus' feels lak prayin' an' cussin' too, at de same time, but it's 'cause I'se so happy. Here I is, I'se nigh 'bout crazy. (Lina Hunter, b. ca. 1848, GA, 266)[43]

The link between song and spirit was inescapable. Since slaves sang spirituals and hymns at work in the fields, people sometimes shouted even there, however inopportunely. "Susie remembers one day when she and her mother were picking cotton when all of a sudden her mother began to sing 'Glory to the Dying Land' and sang so much that 'atter a while she got so happy she couldn't be still and she danced all over Masta's cotton patch and tromped down so much cotton I jest knowed Masta was gwina whup her'" (Susie Johnson, b. ca. 1857, GA, 344).

We didn't have no churches. We went to meetin' at de white folks meetin' house an' wuz allowed to jine. When we jined us wuz made to promise to obey our Masters. We did all ob our real worshipping in de fiel's, out deir we could turn loose in our own way. We could sing, shout an' pray. Dis is one ob de songs we use to sing out in de corn an' cotton fiel's:

Hark from de tomb, it does resound
Years ob tinder cry
Livin', livin' come over de ground
Where we shall lie
Prince in de clay mus' be our end
In spite ob all our power. (Laura Ford,
b. 1852, MS, 757)

Ah jes love ter talk bout when ah wuz a boy. We had a log cabin fuh a church house. In dem days on meetin' Sunday fokes would go ter church and carry de chillun but now not neither the chillun nor dey ma's go either. Fokes would serve de Lord. Dey

would git happy in de fiel' an' fall out choppin, choppin cotton. No sich times as hit wuz now. (Uncle James Tubbs, 1866, AR, child of ex-slaves, 355–56)

We went to church once a month. The slaves had their own little meeting house. Our favorite songs were "Amazing Grace," "Where He Leads Me," and "When I Can Read My Title Clear." I still remember how one of the overseers, a white man, Andy Odom, got so happy that he fell offen a rail fence one day where he was watching the hands as they chopped cotton. They got to singing an finally broke out on "Am I a Soldier of the Cross." Mr. Odom got so happy he went to shouting and fell off the fence. (Preely Coleman, b. 1852, SC, 860)[44]

These transcendent states and experiences are actually the subjects of many shout songs.

I sings an' I shouts wid all my might
To drive away de cold—
An' de bells keep a-ringin' in de gospel light,
Till de story of de Lamb is told.
(Mollie Huff, daughter of James
Green, b. 1841, VA, 1583)

Big bells a-ringin' in de army of de Lord;
Big bells a-ringin' in de army.
I'm so glad I'm in de army of de Lord;
My soul's a-shoutin' in de army. (Minerva
Lofton, b. 1869, AR, child of ex-slaves, 265)

I want to feel my savior near
When soul and body's parting
I want to live a Christian life
I want to die a-shouting
I want to feel my savior near
When soul and body's parting. (Anna Humphrey, b. 1849 or 1850, AL, 1829)

And of all these states and experiences, none was more closely tied to shouting than *getting religion*, that is, a born-again conversion.

After surrender I used to cut cane in the field, and I was converted. The Lord appeared to me in a vision and said, "Go in My name and tell the world that I have sent you to tell the people to be converted from their sins, and sin no more." He took my feet out of the miry clay, and I told everybody and I shouted. The Spirit had on flowin' garments all trailin' 'round Him, and He talked in a human voice. He say, "You will be happy in Heaven." When I come up out of the water, I shouted and sung "On Jordan's Stormy Banks I Stand." (Hennie Ross, b. 1852, LA, 188)

Dere was some Sunday nights when Reverend Chandler would come to our brush arbor to preach and baptize. I never knowed what de shoutin' was 'bout den.

"What yo' shoutin' about?" I'd ask mammy.

"Why, child, when yo' git older and 'fess yo' religion, you'll feel so good, dat yo'll jes' git to shoutin'." (Mary Glover, b. 1854, TX, 1517)

You shoulder seen some ob de niggers get 'ligion. De best way was to carry dem to de cemetery an let dem stand ober a grave. Dey wud start singin' an shoutin' 'bout seein' fire an' brimstone; den dey would sin' some mo' an look plumb sanctified. (Clara C. Young, b. ca. 1842, AL, 2403)

There were numerous established rites to encourage getting religion, all linked to shouting: camp meetings, revivals, protracted services, baptizings, funerals, and the weekly call to the *mourner's bench*, when sinners were summoned to come forward, confess, and repent (as in fig. 16.5). "Dey used to have big 'tracted meetin's in Pierces Chapel nigh Foundry Street and Hancock Avenue. . . . De call to come up to de mourner's bench brought dem Negroes jus' rollin' over one another in de 'citement. Soon dey got happy and dere was shoutin' all over de place. Some of 'em jus' fell out" (Nancy Smith, b. ca. 1857, GA, 299).

For baptizin' we almos' always sung, "On Jordan's Stormy Bank I Stand." De white folks had a big

Baptist church, and I was baptized dere. When de colored folks would hol' church dere I has seen fifty women throwin' demselves 'roun', and shoutin' and singin'. Dere was a big pine thicket near de road to Cuseta, and I've seen at leas' five hundred people in dat grove singin'. (Thomas Johns, b. 1847, AL, 1969–70)[45]

Shouting is always mentioned at camp meetings. "We sho did have church, large meetin'—camp meetin'—with lot of singin' an shoutin' and it was fine!" (Wade Glenn, b. ca. 1860, NC, 38); "De culored peeples uster hab camp meetin's, en dey'd last fer two weeks. Lawd hab mercy did we hab a time at dem meetin's, preachin', singin', en' shoutin'" (Frankie Goole, b. 1853, TN, 23); "I useter go ter camp meetin's. Eve'rbody had a jolly time, preachin', shoutin' en eatin' good things" (Jenny Greer, b. ca. 1853, AL, 27); "We had what they called them old time camp meetings and everybody got happy and shouted" (Parilee Daniels, b. 1846, TX, 1033–34); "W'en I useter go ter camp meetin' dey had big dinnahs en spread hit on de groun'. Dey preached, sung, shouted en eve'ybody had a good time" (Ann Matthews, b. unk., TN, 46); "We use to sing them good old songs, 'It was good enough for our Father's and it was good enough for me.' Yes we had them good old camp meetings and everybody would shout" (Rosa L. Pollard, b. 1844, KY, 3121).[46]

Mass full-immersion baptisms were also scenes of general shouting. "One time I remember a baptizing I went to and saw them shouting. The preacher was old man Thornton Shoalt and when the folks would come out of the water they would be pretty happy and would holler and shout and sing" (Emma Jones, b. 1849, GA, 227). "The first Baptizin' that I remember was on Dix River near Floyd's Mill. Preacher Kemper did the Baptizin' and Ellen Stone, one of our slaves was Baptized there with a number of others—whites and blacks too. When Ellen came up out of the water she was clapping her hands and shouting" (Bert Mayfield, b. 1852, KY, 15). "I was baptised at eleven o'clock by Dave Hill an' I sho' got happy. I shouted an' sung: 'I'se never drunk no whiskey in my life'" (Frank Menefee, b. ca. 1843, AL, 279).

When I got to be a big boy, my Ma got religion at de Camp meeting at El-Bethel. She shouted and sung fer three days, going all over de plantation and de neighboring ones, inviting her friends to come to see her baptized and shouting and praying fer dem. She went around to all de people dat she had done wrong and begged dere forgiveness. She sent fer dem dat had wronged her, and told dem dat she was born again and a new woman, and dat she would forgive dem. She wanted everybody dat was not saved to go up wid her.

De white folks was baptized in de pool first, and den dere darkies. When de darkies time come, dey sung and shouted so loud dat de Patter-rollers come from somewhar, but Marster and Missus made dem go away and let us shout and rejoice to de fullest. . . . My Ma took me wid her to see her baptized, and I was so happy dat I sung and shouted wid her. (Isiah Jefferies, b. 1851, SC, 19)[47]

Children even played at baptismal shouting. "We was more 'ligious than the chillun nowadays. We used to play preachin' and baptizin'. We'd put 'em down in the water and souse 'em and we'd shout just like the old folks" (Dinah Perry, b. ca. 1862, AR, 321). "Marster used to git my sister to shout for him. I kin just see her now, a-twistin' and jumpin' and hollerin' for all de world lak grownup Niggers done at meetin's and baptizin's" (Georgia Johnson, b. 1865, GA, child of ex-slaves, 330).

People also shouted at moments of greatest trial and tribulation, or of greatest joy and illumination. Visions occasioned shouting, as did recovery from illness or other ordeals.

I has tried all my life to liv' a 'spectable life an' serve de Lord; one night when I wuz very sick I ask'd de Lord to do what wuz bes'; I had stuck a black berry thorn in my thum' an' it got infested an' de doctor tol' me hit had to be taken off; when I ask'd de Lord to do what wuz bes' he appeared to me; he had a shinin' light 'round hiz head an' he sed to me: "Joanna dis iz de Savior of de worl'"; get up de

Lord will provide; an' I got up shoutin' an' has been ever since; anudder time I wuz sick an' I went rite up in heaven an' saw de angels playin' on golden strings stretched all over heaven; they wuz singin' "Happy Home; sweet home; where never comes de night." My son cum in 'bout dat time an' heared me talkin' to de angels an' he jus' stud dere a-shakin' an' after he couldn't stop shakin' he started runnin' an' hit de steps so hard dey broke down; an' I aint never been able to fix dem; dat's de reason I hasn't got no front steps today. (Joanna Thompson Isom, b. ca. 1858, MS, 1099–1100)

So dey sarnt down in de woods and all over de plantation er lookin' fer de niggers to come to de Big House 'case dey overseer was dead. En here dey comes a-shoutin' and a-clappin' de han's and a-holl'rin' sumpin' awful.

Ole John Bell is de'd en gone
I hopes he's gone to hell!

En dat was de ones' time I's ever seen dem niggers happy on dat plantation 'tel atter s'render. (Martha Jackson, b. 1850, AL, 223)

Emancipation was greeted by shouting on a mass scale. "When pappy heard dat he was free he was so glad dat he shouted and danced a jig in a pile of ashes" (Mary Glover, b. 1854, TX, 1518). "At surrender I kin remember de niggers wuz all so happy. Dey jes rung bells, blowed horns and shouted like deys crazy" (Hamp Santee, b. ca. 1859, MS, 1918). "When I was 21 years old I was a free boy. I remembers well when the great day come. That day I shouted. . . . We so glad we scatter jus' like partridges. God knows where I went. I was a fiddler. Ever where we have a ball, I set there all night and play for the folks to dance" (Richard Carruthers, b. ca. 1848, TX, 637).

De news come on a Thursday, an' all de slaves been shoutin' an' carryin' on tell ev'ybody was all tired out. 'Member de fust Sunday of freedom. We was

Fig. 13.4. "Arrival of a Federal column at a planter's house in Dixie." Illustration by Thomas Nast. *Harper's Weekly* 7 (April 4, 1863): 219. An early work by Thomas Nast (1840–1902), creator of the modern Santa Claus and bane of Boss Tweed and Tammany Hall. The newly freed slaves surrounding the Federal soldier in the right foreground are shouting. To his right an elderly man and woman execute the traditional shout step in line, while another woman praises with palms upraised. (The small child peeping through the elderly man's legs while grasping his trousers is thereby learning the step in traditional fashion.) To the soldier's left a man bows; the banjo on the ground is presumably his. Elsewhere a boy does handstands, while other children exhibit the fascination with military drums that many ex-slaves described. "I member when de war come through. Oh dem drum; I nebber hear such a drum in my life!" (Tena White, b. ca. 1845, SC, 196).

all sittin' roun' restin' an' tryin' to think what freedom meant an' ev'ybody was quiet an' peaceful. All at once ole Sister Carrie who was near 'bout a hundred started in to talkin':

> Tain't no mo' sellin' today,
> Tain't no mo' hirin' today,
> Tain't no pullin' off shirts today,
> Its stomp down freedom today.
> Stomp it down!

An' when she says, "Stomp it down," all de slaves commence to shoutin' wid her:

> Stomp down Freedom today—
> Stomp it down!
> Stomp down Freedom today.

Wasn't no mo' peace dat Sunday. Ev'ybody started in to sing an' shout once mo'. Fust thing you know dey done made up music to Sister Carrie's stomp song an' sang an' shouted dat song all de res' de day. Chile, dat was one glorious time! (Charlotte Brown, b. ca. 1855, VA, 58–59)

That shouters truly achieved altered states is well established. Many stories tell of believers losing all sense of their own physical safety or the well-being of others. Even babes in arms were forgotten.

> On Sunday morning Aunt Cindy got "happy" at the services and began to throw herself about and shout, the white folks on the seats below hurried to get out from under the edge of the balcony for fear Aunt Cindy would lose her balance and fall over the railing to the floor below. (Isabelle Henderson, b. ca. 1850, MO, 204)[48]

> I had a sister that never went to a meetin' that she didn't get to shoutin' and shout to the end of the sermon. I always tried to get out of the way before I joined because if she got to me, she would beat on me and talk to me. We always tried to get to her, if she had a baby in her arms, because she would jes' throw that baby away when the Spirit moved her. (Tom Mills, b. 1858, TX, 96)

Hagar Brown reported that the day before her interview, she had been holding a grandbaby at church when her daughter was suddenly obliged to rescue the child. "Had to pitch up! Rachel call: 'Git 'um from Grand Ma! Git 'um fore Grand Ma drop!' Fire take the church. Heart commence to turn over! I say, 'Take this child! Take 'um!'" (Hagar Brown, b. ca. 1860, SC, 84).

In the grip of possession, people often did shout in the grip of their neighbors, requiring one or more holders to prevent catastrophe. "When they got religion, they shouted and swooned and fainted and had to be revived. Sometimes it took several persons to hold them" (Frances Lewis, b. 1854, GA, LA, 158). Occasions like baptizings created special complications. "Preacher Langford baptized de niggers jes' lak he did de white folks. Dey had big times too. Big crowds would be dar. Some of 'em would git so happy dey would shout 'til dey fell in de crick" (Olin Williams, b. ca. 1840, GA, 646). Wrote Belle Kearney (1863–1939), daughter of a Mississippi slaveholder: "at the close of the protracted meetings the baptizings begin. Multitudes assemble on the banks of a pond, or creek, or river, and the candidates are led out into the depths by the pastor and the deacons. It requires a heavy squad for the shouters are more unmanageable in the water than in the church."[49]

> [The preacher] and the head deacon would carry the person out in the water that they was gwineter babtize and have all de rest stand around in a circle and shout and sing. They would be quiet til the person comed out of the water and then the noise would start in right. One time they carried a big man in who must have weighed about 240 pounds and he was so heavy he carried them both down with him and all you could see for a minute was footses as black as night scrambling! Youve never seen de like. De shoutin' sure started up right then and if it hadn't been for some of the other men folkses they would've all drowned like rats. (Eugenia Weatherall, b. 1863, MS, 2221)

There is no questioning most shouters' faith, but all of this created the impression that some people were shouting not to praise God but to draw attention to themselves. One narrator boasted that his mother could "out shout all the other mothers at the annual revival meeting" (Charles Harris, b. 1870, KS, child of ex-slaves, 47). An anonymous Tennessee ex-slave reported that at the call to the mourner's bench, church women would "get to rolling and shouting and tell everybody that they had found Jesus and they would shout and shout, and sometimes they would knock the preacher and the deacon down shouting."[50] Civil War–era social worker Lucy Chase complained about such "unseemly" behavior by church women "drowning the voice of the speaker."[51] A song recalled by several ex-slaves mocks a fashionable young lady who gets happy at meeting—though not too happy to mind her stylish clothes and especially her hairpiece (waterfall).

And when a sinner got converted, she used to sing while about to shout:

> You may hold my hat,
> You may hold my shawl,
> But pray don't touch my waterfall. . . .

And then Frances explained that when she was young, negroes wore what was known as a "waterfall." They were made of real hair and had a thin wire to hold them on the head. They were expensive too, she said, and that is why negroes were very careful of them. When they got religion, they shouted and swooned and fainted and had to be revived. Sometimes it took several persons to hold them. They actually sang the "Waterfall" song given above. (Frances Lewis, b. 1854, GA, LA, 158; Lewis was living in New Orleans when interviewed, but evidently learned the piece in her native Georgia)

I got converted when I was young and I've never backslided. We used to sing from our hearts and not from books like they do now. La, if they heard us sing like that now, they'd think we were crazy. I remember when one got religion, we'd clap our hands and sing, "Shout, Sister Phreeny, shout! Shout, Sister Phreeny, shout!" Then she sang:

> It'll take more'n two to hold me,
> And even that can't hold me.
> I'll shout and shout,
> O Sister Phreeny will shout!

Then everybody took hands with her in the lead and shouted. Oh, them was the days! And it generally took more than one man to hold a sister when she got converted. And maybe she didn't want a certain one to do it, so she would sing, "I don't want Brer Jim to hold me. I want Brer Dick to hold me."

In old times women wore waterfalls—they don't do it now—and sometimes they'd sing:

Fig. 13.5. "The sunny South—a negro revival meeting—a seeker 'getting religion.'" Virginia, 1873. Engraving by W. L. Sheppard. *Leslie's* 37 (August 9, 1873): 352.

> You may tetch my hat,
> You may tetch my shawl,
> But don't you tetch my waterfall. (Victoria Williams, b. ca. 1860, MS, 211)

Virginia Clay-Clopton (1825–1915) witnessed similar scenes among Alabama slaves:

> The conversion of the negroes under their own spiritual guides was a bloodcurdling process in those days, for they screamed to Heaven as if the Indians with their tomahawks were after them, or danced, twisting their bodies in the most remarkable manner. As their emotions increased, as they "got feelin'," and the moment of conversion approached, as a rule they all fell in a heap, though in thus "coming through" the wenches were altogether likely to fall into the arms of the best-looking young brother who happened to be near.[52]

Not only did this leave the impression that some people went to service just to show off their fine clothes; it made people with insufficient clothes feel unwelcome even in church.

> Soon atter dey was sot free Niggers started up churches of dey own and it was some sight to see and hear 'em on meetin' days. Dey would go in big crowds and sometimes dey would go to meetin's a fur piece off. Dey was all fixed up in deir Sunday clothes and dey walked barfoots wid deir shoes acrost deir shoulders to keep 'em from gittin' dirty. Jus' 'fore dey got to de church dey stopped and put on deir shoes and den dey was ready to git together to hear de preacher. (Nicey Kinney, b. ca. 1850, GA, 29)

> I belong to de African Met'odist. My preacher, he good but he want lot ob money; dey all do. I miss church sometime, but I hab good reason. W'en my shoes gib out I don't go. Dey people stare an' talk w'en you ain't dress well....

> David got a harp wid a t'ousand string,
> An' w'en 'e touch one de whole Hebben ring.
> Course David's harp gold, can't be nuttin' 'cept gold. (Maria Bracey, b. unk., SC, 66, 67)

> When we lived over yonder where dem tanks is now, me and Molly Murphy use to meet out in de field 'tween our houses at night and stand dere and talk and pray and shout together till de night train come along, sometimes. Den I'd pick up my lantern and say: "Sister Molly, I know I got to git back home." Well, Molly's gone now, but I's still here, and long as I feels de grace o' God in my heart I's goin' shout. De preacher is always glad to see me come to church. "Grandma," he says to me, "we're gwine to have a good meetin' here today 'cause you come." But I ain't git nothin' fittin' to wear to church now. I washed my old dress till it done faded out; jes' any rag won't do for church. I ask the Welfare for a dress to wear last first Sunday; my old shoes I could hide under my skirt, if I could jes' git a print dress or somethin' decent. The Welfare said dey didn't have no dresses. (Mariah Barnes, b. ca. 1856, NC, 2)

Indeed, by the 1930s innumerable ex-slaves insisted that true religion as they had known it had altogether passed from fashion. "Dese last few y'ars dey hab got ter stylish ter shout" (Frankie Goole, b. 1853, TN, 23). "I belongs to de Baptis' church en was baptize wid Jesus when I was twelve year ole. I'se a foot-washin' Baptis', I is, but dey ain't none of dem kind er Baptis' 'roun' here, en I jes goes wid de udder Baptis' en sets in de amen corner, en iffen I wants to shouts, I shouts, en nobody ain't gonner stop me, bless de Lord!" (Roxy Pitts, b. 1855, AL, 316)

Way back yonder we uster have church under a brush arbor and we'd have preaching and shoutin and just raise lots of dust but dem times has changed now and we don't have much shoutin'. I reckon dey're scared dey'll get their clothes dirty. We uster "church" [expel] people for dancin', cussin', and fightin', but now the preacher don't want to lose a member afraid he'll lose a dime, so we don't have no churchin. (Ephom Banks, b. ca. 1865, MS, child of ex-slaves, 104)

I 'fessed religion fifty years ago and jined the Baptist Church. There was forty of us baptized when I was. We all met at the creek and sung "Let's Go Down To Jordan" and then the Reverend preached a sermon. Then we all went into the creek and was baptized. There was plenty of shouting going on. I still shouts at meetings. I don't have nothing to do with it. It hits me just like a streak of lightning and there ain't no holding it. I goes to the camp meetings close to Karnack and trys to behave, but when I gets in the Spirit, I jest can't hold that shouting back. The young fo'ks make fun of me, but I don't mind. Style is crowded all the grace out of religion today. (Ellen Payne, b. 1849, TX, 3043)

Some persons or denominations had never shouted, of course. "I was just Catholic and pray in my house at night. I never got that 'ligion that make you shout and carry on" (Carlyle Stewart, b. 1853, LA, 206). "Some of dem slaves never wanted no 'ligion, and dey jus' laughed at us cause us testified and shouted" (Paul Smith, b. ca. 1863, GA, 329). Such outside pressures multiplied after freedom. Already by Reconstruction, observers were reporting that Blacks would no longer "give way to their wildest gesticulations or engage in their sacred dances before white people, for fear of being laughed at," or that "in the cities, among the

Fig. 13.6. Ellen Payne, ex-slave, Marshall, TX, December 4, 1937. Portraits of African American ex-slaves from the US Works Progress Administration, Federal Writers' Project slave narratives collection, Library of Congress.

'fashionable' negroes, who closely imitate the whites, the 'holy dance' is dying out, and is rather looked down upon; but on the plantations it is still kept up."[53] As ex-slaves testified, these attitudes had intensified by the early twentieth century.[54] And yet believers shout on even today, both as an expression of faith and as a fashion statement.

Yet, in a sense, the ex-slaves were correct that shouting as they knew it had long since vanished. For slaves, that is, shouting was understood not just as the expression of their true religion, but as a divinely inspired alternative to the false doctrines and hollow rites forced on them by slaveholders. That so many slaveholders and their clergy anathematized shouting only confirmed these views.[55] Some whites may have shouted, but more often slaveholders tied shouting not just to irreverence but to insubordination, even insurrection. At the very least, most whites found shouting bothersome, unsettling, or simply indecorous, made plain by a popular joke.

No, honey, colored people didn' have no churches dey own in dem days. Dem ones what didn' go to de white people church, dey would build shelters in de woods for dey churches. Yes'um, colored people went to de same church as dey Massa would go mostly in dat day en time en would set up in de gallery. I remember, Pa used to tell bout one old man, Tom, would all de time be shoutin in church en his boss never like for him to be disturbin de people dat way. En one day his Massa say, "Tom, we gwine to church dis mornin en if you won' shout none in de church, I will give you a spankin new pair of boots." Tom say, "Yes, boss." But de old man Tom, he was very religious en de old fellow set dere en took in what de preacher was speakin en he study bout dem boots. Den he drink in some more en he keep on drinkin in till he get overflowed en he jump up en holler, "Massa boots or no boots, I gwine shout today." (Lizzie Davis, b. ca. 1865, SC, child of ex-slaves, 113–14)

The fact that the promised reward is always fancy footwear underscores that it is the slave's fancy footwork that truly disturbs the white congregation. This was not altogether a joke.

> My grandma was a powerful Christian 'oman, and she did love to sing and shout. Dat's how come Marse Billie had her locked up in de loom room when de Yankee mens come to our plantation. Grandma would git to shoutin' so loud she would make so much fuss nobody in de church could hear de preacher and she would wander off from de gallery and go downstairs and try to go down de white folkses aisles to git to de altar whar de preacher wuz, and dey wuz always lockin' her up for 'sturbin' worship, but dey never could break her from dat shoutin' and wanderin' 'round de meetin' house, atter she got old. (Martha Colquitt, b. ca. 1850, GA, 247)

At the most extreme, whites interpreted shouting as disobedience toward God—or worse, toward slaveholders. "We went to preachin' at de white folks church. De preacher would preach to de white folks furst den he'd call de niggers in an preach to us. He wouldn't read de Bible he'd say: 'Obey yo' Missus an' yo Master.' One ole nigger didn't have no better sense dan to shout on it once" (Lizzie Williams, b. 1849, MS, 2337).

> There wasn't no church of no kind on the place. Neither for the whites nor the colored. In them days they had what you call circuit riders for preachers. The Methodist Circuit Preacher came to our place every once in a while and preached in the old log hall. When the white folks service was over, he talked to the slaves. I always went with my mother. All the children that was big enough went. Every time he started his sermon the same way, "Obey your master and mistress. When they speak to you, move about and be industrious." If the Lord converted your soul, they wouldn't so much as let you shout in the fields. One day my mother got to shouting, and they whipped her to make her stop. They didn't stop her, she went right on after the whipping. She says she is going to praise the Lord Jesus, and she don't care what they do to her and she sure did do it. (Squire Irvin, b. 1849, TN, 1083)[56]

When that happened, it was time to turn the pot down.

Appendix: Shout

The overall importance of shouting, and the surrounding attitudes and beliefs, are further attested to by the large amount of folklore about shouting. (This material thus falls into the broad category of oral tradition Alan Dundes termed *metafolklore*, meaning folklore about folklore. "Metafolklore and Oral Literary Criticism," *The Monist* 50 [1966]: 505–16.) Below are some cases already touched on but deserving further attention.

WHEN FREEDOM CAME. Ex-slaves and other sources all agree that the moment they heard they were free, slaves in multitudes shouted, sang, and prayed, sometimes for days on end. Characteristically, these accounts seem to combine actual experiences with migratory elements. Many narrators, for instance, described spontaneously composing songs for the occasion, but these usually turn out to be well-known folksongs—in fact, one of two well-known folksongs: "No More Auction Block For Me" or "Free At Last." Then again, the versions the ex-slaves gave tend to be highly individualized and may have originated just as they say, even if they were simply adapted for the occasion rather than being created from scratch. These and other parallels in the following accounts should probably be viewed in that general light.

"NO MORE AUCTION BLOCK FOR ME (MANY THOUSANDS GONE)." All of the narrators who gave this item—Fannie Berry, Charlotte Brown, Francis Doby, Harriett Gresham, Bud Jones, and Georgianna Preston—tied it to Emancipation. Charlotte Brown's version appears in the chapter, all others below. Harriett Gresham combined "No More Auction Block" with "Free At Last," Fanny Berry with another well-known item, "Cold Frosty Morning," followed by a third song not found elsewhere. For "No More Auction Block," also see *Cabin Songs* III: 95; Dett, *Hampton*, 233; Higgingson, "Spirituals," 692; Krehbiel, *Folksongs*, 17–20; Lomax, *Ballads*, 577; Lomax, *FSNA*, 455–56; Marsh, *Jubilee Singers*, 146; *Slave Songs*, 48. "No More Auction Block" also appears in the narrative of Harriet Collins, authored by Texas fieldworker Ada Davis; like most of Ada Davis's output, the text is suspicious.

Child, an' her's another one we use to sing. Remember de War don' bin when we would sing dese songs. Listen now:

Ain't no mor' blowin' of dat four-day [before
     day] horn,
I will sing, brethern, I will sing.
A col' frosty mornin',
De nigger's mighty good,

Take your ax upon your shoulder,
Nigger talk [take] to de woods.

Ain't no mor' blowin' of dat four-day horn,
I will sing, brethern, I will sing. . . .

Glory, glory! Yes, child, the Negroes are free, an' when they knew dat dey were free dey—oh baby!—began to sing:

Mammy don't yo' cook no mo',
Yo ar' free, yo' ar' free.

Rooster don't yo' crow no mo',
Yo' ar' free, yo' ar' free.

Ol' hen don't yo' lay no mo' eggs,
Yo' free, yo' free.

Sech rejoicing and shoutin' you never he'rd in your life. (Fannie Berry, b. 1841, VA, 37–39)

After de soldiers—de red and white and blue soldiers—done come down to set us free, all de old niggah folks began to dance and sing:

Oh, de soldiers done set us free,
No more whippin', no more whippin'.
Oh, de soldiers done set us free,
No more spankin', no more spankin'. (Francis
     Doby, b. 1838, LA, 58)

Some left the plantation; others remained to harvest the crops. One and all they remembered to thank God for their freedom. They immediately began to hold meetings, singing soul stirring spirituals. Harriett recalls one of these songs. It is as follows:

T'ank ye Marster Jesus, t'ank ye,
T'ank ye Marster Jesus, t'ank ye,
T'ank ye Marster Jesus, t'ank ye,
Da Heben gwinter be my home.

No slav'ry chains to tie me down,
And no mo' driver's ho'n to blow fer me
No mo' stocks to fasten me down
Jesus break slav'ry chain, Lord
Break slav'ry chain Lord,
Break slav'ry chain Lord,
Da Heben gwinter be my home. (Harriett
    Gresham, b. 1838, SC, 160–61)

A time come when we'd see sojers trompin' by our place. They said it was a war, and then one day old master rang a bell and called all the niggers round and helt up a white flag afore 'em and said, "You listen good to me, 'cause I'm goin' to tell you somethin' you goin' be glad to hear. They ain't no more slavery. You is free." The niggers jumps straight up in the air and dance and sing and shout, "The freedom, oh, praise to Gawd, the freedom! Thank Gawd!" That night down on the flats round the cabins the niggers was millin' all night. They had torches and marched round singin':

No more bullwhips gwine call me,
No more, no more;
Like times a many thousand gone,
No more, no more!

No more bloodhounds gwine run me,
No more, no more;
Like times a many thousand gone,
No more, no more! (Bud Jones, b. ca. 1850,
    VA, 2090–91)

(Georgianna Preston recalls the first night of freedom.) Us young folks carried on somep'n awful. Ole Marse let us stay up all night, an' didn't seem to mind it at all. Saw de sun sot an' befo' we know it, it was a-risin' again. Ole folks was shoutin' an' singin' songs. Dar's one dey sung purty nigh all night. Don't know who started it, but soon's dey stopped, 'nother one took it up an' made up some mo' verses. Lawdy, chile, I kin hear dat song a-ringin' in my haid now:

Ain't no mo' blowin' dat fo' day horn,
Will sing, chillun, will sing,
Ain't no mo' crackin' dat whip over John,
Will sing, chillun, will sing. (Georgianna Preston, b. ca. 1835, VA, 233–34, orig. parentheses)

"FREE AT LAST (SLAVERY CHAIN)." Even today this song, based on a white spiritual, is associated with Emancipation. Ex-slaves Charles Grandy, Jake Green, Annie Harris, Tom Hawkins, Charlie Moses, John Perrier, and Lafayette Price recalled it. Price used the piece to illustrate how slaves improvised spirituals. Others identified it with shouting at freedom. The longest and most unusual versions came from Harris, Green, and Harper, the last combining "Free at Last" and "Come Ye That Love the Lord" (Isaac Watts, 1707). Tom Hawkins, on the other hand, told of a slave who was still afraid to sing "Free at Last" even after she had been emancipated. For other versions, see Robinson, *Log Cabin*, 142; Barton, *Plantation Hymns*, 13, 27, 34; Carter, *Louisiana Negro*, 66–67; Dett, *Hampton*, 112; *Fisk Jubilee Songs*, 23; Kennedy, *Mellows*, 38–39; McIlhenny, *Spirituals*, 95–97, 219; Odum and Johnson, *NHS*, 41, 124; Taylor, *Revival Hymns*, 150; Rosenberg, *Virginia*, 38, 54, 118; Solomon, *Daisies*, 178; Work, *ANSS*, 197. RECORDINGS: Dock Reed and Vera Hall, "Free at Last," field rec., Tuscaloosa, AL, 1950, *Negro Folk Music of Alabama: Volume II: Religious Music*, Folkways LP 4418, 1960; Dr. C. J. Johnson, "Free At Last," *Old Time Song Service: Free At Last*, Savoy LP 14204, 1968; Norfolk Jubilee Singers, "Free At Last" (Decca 7402, 1937); Southern Sons, "I'm Free At Last" (Victor 20–2014, 1942). DISCOGRAPHIES: *Blues & Gospel Records*; *Country Music Resources*, 196; *Gospel Discography*.

We was dancin' an' prancin' an' yellin' wid a big barn fir [bonfire] jus' ablazin' an' de white folks not darin' to come outside de big house. Guess dey made 'em up, 'cause purty soon ev'ybody fo' miles around was singin' freedom songs. One went like dis:

I's free, I's free, I's free at las'!
Thank God A'mighty, I's free at las'!

Once was a moaner, jus' like you,
Thank God A'mighty, I's free at las'!

I fasted an' I prayed tell I came thew,
Thank God A'mighty, I's free at las'! (Annie Harris, b. unk., VA, 128–29)

Slaves was some kind o' glad when dey 'mancipated, all dey sing was:

> Slavery chain is broke at las'
> Chorus Broke at las', broke at las'
> Slavery chain is broke at las'
> Praise God 'till I die.
>
> Come along valiant souls
> Git yo' words all ready
> Verse Ma'ch wid General thoo de fiel'
> Dis ole chatterin' groun'
> Oh! Slavery chain is, etc.

Some o' de slaves didn' hardly b'lieve dey was free. After de war was over, de army had to stay in de Souf twelve months fo' dey could make de niggers know dey was free. An' den jes' kept a wukin' fer de white man fer nuttin. (Charles Grandy, b. 1842, VA, 117)

I can 'member how dey stayed up half de night at Mr. Harper's after de men had read de 'mancipation to us, singing an' shouting. Dat was all dey did, jus' sing an' shout an' go on. I can 'member one of de songs dey sang 'bout dat time. It went something like dis:

> Come thee dat love de Lord,
> Let your jaws be known,
> 'Cause we're free at last!
> Thanks God Almighty,
> We're free at last! (Pierce Harper, b. 1851, NC, 1647)

Some of de niggers done bought an' paid for dey mule an' me an' Pappy was rentin' an' wukkin' on sheers, when here come Parker, jes' hyard 'bout S'render. He say, "Why didn't somebody come tell me 'twas S'render?" Den he start a-singin'

> Slav'y chain, slav'y chain.
> Thank God almighty I'm free at las'.
> Free at las', free at las'.
> Thank God a'mighty I'm free at las'. (Jake Green, b. ca. 1852, AL, 169)

Dey was one song on de place dey uster sing:

> Free at las',
>   Thank God Almighty I's free at las'
> Satan thought he had me fas'
>   Broke his chain, and free at las'.

Atter freedom I nuss Mr. Young' chillen, Walker and Sallie. I jis' hafter play 'roun' wid 'em and see dey git tuck care of. (John Perrier, b. ca. 1860, LA, 3079–80)

Ah can't recollect jes how ole ah wuz in slave time but ah shore can recollect dem yankees riding hosses and ah ask my ma what dey wus doin and she said gatherin up cotton dey made in slave time an ah kin recollect an [w]oman a gin [meaning unclear]. Yo know we had steps made of blocks sawed from trees and she wuz goin ovah em steps er shoutin and singin "Ah am free, at last, ah am free at last, ah'm free at last, thank Gawd a mighty ah'm free at last." She wuz so glad to be free. (Alice Dixon, b. ca. 1856, AR, 153)

I never will forgit de day dey told us de war was over and us was free. One of de 'omans what was down by de spring a washin' clothes started shoutin': "Thank God-a-Moughty I'se free at last!" Marse Tom heared and he come and knocked her down. It was 'bout October or November 'fore he ever told us dat us was free sho' 'nough. Dat same 'oman fainted dead away den 'cause she wanted to holler so bad and was skeered to make a soun'. (Tom Hawkins, b. ca. 1860, GA, 133)

Many other narrators alluded to slaves shouting and singing at freedom, but with no further details. Among the notable exceptions, Nelson Hammock told of a paralyzed slave who miraculously rose and sang her favorite hymn, while Lu Lee remembered that the freed slaves held a big cornshucking (that is, a carnival or celebration); accordingly, they sang a cornshucking song, which like many corn songs was about drinking, calling on slaveholders for refreshment, a fitting taunt under the circumstances. On Susie Melton's Virginia plantation, the emancipated slaves sang a traditional work song as they departed for Union lines, again ironic but fitting.

> Ole Ant Sissy done been par'lyzed fo' years. When de good news came [of the emancipation], slaves shout an' sing so loud dat Ant Sissy got out de baid, hobbled on out de do', an' stood dere prayin' to Gawd fo' his Mercy. Wouldn't let nobody tetch her, wouldn't set down. Stood dere swayin' fum side to side an' singin' over an' over her favorite hymn:
>
> > Oh, Father of Mercy,
> > We give thanks to Thee,
> > We give thanks to Thee,
> > For thy great glory. (Reverend Nelson Hammock, b. 1842, VA, 127, orig. brackets)

> Then one day they tells us we're free. That night we sot up torches and poured tallow in bottles round twisted cloth and lit them all up and had a big corn shuckin'. They drunk whiskey and sung:
>
> > Dram, dram, dram,
> > Old Master David,
> > Old Master Henry,
> > Dram, dram, dram.
> > O, bum-a-licha, bum-a-licha, bum, bum
> > O, bum-a-licha, bum-a-licha, bum, bum ho!
> > Master David.

> I went back to Master Henry's house and he said he'd take me and my sister to the free state of Brazil, where they could keep slaves. I told my sister and we run away to go to grandmammy's. We got out on the prairie and clumb a tree. Next day a uncle of mine come that way, drivin' cattle. He taken us over to my grandmammy. (Lu Lee, b. 1848 or 1849, TX, 2311–12)

> Never will fergit dat night of freedom. I was a young gal 'bout ten years ole, an' we done heared dat Lincum gonna turn de niggers free. Ole missus say dey warn't nothing to it. Den a Yankee soldier tole someone in Williamsburg dat Marse Lincum done signed de 'Mancipation. Was winter time an' moughty cold dat night, but ev'ybody commence gittin' ready to leave. Didn't care nothin' 'bout Missus—was goin' to de Union lines. An' all dat night de niggers danced an' sang right out in de cold. Nex' mornin' at daybreak we started out wid blankets an' clothes an' pots an' pans an' chickens piled on our backs, 'cause Missus said we couldn't take no horses or carts. An' as de sun come up over de trees de niggers all started to singin':
>
> > Sun, you be here an' I'll be gone,
> > Sun, you be here an' I'll be gone,
> > Sun, you be here an' I'll be gone,
> > Bye, bye, don't you grieve arter me,
> > Won't give you may place, not fo' your'n,
> > Bye, bye, don't you grieve arter me,
> > 'Cause you be here an' I'll be gone. (Susie Melton, b. 1853, VA, 212–13)

"PLEASE DON'T TOUCH MY WATERFALL." This song, depicting a stylish young shouter who is none too possessed to mind her fine clothes, doubtless originated in US Black churches. It appears to date from Reconstruction or just after, being known by Blacks throughout the South, in every instance associated with shouting. While collectors and editors have generally failed to connect their versions, this may have been one of the more popular Black church songs of the late nineteenth and early twentieth centuries. Ex-slaves Ellen Godfrey, Frances Lewis, and Victoria Williams gave versions from, respectively, South Carolina, Louisiana by way of Georgia, and Mississippi. (Lewis's text is also excerpted in *Gumbo Ya-Ya*, 473.) Newman I. White (*ANFS*, 128) prints two texts, the first "as heard in eastern North Carolina in the eighteen-eighties."

> Hol' my shaker an hol' my shawl,
> An' tell Bob Jones I'm shoutin' in de cool.

White's second text was "Heard at Negro church in Salisbury, N.C., by Claude and Norman Davis, about 1905. Used to initiate the shouting."

> Hold my bonnet and hold my shawl
> While I shout in the cool, good Lawd.

Byron Arnold titled an Alabama version "A Shout." His informant, Mae Erskine Irvine, recalled it from her Black nurse, who had learned it at her church. "The three miles was the distance she walked to and from meeting."

> Hol' me, sister Betsy, hol' me,
> Hol' me, sister Betsy, hol' me,
> Hol' mah reticule, hol' mah shawl,
> But pray don't tech-a-mah water fall.
> Three miles to walk, three cows to milk,
> Hol' me, sister Betsy, hol' me. (Arnold,
>   *Alabama*, 91)

Arnold adds, "this is a 'shout.' It is spoken instead of sung. The musical notations are intended only as indications for the inflection of the voice. IT IS NOT TO BE SUNG."

A text collected by Dorothy Scarborough in Angelina County, Texas, also mentions Sister Betsy, blending our item with "The Gospel Train." According to Scarborough, performances "end with religious enthusiasm."

> Better git yo' ticket,
> Better git yo' ticket,
> Train's a-comin'.
> Lord-ee-ee, Lord-ee-ee!
> Um-um-um-um-um-um-um-um.
>
> Hold your bonnet,
> Hold your shawl,
> Don't let go that waterfall.
> Shout, Sister Betsy, shout! (Scarborough,
>   *TNFS*, 239)

Thomas Talley (1870–1952) was himself the child of Mississippi ex-slaves; most of his material came from childhood memories and relatives, or from former slaves and their children in Middle Tennessee.

> Hol' my rooster, hōl' my hen,
> Pray don't tetch my Gooshen Ben'.
>
> Hol' my bonnet, hōl' my shawl,
> Pray don't tetch my waterfall.
>
> Hōl' my han's by de finger tips,
> But pray don't tetch my sweet liddle lips.
>   (Talley, *NFR*, 72)

Talley clarifies "Gooshen Bend" as "Grecian Bend," referring "to an angle at which women walked in the era when bustles and wasp waists were in fashion."

Finally, Charles Perdue located a version from an unidentified African American informant (possibly an ex-slave) in the WPA's Georgia folklore collection.

Now Dinah jumps into the aisle rolling from side to side in ecstatic abandon, shouting:

> You kin hol' my bonnet,
> You kin hol' my shawl,
> I'm shoutin' in de cool,
> Thank Gowd! (Charles Perdue, "Don't Let the
>   Devil Out-Talk You: Folk Songs, Rhymes,
>   Chants, and Other Musical Material from the

W. P. A. Collection of Folklore and Ex-Slave Narratives," unpublished paper, 1970, qtd. Rosenberg, *Shout*, 50)

WPA narrators provided the fullest texts by far, four altogether. The versions from Frances Lewis and Victoria Williams appear in the chapter text; the remaining pair are both from Aunt Ellen Godfrey, who describes performing the piece on two very different occasions completely atypical for this tradition, albeit completely comprehensible nonetheless. In her first story, Godfrey was helping to arrange the corpse of a woman (Lavinia) whose widowed husband (Zazarus) actually proposed marriage to Godfrey then and there. She turned him down cold with this song.

Go to writin'!:

> If you want to know my name
> Go to Uncle Amos house.
> Big foot nigger and he six foot high.
> Tryin' to bussin' at my waterfall! (Kissin' her
> waterfall—headdress.)
> Oh, the gay gal
> Settin' on the rider (fence "rider" on "stake and
> rider fence")
>
> Gay gal waterfall.
> Don't tech (touch) my waist
> But bounce my shirt!
> Don't touch my waterfall!

I sing that sing to 'em and man buss out and cry! "My God! You talk ME!" I ain't want him! I kick him with that same word.

They was Zazarus and Lavinia. Dead can't wash for myself. I go wash and lay Lavinia out. And he husband wanter (want to) marry with me. I kick him with that same sing. Hint to wise. If he couldn't understand that he couldn't understand nothing. Mr. Godfrey my last husband, he worth all the two I got. I have the chillun. Wenus, Jane,

Patient, Kate, Harry, Edmund, Jeemes— (Ellen Godfrey, b. 1837, SC, 164–65, orig. parentheses)

During shouting, women reportedly used this song to select the men they wanted to hold them—and to reject others (see Victoria Williams, b. ca. 1860, MS, 211)—so the snub could not have been more pointed. Godfrey's second story is just as good, recounting her liberation by Abraham Lincoln's son, Johnny (there of course being no such person).

I see Abram Lincoln son Johnny! Talk with him! Gimme tobacco. I been to loom. Weave. Sheckle flying—flying sheckle!

> (Singing): Tech (touch) me all round my waist!
> Don't tech my waterfall!
> Gay gal setting on the rider fence!
> Don't tech my waterfall! . . .

I been weave. My loom at door. Six loom on dat side! Six loom on dis side! I see 'em coming. Hat crown high as this. (She measured off almost half of her walking stick—which had a great tarnished plated silver knob.) And I tell 'em "Yankee coming!" I talk with Abram Lincoln own son Johnny and, bless your heart I glad for Freedom till I fool!

> (Singing)
> Freedom forever!
> Freedom evermore!
> Want to see the Debbil run
> Let the Yankee fling a ball
> The Democrack will take the swamp!

Massa been hide. Been in swamp. (Ellen Godfrey, b. 1837, SC, 155–57, orig. parentheses)

The interviewer, Genevieve Wilcox Chandler, added in a note: "This is history. All the old men, too old for the army, hid in Marlboro swamps and were fed by faithful slaves until Yankees passed on. My grandmother and mother gave vivid accounts of this—my mother telling of the sufferings of the women—mental—worrying about her feeble old grandfather down there with the [water] moccasins." Emancipation was, of course, inextricably linked to shouting, explaining why Aunt Ellen found this piece particularly appropriate to these circumstances.

Godfrey may not have provided the most unusual versions, however. That distinction could belong to New Orleans jazz pioneer Ferdinand "Jelly Roll" Morton. During a marathon 1939 session for Alan Lomax and the Library of Congress, Morton recorded takes of "Michigan Water Blues" and "If the River Was Whiskey and You Was a Duck" replacing their usual lyrics with identical passages describing a dancing girl:

> Mama, mama, look at sis, she's out on the levee
>   doing the double twist.
> Mama, mama, look at sis, she's out on the levee
>   doing the double twist.
>
> She said "Come in here, you dirty little sow, you
>   trying to be a bad girl, you don't know how."
> She said "Come in here, you dirty little sow, you
>   trying to be a bad girl, you don't know how."
>
> She said, "Touch my bonnet, touch my shawl, do
>   not touch my waterfall."
> "Touch my bonnet, baby, touch my shawl,
>   please, don't you touch my waterfall." (Jelly
>   Roll Morton, "Michigan Water Blues," AFS
>   1686B, New York, May–June 1939; compare
>   "If the River Was Whiskey and You Was a
>   Duck," AFS 1652B, New York, May–June 1939)

"Don't Touch My Waterfall" was collected from ex-slave Frances Lewis in Morton's hometown New Orleans, though given his peripatetic lifestyle, he might have heard it anywhere. There may be no way to settle that question or to untangle the precise chain of textual associations found in these recordings, except that Morton not only knew the song but tied it to women's possession dancing, or at least to a young lady dancing as if possessed.

"BOOTS OR NO BOOTS." I have not found this story outside the narratives, but it was performed by five ex-slaves from Louisiana, Mississippi, South Carolina, and Virginia. The versions from Lizzie Davis and Emoline Glasgow appear in the chapter text, the remainder below. The texts from Julia Frazier and Sarah Thomas suggest the influence of the *John and Old Marster* trickster-tale cycle, a post–Civil War development, but there is at least the possibility that the tale itself originated during slavery.

One Sunday, dere was a mighty good preacher and one ole 'ligious-hearted cullud man got happy en riz up en shouted twel he 'sturbed the preacher. At dinner Boss say, Uncle yo' must set still this evenin' en not do no shoutin! Ef yo' sets still, I will buy you a bran' new pair of boots. Dat evenin' the old man set still as long as he could. But when the preacher 'gan to tell about heaven en fare-ye-well to this worl', the ole cullud man went wile. He riz up in his seat en yelled, "Boss, boots er no boots, I'se gwine ter shout." (Annie Coley, b. ca. 1860, SC, MS, 439)

There was an old man who would answer the preacher every Sunday meetin'. He made so much noise ole Marsa said, "John, if you stop makin' dat noise in church, I'll give you a new pair of boots." John said, "I'll try, Marse." De nex' meetin' he tried an' tried to be quiet so he could get his new boots, but de spirit got him an' he yelled out, "Glory to God! Boots or no boots, glory to God!" (Julia Frazier, b. 1854, VA, 99)

Dar was a boy on de place dey said wuz Mr. Boley's own son. He wuz very fond of boots, and when de slaves had dere "secret meetin's" day had him out as a "watchman" to see who wuz comin' up on dem. Dey would meet together to sing and pray.

When dey would say somethin' in dere prayers dat suited him, he would jump and begin to shout. Den dey ax him: "John what *will make you do dat*?" "I jes' kaint hep it"—he would say, "Marster promised me a pair 'o boots, but, now, boots or no boots, Glory Halle-lu-yah!" Then John runned away. Every time dey would whup him, he would take out fer de woods. Mr. Boley wouldn't whup him much, because he liked him. He finally sot him free. (Sarah Thomas, b. ca. 1860, LA, 2107–8)

TURNING THE POT DOWN

Dey didn't larn us nothin' an' didn't 'low us to larn nothin'. Iffen dey ketch us larnin' to read an' write, dey cut us han' off. Dey didn't 'low us to go to church, neither. Sometimes us slip off an' have a little prayer meetin' by usse'ves in a ole house wid a dirt flo'. Dey'd git happy an' shout an' couldn't nobody hyar 'em, caze dey didn't make no fuss on de dirt flo', an' one stan' in de do' an' watch. Some fo'ks put dey head in de wash pot to pray, an' pray easy, an' somebody be watchin' for de overseer. Us git whupped fer ev'ything iffen hit was public knowed. (George Young, b. 1846, AL, 433)

We went to a church there on the place. You ought to have heard that "Hellish" preaching. . . . "Obey your Master and Mistress, don't steal chickens, don't steal eggs and meat," and nary word 'bout having a soul to save. All of the slaves had to go to Church. They preached to the whites in the morning and the colored in the afternoon. . . . They used to steal off and pray and turn a washpot upside down to drown the sound. Master track them with dogs and say "Don't you pray." (Wes Brady, b. 1849, TX, 401)

"Speaking of whipping," I said, "What were some of the things that a Negro was whipped for?"

   "Well," she replied, "fer runnin' away, fer prayin', fer singing at night, fer not workin' and fer not takin' orders. Sometimes at night when we wanted to pray and sing, we had to stick our heads in a big iron pot to keep de noise away from de big house." (Lula Cottonham Walker, b. 1824, AL, 432–33) (Following Walker's narrative, conducted by John Morgan Smith, a page of "suggested changes" from an unidentified editor states, "omit account of whipping for 'praying and singing'—preposterous!" Walker's narrative was not sent to the national archives but was retained in the Alabama state files.)

No tale in the narratives seems more inescapable yet more inexplicable than the story of slaves turning the pot down to escape detection. No question it is well known elsewhere.[1] Still, over ninety WPA narrators told

Fig. 14.1. Wes Brady, ex-slave, Marshall, TX, December 4, 1937. Portraits of African American ex-slaves from the US Works Progress Administration, Federal Writers' Project slave narratives collection, Library of Congress.

the tale, more than quadrupling examples from other sources. Yet even some ex-slaves seemed confused by the story if not openly skeptical, younger Blacks and outsiders even more so.

"I used to hear my grandma say that they weren't allowed to have a church service and that they used to go out way off and sing and pray and they'd have to turn a pot down to keep the noise from going out. I don't know just how they fixed the pot" (Cora L. Horton, b. ca. 1880, GA, grandchild of ex-slaves, 322). "So far as serving God was concerned, they had to take a kettle and turn it down bottom upward and then old master couldn't hear the singing and prayin'. I don't know how they turned the kettle to keep the noise from goin' out. But I heard my father and mother say they did it. The kettle would be on the inside of the cabin, not on the outside" (Cyrus Bellus, b. 1865, MS, child of ex-slaves, 142). "I don't know how they found out the iron pot would take up the noise. They had plenty of em settin' round in them days. Somebody found out it and passed it on" (Mary Scott, b. unk., TN, 126–27).

Recalling his ex-slave father's later years, Olympic champion Jesse Owens (1913–1980) wrote: "if Henry Owens never was able to read the words of his religion, at least he didn't have to dig a hole in the ground or put a kitchen pot over his head to pray."[2]

None of this is particularly baffling, however. Even in the pre-electronic period, Black singers in Africa and around the world employed various techniques or accessories to reverberate and distort their voices. Writes Frances Bebey: "the utilization of the voice by musicians in black Africa—its timbres and the different nuances obtained by means of artifices unknown to the rest of the world (stopping the ears, pinching the nose, vibrating the tongue in the mouth, producing echoes by directing the voice into a receptacle, etc.)—largely accounts for the confusion, or rather, the incomprehension that almost inevitably confronts the non-African listener when he at first hears black African music."[3]

More specifically, stories of American slaves singing and praying into pots to conceal sacred mysteries recall African voice disguisers serving the same purpose, often by vocalizing into vessels or containers. Among the BaBembe of the Congo, for example, four hollow, mouthblown wooden effigies speak for a family of spirits.[4] Sacred clowns especially employ such devices. The Hausa *Dan Kama* (jester or juggler) accompanies himself on a single-headed hourglass drum called a *turu*, but "sometimes varies his entertainment by inverting the drum and talking, singing or whistling into the lower open end of the instrument; his voice causes the drumhead membrane to vibrate and to create thus an alternation in the timbre of the vocal sound. The 'snare' probably helps in producing a comic intonation."[5] Performers can accentuate the effect by singing against the drumhead.[6]

Other New World Blacks sang and prayed in pots. In Haiti, writes Harold Courlander, "*canaries* (large clay water vessels) also enter into ritual use. They are sung into, tapped with sticks, and on some occasions are covered with goatskin heads and played like a drum."[7]

By scrambling human speech or channeling the spirits, these devices mask sacred ceremonies, maintaining secrecy by rendering their mysteries unintelligible to outsiders, simultaneously scaring away unbelievers and keeping women and children indoors. Even when employed publicly, they remain shrouded in secrecy, "usually hidden from the women and the uninitiated, who must on no account know how the mystic 'spirit voices' are produced. They form an important accessory in the outfit of many of the [African] secret societies which exercise so dominant an influence."[8]

Thus within the tradition of African voice disguisers, turning the pot down would have been intended not to silence but to encode. When ex-slaves insisted that whites could not hear these ceremonies, they were not nonsensically asserting that these noisy conclaves were inaudible, but that whites could not understand them (and in vernacular English, *hear* and *understand* are synonyms). "Dey go out an' turn de wash pot bottom up 'ards so de echo go under de pot an' de white folks coulden' hear de songs" (George Newton, b. 1867, AR, child of ex-slaves, 2909–10). "During the war we had prayer meetings at the different houses on the plantations. We prayed to be set free. Turned wash pots down in the house to keep the sound down so white folks wouldn't hear us singing and praying to be set free" (Charlie Hinton, b. ca. 1850, NC, 276–77). "De slaves would tek dere ole iron cookin' pots en turn dem upside down on de groun' neah dere cabins ter keep dere white folks fum hearin' w'at dey wuz sayin'. Dey claimed dat hit showed dat Gawd wuz wid dem" (Patsy Hyde, b. unk., TN, 34). Substitute *understand* for *hear* and these statements all still make sense. They actually make more sense, because it was the content of the songs and prayers—and especially the entreaties for freedom—that most incensed slaveholders.

> An' she [mother] sed dey use to have meetin's an' sing an' pray an' de ole paddyrollers would heah dem; so to keep de soun' from goin' out, slaves would put a gra' big iron pot at de do' an' you know some times dey would fergit to put ole pot dar an' de paddyrollers would come an' horse whip ev'ry las' one o' dem, jes' 'cause de poor souls was prayin' to God to free 'em f'om dat awful bondage. (Minnie Folkes, b. 1860, VA, 93)

Fig. 14.2. "Slave preacher leading a Methodist service in the slave chapel of a Port Royal cotton plantation, 1863." *Illustrated London News* 43 (December 5, 1863): 561. Slavery Images: A Visual Record of the African Slave Trade and Slave Life in the Early African Diaspora. slaveryimages.org. This "rude chapel" was built specifically for slave services by the slaveholder, depicted in attendance with his family. The slaves are seated dutifully in the pews, with no evidence of the characteristic African American worship styles described elsewhere.

Any precautions notwithstanding, whites would have been aware of many, probably most of these "secret" meetings, which by narrators' own accounts were sometimes audible for miles. In a milieu where any unobserved or unregulated assembly of Blacks was the subject of rampant paranoia and obsessive vigilance, a nighttime gathering of slaves testifying, trance dancing, and screaming into cookware was likely to attract some attention. A former slave told Dorothy Scarborough "that he had often gone to such services with his mother in his childhood and seen this [turning the pot down] done. He said that, in fact, he believed the white people knew of these gatherings and allowed them, though the Negroes were fearful of being found out."[9] By the logic of African voice modifiers, however, white infidels stayed away or huddled indoors not because they were unaware of these meetings, but because the songs and sermons were incomprehensible, and the spirit voices frightened and kept them at bay.

Prohibitions against independent slave worship did exist at some times and places, but for the most part these decisions were left to individual slaveholders.[10] Some brutally enforced such bans, or forced slaves to attend slaveholder churches and no other. "We didn't have no church in de country for Niggers, an' dey went to church wid deir white folkses, if dey went at tall. De white folks sot in front, an' de Niggers sot in back. All de time dat overseer wuz right dar wid his gun" (Alec Bostwick, b. ca. 1861, GA, 109). Other slaveholders allowed and supported separate slave services, though only under their supervision and surveillance. "Church was what they called it but all that the preacher talked about was for us slaves to obey our masters. Nothin' about Jesus was ever said and the overseer stood there to see the preacher talked as he wanted him to talk" (Charlie Van Dyke, b. ca. 1830, AL, 398). "The sermons they heard were preached by a white preacher and on rare occasions by a colored preacher. Whenever the colored pastor preached there were several white persons present to see that no doctrine save that laid down by them should be preached" (Annie Price, b. 1855, GA, 182). "If you go to church you have to have a pass from the master. The pattyrollers see you and you have to show it to them. . . . They come to church and in all public places like the police stands around now" (William Henry Rooks, b. 1853, MS, 76).

Many whites, however, permitted slaves to worship (or not) as they pleased. Thus if slaveholders let slave congregations be, it was probably because they had given advance permission, or simply did not care. Yet the fact is that Black worship styles—the styles associated with turning the pot down—did frighten and disturb many whites, who barred these displays from their churches or banned them altogether, but in any case avoided slave meetings. In 1864 an escaped slave living in Washington, DC, recalled a plantation camp meeting, when "in the midst of it, the master sent for the leading black man. . . . 'Dick,' said the planter, 'what is the meaning of this hideous noise? If you were whipped by devils, you could not make a more horrible howling. Now, Dick, I can bear a great deal, but more of this I cannot stand.'"[11] The slave claimed Divine sanction, and the service proceeded with whites sequestered at a distance. In this capacity, turning the pot down seems to have completely

Fig. 14.3. "A Negro camp meeting in the South." Engraving by Sol Eytinge Jr., *Harper's Weekly* 16 (August 10, 1872): 620. Blacks just after the war, worshipping in their own way. "When de colored folks would hol' church dere I has seen fifty women throwin' demselves 'roun', and shoutin' and singin'. Dere was a big pine thicket near de road to Cuseta, and I've seen at leas' five hundred people in dat grove singin'" (Thomas Johns, b. 1847, AL, 1969–70). Note that at least three participants—the man standing second from the left, the preacher in the pulpit, and the woman in spectacles kneeling far right—have Bibles or songbooks.

served its practical purpose and fully met participants' expectations.

Whether slaves worshipped in seclusion by choice or necessity, many of the refuges they sought also served as natural echo chambers, creating vocal effects they favored and otherwise contrived. Some ex-slaves linked brush arbors to turning the pot down. "Uncle Anderson said that old man Fields didn't allow them to sing and pray and hold meetings, and they had to slip off and slip aside and hide around to pray. They knew what to do. People used to stick their heads under washpots to sing and pray. Some of them went out into the brush arbors where they could pray and shout without being disturbed" (Will Glass, b. unk., AL, NC, grandchild of ex-slaves, 40). In a perfect turn of phrase, Charles Grandy (b. 1842, VA, 119) referred to a prayer pot by a barn loft as a "hush-arbor."[12]

More generally, of course, these practices illustrate the African American preference for complex, textured sounds, coupled with an acute sensitivity to different acoustic spaces. George Owens (b. ca. 1853, TX, 168) explained *fence-corner church*: "De kind of chu'ch dey have in dem days on dat place was fence-corner chu'ch. Dey go off in de fence corner and sing and pray. Dey feered fer anybody to see 'em." A Louisiana ex-slave described slaves singing and praying in enclosures created by hanging wetted quilts, not unlike sound baffles in recording studios.[13] Slaves also prayed up chimneys. "I 'members dey uster pray in de chim'ly corner. Sometimes dey uster set 'roun' de chim'ly and sing. One of de songs dey uster sing go like dis: / Set knee to knee and look in de place / Hadn' you rather be at home? / Yes, Lawd" (Rosa Green, b. 1852, LA, 1590–91). "My grandmother used to sit by the fireplace and sing: / I'm bound fo' the Promised Land, / I'm bound fo' the Promised Land, / Oh, I'm bound fo' the Promised Land, / Who'll go with me to the Promised Land?" (Mary Edwards, b. 1853, TX, 1282). "We had meetings in the brush arbor when the preacher blew the bugle. In winter time we'd have prayer meetings around the fireplace" (Will Parker, b. 1842, GA, 3018). Evidently the chimney's echo-chamber effect was identical to turning the pot down, functionally and symbolically.

> The first church I went to was under a big mulberry tree there on the place. A white man done the preaching. Master had told us that if we be good Niggers and obey him that we would go to heaven. But I felt all the time that there was something better than that for me. So I kept praying for it till I found the change in my heart. I was by myself down by a spring when I found the Lord.
>
> When the darkies prayed in slavery they daren't let the white fo'ks know 'bout it or they beat them to death. When we prayed we turned a wash pot down to the ground to catch the voice. We prayed lots in slavery to be free and the Lord heard our prayer. We didn't have no song books, the Lord give us our songs. When we sing them at night 'round the fire place it would be just whispering like so the white fo'ks not hear us. We would hum them as we wo'ked in the fiel'. One of our favorite songs went like this:
>
> My knee-bones am aching
> My body's racking with pain

Fig. 14.4. Anderson and Minerva Edwards, ex-slaves, Marshall, TX, August 3, 1937. Portraits of African American ex-slaves from the US Works Progress Administration, Federal Writers' Project slave narratives collection, Library of Congress.

> I really believe I'se a child of God
> This ain't my home cause heaven's my aim.
> (Anderson Edwards, b. 1844, TX, 1262)

In his 1838 memoir, Alabama ex-slave James Williams told of "Uncle David sitting on his stool with his face thrust up the chimney, in order that his voice not be heard by his brutal persecutor. He was praying, giving utterance to these words, probably in reference to his bondage:—'*How long, O Lord, how long*?' 'As long as my whip!' cried the overseer."[14]

There are other North American offshoots of African voice disguisers. The closest relation of the praying pot is the *blowing jug*—a demijohn or large bottle sounded by blowing, humming, or singing into or across its mouth. This instrument gained its greatest fame in the so-called jug bands first documented in the late 1800s. The earliest of these groups consisted entirely of jugs, perhaps with makeshift percussion, but by the 1920s and '30s many Black and white stringbands had incorporated the instrument as a bass substitute.[15] Ex-slave Silas Knox was born in Panola County, Mississippi, and lived his entire life there or in neighboring Tate County. Recalling the postwar period, he appeared to describe an early jug band: "We had parties on Sataday nights and dem whut could would try to dance, and de niggers played on harps and jugs and combs" (Silas Knox, b. ca. 1860, MS, 1288). The harp he names could have been either a harmonica or a set of quills; the comb would have been a makeshift kazoo (in the 1970s David Evans found the paper-and-comb kazoo still in use in Tate and Panola Counties).[16] Knox does not state outright that the jug he recalled was blown—ex-slaves also describe bottles and jugs as struck bell substitutes—but the Tate-Panola County area is only thirty or forty miles from Memphis, a center of the jug band movement, so I think there is a good chance that Knox does provide one of the earliest accounts of an African American jug band. There is little evidence that spirits still spoke through American jugs, but by custom jug players were the groups' comedians, a link perhaps to Africa's sacred clowns and their voice disguisers.[17] The kazoo—the most common African voice modifier—was also a standard feature of jug bands.[18] African American performers also sang and spoke through kazoos (and later harmonicas), but in America these too were comic voices or vocal effects, not spirits.

In North America the spirits did still speak through bottle trees. Derived from African spirit catchers, bottle trees are created by attaching bottles, jars, or jugs to tree branches. They protect homes by trapping spirits, whose voices are heard when the wind whistles through the containers.[19]

Several informants described digging holes under pots, or even to lie in bodily. "When they prayed under the pot, they would make a little hole and set the pot over it. Then they would stick their heads under the pot and say and sing what they wanted" (Will Glass, b. unk., AL, grandchild of ex-slaves, 40). "Niggers was very religious and dey had church often. Dey would annoy de white folks wid shouting and singing and praying and dey would take cooking pots and put over dey mouths so de white folks couldn't hear 'em. Dey would dig holes in de ground too, and lie down when dey prayed" (James Southall, b. 1855, TN, 308). "Massa never 'lowed us slaves go to church but they have big holes in the fields they gits down in and prays. They done that way 'cause the white folks didn't want them to pray. They used to pray for freedom" (Ellen Butler, b. ca. 1860, LA, 177). Athlete Jesse Owens recalled his

father digging a hole in the ground to pray. Earthen pits are sometimes used as resonators in Africa, with similar religious overtones. The *earth bow* or *ground harp* consists of a flexible bow with single string attached to a piece of bark or plank over a hole in the ground. "When the string is plucked or struck, the sound apparently emerges from the bowels of the earth. This explains why it is much used in magic."[20] In Haiti the earth bow evolved into the *tambour maringouin* or mosquito drum, sometimes substituting a tin pail for the earthen pit. In North America, it became the washtub bass.[21]

Slaves also regularly worshipped along river banks and creek bottoms, or in hollows, ditches, and other earthen recesses. This was largely for convenience, shelter, and concealment, but such spaces are excellent sounding chambers, and narrators assigned them the same functions as spirit pots. "I wuz tole dat sum ob de white peeples wuz so mean ter dere slaves dat de slaves would tek a pot en turn hit down in a hollow ter keep dere whites fum yearin' dem singin' en prayin'. De Ku Klux wuz bad on de ex-slaves at fust" (Measy Hudson, b. ca. 1850, TN, 31). "According to 'Aunt' Mary, the Little Negroes were very religious and given to much loud praying and singing, which often so disturbed Dr. Little that he gave orders for them to stop it, and also ordered that all lights in the slave quarters be out at 9 o'clock each night. 'So us tuck to slippin' off to a big gully in de pastur to sing and pray whar de white fokes couldn' hear us'" (Mary Ferguson, b. ca. 1855, GA, 328). "We used to steal off to de woods and have church, like de spirit moved us, sing and pray to our own liking and soul satisfaction and we sho' did have good meetings, honey. Baptize in de river like God said. We had dem spirit filled meetins at night on de bank of de river and God met us dere. We was quiet 'nough so de white folks didn't know we was dere" (Susan Rhodes, b. ca. 1835, NC, 288–89). "At night afte' de white folks wus sleep, sum uf de slaves wud hide down under de hill an' sing an' pray fur de Lord ter cum an' free 'em" (Sarah Felder, b. 1853, MS, 715–16). "All de time dey [slaveholders] wus gone [to war] de slaves kept prayin' to be free; dey would go down under de hill way in de night an' pray hard ter be sot free" (Ebenezer Brown, b. 1852, MS, 249). "We had to steal away at night to have church on de ditch bank, and crawl home on de belly. Once overseers heered us prayin', give us one day each 100 lashes" (Elvira Boles, b. 1843, MS, 107).[22] This is no doubt why spirituals so often describe singing, praying, and getting happy "down under the hill." "See my brudder down de hill; fall down on he knees; / Send up your prayers; I'll send up mine; de good Lord ter please" (Ebenezer Brown, b. 1852, MS, 244); "Went down into the valley to watch and pray, / My soul got happy and I stayed all day" (Mary Gladdy, b. ca. 1853, GA, 25).[23]

Some aspects of praying pots were purely symbolic, as when ex-slaves reported placing them around doors. "Dey would turn a washpot upside-down in front of de door to kill de sound. Den you couldn't hear 'em outside de door" (Lucy Galloway, b. 1863, MS, 804). "When we sang we turned de washpots and tubs in de doors, so dey would take up de noise so de white folks could not hear us" (Chana Littlejohn, b. ca. 1857, NC, 56). "When dey had de prayer meetin's dey shut de do' so won't let de voice out, en dey turn de washpot down at de do'—some say ter keep hit in" (Oliver Bell, b. unk., AL, 55). "A large, iron pot was always placed against the cabin door—sideways, to keep the sound of their voices from 'escaping' or being heard from the outside. Then, the slaves would sing, pray, and relate experiences all night long" (Mary Gladdy, b. ca. 1853, GA, 26–27). This makes little sense acoustically. However, hoodoo or conjure tricks and charms were most often placed in or near doorways; magically, then, doorways were the ideal spots for spirit pots.[24]

Other narrators described pots serving as genuine voice modifiers, however. "They had to slip off and slip aside and hide around to pray. They knew what to do. People used to stick their heads under washpots" (Will Glass, b. unk., grandchild of ex-slaves, AL, NC, 40). A quarter of the ex-slaves who described turning the pot down insisted that they stuck their heads directly in the pot, tub, or barrel to sing, pray, or testify. "Dey would put their heads in barrels or wash pots when praying, to keep the sound from being heard" (Lorena

Thomas, b. ca. 1854, MS, 2096–97). "When we used to pray we put our heads under the wash pot to keep old master from hearin' us" (Robert Wilson, b. 1836, VA, 208). "Mammy bring the wash pot out of the yard and set it in the middle of the floor and she laugh and cry and sing a little, then she puts her head down in the pot clear to her shoulders and mumbles" (John Crawford, b. 1837, MS, 966). "Sometimes dey sneak off an' meet in one ob de other cabins at night. Den each one bring pot an' dey put dere head in de pot to keep de echoes from getting back an' somebody hearing dem. Den dey pray in de pot" (William Mathews, b. 1848, LA, 2614). "I remembah one 'oman had a big mouf. She uster put huh head raight in the pot an' jes' yell an hollah an' you couldn't heah huh more'n three foot away" (Sister Robinson, b. 1836, VA, 242).

> One 'r' d' slaves was a sorter preacher. Sometime d' marster 'low him t' preach t' d' niggers but he hab t' preach wid a tub ober he head co'se he git so happy he talk too loud. Somebudy from d' big house liable t' come down 'n' mek him quit cause he makin' a 'sturbance. (Charlotte Beverly, b. ca. 1847, TX, 285)

Whether or not it needs to be stated, loudly vocalizing with one's head in a large pot—the experiment is simple to reproduce—can in no time create a jarring, incomprehensible sound barrage. With the proper vocalizing, it can be positively unnerving or unearthly. Granted, only a minority of ex-slaves—though a sizable minority—explicitly described this arrangement, but others hint at it. I take this to be the original technique, however, simply because this approach above all others would create a true voice disguiser.[25] This is in fact the gist of Charlotte Beverly's story: without the pot, the slave preacher attracts whites; with his head in the pot, the infidels stay shuttered in the big house.

It also appears, however, that turning the pot down was talked about as much as actually taken up. For every narrator who had personally prayed in pots, another had merely heard about it. "Dey tried to make 'em stop singin' and prayin' durin' de war, 'case all dey'd ask for was to be sot free, but de slaves would get in de cabins and turn a big wash pot upside down and sing into dat, and de noise couldn't get out. I don't remember nothin' about dis ceptin' what mammy say" (Callie Williams, b. 1861, AL, 427). "I never saw them turn no pots down neither; but I have heard of that. They used to sing their songs in a whisper and pray in a whisper" (Lucretia Alexander, b. ca. 1845, MS, 35). "I heard them talk about setting the pot at the doors and having singing and prayer services. They all sung and prayed around the room. I forgot all the things they talked about" (Diana Alexander, b. ca. 1865, child of ex-slaves, MS, 28). "I heard them talk about slipping off and going to some house on the place and other places too and pray for freedom during the War. They turned an iron pot upside down in the room" (Emma Barr, b. 1872, AR, child of ex-slaves, 120). "The Carters didn't mind their Niggers singing hymns and praying but I heard all the time that some of the other places wouldn't let their Niggers worship a-tall. The Niggers had to put their heads in pots to sing and pray" (Cato Carter, b. 1836 or 1837, AL, 645). "Dey go out an' turn de wash pot bottom up 'ards so de echo go under de pot an' de white folks coulden' hear de songs. I've heared mother tell dat a hundred times" (George Newton, b. 1867, AR, child of ex-slaves, 2909–10).

> They used to have prayer meetings. In some places that they have prayer meetings they would turn pots down in the middle of the floor to keep white folks from hearing them sing and pray and testify, you know. Well, I don't know where they learned to do that. I kinda think the Lord put them things in their minds to do for themselves, just like he helps us Christians in other ways. Don't you think so?[26]

Indeed, many accounts of slaves praying in pots can only be understood as folktales far removed from the actual practice. Some narrators described pots being placed *outside* the meeting house or in other nonsensical ways. "Honey, we put a wash pot down in front of de meeten house so's de overseer couldn't hear us a singing and prayin. Dis wash pot caught de sound" (Victoria Randle Lawson, b. ca. 1850, MS, 1307). "When dark cum de men fo'ks wud hang up a wash pot, bottom up'ards, in de little brush chu'ch house us hed, so's it'd catch de noise an de oberseer woulden' hear us singin' an shoutin'" (Clara C. Young, b. ca. 1842, AL, 2402–3). "We often had prayer meeting out in the quarters, and to keep the folks in the 'big house' from hearing us, we would take pots, turn them down, put something under them, that let the sound go in the pots, put them in a row by the door, then our voices would not go, and we could sing and pray to our heart's content" (Harriet Cheatam, b. 1843, TN, 53).

In his 1913 memoir, William H. Robinson wrote that North Carolina slaves "would congregate after the white people had retired, when you would see them with their cooking utensils, pots and kettles, go into a swamp and put the pots and kettles on the fence, with the mouths turned toward the worshippers. They would sing and pray, the kettles catching the sound."[27]

Many former slaves described pots at social dances. "De only fun de young folks had wuz w'en de ole folks had a quiltin'. W'ile de ole folks wuz wukin' on de quilt de young ones would git in 'nuther room, dance en hab a good time. Dey'd hab a pot turned down at de do'er ter keep de white folks fum 'yearin' dem" (Millie Simpkins, b. 1831, TN, 67). "We had dances in the cabins every once in a while. We dance more in winter time so we could turn a pot down in the door to drown out the noise" (Soldier Williams, b. 1839, KY, 191).[28] Like prayer meetings, slave dances were carefully regulated and ruthlessly policed; like slave frolics, private prayer meetings invariably involved dancing, albeit usually called shouting. The transference is thus perfectly logical, but the original function is muddled.

Other cases more conclusively reveal rationalization or simply outright confusion. Several sources describe vessels filled with water, as if there were no other imaginable purpose for the pots or tubs. "Us nebber had no 'musement whilst us wuz slaves, en when prayer meetin' wuz hol' en de cabins dey sot er tub er water en de center en all sot roun' it. Den de tub er water ketch de soun' en kep' it fum goin' out de cabin" (Phoebe Lyons, b. ca. 1855, GA, 402–3). "When de slaves got together an' had prayer an' sang, we put large tubs of water outside of de huts to catch de sounds so we wouldn't bother our marster or missus" (Fannie Nicholson, b. 1848, VA, 217).[29]

There are even purported instances of slaveholders mandating the pot's use, mooting its original purpose of deceiving whites. "When the slaves would hold a religious service in their quarters the mistress would require one of them to turn a tub against the door to catch the sound and absorb it before it got into the mansion" (Nelson Polk, b. ca. 1830, MS, 166). Betty Guwn reported putting the pot against the slaveholder's door: "The slaves had 'meetin'' some nights and her mistress would call her and have her turn a tub against her mansion door to keep out the sound" (Betty Guwn, b. 1832, KY, 98).[30]

That narrators reshaped their experiences around traditional tales or themes comes as no surprise, of course. Many of the patrollers in their stories were all too real, but prayer pots also attracted migratory motifs like the *throwing-coals* or *stringing-grapevine* episodes. And why not: turning the pot down, throwing coals, and stringing grapevines were all widely recognized methods for confounding white vigilantes, if only in wishful thinking.

> My father was once attending a prayer meeting in a house which had only one door. The slaves had turned a large pot down in the center of the floor to hold the sounds of their voices within. (No sounds can escape from a closed room, if a big pot be turned down in the middle of it). But, despite their precaution, the patrolers found them and broke in. Of course, every Nigger present was "in" for a severe whipping, but the Lord must have spoken to my father. Thinking fast and acting quickly (as if he were inspired), my father stuck a big shovel in the fireplace, drew out a peck or more of hot ashes and cinders and flung them broadcast into the faces of them patrolers. The room was soon filled with smoke and the smell of burning clothes and white flesh and, in the confusion

and general hubbub that followed, every Negro escaped. Teasing, and playing pranks on, the patrolers were favorite pastimes of some of the slaves. One of their favorite stunts was to tie a grapevine across some narrow, dark stretch of road where they knew the patrolers would pass. (Rev. W. B. Allen, b. ca. 1850, AL, 7–8)[31]

Mary Kindred told a story resembling the various John and Old Marster trickster tales in which a slaveholder spies on a slave at prayer, with comic complications.[32] This no doubt explains why Kindred or some other storyteller included the pot—another means of misdirecting white eavesdroppers—since it plays no necessary part in the story's plot.

> Dey hab a few cullud preachers in dem day but dey didn' know much. Dey uster hab prayer meetin'. One time dey ax Marse Hadnot iffen dey could hab prayer meetin' dat night. He say to Alf, "Now Alf, I tell you sing one song an' pray one prayer." Dey was lots of niggers dere from de Ryles an' Henderson an' Neylan' plantations, dey was de plantations 'roun' all come to de prayer meetin'. Dey hab a wash pot tu'n bottom up to drown de noise. 'Reckly ol' marster come to de do' (door) an' call, "Alf, didn' I tol' you jes' one song an' one prayer?" Dere he's stan'in' in de do' wid a whip. W'en he say dat dem niggers bust out cause he was gwineter beat dem w'en dey go pas'. Dey rush out so fas' dat dey knock him down an' run right ober him. He didn' git to hit airy one a lick. Dey could jine de chu'ch in dem day iffen dey wanter. An' shout—I he'p you to say dey shout. (Mary Kindred, b. ca. 1855, TX, 2201–2, orig. parentheses)

However, turning the pot down is most often combined with a tale that was almost as popular: the story of slaves being forced to attend segregated white churches, sing white hymns, and listen to whites preach Ephesians 6:5: "Servants, be obedient to them that are your masters according to the flesh, with fear and trembling, in singleness of your heart,

Fig. 14.5. Mary Kindred, ex-slave, Beaumont, TX, June 28, 1937. Portraits of African American ex-slaves from the US Works Progress Administration, Federal Writers' Project slave narratives collection, Library of Congress.

as unto Christ." This is no fiction. Such indoctrination is reported from an early date—it was even recommended by how-to manuals on slavery.[33] Rhode Islander Jehu Grant (1738–1841) ran away to fight in the American Revolution but was later denied a military pension because he technically was still a slave. In his unsuccessful appeal he argued: "had I been taught to read or understand the precepts of the Gospel, 'Servants obey your Masters' I might have done otherwise notwithstanding the songs of liberty that saluted my ear, thrilled through my heart."[34]

Such backhanded paraphrases are rife in the narratives. "Obey de master, obey de overseer, obey dis, an' obey dat" (William Mathews, b. 1848, LA, 2614). "You must be good, don't steal, don't talk back at your marsters, don't run away, don't do dis, don't do dat" (Leah Garrett, b. unk., VA, 15–16). "You may get to the kitchen of heaben if you obey your master, if you don't steal, if you tell no stories, etc'" (Molly Finley, b. 1865, child of ex-slaves, AR, 294). "They sat in the back of the church as the white minister preached and directed the following text at them: 'Don't steal your master's chickens or his eggs and your backs won't be whipped.' In the afternoon of this same day when the colored minister was allowed to preach the slaves heard this text: 'Obey your masters and mistresses and your backs won't be whipped'" (Lewis Favors, b. 1855, GA, 323). "Obey yo' master an' missus an' you will always do right. If you see eggs in de yard take 'em to yo' marster or yo' missus an' put 'em at her feet. If you don't do dis she will needle you well or break bark over yo' head an' de bad man will git you" (Benjamin Johnson, b. unk., VA, 325). "His text was 'Obey your marster and mistress,' and he never told us a word about savin' our souls from hell fire and damnation" (Jake Dawkins, b. ca. 1845, MS, 594–95).

When grandma was fourteen or fifteen years old they locked her up in the seed house once or twice for not going to church. You see they let the white folks go to church in the morning and the colored folks in the evening, and my grandma didn't always want to go. She would be locked up in the seed bin and she would cuss the preacher out so he could hear her. She would say, "Master let us out." And he would say, "You want to go to church?" And she would say, "No, I don't want to hear that same old sermon: 'Stay out of your missis' and master's hen house. Don't steal your missis' and master's chickens. Stay out of your missis' and master's smokehouse. Don't steal your missis' and master's hams.' I don't steal nothin'. Don't need to tell me not to." (Victoria McMullen, b. 1884, AR, grandchild of ex-slaves, 36–37)

'Course we go to church in fair weather. They used to fix up a brush arbor in back of the white-folks meeting house and let the niggers set out there. The white preacher would preach along and then he'ud say, "And you slaves out there, if you want to have the Kingdom Come you got to mind your masters, work hard and don't steal your master's chickens." After I was a plumb old man I read in the papers that there was nine hundred preachers in the penitentiary and I said to myself, "There ought to be nine hundred more there if they would just kech them all." Them preachers and their lefthanded fellowship! (Jack Maddox, b. ca. 1849, TX, 2528–29)

One time when an old white man came along who wanted to preach, the white people gave him a chance to preach to the niggers. The substance of his sermon was this: "Now when you servants are working for your masters, you must be honest. When you go to the mill, don't carry along an extra sack and put some of the meal or the flour in for yourself. And when you women are cooking in the big house, don't make a big pocket under your dress and put a sack of coffee and a sack of sugar and other things you want in it." They took him out and hanged him for corrupting the morals of the slaves. (Waters McIntosh, b. 1863, SC, 18–19)[35]

As popular as the tale of preaching obedience was by itself, numerous versions were combined with turning the pot down. Clearly in the minds of ex-slaves, these stories had some very particular connection.

Black preachers couldn' preach tuh us. Ole boss would tie em tuh a tree an whoop em if dey caught us eben praying. We had er big black washpot an de way we prayed we'd go out an put our mouths to der groun an pray low an de sound wud go up under de pot an ole boss couldn' hear us. De white preacher would call us under a tree Sunday evenin tuh preach tuh us. Dis is whut his text would be: "Mind yo mistress." Den he would 'ceed tuh preach—"Don't steal der potatoes; don't lie bout nothin en don't talk back tuh yo boss; ifn yo does yo'll be tied tuh a tree an stripped neckid. When dey tell yuh to do somethin run an do hit." Dat's de kind uv gospel we got. (Emma Tidwell, b. ca. 1839, AR, 332)

I never saw any slaves auctioned off but I seen dem pass our house chained together on de way to be sold, including both men and women wid babies all chained to each other. Dere was no churches for slaves, but at nights dey would slip off and git in ditches and sing and pray, and when dey would sometimes be caught at it dey would be whipped. Some of de slaves would turn down big pots and put dere heads in dem and pray. My Mistress would tell me to be a good obedient slave and I would go to heaven. When slaves would attempt to run off dey would catch dem and chain dem and fetch 'em back and whip dem before dey was turned loose again. (Sallie Carder, b. ca. 1855, TN, 28)

If a colored man took a notion he wan' to be a preacher, he couldn't preach 'bout de Gospel an' God. Dey didn' 'low him to. All he could preach 'bout was obey. Obey de master, obey de overseer, obey dis, an' obey dat. Dey didn' make no passel of fuss 'bout praying den. Sometimes dey sneak off an' meet in one ob de other cabins at night. Den each one bring pot an' dey put dere head in de pot to keep de echoes from getting back an' somebody hearing dem. Den dey pray in de pot. Dat's de God's truth. (William Mathews, b. 1848, LA, 2614)

We didn't have no colored churches on the place. We went to the white folks Baptist Church. All that preachers teaching to us was, when you serve your master, you is serving God. They didn't allow us to hold no services of our own. We did hold them anyway. We would turn all the pots over so we wouldn't be heared. When pots is turned over in a house they catch all the echo and not a sound can be heard outside. (Julius Jones, b. ca. 1847, TN, 1221)

When they were praying for peace they used to turn down the wash kettles to keep the sound down. In the master's church the biggest thing that was preached was how to serve their master and mistiss. (Alice Wright, b. ca. 1863, AL, 246)[36]

Louisiana ex-slave Roan Barnes (b. unk.) recalled "if dey had a prayer meeting dey would turn a wash pot down to ketch de sound to keep de masters from hearing um. Didn't have no church; sometimes a white man would go around through the quarters preaching to de slaves telling dem to obey de marsters and missus and dey would be good to dem."[37] An anonymous Tennessee ex-slave (b. 1843) remembered:

> white folks have a morning service, and in the afternoon colored folks would go to the same church. The biggest thing I heard them preach about was "Servants, obey your mistress and master." They would tell them not to steal. Very few of them told you about religion. . . . When they had meetings that way [secretly] they came from other men's farms, and they would slip over and keep the padderollers from getting you, and they would turn the kettle down outside the door.[38]

Like turning the pot down, tales of preaching obedience apparently took on a life of their own in oral tradition, representing parables as often as personal experiences. Yet, however they related to real events, these stories obviously held some very special meaning for slaves; beyond that, one tale unquestionably reminded them of the other. Could it be that together these accounts perfectly encapsulated the double lives slaves inevitably led, forever showing one face to whites while reserving their true feelings for fellow captives? Why else would they constantly combine them, or draw so many links to similar conflicts and contradictions? For some ex-slaves, these stories naturally suggested the Jim Crow segregation of their present era. For others they connoted the contrast between carefully selected hymns and highly selective scriptures recited rote in white churches, and the orally composed spirituals and divinely inspired testimonies of the slaves' true religion. More generally, they highlighted slaveholders' own two-faced Christianity, and their concerted efforts to prevent slaves from reading scripture for themselves.

> I heard my parents tell about the Ku Klux come and made them cook them something to eat. They drunk water while she was cooking. I heard them say they would get whooped if they sot around with a book in their hand. When company would come they would turn the pot down and close the shutters and doors. They had preaching and prayed that way. The pot was to drown out the sound. (Lizzie Johnson, b. ca. 1870, MS, child of ex-slaves, 102)

> No, no! you better not be caught tryin' to do somethin' wid a book. Dey would teach you wid a stick or switch. De slaves had secret prayer meetin's wid pots turned down to kill de soun' o' de singin'. We sang a song, "I am glad salvation's free." Once dey heerd us, nex' mornin' dey took us and tore our backs to pieces. Dey would say, "Are you free? What were you singin' about freedom?" While de niggers were bein' whupped they said "Pray, master, pray" (Charity Austin, b. ca. 1852, GA, 62)

John Crawford was raised to address his slaveholder as *grandpappy* and regard him as the image of God.

> Grandpappy don't want the niggers to have learnin' out of books and don't want them to pray. He is scared they will pray for freedom. And he b'lieves they will get [it] if they pray. Better not let Grandpappy ketch you prayin. He reads us out'n the Bible every morning and night. He was a powerful Godly man. Sometimes we little niggers plumb thought he was God . . . . We thought God look jest like Grandpappy.
>
> But at night in our little log cabin in the quarters Mammy bring the wash pot out of the yard and set it in the middle of the floor and she laugh and cry and sing a little, then she puts her head down in the pot clear to her shoulders and mumbles. We chilluns say, "What you sayin' mammy?" She say "Shh, I'm prayin." We say "What you prayin' bout?" She say, "I'm prayin' for the freedom. But if Grandpappy hear you tell it he will birchbark you." (John Crawford, b. 1837, MS, 966)

Like innumerable fellow slaves, John Crawford's mother had come to understand the commandments of Godly slaveholders as mere hypocrisies and lies. Many were further determined to prove it by reading the Bible for themselves.

Appendix: Turning the Pot Down

The following WPA narrators describe turning the pot down: Laura Abromsom, William M. Adams, Diana Alexander, Lucretia Alexander, Rev. W. B. Allen, Charity Austin, Lucy Barnes, Mariah Barnes, Emma Barr, Oliver Bell, Cyrus Bellus, Charlotte Beverly, Emma Blalock, Henry Bobbitt, Siney Bonner, Wes Brady, Lewis Brown, Lucy Brown, Jeff Calhoun, Sallie Carder, Cato Carter, Harriet Cheatam, John Crawford, Anderson Edwards, Eliza Evans, Rachel Fairly, Minnie Folkes, Georgianna Foster, Lucy Galloway, Louisa Gause, Mary Gladdy, Will Glass, Charles Grandy, Henry Green, Betty Guwn, Essex Henry, Gillie Hill, Kitty Hill, Marriah Hines, Charlie Hinton, Cora L. Horton, Measy Hudson, John Hunter, Patsy Hyde, Lizzie Johnson, Julius Jones, Ellis Ken Kannon, Mary Kindred, Victoria Randle Lawson, Chana Littlejohn, Dave Lowry, Phoebe Lyons, Julia Malone, Alice Marshall, William Mathews, Ann Matthews, Stephen McCray, Garland Monroe, Fannie Moore, Rev. John Moore, George Newton, Fannie Nicholson, Wade Owens, Austin Pen Parnell, Dolly Phillips, Nelson Polk, Levi Pollard, Dora Richard, Sister Robinson, Edd Roby, C. G. Samuel, Mary Scott, Lucindy Hall Shaw, Matilda Shepard, Millie Simpkins, James Southall, Lorena Thomas, Emma Tidwell, Lula Cottonham Walker, Sarah Walker, Eliza Washington, Ella Washington, Sylvia Watkins, Andy Williams, Callie Williams, Soldier Williams, Robert Wilson, Alex Woods, Alice Wright, Clara C. Young, George Young.

Below are all of the WPA accounts not given in full in the chapter text or in other sections. (Examples quoted elsewhere are Diana Alexander, W. B. Allen, Charity Austin, Wes Brady, Cyrus Bellus, Charlotte Beverly, Sallie Carder, Cato Carter, Harriet Cheatam, John Crawford, Minnie Folkes, Betty Guwn, Kitty Hill, Cora L. Horton, Measy Hudson, Patsy Hyde, Lizzie Johnson, Julius Jones, Mary Kindred, Alice Marshall, William Mathews, Fannie Moore, Fannie Nicholson, Sister Robinson, James Southall, Emma Tidwell, Lula Cottonham Walker, Callie Williams, Robert Wilson, Alice Wright, George Young.)

Turning the Pot Down

De slaves didn' have no church den, but dey'd take a big sugar kettle and turn it top down on de groun' and put logs roun' it to kill de soun'. Dey'd pray to be free and sing and dance. (William M. Adams, b. ca. 1846, TX, 10)

DISCUSSION: At a prayer meeting, the dancing Adams describes would have been shouting (the terms were used interchangeably), not the social dancing occasionally masked by pots. I have not found the detail of placing logs around the pot anywhere else.

Dey wa'n't 'lowed to meet to pray and shout neither; so dey'd have to slip off atter dark to one o' de houses and hold de prayer meetin's. Dey turned a big wash pot over close to de door, a little off'n de floor, so it'll ketch all de sound. Den de slaves'd shout and pray all dey pleased; every now and den one would slip out side to see if de pot was ketchin' all de sound. Sometimes when one would git so full o' the grace o' God and raise de shout too high, de other slaves'd throw him down on de bed and kiver up his head so he couldn't be heard outside. (Mariah Barnes, b. ca. 1856, NC, 5)

DISCUSSION: Numerous narrators like Barnes described placing magical prayer pots in or near doorways. This arrangement would be most ineffective acoustically; rather, the detail is obviously a later rationalization suggesting the influence of hoodoo or conjure lore, since hoodoo charms were often placed in doorways. For other instances in this appendix, see Laura Abromsom, Oliver Bell, Emma Blalock, Henry Bobbitt, Lucy Brown, Georgianna Foster, Lucy

Galloway, Mary Gladdy, Henry Green, Essex Henry, Chana Littlejohn, Austin Pen Parnell, Nelson Polk, Mary Scott, Sylvia Watkins, Mingo White, Soldier Williams, and Alex Woods. For more examples and discussion, see the chapter text.

Us all b'longed ter Mr. Tresvan De Graffenreid and Miss Rebecca en dey wuz all good ter us en old Marsa en old Miss read de Bible ter us en us got baptized in de river back at Horn's bridge, but dat wa'n't till atter S'render. When dey had de prayer meetin's dey shut de do' so won't let de voice out, en dey turn de washpot down at de do'—some say ter keep hit in. (Oliver Bell, b. unk., AL, 55)

Some of de niggers want to have dere own meetin's, but Lawd chile, dem niggers get happy and get to shoutin' all over de meadow where dey built a bresh arbor. Massa John quick put a stop to dat. He say "if you gwine to preach and sing you must turn de wash pot bottom up"; meanin', no shoutin'. Dem Baptis' at Big Creek was sho' tight wid dere rules too. Turn you out sho' if you drink too much cawn licker, or dance, or cuss. (Siney Bonner, b. ca. 1850, AL, 40)

DISCUSSION: Bonner's was one of several accounts in which slaves turn pots down on orders from, or out of consideration for, slaveholders, forgetting the original function (to fool whites). Compare Henry Bobbitt, Lewis Brown, Betty Guwn, and Nelson Polk.

De marster uz good ter us, in a way, but he aint' 'lowin' no kinds of frolickin' so when we had a meetin' we had ter do it in secret. We'd turn down a wash pot outside de do', an' dat would ketch de fuss so marster neber knowed nothin' bout hit. (Lucy Brown, b. unk., NC, 153)

My mother said she had a hard time getting through. Had to steal half the time; had to put her head under the pot and pray for freedom. It was a large pot which she used to cook in on the yard. She would set it aside when she got through and put her head under it to pray. (Rachel Fairly, b. 1863, MS, 258)

DISCUSSION: Ex-slaves described placing pots in various ways, some of which would have had little or no acoustic impact, obviously representing later elaborations of a little understood detail. A significant number of narrators, however, followed Rachel Fairly, stating that slaves actually put their heads in the pots, which would in fact produce a voice-disguising effect and likely characterizes the original practice. Also see Louise Gause, Will Glass, Charles Grandy, Gillie Hill, Julia Malone, Dolly Phillips, Edd Roby, Lorena Thomas, Ella Washington, and Andy Williams below. For other examples and discussion, see the chapter text.

"Mis' Frances's" niggers wuz free to visit among demselves atter de days work wuz over, and dey could have "meetings" and sing, but usually when de slaves had der meetin's—singin' and prayin', dey would turn a washpot upside-down in front of de door to kill de sound. Den you couldn't hear 'em outside de door. (Lucy Galloway, b. 1863, MS, 804)

De colored people never had no church dey own in slavery time cause dey went to de white people church. Yes, mam, I been dere to de Old Neck Church many a day. In dat day en time, when de preacher would stand up to preach, he would talk to de white folks en de colored folks right dere together. But when de colored people would get converted in dem days, dey never been allowed to praise de Lord wid dey mouth. Had to pray in dey sleeve dem days. De old man Pa Cudjo, he got right one day to de big house en he had to pray wid he head in de pot. (Louisa Gause, b. ca. 1865, child of ex-slaves, SC, 111)

According to Mary Gladdy, ex-slave, 806½—Sixth Avenue, Columbus, Georgia, it was customary among slaves during the Civil War period to secretly gather in their cabins two or three nights each week and hold prayer and experience meetings. A large, iron pot was always placed against the cabin door—sideways, to keep the sound of their voices from "escaping" or being heard from the outside. Then, the slaves would sing, pray, and relate experiences all night long. Their great soul-hungering desire was freedom. (Mary Gladdy, b. ca. 1853, GA, 26–27)

DISCUSSION: This passage appears in a lengthier account of spirit possession and shouting.

Uncle Anderson said that old man Fields [slaveholder in Alabama] didn't allow them to sing and pray and hold meetings, and they had to slip off and slip aside and hide around to pray. They knew what to do. People used to stick their heads under washpots to sing and pray. Some of them went out into the brush arbors where they could pray and shout without being disturbed.

Grandfather Joe [paternal, b. AL] and Grandfather Smith [maternal, b. NC] both said that they had seen slaves have that trouble. Of course, it never happened on the plantations where they were brought up. Uncle Anderson said that they would sometimes go off and get under the washpot and sing and pray the best they could. When they prayed under the pot, they would make a little hole and set the pot over it. Then they would stick their heads under the pot and say and sing what they wanted. (Will Glass, b. unk., AL, NC, grandchild of ex-slaves, 40)

Praying Under Pots

When they'd go to have a church meeting, they turn up the pot so that the noise wouldn't come out. They could go to the white folks' church. But the spirit would come on them sometimes to have service themselves. Then they'd go down to a house at night and turn up those big old iron pots and master never would hear. They wouldn't put the washpot flat on the ground. They'd put

sticks under it and raise it up about a foot from the ground. If they'd put it flat on the ground the ground would carry the sound. (John Hunter, b. ca. 1864, NC, 364)

Yes'm we had meetin at night at one house and next night at a nudder. Honey, we put a wash pot down in front of de meeten house so's de overseer couldn't hear us a singing and prayin. Dis wash pot caught de sound. De next mornin when de bugle blowed we'd slip by and ask de preacher how he feel. De Marster didn't low us to hab no kind ob meetens if'n he knew it. (Victoria Randle Lawson, b. ca. 1850, MS, 1307)

Dere wus no churches on de plantation, an' I doan remember any prayer meetin's. When we sang we turned de washpots an' tubs in de doors, so dey would take up de noise so de white folks could not hear us. I do remember de gatherin's at our home to pray fur de Yankees to come. All de niggers thought de Yankees had blue bellies. The old house cook got so happy at one of dese meetin's she run out in de yard an' called, "Blue bellies come on, blue bellies come on." Dey caught her an' carried her back into de house. (Chana Littlejohn, b. ca. 1857, NC, 56)

She [foster mother] 'splains lots of things to me. I done see de women stick dere heads in de washpot and talk out loud, while us in slavery. She tells me dey prayin' for de Lord to take dem out from bondage. Dey think it right to pray out loud so de Lawd can hear but dey musn't let de massa hear dem. (Julia Malone, b. 1858, TX, 44)

DISCUSSION: Julia Malone's mother was murdered by another slave. After freedom her "foster mammy" explained why Julia had once seen other slaves praying with their heads in pots.

I can remember how my mother used to pray out in the field. We'd be picking cotton. She would go off out there in the ditch a little ways. It wouldn't be far, and I would listen to her. She would say to me: "Pray, son," and I would say, "Mother, I don't know how to pray," and she would say, "Well, just say Lord have mercy." . . .

In slave times, they would have a prayer meeting out in some of the places and they would turn a pot down in front of the door. It would be on a stick or something and raised up a short distance from the ground so that it wouldn't set flat on the ground. It seems that would catch the sound and keep it right around there. They would sing that old song:

We will camp awhile in the wilderness
And then I'm going home.

I don't know any more of the words of that song. (Austin Pen Parnell, b. 1865, MS, child of ex-slaves, 270)

DISCUSSION: W. L. Bost, Lorenza Ezell, and Anna Humphrey also recalled the spiritual "We'll Camp Awhile in the Wilderness." Parnell's narrative again underscores the similar functions ex-slaves assigned to prayer pots and ditches, gullies, river bottoms, and so on.

I heard 'em say they put their heads under big black pot to pray. They sing easy, pray easy. I forgot whut all she [mother] say. (Dolly Phillips, b. ca. 1870, AR, child of ex-slaves, 344)

The slaves loved to pray, they wanted to pray and they did pray. They knew that there was a Supreme Being but the masters would never want to hear any praying. The slaves were told that there was no God. If there was to be any praying the slaves should do it so that they could not be heard or that they should pray under a pot. (C. G. Samuel, b. ca. 1870, IT, child of ex-slaves, 267)

Dey wu'dn't let us shout an' pray eder, an' when ever dey had cumpny de slaves w'ud get out de

big irun pot in de' well house an' roll hit out in de yard an' hav' dere prar meetin' in de big irun pot. (Lucindy Hall Shaw, b. ca. 1850, MS, 1926)

Tell about singing and praying around the black kettle. How did you fix it so your voices could not be heard? Did you ever get caught praying this way?

My mother and other negroes turned the Black Kettle bottom side up, left a hole so voices could not be heard out of the room. Then after all my old Master and Mistress could hear us. Yes I got caught and they stripped all of our close off—and put us up on the whipping block. Beat us so we could not half walk. (Matilda Shepard, b. ca. 1832, GA, 126, int. Barbara Babcock)

DISCUSSION: By Shepard's account, she and other slaves actually experimented with turning the pot down, only to discover that it did not in fact render their meeting inaudible.

On this place dey didn't have no frolics, cause they were Church people. Dey liked to pray & sing. I've heard it said that some over seers wouldn't allow this. Dey would put their heads in barrels or wash pots when praying, to keep the sound from being heard. (Lorena Thomas, b. ca. 1854, MS, 2096–97)

At night when they should have retired forty or fifty would be assembled in a cabin singing and praying with a large kettle turned face downward in the center of the floor to withhold the sound. (Sarah Walker, b. ca. 1855, MO, 280)

Hit was hard back in dem days. Ever' mornin' fo' day break you had to be up an' ready to git to de fiel'. Hit was de same ever' day in de year 'cep' on Sunday, an' den we was gittin' up earlier dan the folks do now on Monday. De drivers was hard too. Dey could say what ever dey wanted to an' you couldn't say nothin' for yourse'f. Somehow or yuther us had a instinct dat we was goin' to be free.

In de event [evening] when de day's wuk was done de slaves would be foun' lock in dere cabins prayin' for de Lawd to free dem lack he did de chillun of 'Is'ael. Iffen dey didn' lock up, de Marsa or de driver would of heard 'em an' whupped 'em. De slaves had a way of puttin' a wash pot in de do' of de cabin to keep de soun' in de house. I 'members once ol' Ned White was caught prayin'. De drivers took him de nex' day an' carried to de pegs, what was fo' stakes drove in de groun'. Ned was made to pull off ever'thing but his pants an' lay on his stomach 'tween de pegs. Den dey whupped him 'twell de blood run from him lack he was a hog. Dey made all de han's come an' see it, an' dey said us'd git de same thang if us was cotched. Dey don't 'low a man to whup a horse lack dey whupped us in dem days. (Mingo White, b. unk., AL, 416)

Us didn't have no prayer meetin' during slavery. De w'ite said dat hit kep' 'em awake fer de slaves ter shout an' sing. So, us would turn de wash pot ober deir heads w'en dey git ter shoutin', ter cotch de soun' w'en de slaves sing an' pray. (Andy Williams, b. 1859, TX, 4070)

Mos' of de time de slaves would be too tired to do anything but go to bed at night, but sometimes dey would set around and sing after supper and dey would sing and pray on Sunday. One of de songs dat was used mos' was Yon Comes Old Marster Jesus. If I remembers rightly, it went somp'n' like dis:

I really believe Christ is comin' again
He's comin' in de mornin'
He's comin' in de mornin'
He's comin' wid de rainbow on his shoulder
He's comin' again bye an' bye.

Dey tried to make 'em stop singin' and prayin' durin' the war, 'case all dey'd ask for was to be sot free, but de slaves would get in de cabins and turn a big wash pot upside down and sing into dat, and de noise couldn't get out. I don't remember nothin'

about dis ceptin' what mammy say. (Callie Williams, b. 1861, AL, 427)

DISCUSSION: This passage comes from the national collection. The draft of Williams's narrative in the state archives (SS1 1 *AL*: 450, 452–53) features slightly different versions of this anecdote and spiritual, which are widely separated in the text. For a similar song, see Perkins, "Spirituals," 224.

De mos' fun we hed was at our meetin's. We hed dem mos' every Sunday an dey lasted way inter de night. De preacher I laked de bes' was name Mathew Ewing. He was a comely nigger, black as night, an he sho cud read out'n his han'. He neber larned no real readin' an writin' but he sho' knowed his Bible an wud hol' his han' out an mek lak he uz readin' an preach de purt'est preachin's you ever heared. De meetins last frum early in de mawnin' 'til late at night; when dark cum de men fo'ks wud hang up a wash pot, bottom up'ards, in de little brush chu'ch house us hed, so's it'd catch de noise an de oberseer woulden' hear us singin' an shoutin'. Dey didn' mind us meetin' in de day time but dey thought if we stayed up ha'f de night we woulden' work so hard de next day, an' dat was de truf. (Clara C. Young, b. ca. 1842, AL, 2402–3)

DISCUSSION: As in many texts, the whites here are fully aware of the slaves' meetings; in this case the pot is introduced only after dark to circumvent curfew. Young also broaches the subject of white opposition to slave literacy.

TURNING THE POT DOWN + OTHER THEMES (PREACHING OBEDIENCE, NIGHT RIDERS, WHITE OPPOSITION TO SLAVE LITERACY, SHOUTING AT FREEDOM, JIM CROW LAWS). Obviously, the tale of turning the pot down could stand alone as a story complete unto itself. However, many ex-slaves tied turning the pot down to other narrative themes, usually to a fairly limited set expressing similar concerns. While some of these texts may recount (or at least reflect) actual events, overall they suggest the prayer pot's evolution from an actual memory into a Black folktale whose symbolic dimensions and logical links to other folktales provided their own reality. Indeed, despite their correspondences, most of these examples appear to have been created independently of one another based on these underlying connotations and understandings, underscoring the pot's importance as a symbolic nexus that outlived the physical object's practical function. There are even hints of these elements in some of the foregoing texts (for example, see Clara Young above), but I have restricted the following section to clearcut cases.

Mama and papa spoke like they was mighty glad to get set free. Some believed they'd git freedom and others didn't. They had places they met and prayed for freedom. They stole out in some of their houses and turned a washpot down at the door. Another white man, not [slaveholder] Alex Rogers, tole mama and papa and a heap others out in the field working. She say they quit and had a regular bawl [ball] in the field. They cried and laughed and hollered and danced. Lot of them run offen the place soon as the man tole 'em. My folks stayed that year and another year. (Laura Abromsom, b. 1863, TN, 9)

DISCUSSION: Like Lucy Barnes (below), Laura Abromsom linked turning the pot down to Emancipation, which, like turning the pot down, was always associated with shouting, prayers, and praise singing.

The niggers didn't go to the church building; the preacher came and preached to them in their quarters. He'd just say, "Serve your masters. Don't steal your master's turkey. Don't steal your master's chickens. Don't steal your master's hawgs. Don't steal your master's meat. Do whatever your master tells you to do." Same old thing all the time. . . . You couldn't tell the difference between Baptists and Methodists then. They was all Christians. I never saw them turn nobody down at the communion, but I have heard of it. I never saw them turn no pots down neither; but I have heard of that. They used to sing their songs in a whisper and pray in a whisper. That was a prayer meeting from house to house once or twice—once or twice a week. (Lucretia Alexander, b. ca. 1845, MS, 35).

DISCUSSION: No other tale was more often combined with turning the pot down than the story of white preachers thumping on Ephesians 6:5: "Servants, be obedient to them that are your masters." Alexander's text takes the typical (and typically amusing) liberties with scripture. Also see Emma Barr, Jeff Calhoun, Anderson Edwards, Charles Grandy, Charlie Hinton, Stephen McCray, Rachel Santee Reed, Eliza Washington, and Alex Woods below. For other examples and discussion, see the chapter text.

I 'members well when ol' Genr'l McGrudder got shot down by de Yankees. Dey shot 'im cause he wuz keepin' us niggers in slavery and said we couldn't be freed. Ole McGrudder had de finest house in Houston, an' a big coach an' gol'en hosses; my, he wuz high an' fine, but de Yankees brought him down. . . . I 'members the fu'nrul—I went 'long to take care ob de chillun. . . . Dat night all de niggers slip out to de creek in de thicket. We take a big wash pot an' turn it fo' a sign to throw our voices 'way from town an' we shouted—we prayed fo' our deliver. (Lucy Barnes, b. ca. 1853, TX, 179)

DISCUSSION: This is another story of shouting at freedom, but with a prayer pot added (see Laura Abromsom above). "Genr'l McGrudder" was General John B. Magruder (1807–1871), commander of the Confederate Department of Texas, New Mexico, and Arizona, who did in fact go to great lengths to keep Blacks in slavery. From his headquarters in Houston, Magruder refused to surrender for two months after Appomattox (April 19, 1865), resisting until Federals finally took control of Texas in June 1865 (Juneteenth).

Union troops did not, however, shoot Magruder, who fled to Mexico, where he and other rebel hold-outs schemed to reestablish the Confederacy under Emperor Maximilian I of Mexico. When Maximilian fell, Magruder returned to Houston, where he died on February 19, 1871. Thomas W. Cutrer, "Magruder, John Bankhead (1807–1871)," *Handbook of Texas*. No doubt many Blacks did rejoice at Magruder's death, which Lucy Barnes conflates with the arrival of Union troops and the first Juneteenth, definitely an occasion for mass celebration, shouting, prayers, and praise singing. The inclusion of the pot is thus on one level perfectly sensible, since prayer pots were inextricably linked to these same behaviors, but this is another case where turning the pot down serves no plot function; to the contrary, an underlying theme of the shouting-at-freedom tales is that Blacks no longer needed to conceal their shouting from whites (or to pray for freedom).

Mama said the preachers told the slaves to be good and bediant. The colored folks would meet up wid one another at preaching same as the white folks. I heard my aunties say when the Yankees come to the house the mistress would run give the house women their money and jewelry and soon as the Yankees leave they would come and get it. That was at Wares [Ware's plantation] in Mississippi.

I heard them talk about slipping off and going to some house on the place and other places too and pray for freedom during the War. They turned an iron pot upside down in the room. (Emma Barr, b. 1872, MS, AR, child of ex-slaves, 20)

No Sir, no readin' an' writin'. You had to work. Ha! Ha! You [better not] let your marster or missus ketch you wid a book. Dat wus a strict rule dat no learnin' wus to be teached. I can't read and write. If it wus not fur my mother wit don't know what would become of me. We had prayer meetings around at de slave houses. I 'member it well. We turned down pots on de inside of de house at de door to keep marster an' missus from hearin' de

singin' an' prayin'. Marster an' his family lived in de great house an' de slave quarters wus 'bout two hundred yards away to the back of de great house. (Emma Blalock, b. ca. 1850, NC, 107)

DISCUSSION: According to ex-slaves, whites preached false doctrine in their churches and tried to prevent the slaves' own meetings, but they also blocked slaves' access to the true Gospel (and knowledge generally) by opposing Black literacy. Thus prohibitions against slaves reading and writing and turning the pot down also connoted each other, and stories of prayer pots frequently describe these bans; see Georgianna Foster, Nelson Polk, Ella Washington, Sylvia Watkins, and Alex Woods below. For other examples and discussion, see the chapter text.

We didn't have many teardowns an' prayer meetin's an' sich, case de fuss sturbed ole missus who wuz kinder sickly. When we did have sompin' we turned down a big washpot in front of de do', an it took up de fuss, an' folkses in de yard can't hyar de fuss. De patterollers would git you iffen you went offen de premises widout a pass, an' dey said dat dey would beat you scandelous. I seed a feller dat dey beat onct an' he had scars as big as my fingers all ober his body. (Henry Bobbitt, b. 1850, NC, 121–22)

DISCUSSION: Not surprisingly, night riders charged with preventing secret slave meetings often figure in accounts of turning the pot down, sometimes matter-of-factly, sometimes as folktale characters. Bobbitt provides a realistic description. Also see Eliza Evans, Henry Green, Essex Henry, Gillie Hill, Marriah Hines, Ellis Ken Kannon, Phoebe Lyons, Garland Monroe, Alex Moore, and Rev. John Moore below. For other examples and discussion, see the chapter text.

The white people had churches in slavery times just like they have now. The white people would have service once a month. But like these street cars. White people would be at the front and colored would fill up the back. They'll quit that after a while. Sometimes they would have church in the morning for the white folks and church in the evening for the colored. They would baptize you just like they would anybody else. I'll tell you what was done in slave time. They'd sing and pray. The white folks would take you to the creek and baptize you like anybody else.

Sometimes the slaves would be off and have prayer meetings of their own—nothing but colored people there. They soon got out uh that. Sometimes they would turn a tub or pot down. That would be when they were making a lot of fuss and didn't want to bother nobody. The white people wouldn't be against the meeting. But they wouldn't want to be disturbed. If you wanted to sing at night and didn't want nobody to hear it, you could just take an old wash pot and turn it down—leave a little space for the air, and nobody could hear it. (Lewis Brown, b. 1855, MS, 295)

DISCUSSION: Like Dora Richard (below), Lewis Brown tied prayer pots and the racial conflicts they encapsulated to the Jim Crow segregation of his present-day surroundings.

De white folks helped de preachah and de driver to read and write a little. Uncle Billy wuz our preachah and de garden tendah. Uncle Billy got in trouble once. He didn't like collads and de missus had three big fine collads in de garden and she all time after Billy to take a good care of dese collads. So'es one Sattidy night aftah church Billy slips out and cuts dem down. De next mornin de cook wuz sent to de garden fer vegetables and some of dese collads fer de misstress but dey wuz gone, de cook hurries to de house and tells de missus. She tells marster, he come in mad and say who done dis, de girl dat is de cook says Billy done it case he dont like collads. He says to get Billy to come here. Billy come to de house, marster says Billy you preachah? Billy says yes sah. He says, Billy you'se cut dem

collads, Billy says yes sah, I'se got some greens. He says now Billy you preachah, git me de Bible and he reads, Thou shall not steal, den he handed Billy de Bible and sayd read dis, he shore hates to, but Marster makes him do it, den he shore tears loose on Billy bout stealin, finally Billy says now marster I can show you in de Bible where I did not steal, he tells Billy to find it and Billy finds it and reads, "You shall reap when you laborth." Marster sayd to Billy get to hell outn here.

We didnt have no church on the plantation, sometimes we went to the white peoples church some time, people would come and preach to us. We would turn a washpot up side down to keep the white people from hearing us, cause dey would run us off. Few of them could read a little. I neber did take to dat too much in dem days. They would baptise in a pond of water, lots of people would come. When der wuz a buryin dey would keep out two [slaves] to do the buryin and de rest of us would go to work just like nothin had never happened. (Jeff Calhoun, b. 1838, AL, TX, 607)

DISCUSSION: Calhoun's tale of Uncle Billy offers a highly original variation on the preaching obedience theme, as well as a novel twist on the literacy question.

The first church I went to was under a big mulberry tree there on the place. A white man done the preaching. Master had told us that if we be good Niggers and obey him that we would go to heaven. But I felt all the time that there was something better than that for me. So I kept praying until I felt the change in my heart. I was by myself down by a spring when I found the Lord.

When the darkies prayed in slavery they darsn't let the white fo'ks know 'bout it or they beat them to death. When we prayed we turned a wash pot down to the ground to catch the voice. We prayed lots in slavery to be free and the Lord heard our prayer. We didn't have no song books, the Lord give us our songs. When we sing them at night 'round the fire place it would be just whispering like so the white fo'ks not hear us. We would hum them as we wo'ked in the fiel'. One of our favorite songs went like this:

My knee-bones am aching
My body's racking with pain
I really believe I'se a child of God
This ain't my home cause heaven's my aim. . . .

When I started preaching, I was a slave and couldn't read or write. Till freedom I had to preach what they told me to. Master made me preach to the other Niggers that the "Good Book" say that if Niggers obey their Master they would go to heaven. I knew there was something better for them but I darsn't tell them so lest I done it on the sly. That I did lots. (Anderson Edwards, b. 1844, TX, 1262, 1266)

DISCUSSION: Besides other details associated with prayer pots (such as white bans on literacy, singing around the fireplace), Edwards's narrative is notable as an example of a slave preacher forced to profess the Ephesian text to other slaves. Ex-slaves Frances Lewis, Henry Lewis, Leo Mouton, and Charley Stewart also gave the spiritual "My Knee-bone's Aching (Heaven Is My Aim)."

Master John Mixon had two big plantations. I believe he owned about four hundred slaves, chillun and all. He allowed us to have church one time a month wid de white folks and we had prayer meeting every Sunday. Sometimes when de men would do something like being sassy or lazy and dey knowed dey was gonna be whipped, dey'd slip off and hide in de woods. When dey'd slip back to get some food dey would all pray for 'em dat Master wouldn't have 'em whipped too hard, and for fear the Patroller would hear 'em they'd put their faces down in the dinner pot. I'd sit and watch out for the Patroller. He was a white man who was

appointed to catch runaway niggers. His name was Howard Campbell. He had a big pack of dogs. The lead hound was named Venus. There was five or six in the pack, and they was vicious too. (Eliza Evans, b. ca. 1850, AL, 92–93)

DISCUSSION: Evans's description of the patroller is obviously based on fact, but her account of slaves feeding runaways, then praying into the dinner pot suggests another latter-day rationalization.

We wore homemade clothes an' shoes wid wooden bottoms. Dey would not allow us to sing and pray but dey turned pots down at de door an' sung an' prayed anyhow an' de Lord heard dere prayers, dat dey did sing an' pray. Mother said dey whupped a slave if dey caught him wid a book in his hands. You wus not 'lowed no books. Larnin' among de slaves wus a forbidden thing. (Georgianna Foster, b. 1861, NC, 316)

In de church de white folks was on one side an' de colored on de other. De preacher was a white man. He preach in a way lak, "Bey yo' marser an' missus" an' tell us don' steal f'om yo' marser an' missus. 'Cose we knowed it was wrong to steal, but de niggers had to steal to git somepin to eat. I know I did. . . .

(Charles Grandy of Norfolk, who saw service during the Civil War says he has been to "hush-arbors.") Whites in our section used to have a service fo' us slaves ev'y fo'th Sunday, but dat twasn't 'nuf fo' dem who wanted to talk wid Jesus. Used to go 'cross de fields nights to a old tobacco barn on de side of a hill. Do' was on de ground flo', an' you could climb up a ladder an' step out de winder to de ground on de other side. Had a old pot hid dere to catch de sound. Sometimes would stick yo' haid down in de pot if you got to shout awful loud. 'Member ole Sister Millie Jeffries. Would stick her haid in de pot an' shout an' pray all night whilst de others was bustin' to take dere turn. Sometimes de slaves would have to pull her haid out dat pot so's de others could shout. (Charles Grandy, b. 1842, VA, 116, 119, orig. parentheses)

DISCUSSION: These stories of preaching obedience and turning the pot down were widely separated in Grandy's transcript but co-present nonetheless.

> The Ku Kluckses come one night. They kept us getting 'em water to run through something under their sheets. The water was running out on the ground. We did see it for a fact, young mistress. We was scared not to do that. They was getting submission over the country, young mistress. They would make you be quiet 'long the roadside, young mistress. They would make you be quiet where you have meeting. They would turn the pots down on the floor at the doors, young mistress. The Ku Kluckses whooped some, tied some out to the trees and left 'em. They was rough, young mistress. (Uncle Henry Green, b. 1848, AL, 88–89)

DISCUSSION: Realistic accounts of night riders often turn up in tales of turning the pot down, but so do many narrative motifs associated with patrollers, for example, the stories of slaves pelting them with hot coals or stringing grapevines across roads to unhorse them. Henry Green's narrative features another popular motif from the night rider tales, that is, the water-drinking trick, in which disguised vigilantes pretend to be parched ghosts just from Hell, compelling Blacks to fetch endless buckets of water.

> Hit's a good thing dat none of de white folkses ain't went to de funerals case iffen dey had de niggers can't sing dere hymns. Does you know dat dey warn't no 'ligion 'lowed on dat plantation. Ole lady Betsy Holmes wus whupped time an' ag'in fer talkin' 'ligion er fer singin' hymns. We sometimes had prayer meetin' anyhow in de cabins but we'd turn down de big pot front o' de door ter ketch de noise. Dey won't gib us no pass hardly, an iffen we run 'way de patterollers will git us. Dey did let us

have some dances do' now an' den, but not offen. (Essex Henry, b. ca. 1854, NC, 396)

> My grandmother told me that they had to chink up the cracks so that the light wouldn't get out to do their washing and ironing at night. When they would hear the overseers or the paterolers coming 'round (I don't know which it was), they would put the light out and keep still till they had passed on. Then they would go right on with the washing and ironing. They would have to wash and iron at night because they were working all day.
>
> She told me how they used to turn pots down at night so that they could pray. They had big pots then—big enough for you to get into yourself. I've seen some of them big old pots and got under 'em myself. You could get under one and pray if you wanted to. You wouldn't have to prop them up to send your voice in 'em from the outside. The thing that the handle hooks into makes them tilt up on one side so that you could get down on your hands and knees and pray with your mouth close to the opening if you wanted to. Anyway, my grandma said they would turn the pots upside down and stick their heads under them to pray. (Gillie Hill, b. unk., AR, grandchild of ex-slaves, 256, orig. parentheses)

DISCUSSION: Hill, granddaughter of Arkansas slaves, gave another unique illustration of the pot's development as narrative theme. Patrollers constantly disrupted dances and prayer meetings, but I have found no other reports of night riders interfering with laundry duty. In fact, as standard practice slave women were assigned to launder and clean for their families on Saturday afternoons (the so-called Saturday half-day). Slave women laundered for whites six to seven days a week (and at night if necessary). Washpots were often turned down, however, suggesting why Hill or some other storyteller created this variation.

> Sundays we went to church and stayed the biggest portion of the day. Nobody had to rush home. On our plantation we had general prayer meeting

every Wednesday night at church. 'Course some of the masters didn't like the way we slaves carried on [so] we would turn pots down, and tubs to keep the sound from going out. Den we would have a good time, shouting, singing, and praying just like we pleased. The paddarollers didn't pay us much 'tention cause they knew how master let us do. Dey would say nasty things 'bout master 'cause he let us do like we did. (Marriah Hines, b. 1835, VA, 141)

DISCUSSION: Hines made it especially clear that slaveholders were fully aware of slave meetings, even barring patrollers from interfering, but that the style of Black worship ("the way we slaves carried on") nonetheless disturbed them, hence the need to turn pots down. Whatever its basis, the ploy worked, since the meetings went on, while whites—including patrollers—stayed away.

Went to white church on plantation. White preachers said, servants, obey your master. I was valued at $800.00. When I was a small boy I lay at marsters feet. He always had shiny shoes and we niggers would keep rubbing them so they would shine more. As I grew older, I cleaned the yard, later helped pick cotton.

I am a Baptist. Have behaved myself. Have prayer meeting at my home. During the war we had prayer meetings at the different houses on the plantations. We prayed to be set free. Turned washpots down in the house to keep the sound down so white folks wouldn't hear us singing and praying to be set free. (Charlie Hinton, b. ca. 1850, NC, 276–77)

Durin' slavery de slaves hadder keep quiet en dey would turn a kittle upside down ter keep de white folks [from] 'yearin dere prayers en chants. W'en a slave wanted ter go ter 'nother plantation he had ter hab a pass. Ef' dey disobeyed dey got a whuppin, en ef dey had a pass widout de Marsters signature dey got a whuppin. *Ef'n dey had ter hab passes now dere wouldin' be no meanness.*

I member de Klu Klux Klan kumin ter mah daddy's home axin fer water en dey would keep us totin' water ter dem fer fifteen ter twenty minutes. Dey didn't whup er hurt any ob us. (Ellis Ken Kannon, b. ca. 1850, TN, 38, orig. emphasis)

DISCUSSION: Besides patrollers checking passes and thirsty Kluxers (see Henry Green above), Kannon's text strongly hints at the preaching obedience theme.

Us nebber had no 'musement whilst us wuz slaves, en when prayer meetin' wuz hol' en de cabins dey sot er tub er water en de center en all sot roun' it. Den de tub er water ketch de soun' en kep' it fum goin' out de cabin.

Slaves nebber got ter visit on other plantations; if dey did so de patrollers ketched em an whipped em. I seed em put slaves on big hogsheads stuck plum full er tenpenny nails, en roll em so de nails done stuck em en tored dey flesh. (Phoebe Lyons, b. ca. 1855, GA, 402–3)

I don't b'leeve in dese mixed white and black families en hit shouldn't be 'lowed. Durin' slavery de white folks didn't want de niggahs ter sing en pray, but dey would turn a pot down en meet at de pot in de nite en sing en pray en de white folks wouldn't 'yer dem. Ef a slave d'ed de white folks wouldn't let no body set up wid de body 'cept de niggers ob dat plantation, but urther slaves would slip in atter dark, set up en den slip back ter dere plantation 'fore day. (Ann Matthews, b. unk., TN, 45)

DISCUSSION: Obviously Ann Matthews opposed race mixing, a separatist agenda that logically suggested another separatist strategy, turning the pot down.

We had church, but iffen the white folks caught you at it, you was beat most nigh to death. We used a big pot turned down to keep our voices down. When we went to hear white preachers, he would say, "Obey your master and mistress." I am a hard shell-flint Baptist. I was Baptized in Pine Bluff,

Arkansas. Our baptizing song was mostly "On Jordan's Stormy Banks I Stand" and our funeral song was "Hark From The Tomb." (Stephen McCray, b. 1850, AL, 208)

Dey had what dey called a stump preacher; ole man Tucker Coles it was. Dey call him a stump preacher 'cause he used to git up on a stump an' preach to de slaves—you see, up dere 'rounst Monticello ole patterollers would keep away, so de slaves ain't bothered to build a hut an' put pots all roun' like dey did in some places. Jus' preached right in de open, an' if de patterollers come, dey would jus' run down de mountain side 'long paths dat de patterollers didn't know nothin' 'bout. (Garland Monroe, b. 1848, VA, 214)

"Durin' slavery times de slaves would hab ter git fum dere marster a pas' 'fore dey could visit dere own peeple on de uther plantations. Ef'n you had no pass you would git in trouble ef caught wid out one which allus ment a good whuppin' w'en dey returned. At dat times menny slaves would run 'way en hide in caves en menny ob dem would go by de 'onderground railroad' ter Canada whar slavery wuz not recognized." (The underground railroad consisted of hiding places throughout the states to Canada; escapees would make the trip under cover from station to station.)

"De slaves would slip out at nite ter private meetin's en turn a pot bottom up on de groun' en leave a little hole under hit so de sound ob dere talkin' would go onder de pot en no one would 'year whut dey wuz talkin' about." (Rev. John Moore, b. ca. 1847, TN, 47, orig. parentheses)

DISCUSSION: Patrollers checking for passes were, of course, habitually tied to turning the pot down, but Moore's text is unique in linking under-the-pot prayers for freedom to the Underground Railroad.

My mother wuz a house girl for de Newtons on her plantation. She say one time ol' massa had a cullud man whut wuz so lazy dat he wen' to de choppin' block an' chop off his own han'. She say cullud folks could fiddle an' dance all dey please, but wa'n't 'lowed t' sing an' pray. She say sometimes dey go out an' turn de wash pot bottom up 'ards so de echo go under de pot an' de white folks coulden' hear de songs. I've heared mother tell dat a hundred times. (George Newton, b. 1867, AR, child of ex-slaves, 2909–10)

DISCUSSION: George Newton's text ties the pot to another act of Black defiance. The logic is unmistakable, but the story of the slave who amputated his own hand rather than work is transparently fictional; tall tales about this sort of unbelievable laziness, many derived from British tradition, are quite common among both Anglo- and African Americans. Newton was born after slavery and attributes these anecdotes to his mother; overall, his text suggests our story's final development from personal experience to traditional narrative.

When the slaves would hold a religious service in their quarters the mistress would require one of them to turn a tub against the door to catch the sound and absorb it before it got into the mansion of the plantation owner. In case they could not find a tub a pot would answer. This practice was also followed on the plantations in Kentucky and Tennessee.

No slave on the Collins plantation was permitted to pick up or open a book, or get curious or anxious about any source of education. Such a stricture of the rules was certain to result in a whipping. (Nelson Polk, b. ca. 1830, MS, 166)

DISCUSSION: Besides prohibitions against literacy, Polk provides another case of pots mandated by the slaveholder (see Henry Bobbitt, Siney Bonner, Lewis Brown, and Betty Guwn).

Dare wuz a church on Mars Charles plantation dat de niggers usta goen sit in de gallary. Dey wuz a white preacher en de white folks sit downstairs.

Niggers have benches in dey house dat dey use when dey have prayer-meetin's. When dey have hit at us house dey take en sit de beds outside en put de benches up en down like in de church. Dey always has a watcher ter look out fo' pattyrollers. Dey turn a pot down sois es [so's as] not ter let de sound go far. (Levi Pollard, b. ca. 1850, VA, 232)

I was a ligious chile in dem days and I'm ligious now too, but colored folks jes naturally had more ligion back dare fore de war. I kin remember when my Ma used to put us chilluns outside de cabin in de quarters and den she would shut de doors and shut de windows tight and sit a tub of water in de middle of floor and kneel down and pray that de yolk of bondage be removed from de nigger's neck. All de niggers done dat, dey did. Ma llus said de sound of dey voices went down into the tub of water and de white folks couldn't hear dem prayin'. . . .

I went to church with my Ma and Pa, to de same church house as de white folks do, cepin' us niggers went in de back door and sot and de white folks dey come in de front and sot. De preacher he preach to us niggers one text I kin allus remember, and dat wuz—"Niggers obey your master and don't lie and steal." (Rachel Santee Reed, b. 1857, MS, 1815, 1816)

DISCUSSION: As in a couple of other cases, the preaching obedience and turning the pot down themes were somewhat separated in Rachel Reed's transcript.

Here's the way I want to tell you. Some of the white people are as good to the colored people as they could be and some of em are mean. My own folks do so bad I'm ashamed of em. So many of the colored of the South have emigrated to the North. I have lived there and I don't know why I'm here now. Some of my color don't like that about the Jim Crow Law, but I say if they furnish us a nice comfortable coach I would rather be with my own people. And I don't care to go to the white folks'

church. My mother used to tell me how they used to hide behind trees so the boss man couldn't see em when they was prayin' and at night put out the light and turn the pot down. (Dora Richard, b. ca. 1860, SC, 35–36)

DISCUSSION: Like Lewis Brown, Dora Richard linked turning the pot down and the racial conflicts it connoted to the Jim Crow laws of the 1930s (which she expressly favored).

Our white Marsa didn't 'low his slaves to read an' 'rite. Went to de white folks church an' den wouldn't low 'em to pray. Would whip 'em when day catched niggers prayin' at home or anywhere else. Dey told me 'bout one old woman (Nigger) on de place dat prayed a heep but she allus put her head down in de pot when she went to pray so as de white folks couldn't hear her. One day dis old woman was a prayin' in de pot an' got so full o' 'ligion 'till she got her head out dat pot an' was jus' a tellin' de news. Old Missus heard her an' went to see what was de matter. Missus, she got happy an' finally Marsa heard 'em an' went to see what de trouble was. Marsa, he got full o' 'ligion too an' dey all had a big time. After dat day dey said dey never did whip 'em fo' prayin' no more. Course dey wouldn't let 'em pray durin' work hours. . . .

I just does 'member my grandma. I never will forget a story she used to tell me 'bout a certain old nigger woman what was owned by some white folks dat didn't low niggers to pray. Dis old nigger woman was down over de tubs washin' one day an' got so full o' ligion she started prayin'. Her Marsa come to find out de trouble an' threatened to whip her fo' disobeyin' his orders. She said: "You can whip me—you can kill dis body but you can't kill my soul." Marsa say: "You God damn fool you ain't got no sense no way." Her marsa made like he didn't believe in ligion but after dat day dis old nigger woman prayed when she wanted to an' wasn't nothin ever said bout it. (Edd Roby, b. 1863, MS, 1864, 1867–68, orig. parentheses)

DISCUSSION: Roby told these two versions of the same tale at two separate interviews, both conducted by Vera Butts of the Mississippi Writers' Project. These items exemplify traditional storytelling in its natural environment, vouching for their authenticity, and for Butts's reliability. Roby was forthright that his accounts came from oral sources not personal experience, and in his texts the variations usually typifying distinct versions of a tale from different narrators occur in different recountings from the same storyteller. (This is not unusual among folk raconteurs and has sometimes occurred in my own fieldwork.) The first rendition touches on restrictive white churches and prohibitions against literacy before proceeding to turning the pot down, all described in the conventional fashion. In the second version, however, a laundress at work over her washtub attracts the slaveholder with her forbidden prayers, a logical transference since washtubs were routinely turned down in place of pots. Of course, the laundress could not turn the tub down as she should have, hence the inevitable confrontation with her slaveholder (in the first version the woman is only beset by whites when she forgets and removes her head from the pot). The different outcomes are also interesting. In the second version the enraged slaveholder, after threatening violence, grudgingly allows the laundress to continue praying her own way, while in the first version the whites, upon investigating, "get happy" themselves and convert to the slaves' ecstatic way of worshiping.

> They never sold any of our set but some on the place was sold. The mothers grieve and grieve over their children bein' sold. Some white folks let their slaves have preachin', some wouldn't. We had a brush arbor and set on big logs. Children set round on the ground. 'Fo freedom I never went to preachin'. I kept Kitty's babies so she went. Mothers didn't see their children much after they was sold.
>
> Fo freedom they would turn a wash pot upside-down at the door and have singin' and prayer meetin'. The pot would take up the noise. They done that when they danced too. I don't know how they found out the iron pot would take up the noise. They had plenty of em settin' round in them days. Somebody found it out and passed it on. (Mary Scott, b. unk., TN, 126–27)

DISCUSSION: The dancing Mary Scott mentions probably refers to shouting at the prayer meetings she describes (not social dancing). The connection she draws between white restrictions on slave worship, the heartless practice of selling slave families apart, and turning the pot down is unique, but also makes perfect sense within the tradition's logic.

> Some of the Niggers went to church then just as they do now, and some of them weren't allowed to go. Reverend Winfield used to preach to the colored people that if they would be good niggers and not steal their master's eggs and chickens and things, that they might go to the kitchen of heaven when they died.
>
> An old lady once said to me, "I would give anything if I could have Maria [former slave] in heaven with me to do little things for me." My mother told me that the Niggers had to turn the pots down to keep their voices from sounding when they were praying at night. And they couldn't sing at all. (Eliza Washington, b. ca. 1860, AR, 53)

DISCUSSION: Eliza Washington gave another secondhand account, no doubt rooted in reality but now brilliantly structured as narrative: the preachers and slaveholders praying out loud for slaves to serve them in heaven provide a perfect foil for slaves praying secretly into pots for earthly freedom.

> Once in a while Jim Ross let us go to de Catholic Church in Marion. Dat was right close to de plan'ation where we is at. Dey wouldn't let us pray or hol' prayer meetings by ourself. But we use to sneak off an' have "pot praying." Two men use to carry de great big hog pot dey use to scald hogs in 'way out in de woods an' put it down an' us'd come an' stick our heads down in it an' pray. All de noise

use to go down inside de pot an' you couldn't hear nothing outside. Course dey didn't have no schools or nothing like dat. Nobody know how to read an' write den. (Ella Washington, b. 1855, LA, 3971)

De white folks wouldn't let de slaves hab a book er papah fer fear dey'd l'arn sumpin', en ef dey wan'ed ter pray dey'd tu'n a kettle down at dere cabin do'er. I member yearin' mah mammy pray "Oh father op'n up de do'ers en sho us lite." I'd look up at de ceiling ter see ef he wuz goona op'n up sumpin'; silly, silly me thinkin' such. I's 'longs ter de Missionary Baptist chuch but I don't git ter go very off'n. (Sylvia Watkins, b. ca. 1847, TN, 77)

DISCUSSION: Watkins's text underscores the mystical associations of doorways, where pots were often placed.

I learned to read an' write since de surrender by studying in spare time. Dey wouldn't let any slaves have books in slavery time. Mother had a book she kep' hid. Dey would whup a slave if dey caught him wid a book.

Dere were between twenty-five and thirty slaves on de plantation but dere wus no church. Dey would not allow us to have prayer meetings in our houses, but we would gather late in de night and turn pots upside down inside de door to kill de sound and sing and pray for freedom. No one could hear unless dey eavesdropped.

The patteroller rode around to see after de slaves and whipped 'em when dey caught 'em away from home. I have seen slaves whipped. Dey took them into the barn and corn crib and whipped 'em wid a leather strap, called de cat-o'-nine tails. Dey hit 'em ninety-nine licks sometimes. Dey wouldn't allow 'em to call on de Lord when dey were whippin' 'em, but dey let 'em say "Oh! pray, Oh! pray, marster." Dey would say, "Are you goin' to work? Are you goin' visitin' widout a pass? Are you goin' to run away?" Dese is de things dey would ask him, when dey wus whuppin' him. . . .

Sometimes we went to the white folkses church. De preacher would tell us to obey our missus and master. Dat's what de preacher tole us. Dey would take us back home and give us plenty to eat after preachin' was over, and tell us to do what de preacher said. Dey tasked us Saturday mornings, and if we got done we go to de branch on a flat rock and wash our clothes. (Alex Woods, b. 1858, NC, 416, 417–19)

DISCUSSION: Woods practically inventoried various themes associated with turning the pot down, including bans on literacy, patroller surveillance, the flogged slave compelled to pray not to God but to his persecutor, and, of course, preaching obedience. This is another case where the tales of turning the pot down and preaching obedience were somewhat separated in the transcript, nonetheless confirming their presence in the same narrative universe.

TURNING THE POT DOWN AT DANCES. Although turning the pot down was tied almost entirely to religious observances, ex-slaves and other sources occasionally describe the practice with social dancing. The texts from narrators Millie Simpkins and Soldier Williams nonetheless retain religious touches, and this variation as a whole suggests a later narrative development reinterpreting (or misinterpreting) prayer pots, which typically masked shouting (holy dancing). Soldier Williams might actually describe shouting, which was sometimes simply called dancing (see William M. Adams and Mary Scott above). The other accounts (Lowry, Owens, Simpkins) definitely place pots in secular contexts, however.

De slaves from Lowry side of de road usto stealed over on de Free State side, sometimes, to see de er pretty gals. Sometimes de Free State gals would have a dance. De would turn down a pot near de door to catch de sound. Because if de patrolers were to catch de slaves over on de Free State side, de would beat dem. (Dave Lowry, b. 1857, VA, 198)

De patrollers would come to de colored frolic an' one time a han' slipped off an', gentlemen, didn't he give 'em trouble to ketch him an' dey didn't. When dey had dem Saddy night frolics an' dance all night long an' nearly day when hit was goin, dey would turn de pot upside down in de floor to hold de soun' in. My daddy pick de banjo. At de cornshuckings dey'd sing *All 'Roun' de Corn Pile Sally*, an' dey had whiskey an' gin. (Wade Owens, b. 1863, AL, 307, orig. emphasis)

De only fun de young folks had wuz w'en de ole folks had a quiltin'. W'ile de ole folks wuz wukin' on de quilt de young ones would git in 'nuther room, dance en hab a good time. Dey'd hab a pot turned down at de do'er ter keep de white folks fum 'yearin' dem. De white folks didn't want us ter l'arn nothin' en ef a slave picked up a lettle piece ob papah, dey would yell "put dat down you—you wan't ter git in our business." De white folks wouldn' let de slaves pray, ef dey got ter pray hit wus w'iles walkin' 'hind de plow. White folks would whip de slaves ef dey 'yeard dem sing and pray. (Millie Simpkins, b. 1831, TN, 67)

DISCUSSION: Although she described pots at work parties with social dancing, Millie Simpkins also linked them to white prohibitions against slave worship and literacy, details recalling the pot's original significance. An ex-slave interviewed by Fisk University also recounted pots at quiltings (Anon. ex-slave [b. ca. 1850, TN], *Unwritten History*, 300).

Ma was Margarett Ball. Pa was William Anderson. Ma was a cook and pa was a field hand. They whooped plenty on the place where I come up. Some of 'em run off. Some they tied to a tree. Bob Ball didn't use no dogs. When they got starved out they'd come outen the woods. Of course they would. Bob Ball raised fine tobacco, fine Negroes, fine horse. He made us go to church. Four or five of us would walk to the white folks' Baptist church. The master and his family rode. It was a good piece. We had dances in the cabins every once in a while. We dance more in winter time so we could turn a pot down in the door to drown out the noise. (Soldier Williams, b. 1839, KY, 191)

DISCUSSION: Williams might seem to describe social dancing, but there is a definite intimation of holy dancing (shouting) as well, contrasted with restrictive slaveholder church services in the conventional fashion.

WHEN I CAN READ MY TITLE CLEAR

Hymns

To give variety and interest to the exercises of the Sabbath school, it is proper to teach the scholars *hymns and psalms, and how to sing them.* They [slaves] are extravagantly fond of music; and this taste may be turned to good account in their instruction. *Watts* will furnish a great number of suitable psalms and hymns, and they may be selected from various other authors. . . . One great advantage in teaching them good psalms and hymns, is that they are thereby induced to lay aside the extravagant and nonsensical chants, and catches and hallelujah songs of their own composing; and when they sing, which is very often while about their business or of an evening in their houses, they will have something profitable to sing. (Charles C. Jones, *The Religious Instruction of the Negroes in the United States* [Savannah: Thomas Purse, 1842], 265–66, orig. emphasis)

"None of us learned to read an' write in slave days. I didn' go to school atter freedom, we didn' have time then, we had to get out an' scratch for our bread. . . . The preacher read the Bible to us, and so did my master, Bill Ramsay. What songs did we sing? Gal, get me my old mistis' hymnbook." (The girl brought a much worn book of classic hymns.) "Why these are just the same hymns the white folks sang." "Of course they is, how would we niggahs know any others?" Here the wife spoke up. "We did have the melodies we made up ourselves, but I can't remember any of them. My mother used to sing, 'I'm going home to die no more' that was one of her favorites." (George Washington Ramsay, b. 1854, MS, and Amy Ramsay, b. 1868, MS, child of ex-slaves, 1779–80, orig. parentheses)[1]

The baby had Alphabet Blocks to play with and I learned my letters while she learned hers. There was a Blue Back Speller there too and one day the master caught me studying it, and he struck me with his muddy boot. Col. Myers was a hard master, not kind like many of them.

Fig. 15.1. "Primary School for Freedmen, In Charge of Mrs. Green, and Vicksburg, Mississippi." Engraving from a sketch by A. R. Waud. *Harper's Weekly* 10 (June 23, 1866): 392.

I found a Hymn book one day and spelled out, "When I Can Read My Title Clear" [Isaac Watts, 1707]. I was so happy when I saw that I could really read, that I ran around telling all the other slaves. After the War I went to Gill's School in Holly Springs. That was a school run by northern white people....

I joined the Methodist Church in 1867 and have been a church worker ever since. I taught in Sunday School for thirty years.... I taught in the Negro school here in Holly Springs until my daughter graduated in '91, then I thought it was time to quit. I have been writing the Negro Section of the county paper, The South-Reporter, now for the past ten years and guess I'll keep it up as long as I can see to write. (Belle Caruthers, b. 1847, MS, 365, 367–68)

All during North American slavery, restrictions on, or prohibitions against, teaching slaves to read and write were commonplace, whether these entailed actual legal statutes or merely the opposition of individual slaveholders. Yet slaves everywhere were surrounded by literature and literacy, whose effects and influences are self-evident. As one token, the individual songs most often mentioned by WPA narrators are not the famous spirituals, worksongs, or slavery laments but eighteenth-century Protestant hymns by Isaac Watts (1674–1748), Charles Wesley (1707–1788), and church-schooled composers of their kind, disseminated by mass print, organized worship, and scripted chorusing. Exactly how and why these seeming contradictions came to pass is this chapter's subject.

The campaigns against Black education were to a great extent successful. From the early 1800s through Emancipation, slave illiteracy is estimated at or above 90 percent. Those figures dropped precipitously in the generations born after freedom, but for persons born before 1865 these levels remained relatively constant throughout their lifetimes.[2] The South has always led the nation in illiteracy, the highest incidences being among Blacks and poor whites in the cotton-producing regions of the Southeast and lower Mississippi. Not all slaveholders were fully literate, in fact. As G. W. Pattillo remarked, "the Ingram slaves were not given passes by their owner to go any place, consequently they were known as 'Old Ingram's Free Nigger's.' Master Ingram could not write but would tell his slaves to inform anyone who wished to know, that they belonged to J. D. Ingram" (G. W. Pattillo, b. 1852, GA, 167).[3]

Then again, bans on slave education were never universal, nor were they ever universally observed or enforced. In 1887 James Lane Allen (1849–1925) remembered Kentucky slaveholders openly educating their slaves, "for the teaching of negroes was not forbidden in Kentucky."[4] During her 1838–39 residence on a Georgia plantation, Fanny Kemble (1809–1893) secretly gave one of her husband's slaves reading lessons, even knowing that "the penalties for teaching them are very severe—heavy fines, increasing in amount for the first and second offense, and imprisonment for the third."[5] Frederick Douglass (1818–1895) was instructed by another slaveholder's wife until the woman's husband found out and

> promptly forbade the continuance of her instruction; telling her, in the first place, that the thing itself was unlawful; that it was also unsafe, and

could only lead to mischief. To use his own words, further, he said, "if you give a nigger an inch, he will take an ell"; "he should know nothing but the will of his master, and learn to obey it." "Learning would spoil the best nigger in the world"; "if you teach that nigger—speaking of myself—how to read the bible, there will be no keeping him."[6]

Douglass was already spoiled, of course, going on to become one of the nineteenth century's best-selling antislavery authors.

Even if 90 percent of slaves were illiterate, 10 percent were not—a small but not insignificant figure by the standards of the day—and period sources constantly refer to literate Blacks. A 1778 advertisement describes Joe, a Virginia runaway who "can read a little, is fond of singing hymns, and exhorting his brethren of the Ethiopian tribe."[7] In the 1820s Timothy Flint traveled among slaves along the lower Mississippi: "They learn easily to read, to sing, and scrape the fiddle."[8] L. J. Coppin was born a slave in Maryland in 1848: "There was a Bible and hymn book in our home ever since I can remember any thing."[9] Recalling slaves on her family's Virginia plantation, Letitia Burwell agreed "many could read, and in almost every cabin was a Bible."[10]

The WPA materials support this mixed view. Narrators regularly mention objections to slave education but seldom legalities. In their accounts, opposition sprang partly from custom but mainly from the intolerance of individual slaveholders. "Us chaps did not learn to read and write, dat is why I can't read and write today. Marse wouldn't allow us to learn. Once he saw me and some other chaps, white chaps, under a tree playing wid letter blocks. Dey had de A B C's on dem. Marse got awful mad and got off his horse and whipped me good" (Milton Marshall, b. ca. 1855, SC, 173). Yet narrators also recalled whites who encouraged slaves to learn even as others opposed it.

My young Mistress Bessie liked me and tried to learn me to read and write. She would slip to my room, and had me doin' right good. I learned

Fig. 15.2. Susan Merritt, ex-slave, Marshall, TX, August 3, 1937. Portraits of African American ex-slaves from the US Works Progress Administration, Federal Writers' Project slave narratives collection, Library of Congress.

the alphabet. One day Mistress Jane catch her "schoolin'" me, and lammed me over the head with the butt of a cowhide whip and tell Miss Bessie that she would cowhide her if she caught her learnin' me anything. "Niggers don't need to know anythin'," she said. That white woman was so rough that one day we was makin' soap and some little chickens got in the fire 'round the pot and burned to death. She said I let them do it and made me walk barefoot through a bed of coals several times. (Susan Merritt, b. 1851, TX, 2643–44)[11]

In other cases, individuals were thwarted not by slaveholding thugs or legal codes but by the basic laws of supply and demand.

I learned to fiddle after the fiddler on the place. Uncle Jim was the fiddler. Andy Jackson, a white boy, raised him. He learned him to read and write in slavery. After slavery I went to learn from a Negro man at night. I learned a little bit. My master wouldn't cared if we had learned to read and write but the white folks had tuition school.

Some had a teacher hired to teach a few of them about. I could learned if I'd had or been 'round somebody knowed something. He read to us some. He read places in his Bible. Anything we have and ask him [to read]. We didn't have books and papers. I loved to play my fiddle, call figures, and tell every one what to do. I didn't take stock in reading and writing after the War. (William Gant, b. 1837, TN, 12)[12]

Yet even in the face of such barriers, some slaves managed to steal a little learning. "Ah didn go to school. Ah wuz awful sly. Ah wanted tuh learn tuh read so ah hung aroun ole mistess when she wuz teachin huh chillun tuh read. Ah listened an when she put de book down an went out ah got de book. Ah kep' it up till ah learnt tuh read. Ah been teachin one Bible class in Curtis 42 years" (Emma Tidwell, b. ca. 1839, AR, 332). "The only book learning we ever got was when we stole it. Master bought some slaves from Cincinnati, that had worked in white folks houses. They had stole a little learning and when they came to our place they passed on to us what they knew. We wasn't allowed no paper and pencil. I learned all my A.B.C.'s without it" (Mark Oliver, b. 1856, MS, 1664).

And some slaves did not have to steal their learning at all. "Sich niggers dat wants to larn to read an' write, de Marster's girls an' boys larns 'em" (Betty Bormer, b. 1857, TX, 342). "Old Burgess' children helped me learn to spell. De Boss would make me spell words backwards" (Jane Thompson, b. ca. 1850, MS, 353). "My young Mistess Nannie helped us some to get our A.B.C.'s and to write" (Campbell Davis, b. 1852, TX, 1065). "Our white chillun taught us slaves to read an' write at night. I never paid much 'tention, but I can read my Testament now, but I can't write to do no good" (Green Cumby, b. 1851, TX, 1004).

The white boys taught the Negroes to read and write at night and on Sunday. We went to church every Sunday. Master Dave give the colored fo'ks their own church and let them have their own preacher. They preached to us not to steal and to

Fig. 15.3. Bert Strong, ex-slave, Marshall, TX, October 5, 1937. Portraits of African American ex-slaves from the US Works Progress Administration, Federal Writers' Project slave narratives collection, Library of Congress.

obey our Master and Mistress, but they preached the gospel too. My favorite song was:

> Dark was the night and cold
>   was the ground
> On which my Lord did lay, as
>   sweat like drops of blood
> Did run down, and in agony
>   he did pray. [Thomas Haweis, 1792]
>   (Bert Strong, b. 1864, TX, 3757)

On Clara C. Young's Alabama plantation, a slave was the teacher. "Dey had a nigger woman to teach all de house darkies how to read en write en I larned how to sign my name en got as fur as b-a-k-e-r in de Blue Back Speller" (Clara C. Young, b. ca. 1842, AL, 2401). Stephen Varner came from another Alabama plantation, where slave children "went to school in the same building that they went to church. They were allowed to go to school only until they were old enough to go the field. They were taught to read and write" (Stephen Varner, b. 1852, AL, 402).

Slaveholders' motives in this were sometimes purely practical. "There warn't no school on our place, but Marster Bill teached certain of his darkies to read and write and figure so he could use them booking cotton in the field and sich like" (Simp Campbell, b. 1860, TX, 614). "Marse wanted his slaves to hab some book learnin' so's us wuz taught to read an' write an' figer" (Simon Durr, b. 1847, MS, 656). "My young mistress taught me how to read and write, and spell some, and keep talley" (James Augustus Holmes, b. 1843, GA, 1045).

However, the most commonly expressed motives of slaves and slaveholders alike were religious illumination, education, or indoctrination. "How did I learn to read? Atter de war I studies. I wonts to read de hymns an' songs" (Joe High, b. 1857, NC, 415). "I jined de Baptist church when I lived at Chatawa en atter I cum here [McComb] I wurk for Mr Heber Craft. His son taught me how ter read en play de piany en fiddle. Den I went to school here in dis town. I wanted ter learn to read so I could read de Bible en learn de Holy Writ" (James W. Washington, b. 1854, MS, 2202). The Bible was obviously the primary objective, but this was not without considerable controversy. Slaveholders struggled mightily to obscure or abridge scripture's millennial visions and insurrectionist suggestions even as they alleged its support for their status quo, and numbers of ex-slaves insisted they heard nothing from the Bible but "servants, be obedient to them that are your masters" (Ephesians 6:5). Knowing they were being fed doctored texts and false doctrine, they recognized literacy as their only remedy, and with or without assistance, encouragement, or permission slaves obsessively read the Bible. "It was from our white folks that I learned to read and write. Slaves read the Bible more than anything else" (John F. Van Hook, b. 1862, NC, 78). "He [white preacher] larnt us to read de Bible, but on some of de plantations slaves warn't 'lowed to larn how to read and write" (Alice Green, b. ca. 1862, GA, 42).[13] Others, however, were consigned to ignorance. "We didn't know nothing bout the Bible, and if we had a Bible none of us knowed how to read it" (Sally Dixon, b. unk., MS,

628). "Good Lord, Miss! Slave folks warn't 'lowed no time for to larn readin' and writin'. Deir time was all tuk up in de field at wuk. Slaves went to de white folks' church, but one thing sho' dey couldn't read de Bible for deirselfs and couldn't write none" (Anderson Furr, b. ca. 1850, GA, 349).

As a whole, slaveholders may have been more comfortable with hymn singing than Bible study, or at least with singing carefully selected, suitable psalms and hymns. Period accounts somewhat support that view. So do the memories of ex-slaves. Whether or not they knew their scripture, whether or not they were literate, scores of ex-slaves faithfully reproduced dozens of formally composed, published Anglo-Protestant hymns—part or whole—sometimes decades after they had last sung them at worship.

One reason for this was simple and self-evident: slaves had learned to sing these hymns because they were forced to, and many discontinued singing such songs as soon as white people stopped making them (or at least until white people from the WPA requested them again). There is more to it than that, however. These texts and tunes were major resources in the evolution of African American spirituals, and if they figure at all in discussions of nineteenth-century Black folksong, it is in that capacity. Yet that Black singers and songmakers took so many of these pieces so thoroughly to heart indicates they appreciated them for their own sake as well, and some ex-slaves flatly stated that they preferred white hymns to Black spirituals. For them, these songs were anything but foreign literature or white mind-control: they were majestic expressions of true faith voicing their deepest hopes and beliefs. After the war some Black congregations continued to sing *Watts hymns* (the South's generic term for these songs, whether or not Dr. Watts composed them); and while they have obviously faded from the forefront of Black religious music, Watts hymns are still included in songbooks produced for and by Black churches, and are still regularly sung at worship, performed in concert, and recorded, broadcast, or filmed.

Traditional Black choral genres—the spiritual, for instance—are characterized not just by oral composition and transmission but by improvisation, spontaneity, and individual contributions. By contrast, in formal white hymnody singers adhere to a fixed text and tune regulated by a printed standard. The simplest method of coordinating such material is to sing directly from print, something that would have been unthinkable on some plantations or in certain regions. "You should o' seen us in our Sunday bes' goin' ter church 'hind de missus coach, wid ole Uncle Mose high on de box. We can't read de hymns eben iffen we had a book 'cause we ain't 'lowed ter have no books, but we sung jist de same" (Henrietta McCullers, b. ca. 1850, NC, 74).

However, throughout the antebellum period there are reports of literate slaves singing directly from hymnals. "I used to sing but I forgot all the songs. We had song books. I joined the church when I was twelve years old" (Warren McKinney, b. ca. 1850, SC, 29). "Dey sing 'Amazin' Grace,' 'n' 'O Ship 'r' Zion' mos'. Some 'r' de cullud folks could read de hymns in de hymn book. Young mistis she learn 'em" (Andrew Moody, b. ca. 1855, TX, 2722). "What did we sing? I jes' can't member what the himes (hymns) was any more. My daddy used to have pr'ar meetin's at our house, ef I could read, I could find the himes in our book. One was 'Hark from the tomb, a doleful sound'" (Mandy Jones, b. ca. 1857, MS, 1232–33, orig. parentheses). "Dey would sing anything they could make a noise wid. Some of dem could read out de hymn book en some couldn' tell one word from de other. Yes, mam, some of de young Massa would steal off to de woods wid dey colored mate on a Sunday evening en learn dem to read" (Sallie Paul, b. ca. 1856, SC, 239).[14]

> I went to a Methodist Church in slavery times. It was up the road just a mile from where I live now. It had two floors, one for the whites and one for the slaves. Most of the preaching was done by white preachers. Just before the war they begin to let the Negroes preach, and allowed them to have books, especially hymn books and the Bible. During the Civil War the children were reading anything they could find to read. (A. M. "Mount" Moore, b. 1846, TX, 2732)

The slaves 'tended church with their marsters and after their service was over they would let the slaves hold service. They always left their pastor to preach for us and sometimes they would leave one of their deacons. When they left a deacon with us one of our preachers would preach. They only had two kinds of song books: Baptist Cluster, and Methodist Cluster. I kept one of these 'til a few years ago. Our preachers could read some, but only a few other slaves could read and write. If you found one that could you might know some of his marster's chillun had slipped and learned it to him 'cause one thing they didn't 'low was no colored folk to learn to read and write. Us had singin' classes on Sunday, and at that time everybody could really sing. People can't sing now. (Anon., b. unk., GA, 363–64)

No man, I nevva could sing. Ah can't recollect dese made up songs, all I sing I do out de hymnbook, but I do member one goes [like] dis:

> 1821 Jesus work is just begun
> 1822 Jesus brought the sinna through
> 1823 Jesus sot de prisoner free
> 1824 Jesus preached among de poor
> 1825 Jesus brought de dead to life
> 1826 Jesus had all things fixed
> 1827 Jesus rose and went to heben
> 1828 Jesus made de plain way straight
> 1829 Jesus turned de blood to wine. (Ruben
>   Woods, b. ca. 1853, AL, 4276)[15]

Obviously, singing from print was not the norm among slaves, but in this period hymnals were often unknown even in white congregations. Lacking printed aids, hymn singers were forced either to memorize their material or rely on some other prompt. Ex-slave author L. J. Coppin (1848–?) remembered: "the old church leaders, as a rule, did not know many hymns by heart. They used to call them 'hymes.' My mother had this advantage of them, she could read, and would learn hymn after hymn, and sing them from memory."[16] Some whites coached slaves directly from print while steadfastly denying them the right to read for themselves. "Yes, dey sho' did have a Sunday school. A white lady she was de teacher. She teach us 'bout de Bible and right and wrong. Dey didn' teach us to read any time though. I don' 'member de preacher' name but I useter t'ink he was a good preacher. I 'member de ol' songs dey uster sing, ''Mazin' Grace' and 'On Jordan's Stormy Banks I Stan', and 'When I kin read my title clear'" (Clara Brim, b. ca. 1837, LA, 430). "Preacher had a Blue Back Speller an' a Bible. Dat was when I learn: 'I kin read my titles clear'" (Simon Hare, b. 1849, NC, 914).

"Used to have Sabbath School in de white people's house, in de porch, on Sunday evening. De porch was big and dey'd fill dat porch! They never fail to give de chillun Sabbath School. Learn them de Sabbath catechism. We'd sing a song the church bells used to ring in Beaufort. You never hear it any more. But I remembers it." The old woman sang the song for me as melodiously and beautifully as any young person. The words are:

> I want to be an angel, and with the angel stand,
> A crown upon my forehead, a harp within my
>   hand.
> Right there before my Saviour, so glorious and
>   so bright,
> I'll hear the sweetest music, and praise Him day
>   and night. [Sidney P. Gill, 1845] (Rebecca Jane
>   Grant, b. ca. 1843, SC, 185)

My mistress made all the children, both girls and boys, come to her every Sunday, and she taught Sunday School. The book used was the old fashioned Catechism:

> Jesus keep me near the cross,
>   There's a precious fountain,
> Free to all a healing stream,
>   Flows from Cavalry's mountain. [Fanny
>   Crosby, 1869]

It was against the law for them to learn to read and write, so she taught them the Lord's prayer and a few other things in the book. . . .

> Am I a soldier of the cross,
>   A follower of the lamb,
> And shall I to own his cause,
>   Or blush to speak his name. [Isaac Watts,
>   1724] (Rev. W. E. Northcross, b. 1840, AL,
>   299)[17]

Another common solution was *lining* hymns (aka *leading*, *deaconing*, *hoisting*, or *wording*): having a song leader read, recite, or sing an individual line or verse to be repeated by the entire congregation, proceeding then to the next passage and so on. "Some o' de songs wuz sung long by de preacher or leader fust calling out a line, den de darkies would sing dat, den he would call out another line an' den dey would sing dat, an' so on through de song" (Sylvia Floyd, b. ca. 1852, MS, 744). "Quick as de funeral start, de preacher give out a funeral hymn. All in de procession tuck up de tune and as de wagons move along wid de mules at a slow walk, everybody sing dat hymn. When it done, another was lined out, and dat kept up 'till we reach de graveyard" (Gus Feaster, b. ca. 1840, SC, 51). "De fus time I went to chu'ch, missus tuk me and anuther gal to min' de chillen. I never heerd a preacher befo'. I 'member how de preacher word de hymn: / Come, ye sinners, po' an' needy, / Weak an' wounded, / sick an' po' [J. Hart, 1759]" (Rosa Green, b. 1852, LA, 1593). "We hed church under a arbor. De preacher read de bible and he told us what to do to be saved. I 'member he lined us up on Jordan's bank [that is, 'On Jordan's Stormy Banks'] and we sung behind him" (Thomas McMillan, b. unk., AL, 67).

Dere wuz preachin' down in de Quarters, but dat wuz at night an' wuz led by de colored preachers. I recollects one night dare wuz a service gwine on in one of de cabins an' all us wuz dare an' ole Uncle Alex Frazier wuz up a linin' off a hymn 'bout

Broad is de road dat leads ter Death
An' there an' here we travel. [Isaac Watts, 1707]

when in come some mens atter a colored feller whut had stole some sheep an' hogs. Dey kotch 'im, but sho broke up de meetin'. (Jane Mickens Toombs, b. ca. 1855, GA, 33)[18]

Preachers in that day conducted the services in the following manner. He would word out their song two lines at a time, the congregation committing this to memory would sing these two lines, then two more lines were worded out and so on until that song was ended. One of the songs used worded out as follows:

1. Come let us now forget our birth and think that we must die—all sing.
2. What are our best delights on earth, compared with those on high—all sing.
3. O here the mortals weep no more and there the weary rests. (Charles Butlington, b. ca. 1846, MO, 156–57)

This is the only mention in the narratives of Jane Taylor's "Come Let Us Now Forget Our Mirth" (ca. 1810), but Butlington quotes the entire first stanza and the last two lines of the fifth.

However, many slaves would have learned these songs simply as a result of being forced weekly to attend white churches, sit in segregated galleries, and listen to lectures about obeying their masters. "It was at this church where 'de niggers prayed in de back and de whites in de front' that she learned another song to add to her repertoire: / How sweet the name of Jesus sounds / To a believers ears; / It sootheth sorrow, healeth wounds, / And drives away all fears [Newton, 1774]" (Katie Phoenix, b. ca. 1857, TX, 3085). "Us slaves went ter de white church en set in de gallery, your white preacher read de Bible and sung dat good ole song 'Jesus lover of my soul' [Wesley, 1740], en den us had baptizing by de white preacher at Hill's Pond and my, didn' dem niggers shout and holler and sing

nother good ole song, 'Dark wus de night, cold wus de groun', which de Lord laid his haid' [Haweis, 1792]" (Sara Benton, b. 1846, AL, 62). "We uster go t' d' w'ite folks chu'ch. If us couldn' git inside d' chu'ch house we stan' 'roun' by d' do' (door) 'n' winder. Us uster sing, / Hallelujah, we mus' be bo'n 'r' God, / Hallelujah, we mus' be bo'n ag'in . . . Dey sing some 'r' d' w'ite folks hymns too. Dey sing, 'An' am I bo'n t' die?' [Wesley, 1763] 'n' 'Ol' Ship 'r' Zion' 'n' udders" (Charlotte Beverly, b. ca. 1847, TX, 282, orig. parentheses). "My white folks attended church at Concord Presbyterian Church. Us went dere too, and us set up in de gallery. Yes, they asked us. De preacher asked us to jine in some of de hymns, especially 'De Dyin' Thief' and 'De Fountain Filled Wid Blood' [William Cowper, 1772] and dat one 'bout ''Mazing Grace How Sweet de Sound Dat Save A Wretch Like us' [Newton, 1779]" (Aleck Woodward, b. ca. 1854, SC, 254).[19]

Finally, hymns were recomposed to enable or encourage spontaneous choral performance. Whether by editorial design or folk process, the American versions of many English hymns acquired repetitive, formulaic refrains allowing even unversed singers to join in. These singalong choruses were especially popular (and effective) at camp meetings, baptizings, funerals, and other mass events, and in fact, the two most frequently named hymns in the narratives were tied to baptizings and funerals. "Our baptizing song was mostly 'On Jordan's Stormy Banks I Stand' and our funeral song was 'Hark From The Tomb'" (Stephen McCray, b. 1850, AL, 208). "Our favorite funeral song was 'Hark From the Tomb'" (Jane Montgomery, b. 1857, LA, 228). "Dey dipped de white folkses fust, and den de Niggers. You could hear 'em singin' a mile away dem old songs lak: *On Jordan's Stormy Banks I Stand*" (Cordelia Thomas, b. ca. 1855, GA, 18, orig. emphasis). "Right now I can't rekelleck no song we sung at funerals cep'n 'Hark from the tombs a doleful sound'" (James Bolton, b. 1852, GA, 98). "We had what they called them old time camp meetings and everybody got happy and shouted, then we would all go down to the nearest creek while they baptised the white people first, we negroes sang 'On the Stormy Banks of Jordan'" (Parilee Daniels, b. 1846, TX, 1033–34). "Our baptizing song was 'On Jordan's Stormy Bank I stand' and 'Hark from the Tomb.' Now all dat was before de War. We had all our funerals at the graveyard" (Harriet Robinson, b. 1842, TX, 272).

Samuel Stennett's "On Jordan's Stormy Banks I Stand" (1787) was early and regularly remarked among American slaves. In May 1817, a Kentucky slavedriver taking a fleet of flatboats to New Orleans put ashore for the Sabbath on the banks of the Cumberland, where his human cargo attended services in chains. Included was a performance of "On Jordan's Stormy Banks."[20] An 1847 memoir describes a slaveholder performing this item on request at a slave's deathbed.[21] In 1880 it was featured at the funeral of former slave Susan Green, wife of prominent Black Baptist the Rev. Elisha W. Green (1815–1893), also an ex-slave.[22] WPA narrators, however, most often remembered "Jordan's Stormy Banks" as a baptismal hymn. "They would go down on the creek and we would sing 'On the Stormy Banks of Jordan,' and the preacher would baptize the white folks first and then the negroes" (Rosa L. Pollard, b. 1844, KY, 3121).

> Now when we'd baptize, it would be,
>
> On Jordans stormy banks we stand.
> And cast a wistful eye
> To Caanons happy land
> Where my possessions lie.
>
> That generous fruit that never fails
> On trees of mortal glory. (Henry Gibbs, b. 1852, MS, 827)

Stennett's text is among the most widely adapted in Anglo-American hymnody—George Pullen Jackson identified three major branches, with numerous offshoots—but most ex-slave versions derive from an arrangement published in the 1830s by South Carolina–born, Georgia-based author, composer, and music teacher Matilda T. Durham (1815–1901). Durham's main contribution was a singalong camp-meeting

Fig. 15.4. "Hark from the Tombs (A Funeral Thought)" (1707), Isaac Watts (1674–1748). From William Walker, *The Southern Harmony, and Musical Companion* (1854 ed.).

chorus, so that the hymn is now often known after that chorus as "I Am Bound For the Promised Land."

My grandmother used to sit by the fireplace and sing:

> I'm bound fo' the Promised Land,
> I'm bound fo' the Promised Land,
> Oh, I'm bound fo' the Promised Land
> Who'll go with me to the Promised Land? (Mary Edwards, b. 1853, TX, 1282)

Isaac Watts's "Hark From the Tombs a Doleful Sound" (1707) was the most popular funeral hymn for both Blacks and whites in the 1800s South, sung to the tune "Plenary" (aka "Auld Lang Syne"). Watts himself titled the piece "A Funeral Thought," but it was always known after its opening line.

> Hark! from the tombs a doleful sound,
> Mine ears, attend the cry;
> Ye living men, come view the ground
> Where you must shortly lie.
>
> Princes, this clay must be your bed,
> In spite of all your towers;
> The tall the wise the reverend head
> Must lie as low as ours. (Watts, 1707)

This is another of the songs most often mentioned in the narratives, its Black currency fully vouched by other sources. In 1836, a freed slave called Grandfather Sol, then reputed to be a hundred years old, was interviewed in Cincinnati. Sol had been kidnapped from Africa sometime in the 1700s and taken to Virginia and then Kentucky. Asked for his favorite hymn, he performed "Hark From the Tombs," learned from a slaveholder.[23] Sometime around 1828 near Mayslick, Kentucky, Elisha Green observed a southbound slave coffle consisting of "forty or fifty men, chained" and "five or six wagons loaded with women and children. The foremost man looked to be about seventy years old, and he was singing: 'Hark from the tomb.'"[24] The piece was more often used to lead funeral processions; evidently the man had not lost his sense of humor. Robert Todd described this song opening Black camp meetings on the Delaware-Maryland-Virginia Peninsula in the 1850s.[25]

By virtually all accounts, "Hark from the Tombs" was a funeral hymn. Austin Steward (1794–1860) recalled it from the funeral of a Virginia slave when he was around eight (ca. 1802).[26] Ex-slave authors L. J. Coppin (1848–?) and Irving Lowery (1850–?) learned it somewhat later at funerals in, respectively, Maryland and South Carolina.[27] Harriett Beecher Stowe depicted "Hark From the Tombs" at a Virginia slave burial in her 1856 novel *Dred*.[28] Around 1870 Ella B. Washington encountered it at a Charleston funeral.[29] The title was still a standby in some communities three decades later when Susan Showers heard it lined out at a Black burying in rural Alabama.[30]

Given its theme, "Hark From the Tombs" was rather ill-suited to most settings other than memorials. "Preacher Morris, white man, made us husband and wife. I 'members de song de white folks sung dat day. 'Hark from de tomb a doleful sound.' Don't you think dat a wrong song to sing on a weddin' day?" (Aleck Woodward, b. ca. 1854, SC, 255). Almost all narrators who specified remembered the song from buryings or funerals (the two events were distinct rituals, sometimes separated by months): "Dey jus' had a prayer when dey buried plantation slaves, but when de crops was laid by, maybe a long time atter de burial, dey would have a white man come preach

Fig. 15.5. "A Negro Funeral in Virginia," *Harper's Weekly* 24 (February 21, 1880): 124.

a fun'ral sermon and de folks would all sing: *Harps (Hark) From De Tomb* and *Callin' God's Chillun Home*" (Nancy Smith, b. ca. 1857, GA, 300, orig. parentheses and emphasis).[31] "When de waggin cum ter take de body ter de buryin' groun' ev'ybody went out behin' de corpse singin' some good ole song lak 'Amazin' Grace' an' 'Hark Frum De Tomb'" (Manuel Johnson, b. ca. 1863, GA, 340). "When niggers died you could hear someone goin' on de road singin': 'Hark From de Tomb de Mournful Sound'" (Lizzie Williams, b. 1849, MS, 2337–38). "I 'members dat when dey would be a funeral, us'd sing; marching de body 'fore us'd get to de grave an singin', 'Hark come de tune a mournful sound, my years a tender cry; a livin' man come view de ground where you may shortly lie'" (Jim Gillard, b. ca. 1850, GA, 155). "Did you ask somethin' 'bout old time songs? Sure did have purty music dem days. It's so long, honey, I jest can't 'member the names, 'excusing one. It was 'Hark, from the Tombs a Doleful Sound.' It was a burying song; wagons a-walking slow like; all that stuff. It was the most onliest song they knowed" (Aunt Mittie Freeman, b. 1851, MS, 352).

De hymn dey sang for my mother's funeral went like dis:

> Back from de doleful sound,
> My ears intend to cry;
> De livin' men, come view de ground
> Prince say de clay must be your bed

In spite of all your toils,
De clay must be your bed.

Reverend Heywood, who is in charge of the home, was in the room when Catherine sang the hymn. He very obligingly got an old hymnbook, which, he said, "is well over a hundred years old." The hymn she sang was in it. (Catherine Cornelius, b. ca. 1836, LA, 45–46, int. Robert McKinney)

In sum, simply given the basic circumstances of their captivity, most slaves could not have escaped hearing and learning the songs of Watts and his brethren, and some narrators reported little or no exposure to any other sacred music. "Most of the churches being white, the Spirituals were not sung. My favorites are common hymns. Short and long meter. 'Hark from the Tomb' etc. I only remember going to two funerals and that in S. C. Old 'Uncle Dick' sang 'Hark from the Tomb'" (George Washington Miller, b. 1856, SC, 1489). Others even expressed an outright preference for white hymns, and the more restrained, regulated singing styles and worship practices tied to these. "We sang old Dr. Watts hymns. They didn't sing these hear [here] little gig hymns and jump up songs like they sings now. The words was beautiful" (Virginia Harris, b. ca. 1855, MS, 940–41). "I don't like them old spiritual songs what they used to sing. When they carries me to church, and they sings them, I don't join in with them, but my voice rings out, loud as the next one, when they sings some beautiful hymn out of the book like 'How firm the Foundation ye Saints of de Lord'" [Robert Keene, 1787] (Dempsey Pitts, b. 1830, NC, 1723–24). "You know, miss, I like Dr. Warts' songs. We always have to get up and sing a song and tell the pastor our 'termination" (Eva Reed, b. 1863, LA, 184).

In church music I hold that the good old hymns of John and of Charles Wesley are the best to be had. I don' like shouting "Spirituals" showoff and carrying on—never did encourage it! Inward Grace will come out in your singing more than anything else you do, and the impression we carry away from

your song and from the singer are what I count. Read well, sing correctly, but first, last, remember real inward Grace is what shows forth the most in singing. . . .

Some of the spirituals are fine but still I think Wesley hymns are best. I tell my folks that the good Lord isn't a deaf old gentleman that has to be shouted up to or amused. I do think we colored people are a little too apt to want to show off in our singing sometimes. (Reverend Charles Williams, b. 1859, WV, 111, 112)

Us didn't go to no nigger church, caze dere warn't none. I was babtized in Jones Creek, an' Dr. Edmon's a white preacher, j'ined me to de Jones Creek Babtist Church long fo' de war, an de song I lacked bes' was a white folks song. Twarn't no nigger song. It was lack dey sing it now, 'cep' mo' lovely, Miss, mo' lovely.

Dark was de night
Col' was de groun'
On which my Savior lay
Blood in draps of sweat run down
In agony he pray.

Lawd, move dis bitter cup
If sich dy sacred will
If not content I'll drink it up
Whose pleasure I'll fulfill. [Haweis, 1792] (Amy
Chapman, b. 1843, AL, 59)

Yet if some slaves preferred hymns, others remained unconverted, rejecting white hypocrisies sung rote from print, or lined out by lying preachers in segregated churches. These believers favored their own songs of true faith, spontaneously revealed in authentic spirit-filled meetings, even when that meant turning the pot down. "Us went ter meetin' 'bout once a month to de white folks meetin' house, but us didn't jine in wid de services. De service was good but us liked our own whar us could git in de spirit an' pray, sing an' shout" (Isom Weathersby, b. 1847, MS, 2237).

"In church we sat in de gallery. De white man preached all de sermons. But we could jine in de singin'. De white folks word off de hymns an' we follow 'long. 'Deed old folks was good dem days, dat is, our parents was. Dey sure oughter go to Heaven. Dey git together at night, turn down dem pots an' 'pray de wild' (while?)" (Alice Marshall, b. ca. 1850, VA, 202–3, orig. parentheses).

> We wasn't 'lowed to go to regulah Sunday School, but we had a diff'unt Sunday School. We had a catechism to learn. This wuz it: "Be nice to massa an' missus, don't tell lies, don't be mean, be obedient, an' wuk hard." That wuz our catechism.
>
> Sometimes us slaves could go to meetin' houses an' sometimes us slaves could 'ave meetin's to ourselves at our houses wif purmission, but every once in a while we'ud slip an' have meetin's at our houses. Wen dey had these the men an' women 'ud come slippin' in fust one den 'nothah until they wuz all in. Then dey'd turn a big pot down at the do' sill so's ta catch the noise wen dey shouted an' hallahed. I remembah one 'oman had a big mouf. She uster put huh head right in the pot an' jes' yell an hollah an' you couldn't heah huh more'n three foot away. (Sister Robinson, b. 1836, VA, 241–42)

White hymns were also sung at slave meetings, but in these contexts slaves often mistook them for their own creations. "Dey was lots of ch'uch songs w'at de cullud folks mek deyse'fs. Dey warn't outen no books 'cause us couldn' read nor write. Dey say lots of dem song' like 'Mazin' Grace' [Newton, 1779] and 'Am I bo'n to die?' [Wesley, 1763] was tuk up by de w'ite folks later on" (Lorenza Ezell, b. ca. 1850, SC, 1319–20). "Dey wuz allowed ter pray and shout sometimes, but dey better not be ketched wid a book. De songs dat dey sung den, dey hardly ever sing 'em now. Dey were good ole songs. 'Hark from de tomb de doleful sound.' 'My years are tender,' 'Cry, You livin' man,' 'Come view dis groun' where we must shortly lie'" (Parker Pool, b. 1851, NC, 187).

> They never had larnt to read the songs they sung at funerals and at meetin'. Them songs was handed

down from one generation to another and, far as they knowed, never was writ down. A song they sung at the house 'fore they left for the graveyard begun:

> Why do we mourn departed friends,
>   Or shake at death's alarm. [Watts, 1707]

At the grave they sung, *Am I Born to Die. To Lay This Body Down?* [Wesley, 1763] (Jefferson Franklin Henry, b. ca. 1860, GA, 186–87, orig. emphasis)

None o' the niggers have any learnin', warn't never 'lowed to as much as pick up a piece of paper. My daddy slip an' get a Webster book and den he take it out in de fiel and he larn to read. De white folks 'fraid to let de children learn anythin'. They 'fraid dey get too sma't and be harder to manage. Dey nebber let em know anything about anythin'. Never have any church. Effen you go you set in de back of de white folks chu'ch. But de niggers slip off an' pray and hold prayer-meetin' in de woods den dey tu'n down a big wash pot and prop it up wif a stick to drown out de soun' ob de singin'. I 'member some of de songs we uster sing. One of dem went somethin' like dis:

> Hark from de tomb a doleful soun'
> My ears hear a tender cry.
> A livin' man come through the groun'
> Whar we may shortly lie.
> Heah in dis clay may be you bed
> In spite ob all you toil
> Let all de wise bow revrant head
> Mus' lie as low as ours. (Fannie Moore, b. 1849,
>   SC, 132–33)

It is easy to see why slaves would claim many of these items. Fannie Moore's version of Dr. Watts's text has been completely recomposed, and Black singers made these songs their own in other ways. Even without recordings, WPA interviewers managed to convey the characteristic African American vocal style, full of melisma, bends, moans, cries, shouts, and other effects—exactly the approach Reverend Williams dismissed in favor of more staid white hymn singing.

Jane said a favorite song for revivals when they called for "Mourners" to come to the bench was:

On Jordin's Stormy Banks I Stand

On jo-r-dins stormy b-a-n-k-s I stan'
An' cast a *wishful* eye—
O—h, wh—o-o-o will come
An' go wid mee—?
I'se boun' fer de prom-i-se lan'. (Jane Sutton,
    b. ca. 1853, MS, 2093, orig. emphasis)

African American singers almost always added choruses or refrains where they did not exist, and sometimes substituted their own when they did. In 1870 Elizabeth Kilham observed:

The colored people scarcely ever sing a hymn without a chorus, their favorite being, "Shall we know each other there?" This they sing with almost everything, sometimes in rather startling association, as, . . .

"Hark from the tombs a doleful sound,—
Chorus—Shall we know each other *there*?"[32]

Texts could also be expanded or personalized, perhaps spontaneously in performance, by simple repetition.

It was like a picnic when a slave would die and Reverend Nelson would preach de funeral. De funeral song dat I liked best was:

Out from de tomb a doleful sound
Out from de tomb a doleful sound
And I heard a tender cry
Out from de tomb a doleful sound
A livin' man came viewed de ground
Of every sinful heart, of every sinful heart.
    (Elizabeth Ross Hite, b. ca. 1850, LA, 105)

Oh! I know de spiritual—but Missis, my voice too weak to sing—dey aint in books; if I hear de name I can sing—"The Promise Land," Oh, how Mas Joel Easterling (born 1796) use to love to sing dat!

I am bound for de Promise Land!
Oh! who will arise an go with me?
I am bound for de Promise Land!
I've got a mother in the Promise Land,
My mother calls me an I mus go,
To meet her in de Promise Land! [Stennett, 1787–
    Durham, ca. 1830] (Mary Frances Brown, b. ca.
    1847, SC, 132–33, orig. parentheses)

Combining elements from different hymns was another common approach. Sylvia Cannon (b. ca. 1857, SC, 196) gave a "Funeral Song" blending "Hark From the Tombs" and "Come Ye That Love the Lord" (Watts, 1707) with the chorus of William Steffe's "On Canaan's Happy Shore" (ca. 1850). Sally Murphy joined "Hark From the Tombs" to a couple of lines from "And Must I Be to Judgment Brought" (Charles Wesley, 1763): "I did think 'Hark from the Tomb in doleful sound, How careful, how careful den ought I to live, wid whut Religious Fear,' wus de prettiest thing, and I show did love to hear dem sing it" (Sally Murphy, b. 1857, GA, 267). Robert Franklin also linked these items: "De cemetery wuz on de plantation, de funeral songs was 'Hark From The Tomb The Doleful Sound' an' 'Must I be to Judgement Brought to Answer on That Day'" (Robert Franklin, b. 1851, MS, 1419).

Sometimes such associations resulted in distinct strains or subtypes. Slaves most often linked "Hark From the Tombs" to two other titles overlapping in theme, context, and function: "And Must This Body Die" (1707), also by Watts, and Charles Wesley's "And Am I Born to Die" (1763). All three were designated as funeral hymns—"Am I Born to Die" and "Must This Body Die" are printed back-to-back in many hymnals—and several ex-slaves remembered them either being performed together or variously combined. "When de funeral was done preached, dey sung *Harps From De Tomb*. Den dey put de coffin in a wagon an driv slow and keerful to de graveyard. De preacher prayed at de grave and de mourners sung, *I'se Born to Die and Lay This Body Down*" (Robert Shepherd, b. ca. 1845, GA, 252, orig. emphasis).

One we used to sing was Am I Born to Die.

> Am I born to die and lay this body down
> And must my trembling spirit fly
> Into a world unknown.
> Oh am I born to die, to die-e-e.

The prettyiest song of all was Hark From the Tomb.

> Princes this clay must be your bed
> In spite of all your towers
> The tall, the wise, the reverent head
> Must lie as low as ours. (William Moore, b. 1855, TX, 2766)

I 'members two songs dey sung at my grandpa Gloster's funeral:

> Am I bo'n to lay this body down
> And must my trembling spirit fly into world's unknown.

The other was:

> Hark from the tomb my ears a tender cry
> A living man can view the ground where I may shortly lie,
> And must this body die and this frame decay,
> And these active limbs of mine lay molten in the clay.

My old Master called himself a preacher. He went after a colored preacher when my grand-people died, but he preached too. (Bert Strong, b. 1864, TX, 3757)

Yessim everybody ought to be religious if they expects to see the Fathers face in peace. Dey have to be bawned again. I belongs to de Baptist Church and I sho loves de Lawd and I loves to sing dis song.

> I'm bowned to die, to Lay dis body down
> Must my trembling spirit fly to a world unknown
> Must des active limbs of mine lay
> Moulding in de clay. (Harriet Sanders, b. 1867, MS, child of ex-slaves, 1915) (The first two lines are from "Am I Born to Die," the last two from "Hark from the Tomb")

Some slaves may have learned these items from white hymnals, but for others they had been completely naturalized as Black folklore, not just as songs but as proverbial wisdom, inside jokes, and figures of speech. An ex-slave interviewed by Fisk remembered that, in his childhood, "we used to sing to the rabbits. Yes, we would be out playing in the field, and turn around and out jumped two or three rabbits, and we would catch the rabbits and sing to them. We would tell the rabbits to 'Harken from Tomb the Doleful Sound'" (Anon. ex-slave, b. ca. 1850, TN).[33] In 1894 Mr. Baytop of Gloucester County, Virginia, sent the *Southern Workman* a story he had heard around 1888: a Black man driving past a cemetery feels and hears someone getting into the buggy but sees nothing. "He tried to sing, hoping to frighten away his supernatural and unseen guest. The only hymn he could think of was, 'Hark from the tomb a doleful sound.' He opened his parched lips but no sound came forth. His vocal organs refused to vibrate. He felt the cold breath of his unseen companion, who, apparently peering in his face uttered mockingly, 'Hark! hark! hark!'" Farther on, "that invisible companion departed without even thanking the man, much less paying for his ride."[34]

Other textual variations may stem from individual singers' personal tastes, talents, interpretations (or misinterpretations), or failing memories, a fact many narrators freely admitted. Then too, some could reflect writers' or editors' condescension or poor attempts at humor, and it is not always clear which is which. In "Hark From the Tombs," *hark* often becomes *harp*, the instrument upon which dead people in hymns customarily play tunes, so that *tomb* may accordingly become *tune*. "I don't have no fav'rite spiritual. All of them's good ones. Whenever they'd baptize they'd sing: / Harp From the Tune the Doleful Sound / Which starts like this: / Come live in man and view this ground / where we must sho'ly lie" (Red Richardson, b. 1862, TX, 264). "De preacher talked a little and prayed; den atter de mourners had done sung somepin on de order of *Harps From De Tomb*, dey shovelled in de dirt over de coffin" (Cordelia Thomas, b. ca. 1855, GA, 20). "One ob de songs dey usta sing at de funerals wuz: / Hark! frum de tune ob dornful sorrow / Mah years a tender cry / He livin' man cum an' view dis groun' / Whar yo' mus' shortly lie! / Lor' us sho' did hab plenty ob singing ob dem good ol' hymns, an' shout an' pray" (Henry Barnes, b. 1858, AL, 41). "Marsa used to sing dem good ole songs, My heart frum de tomb, a doleful sound, My ears attend to cry, and Amazing grace how sweet it sounds" (Wade Owens, b. 1863, AL, 307). Whether these recomposed texts represent corruptions or improvements is open to debate.

Within a decade of freedom, Black composers were themselves appearing regularly in print. Religious songbooks for and by African Americans had existed since 1801, when Richard Allen (1760–1831) published his first collections of *Spiritual Songs* and *Hymns*.[35] Allen was based in the Northeast, however; he had purchased his freedom in Philadelphia in 1783, going on to become the African Methodist Episcopal Church's first bishop (1816). Developments in the South lagged until war's end, but by the 1870s the region's Black composers, scholars, and educators were turning out landmark collections of slave spirituals and hymns, often under the auspices of Black colleges and their jubilee groups.

For the most part, these collegiate composers fell within the literary tradition of Wesley and Watts, but by this period ballads or *ballets* (Black broadsides, mainly religious) had become, and would for decades remain, fixtures among semiliterate worshippers in rural and neighborhood churches, interacting more directly with oral traditions.

In de old days, if de people had a song, dey would put it down on a long strip called a ballad, but honey, I been through de hackles en I can' think of nothin like I used to could. Is anybody sing dis one for you, Miss Davis? It a old one, too, cause I used to hear Pa turn dat one many a day.

> One for Paul,
> En one for Sidas,
> One to make so joyous.
> Sisters, don' you hear de lambs a cryin?
> Oh, good Shepherds, feed my sheep.
> (Repeat over and over) (Lizzie Davis, b. ca. 1865,
>   SC, child of ex-slaves, 110, orig. parentheses)

By the late 1800s, these ballets were being printed in the hundreds of thousands by presses large and small, bringing them within the means of many local songmakers or small entrepreneurs. In 1924 R. Emmet Kennedy (1877–1941) reported that in South Louisiana, "the spirituals, or hymns, or 'ballets' of the Southern Negroes, are original productions which the authors go about singing from church to church, the congregations learning them by word of mouth. If they become popular, the authors have them printed on narrow strips of paper, and they are sold to the church members at five cents each."[36]

Certainly by the turn of the twentieth century, African Americans had helped establish a truly American idiom in sacred song, and from that period to present Black artists have introduced many, arguably most major innovations in American religious music. America's premier fin de siècle hymnist was Charles A. Tindley (1851–1933), the child of an enslaved man and free Black woman whose compositions—"I'll Overcome Someday [We Shall Overcome]" (1900), "What Are They Doing in Heaven?" (1901), "Stand By Me" (1905), "(Take Your Burden to the Lord) And Leave It There" (1916)—became standards on a par with anything by Watts or Wesley.[37] Yet Watts hymns persevered, especially among rural congregations, older church members, and other more conservative elements. In the familiar pattern, young people and city dwellers might avidly follow new musical fashions, but other worshippers found solace in perennials reminding them of family, community, and tradition. Around 1898 Susan Showers attended a Black burying in rural Alabama:

> The hymn singing would have been a novelty to one not accustomed to the same in the back country churches. The preacher "lined off" the hymn, a couplet at a time: "Hark from the tomb a doleful sound," etc. It was indeed a "doleful sound" that ascended from the cemetery hill when the people took up the refrain. Many stanzas were sung in a slow, dragging measure; and each couplet was read out laboriously beforehand by the preacher. I have often stood in a country church while the people sang in this way as many as twenty stanzas of some dismal hymn in long meter, without apparent fatigue, while I was ready to drop.[38]

In the four decades separating Showers's report from the WPA project, even more had changed in Black religious music. By the time the ex-slaves sat for their interviews, the focus had long since shifted from eighteenth-century hymns and congregational singing to records, radio, and professional jubilee groups. New secular styles like blues and jazz, new venues of popular entertainment, and radically altered moral standards had distracted still more young people. Yet Watts hymns remained points of reference even among young urbanites, and not just the church members. One case in point is the recorded drama "The Death of Holmes' Mule—Parts 1 & 2" (Paramount 12793, 1931) by Charlie Turner and Winston Holmes, Prohibition-era entertainers from wide-open Kansas City. As the skit begins, Turner pretends to stumble across his partner "burying a mule" (possibly a reference to moonshining or bootlegging).[39]

> Charlie Turner: Burying a mule without prayer, you can't do that! Why—
> Winston Holmes: You know I can't sing nor pray.
> CT: Can't sing or pray? Why, I can't either, but probably my old guitar can.

> WH: You don't mean to tell me that that old guitar can sing and pray?
> CT: Why certainly.
> WH: All right, let's hear one of them old long meter numbers.
> CT recites:

> > Hark from the tune, a long-eared coon,
> > I hope my dog'll catch him soon. (*He responds with his slide guitar like a leader and congregation lining out a hymn.*)

> WH: (*laughs*) Boy, that sure is it, ain't it? Well, sir, listen at that fool.
> CT recites:

> > Hark from the tune a toneful sound,
> > Someone stole my demijohn. (*slide guitar response*)

The skit continues with running jokes about illicit alcohol (the second part even names notorious Kansas City bootlegger and music patron Burton Ellis and his Yellow Front Café) and more hymn parodies: "Hark I see and I'll pursue," Turner declares at one point, "I'll find my jug and whiskey too." For the magisterial first stanza of Watts's "Am I a Soldier of the Cross" (1724)—

> Am I a Soldier of the Cross,
> A follower of the Lamb?
> And shall I fear to own his cause
> Or blush to speak his name?

—Turner and Holmes substitute

> Am I a shoulder of a horse,
> A foreleg of a lamb?
> Shall I shave my mustache off,
> Or go just as I am? (*slide guitar response*)[40]

Turner and Holmes were making fun of the songs of their parents' and grandparents' generations, and doing a very good job of it. "De ole songs I member ez: 'Harp fum de Tomb dis Mournful Sound.' 'Am I a Soldier ob de Cross'" (Emma Grisham, b. ca. 1847, TN, 30). "I didn't sing much at meeting 'cause I was too little, but the others sang 'Hark from the Tomb,' and 'I am a Soldier of the Cross'" (Tishey Taylor, b. ca. 1860, MO, 344). Then again, Turner and Holmes were obviously familiar with these items, and assumed their listeners were too. Little is known of the pair's later lives, but if they followed one common trajectory, they may have eventually foresworn the Devil's music and sporting life, entered the church, and turned to singing classics like "Hark From the Tombs" and "Am I a Soldier of the Cross?" in earnest.

The ads for "The Death of Holmes' Mule" credited the record to Charlie Turner and His Praying Guitar, a reference to the way that Turner, in his own words, makes his slide guitar "sing and pray." Beginning in the antebellum period, Black instrumentalists made a habit of adapting hymns and spirituals to fiddles, banjos, guitars, harmonicas, and trumpets, imitating the cadences and inflections of Black sacred singing and singing styles. This process was in fact essential to the development of, and remains fully audible in, jazz, blues, and other Black-derived instrumental styles. James "Jim" Davis was evidently an early exponent of the approach.

I used to be a banjo picker in Civil War times. I could pick a church song just as good as I could a reel. . . . I used to pick

Dark was the night
Cold was the ground
On which the Lord might lay.

I could pick anything.

Amazing grace
How sweet it sounds
To save a wretch like me.

Go preach my Gospel
Says the Lord,

Bid this whole earth
My grace receive;
Oh trust my word
Ye shall be saved. (James Davis, b. 1840, NC, 114)

As Charlie Turner demonstrates, the bottleneck or slide guitar techniques that fully emerged after 1900 were especially effective for mimicking the vocal nuances of Black sacred singing, and today "Dark Was the Night" may be best known from a slide guitar rendition by East Texas street evangelist Blind Willie Johnson (1902–1947) ("Dark Was the Night—Cold Was the Ground," Columbia 14303D, 1927). Blind Willie McTell (1898–1959) rendered "Amazing Grace" this same way, letting his slide guitar "give it out."[41] Well into the 1960s, Georgia-born street musician Jesse Fuller (1896–1976) performed "Hark From the Tombs" as a slide guitar instrumental, sometimes paired with "I'm So Glad Salvation's Free" (Isaac Watts, ca. 1810).[42]

Thus many vestiges of the old Watts hymns still surrounded ex-slaves, just as some still resound today. Often narrators remembered these songs remarkably well, and at a time when many other church members seemed to be forgetting them. Of course, only a small percentage of ex-slaves remained active performers, but if narrators were still singing publicly at all, they were probably singing in church. Sadly, with the passage of time, a few ex-slaves no longer felt welcome even there, being uncomfortable with the new singing and preaching, and the stylish young people who laughed at their shouting and old-fashioned songs and whispered about their ragged clothes and worn-out shoes. Moreover, the dozens of narrators who were yet singing at worship were not always singing Watts hymns. While ex-slaves may have named more hymn titles, the songs they actually sang the most for interviewers were spirituals.

Appendix: Hymns

Better than any other source, the WPA ex-slave narratives establish the absolute centrality of published

Anglo-Protestant hymns to slave music. Following are all items I have identified in the narratives.

"ALL THE WAY MY SAVIOR LEADS ME" (1875), Fanny Crosby (1820–1914). TITLE: James Augustus Holmes (from mother). OTHER SOURCES: *DNAH*. Obviously this composition dates from long after freedom; Holmes (b. 1843), who attributed it to his mother in the antebellum era, may have confused it with another song. Crosby's song is reported from other ex-slaves, however. See Albert, *Charlotte Brooks*, 43–45.

"AMAZING GRACE (HOW SWEET THE SOUND)" (1779), John Newton (1725–1807). TEXTS: James Davis, Fanny Sellers, Melvin Smith, Neal Upson. TITLE/FIRST LINE: Frank L. Adams, Charles Gabriel Anderson, Arrie Binns, James Bolton, Clara Brim, Thomas Brown, Charles Butlington, Julia Casey, Susan Castle, Preely Coleman, William Davis, Sarah Douglas, Lorenza Ezell, Robert Franklin, Maria Hadnot, Virginia Harris, Manuel Johnson, Miemy Johnson, Lu Lee, Andrew Moody, Wade Owens, Ellen Payne, Harriet Miller, Will Rhymes, George Selman, Samuel Smith, John Sneed, Patsy Southwell, Gus Williams, Aleck Woodward. OTHER SOURCES: *DNAH*; Barton, *Plantation Hymns*, 12; Jackson, *Down-East*, 140; Jackson, *Early*, 153; Jackson, *Sheaf*, 239; Hallowell, *Calhoun*, 50; Mellinger E. Henry, "Negro Songs From Georgia," *JAF* 44 (1931): 444–45; Gainer, *West Virginia*, 203; Lomax, *Ballads*, 573–74; McDowell, *Camp*, 67; Rosenberg, *Virginia*, 2; *Sacred Harp*, 45; *Social Harp*, 190; *Southern Harmony*, 8; White, *ANFS*, 105–6. RECORDINGS: Fred McDowell with the Hunter's Chapel Singers, "Amazing Grace," Chicago, February 6, 1966, *Fred McDowell: Amazing Grace*, Testament CD 5004, 1994; Mahalia Jackson, "Amazing Grace" (Apollo A194, 1947); Rev. H. R. Tomlin, "Amazing Grace" (OKeh 8378, 1926). DISCOGRAPHIES: *Blues and Gospel Records*; *Country Music Records*; *Country Music Sources*, 615–16; *Gospel Discography*. VIDEOS: Aretha Franklin with James Cleveland and the Southern California Community Choir, "Amazing Grace," New Temple Missionary Baptist Church, Los Angeles, January 1972, *Amazing Grace*, dir. Alan Elliott, Sydney Pollack, Universal DVD, 2019. DISCUSSION: The ex-slaves usually recalled this item from worship services: Adams, Brim, Miemy Johnson, Samuel Smith, Woodward (white churches); Castle (joining church); Coleman (slaves' own meeting house); Lee, Miller, Moody, Payne, Sneed, Upson (meetings in quarters); Binns (white churches, meetings in quarters); Douglas (missionary meeting); Butlington, Casey (camp meetings); Bolton, Melvin Smith, Southwell (baptizings); Manuel Johnson (funerals); Brown (from mother); Sellers (from father); Owens (from slaveholder); Rhymes, Selman (favorite song); James Davis (sung and played on banjo); Ezell (attributed to Black tradition); Anderson, Franklin, Hadnot, Williams (no context). By the time he composed America's best-known hymn, Englishman John Newton had lived a checkered life in which he had been both a slaver and a slave. This title has always been a favorite of African Americans and is among the most-named items in the narratives. It was more often named than actually rendered, however, and texts even of this familiar item were recomposed or incomplete. Melvin Smith's first verse features additions found in some later versions (*DNAH*, "'Amazing Grace!' Folk Process Accretions"), while his second stanza combines the first two lines of Newton's fourth stanza with the last two lines of the first. Fanny Sellers contributed a unique text whose second stanza employs a wandering commonplace not usually associated with "Amazing Grace." James Davis and Neal Upson gave only Newton's first two lines.

"The niggers had a church in the brush arbor right thar on the place. . . . The preacher was the oniest one that could read the Bible. When a nigger joined the church he was baptized in the creek near the brush arbor." And in a low tone he began to speak the words of the old song though he became somewhat confused:

> Lord, remember all Thy dying groans,
>> And then remember me.
> While others fought to win the prize
>> And sailed through bloody sea.

> Through many dangers, toils an' snares,
>> I have already come.
> I once was lost but now am found,
>> Was blind but now I see.

I've knowed that song for a long time. I been a member of the church for sixty year. (Melvin Smith, b. 1841, SC, 291)

My daddy's favorite hymn was:

> Amaze in Grace,
> How sweet they sound,
> I once was blind but now I see.

> The wind blows east,
> The wind blows west,
> The wind blows shady way. (Fanny Sellers, b. unk., TN, 348)

"AM I A SOLDIER OF THE CROSS" (1724), Isaac Watts (1674–1748). TEXTS: John Crawford, Catherine Eppes, Cornelius Garner, Nancy Jackson, W. E. Northcross. TITLE: George Conrad, Emma Grisham, Patsy Hyde, Laurie Ramsey Parker, Mariah Snyder, Tishey Taylor, Easter Wells. OTHER SOURCES: *DNAH*; Richard Allen, *A Collection of Hymns and Spiritual Songs* (Philadelphia: T. L. Plowman, 1801), 18; Barton, *Plantation Hymns*, 12, 29; Brown, "Songs," 618; Clinkscales, *Plantation*, 100–101; *Colored Harp*, 3; Coppin, *History*, 23; Fauset, "Folk Tales," 300; Hallowell, *Calhoun*, 47; Jackson, *Sheaf*, 41, 126; *New Harp*, 141–42; *Sacred Harp*, 57, 166, 309; *Southern Harmony*, 10, 45; White, *ANFS*, 47–48, 105–6. RECORDINGS:

Richard Allen Singers with Theodore King, "Am I a Soldier of the Cross?" *Wade In the Water, Vol. II: African-American Congregational Singing*, Smithsonian/Folkways CD 40073, 1994; John and Lovie Griffins, "Am I a Soldier of the Cross," field rec., Perry Co., AL, April 1954, *Music From the South Vol. 7: Elder Songsters No. 2*, Folkways LP 2656, 1956; Original Gospel Harmonettes, "Am I a Soldier" (Specialty 904, 1956); Wilton Jennings, leader, "Am I a Soldier of the Cross," field rec., Ezion United Methodist, Queen Anne's Co., MD, August 1991, *Singing and Praying Bands of Tidewater Maryland and Delaware*, Global Village CD 225. DISCOGRAPHIES: *Blues and Gospel Records*; *Gospel Discography*. DISCUSSION: Crawford, Jackson, Northcross, and Taylor remembered this song at meetings. Eppes and her neighbors performed it for the interviewer, Susie R. O'Brien. The others did not specify contexts. In Black oral tradition this item is represented almost entirely by its first verse, which wanders into numerous other songs. For examples, see Barton, *Plantation Hymns*, 12 (with "Amazing Grace," "Traveling to the Grave," "Jesus My All to Heaven Is Gone," "Must Jesus Bear the Cross Alone"), 29 (with "All Hail the Power"); Hallowell, *Calhoun*, 47 (with "And Am I Born to Die"); White, *ANFS*, 105–6 (with "Dark Was the Night," "Amazing Grace"). Ex-slaves Northcross and Garner simply gave the first stanza, Eppes added a sing-along chorus, Crawford a unique ending. Jackson combined "Am I a Soldier" with the spiritual "Stand Your Storm (Stem the Storm)," for which see Mrs. Mary Dickson Arrowood and T. F. Hamilton, "Nine Negro Spirituals, 1850–61, From Lower South Carolina," *JAF* 41 (1928): 582; Dett, *Hampton*, 189; Jackson, *WNS*, 187, 325; Marsh, *Jubilee Singers*, 154; Stuart, "Camp-Meeting," 100; Work, *ANSS*, 130, 161. RECORDINGS: Shirley Caesar, "Stand the Storm" (Hob 13010, 1975); Singing Crusaders, "Stand the Storm" (MGM 10233, 1948); Sister Rosetta Tharpe, "Stand the Storm" (Decca 48332, 1953). DISCOGRAPHIES: *Gospel Discography*. In a memoir, J. G. Clinkscales (1855–1942) described holding mock funerals for dead chickens on his family's Virginia plantation, with "a funeral procession consisting of half a hundred pickaninnies. . . . A song and a prayer preceded the oration. . . . From my sisters we had caught Dixie and the Suwanee River; and from the grownup negroes, 'Am I a Soldier of the Cross.'" Clinkscales, *Plantation*, 100–101.

Some of de ole tunes we use to sing is:

> Am I a soldier of de cross, a follower of de lamb,
> And shall I fear to own His cause er blush to
>   speak His name?

Sing dat in long meter—you know dat don't you? (Cornelius Garner, b. 1846, MD, 100)

I b'longs to de Baptis' Church, an' dey calls me Ma Eppes 'ca'se I's de mother of de church. I loves to sing de gospel Hymns. She began to sing in a high, cracked voice, her body swaying with the rhythm. The song rose until her neighbors had gathered to form quite an audience. With much moaning between every line, she sang:

> I am a sojer of de Cross,
>   A follower of de Lam'.
> I'm not afeared to own His name,
>   Nor to 'fen' His cause.
>   (Chorus)
> I wan' you to come,
>   I wan' you to come,
> I wan' you to come
>   An' be saved.

She was still singing as I left her, the neighbors joining in the choruses. (Katherine Eppes, b. ca. 1850, AL, 120–21)

> I am a soldier of the cross
> A follower of the lamb.
> And why should I fear to speak

That pleasant Man's name
When I been there 10,000 years.
Please jine the Sunday sont [saint?] (John Crawford, b. 1837, MS, 977)

> Stand your storm, stand your storm, stand your storm,
>   Till the wind blows over
> Stand your storm, stand your storm, stand your storm,
>   I am a soldier of the cross, a follower of the Lamb
> Stand your storm, stand your storm, stand your storm,
>   Till the Christians done gain the day
> Stand your storm, stand your storm, stand your storm,
>   I am a soldier of the cross, a follower of the Lamb. (Nancy Jackson, b. 1830, TN, 1912)

"AND AM I BORN TO DIE?" (1763), Charles Wesley (1707–1788). TEXTS: Charlie Davis, Jesse Davis, William Moore, Harriet Sanders, Millie Ann Smith, Bert Strong. TITLE/FIRST LINE: Frank L. Adams, Jim Allen, Charlotte Beverly, Arrie Binns, Isabella Dorroh, Callie Elder, Ann Ulrich Evans, Lorenza Ezell, Maria Hadnot, Simon Hare, Jefferson Franklin Henry, Ed McCree, Calvin Moye, Laurie Ramsey Parker, Robert Shepherd, Paul Smith, Neal Upson, Gus Williams. OTHER SOURCES: *DNAH*; Bruce, *Hallelujah*, 100–101; Jackson, *Early*, 155–56; Jackson, *Spirituals*, 240; Jackson, *WNS*, 169; Hallowell, *Calhoun*, 31; Lomax, *FSNA*, 238–39, 246; Owens, *Texas*, 164; *Sacred Harp*, 47, 428; *Southern Harmony*, 31, 281; *Social Harp*, 55; Harriet Beecher Stowe, *Old Town Folks and Sam Lawson's Fireside Stories*, 2 vols. (1869, 1871; rpt. Stowe, *Writings*, vol. 9), I: 41; Todd, *Methodism*, 179; White, *ANFS*, 47–48. RECORDINGS: Golden Gate Jubilee Quartet, "Lord, Am I Born to Die" (Bluebird B7994, 1938); H. R. Tomlin, "And Am I Born to Die" (OKeh 8375,

1926). DISCOGRAPHIES: *Gospel Discography*. DISCUSSION: McCree, Shepherd, Paul Smith, Elder, Henry, and Strong described this song at funerals; Adams, Beverly, and Rhymes in white churches; Hadnot, Moye, and Upson at meeting; Binns and Moore at meetings in the quarters; Dorroh as learned from slaveholder's son; Evans in the field; Millie Ann Smith at meeting or in the field. Davis named it as his favorite hymn. Allen, Ezell, Hare, Parker, Sanders, and Williams did not specify contexts. Sanders combined this item with Watts's "And Must This Body Die" (1707), Jesse Davis with Charles Wesley's "A Charge I Have to Keep" (1762). Charlie Davis quoted the first stanza's second line: "Does I b'lieve in spirits and hants? My answer to dat question is dis: 'Must my tremblin' spirit fly into a world unknown?' When a person goes 'way from dis world, dere they is, and dere they is gwine stay, 'til judgment" (Charlie Davis, b. ca. 1849, SC, 253).

"AND MUST I BE TO JUDGEMENT BROUGHT" (1763), Charles Wesley. TEXTS: Sina Banks. TITLE: Jim Allen, Robert Franklin. OTHER SOURCES: *DNAH*. For another ex-slave text, see Coppin, *History*, 28; also Brown III: 653; Jackson, *Down-East*, 213–14. RECORDINGS: Marion Williams, "Must I Be To Judgement Brought," *Born To Sing the Gospel*, Shanachie CD 6009, 1989. DISCUSSION: Franklin named this as a funeral song, Allen gave no context. Banks performed the first stanza, learned at a white church: "And must I be to judgement brought, / And answer in that day, / Yes, every secret of my heart / And every word I say" (Sina Banks, b. ca. 1851, MO, 13). She alters Wesley's original third line—"For every vain and idle thought"—but quotes accurately otherwise.

"AND MUST THIS BODY DIE?" (1707), Isaac Watts. TEXTS: Harriet Sanders, Bert Strong. OTHER SOURCES: *DNAH*; Stowe, *Old Town Folks*, 41; Jackson, *Sheaf*, 192; Rosenberg, *Virginia*, 2. DISCUSSION: Both Sanders and Strong gave recomposed versions. Sanders combined lines 3–4 from this item's first stanza with the opening two lines of "And Am I Born To Die?" Strong combined this song with "Hark From the Tombs."

"AROUND THE THRONE OF GOD IN HEAVEN" (1855), Anne Houlditch Shepherd (1809–1857). TEXT: Mary Colbert. OTHER SOURCES: *DNAH*. DISCUSSION: Colbert remembered the first two lines of this Sunday school song: "My favorite song began: / 'Around the Throne in Heaven, / Ten thousand children stand'" (Mary Colbert, b. 1854, GA, 220).

"BECAUSE HE FIRST LOVED ME" (1909), William M. Kendall. TITLE/FIRST LINE: Nettie Van Buren. OTHER SOURCES: *DNAH*; Jackson, *WNS*, 323. RECORDINGS: Cassietta George, "Oh How I Love Jesus (Because He First Loved Me)" (Audio Gospel 110, 1966). DISCOGRAPHIES: *Gospel Discography*. DISCUSSION: The child of ex-slaves, Van Buren stated, "my Mother's favorite song was 'Oh How I Love Jesus Because He First Loved Me'" (Nettie Van Buren, b. ca. 1870, AR, child of ex-slaves, 5) (the rhyming line is "And purchased my salvation on Calv'ry's tree"). Obviously this was long after slavery.

"THE BLUEBIRD'S TEMPERANCE SONG (OH! I'M A HAPPY BLUEBIRD)" (1862), Mary A. Kidder (1820–1905). TEXTS: Letha Johnson. OTHER SOURCES: *DNAH*. Kidder's title was first published in *Bradbury's Golden Showers of S. S. Melodies* (New York: Ivison, Phinney, 1862), 57–59, occasionally reprinted in other Sunday school songbooks. Johnson (b. ca. 1861) gave the first stanza, which she had learned at a Reconstruction-era school.

I used to go to a schoolteacher named Thomas Jordan. I remember he used to have us sing a song:

> I am a happy bluebird
> Sober as you see;
> Pure cold water
> Is the drink for me.
>
> I'll take a drink here
> And take a drink there,

Make the woods ring
With my temperance prayer.

We'd all sing it; that was our school song. I believe that's the onliest one I can remember. (Letha Johnson, b. ca. 1861, MS, 98–99)

"BREAD OF HEAVEN" (1824), Josiah Conder (1789–1855). TITLE: Bud Dixon. OTHER SOURCES: *DNAH*. DISCUSSION: Dixon named this title from baptizings and funerals; it also is possible, however, that he was quoting this phrase from a stanza found in some Black versions of "Guide Me, O My Great Redeemer" (1745, William Williams). For example, see Kennedy, *Mellows*, 108–12.

"BRINGING IN THE SHEAVES" (1874), Knowles Shaw (1834–1878). TITLE: Dennis Simms. OTHER SOURCES: *DNAH*. DISCUSSION: Simms recalled this familiar Reconstruction-era title being sung "to the accompaniment of a Jew's harp and fiddle, or banjo" (Dennis Simms, b. 1841, MD, 61–62).

"BROAD IS THE ROAD THAT LEADS TO DEATH" (1707), Isaac Watts. TEXTS: Jane Mickens Toombs. OTHER SOURCES: *DNAH*; Jackson, *Down-East*, 106–7; Jackson, *Sheaf*, 120; *New Harp*, 18; *Sacred Harp*, 38; *Social Harp*, 118; *Southern Harmony*, 48. DISCUSSION: Toombs recalled the first two lines.

"A CHARGE TO KEEP I HAVE" (1762), Charles Wesley. TEXTS: Jesse Davis, Alex Humphrey. TITLE/FIRST LINE: Railroad Dockery, Robert Franklin, Susannah Wyman. OTHER SOURCES: *DNAH*; Brown III: 579–80; Jackson, *Down-East*, 158; McDowell, *Camp*, 66. RECORDINGS: Blue Spring Mississippi Baptist Association Delegation, "A Charge To Keep I Have," Washington, DC, February 1989, *Wade In the Water, Vol. II: African-American Congregational Singing*, Smithsonian-Folkways CD 40073, 1994; John and Lovie Griffins, "A Charge To Keep I Have," field rec., Perry Co., AL, April 1954, *Music From the South Vol. 7: Elder Songsters No. 2*, Folkways LP 2656; Dr. C. J. Johnson, "A Charge To Keep I Have," *Old Time Song Service: Free At Last*, Savoy LP 14204,

1968; Rev. Cleophus Robinson With The Spirit of Memphis, "A Charge To Keep I Have" (Peacock 1733, 1954); Union Jubilee Quartet, "A Charge to Keep I Have," field rec., Silent Grove Baptist Church, Clarksdale, MS, July 25, 1942, *Negro Religious Field Recordings*, Document CD 5312. DISCOGRAPHIES: *Gospel Discography*. DISCUSSION: The first stanza of Wesley's original runs, "A charge to keep I have, / A God to glorify; / A never-dying soul to save, / And fit it for the sky." Alex Humphrey gave a slightly recomposed version: "I professed religion fifty-seven years ago and was baptized in a creek. My favorite song is: / A charge to keep, I have, / A God to glorify, / And every shape, every look is / Toward Heaven Divine" (Alex Humphrey, b. 1864, TX, 1823–24). Jesse Davis combined this item with another Wesley title, "And Am I Born To Die?": "What's my favorite song? None better than de one dat I'll h'ist right now. Go ahead? I thanks you. Listen: / Am I born to die / To lay dis body down / A charge to keep I have / A God to glorify" (Jesse Davis, b. ca. 1850, SC, 265). Ex-slave author William H. Robinson (1848–?) prints a parody titled "The Slave Holders' Hymn to Be Sung at Evening Prayers": "A charge to keep I have, / A negro to maintain. / Help me, O Lord, whilst here I live, / To keep him bound in chains" (*Log Cabin*, 83–84).

"CHILDREN OF THE HEAVENLY KING" (1743), John Cennick (1718–1755). TEXTS: Julia Frances Daniels. TITLE: Will Rhymes. OTHER SOURCES: *DNAH*; *Colored Harp*, 40; Jackson, *Down-East*, 195, 252; Jackson, *Early*, 235–36; Jackson, *Sheaf*, 97, 108; *Sacred Harp*, 405; *Social Harp*, 20, 33; "Songs of the Blacks," *Dwight's* 9 (November 15, 1856): 52; *Southern Harmony*, 6, 165. DISCUSSION: Will Rhymes named this as his favorite hymn. Daniels performed its first stanza with lines 1–2 of the second stanza and line 2 of the third:

We'd ask the Niggers from other farms to come to the meetin's and I used to say: I likes a meetin' just as good as I likes a party. We used to sing:

Children of the Heavenly King
As we join and let us sing
Sing our savior, worthy of praise.
Glory in His Works and ways.
We are traveling home to God
In the way our fathers trod.
Christ our advocate is made. (Julia Frances Daniels, b. 1848, TX, 1022)

"COME LET US NOW FORGET OUR MIRTH, AND THINK THAT WE MUST DIE" (ca. 1810), Jane Taylor (1783–1824). TEXTS: Charles Butlington. OTHER SOURCES: *DNAH*. DISCUSSION: Butlington remembered this item being lined out in church.

"COME, SAINTS AND SINNERS, HEAR ME TELL" (ca. 1806), Anon. TEXTS: Bert Mayfield. OTHER SOURCES: *DNAH*; Jackson, *Another*, 198; Jackson, *Early*, 67–68. DISCUSSION: This early 1800s title is sometimes erroneously attributed to Black hymnist Charles A. Tindley (1851–1933). Mayfield recalled its first stanza from an 1860s baptizing: "One of the songs I remember on this Baptizing was: / Come sinners and saints and hear me tell / The wonder of E-Man-u-el, / Who brought my soul with him to dwell / And give me heavenly union" (Bert Mayfield, b. 1852, KY, 15–16).

"COME, YE SINNERS, POOR AND NEEDY (WRETCHED)" (1759), J. Hart (1712–1768). TEXTS: Rosa Green, Nancy Jackson, Will Rhymes. TITLE: Mary Colbert. OTHER SOURCES: For another ex-slave version, see Coppin, *History*, 49–50. Also see *DNAH*; Jackson, *Early*, 232–23; Jackson, *WNS*, 168, 204, 224, 322; Asbury and Meyer, "Old-Time," 172, 182; Gainer, *West Virginia*, 201; McDowell, *Camp*, 54; McDonald, *Virginia*, 278; McNeil, *Folksongs*, 115–17; Owens, *Texas*, 163; Randolph, *OFS* IV: 61; Rosenberg, *Virginia*, 53. DISCUSSION: Green and Jackson remembered this piece from baptizings, Colbert from funerals, Rhymes from his mother. Green gave the first two lines, Rhymes the chorus: "My mudder she lots of time sing: / I

will arise and go to Jesus, / He will embrace me in his arms; / In the arms of my deah Saviour, / Oh, dere are ten t'ousand charms" (Will Rhymes, b. 1853, LA, 3301). Jackson's contribution is completely recomposed: the Hart text supplies the third line of each stanza, while stanzas 2–4 each begins with a different line from the first stanza of "Jesus My All to Heav'n Is Gone" (John Cennick, 1743), all interspersed with a repetitive refrain ("come to the water side") typical of baptizing spirituals.

When we went forth to baptise, we first kneeled by the water side and pray, then we all rise and sing:

This baptizing shall go on
Come to the water side, come to the water side,
Come all you poor, needy, and tired
Come to the water side, come to the water side.

Jesus my all the heaven is gone
Come to the water side, come to the water side,
Come all you poor, needy, and tired,
Come to the water side, come to the water side.

This path I see and now I pursue
Come to the water side, come to the water side,
Come all you poor, needy, and tired
Come to the water side, come to the water side.

The narrow way to heaven now I view
Come to the water side, come to the water side,
All ye poor and needy and tired,
Brother, come to the water side, come to the
water side. (Nancy Jackson, b. 1830, TN, 1912)

"COME YE THAT LOVE THE LORD" (1707), Isaac Watts. TEXTS: George Briggs, Sylvia Cannon, Henry Gibbs, Pierce Harper. TITLE/FIRST LINE: Wash Armstrong, Julia Bunch, Cicely Cawthorn, Elisha Doc Garey, Ann May, Solomon P. Pattillo, Will Rhymes, George Selman, Smith Simmons, Patsy Southwell. OTHER SOURCES: *DNAH*; Asbury and Meyer, "Old-Time," 175–76; *Country Music*

Sources, 607; *Colored Harp*, 45; Ebenezer Davies, *American Scenes, and Christian Slavery* (London: John Snow, 1849), 262; Jackson, *Early* 107–8; K. G. S., "Negroes' Spirituals," *Lippincott's* 7 (March 1871): 333; *New Harp*, 12, 44; Mary W. Porter, "In Memoriam," *The Independent* 30 (September 19, 1878), 1; *Sacred Harp*, 52; *Social Harp*, 49, 119. RECORDINGS: H. R. Tomlin, "Come Ye That Love the Lord" (OKeh 8421, 1926). DISCUSSION: Cannon and Bunch recalled this song from funerals; Gibbs at foot washings; Southwell at baptisms; Armstrong and Garey at services; Pattillo at secret meetings; Simmons from his mother; Cawthorn from a slaveholder. Rhymes and Selman named it as a favorite song. May gave no context. Gibbs's text stayed closest to Watts's original, which is: "Come, ye that love the Lord, / And let your joys be known; / Join in a song of sweet accord. / And thus surround the throne" (Watts, 1707). "When de folks was washing dey would sing. 'Come ye that love de Lawd.' Den dis one too. / Let your joys be known / Join in de songs with sweet accord / And thirst around de throne" (Henry Gibbs, b. 1852, MS, 827). Harper described this item, combined with "Free at Last," being shouted on the first night of freedom. Briggs inserted this hymn's opening lines in the spiritual "Listening All the Day," while Cannon combined it with "Hark From the Tombs":

I can 'member how dey stayed up half de night at Mr. Harper's after de men had read de 'mancipation to us, singing an' shouting. Dat was all dey did, jus' sing an' shout an' go on. I can 'member one of de songs dey sang 'bout dat time. It went something like dis:

> Come thee dat love de Lord,
> Let your jaws be known,
> 'Cause we're free at last!
> Thanks God Almighty,
> We're free at last! (Pierce Harper, b. 1851, NC, 1647)

"DARK WAS THE NIGHT, AND COLD THE GROUND" (1792), Thomas Haweis (1734–1820).

TEXTS: Alec Bostwick, Amy Chapman, Ann Ulrich Evans, Rebecca Fletcher, Precilla Gray, Turner Jacobs, Anna Mitchel, Bert Strong. TITLE: Sara Benton, Bert Luster, Ann Matthews, Jane Montgomery, Millie Simpkins, John Sneed. OTHER SOURCES: *DNAH*; Brown III: 584–85; Brown and Owens, *Toting*, 82; *Cabin* III: 147; Dett, *Hampton*, 105; Hallowell, *Calhoun*, 31; Jackson, *WNS*, 199; Odum and Johnson, *Workaday*, 195–96; Rosenberg, *Virginia*, 24; White, *ANFS*, 105–6. RECORDINGS: John and Lovie Griffins, "Dark Was the Night and Cold the Ground," field rec., Perry Co., AL, April 1954, Mary Price, "Dark Was the Night," field rec., Angola, LA, June 1954, Rev. Lewis Jackson and Charlotte Rucelle, "Dark Was the Night," field rec., New Orleans, May 1954, *Music From the South Vol. 7: Elder Songsters No. 2*, Folkways LP 2656, 1956; Blind Willie Johnson, "Dark Was the Night— Cold Was the Ground" (Columbia 14303-D, 1927); Marion Williams, "Dark Was the Night," *Prayer Changes Things*, Atlantic LP 18142, 1975. DISCOGRAPHIES: *Blues and Gospel Records*; *Gospel Discography*. DISCUSSION: Haweis's dramatic recreation of the Agony in the Garden (Luke 22:44) was another favorite of slaves. Chapman performed the first and second stanzas; Bostwick, Evans, Fletcher, Jacobs, Mitchel, and Strong the first; Gray lines 3–4. Chapman and Strong described the piece in white churches; Benton, Bostwick, and Jacobs at funerals; Evans in the field. Gray, Matthews, Mitchel, Montgomery, and Simpkins gave no context. Rebecca Fletcher had learned it from another slave working in the big house kitchen. James Davis recalled playing this hymn on the banjo.

The old slave woman in the kitchen used to sing hymns—you call 'em "spirituals," now—but anyhow, she would sing. And soon, even the littlest one learned from her and joined in. One of these was:

> Dark was the night and cold the ground
> On which our Lord was laid.
> Great drops of sweat-like blood poured down,

And anchored, kneeled, He prayed. (Rebecca Fletcher, b. 1842, MS, 65)

"DAY IS PAST AND GONE" (1792), John Leland (1754–1841). TITLE/FIRST LINE: Peter Mitchell. OTHER SOURCES: *DNAH*. DISCUSSION: Mitchell remembered Leland's first line from white baptizings: "Dem white people hab a big pool 'bout fifty yard' from de house w'er dey was baptise'. I 'member dem sing, / Day is pas' an' gone, / Evenin' shades appear!" (Peter Mitchell, b. 1862 or 1863, TX 2719).

"DEATH HAS BEEN HERE, AND BORNE AWAY" (ca. 1825), Jane Taylor (1783–1824). TEXTS: Alice Hutcheson. OTHER SOURCES: *DNAH*. DISCUSSION: Like much of Jane Taylor's work, this item was directed primarily at young people, appearing in Sunday school books and other juvenilia. Ex-slave Hutcheson gave the first, second, and fourth stanzas; her third stanza is from William Hiley Bathurst's "O For a Faith That Will Not Shrink" (1831).

White men preached de fun'rals. When dey buried a Nigger dey mos'ly had prayer, a little talkin' and some songs. Parts of de songs went like dis:

Death has been here and
Tore away a sister from our side,
Jus' in de mornin' of 'er day
As young as us, she had to die.

Not long ago she filled 'er place
And sot us free to larn,
But she done run 'er mortal race
And nevermore can she return.

Us can't tell who nex' may fall
Underneath de chasen' rod,
One maybe fus', but let us all
Prepare to meet our God.

And needful help is thine to give
For Grace our souls to Thee apply,

To learn us how to serve and live
And make us fit at las' to die. (Alice Hutcheson, b. ca. 1860, GA, 286–87)

"DID CHRIST O'ER SINNERS WEEP?" (ca. 1790), Benjamin Beddome (1717–1795). TEXTS: Frank Hughes. OTHER SOURCES: *DNAH*; Jackson, *Early*, 163; Jackson, *Sheaf*, 159; *New Harp*, 68; *Sacred Harp*, 33, 396; *Southern Harmony*, 7. RECORDINGS: Dr. C. J. Johnson, "Did Christ O'er Sinners Weep," *Save a Seat For Me*, Savoy LP 14261, 1969; Testerina Primitive Baptist Church, "I Don't Know What I'd Do Without the Lord/Did Christ O'er Sinners Weep? (The Weeping Savior)," field rec., Leon Co., FL, May 1980, *Drop on Down in Florida: Field Recordings of African American Traditional Music 1977–1980*, Dust-To-Digital CDs 24. DISCUSSION: Hughes recalled two-and-a-half of Beddome's original four stanzas.

In dat day of course dere was some rough bad singin goin on. De kind I like is of de spirit.

Did Christ over sinners weep?
And shall our cheeks be dry
Let floods of penitence grief
Burst forth from every eye.
The son of God in tear the wondering Angel see,
Be thou astonished Ole my soul,
He shed those tears for me.
In heaven above, no sin is found
There's no weepin' there. (Frank Hughes, b. 1858, AL, 1062)

"GO PREACH MY GOSPEL, SAITH THE LORD" (1709), Isaac Watts. TEXTS: James Davis. OTHER SOURCES: *DNAH*. DISCUSSION: Davis quoted from this title while describing hymns played on the banjo, giving the original's first two lines with his own concluding line.

"GOOD SHEPHERD" and "LET THY KINGDOM, BLESSED SAVIOR" (ca. 1815), attr. John Adam Granade (1770–1807). TEXTS: William Banjo,

Madison Bruin, Lizzie Davis, Frank Gill. OTHER SOURCES: For "Good Shepherd," see Eliza Frances Andrews, *The War-Time Journal of a Georgia Girl, 1864–1865* (New York: D. Appleton, 1908), 90; Ballanta, *St. Helena*, 30; Fauset, "Folk Tales," 295–96; *Cabin* I: 210–11; *Cabin* III: 38–39; Dett, *Hampton*, 224–25; Harris, *Friends*, 199–200; Ruth Crawford Seeger, *American Folk Songs for Christmas* (New York: Doubleday, 1953); *Slave Songs*, 16–17; Taylor, *Revival Hymns*, 245–46; Work, *Spirituals*, 114. RECORDINGS: Alphabetical Four, "Shepherd Go Feed My Sheep," Decca 7845, 1941; Paul Robeson, "Hear De Lam's A Cryin'/Going To Ride Up In De Chariot," concert rec., New York, November 25, 1947, *The Power and the Glory*, Columbia/Legacy CD 47337, 1991; Jimmie Strothers, "Keep Away from the Blood-Strained Banders," field rec., State Farm, VA, 1936, *Treasury of Field Recordings*, Rounder CD 1500, 1997. DISCOGRAPHIES: *Blues and Gospel Records*; *Gospel Discography*. Strothers's version was later rearranged by the Jefferson Airplane among others (Jefferson Airplane, "Good Shepherd," *Volunteers*, RCA Victor LP 4238, 1969). For "Let Thy Kingdom," see *DNAH*; Taylor, *Revival Hymns*, 71–72; Richard Hulan, "John Adam Granade: The 'Wild Man' of Goose Creek," *WF* 33 (1974): 77–87. DISCUSSION: This item, known to three ex-slaves, alludes to John 21:17: "He saith unto him the third time, Simon, son of Jonas, lovest thou me? Peter was grieved because he said unto him the third time, Lovest thou me? And he said unto him, Lord, thou knowest all things; thou knowest that I love thee. Jesus saith unto him, Feed my sheep." By all appearances the piece originated and developed in Black tradition as an independent song, but it parallels a white hymn also based on John 21:17, "Let Thy Kingdom, Blessed Savior," conventionally credited to South Carolinian John Adam Granade. Even after thorough research, Richard Hulan was unable to confirm the attribution, but "found nothing to indicate this text could not have been by Granade." Hulan, "John Adam Granade," 77–87. In any case, aside from Marshall Taylor's *Revival Hymns*, "Let

Thy Kingdom" does not appear in Black sources, and its relation to "Good Shepherd" may be coincidental.

Back in slavery times on Sunday I uster to go 'long to chu'ch wid de w'ite folks to open de gate. Dey uster go to de Christian Chu'ch. Us uster sing on de plantation . . .

> I'm clim'in Jacob's ladder
>> Over on de other sho'
> Don't you hear de lam's a-cryin'?
>> Oh, Good Shepherd, feed my sheep.

> Dere's some for Paul
>> And some for Silas
> And some to mek my heart rejoice,
>> Don't you hear de lam's a-cryin'?
> Oh, Good Shepherd, feed my sheep.
> I'm a-clim'in' higher, higher
>> On de other sho'. (Madison Bruin,
>> b. 1856, KY, 509–11)

Dere was plenty old songs us useta to sing, but I can't 'member 'em. Dere is dis one dat goes—

> Wonderful Peter,
> Wonderful Paul,
> Wonderful Silas,
> Who for to make a
> Mah heart rejoice.
> Oh Good Shepherds, feed a' mah sheep.
> Don't you hear de young lambs a bleatin'?
> Don't you hear de young lambs a bleatin'?
> Don't you hear de young lambs a bleatin'?
> Oh! Good shepherds feed a' mah sheep. (Frank
>> Gill, b. ca. 1845, MS, 152–53)

"GUIDE ME, O MY GREAT REDEEMER (JEHOVAH)" (1745, Welsh), William Williams (1717–1791), (1771, English trans.), Peter Williams. TITLE: Willis Cofer, Robert Shepherd, Nancy Smith, Georgia Telfair, Cordelia Thomas, Emma Virgel. OTHER SOURCES: For other ex-slave versions, see Albert,

Charlotte Brooks, 9; Rev. J. P. Robinson (1856–?) *Sermons and Sermonettes* (Nashville: National Baptist Publishing Board, 1909), 208–9. Also see *DNAH*; Kennedy, *Mellows*, 108–12; *New Harp*, 145. RECORDINGS: Ike Caudill and congregation, "Guide Me O Thou Great Jehova," field rec., Mt. Olivet Old Regular Baptist Church, Blackey, KY, September 1959, *Voices from the South*, Rounder CD 1701, 1997; Mahalia Jackson, "Guide Me, Oh Thou Great Jehovah," *Mahalia Sings the Gospel Right Out of Church*, Columbia 9813, 1969. DISCOGRAPHIES: *Gospel Discography*. DISCUSSION: In Black tradition this item is sometimes known, after its chorus, as "Where the Healing Waters Flow" ("Open now the crystal fountain / Where the healing waters flow"). A half dozen Georgia narratives refer to it this way, but all of these interviews were conducted by the same fieldworker, Grace McCune, and their overall correspondences strongly suggest that this is another case of a writer repeating material. The piece's currency among Blacks is documented by period sources, however.

"HARK FROM THE TOMB" (1707), Isaac Watts. TEXTS: Henry Barnes, Sylvia Cannon, Jeptha Choice, Catherine Cornelius, Laura Ford, Elisha Doc Garey, Jim Gillard, Elizabeth Ross Hite, William Moore, Sally Murphy, Parker Pool, Red Richardson, Bert Strong. TITLE/FIRST LINE: Frances Batson, James Bolton, Cicely Cawthon, Willis Cofer, Robert Franklin, Mittie Freeman, Alice Green, Emma Grisham, Carrie Hudson, Manuel Johnson, Mandy Jones, Julia Larken, Stephen McCray, George Washington Miller, Jane Montgomery, Calvin Moye, Lewis Mundy, Wade Owens, Bob Potter, Harriett Robinson, Robert Shepherd, Nancy Smith, Patsy Southwell, Tishey Taylor, Cordelia Thomas, Addie Vinson, Emma Virgel, Lizzie Williams (MS), Aleck Woodward, Caroline Wright. OTHER SOURCES: For other ex-slaves, see Anon. ex-slave (b. ca. 1850, TN), *Unwritten History*, 248; Coppin, *History*, 57–58; Green, *Life*, 2–3; Lowery, *Plantation*, 208; Steward, *Slave*, 39. For other period sources, see Brown, "Songs," 618;

David W. Guion, *Darkey Spirituals: Hark, From De Tombs* (New York: M. Witmark & Sons, 1918); Kilham, "Sketches. Fourth," 309; Showers, "Weddin' and Buryin'," 482; Harriet Beecher Stowe, *Dred: A Tale of the Dismal Swamp*, 2 vols. (1856; rpt. Stowe, *Writings*, vols. 3 & 4), II: 168; Todd, *Methodism*, 179; Washington, "Funeral," 243. Also see *DNAH*; Davis, *Folk-Songs*, 322; Jackson, *Early*, 147–48; Jackson, *Sheaf*, 20; McDowell, *Camp*, 16, 63; Randolph, *OFS* IV: 76–77; *Sacred Harp*, 162; *Social Harp*, 123; *Southern Harmony*, 262. RECORDINGS: Pace Jubilee Congregation, "Hark From the Tomb" (Black Patti 8042, 1927); Jesse Fuller, "Hark from the Tomb," *Frisco Bound*, Arhoolie LP 360, 1968. DISCOGRAPHIES: *Blues and Gospel Records*. VIDEO: Jesse Fuller, "I'm Glad Salvation's Free"/"Hark from the Tomb" (medley), *Masters of Bottleneck Blues Guitar*, Vestapol DVD 13002, 2002. DISCUSSION: This was without question the South's favorite funeral hymn. Watts actually titled the piece "A Funeral Thought," but in the South it was universally known by its first line. Ex-slaves recalling it from funerals included Barnes, Bolton, Cawthon, Cannon, Choice, Cofer, Cornelius, Franklin, Freeman, Garey, Gillard, Hite, Hudson, Johnson, Larken, McCray, Miller, Montgomery, Pool, Robinson, Shepherd, Smith, Strong, Thomas, Vinson, Virgel, and Williams. Jones, Moye, Potter, and Taylor remembered it from church services; Richardson and Southwell at baptizings; Moore in the cabins at night; Green from mother; Owens from a slaveholder; Woodward as sung by white folks at his wedding. Ford described it being sung and shouted in the fields. Batson, Grisham, Mundy, Murphy, and Wright did not specify. Of those providing texts, Henry Barnes, Jeptha Choice, Elisha Doc Garey, Sally Murphy, Parker Pool, and Red Richardson gave variants of the first stanza; William Moore the second. Catherine Cornelius and Laura Ford gave parts of both. Bert Strong performed a recomposed version of the first stanza, Sylvia Cannon combined the first stanza with Watts's "Come Ye That Love the Lord."

"HARK THE VOICE OF JESUS CALLING" (1863), Daniel March (1816–1909). TEXTS: W. E. Northcross. OTHER SOURCES: *DNAH*. DISCUSSION: Rev. Northcross quoted the first stanza while describing his postwar pastorship of various Alabama churches: "Hark the voice of Jesus calling, / Who will [come] and work today? / Fields are white and harvest waiting, / Who will bear the sheaves away" (Rev. W. E. Northcross, b. 1840, AL, 303).

"HOW FIRM A FOUNDATION, YE SAINTS OF THE LORD" (1787), Robert Keene. TEXTS: Mary Anngady, Aron Carter. TITLE: Dempsey Pitts. OTHER SOURCES: For another ex-slave version, see Albert, *Charlotte Brooks*, 81. Also see *DNAH*; Jackson, *Down-East*, 155; Jackson, *Sheaf*, 99–100, 109–10, 158, 168; *New Harp*, 57; *Sacred Harp*, 72; *Social Harp*, 22, 204; *Southern Harmony*, 69, 101. DISCOGRAPHIES: *Country Music Records*; *Country Music Sources*, 615. DISCUSSION: Pitts named this item from church, Carter remembered the first two lines: "Now les see, iffen ah' recalls some o' de songs we use to sing. Manda yo' members some? Less' see now, hmmmmmmm, now jest what wuz some o' de 'propriate songs den? / Da, de da, de, How firm a Foundation, / What more kin' ah see?" (Aron Carter, b. 1857, MS, 359). Mary Anngady, at one time a professional entertainer married to her African stage partner, gave a Bakuba-language text set to this tune, learned from a missionary hymnal (Mary Anngady, b. ca. 1857, NC, 36–8): *Nkana mu Ncema* (Ibanj, Democratic Republic of Congo: American Presbyterian Mission, 1909; Rev. and enl. ed. of Lucy G. Sheppard, *Masamba wa Nzambi*, n.d.), 9. Presbyterian Historical Society, Pearl Digital Collection, digital.history.pcusa.org/islandora /object/islandora:15798#page/1/mode1up.

"HOW HAPPY EVERY CHILD OF GRACE" (1759), Charles Wesley. TITLE: Aaron Ray (favorite song). OTHER SOURCES: *DNAH*.

"HOW SWEET THE NAME OF JESUS SOUNDS" (1774), John Newton. TEXTS: Katie Phoenix. OTHER SOURCES: For a period example, see Schoolcraft, *Gauntlet*, 85. Also see *DNAH*; Jackson, *Sheaf*, 140, 147; *Sacred Harp*, 56, 283; *Social Harp*, 190; *Southern Harmony*, 12.

"HOW TEDIOUS AND TASTELESS THE HOURS" (ca. 1779), John Newton. TEXTS: Ellen Nora Ford. OTHER SOURCES: *DNAH*; Randolph *OFS IV*: 62–63; Sandburg, *Songbag*, 154. RECORDINGS: Juanita McDonald, leader, "How Tedious and Tasteless the Hours," field rec., John Wesley United Methodist, Dorchester Co., MD, June 1988, *Singing and Praying Bands of Tidewater Maryland and Delaware*, Global Village CD 225; Sallie Martin Singers, "How Tedious and Tasteless," *God Is Here*, Vee Jay LP 5041, 1963. DISCOGRAPHIES: *Gospel Discography*. DISCUSSION: Ford recalled the second half of Newton's first stanza:

I was baptized October 14, 1872. I remember one of the hymns we used to sing, part of it went:

> The midsummer sun shines but dim,
> The fields strive in vain to look gay,
> But when I am happy in Him,
> December is pleasant as May. (Ellen Nora Ford, b. ca. 1855, TX, 1356–57)

"I HEARD THE VOICE OF JESUS SAY, 'COME UNTO ME AND REST'" (1846), Horatius Bonar (1808–1889). TEXTS: William Banjo, Susan Merritt, Steve Stepney. FIRST LINE: Molly Ammonds. OTHER SOURCES: *DNAH*; Robinson, *Sermons and Sermonettes*, 69. RECORDINGS: Biddleville Quintette, "I Heard the Voice of Jesus Say Come Unto Me And Rest" (Paramount 12396, 1926); Four Girls, "I Heard the Voice of Jesus Say," field rec., Clarksdale, MS, 1942, *Field Recordings, Vol. 4*, Document CD 5621; United Southern Prayer Band of Baltimore, Washington, and Virginia, "I Heard the Voice of Jesus Say," Washington, DC, February 1989, *Wade In the Water, Vol. II: African-American Congregational Singing*, Smithsonian/Folkways CD 40073, 1994. DISCOGRAPHIES: *Blues and Gospel Records*; *Gospel Discography*. DISCUSSION: Bonar's complete hymn was well-known in Black churches; its first stanza was also among the most popular wandering verses in Black religious song. Excepting Ammonds's example, all WPA texts were recomposed to some degree. Merritt performed the first stanza, slightly altering the first line, while Banjo, who accompanied himself on accordion, combined this item and "Good Shepherd (Feed My Sheep)." Stepney inserted Bonar's first stanza in the spiritual "Shine On Me," which is typical for that piece. Ammonds remembered the song at preaching, Stepney in the field; Banjo and Merritt did not specify contexts. This title was also the subject of a popular Black parody, "I Heard the Voice of a Porkchop Say 'Come Unto Me and Rest,'" Blind (Bogus) Ben Covington (Paramount 12693, 1928); Jim Jackson (Victor 21387, 1928).

I 'member one favorite song was:

> I heard the voice of Jesus saying
> "Come unto me and live"
> Lie down, lie down weeping one
> And rest they head on my breast
> I come to Jesus as I was
> Weary, lone, tired and sad
> I found him in a resting place
> And he has made me glad. (Susan Merritt,
>   b. 1851, TX, 2642)

"I LOVE THE LORD; HE HEARD MY CRY" (1719), Isaac Watts. TEXTS: William Hawes. OTHER SOURCES: *DNAH*. RECORDINGS: Reverend R. C. Crenshaw and congregation of New Brown's Chapel, "I Love the Lord," field rec., Memphis, 1959, *Sounds of the South* 1. DISCOGRAPHIES: *Gospel Discography*. DISCUSSION: Hawes gave the first stanza: "My favorite spiritual is: / I love the lord he hears my cry. / He pitied my groans. / Long as I live when trouble arise, / I'll hast'en to his throne" (William Hawes, b. 1864, KY, 326).

"I LOVE THY KINGDOM, LORD" (1800), Timothy Dwight (1752–1817). FIRST LINE: Tom Scott (mother's favorite song). OTHER SOURCES: *DNAH*.

"I THINK WHEN I READ THAT SWEET STORY OF OLD" (1841), Jemima Luke (1813–1906). TEXTS: Hannah Davidson. OTHER SOURCES: *DNAH*. DISCUSSION: Luke's piece is one of the most reprinted children's hymns in the English-speaking world. Davidson faithfully reproduced the first three verses, omitting the original's fourth, concluding stanza.

School? We never seen the inside of a schoolhouse. Mistress used to read the Bible to us every Sunday morning. We say two songs I still remember.

> I think when I read that sweet story of old,
> When Jesus was here among men,
> How he called little children like lambs to his fold,
> I should like to have been with them then.

> I wish that his hands had been placed on my
>   head,
> That his arms had been thrown around me,
> That I might have seen his kind face when he said,
> "Let the little ones come unto me."

> Yet still to his footstool in prayer I may go
> And ask for a share of his love,
> And that I might earnestly seek Him below
> And see Him and hear Him above. (Hannah
>   Davidson, b. 1852, KY, 29–30)

"I WANT TO BE AN ANGEL" (1845), Sidney P. Gill. TEXTS: Mary Colbert, Hannah Davidson, Rebecca Jane Grant, Georgia Telfair. OTHER SOURCES: *DNAH*. John Battle Avirett (1835–1912) recalled slave children on his family's North Carolina plantation singing this title. Avirett, *Plantation*, 139. For obscene parodies, see Randolph, *Roll Me*, 324. DISCUSSION: Gill, a Philadelphia infant school teacher, composed this piece as a memorial to one of her pupils. Colbert, Grant, and Davidson all remembered it from Sunday schools taught by slaveholders. Telfair gave no context. Telfair and Colbert gave the opening lines, Grant and

Davidson the first stanza (divided into two stanzas in Davidson's text).

I want to be an angel
And with the angels stand
With a crown upon my forehead
And a harp within my hand.

And there before my Saviour,
So glorious and so bright,
I'd make the sweetest music
And praise him day and night. (Hannah Davidson, b. 1852, KY, 30)

"I WOULD NOT LIVE ALWAY; I ASK NOT TO STAY" (ca. 1830), William Augustus Muhlenberg (1796–1877). TITLE/FIRST LINE: Patsy Hyde. OTHER SOURCES: *DNAH*; McDowell, *Camp*, 16; J. Thornton Randolph, *The Cabin and Parlor; Or, Slaves and Masters* (Philadelphia: T. B. Peterson, 1852), 305; Randolph, *OFS* IV: 68–69. DISCUSSION: Hyde listed this item with "Am I a Soldier of the Cross": "De songs I member ez: / I'se a Soldier ob de Cross. / Follow de Lamb. / I Would not Live Allus. / I Axe Not ter Stay" (Patsy Hyde, b. unk., TN, 34).

"IF I MUST DIE, O, LET ME DIE, WITH HOPE" (1794), Benjamin Beddome. TEXTS: James R. Sutton. OTHER SOURCES: *DNAH*. DISCUSSION: Sutton gave the entire second stanza followed by the opening lines of the first: "I remembers one song dey ust-a sing when I was a chile. It went like dis: 'Ef I mus' die—Oh let me die in peace wid all mankind; An' change my fleetin' joy below for pleasure more refined. Ef I must die, Oh let me die in hope in Jesus' blood. . . .' (Could not remember last line)" (James R. Sutton, b. 1866, NC, child of ex-slaves, 2081–82, orig. parentheses and ellipsis).

"I'M GLAD SALVATION'S FREE" (ca. 1810), Isaac Watts. TEXTS: Sara Crocker, Gus Feaster. TITLE: Charity Austin, Mary Veals, Olin Williams. OTHER SOURCES: *DNAH*. VIDEOS: Jesse Fuller, "I'm Glad Salvation's Free"/"Hark from the Tomb" (medley), video ca. 1970, *Masters of Bottleneck Blues Guitar*,

Vestapol DVD 13002, 2002; Mahalia Jackson, "I'm Glad Salvation Is Free" (Apollo 222, 1950). DISCOGRAPHIES: *Gospel Discography*. DISCUSSION: Austin mentioned this title in her account of turning the pot down, while Crocker remembered it at an Emancipation celebration. Williams associated it with baptisms, Feaster with his own born again experience.

"I'M PRESSING ON THE UPWARD WAY" (ca. 1900), Johnson Oatman (1856–1922). TITLE: James Augustus Holmes (from mother). OTHER SOURCES: *DNAH*. Although Holmes (b. 1843) described hearing this turn-of-the-century hymn in the antebellum period from his slave mother, he was obviously misremembering.

"IN EVIL LONG I TOOK DELIGHT" (1779), John Newton. TEXTS: Amy Chapman. OTHER SOURCES: *DNAH*. DISCUSSION: Chapman gave the first four stanzas of Newton's eight-stanza text with some changes. (Compare her first verse to Newton's original: "In evil long I took delight, / Unaw'd by shame or fear / Till a new object struck my sight, / And stopt my wild career.")

An' anudder one us niggers useter sing was mighty pretty:

In evil long I tuk de light
An' led by shame an' fear
When a new object stopped my flight
An' stopped my wild career.

I saw him hangin' on a tree
In agony an' blood
He fixed his languid eyes on me
As near his cross I stood.

Sho' never till my latter breath
Kin I forgit dat look
He seemed to change me wid his death
Yit not a word he spoke.

My conscience felt an' owned de guilt
An' plunged me in despair

I saw my sins his blood had spilt
An' helped to nail him dere. (Amy Chapman,
   b. 1843, AL, 59–60)

"IN MERCY, NOT IN WRATH, REBUKE ME, GRA-
CIOUS GOD!" (1779), John Newton. TEXTS: Dellie
Lewis. DISCUSSION: Lewis quoted Newton's hymn
to illustrate her faith, but did not specify where,
when, or from whom she learned it.

I is always been a 'piscopalian in belief, white folks.
I ma'ied Bill Lewis when I was fifteen year old in
Montgomery an' us had three chilluns. I is strong
in my faith.

In mercy, not in wrath,
   Rebuke me, gracious Lawd
Les' when Dy whole displeasure rise,
   I sink beneath Dy rod. (Dellie Lewis,
      b. unk., AL, 256–57)

"JESUS KEEP ME NEAR THE CROSS" (1869), Fanny
Crosby. TEXTS: W. E. Northcross. TITLE: Bud
Dixon. OTHER SOURCES: *DNAH*. RECORDINGS:
Prof. Alex Bradford and Singers, "Jesus Keep Me
Nearer the Cross" (Apollo 287, 1952); Rev. Cleophus
Robinson, "(Keep Me) Near the Cross," Chicago,
September 1963, *Someone to Care: The Battle Ses-
sions*, Specialty CD 7055, 1994. DISCUSSION: Dixon
named this postwar title from baptizings and funer-
als. Northcross recalled learning it from his mother.
"JESUS, LOVER OF MY SOUL" (1740), Charles
Wesley. TITLE: Sara Benton. OTHER SOURCES:
DNAH; Gainer, *West Virginia*, 205; Virginia Jo Hur-
dle and Herbert Halpert, "Folklore of a Negro Cou-
ple in Henry County," *Tennessee Folklore Society
Bulletin* 19 (1953): 78; *New Harp*, 65, 103. RECORD-
INGS: Uncle Dave Macon, "Jesus, Lover of My
Soul" (Vocalion 5316, 1928); Smith's Sacred Sing-
ers, "Jesus Lover Of My Soul" (Columbia 15593-D,
1930). DISCOGRAPHIES: *Country Music Records*;
Country Music Sources, 609. For Black parodies, see
White, *ANFS*, 133.

"JESUS MY ALL TO HEAV'N IS GONE" (1743), John
Cennick. TEXTS: Jerry Eubanks. TITLE: Aunt
Adeline, Aron Carter, Fannie Hughes, Anna Hum-
phrey, Mariah Snyder. OTHER SOURCES: Also
see *DNAH*; Barton, *Plantation Hymns*, 13; Bruce,
Hallelujah, 90; Fauset, "Folk Tales," 302; Jackson,
Another, 166; Jackson, *Down-East*, 237, 274–75;
Jackson, *Early*, 197–98, 204, 222, 228, 231–33, 239;
Jackson, *Sheaf*, 48, 50, 203; Jackson, *WNS*, 174,
222; Odum and Johnson, *Workaday*, 200; Taylor,
Revival Hymns, 243–44; *Sacred Harp*, 53, 88, 160,
324; *Social Harp*, 21, 28, 34, 47, 52, 56, 73, 79, 99, 102,
105, 108, 139; *Southern Harmony*, 11, 312, 326; Wyeth,
Sabre, 34. DISCUSSION: In the South this item
usually appears with an added chorus or otherwise
recomposed around spiritual commonplaces. The
version from ex-slave Jerry Eubanks is brief but typical, opening with Cennick's first two lines, adding
an original concluding couplet, then repeating the
second line. Eubanks, Humphrey, and Snyder gave
no contexts; Carter and Hughes named the song at
baptizings. "A colored preacher did the baptizin'.
When the shoutin' would quiet down a little they'd
sing 'Jesus an' I All to Heaven Are Goin' " (Fannie
Hughes, b. ca. 1854, GA, 331). Aunt Adeline recalled
singing the song as a child at play, with a make-
believe hymn book.

I can give you part of de verses of a song. One is dis.

   (1) Jesus My all to heaven is gone,
      Whom I place my hopes upon
      Den will I tell de sinner around
      What a dear Savior I'm found.

      ———

   (2) He whom I place my hopes upon

My mind ain't on it—Jes have to cut it out. (Jerry
Eubanks, b. 1846, MS, 692–93)

When my mother's master came to Arkansas
[from Tennessee] about 1849, looking for a country residence, he bought what was known as the

old Kidd place on the Old Wire Road, which was one of the Stage Coach stops. I was about one year old when we came. We had a big house and many times passengers would stay several days and wait for the next stage to come by. It was then that I earned my first money. I must have been about six or seven years old. One of Mr. Parks' daughters was about one and a half years older than I was. We had a play house in back of the fireplace chimney. We didn't have many toys; maybe a doll made of a corn cob, with a dress made of scraps and a head made from a roll of scraps. We were playing church. Miss Fannie was the preacher and I was the audience. We were singing "Jesus my all to Heaven is gone." When we were about half way through with our song we discovered that the passengers from the stage coach had stopped to listen. We were so frightened at our audience that we both ran. But we were coaxed to come back for a dime and sing our song over. I remember that Miss Fannie used a big leaf for a book. (Aunt Adeline, b. ca. 1848, AR, 11–12)

"THE LITTLE BOY'S SONG TO HIS MOTHER" (ca. 1857), Anon. TEXTS: Georgia Telfair. OTHER SOURCES: *DNAH*. DISCUSSION: Telfair quoted a single line from a song published anonymously under this title in various Sunday school songbooks, ca. 1857–59 (*DNAH*): "Little chillun wuz larnt to sing, 'How Sweetly do de Time Fly, When I Please My Mother,' an' us chillun' sho would do our best a singin' dat little old song, so Preacher Cobb would praise us" (Georgia Telfair, b. 1864, GA, 4).

"MUST JESUS BEAR THE CROSS ALONE" (1693), Thomas Shepherd (1665–1779). TEXTS: Mary Ferguson, Abram Harris, Eva Strayhorn, Annie Young. OTHER SOURCES: *DNAH*; Gainer, *West Virginia*, 204. RECORDINGS: Bells of Joy, "Must Jesus Bear the Cross Alone," *The Bells of Joys*, Checker LP 10001, 1959. DISCOGRAPHIES: *Country Music Sources*, 620; *Gospel Discography*. DISCUSSION: Ferguson gave the original's first and third stanzas, Strayhorn the first. Young gave the first stanza's opening line and the complete third verse. Abram

Harris's version has been recomposed. Strayhorn learned the song from whites at integrated camp meetings or Sunday services, Young at church. Ferguson and Harris did not specify contexts.

> Must Jesus bear the cross alone
>   and all the world go free?
> No, there is a cross for every one;
>   there's a cross for me;
> This consecrated cross I shall bear til
>   death shall set me free.
> And then go home, my crown to wear;
>   there is a crown for me. (Mary Ferguson,
>   b. ca. 1855, GA, 331)

> Mus Jesus bear de cross alone
> and all de worl go free?
> Oh Brother don't stay away
> Oh Backslider, don't stay away. (Abram Harris,
>   b. 1845, SC, 175)

"O FOR A FAITH THAT WILL NOT SHRINK" (1831), William Hiley Bathurst (1796–1877). TEXTS: Alice Hutcheson, Gussie Shelby. OTHER SOURCES: *DNAH*. DISCUSSION: Shelby somewhat reorders four out of five stanzas of Bathurst's original, while Hutcheson combined this item with Jane Taylor's "Death Has Been Here." The traditional sermons that Shelby names probably originated long after slavery, but they were preached in Black churches for decades, later appearing on commercial recordings. Especially popular was "Dry Bones in the Valley" (from Ezekiel 37), on which see Bruce A. Rosenberg, *The Art of the Folk Preacher* (New York: Oxford University Press, 1970), 28, 62–63, 200–208. RECORDINGS: Calvin P. Dixon (Black Billy Sunday), "Dry Bones in the Valley—Parts I & II" (Columbia 14089D, 1925); Rev. J. M. Gates, "Dry Bones in the Valley" (Victor 35810, 1926); Rev. Leora Ross, "Dry Bones in the Valley" (OKeh 8486, 1927). Psalms 91:2 (Shelby's favorite verse) reads "I say of the LORD, *He* is my refuge and my fortress: my God; in him will I trust."

My favorite verse in the Bible is Psalms, 91:2 verses. I say it every night before I go to bed and every morning when I wake up. My favorite hymn is:

> Oh for a faith that will not shrink
> Beneath the chastening rod,
> That will not murmur nor complain,
> But in the hour of grief and pain,
> Will lean upon its God,
> Its faith that keeps the narrow path,
> Till life's last hours are fled,
> And in the pure and heavenly ray,
> In illness and the dying bed,
> Lord give me such a faith as this,
> And then what er'e may come,
> Of thy eternal sun.

My favorite sermons are "Dry Bones in the Graveyard," and "And they played on the Harp of a Thousand Strings," and the "Spirits of Men were Made Perfect." (Gussie Shelby, b. 1865, MO, child of ex-slaves, 351–52)

"O FOR A THOUSAND TONGUES TO SING" (1739), Charles Wesley. TITLE/FIRST LINE: Leah Garrett, Solomon P. Pattillo, Charlie Powers. OTHER SOURCES: W. S. B. Mathews heard this hymn from slaves ca. 1862. "The Jubilee Slave-Songs," *New York Musical Gazette* 7 (October 1873): 147. Also see *DNAH*; Jackson, *Early*, 145; Jackson, *Sheaf*, 114, Jackson, *WNS*, 182; *New Harp*, 33; *Sacred Harp*, 88. RECORDINGS: Shirley Caesar, "O For a Thousand Tongues," *He's Working It Out For You*, Word/Epic CD 48785, 1991; Victory Chorale Ensemble, "O For a Thousand Tongues," *O For a Thousand Tongues*, Spire LP 5501, 1965. DISCOGRAPHIES: *Gospel Discography*. DISCUSSION: Slaveholders generally encouraged hymn singing, except those items conventionally likening *sin* and *salvation* to, respectively, *slavery* and *freedom*. "O For a Thousand Tongues" was one such title, its fourth stanza—"He breaks the power of cancelled sin, / he sets the prisoner free"—being especially

provocative. Pattillo quoted the first line ("Oh for a thousand tongues to sing my Great Redeemer's praise"), which he described at secret meetings (Solomon P. Pattillo, b. 1868, AR, child of ex-slaves, 294). Leah Garrett and Charlie Powers gave anecdotes incorporating this title.

De preachers always preached to de white folks first, den dey would preach to de slaves. Dey never said nothin' but you must be good, don't steal, don't talk back at your marsters, don't run away, don't do dis, don't do dat. Dey let de colored preachers preach but dey give 'em almanacs to preach out of. Dey didn't 'low us to sing such songs as "We Shall Be Free" and "O For a Thousand Tongues to Sing." Dey always had somebody to follow de slaves to church when de colored preacher was preachin' to hear what wuz said and done. Dey wuz 'fraid us would try to say something 'gainst 'em. (Leah Garrett, b. unk., MD, 15–16)

Another thing my grand pappy uster tell 'bout back in North Carolina wuz 'bout my grand mamy alwa's laked to sing an' shout an' praise de Lord. De white folks wouldn't 'low 'em to make much racket. Dey would come and quiet 'em off right now. So one day my grand mamy wuz a feelin' happy an' a singin' dat ole song "O Fer a Thousand Tongues." She wuz a singin' purty loud an grand pappy call out "yo has got one too many now, fer if you don't watch out yo' will make de white folks hear yo' wid de one ye got."

My grand parents say dat dey lived an' wuz raized up 'bout lak a bunch ob pigs, jes any ole way. Yo' might say jes' fed an' wuked an' slept, but dey wuz powerful strong an' lived to be mighty ole. (Charlie Powers, b. ca. 1851, MS, 1751)

"O HAPPY DAY, THAT FIXED MY CHOICE" (1755), Phillip Doddridge (1702–1751). TEXTS: Sarah Felder. TITLE: Elisha Doc Garey, Henry Green. OTHER SOURCES: *DNAH*. For other slave versions, see Albert, *Charlotte Brooks*, 37; Mathews, "Jubilee Slave-Songs," 148. DISCUSSION: From the time of its posthumous publication, Doddridge's piece was a popular English and American baptismal hymn. Felder and Garey both remembered it from postwar baptizings. Garey used the original title: "Oh, Happy Day dat Fixed My Choice." Felder gave the chorus. Arkansas fieldworker Watt McKinney reported that "Uncle Henry Green, an ex-slave ninety years of age, is affectionately known throughout a large part of Phillips County as 'Happy Day' . . . on account of his love for the old religious song 'Happy Day'" (Henry Green, b. 1848, AR, 90). This item remained popular in twentieth-century Black tradition. In 1969 Oakland's Edwin Hawkins Singers scored an international hit with a contemporary arrangement ("Oh Happy Day," Pavilion 20001). Also see DISCOGRAPHIES: *Gospel Discography*.

We bofe [she and her husband of fifty-nine years] jined de Baptist Church an' wus baptised at de same time. Dar wus a big crowd ter be baptized wid us an' wus rainin' but we wus all so happy dat we didnt keer one bit fur de rain; we jes kept singin an' sum uf dem shouted. We wus baptized in de creek. I 'member er song dat sung wus—

> O happy day, O, happy day!
> When Jesus wash'd our sin er way.
> He taught me how ter sing an' pray
> An' be rejoicin' ebery day,
> O, happy day, O, Happy Day!
> When Jesus wash'd my sin er way. (Sarah Felder,
> b. 1853, MS, 721–22)

"ON JORDAN'S STORMY BANKS I STAND" (1787), Samuel Stennett (1727–1795). TEXTS: Mary Frances Brown, Catherine Cornelius, Mary Edwards (TX), Henry Gibbs, Martha Jones, Oliver Jones, Jane Sutton, Neal Upson, Parson Rezin Williams. TITLE ("On Jordan's Stormy Banks I Stand"): Willis Bennefield, Clara Brim, Cicely Cawthon, Eli Coleman, Jake Compton, Parilee Daniels, William Davis, Ann Ulrich Evans, George Govan, Measy Hudson, Precilla Gray, Thomas Johns, Steve Johnson, Anna

Lee, John McAdams, Stephen McCray, Thomas McMillan, Harriet Miller, Patsy Moses, Grundy Patton, Rosa L. Pollard, Harriett Robinson, Hennie Ross, Polly Shine, Cordelia Thomas, Olin Williams. TITLE ("I Am Bound for the Promised Land"): Cicely Cawthon, Ellen Lindsey, Anna Mitchel, Lewis Mundy, Amanda Oliver, Mattie Stenston, Eva Strayhorn, Elias Thomas, Jane Thompson. OTHER SOURCES: *DNAH*. For other ex-slave examples, see Anon. ex-slave (b. unk., TN); Anon. ex-slave (b. unk., TN), *God Struck*, 17, 91; Anon. ex-slave (b. unk., TN), Anon. ex-slave (b. 1855, TN), *Unwritten History*, 47, 80; Aleckson, *Before the War*, 278; Green, *Life*, 51. Also see Asbury and Meyer, "Old-Time," 172; Ballanta, *St. Helena*, 36–37; Brown III: 629–30; Bruce, *Hallelujah*, 90, 103; Fauset, "Folk Tales," 302; Charles Hofmann, "Florida Folklore—Summer 1945," *JAF* 59 (1946): 68; Jackson, *Down-East*, 115–16, 235; Jackson, *Early*, 113, 230, 238; Jackson, *Spirituals*, 219–20; Jackson, *WNS*, 186, 208, 209; McDowell, *Camp*, 59; Lucy McKim, "Songs of the Port Royal Contrabands," *Dwight's* 21 (November 8, 1862): 255; *New Harp*, 26, 177; Randolph, *Ozark* IV: 62; *Sacred Harp*, 65, 117, 128, 302, 310, 378; *Social Harp*, 114, 166; Solomon, *Daisies*, 129; *Southern Harmony*, 51, 137, 253, 318; Thomas, *Devil's Ditties*, 39–43, 116–17. RECORDINGS: Sylvester "Deacon" Jones and group, "Bound for the Promised Land," New Zion Baptist Church, Knight Post Office, LA, May 17, 1939, Library of Congress Celebrates Songs of America. hdl.loc.gov.loc.afc.afcss39.2672a1; The Charioteers, "I'm Bound for the Promised Land" (Columbia 35787, 1945); Alfred G. Karnes, "I Am Bound for the Promised Land" (Victor 20840, 1927); The Seventh Day Adventist Choir, "On Jordan's Stormy Banks We Stand" (Columbia 14178-D, 1926); Turkey Mountain Singers, "I Am Bound for the Promised Land" (Victor 20942, 1927); Albertina Walker, "On Jordan's Stormy Banks I Stand," *Come By Here*, Gospel LP 3071, 1967; Clara Ward and the Famous Ward Singers, "On Jordan's Stormy Banks," *A Vision of Truth*, Nashboro LP 7103, 1971; Wright Brothers Gospel Singers, "Jordan's Stormy

Banks" (OKeh 05700, 1940); Hank Williams, "I Am Bound for the Promised Land" (1951 radio broadcast), *Live, Rare and Inspirational*, Readers Digest CDs SSTC07713, 2011. DISCOGRAPHIES: *Blues and Gospel Records*; *Country Music Records*; *Country Music Sources*, 614–15; *Gospel Discography*. DISCUSSION: This is another of the songs, sacred or secular, most often named by ex-slaves. Coleman, Compton, Daniels, Gibbs, Johns, Johnson, Lee, McAdams, McCray, Pollard, Robinson, Ross, Shine, Stenston, Thomas, Thompson, and Williams described the song at baptizings. Edwards described it in slave cabins; Miller and Evans in the fields; Davis, Oliver Jones, McMillan, Strayhorn, and Upson at church or meeting; Sutton at revivals; Patton and Thomas at harvest celebrations. Lindsey learned the song from her mother; Cawthon listed both titles among her "Mistis' favorite songs." Bennefield, Brim, Brown, Cornelius, Govan, Gray, Hudson, Martha Jones, Mitchel, Mundy, Oliver, and Williams did not specify contexts.

"THE POOL AT BETHESDA (BESIDE THE GOSPEL POOL)" (ca. 1780), John Newton. TITLE/FIRST LINE: Perry Sid Jemison. OTHER SOURCES: *DNAH*; Jackson, *Down-East*, 116; Jackson, *Sheaf*, 113; Rosenberg, *Virginia*, 6. DISCUSSION: Jemison recalled this item's first line: "I remember one of de baptizing. De men dat did it was Emanuel Sanders. Dis wuz de song dat dey sing: 'Beside de gospel pool, Appointed for de poor.' Dat is all I member of dat song now" (Perry Sid Jemison, b. ca. 1858, AL, 52).

"RETURN, O GOD OF LOVE, RETURN" (1707), Isaac Watts. TEXTS: Betty Massingale Bell. OTHER SOURCES: *DNAH*; *Sacred Harp*, 54; *Southern Harmony*, 72. DISCUSSION: Bell recalled three out of four stanzas of this Watts item, which she knew as "Georgia," its usual title in shape-note books (after the most common tune). Bell was literate.

I 'members, too, on a summer's night de slaves wud git together in de quarters an' sing altogether "Old Georgia." Dis song wuz sho' a pretty thing. . . .

OLD GEORGIA

Return, O god of love, return—
 Earth is a tir'sum place;
How long shall we, Thy chillun m'urn
 Our absence frum Thy face?

Let heaven succeed our painful years,
 Let sin an' sorro' cease;
An' in propo'tion tu our tears,
 So make our joys increase.

Thy wonders tu Thy servants sho',
 Make Thy own wuk complete;
Den shall our souls Thy glory kno',
 An' own Thy love wuz great. (Bettie
  Massingale Bell, b. ca. 1857, AL, 50–51)

"ROCK OF AGES" (1776), Augustus Toplady (1740–1778). TITLE: Cornelius Garner, Anna Lee, Aaron Pinnacle, Mollie Watson. OTHER SOURCES: *DNAH*; Brown III: 605; Gainer, *West Virginia*, 202; Kennedy, *Mellows*, 90; White, *ANFS*, 89–90. DISCUSSION: Watson recalled this title from a slaveholder, Lee at camp meetings; Garner and Pinnacle gave no contexts.

"SHALL WE GATHER AT THE RIVER" (1864), Robert Lowry (1826–1899). TITLE: Bill Reese (joining church). OTHER SOURCES: *DNAH*.

"SHOW PITY, LORD, O LORD FORGIVE" (ca. 1740), Isaac Watts. TEXTS: H. B. Holloway, Lu Lee, Henry Ryan. TITLE: Chana Littlejohn. OTHER SOURCES: For a period example, see Schoolcraft, *Gauntlet*, 85. Also see *DNAH*; Jackson, *Sheaf*, 157; McDowell, *Camp*, 56; Randolph, *OFS* IV: 70–71; *Sacred Harp*, 73; *Social Harp*, 33, 189; *Southern Harmony* 172. RECORDINGS: Biddleville Quintette, "Show Pity Lord" (Paramount 12424, 1926). DISCUSSION: Henry Ryan performed the first stanza with the first line of the third stanza; Holloway and Littlejohn quoted this item in folktales. Lee gave a recomposed version of the first stanza:

We didn't ever hear no preachin' in the place a'tall. But we used to have prayings in the different cabins. They sang at the prayings. I never did perfess religion though, 'til I was 'bout eighteen year old. They used to sing "Amazing Grace" and a real pretty tune called "Pity Lord."

> Show pity Lord
> Oh Lord forgive.
> Show pity Lord
> Oh Lord forgive.
> And let every penitent sinner live.

We didn't know nothing 'bout Sundays 'cept that was the day the niggers didn't go to the fields and we washed and ironed our clothes—leastways the old women did. (Lu Lee, b. 1848 or 1849, TX, 2296–97)

We didn't learn to read and write; but we had a prayer house on de plantation where we could go to sometimes, until freedom come, then we went on to it just the same. Old man Bennefield, a nigger preacher, talked to us there. I can 'member one of de favorite songs we sung:

> Show pity, O Lord, forgive,
> Let e'er repentant sinner live;
> Are not they mercies large and free,
> May not a sinner trust in Thee.
>
> My crimes are great, and can't surpass. (Henry Ryan, b. ca. 1854, SC, 72)

I used to see Niggers in Georgia share cropping. Nigger work all the year. Christmas eve night they would be going back to the plantation singing—done lost everything—sitting on the wagon singing:

> Sho' pity Lawd forgive
> That a r'pentant rebel live.

Then they would have to get clothes and food against the next year's crop. Then you'd see 'em on the wagon again driving back to the plantation loaded down with provisions, singing:

> Lawd revive us agin
> All our increase comes from thee. (H. B. Holloway, b. 1849, GA, 297) (For the second stanza, see Jackson, *WNS*, 323.)

When de overseer whupped one o' de niggers he made all de slaves sing, "Sho' pity Lawd, Oh! Lawd forgive!" When dey sang awhile he would call out one an' whup him. He had a sing fur everyone he whupped. Marster growed up wid de niggers an' he did not like to whup 'em. If dey sassed him he would put spit in their eyes and say "now I recon you will mind how you sass me." (Chana Littlejohn, b. ca. 1857, NC, 56–57)

"THERE IS A FOUNTAIN FILLED WITH BLOOD" (1772), William Cowper (1731–1800). TITLE: Ellen Payne, John Sneed, Ned Walker, Aleck Woodward. OTHER SOURCES: *DNAH*; *New Harp*, 64; *Sacred Harp*, 368. RECORDINGS: Kings of Harmony Quartette, "Fountain of Blood" (King Solomon 1001, 1943); Five Blind Boys of Alabama, "There Is a Fountain" (Specialty 876, 1955); Aretha Franklin, "There Is a Fountain Filled with Blood," New Bethel Baptist Church, Detroit, 1956, *You Grow Closer*, MCA CD 1108, 1998. DISCOGRAPHIES: *Blues and Gospel Records*; *Country Music Records*; *Country Music Sources*, 611–12; *Gospel Discography*. DISCUSSION: Payne, Sneed, and Woodward named this piece from church, Walker from funerals.

"TRY US, O GOD, AND SEARCH THE GROUND" (1742), Charles Wesley. TEXTS: Ben Horry. OTHER SOURCES: *DNAH*. DISCUSSION: Ex-slaves constantly insisted that their religious songs and singing were inspired by divine visions. Ben Horry provided one fascinating example with his version of another Wesley perennial. (Though well represented in American hymnals, it is not especially common in oral tradition.)

Religion? Reckon Stella got the morest of it. I sometimes a little quick. Stella, she holds one course. I like good song. One I like best?

Try us, Oh Lord,
And search the ground
Of every sinful heart! (Uncle Ben stopped to think).
What 'eer of sin
In us be found
Oh, bid it all depart!

Reason I choose that for a favorite hymn, I was to Brookgreen doing some work for Dr. Wardie Flagg and I had to climb as high as that live oak tree, and I feel high as that tree! I lay there till I doze off in sleep. And I tell you what happen to me curious. While I was sleep I seen two milk white chickens. You know what them two white fowl do? They gone and sit on my mother dresser right before the glass and sing that song. Them COULD sing! And it seem like a woman open a vial and pour something on me. My spiritual mother (in dem day every member in the church have what they call a spiritual mother) say, "That not natural fowl. That sent you for a token." Since that time I serve the choir five or six years and no song seem strange to me since that day. God ain't ax about you color; God ax about you heart. (Ben Horry, b. ca. 1850, SC, 313–14, orig. parentheses)

"THE UNDERGROUND RAIL CAR, OR, SONG OF THE FUGITIVE" (1854), George N. Allen (1812–1877). TEXTS: Parson Rezon Williams. OTHER SOURCES: Sarah H. Bradford, *Scenes in the Life of Harriet Tubman* (Auburn, NY: W. J. Moses, 1869), 32–33; J. D. Green, *Narrative of the Life of J. D. Green* (Huddlesfield: Henry Fielding, 1864), 12. DISCUSSION: Though not a hymn in the strictest sense, Allen's homily, which besides sheet music and broadsides turns up in various antislavery publications, definitely borrows the Protestant hymn's style and diction. The original

was dedicated "To Fred. Douglass Esq.," America's most famous fugitive slave.

Still another favorite of "Parson" Williams, which he composed on Col. Bowie's plantation just before the Civil War, a sort of rallying song expressing what Canada meant to the slaves at that time, runs thus:

I'm now embarked for yonder shore
There a man's a man by law;
The iron horse will bear me O'er
To shake de lion's paw,
Oh, righteous Father, will thou not pity me
And aid me on to Canada, where all the slaves are free.

Oh, I heard Queen Victoria say
That if we would forsake Our native land of slavery,
And come across de lake
Dat she was standin' on de shore
Wid arms extended wide,
To give us all a peaceful home
Beyond de rollin' tide. (Parson Rezin Williams, b. 1822, MD, 72–73)

"WE SHALL SLEEP BUT NOT FOREVER" (1878), Mary A. Kidder. TITLE: James Augustus Holmes (from mother). OTHER SOURCES: *DNAH*. Like the other songs Holmes (b. 1843) attributed to his slave mother, this was a postwar composition; possibly he was remembering a similar antebellum song.

"WHEN I CAN READ MY TITLE CLEAR" (1707), Isaac Watts. TEXT: Simon Hare, Levi Pollard, Rube Witt. TITLE/FIRST LINE: Frank L. Adams, Anne Bell, Clara Brim, Belle Caruthers, Wade Glenn, Eva Strayhorn, John Thompson. OTHER SOURCES: For other slave versions, see Richard Allen (1760–1831), *Collection of Hymns*, 33; William Wells Brown (1814–1884), *Clotel; Or, the President's Daughter* (London: Partridge & Oakey, 1853), 98; Coppin (1848–?), *History*, 23; Lowery (1850–?), *Plantation*, 208; Levin Tilmon (1807–1863), *A Brief*

Miscellaneous Narrative of the More Early Part of the Life of L. Tilmon (Jersey City: W. W. & L. A. Pratt, 1853), 90. Also see *DNAH*; *Colored Harp*, 37–38; Gilman, *Recollections*, 122; Jackson, *Another*, 16, 54, 89, 103, 15; Jackson, *Down-East*, 123, 283; Jackson, *Early*, 227; Jackson, *WNS*, 218; Kilham, "Sketches. Fourth," 306; McDowell, *Camp*, 65; *Sacred Harp*, 47; *Social Harp*, 24, 45, 50, 115, 121; Randolph, *Cabin and Parlor*, 303; Solomon, *Daisies*, 134; "Songs of the Blacks," 52; Joseph Sturge, *A Visit to the United States in 1841* (London: Hamilton, Adams, 1842), xlii–xliii; *Southern Harmony*, 27, 104, 250, 293; Rev. E. W. Warren, *Nellie Norton; Or, Southern Slavery and the Bible* (Macon, GA: Burke, Boykin, 1864), 21–22; Wilson, "Old Plantation—I," 122. RECORDINGS: Rev. J. B. Crocker (The Singing Preacher), "When I Can Read My Title Clear" (King 4350, 1950); John and Lovie Griffins, "When I Can Read My Title Clear," field rec., Perry Co., AL, April 1954, *Music From the South Vol. 7: Elder Songsters No. 2*, Folkways LP 2656; Vera Hall and Dock Reed, "When I Can Read My Title Clear," field rec., Livingston, AL, May 27, 1939, Library of Congress Celebrates Songs of America. hdl.loc.gov.loc.afc .afcss39.2686a2; Rev. Cleophus Robinson, "When I Can Read My Title Clear" (Peacock 1719, 1953). DISCOGRAPHIES: *Blues and Gospel Records*; *Country Music Records*; *Country Music Sources*, 607; *Gospel Discography*. DISCUSSION: This is yet another Watts title well documented among slaves from an early date. Ex-slave Belle Caruthers recalled it from a hymn book, Brim from church, Strayhorn from white camp meetings and churches, Hare and Pollard from Sunday school, Witt from baptizings. Glenn had heard his mother sing it as a spinning song; Thompson named it as his mother's favorite song. The version performed by Rube Witt, his wife, and their friend Deacon Wilson features the three stanzas included in the *Sacred Harp* and most other shape-note books, although their third stanza is significantly rearranged.

I was baptized in 1868 by a colored preacher, in a creek. I don't believe in these pools like they have in churches now. Religion ain't what it was when I was a boy . . . there's too much style now. I 'members when we had preaching and baptizing down by the side of the creek. My favorite song went like this: (Rube and his wife and Deacon Wilson all sing)

> When I can read my title clear
> To mansions in the sky
> I'll bid farewell to every fear
> And wipe my weeping eye.
> Should earth against my soul engage,
> And fiery darts be hurled;
> Then I can smile at Satan's rage,
> And face a frowning world.
> So if I but safely reach my home.
> My heaven, my God, My all
> Not a wave of trouble shall roll
> Over my peaceful soul. (Rube Witt, b. 1850, TX, 4263, orig. parentheses)

"WHY DO WE MOURN DEPARTING FRIENDS" (1707), Isaac Watts. TITLE: Jefferson Franklin Henry. OTHER SOURCES: *DNAH*; Jackson, *Down-East*, 129; Jackson, *Early*, 157; Gilman, *Recollections*, 83; Washington, "Funeral," 243. DISCUSSION: This is another of Watts's funeral selections. Ex-slave Jefferson Franklin Henry recalled it at funerals, with "And Am I Born To Die." Authors Caroline Gilman and Ella Washington also heard it at Black funerals, both in South Carolina, Gilman in 1838, Washington in 1871.

"WHY DO YOU WAIT, DEAR BROTHER" (ca. 1870), George F. Root (1820–1895). TEXTS: Tom McGruder. OTHER SOURCES: *DNAH*. DISCUSSION: McGruder gave the first stanza. "Why do you wait, dear brother, / Oh, why do you tarry so long? / Your Saviour is waiting to give you / A place in His sanctified throng" (Tom McGruder, b. unk., TN, 77).

SPIRITUALS

The favorite song in camp was the following,—sung with no accompaniment but the measured clapping of hands and the clatter of many feet. It was sung perhaps twice as often as any other. That was partly due to the fact that it properly consisted of a chorus alone, with which the verses of other songs might be combined at random.

I. HOLD YOUR LIGHT

"Hold your light, Brudder Robert,—
    Hold your light,
Hold your light on Canaan's shore.

"What make ole Satan follow me so?
Satan ain't got nothin' for do wid me.
    Hold your light,
    Hold your light,
Hold your light on Canaan's shore."

This would be sung for half an hour at a time, perhaps, each person present being named in turn. (Thomas Wentworth Higginson [1823–1911], Colonel, First South Carolina Colored Union Volunteers, "Negro Spirituals" [1867], 685)[1]

FUNERAL SONG

Star in de east en star in de west,
I wish de star was in my breast.
Mother is home, sweet home,
Mother is home, sweet home,
Want to join de angel here.
What a blessed home, sweet home,
What a blessed home, sweet home,

385

Want to join de angel here.
(You can sing bout father, brother, sister en all.)
(Sylvia Cannon, b. ca. 1857, SC, 195, orig. parentheses)

The "Art" of Singing

"Singin'," says "Aunt" Callie, "ain't knowin' lines an' words, but bein' able to care (carry) a chune (tune). I has sung all my life—dat is, up n'til my husbant died two yayers (years) ago," she continued, "but ain't never knewed by heart hardly none o' de songs I has sung. 'Cose, cullud fokes don't have to have no words an' lines to sing by; all dey needs to do is to learn de chune an' dey makes souns for words. Furrer moe, if a cullud pusson raley wants to sing, an' raley kin sing, all he gotta do is open his mouth and a song jes' nachally drops out." (Callie Chatman, b. 1851, GA, 195, orig. parentheses)

For ex-slaves, spirituals were the antithesis of white hymns sung rote from songbooks in segregated churches.[2] Instead, spirituals were divinely inspired and spontaneously composed, preferably well beyond the bounds of slaveholders' religious and social restrictions. Their mysteries were by custom concealed from infidels, rendered indecipherable by turning the pot down. They in turn inspired shouting, testifying, and holy visions. They were performed at worship, at work and play, and in private reveries; at meeting, in the fields, within the family and home, and in personal solitude; at times of greatest joy and direst sorrow, trial, and tribulation. They were the deepest reservoir of Black resolve, resilience, and resistance.

This was the ideal, anyway. In reality, whites also sang spirituals and shouted, and many of the spirituals slaves sang were well known to slaveholders; many were of white origin, appearing in songbooks alongside Anglo-American hymns. Then too, slaves often based their spirituals on textual or melodic ideas borrowed from white sources. Some ex-slaves even mistook their adaptations of formally composed white hymns for Black creations, though some had been so thoroughly recomposed that they practically were. Nor did slaves completely conceal their own sacred songs from slaveholders. In fact, many WPA narrators described gladly singing their spirituals for or with their captors in true Christian fellowship, even in the most hellish convocations imaginable.

Yet allowing all this, ex-slaves also insisted that true spirituals were, in origin and essence, African American, proceeding not from the invariant printed texts of formally preconceived compositions, but from divine revelations spontaneously recounted. "Spiritual songs dey come through visions. Dat's why de cullud folks kin mek dem and sing dem better dan de w'ite folks" (Jacob Branch, b. ca. 1851, TX, 411). "It looked lak de songs in them days was revealed to the folks. A lot of times they didn't need no song book to help them along" (Sam Meredith Mason, b. 1858, TX, 2600). "We didn't have no song books, the Lord give us our songs" (Anderson Edwards, b. 1844, TX, 1262). "God jes' give me song en words. I sho b'lieve en dat ole song, 'Where You Go I'll Go With You; Open Your Mouth en I'll Speak Fer You,' kaze dat's what He's done fer me. I'se been all roun' dese parts preachin' God's words" (Lucy Ann Warfield, b. ca. 1824, KY, 456). "I takes de white chillun to church sometime, but dey couldn't learn me to sing no songs 'cause I didn' have no spirit" (Sarah Ashley, b. 1844, TX, 35).

These were far from anecdotal asides: the narratives and similar sources abound in compositions inspired by visions, dreams, spirit possessions, illnesses, and other extraordinary states.

Aunt Reiny Thatcher, another old negro, who lived to be 119 years old (I saw her when she was 110 years old and she lived 9 years after that) said when she had her "experience" that the angels came right out of heaven and taught her the words and tune to this spiritual. "She taught it to my mother who taught it to me," says Mrs. Merrill. She would say, "oh Elvira, I saw them angels with these old eyes a'mine, and ah could hear them jest as plain":

One day, one day,
Old Satan went abroad
And so my soul flew to God
Glory be to King Immanuel
To my King Immanuel
To my King Immanuel,
Glory be to King Immanuel
Old Satan went a howling
Just like a howling dog,
Glory be to my King Immanuel.

And old Satan sure did howl when he found he couldn't have my spirit no more. Another colored ladies' experience song went like this:

All around my house was walled with brick
And in the middle was steel
King Jesus arose and fought in blood,
And conquered till he fell.
Ah'm gwine to Glory, hallelujah!
Oh, praise ye my Lord,
Ah'm gwine to Glory, hallelujah!
Love and serve the Lord. (Sarah Emery
    Merrill, b. unk., KY, child of ex-slaves,
    127–28)

'Member vision I had after I got 'ligion. Was lyin' in bed fas' asleep. Ole Ship of Zion was comin' 'long loaded up wid de pretties angels all dressed in white an' dey jes' a-singin':

O sister have you got yo' counts conceal?
No man can hinder!

I had my counts conceal befo' I lef de fiel,
No man can hinder!

Ride on conquerin' king,
No man can hinder!

Lawd! When dat ship come pass me, I jumped an' tried for to git on it, an' when I come to, I had fell in de flo' an' most bust dis hip open. Ain' been

able to use dis side much since. (Nancy Williams, b. 1847, NC, 321)[3]

I hab a beautiful slumbering sleep las' night. Dat's when you trabble (travel) wid God or wid Satan. I trabble wid God when dat slumber come on me— jes' 'bout half way sleep. Las' night I walk an' I talk wid de Lord, an' I nebber see befo' how dat music did swell up an' down, high an' low an' de angel in dem beautiful robe wid de gold tags hanging 'bout dem. I nebber see sech a sight. O! I know de Lord go hab mercy on me till I git dere. He ain't gwine left me out. We all is go be like, all white togedder, all talk 'like. No mo' slight, no mo' scorn, no mo' driving. O Jesus! I jes' waitin' to jine in wid you all up dere an' let me boice (voice) he'p swell dat sweet music I hear.

On dat shore will I rest
My weary soul on thy breast,
On thy breast, on thy breast,
On dat shore will I rest. . . . (Ophelia Jemison,
    b. ca. 1868, SC, child of ex-slaves, 215, orig.
    parentheses and ellipsis)

Yuh know dere spirituals hymns en dere reels. I e'n sing one uv dem dat I use'er sing in my slumberin' hours. It go lak dis:

Chillun, wha' yuh gwinna do in de jedgment
    mornin'?
Chillun, wha' yuh gwinna do in de jedgment
    mornin'?
Oh Chillun, wha' yuh gwinna do in de jedgment
    mornin'
When ole Gable [Gabriel] go down on de
    seashore?

He gwinna place one foot in de sea
En de other on de land,
En declare tha' time would be no more,
Chillun, wha' yuh gwinna do? [repeat both
    verses]

Now de angels sing dat to me in my slumberin' hour en dey sing it dat I might gi'e it to de libin' heah on dis earth. Well, I know right smart uv dem song cause accordin' to my 'sperience, de hymn book wha' to fence de human family in. I got uh good set uv lungs en I wuz de one lead de flock den. Dere jes one grand reason why I can' sing right well dis a'ternoon, yuh is take me on de surprise lak. (Washington Dozier [Dosier], b. 1847, SC, 332)

Concerning ex-slave Mary Gladdy, interviewer J. R. Jones wrote: "she is a Seventh Day Adventist; is not a psychic, but is a rather mysterious personage."

For more than thirty years, the Lord has been revealing his work, and many other things, to Mary Gladdy. For more than twenty years, she has been experiencing "visitations of the spirit." These do not occur with any degree of regularity, but they do always occur in "the dead hours of the night" after she has retired, and impel her to rise and write in an unknown hand. These strange writings of hers now cover eight pages of letter paper and bear a marked resemblance to crude shorthand notes. Offhand, she can "cipher" (interpret or translate) about half of these strange writings; the other half, however, she can make neither heads nor tails of except when the spirit is upon her. When the spirit eases off, she again becomes totally ignorant of the significance of that mysterious half of her spirit directed writing. (Mary Gladdy, b. ca. 1853, GA, 18–19, orig. parentheses)

Jones does not communicate any of Gladdy's spirit writings, but he did take down three of her wonderfully original spirituals, "The Gospel Train," "My Sister, I Feels 'Im," and "Keep the Fire Burning While Your Soul's Fired Up."

Fire, fire, O, keep the fire burning while your soul's
    fired up,
O, keep the fire burning while your soul's fired up;

Never mind what satan says while your soul's
    fired up,
You ain't going to learn how to watch and pray.
Less you keep the fire burning while your soul's
    fired up.

Old satan is a liar and a cunjorer, too;
If you don't mind, he'll cunjor you;
Keep the fire burning while your *soul's fired up.*
Never mind what satan says while your soul's
    fired up. (Mary Gladdy, b. ca. 1853, GA, 24,
    orig. emphasis)

The second stanza's opening lines—"Old satan is a liar and a cunjorer, too; / If you don't mind, he'll cunjor you"—are among the most popular of all wandering spiritual commonplaces.[4] Otherwise this particular item appears unique to Gladdy and her mystical outlook. Gladdy's song may be unique, but her example is not. Journalist Edward King (1848–1896) observed spiritual making in 1870s Virginia:

The improvisations are in some cases remarkable. A student at the Hampton Normal School has given to the public a long rhapsody on the judgment day, improvised by an old slave who was densely ignorant, but who embodied his dreams in song, as follows:

I'm a gwine to tell yo' bout de comin of
    de Savior,
        Far' you well, Far' you well;
Dar's a better day a comin',
        Far' you well, Far' you well;
When my Lord speaks to his Fader,
        Far' you well, Far' you well;
Says Fader, I'm tired of bearin',
        Far' you well, Far' you well;
Tired o' bearin' for pore sinners,
        Far' you well, Far' you well;
Oh! preachers, fold your Bibles,
        Far' you well, Far' you well;
Prayer makers, pray no more,

Far' you well, Far' you well;
For de last soul's converted,
Far' you well, Far' you well;
In dat great gittin'-up mornin',
Far' you well, Far' you well.[5]

Even under less mysterious circumstances, ex-slaves constantly describe extemporaneous composition, which they regarded as a distinctly Black practice. "We didn't hab no song books nor couldn't read if we had 'em, we sorter made 'em up 'long as us went" (Steve Weathersby, b. ca. 1856, MS, 2247). "In de evening when de work was done we would sit 'round and play marbles and sing songs. We made our songs up as we went along" (William Black, b. ca. 1850, MO, 32). "We made up our own tales an' songs. Some ob 'em wuz purty too sung out in de fiel' or in de moon lit 'round de cabins" (Albert Cox, b. ca. 1851, MS, 515). "Niggers jes' makes dey own verses, jes' naturally comes to us, an' we make our own rhyme as we go" (Filmore Taylor Hancock, b. 1851, MO, 188). "Dey mos' always made 'em up as dey go an' singing 'em lack niggers do" (Julia Cox, b. 1850, MS, 520).[6]

Moreover, these improvisations did not proceed solely from otherworldly visions, divine inspiration, or spirit possession but rather relied on far more practical methods and means enabling singers to create or recreate spiritual texts in the moment, in ways both large and small. Far from merely describing this spontaneous songmaking, ex-slaves appear to have improvised dozens of spirituals, at least in part, at their interviews.

That alone indicates that the spirituals that slaves knew differed fundamentally from the Negro spiritual as now known to the world. Few genres of folksong are presently more famous, nor more closely associated with North American slavery, but today's familiar titles and arrangements—"Swing Low, Sweet Chariot," "Didn't It Rain," "Down By the Riverside," "Sometimes I Feel Like a Motherless Child"—come not from nineteenth-century oral tradition but from Black collegiate choirs, popular songbooks, concert singers, jubilee quartets, the Civil Rights movement, and the urban folksong revival. Granted, many currently familiar items were known to slaves—or at least to their children and grandchildren—but not always as well known as now, and some of the best-known examples actually originated decades after slavery's abolition. Nor did these titles necessarily denote the same songs as today; to the contrary, the idea of spirituals as fixed, repeatable songs identified by specific titles was generally foreign to nineteenth-century Black folksingers.

Yet while slaves seldom performed a given spiritual the same way twice, they seldom created it completely anew. There is no mistaking the folk spiritual's incredibly repetitive, formulaic manner of expression, reiterating a handful of themes with a remarkable economy of language and imagery. This stylization served as a mnemonic aid but also as a generative grammar or native idiom of sorts, enabling fluent tradition bearers to produce spiritual texts even on the spot.

If spirituals are visionary, their visions are first and foremost millennial, in fact fully apocalyptic. "John saw the number in the middle of the air, / The number counted 144,000 and then it couldn't be counted" (Frances Lewis, b. 1854, GA, 158). "W'en Gabriel mek his las' alarm, / I want to be rollin' in Jesus' arm', / Becase I don' wanter stay yere no longer" (Lorenza Ezell, b. 1850, SC, 1320). "The greatest day I ever saw / Angels weep over Zion's hill / Now your troubles soon be over / And get your Jesus / And hold him fast" (John Crawford, b. 1837, MS, 976–77).

Spirituals ever and always anticipate that Last Day, the reunion of the righteous, and the sinner's final doom. "I will meet my Massa Jesus, / O Glory Hallelujah! Hallelujah!" (Mary Frances Brown, b. 1859, SC, 88). "The wind blows east and the wind blows west, / It blows like Judgment Day. / And all them sinners who never have cried, / Will surely cry that day" (Estella Jones, b. ca. 1855, GA, 349). "Mother where shall I meet you, / Bye and bye, bye and bye. / I will meet you over in Canaan" (Mary Frances Brown, b. 1859, SC, 87). "My ol' gray headed mudder, / You t'ink you mighty gran', / You ain' fitten t' face yo' God, / You ain' fitten fo' t' die" (Delia Barclay, b. unk., TX, 158). "But I'll meet my mothah and fathah dar, / To walk in Jaruselum, jes like John" (Lizzie Williams, b. ca. 1847, AL, 395). "My fat-h-er id-l-ed his t-i-me aw-a-y, / An' went do-w-n to he-l-l!" (Charley Stewart, b. 1852, AL, 2046). "Too late, sinner, too late, the train's done gone; / Never seen the like since I've been born" (Mary Gladdy, b. ca. 1853, GA, 25–26). "I may be blind, and I can not see, I may be crippled and I can not walk, / But I'll meet you at the Station when the train comes along" (Mintie Gilbert Wood, b. 1847, TN, 377).

Of course, *meeting* presupposes leaving and going away. "I'm sorry I'm gwine to lebe you, / Farewell, oh farewell / But I'll meet you in de mornin / Farewell, oh farewell" (Parson Rezin Williams, b. 1822, MD, 72). "I'm a-goin' home, I'm a-goin' home, I'm a-goin' home, / To die no more. / Glory—Glory—Hallelujah!" (Mary Frances Brown, b. 1859, SC, 89). "Hold out true believer, hold out 'till the last day, / Hold out 'till Jesus call me; / Take up my cross, I'm a-goin' home" (Affie Singleton, b. ca. 1849, SC, 283). "Praying time will soon be over, / I'm going to live with Jesus—after while" (Rev. W. B. Allen, b. ca. 1850, AL, 9).[7] "I'm goin' away, I'm goin' away, / I'm goin' away to live forever, / I'll never turn back no mo'" (Mary Ella Grandberry, b. ca. 1845, AL, 161). "I'm going, / I'm going, / I'm going away to the city, / I'm going, / I'm going away out of sight, / 'Cause my Jesus calls me, / Calls me for to come to him" (Lu Perkins, b. ca. 1850, MS, 3057).

And that departure entails a terrifying passage and doleful pilgrimage.

> Jesus listening all de day long to hear some sinner
> pray.
> De winding sheet to wrop (wrap) dis body in,
> De coffin to hold you fast;
> Pass through death's iron do'.
> Come ye dat love de Lawd and let your joy be know'd;
> Dis iron gate you must pass through, if you gwine
> to be born agin. (George Briggs, b. 1849, SC, 86,
> orig. parentheses)[8]

If the Black folk spiritual's underlying tone is apocalyptic, its overarching narrative is the pilgrimage to that End Time. Ready for Judgment, seeking personal salvation and family reunion, lonely pilgrims journey ceaselessly through a landscape of Biblical proportions and plainspoken symbolism: bidding farewell, leaving, going away, crossing over, passing through, moving along, climbing higher, traveling on, never turning back, till finally they meet in Heaven. Mountains and hills are obstacles but also ascents. "'Cause I reach over Zion's Hill. / 'Cause I'm been done with all things here. / Sisters wont you please help me bear my cross / Up over Zion's hill-l-l-l" (Mose Hursey, b. ca. 1855, LA, 1833). "Peter spied the promised land / On the hill of Cavalry / The Great Jehovah spoke / Sanctify to God upon the hill" (Abbie Lindsay, b. 1856, LA, 258). Valleys are depressions but also refuges. "I was low down in the valley, / When I first found the Lord" (Fannie Gibson, b. ca. 1850, AL, 147). "Went down into the valley to watch and pray, / My soul got happy and I stayed all day" (Mary Gladdy, b. ca. 1853, GA, 25). Rivers and seas are the source and boundary of eternal life, which awaits over on the other bank or shore. "Down to de water, River of Jordon; Dere my Savior was baptized. . . . / Come along, come along, my dear loving brother. / Come along and let's go home. / Down into de River where my Savior was baptized" (Caroline Farrow, b. ca. 1857, SC, 40–41).[9] "I'm gonna lay down my burden, down by the river side, / Ain't gonna study war no more" (Phannie Corneal, b. 1864, MO, 313). "If you don't 'lieve I's a chile of Gawd, / Jis' meet me on dat other shore" (Henry Lewis, b. 1831, TX, 9–10).

The trials and tribulations of those who hold to the gospel road metaphorically suggest or even bodily summon Biblical parallels: Jesus, Moses, Satan, et al. "I'll go, I'll go if it's raining, / I'll go, I'll go if it's stormy, / I'll go, King Jesus is my Captain, / And He's gone on befo'" (Frances Lewis, b. 1854, GA, 157). "Oh Chillun, wha' yuh gwinna do in de jedgment mornin' / When ole Gable [Gabriel] go down on de seashore? / He gwinna place one foot in de sea / En de other on de land, / En declare tha' time would be no more" (Washington Dozier or Dosier, b. 1847, SC,

Fig. 16.1. Mose Hursey, ex-slave, Dallas, December 1, 1937. "I heard them git up with a powerful force of spirit clapping hands and walking 'round the place. They shout 'I got the glory.' 'I got that old time religion in my heart.' I seen some powerful figurations of the spirit in them days" (Mose Hursey, b. ca. 1855, LA, TX, 1833). Portraits of African American ex-slaves from the US Works Progress Administration, Federal Writers' Project slave narratives collection, Library of Congress.

332). "David, David is a 'bediant young boy, / He kilt Goliah, and shouted fer joy. / God, gimme rashions from on high! (very high pitch) / Dats gon-na last me till—I—die" (Jane Sutton, b. ca. 1853, MS, 2091, orig. parentheses). "If I could, I surely would; Set on the rock where Moses stood—first verse or stanza. All of my sins been taken away, taken away—chorus" (Sarah Pittman, b. ca. 1855, LA, 353).[10] "De rough rocky road w'at Moses done trabble, / I's boun' to carry my soul to the Lawd. / It's a mighty rocky road but I 'mos' done trabble it" (Lorenza Ezell, b. ca. 1850, SC, 1320).[11] "Old Satan mighty busy; / He rolls rocks in my way. / King Jesus mighty good friend, / Like bosom friend; / He rolls them out of my way. / Free me, Lord; / Free me, Lord; / Walking in the Heaven's highway. / Oh, free me, Lord, / Free me, Lord" (Lu Perkins, b. ca. 1850, MS, 3057–58).[12]

Still, true believers are bound to travel on if only an inch at a time.

Inching Along

(Chorus)

I'm inchin' along, inchin' along,
Jesus is comin' bye and bye,
Like de po' lowly worm,
I'm inchin' along,
Jesus is comin' bye and bye. . . .

I went on de wall to repent and pray,
Jesus is comin' bye and bye.
And I know my sin must be washed away,
Jesus is comin' bye and bye.

(Repeat Chorus)
When I got dere, old Satan dere, but
Jesus is comin' bye and bye.
He say to me, "You too young for prayer."
Jesus is comin' bye and bye.

Den I heard a voice I could not see,
Jesus is comin' bye and bye.
My sin's forgiven, my soul's set free,
Jesus is comin' bye and bye.

So I made old Satan out a liar,
Jesus is comin' bye and bye.
I kept on prayin' my way up higher,
Jesus is comin' bye and bye. (Ceceil George, b. 1846,
    LA, 86–87, orig. parentheses)[13]

In such company any misstep can spell damnation, provoking echoes of Biblical commandments, prohibitions, prescriptions, and parables. "I don't go out much 'cept to church—folks is so critical. / You have to mind how you walk on the cross; / If you don't your foot will slip, / And your soul will be lost" (Gracie Mitchell, b. unk., AL, 108). "Come old sheep, / Old sheep you know the way, / Old sheep know the way, / Young must learn the way" (Frances Lewis, b. 1854, GA, 158).[14] "Repent, believe, and be baptized, / Let's go down to Jordan, Let's go down to Jordan, / This baptizing shall go on" (Rube Witt, b. 1850, TX, 4264). "In dis life of heaby load / Let us share [cheer] de weary traveler / Along de heabenly road" (Fannie Moore, b. 1849, SC, 133).[15] "In dat mawnin' Away down yonder by de river's banks, / Twenty-four elders, all in ranks— / An' I'm bound to cross Jordin, in de mawnin'" (Jane Sutton, b. ca. 1853, MS, 2093).

> Raise de Heaven as high as de sky;
> Fall down on your knees;
> Send up yer prayers; I' send up mine;
> De good Lord ter please.
>
> See my brudder down de hill;
> Fall down on your knees;
> Send up yer prayers; I'll send up mine;
> De good Lord ter please. (Orris Harris, b. ca. 1858, MS, 932)[16]

Obviously spirituals are also overtly self-referential, describing the worship and prayer that surrounds them, naming participants (whether earthly or otherworldly), demanding their devotion and involvement, recasting ritual as a heavenward journey. "I can't think o' but one ob de ole songs whut we made up an' hit went lak dis— / Going to de meetin house to hear de people pray, / Going to lead de ole sheep along / Going to lead de ole sheep along" (Tom Floyd, b. ca. 1842, MS, 749). The structure of Black worship often did parallel the pilgrimages depicted in spirituals: members performed these songs while marching or shouting around church houses, parading through camp grounds, processioning to river banks for baptizings, or to graveyards for buryings:

> The first funeral I ever saw was that of Gran'pap Holden. . . . They put the coffin in the spring wagon and took the long way round by road up to the burying ground on the hill. A young girl, Melindy Leaper, walked behind the wagon singing:
>
> *We're travelin' to the grave,*
> *We're travelin' to the grave,*

Fig. 16.2. "A Southern baptism, Aiken, South Carolina," 1906. Detroit Publishing Co. Collection, Library of Congress, Prints and Photographs Division.

> *We're travelin' to the grave,*
> To lay this pore body down. (Rachel Cruze, b. 1856, TN, 317, orig. emphasis)

I kin see dem folkses now, a-marchin down to de crick, back of de church, and all de can-i-dates dressed in de whites' white clothes, what was de style den. Evvybody jined in de singin', and de words was lak dis:

> Marchin' for de water
> For to be baptized.
> De Lord done lit de candle
> On de other side
> For to see his chilluns
> When dey gits baptized. (Carrie Hudson, b. ca. 1860, GA, 215–16)[17]

FUNERAL SONG

> Come ye dat love de Lord,
> En let your joys be known.
> Hark from de tomb,
> En hear my tender voice.
> By de grace of God I'll meet you
> On Canaan Happy Shore.
> Oh, mother, where will I meet you on Canaan Happy Shore?
> En by de grace of God I'll meet you on Canaan Happy Shore.

(Shaking hands, marching around grave. White en Colored marched from church to graveyard. Old people in de ox cart en young people walking) (Sylvia Cannon, b. ca. 1857, SC, 196, orig. parentheses)[18]

White spirituals employ these same themes and poetics, of course, which derive largely from the Anglo-American line. (Most obviously, the pilgrimage has an especially long and venerable history in English-language folklore and literature.) These borrowings assumed new forms among slaves, however, whose innovations in turn profoundly influenced their white counterparts. (It is well-established, for instance, that the characteristic call-and-response structure of American spirituals—Black or white—derives from African and African American musical practice.) Moreover, the same elements clearly held very different meanings for Black and white singers. Given the spiritual's millennial subtext, themes that for whites reaffirmed the status quo were instantly incendiary or insurrectionist in Black mouths, none more so than the topic of freedom.

Ironically, this element is also originally white: Anglo-American Protestant hymns and spirituals conventionally equate sin with slavery and salvation with freedom. When sung by slaves, such pieces might suggest this world more than the next, however, and slaveholders were most mindful of these potential subversions. Charles Wesley was generally an approved source, but not his "O For a Thousand Tongues to Sing" (1739) ("He breaks the power of cancelled sin, / he sets the prisoner free"). "We Shall Be Free (When the Good Lord Sets Us Free)" was more inflammatory yet.[19] "Dey didn't 'low us to sing such songs as 'We Shall Be Free' and 'O For a Thousand Tongues to Sing.' Dey always had somebody to follow de slaves to church when de colored preacher was preachin' to hear what wuz said and done. Dey wuz 'fraid us would try to say something 'gainst 'em" (Leah Garrett, b. unk., MD, 15–16). Whites too sang Isaac Watts's "I'm Glad Salvation's Free" (ca. 1810), but slaves were well advised to sing it secretly. "We sang a song, 'I am glad salvation's free.' Once dey heerd us, nex' mornin' dey

took us and tore our backs to pieces. Dey would say, 'Are you free? What were you singin' about freedom?'" (Charity Austin, b. ca. 1852, GA, 62). Slaveholders were not just being paranoid: slaves were not questing for spiritual freedom alone.

The slaves were glad to be freed and many of the women began to sing songs of praise. Sara's daughter, who was just a child at the close of the War, said she remembered hearing them sing and thought they "wuz having meetin'." She began to sing one of the songs she remembered:

> I am glad salvation is free for us all,
> I am glad salvation is free. (Sara Crocker, b. ca.
> 1835, GA, 228)[20]

As events unfolded and millennial vision became earthly reality, Black troops marching south sang the same spirituals they had previously performed on the way to baptismal pools or graveyards.

When I was with the Yankees, I done some livin'. . . . I used to be in a brass band. I like a brass band, don't make no difference where I hear it. There was one song we played when I was in the army. It was:

> Rasslin Jacob, don't weep
> Weepin' Mary, don't weep.
> Before I'd be a slave
> I'd be buried in my grave,
> Go home to my father and be saved.

The Rebels was hot after us then. Another one we used to sing was:

> My old mistress promised me
> When she died, she'd set me free. (Tom Windham, b. 1845, GA, 211)[21]

The identification of Gabriel's apocalyptic trumpet with Union brass bands seems almost inevitable. James

Calhart James was born August 23, 1846, on a 4,000-acre South Carolina rice plantation with 300 slaves. "My master was my father; he was kind to me but hard on the field hands who worked in the rice fields."

> One of the songs sung by the slaves on the plantation I can remember a part of it. They sang it with great feeling of happiness—
>
> > Oh where shall we go when de great day comes
> > An' de blowing of de trumpets and de bangins of
> > de drums
> > When General Sherman comes.
> > No more rice and cotton fields
> > We will hear no more crying
> > Old master will be sighing.
>
> I can't remember the tune, people sang it according to their own tune. (James Calhart James, 1846, SC, 34, 35–36)[22]

The spiritual's pilgrimage, then, is a quest for freedom as much as salvation, though the two are ultimately one and the same. It is no exaggeration to say that in the slaves' spirituals, earthly liberty was as much the goal as heavenly repose. If slaves also borrowed this slavery–freedom trope from whites, they obviously understood it very differently, and employed it to far different effect.

> High! You cain' git over him,
> Low! You cain' git under him,
> Broad! You cain' git 'roun' him,
> Must go in through an by him,
> He's de way an' ther's no other.
>
> Cain' sing yo'self to heaven,
> But you kin sing yo'self to hell,
> God give up his soul,
> To unslave de bodies,
> I help fight in de fiel! (Nancy Williams,
> b. 1847, NC, 321)

Having mastered these basic poetics—or simply memorized a selection of skeletal phrases, lines, and stanzas—singers utilized other established patterns momentarily to expand a few stylized statements into complete song-texts. In the simplest scenario, singers needed only to substitute individual words in an incremental sequence.

> Oh, mother lets go down, lets go down, lets go
> down, lets go down.
> Oh, mother lets go down, down in the valley to
> pray.
> As I went down in the valley to pray
> Studyin' about that good ole way
> Who shall wear that starry crown.
> Good Lord show me the way.

Then the other part was like that except it said "father" instead of "mother," and then "sister" and then "brother." (W. L. Bost, b. ca. 1850, Newton, NC, 143–44)[23]

> My brother, where were you,
> My brother, where were you,
> My brother, where were you,
> > When you found the Lord?
>
> I was low down in the valley,
> I was low down in the valley,
> I was low down in the valley,
> > When I first found the Lord.
>
> My sister, where were you,
> My sister, where were you,
> My sister, where were you,
> > When you found the Lord?
>
> I was low down in the valley,
> I was low down in the valley,
> I was low down in the valley,
> > When I first found the Lord.

This song can be extended indefinitely by addressing the question to various members of one's family, and to friends. (Fannie Gibson, b. ca. 1850, AL, 147)

Estella Jones gave three successive texts illustrating this approach in three slightly different forms:

I still 'members some of de songs dey used to sing at frolics and at church too: . . .

You'd Better Be Praying

You'd better be praying while you're young,
You'd better be praying while you're young,
You'd better be praying without waiting any
 longer,
You'd better be praying while you're young,

You'd better seek religion while you're young,
You'd better seek religion while you're young,
You'd better seek religion without waiting
 longer,
You'd better seek religion while you're young.

Come Change My Name

Bright Angel, bright angel, come change
 my name,
O angel come change my name.
Come change my name from Nature to Grace,
O angel come change my name.

Sweet Jesus, sweet Jesus come change my name,
O Jesus come change my name.
Come change my name from Nature to Grace,
O Jesus come change my name.[24]

I'm On My Way

If a seeker gets to Heaven before I do,
Look out for me, I'm on my way too.

Shout, shout the Heaven-bound King!
Shout, shout I'm on my way!

If a brother gets to Heaven before I do,
Look out for me, I'm on my way too.
Shout, shout the Heaven-bound King!
Shout, shout I'm on my way! (Estella Jones,
 b. ca. 1855, GA, 348–50)

Elizabeth Kilham observed the technique in a Southern Freedman's camp ca. 1865. Singing "Roll Jordan Roll," recently liberated slaves began by naming Biblical heroes (King Jesus, Gabr'el, Moses, 'Lijah), "till prophets and apostles, in successive verses, are gathered on the 'tree of Life.' To this company they join their own friends, living or dead, it matters not: / 'My fader sittin' on de tree ob life, / Roll, Jerden, roll, / My mudder sittin' on de tree ob life, / Roll, Jerden, roll.'" Eventually sister, "brudder," Abe Lincoln, "Gen'l Howard," and "Gen'l Butler" were added.[25] Around the same time in South Carolina, Thomas Wentworth Higginson recorded several spirituals in which "the name of every person present successively appears."[26] The technique of enrolling the full family circle was also routine in white spirituals, its popularity and emotional impact obviously proceeding from the fact that many persons so named truly would have been dead and gone. Again, however, calling the eternal roll of family members in Glory would have had additional meaning for slaves whose families had been (or could be) sold apart, and this may be the most common of all improvisational patterns in spirituals. In 1855 former slave Peter Randolph (ca. 1825–1897) wrote:

in parting with their friends at the auction-block,
the poor blacks have the anticipation of meeting
them again in the heavenly Canaan, and sing—

"O, fare you well, O, fare you well!
God bless you until we meet you again;
Hope to meet you in heaven to part no more.

Fig. 16.3. "Family of Slaves at the Gaines' House." William F. Gaines plantation, Hanover Co., VA, 1862. Photo by G. H. Houghton. Library of Congress, Prints and Photographs Division.

> Chorus—Sisters, fare you well; sisters, fare you well;
> God Almighty bless you, until we meet again."[27]

In a slightly more involved approach, entire lines or phrases might be exchanged, altered, or rearranged.

> A sister on the road, she almost done travelin',
> It's a rough and rocky way,
> But I almost done travelin'.
> Heaven is so high and I is so low,
> I fear I'll never get there.
>
> I 'most done travelin', I bound to carry my soul to the Lord.
> I 'most done travelin', it's a rough and rocky way.
> I 'most done travelin', my soul to the Lord.
> I 'most done travelin', moanin' on the road.
> I 'most done travelin', I 'most done travelin'.
> (Frances Lewis, b. 1854, GA, 157–58)

Most of de old people sing bout:

> O Heaven, sweet Heaven,
> When shall I see?
> If you get dere fore me,
> You tell my Lord I on de way.
> O shall I get dere?
> If you get dere fore I do,
> You tell my Lord I on de way.
> O Heaven, sweet Heaven,
> When shall I see?
> Oh when shall I get dere?

Oh, dat be a old song what my grandmmamy used to sing way back dere. (Sylvia Cannon, b. ca. 1857, SC, 180)[28]

> Ask my Lord for mercy,
> Good Lord, gimme religion,
> Good Lord, gimme a heart to b'lieve,
> Dis is de buryin' groun'.
> Amen, Hallelujah. Dis is de buryin' groun'.
>
> Tell your mother,
> Tell your father,
> Dis is de buryin' groun'.
> Tell all you neighbors,
> Tell all your neighbors chillun,
> Dis is de buryin' groun'.

Repeat: Ask my Lord for mercy and etc. Also: Goin' on to Glory, and etc. This song is repeated over and over—with such changes in the ending as: Everybody! Hallelujah—Glory! Hallelujah—to suit the fancy of the singer. (Filmore Taylor Hancock, b. 1851, MO, 188)

Ten of the twelve lines of Fannie Gibson's "Going Home to Live With the Lord" reiterate just two well-traveled commonplaces—"I's goin' home soon in de mornin' (so soon)," and "I's goin' home to live with de Lord"—both of which are intimated by the remaining two lines ("De Lord is a-waitin' for me," repeated). The result is minimalist but brilliant, wringing every nuance out of a couple of formulaic but fairly profound propositions.

> Goin' home soon in de mornin',
> Goin' home soon in de mornin',
> I's goin' home to live with de Lord.

In de mornin' so soon,
In de mornin' so soon,
I's goin' home to live with de Lord.

I's goin' home to live with de Lord,
I's goin' home to live with de Lord,
I's goin' home soon in de mornin'.

O, de Lord is a-waitin' for me,
O, de Lord is a-waitin' for me,
I's goin' home soon in de mornin'. (Fannie Gibson, b. ca. 1850, AL, 146)[29]

Besides providing a basic improvisational grid, these constant repetitions also served as stalls, giving improvisers time to think and adapt. In 1899 William E. Barton (1861–1930) observed "many songs have a line three times repeated, with a fourth but little changed, and thus build a song out of meagre material."[30] Typically, the fourth line does not rhyme—often it is an all-purpose wandering refrain—allowing singers to extemporize full stanzas from single formulaic statements ad infinitum. A sizable portion of the spirituals sung by ex-slaves follow this AAAB pattern, and many plausibly could have been improvised wholly or in part on the spot.

Anudder one we uster like to sing, go like dis:

Ain't you weary trablin'?
Ain't you weary trablin'?
Ain't you weary trablin'?
Come and join de ban'.

God's house is a house
God's house is a house
God's house is a house
Come and join de ban'. (George Rivers, b. ca. 1850, TX, 3328)[31]

By'm by don' you griebe atter me
(This line repeated four times)

II

Wen I'm gone don you griebe atter me
* * * * * * * *
* * * * * * * *
By'm by don you griebe atter me.

III

De Lawd has prepared de way an
has carried my soul away
(This line repeated three times)
By'm by don' you griebe atter me.

IV

Wen I'm dead don' you griebe atter me
(This line repeated three times)
By'm by don' you griebe atter me. (Aunt Ann Stokes, b. 1844, MO, 337. orig. asterisks and parentheses)[32]

Don't you hear Jesus call?
Don't you hear Jesus call?
Don't you hear Jesus call?
Yes, I hear Jesus call my soul.

Don't you hear the turtledove?
Don't you hear the turtledove?
Don't you hear the turtledove?
Yes, I hear the turtledove in my soul.

Don't you hear the angel call?
Yes, I hear the angel call,
I got the witness in my heart,
And the glory in my soul. (Frances Lewis, b. 1854, GA, 157)

Choruses and choral refrains served the same purpose. In the summer of 1862 on South Carolina's Wakamah River, Reverend William Wyndham Malet heard slave rowers singing "a kind of epic hymn, improvised by one of the boatmen, going on for at least ten minutes. I marked down the following words:— / The Jews killed my Jesus. (*Chorus*)—Hallelujah! / Upon the cross they stretched Him—Hallelujah! / They laid him in the Sepulchre—Hallelujah! . . . / The hallelujah is prolonged so as to give the singer time to remember or improvise the next line."[33] Most of the preceding items could be sung in the call-and-response pattern typical of spirituals, but some texts self-evidently feature responsorial refrains.

> Way over in the promised land,
> O Glory Hallelujah! Hallelujah! (pronounced
>   Halle-lool-yah)
> Way over in the promised land,
> O Glory Hallelujah! Hallelujah!
>
> I will meet my Massa Jesus,
> O Glory Hallelujah! Hallelujah!
> I will meet my Massa Jesus,
> O Glory Hallelujah! Hallelujah!
>
> I will tell the world good bye,
> O Glory Hallelujah! Hallelujah!
> I will tell the world good bye,
> O Glory Hallelujah! Hallelujah!
>
> I will live with my Jesus,
> O Glory Hallelujah! Hallelujah!
> I will live with my Jesus,
> O Glory Hallelujah! Hallelujah! (Mary Frances
>   Brown, b. 1859, SC, 88, orig. parentheses)

Ol' man Hutchins he hire a man to come out and preach to us at de camp groun'. Dey uster sing along like dis:

> We will cross de ribber of Jordan,
>   So happy, so happy.
> We will cross de ribber of Jordan,
>   So happy in de Lawd.
>
> O, who will come and go wid me,
>   So happy, so happy.

Fig. 16.4. John Crawford of Austin, ca. 1937–38. Portraits of African American ex-slaves from the US Works Progress Administration, Federal Writers' Project slave narratives collection, Library of Congress.

> O, who will come and go wid me,
>   So happy in de Lawd. (Ellen Rogers,
>   b. ca. 1837, TX, 3361)

My mammy got converted to the song:

> Way down yonder by myself
> Couldn't hear nobody pray
> Way down yonder in the valley
> Couldn't hear nobody pray
> Had to pray myself
> Jest had to pray myself. (John Crawford, b. 1837,
>   MS, 976)[34]

Singers and songmakers also created new songs from old, piecing together set passages from established spirituals and hymns or from the vast pool of so-called wandering stanzas or floaters, all-purpose lines and verses with no one particular home, manipulated in infinite ways. Lafayette Price expressly improvised a new piece by combining two well-known spirituals—"Inching Along" and "Free At Last"—with a floater warning listeners to "mind how you walk on the cross."

You know niggers lub to sing. Dey kin jis' mek dey song w'ile dey go 'long.

> My sister, you better min' how you walk on de cross
> Foot might slip and your soul git los'.
> Come inchin' long,
> Come inchin' long,
> Like a po' inchin' (measuring) worm
> Marse Jesus come bye-and-bye.
>
> Ol' Satan though he had me fas',
> Broke his ol' chain an' free at las'.
> (Repeat Chorus)
>
> (Lafayette Price, b. ca. 1850, AL, 3175–76, orig. parentheses)

This "walk on the cross" warning easily qualifies as one of the most popular rhymes in African American folksong.[35] WPA narrators contributed over a half dozen versions. Rebecca Fletcher (b. 1842, MS, 65–66) and Gracie Mitchell (b. unk., AL, 108) simply gave the basic couplet (Fletcher remembered it from an older slave in the kitchen; Mitchell did not specify). Most narrators followed Lafayette Price, however, joining the figure to other material. Joanna Thompson Isom (b. ca. 1858, MS, 1097–98) inserted it in her version of "Dese Bones Gonna Rise Again." Lizzie Davis combined it with another commonplace (the *Sunday band*) in a unique creation. Orelia Alexie Franks was born near Lafayette on Valerian Martin's sugar plantation. "I was raise' w'er eb'rybudy talk' French. I talks 'Merican but I talks French goodes'" (Orelia Alexie Franks, b. unk., LA, 1423). She employed the couplet's last line only in another highly original composition. Elizabeth Ross Hite, by contrast, created an entire spiritual from this commonplace alone.

> Oh, my sister,
> How you walk on de cross?
> Sunday mornin band!
> Oh, your feet might slip

> En your soul get lost.
> Sunday mornin band!
> Oh, what band,
> Oh, what band,
> Do you belong?
> What band! What band!
> Sunday mornin band! (Lizzie Davis, b. ca. 1865, SC, child of ex-slaves, 113)

Another song dey uster sing was:

> Sinner blin'
> Johnnie can't you ride no mo'?
> Sinner blin'
> Yo' feet may be slippin'
> Yo' soul git loss,
> Johnnie can't you ride no mo'?
> Yes, Lawd,
> Day by day you cannot see,
> Johnnie can't you ride no mo'?
> Yes, Lawd. (Orelia Alexie Franks, b. unk., LA, 1424)

Yea, we sang spirituals. My favorite one was "Better Mind How You Walk On De Cross." Yea, we shouted all night. Church lasted all night and way into de mornin'. Dis is de way "Better Mind How You Walk On De Cross" goes:

> Better mind how you walk on de cross
> Better mind how you walk on de cross
> Your foot might slip and your soul get lost
> Better mind how you walk on de cross
> Better mind how you walk on de cross
> How you walk and talk about Jesus
> How you lean, walk, talk about de cross
> How you walk on de cross, walk on de cross
> I am leanin' on Jesus, leanin' on Jesus
> Better mind how you walk on de cross.

We got happy when dat hymn was sung. De darkies would sing and you ought to er heard dem. De old preacher would stomp his foots, and all de people would pray and shout. (Elizabeth Ross Hite, b. ca. 1850, LA, 103–4)

In performance, spirituals were wholly inclusive and maximally participatory, but there were recognized song leaders and acknowledged songmakers. Where some narrators who professed to love spirituals could scarcely recall a full verse or stanza, others were storehouses of unique, often lengthy texts built on traditional idioms or themes, many of which I believe to have been at least partly improvised for the WPA interviewers. Mary Frances Brown, Sylvia Cannon, Lizzie Davis, Fannie Gibson, Mary Gladdy, Estella Jones, Frances Lewis, Lafayette Price, and Rosa Thomas all deserve special mention in this regard, but many others contributed one or two texts of this kind.

These singers and their communities obviously did not conceive authorship in the modern legalistic sense, but the concept was current. Recalling "more than a half century of collecting," John W. Work (1901–1967) observed "many churches have spirituals which are led exclusively by special singers. Thus, within a church a spiritual may be designated as 'Brother Jones' song,' or 'Sister Mary's song.' Such songs may have been composed, or merely introduced into the church singing by the leader. The 'ownership' of such a song carried with it the indisputable ability to sing it effectively."[36] WPA narrators frequently attributed spirituals to specific individuals. Parents were most common, but many also named preachers or other acquaintances.

When Tom Knight git going good his sermon, he 'mence to sing:

> We gwan have a moughty bounty,
> Bounty! A moughty bounty,
> We gwan have a moughty bounty.

> Golden slippers all on my feet,
> De golden lace aroun' my waist,
> We gwan have a moughty bounty!

> Bounty, yes bounty!
> We gwine have a moughty bounty!

> Golden crown all on my head,
> We gwan have a moughty bounty!
> By king Jesus we'll be fed,
> We gwan have a moughty bounty. (Alice Marshall, b. ca. 1850, VA, 203)

Dere wus a cullud church fifteen miles from Mt. Pleasant we're we went to service. De preacher wus name' John Henry Doe. I use to like to sing dis song:

> Run away, run away
> Run away, run away
> Sojus of the cross.
> CHORUS
> Hole on, hole on
> Hole on, hole on
> Hole on, hole on
> Hole on, sojus of the cross. (Thomas Goodwater, b. 1855, SC, 168)

Familiar old spirituals were composed by "Parson" Williams, including *Roll De Stones Away*, *You'll Rise in De Skies*, and *Ezekiel, We'se Comin Home*. Following is one of Williams's spirituals:

> When dat ole chariot comes,
> I'm gwine to lebe you:
> I'm bound for de promised land
> I'm gwine to lebe you.

> I'm sorry I'm gwine to lebe you,
> Farewell, oh farewell
> But I'll meet you in de mornin
> Farewell, oh farewell. (Parson Rezin Williams, b. 1822, MD, 72)

Obviously too, slaves did not equate authorship with complete originality or novelty. Every line in Parsons Williams's text is a popular commonplace, but I am sure this precise combination is his, the same being generally true of Marshall's and Goodwater's texts. Sam Meredith Mason credited the ubiquitous "Down in the Valley to Pray" (possibly of white origin) to his father. (The father, or possibly Mason himself did radically rearrange the piece, even altering its usual stanzaic structure.)

> Pappy would work out, too. He took a great interest in education, but he jes' couldn't learn nothin'. That's about the way it is with ninety-nine percent of my race. But pappy liked to make up some words to fit a song. He used to chant this:

>> I went down in the valley,
>> Shoutin' about the good old way,
>> Shoutin' about the good old way,

>> I went down in the valley—to pray—
>> Good Lawd, show me the way
>> Good Lawd, show me the way

> It looked lak de songs in them days was revealed to the folks. A lot of times they didn't need no song book to help them along. (Sam Meredith Mason, b. 1858, TX, 2600)

Even without sound recordings there is ample testimony that, in the nineteenth century as in the twentieth, spirituals were performed in an emotional, highly expressive style featuring the characteristic Black vocal techniques described as moaning, groaning, growling, crying, hollering, and so forth. Sometimes *shouting* refers to singing rather than dancing, precisely the approach derided by advocates of more decorous white hymnody. "Some of the Spirituals are fine but still I think Wesley hymns are best. I tell my folks that the Good Lord isn't a deaf old gentleman that has to be shouted up to or amused. I do think we colored people are a little too apt to want to show off in our singing sometimes" (Reverend Charles Williams, b. 1859, WV, 112).

Many interviewers went to great lengths to suggest melisma, slurs, bends, and other vocal effects docu-

mented in twentieth-century recordings of Black religious singing. Period descriptions also refer constantly to such vocal tricks, like "the intangible *portamentos* (or slides), which it is impossible to represent in notes."[37]

My mother wuz quiet. She didn't have much to say to nobody. I don't remember hearin' her sing much, but one of them was:

> My knees is worn, a'waggin' up Zion hill!
> A w-a-gg-i-n' u-p Zion Hi-l-l!

Anudder one wuz:

> My fat-h-er id-l-ed his t-i-me aw-a-y,
> An' went do-w-n to he-l-l! (Charley Stewart, b. 1852, AL, 2046)

My daddy wuz a "rank sinner" but my mother wuz a good old church woman. She usta sing some good old songs, but I kaint member much about dem now. One of dem went like dis:

> I'm in dis fiel' of battle—I'm on my w-a-y!
> Give back, give back—ye hosts of hell;
> I'm on my w-a-y!
> Let God's chillun—take de fiel'
> I'm on my w-a-y! (Nep Jenkins, b. 1853, AL, 1150)

By de handle of me soul, come a'bolting along, through by me——. Mother whar have ye been, all so long——Dis long time ye jest come in?

> Mother, whar have ye been—dis long time—I called ye,
> An' ye jes' now come in? By de handle of me soul,
> Come bolting along—through by me. I'll fight it through danger, all danger and deaths 'against pore me.
> Sister, preacher, w-h-a-r have ye been so lo-n-g!
> Dis long time I called ye, and ye jes' now com-i-n' i-n!

By de handle of my soul, come bolting along,
    through by through,
I'll fight through all danger till death is against
    po'——me!

Dem old song jes' come to me sometimes. I can't
say 'em off. I jes' has to sing 'em to mysef. (Rosa
Thomas, b. 1861, AL, 2101)

Rosa Thomas is described as "singing in a low mellow
voice" (Rosa Thomas, b. 1861, AL, 2101), placing her
in a long line of gospel contraltos. Other accounts
appear to describe falsetto singing, another characteristic African American vocal technique.[38]

Jane seems to have "raised" her daughters better
than the general run, as they are neat, industrious
and very thoughtful of their old mother. She is
very deaf, so they sit near her and tell her what is
said if she fails to understand. They said she had
been a leader in their church singing and could
still sing well, and these are some of the songs she
sang for the writer:

David and Goliath

David, David is a 'bediant young boy,
He kilt Goliah, and shouted fer joy.
Shoutin' about the good old way,

God, gimme rashions from on high! (very high
    pitch)
Dats gon-na last me till—I—die.
Shoutin' about the good old way,

David, David, don't git lost.
Strech a rod and come—ac-r-o-ss! (Jane Sutton,
    b. ca. 1853, MS, 2091, orig. emphasis and
    parentheses)

Mary Frances was asked if she could sing spirituals. The following is one that she sang in a very

high-pitched wavering voice and then she complained of shortness of breath on account of her
heart.

We got a home ober dere,
Come an' let us go,
Come an' let us go,
Where pleasure neber (never) die.
Chorus: Oh! let us go where pleasure neber die,
    Neber die,
    Come and let us go,
    Where pleasure neber die, neber die.
Mother is gone ober dere,
Mother is gone ober dere,
Where pleasure neber die,
Where pleasure neber die.
Chorus.
[Repeated three times with substitution of
    Father, Sister, and Brudder for Mother.]
    (Mary Frances Brown, b. ca. 1847, SC, 135–36,
    orig. parentheses)

There are also hints of the distinctive rhythmic qualities of Black singing that utterly transformed the spiritual genre and American music generally. "Then with
a beautiful and peculiar rhythm only attained by the
southern Negro, she chanted: 'Come-ye-dat-love-de-
Lord / And-let-your-joys-be-known'" (Julia Bunch,
b. 1853, SC, 158). "The notes of our music are peculiarly
shaped because . . . it was written not according to a
fixed rule but according to the rhythmical nature of
our race" (Sarah Emery Merrill, b. unk., KY, child of
ex-slaves, 127).

Some ex-slaves insisted that, like shouting (holy
dancing), true spiritual singing required full possession, and that true spiritual singers actually channeled
spirit voices.

I wants to go to Hebben now an' when de roll is
call up dere an' I be dere, de Lord, he find a hiding
place for me. I goes to chu'ch when I kin an' sing
too, but ef I sing an' it doan mobe (move) me any,

den dat a sin on de Holy Ghost; I be tell a lie on de Lord. No I aint sing when it doan mobe me. You mus'n ax me to do dat. (Emma Fraser, b. ca. 1857, SC, 87, orig. parentheses)

I was plumb growed up fo' I eber went t' chu'ch. I go t' Sunday school wid d' w'ite chillen t' tek care 'r' 'em. Dey couldn' learnt me t' sing no songs cause I didn' hab d' spirit. I hear dem sing, "Let d' light shine." Nobudy can't sing w'en dey ain' got d' spirit t' sing. I neber learnt no edication. Books don' mean nuthin' t' me 'cept so much black 'n' w'ite. (Sarah Ashley, b. 1844, MS, 89)

In congregation, this spirit-filled singing was further enlivened by the interplay between rotating song leaders and ecstatic responders, all supported by handclapping and foot stamping that rattled and shook church houses or echoed off hillsides and riverbanks.[39] As the spirit really took hold, some members shouted all about until they fell out, convulsing in others' arms or on the ground, screaming incomprehensibly or speaking in tongues. In such settings, even the most repetitive spiritual was spontaneously, polyvocally recomposed into something defying written representation, often at earsplitting volume. "Forty-seven other people was baptized with me—at the same time, and you could have heared Niggers shoutin and moanin and singin for two miles!" (Mary Carpenter, b. 1851, GA, 145). "When dey started to the burial ground with the body every body in the whole procession would sing hymns. I've heard 'em 'nough times clear 'cross the fields, singin' and moanin' as they went" (Arrie Binns, b. ca. 1845, GA, 77). "When folkses would git 'ligion dey would holler and shout a-testifyin' for de Lord. Atter de meetin' dey dammed up de crick and let it git deep enough for de baptizin'. Dey dipped de white folkses fust, and den de Niggers. You could hear 'em singin' a mile away dem old songs lak: *On Jordan's Stormy Banks I Stand,—Roll, Jordan Roll,—All God's Chilluns is a goin' Home*, and—*Whar de Livin' Waters Flow*" (Cordelia Thomas, b. ca. 1855, GA, 18, orig. emphasis).

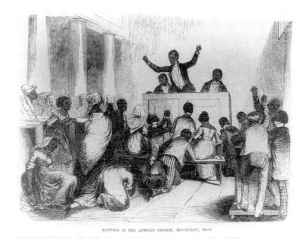

Fig. 16.5. "Meeting in the African Church, Cincinnati, Ohio," *Illustrated London News* 22 (April 30, 1853): 276. Slavery Images: A Visual Record of the African Slave Trade and Slave Life in the Early African Diaspora. slaveryimages.org. An antebellum Black church service, with a clear view of the *mourner's bench* (and the mourners) just in front of the pulpit.

If ex-slaves improvised many spiritual texts whole or in part for interviewers, they most likely did so because this was the only way they knew how to sing them. Some narrators may have even created pieces they had never sung before merely to oblige the fieldworkers. True, the song titles that most often crop up in the narratives are Protestant hymns, whose rigidly demanding words required rote memorization or written prompts, which explains why ex-slaves provided far more hymn titles than texts, and then a high proportion of fragments. By contrast, spirituals were not invariant set pieces distinguished by standard titles and fixed texts. Rather, these songs were gifted in the moment, and some ex-slaves could seemingly create them almost at will to any desired length, so that by word count spiritual texts far outdistance hymns or any other genre of song in the ex-slave narratives, sacred or secular.

Not all spirituals were personal creations or spontaneous improvisations, however. Even impromptu performances were typically pieced together from prefabricated lines and stanzas, while many other spirituals known to slaves were distinct, well-established songs with recognized titles, familiar to nearly everyone, identifiable even in their most extreme or unusual versions. Many of these are still well known today: "Swing Low, Sweet Chariot," "Didn't It Rain," "Roll Jordan Roll," "The Old Ship of Zion." Yet even at their most stable, most nineteenth-century manifestations bear only passing resemblances to latter-day adaptations. Before the war, Thomas Wentworth Higginson, colonel of a Black regiment composed of ex-slaves from southeastern states, "had been a faithful student of the Scottish ballads," who "had always envied Sir Walter [Scott] the delight of tracing them out amid their own heather." With that inspiration, he became an especially keen and perceptive observer of spiritual singing and songmaking among his troops.

> The individual songs rarely coincided; there was a line here, a chorus there,—just enough to fix the class, but this was unmistakable. It was not strange that they differed, for the range seemed almost endless, and South Carolina, Georgia, and Florida seemed to have nothing but the generic character in common, until all were mingled in the united stock of camp melodies. . . . Among the songs not available for marching, but requiring the concentrated enthusiasm of the camp, was "The Old Ship of Zion," of which they had three wholly distinct versions, all quite exuberant and tumultuous.[40]

WPA narrators provided four versions of "The Old Ship of Zion," as distinct from one another as they are from each of Higginson's three texts. This item would eventually be standardized by collegiate songbooks and gospel quartets, but there was no such single standard among slaves.

> My pappy's name was Jacob Keller and my mother was Maria. They's both dead long ago, and I'm waiting for the old ship Zion that took my Mammy away, like we use to sing of in the woods:
>
> > It has landed my old Mammy,
> > It has landed my old Mammy,
> > Get on board, Get on board,

> 'Tis the Old Ship of Zion—
> Get on board! (Isabella Jackson, b. ca. 1858, LA, 154)

> Ole Ship O' Zion come here
> Ole Ship O' Zion come here
> Ole Ship O' Zion come here
> Halleluiah she has landed
> And will land ever more. (Temple Wilson, b. ca. 1857, MS, 2371)

> I 'member one song they used to sing
>
> > We'll land over shore
> > We'll land over shore;
> > And we'll live for ever more.

> They called it a hymn. They'd sing it in church, then they'd all get to shoutin'. (Dinah Perry, b. ca. 1862, AR, 320)

> "De Ol' Ship of Zion" was anudder. It go:
>
> > What ship is dat sailin' so slow?
> > Tis de ol' ship of Zion
> > She has landed many thousand
> > And she can land as many more.
> >
> > Wonder who de captain is
> > As she moves along
> > King Jesus is de captain
> > As she moves along. (George Rivers, b. ca. 1850, TX, 3328)[41]

Ex-slaves were in fact aware that their spirituals differed from the Negro spirituals most people knew by the 1930s.

> Us sing "Swing Low, Sweet Chariot," but dey didn' sing it like dey does dese days. Us sing:
>
> > Swing low, sweet chariot
> > Freely let me into res',

Fig. 16.6. Lorenza Ezell, ex-slave, Fort Worth, TX, November 9, 1937. Portraits of African American ex-slaves from the US Works Progress Administration, Federal Writers' Project slave narratives collection, Library of Congress.

> Becase I don' wanter stay yere no longer.
> Swing low, sweet chariot
> W'en Gabriel mek his las' alarm,
> I want to be rollin' in Jesus' arm',
> Becase I don' wanter stay yere no longer.
> (Lorenza Ezell, b. 1850, SC, 1320)

Few spirituals are now as well known as "Swing Low, Sweet Chariot," which may have been familiar to slaves, though the earliest published notices are from the early 1870s. Some are from oral sources, some from Black collegiate songbooks. All attribute the piece to the slaves, but antebellum evidence is frankly lacking. (Lorenza Ezell describes the war years.) Oral versions usually share only the *swing low* refrain, combined with various floaters.[42] Ezell and Hilliard Johnson gave it that way.

> And another one, dey is so many, let me see. Here one but I jes' can't call to mine a heap of verses:
>
> Trouble here and dey's trouble dere,
>   I really do believe dere's trouble
>   ev'ywhere.
> Swing low, chariot, I'm gwine home.
>   Swing low, chariot, I'm gwine home.
>
> Den hit goes on and tell 'bout de moaner, says:
>
> Oh, dey's a moaner here, dey's a moaner dere,
>   I really do b'lieve dey's a moaner
>   ev'ywhere
> Swing low, chariot, I'm gwine home.
>   Swing low, chariot, I'm gwine home.
>
> Oh dey's a sinner here, dey's a sinner dere,
>   I really do b'lieve dey's a sinner
>   ev'ywhere
> Swing low, chariot, I'm gwine home.
>   Swing low, chariot, I'm gwine home.
>
> Oh, dey's a Christun here, dey's a Christun dere
>   I really do b'lieve dey's a Christun
>   ev'ywhere
> Swing low, chariot, I'm gwine home.
>   Swing low, chariot, I'm gwine home.
>
> Den dey's a heap of 'em to dat song lac a "deacon" and a "member" and a "prayer" and a "singer," jes' a whole passel dem verses, but I reckon dem will do today. (Uncle Hilliard Johnson, b. ca. 1857, AL, 230)

The arrangement of "Swing Low, Sweet Chariot" universally recognized today derives from a single source, the Fisk Jubilee Singers, as included in the first edition of their *Jubilee Songs* (1872) and much performed, reprinted, and copied thereafter. By the late 1930s this version was also circulating on dozens of commercial recordings by gospel quartets and choirs (mainly Black, a few white), constantly figuring in their radio broadcasts and live performances as well. This is the true wellspring of the song's present fame, and its current standardized form.[43] A dozen-and-a-half narrators named "Swing Low, Sweet Chariot," but besides Lorenza Ezell and Hilliard Johnson only one ex-slave other gave a text, and then a questionable fragment.[44] Several narrators who named it were apparently asked specifically about the song, which by the late 1930s was quite well known.

"Roll Jordan Roll," another renowned Negro spiritual, is well documented in the antebellum period, though not so thoroughly as its later fame might predict.[45] It was named by fewer than a dozen narrators, and only one gave a text. Lizzie Davis's rendition is typical of oral versions, simply joining the "Roll, Jordan" refrain to wandering stanzas (in her case verses not usually associated with this item):

1. I went over Jordan
   To make one prayer,
   En to hear sweet Jordan roll.
   Roll Jordan, roll!
   Roll Jordan, roll!

2. When I got dere, old Satan was dere,
   What did you reckon he said to me?
   You too young to pray en you too young to
       die.

3. I made old Satan out a liar,
   En I went on my way.
   Roll, sweet Jordan, roll. (Lizzie Davis, b. ca. 1865,
       SC, child of ex-slaves, 111)[46]

If millions of people around the world now recognize "Didn't It Rain," most credit goes to gospel superstar Mahalia Jackson (1911–1972), who prominently featured (and frequently recorded) the song throughout her career; even before then it had been popularized (and somewhat standardized) through recordings by the Biddleville Quintette (Paramount 12848, 1929), the Heavenly Gospel Singers (Bluebird B6094, 1935), the Golden Gate Quartet (OKeh 6529, 1941), and others.[47] The piece is almost certainly a Black creation but may also date only to the postwar period. It does not appear in antebellum sources and is comparatively rare in traditional collections generally, where in the usual pattern the "didn't it rain" refrain more often appears in otherwise unrelated songs. Commercial recordings and popular rearrangements invariably tell the story of Noah and the Flood in some detail. Traditional versions may or may not narrate. Oral texts that can be grouped as a distinct song share at least two of three traits: the refrain "didn't it rain"; some indication that for forty days the rain kept dropping (without stopping); and mention of an angel singing, crying, or moaning.[48] These elements may be combined with wandering verses or refashioned in unique ways. (Noah is seldom mentioned.) Martha Kelly's version is thus both somewhat unusual and completely representative:

I don' know whe' if I could remember dat other one or no. Seem like it go something like dis:

Oh, didn' it rain?
It rain 40 days,
En it rain 40 nights,
It ain' never stop a droppin yet,
En I heard de angel in de mornin sing,
Oh, didn' it rain?

But down by de graveyard,
Me en my Lord gwine stand en talk,
Up on de mountain fire en smoke,
I wouldn' be so busy bout de fire en smoke.
I heard de angel in de mornin sing,
Oh, didn' it rain?
[First verse repeats, second verse repeats, first
    verse repeats, with slight variations] (Martha
    Kelly, b. unk., SC, 85–86)[49]

Similar circumstances surround other latter-day favorites. "Nobody Knows the Trouble I've Seen" is now as famous as "Swing Low, Sweet Chariot." Its slave origins and antebellum currency seem beyond dispute, but it is not one of the better-documented early spirituals and barely figures in the narratives: only two ex-slaves named it; a third interview contains a plagiarized text.[50] Over two dozen ex-slaves named the perennial "Old-Time Religion" but only half a dozen gave texts, and those were fragments. "I loved that old song that goes like this: 'It was good for our Father's and it is good enough for me.' Then another (I'se forgot the words, but this is the name), 'It's the old Time Religion'" (John McAdams, b. 1849, TN, 2466). "We all went ter church an' den dey wud sing—Old time 'ligion, old time 'ligion, / It's good 'nouf fur me" (Ann Drake, b. 1855, MS, 646). "Give me that old time religion. It is good enough for me. It is good when I am dying, it has lan'd many a thousand will land many a more, it is good when I am in trouble, it is good enough for me" (Matilda Shepard, b. ca. 1832, GA, 126).[51] The longest text is actually a traditional joke.

> One time de preacher wuz in de river fixin' ter baptize a man. Eve'ybody wuz singin' ole' time 'ligion. A 'oman sung, "I don' lak dat thing 'hind you." Bout dat time de pahson en de udder man se'd an alligator. De parson sez, "No-By-God I Don't Either." He turned de man loose en dey both run 'way. (Ann Matthews, b. unk., TN, 46)

The punchlines from the woman and preacher are sung to the tune of "Old-Time Religion" (which was often performed at baptizings).[52]

Granted, improvisation was fundamental to early spirituals, but even then various levels of memorization or rote repetition were often involved. In the postwar period, however, and even more so after 1900, a new wave of Black sacred songs appeared, many composed by professional songwriters and featuring stanzaic structures, rhyme schemes, and literary diction that had to be committed to memory. Ex-slaves even gave a few such items, Jesse Davis for one:

> All de medicine you may buy
> All de doctors you may try
> Ain't gonna save you from de tomb
> Some day you got to lay down and die.
> De blood of de Son can only
> Save you from de doom!
> Some day you got to lay down and die.

You lak dat one? You just ought to hear my wife, Zingo, and Me, singin' dat 'round de fire befo' us go to bed. (Jesse Davis, b. ca. 1850, SC, 266)

As its form suggests, the stanza is definitely postwar and quite likely post-1900, otherwise known from sound recordings.[53] Ex-slaves could have absorbed such newer material from any of many sources, including children, grandchildren, or others around them. Many narrators were still attending church. A few admitted enjoying records and radio (and especially sacred recordings and broadcasts); a few others mentioned what sound like songbooks from Black colleges or popular presses, which were in wide circulation by the 1930s.

> Yes, we sung at the buryins, en in church, en while we was at wuk. Dem ole black folks jes' studied up deir songs in dey head. How did we 'uns do it. I heered a Bishop say dat God gave the black folks wisdom to study out dem songs. Queenie, get the book for the lady, with all dem ole time songs in it, us cullud folks loves to sing. (Annie Coley, b. ca. 1860, SC, 446)

> I don't 'member so many of dem old songs what dey uster sing. I got a red book with lots of 'em in it what somebody fix up. One song dey uster sing was:
>
> > I'm comin', I'm comin'
> > Glory, Hallelujah
>
> You know how de niggers uster make dem songs right from de heart. (Harrison Beckett, b. ca. 1860, TX, 235–36)

Individual cases vary, but as a general rule, traditional singers learn their songs relatively early in life, their repertoires generally being fixed by early adulthood. That was definitely the case with most WPA narrators, especially where sacred songs were concerned, religious traditions being especially conservative. At the time they were interviewed, many ex-slaves had apparently not learned any new songs for a half a century or more. Some had not performed their existing repertoires during much of this time, but others were still singing at meeting, or for themselves, their family, and friends. Indeed, if ex-slaves were performing at all in the 1930s, they were probably singing church songs, possibly having foresworn all others. Yet even then, most insisted on singing items they had learned in their youths.

That said, ex-slaves did know many religious songs from the late nineteenth or even early twentieth centuries. In 1926 Howard Odum and Guy Johnson reported that "the song 'Give me Jesus' was said to have been the product of 'over-free spirit and super-religiousness' just after the Civil War. The Negro claims that the white man took him at his word when he sang 'Give me Jesus, You can have all this world,' and has left him nothing in this world but Jesus."[54] Though based on an older white hymn, "You Can Have All the World But Give Me Jesus" was in fact widely adopted by Blacks during Reconstruction, and this was indeed a traditional Black joke. Ex-slaves knew both.

I don't 'member much 'bout the songs they sung just after the war. Fo'ks can't holler and sing in town like they do in the country. I recalls a fellow saying just after the war: "All the Niggers are singing, 'You Can Have All the World, But Give Me Jesus,' but the white fo'ks done grabbed up the world, so the Niggers don't have the world or Jesus either." (Charley Mitchell, b. 1852, VA, 2716)

In the mornin',
In the mornin',
In the mornin', when I arise,
Give me Jesus
You can have this world when I die,
You can have this world when I die,
But give me Jesus,
Give me Jesus,
You can have this world when I die. (Lu Perkins,
   b. ca. 1850, MS, 3057–58)[55]

Yet like older people everywhere, the ex-slaves were not wholly approving of newer music, even newer religious music. By the Depression, many were expressly disgusted. "I do not like the way they have messed up our songs with classical music. I like the songs 'Roll Jordan Roll,' 'Old Ship of Zion,' 'Swing Low Sweet Chariot.' Classical singers ruin them, though" (Reverend Squire Dowd, b. 1855, NC, 269).

We went over to Flat Rock to church, and de singin' was gran'. All day long we'd be at preachin' and singin'. Singin' dat good ole spiritual song about You shan't be slaves no more since Christ has made you free! I lay hear yesterday and heard all those foolish songs and jubilee songs that came over the radio—then some of those good ole time spirituals came and it jest made me feel like I was in ole times. (Fannie Yarborough, b. ca. 1854, TX, 4293)

Niggers don' have as much 'ligion as they use ter. Ah went to a missionary meeting at one sister's house an she said ter me: "Sister Douglas, start us off wid a song" an ah started off with "Amazing Grace" [John Newton, 1779]. Sang bout half of de first verse an noticed none of them j'ined in but ah kept right on singin' an wuz gettin full of de sperit when that sister spoke up and said: "Sister Douglas, don' yo know that is done gone out of style?" an selected "Fly Away" [probably "I'll Fly Away," Albert E. Brumley, 1932] an den all them sisters j'ined in an sung "Fly away, fly away" an it sounded jes like a dance chune. (Sarah Douglas, b. ca. 1855, AR, 197)

Besides introducing new vocal approaches, concert, radio, and recording artists added instruments and instrumental styles associated with sinful music, decreasing or altogether eliminating improvisation and collective composition. Concert singers and their accompanists sang and played by rote from scores. Jubilee quartets emphasized lockstep precision reflecting grueling rehearsals. It is no mystery why ex-slaves steeped in oral spirituals found these innovations, so exciting for younger generations, sterile and foolish. They also realized that young people now considered their own sacred songs laughably old-fashioned.

> Ma sung some of de oldest hymns dat I is ever heard: (He sang) "O, Zion, O, Zion, O, Zion, wanta git home at last." (Another) "Is you over, Is you over, Is you over" and the bass come back, "Yes thank God, Yes thank God, Yes thank God, I is over." "How did you cross?" "At de ferry, at de ferry, at de ferry, Yes, thank God I is over." If I sing dem now folks laughs at me, but ma sho' teached dem to her chilluns. (Gus Feaster, b. ca. 1840, SC, 51, orig. parentheses)

> Yes'm, I remember old religious "himes" they used to sing, but they don't sing 'em anymo'. They'd think you were crazy if you did. Did you ever hear this one?

> > O Sister Mary, who's on the Lord's side?
> > Mary wept and Martha mourned,
> > Who's on the Lord's side?
> > I let you know befo' I go
> > Who's on the Lord's side. (Frances Lewis, b. 1854, LA, 155)

However they responded, by the 1930s ex-slaves were surrounded by this new sacred music. In Ella Stinson's case, her teenaged granddaughter Laura (b. ca. 1920) was actually present at Stinson's interview.

> "Lil' Laura kin sing good," she said. "Come on honey, sing a song for de lady." So the 16 year old girl sang in a beautiful soprano voice the "Jubilee songs" which [Stinson] said were sung on plantations around Augusta.

> > Oh, hand me down,
> > Hand me down,
> > Hand me down,
> > Hand me down,

> > Hand me down de silver trumpet, Gabriel!
> > Knock it down,
> > Throw it down,
> > Any way you can get it down,
> > Hand me down de silver trumpet, Lawd!

> Then she sang "My Lawd is so High."

> > My Lawd is so high,
> > You can't come over him
> > So low, you can't go under him,
> > So wide, you can't go 'round him
> > You have to come in by de door. (Ella Stinson, b. ca. 1857, SC, 598–99)

"Hand Me Down the Silver Trumpet, Gabriel" may resemble spirituals Stinson had heard on Reconstruction-era plantations, but best evidence suggests her granddaughter learned both of these items from records or radio broadcasts by Black jubilee groups, or from someone who had. Gabriel and his apocalyptic horn are fixtures in nineteenth-century spirituals, but "Hand Me Down the Silver Trumpet, Gabriel" can be traced back no further than 1920s recordings by Black quartets and choirs.[56]

"Hand Me Down the Trumpet" may recall an earlier day in Black religious song, but "My Lord Is So High (You Have to Come in By the Door)" looks only ahead. Ex-slave Nancy Williams also gave a version, but aside from these two WPA texts, "So High" is known from professional sources and commercial media. The earliest example comes from Newman I. White's *American Negro Folk-Songs* (1928), "reported from Auburn, Ala., 1915–1916. MS. of T. M. Brannon, as from Barbour, Ala. 'Sung by Negro comedian.'" It consists of this item's chorus (given by Stinson's granddaughter), combined with the chorus of "Swing Low, Sweet Chariot."[57] By the 1920s and '30s, however, "So High" was appearing regularly on recordings by gospel quartets, mainly Black, a few white.[58] These are most likely the sources of the WPA versions. They were certainly the basis for the self-perpetuating professional strain. Elvis Presley modeled his 1966 version on the

Heavenly Gospel Singers' 1938 recording. LaVern Baker followed 1950s R&B fashion by recasting this gospel standard as a romantic love song. As late as the 1980s, North Carolina singer-guitarist Doc Watson still featured the item in concert performances.[59]

Like Anglo-American Protestant hymns, oral spirituals as ex-slaves recalled them had not wholly disappeared by the 1930s, but times were definitely changing. The momentum belonged to a new generation of Black singers and songmakers, some still in their teens. In the decades immediately following, Ella Stinson's granddaughter and her peers would create modern Gospel music.

Appendix: Spirituals

By far, the greatest amount of song material in the narratives consists of spiritual texts, quoted copiously in this and other chapters but still not exhausted. Below are examples not covered elsewhere.

"AIN'T I GLAD I'VE GOT OUT OF THE WILDERNESS (LEANING ON THE LORD)." TEXTS: Affie Singleton, Susan Snow. OTHER SOURCES: *DNAH*; *Slave Songs*, 14. RECORDINGS: Edwards' Luling Dixie Singers, "How Did You Feel When You Come Out the Wilderness?" field rec., Luling, TX, February 27, 1936, *Field Recordings, Vol. 14*, Document CD 5630; The Hunter's Chapel Singers, "When You Come Out of the Wilderness," Chicago, February 6, 1966, *Fred McDowell: Amazing Grace*, Testament CD 5004, 1994; Selah Jubilee Singers, "How Did You Feel When You Come Out the Wilderness" (Decca 7876, 1941). DISCOGRAPHIES: *Gospel Discography*. DISCUSSION: Indisputably originating in the antebellum period, this spiritual is best known today through the minstrel parody "The Old Grey Horse Came Tearing Out the Wilderness" and its offshoot, "The Old Grey Mare (She Ain't What She Used to Be)." Ex-slaves Ned Chaney, Steve Jones, and Mary Kindred mentioned "The Old Grey Horse Came Tearing Out the Wilderness." Affie Singleton's inter-

viewer, Robert L. Nelson, appears to credit the text in Singleton's narrative to another (anonymous) ex-slave, and the passage may be from a secondary source, which is definitely the case with other material in Singleton's interview.

I didn't go to church much, cause I didn't have religion den, but I never will forgit one song dey sung when dey buried Mr. Lude. He was my mistis' sister's husband, an' he was sick from a nail stuck in his foot. Dey tried to carry him home, but dey had to bring him back an' he died. An' ol' colored man preached de funeral, an' dey sung dis song:

> My mother prayed in de wilderness,
> In de wilderness,
> In de wilderness,
> My mother prayed in de wilderness,
> An then I'm a goin' home.
> Then I'm a goin' home
> Then I'm a goin' home
> We will all make ready, Lord,
> An' then I'm a goin' home.
>
> She plead her cause in de wilderness,
> In de wilderness,
> In de wilderness,
> She plead her cause in de wilderness,
> An' then I'm a goin' home.

Ol' marster, mistis, an' all of 'em cried, an' us children cried too. (Susan Snow, b. 1850, AL, 2009)

The masters and mistresses used to beat the slaves, says Affie Singleton, so that at night they would resort to singing spirituals. Rough treatment says an ex-slave, made them put greater expression into their songs. They would often go out into the forest and would come out singing:

> Didn't my soul feel happy when I come out the wilderness leaning on the Lord. (Affie Singleton, b. ca. 1849, SC, 283)

"DOWN BY DE RIVERSIDE." TEXTS: Phannie Corneal, Ellen King. TITLE: Sylvia Watkins. There is also a text of doubtful authenticity in the narrative of Annie Little, produced by Texas fieldworker Effie Cowan. SOURCES: Barton, *Plantation Hymns*, 13; Brown III: 619–20; Dett, *Hampton*, 74–75; Diton, *South Carolina*, 24–25; Fauset, "Folk Tales," 297; Jackson, *WNS*, 192–93; Johnson, *Utica*, 16–19; Odum and Johnson, *NHS*, 101; Sandburg, *Songbag*, 480–81. RECORDINGS: Elkins-Payne Jubilee Singers, "Down By the Riverside" (Paramount 12071, 1923); Lead Belly, "Ain't Gonna Study War No More," Washington, DC, August 1940, *Go Down Old Hannah*, Rounder 1099, 1994; Morehouse College Quartet, "Down By the Riverside" (OKeh 4887, 1923); Sister Rosetta Tharpe with the Dependable Boys, "Down By the Riverside" (Decca 48106, 1948). DISCOGRAPHIES: *Blues and Gospel Records*; *Country Music Records*; *Country Music Sources*, 582; *Gospel Discography*. DISCUSSION: The "down by the riverside" refrain once occurred in numerous American religious songs but is now firmly associated with this Black spiritual, standardized in the 1900s by gospel quartets and concert singers. Phannie Corneal gave that form; Ellen King's text suggests the older tradition.

My favorite Gospel hymn:

> I'm gonna lay down my burden, down by the
> river side,
> Down by the river side,
> Down by the river side,
> I'm gonna lay down my burden, down by the
> river side,
> Ain't gonna study war no more. (Phannie Corneal, b. 1864, MO, 313)

Aunt Ellen firmly believes the old-time religion was best for all, and tried to sing in a wavering voice the following:

> Down by the river side,
> Jesus will talk and walk,

Ain't going to study the world no more,
Ain't going to study the world no more,
Down by the river side,
Jesus will walk and talk. (Ellen King, b. 1851,
    MS, 235)

"DRINKING OF THE WINE." TEXTS: James Lucas. OTHER SOURCES: Parrish, *Sea Islands*, 249–51; Odum and Johnson, *NHS*, 136; Solomon, *Daisies*, 167.

De songs has all left me. When you is gone I'll think ob dem but only one I kin rickolict is "Drinkin ob De Wine."

> Ought to have been to heavin three thousand
>   years.
> A drinkin' ob dat wine, a drinkin' ob dat wine.
>   (James Lucas, b. 1833, MS, 1344)

"GLORY, GLORY, HALLELUJAH, WHEN I LAY MY BURDENS DOWN." TEXTS: Henry Reed. OTHER SOURCES: Odum and Johnson, *Workaday*, 188, 200–201. RECORDINGS: The Hunter's Chapel Singers, "When I Lay My Burden Down," Chicago, February 6, 1966, *Fred McDowell: Amazing Grace*, Testament CD 5004, 1994; Will Slayden and Emma Slayden, "Glory, Glory Hallelujah," field rec., Shelby Co., TN, Summer 1952, *Will Slayden*. DISCOGRAPHIES: *Blues and Gospel Records*; *Country Music Sources*, 591; *Gospel Discography*. DISCUSSION: This commonplace or title stanza, probably postwar, was extremely popular well into the twentieth century.

Well, dis is my favorite song:

> Glory, Glory Hallelujah
> When I lay my burdens down
> When I lay my burdens down
> No more Monday, no more Tuesday.
> Glory, Glory Hallelujah
> Howdy, Jesus, Howdy

No more sorrows, no more weeping
When I lay my burdens down. (Henry Reed,
  b. 1853, LA, 186)

"THE GOSPEL TRAIN (I)." TEXTS: Hagar Brown, Benny Dillard, Mollie Hatfield, Lizzie Williams (AL). TITLE: William Emmons. OTHER SOURCES: Brown III: 588–89; *Cabin* III: 134; Cohen, *Rail*, 619–24; Fauset, "Folk Tales," 299; Jackson, *WNS*, 210–11; Marsh, *Jubilee Singers*, 150–51; McIlhenny, *Spirituals*, 107–9; Odum and Johnson, *NHS*, 113–15; Odum and Johnson, *Workaday*, 202; Solomon, *Daisies*, 159; Taylor, *Revival Hymns*, 158–59; White, *ANFS*, 64–65. RECORDINGS: Belleville A Capella Choir, "The Gospel Train," field rec., Belleville, VA, April 1960, *Voices from the American South*, Rounder CD 1701, 1997; Silver Leaf Quartet, "Gospel Train," field rec., Ark, VA, April 1960, *Velvet Voices*, Rounder CD 1708, 1997. DISCOGRAPHIES: *Blues and Gospel Records*; *Country Music Records*; *Gospel Discography*. DISCUSSION: There are many unrelated songs titled "The Gospel Train" (see Mary Gladdy following). Brown, Dillard, and Hatfield all gave the best-known, first published in the *Fisk Jubilee Songs* (1872); rpt. Marsh, *Jubilee Singers*, 150–51. Lizzie Williams (AL) probably quotes this song's chorus ("Git on bo'd, little chillun, git on bo'd"), as sung by her father in the fields, though this line sometimes appears in other pieces. William Emmons simply named this title, so it is also unknowable exactly what song he intended (but most likely this one).

In hot weather chillun played on de crick and de best game of all was to play lak it was big meetin' time. White chillun loved to play dar too wid de little slave chillun. Us would have make-believe preachin' and baptizin' and de way us would sing was a sight. . . . When us started playin' lak us was baptizin' 'em, us th'owed all us could ketch right in de crick, clothes and all, and ducked 'em. Whilst us was doin' dat, us was singin':

Git on board, git on board
For de land of many mansions,
Same old train dat carried
My Mammy to de Promised Land. (Benny Dillard, b. ca. 1858, GA, 290)

De song I sings all de time when I here by myself is.

De Gospel train is a comin
I hear it jes at hand,
The four wheel charriot is a movin,
She's carryin us all through dis land. (Mollie Hatfield, b. ca. 1860, AL, 955)

Hope duh Lord will forgive me for short remembering.

Oh, git on board
The gospel train is coming
Some of these morning!
Git on board!
Yeddy? Be here in the morning! (Hagar Brown, b. ca. 1860, SC, 81)

"THE GOSPEL TRAIN (II)." TEXTS: Mary Gladdy. DISCUSSION: Mary Gladdy, the "rather mysterious personage" who produced automatic spirit writings, provided this and two other unique pieces—"Keep the Fire Burning While Your Soul's Fired Up" and "Sister I Feel 'Im"—probably all her own creations. Whatever its origins, Gladdy's "Gospel Train" is not the song usually known by that name. The second stanza's opening lines are a wandering commonplace, but I have found no other direct parallels.

THE GOSPEL TRAIN

Never seen the like since I've been born,
The people keep a-coming, and the train's done gone;
Too late, too late, the train's done gone,
Too late, sinner, too late, the train's done gone;

Never seen the like since I've been born,
The people keep a-coming, and the train's done
    gone;
Too late, too late, the train's done gone.

Went down into the valley to watch and pray,
My soul got happy and I stayed all day;
Too late, too late, the train's done gone;
Too late, sinner, too late, the train's done gone;
Never seen the like since I've been born,
The people keep a-coming and the train's done
    gone;
Too late, too late, the train's done gone. (Mary
    Gladdy, b. ca. 1853, GA, 25–26)

"HOW LONG (OH LAWD, HOW LONG?)." TEXTS: Mary Homer. OTHER SOURCES: K. J. Holzknecht, "Some Negro Song Variants from Louisville," *JAF* 41 (1928): 559; Kennedy, *Mellows*, 93–94; Lomax, *Ballads*, 586–87; Parrish, *Sea Islands*, 220; Perkins, "Spirituals," 224; Randolph, *OFS* IV: 51; Taylor, *Revival Hymns*, 63–65; Work, *ANSS*, 127. RECORDINGS: Rev. Edward Clayborn, "This Time Another Year You May Be Gone" (Vocalion 1221, 1928); Odette and Ethel, "Befo' This Time Another Year" (Columbia 14169-D, 1926); Grace Outlaw with the Florida Jubilee Singers, "In Some Lonesome Graveyard" (Paramount 12414, 1926). DISCOGRAPHIES: *Blues and Gospel Records*; *Gospel Discography*. DISCUSSION: This item first appears in Marshall Taylor's *Revival Hymns and Plantation Melodies* (1882) but may be older. Almost all versions are Black. Like many WPA texts Mary Homer's version was evidently recited rather than sung.

Yas Sar, I's will says de words ob one ob de songs
fo' yous. Here 'tis,

    W'en de clouds hang heavy
    an' it looks lak rain, Oh Lawd
    how long will de sun draw wautah
    f'om every vein, Oh Lawd, how long?

    'Bout dis time a tudder yeah,
    I's may be in some lonely grave,
    Oh Lawd, how long? (Mary Homer, b. 1856,
      TN, 1793–94)

"HOW LONG US HAFTA LINGER." TEXTS: Lafayette Price. DISCUSSION: Spiritual parodies in this vein are commonplace. For example, see White, *ANFS*, 132–33, whose examples include the following: "I went down in the valley to pray. / I got drunk and stayed all day."

    Sometime dey sing dis one:
    How long us hafter linger?
    How long us hafter linger?
    How long us hafter linger?
    We hafter linger on de way.

    Brudder got a light and gone to hebben,
    Brudder got a light and gone to hebben,
    Brudder got a light and gone to hebben,
    We hafter linger on dey way.

De sinners uster change it and sing:

    Oh yes, we hab some licker
    Oh yes, we hab some licker
    Oh yes, we hab some licker
    We hab some licker on de way. (Lafayette Price,
      b. ca. 1850, AL, 3175)

"I AM A BAPTIST BORN." TEXTS: Fannie Jones. OTHER SOURCES: Odum and Johnson, *NHS*, 103.

When she was asked to sing, the cracked voice
broke into this song:

    I am a Baptist born,
    And my shoes cried,
    And my eyes batted,
    And when I'm gone
    Dere is a Baptist gone. (Fannie Jones, b. 1853,
      GA, 355)

"I AM BOUND TO CROSS JORDAN." TEXTS: Jane Sutton. DISCUSSION: As with Sutton's other performances, the interviewer, Mrs. J. H. Walsh, took pains to suggest characteristic African American vocal effects and inflections. Sutton's text combines various commonplaces in a completely original composition, probably her own, possibly improvised during performance.

Her daughters tried to recall to her mind a "very pretty" song she sometimes sings but she could not remember. They promised to write down the words for the writer and give them to her when she came again. Another song which they called a "Spiritual" was:

I'm Bound To Cross Jordan.

One of dese mawnin's, bright and fair,
I'm ago-na hitch on my wings an' try de air,
I'm bound to c-r-o-s-s Jo-r-din!
In dat mawnin' Away down yonder by de river's
    banks,
Twenty-four elders, all in ranks—
An' I'm bound to cross Jordin, in de mawnin'
I'm boun' to cross Jordin in dat mawnin'
O—h, lets git ready, lets get ready,
I'm boun' to cross Jordin—in—dat—mawnin'—!
    (Jane Sutton, b. ca. 1853, MS, 2093)

"I BELONG TO THE BAND." TEXTS: Judia Fortenberry. DISCUSSION: Fortenberry's chorus is from the well-known "Steal Away," combined with the commonplace of the Christian band. Apparently this was another text recited rather than sung.

1

I belong to the band
That good old christian band
Thank God I belong to the band.
    Chorus

Steal away home to Jesus
I ain't got long to stay here.

2

There'll I'll meet my mother,
My good old christian mother,
Mother, how do you do;
Thank God I belong to the band.

I can't remember the music. But that's an old song we used to sing 'way back yonder. I can't remember any more verses. You got enough anyhow. (Judia Fortenberry, b. 1859, AR, 330)

"I GOT 'LIGION." TEXTS: Eva Reed. DISCUSSION: Eva Reed performed this item, probably her own creation, while describing the church she had established.

When I start dis in church, the sisters catch it and carry it on. Den I gets up and tells my 'termination. Now tonight, when the pastor comes to my home, he will bless the bread and wine just like they did at the Lawd's Supper. We eat it with clean hands and clean hearts. And whoever eats and drinks of this Cup unworthy, you eats damnation when not deserving the Lord. Then the pastor preaches.

I got 'ligion
Oh, I got 'ligion
It's all in my soul.

Oh, it makes me happy
Oh, it makes me happy
Lawd, it's all in my soul.

Oh, I'm determined
Oh, I'm determined
It's all in my soul. (Eva Reed, b. 1863, LA, 184)

"I KNOW (FEEL) MY TIME AIN'T LONG." TEXTS: Lizzie Davis. DISCUSSION: Another wandering line elaborated into a complete song (compare Work, *ANSS*, 135).

> Lord, I know dat my time ain' long,
> Oh, de bells keep a ringin,
> Somebody is a dying,
> Lord, I know dat my time ain' long.
> > (Repeat three times)
> Lord, I know dat my time ain' long,
> Oh, de hammer keep a knockin,
> Keep a knockin on somebody coffin,
> Lord, I know dat my time ain' long.
> > (Repeat three times)

Lizzie—Lord, I sho know my time ain' long. De Lord say de way of de righteous prevaileth to eternal life en I know I right, people. Lord, I know I right. 'Sponsibility or no 'sponsibility, Lord, I seekin de Kingdom. (Lizzie Davis, b. ca. 1865, SC, child of ex-slaves, 287, orig. parentheses)

"I WANT TO BE READY (WALKING IN JERUSALEM JUST LIKE JOHN)." TEXTS: Lizzie Williams (AL). OTHER SOURCES: Ballanta, *St. Helena*, 46–47; Barton, *Plantation Hymns*, 35; Norm Cohen, booklet accompanying *Minstrels and Tunesmiths*, JEMF LP 109, 1981, 19–20; Dett, *Hampton*, 33; Diton, *South Carolina*, 50; Fauset, "Folk Tales," 296; Johnson, *Utica*, 124–27; Scarborough, *TNFS*, 11; White, *ANFS*, 104. RECORDINGS: Tuskegee Institute Singers, "I Want to Be Ready" (Victor 18446, 1916); Bill Monroe & His Bluegrass Boys, "Walking In Jerusalem" (Decca 28608, 1952). DISCOGRAPHIES: *Blues and Gospel Records*; Cohen, *Minstrels and Tunesmiths*, 20; *Gospel Discography*. DISCUSSION: This item first appears in Black collegiate songbooks from the late 1800s; Lizzie Williams (AL) was mistaken when she attributed it to the antebellum era (the other item Williams quotes, "The Gospel Train," is also from the postwar period). Beginning in 1916, "I Want to Be Ready" was frequently recorded by Black quartets; after World War II, it became a favorite of white bluegrass groups.

All de niggahs have to go to church, jes lik' de white fokes. Dey have a part of de church for demselfs. After de wah we hab a church of our own. All de niggahs love to go to church an' sing. I mind a lot of de songs we used ter sing in de fiel's. I mind my pappy used ter sing in de fiel'. "Git on bo'd, little chillun, git on bo'd." Sometimes dey baptiz in de ribber. Den dey sing:

> I wanna be ready
> I wanna be ready
> I wanna be ready good Lawd to walk in
> > Jaruselum jes like John.
> John say de city was jes four square,
> To walk in Jaruselum jes like John.
> But I'll meet my mothah and fathah dar,
> To walk in Jaruselum, jes like John. (Lizzie Williams, b. ca. 1847, AL, 395)

"I WONDER WHERE IS GOOD OLD DANIEL (THE HEBREW CHILDREN)." TEXTS: Mary Ella Grandberry, Lu Lee. OTHER SOURCES: Arnold, *Alabama*, 164; Brown III: 678; *Cabin* III: 107; Hague, "Blockaded Family," 127–28; Jackson, *WNS*, 202–3; Owens, *Texas*, 163; Sandburg, *Songbag*, 92–93; *Southern Harmony*, 266; Stuart, "Camp Meeting," 99; White, *ANFS*, 429. DISCUSSION: "I Wonder Where Is Good Old Daniel (The Hebrew Children)" appears in shape-note songbooks beginning in the 1840s, but not as Grandberry and Lee recalled it, their contrasting versions typifying the Black oral tradition. Although Grandberry describes her father reading, her version definitely did not come from a book. Most have assumed white origins, but Carl Sandburg suggested the piece was "borrowed, possibly, from the negroes" (*Songbag*, 92). Either scenario is plausible.

A few years 'fo' de war my pappy learnt to read de Bible. (Mary Ella apparently forgot her previous comment on penalties for learning to read.) Whenever we would go to chu'ch he would read to us an' we'd sing. 'Bout de mos' two pop'lar songs dey sung was *Steal Away* an' *I Wonder Whar Good Ol' Dan'el Was*. *Steal Away* is sech a pop'lar song what ever'body knows hit. De yuther one is done mought' played out, so I'll sing hit for you. It goes lack dis:

> I wonder whar was good ol' Dan'el,
> > I wonder whar was good ol' Dan'el,
> I wonder whar was thankin' (thinking) Peter,
> > I wonder whar was thankin' Peter.
>
> > (Chorus)
> > I'm goin' away, goin' away.
> > I'm goin' away, goin' away,
>
> I wonder whar was weepin' Mary,
> > I wonder whar was weepin' Mary,
> I'm goin' away, I'm goin' away,
> > I'm goin' away to live forever,
> I'll never turn back no mo'. (Mary Ella Grandberry, b. ca. 1845, AL, 160–61, orig. italics and parentheses)

When old man Davy [slaveholder] had company he would call us in to sing for them. His special song for us was:

> Way down is the good old Daniel
> Way down is the good old Daniel
> Way down is the good old Daniel
> We live in the Promised Land
> Bye and Bye
> Bye and Bye
> We will go there to see him
> We will go there to see him
> We will go there to see him
> And live in the Promised Land. (Lu Lee, b. 1848 or 1849, TX, 2296)

"IF RELIGION WAS TO BUY." TEXTS: George Womble. OTHER SOURCES: Arnold, *Alabama*, 173; Bales, "Negro Folk-Songs," 97; Brown III: 401; *Cabin Songs* III: 102; Louise-Clarke Pyrnelle, *Diddie, Dumps, and Tot: Or Plantation Child-Life* (New

York: Harper & Brothers, 1882), 25; McIlhenny, *Spirituals*, 73; White, *ANFS*, 101–2. DISCUSSION: This floating stanza, recalled by George Womble, probably did originate in slavery or just after.

The following song is one that used to be sung in slavery:

> If religion was to buy,
> The rich would git it all
> And the po' would die,
> But it ain't that way,
> Thanks the Lord. (George Womble, b. 1843, GA, 655)

"IF YOU GET THERE BEFORE I DO." TEXTS: Mary Frances Brown, Sylvia Cannon, Sarah Felder, Estella Jones, Frances Lewis. OTHER SOURCES: *Slave Songs*, 31; Barton, *Plantation Hymns*, 10; Bass, "Negro Songs," 424; Brown III: 591, 620; Hallowell, *Calhoun*, 18; Jackson, *WNS*, 319; Scarborough, *TNFS*, 12; White, *ANFS*, 72, 111. DISCUSSION: This is another wandering rhyme variously rephrased in otherwise unrelated songs, as illustrated by the WPA examples. Cannon's and Jones's contributions are quoted in the chapter text, Mary Frances Brown's with "We Are Slipping Through the Gates," Frances Lewis's with "Zion's Hill." Sarah Felder's text is unique and may be her own.

> I'is gwine ter heaven when I die,
> I'is gwine ter heaven when I die,
> Iffen you git dar 'fore I do,
> Tell de Lord I'is cumin' too,
> Fur I'is gwine ter heaven when I die. (Sarah Felder, b. 1853, MS, 722)

"I'LL NEVAH TURN BACK NO MOAH." TEXTS: Rosa Thomas. DISCUSSION: This is another case of a widespread commonplace (see Brown III: 404–5, 620; Jackson, *WNS*, 222–23) elaborated into a unique composition. Mary Ella Grandberry used this line in her version of "I Wonder Where Is

Good Old Daniel." Several narrators recited their texts for interviewers, but Thomas was among those who insisted they could not recite but had to sing their songs.

I wuz too small to remember anything dat happened during slavery times but I do remember some of de songs my mother used to sing. I can sing 'em to you, but I fergits de words when I tries to say 'em over to you. One of dem wuz: (singing in a low mellow voice)

No moah, no moah, My Lawd, I'll nevah turn back no moah!
No moah, No moah, My Lawd, I'll nevah turn back no moah!
Sometime, I'm up, Sometime I'm down, I'll nevah turn back no moah! (Rosa Thomas, b. 1861, AL, 2101, orig. parentheses)

"JACOB'S LADDER." TEXTS: Rose Adway, Madison Bruin, Eliza Holman, Thomas Johns. TITLE: Lucy Ann Warfield. OTHER SOURCES: Ballanta, *St. Helena*, 61; Brown III: 585–86, 594–95; *Cabin Songs* III: 118; *Country Music Sources*, 581–82; Dett, *Hampton*, 118; Hallowell, *Calhoun*, 33; Johnson, *Spirituals* I: 59; Leigh, *Georgia Plantation*, 60; Lomax, *FSNA*, 453; Odum and Johnson, *Workday*, 111–12; Pearson, *Letters*, 28; Perkins, "Spirituals," 233; Randolph, *OFS* II: 336; Rosenberg, *Virginia*, 58; Sharp, *EFSSA* II: 295; *Slave Songs*, 95, 96; Solomon, *Daisies*, 160; White, *ANFS*, 59–60. RECORDINGS: Golden Gate Quartet, "We Are Climbing Jacob's Ladder," Washington, DC, December 1940, *Freedom*; Harrod's Jubilee Singers, "Jacob's Ladder" (Black Swan 2057, 1922); Clara Ward and Her Singers, "Jacob's Ladder," *Come In the Room*, Vanguard LP 9101, 1961. DISCOGRAPHIES: *Blues and Gospel Records*; *Country Music Sources*, 581–82; *Gospel Discography*. DISCUSSION: Ex-slave variants of this well-known spiritual are typical of oral versions, incorporating the most common refrains: "soldiers of the cross" or "for the work is almost done." Like most traditional texts, however, the WPA examples are otherwise quite varied. Eliza's Holman's version is the most personalized. Madison Bruin combined "Jacob's Ladder" and "Good Shepherd." Actually, however, "Jacob's Ladder" is more closely associated with another nineteenth-century Black spiritual, "Keep Your Lamp Trimmed And Burning" (below), which often features the "don't you get weary, for the work is almost done" stanza found in Rose Adway's and Thomas Johns's "Jacob Ladder" texts (and numerous others).

I am climbin' Jacob's ladder
I am climbin' Jacob's ladder
I am climbin' Jacob's ladder
For the work is almost done.

Every round goes higher and higher
Every round goes higher and higher
Every round goes higher and higher
For the work is almost done.

Sister, now don't you get worried
Sister, now don't you get worried
Sister, now don't you get worried
For the work is almost done.

My mother used to sing dat when she was spinnin and cardin'. They'd spin and dye the thread with some kind of indigo. (Rose Adway, b. ca. 1862, MS, 18)

My favorite song was "De Ol' Time Religion." I kin sing dat song now, and bring folks up singin' or shoutin'. We liked to sing, too, "Swing Low, Sweet Chariot," and others. My mother's favorite song went like dis:

We are climbin' Jacob's ladder (repeated three times), For de work is mos' done.
Brother in Heaven just before you (repeated three times) for the work is mos' done.

Brethern, don't get weary (repeated three times),
    for de work is mos' done. (Thomas Johns,
    b. 1847, AL, 1969, orig. parentheses)

Do I's know any ol' songs? Shucks. I's use to know lots ob dem an' I's use to could sing too but I's can't do it any mo'. Yas, I's will tell yous de one dat I's lak bes' an' it 'spresses my feelin's 'zactly. I's will tell yous de wo'ds:

> I's am climbin' Jacob's laddah, laddah,
> I's am climbin' Jacob's laddah, laddah,
> Soldier ob de cross: Oh-h-h! Rise, shine,
> Give God de glory, glory, glory! in de yeah ob de
>   Jubilee.
> I's want to climb up Jacob's laddah, laddah,
> Jacob's laddah 'til I's gits in de new Jeru-sa-lem!

Marster, dat's jus' how I feel. (Eliza Holman, b. ca. 1855, MS, 1778)

"JES' CARRY ME AND BURY ME." TEXTS: Hilliard Johnson. The interviewer, Ruby Pickens Tartt, was obviously taken with Johnson's image of the pale white horse, which appears to conflate two of the Four Horsemen of the Apocalypse (John 6): Death, who rides a pale horse, and the conquering figure on a white horse, usually identified as Christ.

"Well, here's one you ain't got, 'ca'se hit's a really old sperichel my gran'maw use to sing. I'se sorter hoarse today, but hit go:

> "Jes' carry me and bury me
>   I'll rise at de comin' day
> Jes' carry me and bury me,
>   I'll rise at de comin' day.

"Now dat's jes' de chorus and de verse say:

> "When I was in my worldly ways
>   Nobody had nothin' to say.

> Now I'm ridin' de pale white hoss
>   Ev'ybody got something to say.

"Den de chorus ag'in, and hit's a pretty one sho's you bawn." I mentioned the figure of speech "pale white hoss," but he "didn't know nothin' 'bout no figures!" (Uncle Hilliard Johnson, b. ca. 1857, AL, 227–28, int. Ruby Pickens Tartt)

"JESUS IS A ROCK IN A WEARY LAND." TEXTS: Ellen Broomfield, Eva Strayhorn. OTHER SOURCES: Hallowell, *Calhoun*, 51; Parrish, *Sea Islands*, 18, 161–63; Randolph, *OFS* IV: 94; Taylor, *Revival Hymns*, 209–10. RECORDINGS: Belmont Silvertone Jubilee Singers, "My Lord's a Rock in the Weary Land" (Decca 7674, 1939); Biddleville Quintette, "Jesus Is a Rock In the Weary Land" (Paramount 12937, 1929); Charioteers, "Jesus Is a Rock In a Weary Land" (Associated 60,597, 1944); Peter Davis and Sea Island Singers, "Rock in the Weary Land," field rec., St. Simmons Island, GA, 1959, *Georgia Sea Islands: Biblical Songs and Spirituals*, Rounder CD 1712, 1998; Five Blind Boys, "Jesus Is a Rock in a Weary Land" (Peacock 1723, 1953); Original Gospel Harmonettes, "Jesus Is a Rock In a Weary Land" (RCA Victor 22/50-0081, 1949); Pace Jubilee Singers, "Jesus Is a Rock In a Weary Land" (Victor 38361, 1929); Selah Jubilee Singers, "King Jesus Is a Rock in the Weary Land" (Decca 7884, 1942). DISCOGRAPHIES: *Blues and Gospel Records*; *Gospel Discography*. DISCUSSION: This is probably a Black creation from just after the war; in the twentieth century it became a favorite of quartets. Broomfield and Strayhorn both gave its chorus.

> My Jesus is a rock in a weary land,
> A weary land, a weary land.
> My Jesus is a rock in a weary land,
> A shelter in the time of storm. (Ellen Broom-
>   field, b. 1853, LA, 32)

"KEEP YOUR LAMP TRIMMED AND BURNING." TITLE: Rachel Hankins. OTHER SOURCES:

Arrowood and Hamilton, "Negro Spirituals," 582; *Cabin* III: 41; Dett, *Hampton*, 199–98; Higginson, "Spirituals," 687; Jackson, *WNS*, 157; Marsh, *Jubilee Singers*, 190. RECORDINGS: Rev. Pearly Brown, "Keep your Lamp Trimmed and Burning," KPFA radio, Berkeley, CA, September 1974, *You're Gonna Need That Pure Religion*, Arhoolie CD 9025, 2002; Blind Willie Johnson, "Keep Your Lamp Trimmed and Burning" (Columbia 14303-D, 1928); Reverend Gary Davis, "Keep Your Lamp Trimmed and Burning," *Gospel, Blues and Street Songs*, Riverside LP 148, 1956; Fred McDowell, "Keep Your Lamp Trimmed and Burning," field rec., Como, MS, 1959, *Southern Journey*. (Davis and McDowell both rerecorded the song many times.) DISCOGRAPHIES: *Blues and Gospel Records*; *Gospel Discography*. DISCUSSION: This spiritual was known to whites—Hankins identified it with a slaveholder—but it may be a slave creation and in any case is most probably African American. It is closely related to another Black spiritual, "Jacob's Ladder" (above). In the twentieth century, "Keep Your Lamp Trimmed And Burning" was one of several sacred songs transformed into "talking guitar" showpieces.

Master Columbus would call us niggers up on Sunday evening and read the Bible to us and tell us how to do and he taught us one song to sing and it was this "Keep Your Lamp Trimmed and Burning" and he'd have us to sing it every Sunday evening and he told us that that song meant to do good and let each other see our good. When it rained we did not have meeting but when it was dry we always had meeting. (Rachel Hankins, b. 1850, AL, 155)

"LAND OF CANAAN." TEXTS: Mary Frances Brown. DISCUSSION: This item employs the ubiquitous "by and by" refrain, and may draw from William Steffe's "On Canaan's Happy Shore" (ca. 1850), but like Brown's other contributions, her arrangement of these elements is quite original, possibly even improvised at the interview.

THE LAND OF CANAAN

Mother where shall I meet you,
Bye and bye, bye and bye,
Mother where shall I meet you,
Bye and bye, bye and bye.

I will meet you over in Canaan,
Bye and bye, bye and bye,
I will meet you over in Canaan,
Bye and bye, bye and bye.

Then my troubles will be over,
Bye and bye, bye and bye,
Then my troubles will be over,
Bye and bye, bye and bye.

I will sit 'long side of my Jesus,
Bye and bye, bye and bye,
I will sit 'long side of my Jesus,
Bye and bye, bye and bye. (Mary Frances Brown,
    b. 1859, SC, 87)

"LET'S GO DOWN TO JORDAN." TEXTS: Amy Else, Eison Lyles, Andrew Moody, Rube Witt. OTHER SOURCES: Arnold, *Alabama*, 182; Barton, *Plantation Hymns*, 31; Bass "Negro Songs," 423; Carter, *Louisiana Negro*, 67–68; Gordon, *Folk-Songs*, 25–26, 29; King, *Great South*, 619–20; Lomax, *Ballads*, 582–83; McIlhenny, *Spirituals*, 164–66; Odum and Johnson, *NHS*, 124, 147. DISCUSSION: The River Jordan often appeared in baptizing songs. Samuel Stennett's "On Jordan's Stormy Banks I Stand" (1787) was the most popular of these, but ex-slaves named or performed several others: "Cross De Riber Jordan" (Naisy Reece); "Crossin' de River Jordan" (Emma Virgel); "On de udder side ob Jordan" (Louis Fowler); and so forth. Collections abound in similar examples. Many of these items were probably independent creations, but "Let's Go Down to Jordan" represents an established (if somewhat diffuse) tradition, distinguished by that title (which may also serve as refrain) and the statement "religion is so sweet." Else, Lyles, and Witt all described it at baptisms, as do most other sources.

Dey sing "Amazin' Grace," 'n' "O Ship 'r' Zion" mos'. Some 'r' de cullud folks could read de hymns in de hymn book. Young mistis she learn 'em. Dey uster sing hymns de cullud folks mek. Dey sing:

> Jerd'n ribber so still 'n' col',
>> Le's go down t' Jerd'n.
> Go down, go down,
>> Le's go down t' Jerd'n. (Andrew Moody,
>> b. ca. 1855, TX, 2722)

Parson Clemmons was the pastor of the church when I 'fessed religion, and he baptized me. My mama made me a long, white robe to be baptized in. I still 'members the song they sung:

> Let's go down to Jordon,
> Religion is so Sweet
> Let's go down to Jordon
> Christ said, Baptizing must go on.
> Let's go down to Jordon. (Amy Else, b. 1848,
> TX, 1302)

Atter dat [the earthquake of 1886] us built St. Luke, and we had logs for seats. We marched together and sang: "Let's go down to de water and be baptized. I promised de Lawd dat I'd be baptized when St. Luke was finished. 'Ligion so sweet, 'ligion so sweet."

Little boys watched us while us was building St. Luke's. Dey would play in de branch and sing: "Little boy wouldn't swim, kaise leather tacked to his shoe." Den dey would catch hands and jump up and down on de bank and sing: "Loop de la—loop de loop de la; Deacon coming out, deacon coming out." Den all would run to de shade trees and put on deir clothes.

And when us finished St. Lukes, such a baptizing as us had! All of us marched down to de pool while we sung:

> 'Les got down to de water and be baptized.
> 'Ligion is so sweet, I's promised de Lord I'd be
> baptized;
> 'Ligion is so sweet, and I's promised de Lord I'd
> be baptized. (Eison Lyles, b. ca. 1865, child of
> ex-slaves, SC, 138)

"THE LILY OF THE VALLEY." TEXTS: Annie Bridges. OTHER SOURCES: F. A. Clark, ed., *Songs of the Pilgrim Way* (Philadelphia: A. M. E. Book Concern, 1915), d16; Dett, *Hampton*, 145; Marsh, *Jubilee Singers*, 163. RECORDINGS: Texas Jubilee Singers, "He's the Lily of the Valley" (Columbia 14445-D, 1928). DISCUSSION: Though not well known, this item did occasionally appear in postwar songbooks and later on records.

(One of the religious songs used to be):

> Jesus in his chariot rides
> He had three white horses side by side
> When Jesus reached the mountain top
> He spoke one word, the chariot stop
> He's the lily of the valley, O my Lord.
> (Annie Bridges, b. 1855, MO, 46,
> orig. parentheses)

"LITTLE BABY'S GONE TO HEAVEN." TEXTS: Mary Jane Drucilla Davis. DISCUSSION: Of ex-slaves Davis alone performed this item, an infant's funeral song, but such pieces are reported elsewhere. Describing Black spirituals in wartime South Carolina Thomas Wentworth Higginson wrote, "of 'occasional hymns,' properly so called, I noticed but one, a funeral hymn for an infant, which is sung plaintively over and over, without variety of words. . . . 'De little baby gone home.'" Higginson, "Negro Spirituals," 689.

> Little baby's gone to heaven
> To try on his robe
> Oh, Lord, I'm most done toiling here
> Little baby, mmm-m-mm.

Oh, it was so mournful. And let me tell you what they'd do. They'd all march one behind the other and somebody would carry the baby's casket on their shoulder and sing that song. That's the first song I remember. I was three years old and now I'm seventy-three and crippled up with rheumatism. (Mary Jane Drucilla Davis, b. ca. 1865, GA, child of ex-slaves, 124)

"LITTLE WHEEL ROLLING IN MY HEART." TEXTS: Madison Bruin. OTHER SOURCES: Brown III: 675; *Cabin Songs* III: 100; Dett, *Hampton*, 168; Perkins, "Spirituals," 235.

Back in slav'ry times on Sunday I uster to go 'long to chu'ch wid de w'ite folks to open de gate. Dey uster go to de Christian Chu'ch. Us uster sing on de plantation:

> Little wheels rollin' in my heart" (Madison
> Bruin, b. 1856, KY, 509–10)

"MOTHERLESS CHILDREN (SEES A HARD TIME)." TEXTS: Laura Clark, Gus Feaster. DISCOGRAPHIES: *Blues and Gospel Records*; *Gospel Discography*. DISCUSSION: Often misattributed to the slavery era, this is evidently a twentieth-century creation, though two ex-slaves had heard it.

I sets cross de road here from dat church over yonder and can't go 'ca'se I'm cripple' and blin', but I heers um singin':

> A motherless chile sees a hard time
> Oh, Lord he'p her on de road
> Er sister will do de bes' she kin
> Dis is a hard world, Lord, for a mother-
> less chile. . . .

I can't read no songs to comfort me, jes' ketch 'em from de preacher on de stan' an' hole 'em, dat's de way I ketch my larnin'. (Laura Clark, b. ca. 1850, AL, 73, 75)

"Motherless chilluns sees hard times; just ain't got no whar to go; goes from do' to do'," dat's de song dey got up. I doesn't know whar it come from. (Gus Feaster, b. ca. 1840, SC, 46)

"MY KNEE-BONE'S ACHING (HEAVEN IS MY AIM)." TEXTS: Anderson Edwards, Frances Lewis, Henry Lewis, Leo Mouton, Charley Stewart. OTHER SOURCES: Fauset, "Folk Tales," 301; Higginson, "Spirituals," 688; King, *Great South*, 615; Perkins, "Spirituals," 228–29; Porter, "Negro Songs," 1; *Slave Songs*, 72; White, *ANFS*, 86–87. RECORDINGS: Viola James and congregation, "Tryin' to Make Heaven My Home," field rec., Independence Church, Tyro, MS, September 1959, *61 Highway Mississippi*, Rounder CD 1703, 1997. DISCUSSION: This piece is quite well documented in period sources and almost certainly originated during slavery. Highly variable, it is distinguished by five elements, at least two of which appear in most versions: these are the statements 1) that the singer is done (tired of) wagging crosses; 2) that their knee-bone is aching, their body racked with pain; 3). that they call themselves a child of God; 4) that someone called and someone else refused to answer; and 5) that heaven is their aim (home). In addition to the texts below, Anderson Edwards included a version in his account of turning the pot down, while Charley Stewart had heard it from his mother.

> The Lord called Adam, and Adam 'fused to
> answer.
> The second time he answered, "Hear me Lord,
> I almost done waggin' with crosses,
> My knee-bone is aching, my body racked with
> pain,
> I call myself a Child of God, and heaven is my
> aim." (Frances Lewis, b. 1854, GA, 157)

Old massa 'low us praise Gawd but lots of massas didn't 'low dem to git on de knees. Us have church-house and de white folks go in de mornin' and us go after dinner. Us used to sing:

My knee bones achin',
My body's rackin' with pain,
I calls myself de chile of Gawd,
Heaven am my aim.

If you don't 'lieve I's a chile of Gawd,
Jis' meet me on dat other shore,
Heaven is my home.
I calls myself a chile of Gawd,
I's a long time on my way,
But Heaven am my home. (Henry Lewis, b. 1831,
    TX, 9–10)

Dey uster sing d' song d' w'ite folks sing 'n' den had
some dey mek deyse'f. One 'r' dem went like dis,

Little chillens, y' better b'lieve,
        I's gittin' tired 'r' waggin' d' cross.
Little chillens, y' better b'lieve,
        My bones is achin' 'n' my body's feelin'
            pain.
Call yo'se'f d' chillen 'r' God
        Heben gwinter be my home.
Sister Mary call Marthy,
        An' Marthy refuse' t' answer,
Call yo's'ef, d' chillen 'r' God,
        O, Heben gwinter be my home. (Leo
            Mouton, b. ca. 1860, LA, 2812–13)

"MY SISTER, I FEELS 'IM (OLD SLAVE CANTI-
    CLE)." TEXTS: Mary Gladdy. DISCUSSION: This
    is the last of three texts from Mary Gladdy, the
    "mysterious personage" who regularly communi-
    cated with spirits. According to Mary, this song
    accompanied the concluding handshake at slave
    experience meetings, which were masked by turn-
    ing the pot down.

OLD SLAVE CANTICLE.

My sister, I feels 'im, my sister, I feels 'im;
All night long I've been feelin' 'im;
Jest befoe day, I feels 'im, jest befoe day I feels 'im;

The sperit, I feels 'im, the sperit I feels 'im!

My brother, I feels 'im, my brother, I feels 'im;
All night long I've been feelin' 'im;
Jest befoe day, I feels 'im, jest befoe day I feels
    'im;
The sperit, I feels 'im! (Mary Gladdy, b. ca. 1853,
    GA, 26)

"ON THE HILL OF CAVALRY." TEXTS: Abbie
    Lindsay. DISCUSSION: Like many narrators,
    Abbie Lindsay excused her failing memory, and
    interviewer Samuel S. Taylor included the nota-
    tion "(FRAGMENT)" with the two other pieces
    she sang. This was by far the longest text that she
    provided, though it was still incomplete by her
    reckoning.

The ark was seen at rest upon the hill
On the hill of Cavalry
The Great Jehovah spoke
Sanctify to God upon the hill.

                                    (First verse)
Peter spied the promised land
On the hills of Cavalry
The Great Jehovah spoke
Sanctify to God upon the hill.

                                    (Second verse)

There was lots more that they sung. (Abbie Lind-
    say, b. 1856, LA, 257–58, orig. parentheses)

"REMEMBER ME." TEXTS: William Oliver, Cath-
    erine Scales. TITLE: Lewis Mundy, James Wil-
    son. OTHER SOURCES: Higginson, "Spirituals,"
    689–90; Jackson, *WNS*, 165, 179, 324; King, *Great
    South*, 618–19; Lomax, *Ballads*, 610–11; McIlhenny,
    Spirituals, 82–84, 186; Odum and Johnson, *NHS*,
    92; Odum and Johnson, *Workaday*, 188; Parrish,
    Sea Islands, 226, 228–31; *Slave Songs*, 12; Spaulding,
    "Palmetto," 198. RECORDINGS: Jimmie Strothers
    and Joe Lee, "Do Lord, Lord, Remember Me," field
    rec., Lynn, VA, June 1936, *Field Recordings, Vol-*

ume 1: *Virginia*, Document CD 5575; Williams Family, "Do, Lord, Remember Me," field rec., Jonesville, FL, May 1978, *Field Recordings of African American Traditional Music 1977–1980*, Dust-to-Digital CDs 24. DISCOGRAPHIES: *Blues and Gospel Records*; *Country Music Sources*, 587; *Gospel Discography*. DISCUSSION: Catherine Scales's version of this well-known spiritual is one of two items in the WPA narratives with a tune transcription (the standard melody). William Oliver gave a highly original version: "I remember one song my mother sang: / Do, Lord, remember me! / Remember me when the year go round! / Do, Lord, remember me! / Why can't you die / Like Jesus died? / He laid in His grave! / He crippled some. / Some He saved. / I can't get it all" (William Oliver, b. unk., SC, 218).

One slave woman wuz sold way fum home—had three chillun, and daze six an eight an ten yuhs ole. She sang a song juss fo dey tuk huh off. She put her three children between her knees. She sung, "Lord, Be With Us."

> [tune transcription]
> do - me - sol - re - do - sol - te - sol - me - do - do - sol -
> Remembuh me Remembuh me Oh Lord
> fa - me - sol - do
> remembuh me

This was sung full of quavers and pathos, and entreaty. Den she cried! An dey took huh off, and de chillun never saw her no more. (Catherine Scales, b. ca. 1855, NC, 248–49)

"SHINE ON ME." TEXTS: Martha Kelly, Steve Stepney. TITLE: Minerva Bratcher ("Let the Light Shine on You"), Bob Potter ("Let Our Light Shine"). OTHER SOURCES: Dett, *Hampton*, 44–45. RECORDINGS: Rev. Johnny Blakey, "Let the Light Shine On Me" (OKeh 8758, 1928); Cliff Carlisle Quartet, "Shine On Me" (Bluebird B-6855, 1936); Famous Garland Gospel Singers, "Shine On Me" (Banner 32726,

1931); Blind Willie Johnson, "Let Your Light Shine On Me" (Columbia 14490-D, 1929); Jubilee Gospel Team, "Let the Light from the Lighthouse Shine on Me" (Paramount unissued, 1930); Lead Belly, "Let It Shine On Me," Washington, DC, 1940, *Let It Shine On Me*, Rounder CD 1046, 1991; Ernest Phipps & His Holiness Singers, "Shine On Me" (Bluebird B-5540, 1928); Swan Silvertones, "Heavenly Light Shine On Me," ca. 1954, *Love Lifted Me*, Specialty LP 2122, 1970. DISCOGRAPHIES: *Blues and Gospel Records*; *Country Music Records*; *Country Music Sources*, 597; *Gospel Discography*. DISCUSSION: This latter-day piece was extremely popular with choirs and quartets, where it probably originated. Like most versions, Steve Stepney's text incorporates the opening stanza of Horatius Bonar's "I Heard the Voice of Jesus Say" (1846). (Stepney's text was actually communicated by his grandchildren and definitely suggests the twentieth-century tradition.)

The Lighthouse

> Shine on mee, Shine on me,
> I wonder if the lighthouse shine on me.
> Shine on mee, shine on me,
> Let the power o' th' lighthouse
> Shine on me.
>
> I heard th' voice of Jesus say
> Come unto me and rest.
> Lie down, lie down O weary one,
> Thy head upon my breast.
>
> Chorus: Shine on mee etc.

Remarks: Almost without exception a song in the field is begun by someone signing the chorus. (Steve Stepney, 1840–1935, MS, communicated by his grandchildren, 2039–40)

Some of de peoples used to sing dere, but I wouldn' never bear much along dat line. Didn' have no voice much to sing. Is you got dis one?

Lord, I wonder,
Lord, I wonder,   (Repeat
Lord, I wonder,   ——3
When de lighthouse   Times)
Gwine shine on me.
Dat all dere be to dat one. (Martha Kelly, b. unk., SC, 83, orig. parentheses)

"SIT DOWN, CHILD (SERVANT, SISTER, MEMBER, and so on) (I CAN'T SIT DOWN)." TEXTS: Emma Crockett, Rebecca Fletcher. OTHER SOURCES: Arnold, *Alabama*, 176; Bruce R. Buckley, "'Uncle' Ira Cephas—A Negro Folk Singer in Ohio," *Midwest Folklore* 3 (1953): 16; Lomax, *Ballads*, 584–86; McIlhenny, *Spirituals*, 174–77; Solomon, *Daisies*, 171; Work, *ANSS*, 65. RECORDINGS: Blue Spring Mississippi Baptist Association Delegation, "Sit Down Servant," Washington, DC, February 1989, *Wade In the Water, Vol. II: African-American Congregational Singing*, Smithsonian Folkways CD 40073, 1994; Rev. Timothy Hayes and group, "Sit Down Servant," field rec., Glass, VA, 1979, *Virginia Work Songs*; Dr. C. J. Johnson, "Sit Down Servant, Sit Down" *Old Time Song Service: Free At Last*, Savoy LP 14204, 1968; Norfolk Jubilee Quartet, "Sit Down Sit Down I Can't Sit Down" (Paramount 12301, 1925); Rosetta Tharpe, "Sit Down" (Decca 8538, 1941); Swan Silvertones with Dorothy Love Coates and the Original Gospel Harmonettes, "Medley (Live): Sit Down Servant/Amen," unk. location, ca. 1954, *The Swan Silvertones: Heavenly Light*, Specialty CD 7044, 1993. DISCOGRAPHIES: *Blues and Gospel Records*; *Country Music Sources*, 583; *Gospel Discography*. DISCUSSION: This floater addresses one or more spiritually possessed persons (children, servants, members, relations) who for that reason simply can't sit down. Some texts are devoted entirely to this incremental sequence; others, like Rebecca Fletcher's, include additional lyrics. The commonplace wanders into other songs as well (Emma Crockett included it in her version of the shout "Rock Daniel"). Fletcher also communicated the African American folk belief that the jaybird visits hell every Friday to take the Devil a grain of sand, a drop of water, or more kindling. South Carolina ex-slave Charlie Robinson also expressed this belief, for which see Brown VII: 394–95; "Folk-Lore and Ethnology," *Southern Workman* 23 (1894): 15; Collins Lee, "Some Negro Lore From Baltimore," *JAF* 5 (1892): 111; Sadie Price, "Kentucky Folk-Lore," *JAF* 14 (1901): 33; Puckett, *Folk Beliefs*, 549–50; Susan B. Showers, "Alabama Folk-Lore," *Southern Workman* 29 (1900): 180.

When I was little, I heard 'em sing:

Sit down child, sit down
Sit down child, sit down
Sit down child, sit down
O Lord, I can't sit down!

O Lord, I fold up my arms and I wonder
And I wonder, Lord, I wonder
I fold up my arms and I wonder to see
How far I am away from my Home.

Another was like this:

I saw the light coming down
I saw the light coming down
It's a mighty pretty light coming down
Way up in the heavens coming.

They don't have singin' that way anymore. There's another verse about "I can't sit down, I want my starry crown." Friday is the day the jaybird carries a grain of sand to the Bad Man to torment you if you died bad. If you lived without thinkin' about God, those sands will help to worry you, for they are hot and will burn your feet. (Rebecca Fletcher, b. 1842, MS, 68)

"STEAL AWAY TO JESUS." TEXTS: Madison Bruin, George Rivers. TITLE: Frances Banks, Benjamin Russell. OTHER SOURCES: Anon. ex-slave (b. unk., TN), *Unwritten History*, 13; Dett, *Hamp-*

ton, 111, VII; Johnson, *Utica*, 116–17; Odum and Johnson, *NHS*, 139; Marsh, *Jubilee Singers*, 147; Perkins, "Spirituals," 245–46; White, *ANFS*, 55–56; Work, *ANSS*, 123. RECORDINGS: Fisk University Male Quartette, "Steal Away To Jesus" (Columbia A2803, 1915). DISCOGRAPHIES: *Blues and Gospel Records*; *Country Music Sources*, 583; *Gospel Discography*. DISCUSSION: This is another famous Negro spiritual that probably originated among slaves, but that is best known through later arrangements and adaptations. George Rivers's text suggests that modern strain, Madison Bruin's the older tradition. There is also a text in the narrative of Harriet Collins, produced by Texas fieldworker Ada Davis. This particular example may be authentic, but all of Davis's materials demand caution.

I 'members some of de song us uster sing. One was:

> Steal away—steal away
> Steal away to Jesus
> Steal away—steal away
> I ain't got long to stay here.

> W'en my Lord calls me
> He calls me by de lightnin'
> He calls me by de thunder
> I ain't got long to stay here.
> > (Repeat chorus) (George Rivers, b. ca.
> > 1850, TX, 3327–28, orig. parentheses)

> Steal away, steal away, steal away to my Jesus
> Steal away, steal away, steal away
> > I ain't got long to tarry.
> > Tell my mudder if she want to see me,
> > Look on de hoss on de battlefiel'. (Madison Bruin, b. 1856, KY, 509–10)

"THE SUN GOIN' RISE TO SET NO MO'." TEXTS: Frances Lewis. DISCUSSION: The final stanza's last two lines are from "Down in the Valley to Pray," while the third stanza's last line suggests "The Angels Changed My Name," for which see Marsh, *Jubilee Singers*, 227; McIlhenny, *Spirituals*, 45–46; Rosenbaum, *Shout*, 120–21; "Silhouettes," *Southern Workman* 20 (April 1891): 172. Compare Blind Gary, "I Am the Light Of the World" (ARC 5-12-66, 1935). Like Lewis's other contributions, however, the whole is quite original, possibly her own creation cobbled together at the interview. (Supporting that view, she included the first stanza in another of her performances, "Zion's Hill" below.)

> The sun goin' rise to set no mo',
> King Jesus is my Captain.
> He gave me His orders, and He told me not to
> > fail,
> The sun goin' to rise to set no mo'.

> The sun goin' rise to set no mo',
> The sun goin' rise to set no mo',
> The sun goin' rise to set no mo'.

> I know I've been converted,
> God knows I ain't ashamed,
> The Holy Ghost is my witness,
> And the angels done sign my name.

> The sun goin' rise to set no mo',
> The sun goin' rise to set no mo',
> The sun goin' rise to set no mo',
> On that Resurrection Day.

> I went to the Valley, and I didn't go to stay,
> My soul got happy, and I stayed all day.
> The sun goin' rise to set no mo',
> The sun goin' rise to set no mo',
> The sun goin' rise to set no mo'. (Frances Lewis,
> > b. 1854, GA, 156)

"THEM BONES OF MINE." TEXTS: Susan Forrest. OTHER SOURCES: Barton, *Plantation Hymns*, 11.

Dey uster sing lots of songs, but I ain't got my singin' min' now. I 'member one start like dis:

Dem bones of mine,
Comin' togedder in de morning.

My daddy he teached me how to shout. (Susan Forrest, b. ca. 1862, GA, 1379)

"WE ARE SLIPPING THROUGH THE GATES." TEXTS: Mary Frances Brown. DISCUSSION: Mary Frances Brown contributed several songs that truly convey a sense of spontaneous oral performance. Like the other religious titles, "We Are Slipping Through the Gates" is in the familiar spiritual idiom but seems to be Brown's original creation otherwise, possibly composed in performance. It may be telling that another of Brown's texts, "Land of Canaan," also employs the "by and by" commonplace, while two of her other performances ("The Promise Land," "I'm A-Goin' Home to Die No More") use the "Glory, Hallelujah!" refrain.

> We are a-slippin' through the gates, we are
> a-slippin' through the gates, we are a-slippin'
> through the gates,
> Oh Lord! Oh Lord!
> In the new Jerusalem I'm goin' to rest,
> Oh Lord! Oh Lord!
> Inside the pearly gates my Savior waits for me,
> Oh Lord! Oh Lord!
> My Saviour wont you come for me when I die?
>
> Oh! Mother wont you come for me, when I die?
> Oh! Mother wont you come for me, when I die?
> Bye and bye - bye and bye!
> Oh Lord! Oh Lord!
> Glory - Glory - Hallelujah! Glory - Glory
> - Hallelujah!
> Glory - Glory - Hallelujah! (Mary Frances
> Brown, b. 1859, SC, 89–90)

"WHEN THE TRAIN COMES ALONG." TEXTS: Liza Jones, Mintie Gilbert Wood. OTHER SOURCES: Ballanta, *St. Helena*, 12; John Nelson Clark Cog-

gin, *Plantation Melodies and Spiritual Songs*, 3rd ed. (Philadelphia: Hall Mack, 1927); Cohen, *Rail*, 633–35; *Country Music Sources*, 589; Diton, *South Carolina*, 4–5; Odum and Johnson, *NHS*, 111; Seale, "Easter Rock," 214; Work, *ANSS*, 94. RECORDINGS: Gary Davis, "I'm Gonna Meet You at the Station" (Lenox 520, 1949); Rev. Charlie Jackson, "All Aboard" (Jackson 102, 1970); Rollie Lee Johnson, "When the Train Comes Along," field rec., Richmond, VA, May 1938, *Field Recordings, Vol. 12*, Document CD 5614; Lead Belly, "When the Train Comes Along," Washington, DC, 1940, *Go Down Old Hannah*, Rounder CD 1099, 1994; Uncle Dave Macon, "When the Train Comes Along" (Champion 16805, 1934); Odette and Ethel, "When the Train Comes Along" (Columbia 14169-D, 1926); Will Slayden, "When the Train Comes Along," field rec., Shelby Co., TN, Summer 1952, *Will Slayden*; Henry Thomas, "When the Train Comes Along" (Vocalion 1140, 1927); Brother Williams Memphis Sanctified Singers, "I Will Meet You at the Station" (Vocalion 1482, 1930). DISCUSSION: "When the Train Comes Along" is another late nineteenth-century piece of obvious Black origin. (The sole white version is from Uncle Dave Macon, whose repertoire was much indebted to Black tradition.) As Mintie Wood suggests, though, it dates to around 1900, long after slavery. The other titles Wood mentions—"God Will Take Care of You, Be Not Afraid" (Fanny Crosby, ca. 1870) (*DNAH*), and "Life's Railway to Heaven" (M. E. Abbey and Charles D. Tillman, 1890) (Cohen, *Rail*, 611–18)—are obviously also later. Liza Jones's text may have crossed with another item. Her second stanza ("Some come cripplin' / Some come lame") occurs in most versions of "When the Train Comes Along" but also other songs, such as Brown III: 631; Fauset, "Folk-Tales," 300–301; Gordon, *Folk-Songs*, 25; Kennedy, *Cameos*, 159–60, Kennedy, *Mellows*, 38–39; Krehbiel, *Folksongs*, 158; White, *ANFS*, 68, 85. For Liza Jones's first verse, see White, *ANFS*, 118.

All my old favorite songs us slaves use to sing, I can't separate 'em anymore. I try to think of 'em, so I can sing 'em, but I jest find myself mixin' 'em up, and can't tell one from the other. Just singing. But the songs I like best dis day and time is "Life Is Like a Mountain Railroad," "God Will Take Care of You," and "I maybe blind, and I can not see, I may be crippled and I can not walk, But I'll meet you at the Station when the train comes along." (Mintie Gilbert Wood, b. 1847, TN, 377)

Den dey was anudder one:

> Heavenly land,
> Heavenly land,
> Heavenly land,
> I's gwinter beg God
> For dat Heavenly Land
>
> Some come cripplin'
> Some come lame
> Some come walkin'
> In Jesus' name. (Liza Jones, b. 1856, TX, 2119)

"THE WIND BLOWS EAST, THE WIND BLOWS WEST." TEXTS: Estella Jones. DISCUSSION: These stanzas occasionally occur in "Didn't My Lord Deliver Daniel" (such as Marsh, *Jubilee Singers*, 134–35), but the "wind blows east, wind blows west" line also crops up independently in many sacred and secular songs. Fanny Sellers (b. unk., TN, 348) included it in "Amazing Grace" (John Newton, 1779).

The Wind Blows East

> The wind blows east and the wind blows west,
> It blows like Judgment Day.
> And all them sinners who never have cried,
> Will surely cry that day.
>
> Let me tell you, sure to cry that day, sure to cry that day,

> All them sinners who never have cried
> Will surely cry that day. (Estella Jones, b. ca. 1855, GA, 349)

"WITNESS FOR MY LORD." TEXTS: Henry Garry. OTHER SOURCES: Gordon, *Folk-Songs*, 38–39; Hallowell, *Calhoun*, 72; Jackson, *Dead Man*, 176–84; Johnson, *Spirituals* I: 130–33; Johnson, *Utica*, 131–43; Odum and Johnson, *NHS*, 132–33; Perkins, "Spirituals," 230–31; Work, *ANSS*, 177–79. RECORDINGS: Christian and Missionary Alliance Gospel Singers, "A Witness For My Lord" (Columbia 46-P, 1924); Jubileers, "Daniel Was a Witness for My Lord" (Beacon 7002, 1943); Lead Belly, "Witness For My Lord," Washington, DC, August 1940, *Leadbelly, Vol. 5*, Document CD 5595; Silver Leaf Quartet, "Witness For My Lord," field rec., Ark, VA, April 1960, *Velvet Voices*, Rounder CD 1708, 1997; Roxie Threadgill and group of women, "Witness For the Lord," field rec., Moorehead Plantation, Lula, MS, August 1942, *Rock Me, Shake Me*, Document CD 5672. DISCOGRAPHIES: *Blues and Gospel Recordings*; *Gospel Discography*. DISCUSSION: As Henry Garry (b. ca. 1865, child of ex-slaves) indicates, this well-known item is likely a postwar creation. There is also a version in Kate Curry's narrative, authored by Texas fieldworker Effie Cowan. As usual with Cowan, the text appears highly embellished.

Yo' ax me 'bout de old songs de slaves useter sing. Well, I don't 'members many of dem. Atter de S'render all de ole slaves what stayed on de plantations 'roun' Gainesville [AL] useter gather at de landin' dar waitin' to see de steamboats pull in from down de Tombigbee on dere way to Columbus (Miss.), an' somebody'd start a song, an', Law man, how dem niggers sing. Here one I heerd my mammy sing so much I learnt it:

> Read in de bible, understan'
> Methuselah was de oldes' man.
> He lived nine hundred an' sixty nine

Den died an' go to Heben in de Lawd's
  due time.

Methuselah was a witness
For my Lawd,
For my Lawd.

Read in de Bible, Understan'
  Samson was de stronges' man.
Went down to battle to fight one time
  Killed a thousan' of de Philistines.

Samson was a witness
For my Lawd,
For my Lawd.

Daniel was a Hebrew chile,
  Went to de Lawd to pray a while.
De Lawd tole de angels de lions to keep.
  So Daniel lay down an' went to sleep.

An' dat's anoder witness
For my Lawd,
For my Lawd. (Henry Garry, b. ca. 1865,
  AL, child of ex-slaves, 141, orig. pa-
  rentheses)

"YOU MUST BE BORN AGAIN." TEXTS: Madison
Bruin. OTHER SOURCES: Fauset, "Folk Tales,"
301. This is yet another item whose form indicates
postwar, possibly even twentieth-century origins.

Anudder one w'at dey uster like to sing was:

Oh, you mus' be born ag'in,
Oh, you mus' be born ag'in,
Oh, you mus' be born ag'in,
Without a change you can't be saved
Oh, you mus' be born ag'in. (Madison Bruin,
  b. 1856, KY, 510)

"ZION'S HILL." Mose Hursey, John Crawford, Frances Lewis. OTHER SOURCES: Barton, *Plantation
Hymns*, 20; Brown III: 662–63; Jackson, *WNS*, 182–

83; White, *ANFS*, 87. DISCUSSION: It is unclear
whether these are all versions of the same song, or
simply three instances of the same theme or image.
Mose Hursey's text seems to bear the influence of
"My Knee Bone's Aching" (above). Frances Lewis
titled her contribution "Almost There." Its second
stanza is a well-known floater (above), while she
included a variant of the fourth verse in another
song, "The Sun Goin' Rise to Set No More" (also
above). Like Lewis's other texts, I believe this item
was at least partly improvised at the interview.

I'm almost over and I soon will be there,
I'm climin' up Zion's hill,
I'm almost there.
I'm goin' up Calvary and soon will be there,
I'm climin' up Zion's hill.

If you get there befo' I do,
Tell Jesus I'll soon be there,
And tell Him that I'm comin' too,
I'm climin' up Zion's hill.

One day when I was walkin' 'round,
I heard a reason from on high,
It spoke and it made me happy and cry,
It said my sins are forgiven and my soul set free.

Jesus is my Captain and He gone on befo',
And He gave me His orders,
And He told me not to fear,
I'm on my journey and I'll soon be there. (Fran-
  ces Lewis, b. 1854, GA, 155)

Sisters wont you help me bear my cross,
Sisters wont you help me bear my cross.
Help me to bear my cross—
Help me to bear my cross—
I'm been done wear my cross.
I'm been done wear my cross.
I'm been done with all things here.
I'm been done with all things here.
'Cause I reach over Zion's Hill.

'Cause I reach over Zion's Hill.
'Cause I'm been done with all things here.
Sisters wont you please help me bear my cross
Up over Zion's hill-l-l-l. (Mose Hursey, b. ca.
   1855, LA, 1833)

Nuther song was:

The greatest day I ever saw
Angels weep over Zion's hill
Now your troubles soon be over
And get your Jesus
And hold him fast
Faster and tighter than iron bands
Hold on out
Cause your troubles soon be over. (John Craw-
   ford, b. 1837, MS, 976–77)

INDIVIDUAL STANZAS NOT IDENTIFIED WITH SPECIFIC SPIRITUALS. The narratives also contain many stray spiritual verses not conclusively identified with any of the preceding items. A few hint at known spirituals or established commonplaces, but most have no obvious parallels in other sources and may have been original to the ex-slaves and their communities.

"ADAM'S FALLEN RACE." "Us uster sing lots dem chu'ch songs what was mek by de cullud folks like: / Adam's fallen race, / Good Lawd, hang down my head and cry. / Help me to trust Him, / Help me to trust Him, / Help me to trust Him, / Gift of God. / Help me to trust Him, / Help me to trust Him, / Help me to trust Him, / Eternal life. / Had not been for Adam's race, / I wouldn' been sinnin' today" (Liza Jones, b. 1856, TX, 2118–19).

"ALL MY SISTERS GONE." "All my sisters gone, / Mammy and Daddy too / Whar would I be if it weren't / For my Lord and Marster" (Benny Dillard, b. ca. 1858, GA, 286).

"BOAT AM COMIN' AND US STAN'IN' ON DE BANK." "W'en us was comin' to Lou'siana us hafter cross a big ribber. It was sho' a turrible t'ing to git 'cross dat ribber. W'en dey all git 'cross safe, us so t'ankful us sing: / Jesus has been wid us / Yet still wid us / He's promised to be wid us / To de en'. / De boat am comin' and / Us stan'in' on de bank / Waitin' for de boat / Praise de Lord. / It favers werry good to anybody w'at has met wid conflicks and has come t'rough and goes in dis d'rection" (Lafayette Price, b. ca. 1850, LA, 3174).

"CHRIST HE DONE HUNG ON D' CROSS." "Den dey uster sing one dat d' cullud folks mek deys'efs 'bout dat Christ he done hung on d' cross fo' 160 minutes fo' our sins, but I don' 'zactly 'member how it went" (Jim Barclay, b. 1855, TX, 163).

"CLIMB UP THE WALLS OF ZION." "Dis is a spiritual dey use to sing durin' slavery: / Climb up de walls of Zion / Ah, Lord, / Climb up de walls of Zion / Ah, Lord, / Climbin' up de walls of Zion / Ah, Lord. / Climbin' up de walls of Zion / Ah, Lord, / Great camp meetin' in the promise lan'" (Thomas Goodwater, b. 1855, SC, 169).

"COME ON CHARIOT AND TAKE HER HOME." "When a slave died, there was a to do over dat. . . . A song we used to sing was 'Come on Chariot and Take Her Home, take Her Home' / Here come Chariot, les ride, / Come on Les ride. / Come on Les ride" (Jim Allen, b. ca. 1850, AL, 60–61).

"DANIEL IN DE LION'S DEN." "Yes, the old-time religious songs—I sure remember some of them! Used to be able to sing lots of em, but have forgotten the words of many. Let's see: / I'm a-goin' to tell my Lord, Daniel in de lion's den; / I'm a-goin' to tell my Lord, I'm a-goin' to tell my Lord, Daniel in de lion's den" (Aunt Minerva Lofton, b. 1869, AR, child of ex-slaves, 265).

"DAT OLD WHEEL BEGINS TO TURN." "Lina went back to her chair, and as she sat down started singing. With each note her tones grew louder. The words were something like this: / 'God A'mighty, when my heart begins to burn / And dat old wheel begins to turn, / Den, Oh, Lord! Don't leave me here.' / It seemed from the length of her chant that the wheels would turn indefinitely, but no sooner had she finished that song, than she started another" (Lina Hunter, b. ca. 1848, GA, 265).

"FIRST TO DE GRAVEYARD." "Befo' breakfast, here is de words of praise I lifted to de Lawd, over dar on Tosch. You set down de coser (chorus): 'First to de graveyard; den to de Jedgement bar!' Is you got dat verser? Den git dis: 'All de deacons got to go; all de members got to go; all de sinners got to go.' Mo' 'longs to it, but dat's all I takes when I is praising Him fer relieving pain through me. (He sings each line five times. He takes off his hat; bows; holds his hands over head, and closes his eyes while singing. His hair is snow hair.) Lawd, help me dis morning! Here's another first line to one of our songs: 'All dem preachers got to go'" (George Briggs, b. 1849, SC, 83–84, orig. parentheses).

"GOD IS MY SHEPHERD." "Another one went lak dis / God is my shepherd I cannot want / He lives in my house my brethern / He lives in my house my brethern / He lives in my house my brethern / We are in Beaulah land" (Temple Wilson, b. ca. 1857, MS, 2370–71).

"GOIN' TO CARRY DIS BODY TO THE GRAVE-YARD." "Fun'rals was at night an' w'en ready to go to the graveyard every body would light a lightud [lightwood, or dried pine] knot as torch while every body sing. This is one of the songs wen' use to sing, / Goin' to carry dis body / To the graveyard / Grave-yard don' you know me? / To lay dis body down" (Adele Frost, b. 1844, SC, 89).

"THE HARDSHELL SHIP." "I went to de Hardshell Baptist Church with Miss Tea Kelly en Marse Kelly. Dey uster sing er song I nebber ain't forgot yet: / Oh, de Hardshell ship is er moughty good ship; / She is safe en sound. / Who woan go on de Hard-shell ship? / For de Glory Land she's bound" (Sallah White, b. ca. 1845, TN, 462).

"I AM GOING TO PREACH MY GOSPEL." "Most pretty song was: / I am going to preach my gospel / Said the Lord / Said the Lord / Said the Lord / Going to preach my gospel / And lead my great commission on / Dont be damned by wronging / And let my Gospel go on / And I'm going to be with my father / In that holy land" (John Crawford, b. 1837, MS, 977–78).

"I BAPTIZE YOU IN DE RIBBER JORDAN." "I baptize you in de ribber Jordan / I baptize you in de ribber Jordan / Halleluiah, Halleluiah, Halleluiah Lord. / Children, come a-runnin' come a-runnin' / I baptize you in de ribber Jordan / I baptize you in de ribber Jordan / Children, come a-runnin', come a-runnin'" (Elizabeth Ross Hite, b. ca. 1850, LA, 104).

"I BEEN LONG WAYS TO HEAR THE GOSPEL." "I been long ways to hear the gospel preached—Hal-lelujah. But the warfare will soon be over—Halle-lujah" (Roxy Pitts, b. 1855, AL, 296).

"I TELL YOU, SISTER." "I tell you sister what's a natu-ral fact, / It's a mighty bad thing to ever look back" (Frances Lewis, b. 1854, GA, 156–57).

"I WANT TO GO TO HEAVEN WHEN I DIE." "She is deeply interested in the old age pension, but was told that she would have to prove her age. She would not talk of superstitions; the only thing the writer could get from her was this song: / When I go to heaven, gonna live always; / Want to go to heaven, by and by, / To feast on the milk and honey and the wine; / And I want to go to heaven when I die" (Lonie Knox, b. unk, SC, 237). Julia Ann James (b. ca. 1858, NC, 388) named "I Want Ter Go Ter Heaven When I Die," which may or may not be the same song.

"I WISH I WAS IN HEAVEN." "I wish I was in heaven / To see my mother when she entered, / To see her try on her long white robe and starry crown. / I wish I was in heaven to see my mother / In her long white robe and starry crown" (Frances Lewis, b. 1854, GA, 157). "One of de songs I r'member my mama singing to us wuz: / I wished I wuz in de Heaven, / To see my mother when she enter; / To see her try on de long white robe; / P-r-ay—let my mother be the one!" (Dora Jackson, b. 1858, MS, 1111).

"I'LL BE THERE AT GETTING UP MORNING." "Say boss I want to sing you a song that go like this: / The Bible tell me here below, think up yonder is white as snow, / And I'll be there at getting up morning" (Harre Quarls, b. 1841, TX, 3216).

"I'M BOUND FOR THE PROMISED LAND." "I remember too that my mother use ter pray and sing. One song she specially laked wuz this: / I'm bound fer the promise Land / I'm bound fer the promise Land / Thars a better day acoming by and by. / Anudder song, I don't know all the words ter it, but it went somethin' lak this: / I'm gwine ter tell the Lord all about it / I'm gwine ter tell the Lord all about it, / When I reach the promise Land" (Ellen Lindsay, b. ca. 1853, GA, 134). This is an alternate title for "On Jordan's Stormy Banks I Stand" (Samuel Stennett, 1787), but Lindsay seems to give a different song.

"LIE ON HIM IF YOU SING RIGHT." "Lie on him if you sing right / Lie on him if you pray right / God knows that your heart is not right / Come, let us go to heaven anyhow. (Fragment)" (Abbie Lindsay, b. 1856, LA, 257, orig. parentheses).

"LITTLE CHIL'REN, I AM GOING HOME." "Little Chil'ren, I am going home / Going away to another brighter world / Little Chil'ren, I am going home / I have fought the battle and won the crown / Little Chil'ren, I am going home" (Simp Campbell, b. 1860, TX, 615).

"OH, WHERE IS HE." "Here is another hymn we sang in slavery: / Oh, where is He, Oh, where is He / Born de King of Jews? / Oh, where is He wid dat good news? / May Jesus wash my sins away. / Born de King of Jews / Oh, where is He wid dat good news? / Oh, where is He born de King of Jews? / I am standin' on de ladder washing my sins away / I am standin' here wid a heart dat will stay / Waitin' for my Lord / Oh, where is He born de King of Jews? / Oh, where is He wid dat good news / And born de King of Jews?" (Elizabeth Ross Hite, b. ca. 1850, LA, 105).

"PUT ON MY LONG WHITE ROBE." "Gosh fo'mighty, what youse want next, now tis fo' me to sing. Well youse can' put de bluff on dis nigger here it am: / Put on my long white robe, / Put on de golden crown / Put on my golden slipper / an' fo' ever be Jesus Lam'" (Philles Thomas, b. 1860, TX, 3818).

"READ IN THE GOSPEL OF MATTHEW." "Gwan, gwan. No sar! Ise aint gwine sing yous no song. If 'twas 40, or mo' yeahs ago, Ise could sho sing fo' yous but now, my voice sounds lak de voice of de diein' calf. Now, Ise will tell de words of one dat Ise always lak best: / Read in de Gospel of Math-yew, de Gospel of Luke an' John. Read in de Gospel an' larn de news. How de little boy Chil's was bo'n. Read 'bout Mary an' Joseph come a-ridin' f'om far. Poor little Jesus, Hail Lawd, Chil' of Mary. Hail Lawd, bo'n in de stable, Hail Lawd, aint dat a shame" (Leithean Spinks, b. 1855, MS, 3724).

"RESURRECTION DRAWIN' NIGH." "O John! / O John! / O John! / Resurrection drawin nigh! / Resurrection drawin nigh! / Resurrection drawin nigh! / John look way down to de wheel of time, / Resurrection drawin nigh! / Never see nothin but a human kind, / Resurrection drawin nigh!" (Lizzie Davis, b. ca. 1865, SC, child of ex-slaves, 110–11).

"RISE, SHINE." "Now, thar am tudder one dat Ise lak best, one weuns all sings on Sunday lots. It goes lak dis, Rise, Shine, give God de Glo-r-r-y, in de yeah of de Jubi-le-e-e" (Leithean Spinks, b. 1855, MS, 3724). Probably another postwar example.

"SAW MY MOTHER FLYING BY DE SKIES." "I can jes' remember one verse uv de songs my mother used to sing t'me: / Saw my mother flying by de skies, / Saw my mother flying by de skies, / Saw my mother flying by de skies, / To ring Jerusalem" (Andrew Jackson Jarnagin, b. 1853, MS, 1129).

"SEE WHEN HE RISE." "My pa use to sing dis song: / See w'en 'e rise / Rise an' gone, / See w'en 'e rise / Rise an' gone. / Gone to Galilee on a Sunday morning. / Oh, my Jesus rise an' gone to Galilee / On a Sunday morning" (Thomas Goodwater, b. 1855, SC, 169–70).

"SINCE I BEEN IN THE LAND." "Howdy, my brethern, Howdy yo' do, / Since I bin in de lan' / I do mi'ty well, an' I thank de Lord, too, / Since I bin in de lan' / O yes, O yes, since I bin in de lan' / O, yes, O yes, since I bin in de lan' / I do mi'ty well an' I thank de Lord too, / Since I bin in de lan'—" (Ebenezer Brown, b. 1852, MS, 244). "Howdy my brethern, How d' yer do, / Since I'se bin in de lan', / I do mighty po', but I thank de Lord sho' / Since I'se been in de lan'. / O, yes! O, yes! Since I'se bin in de lan'" (Laura Montgomery, b. 1850, MS, 1554). Brown and Montgomery were both interviewed by Mrs. Wm. F. Holmes, who tended to repeat material between interviews. This may be a single song text that has been divided, but I deem the material genuine nonetheless.

"THERE IS A HAPPY LAND." "My mistress name Nancy. Her was of de quality. Her voice was soft and quiet to de slaves. Her teach us to sing: / Dere is a happy land, far, far 'way / Where bright angels stand, far, far 'way, / Oh! How them angels sing! / Oh! How them bell ring! / In dat happy land, far, far 'way!" (Anderson Bates, b. 1850, SC, 43).

"TROUBLE WATER TODAY." "We was Baptist and baptized by immersion. An old Baptist song that was sung at the baptism was: 'Trouble water today, trouble water today. He will save you, He will save you; come to Jesus today, come to Jesus today, come to Jesus today. He will save you, He will save you, just now'" (William Pratt, b. 1860, SC, 278).

"WASN'T FOR OLD SATAN." "We use to sing dis in experience meetin's: / Go round, go round / Look at the mornin' star, / Go round, go round / Got a soul to save. / CHORUS / Wusn' for old satan / I wouldn' have to pray, / Satan broke God's Holy Law / I got a soul to save" (Thomas Goodwater, b. 1855, SC, 170).

"WHO BUILT THE ARK?" "Who built the Ark? / Norah built the Ark. / He built it on a sandy land, / Norah built the Ark. / Some call Norah a foolish man / To build the Ark on sandy land" (Frances Lewis, b. 1854, GA, 158).

"WHO IS DAT COMING." "De songs wuz ole ones lak 'Ole Time Religion' an' 'De Ole Ship O' Zion' an' some dat dey made up de words an' de tunes. One ob dese dat I can recollect my pappy an' mammy a singing went lak dis / What is dat a coming? / Who is dat a coming? / Who is dat a coming? / It looks lak Jesus, / It looks lak Jesus, / It looks lak Jesus, / Oh, Oh, Oh" (Temple Wilson, b. ca. 1857, MS, 2370).

"YON COMES OLE MARSTER JESUS." "When asked about old songs Callie did not know any of those we are trying to locate, but sang the following hymn: / 'Yon Comes Ole Marster Jesus / Ah really believe Christ is comin' agin / He's comin' in der mornin' / He's comin' in der mornin' / He's comin' wid der rainbow on His shoulder / He's comin' agin bye an' bye'" (Callie Williams, b. 1861, AL, 452–53).

SECULAR SONG

SINGING GAMES

Judge Maddox settled near Mount Enterprise and built him a good frame house and little double room log houses for the niggers. My first real hard work was gathering brush in the fields. Life was pretty hard. There was a cowhide to get you every time you turned your head out of time. They got us up for the fields before day. We used to go to the fields singin'—

Chicama - chicama craney - crow
Went to the well to wash my toe
When I got back all my chickens was gone.
It's one o'clock old witch.

We had an overseer. He thought three o'clock the time to get up. Then there was a nigger man was a leader or driver. When they put me to work that ended my play days. . . . I used to see the little niggers playin' and I wanted to play too, but I'd have to tote water or somethin'. They played base, puss wants a corner and a game about a old hen fluttering 'round to keep the little chickens from the hawks. They say, "Shoo, shoo." They called it playing shoo. What I always like when I used to play was William, William Tremble Toe. It goes:

William, William Tremble Toe
He's a good fisherman.
He catches hens
Puts them in pens
Some lay eggs
Some lay none.
Wire briar
Limber lock
Three geese in a flock
One flew east
One flew west

One flew over the cuckoo's nest.
But o-u-t spells out.
So begone
You dirty trout.
You.

We learned some of them games from Judge Maddox's chilluns.[1] He had eight of them. They were fair to middlin' good chilluns. I can remember them tryin' to comfort me sometimes when the old lady cut me with the cowhide she kept by her. We didn't see them enough to really get to know them though. (Jack Maddox, b. ca. 1849, TX, 2527–28)

Marse Ben Prescott . . . was Lucy's and my marster, and he and Mis' Adie, what was his wife, raised [us] up right in dere house, 'cause we don't have no mama and 'sides we is de only twins what was on de place. . . . Course we has to call de white folk's chillen "young Marse" or "young Mis" 'pending iffen it a boy or girl, but we plays ring games with 'em like "Choose your Partner" and "Catch Liza Jane," and sociates with 'em every day. (Lydia Jefferson, b. 1851, LA, 1941)

I heared tell dey had Christmas fixin's and doin's on other plantations, but not on Marse Frank's place. All corn shuckin's, cotton pickin's, log rollin's, and de lak wuz when de boss made 'em do it, an' den dere sho warn't no extra sompin t' eat. De onliest game I ever played wuz to take my doll made out of a stick wid a rag on it and play under a tree. When I wuz big 'nough to wuk, all I done wuz to help de cook in de kitchen and play wid old Mist'ess' baby. (Easter Brown, b. 1860, GA, 138–39)

Compared to many folklore collections, the ex-slave narratives contain relatively few children's traditions, the main reason being painfully obvious: maintained only as laborers, slaves generally enjoyed relatively little that could be considered childhood, even by nineteenth-century standards. "My fust wuk in de fields wuz when I wuz 'bout five years ole'. I wuz put to hoeing out de fence corners an' pulling up grass an' den on to heavier wuk as I growed bigger" (George Weathersby, b. 1852, MS, 2233–34). "I went to work in the field hoeing when I was nine years old and has worked in the field ever since till 'bout three years ago" (Lucy Thomas, b. 1851, TX, 3800–801). "I b'leeve I was 'bout nine or ten year' ol' when freedom come 'cause I was nussin' for de white folks" (Susan Smith, b. ca. 1855, LA, 3663). "As a youngster Mr. Wright had to pick up chips [kindling] around the yard, make fires and keep the house supplied with water which he got from a well. Then when he was ten years of age he was sent to the field as a plow boy" (Henry Wright, b. 1838, GA, 195). "I wuked 'round de house 'tel I wuz 'bout ten y'ars ole en de Marster put me ter wuk in his big whiskey house" (Dan Thomas, b. 1847, TN, 74). "By the time I was twelve, I could break horses along side the best of 'em" (Bill Green, b. 1851, TX, 1595). "I can't think uv no games, case we ain't neber played none" (Tom Wilcox, b. 1856, NC, 378). "Where I was, there warn't no playing done, only 'mongst the little chillun, and I can't remember much that far back" (Susan McIntosh, b. 1851, GA, 84).

The slave children who played the most were usually assigned to the task, if only temporarily. "I didn't do no work back in dem times—nuttin' but play. Me and my sister belonged to de youngest boy (dey was seven boys in dat family) and we just climbed trees and frolicked all de time" (Shang Harris, b. ca. 1840, GA, 117, orig. parentheses).

Marse Tumlin had a farm 'bout four mile from town, and a overseer, and I seed him buckle the niggers crost a log and whip them. Marse lived in Jefferson, heself, and when he'd go to the farm he allus took his boy with him. We'd be playin' in the barn and Marse call from the house, "Come on, Jimmie, we're gwine to the farm." Jimmie allus say to me, "Come on, nigger, let's ride round the farm." I'd say, "I ain't no nigger." He'd say, "Yes, you is, my pa paid $200 for you. He bought you for to play with me." (Francis Black, b. ca. 1850, TX, 88)

Fig. 17.1. "Domestic Life in South Carolina." *Illustrated London News* 42 (May 23, 1863): 4. Slavery Images: A Visual Record of the African Slave Trade and Slave Life in the Early African Diaspora. slaveryimages.org.

Numerous ex-slaves reported having been temporary *pets* for slaveholders. "I was Marse Allens' pet nigger boy. I was called a 'stray.' I slep on de floor by ole Miss and Marse Bob. I could a slep on de trundle bed, but it was so easy jist to roll over and blow dem ashes and make dat fire burn" (Jim Allen, b. ca. 1850 AL, 55). "My old Miss, I called her Miss Mary, took care of me 'till I was eight year old. . . . Old Miss jest wanted me to be in th' room with her an' I slep' on a pallet right near her bed. In the daytime I played in th' yard an' I pick up chips for old Miss. Then when I got most big enuff to work she give me back to my ma" (Melvin Smith, b. 1841, SC, 288). Smith's case was not atypical: children as young as eight years old were widely considered big enough for hard labor. "I was a boy in slavery. Now you talk about hard times, I have had hard times. I started plowing at eight years old" (Anon. ex-slave, b. unk, TN).[2]

It is hardly surprising, then, that so many of the singing games known to ex-slaves were—as they recognized—borrowed from white children. In fact, those most often mentioned—"Frog in the Mill Pond," "Molly Bright (How Many Miles to Babylon)," "Old Witch (Chick-A-Ma, Craney Crow)," "William Trimbletoe"—were British perennials known to English-speaking children the world over. There are occasional glimpses of the African American children's clapping games, ring plays, and jump rope rhymes that in the twentieth century emerged as world-famous folk art, but only intimations. Again the cause is fairly obvious: the average slave's childhood was so constricted that the bulk of Black children were given time to play in their own way only after freedom.

Children's singing games—dramatic or mimetic movements or formations, or imitations of adult dances accompanied by song—are an incredibly rich and complex topic permitting fairly detailed classifications. For our purposes, however, it is enough to state that most of the singing games played by slave children—and the focus here is only on games with song—were true contests, either involving teams, or pitting a single player—the *it*—against the group in a competitive musical drama. As is customary, the *it* was usually selected either by the outcome of the preceding match, or through a counting-out rhyme. "*Hiding de Switch* was de one whar you counted 'em out; dat countin' run lak dis: 'Ten, ten, double-ten, forty-five, fifteen.' Gentlemen! I could run lak a snake" (Dosia Harris, b. 1860, GA, 110, orig. emphasis). "Sometimes us played what us called de 'Crow' game. Us spread our fingers out, side by side and counted 'em out wid a rhyme. De one de last word of de rhyme fell on had to be de crow. I didn't love to be counted out and made de crow, but it was a heap of fun to count de others out" (Callie Elder, b. ca. 1860, GA, 307).

Us uster tie butter weeds at d' top t' mek dolls t' play wid. Dey hab little skirts on dem like little ladies. Den dere was lots 'r' games we play befo' us git big. One game say,

Doll, doll,
    Young lady,
Doll, doll,
    All 'roun'.

Atter we sing dis we all tu'n (turn) a-loose han's, clap han's 'n' tu'n 'roun' 'n' 'roun'. Iffen anybudy too slow dey hafter be d' "it" nex' time. (Delia Barclay, b. unk., TX, 154, orig. parentheses)

D' boys 'n' gals hab anuder game w'at dey choose sides fo'. Den dey sing out,

> Lincoln Board, Lincoln Board,
>   Don' fool me.
> I'll trabble back.
>   I'll trabble back.
> T' d' gal I lub (love),
>   BEHIN' ME.

D' gal w'at was behin' d' boy den was he gal fo' d' nex' game. (Delia Barclay, b. unk., TX, 155, orig. parentheses)

Teams chosen or the *it* selected, games tended to follow one or both of two patterns: the prisoner-in-a-ring or the chase. Among the more intriguing titles in Thomas Talley's landmark *Negro Folk Rhymes* is "Frog in a Mill (Guinea or Ebo Rhyme)."[3] Actually, what Talley mistook for West African pidgin languages are nonsense refrains from a popular English singing game epitomizing the prisoner-in-a-ring form: "Frog in the Mill Pond (Middle) (And Can't Get Out)." British origins notwithstanding, in North America this game was most commonly collected from Black children.

One of the favorite games was "Frog in the Mill Pond Can't Jump Joseph." This was played in a circle, one person being in the center, and trying to get out while the others marched around him singing. Then they danced the cotillion and sang any number of their favorite songs. (Caroline Malloy, b. ca. 1840, GA, 412)

> "Frog in the middle and can't get out,
> Take a stick and punch it out."

Fig. 17.2. Abe Livingston, ex-slave, Beaumont, TX, September 10, 1937. "Freedom didn' mean much. I didn't know d' difference. I did well anyhow" (Abe Livingston, b. 1854, TX, 2402). Portraits of African American ex-slaves from the US Works Progress Administration, Federal Writers' Project slave narratives collection, Library of Congress.

All walk around with eyes closed singing above two lines. The frog takes a chance to get out between two of those walking around and hides. When it is found that the frog is out all go to hunt him. The one who catches him is frog next time.[4]

Still more popular was "Molly Bright (How Many Miles to Babylon)," another British title usually described as a variety of tag or hide-and-go seek.

Us boys, d' w'ite boys 'n' me had lots 'r' fun w'en us growin' up. I 'member d' game us play 'n' sing dis,

> Marly Bright, Marly Bright,
>   Three score 'n' ten.
> Kin you git dere by candlelight?
>   Yes, iffen your legs
> 'R' long, 'n' limber 'n' light,
>   Watch out fo' d' ol' Blue Witch on d' Road.

Den d' boys run t' git t' d' base fo' d' Witch kotch 'em. W'en us beat d' witch t' d' base d' game was all ober. Us play lots dat way. (Abe Livingston, b. 1854, TX, 2400–401)

When us played our hidin' game, us sung somepin'
lak dis:

> Mollie, Mollie Bright
> Three score and ten,
> Can I get there by candlelight?
> Yes, if your laigs is long enough! (Callie Elder,
>   b. ca. 1860, GA, 307)

We played "Frog in de Middle," an' "Jack in de
Bush" an' "Molly Bright." We'd play dat on moon-
lite nites; dey had sides an' de sides wud draw a
line in de dus' an' dare ennybody to cross de line;
you wuz a coward ef you tuk a dare an' when you
crost dat line you eder had to run or pay a pawn;
sumtimes we'd run a mile frum home in de moon-
lite. (Jane McLeod Wilburn, b. ca. 1850, MS, 2293)[5]

The pawn—a forfeit or penalty such as a kiss or article of clothing—was another English game custom
widely adopted by African American children.[6] As in
the foregoing examples, "ringing up" almost always
preceded chasing an escaped prisoner.

I never was any hand to play any games 'cept
"Chick, Chick." You'd ketch 'hold a hands and
ring up. Had one outside was the hawk and some
inside was the hen and chickens. The old mother
hen would say:

> Chick-a-ma, chick-a-ma, craney crow,
> Went to the well to wash my toe;
> When I come back my chicken was gone,
> What time is it, old witch?

One chicken was s'posed to get out and then
the hawk would try to ketch him. (Dinah Perry,
b. ca. 1862, AR, 320–21)[7]

Den we used to play Ti Balai (Little Broom). We
used to pick an old broom dat lay around in de
camp, and de chilens all sit on de grass in a circle.

One of dem take de little broom and sing, going
around outside de circle of de chilens:

> Tringue, Tringue,   I drag, I drag a
>   ti balai   small broom
> Ti mouton la queu   Lil lamb wid its tail
>   coupe   cut off
> Cha po ti bam bail   Lookin' for its tail
>   all around
> Cha po ti bam bail.   Lookin' for its tail
>   all around.

Den dey drop dat piece of old broom just back of
someone, and keep on a-goin', saying, "Cha po ti
bam bail. Cha po ti bam bail." When one of dem
chilen notice like dat, dat de gal goin' around had
done lost de broom, all de chilen begun to look
around in de back. And de one who find de broom
got to get up quick, and take de broom and chase
de gal doin' de runnin', and hit her with it. Den
everybody sits on de ground again, and de one
what find de broom, den its her turn to be goin'
around and around. (Francis Doby, b. 1838, LA,
52–53, orig. translation)

Black children also created their own routines,
albeit often modeled on English singing games. "When
us was chillun in de quarters we did a mighty lot of
playin'. Us useta play 'Sail away Rauley' a whole lot.
Us would hol' han's an' go 'roun' in a ring, gittin' faster
an' faster an' dem what fell down was outa de game"
(Katherine Eppes, b. ca. 1850, AL, 120). "'Us chilluns
useta have a good time singin' and a-playin'," he said.
'I 'members one of our little verses run somethin' lak
dis: / 'Shoo, shoo, shoo gander / Th'ow yo' feathers
'way yander'" (Oliver Bell, b. unk., AL, 28). Madison
Bruin and Gracie Stafford both recalled games of chase
resembling "Chick-A-Ma Craney Crow" (which Bruin
knew too). The British game might even have been
their inspiration, but their examples are almost certainly original African American creations and likely
independent of one another at that.

Us play pitchin' hoss shoes, and marbles, den us play a game w'ere us choose sides and den sing:

> Can, can, candio,
> Ol' man dandio,
> How many men you got?
> More'n you able to ketch.

Den dem on one side try to ketch dem on de other side. Den us uster play "hide de switch." Endurin' de war us git whip' many a time for play wid shells us fin' in de woods and dey ain't bus' and us boys play wid 'em. Us git whip' for dat 'cause de ol' folks say ain't no tellin' w'en one might bus' and kill us. (Madison Bruin, b. 1856, KY, 507–8)

They don't play like we did. We used to sing:

> Shoo, chicken, shoo,
> You feed my chicken?
> Yes, ma'am.
> You brown my biscuit?
> Yes, ma'am.

Then the leader would raise his hands and say, "Shoo, chickens, shoo," and everyone would run just like chickens do when they are bein' shooed. (Gracie Stafford, b. ca. 1860, LA, 198)

Two other popular games, "In Some Lady's Garden" and "King George and His Army," are probably also African American, yet they not only employ the prisoner-in-a-ring format but also the feudal and pastoral Mother Goose imagery of English singing games.

The boys would play ball and marbles. We-all would play ring-games. Both boys and girls would play the ring-games. We'd form a ring and somebody had to sit in the center. We'd ask:

> "Why didn't yo'-all do this?"

The one in the ring would say:

> "Jake grinned at me!"

We'd keep that up fo' a long time. At other times, the boys and girls would stand up, then hold up their hands and start skippin'. We'd say:

> Hold up the gates, as high as the sky,
> And let King George and his army pass by.
> (Mary Edwards, b. 1853, TX, 1282–83)[8]

Ring plays too. Sometimes when they wanted to amuse themselves, they would play ring plays. They all take hands and form a ring and there would be one in the center of the ring. Now he is got to get out. He would come up and say, "I am in this lady's garden, and I'll bet you five dollars I can get out of here." And d'reckly he would break somebody's hands apart and get out. (Claiborne Moss, b. 1857, GA, 162)

Every night the Judge and the old missus had the niggers come to the big house and stand in rows in they clean lowerings clothes with white handkerchiefs tied 'round they heads and have play-party songs. They used to sing:

> I'm in some lady's garden,
> Le' me out of here.
> I'm in some lady's garden,
> Poor old Reuben,
> Poor old boy.
> I'm in some lady's garden;
> Pray so hard to get me out of here. (Lu Perkins,
> b. ca. 1850, MS, 3060–61)

"I'm in Some Lady's Garden" usually features the prisoner-in-a-ring described in the title, but Delia Barclay remembered a catching game similar to "London Bridge."

Anudder game us like was play' by makin' a arch up wid two chillren hol'in' han's. D' uder chillren

Fig. 17.3. "Noon at Primary School for Freedmen, Vicksburg, Mississippi." Engraving from a sketch by A. R. Waud. *Harper's Weekly* 10 (June 23, 1866): 392. Besides jump-rope (far left) and chase games, children are ringing up or squaring off in various spots on the playground.

pass under d' arch in a row 'n' den sometime' dey git kotch 'n' hol' tight. D' song fo' dis game go,

> Winsome lady's gyarden (garden),
> Back do' (door)'s lock'
> 'N' d' uder ones prop'
> Winsome lady's gyarden. (Delia Barclay, b. unk., TX, 154, orig. parentheses)

There is considerable variation in the accompanying song, the only constant being some form of the statement "I'm in some lady's garden." "One of the ring games dat we played more dan any other was 'Bald Horse.' We would all form a ring and puts one in de middle and starts goin around and singin, 'Bald horse buried in de turnip patch, de buzzards are after me. Do let me out me of here, I'se in some ladies garden.' Another little song we sung a lot was 'Up de hill, Down de level, Grandmas little dog treed de devil'" (Mollie Dawson, b. 1852, TX, 1133).[9]

A few items recalled by ex-slaves are more distinctively African American, perhaps even the products of the informants' own play groups.

> Rachel remembered a few children's games, but not the exact pattern of play.

FISH

> I'll be de head.
> You be de back.
> You be de side.
> You be de fin.
> You be de eye.

Old head wants to go. Old side wants to go. Old eye wants to go. Repeat everything. When it run out to de las' one, de old tail. Do it three times. De one what is tail las' time must pay a pawn. Den all ring up and go round and if old tail don't remember who he is, he have to pay another pawn. Den de pawn is sell, and you pay with a kiss whosoever de pawn belongst to.

COONSY

One, old woman; one, old man; ring up. I'll say I'm old woman, another old man, one old Coonsy. You count up to ten data-way. I'll turn old Coonsy, old Coonsy turn next one, do it three times, de las' one pay a pawn.

HANDS UP AND GO ROUND, OLD GEORGIA RABBIT WHO?

I steal a partner, you steal another, then I'll steal your partner and you steal another. (Rachel McCoy, b. 1863, GA, 398–99, orig. italics)

One t'ing dey didn' mek us li'l ones do no heaby wuk. Us mos'ly play. Dey was one li'l song w'at go'd:

> Ol' 'possum in a holler log
>   Sing high de loo,
> Fatter dan a ol' green frog
>   Sing high de loo,
>   Whar 'possum?

Den us play: "Ol' Bella, ol' Bella, tu'n 'roun' and 'roun'"—and—"Take a home, take a home," dat kinder like "gwine 'roun' de rosebush" is now. (Mary Johnson, b. ca. 1858, VA, MS, LA, 2025)

Strikingly, one of the most fundamental aspects of modern Black child's play is largely absent in ex-slave descriptions and other accounts: handclapping. Indeed, many modern African American singing games are more properly called singing-and-clapping games. Considering that handclapping is basic to African children's games but uncommon (if not unknown) in British singing games, the rarity of body percussion among slave children most plausibly reflects the prevailing English influence. In any event comparatively few ex-slaves mentioned handclapping with children's games; moreover, when it did appear it was usually in imitation adult activities like patting or shouting.

> Most of de time, we didn' play wid things, we jes play; sing an' march aroun' an' pat an' clap hands dis-er-way:
>
> > Oh, yes, we'll gain de day,
> > Oh, yes, we'll gain de day,
> > Oh, yes, we'll gain de day,
> > Po' sinners, flockin' home!
>
> Old Miss liked ter hear de chullun sing, make 'em line up in de yard, say dey ought ter be let shout like de grown people. She make 'em sing:
>
> > Don' you see dem sixteen of chullun,
> > Way over in de promised land?
>
> Den dey'd shout! (Sam Broach, b. 1848, MS, 223–24)

Still, narrators occasionally described clapping games that may have originated among slave children.

> We'd watch the doodle bugs build their houses. We'd sing, "Doodle, Doodle, your house burned down." Those things would come up out of their holes just a-shakin'. One game I remember was, "Skip frog, Skip frog, Answer your Mother, she's callin' you, you, you." We'd stand in a circle and one would be skip frog. We'd slap our hands and skip frog would be hoppin' just like frogs do. Oh, I wish I could call them times back again. I'd go back tomorrow. But I'm tryin' to live so I can meet 'em once again. (Hagar Lewis, b. 1855, TX, 7)[10]

A play or ring song they used to sing was:

> *Rabbit and Peavine*
>
> Rabbit, Rabbit, in de peavine.
> I axed whar was he gwine, He said—
> I'm gwine on down by de Vicksburg town——
> And ain't got long to tarry.
> *Git up*, in *de peavine*!
>
> (To play this the children form a ring, with one in the middle, who sits on the ground while the others sing and march around him. When they ask where he is going he begins to hop like a rabbit and slaps his hips with his hands with his feet extended out to front. When they get to the part "We're gwine on down to Vicksburg town"—they all get down on the ground and hop around the ring singing and slapping their thighs—imitating rabbits.) (Jane Sutton, b. ca. 1853, MS, 2092, orig. emphasis and parentheses)[11]

> Wen we were young we uster hev parties called "Dideoos," de banjo would play en den de girls would line up on one side of de cabin en de boys on de tother side while the folks war a clappin en er playing why [while] de boys en girls wuld choose dar partners den weuns sing:
>
> > Ole Brer Rabbit,
> > Shake it, shake it,
> > How I love you,
> > Shake it, shake it.

I'd ruther play dat game dan to eat. (Mary Wright, b. 1865, KY, child of ex-slaves, 62–63)[12]

Granted, it is not entirely clear whether Mary Wright is describing a children's game or an adult dance. Significantly, many of the same games played by children were *danced* by adults with fiddles and banjos at Saturday night frolics, cornshuckings, and log rollings, where patting and body percussion were always present.

I only 'members part of the wo'ds to two of the ring plays we played at dances in slavery times. One was:

London Bridge is washing away
Oh, boys remember me
London Bridge is washing away.

The other one was:

I'm in some lady's garden, I'm in some lady's
    garden,
So let me out for I'm suffering for water and wine
I'm in some lady's garden, I'm in some lady's gar-
    den. (Mariah Snyder, b. ca. 1848, TX, 3710)[13]

Hannah Murphy and Lizzie Farmer both gave texts of the game song "Mary Jane." Murphy, however, remembered playing it as a child, while Farmer had danced it at adult work parties.

We would have dances and play parties and have sho' nuff good times. We had "ring plays." We'd all catch hands and march round, den we'd drop all hands 'cept our pardners and we'd swing round and sing:

You steal my pardner, and I steal yours,
Miss Mary Jane.
My true lover's gone away,
Miss Mary Jane!

Steal all round and don't slight none,
Miss Mary Jane.

He's lost out but I'se got one,
Miss Mary Jane!

We always played at log rollin's and cotton pickin's. (Lizzie Farmer, b. ca. 1857, TX, 98–99)

After emancipation, Black adults would abandon these selections for a rapid succession of other dance styles and accompaniments, so that by the twentieth century "London Bridge," "In Some Lady's Garden," "Mary Jane," "Skip to My Lou," "Polly Put the Kettle On," "Shoo Fly," and many other items ex-slaves recalled from adult frolics were regarded entirely as child's play. Most telling of all, after 1900 "Patting Juba" was rarely collected except as a children's game.[14] Obviously slave children found some opportunities to play; but during slavery, playing—like patting—was mainly an adult activity, and accounts of child's play barely make a ripple in the ex-slave narratives compared to Saturday night frolics and work parties rewarding adult laborers who could pull their full weight through grueling week after week, season after season. Perversely, this may explain both the relative absence of handclapping in slave children's games and its resurgence in subsequent generations. By all appearances, slavery and the brutalization of slave children obliterated African clapping games, English equivalents occasionally filling the void. The fundamental role of handclapping in modern African American child's play more likely derives from the body percussion of adult slaves, as picked up and preserved by subsequent generations of Black children. That these children also perpetuated much of the adult slave dance repertoire obviously supports this view. Nor can it be wholly irrelevant that the so-called adults at Saturday night slave-labor frolics were so often no more than children.

Appendix: Lullabyes and Other Nursery Songs

Sung by a "mighty clevah woman" to her lover. The negro woman is at home rocking her baby, her husband is sitting not far away. A weird little whistle is heard. The negro woman sings to warn her lover of danger.

> Oh, de win's in de wes',
> An' de cuckoo's in de nes',
> No lodgin' hyar foah you,
> By you baby by yoo.

> Oh, de devil's in de man,
> Cain't you unnerstan',
> No lodgin' hyar foah you,
> By you baby by yoo.

(Repetition of the first verse.) (Aunt Ann Stokes, b. 1844, MO, 337, orig. parentheses)

Old timey sing?

> 1. Wish I had a hundred dog
>   And half wuz hound!
>   Take it in my fadder field
>   And run the rabbit down!
>   Chorus: Now he hatch
>   He hatch!
>   He hatch!
>   And I run the rabbit down!

> 2. I wish I had a hundred head o' dog
>   And half of them wuz hound!
>   I'd take 'em back in my bacco field
>   And run the rabbit down.
>   Chorus: Now he hatch—he hatch!
>   He hatch—he hatch!
>   Now he hatch—he hatch!
>   And I run them rabbit down!

That wuz a sing we used to have on the plantation. Then we make up sing—we have sing fer chillun. Make 'em go sleep. Every one have his own sing.

> Bye-o-baby!
> Go sleepy!

> Bye-o-baby!
> Go sleepy!
> What a big alligator
> Coming to catch
> This one boy!
> Diss here the Watson one boy child!
> Bye-o-baby go sleepy!
> What a big alligator
> Coming to catch this one boy! (Mom Louisa
> Brown, b. ca. 1860, SC, 116–17)

Den old Granma come along and sing dis for us to go to sleep:

> Sizette, te ein bell femme   Sizette is a beautiful woman
> Mo chere amie-aie   Ah dear one-aie
> Mo achete ban-ban   I buy pretty things
> Ce pou nou marie   For us to get married. (Francis Doby, b. 1838, LA, 52)

In their notes to America's two best-known lullabyes, the editors of the *Brown Collection of North Carolina Folk Songs*, Henry M. Belden and Arthur Palmer Hudson, reflected on the lullaby's underrepresentation in anthologies like theirs. Of "Bye Baby Bunting," they wrote, "perhaps because it is so very widely known and sung, this old English lullaby . . . does not often appear in collections of traditional folk song." Of its companion, "Rock-A-Bye Baby," they observed: "like 'Bye Baby Bunting,' this old English lullaby . . . seldom appears in collections of traditional folk song. . . . It appears a dozen times in our collection, in localities all the way from the mountains to the sea. The texts vary but little." Brown III: 148. In truth, America's best-known lullabyes are simply so familiar that many fieldworkers evidently saw small point in collecting and publishing them.

John A. Lomax's guidelines for interviewers advised asking, "Can you give the words or sing any lullabyes?" Obviously some fieldworkers asked, and some ex-slaves responded. Still, like most folksong collections, the ex-slave narratives contain relatively few lullabyes, especially considering that slave women spent so much time rocking babies, their own or others. Many spent their working lives—during and after slavery—as nursemaids to white children. Indeed, slave mammies were among the icons of the Old South, and by the turn of the century, the contrived "slave mammy's lullaby" was a major subgenre of "coon song" publishing. Millie Evans gave one of the better-known examples, "Mammy's (Daddy's) Little Carolina Coons" (R. C. Young and E. S. S. Huntington, 1916):

> Ev'y ev'nin at three 'clock ol' mistress would call all we litsy bitsy chillun in an we would lay down on pallets an have to go to sleep. I can hear her now singin' to us piccaninnies:
>
>> Hush-a-bye, bye-yo'-bye, mammy's piccaninnies
>> Way beneath the silver shining moon
>> Hush-a-bye, bye-yo'-bye, mammy's piccaninnies
>> Daddy's little Carolina coons
>> Now go to sleep yo' little piccaninnies. (Millie Evans, b. 1849, NC, 241)

Needless to say Evans's example is an anachronism, perhaps performed to please the interviewer, Carol N. Graham. Newman I. White noted, "this song has long been sung among white people in the South, and is obviously one of the many songs about the Negro composed by popular songwriters of the white race." White, *ANFS*, 397–98; also Brown III: 151–52. For a similar item, see Katie Sutton (b. unk., IN, 195). Such influences proved far-reaching: DuBose Heyward's lyrics for George Gershwin's "Summertime" (1935)—still one of the most frequently performed pop songs on the planet—imitate a Black lullabye.

The narratives do contain numerous real lullabyes, and even more references to slaves nursing white children, typically the first and often only work assigned females.

> I uster have ter tend to de chillun all de time, and I could git dem ter sleep bettern den der mama

Fig. 17.4. "African American woman holding a white child," Arkansas, ca. 1855. "Modern handwritten note in case: Slave nanny/white child image came from an estate sale somewhere in the flat lands delta area of Arkansas. Likely from one of the following Arkansas towns: Helena, West Memphis, Forrest City, Elaine, Brinkley, Cotton Plant, Clarendon, Pine Bluff." Library of Congress, Prints and Photographs Division.

> could when I would sing. I'd pat mah foot and pat dem on de back a little, rock and sing, "Laugh and play till pappy comes. He'll take good care of baby." Dey would go right ter sleep. (Vina Moore, b. 1845, MS, 2759)

> My job wuz mindin' massa's and missus's chilluns all day long, and puttin' dem ter baid at night; dey had ter habe a story told ter dem befo' dey would go ter sleep; and de baby hed ter be rocked; and I had ter sing fo' her "rockaby baby close dem eyes befo' ole san man comes, rockaby baby don' let ole san man cotch yo peepin'" befo' she would go ter sleep. (Susan Kelly, b. ca. 1856, VA, 189)

> Sho', I remembers de slavery days! I was a little gal but I can tell you lots of things about them days. My job was nussing de younguns. I took keer of

them from daylight to dark. I'd have to sing them
to sleep too. I'd sing:

By-lo Baby Bunting
Daddy's gone a-hunting
To get a rabbit skin
To wrap Baby Bunting in.

Sometimes I'd sing:

Rock-a-bye baby, in a tree top
When de wind blows your cradle'll rock.
When de bough breaks de cradle'll fall
Down comes baby cradle'n all. (Lou Smith,
    b. ca. 1854, SC, 300)

In keeping with the general trend, "Rock-A-Bye Baby"
and "Bye Baby Bunting" were the items most commonly
mentioned by ex-slaves. Seven narrators (Frank L.
Adams, John Finley, Ellen Godfrey, Frank Hughes,
Susan Kelly, Lou Smith, and Narcissus Young) gave
texts of "Rock-A-Bye Baby" (Delia Barclay, James
Bolton, and Maria Hadnot simply named it), and
their contributions actually vary more than one might
expect (for other texts and references, see Brown III:
148–49; Halliwell, *Nursery Rhymes*, 209).

Dere used to be a baby song what my mammy sung.

Go to sleep, go to sleep little baby
Rock a by baby, rock a by baby. (Frank Hughes,
    b. 1858, AL, 1062)

We sung de' babies to sleep wid,
Rock-a-bye baby, on de tree top,
W'en de win' blow, de cradle will rock;
W'en de bough break, de cradle will fall,
An' down come rock-a-bye baby an' all.
Go to sleep, li'l baby. (Frank L. Adams, b. 1853,
    TX, 2)

Ellen Godfrey's text had crossed with "Patty Cake."

Rock-a-bye!
Rock-a-bye!
Down come baby cradle and all!
Roll'em! Roll'em! Roll'em!
Roll'em and boll'em!
And put'em in the oven! (Aunt Ellen Godfrey,
    b. 1837, SC, 164)

John Finnely's example recalls "Rock-A-Bye Baby"
but had strayed even further from the original.

Thar am some powe'ful good singin' on de Marster's place allright, allrght. I's jus' tell de wo'ds ob
me. It am dis away:

De moonlight, a shinin' star. De big owl a hootin'
in de tree. Oh by my baby, aint you gwine to
sleep a rockin' on my knee? By, oh my honey
baby, a rockin' on my tree. Yes, she gone to sleep,
honey baby sleep a rockin' on my, a rockin' on
my knee.

Thar 'tis, an' dat's all. (John Finnely, b. ca. 1850,
AL, 1347)

"Bye Baby Bunting" ranked just behind "Rock-a-
Bye Baby." Lou Smith (b. ca. 1854, SC, 300), Chaney
Mack (b. ca. 1864, GA, 1422–23), and C. B. McRay all
gave the standard verse.

Mother's fav'rit lullaby was,

Bye-o-Baby Buntin', Daddy's Gone a huntin',
To git a little rabbit skin
To wrop my Baby Buntin' in. (C. B. McRay,
    b. 1861, TX, 2518)

Narcissus Young combined "Baby Bunting" with
"Rock-a-Bye Baby": "I member de ole song back
dere, 'Rock a Bye Baby, Yo Daddy's gon' a Huntin'
ter git a Rabbit Skin ter put de Baby in'" (Narcissus
Young, b. 1841, TN, 80). For other "Bunting" texts

Fig. 17.5. C. B. McRay, ex-slave, Ft. Worth, TX, June 19, 1937. Portraits of African American ex-slaves from the US Works Progress Administration, Federal Writers' Project slave narratives collection, Library of Congress.

and references, see Brown III: 148; Halliwell, *Nursery Rhymes*, 210.

Another reason lullabyes have been relatively little noted may be that many of their key aspects are frankly difficult to observe and document. *To lull* and *lullaby* derive from the nonsense syllables characteristic of *lulling* (*lululul*), and in context lullabyes may be mere snatches of song interspersed with baby talk and silly sounds, humming and lulling, rocking, walking, patting, rubbing, and so on, all in an intensely personal, private context (for example, see Jones and Hawes, *Step It Down*, 3–15). Some of the foregoing accounts suggest these dynamics, but even more than other folksong genres, true lullabyes defy written transcriptions.

Not all lullabyes were brief rhymes or improvisations, however. "Poor Little Black Sheep" is by general agreement African American in origin, maybe even a slave creation. It is also an especially graphic expression of the lullaby's double-vision, which alternates between soothing, protective, and fantastic images on the one hand and themes of violence, death, and disorder on the other (such as babies plummeting from treetops, or people killing and skinning bunnies; see Barre Toelken, "Ballads and Folksongs," *Folk Groups and Folklore Genres: An Introduction*, ed. Elliott Oring [Logan: Utah State University Press, 1986], 163–65). In this vein, "Poor Little Black Sheep" put babies to sleep with a description of a little lamb's decomposing remains. In an interesting twist, Joanna Thompson Isom joined "Little Black Sheep" to another description of rotting carcasses. Based on Ezekiel 37:1–11, "Dese Bones Gonna Rise Again" originated as a minstrel parody, but Isom's text has been orally recomposed.

I hav' been midwife, an' nuss, an' washerwoman; when I wuz little my granny taught me some ole, ole slave songs dat she sed had been used to sing babies to sleep ever since she wuz a chile. I used to sing dis one:

> Little black sheep, where's yo' lam'
> Way down yonder in de meado'
> The bees an' de butterflies
> A-peckin' out hiz eyes
> The poor little black sheep
> Cry Maa-a-my.

Anudder one I sings to de chilluns goes lak dis:

> I know, I know dese bones gwine rize agin
> Dese bones gwine rize agin
> I heared a big rumblin' in de sky
> Hit mus' be Jesus cummin' by
> Dese bones gwine rize agen
> Dese bones gwine rize agen'.
>
> I know, I know dese bones gwine rize agen
> Dese bones gwine rize agin
> Mind my brothers how you step on de cross
> Yo' rite foot's slippin's an' yo' soul will be los'
> Dese bones gwine rize agin
> Dese bones gwine rize agin. (Joanna Thompson Isom, b. ca. 1858, MS, 1097–98)

For "Little Black Sheep," see Arnold, *Alabama*, 97; Brown I: 183; Brown III: 152–53; Owens, *Texas*, 179; Puckett, *Folk Beliefs*, 74; Randolph, *OFS* II: 345–46; Scarborough, *TNFS*, 147–49; *Solomon*, Daisies, 53. RECORDINGS: Nathan Frasier (banjo, vocal), Frank Patterson (fiddle), "Po Black Sheep," field rec., Nashville, TN, March 1942, *Altamont*. Jane Sutton gave what may be a fragment: "Sixteen blackbirds, / Picking on a sheep-hide—(Couldn't remember words)" (Jane Sutton, b. ca. 1853, MS, 2092). For "Dese Bones," see Arnold, *Alabama*, 148–49; Barton, *Plantation Hymns*, 32; Brown III: 580–81; Fauset, "Folk Tales," 300–301; Lomax, *Ballads*, 597–600; Lomax, *FSNA*, 476; McIlhenny, *Spirituals*, 62–63; Odum and Johnson, *NHS*, 102; Perkins, "Spirituals," 242; Sandburg, *Songbag*, 470–71; White, *ANFS*, 83–85. RECORDINGS: Golden Gate Jubilee Quartet, "Dese Bones Gonna Rise Again" (Bluebird B8123, 1939); Jubilee Gospel Team, "These Bones Gonna Rise Again" (QRS R7013, 1928). DISCOGRAPHIES: *Country Music Records*; *Country Music Sources*, 68–69.

Joanna Isom suggests another explanation for the relative absence of lullabyes from folksong collections: that is, they are not absent at all, merely unrecognized or unacknowledged. In practice, all types of songs are pressed into service as lullabyes (see Bess Lomax Hawes, "Folksongs and Functions: Some Thoughts on the American Lullaby," *JAF* 87 [1974]: 140–48). Numerous narrators recalled mothers rocking them and their siblings to sleep with spirituals and hymns, which, song for song, may have been the most common slave lullabyes. "I 'members my mammy singing 'Swing Low Sweet Chary-ot' and she rock me to sleep, she would sing: 'I Dont Care Whar Dey Bury My Body—But O! My Lil' Soul is Gwine ter Rise and Shine'" (James Claiborne, b. 1860, MS, 400–401). For the second item, also see Marsh, *Jubilee Singers*, 220; Perkins, "Spirituals," 224; Work, *ANSS*, 141.

My mudder she lots of time sing:

> I will arise and go to Jesus,
> He will embrace me in his arms;

In the arms of my deah Saviour,
Oh, dere are ten t'ousand charms.
and, "Bye O Bye go to sleep." (Will Rhymes,
b. 1853, LA, 3301)

Ex-slaves also described ballads, minstrel songs, reels, worksongs, war songs, and others being sung as lullabyes.

By the same token many songs conventionally classified as lullabyes were put to other uses. "The Gray Goose (Go Tell Aunt Nancy, Patsy, Rhody, and so on)" probably originated as a cradle song, which is how it usually appears in collections. The piece shows up in numerous contexts, however. Tempie Cummings had sung it as a lullaby, but John C. Bectom named it as a dance song, Laura Montgomery as a singing game.

I don' 'member none 'r' d' wuk songs. I tuk care 'r' d' little w'ite chillun an' uster sing dem t' sleep wid:

> Go tell Aunt Nancy
> Go tell Aunt Nancy
> Go tell Aunt Nancy
> Her ol' gray goose is dead.
> D' one she was savin'
> D' one she was savin'
> D' one she was savin'
> T' mek a feather bed. (Tempie Cummins,
> b. ca. 1862, TX, 1010–11)

Also see Brown III: 177–78; *Country Music Sources*, 112; Gordon, *Folk-Songs*, 85; Mellinger E. Henry, "Nursery Rhymes and Game-Songs from Georgia," *JAF* 47 (1934): 336; Perrow, "South" (1913), 130; Randolph, *OFS* II: 347–49; Scarborough, *TNFS*, 8, 195–96; Sharp, *EFSSA* II: 345; Solomon, *Daisies*, 115.

Ex-slaves mentioned a few other nursery songs and rhymes, but for whatever reasons children's traditions are but a small part of the WPA collection. A final pair of examples are actually most interesting for what they illustrate about the project's editorial methods.

Dey hab some co'n hollers. One was sump'n like dis "Rabbit gittin' up in a holler fo' niggers kotch fo' bre'kfas"—"Ol' cow Piedy, Ol' cow Piedy." Some-time' my mudder sing t' d' li'l pick'ninnies. She jump dem up in d' air 'n' sing. She sing 'nudder one:

Sugar in d' gou'de (gourd),
  Sugar in d' gou'de.
Iffen you wanter git
  D' sugar out—
Rr-o-o-ll d' gou'de ober.

'N' all d' time she jumpin' dem right straight up in de air. (Dennis Grant, b. ca. 1850, TX, 1550, orig. parentheses)

Sometimes we hollers de corn hollers. One was somethin' like this: "Rabbit gittin' up in a holler for niggers kotch for breakfast." Sometimes my mudder jump up in de air and sing.

Sugar in de gourd.
Sugar in de gourd,
Iffen you wanter git
    De sugar out—
R - o - o - l - l de gourd over.

And all de time she shoutin' dat, she jumpin' right straight up in de air. (John Moore, b. 1843, LA, 127)

Dennis Grant accurately describes a *dandling song* (a song for bouncing a baby), with the mother "jumping" (dandling or bouncing) the baby up in the air. The description in John Moore's narrative, in which the mother herself jumps straight up in the air, is utterly absurd, but this did not come from Moore; it was obviously copied from Grant's interview, and copied very badly. Dennis Grant was interviewed by Letha K. Hatcher, John Moore by Fred Dibble and Bernice Grey—all prolific interviewers whom I regard as reasonably reliable—and circumstantial evidence indicates the fieldworkers had nothing to do with this fiasco. The bungled passage is found only in the version of John Moore's interview sent to the Library of Congress (S1 5 *TX* 3: 125–27), not the draft originally deposited by Hatcher with the state office (SS2 7 *TX* 6: 2736–42). Dennis Grant's narrative appears only in the state materials (SS2 5 *TX* 4: 1546–52); the state office did not forward it to the national collection. The obvious conclusion, then, is that someone within the state organization's editorial process moved this passage from Dennis Grant's narrative to the revised draft of John Moore's narrative that was forwarded to Washington, botching the quote in the process. Grant's narrative and the state draft of Moore's narrative both seem genuine; the official version of Moore's narrative housed since 1941 in the Reading Room of the Library of Congress (S1 5 *TX* 3: 125–27) is a preposterous aberration.

REELS AND RING PLAYS

We used to sing songs too, on Dr. Andrew's place. But I can't never 'member the words. We used to sing songs and kinda imposed the words as we went. "Christmas Time" was the name of a dance song. "Christmas time, Christmas Time, it's almost day." That's all I can remember but it was a good dance song that we used to sing in the hugging up dances. (Rosa Maddox, b. 1848, LA, 2533)

Cawnshucking and candy pullins was common in dem days. We played a song like dis:

> Sweet, sweet, I don' know where Miss __(Mary)__ go, sweet, sweet.

We'd ring up, dance in er circle to de music and call de name er de one to come to de center. (Rose Brown, b. 1853, AL, 285, orig. parentheses and emphasis)

When the crops is laid by is when we have the most parties. We used to dance and sing and have play-games. The reels was what I used to like but I done quit that foolishness many years ago. I used to cut a step or two. I remembers a reel called the Devil's Dream. It was a fast song.

> Oh! de devil dreampt a dream
> He dreampt it on a Friday—
> He dreampt he caught a sinner—

Then somebody would call out real loud:

> Oh! de devil he dreampt a dream—. (Julia Frances Daniels, b. 1848,
> TX, 1023)[1]

Even when instruments were available, singing and body percussion provided much of the accompaniment for slave dancing. When instruments were not to be had, this was the only alternative, but for jig dances instrumental accompaniment might be suspended anyway in favor of vocals and patting. Under any circumstances, dance songs especially reflected the Black penchant for improvisation, many being recomposed to fit each and every new occasion. "Weuns have lotsa dances dem days, an' wid jus one fiddle, why, de niggers have so much music an' swing to it dat weuns jus' loves to sing an' dance. 'Twas a numbah of tudder songs, but de words am mos'ly made up right den" (Willie Blackwell, b. 1834, NC, 311–12). "My biggest job was keeping flies off'n the table at the Big House. When time come to go in for the day we would cut up and dance. I can't remember any of the songs jest now, but we had some that we sung. We danced a whole lots and jest sung 'made up' songs" (Hal Hutson, b. 1847, TN, 146–47). "We got in groups in front of the cabins and sang and danced to the music of banjoes until the overseer would come along and make us go to bed. No, I don't remember what the songs were, nothing in particular, I guess just, some we made up and we would sing a line or two over and over again" (Susan Bledsoe, b. 1845, TN, 7).

Dey would hab parties whar dey'ud play games lak thimble an' cross questions an' crooked answers an' de lak. Den dey would sing songs. One song I recollect wuz—

Hulla, Hulla, Hulla,
Hand me a gourd to drink water

We would sing dis over an' over an' keep a addin' to it. (Wright Stapleton, b. 1850, MS, 2022)

Some spontaneous compositions were passing commentaries or makeshift mouth-music, performed once and never again; others were established songs whose incremental structures allowed singers to particularize them for each performance.

(A song permitting of unlimited variation is the "Johnson Gal," described by Della Harris:)

Fig. 18.1. "Piccaninnie Dance Down in Dixie." Anniston, AL: Russell Bros., 1895. Library of Congress, Prints and Photographs Division.

Hi, ho, Johnson gal, Johnson gal, Johnson gal,
Hi, ho, Johnson gal,
Johnson gal is de gal fo' me

You see, dey wasn't no sech person as de Johnson gal. De boys jus' start dat way to git all de gals to perkin' up. When dey hear dat, dey know dey gonna start callin' real names de nex' time. Arter dey sing Johnson gal three or fo' times—never know how many times dey gonna sing it—den some one change it to:

Hi, ho, de Henry gal, Henry gal, Henry gal,
Hi, ho, de Henry gal,
Henry gal is de gal fo' me.

Dat mean de Henry gal come fo'ward an' do her steps in de ring, an' when she done all she know dey call for some other gal de same way. Mos' times dey call all de gals, but sometime dey leave out one gal jus' fo' meanness. An' any gal dat's left out feel mighty po'ly 'bout it, too. (Della Harris, b. ca. 1852, NC, 131–32, orig. parentheses)[2]

One of the songs that the slaves on the House plantation used to sing at their parties runs as follows:

Oh, I wouldn't have a poor girl,
  (another version says, "old maid")
And I'll tell you the reason why,
Her neck's so long and stringy,
I'm afraid she'd never die. (Henry Wright,
  b. 1838, GA, 200, orig. parentheses)[3]

And a nudder song dey uster sing and dance wus—

Come 'long gals an' let's go to Boston,
Come 'long gals an' let's go to Boston,
Come 'long gals an' let's go to Boston
Early in de mornin'.
Jack, Jack, Jack, I'll tell you' daddy,
Jack, Jack, Jack, I'll tell you' daddy,
Jack, Jack, Jack, I'll tell you' daddy
Whar yo' go a courtin'.
Reckin I keer if yo' tell my daddy,
Reckin I keer if yo' tell my daddy,
Reckin I keer if yo' tell my daddy,
Whar I go a courtin'—

Dem was good times an' ebery body liked it. Some
uf dem men folks wud git a lit'l too much to drink
but dey never done no mischief. (Rina Brown,
b. 1853, MS, 280)

At other times slaves did perform prearranged
dance songs with relatively fixed texts and tunes tied
to prearranged figures or steps. "One song I remember
is, 'would like to catch-a-feller looking like me.'
Another was, 'I feel as happy as a big sunflower' (Charlie
can sing them both, and dance accompaniment)"
(Charlie Giles, b. ca. 1840, SC, 116, orig. parentheses).
Often these items were shared by Blacks and whites
and straddled instrumental and vocal traditions, being
alternately sung or played on various instruments,
especially the fiddle. Many fall into the *fiddle tune*
genre and probably originated as instrumentals with
words added later. However, dance singers and instrumentalists
adapted vocal music from any imaginable
source: children's games, worksongs, ballads and love
lyrics, minstrel and Tin Pan Alley pieces, spirituals

and hymns. They also created new and original items.
The most common terms for these dance songs were
ring plays or *reels*, but there were others (*songs*, *games*,
play-parties, and more).[4] In any case, a high proportion
of the dance accompaniments known to ex-slaves
led multiple lives: they were played instrumentally,
played and sung, and sung a cappella.

Period accounts and later recordings give a good
idea of how this dance singing sounded. First and
foremost, it was loud, and had to be to be heard over
the general tumult, performed in a full-throated,
declamatory holler replete with percussive grit and
other effects. "Tom and Gilbert played de fiddle an' we
chilluns down in de quarters cud hear dem stampin'
deir feet an' shoutin' an' singin'" (Adam Singleton,
b. 1858, AL, 1950). Just as instrumentalists imitated
voices and vocal music, vocalists imitated musical
instruments and instrumental music, verbally or nonverbally.
Obviously too, such singing was rhythmically
structured to provide a danceable beat. Many of the
dance songs recalled by ex-slaves were cast in a call-
and-response pattern; in any case, singing at slave
dances was wholly inclusive, possibly led by callers
or musicianers but demanding the whole crowd's participation.
"We was let off Sadday at noon and could
go to the fiddlin's and dance all night. You could hear
the niggers dancin' a mile away. The same man called
for us that called fer the white folks. . . . I don't recollect
none of the words of the tunes" (Charles Willis,
b. ca. 1845, MS, 399). While almost anything could
be turned into a dance song, there were established
categories or favored sources.

DANCE CALLS. Sometimes dance lyrics were sung
by instrumentalists, sometimes by dancers, sometimes
by any and all persons so moved. Still, dance callers
were the most important vocalists at many gatherings,
customarily interspersing dance prompts with
sung passages, perhaps singing the prompts as well.
"'Twas de quadrille dance weuns does. Deys have de
fiddles fo' music, an' Uncle John am de prompter. He
sings all de way through de dance. . . . 'Swing youse
partner, aint she sweet, swing her off her feet. All jine
hands an' circle 'round, watch youse step an' don't fall

down. Swing de gal to youse left, make it swift or youse git left'" (Tob Davis, b. 1857, TX, 1083). Many dance songs give direct instructions in this manner; others describe accompanying movements metaphorically or dramatically:

At d' dance dey hab a man t' call d' parts,

> Swing yo' corner, 'n'
> yo' pardner.

Den dey sorter sing fo' d' dancin'. Dey dance by d' singin'. Dey sing:

> My ol' mistus promise me,
> Shoo a la a day,
> W'en she die she set me free,
> Shoo a la a day,
> She lib so long 'til her head git bal' (bald)
> Shoo a la a day,
> She gib up d' idea 'r' dyin' a-tall,
> Shoo a la a day. (Jake Desso, b. 1863, TX, 1196,
> orig. parentheses)[5]

One thing I can remember de slaves use ter do, dat wuz ter light candles when de nite wuz dark an' go off in de woods an' build big fires an' play games by de firelight. One game wuz ter ketch hands an' go 'round in a circle an' sing some ole song dat dey would make up, lak dis.

> Run Liza Jane an' take her home,
> Run Liza Jane an' take her home,
> Run Liza Jane an' take her home,
> Run, run, run.

A boy would be a running his gal, an' when he kotch her a nuther couple would run. (Lawerence Evans, b. 1858, MS, 704–5)[6]

All would line up to dance, every one would have a parner, den de head lady would say, "Paunt your swing." That means go round, Den she say,

"Cross Swing." That means every one would cross over and [get] a new parner. Den she would say, "Cashing the ring." That means de head lady would dance around de ring to everybody. Den de next one, and so on. Den de would have some love songs, while dancing, as dese flip, jack flip a jas.

> Set up again.

> Back Cherter old tones love.
> Back ole agger sinder loving summer day.

> Rule over, rule under, give me a glass of drink
>   wine,
> Don't want no more snow water.

That means all would stop dancing and take a drink of wine. (Dave Lowry, b. 1857, VA, 198, orig. brackets. The text is given exactly as transcribed.)

FIDDLE TUNES WITH WORDS. So-called fiddle tunes also draw on every imaginable source (and are not always played on fiddles), but the core of the Southern fiddle-tune repertoire derives from two sources: 1) a vast stock of traditional fiddle and pipe tunes imported from England, Scotland, and Ireland; and 2) an equally large repertoire created by Anglo and African American fiddlers in the same pattern. Typically, that structure involves two melodic phrases of equal length, distinguished in range as low, the so-called "coarse" part, and high, the "fine" part. British fiddle tunes usually do not have lyrics, but African American fiddle tunes often do, closely corresponding to the tune's rhythmic pattern, with the coarse part serving as the verse, the fine part as chorus. The idea that a melody invariably represents a verbal phrase (or vice versa) is fundamentally African, reflecting the identification of language and music throughout Africa, but especially in areas where tonal languages are spoken. Southern white fiddle tunes (and particularly those shared with Blacks) sometimes also have words, but this may be an African American innovation, yet another expression of the African-based beliefs that instruments have voices and speak, but also that human voices are instruments.

To verbalize fiddle tunes, or to create new dance songs in that pattern, songmakers sometimes simply drew on readymade wandering stanzas, but other lyrics are particular to specific items. The words might or might not be sung with instrumental renditions but could always substitute when instruments were not available. "Cinto don' know how to do no step, but he could sho nuff fiddle. He play fo' all de dancin'. . . . Den dey wah a ol' song which come back to me, 'High-heel shoes an' Cal'co Stockings.' It go somethin' like dis: / Fare you well Miss Nancy Hawkins, / High-heel shoes and cal'co stockings" (Lucy Lewis, b. unk., TX, 2364). "Marse William whistle like a partridge; den Miss Nellie play her pianny. I dance and Marse send fer me a sugar and butter biscuit. Marse git his banjo and he pick it fer me to sing 'Oh, Bob white, is your wheat ripe? No, no, not quite.' Dat when I lived as a little gal on Marse William's home tract, called Musgrove Tract" (Cordelia Anderson Jackson, b. ca. 1859, SC, 7). "We used to dance and sing and have play-games. . . . I used to cut a step or two. I remembers a reel called the Devil's Dream. It was a fast song. / Oh! de devil dreampt a dream" (Julia Frances Daniels, b. 1848, TX, 1023).[7]

> I can hear 'em yet hollerin', "swing yo' pardner," on over in a co'ner de fiddles a playin' . . .

> > Wuked all de year to make a bale o' cotton
> > Gib it all away to see Sally Goodun.
> > Looked down de road and seen Sall a commin'
> > Thought to my soul I'd kill mysef a runnin'.
> > (Anda Woods, b. ca. 1841, AL, 2389–90)[8]

Few Southern fiddle songs have been as popular as "Hop (Step) Light (High), Lady (Ladies) (The Cake's All Dough)," also known as "Did You Ever See the Devil (Go to Meeting), Uncle Joe." It is well documented among Blacks from an early date; Joel Chandler Harris collected a version in Putnam County,

Georgia, in 1856, described as a "Plantation Play-Song."[9] It is frequently sung unaccompanied, but borrows the melody of the British fiddle tune "Miss McLeod's Reel," which is also played purely instrumentally, whether under that name or as "Hop Light, Lady." Blacks probably introduced the lyrics, however. A variant of this same melody is used for "Jump Jim Crow," definitely a slave creation. Seven ex-slaves remembered "Hop Light, Lady." Barney Alford, Georgia Baker, Delia Barclay, and Mary Ann Brooks described it being sung unaccompanied; Campbell Davis, Frances Lewis, and Adam Singleton recalled it played on the fiddle but with lyrics; all seven gave similar versions of the title stanza. The most unusual example came from Delia Barclay, who remembered "Hop Light, Lady" accompanying children's hopscotch games, unique but appropriate.

> I was a mighty dancer when I was young—danced all night long. Paddyrollers run us home from dancin' one night. I member one song we used to sing:

> > Hop light lady
> > Cake was all dough—
> > Never mind the weather,
> > So the wind don't blow. (Mary Ann Brooks,
> > b. 1848, AR, 254)

> Befo' I got converted I went to dances. We danced by a fiddle and the fiddler kept time with a song:

> > Hop light, ladies,
> > The cake's all dough.
> > Don't mind the weather
> > So the wind don't blow. (Frances Lewis, b. 1854,
> > GA, 161)

> All d' middle size chillren like d' hoppin' game d' bes'. Us mark out diff'runt plots on d' groun' 'n' den hab a caller. D' chillren tek tu'ns 'n' d' caller sing out,

Hop light, ladies,
D' cake's all dough,
Ne'mine d' wedder (weather),
So's d' win' don' blow. (Delia Barclay, b. unk., TX, 155, orig. parentheses)

The lyrics for some fiddle tunes went to great lengths and varied considerably, but other items featured just one or two stanzas repeated rote. Even items of this sort allowed for improvisation, though. Byron Arnold's informant Jennie Chandler had learned the fiddle-tune-with-words, "Sally Ann," on her father's Alabama plantation. "A family of twenty-two Negroes named Big John, Lil John, Sweetie John, etc., had a family band which would play for dances both white and colored. It would amuse the Negroes for the whites to sing 'Sally Ann' with them. There were many verses made up to suit the occasion or the steps of the dance."[10]

CHILDREN'S SINGING GAMES. Some of the dances performed at adult recreations also functioned as children's singing games, not surprising considering that participants at "adult" dances were often preadolescents or not far removed. Many of these items had long led double lives as children's songs and fiddle tunes with words. "Polly (Molly, Jenny) Put the Kettle On" is a well-known nursery rhyme reported as a singing game and fiddle tune in Britain and North America from around 1800. It was especially well remembered by ex-slaves, but only Chaney McNair associated it with children. Lucy Donald, Hattie Jefferson, and Primous Magee all described it as a fiddle tune (Jefferson briefly quoted the rhyme). W. S. Needham Jr. (b. 1854), a slaveholder's child, had learned to fiddle the piece from a Mississippi slave named Mance. Mississippi ex-slave Mollie Williams recalled it as a reel, apparently sung unaccompanied and danced by adults:

Gennie, put de kittle on,
Sallie, boil de water strong,
Gennie, put de kittle on

An' le's hav tea! (Mollie Williams, b. 1853, MS, 2348)[11]

Based on another English singing game, "Pop Goes the Weasel" is widespread in America as a nursery rhyme, play party, fiddle song, and jack-in-the-box tune. Mollie Williams again:

Dey danced reels an' lak in de moonlight:

Mama's got de whoopin' cough,
Daddy's got de measles,
Dat's whar de money goes,
Pop goes de weasel. (Mollie Williams, b. 1853, MS, 2348)[12]

A 1970s field recording by Black fiddler Cuje Bertram (1894–ca. 1980) includes the same stanza.

PLAY PARTIES. Though practically unavoidable, the term *play-party song* is somewhat misleading, since play-parties were more properly events, literally parties where people played (danced) to singing only. The games played on these occasions were also called play-parties. Some of the accompanying songs were original to these events, but they might come from anywhere, or spread from play-parties to other genres, so that so-called play-party songs were often performed on occasions or in styles that participants definitely did not consider play-parties. Allowing, however, that there are exceptions to virtually any generalization about the play-party, as a distinct institution, play-parties were carefully organized and chaperoned social occasions, mainly for adolescents and young adults, maintaining a rigid decorum in deliberate contrast to behaviors associated with recreational dancing. Musical instruments and especially the fiddle were forbidden. Alcohol was never served. Favored routines self-consciously excised social dancing's more disreputable or dangerous elements (vulgar lyrics, the waist swing and other suggestive movements, couple dances, and so on). The fancy footwork and bumping-and-grinding associated with sinful dances were thus forgone in favor of marching, skipping, trotting, galloping, hopping, and other innocuous movements described in metaphoric, idyllic lyrics echoing the singing game's nursery-rhyme style.

> Play parties were the usual form of amusement the county afforded. Later in the German Cat holies [Catholics] settlement of Clark County square dances were given—usually in the vicinity of St. Joe. There were no musical instruments at the play parties. The people would sing songs that accompanied the games they played. The guests, in wagons or on horse back, would gather at the host's home by sundown. The young gallant would bring the lady of his heart behind him on his favorite plow-horse. The husband would bring his wife and children in the wagon. After they arrived the children would soon go to sleep across the bed where the wraps were laid. Both young and old played "Skip to My Lou," "Weevily Wheat" and such games until it was time to go home, which was about twelve o'clock. (George Thomas, ca. 1855–1937, IN, 224)[13]

(Following, is a "Love Song" she sang—which she learned as a girl when attending play-parties):

> I'm wandering down to Graybrook Town,
> Where the drums and fifes are beating
> The American have gained the day
> And the bridges [handwritten in margin: British?] are retreating.
>
> My pretty little pink,
> I used to think that you and I would marry,
> But since you told me so many faults
> I care nothing about you.
>
> I'll take my knapsack on my back
> My rifle on my shoulder
> I'll open up a ring and choose a couple in
> To relieve the broken hearted. (Annie Bridges, b. 1855, MO, 46, orig. parentheses)[14]

Fig. 18.2. Litt Young, ex-slave, Marshall, TX, September 7, 1937. Portraits of African American ex-slaves from the US Works Progress Administration, Federal Writers' Project slave narratives collection, Library of Congress.

Litt Young actually identified "Coffee Grows On White Oak Trees" (another marching play-party song) with Union troops marching out of Vicksburg.

> We had small dances on Saturday night and play ring plays, and have banjo and fiddle playing and knock bones together. There was all kinds of fiddles made from gourds and things. They made the banjoes from sheep hides. It's been so long I can't 'member the names of the ring plays, 'cept the one that goes like this: "Coffee grows on white oak trees, River flows with brandy-o." That song was started there in Vicksburg by the Yankee soldiers when they left to go home, 'cause they was so glad the war was over. (Litt Young, b. 1850, MS, 4302)[15]

The play-party was often motivated by religious objections to dancing and dance music, but not always; sometimes people played these games only because instruments were unavailable, or, even when instruments were available, simply because they enjoyed them. On the other hand, persons who objected to dancing on religious grounds usually objected to any and all dancing, with or without instruments; in practice, instrumental music and play-parties were so completely intertwined and completely interchangeable that for church members they were equally wicked. The play-party was adopted by some Blacks, and ex-slaves occasionally use "ring play" to describe sedate gatherings and games more or less equivalent to play-parties. For most narrators, ring plays were sinful dances no different from reels. In any event, ex-slaves had occasionally attended play-parties, and knew many dance lyrics often classed as play-party songs (such as "Hop Light, Lady"), but in their cases this is usually not the best description.

MINSTRELSY AND TIN PAN ALLEY. Dancing and dance songs were major attractions of blackface minstrelsy, and an important link to African American folk tradition. Minstrels often borrowed Black dances and their accompaniments, and their caricatures sometimes counter-influenced the original sources. However, the process was incredibly complex and variable and many of the dance songs Black communities shared with minstrels show little or no blackface influence, indicating Blacks sometimes preserved their original traditions unaltered by professional adaptations. There is no question that blackface performers borrowed "Little Liza Jane" from slaves, or that their renditions in turn impacted Black tradition.[16] Ex-slave texts occasionally suggest minstrel influences—see especially Lucy Thurston's version below—but more often the folk process, differing greatly in particulars. Marshal Butler, Dosia Harris, Lina Hunter, Hannah Jameson, and Anda Woods named "Little Liza Jane" as a dance song. Harris, Hunter, and Jameson described it a cappella; and Butler and Woods recalled it with fiddles but also vocals. Alice Hutcheson (and possibly Frank Menefee) recalled it as a cornshucking song, Hannah Jameson at cornshucking dances, and Lucy Thurston as a field song. Bryant Huff gave a Confederate camp song incorporating a verse from "Liza Jane," while Lawrence Evans, Lydia Jefferson, and Eliza Overton described another offshoot, the African American children's singing game variously called "Run Liza Jane," "Swing Ole Liza Single," "Catch Liza Jane," or "Steal Liza Jane." This piece was sometimes played with fiddling at adult dances as well.

Dem dances was grand. Ev'y body would be enjoyin' dey se'ves den. I can hear 'em yet hollerin', "swing yo' pardner," an' over in a co'ner de fiddles a playin' de ole rag times an' dem singin' snotches of songs lak dis:

> You go down de new cut road
> I'll go down de lane,
> If yo' git deir befo' I does
> Kiss Miss Liza Jane. (Anda Woods, b. ca. 1841, AL, 2389–90)

Dey danced, frolicked, and cut de buck in gen'ral. Dey didn't have no sho' 'nough music, but dey sho' could sing it down. One of de dance songs went somepin' lak dis:

> Oh! Miss Liza, Miss Liza Jane!
> Axed Miss Liza to marry me
> Guess what she said?
> She wouldn't marry me,
> If de last Nigger was dead. (Dosia Harris, b. ca. 1860, GA, 109–10)

Marster Dickey took me to Covington, La. an I wuk out in the fiels. Finally I got happy an sang wid de res'. I member one song us used to sing mos' of all wuz—

> Ohoooooooo lil Liza, lil Liza Jane,
> Ohoooooooooooooo lil Liza, lil Liza Jane.
> Hair as blak as coal in de mi-ine,
> Lil Liza Jane,
> Eyes so large an' big an' fin'
> Lil Liza Jane.
> Ohoooooooo lil Liza, lil Liza Jane,
> Ohoooooooo lil Liza, lil Liza Jane.

Mouse in de hol and de cats' gwine git it,
Lil Liza Jane,
Cats in de' tree an' de dawg gwine git it,
Lil Liza Jane.
Ohoooooooo lil Liza, lil Liza Jane,
Ohhhhhhhh lil Liza, lil Liza Jane. (Lucy Thurston, b. ca. 1836, LA, 2113)

The professional origins of other songs danced in Black communities are, by contrast, beyond dispute.

War come on, my marster went out as a captain of de Horse Marines. A tune was much sung by de white folks on de place and took wid de niggers. It went like dis:

I'm Captain Jenks of de Horse Marines
I feed my horse on corn and beans.
Oh! I'm Captain Jenks of de Horse Marines
And captain in de army! (Charley Barber, b. ca. 1856, SC, 31)

"Captain Jinks of the Horse Marines" (T. Maclagan) was an 1860 English music hall hit popularized in America by British comic, singer, and female impersonator William H. Lingard (1837–1927). Ex-slaves Charley Barber and Mollie Williams both attributed the song to whites; it was later collected mainly but not entirely from Anglo-Americans. Barber mentions only vocals, but Williams describes the piece being fiddled, sung, and danced.[17]

ROWDY AND VULGAR SONGS. Church people objected to dance songs not only because they accompanied dancing but because of their vulgarity and worldliness, celebrating the hedonism, vice, and dissolution that often surrounded their performance. Obscene or off-color folksongs have always been notoriously difficult to collect, and the scant material ex-slaves provided seems incredibly mild by today's standards, but they were definitely familiar with such items.

Dey uster hab lotser dances. Dey hab fiddle player and 'corjun (accordion) player. Dey sing "Swing

your partner, promenade." Dey uster hab a l'il song dat started out,

Dinah got a meat skin lay away,
Grease dat wooden leg, Dinah,
Grease dat wooden leg, Dinah.
Dinah got a meat skin lay away,
Shake dat wooden leg, Dinah,
Shake dat wooden leg, Dinah. (Mary Kindred, b. ca. 1855, TX, 2204, orig. parentheses)

The significance of Dinah, Sal, Sally, and so on greasing the singer's wooden leg with her meatskin escaped no one, and this dance lyric was extremely popular with Blacks and whites alike. William M. Adams named it with fiddle and bones. In his autobiography, W. C. Handy (1873–1958) described beating straws while his ex-slave uncle Whit Walker (b. ca. 1800) fiddled and sang the piece; Huddie "Lead Belly" Ledbetter (1889–1949) recalled playing it on the accordion.[18] William Pratt had heard it with jigging and a couple dance known as the hack-back or hack-a-back, but also sung in the fields: "We used to dance jigs by ourself, and we danced the 'hack-back,' skipping backwards and forwards facing each other. When one danced a jig he would sing, 'Juber this, Juber that, Juber kills a yellow cat.' My brother used to sing a cotton picking song: 'My mammy got meat skin laid away; grease my belly three times a day'" (William Pratt, b. 1860, SC, 278).[19]

"Buffalo Gals" unquestionably owes much of its popularity to minstrel sources, but this is likely another case of minstrels borrowing from Black tradition with debatable counter-influence.[20] The piece, which was also well known among whites, occurs both as an unaccompanied dance song and fiddle tune with or without words. The gals' location changes constantly, and textual variation is high overall. Mollie Williams called the piece a reel; Gus Feaster remembered it as a "vulgar song," both of them describing vocal performances. In the nineteenth century, the song did have a decidedly sordid reputation, being particularly tied to prostitutes. The *Alabama Planter* for December 10, 1846, reported that lately in Mobile, "a flower, innocent and beautiful but long since torn from its stem, trampled, soiled, and desecrated was arrested for drunkenly singing 'Mobile Gals, Won't You Come Out Tonight?' on the streets."[21] Feaster's vulgar text is truncated but still suggestive (as is its context), and may have been more so in full: Ozark folklorist Vance Randolph (1892–1980) collected several obscene versions of the song, some dating as far back as the 1800s.[22]

> Thar was plenty dancin' 'mong'st darkies on Marse George's place an' on ones nearby. Dey danced reels an' lak in de moonlight. . . .
>
> > Buffalo gals, can't you come out tonight,
> > Come out tonight, an' dance by de light of de
> > moon? (Mollie Williams, b. 1853, MS, 2348)

> When boys and gals gits up some size dey feels deyselves. At dat age, we went bird thrashing in de moon light. Den we sing dis vulgar song, "I'll give you half-dollar if you come out tonight; I'll give you half-dollar if you come out tonight." (Gus Feaster, b. ca. 1840, SC, 51)

AFRICAN AMERICAN DANCE SONGS. Numerous dance accompaniments recalled by ex-slaves can with some certainty be ascribed to Black songmakers. Not surprisingly, animal tricksters were popular subjects.

> About all I remember about the dances was when we danced the cotillion at regular old country breakdowns. Folks valued their dances very highly then, and to be able to perform them well was a great accomplishment. *Turkey in the Straw* is about the oldest dance tune I can remember. Next to that is *Taint Gonna Rain No More*, but the tune as well as the words to that were far different from the modern song by that name. *Rabbit Hair* was another favorite song, and there were dozens of others that I just never tried to remember until you

asked me about them. (John F. Van Hook, b. 1862, NC, 83, orig. italics)

As Van Hook states two distinct songs are now known as "(It) Ain't Gonna Rain No More," the item most familiar today having been popularized through a 1923 recording (Victor 19171) by vaudevillian Wendell Hall (1896–1969).[23] Ex-slaves used this title for an older, nineteenth-century piece recognized as a Black creation.[24] Texts are usually composed of wandering stanzas concerning the doings of the crow, hawk, and buzzard, interspersed with the ain't-gonna-rain refrain. These verses are also associated with the ring play "Jim Crow," and sometimes other songs.[25] Van Hook remembered "Ain't Gonna Rain No More" as an adult dance song, Annie Bridges as a children's singing game.

> (Following is a song she learned as a child)
>
> > Rain, rain, rain all around
> > Ain't goin' rain no more
> > And what did the blackbird say to the crow
> > You bring rain, and I'll bring snow
> >
> > Rain, rain, rain all around
> > Ain't goin' a-rain no more
> > Old Hawk and buzzard went to roost
> > The hawk came back with a loosened tooth
> >
> > Rain, rain, rain all around
> > Ain't goin' a-rain no more
> > I had an old hat and it had a crown,
> > Look like a duck's nest sittin' on the ground.
> >
> > Rain, rain, rain all around
> > Ain't goin' a-rain no more. (Annie Bridges,
> > b. 1855, MO, 47)

Improvisation figured in most slave singing, but there is agreement from all quarters that dance songs might be entirely extemporaneous. "One song I recollect wuz— / Hulla, Hulla, Hulla, / Hand me a gourd to drink water / We would sing dis over an' over an' keep a addin' to it" (Wright Stapleton, b. 1850, MS, 2022). Some items had incremental structures or other formal features facilitating recomposition or improvisation. Some were actually created in the moment, in response to the immediate occasion or some topical concern. Dance songs were also especially likely to incorporate wandering stanzas, or to cross and combine with other songs. As a result, many dance titles exist not so much as discrete songs but as loose chains of thematic associations tracing diverging streams of consciousness. In isolation, any two links may appear completely unrelated, their connection revealed only by their place in the whole. In that regard, the ex-slave narratives unearth a couple of missing links revealing how fascinating yet frustrating tackling these song complexes can be.

The subjects in this case are, on the one hand, a description of a dead cow in a creek branch, and, on the other, a song about drinking cold water from a gourd. Both pieces were usually named as game or dance accompaniments, though Betty Curlett recalled "The Old Cow Died" as a lullaby.

Song her Mother and Grandmother sang:

> Old cow died in the fork of the branch
> > Baby, Ba, Ba.
> Dock held the light, Kimbo skinned it.
> > Ba, Ba, Ba.
> Old cow lived no more on the ranch and drank no
> > more from the branch, Kimba a pair of shoes,
> > he sewed from the old cow hide he had tanned.
> > Baby, Ba, Ba. (Betty Curlett, b. 1872, MS,
> > child of ex-slaves, 80)

Usually the old cow drowns, but even this varies. In some texts the other animals celebrate her death; in others they too become casualties. "De ole cow died in de head of de branch, / De jay birds whistled and de buzzards danced" (Auburn, AL, 1915–1916).[26] "The old cow died in the forks of the branch; / The racoon fiddled and the 'possum danced" (Peedee region, SC, early 1900s).[27] "'Way down yonder, in de forks o' de creek, / De ole cow died in de middle o' next week"

(Auburn, AL, 1915–1916); "Way down yonder in de growin' corn, / De old cow died wid de holler horn" ("Sung by an ex-slave," Mobile Co., AL, 1915–1916).[28] "Ladies an' gentl'men, I tell you de fac' / De ole caow died in de fodder stack" (VA, 1909).[29]

> Ole cow died at the mouth of the branch
> 'T'ain't gwine rain no mo'.
> The buzzards had a public dance
> 'T'ain't gwine rain no mo'. (TX, ca. 1900)[30]

> Run nigger run, the patterol'l ketch yuh,
> Run nigger run, it's almost day, . . .
> Ol' cow died in the fowk of the branch,
> Jay bird whistle an' the black bird dance,
> Creek's all gone, pond's all dry,
> If t'want for the tadpole, we'd all die. (AL slaves)[31]

Sum uf de slaves wus jes standin' round singin' and sum pattin' lak dancin' . . .

> Jay bird died wid de whoopin' couf
> 'Possum died wid de colic.
> 'Yon er leetle boy wid fiddle on his back.
> Jes ter have er frolic. (Ann Drake, b. 1855,
> > MS, 643)[32]

> Old cow died of whooping cough,
> Baby cow died of measles,
> Father died with a spoon in his mouth,
> And carried it off to Jesus. (AL, white, 1952)[33]

At these same gatherings, slaves often danced and sang "A Gourd of Cold Water," described in a 1894 *Southern Workman* article:

> Girls all face one way and boys the other. Form a line holding each other's hand with arms raised. The leader leads the long line in and out between each other's upraised arms, all singing—

> "Reg'lar, reg'lar, rolling under,
> Gimme de go'rd to drink water.

Don't want no more de ice water
Gimme de go'rd to drink water.
You bring rain and I bring thunder,
Gimme de go'rd to drink water
Reg'lar, reg'lar, rolling under
Gimme de go'rd to drink water."

Whenever the leader sings the others repeat "Gimme de go'rd to drink water."[34]

Apparently this piece varied almost as much as "Old Cow." Wright Stapleton remembered the chorus as "Hulla, Hulla, Hulla, / Hand me a gourd to drink water" (Wright Stapleton, b. 1850, MS, 2022), Dave Lowry as "Rule over, rule under, give me a glass of drink wine, / Don't want no more snow water" (Dave Lowry, b. 1857, VA, 198). In Mississippi or Tennessee, Thomas Talley heard it as "Rule, rule, rule over / Draw wine but drink water."[35]

And for some reason, several texts combine "A Gourd of Cold Water" with "The Old Cow Died." "I only remember part of the words to one play. That was 'Rolling river, roll on, the old cow die in cold water . . . now we'se got to drink bad water cause the old cow died in cold water'" (Susan Merritt, b. 1851, TX, 2640, orig. ellipsis).

Comes to me sometimes little play-game songs. We played somethin' we called "Reglar, reglar, roll over." We sing:

Reglar, reglar
All roll over
Old cow died for want of cold water.
Reglar, reglar—
All roll over. (Rosa Maddox, b. ca. 1848,
    LA, 2524)

Red Morroco

Red Morroco, cool over
Red Morroco, cool over.
Give me a drink uv cool water.

Ask young lady thru yonder
Give me a drink uv cool water.

Reel er Reel

Reel er reel er reel over
Give me er gourd of cool water
Reel er reel er reel over
Give me a gourd of cool water.

Old cow shiverin' in de cool water
Give me a drink uv cool water.
Old cow suckin' in de cool water
Give me er gourd uv cool water.

Hoist dem windows over yonder.
Give me er drink uv cool water.[36]

The connection between a dead cow in a cold creek and a gourd of cold water is as obvious and sensible as it is surrealistic or just plain silly, and texts combining the themes may even have been created independently. In 1940 in East Texas, John Lomax recorded the following from local African American songster Arthur "Brother in Law" Armstrong:

Saw a mule in the corner of the fence,
He ain't quite dead but he got no sense.

Singing hallé-, hallé-, hallelu!
We'll sing hallé-, hallé-, hallelu!
Sing hallé-, hallé-, hallelu!

Old King Buzzard flew so high,
Prayed to the Lord some cow might die.

Singing hallé (etc.)

The old cow died, and the little calf cried,
The old bull laughed 'til he had a pain in his side.[37]

Intriguingly, the first half of Armstrong's chorus— "hallé-, hallé-, hallelu"—suggests that his version of

"The Old Cow Died" might also have crossed with "A Gourd of Cold Water." There is no question that Armstrong sings the gospel "hallelu" in his chorus, but in this context there is also no escaping the resemblance between Armstrong's "hallé-, hallé-, hallelu" and Wright Stapleton's "hulla, hulla, hulla," his reinterpretation of "reglar, reglar, all roll over": "Hulla, Hulla, Hulla, / Hand me a gourd to drink water" (Wright Stapleton, b. 1850, MS, 2022). Armstrong's "hallelu" could thus have no religious significance whatsoever, simply being another reinterpretation of "reg'lar, reg'lar, rolling under," "rule over, rule under," and so on. To complicate matters, in the early 1900s Black fieldhands around Lynchburg, Virginia, were overheard singing:

> Old King Buzzard floating high,
> "Sho do wish old cow would die."
> Old cow died, old calf cried,
> "Oh mourner, you shall be free."[38]

The opening lines are the closest parallels to Arthur Armstrong's "Buzzard Song" that I have found anywhere. The last line is from "(Shout) Mourner, You Shall Be Free," a minstrel parody of the slave spiritual "You (We) Shall Be Free." The remaining two lines are from "The Old Cow Died." Perhaps Armstrong sings the Gospel *hallelu* after all. Or perhaps the religious touches in the Virginia text have another explanation, including pure coincidence.

One can chase such textual associations almost endlessly. Dorothy Scarborough prints a specimen combining "A Gourd of Cold Water" with the singing game "I'm In Some Lady's Garden," most likely also a slave creation. (Scarborough's white informant described it as a game song "her mother . . . heard the children on plantations in Louisiana sing in the early days.") The first line offers yet another variation on "roll (rule) over, roll under":

> Ransum scansum, through yonder,
> Bring me a gourd to drink water,
> Dis way out and t'other way in,
> In my lady's chamber.
> Dis way out and t'other way in,
> In my lady's chamber.[39]

This association may then explain Mollie Dawson's unusual version of "I'm In Some Lady's Garden," which hints at our tradition but substitutes a bald horse for the old cow, and a turnip patch (the garden) for the cold rolling river.

> One of the ring games dat we played more dan any other was "Bald Horse." We would all form a ring and puts one in de middle and starts goin around and singin, "Bald horse buried in de turnip patch, de buzzards are after me. Do let me out of here, I'se in some ladies garden." (Mollie Dawson, b. 1852, TX, 1133)

As a basic condition of their function, these lyrics were forever works in progress, never reaching any logical conclusion. Most likely any given singer rendered their individual version in dozens or more different ways over a lifetime. The occasional traces in print or on sound recordings are skeletal remains, since the songs themselves only came alive in performance, where they might be wholly reimagined in the blink of an eye. In sum, the singing at slave frolics often required mental agility and verbal dexterity on a par with the physical demands of the dance steps.

WORKSONGS

As they followed their leader down the row "chopping out" cotton, or, when later they worked in gangs at picking it, it was their custom, seeming to act from instinct in the matter, to sing. One voice usually began the song, then another would join him, and then another, until dozens of voices blended in weird and melodious harmonies that floated from the distant cotton fields to the house of the master. (Virginia Clay-Clopton [1825–1915], *A Belle of the Fifties: Memoirs of Mrs. Clay of Alabama* [New York: Doubleday, Page, 1904], 220–21)

Pick Dat Cotton

Ole Massa say, (oratorical) Pick dat cotton!
(In whining, canting tone) Can't pick cotton, Massa, (triumphant)
    Cotton seed am rotten!
          Ha! Ha! Ha!

Remarks: The laugh is at ole massa. "He think he got a big crop, but he ain't." This song will be sung singly, in groups, over and over, until some one tires and starts another. . . . Almost without exception a song in the field is begun by someone singing the chorus. (Steve Stepney, 1840–1935, MS, communicated by his grandchildren, 2039–40, orig. parentheses and italics)[1]

De people dat owned de plantation near us had lots of slaves. Dey owned lots uv mah kin folks. Dey marster would beat dem at night when dey come fum de fiel' an lock em up. He'd whoop um an' send um tuh de fiel'. Dey couldn' visit no slaves an no slaves was 'lowed to visit em. So mah cousin Sallie watched him hide de key so she moved dem a li'l further back so dat he had tuh lean ovah tuh reach dem. Dat mawnin soon when he come tuh let em out she cracked him in de haid wid de poker an made little Joe help put his haid in de fiuh place. Dat day in de fiel' Little Joe made er song: "If yo don' bleave Aunt Sallie kilt Marse Jim de blood is on

Fig. 19.1. "African American man with a horse cultivating cotton with plow, N.C." Photo by D. A. Tompkins, ca. 1902. Library of Congress, Prints and Photographs Division.

huh under dress." He jes hollered hit. "Aunt Sallie kilt Marse Jim." Dey zamined Aunt Sallie's under dress so dey put huh in jail till de baby come den dey tried huh an sentenced huh tuh be hung an she wuz. (Charity Morris, b. unk., NC, 149–50)[2]

I can recollect hearin' the folks hollerin' when the Yankees come through and singin' this old cornfield song

> I'm a goin' away tomorrow
> Hoodle do, hoodle do.

That's all I can recollect. (Alice Wise, b. 1858, SC, 216)

Worksongs have always provided one of the clearest links between Africa and African Americans. Singing while working is not a global practice, though it does occur widely. Nonetheless, the integral connection between labor and song in the Black world is truly singular, and from the colonial era white observers fixated on the singing of African American sailors, stevedores, rowers, animal handlers, crop pickers, tree cutters, hoe wielders, ditch diggers, street vendors, cornshuckers, road and rail construction teams, and the like. The tradition's source was never much in doubt; by this period, other white colonizers had described generations of Africans singing exactly the same kinds of songs—rhythmic, call-and-response cadences coordinating group efforts, melismatic solo calls for signaling or self-expression—during precisely the same activities: agriculture; herding, hunting, and gathering; building, development, and extractive projects; transportation and shipping; cottage industries and factory production.

Whether in Africa or the New World, Black worksong was also renowned for putting true musical artistry to utilitarian ends, timing the rhythms of work as precisely as dance movements. In work settings, antiphony—the rhythmic call-and-response intrinsic to African-based music and song—calibrated individual exertions like interlocking gears. Characteristic Black vocal tricks like falsetto or declamatory wailing were ideal for reaching remote fellow workers, white bosses, water carriers, loading teams, riverboat crews, or landing parties. The texts of many worksongs were in effect instruction manuals, describing or directing the tasks underway.[3]

Judging from period descriptions, slaves seldom worked without singing. For their part, most slaveholders permitted, encouraged, in some cases even demanded these songs, recognizing that they promoted speed and efficiency while also serving for surveillance. "De slave owners us'ter say when he had a bunch wukin' in de fields, as long as dey could hear 'em singin' dey knowed dem niggers wuz a workin' but when dey got quiet dey had ter go put 'em back to wuk fer when dey stopped singin' dey stopped wuk too" (Steve Weathersby, b. ca. 1856, MS, 2247). "When old Master come to the lot and hear the men singin' like that, he say 'The boys is lively this mornin', I's gwine git a big day's plowin' done.' They did too, cause them big Missouri mules sho' tore up that red land" (Lizzie Hughes, b. 1848, TX, 167).

Some slaves were allowed to sing only while laboring. "An at night time us jes' went to our cabins an' went tuh bed, 'cayse us betta not hab any noise down

dar. De mos' ob de singin' us done wuz in de fiel'"
(Henry Cheatam, b. 1851, MS, 92). Rosa Tims "had
a very cruel master who whipped his slaves often to
keep them smart. The slaves were allowed to sing
while working; but they had to turn down a washpot
to retain the sound when they sang and prayed at
home. They were not allowed to visit without a pass.
If they slipped off, the hounds found them, then a
dreadful whipping followed."[4] Frederick Douglass
(ca. 1817–1895) wrote:

> slaves are generally expected to sing as well as
> to work. A silent slave is not liked by masters or
> overseers. "*Make a noise*," "*make a noise*," and
> "*bear a hand*," are the words usually addressed to
> the slaves when there is a silence amongst them.
> This may account for the almost constant singing
> heard in the southern states. There was, generally,
> more or less singing among the teamsters, as it
> was one means of letting the overseer know where
> they were, and that they were moving on with
> the work.[5]

The narratives touch on most major African American worksong traditions, but they do omit or slight
a few important occupations and activities. The rowing songs of coastal Georgia and Carolina slaves were
among the first American folksongs to be noted in
large numbers, but these are absent.[6] There are many
examples from steamboat and dock workers but few
other worksongs from urban or industrial slaves.[7]
Songs associated with domestic work or household
chores are not nearly as well represented as field songs.
Overall, however, the narratives do give a fairly complete accounting.

Like horns and bells, hollers and worksongs were
audible everywhere constantly throughout the plantation South. "When de slaves was workin you could
hear dem singin fer miles, each one singin a different
song" (Vina Moore, b. 1845, MS, 2759). "Evvybody was
up so early dat by sunrise dey was out in de fields, jus' a
whoopin' and hollerin'" (Charlie Hudson, b. 1858, GA,
225). "Sing—I say dey did sing. Sing about the cooking

and about the milking and sing in de field" (Hannah
Hancock, b. ca. 1855, SC, 145). "Eberthing kept in a stir
'round de plantation wid 'bout fifty slaves. Some wuz a
wukin' while uders wuz a spinnin' and knittin, quilten,
makin' soap and tendin' to de chickens an' de stock.
Deir wuz singin', hollerin' an action all ob de time"
(Chaney Moore Williams, ca. 1852–1937, MS, 2304–5).
"Marster lak to see his slaves happy and singin' 'bout
de place. If he ever heard any of them quarrelin' wid
each other, he would holler at them and say: 'Sing! We
ain't got no time to fuss on dis place'" (Junius Quattlebaum, b. ca. 1853, SC, 283).

There were songs for every job or task, but most
can be divided between two basic categories, solo
hollers and *gang songs*. Metrically free but rhythmically intense, hollers are typically performed at the
top of a singer's register with considerable use of melisma, falsetto, and similar effects: growling, moaning,
whooping, yelping, and, of course, hollering. Texts
might be precomposed, or improvised or adapted to
suit immediate circumstances; some consisted partly
or entirely of nonsense sounds (such as "hoodle do,
hoodle do").

Ex-slaves were insistent on two other points:
1) hollers could be heard at remarkable distances; and
2) they could convey very specific information, even
nonverbally. "They has field calls and other kind of
whoops and hollers that has a meanin' to them" (Cato
Carter, b. 1836 or 1837, AL, 641). "En us had ole 'corn
hollers,' but I fergits um now, yer c'ud hya um er mile"
(Oliver Bell, b. unk., AL, 56). "When de niggers would
work dey would all sing de same song. Sometime all
hands was singin' at de same time. Each plantation
had a different hollin. I jes can't get ours, now, do, I'm
hoarse" (Jerry Eubanks, b. 1846, MS, 697).

> Us allus gits us groceries by steam boat. De wagons
> go down de ol' Bevilpo't road to de steam boat
> landin'. Dat was on de Ang'leen [Angelina] Ribber.
> De boats dat come up de ribber us knowed dem
> by dey holler comin' 'roun' de ben'. One of de bigg_'
> boats was Cap'n Bryce Hadnot, de "Ol' Grim."
> (Mary Kindred, b. ca. 1855, TX, 2203)

Mr. Denman had a boy that killed squirrels and throwed them in the kitchen. The white folks et them. You ain't never seen no white folks then that would eat rabbit. But I had a brother who hunted every time he gets the chance. Mostly on Sundays. He would leave for the swamps afore daybreak and we would know when we hear him callin', "OooooooOOOooo-da-dah-dah-ske-e-e-e-t-t-t-ttt," that he had sumpin'. That was just a makeup of his own, but we knowed they was rabbits for the pot. (Julia Frances Daniels, b. 1848, TX, 1022)

Dere am anudder thin' 'bout de parties dat Ise wants to tell dats diffe'nt f'om now. De cullud fo'ks don' let de younguns pester 'roun' all night lak Ise see now, sometimes 'til two or three in the mo'nin', gittin' all diseased up. No sar! W'en de certain time come, yous would heah fust one, den de udder, holler way off, WOOOEE, den de udder WOOOEE. Dat means, come home. (Penny Thompson, b. ca. 1851, AL, 3873)

Other hollers allowed workers to vent, or simply to amuse themselves and others. "We allus had a leader when we wuz workin and we allus likes to sing, you'n could hear dem fer three miles. The leader would sing, 'Whos been here while I wuz gone', and 'Purty little girl wid the red dress on' and 'Purty little Sally', and 'Look at dem eyes.' . . . One plantation holler wuz, Uh, Uh, Uh, Uh, Uh, Uh" (Jeff Calhoun, b. 1838, AL, TX, 609, 610).

I 'members a few of de "hollers." "Tea in de teakettle nine days ol'," was de startment of one "holler." A song 'gin, "My ole Missus, she promise me, w'en she die, she sot me free." Another was "Ole Lou'siana niggers et hot mush," Ole Virginny niggers say, "Good Lawd, hush." (Dey say de las' line was 'cause de moufs was so full of hot mush dey couldn' talk). I's shame to tell you dese 'cause dey jes' foolishness. (Jack White, b. 1857, TX, 4036, orig. parentheses)[8]

Perhaps because they were sung in remote settings, or in circumstances where whites were inclined to indulge laborers so long as they labored, field songs and hollers provide some of the more striking instances of overt protest or complaint in slave songs. "Some ob de folks was putty happy in de fields and would sing: / Oho, I'se gwine home, / and cuss out de ole overseer" (Mary Kincheon Edwards, b. 1810, LA, 1280). "The niggers sung songs in the field when they was feeling good and wasn't scart of old massa. Sometime they'd slack up on that hoe and old mass holler, 'I's watchin' yous.' The hands say, 'Yes, suh, us sees you, too.' Then they brightened up on that hoe" (Martin Ruffin, b. 1854, TX, 266).

I wuk in field on Maussa Johnnie Fripp plantation. Sometime we sing w'en us wuk. One song we sing been go lak dis:

> Go way, Ole Man
> Go way, Ole Man
> W'ere you bin all day
> If you treat me good
> I'll stay 'till de Judgment day,
> But if you treat me bad,
> I'll sho' to run away. (Sam Polite, b. ca. 1844, SC, 274–75)

I's 'member dat whin we'ns in de fiel' we'ns sang somethin' lak dis,

> Massa sleeps in de feathah bed,
> Nigger sleeps on de flooah,
> Whin we'ns all git to Heaven,
> Dey'll be no slaves no mo.

Dats 'bout all I's know of dat song, but I's know a little of some mo'. Yere one dey sang 'lots.

> Rabbit in de Briar patch
> Squirrel in de tree
> Wish I could go huntin',
> But I ain't free.

Rooster's in de hen house
Hen's in de patch
Love to go shootin'
But I ain't free. (Millie Williams, b. 1851, TX, 4113)

I forgot our plough songs:

I wonder where my darling is.

Nigger makes de cotton and de
White man gets the money.

Everybody used to sing. We worked from sun to sun.... About four o'clock we all start up singing. Sing till dark. (John Patterson, b. ca. 1860, KY, 285)

Patterson's white-man-gets-the-money line usually concludes a wandering stanza probably originating during slavery or just after.

I can't read an' write but dey learned us to count. Dey learned us to count dis way. "Ought is an' ought, an' a figger is a figger, all for de white man an' nothin' fer de nigger." Hain't you heard people count dat way? . . . In slavery time they kept you down an' you had to wurk, now I can't wurk, an' I am still down. Not allowed to wurk an' still down. Its all hard, slavery and freedom, both bad when you can't eat. *The ole bees makes de honey comb, the young bee makes de honey, niggers makes de cotton an' corn an' de white folks gets de money.* Dis wuz de case in Slavery time an' its de case now. De nigger do mos' de hard wurk on de farms now, and de white folks still git de money dat de nigger's labor makes. (Andrew Boone, b. 1857, NC, 133, 137, my emphasis)[9]

Boone's ought-is-an-ought verse is, in turn, another popular floater sung in the fields and elsewhere.

When de chillun come on, us try rentin' a farm and got our supplies on a crop lien, twenty-five percent on de cash price of de supplies and paid in cotton in de fall. After de last bale was sold, every year, him come home wid de same sick smile and de same sad tale: "Well, Mandy, as usual, I settled up and it was—'Naught is naught and figger is a figger, all for de white man and none for de nigger.'" (Manda Walker, b. 1857, SC, 173)[10]

Some slaveholders did give license for mild protest so long as workers met their quotas. This was especially so during the cornshucking carnival, when songs mocking slaveholders or complaining of want and mistreatment were just a few among many customary rites of reversal. No doubt, too, such material is grossly underreported. Having traveled the South in the 1850s, John Dixon Long (1817–1894) cautioned that slaves truly expressed themselves only when "unobserved by any white man": "You must catch him at work. Listen to his songs while seated on his oxcart hauling wood, or splitting rails. You must overhear his criticisms in the quarters—his holiday songs and self-made hymns. His songs do not always indicate a happy state of mind. He resorts to them in order to divert his thoughts from dwelling on his condition."[11] English actress Frances Kemble lived on a Georgia plantation in the 1830s: "I have heard that many of the masters and overseers on these plantations prohibit melancholy tunes or words, and encourage nothing but cheerful music and senseless words, deprecating the effect of sadder strains upon the slaves, whose peculiar musical sensibility might be expected to make them especially excitable by any songs of a plaintive character, and having any reference to their particular hardships."[12]

In remote worksites, however, slaves definitely sang about their particular hardships, and mocked and vilified the responsible parties.

Mind you, never would sing it when Marsa was roun', but when he wasn't we'd swing all roun' de cabin singin' 'bout how old Marsa fell off de mule's back. Charlie had a bunch of verses:

Jackass stamped,
Jackass neighed,
Throwed ole Marsa on his haid.

Don' recollec' all dat smart slave made up. But ev'ybody sho' bus' dey sides laughin' when Charlie sung de las' verse:

Jackass stamped,
Jackass hupped,
Marsa hear you slave, you sho' git whupped.
(Julia Frazier, b. 1854, VA, 98–99)[13]

Some songs and hollers were more practically purposed, used to goad, direct, or summon draft animals and livestock. "Me sho' did like ter git behind de ox-team in de co'n-field, fo' I could sing and holler all de day. 'Gee thar Buck, whoa thar Peter, git off dat air co'n, what's de matter wid yo' Buck, can't yo' hear, gee thar Buck'" (Simon Stokes, b. ca. 1939, VA, 281). "Yous want me to sing some ob de songs dat de cowboys sing on de range? Now, I's sho lak to do dat, but I's never could sing much an' now I's old, I's can't sing atall, but I's can holler yip, yip, yi. I's could always do dat loud an' rope de critters an' ride de hosses" (Sam Jones Washington, b. 1849, TX, 3990). "We used to call de cows on de plantation like dis: 'co-winch, co-winch.' We called de mules like dis: 'co, co,' and de hogs and pigs, 'pig-oo, pig-oo.' We had dogs on de place, too, to hunt wid" (John N. Davenport, b. 1848, SC, 242).

I members when de old major won a bet from another neighbor. He bet his friend dat his cow driver, Sampson, could call all de cows by name and get dem to come to him. Sampson did dis by singin' a song dat went somethin' like dis.

Cherry Bound and Durham, you,
Dotty Old Milly, too,
Oh you little Georgiana
Oh, you Durham, come on follow.
'Cause I love you

Fig. 19.2. "Colored army teamsters, Cobb Hill, VA, 1864." Photo by John C. Taylor. Gladstone Collection of African American Photographs, Library of Congress, Prints and Photographs Division.

Yes, I love you
As I love my life.

De cows and bulls all come arunnin' fast and de Major won his wager. All de rest of dem had been taught to follow Cherry Bound, Durham, Dotty Red, Old Milly, and Georgiana. (John I. Young, b. 1855, SC, 486)

Since the 1800s, hog calling has been practiced by both Blacks and whites, but it may be another African American innovation. Certainly the vocal properties epitomize African American (and African) singing and field songs. In 1838 English naturalist Philip Henry Gosse (1810–1888) was employed as a teacher on various Alabama plantations, later authoring one of the earliest accounts.

Long whoops . . . begin to be heard from every quarter. . . . The sun has set, and the negroes on the plantations have begun to call home the hogs. Some negroes from long practice have acquired great power of voice; they will utter a continued unbroken shout, lasting nearly a minute, which may be heard at the distance of a mile. . . . The hogs are turned out in the morning to forage in the woods for themselves, and in the evening are summoned home by this call, which they well understand, to food and rest. I have been near hogs rooting and grazing in the woods, when suddenly the shout of the distant negro has pealed along the air; instantly they are all attention, every head is raised; they listen a moment, then all is bustle; with a responding grunt, they scamper away towards home, and each races to be foremost.[14]

Ex-slaves occasionally described hog-calling whites, but most remembered it as their own custom.

De hogs and pigs was allowed to roam over de woods. When de time come to feed 'em, pappy would jes' shout:

Pig-o-o-o
Come on - on - on
Pig-o-o-o!

Hogs and pigs would come runnin' through de woods, all a runnin' and a squealin'. If pappy wouldn't sing to 'em lak dat dem hogs an' pigs wouldn't come a runnin'. (Harriet Millett, b. 1854, MS, TX, 2696–97)

It was real funny to hear the darkies call their stock. They'd say: "Soo-oo-oo-k, Janey! Soo-oo-oo-k, Spot! Whoo-oo-ie! Whoo-oo-oo-ie! Come on to your breakfast! Come on to your supper!" and every man's hog would go to its place, and cows too. When Uncle Ponder stood there and called at the drawbars, they didn't have no fences then, they'd all come running and every one knowed where its stall was. Sometimes four or five men would milk. (Cicely Cawthon, b. 1859, GA, 188–89)

I did inji gwine to de pens wid big bucket ob slop an' hear dozens ob dem hogs a squeelin' an

runnin' lak some 'em wild. Yo' could hear 'em a mile. Ole Marse, he could talk to 'em, hit seemed lak dey could under stand eber thing he say. I soon learned to gib dat ole hog holler. I did love to hear de sound ob dat call a rollin' thro' de woods an' 'cross de pasteur an fiel's. (Robert Laird, b. 1854, MS, 1291).

Other hollers imitated animals or birds. "Den I was one of de grandest hollerers you ever hear tell bout. Use to be just de same as a parrot. Here how one go: O - OU - OU - O - OU, DO - MI - NICI - O, BLACK - GA - LE - LO, O - OU - OU - O - OU, WHOOOUOU. Great King, dat ain' nothin" (Hector Godbold, b. 1850, SC, 146). "Our work song was, 'John Henry was a man; he worked all over dis town.' Dey still uses dat song. In slavery some holler when dey be in de field like owls; some like crows; and some like peafowls" (Gus Feaster, b. ca. 1840, SC, 52).

I use to holler a heap in late years but after I lay it down, all dat leave me.

Bulldogs a barkin,
Howl! Howl!
Bulldogs a barkin,
Howl! Howl!
Bulldogs a barkin,
Howl! Howl!
Ah - codle - codle - ou,
Ah - codle - codle - ou,
Ah - ou - ah - ou.
Ah - codle - ou,
Ah - ou - ah - ou,
Ah - codle - codle - ou. (Hector Smith,
   b. ca. 1858, SC, 109)

There were signal hollers for waiters and water boys. "When I was a young boy, durin' de time when folks called me Boy, Willie and Buck, I had to help tote water to de field hands. I got de water f'om de springs on de plantation, and den I had to tote de cedar bucket to de field. When a worker wanted me to bring de water, he would shout, 'Yip-yip-yip-ee-ee!'" (William Smith, b. 1845, LA, 3691)

Pappy was a sort of ruler over de other slaves.... Pappy had a way of lettin' folks know when he wanted somethin'. When it was near dinner time and de food was brought to de fields, he would chant:

Oo-oh, little Mary,
I want my dinner,
Oo-oh, I'm so hongry,
And I want my dinner.

And he chanted so loud, dat even de mules in de fields would staht brayin', Sometimes de other slaves would sing de song while in de fields. Durin de cotton pickin' season de slaves got up befo' daylight. Pappy would sing out:

De mawnin' star is risin'
De mawnin' star is risin'
Oh, de mawnin' star is risin',
Day is breakin'——
Breakin' in my soul.

If de hands needed some water, pappy would sing out:

Oh, little Mary, I want some water,
I'm so thirsty for some water.

And de waterboy up at de house would git his cedar bucket and gourd dipper and bring de water to de field. (Harriet Millett, b. 1854, MS, TX, 2695–97)[15]

No'em, never wuz no singer, no time. Not on steamboats, nor nowheres. Don't member any songs, except maybe the holler we use to set up when dey wuz late wid dinner when we wuked on de steamboat;—Dey singsong lak dis:

Fig. 19.3. "Negro stevedores eating on stern of boat. Food supplied to crew consists almost entirely of carbohydrates with some of the cheaper cuts of meat. Sleeping quarters are not provided for stevedores, who sleep in any available space." *El Rito*, Pilottown, LA, September 1938. Photo by Russell Lee. Farm Security Administration/Office of War Information Photograph Collection, Library of Congress, Prints and Photographs Division.

Ol hen, she flew
Ovah de garden gate,
Fo' she wuz dat hungry
She jes' couldn't wait.—but den dat ain't
    no real song. (Samuel Sutton, b. 1854, KY, 96)

Special warning hollers alerted other slaves to the presence of whites, who were presumably unable to distinguish these within the constant flow of worksongs. "When we's in de fields and sees de padder roller ride by, we starts murmerin' out loud, 'Patter de pat, patter de pat.' One after 'nother took it up and purty soon everybody murmerin'. We allus do dat to let everybody know de padder roller 'round" (Millie Williams, b. 1851, TX, 4114).

I was a sort of lot man. They about 200 oxen, mule, goat, sheep and cow to slop and feed. I keep a eye on the niggers down in the cotton patch. Sometime they lazy around and if I see the overseer comin' from the big house I had a song I sing to warn them, so they git to work and not be whipped. The song go like this:

Hold up, hold up, American Spirit!
Hold up, hold up, Hooooooooooooooo!

When the niggers hear that they sure grab that old hoe. (Richard Carruthers, b. ca. 1848, TX, 631)

Dere wuz always a leader in de fiel's to warn ebery one if de overseer's wuz comin'. On our plantation de leader wuz Aunt Dinah who sung all de time whilst wurkin'. Dis wuz her warnin' song to de niggers. "Walk indepen'ent, walk bold, Marster in de fiel' run leader an' carry de news home, master in de fiel'." De leader would sta'at chantin' dis song an' de ones nearby 'ud take it up an in no time 'tall de ones fuddrest away would hear it an git chantin' it an' workin'. Ef de ober seer katched a nigger sittin' in de corn row or lyin in de shade ob a tree dat nigger sho gwine git forty lashes on he bare back. (Robert Franklin, b. 1851, MS, 1419)

De reason we was always on de watch fo' de Colonel was 'cause ob somethin' dat always took place in de fields. De mawster never did care if we held night school in our cabins, but when we was in de fields, he wanted us to work. But George, his boy, when out in de field would try to learn our A B C's, right out in de fields. Mawster George would take a blue back speller and learn us. De workers would watch out fo' de comin' ob Mawster Pratt Washington, and when dey saw him a ridin' down de hill toward de fields, dey would staht singin' out—"Ole hog 'round de bench——Ole hog 'round de bench!" Dat was de signal, and den dey would staht workin' lak dey had been workin' hard all ob de time. (Rosina Hoard, b. 1859, TX, 1732)

Some worksongs were original to their tasks, others adapted from other genres, especially spirituals or hymns. "Yes, I 'member a field song. It wuz 'Oh! come let us go where pleasure never dies. Great fountain gone over.' Dat's one uv 'em" (Louisa Adams,

b. ca. 1856, NC, 5). "Mack Mullens [Mullen] says that some of the most beautiful spirituals were sung while they labored" (Mack Mullen, b. 1857, GA, 235). They might direct the task underway, or describe the natural world surrounding workers as they sang. "De onliest song I ever heared de niggers sing in de fields run somepin lak dis: 'Tarrypin, Tarrypin, (terrapin) when you comin' over, For to see your wife and fam-i-lies.' Dey must a been wantin' to eat turkle (turtle), when dey was a-singing' dat song" (Dosia Harris, b. ca. 1860, GA, 111, orig. parentheses).[16]

"We're marching home day by day, marching to the beautiful land of God." In response to our request for some "way back yonder" songs, this old negro, who says he is trying to forget all those horrible days of slavery, sings these lines which were used in the field while coaxing the mules along. . . . "They used to whip slaves if they didn't pick enough cotton. They put four pegs in the ground and tied one leg to one peg, the other to the other, and the arms were tied together. They were stripped of all clothing and whipped with a rawhide, 'Do pray marster, do pray marster, hi-yi hi yi' until their cries almost died away. Then they'd put to picking cotton with all that suffering. . . . We sang when we went to church and when we were at work and all the time, it seems like. We worked 'taters, sweet 'taters." Then he broke out with:

"Grasshopper sittin' on sweet tater vine,
Old turkey-gobbler come struttin' up behind,
Snipped grasshopper off sweet 'tater vine.

"We were called lazy and it seem like we never could get enough sleep, so lots of times, 'specially in warm weather, we just naturally dozed. Then we'd hear maybe that old field lark a-singin':

"Laziness 'll kill you.
Laziness 'll kill you.

Fig. 19.4. Mariah Snyder, ex-slave, Marshall, TX, October 5, 1937. Portraits of African American ex-slaves from the US Works Progress Administration, Federal Writers' Project slave narratives collection, Library of Congress.

"'Twas alright for that old bird to reprimand us if he hadn't been havin' the easiest life of anything. Birds got lots of sense, more'n some people. That old shivareein' owl, sometimes called the 'death-bird,' knows just when somebody will die, and where. We used to sing:

"Of all the varmints in the woods,
I'd rather be a coon,
And carry my tail curled up my back,
And get up in the mornin'—soon." (Shack Wilson, b. ca. 1860, LA, 213–14)[17]

The Negroes most allus sung while they was working in the fiel' when they was happy. One of the songs was:

When I'm here you'll call me honey, but
When I'm gone you'll honey everybody.

Another one was:

The Raccoon is a funny thing

Ramblin 'round in the dark. (Mariah Snyder, b. ca. 1848, TX, 3710)[18]

Yes, mam, de darkies wud sing: dey wud sing whilst dey wus at wurk an' dat made 'em wurk de better. Here is one chune.

Shoo fly, don't yer bother me,
Shoo fly, don't yer bother me,
Shoo fly, don't yer bother me,
Fur I b'long to com'ny "G."

Cum 'long boys an' lets go er huntin',
Cum 'long boys an' lets go er huntin',
Cum 'long boys an' lets go er huntin',
Fur I heerd de dogs bark,
An' I knowd dey treed sumptin'. (Jim Martin, b. 1857, MS, 1441–42)[19]

Most slaves worked from dawn to dusk—sun to sun—so the sun was a constant reference in field songs. "When de slaves wus wurkin' good dey wud sing like dis— / 'Watch de sun; see how she run; / Niver let her ketch yo' wid yer wurk undun'" (Ebenezer Brown, b. 1852, MS, 243).

I members hearin' my mammy come in out'n de field singin' every afternoon. She allus would sing de same song. It went sompin' like dis:

Sun Gwine down, Oh Lord
　　De Sun gwine down
Sun Gwine down Lord
　　De sun Gwine down! (William Wheeler, b. ca. 1855, MS, 2274–75)

Master Driver had four children, Mary, Julia, Frank and George. Every one of them children kind and good just [like] the old Master. They was never mean and could I find some of 'em now hard times would leave me on the run! They'd help this old man get catched up on their eating! Makes me think of that old song we used to sing:

Don't mind working from Sun to Sun,
Iffen you give me my dinner—
When the dinner time comes!

Nowadays I gets me something to eat when I can catch it. The trouble is sometimes I don't catch! But that ain't telling bout the slave days. (Andrew Simms, b. ca. 1857, TX, 296)

Across the South, slaves sang "Rain Come Wet Me, Sun Come Dry Me" as they worked nonstop through rain showers.

Yes, I knows that little song. I can even tell you where it started from:

Rain come wet me,
Sun come dry me.
Stand back, nigger man,
Don't come nigh me.

Dat's all I ever did hear of it. You see, when I was young we would be out in de canefields, it would come up a shower of rain. You would see the buzzard sailin' around, den dey would light in some dead tree. Us just made de song; we would call him "nigger man." (Lindy Joseph, b. 1866, LA, child of ex-slaves, 144)

We just sits down sometimes and talks about how we used to cut dat cane in them fields, in de heat and cold. I knows it was happier times than now, hearing all them Negro singing them old corn songs. They kindly went like this:

Rains come wet me,
Sun comes dry me.
Stand back boss-man
Don't come nigh me.

I forgot just how it did go. We used to sing dat song about "Plow, Gang, Plow in the Lowland," but so much trouble has done went over dis head

Fig. 19.5. "Cutting Sugar Cane in Louisiana." Photo by William Henry Jackson, ca. 1880–1897. Detroit Publishing Co. Collection, Library of Congress, Prints and Photographs Division.

I just can't think. (Annie Flowers, b. ca. 1860, LA, 71)[20]

Slaves sang constantly in the fields but also going to and fro. "One of dem went like dis when dey wus cumin' frum de fiel' late in de evenin'—We is gwine er round—O, de las' round— / We is gwine er round—De las' round—Aint yo' glad we gwine round de las' round / We is gwine home" (Barney Alford, b. ca. 1850, MS, 46–47). "I can see raght now dem niggers a-sweatin' in de fiel's an' de roustabouts a-loadin' cotton. I can hear de voices of de tired folks comin' home singin' atter de sun done sunk behin' de mountain" (Aunt Clussey, b. ca. 1845, AL, 21).

Dis am one deys sing lots w'en deys gwine to wo'k in de mo'nin':

Old cotton, old co'n, see yo' ever' mo'n,
Old cotton, old co'n, see yo' since I's bo'n.
Old cotton, old co'n, see yo' ever' mo'n,
Old cotton, old co'n, hoe yo' 'til dawn,
Old cotton, old co'n, what fo' yo' bo'n. (Pauline Grice, b. ca. 1856, GA, 1602)

I's can hear dem darkies now, goin' to de cotton patch way 'fore day a singin':

Peggy, does you love me now?

One ole man he sing:

> Sat'day night and Sunday too
> Young gals on my mind,
> Monday mornin' way 'fore day
> Ole marster got me gwine.
> Chorus:
> Peggy, does you love me now?

Den he whoops a sort of nigger holler, what nobody can do jes' like dem ole time darkies. (Jenny Proctor, b. 1850, AL, 214–15)[21]

Since any movement of slaves was obsessively regulated by whites, slaves on the move were expected to sing *walking songs*, marching cadences keeping them in line or in step while audibly registering their progress and position.

> Dey loads 15 or 20 wagons, less dan a week after de weddin' an' we stahts fo' Texas. Weuns travel f'om daylight to dahk, wid mos' ob de niggers wa'kin'. Weuns cook de meals over de camp fiah an' slep' on de groun'. Of course, 'twas hahd, but weuns all 'joy de trip. Dere was one nigger, called Monk, Him knows a song an' he larned de udder niggers to sing it. It's something lak dis:
>
> Walk, walk, you nigger walk, walk!
> De road am dusty, de road am tough.
> Dust in de eye, dust in de tuft:
> Dust in de mouth, yous can't talk—
> Walk, yous niggers, don't you balk.
>
> Walk, walk, you nigger walk, walk!
> De road am dusty, de road am tough.
> Walk 'til we reach dere, walk or bust—
> De road am long, we be dere by and by.
>
> Now, mos' ob weuns was a follerin' behin' de wagins, an' weuns sung it to de slow step ob de ox. Weuns don' sing it many times 'til de Missy come an' sit in de back ob de wagin, facin' weuns. She den began to beat de slow time an' sing wid weuns. Dat please de Missy Mary, an' she laugh an' laugh when weuns sing. (Bill Homer, b. 1850, LA, TX, 1785–86)

Grimly, walking songs are often reported with coffles—shackled slaves being marched to auction—the chains requiring them to move in lockstep. "I seen some niggers chained in a line that they was a-driftin' to the west. They swing they ankle chains and it clinks to most a music and they champs a song, 'Yo-o-o-o-o, Yoho-ho-ho-ho—, Swing long my bullies, swing, swin-n-g long my bullies.' They didn't have no hair on they heads" (John Crawford, b. 1837, MS, 978). In 1828 Elisha Green encountered a line of "forty or fifty men, chained" and "five or six wagons loaded with women and children" moving south through Kentucky. Leading the coffle, a slave who "looked to be about seventy years old" was singing "Hark From the Tombs," ordinarily used in funeral processions.[22] Having observed Mississippi slave traders in the 1840s, Rev. Charles Elliott wrote that "the slavedrivers, aware of this disposition in the unfortunate negroes, endeavor to mitigate their discontent by feeding them well on the march, and by encouraging them to sing 'Old Virginia never tire,' to the banjo."[23]

Beginning in the 1860s, ex-slaves in the Union army's Black regiments transformed their walking songs into military marching cadences, a tradi-

Fig. 19.6. "The Coffle Gang." George Washington Carleton, *The Suppressed Book About Slavery!* (New York: Carleton, 1864), fac. 49. A slave coffle near Paris, Kentucky, 1850s. Library of Congress, Prints and Photographs Division.

tion that has since been institutionalized by the US armed services.

Slaves also sang to coordinate their movements while tilling, threshing, or chopping, with the beat of axes, hoes, hammers, or flails timed to the call-and-response. "Work songs? Yes, ma'am we had 'em—songs that ud move wid de work, but I don't know any of 'em now. Dere was plenty of singin' allers—aftah sundown, on Sundays, in de fiel'—mos' any old time. But I don' know any of 'em now" (Hanna Fambro, b. 1850, GA, 341).

Well, when de railroad come to Appomattox dey hire de niggers and Miss Sarah Ann hired her'n to 'em too. . . . De niggers start to sing:

> A col' frosty mo'nin',
> De niggers mighty good,
> Take yo' ax upon yo' shoulder,
> Nigger, TALK to de wood.

An' de woods jes' ringin' wid dis song. Hundreds of dem jes' asingin' to beat de ban'. Dey be lined up to a tree, an' dey sing dis song to mark de blows. Fust de one chop, den his pardner, an' when dey sing TALK dey all chop together; an' perty soon dey git de tree ready to fall an' dey yell "Hi" an' de niggers all scramble out de way quick 'cause you can't never tell what way a pine tree gonna fall. (Fannie Berry, b. 1841, VA, 39)

Old Jerry am de leader. What weuns sing? Lawdy Man! 'Twas so many diffe'nt songs him have. Let me see. I's m'ybe 'membahs de words ob one. Dis am one, an' de way deys do, am dis away, w'en dey raise de axe, or de grubbin' hoe, dey says "Hi." W'en deys swing it down, dey says, "Ho," an' w'en de axe hits, deys says, "Ug," so de song goes:

> Hi, Ho, Ug, Hi, Ho, Ug,
> De sharp bit, de strong ahm,
> Hi, Ho, Ug, Hi, Ho, Ug,
> Dis tree am done 'fo' weuns am wahm. (Giles Smith, b. ca. 1858, AL, 3604–5)

Around the start of the war, Robert Quarterman Mallard (1840–1904) observed Georgia slaves singing while threshing rice. "The rhythmical beat of numerous flails is accompanied by a recitative and improvised song of endless proportions, led by one voice, all joining in the chorus, and can be heard a mile away."[24]

The majority of work and worksongs described by ex-slaves were tied to the antebellum South's primary cash crops: rice, tobacco, sugar cane, corn, but especially cotton, the most labor-intensive of all. From the time they set the cotton seed, the slaves were constantly in the fields, guarding the ground, tending the plants, thwarting pests, and *chopping out*—the grueling task of weeding hundreds, possibly thousands of acres with handheld hoes—all in preparation for the frenetic fall harvest. Songs were essential to the labor's breakneck pace. "When de darkies wus in de field at wuk dey allus sung to keep time wid de hoe en dat wuld mek 'em wurk faster, en dey sung de ole time songs sich as 'On Jordan's Stormy Banks I Stand'—I doan remember dem singin eny udder songs, but they sho prayed to be sot free" (Harriet Miller, b. 1859, MS, 1502).

All the hands went off to the field singing:

> This ain't Christmas morning, just a long summer day
> Hurry up yellow boy and don't run away
> Grass in the cotton and weeds in the co'n
> Get in the field ca'se it'll soon be morn. (Lizzie Hughes, b. 1848, TX, 1816)

Chopping out was in fact one of the most routine yet wholly miserable and utterly exhausting tasks assigned field slaves, especially in subtropical areas where weeds (grass) ran rampant. In the 1830s Frances Kemble overheard Georgia slaves singing

an extremely pretty, plaintive, and original air, there was but one line, which was repeated with a sort of wailing chorus—

Oh! my massa told me, there's no grass in Georgia.

Upon inquiring the meaning of which, I was told it was supposed to be the lamentation of a slave from one of the more northerly states, Virginia or Carolina, where the labor of hoeing the weeds, or grass as they call it, is not nearly so severe as here, in the rice and cotton lands of Georgia.[25]

Weeding was a continual priority, but for cotton planters the fall harvest was an existential issue, and slaveholders drove their chattel mercilessly throughout the picking season. The most commonly cited cotton-picking quota for field slaves (from preadolescents to geriatrics) was three hundred pounds a day, sometimes adjusted to an individual's age, experience, and ability. "De most cotton dat I could pick was about three hunnert pounds a day. Dat wasn't much 'cause others could pick twice dat much" (Rebecca Thomas, b. 1825, AR, TX, 3822). "Later in life, about de most cotton dat I picked was five hunnert pounds a day. I could pick dat much a day and I could den go out at night to dance and jump around. I used to be a fiddler-player in dem early days. I would fiddle and de prompter would call" (William Smith, b. 1845, LA, TX, 3692).

I was never bothered wid a backache in my life. I picked two and three hunnert pounds ob cotton a day, and one day I picked about four hunnert pounds. Sometimes a prize was give by the owner ob a plantation to de slave whut could pick de most cotton fo' one day. De prizes was a big cake or a suit fo' a man and a dress fo' a woman. Pickin' cotton at dat time wasn't so bad, 'cause we was used to it. We had a fine time ob it. One time I won a fine dress and another time a pair ob shoes fo' pickin' de most cotton fo' de day. I'd be so fast dat I could take two rows at a time.... Some ob de folks was putty happy in de fields and would sing:

Oho, I'se gwine home,
and cuss out de ole overseer. (Mary Kincheon Edwards, b. 1810, LA, 1280)

Fig. 19.7. Mary Kincheon Edwards, ex-slave, Austin, TX, August 5, 1937. Portraits of African American ex-slaves from the US Works Progress Administration, Federal Writers' Project slave narratives collection, Library of Congress.

Slaves who failed to make their weight were routinely beaten and tortured. "I never git whip, 'cause I allus git my 300 pound. Us have to go early to do dat, when de horn goes early, befo' daylight" (Sarah Ashley, b. 1844, TX, 35).

Slaveholders sometimes used competitions to spur cotton pickers, especially when moonlight allowed them to work their slaves around the clock. Occasionally slaves even picked cotton by bonfire, torch, or candlelight. "I was ten years old when the war ended. I had to carry matches and candles to the cotton pickers. It would be too dark to weigh up. They couldn't see. They had tasks and they would be picking till late to git their tasks done. Matches and candles come from the big house, and I had to bring it down to them. That was two years before the war" (Lewis Brown, b. 1855, MS, 293). All-night cotton pickings might even acquire a somewhat festive air, but the food, drink, and prizes were transparently intended only to fuel the relentless labor, and slaves definitely did not look forward to cotton pickings as they did corn-

Fig. 19.8. "Picking Cotton on a Georgia Plantation." *Ballou's Pictorial* 14 (1858): 16. Slavery Images: A Visual Record of the African Slave Trade and Slave Life in the Early African Diaspora. slaveryimages.org.

shucking carnivals. "Cotton pickin's warn't planned for fun and frolic lak cornshuckin's. If Marse Billy got behind in his crops, he jus' sont us back to the fields at night when de moon was bright and sometimes us picked cotton all night long. Marster give de 'oman what picked de most cotton a day off, and de man what picked de most had de same privilege" (Callie Elder, b. ca. 1860, GA, 312). "Some times dere would be cotton pickin at night too. Dis would be when dere was a moon shinin bright. I went to many a one. Dis would be a big to do and plenty of whiskey and eats after ten or eleven oclock. Dancing is goin on too. Dere was a big house to dance in" (Jerry Eubanks, b. 1846, MS, 696). "De cotton pickin's was on nights when de moon was extra bright 'cause dey couldn't do much lightin' up a big cotton field wid torches lak dey did de places where dey had de cornshuckin's.... Us danced in de moonlight when de cotton was picked and de prize done been give out to de slave what picked de most" (Carrie Hudson, b. ca. 1860, GA, 216–17).[26]

In any event, all cotton pickers sang as they raced through the fields gathering bolls. "In cotton pickin' time dey would pick in groups, an' sing, holler an' shout" (Salem Powell, b. ca. 1857, MS, 1748). "I wuz too little to wuk fiel's. I can recollect seein' de fiel's white wid cotton an' dem full ob slaves a pickin' hit an' a singin' an' a hollerin'" (Lawrence Evans, b. 1858, MS, 704). "There was lots of jest makeup songs. Niggers like to sing and make up songs. In the fields when they pick cotton a bunch a-going one side lift up they head and roll out 'uhm-m-mmm, yo-o-o-o', and then those on tuther side pick it up and go the same way and jest put some makeup words to it" (John Crawford, b. 1837, MS, 978).

We had to work purty hard durin' de early days, and dere was de time when de cotton pickers would sing out:

> I killed an old gray goose,
> Ho-ho, put him on to cook—
> Took eleven months to cook him,
> Ho-ho, the old gray goose.[27]

And den another one:

> Its a crane,
> De same old crane,
> But a lame, tame crane,
> De same old crane,
> It's a crane,
> De same old crane,
> Lame, tame, crane! (Henry Owens, b. 1843, TX, 3011)

My job was to tote water to de field hands, and den I done a little cotton pickin'. But I never was a good cotton picker. About de most dat I ever picked was about two hunnert pounds a day. De older folks would pick de cotton and moan out a song:

> Oh, rock along, Susie, Oh, Oh, rock along,
> Oh, rock me, Susie, rock me,
> Oh, rock along, Susie, Oh, Oh, rock along.
> (J. W. King, b. 1854, TX, 2213)

Dey had a ol' lady what ten' to de chillun when dey in de fiel' pickin' cotton. Sometime she uster sing:

Fig. 19.9. "Port Royal, SC. African-Americans preparing cotton for the gin on Smith's plantation." Photo by Timothy H. O'Sullivan. Photograph of the Federal Navy, and seaborne expeditions against the Atlantic Coast of the Confederacy, specifically of Port Royal S.C., 1861–1862. Selected Civil War Photographs 1861-1865, Library of Congress, Prints and Photographs Division.

> My Lord say dey's room enough,
> Room enough in hebben for us all.
>
> And eb'ry now and den she stop and retch (reach) over and fotch (fetch) 'em a whack on de head and say:
>
> Come 'long wid dat row. (Aleck Trimble, b. 1861, TX, 113–14, orig. parentheses)

Describing South Carolina cotton pickers in autumn 1853, a Northern correspondent wrote:

> The negroes were at work in the fields, picking cotton, and stowing it in long baskets. They worked in gangs, or companies, men, women and children, selected and classified according to age and physical ability—each slave being required to pick as many pounds of cotton in a day as his master, or overseer, had prescribed. . . . While at work in the cotton fields the slaves often sing some wild, simple melody, by way of mutual cheer, which usually ends in a chorus, in which all join with a right hearty good will, in a key so loud as to be heard from one plantation to another. In singing the chorus, one plantation responds to another, and the welkin is made to ring for miles with musical echoes. . . . I could not comprehend the words of the songs or chorus.[28]

Slaveholders definitely appreciated the field song's function. A Mississippi slaveholder stated outright: "when at work I have no objection to their whistling or singing some lively tune, but no *drawling* tunes are allowed in the field, for their motions are almost certain to keep time with the music."[29] And there were other methods for ensuring slaves met their quotas. "They used to whip slaves if they didn't pick enough cotton" (Shack Wilson, b. ca. 1860, LA, 213). "Marse Bill had no overseer dat I remember; he an' young Marse Russ toted de whip, an' wud ride ober de fiel' an' make de slaves wurk an' dey wud shore whup iffen dat wurk wusnt dun" (Ebenezer Brown, b. 1852, MS, 243). Ex-slave author Moses Roper (ca. 1815–1891) was born in North Carolina and trained as a domestic, but around 1835 he was sold to a South Carolina planter. "He treated me very kindly for a week or two, but in summer when cotton was ready to hoe, he gave me task work connected with this department, which I could not get done, not having worked on cotton farms before. When I failed in my task, he commenced flogging me, and set me to work without any shirt, in the field in a very hot sun, in the month of July."[30]

In Africa and much of the New World, instrumentalists commonly accompanied labor. The practice was rarer in North America, but not unknown.[31] "Judge Maddox bought a nigger man who had a three string fiddle. I used to hear him play and sing. We had to work at night too. When I was ten or eleven years old I had to plate [plait] hats out of rice straw and other straw. If we younguns didn't get as much done as we ought to they would beat us. But this nigger would play to us as we worked" (Jack Maddox, b. ca. 1849, TX, 2531–32). In the 1890s Julian Ralph watched roustabouts at Chester, Illinois, loading flour barrels on a New Orleans–bound steamer: "As a happy makeshift a negro came out and sat on a barrel and played a jewsharp. . . . He turned his genius upon a lively tune, and the serpentlike stream of barrels began to flow faster under the negroes' hands, as if it were a current of molasses and the music had warmed it."[32] At work parties like cornshuckings, instruments were almost always on hand for the concluding frolic, and there are occasional accounts of fiddlers and banjo players accompanying the work. Call-and-response corn songs were always sung as well, however, and instrumentalists were usually held in reserve for the frolic.

People also sang with household tasks, and WPA interviewers caught ex-slaves still singing as they went about their chores.

> As the interviewer approached the house she could hear Alice singing, "Good mornin' to you! Howdy you do?" and through the open window the old woman could be seen busily engaged in household duties. Her broom, moving in rhythm with the song, did not miss a stroke when the tune changed to, "Lord I'se a comin' Home." (Alice Hutcheson, b. ca. 1860, GA, 282)

> > Dar's golden streets and a pearly gate somewhars,
> > Dar's golden streets and a pearly gate somewhars,
> > I gwian ter keep on searchin' till I finds hit,
> > Dar's golden streets and a pearly gate somewhars.
> >
> > Dar's perfect peace somewhars,
> > Dar's perfect peace somewhars,
> > I gwian ter keep on searchin' till I finds hit,
> > Dar's perfect peace somewhars.

> Good mornin' Missie! Glad to see you again. I is workin' on chairs again. Got these five to bottom for Mr. Brown and I sho can talk while I do this work. (Marion Johnson, b. ca. 1848, LA, 115)

> Paul Smith's house stands on China Street, a narrow rutted alley [in Athens, GA] deriving its name from the large chinaberry tree that stands at one end of the alley. Large water oaks furnish ample shade for the tidy yard where an old well, whose bucket hanging from a rickety wooden frame, was supplying water to two Negro women, who were leaning over washtubs. As they rubbed the clothes against the washboards, their arms kept time to the chant of *Lord I'se Comin' Home*. Paul and two Negro men, barefooted and dressed in overalls rolled to their knees, were taking their ease under the largest tree, and two small mulatto children were frolicking about with a kitten. (Paul Smith, b. ca. 1863, GA, 321, orig. italics)

Slave women were invariably tasked with the plantation's laundry—many ex-slaves continued to earn their livings washing and ironing for whites—and several narrators recalled wash songs.

> De cabins was a long ways off from de big house, close by de big old spring whar de wash-place was. Dey had long benches for de washtubs to set on, a big old oversize washpot, and you musn't leave out 'bout dat big old battlin' block whar dey beat de dirt out of de clothes. Dem Niggers would sing, and deir battlin' sticks kept time to de music. You could hear de singin' and de sound of de battlin' sticks from a mighty long ways off. (Paul Smith, b. ca. 1863, GA, 325)

> Tubs had been hauled to de bank ob de river, fires was made and de washin' was done right dere. De washed clothes was den brought back to de big house and hung up to dry. The Guadalupe was a very dangerous-lookin' river, and de water was very blue. While de wimmen was washin' de clothes dey would sing songs. Some ob 'em made up songs while dey washed, but I don't remembah none ob de words. Pappy and mammy was good singers. (Fannie McCulloh Driver, b. 1857, TX, 1233)

Fig. 19.10. "African American woman doing laundry with a scrub board and tub," ca. 1900. Library of Congress, Prints and Photographs Division.

Spinning and weaving were essential activities on most plantations as well, whether for their own needs or outside markets, since some slaveholders operated cottage textile factories staffed by slaves tasked with mass production quotas. Spinning wheels and looms were also regulated by song, then, at a pace as relentless as gathering the cotton.

Mammy sang a lot when she was spinning and weaving. She sing an' that big wheel a turnin!

When I can read my title clear,
Up Yonder, Up Yonder, Up Yonder!

—and another of her spinnin' songs was a humin'—

The Promise of God Salvation free to give.
(Wade Glenn, b. ca. 1860, NC, 38)

Mother was let off some days at noon to git ready fo' spinnin' dat evening. She had to portion out de cotton dey was gonna spin an' see dat each got a fair share. When mother was goin' 'round countin' de cards each had spun she would sing dis song:

Keep yo' eye on de sun,
See how she run,
Don't let her catch you with your work undone,
I'm a trouble, I'm a trouble,
Trouble don' las' always.

Dat made de women all speed up so dey could finish fo' dark catch 'em, 'cause it mighty hard handlin' dat cotton thread by firelight. (Bob Ellis, b. 1849, VA, 88–99)[33]

Mother died in 1882, but I never has forgot dis song she used to sing. Mother said dey would always spin in pairs—one would treadle whilst de other would wind de ball. You got to wind it fast, too, an' take de thread right off de spindle, else it git tangled up. An' mama tol' me dey would all pat dey feet an' sing:

Wind de ball, wind de ball,
Wind de ball, lady, wind de ball,
Don't care how you wind de ball,
Wind de ball, lady, wind de ball,
Ding, ding, ding,—wind de ball,
Wind de ball, lady, wind de ball. (Mildred
    Carter, b. 1856, VA, 70)

Seaports were the South's first cities, while river ports and landings marked the beginnings of broader urban development, and many ex-slaves worked as roustabouts, the umbrella term for the deckhands and shore crews who manned boats and loaded cargos. Jim Archer had rousted on Vicksburg's riverfront.

This song Uncle Jim learned while working with the roustabouts. He heard it sung by the captain who stood on the boiler deck and the mate who was in charge of the laborers. Learned probably in the 1880's. According to [Herbert] Halpert this song may have originated as a sea shanty. The story, as much as Archer sings, indicates that it is the story of the seaman who wooed the captain's daughter and promised to marry her over the water.

> Captain, Captain, give me your daughter
> Rango, rango
> I'll marry her on the water
> Rango, rango. (Jim Archer, b. ca. 1860,
>   MS, 74–75, int. Ferriss, Halpert)

Roustabouts had songs for entertainment and self-expression, to identify or advertise boats, to signal or sound an alarm, to boost esprit de corps, and to attract and entertain crowds at landings; however, the most widely noted roustabout items were *chanteys*, call-and-response group songs coordinating various duties. "Rango" or "Ringo" (aka "Reuben Ranzo") was in fact one of the most popular of all nineteenth-century chanteys, sometimes said to be English, sometimes Anglo-American, though there is a strong case for African American origins.[34] The custom of chanteying itself was indisputably introduced by African sailors, appearing only after Europeans and Africans began regularly crewing together in the fifteenth century. On America's docks and landings, chanteys were sung almost exclusively by Black roustabouts. In 1817 Whitman Mead toured Savannah's waterfront: "Along the wharves they [slaves] are to be seen transporting the cargoes of ships to and from the warehouses. They accompany all their labour with a kind of monotonous song, at times breaking into a yell, and then sinking into the same nasal drawl."[35] Twenty years later, Philip Henry Gosse observed slaves loading cotton on an Alabama River steamboat:

> The men keep the most perfect time by the means of their songs. These ditties, though nearly meaningless, have much music in them, and as all join in the perpetually recurring chorus, a rough harmony is produced, by no means unpleasing. I think the leader improvises the words, of which the following is a specimen; he singing one line alone, and the whole then giving the chorus

at every line, till the general chorus concludes the stanza:—

> "I think I hear the black cock say,
>   Fire the ringo, fire away!
> They shot so hard I could not stay;
>   Fire the ringo, fire away!"[36]

This appears to be the earliest published text of "Rango," incidentally.

By reputation roustabouts came from the lowest ranks of rootless, unskilled workers, driven by desperation to this last resort. Most were very young, and lasted only a few years.

> I was treated most harshly 'mongst a group of just white people and who seemed to think me de old work ox for all de hardest work. De nearest other negro slaves were 'bout 15 or 20 miles from me. When I was grown I ran away one night and walked and rode de rods under stage coaches to Paducah, Kentucky. I got me a job and worked as a roustabout on a boat where I learned to gamble wid dice. I fought and gambled all up and down de Mississippi River, and in de course of time I had 'bout $3,000, but I lost it. (Ben Lawson, b. ca. 1850, IL, 177)

The roustabout's lifestyle had a certain appeal, however, and many signed on by choice. The pay (in cash) was comparatively good, the food poor but plentiful. Added to this were freedom and mobility, male comradery (prominently featuring singing and songs), some measure of public recognition and respect, and regular stopovers in major vice centers (as ports always are).

> I steamboated six years on de Mississippi between St. Paul and New Orleans. I got $1 a day and board, and we sure could pack dem sacks and sing dem songs. De old mate would holler at us: "Give me a song boys." And den we would start out. It 'peared

like de work went easier when we was singin'. It would take us four weeks to make de rounds before we got back to St. Louis. We hauled potatoes, sheep, wheat, corn, cattle, horses, and cotton. There was 45 of us altogether. (Robert Bryant, b. ca. 1862, MO, 65)

Dissipation was expected, accepted, and to a certain extent encouraged. "The life of the roustabout varied some with the habits of the roustabout and the disposition of the mate. We played cards, shot dice and talked to the girls who always met the boats" (George Fortman, b. ca. 1850, KY, 93). Few descriptions of roustabouts fail to mention their constant singing but also their incessant gambling and drinking. "By Jingoes, cose I can tell you something bout de days I spent on de river boats. I is spent many a day from sunup til sun down a working on one of de government boats and from sun down til de next mornin' a singin' and a shootin craps wid de rest of de niggers working dere.... Most of us would spend a weeks wages on corn likker. But we felt like we deserved our fun and took things as they come. We wasn't looking for a dark day to come then" (Frank Williams, b. 1852, MS, 2320). "Uncle George said that food was always plentiful on the boats. Passengers and freight were crowded together on the decks. At night there would be singing and dancing and fiddle music. 'We roustabouts would get together and shoot craps, dance or play cards until the call came to shuffle freight'" (George W. Armstrong. b. 1861, TN, 5). Then too, roustabouts did more than just talk to some of the girls who met the boats, and whoring, along with gambling, drinking, and doping, was also part of the package. America's rivers afforded some of history's most notorious vice dens, the Mississippi especially: St. Louis, Cairo, Memphis, Natchez-Under-The-Hill, Vicksburg, New Orleans. In 1907 Harris Dickson (1868–1946) described Vicksburg's riverfront dives as they were in the late 1800s, before the Reformers shut them down.

In these whiskey was sold indiscriminately to white and black, men and women, adults and

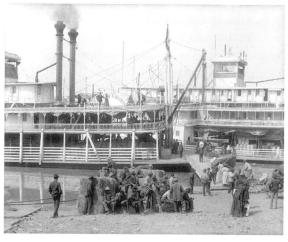

Fig. 19.11. "The Steamboat Landing, Vicksburg, Miss.," ca. 1900–1910. Roustabouts on the Mississippi at Vicksburg. Detroit Publishing Co. Collection, Library of Congress, Prints and Photographs Division.

children. Any person could step up to the bar, buy a glass of beer, sprinkle in the cocaine, and join the revelry.

Back of the bar was a dancehall: a negro "professor" banged away on his battered piano. Everybody danced; formalities were waived, and there were no rules of etiquette. Negroes played craps and poker on the tables in the corner; generally negroes, but sometimes white men.[37]

Vicksburg's dives had grown up to serve the river trade, but they were eventually closed partly because they so disrupted it. Harris reports that after the boats were unloaded and the roustabouts paid, they would disappear into the dives, only returning to work when their money was gone. If enough of them were lucky at the gaming tables, crewless boats could be tied up for days, even weeks.

While some landed citizens regarded roustabouts mainly as social problems, others appreciated the essential service they provided, or envied their carefree, reckless lifestyle. Strapping young males in their prime, they cut romantic figures. They were also widely admired for their singing, which served as major public entertainments in river towns. Besides their indispensable work, their status as musical performers may explain much of the forbearance for their misbehavior. Somewhat ironically, spirituals and hymns provided the greatest number of roustabout songs not originating with the river trade itself.

In 1883 I left the Wilson home and began working and trying to save some money. River trade was prosperous and I became a "Roustabout." The life of the roustabout varied some with the habits of the roustabout and the disposition of the mate. We played cards, shot dice and talked to the girls who always met the boats. The "Whistling Coon" was a popular song with the boatmen and one version of "Dixie Land." One song we often sang when nearing a port was worded "Hear the trumpet Sound"—

Hear the trumpet sound,
Stand up and don't sit down,
Keep steppin' 'round and 'round,
Come jine this elegant band.

If you don't step up and jine the bout,
Old Missus sure will fine it out,
She'll chop you in the head wid a golden ax,
You never will have to pay de tax,
Come jine the roust-a-bout band. (George Fortman, b. ca. 1850, KY, 93)

"Hear the Trumpet Sound" is more precisely a spiritual parody, almost certainly of minstrel origin. W. C. Handy (1873–1958) described his quartet singing the piece for riverboat excursion parties during the same period. It was, he recalled, "one of the songs that scored wherever we sang." ("Whistling Coon," which George Fortman also mentioned, was composed by blackface banjoist Sam Devere, frequently appearing in minstrel songbooks of the 1890s and later on records.)[38] "Dixie" was claimed by minstrel pioneer Dan Emmett (1815–1904), but there is no question the piece originated in black tradition, reportedly sung by roustabouts among others. George Taylor Burns had spent seventy years working various rivers.

When asked if he knew many songs sung by boatmen in earlier days, George Taylor Burns said that the songs varied as different boatmen sang the same songs to different tunes. Many boat songs were put to the tune of "Dixie"; also a number of songs mentioned the name of Captain, or some craft. Thus Dixie was sung on any craft where W. H. Daniels was Captain.

Oh, I was a slave in the land of Dixie
But Captain Daniels saw I was Pert and frisky,
Now I'm glad I'm a steamboat man (George Taylor Burns, b. ca. 1830, MO, 28)

Some chanteys described or directed work, literally or metaphorically. Gambling, alcohol, and women were other common topics, along with the relative vices and virtues of different riverboats, their captains, mates, and crews. Isaam Morgan was born near Alabama's Tombigbee River. "'Marster Morgan,' said Isaam, supplied the steamboats with firewood and sent the slaves out to cut the timber, then later they cut and split the wood the required size. Isaam also said any slave that worked overtime and cut more wood than required of them, Mars'er Morgan paid them for their extra work" (Isaam Morgan, b. 1835, AL, 261).

Isaam worked at different jobs and was a roust-a-bout on different steamboats, among them the old "May-Boyd," "Lula D," and the "Gardner." One of the old songs on the boats he recalled for the writer, is as follows:

The John T. Moore,
The Lula D.
And all them boats are mine,
If you can't ship on the Lula D.
You ain't no man o' mine. (Isaam Morgan, b. 1835, AL, 263)

William H. McCarty was born December 12, 1835, in Hancock County, Mississippi, his background and legal status somewhat confused. His narrative states that "his father was Elondus Serellus a Portugeese," while "his mother, Clara McCarty, was of the Cancousal race," an obvious misspelling of Caucasian (William H. McCarty, b. 1835, MS, 1371). This may also intend that Elondus Serellus was Afro-Portuguese (Cape Verdean? Brazilian?), but there is no indication that either Serellus or Clara McCarty was a slave. For whatever reason, their son William was regarded as colored, and at age ten was bonded to the Hancock County Sheriff, who then sold him to local merchant-planter W. J. Portivant. Besides his plantation and seventy-five slaves, Portivant owned five large general stores served by three steamboats. From 1848 until around 1862, William McCarty worked on these and other boats, shipping on the Pearl, Alabama, Tombigbee, and Red Rivers; on Lakes Ponchartrain and Borgne; in the Gulf of Mexico; and on the Mississippi between New Orleans and St. Paul. Boats he crewed included the *Virginia Pearl, Ruby, Madison, J. J. Warren, Belle Lee, Rover, Womac,* and *Natchez.*

"Nothing was more picturesque on the old time Steamboats in the golden years of steamboating than the negro workmen." Seldom did they make a trip without composing a song for the Steamer. If they liked or disliked a boat, their song expressed their feelings. As a steamboat cast off lines and swing out into the Mississippi, black smoke curling up from her tall stacks and her boilers sizzling, her gang gathered on the forward deck and sang these old songs.

> De Dandy Womac am a backin' boat:
>> An every boat we meets en route
> Mus' take de bank else bees pass'
>> Ez sho' ez y"re bo'n.
> Dis am de boat dat none can pass,
>> We allus in de lead:
> What evah am ahead we allus pass,
>> Ez we goes by wid our speed.

> De Pearl; she am de fines' boat.
> Treats niggahs bes' when she am float,
> An she hef a white man's crew
> Who knows niggahs an' sees dem frew.
> "The Chorus"
> De Cap'n am a white man,
>> De mate he treat us right
> De Cook he feeds a plenty,
>> Dat why we works day and night

> Hopping Mad'son backs out on time
>> An leaves big Injun here behin'
> Good bye niggahs, good bye all
>> See yo' at de nex' big ball
> Robert E. Lee got Railroad time—
>> Her crew am all de superfine—
>> Who'a, Gals, whoa:

> Ah Cuss dat Steamboat Rover,
>> Ah Cuss him all de way:
> Ah Cuss and Cuss de Thompson Dean,
>> Beckase she tuck my Lula 'way. (William
>> H. McCarty, b. 1835, MS, 1373–75)[39]

Operating on irregular schedules, riverboats depended on the singing of deckhands, bells, steam whistles, calliopes, even brass bands to announce their arrivals. When they heard the music, merchants and tradespeople, innkeepers, whores, bootleggers, and thieves all flocked to docks, levees, and landings, but the whole town (including families) might turn out just to take in the scene and listen to the roustabouts sing.

Now when I wuz young, de most pleasuring I had wuz meeting de steam boats. When us nigger gals would heard dem three long whistles, Lawd we would hot foot hit down to de wharf. Lawd, how dem niggers would sing; sing and work, toating off de freight. I kin hear 'em now. Dey wuz de good old days. Didn't have no time to "court," though.

Us gals would jist be flutatious lak. (Savannah Rice, b. ca. 1850, AL, 319)

Honey, yo' jest oughta have been livin' up de river, when I wuz a girl coming on. De darkies sho' sang some putty songs, an' dey all keep time when dey work. Honey, yo' oughta see de river when dey over flows de bluffs. Dere's cotton an' pumpkins an' cattle floatin' ebery whar, an' eben 'taters and ears of corn. Lor', chile, how de rivers up en Alabamy do flows over when de spring rains come down. Hit looks like de steamboats float 'way 'bove de bluffs, de water be so high. (Clara Davis, b. 1865, AL, child of ex-slaves, 123–24)

A boatman's life is a life of pleasure
Plenty to eat and money to treasure
Oh, who would go back to Dixie Land?

The rousters are always dancin and singin
Boat horns a blowin and bells a ringin
Oh, who would go back to Dixie Land?

Pretty gals come crowdin where boats are landin
Smile at de Cap'n where he is standin
And smile at de darkey from Dixie Land.
(George Taylor Burns, b. ca. 1830, MO, 28–29)

Traveling the Mississippi in the 1850s, T. B. Thorpe (1815–1878) wrote that deckhands' "custom of singing at all important landings, has a pleasing and novel effect, and if stimulated by an appreciative audience, they will roll forth a volume of vocal sounds that, for harmony and pathos, sink into obscurity the best performances of 'imitative Ethiopians.'"[40] Other steamboats had calliopes as well, or string bands or orchestras to entertain passengers, crew, and onshore spectators. Robert Everest took passage on an Ohio River steamship in the 1850s. "We had again a long, handsome saloon on the upper deck, and a large party, principally Kentuckians, among whom we had an opportunity of observing the manners of the South.

Card-tables were usually laid out after breakfast, and dancing took place in the evening to the sound of a banjo, played by a negro."[41] Besides music and song, professional gambling was another major attraction of riverboats, which operated outside normal jurisdictions. Over the winter of 1853–54, Fredrik Olmsted (1822–1903) traveled aboard the Alabama boat *Fashion*. "Sunday was observed by the discontinuance of public gambling in the cabin and in no other way. At midnight gambling was resumed, and during the whole passage was never at any other time discontinued, night or day, so far as I saw."[42] Roustabouts are not described observing the Sabbath in any fashion.

Ex-slaves did not long for the cotton field no matter how fondly they recalled the singing and fellowship. For some young men, though, the riverboat whistle was an irresistible summons, and river work, no matter how difficult and dangerous, was as addictive as gambling, whiskey, and cocaine.

We sure could pack dem sacks and sing dem songs. De old mate would holler at us: "Give me a song boys." And den we would start out. It 'peared like de work went easier when we was singin'. It would take us four weeks to make de rounds before we got back to St. Louis. We hauled potatoes, sheep, wheat, corn, cattle, horses, and cotton. There was 45 of us altogether. I never got hit but one time on de boat. De mate with [brass] knucks on hit at another feller for 'cause he was loafin' and hit me and knocked me and my load in de river. I couldn't swim but dey fished me back in de boat and rolled me over and over to run dat water out of me. I run on de "Bald Eagle" and de "Spread Eagle." My mama got after me to quit and when I got hit she got uneasy about me, but I would hear dat whistle blowin' and my feet'd begin to itch and I could not help but go down to the old boat again. De old mate had my name "doubled-up." It was Bob Rob. (Robert Bryant, b. ca. 1862, MO, 65)

MINSTRELSY

"You know its a funny thing, de white folks took everything from us niggers, even try to take our old songs and have dem on de radio. We niggers say 'de white folks take everything, dis, dat, an' 'tother, but what we got is jes' natural borned to us.

"I knocks a tambourine jes' like de Georgia niggers played a tambourine, 'fore de Civil War. Dem Georgia minstrels was taken over to England to perform 'fore de Queen Victoria, way 'fore Civil War. Folks from way up East got 'em an' took 'em. Dey ain't many plays like dem anymore."

"Uncle" Fil, as he was familiarly known in Rolla, played for the Folk Festival in Rolla and received so much applause, he had to be helped off the stage. He is exceedingly active. He plays the old tambourine, (he owned so many years) under and over his legs, behind his head, bouncing it and catching it, never losing the rhythm an instant. (Filmore Taylor Hancock, b. 1851, MO, 159, int. Mabel E. Mueller)

My father was a full blood African. His parents come from there and he couldn't talk plain. . . . He was a quill blower and a banjo picker. They had two corn piles and for prizes they give them whiskey. They had dances and regular figure callers. This has been told to me at night time around the hearth understand. I can recollect when round dancing come in. It was in 1880. Here's a song they sung back in Virginia: Moster and mistress both gone away. Gone down to Charleston / to spend the summer day. I'm off to Charleston / early in the mornin' / to spend another day. (Ellis Jefson, b. ca. 1861, VA, 43–44, orig. slashes) (E. P. Christy, "I'm off for Charleston," *Christy's Plantation Melodies* [1851], 51–52)

When I was eight or nine years old I went to a tent show with Sam and Hun, my brothers. We was under the tents looking at a little Giraffe; a elephant come up behind me and touched me with its snout. I jumped back and run under it and between its legs. That night they found me a mile from the tents asleep under some brush. They woke me up hunting me with pine knot torches. I had cried myself to sleep. The show was "Dan

Fig. 20.1. Minstrel poster, Alabama. August 1936. Photo by Walker Evans. Farm Security Administration/Office of War Information Photograph Collection, Library of Congress, Prints and Photographs Division. Among the minstrel stereotypes depicted, in the upper right, a dandy serenades a girl with his banjo while her mother douses him with water; a razor-toting rival leans from another window. To their left, a bulldog bites the butt of a watermelon thief while a second dog snaps at his companion. In the foreground, a farmer and policeman pursue a chicken thief who has set off a kicking mule and upset a laundress and her washtub.

Rice and Coles Circus" at Dedneh [?], Mississippi. They wasn't as much afraid of snakes as wild hogs, wolves and bears. (Lizzie Luckado, b. 1867, MS, child of ex-slaves, 304)

As a captive audience—literally—slaves were avid consumers of the fledgling American entertainment industry; indeed, they were the ostensible subjects of its first great success, so-called "Ethiopian minstrelsy." From the first they also actively participated in American popular music as performers, creators, and composers. Not that any of this access or activity was unrestricted or unregulated, even after slavery. Nevertheless, the WPA narrators between them describe almost the full-range of nineteenth-century popular music, most of it related to minstrelsy.

The true character of blackface minstrelsy—America's first and for half a century dominant mass entertainment—is a longstanding dispute beyond this study's scope. Suffice it to say that minstrel shows were in large measure racist travesties (or just bizarre fantasies), yet they also drew (if selectively or capriciously) from authentic African American folklore and folklife, especially music, song, and dance. Minstrelsy's enormous appeal to Black audiences—as well the active participation of thousands of Black artists—defies pat judgments or generalizations, and minstrels influenced almost all American music that followed, including subsequent Black innovations.[1]

There is also overwhelming evidence that, their status notwithstanding, large numbers of slaves regularly enjoyed minstrelsy and other professional entertainments. As standard practice, antebellum theaters, circuses, and showboats provided separate seating and admission prices for slaves and free Blacks.[2] From 1835 to 1851 the diary of William Johnson (d. 1851), a manumitted Mississippi slave living at Natchez, describes a continual array of concerts and shows (including "Ethiopian Singers") in the city's theaters and halls.[3] As a slave, James Thomas (1827–1913) had lived in Nashville, then already a musical hub. He later recalled how in 1842 white minstrel star John Diamond came to town with a circus and stole the show by dancing on a board. "When he came again, he had a fiddler in back to sit on the ring along the side [of] the board. They soon added a banjo player, then tamborine."[4] (Thomas, a fiddler himself, described many of the city's other prewar entertainments, including the 1851 visit of Swedish opera singer Jenny Lind, and an 1853 appearance by Norwegian violinist Ole Bull.) Black theater attendance only increased in the postwar years, when the obligatory segregated upper gallery became known as "Nigger Heaven."[5]

Excepting river or sea ports (and vice centers) like Natchez, Nashville, and New Orleans, theaters were scarce in the antebellum South, and standalone minstrel troupes did best in Northeastern or Midwestern population centers. For plantation slaves, any direct exposure most likely came through traveling shows such as circuses, where minstrels would have been just part of the program. "We wuz let go to shows when dey come to Carlisle. I member goin' to see Dan Rice's

Circus dat use to come to Carlisle ever yeah" (William Emmons, b. ca. 1848, KY, 328). "Doctor Lyles would call us and give us money on Christmas and holidays. When de showboats would come to town, he'd give us fifty cents. Shucks, we didn't need no money in dem days" (Catherine Cornelius, b. ca. 1836, LA, 46). "When a celebration or circus came through he [slaveholder] give us all twenty-five or thirty cents and told us to go" (Charles Anderson, b. ca. 1860, KY, 46). "We ain't had but two meals a day an' dey wus scant. We had a few frolics, dances an' sich lak onct in a while an' onct a year we all went ter a show, sorter lak a circus" (Anna Mitchel, b. 1862, NC, 114–15).

> They had neighborhood parties for corn-shuckings, cotton pickings, quiltings and other things. The host and hostess always have some good suppers at these parties, with whiskey. They would sometimes have square dancing or cake walks, with fiddlers.
>
> School exhibitions were common where they would have picnics or barbecues, and popular speakers would participate.
>
> School boys had great delight in seeing circuses, and once some of them walked three miles to see the elephants tracks. (Henry Gray Klugh, b. ca. 1850, SC, 233)

> Every time a circus come to town I'd run off and they wouldn't see me again all day. Seemed like I just couldn't help it. I wouldn't take time to git permission to go. One time to punish me for running off he [slaveholder] tied me up by my thumbs, and I had to stay home while de rest went. I didn't dare try to git loose and run off for I knowed I'd git my jacket tanned if I did. (Morris Hillyer, b. ca. 1850, GA, 140)[6]

Minstrelsy and the American circus developed in tandem, P. T. Barnum (1810–1891) being an essential early patron of both. Today Dan Emmett (1815–1904) is celebrated for codifying the minstrel show as a self-contained theatrical format, but that was a brief

Fig. 20.2. *Old Dan Emmit's Original Banjo Melodies*, 2nd series (Boston: Keith's Music Publishing House, 1844). American Minstrel Show Collection, 1823–1947, Houghton Library, Harvard University. Dan Emmett as he appeared in real life (center), and costumed in blackface with the Virginia Minstrels (clockwise from upper right): Emmett, fiddle; Dick Pelham, tambourine; Bill Whitlock, banjo; Frank Brower, bones.

interlude in a long career mainly spent performing solo in circus big tops or sideshows. Showboats—initially dryland circuses transported by boat, eventually floating theaters as well—were a response to the challenges of touring pre-railroad rural America, providing minstrels another niche among a motley range of entertainers and entrepreneurs. Not only circuses and showboats but carnivals, fairs, markets, medicine shows, dime museums, freak exhibitions, school programs, political rallies, educational lectures, and other traveling diversions or community events regularly employed blackface singers, instrumentalists, and dancers. All in all, far more Americans saw variety shows featuring minstrels than minstrel shows per se, and as the premier nineteenth-century rural-and-smalltown variety show, the circus was indispensable in spreading minstrelsy outside cities.

From their advent in the 1830s, circuses worked the South, harnessing the rivers to saturate the region. The diary of Natchez free Black William Johnson notes over a dozen visiting circuses between 1835 and 1851.

On November 23, 1837, "the Grand Carravan of Animals arrived in town, the Musicians was on the back of the Elephant as they past through the Streets."[7] The circuses paraded up from the Mississippi after arriving by boat, their only conceivable means of then reaching Natchez. (It is doubtful even Hannibal could have descended the mythically perilous Natchez Trace with elephants.)

Simply presenting shows aboard their water transports was an obvious next step. Born in Missouri in the mid-1830s, George Taylor Burns was taken to Indiana around 1840 and indentured to a flatboat captain. "My life for the next 70 years was spent on the different rivers" (George Taylor Burns, b. ca. 1835, MO, 27). He had regular encounters with theater showboats, including one of the most famous, the *Banjo*.

Speaking of showboats, Honey, you should have seen the BANJO. It sure was a beautiful sight. I was working on the Gray Eagle when the Banjo used to pass up and down the river. The captain would keep the calliope playing and the roustabouts (all of them negroes) would be out on the deck dancing and shouting to the roustabouts on the Gray Eagle.

Some of the shows the Banjo staged were East Lynn and Ten Nights in a Barroom. Uncle Tom's Cabin was staged on that boat during a period from 1857 to 1860 and maybe for a longer time.

When the showboat, with its deck ablaze with kerosene lamps and with every kind of gay banners and flags strung around its texas [the large upper-deck stateroom] and sides passed up and down the streams, people white and Black would come flocking to river's banks.

The Banjo showed at New Orleans, and at Cairo regularly. I remember it lay off the old wharf boat at Evansville, July 18, 1860 and people from all over this part of the country went to the show. The Gray Eagle was due to leave the wharf the next afternoon at 4:00 o'clock. Captain W. H. Daniels was in command. Captain Daniels never put any hard work on me because I was crippled. I was an assistant on the boat and only had light work to do. That day the Captain said I could go on the Banjo and help awhile, if I cared to, and of course I did.

The next time we saw the Banjo she was laid up at New Orleans for repairs of some sort, but crowds were flocking to her as fast as ever. (George Taylor Burns, b. ca. 1835, MO, 32, orig. parentheses)

The *Banjo* was the upper Mississippi's principal pre–Civil War showboat, one of several owned by circus impresario G. R. Spaulding. Eighty feet with a fully equipped theater seating two hundred, its programs were devoted to the blackface minstrelsy suggested by its name. The *Banjo* was first reported at Cape Girardeau in 1849, last documented a decade later at St. Paul. (New Orleans was outside its known circuit, so Burns may have been remembering another boat there.)[8] That "Uncle Tom's Cabin" was acted onboard the *Banjo* might almost be guessed. Harriett Beecher Stowe's novel (1852) was instantly adopted by minstrels, who produced dozens of adaptations and parodies (many from a proslavery perspective). The melodramas "East Lynn(e)" and "Ten Nights in a Barroom" gained similar popularity decades later, after the *Banjo*'s disappearance. (Again, Burns seems to have merged his memories, but based on firsthand familiarity with showboat programs.)[9] The *Banjo*'s dancing deckhands were immortalized in a famous routine by blackface star Dave Reed (1830–1906). According to the 1877 *New York Herald*, Reed based his stage sensation "Sally Come Up" on a step he had learned "from the Negroes when he used to dance on the steamboat *Banjo* on the Mississippi."[10]

However, the most important circus promoter in the mid-nineteenth century South was Dan Rice (1823–1900), who was recalled by several ex-slaves.[11] Born Daniel McLaren in New York City, January 25, 1823, Rice made his professional start as a horse trainer and wrestler with P. T. Barnum before going to work briefly for his later archrival G. R. Spaulding, of *Banjo* fame. Rice operated along the Mississippi from 1851 to 1886, with a break from 1865 until 1868 (he was reputedly the first to resume river shows after the war). He was always especially active in the South, remaining there even during the early war years. His *New York Sun* obituary (February 22, 1900) stated that Rice required his performers to read to him from the Bible on Sundays, "an eccentricity akin to that which prompted him to build meetinghouses for the colored people down South. He is said to have built half a dozen meetinghouses. From 1860 to 1862 he was in the South."[12]

Rice returned South after 1868. Lyttleton Dandridge saw his program during the brief period when he actually staged it aboard his boat. "I remember two shows I saw. They was the Daniel Rice shows. They was animal shows but they had em on a boat, kind of a flatboat. We didn't have trains and things like that—traveled on the big waters" (Lyttleton Dandridge, b. 1857, LA, 88). Most of the time Rice followed the older practice of simply transporting his circuses by boat, then pitching his tents onshore.[13] (This is how Lizzie Luckado and William Emmons remembered him.)

Rice's retinues invariably featured blackface minstrels and other musical performers (including several celebrities over the years), but the ex-slave narratives suggest his menageries made far greater impressions. In fact only a couple of the WPA narrators recalling circuses mentioned musicians, singers, or dancers, though most of these programs would have featured minstrels as well as brass bands, steam pianos, and other musical entertainments.[14] In any event, ex-slaves insisted circuses were so popular that they became effective tools in postwar voter suppression.

> Git rid of de carpetbaggers? Oh, Yassah, dey vote 'em out. Well sah, tell you how dey done dat. De 'publicans done paid all de niggers' poll tax, an' gib 'em a receipt so dey could vote same as de whites. Dey made up to 'lect de officers at de co'te house all niggers an' den sen' yuther ones to Montgomery to make de laws. Same day de 'lection come off dar was a circus in Livingston an de Demmycrats 'suaded de boss man of de circus to let all Sumter

County niggers in de show by showin' dere poll tax receipts. Yassah, when de show was ober de 'lection was ober too, an' nobody was 'lected 'cepin' white Demmycrats. (Henry Garry, b. ca. 1865, AL, child of ex-slaves, 140–41)

Narrator Pen Eubanks described how South Carolina Red Shirts used this same ploy in the infamous 1876 election.

With few exceptions, early minstrels were whites in blackface. Proper Black minstrel troupes first began forming in the 1850s, and proliferated after 1865, when several groups simultaneously appeared billing themselves as the Georgia Minstrels, thereafter a synonym for colored minstrels (Blacks in blackface). These various Georgia Minstrels also set the pattern for early Black troupes by emphasizing plantation traditions and the performers' credentials as actual ex-slaves. Fil Hancock (above) may have been thinking of Sam T. Hague's Georgia Slave Troupe Minstrels, the first to tour England (1866), but they were soon followed there by many others who had adopted the Georgia Minstrel brand.[15] Showboats started using Black musicians, singers, and dancers around this same time.[16] Circuses lagged a little behind, with most admitting Black performers to the big tent only in the 1880s; before that (and sometimes even after), Black minstrels were relegated to sideshows and midways.[17]

By the late 1800s, Black minstrels and minstrelsy were booming throughout the United States and the American South. Sam Scott had worked as a minstrel stagehand, prop manager, promoter, and sometime performer around northwest Arkansas in the 1880s and '90s.

> No, I never did dance, but I sure could play baseball and make de home runs! My main hobby, as you calls it, was de show business. You remember de niggah minstrels we used to put on. I was always stage manager and could sing baritone a little. Ed Williamson and Tom Nick was de principal dancers, and Tom would make up all de plays. . . . Yes,

Fig. 20.3. "Original Georgia Minstrels Are Coming." Lithograph. Cleveland, OH: O. V. Schubert, 1876. Library of Congress, Prints and Photographs Division. A postwar poster for the premier Black minstrel troupe, the elephant evoking the ongoing association between minstrelsy and circuses. Depicted on the elephant's head is a banjo soloist; just below and to the right, in the white shirts, is a male dance team. The animal's torso is occupied by a large ensemble typical of the late nineteenth century, with two violins, two clarinets, trumpet, string bass, and drum (but no banjo); as was always customary, Tambo and Bones (the tambourine and bones players) are seated at opposite ends (far right and far left, respectively). The four men without instruments (center left) may be vocalists, comedians, and/or dancers. On the elephant's right hind leg and in the background underneath, minstrels accompanied by spectators are parading (or stampeding), some with brass band instruments (though one man carries a string bass over his shoulder and the figure in the lead is holding a banjo). In his journal, free Black William Johnson described an 1837 circus parade in Natchez where the musicians actually did ride on an elephant's back.

I still takes out a show occasionally to de towns around Pope and Yell and Johnson Counties, and folks treat us mighty fine. Big crowds—played to $47.00 clear money at Clarksville. Usually take about eight and ten in our comp'ny, boys and gals—and we give em a real hot minstrel show.

De old show days? Never kin forgit em! I was stage manager of de old opry house here, you remember, for ten years, and worked around de old printin' office downstairs for seven years. No, I don't mean stage manager—I mean property man—yes, had to rustle de props. And did we have road shows dem days! Richards & Pringle's Georgia Minstrels, de Nashville students, Lyman Twins, Barlow Brothers Minstrels, and—oh, ever so many more—yes, Daisy, de Missouri Girl, wid Fred Raymond. Never can forgit old black Billy Kersands, wid his mouf a mile wide!

De songs we used to sing in old days when I was a kid after de War wasn't no purtier dan what we used to sing wid our own minstrel show when we was at our best twenty-five and thirty years ago; songs like "Jungletown," "Red Wing," and "Mammy's L'il Alabama Coon." Our circuit used to be around Holla [Hollow] Bend, Dover, Danville, Ola, Charleston, Nigger Ridge, out from Pottsville, and we usually started off at the old opry house in Russellville, of course. (Sam Scott, b. 1859, AR, 131–32)

Judging from their bill, the Russellville Opera House belonged to the emerging network of premier Black venues eventually dubbed the chitlin' circuit. Superstar singer-comedian Billy Kersands was the chief attraction in Richard & Pringle's Georgia Minstrels, the most important latter-day troupe still using the Georgia Minstrels title. Several groups also billed themselves as Nashville Students, calculated to suggest a connection to Nashville's Fisk University and its Fisk Jubilee Singers. Scott may have remembered P. T. Wright's Nashville Students Concert Company, really a minstrel variety show based in nearby Kansas City.[18] By this period, most Black minstrels included concert arrangements of spirituals and other religious songs in their portrayals of plantation life. Authentic college jubilees like the Fisk Singers were usually obliged to stage their fundraisers outside the former Confederacy, finding some of their greatest successes abroad. Hampton College in Virginia also fielded an internationally renowned jubilee choir.

No ah nevuh went to Hampton, but my chillun was some o' de fus to go dah. I had one o' de yellines' daughters you ever heah. She was a contralto. An' she could make noise! Dey say at dat time she was de contralto "by de world." She useta go roun like Mr. Wainwright does, an' dey took her ev'ywhere. Even went to Australia an' back. Dat's when dey said she de bes in de worl. She taken sick an' died, but I got anothuh daughter what kin yell too. (Matilda B. Laws, b. 1854, VA, 193)[19]

Back in America another minstrel group—the Hamtown Students— attempted to capitalize on the Hampton Singers' success.[20]

Mary Anngady took part in one of postwar minstrelsy's more intriguing developments, the African Prince phenomenon of the 1890s. Anngady was born in Chapel Hill, North Carolina, where her mother was cook for a city merchant who after freedom encouraged Mary's formal education.

I married Aaron Stallings of Warrenton, North Carolina while at Shaw [College]. He died and I married Rev. Matthews Anngady of Monrovia, west coast of Africa, Liberia, Pastor of First Church. I helped him in his work here, kept studying the works of different authors, and lecturing and reciting. My husband, the Rev. Matthews Anngady died, and I gave a lot of my time to the cause of Charity, and while on a lecture tour of Massachusetts in the interest of this feature of colored welfare for Richmond, Va., the most colorful incident of my eventful life happened when I met Quango Hennadonah Perceriah, an Abyssinian Prince, who was traveling and lecturing on the customs of his country and the habits of its people. Our mutual interests caused our friendship to ripen fast. . . . We were married in Raleigh by Rev. J. J. Worlds, pastor of the first Baptist Church, colored.

P. T. Barnum had captured my husband when he was a boy and brought him to America from Abyssinia, educated him and then sent him back to his native country. He would not stay and soon he was in America again. He was of the Catholic faith in America and they conferred the honor of priesthood upon him but after he married me this priesthood was taken away and he joined the Episcopal Church. After we were married we decided to go on an extensive lecture tour. He had been a headsman in his own country and a prince. We

took the customs of his people and his experiences as the subject of our lectures. I could sing, play the guitar, violin and piano, but I did not know his native language. He began to teach me and as soon as I could sing the song *How Firm a Foundation* in his language which went this way:

Ngama i-bata, Njami buyek
Wema Wemeta, Negana i
bukek diol, di Njami,
i-diol de Kak
Annimix, Annimix hanci

Bata ba Satana i-bu butete
Bata ba Njami i bunanan
Bata be satana ba laba i wa,
Bata ba Njami ba laba Munonga

We traveled and lectured in both the north and the south and our life, while we had to work hard, was one of happiness and contentment. I traveled and lectured as the Princess Quango Hennadonah Perceriah, wife of the Abyssinian Prince. (Mary Anngady, b. ca. 1857, NC, 36–38)

Anngady employed *Abyssinia* in one of its early senses as a generic term for Africa (not to denote a specific nation). Her husband was actually a member of the Congolese Bakuba, as described in lectures emphasizing witch doctors, human sacrifice, and cannibalism (all summarized in Anngady's narrative). "My husband was a cannibal headsman and performed this duty of cutting off persons heads when a boy and after being civilized in America this feature of his early life bore so heavily upon his mind that it was instrumental in driving him insane. By custom a prince was born a headsman and it was compulsory that he execute criminals. He died in an insane ward of the New Jersey State Hospital" (Mary Anngady, b. ca. 1857, NC, 43).

As fantastic as all that seems, Mary's song is in plain fact a Bakuba-language text of Robert Keene's hymn "How Firm a Foundation, Ye Saints of the Lord"

(1787), or at least a Bakuba text set to that tune, and we can pinpoint its source precisely. In 1892 William H. Sheppard (1865–1927), the child of ex-slaves and a graduate of Virginia's Hampton Institute, established the first Protestant mission in the Belgian Congo. Shortly afterwards his wife, Lucy Gantt Sheppard (1867–1955), compiled and published the first Bakuba-language hymnal, successively revised and enlarged. Anngady's text reproduces exactly Lucy Sheppard's version of "How Firm a Foundation," stanzas one and three to be exact:

Tune—*How Firm a Foundation (Protection.)* P. & H. 325.

1. Ngana i bata, Njami buyĕk,
   Wena wemĕata ngana i bukĕk,
   Dioi di Njămi, i-dioi de kok,
   Animix, animix, animix hanci. . . .
3. Bata ba Satana i bu butĕte.
   Bata ba Njămi i bunananan,
   Bata be Satana ba lăba iwa,
   Bata ba Njămi ba laba muonya.[21]

Whatever role Quango played in teaching Mary to speak Bakuba, this is obviously where she really learned her song. In fact, it seems doubtful whether Anngady's interviewer, T. Pat Matthews, could have so closely matched Sheppard's text by transcribing phonetically, suggesting Mary still had the original close at hand. Prince Quango himself belonged to a wave of self-styled African princes touring America in the 1890s, just one of several in P. T. Barnum's employ, though even Buffalo Bill Cody's Wild West Show for a time featured Prince Oskazuma, "African Warrior, Lecturer, Mimic, Fire Fiend."[22] Obviously, P. T. Barnum did not capture Quango in Africa. Mary identifies him as a Catholic, so he was probably a product of the Belgian Congo's earlier Catholic missions (he was already or soon would be in the United States by the time the Sheppards and Protestantism arrived in the Congo). Virtually all African missions raised funds and recruited in the United States (that was definitely

how Mary met her second husband, the Reverend Anngady), and this is a much more plausible explanation for how Quango (Mary's third husband) arrived in America and met P. T. Barnum.

In the war's aftermath thousands of ex-slaves sought better lives in the American West. The mining camps in and around Denver (Central City, Leadville, Cow Creek) also provided especially good opportunities for aspiring musicians, singers, and dancers, including access to traveling shows. White banjo player and entrepreneur Frank Converse took a minstrel troupe to Denver City in 1861, by his reckoning the first public entertainment there.[23] In short order, the area was a major center for minstrelsy and its new competitor, the Wild West Show. Henry "Uncle Eph" Bufford was born in Georgia around 1850 and came to Denver in 1868.

> Ed. Sanderline opened his barber shop on Larimer Street between Fifteenth and Sixteenth Streets, and it was the leading barber shop of that day. Eph was head porter and bouncer around the place and matched fists with all the bad gamblers of the Cow Creek district. . . . He traveled in this country and Europe with Buffalo Bill and his Wild West Show. After leaving that outfit he went with Ringling Bros., where he remained until his poor eyesight forced him to come back to Denver. (Henry "Uncle Eph" Bufford, b. ca. 1850, CO, 33–34)

Anna Clark and Susan Harris had lived very similar lives. Anna Clark was born in Georgia on April 5, 1847, and arrived in Central City around the same time as Eph Bufford. Susan Harris was actually born in Leadville.

An excellent cook and pie maker her services were sought for by the best families. She not only excelled in this line but was known as an expert buck and wing dancer and on pay days in the mining camp she was the star of attraction. It was on one occasion that she met Dan Clark, the fiddler and it was love at first sight. They married and as she told this writer they both got religion and stopped dancing, drinking gin and playing cards. (Anna Clark, b. 1847, CO, 38)

Her father was the mine blacksmith . . . Her mother keeper of the boarding house, was an expert at blackjack and poker. . . . At fifteen she was playing and dancing in the town dance hall and ever so often with her father she would go to Central City and Denver. It was on one of these trips to Denver that she met George Walker, a minstrel man, he at once saw in her a meal ticket in the dance game and under the direction of her father they formed the team of Walker and Snow which was her maiden name, tap dancers. They traveled for a year with a medicine show. (Susan Harris, b. 1872, CO, child of ex-slaves, 52–53)

After reforming, Clark became a prominent churchwoman, representing her Baptist congregation in various local, state, and national offices. Harris eventually finished high school in Kansas City, "specialising in music," completed missionary training in Chicago, then traveled to Liberia where she met and married a clergyman before returning to church work in Colorado.

There is no question, then, that Blacks were directly exposed to professional minstrelsy even before slavery's end, when legions actually began performing in minstrel troupes and similar shows, and even more began attending. Through no mystery, in later years the persons best-versed in minstrel materials tended to be former minstrels or urban Blacks. The influence of minstrelsy among the general population, and especially plantation slaves and subsequent generations of rural Blacks is more problematic and nuanced. While some plantation slaves were treated to shows, many were not. Minstrels usually figured in such programs, but they were not the main attraction, and judging from the anecdotal evidence, they may not have had as much impact as often assumed. During the war, Thomas Wentworth Higginson commanded a regiment of former slaves from South Carolina,

Georgia, and surrounding states. "A few youths from Savannah, who were comparatively men of the world, had learned some of the 'Ethiopian Minstrel' ditties, imported from the North. These took no hold upon the mass."[24]

Higginson's comments appear more widely applicable. Despite some cross-influences, the instrumental music of slaves probably affected antebellum minstrels more than the reverse. Minstrel dances may have been complete novelties to white audiences, and sometimes did influence African Americans, but Blacks needed no introduction to dances borrowed from their own repertoires.

Oh, them old-time dances, I could die a cryin' thinkin' of 'em. I'd put on my Sunday dress and Columbus would come and took me. There was awful lot of good violin music. Don't know how they learned it, but you know how colored folks can play. We'd dance the Georgia Minstrel. Didn't you ever see the Georgia Minstrel? They don't never dance it anymore. They danced it with their feet and twist just like this. Sometimes we dance on a platform; sometimes just on the ground. (Chaney McNair, b. 1852, IT, 219)

McNair gives no indication why she associated this dance with ex-slaves performing in blackface (the Georgia Minstrels). Perhaps she and her neighbors learned it from stage minstrels, perhaps not, but the twisting and clogging she describes are typical of Black folk dancing generally and do not necessarily indicate any minstrel contribution.

Reams of published material do establish beyond a doubt that by the postwar period Black singers had adopted dozens of songs by minstrel composers. Jim Threat recalled a piece otherwise known only from blackface songbooks:

Ha! Ha! white folks going for to see,
Ha! Ha! White folks going for to see,
Going for to tell you this, that and 'tother,
Fell in love with a great waterfall.

Fell in love with Dinah Crow,
Teeth was shining like banks of snow,
Eyes as bright as rings of the moon,
Teeth as sharp as a 'possum or a coon.
(Dat nigger's teeth was plenty sharp—
Great consolation between us niggers.)

Ask Miss Dinah to be my bride,
She bit my arm, she tore my coat,
Give such a rash-tash—
She mashed her d— nose.
(Dat nigger's temper was plenty rash—
Great consolation between us niggers.) (Jim
   Threat, b. 1851, AL, 340–41)[25]

Harre Quarls gave the best-known stanza of C. A. White's "Walk in the Parlor" (1847):

Say boss, I want to sing you another song before you go:

Walking in the parlor, lightning is a yellow gal,
She lives up in the clouds, Thunder he is
   black man
And he can holler loud, when he kisses
   lightning,
She dart up in a wonder, he jump up and grate
   the clouds
that what make the thunder. (Harre Quarls,
   b. 1841, TX, 3216)[26]

Uncle Fil Hancock, a stage performer himself, contributed an unusual version of "Rock The Cradle, John," adapted from an English music hall ditty, while Julie Woodbury gave a rearranged version of Stephen C. Foster's "Uncle Ned" (1848).

One of the numerous songs, a favorite of his goes:

You, by word, now all we go,
In fact we spoke both high and low,
In the house and out of doors,
Evening in the baby's nose.

When I was young an' in my prime,
I'se a courtin' them gals,
Most all de time.
Now I'm old and you will see,
I'm not as young as I used to be.

Now when the elephant moves aroun'
The music begins to play,
Oh, the boys aroun' dat monkey's cage
I'd better keep away.
Rock, the cradle John.
Rock, the cradle John.
Many a man is rockin' another man's son
When he thinks he's rockin' his own. (Filmore
   Taylor Hancock, b. 1851, MO, 188–89)[27]

I recollects, way back yonder, Pa would sing:

Dey ain' had no eyes for to see,
Dey ain' had no teeth for to eat,
En dey had to let de corncake go,
Gwine whe' all de good niggers go.

Dat was my father's piece dat he used to sing in slavery time. Dat right cause I could remember back more so den I can forward. (Julia Woodberry, b. ca. 1865, SC, child of ex-slaves, 246)[28]

No one can dispute, then, that minstrels contributed dozens of songs to American folk tradition, which then passed by word of mouth to legions who never saw a minstrel show or songbook.[29] To accommodate this repertoire, twentieth-century folksong collections often have sections devoted specifically to blackface material. In the 1920s and '30s innumerable minstrel songs were also field recorded or released on commercial records. Some of the artists had never performed outside their families or communities, but others were veterans of circuses, medicine shows, vaudeville, street theater, or other vestiges of minstrelsy. Many had actually worked in blackface.[30]

On the other hand, many of the best-known titles credited to minstrels—"Jim Crow," "Old Dan Tucker,"

"Dixie"—were actually based on Black folksongs, and in many cases ex-slaves appear to have known the Black folksongs minstrels copied rather than their adaptations.

> Yes Sir, Cap'n, I kin tell yo sum er dem old songs whut de niggers used ter sing in de slabery times. Dis is sum of em: . . .
>
> > Wheel er bout en do er bout
> > en Jump Jim Crow.
> > Every time I do er bout
> > I do jes so. (Abram Harris, b. 1845, SC, 174–75)

No artifact of minstrelsy is more infamous than T. D. Rice's "Jim Crow" song-and-dance routine, which beginning in the 1890s lent its name to American apartheid. Concerning its inspiration, there was apparently never a single story even at the time, but possibly as early as 1828, or as late as 1833–35, in Pittsburgh, Cincinnati, or Louisville, actor Thomas D. Rice (1808–1860) saw a Black stagecoach driver, or stable hand, or theater stage hand (who may have been lame) perform a traditional Black dance song that Rice immediately appropriated and turned into an international sensation. Rice began performing "Jim Crow" onstage sometime during this same stretch, and had taken it to London by 1836. He may have had the song published around then as well, though no such printing has survived.[31] Published versions from around 1840 and later do exist, some credited to Rice, some not. In the established pattern, the success of the original "Jim Crow" also inspired numerous sequels, parodies, and topical adaptations ("De Original Jim Crow," "De Lates Jim Crow," "Jim Crow's Ramble," and so on).

Much of the attention to "Jim Crow" has focused on Rice's dance (which in descriptions did closely resemble slave dances like the heel-and-toe and buzzard lope), the costume and character he developed to go with it (racist caricatures typical of minstrelsy), and the contribution of such degrading blackface stereotypes to the fin-de-siècle white-supremacist police state also called Jim Crow. Yet the accompanying song provides the most definite link to slave music, as well as making the case that minstrel adaptations had debatable impact on the African American tradition they borrowed. Most early print versions of "Jim Crow" are based in part on the Black folksong as subsequently documented, but they are clumsily rewritten in the minstrel manner; somewhat predictably, later minstrel texts suggest a self-perpetuating professional fad with no direct connection to oral tradition. In any case, texts of "Jim Crow" from traditional singers seldom resemble minstrel versions, whose style can be gauged by the following:

> Weel about and turn about and do jis so,
> Eb'ry time I weel about and jump Jim Crow
>
> Oh I'm a roarer on de fiddle,
> And down in Old Virginny;
> They say I play de skyentific
> Like Massa Paginnini.

The source in this case is a song sheet "Jim Crow" (New York: Firth & Hall), undated but probably from around 1840, the mention of Italian violinist Niccolò Paganini (1782–1840) being one clue. The full text features forty-four verses in this style. A few have parallels in folk sources; most never occur in oral tradition.[32]

T. D. Rice always acknowledged borrowing "Jim Crow" from a Black folksinger, and the evidence definitely supports him there. Around the same time he picked up the song, James French may have heard it from another slave. In French's novelization *Sketches and Eccentricities of Col. David Crockett of West Tennessee* (1833), a Black banjo player is depicted entertaining a dance party ca. 1805.

> While Ben with his banjo and feet kept time, he sung the following lines:
>
> > "My old misses she don't like me,
> > Bekase I don't eat de black eye pea;
> > My old misses she don't like me,
> > Bekase I don't eat de black eye pea.

"My old misses long time ago,
She took me down de hill side to jump Jim Crow;
'Fus 'pon de heel tap, den 'pon de toe,
Eb'ry Monday morning I jump Jim Crow.

"Oh Lord, ladies, don't you know
You nebber get to Heben till you jump Jim Crow."
(Repeat—"My old misses," &c.) . . .

And not one of all that crowd danced more, got in a love scrape sooner, drank more whiskey, saw more fun, or sat up later than David Crockett.[33]

James Strange French (1807–1886) was a Virginia novelist, attorney, and inn keeper. In his most famous court case (1831) he defended slave insurrectionist Nat Turner and his coconspirators. *Sketches and Eccentricities* so enraged Davy Crockett (1786–1836) that he immediately produced his own *Narrative*. French's account is highly fictionalized (the dance he describes is set two years before he was born), but drew on French's real-life experiences, including firsthand familiarity with slaves and slave music. His version of "Jim Crow" also suggests some authorial tampering but is generally consistent in style and content with traditional versions. It is at least conceivable that French had already come in contact with Rice's hit, which, depending on what story we accept, may or may not have been onstage or in print when French's 1833 book went to press. Again, though, Rice was always completely forthright about borrowing "Jim Crow," and more likely French simply heard another slave performing the same traditional dance song. Anyway, there are other proofs that "Jim Crow" was by then established in African American tradition. In the 1880s ex-slave Bethany Veney (1813–1915) wrote of singing and dancing the piece around age seven (ca. 1820) on a Virginia plantation.

My old master, who at times was inclined to be jolly, had a way of entertaining his friends by my singing and dancing. Supper over, he would call me into his room and, giving me to understand what he wanted of me, I would, with all manner of grotesque grimaces, gestures, and positions, dance and sing:

Where are you going, Jim?
Where are you going, Sam?
To get a proper larning,
To jump Jim Crow.[34]

Veney's verse is somewhat novel for suggesting human characters. "Jim Crow" texts usually concern the antics of various animal tricksters—the hawk, buzzard, and crow—in a freshly plowed and planted field.

Cose we chillen used to sing some, jes' foolish things. I rec'lecs one 'bout de buzzard—

Whar you goin' buzzard,
Whar you goin' to go?
I'se goin' down to new ground
To hunt Jim Crow. (Sarah Ford, b. ca. 1850, TX, 1362)

Fig. 20.4. Sarah Ford, ex-slave, Houston, March 9, 1937. Portraits of African American ex-slaves from the US Works Progress Administration, Federal Writers' Project slave narratives collection, Library of Congress.

This in fact settles the much-debated identity of Jim Crow and attempts to tie him to a historical individual surnamed Crow: originally, Jim Crow was a *crow*—literally—a crony or adversary of the hawk and buzzard (and sometimes the blackbird and duck). Nor do African American versions suggest any particular racial significance.

There was anodder song that Caleb would sing; it goes like dis.

> Whar yer gwine buzzard, whar yer gwine crow
> Gwine down ter tivver [the river] ter do jest so.

There was a whole lot more ter dat song but I done fergot it. Anodder song that comes ter my mind is:

> Hawk and der buzzard went down ter der law
> When der hawk got back her had er broken jaw
> Lady's pocketbook on der judges bench
> Haden had no use fer a pocketbook since. (William Henry Towns, b. 1854, AL, 410)[35]

Georgia Sea Islands singer Bessie Jones (1902–1984) had played "Jim Crow" as a child in the early 1900s.

> Where you going, buzzard?
> Where you going, crow?
> I'm going to the new ground
> To knock Jim Crow.

In the 1960s Jones told Bess Lomax Hawes, "when I was a little girl, I thought Jim Crow might have been a bird, because it was 'going down to the new ground,' and they always shoot them birds out of the corn. 'New ground' is ground where the trees have been cut off, but it's never been planted in. So that was what I understood at the time, that was my idea. But we don't know what the old folks meant, we sure don't."[36] I think Bessie Jones understood the song and its original meaning perfectly.

All of this evidence argues, moreover, that "Jim Crow" developed organically within Black tradition with no necessary minstrel influences. The dance is based on the heel-to-toe step and jigging always mentioned with slave dancing; the accompanying song is set to the tune of "Hop Light Ladies" (known to a half dozen ex-slaves), with which "Jim Crow" sometimes exchanges verses.[37] The buzzard, hawk, and crow stanzas dominating traditional texts also circulate independently or in other Black songs, including "Ain't Gonna Rain No More," another ring play known to ex-slaves.

And in Black tradition, "Jim Crow" was first and foremost a ring play. "Some of de dances de niggers had was, 'Jump Jim Crow'; one nigger would jump up and down while tripping and dancing in de same spot. Sometimes he say, 'Every time I jump, I jump Jim Crow'"(John N. Davenport, b. 1848, SC, 242). On a plantation on Bayou Lafourche, "frequently these slaves were permitted to have a ball or dance. Some would play ring plays, such as 'Git around Napper and git out ob de way' or 'Where yo gwine buzzard, Where you gwine crow? Ise gwine down to de new groun to jump Jim Crow? Wheel aroun and turn aroun and do jes so. Evy time you turn aroun, you jump Jim Crow.'"[38]

One assumes ex-slaves interviewed in the 1930s could not help being acquainted with Jim Crow as a euphemism for excluding legal citizens, suppressing Black votes, violating basic human rights, and burning innocent people alive. A few actually employed the term in its contemporary sense. Yet most ex-slaves still thought of "Jim Crow" as a singing game. Liza Jones even used Jim Crow as a synonym for ring play.

When dey wasn' no task, us chillun all play, w'ite chillun and all. Oh, yes, any ol' kind of Jim Crow play. Dey was one song us sung:

> Don't steal,
> Don't steal,
> Don't steal my sugar
> Don't steal,

Don't steal,
Don't steal my candy,
I's comin' roun' de mountain. (Liza Jones, b. 1856,
TX, 2118)

Amazingly, Black children who played "Jim Crow" well into the age of Jim Crow society appear to have ignored that fact, maintaining the song's original function and meaning. Nor did they relate the song at all to minstrelsy.[39]

"Old Dan Tucker" was one of the first great minstrel hits and remains one of America's best-known songs. It was initially claimed by Daniel Decatur Emmett (1815–1904), who debuted his arrangement on February 6, 1843, at the Bowery Theater in New York; within the year at least three publishers in Boston and New York had issued the song with different composer credits.[40] In 1844 Bishop Henry Benjamin Whipple reported hearing "Dan Tucker" being sung by slaves on the streets of Mobile, and similar accounts soon followed.[41] By 1855 a correspondent for the journal *Putnam's* could write: "the most searching test of popularity can be applied to 'Ole Dan Tucker' with perfect confidence. It has been sung, perhaps, oftener than any melody ever written."[42] Not all of this popularity can be credited to Emmett or other minstrels. Emmett later asserted that he had composed "Dan Tucker" in 1830 when he was fifteen or sixteen. Perhaps so, but the song's key elements indisputably predate Emmett's version or even Emmett himself, and more likely, Emmett was merely the first white opportunist to rearrange and publicize another well-known Black folksong, closely followed by others. In the pattern of "Jim Crow," these popularizers emended and expanded the material they borrowed in the bombastic, buffoonish minstrel style, but with debatable counterinfluence on Black versions, which mainly suggest a completely oral milieu, exhibiting a high degree of variation even for dance lyrics.[43]

When I got ligion I asked de Lawd to take all de foolishness out of my head and make room for his

word and you know since den its the hardest thing in de world for me to remember dose songs we useter dance by. I do 'member a few tho' lak "Shoo, Fly," and "Old Dan Tucker" and "Run, Nigger, Run, de Pateroller Catch You." . . . Now I does member a little of "Old Dan Tucker," it went dis way:

Old Dan Tucker was a mighty mean man
He beat his wife with a fryin' pan.
She hollered and she cried, I'm gwineter go,
Dey's plenty a men, won't beat me so.

Get out of de way, Old Dan Tucker,
You've come too late to get your supper

Old Dan Tucker, he got drunk,
Fell in de fire, kicked up a chunk
Red hot coal got down his shoe
Oh, Great Lawd, how de ashes flew!

Get out of de way, old Dan Tucker,
You've come too late to get your supper. (Dora
Franks, b. ca. 1837, MS, 791–92)

Sum uf de slaves wus jes standin' round singin' and sum pattin' lak dancin'. Yes, sum uf de songs wus—

Git out 'er de way fur old Dan Tucker;
Cum too late ter git his supper.
Old Dan Tucker, he got drunk,
Fell in de fire an' kick'd up er chunk,
Git out 'er de way fur Old Dan Tucker;
Cum too late ter git his supper. (Ann Drake,
b. 1855, MS, 643)

Oh, Daniel Tucker on the railroad track,
    Pinnin' the engine to his back,
Trimmin' the corners of the railroad wheel,
    Give him the toothache in his heel.
            Chorus
Oh, Sambo, pore boy,
    Oh, Sambo, pore boy!

The frog wanted to come,
　　But he didn't have the chance.

The cricket played the fiddle,
　　An' the tadpole danced.
The frog wanted to come,
　　But he didn't have the chance. ("A song
　　　　given by Josephine Pankey of Little Rock,
　　　　Arkansas, which was sung by slaves
　　　　before the war and was 'fiddled' for the
　　　　Negro dancers.")[44]

Most Black texts of "Tucker" follow this pattern, combining wandering stanzas around a chorus telling supperless Dan to get out of the way. Many of these floaters are regularly attached to other Black folksong characters ("Old Man Baker," "Captain Dime," "Old Aunt Dinah," "Ole Granny Grunt").[45] Some more properly belong to other songs. The variations between texts can be extreme, but most incorporate what Constance Rourke described as "those brief and cryptic bird and animal fables that have proved to be a consistent Negro creation."[46] "We sang 'Old Dan Tucker.' Git outen de way, ole Dan Tucker, Sixteen Hosses in one stable, one jumped out an' skined his nable an' so on" (Jane Arrington, b. 1852, NC, 48). In the antebellum period, "Old Dan Tucker" was an unparalleled triumph in print and onstage, indisputably accounting for much of the song's remarkable currency, including some later Black versions. Nonetheless, it appears that, as with "Jim Crow," the original "Dan Tucker" (or its constituents) continued to coexist independently within a Black oral tradition still familiar to some ex-slaves.

Dan Emmett's success with "Old Dan Tucker" was eclipsed many times over by his most famous title, "Dixie." Here again, Emmett's composer claim was never universally accepted even in his lifetime; lyrics aside, it is certain that he did not create the tune. Despite his own conflicting statements about the song's origins, Emmett indisputably debuted his version in New York City on April 4, 1859, listed in the program as "'Way Down Souf in Dixie,' a 'Corn-shucking Dance.'"[47] The title's success was immediate

and spectacular. Abraham Lincoln used it in his 1860 presidential campaign, Jefferson Davis shortly thereafter at his inauguration as Confederate president. Today, it is one of the most recognized melodies in the United States and the world, and in this instance the evidence overwhelmingly indicates that "Dixie's" instant and enduring celebrity can be credited mainly to Dan Emmett and blackface minstrelsy. Tellingly, most ex-slaves who named "Dixie" identified it with whites and the war years.[48]

However, Emmett himself acknowledged "Dixie" as a Black folksong, and others agreed. In 1861, responding to Emmett's success, a correspondent for the *Mobile Register* wrote of "Dixie" that "its real origin is of much older date. Those who have traveled much on Western rivers must often have heard it, among the firemen and deckhands of the river steamers."[49] The WPA narratives corroborate the *Register*'s report; several ex-slaves recalled "Dixie" as an antebellum riverboatman's song. Alfred Jones (b. 1833, AL, 224) remembered "Dixie" being played on an Alabama riverboat's calliope in the 1840s. In the 1880s George Fortman signed on as a Mississippi riverboat roustabout: "The 'Whistling Coon' was a popular song with the boatmen and one version of 'Dixie Land'" (George Fortman, b. ca. 1850, KY, 93).[50] George Taylor Burns had crewed Ohio and Mississippi riverboats in the 1840s.

> I was still a young child, possibly seven years of age when we came to Indiana. That may have been in the year 1839 or 1840, but within one month of landing at Troy, I had been indentured to a flatboat captain and my life for the next 70 years was spent on the different rivers. . . .
>
> When asked if he knew many songs sung by boatmen in earlier days, George Taylor Burns said that the songs varied as different boatmen sang the same songs to different tunes. Many boat songs were put to the tune of "Dixie"; also a number of songs mentioned the name of Captain, or some craft. Thus Dixie was sung on any craft where W. H. Daniel was captain.

Oh, I was a slave in the land of Dixie
But Captain Daniels saw I was Pert and frisky,
Now I'm glad I'm a steamboat man.

Old missus called me fat and lazy
But after I left her, she went plum crazy
She missed me so from Dixie Land.

A boatman's life is a life of pleasure
Plenty to eat and money to treasure
Oh, who would go back to Dixie Land?

The rousters are always dancin and singin
Boat horns a blowin and bells a ringin
Oh, who would go back to Dixie Land?

Pretty gals come crowdin where boats are
    landin
Smile at de Cap'n where he is standin
And smile at de darkey from Dixie Land.

Some time its stormy winds keep blowin
Then its hard to keep the steamboat goin
Still I wouldn't go back to Dixie Land. (George
    Taylor Burns, b. ca. 1830, MO, 27, 28–29)

Though obviously distinct from "Dixie" as now widely recognized, as Burns states, his text can easily be sung to the well-known tune, also following the familiar pattern of short couplets alternating with a Dixie-Land refrain: "I wish I was in de land ob cotton / Old times dar am not forgotten / Look away! Look away! Look away! Dixie land" (Dan Emmett). "Old missus called me fat and lazy / But after I left her, she went plum crazy / She missed me so from Dixie Land" (George Taylor Burns). Unlike Emmett's version, the protagonist in Burns's text—evidently a former plantation slave, now a riverboatman—definitely does not wish to go back to Dixie and the land of cotton! (Apparently his old times there were best forgotten.) Burns's comments also indicate that the song was constantly recomposed, possibly in performance. If, as reported, the Black folksong that Dan

Emmett borrowed for "Dixie" was previously common among Black riverboat workers, Burns's text has a strong claim as one possible instance.

Other ex-slaves also hinted at a pre-Emmett tradition. Dan Emmett actually subtitled "Dixie" a "Corn-shucking Dance." Carrie Davis had sung "Dixie" at Georgia cornshuckings in the 1850s. "Corn-shuckings, they wuz a nuther good time, most uv em would be tight and sing and holler, 'Sheep's in cotton patch, got em out Monday. Had er been a white man, got em out Sunday.' Kid Kimbrough wuz our leader, would sing Dixie too" (Carrie Davis, b. ca. 1850, GA, 119). George Fleming and Susan McIntosh recalled slaves playing "Dixie" for dancing on quills. Katie Arbery and William Little identified it as a fiddle song, Lu Perkins as a play-party:

> Every night the Judge and the old missus had the niggers come to the big house and stand in rows in they clean lowerings clothes with white handkerchiefs tied 'round they heads and have play-party songs. They used to sing . . .
>
> > Went to war with Captain King,
> > And 'tach my horse to a hickory limb.
> > Look away, look away
> > In the south of Dixie.
> > I take my rasher on my back
> > And march south to the Rio Grande,
> > I wish I was in the south of Dixie—
> > Don't you? Don't you? (Lu Perkins, b. ca. 1850,
> >   MS, 3061)

As America's first mass entertainment, minstrelsy eventually reshaped all of American music, including African American music. Yet apparently even minstrelsy could not penetrate some isolated pockets of the feudal antebellum South. That was about to change. Most ex-slaves who named "Dixie" were obviously recalling Dan Emmett's hit; moreover, almost all of them remembered "Dixie" from the war years, played by military bands or sung by marching and marauding soldiers.

BALLADS

I remember that I used to hear some old love songs, "Barbra Allen," and one about "Oh to me the time seems long, since you and I did part." (Stearlin Arnwine, b. 1853, TX, 84)

Our work song was, "John Henry was a man; he worked all over dis town." Dey still uses dat song. In slavery some holler when dey be in de field like owls; some like crows; and some like peafowls. (Gus Feaster, b. ca. 1840, SC, 52)

Protracted Meeting Ball

At certain times of the year, all of we niggers would go on a months spree of dancing, eating and drinking. This was at Varner, on Bob Rice's place, you know he was one of the big sportin' men. Had race horses and his own race track. For one solid month, we would do nothin but have a big time. We all bought our food at de "bar," and also our drinks. This bar belonged to Mr. Rice. I can't sing any of de songs because they was bad and rowdy. When asked about the boll weevil, he said he only knew a line or two. "Boll weevil leads a sporting life." (John Cottonham, b. 1866, AR, child of ex-slaves, 60)

With slave spirituals, the study of medieval British ballads marked the birth of American folksong scholarship, all to the credit of Francis James Child (1825–1896), a Harvard professor with little interest in American folksong per se, but some interest in African Americans. Born and raised in Boston, Child was a Union man and devoted abolitionist who during the war edited the prowar, antislavery songbook *War-Songs for Freemen* (1862), which included some of his own compositions.[1] He was to achieve immortality, however, through the corpus of English and Scottish narrative songs bearing his name, the Child ballads. Completed over the course of half a century, published serially (the last part posthumously), *The English and Scottish Popular Ballads* (1882–98) instantly became the starting point of all Anglo-American folksong scholarship.[2] Child relied entirely on published or manuscript sources for his definitive classification and compilation of 305 English and Scottish ballads composed ca. 1400–1700, but the realization that many of these songs were still being sung in Britain and America spurred an unparalleled program of fieldwork and publication on both sides of the Atlantic. Professor Child personally had no interest in folksong collecting, but his volumes do include a few field texts sent by American friends and admirers, among them a pair from African Americans.[3]

The ballad, a quintessential Western European genre, would come to play an especially important role among North American Blacks, whose African heritage included various narrative song-types. Surprisingly, narrative folksongs do not occur globally, and Africans thus arrived in America distinctly primed for English-language stories-in-song. Where Blacks first heard British ballads is no mystery. Louise Neill was the daughter of a slave woman and white overseer. "My fathah was good and when we got freedom he took us all and moved to another fahm. He used to come to our cabin in the afternoon when he was restin' and set on the front po'ch and sing a song that went like this: I wish—I wish—I wish, I wish I was young again.' He sang some other songs which I don't remember" (Louise Neill, b. ca. 1860, GA, 2890). We can only guess at the other songs Neill's father sang, but the verse she quotes is associated with numerous Anglo-American songs, including the ballad "Love Has Brought Me to Despair" (Laws P 25) and a related love lyric sometimes actually called "I Wish, I Wish."

> O I wish, I wish, O I wish in vain,
> O I wish I was a maid again.
> But a maid again I will never be,
> Till a apple it grow on a orange tree.[4]

Even when the slaves' sources must be inferred, they are self-evident. British ballads were sung throughout the US and Canada, but the South was a major bastion of Child ballads and British and Irish folksongs generally. In later years, collectors gathered dozens of Child numbers from surviving slaveholders, their children, and grandchildren. In a turnabout, a few had even learned them from slave mammies or other Blacks. Some ex-slaves reported little or no contact with poor whites—and for many ex-slaves poor whites meant any whites except slaveholders—but others had regularly interacted with Anglo-American merchants, doctors and attorneys, educators, tradespeople, small farmers, laborers, itinerants, squatters, and vagrants, as well as plantation hirelings like overseers and mechanics. Ballads were well known to these and virtually all other whites as well. Ex-slaves also heard ballads and folksongs from soldiers of both armies during the war. The Civil War was a watershed for the American ballad generally, and in some cases for Black participation. However, African American balladry would not truly come into its own until the late 1800s, the first known Black ballads—"Stewball" (Laws Q 22), "John Henry" (Laws I 1), "The Boll Weevil" (Laws I 17), "The Bully of the Town" (Laws I 14)—being composed by the slaves' children but more often their grandchildren; for most slaves, ballads were an Anglo-American tradition they observed and occasionally affected but seldom made completely their own.

That notwithstanding, ballads, including medieval or Child ballads, were known to slaves. Texas ex-slave Stearlin Arnwine named "Barbara Allen" (Child 84), easily the most popular Child title in America. There is, however, only one actual medieval ballad text in the narratives, but it is an especially intriguing one, appearing in a compilation of conjure beliefs and practices. Titled "*FOLKLORE* (Negro)" (S2 13 *GA* 4: 261–68), the materials were assembled from the Atlanta interviews of Edwin Driskell, a Black fieldworker with the Georgia ex-slaves project.

> Says Mr. Holmes: "If anybody comes to your house an' you don't want 'em dere, when dey leaves you take some salt an' throw it at 'em, when dey gits out of hearin' you cuss at 'em an' dey won't ever come back again." Following are some songs that used to be sung about conjure, etc.:

SON: "Mother make my bed down
I will freely lie down,
Mother, make my bed down
I will freely lie down"
MOTHER: "Ransom, my son, what did she
give you to eat?
Ransom, my son, what did she give
you to eat?"
SON: "Red head (parched lizard) and
speckle back
Oh, make my bed down I will freely
lie down."
"I'm goin' to pizen (poison) you, I'm
goin' to pizen you,
I'm jus' sick an' tired of de way you do,
I'm goin' to sprinkle spider legs 'roun
yo' bed
an' you gonna wake up in de mornin'
an find youself dead.

"You beat me an' you kick me an' you
black my eyes,
I'm gonna take dis butcher knife an'
hew you down to my size,
You mark my words, my name is Lou,
You mind out what I say, I'm goin'
to pizen you." (S2 13 *GA* 4: 265,
orig. parentheses)

Driskell writes in a headnote: "the Negro folklore as recounted below was secured from the following: Mrs. Julia Rush (an ex-slave) who lives at 878 Coleman Street, S. W.; Mr. George Leonard (a very intelligent elderly person) whose address is 148 Chestnut Avenue, N. E.; and Mr. Henry Holmes (an ex-slave); Mr. Ellis Strickland; Mr. Sam Stevens and a young boy known only as Joe" (S2 13 *GA* 4: 261). He does not, however, credit several of the individual items, including this song text, which actually contains two thematically similar songs run together (the division is between the lines "Oh, make my bed down I will freely lie down" and "I'm goin' to pizen you"). Another copy of the second song ("I'm goin' to pizen you")

was discovered in the WPA folklore files for Georgia (separate from the ex-slave narratives), attributed to Julia Rush (b. 1828, GA), so she is definitely its source.[5] However, neither of these song texts appears in Rush's individual narrative (S2 13 *GA* 3: 229–31), or in any other individual ex-slave narrative. Henry Holmes obviously offered the opening comments; Driskell's compilation represents his only appearance in the narratives (he did not provide an individual interview that has survived). Holmes and Rush are quoted by name throughout Driskell's compilation, providing much of the other material. The best guess (but only a guess) is that Rush also gave the first of these two song texts, a unique version of "Lord Randall" (Child 12).

"Lord Randall" is one of the more popular Child numbers in both Britain and the United States, relating a conversation between mother and son that ends in the realization that the son (Lord Randall) has been poisoned by his wife or lover.[6] The ex-slave narratives contain the only traditional North American Black text that I have found, which is singular as well for incorporating conjure lore: Randall hasn't been drugged, he's been hoodooed![7] In American white texts, Randall is most often poisoned by striped, streaked, blackback, or speckled-belly eels cooked in butter (batter) or eel broth. Sometimes snakes or other reptiles are substituted for eels:

"Have you been to your dinner, my rambling
young son?
Have you been to your dinner, my handsome
young man?"
"Yes I've been to my dinner and ate half a
snake's head,
And I'm sick to my heart, and I wish to lie down."[8]

To African Americans this would immediately indicate conjure, since snakes, lizards, and other reptiles—live, freshly killed, or parched (dried and powdered)—were among the most common ingredients in conjure tricks and charms, their heads being especially efficacious. Conjure-related deaths were quite often ascribed to "snakes and lizards in the body." Snakes, lizards, and toads also served as familiars or agents of hoodoo doctors.[9]

> In slavery an old man was said to be a conjurer, who had all kinds of snakes and insects. He took sick and died and the saying is that after he had died one night he came back and carried his box of insects and snakes out of his house and set them down an nobody could even go and get his body as these insects and snakes would come up and run them away. (George W. Harmon, b. 1854, TX, 142)

This also explains why "Ransom, My Son" was included in a collection of African American conjure lore and joined to the second item, which typifies the tongue-in-cheek hoodoo songs current beginning around the turn of the twentieth century, both in Black oral tradition and blackface stage parodies.[10] "I'm Goin' To Pizen You" may be connected to the professional fad but has ties to oral texts too.[11]

Julia Woodberry performed another venerable British title, "The Twelve Blessings of Mary" (aka "Seven Joys of Mary," "The Vessel Cup"), a fifteenth-century carol well-known to both Anglo- and African Americans.

> Well, I used to know a heap of dem songs dat I hear my auntie en my grandmammy sing dere home when I was comin up. Let me see, child, dey was natural born song too.
>
> > I got somethin to tell you,
> > Bow - hoo, oo - hoo, oo - hoo.
> > I got somethin to tell you,
> > Bow - hoo, oo - hoo, oo - hoo.
> > En a bow - hoo, oo - oo - hoo.
>
> > Way cross de ocean,
> > 'Mongst all dem nation,
> > Massa Jesus promise me,
> > He gwine come by en by,
> > He gwine come by en by.

> > Dere many miles round me,
> > De curried be so bold,
> > To think dat her son, Jesus,
> > Could write widout a pen,
> > Could write widout a pen.
>
> > De very next blessin dat Mary had,
> > She had de blessin of two,
> > To think dat her son, Jesus,
> > Could bring de crooked to straight,
> > Could bring de crooked to straight.

> Dat was my auntie's grandmother Eve piece way back yonder in slavery time. Dat was her piece. (Julia Woodberry, b. ca. 1865, SC, child of ex-slaves, 239–40)

Woodberry attributes her version, which has been completely recomposed, to her aunt's grandmother, providing no other context; but among African Americans this piece was typically used as a shout song. In the 1870s Mary Porter printed a text combining "The Blessings of Mary" with the shout "Joshua Fought the Battle of Jericho." Half a century later in South Carolina, Robert Winslow Gordon found "The Blessings" still used for shouting.[12] Porter's Louisiana version, which inventories all twelve blessings, exemplifies the usual incremental pattern (I quote the first two joys).

> > De very first blessing Sister Mary had,
> > > It was de blessings of one,
> > To think that her Son Jesus Christ
> > > Was suckled at the breast so young
> > > > *Chorus.*—Oh! Joshuay, etc.
>
> > De very next blessing Sister Mary had,
> > > It was de blessings of two,
> > To think that her Son Jesus Christ
> > > Could read dat Bible through.[13]

As one might deduce, making the crooked ways straight and writing without a pen (both included in Julia Woodberry's version) usually serve as blessings eight and ten, respectively.

British folksongs featuring anthropomorphic animals were particularly attractive to slaves steeped in African and African American animal trickster tales. John Van Hook gave the two best-known examples.

When asked if he remembered any of the tunes and words of the songs he sang as a child, John was silent for a few moments then began to sing:

A frog went courtin'
And he did ride
Uh hunh
With a sword and pistol
By his side
Uh hunh

Old uncle Rat laughed,
Shook his old fat side;
He thought his niece
Was going to be the bride.
Uh hunh, uh hunh.

Where shall the wedding be?
Uh hunh
Where shall the wedding be?
Uh hunh

Way down yonder
In a hollow gum tree.
Uh hunh, uh hunh.

Who shall the waiters be?
Uh hunh
Granddaddy Louse and a Black-eyed flea.
Uh hunh, uh hunh, uh hunh.

Laney [Van Hook's wife] reminded him of a song he used to sing when their child was a baby. "It is hard for me to formulate its words in my mind. I just cannot seem to get them," he answered, "but I thought of this one the other night and promised myself I would sing it for you sometime. It's *Old Granny Mistletoe*."

Old Granny Mistletoe,
Lyin' in bed,
Out the window
She poked her head.

She says, "Old Man,
The gray goose's gone.
And I think I heard her holler,
King-cant-you-O, King-cant-you-O!"

The old fox stepped around,
A mighty fast step.
He hung the old gray goose
Up by the neck.

Her wings went flipflop
Over her back
And her legs hung down.
Ding-downey-O, ding-downey-O.

The old fox marched
On to his den.
Out come his young ones,
Some nine or ten.

Now we will have
Some-supper-O, some-supper-O.
Now we will have
Some-supper-O, some-supper-O. (John F. Van
    Hook, b. 1862, NC, 87–88)

"The Fox Went A-Hunting" also originated in the middle ages. There are other reports of slaves singing the piece, which remained current among African Americans well into the twentieth century.[14] "Froggie Went A-Courting" dates to at least November 21, 1580, when "A Moste Strange Weddinge of the Frogge and the Mouse" was registered with the London Company of Stationers. It was even more popular among Blacks (and Americans generally) and remains well known today.[15]

Britain's large repertoire of bawdy songs fared well in parts of Canada, but far less so in Puritan New

England and the fundamentalist South and Midwest. They were definitely known, however. Anda Woods recalled slaves fiddling and dancing to "The Cuckoo's Nest," a popular English song of seduction: "O' she ruffled up her feathers an' she turnt up her toes / An' hopped right over in de coo-coo's nest" (Anda Woods, b. ca. 1841, AL, 2390). The sexual associations of cuckoos are given, besides which in British and Irish folksongs birds' nests customarily connote female genitalia. Longer versions of this item leave no doubt that this is what the cuckoo's nest represents.[16]

Mary Kindred gave another English seduction ballad rarely collected in North America, "Raking the Hay."

My Gramma was a ol' midwife. Us chillen uster ax her w'er she git de babies an' she tell us she treed dem in holler logs. We'd git de dogs an' chase through de woods but de oni'es' t'ings we ebber tree' was rabbits. So we go'd back to her an' tol' her we tuk de dogs an' couldn' tree no babies. Den she say she ketch dem on a hook so den we git hooks an' go fishin' but all we ketch was minner perches. Fin'lly I say, "I kaint ketch no baby wid dis hook. Gimme de kinder hook w'at you ketch dem wid." Well, right dere w'en I ax her dat I jammed her. So she went to de trunk w'at we call her med'cine ches' an' move t'ings 'roun' 'til she fin' a hook an' line dat she hab all ready fix an' give it to me. I tuk it an' go fishin'. But I ain' ketch no babies too dis mawnin'. Not wid dat kinder hook. She uster sing us a l'il song too. Went like dis;

One mawnin', one mawnin' in May.
I spy a bootiful (beautiful) dandy,
A-rakin' 'way de hay.
I ask her if she marry me,
So scornful she say "No."
But befo' six mont's
Come rollin' by—
Her apron strings
Dey wouldn' tie.
She wrote me a letter,

She marry me bye an' bye.
I wrote her anudder an' said,
"No, no, my gal, not I." (Mary Kindred,
    b. ca. 1855, TX, 2200–201, orig. parentheses)

Mary's grandmother may have dissembled and teased, but the song makes no secret of how a girl really catches a baby, haystacks carrying the same connotations as cuckoo nests; unfortunately, that is all the hay-raker snares in her apron strings, having failed to tie up the father. The text differs considerably from most English versions of "Raking the Hay." In 1918 in Virginia, however, Cecil Sharp (1859–1924) collected three Anglo-American examples, all beginning like the following from Willie Hughes of Buena Vista:

One morning, one morning, one morning in May,
I spied a fair damsel a-raking of hay.
I asked her if she'd marry me,
Marry me by and bye.
The answer that she made me
Was: O no, my boy, not I.

Sharp evidently regarded these items as fragmentary and so did not include them in *English Folk Songs from the Southern Appalachians*, but they conclusively identify Mary Kindred's text with an American subtype of "Raking the Hay."[17]

Medieval ballads and related British traditions obviously achieved some currency among African Americans, but the Child ballad's late medieval subject matter and worldview, dispassionate, laconic narrative style, and formulaic, archaic diction understandably limited its overall acceptance. The Child numbers best known to North American Blacks—"The Maid Freed From the Gallows" (Child 95) and "Our Goodman" (Child 274)—both possessed incremental structures easily recast in the African American vernacular, expressing themes otherwise commonplace in Black folksong (crime and punishment for "The Maid," alcoholism and marital infidelity for "Our Goodman").[18]

Beginning around 1700 medieval ballads were displaced even in Britain by broadside ballads, which took their name from the mass-printed songsheets through which many originated and circulated. Quite a few of these items also passed into oral tradition, however, and the broadside press thereby introduced a new narrative style that was then employed in numerous ballads never appearing in print: explicit, sensationalistic, and journalistic, topically current and circumstantially detailed, didactic and moralistic, cast in the current vernacular.[19] Broadsides were fixtures in America from the colonial period, their highly subjective first-person narrators and harshly judgmental Protestant subtexts making them especially well suited to social commentary, timely causes, moral pronouncements, and Black styles of expression. In the antebellum period, free Blacks occasionally employed the format, more so their abolitionist allies, but in the postwar era, broadsides (or *ballets*) flooded Black communities, especially churches. Only a few contained ballads, of course, but many late nineteenth-century African American ballads that were never printed employed the broadside style.[20]

Ex-slaves were definitely acquainted with Anglo-American broadside ballads, mainly from the war years, when the format flourished north and south. Rachel Bradley gave a stanza from "The Battle of Elkhorn Tavern (The Pea Ridge Battle)" (Laws A 12), otherwise documented only among Ozark whites. (Bradley was from the immediate vicinity, Farmerville, in far northwestern Louisiana near the Arkansas line.)

> Who is Price a fightin'?
> He is a fightin', I do know.
> I think it is old Curtis,
> I hear the cannons roa'. (Rachel Bradley,
>   b. ca. 1830, LA, 236)[21]

The references are to Confederate General Sterling Price (1809–1867) and Union General Samuel Ryan Curtis (1805–1866), who defeated Price in the Ozarks at Pea Ridge (Elkhorn Tavern) (March 7–8, 1862) and then, decisively, at the Battle of Westport (October 21–23, 1864).[22] No print copy has come to light, but the ballad is firmly in the broadside style.

"Joe Bowers" (Laws B 14) originated during the California Gold Rush but was based on an older British broadside, "The Girl I Left Behind Me" (Laws P 1 B). It became one of the most-reprinted titles of the 1860s, when it was adopted by Confederate troops, which was how Lucy Gallman heard it. Southerners also borrowed its melody for "I'm a Good Old Rebel."[23]

When the soldiers was here, I 'member how they would sing:

> I'm all de way from Georgia,
> I'm all the way to fight,
> I left my good old mother,
> To come here to fight.

> Joe Bowers, Joe Bowers,
> He had another wife,
> He's all de way from Missouri,
> To come here to fight.

I didn't like slavery. I'd rather live like now. (Lucy Gallman, b. 1857, SC, 102)

However, no broadside theme dominated the war years like the battlefield testament, in which a dying solider bids comrades farewell and imparts messages to loved ones back home. Among the better-known was "Brother Green (The Dying Soldier)," which the narrator named only as Mrs. Hunter had learned from her ex-slave mother. Such items may strike contemporary readers as maudlin and contrived, but they sprang from a practical and personal horror that gripped the entire nation. No one, that is, had anticipated the carnage of America's first Industrial Age war. Primitive medical and mortuary services were overwhelmed, and Civil War battlefields were left blanketed with thousands of untended mangled, dead, and dying men, likely then to be buried anonymously in mass graves, their fates forever unknown to their families. Throughout the war, soldiers of both armies agonized not only that they would be butchered, but that their mothers, wives, and children would never know what became of them. A Mississippi version of "The Battle of Shiloh Hill" (Laws A 11) concludes "The wounded men were crying / For help from everywhere, / While others who were dying / Were offering God their prayer: / 'Protect my wife and children / As consistent with Thy will.' / Such were the prayers I heard / That night on Shiloh Hill."[24] On the night before another infamous bloodbath, the Battle of Cold Harbor (June 3, 1864), Colonel (later General) Horace Porter (1837–1921) passed through the Union camp.

> As I came near one of the regiments which was making preparations for the next morning's assault, I noticed that many of the soldiers had taken off their coats, and seemed to be engaged in sewing up rents in them. This exhibition of tailoring seemed rather peculiar at such a moment, but upon closer examination it was found that the men were calmly writing their names and home addresses on slips of paper, and pinning them on the backs of their coats, so that their dead bodies might be recognized upon the field, and their fate made known to their families at home.[25]

Long after the war, night riders masquerading as Confederate ghosts played on these accounts, while people remembered the stories and songs well into the twentieth century. However overwrought items like "Brother Green" may seem today, their appeal to Civil War–era soldiers and civilians alike was profound. This, of course, included slaves and former slaves, who faced these circumstances themselves in various capacities. "During this time masters suffered as well as their slaves, for many of their sons went gaily forth to battle and were never heard of again. Simpson Rigerson, son of 'Marse' Jesse Rigerson, was lost to his parents" (Bryant Huff, b. unk., GA, 241). "My father was suppressed. He belong to Master Erman. He run off and went on with the Yankees when they come down from Virginia. We think he got killed. We never heard from him after 1863" (Ellis Jefson, b. ca. 1861, VA, 43–44). "Den I wuz put to burying Yankee soldiers. When nobody wuz lookin I stript de daid ob dey money. Sometimes it wuz in a belt around dey bodies. Soon I got a big roll ob greenbacks den I come trampin back home" (James Lucas, b. 1833, MS, 1341). "Brother Green" was sung to the tune of "Barbara Allen."[26]

Fig. 21.1. "Cold Harbor, VA. African Americans collecting bones of soldiers killed in the battle." April 1865. Photo by John Reekie. Selected Civil War Photographs 1861–1865, Library of Congress, Prints and Photographs Division. "Den I wuz put to burying Yankee soldiers. When nobody wuz lookin I stript de daid ob dey money" (James Lucas, b. 1833, MS, 1341).

> My mama was a slave, and she used to sing this song. She say a dead soldier used to sing it on de battlefield.
>
> O Brother dream [Green] do come to me
> For I am shot and bleeding.
> Oh, I must die no more to see
> My wife and little children.
>
> The Southern forehead had [foe had laid] me low
> On this cold ground to suffer.
> O Brother stay and lay me away
> And write my wife a letter.
>
> Tell her I am prepared to die
> And I hope we'll meet in heaven.
> My poor little babes—
> I love them well. (Mrs. Hunter, b. unk., LA, 123)

Fig. 21.2. "My God! What Is All This For?" America Singing: Nineteenth-Century Song Sheets, Library of Congress, Prints and Photographs Division. A Civil War–era broadside exemplifying the battlefield testament. Like many, this item seems never to have achieved any currency beyond its limited print circulation. The antiwar message is not unusual for such pieces.

Narrator Lafayette Price was himself among the thousands of slaves actually serving in Confederate ranks as substitutes or conscripts. Price was born around 1850 in Alabama, but after the deaths of his enslavers, he became orphan children property and was sent with their minor heirs to James and Robert Carroll's plantation in northwest Louisiana, only two or three miles from where the Battle of Mansfield (Sabine Crossroads) was shortly fought (April 8, 1864). In the battle's aftermath the Carroll brothers were conscripted into Confederate service, and Price with them.

> One night right where de battle was fought we had to camp. It was rainin' and sleetin' and snowin'. I said "W'at you goin' to do tonight?" Mr. James Carroll say "We jus' hafta stan' were we camp. Jus' stack de guns and put out, w'at you call de watchman." Dey had w'at you call de relief. Dey wasn' in bed, dey was out under a tree in de col'. Ev'ry hour dey walk 'em out 'long a runway to walk guard. It

was a wunnerful distressin' time. De sojers had a li'l song dey sung:

> Eat w'en you're hungry,
> Drink w'en you're dry,
> Effen a tree don' kill you,
> You'll live 'til you die.

Dis was 'cause dey had to stan' under trees and w'en de Yankees shoot cannon dey knock off lim's and tops of trees and them under de trees might git kill' from de fallin' branches. Anudder song was:

> It was on de eighth of April,
> Dey all remember well,
> W'en fifes and drums was beatin'
> For us all to march—away. (Lafayette Price, b. ca. 1850, LA, 3181–82)

Price's second example quotes "The Battle of Shiloh Hill" (Laws A 11).

> It was on the sixth of April, just at the break of day.
> The drums and fifes were playing for us to march away;
> The feeling of that hour I do remember still,
> For the wounded and the dying that lay on Shiloh Hill.[27]

Credited to M. B. Smith (Company C, 2d Regiment, Texas Volunteers), the earliest version of "Shiloh Hill" I have found is in *Allan's Lone Star Ballads* (1874), which was compiled mainly from war-era songbooks and broadsides. The Second Texas definitely fought at Shiloh (Pittsburg Landing) (April 6–7, 1862), and Smith was presumably there, probably composing the piece not long after.[28] Very likely his song appeared in print during the war. It achieved only limited oral circulation, but epitomizes the broadside style.

Lafayette Price did not exaggerate soldiers' dread of shells exploding in treetops, which showered shrapnel but also splintered the trees, impaling or crushing

Fig. 21.3. "Battle-field of Chancellorsville: Trees shattered by artillery fire on south side of plank road near where Gen. Stonewall Jackson was shot." 1865. Civil War Photograph Collection, Library of Congress, Prints and Photographs Division. The Battle of Chancellorsville (Spotsylvania Courthouse) took place two years before this photo was taken, from April 30 to May 6, 1863. Some of the heaviest fighting occurred around this location, where Jackson was mortally wounded on May 2.

those below. His other example—"Eat w'en you're hungry, / Drink w'en you're dry, / Effen a tree don' kill you, / You'll live 'til you die"—was many times more popular than "Shiloh Hill." It often appears in another ballad found in *Allan's Lone Star Ballads*, "The Rebel Soldier (Prisoner)," and even more often in the related lyric, "Jack of Diamonds (Rye Whiskey)." "The Rebel Soldier" was itself fairly popular with whites (and especially rebel soldiers), but I have found only one African American example, from Arkansas ex-slave R. C. Smith, who had learned it directly from Confederate troops. For comparison and completeness, I also include the 1874 *Lone Star Ballads* text.

> One morning in May
> I heard a poor rebel say;
> "The federal's a home guard
> Dat called me from home. . . ."
>
> I wish I was a merchant
> And could write a fine hand,
> I'd write my love a letter
> So she would understand.

> I wish I had a drink of brandy,
> And a drink of wine,
> To drink wid dat sweet gal
> How I wish dat she was mine.
>
> If I had a drink of brandy
> No longer would I roam,
> I'd drink it wid dat gal of mine
> Dat wishes me back home.

I've heard the soldiers sing that song a heap of times. They sung it kind of lonesome like and I guess it sort of made them home sick to sing it. Us niggers learned to sing it and it is about the only one I can sing yet. (R. C. Smith, b. ca. 1840, AR, 280, orig. ellipsis)

> One morning, one morning, one morning
>   in May,
> I heard a poor soldier lamenting, and say,
> I heard a poor soldier lamenting, and say,
> "I am a rebel prisoner, and Dixie is my home!
>
> "O Mollie! O Mollie! it was for your sake alone
> That I left my own country, my father to moan,
> That I left my poor mother far away to roam—
> I am a Rebel prisoner, and Dixie is my home!
>
> "With a bottle of good brandy and a glass of wine,
> You can drink with your own true love, while I
>   weep for mine,
> You can drink with your own true love, while I
>   weep and moan;
> I am a rebel prisoner, and Dixie is my home!
>
> "Altho' my body's absent my heart is always true,
> There is no one in this wide world I love so well
>   as you,
> There is no one in this wide world I love so well
>   as you,
> I am a Rebel prisoner, and what shall I do?
>
> "Go build me a cottage on yonder mountain high,
> Where old General Price will help me to cry,

Where Southern boys will greet me and help me
to mourn—
I am a rebel prisoner, and Dixie is my home!

"Farewell to old Texas! I could no longer stay,
For hard times and the Federals drove me away,
Hard times and Abe Lincoln have caus'd me to roam—
I am a Rebel prisoner, and Dixie is my home!"
(*Allan's Lone Star Ballads* [1874], 80–81)[29]

"The Rebel Soldier" actually derives from an earlier English broadside variously titled "The Poor Stranger," "The Poor Girl," "The Poor Strange Girl," and so forth. "The Poor Stranger" was once among the British broadside ballads better known to American whites, overlapping in text, and sharing its tune, with the prodigious Anglo-American folk lyric complex that includes "The Cuckoo," "The Wagoner's Lad (On Top of Old Smokey)," and "Pretty Saro." It relates a typical broadside tale of forsaken love: roving out one May morning, the narrator spies a lamenting maid who, having been lured away from parents and home by William (Willie), ruined then discarded in a strange land, now wanders heartbroken, all to the refrain, "I am a poor strange girl (stranger) far from my home."[30]

Some editors have treated "The Rebel Soldier" as a mere variant of "The Poor Stranger," and their overlap is considerable, but "The Rebel Soldier" is a distinct ballad telling a completely different story. Most obviously, the poor strange girl has become a Confederate field soldier, with other necessary adjustments (Willie has become Molly, Polly, Lillie, and so on).[31] The *Lone Star Ballads* text probably reprints an item from the war years, and the piece was definitely in oral circulation by then. Vance Randolph published a text dated January 6, 1942, "given to Mrs. Clara Robinson, Kingston, Ark., by a Mr. Salter who lived at Higdon, Ark., and was in the rebel army, fighting in a battle at Cane Hill."[32] The Battle of Cane Hill took place November 28, 1862, in ex-slave R. C. Smith's native Washington County, Arkansas, where, perhaps not coincidentally, he remembered hearing rebel soldiers sing the song around this time.[33]

More particularly, in contrast to "The Poor Stranger," which portrays a female debilitated by heartbreak and loneliness, "The Rebel Soldier" depicts a male coping with the trauma of war, and later versions focus largely on the singer's self-destructive drinking, gambling, and drifting. "The Rebel Soldier" in fact tells the story of untold numbers of real Rebel soldiers, and American veterans generally. Against the pleas of his parents, or because his true love and her parents reject his poverty and rowdy ways, or to impress his sweetheart and for her sake alone, the young man enlists. In some texts he is drawn to a charismatic commander (mentioned are Generals Sterling Price and John H. Morgan, both known for winning personal glory by leading their men into disaster).[34] In other cases the Union men, Yankees, Federals, Abe Lincoln, hard times, and so forth have forced the singer away from home. Ex-slave R. C. Smith faults Federals and the home guard, the latter suggesting that the narrator is a conscript, or a deserter returned to the ranks. Whatever the cause, he is cannon fodder and soon knows it.

It's grape shot and musket, and the cannons
lumber loud,
There's a many a mangled body, the blanket for
their shroud;
There's a many a mangled body left on the
fields alone,
I am a rebel soldier and far from my home.[35]

To cope with the knowledge that very likely he himself will be mangled by grapeshot or musket (or splintered trees) the soldier drinks whiskey like water and gambles compulsively: "If the ocean was whiskey, and I was a duck, / I'd dive to the bottom to get one sweet sup. / But the ocean ain't whiskey, and I ain't a duck, / So I'll play Jack o' Diamonds and try to change my luck."[36] In fact, by the end of his ordeal the rebel soldier is suffering from various conditions associated with what is now recognized as post-traumatic stress disorder: alcoholism, gambling, and other addictions, alienation from loved ones, suicidal depression, homelessness: "Oh baby, oh baby, I've told you before. / Do make me a pallet, I'll lay on the floor." "Jack o' Diamonds, Jack o' Diamonds, I known you of old, / You've robbed my poor pockets of silver and gold." "Rye whiskey, rye whiskey, rye whiskey, I cry, / If you don't give me rye whiskey I'll lay down and die."[37] This was the real-life predicament of untold thousands of Civil War soldiers by war's end and in the decades following, and "The Rebel Soldier" graphically and poignantly describes their condition and experiences.

That specificity may also explain "The Rebel Soldier's" somewhat limited circulation, particularly among African Americans. However, sometime during or just after the war, the verses describing the rebel soldier's debauchery, dissolution, and wanderlust took on a life of their own as one of America's most popular folk lyrics; under such titles as "Jack of Diamonds," "Rye Whiskey," or "Drunken Hiccoughs" the piece is still familiar to country and bluegrass fans, but it was once just as well known in Black tradition.[38] Nor is that at all surprising. Obviously, few African Americans could or would identify with "The Rebel Soldier," but "Jack of Diamonds" features themes that proved especially appealing to Black singers and songmakers in the postwar period and after: drinking, gambling, womanizing, rambling. Indeed, besides generally anticipating much twentieth-century Black music, "Jack of Diamonds" has some very specific links to later Black creations and innovations.[39] The piece was familiar to several ex-slaves, all of whom associated it with the war years. Annie Bridges (b. 1855) had learned it "as a child" in Missouri; like many texts, her version adds fiddling to the singer's sins.

> I'll tune up my fiddle
> I'll rosin my bow
> I'll make myself welcome
> Wherever I go
>
> Rye whiskey, rye whiskey,
> Ain't no friend of mine,
> He killed my old daddy,
> And he injured my mind. (Annie Bridges, b. 1855,
>   MO, 46–47)

Jim Davis (b. 1840) had played "Jack of Diamonds" as "a banjo picker in Civil War times."

> Farewell, farewell, sweet Mary;
> I'm ruined forever
> By lovin' of you;
> Your parents don't like me,
> That I do know
> I am not worthy to enter your do. (James Davis,
>   b. 1840, NC, 114)

An anonymous Georgia ex-slave gave the following:

> Farewell, sweet Mollie
> I bid you adieu;
> I am ruined for a-loving you.
> I eat when I'm hungry;
> I drink when I'm dry.
> And think on sweet Mollie,
> And sit down and cry.[40]

Finally, following his own Confederate conscription, Lafayette Price had heard soldiers sing another verse found both in "The Rebel Soldier" and "Jack of Diamonds."

> De sojers had a li'l song dey sung:
>
>> Eat w'en you're hungry,
>> Drink w'en you're dry,
>> Effen a tree don' kill you,
>> You'll live 'til you die.
>
> Dis was 'cause dey had to stan' under trees and w'en de Yankees shoot cannon dey knock off lim's and tops of trees and them under de trees might git kill' from de fallin' branches. (Lafayette Price, b. ca. 1850, LA, 3181–82)

Whether Price heard the verse as part of "Jack of Diamonds" or "The Rebel Soldier" is unknowable, but the stanza's wartime provenance is well established.[41] Arthur Palmer Hudson relayed a report of a drunk singing the verse as "if a tree don't fall on me" in the 1860s on the street of a North Mississippi town. A Tennessee variant declares "I'll eat when I'm hungry, / I'll drink when I'm dry. / If the Yankees don't kill me, / I'll live till I die."[42] During the 1860s Yankees and falling trees did in fact kill tens of thousands of Southern soldiers and civilians in Northern Mississippi and Tennessee. The detail also proved surprisingly tenacious: in twentieth-century texts of "Jack of Diamonds (Rye Whiskey)" making no other mention of the war, the singer continues to worry that a tree might kill him. Later versions occasionally mention hard times, moonshine, women, and so forth as threats, but even so, traditional texts of "Jack of Diamonds" name trees five times more often than any other danger![43] In 1948, nearly a century after the war, cowboy singer and actor Tex Ritter (1907–1974) took "Rye Whiskey" (Capitol 40084) to #9 on the Country and Western charts; in it he sings "If a tree don't fall on me, I'll live till I die."[44] Whether most listeners still understood the detail in its original sense is, of course, doubtful, but into the mid-twentieth century some Southern whites still recognized "Jack of Diamonds" as a Civil War song.[45] By then, Blacks had usually recomposed the piece in ways wholly obscuring its origins. In the early 1900s, Thomas Talley collected the following from an unidentified Black in Mississippi or Middle Tennessee.

> I'll eat when I'se hongry,
> An' I'll drink when I'se dry;
> An' if de whitefolks don't kill me,
> I'll live till I die.[46]

By this time Blacks were also composing their own ballads, and in fair numbers. The first began appearing in the nineteenth century's final decades, and two of the most famous—"John Henry" (Laws I 1) and "The Ballad of the Boll Weevil" (Laws I 17)—do figure in the narratives, but just barely. Gus Feaster (b. ca. 1840, SC, 52) named "John Henry," but described it as an antebellum worksong, in which case he was confused (or thinking of a different song), because the world-famous "John Henry" dates to the late 1800s.[47] John Cottonham (b. 1866, AR, child of ex-slaves, 60) briefly quoted "The Boll Weevil." His example is also interesting for his description of the Protracted Meeting Ball, a monthlong spree of dancing, eating, and drinking with "bad and rowdy songs." A *protracted meeting* was ordinarily an extended religious revival, so these profane gatherings expressly parodied religious observances (a well-established European and American custom). The reference to the boll weevil and his sporting life dates the sprees to the 1890s or after, when boll weevils entered the United States from Mexico, and when "The Ballad of the Boll Weevil" is known to have originated. The earliest text was collected from Black tenants in South Texas in 1897.[48]

"John Henry" and "The Boll Weevil" embodied a uniquely American ballad type that emerged in this very period: the blues ballad, which recalled the chronological narrative technique of Anglo-American ballads while anticipating the nonlinear, associational approach of African American blues (a still later development).[49] Composed by both Blacks and whites (the earliest known instances are actually Anglo-American), blues ballads were transmitted orally, of course, occasionally in print. Unlike earlier ballads, however, in performance blues ballads were usually accompanied instrumentally (banjos and guitars being most common), employing a range of new vocal and instrumental styles then sweeping the South. Eventually too, blues ballads found a home in a mass medium actually capable of capturing and communicating those musical performances: the phonograph record. African American balladry had definitely arrived. This was all beyond the ken of most ex-slaves, however. Judging from their recollections, ballads were for them minor musical diversions occasionally overheard from whites, yet comparatively insignificant in their own repertoires. That said, their memories do provide an intriguing prelude to the Black ballad-making that would explode in the late 1800s. First, however, there was a war.

THE WAR

I'se gwine tell dis story on myse'f. De white chillun was a-singin' dis song:

> Jeff Davis, long an' slim,
> Whupped old Abe wid a hick'ry limb.

> Jeff Davis is a wise man, Lincoln is a fool,
> Jeff Davis rides a gray, an' Lincoln rides a mule.

I was mad anyway, so I hopped up an' sung dis one:

> Old Gen'l Pope had a shot gun,
> Filled it full o' gum,
> Killed 'em as dey come.

> Called a Union band,
> Make de Rebels un'erstan'
> To leave de lan',
> Submit to Abraham.[1]

Old Mis' was a-standin' right b'hin' me. She grabbed up de broom an' laid it on me. She made *me* submit. I caught de feathers, don't you forgit it. I didn't know it was wrong. I hear'd de Niggers sing it an' I didn' know dey was a-singin' in dey sleeves. I didn' know nothin' 'bout Abe Lincoln, but I hear'd he was a-tryin' to free de Niggers an' my mammy say she want to be free. (Susan Snow, b. 1850, AL, 138–39, orig. emphasis)

[Jimmie Green declares] de history books is wrong. 'Twas Abe Lincoln an' Jeff Davis dat met under de ole apple tree. Lincoln stuck a shotgun in Jeff Davis' face an' yelled, "Better surrender, else I shoot you an' hang you." Davis tole him, "Yessir, Marse Lincoln, I surrender." An' de soldiers heard it, an' made up a song 'bout it. Ain't you never heard dat song? "Hang Jeff Davis to a sour apple tree." Dat's de song an' dat's what de soldiers yelled at

Lincoln to do, but he was too kind. (Jimmie Green, b. 1845, VA, 127, orig. brackets)

The Northern soldiers come to town playing Yankee Doodle. When freedom come, they called all the white people to the courthouse first, and told them the darkies was free. Then on a certain day they called all the colored people to the parade ground. They had built a big stand, and the Yankees and some of our leading colored men got up and spoke, and told the Negroes: "You are free now. Don't steal. Now work and make a living. Do honest work, make an honest living to support yourself and your children. No more masters. You are free." Eugene said when the colored troops come in, they sang:

> Don't you see the lightning?
> Don't you hear the thunder?
> It isn't the lightning,
> It isn't the thunder,
> But its the button on
> The Negro uniforms!

The slaves that was freed, and the country Negroes that had been run off, or had run away from the plantation, was staying in Augusta in Guv'ment houses, great big ole barns. They would all get free provisions from the Freedmen's Bureau, but people like us, Augusta citizens, didn't get free provisions, we had to work. It spoiled some of them. When the small pox come, they died like flies [crossed out in original] hogs, all over Broad Street and everywhere. (Eugene Wesley Smith, b. 1852, GA, 234–35)

The American Civil War held an obvious interest for slaves, who were generally aware that they (not "states' rights") were the true cause, and that the war was in fact a fight for their freedom. Beyond that, their experiences differed widely. Some were forced to confront the conflict firsthand. Others knew the war only through partisan rumor, folksong, and legend.

Fig. 22.1. "The War in Mississippi—The 1st Mississippi Negro Cavalry Bringing into Vicksburg Rebel Prisoners Captured at Haines' Bluff." From a sketch by Frederic B. Schell. Mid-Manhattan Library Picture Collection, New York Public Library.

I wuz nine when de war commence. Durin' de war an' I wuz workin' in de fiel', long wid de fifty or sixty other slaves. Dar wuzn't nary a Yankee track made in our section, an' we ain't knowed much 'bout de war.... No mam, we ain't liked Jeff Davis, but we did like Mr. Lincoln. I 'members a verse uv a song dat we sung durin' de first uv de war. It goes dis way.

> Jeff Davis is a rich man,
> Lincoln is a fool,
> Davis rides a big fat horse,
> Lincoln rides a mule.
> Knick knack dey say
> Walk ole Georgia row. (Tom Wilcox, b. 1856, NC, 377–78)

He said the colored people did not know much about Jeff Davis or Abraham Lincoln except what they heard about them. All that he remembered was a song that his Missus used to sing:

> Jeff Davis rides a big gray horse,
> Lincoln rides a mule;

Jeff Davis is a fine old man,
And Lincoln is a fool. (George Woods,
    b. ca. 1842, SC, 250)

Just 'bout the close of the war I got hold of a song I thought was pretty and was allus singing it, but didn't know what it meant. It went like this:

Old River ain't you sorry as you can be
We go marching home, we go marching home
Cause we hung Jeff Davis to a sour-apple tree.

I went through the house singing it one day and Mistress heard me and hollered, "Lucy, hush your singing that song." I had a good voice and she allus like to hear me sing so I didn't know till I was grown why she made me hush singing it. I found out it was a Yankee soldier song they sung after the surrender at the Battle of Mansfield. (Lucy Thomas, b. 1851, LA, 3804)

Thomas's slaveholder may have mainly objected to disparaging Jeff Davis; the Battle of Mansfield (Sabine Crossroads) (April 8, 1864) was a Confederate victory during the Union army's unsuccessful Red River Campaign, probably explaining the "Old River" in the song text.[2] The mention of surrender refers to the unusually high number of Union prisoners taken at Mansfield; apparently those Yankee prisoners (or their Confederate captors) sang this song afterwards in mockery or jest, a well-established custom. Griffin Frost was a member of the Missouri State Guard (Confederate), taken prisoner in Arkansas in 1862, paroled, then captured again in 1863, after which he spent the rest of the war in a Union prison at St. Louis. There he authored a memoir describing his confinement: "The Yankee officers are quite sociable, they call on us for a song, we give them 'Old John Brown'; they reply with 'We'll hang Jeff Davis on a sour apple tree,' &c."[3] The exchange was especially pointed, since these two items share a tune and many of the same words; frequently they are simply different verses in the same song.

Fig. 22.2. Lucy Thomas, ex-slave, Marshall, TX. December 4, 1937. Portraits of African American ex-slaves from the US Works Progress Administration, Federal Writers' Project slave narratives collection, Library of Congress.

There is no question, moreover, that the ex-slaves' memories were entirely accurate, and that soldiers and civilians North and South sang incessantly throughout the war. On April 26, 1863, an English envoy to the Confederacy, Sir Arthur James Lyon Fremantle, "spent a very agreeable evening" dining with Confederate officers in San Antonio. "One of the officers sang the abolition song, 'John Brown,' together with its parody, 'I'm bound to be a soldier in the army of the South,' a Confederate marching-song, and another parody, which is a Yankee marching song, 'We'll hang Jeff Davis on a sour-apple tree.'"[4] In 1865 J. Clement French described emancipated slaves in Charleston performing "John Brown's Body" and "Hang Jeff Davis," accompanied by a "shout" or "'breakdown' dance."[5] Of contraband Union army recruits training in Georgia, a New York Times correspondent wrote: "a large part of the exercises seem to consist of singing the celebrated song in which it is promised to hang Jeff. Davis on a sour apple tree, etc."[6] Following the fall of Confederate capital Richmond, former slaves, Union soldiers, and other supporters celebrated the Fourth of July in Davis's former residence. "We ate, we drank, we made speeches and cheered sentiments, we sang the rankest abolitionism under the portals of the traitor, and there were those who sung 'We'll Hang Jeff. Davis on a Sour Apple Tree.' "[7]

For soldiers, civilians, and slaves alike, the Civil War was a singing, musical war. In the pattern of premodern conflicts globally, combatants and noncombatants made music and vocalized even in the midst of conflict, chaos, and carnage.

> I was just about eleven years of age when Sherman's Brigade went marchin' through Georgia. It looked like a million men and maybe there was that many; I don't know. The soldiers wore blue jackets with brass buttons, and there was dead and dyin' men all over the roads and the fields—everywhere you went you saw them—and blood was just a runnin'. The soldiers sang "Yankee Doodle Dander," but I don't see how they could sing or have music when dead was all around—husbands and fathers and sons gone from they loved ones. Maybe they were just tryin' to keep up courage. (Frances Lewis, b. 1854, GA, 154)

Soldiers sang while recruiting, mustering, and drilling; on the march, the mount, or the rails; on parade or maneuver; in camp and on sentry duty; during furloughs on city streets and in restaurants, saloons, and brothels; even on battlefields. "We could hear soldiers singin' on de trains at Cuseta goin' to de war, from our place three miles away" (Thomas Johns, b. 1847, AL, 1970). "De old master and 'most all de white men of de neighborhood, 'round 'bout us, march off to de war in 1861. One day I see them ridin' down de big road on many hosses and they wavin' deir hats and singin': 'We gwine to hang Abe Lincoln on a sour apple tree!' and they in fine spirits" (Alfred Sligh, b. 1837, SC, 92).

> Now den, jus' below Marster Ellis's plantation, der waz a army camp. I's don' know whut de name of it waz, but I guess der waz over 1000 soldiers in dis camp. We'ns hear 'em shout, "March, Halt, March,

Fig. 22.3. Millie Williams, ex-slave, Fort Worth, TX. June 26, 1937. Portraits of African American ex-slaves from the US Works Progress Administration, Federal Writers' Project slave narratives collection, Library of Congress.

> Halt." It waz jus' lak dat all day long. We'ns see 'em ride by de plantation wid a big sword by der side. Der waz a little song dey sung,
>
> > Lincoln's not satisfied,
> > He wants to fight again,
> > All he's got to do,
> > Is hustle up his men. (Millie Williams, b. 1851, TX, 4115)

The men who signed up to go as volunteers were given their uniforms and the officers who had come from headquarters to organize and drill such men soon called them to form a line. A Mr. Zeb Patrick was placed head as drummer, a Mr. Thomas Huff (old Elsie informed me that Mr. Huff was my husband's father) was placed on a nearby stand to fiddle and a Mr. Bill Cranford was assigned to play the flute. At the officer's command the drummer threw back his head and proudly stepped forward with the ratatat-tat, the men clad in their crisp new uniforms swung into motion and the officer's call of, "Forward, left, right," could be heard above the clank of the guns. When the marching slowed up the whole crowd would sing:

> We will keep our niggers all at home,
> To raise our cotton and our corn,
> We will show them (meaning Yankees) to the
> cannons mouth,
> They cannot come it on [deceive, exploit] the
> South. (Elsie Posey, b. ca. 1840, MS, 1736–37,
> int. Ruby Huff, orig. parentheses)

I recollects clearly when Marse Young's sons and all de white boys old enough around wuz gettin' ready to go to war. I members seein' the major, his sons and others in de neighborhood ridin' away to war on dere fine horses. One of dere war songs went like dis:

> De Louisiana Tigers bound to win.
> De Mississippi Rifles bound to win.
> Fly, ball, fly,
> I'd rather be a Rebel
> To pull de Rebel triggah
> Dan be a dirty Yankee
> And fight to free de niggah.
> Off for Richmond so early in de mornin',
> Off for Richmond I hear de Yankee say. (John I.
> White, b. 1855, SC, 484)

When the cannons went to popping the folks went arunning—hard to tell who run the fastest, the whites or the blacks! Almost the town was wiped out.[8] Buildings was smashed and big trees cut through with the cannon balls. And all the time the Yankee drums was a-beating and the soldiers singing:

> We'll hang Jeff Davis on a sour apple tree,
> As we go marching on! (John White, b. 1816,
> TX, 326–27)

A Union veteran of First Bull Run (First Manassas) (July 21, 1861) recalled Federal troops' initial success in the battle (they were ultimately routed). "The next thing I remember was the order to advance, which we did under a scattering fire; we crossed the turnpike, and ascending a little way, were halted in a depression or cut in the road which runs from Sudley's ford. The boys were saying constantly, in great glee: 'We've whipped them.' 'We'll hang Jeff Davis to a sour apple tree.' 'They are running.' 'The war is over.'"[9]

Opposing armies sang for or with one another. Slaves especially recalled soldiers singing as they marauded, commandeered, and looted. "The [Confederate] sojers used to pass and all the whoopin' and hollerin' and carryin' on you ain't never heard the likes. They hollers, Who-oo-oo-oo, Old Man Denman, hows' your chickens? And they chunks and throws at them til' they cripples them up and can put them in the bags for cookin'. Old Man Denman cussus at them something powerful" (Julia Frances Daniels, b. 1848, TX, 1024). "I seed the Yankees come through. I seed that. They come in the time old master was gone. He run off—he run away. He didn't let 'em git him. I was a little child. They stayed there all day breaking into things. . . . The soldiers tickled me. They sung. The white people's yard was just full of them playing 'Yankee Doodle' and 'Hang Jeff Davis on a Sour Apple Tree'" (Evelina Morgan, b. ca. 1855, NC, 136).

I member when de Yankees came ter my mother's house on de McKnight plantation near Louisburg an' dey went inter her things. When de Yankees came down my brother Buck Perry drug me under de bed and tole me to lie still or de Yankees would ketch me. I member de sweet music dey played an' de way dey beat de drum. Dey come right inter de house. Dey went inter her chist; they broke it open. Dey broke de safe open also. Dey took mother's jewelry. But she got it back. Missus went ter de captain an' dey give back de jewelry. (Celia Robinson, b. ca. 1855, NC, 217–18)

I wuzn't more dan five years ole when de yankees burnt Mister Jacob Thompson's fine house, but I remember well seein' dem, an' I have heared my gran' mammy tell how dey raided hit. . . . Dey didn't hav' no bizness to take Miss Sallie's bes' homespun blankets, an' put 'em on dere hosses fer saddle-blankets, an' dey tuk her fine silk dresses an' put dem on deyselves wid hoop skirts an' all, an' den dey hopped on dey hosses an' rid away, whoopin' an' hollerin' an' singin'—

> Yankee Doodle dandy
> Buttermilk and brandy.

I didn't know no better dan to think hit wuz funny, an' I tho't dey wuz jus' havin' some fun, an' I laughed at dem; I couldn't understand why ever'body wuz cryin'. (Joanna Thompson Isom, b. ca. 1858, MS, 1095–96)[10]

Civilians sang their soldiers off to war, then sang to raise homefront spirits or fan partisan flames at rallies and fund drives, in parlors and cabins, at funerals, and in endless commiseration and grief. "When the husbands and brothers and sweethearts were gone to war the white ladies would sing. Annie Ellis and Mag Thomas would sing these pitiful songs. 'Adieu my friends, I bid you adieu, I'll hang my heart on the willow tree and may the world go well with you'" (Hattie Rogers, b. 1859, NC, 230).[11] "My mistress was a good Christian woman. . . . Her house, durin' de war, always had some sick or wounded soldier. I 'member her brother, Zed, come home wid a leg gone. Her cousin, Theodore, was dere wid a part of his jaw gone. My mistress could play de piano and sing de old songs" (Adeline Jackson, b. ca. 1849, SC, 3).

Then the war come. I heared them talking 'bout it and the Second and Third Infantry Cavalry camped on the place before they go off East. The people come from fur and near. I seen them when they went off. They was thousands of sojers. They went off singing, "Goodbye mother; goodbye sister. Farewell, farewell." Lots of people weeped. Then they got to singin' war songs. (Lu Perkins, b. ca. 1850, MS, 3060)

Us see lots of tents out by Liberty and dey say it sojers. I tag long wid de big boys, dey sneaks out de spades and digs holes in de prairie in de knolls. Us plannin' to live in dem holes in de knolls. When dey say de Yankees is comin' I sho is 'fraid and I hear de cannons say, "Boom, boom," from Galveston to Louisiana. De young white missy, she allus sing de song dat go:

> We are a band of brothers, native to de soil,
> Fightin' for our liberty with treasure, blood,
>   and toil.
> And when us rights was threaten', de cry rise
>   near and far,
> Hurrah for the Bonnie Blue Flag what bears a
>   single star. (John Price, b. ca. 1860, TX, 199)

Children's singing games have always imitated marching or mounted soldiers and were adapted accordingly. "We'se had play songs such as 'The Old Gray Horse Came Tearing Through The Wilderness,' and 'When Sherman was Marching Through Georgia He Was Fought a Thousand Strong'" (Steve Jones, b. 1849, SC, 2141).

De Yankees stays around dar fer a little while, an' dey gathers rations, den dey goes atter [Confederate General Joseph] Wheeler. We uster sing a song 'bout Wheeler's Cavalry but I only 'members dat it went lak dis:

> Wheeler's Cav—al—ry,
> Marchin' on de battlefield
> Wheeler's Cav—al—ry,
> Marchin' on de battlefield.

It wuz really a game we played, while we marched an' pranced an' beat on tin pans. De missus ain't carin' case we is bein' true ter de south she thinks. Shucks we doan care nothin' 'bout Wheeler 'cept what we hyar, an dat ain't so good. We doan keer 'bout de Yankees nother, case we is skeered of dem. (Emma Stone, b. ca. 1860, NC, 325–26)[12]

Soldiers and civilians also sang for one another. "Dey [Federal soldiers] larn't us a song: 'If I had ole Abe Lincoln all over dis world, but I know I can't whip him; but I fight him 'till I dies.' Dey low'd 'we freeded you alls'" (Gus Feaster, b. ca. 1840, SC, 45). "When de Yankee sojers march by one day to de Five Forks, dat we hide, b't some didn't run, an' when de sojers saw dem pore creeturs dey jess emptied dere 'sacks o' all de eatin's dey had. 'Here! take dis!' dey kep' a shoutin', an' off dey went so happy, a singin' 'Old John Brown.'"[13] In a widespread ritual of defeat, humiliation, and subjugation, Southern civilians but also slaves were often compelled to perform for Federal troops at gunpoint. "When de Yankees come . . . de fust thing they ask, was: 'You got any wine?' They search de house; make us sing: 'Good Old Time 'Ligion.'; put us to runnin' after de chickens and a cookin'. When they leave they burnt de gin house and everything in dere. They burn de smokehouse and wind up wid burnin' de big house" (Anne Broome, b. ca. 1850, SC, 105–6).

The war was an absolute boon for minstrelsy, music publishing, and brass band music. Considering the impetus the war gave brass bands, it is no exaggeration that ragtime and jazz would not have happened the way they did without the Civil War. "The first band of music I ever herd play the Yankees wuz playin' it. They were playin' a song, 'I am tired of seeing de homespun dresses the southern women wear'" (Hannah Crasson, b. 1853, NC, 193). "I member when de war come through. Oh dem drum; I nebber hear such a drum in my life! De people like music; dey didn't care nothing bout de Yankees, but dem bands of music!" (Tena White, b. ca. 1845, SC, 196).

I 'members de day well when Marster told us was free. I was glad and didn't know what I was glad 'bout. Den 'bout 200 Yankee soldiers come and dey played music right dar by de roadside. Dat was de fust drum and fife music I ever heared. Lots of de Niggers followed 'em on off wid just what dey had on. None of our Niggers went and lots of 'em stayed right on atter freedom. (Julia Bunch, b. 1853, SC, 158–59)

Bugles, fifes and drums, and brass bands coordinated marches and troop movements, identified friend and foe on smoke-filled battlefields, and, in the absence of wireless electronics, signaled and messaged. Afterward they paid tribute to the dead. Experienced horn players, fifers, and drummers were suddenly in demand in both armies, but even soldiers with little or no experience—including contraband recruits and conscripts—might be pressed into marching bands. "When the Yankees come to Atlanta they just forced us into the army. . . . I used to be in a brass band. I like a brass band, don't make no difference where I hear it" (Tom Windham, b. 1845, GA, 210, 211). "Papa went to the War. He could blow his bugle and give all the war signals" (Nancy Anderson, b. ca. 1870, child of ex-slaves, MS, 50). "When he was fourteen years old he did Guard Duty for the Rebels and when he was about fifteen years old the Union soldiers came by and wanted him to go with them as a drummer boy. But he didn't go with them" (Joseph Allen, b. 1851, KY, 2).

I was a drummer in the Civil War. I played the little drum. The bass drummer was Rheuben Turner. I run off from home in Drew County. Five or six of us run off here to Pine Bluff. We heard if we could get with the Yankees we'd be free, so we run off here to Pine Bluff and got with some Yankee soldiers—the twenty-eighth Wisconsin. Then we went to Little Rock and I j'ined the fifty-seventh colored infantry. I thought I was good and safe then. (John Young, b. ca. 1845, AR, 257)

Mack allways liked music. So when he ran away and got with the "Yankees" he was taught to blow the bugle, this he played thruout the time he spent with the Union army. He never carried a gun. Today Mack still looks like a man around seventy five altho he is much older (does not know age) but for years he has played his horn and taken an active part in the May 30th Memorial Services at the National Cemetary Celebration [in Vicksburg].

"The reason I ran away to the Yankees says Mack is because I wanted to be free, I wont talk

Fig. 22.4. "Band of 107th U.S. Colored Infantry." Arlington, VA, November 1865. Photo by William Morris Smith. Civil War Photograph Collection, Library of Congress, Prints and Photographs Division. Note that the men are holding books in their left hands, presumably musical scores.

of slavery, it is too long past.... If any one wants to know what I did in the Army tell them I blew the horn. And I don't talk to nobody about what went on in the Army, it was a secret then and to me it is a secret now." (Mack Henderson, b. unk., MS, 972–73)

Off the battlefield, military bands gave concerts and parades and serenaded civilians and fellow soldiers. "The Yankees done us no harm. They done all right in Raleigh. They did not take nothing around home. They put out guards around the homes by the time they got in. We were not afraid of 'em, none of us children, neither white nor colored; they played such purty music and was dressed so fine. We run after the band to hear 'em play" (Catherine Williams, b. 1851, NC, 382–83). "Whar de Buena Vista schul ez hit uster be a Yankee soldiers Barrick. Eber mawnin' dey hadder music. We chilluns would go on de hill, (whar the bag mill ez now) en listen ter dem. I member a black hoss de soldiers had, dat ef you called 'im Jeff Davis he would run you" (Frances Batson, b. ca. 1850, TN, 1, orig. parentheses). "De Yankees played songs o' walkin' de streets of Baltimore an' walkin' in Maryland. Dey really played it. Dey slaughtered cows and sometimes only et de liver. I went to de camp atter dey lef' an' it wuz de awfulest stink I ever smelled in my life" (Parker Pool, b. 1851, NC, 190). Pool quotes the first stanza of "Maryland! My Maryland" (James Rider Randall, 1861), which expressed Southern outrage at the Union occupation of Maryland (a slave state that never seceded): "Avenge the patriot gore / That flecked the streets of Baltimore, / And be the battle queen of yore, / Maryland! My Maryland!" The tune (aka "O Tannenbaum") became a favorite with brass bands of both armies. "Maryland! My Maryland!" also became the state song of Maryland.[14]

Florida ex-slave Willis Williams recalled that after the war, Tallahassee was occupied

> by a colored company; the 99th infantry. Their duty was to maintain order within the town. An orchestra was with the outfit and Willis remembers that they were very good musicians. A Negro who had been the slave of a man of Tallahassee was a member of the orchestra. His name was Singleton and his former master invited the orchestra to come to his house and play for the family. The Negroes were glad to render the service, went, and after that entertained many white families in their homes. (Willis Williams, b. 1856, FL, 352)

Fiddles and banjos were played in camp but even on the move or on the march. "I sho hear dem guns at Fort Sumter dere an I remembers when dem soldiers come through dis way dat de elements was blue as indigo bout here. Had parade bout five miles long wid horses dancin bout en fiddles just a playin" (Hector Godbold, b. 1850, SC, 147). "I was there when the Yankees come through. That was in slave time. They marched right through old man Madden's grove. They were playing fifes and beating the drums. And they were playing a fiddle. Yes sir, they were playing the fiddle too. It must have been the fiddle; it sounded just like one. The soldiers were all just a singin'" (Perry Madden, b. ca. 1858, AL, 44).

Talk 'bout being brave. De bravest thing I ever see was one day at Ashepoo junction. Dat was near de end of de war. Grant was standing up before Richmond; Sherman was marching tump-tump through Georgia. I was a stripling lad den and boy-like I got to see and hear everything. One day more than all, de overseer sent my pappy to Ashepoo junction to get de mail. I gone 'long wid him. Seem like I jest had to go dat day. I member dat morning well. When I got to de junction de train start to come in. What a lot of train! De air fair smoke up wid dem. They come shouting in from Charleston, bound upcountry. I stand wid my pappy near de long trestle, and see de trains rock by. One enjine in front pulling one in de back pushing, pushing, pushing. De train load down wid soldier. They thick as peas. Been so many a whole ton been riding on de car roof. They shout and holler. I make big amaze to see such a lot of soldier—all going down to die. And they start to sing as they cross de trestle. One pick a banjo, one play de fiddle. They sing and whoop, they laugh; they holler to de people on de ground, and sing out, "Goodbye." All going down to die. . . . One soldier man say in a loud voice: "Well, boys we going to cut de Yankee throat. We on our way to meet him and he better tremble. Our gun greeze up, and our bayonet sharp. Boys we going to eat our dinner in hell today." (William Rose, b. ca. 1856, SC, 48–49)

The nation's complete mobilization also expanded minstrelsy's audience exponentially. Off-duty soldiers, civilians, slaves, and contrabands flocked to theaters to see and hear minstrels, who alternately toured Union and Confederate camps and hospitals, where amateur minstrel shows staged by troops were common diversions.[15] Some of the best-known war songs were composed by minstrels, then disseminated on stage as well as in print and person-to-person.

With the war as a topic, the American folk ballad also came into its own during this period. In fact, the

Fig. 22.5. "Coming into the lines." Drawing by Edwin Forbes. Morgan Collection of Civil War Drawings, Library of Congress, Prints and Photographs Division. A contraband leads his family to freedom, his fiddle tucked safely under his arm.

Civil War was a watershed in American folk and popular music as a whole. In a country still riven by slow and unreliable communication and transportation, where most people lived and died within a few miles of their birthplaces, where literacy was low and professional entertainment little known outside cities, the conflict brought together millions of persons, Black and white, who would have otherwise had no contact, and who then spent a significant amount of their time singing and making music.

This was especially true of slaves and free Blacks, whose roles as performers were already institutionalized. Those who accompanied slaveholders to war, escaped and fled to Union lines, or enlisted in either army served as entertainers in camp. "I was Doctor Charles body 'tendant an' den I cooks for him an' nine other gen'men. Sometimes when de guns was quiet us niggers would git out an entertain de camp. Den we would all git to laughin' an' be right jolly. But mos' de time it was serious talk. We was losin' too many men" (Elodga Bradford, b. 1845, MS, 185). "Nuddah thing ah members right peertly, dem sodjahs paid us niggers whut went wid usses mahstahs ez luckey-boys aw boddy suvvants, ter sing—'hang Jeff Davis awn er sow appah tree,' an' us sunged hit kase hit soun' funny" (Addison Ingram, b. 1830, AL, 202). "De white folks

Fig. 22.6. "A breakdown in the wagoner's camp, May 6, 1863." Drawing by Edwin Forbes. Morgan Collection of Civil War Drawings, Library of Congress, Prints and Photographs Division.

'fore de war had w'at dey called 'Muster' en I would go down wid dem. I would dance en de folks would gib me money er gib me candy en durin' de war de soldiers wuz de prettiest things" (Measy Hudson, b. ca. 1850, TN, 31). "Dar was a old Abraham Lincoln song dat went like dis: 'Oh, Abe Lincoln, I'm gwine away; I'm gwine to Virginia, for to turn de Yankees back.' Some of de old niggers and some of de young ones went with deir marsters to de army. Dey acted as deir bodyguards and helped dem. Dey thought de Southern cause was right" (Maggie Wright, b. ca. 1855, SC, 318).

Just after the war, author, journalist, and Union veteran James Franklin Fitts (1839–1890) described army camps filled with fugitive slaves, where "the sound of a violin would instantly draw scores of them to the spot; and, forming a ring of ten feet diameter, they would disport themselves to the infinite delight of crowds of soldiers, gathered around to witness the performance."[16]

Some of the Civil War songs slaves sang were their own, but they did not make up many and probably most of the items they knew, picking them up instead from soldiers, slaveholders, or other whites. "There wasn't no fightin' in Union County but I 'member when the Yankees was goin' through and singin' / 'The Union forever, hurrah, boys, hurrah / We'll rally 'round the flag, boys / Shouting the battle cry of freedom.' (She sang this—ed.)" (Katie Arbery, b. 1857, AR, 64, orig. parentheses). "De young white missy, she allus sing de song dat go: / We are a band of brothers, native to de soil, / Fightin' for our liberty with treasure, blood, and toil" (John Price, b. ca. 1860, LA, TX, 199). "When I was three years old I remember hearing this song. 'Old Beauregard and Jackson came running down to Manassas, I couldn't tell to save my life which one could run the fastest, Hurray boys, hurray!'" (Hattie Rogers, b. 1859, NC, 230–31).[17] "He said that he had heard that the Yankees taught the song to the Negroes. / Old massa's gone away / The darkies stayed at home" (Jim Archer, b. ca. 1860, MS, 75).[18]

By no great mystery, slaves did not entirely understand many of these songs, since slaveholders typically restricted their knowledge of current events, and especially any news of the war and the prospect of freedom. "The slaves didn't carry news from one place to another cause they didn't have no news to carry. If the white fo'ks wanted to carry news anywhere, they put a boy on a mule and send him with it" (Ellen Payne, b. 1849, TX, 3041). "Sometimes de slaves toted news back and forth, but dey had to be mighty careful not to let de white folks hear 'bout it. Dey wuz purty close-mouf' dem days" (James Augustus Holmes, b. 1843, GA, 1045). "The attitude of the slaves toward freedom varied and as they were not allowed to discuss it, their hope was veiled in such expressions as the 'LORD will provide'" (Bryant Huff, b. unk., GA, 241).

The ex-slaves themselves often confessed they were clueless about partisan causes. "Us kids used to sing a song 'Gonna hang Jeff Davis to a sour apple tree as we go marchin' home.' I didn't know what it meant at the time" (Hannah Davidson, b. 1852, KY, 31). "I remember one time Old Joe wus singin' / 'Hang Jeff Davis ter de sour apple tree / As we go marchin' by—' / an' Marse Anderson heard him an' made him quit singin' dat song, an' sed dat wus de finest man dat ever lived" (Ann Drake, b. 1855, MS, 646–47). "The only thing I ever hearded bout Jeff Davis was a song the folks sang. The words was 'Going to hang Jeff Davis to a sour apple tree.' There was another song they sang too about 'Greely and Grant went up north.

Greely stopped Grant, wearing broadcloth'" (Ruben Fox, b. ca. 1853, MS, 778). It appears doubtful whether Ruben Fox knew much more about Ulysses S. Grant (1822–1885), Horace Greeley (1811–1872), and the 1872 US presidential election than he did about Jefferson Davis. In point of fact Grant stopped Greeley (the song's correct form): not only was Grant reelected in a landslide, but Greeley died before the Electoral College could even meet.

Yet as often as not, slaves understood their war songs more clearly, deeply, and personally than anyone. "The mistress wouldn't let any of the slaves sing about Yankee songs. They let us have church meetings but no singing about the Yankees. One slave girl got a whipping for sometimes singing about that John Brown. They tied her to a tree and the lashing bloodied up the tree all around" (Plomer Harshaw, b. 1852, MS, 170).

"Oh, Lordy, how we used to sing:

"We'll hang Jeff Davis on a sour apple tree
Hang Jeff Davis on a sour apple tree
Hang Jeff Davis on a sour apple tree
As we go marchin' on."

"Would you have done it?" we asked.
"Oh, Lordy, no ma'am. We wouldn't a harmed him, but he was a tiger. He was bad 'cause he wanted to keep us in slavery, and that was mean in him." (Hunton Love, b. ca. 1840, LA, 164, int. unk.)

The old man was pressed further and was asked if he could remember any songs the Negroes sang in Civil War days. This was the only one he could recall:

Old moster eats beef and sucks on de bone,
    And gives us de gristle—
To make, to make, to make, to make,
    To make de nigger whistle.

The song ended, accompanied by gay laughter from Lizzie [his wife]. (James Green, b. 1841, VA, 1582)[19]

Another event that brought smiles to the face of Mrs. Blakely was the day the Yankee soldiers destroyed the home of the Rev. Murray [slaveholder]. As the Yankees rifled through his belongings, an old slave man sang to the top of his voice the following words which were clearly heard by all, "Short steady, I am running from the fire, old satans mad and I'm glad." After destroying the house and everything in their sight the soldiers carried off the slaves. (Sallie Blakeley, b. ca. 1858, GA, 66)[20]

Ex-slaves were always asked about the war, and music and song supplied many of their clearest wartime memories. For quite a few, song lyrics provided almost all they knew about the American Civil War. Many pieces were originally the products of professional tunesmiths or citizen and soldier poets, circulated through broadsides, songbooks, newspapers,

Fig. 22.7. Druella Jones or Aunt Jones, Alabama, 1915. "Photograph of ex-slave Jones at the age of 94. She and two others were the only old slaves I found who were not loyal to their owners. During the war she tried to burn her master's house." Essie Collins Matthews, *Aunt Phebe, Uncle Tom and Others: Character Studies Among the Old Slaves of the South, Fifty Years After* (Columbus, OH: 1915). Slavery Images: A Visual Record of the African Slave Trade and Slave Life in the Early African Diaspora. slaveryimages.org.

and magazines. The most successful instantly entered oral tradition, however, and regularly turn up in later folksong collections. Some of these items remained forever associated with the war; others were adapted to new topics and events. Black versions especially show signs of oral transmission and recomposition—and occasionally even subversion.

Several narrators knew the Confederate anthem "The Bonnie Blue Flag" or its parody, "The Homespun Dress." The words for "Bonnie Blue Flag" (New Orleans: A. E. Blackmar, 1861) were composed by expatriate English music hall singer and Confederate soldier Harry McCarthy, who set them to a traditional Irish tune, "The Jaunting Car" (also used for "The Homespun Dress"). "De young white missy, she allus sing de song dat go . . . Hurrah for the Bonnie Blue Flag what bears a single star" (John Price, b. ca. 1860, TX, 199). The flag referred to in the song does not describe any official Confederate standard and is subject to conflicting stories. It may be the product of McCarthy's imagination, but his song was a complete sensation. By consensus, the words to "The Homespun Dress," a defiant declaration of Confederate women's willing sacrifices, were written in 1863 by Carrie Bell Sinclair, though some sources state that one Lieutenant Harrington of Alabama composed them the previous year.

> She sang for me in a quavering voice the following songs reminiscent of the war:
>
> > Homespun dresses plain I know,
> > And the hat palmetto too.
> > Hurrah! Hurrah!
> > We cheer for the South we love so dear,
> > We cheer for the homespun dresses
> > The Southern ladies wear! (Rachel Bradley,
> >   b. ca. 1830, LA, 236)

This item was itself much recomposed and parodied; ex-slave Hannah Crasson remembered hearing Union troops playing and singing, "I am tired of seeing de homespun dresses the southern women wear." ("The Jaunting Car" melody was adopted by brass bands of both armies.)[21] Caroline Smith combined "The Homespun Dress" with another Civil War–era piece, "Whole Hog or Die," aka "Root, Hog, or Die," a figure of speech for making do during difficult circumstances that perfectly matches the theme of "The Homespun Dress."[22] The line refers to the Southern custom of turning hogs loose to forage over winter, then rounding the survivors up in the spring. Many ex-slaves used the expression, most associating it with the war years. "We thought sure the Yankees would make way to take care of ex-slaves after they freed us, instead they turned us out like a bunch of hogs. We could root hog or die, for all they cared but Master he held me long years after the war" (Frank Bell, b. 1851, LA, 240). "Master calls up all the slaves and says we was free, but if we stayed and worked for him we'd have plenty to eat and wear, and if we left, it'd be root, hawg or die" (Rube Witt, b. 1850, TX, 209).

> I was a big girl durin' the war. My job was to card and spin. . . . I remember seeing the soldiers come through during the war. They come by droves stealing horses, setting the cotton on fire and taking sumpin to eat, too. Yes, I does still member the songs we sung durin' the war but I've got the asthmy and ain't got much wind for singin'.
>
> > You want to know the reason,
> > You want to know the reason,
> > You want to know the reason, I'll tell you why,
> > We'll whip them Yankees, whole hog or die.
> >
> > Hooray, Hooray, Hooray, for the Southern Girl.
> > Hooray for the homespun dress the Southern
> >   ladies wear.
> > My homespun dress is plain I know,
> > I glory in its name;
> > Hooray for the homespun dress the Southern
> >   ladies wear.
>
> I've got the asthmy honey and jest caint sing no more. (Caroline Smith, b. ca. 1850, AR, 178–79)

Texas ex-slave Maggie Whitehead Matthews combined "The Bonnie Blue Flag" and "The Homespun Dress." In another turnabout, she recalled this arrangement being performed by emancipated slaves at the first Juneteenth; accordingly, her text substitutes "colored wimmen" for the original "Southern ladies," and adds "radical girl" (meaning radical Republican, a proponent of Reconstruction). She also cleverly substitutes "Blue Bonnet" for "Bonnie Blue." (The bluebonnet is the state flower of Texas, but "bonnet" also goes well with "homespun dresses." This is likely a later detail, however, since the bluebonnet [*Lupinus subcarnous*] did not become the state flower until 1901.)

> About six months befo' freedom Parson Herron died, his boys den took care of de big plantation. We was den willed to Ferdinand and Mattie Rogan at Lockhart. . . . It was Mawster Rogan dat told us on June 19, 1865 dat we was free. I remembah den how our first Nineteenth was celebrated on June 19, 1866, and de song we sung was
>
> > De Blue Bonnet Flag
> > Hurrah fo' de Blue Bonnet Flag,
> > Hurrah fo' de homespun dresses
> > Dat de colored wimmen wear;
> > Yes I'm a radical girl
> > And glory in de name—
> > Hurrah fo' de homespun dresses
> > Dat de colored wimmen wear. (Maggie White-
> > head Matthews, b. 1857, TX, 2625)

Popularly known as "Rally 'Round the Flag," the Union anthem "The Battle Cry of Freedom" (Chicago: Root & Cady, 1862) was composed by George F. Root and debuted on the Chicago stage on July 24, 1862. In this case there is no doubt about the flag in question. The song became an absolute sensation in the North. Union troops are reported singing it constantly in camp, on the march, and in battle (there were also less successful Southern versions).[23] Ex-slaves associated the song with Northern soldiers. "W'en dey wuz fightin' at Fort Negley de cannons would jar our

house. De Soldier's ban' play on Capitol Hill, en play 'Rally 'roun' de Flag Boys, Rally 'roun de Flag'" (Patsy Hyde, b. unk., TN, 34). "Although the Heard farm was in the country the highway was very near and Mrs. Avery told of the long army of [Union] soldiers marching to La Grange singing the following song: 'Rally around the flag boys, rally around the flag, joy, joy, for freedom'" (Celestia Avery, b. 1862, GA, 26–27).

> "Yes, I'm tellin' yo' 'bout that fast as I kin. The end of the war it come jus' like that—like yo' snap yo' fingers."
> "How did you know the end of the war had come?" asked the interviewer.
> "How did we *know* it? Hallelujah broke out—
>
> > "Abe Lincoln freed the Nigger
> > With the gun and the trigger;
> > And I ain't a-goin' to get whipped any more.
> > I got my ticket,
> > Leavin' the thicket,
> > And I'm a-headin' for the Golden Shore!
>
> "Soldiers all of a sudden wuz everywhar— comin' in bunches—crossin' and walkin' and ridin'. Everyone was a-singing. We wuz all walkin' on golden clouds. Hallelujah!
>
> > "Union forever,
> > Hurrah, boys, hurrah!
> > Although I may be poor,
> > I'll never be a slave—
> > Shoutin' the battle cry of freedom." (Felix Haywood, b. 1845, TX, 1693)[24]

Katie Arbery also recalled the chorus from Union troops; Patsy Hyde knew the tune from Yankee brass bands. Minnie Davis and Fannie McCulloh Driver described the song actually being performed around flag poles by emancipated slaves.

> On the day we learned of the surrender, the Negroes rallied around the liberty flag pole that

Fig. 22.8. Felix Haywood, ex-slave, June 16, 1937, San Antonio, TX. Portraits of African American ex-slaves from the US Works Progress Administration, Federal Writers' Project slave narratives collection, Library of Congress.

they set up near where the [Athens] city hall is now. All day long they cut up and there was a song they sung that day that went something like this:

We rally around the flag pole of liberty,
The Union forever, Hurrah! Boys Hurrah!

Next morning when the Negroes got up the white folks had cut that pole down. We were mortally afraid of the Yankees when they appeared here a short time after surrender. We were afraid of the Klu Klux Klan riders too. The Negroes did act so bad; there were lots of killings going on for a long time after the war was supposed to be over. (Minnie Davis, b. ca. 1860, GA, 262)

I had a chance to go to school after slavery. School was held in a old house. De teacher's name was Britton, a nigger. He was fine to me and was good to all ob de chillun. Every Friday afternoon, Britton would make us march out ob de school and around de flag pole. We'd sing:

We will rally around de flag pole,
Union forever, hurrah, boys, hurrah!
We will rally around de flag pole,
Rally once again.

We will shout de battle cry,
We will shout fo' freedom.
We will rally around de flag pole,
Rally once again.

I was a poor child, but now I'll never be a
  slave again,
Shout to de battle cry ob freedom!
We will rally around de flag pole, once again.
But, wel' never be a slave again.

After we marched around de flag pole and done our singin' we was ready to go home till de next Monday. (Fannie McCulloh Driver, b. 1857, TX, 1235–36)

One of the war's most enduring hits, "Kingdom Coming" (Chicago: Root & Cady, 1863), was composed by Henry Clay Work (1832–1884), author of "Babylon is Fallen" (1863), "Wake Nicodemus" (1864), "Marching Through Georgia" (1865), "My Grandfather's Clock" (1876), and other minstrel hits. It was introduced to the public by the Christy Minstrels in Chicago on April 23, 1862, and published early the following year, instantly catching on in the North. Related from the perspective of a plantation slave, the piece most humorously describes a slaveholder fleeing in panic at the Union army's approach. Federal troops especially liked the song. Jim Archer "had heard that the Yankees taught the song to the Negroes" (Jim Archer, b. ca. 1860, MS, 75). Ex-slave Jacob Stroyer (1846–?) described assembled freedmen performing it in Columbia, South Carolina, in Spring 1865; Vance Randolph cites an 1889 account of Black Union troops singing "Kingdom Coming" as they marched into Richmond, the fallen Confederate capital.[25] It was also current on plantations. Elijah Green remembered performing the piece mockingly behind his slaveholder's back; Lorenza Ezell insisted that his uncle and other slaves had actually composed it.

Durin' the seven days fight the battle got so hot 'til Mr. William Jones made his escape. . . . He went up in the attic an' stay' there 'til the war was end'. I carry all his meals to him an' tell him all the news. Master show a frighten' man; I was sorry for him. That battle at Richmond, Virginia was the wors' in American history. . . .

One song I know I use to sing to the slaves w'en master went 'way but I wouldn't be so fool as to let him hear me. What I kin 'member of it is:

Master gone away
But darkies stay at home,
The year of jubilee is come
An' freedom will begun. (Elijah Green, b. 1843, SC, 196, 197)[26]

W'en Genr'l Sherman come 'cross de Savannah Riber in Sou'f Car'lina, some of his sojers come right 'cross us plantation. All de neighbors hab brung dey cotton and stack it in de thicket on de Lipscomb place. Sherman' men fin' it and sot it on fire. Dat cotton stack was big as a li'l co'house (courthouse) and it was two mont's a burnin'.

My ol' marster run off and stay in de woods a whole week w'en Sherman' men come t'rough. He didn' need to worry 'cause us tek care of eb'ryt'ing. Dey was a funny song w'at us mek up 'bout him runnin' off in de woods. I know it was mek up 'cause my uncle hab a han' in it. It went like dis:

W'ite folks hab you seed ol' marster
Up de road wid he mustache on?
He pick up he hat and he lef' real suddent
And I b'leeb he's up and gone.
    (Chorus)
Ol' marster run away
And us darkies stay at home

Fig. 22.9. "The Burning of Columbia, South Carolina, February 17, 1865." Engraving from a sketch by William Waud. *Harper's Weekly* 9 (April 8, 1865): 217. Library of Congress, Prints and Photographs Division. In the lower right foreground, two Federal soldiers flourish looted liquor bottles: one is singing and dancing while a companion claps and sings along; to the right of them a second tippler is singing to (or toasting) a line of fleeing women with small children in tow.

It mus' be now dat de Kingdom's comin'
And de year ob Jubilee.

He look up de ribber and he seed dat smoke
W'er de Lincoln gunboats lay
He big 'nuff and he ol' nuff and he orter know
    better
But he gone and run away.
    (Repeat chorus)
Now dat overseer want to give trubble,
And trot us 'roun' a spell,
But we lock him up in de smokehouse cellar
Wid de key done throwed in de well.
    (Repeat chorus)
    (Lorenza Ezell, b. ca. 1850, SC, 1323–24,
        orig. parentheses)[27]

Work followed the success of "Kingdom Coming" with "Babylon Is Fallen" (Chicago: Root & Cady, 1863). Set to the same tune, it describes Black Union soldiers on the march in nothing less than apocalyptic terms, underscored by the allusion to Revelation: "And there followed another angel, saying Babylon is fallen, is fallen, that great city, because she made all nations drink of the wine of the wrath of her fornication"

(Revelation 14:8; also see 18:1–2). Of the two compositions, "Babylon Is Fallen" was the preferred marching song of Black regiments.[28] All of the ex-slaves giving examples recalled the piece from Black troops. Harriett Gresham associated it with the Federal occupation of Charleston and performances by her future husband's regimental band. Eugene Wesley Smith remembered that white Union troops entered Augusta playing "Yankee Doodle," while Black soldiers came in singing "Babylon Is Fallen." William L. Bethel had learned the song during his own military service.

> At the age of about 18 years I went to Bristow, Virginia, enlisted in the Army, and then I went to Richmond, where we went over breast works. One of our favorite songs was: "Look over in the valley, don't you see it lighten [lightning], looks like we are going to have a storm, but altho you are mistaken, 'tis the darky soldier's buttons shining on the uniform." After surrender we went to Raleigh, North Carolina, where we mustered out. (William L. Bethel, b. 1844, NC, 60)

William Patterson remembered another famous marching song, and one of the war's most enduring legends. On May 10, 1865, Confederate President Jefferson Davis was captured by Federal cavalry at Irwinsville, Georgia. Hoping to slip away unrecognized, he had thrown his wife's shawl over his head, but stories that he was dressed completely in woman's clothing (including undergarments) immediately took hold North and South. "I doan think much of Mr. Jeff Davis. Dey used to sing songs uv hanging him to a sour apple tree. Dey say he libed a long time atter de war dressed like a 'oman, he wuz so skeered" (Sarah Harris, b. 1861, NC, 378). Newspapers hawked the story, which spread word-of-mouth as well; wartime hitmakers Henry Tucker and George Cooper rushed out "Jeff in Petticoats" (New York: William Pond, 1865). Decades later the tale was still circulating.[29]

> Sherman's army came through there [Houston Co., GA] looking for Jeff Davis, and they told me that they wasn't fightin' any more,—that I was free. They said, "You ain't got no master and no mistress." They et dinner there. All the old folks went upstairs and turned the house over to me and the cook. And they et dinner. One of them said, "My little man, bring your hat 'round now and we are going to pay you," and they passed the hat 'round and give me a hat full of money. I thought it wasn't no good and I carried it and give it to my old mistress, but it was good. They asked me if I had ever seen Jeff Davis. I said "No." Then they said, "That's him sittin' there." He had on a black dress and a pair of boots and a mantilla over his shoulders and a Quaker bonnet and a black veil.
>
> They got up from the dining table and Sherman ordered them to "Recover arms." He had on a big black hat full of eagles and he had stars and stripes all over him. That was Sherman's artillery. They had mules with pots and skillets, and frying pans, and axes, and picks, grubbing hoes, and spades, and so on, all strapped on these mules. And the mules didn't have no bridles, but they went on just as though they had bridles. One of the Yanks started a song when he picked up his gun.

> Here's my little gun
> His name is number one
> Four and five rebels
> We'll slay 'em as they come
> Join the ban'
> The rebels understan'
> Give up all the lan'
> To my brother Abraham
> Old Gen'l Lee
> Who is he?
> He's not such a man
> As our Gen'l Grant
> Snap Poo, Snap Peter
> Real Rebel eater
> I left my ply stock
> Standin' in the mould
> I left my family
> And silver and gold

Fig. 22.10. "Jefferson Davis as an unprotected female! He is one of those rare types of humanity born to control destiny, or to accept without murmur, annihilation as the natural consequence of failure—*N.Y. Daily News*, May 15, 1865." *Harper's Weekly*. Mid-Manhattan Library Picture Collection, New York Public Library.

Snap Poo, Snap Peter
Real Rebel eater
Snap Poo, Snap Peter.

And General Sherman gave the comman', "Silence," and "Silence," roared one man, and it rolled down the line, "Silence, silence, silence, silence." And they all got silent. (Frank A. Patterson, b. 1850, NC, 279–80)

The song Patterson recalled, "Snapoo," has a long and venerable history; some elements date back several centuries to Britain, Ireland, and the Continent. It employs an Irish folk tune best known from Patrick S. Gilmore's wartime hit "When Johnny Comes Marching Home" (Boston: Henry Tolman & Co., 1863). Gilmore (1829–1892), the bandmaster of the Union army's New Orleans occupation force, attributed the melody to one of that city's Black dock workers, even misidentifying it as a traditional *Negro air*. Ed Cray has convincingly argued that what Gilmore probably heard was "Snapoo," commonly reported as an antebellum shanty.[30] During the war "Snapoo" was commonly sung by soldiers of both armies as a marching cadence. Besides Frank Patterson, ex-slave Susan Snow (b. 1850, AL, 138–39) gave a couple of stanzas, the first referring to Union general John Pope, the second (corresponding to lines 5–8 of Patterson's text) to Abraham Lincoln. Mingo White had heard another version from older slaves.

De only games dat I played when I was young was marbles an' ball. I use to sing a few songs dat I heard de older folks sing lak:

Cecess ladies thank they mighty grand,
    Settin' at de table, coffee pot of rye,
O' ye Rebel union band, have these ladies understan'
    We leave our country to meet you, uncle Sam. (Mingo White, b. unk., AL, 419)

"When Johnny Comes Marching Home" is in turn among the most parodied songs in American history. One of the earliest takeoffs was "Johnny, Come Fill up the Bowl (In Eighteen Hundred and Sixty-One)," really several parodies. Published texts began appearing in 1863 (the very year Patrick Gilmore issued the original "Johnny"), multiplying rapidly. These included both Northern and Southern versions.[31] In the twentieth century, the song was collected mainly from whites, but five ex-slaves gave four texts (Fannie Berry, Pauline Johnson and Felice Boudreaux, Sally Nealy, Tom Wilcox), their variations suggesting that print played little role.

"Johnny, Come Fill up the Bowl" provides a year-by-year account of the war's progress in the form of a drinking song. Fanny Berry gave only the usual first verse: "Lord, Lord, honey! Squeeball an' I use to sing dis song: / 'Twas 1861, the Yankees made de Rebels run, / We'll all go ston' blin', / When de Johnny's come a-marching home" (Fannie Berry, b. 1841, VA, 37). Other WPA versions count as high as 1867. Usually the refrain of "When Johnny Comes Marching Home" ("We'll all be glad / When Johnny comes marching home") is recast as a toast: "We'll all drink stone blind / Johnny, come fill up the bowl." The "hurrah, hurrah" of "Johnny Comes Marching Home" accordingly became "for bowls, for bowls," but was then reinterpreted as "footballs," "for bales," "shrew ball," "skebaugh," "pas bonne," and more. Arkansas fieldworker Bernice Bowden, who interviewed ex-slave Sally Nealy, noted with Nealy's version that

> The word "football" doesn't sound right in this song, but I was unable to find it in print, and Sally seems to think it was the right word. Sally is a very wicked old woman and swears like a sailor, but she has a remarkable memory. She was "born and bred" in Rusk County, Texas and says she came to Pine Bluff when it was "just a little pig." Says she was sixteen when the Civil War began. (Sally Nealy, b. ca. 1845, AR, 187)

As odd as it may seem, "football" shows up in sheet music as early as 1863, and in other traditional texts.[32]

FOLKLORE SUBJECTS—Songs of Civil War Days

(1)
In eighteen hundred and sixty-one
Football (?) sez I;
In eighteen hundred and sixty-one
That's the year the war begun
We'll all drink stone blind,
Johnny, come fill up the bowl.

(2)
In eighteen hundred and sixty-two
Football (?) sez I;
In eighteen hundred and sixty-two
That's the year we put 'em through
We'll all drink stone blind,
Johnny, come fill up the bowl.

(3)
In eighteen hundred and sixty-three
Football (?) sez I;

In eighteen hundred and sixty-three
That's the year we didn't agree
We'll all drink stone blind,
Johnny, come fill up the bowl.

(4)
In eighteen hundred and sixty-four
Football (?) sez I;
In eighteen hundred and sixty-four
We'll all go home and fight no more
We'll all drink stone blind,
Johnny, come fill up the bowl.

(5)
In eighteen hundred and sixty-five
Football (?) sez I;
In eighteen hundred and sixty-five
We'll have the Rebels dead or alive
We'll all drink stone blind,
Johnny, come fill up the bowl.

(6)
In eighteen hundred and sixty-six
Football (?) sez I;
In eighteen hundred and sixty-six
We'll have the Rebels in a hellava fix
We'll all drink stone blind,
Johnny, come fill up the bowl.

(7)
In eighteen hundred and sixty-seven
Football (?) sez I;
In eighteen hundred and sixty-seven
We'll have the Rebels dead and at the devil
We'll all drink stone blind
Johnny, come fill up the bowl. (Sally Nealy, b. ca. 1845, AR, 186–87, orig. parentheses)

Earlier in her interview, Nealy gave a verse not found in the text above (or any other I have seen). In it, "football" ("for bowls") becomes "by fall."

I 'member one song they sung durin' the war

The Yankees are comin' through
By fall sez I
We'll all drink stone blind
Johnny fill up the bowl. (Sally Nealy, b. ca. 1845,
    AR, 185)

Tom Wilcox's version condenses the usual countdown.

Hyar's de song do' de best I 'members it an' it wuz
sung atter de war.

Ole Confederate has done played out,
    Shrew ball, shrew ball,
Ole Confederate has done played out
    Shrew ball say I,
An' ole Gen'l. Lee can't fight no mo';
We'll all drink stone blind
Johnnies go marchin' home.

I bought me a chicken fur fifty cents,
    Shrew ball, Shrew ball,
I bought me a chicken fur fifty cents
    Shrew ball say I,
I bought me a chicken fur fifty cents
An' de son uv a bitch done jump de fence,
We'll all drink stone blind
Johnnies go marchin' home.[33]

Eighteen hundret an' sixty one
    Shrew ball, shrew ball,
Eighteen hundret an' sixty one
    Shrew ball say I,
Eighteen hundret an' sixty one
An' dat's de year de war begun
We'll all drink stone blind
Johnnies go marchin' home.

Eighteen hundret an' sixty-five
    Shrew ball, Shrew ball,
Eighteen hundret an' sixty-five
    Shrew ball say I,
Eighteen hundret an' sixty-five
De Yankees et ole Lee alive;

We'll all drink stone blind
Johnnies go marchin' home." (Tom Wilcox,
    b. 1856, NC, 379)

There is even a bilingual text (but just barely) from
sisters Pauline Johnson (née Boudreaux, b. 1853) and
Felice Boudreaux (b. 1859), Louisiana Creoles then
living in Beaumont, Texas. "In slav'ry time mos' eb'rybudy 'roun' Opelousas talk Creole. Dat w'at mek de
words hard to come sometime'. Us bofe talk better
dat way dan English" (Pauline Johnson, b. 1853, LA,
2039–40).

Us seed de bofe kindser sojers. Dey was Zouaves
dat pass on foot. Dem hab bright red dress. Den us
seed de Yankees comin' through wid dey cannon
an' de band playin'. Of all dem mens w'at come
back from de war dey's all dead now. Slightly
embarrassed at being so undignified, the two managed between them to recall one of the wartime
songs. After they began singing it they both joined
in the spirit of the thing and giggled and laughed,
seeming to enjoy their lapse from grace. The song
ran, in part:

O, de Yankee come to put de nigger free,
    Sez I, sez I "Pas boune" [pas bonne]
In eighteen-sixty t'ree,
    De Yankee git out dey gun an' say,
"Hurrah," le's put on a ball. (Pauline Johnson,
    b. 1853, Felice Boudreaux, b. 1859, LA,
    2040–41)

Many of Louisiana's Zouaves were French-speaking (white) Creoles, so if Pauline and Felice learned
this item from passing soldiers, the Zouaves would
seem likely suspects. On the other hand, *pas bonne*
(no good) could just be their misunderstanding of
"for bowls" (or "footballs," "shrew ball," and the like).

Ex-slaves also frequently mentioned soldiers
performing "Yankee Doodle" and "Dixie," ostensibly expressing partisan viewpoints: "The Southern
soldiers' song was 'Look Away Down in Dixie' and

Fig. 22.11. Felice Boudreaux and Pauline Johnson, ex-slaves, Beaumont, TX, July 3, 1937. Portraits of African American ex-slaves from the US Works Progress Administration, Federal Writers' Project slave narratives collection, Library of Congress.

the Northern soldiers' song was 'Yankee Doodle Dandy'" (Rachel Hankins, b. 1850, AL, 155–56). Actually, ex-slaves describe Northern soldiers singing and playing "Dixie" far more often than "Yankee Doodle," even if they tended to perform it as a taunt. "I know a heap o' sojus had on nice buttons an' had plumes in dere hats. Dey wus singin' an' playin' on a flute dis song, 'I wish I wus in Dixie,' an' dey went in de big house an' broke up ebery thing. Dey say to me, 'you are free as a frog,' an' dey say to my pa, 'all your chillun are free.' Dey say 'little niggers is free as a frog' an' we holler much" (Dave White, b. ca. 1842, SC, 191). "On one occasion the Yanks came to our plantation, took all the best mules and horses, after which they came to my mother's cabin and made her cook eggs for them. They kept so much noise singing, 'I wish I was in Dixie' that I could not sleep" (Charlie Pye, b. 1856, GA, 187–88). "Hannah said the Yankees came through the plantation on a Sunday. 'I'll never forget dat!' she exclaimed. 'Dey was singing Dixie. 'I wish't I was in Dixie, look away!' Dey was all dress in blue. Dey sot de gin house afire, and den dey went in de lot and got all de mules and de horses and ca'y 'em wid 'em" (Hannah Murphy, b. ca. 1857, GA, 469).

Yes, when Lee surrendered, I was hired out. De Yankees came and give all de slaves meat meal an' everything dey wanted. I went to Richmond an' stayed dar wid my Ant. Dar I stood out on de street when soldiers fit in Petersburg; soldiers was as thick as fleas. Dar was all kinds of music playin'. I never will ferget er hearin' dem soldiers sing dis "Dixie Land the land of clover. When I died I died all over. Dixie Land is the land of clover. Long as I live, I'll die in Dixie Land." Played dis music on a gra' big thing I donna what 'twas. I could smell tobacco burnin' all day. (Jennie Patterson, b. ca. 1846, VA, 220)

The days after the War—called Reconstruction days, I believe—were sure exciting, and I can "mind" a lot of things the people did, one of them a big barbecue celebration commemoratin' the return of peace. They had speeches, and music by the band—and there were a lot of soldiers carrying guns and wearing some kind of big breastplates. The white children tried to scare us by telling us the soldiers were coming to kill us little colored children. The band played "Dixie" and other familiar tunes that the people played and sang in those days. (Mary Jackson, b. ca. 1860, TX, 20)[34]

On October 2, 1859, radical abolitionist John Brown (1800–1859) attacked the Federal Arsenal at Harpers Ferry, Virginia, with a force of eighteen men including his sons and five free Blacks. He hoped thereby to incite a general slave revolt across the South but was quickly captured, tried, and hanged on December 2. The episode made Brown an archvillain to slavery's supporters but a martyr to abolitionists and slaves. "Happy Land of Canaan" most likely originated immediately following Brown's raid (it parodies the spiritual genre but does not appear to take off on any specific spiritual). The piece was popular in print as well as oral tradition, originally pro-Southern and most often attached to John Brown, but adapted to other persons and partisan issues (there are also pro-Northern versions).[35] Fannie Berry lived not far from Harpers Ferry at the time of the Raid and had heard the song from her slaveholder, as well as the legend that en route to execution Brown paused to bless a slave child in its mother's arms.[36]

> An' den come de time ole John Brown raised all dat ruckus up at Harpers Ferry, I member ole Marser comin' home an' sayin' dat on his way to de gallows ole John stopped an' kissed a little nigger chile. How come I don't 'member? Don't tell me I don't, cause I do. I don't keer if it's done been a thousin' years. I know what Marser say an' it's as fresh in my mind as it was dat day. Anyhow ole Marster started to sing dis song an' all de little nigger chillun used to sing it wid him.

> > Old John Brown come to Harper Ferry town,
> > Purpose to raise an insurrection,
> > Ole gov'nor Wise put de specks upon his eyes,
> > An' showed him de happy lan' of Canaan.

> > Old John Brown come to Harper Ferry town,
> > Purpose to steal our chickens,
> > They walked him up a slope, an' they hung him
> > > wid a rope,
> > An' showed him de happy lan' of Canaan. (Fannie Berry, b. 1841, VA, 41–42)

Henry A. Wise (1806–1876) was Virginia's governor at the time of the Harpers Ferry Raid, and played an active role in Brown's prosecution and execution. During the war that followed, Wise's political connections earned him an appointment as brigadier general in the Army of Northern Virginia. Like many "political generals," his performance was generally subpar, as remarked in other versions.

> Dese songs was 'bout de soldiers an' de war. There was one 'bout ol' General Wise what went:

> > O'l General Wise was a mighty man,
> > > And not a wise man either,
> > It took forty yards of cloth to make a uniform,
> > > To march in de happy land of Canaan.

> > Chorus:
> > Haha, ha-ha, de south light is comin',
> > > Charge boys, charge, dis battle we mus' have,
> > To march us in the happy land of Canaan.
> > > (Mingo White, b. unk., AL, 419)

There were also Northern versions. Lizzie Samuels and Edward Glenn had both learned "Land of Canaan" from Union troops. Samuels's text describes the death of the mysterious Saul Crawford, which sounds like a soldiers' inside joke. The concluding description of wartime shortages may be from a different song. Glenn recalled Union soldiers singing "Happy Land of Canaan" mockingly as they marched into the South.

> Lizzie learned this song from the soldiers:

> > Old Saul Crawford is dead,
> > And the last word is said.
> > They were fond of looking back
> > Till they heard the bushes crack
> > And sent them to their happy home
> > In Canaan.
> > Some wears worsted
> > Some wears lawn
> > What they gonna do
> > When that's all gone. (Amanda Elizabeth Samuels, b. ca. 1857, TN, 174)

> One morning I saw a blue cloud of Yankees coming down the road. The leader was waving his arms and singing:

> > Ha, ha, ha! Trabble all the day!
> > I'm in the Rebel's Happy Land of Canaan.
> > Needn't mind the weather,
> > Jump over double trouble,

I'm in the Rebel's Happy Land of Canaan.
(Edward Glenn, b. unk., GA, 349)

John Lomax's guidelines specifically recommended asking ex-slaves about Abraham Lincoln and Jefferson Davis; in a striking number of cases, the ex-slaves responded with folksongs. "I member folks singin' er song bout, 'Ole Jeff Davis T'inks He's Mighty Smart,' en de name of Abra'm Lincum wuz poplar den en folks t'ink he wuz a moughty big man" (Susie Hawkins, b. ca. 1860, NC, 355).

(Following is a song of Abraham Lincoln, she sang):

If it hadn't been for Uncle Abraham
What would we a'done?
Been down in de cotton field,
Pickin' in de sun. (Annie Bridges, b. 1855, MO, 50–51, orig. parentheses)

When war come dey come and got de slaves from all de plantations and tuk 'em to build de breastworks. I saw lots of soldiers. Dey'd sing a song dat go something like dis:

Jeff Davis rode a big white hoss,
Lincoln rode a mule;
Jeff Davis is our President,
Lincoln is a fool. (William M. Adams, b. ca. 1846, TX, 10)

More than a dozen ex-slaves recalled this last verse, sometimes by itself, sometimes in longer songs. The rhyme is indisputably a Southern white wartime creation. Ironically, the earliest example I have found (1862) was printed in the abolitionist newspaper *The Liberator*, defiantly contributed by a "Nashville rebel."[37] It can be sung to the "Jaunting Car" tune used for "The Bonnie Blue Flag" and "Homespun Dress" and may even appear in those songs. Sam Word (b. 1859, AR, 235) included it in "The Bonnie Blue Flag," Virginia Yarborough in "The Homespun Dress."

Songs? gosh fo' mighty, what next? Ise tell de words of one 'bout de wah:

No'then goods am outter date
since old Abe's blockade
Jeff Davis rides a big white hoss
Abe Lincoln rides de mule.
Jeff Davis sats in a rockin' chaiah
Lincoln sats on a stool.
Hurrah, hurrah, fo' de sunny South so dear
Three cheers fo' de homespun dress
Southland ladies wear.

Youse see 'twas hard fo' to buy store goods durin' de wah so de big ladies have to wear homespun laks de niggers use. Dats how come fo' someone to make up dat song. (Virginia Yarborough, b. ca. 1860, LA, 4299)

Textual variations are fairly limited. The butt of the rhyme (usually Lincoln) is always a fool who rides a mule, the hero (usually Davis) is a fine man, smart man, gentleman, or President who rides a fine horse, a big white horse, a gray horse, a milk white steed, and so on. Slaves sometimes reversed the roles, however.

I can't say much 'bout Abe Lincoln. He was a republican in favor of de cullud folk being free. Jeff Davis? Yeah, the boys usta sing a song 'bout 'im:

Lincoln rides a fine hoss,
Jeff Davis rides a mule,
Lincoln is de President,
Jeff Davis is de fool. (Amanda Oliver, b. 1857, MO, 231)

Old Jeff Davis was a Rebel and he rode a fine horse. Abe Lincoln come there, wid a mule. De slaves made up a song 'bout how old Abe Lincoln got hold of Jeff Davis in de army and Abe Lincoln took and road [rode] Jeff Davis' big fine horse and Jeff Davis had to ride de mule. Abe Lincoln was United

States president and Jeff Davis was de fool. (Lou Griffin, b. ca. 1840, AR, 144)

Things is all peaceful now, but the world was sure stirred up when Abraham Lincoln was elected. I remember well when they killed him. We had a song about him that went like this:

Jefferson Davis rode the milk white steed,
Lincoln rode the mule,
Jef Davis was a mighty fine man,
And Lincoln was a fool.

One of the little girls was singing that song one day and she mixed them names up. She had it that Davis was the fool. I have laughed about that a many a time. When Misses finished with her she had sure broke her from sucking eggs. (Prince Johnson, b. 1847, MS, 1175–76)

Even examples lauding Davis sometimes suggest backhanded compliments (Virginia Yarborough's text, for example, ties him to wartime shortages). Jefferson Davis was never widely popular in the Confederacy, blamed during the war for military defeats and home-front hardships, then forever scapegoated and reviled for the Lost Cause. Two other ex-slaves, Bryant Huff and George Woods, recalled a popular Confederate camp song sometimes including this stanza.

During this time masters suffered as well as their slaves, for many of their sons went gaily forth to battle and were never heard of again. Simpson Rigerson, son of "Marse" Jesse Rigerson, was lost to his parents. A younger son, who lost his right hand while "helping" feed cane to a grinder, is the only member of the family now living [because he was exempted from Civil War service and thus survived]. Sorrow did not break this slaves group and they soon learned to sing away their troubles. One song which gives some light on their attitude toward the government went as follows:

I. Jeff Davis rode the gray horse
Ole Lincoln rode the mule
Jeff Davis is the gentleman
Ole Lincoln is the fool

Chorus:
I'll lay ten dollars down
I'll count it one by one.
I'll give ten dollars to know the man
Who struck Peter Butler's son.

II. I lay down in my bed
I lay down in no dread
Conscript come and took me
And dragged me from my bed.

III. I went down a new cut road
She went down the lane
I turned my back upon her
And 'long come Liza Jane. (Bryant Huff, b. unk., GA, 241)

He said the colored people did not know much about Jeff Davis or Abraham Lincoln except what they heard about them. All that he remembered was a song that his Missus used to sing:

Jeff Davis rides a big gray horse,
Lincoln rides a mule;
Jeff Davis is a fine old man,
And Lincoln is a fool.

Another song was:

I'll lay $10 down and number them one by one,
As sure as we do fight 'em.
The Yankees will run. (George Woods, b. ca. 1842, SC, 250)

This is another war song the slaves obviously did not make, and apparently few learned to sing it, but they may have heard the piece often, since the song that I will for convenience call "Peter Butler's Son" was reportedly among the more popular items originating within the Confederate ranks.[38] Born in Georgetown, Kentucky to a slaveholding family, Basil W. Duke (1838–1916) would go on to become a prominent Confederate officer and, later, a respected author and Civil War historian distinguished by his extensive firsthand knowledge and experience. In a 1911 memoir Duke even gave a remarkable comparative description of this item and its wartime tradition.

> Every ex-Confederate must recall one such song, the most popular of all, which was raised in quaint, jingling tune whenever and wherever a half-dozen ragged rebels were gathered together.
>
> The rollicking refrain, captivating in its very absurdity, ran as follows:
>
> > "I'll lay ten dollars down,
> >   And count it up one by one.
> > Oh, show me the man, so nigh as you can,
> >   Who struck Billy Patterson."
>
> Innumerable verses were composed and sung to this refrain. The Army of Northern Virginia, the Army of Tennessee, and the Army of the trans-Mississippi had each its history rudely chronicled, as fast as made, in this rough minstrelsy. No one man knew, or could possibly have known, the whole of it, for new stanzas were constantly added. Every corps and command contributed some commemorative quatrain. The events of campaigns were told in this improvised verse as rapidly as they occurred, and thereafter were sung or recited by the rhapsodist who professed to know that much of the fragmentary epic. The wits and wags of the camp sought to make caustic criticism more effective by embodying in it lines which might be heard throughout the Confederacy.[39]

Duke was the brother-in-law of fellow Confederate General John H. Morgan (1825–1864), with whom he served, taking part in Morgan's Raid (1863) and later writing a book on the fiasco.[40] With many other exploits, following the fall of the rebel capital Richmond, Duke was among the bodyguards who escorted Jefferson Davis to safety. Aside from Duke's *Reminiscences* and the ex-slave versions, "Peter Butler's Son" survives in a mere handful of published texts, but we have every reason to accept Duke's account of its wide currency within Confederate ranks, as he was definitely in a position to know. Moreover, Duke supports his claims by quoting a dozen select verses from different theaters, battles, and campaigns, providing a virtual roster of celebrated Confederate commanders (and a few of their Union foes).[41] Most examples, however, also express the "caustic criticism" Duke acknowledges; typically too, they are quite localized and personalized, famous generals and great battles figuring mainly by allusion. Overall, "Peter Butler's Son" is less concerned with the glorious Southern Cause than the misfortunes of common soldiers who became casualties of the Confederate Officer Corps' legendary daring and risk-taking. Aside from the deadly risks and terrors of combat, and the hardships and privations of any soldier's life, capture and mistreatment by the Yankees are the most common outcomes for the singer.

> "Gen. Lee, he said, 'My soldiers,
>   You've nothing now to fear,
> For Longstreet's on the right of them
>   And Jackson's in their rear.'" . . .
>
> "Oh, Morgan crossed the river,
>   And I went across with him;
> I was captured in Ohio
>   Because I couldn't swim."[42]
>
> Old Burnside tuck me prisoner;
> He used me rough, 'tis true;
> He stole the knapsack off my back,
> And he did my blanket too.

The first verse refers to the Seven Days Battles (June 25–July 1, 1862) (a pyrrhic Confederate victory), the second to Morgan's Raid (June 11–July 26, 1863) (a costly, needless military disaster precipitated by a vainglorious commander). The third stanza is from a North Carolina text describing another Confederate thrashing; as editors Henry M. Belden and Arthur Palmer Hudson observe, "the unknown composer of this ballad was probably a soldier under the command of General Laurence O'Brien Branch, defender of New Bern, [NC], when the city was captured, on March 14, 1862, by General A. E. Burnside, after an engagement in which the Confederates lost about 578 killed, wounded, and captured."[43] Taken together, these examples also typify the song's *caustic criticisms*, expressing the common soldier's complaints, and definitely giving "some light on their attitude toward the government," as ex-slave Bryant Huff put it (Bryant Huff, b. unk., GA, 241). In Huff's version, the singer-soldier is only in his predicament because he was conscripted, and he names the person most Southerners blamed at times like this: Jefferson Davis.

Ordinary soldiers and wartime civilians seldom have unvarnished praise for their leaders, and none of the august personages singled out in this song come off particularly well. As usual, though, Jeff Davis fares worst of all. Huff namechecks the Confederate president just before a conscription officer drags the singer from bed. A Florida white text recounting yet another humiliating Confederate defeat makes similar mention (the annotations are from editor Alton C. Morris):

"I CAN WHIP THE SCOUNDREL." Text and musical notation secured From Mrs. J. E. Maynard, Micanopy, who wrote it down from firsthand knowledge of the song as it was sung in Micanopy after the Civil War. There were many more stanzas, she wrote:

The Yankees came to Baldwin;
They came up in the rear;
They thought they'd find old Abner,
But old Abner was not there.

Chorus
So lay ten dollars down,
Or twenty if you choose,

For I can whip the scoundrel
That stole old Abner's shoes.

Jeff Davis was a gentleman;
Abe Lincoln was a fool.
Jeff Davis rode a dapple gray;
Abe Lincoln rode a mule.

This Civil War song records a historical occurrence made somewhat more heroic by Florida partisanship for the Southern cause. On February 9, 1864, a contingent of the Fortieth Massachusetts Mounted Infantry, commanded by Colonel G. V. Henry, marched into Baldwin at daybreak, captured large supplies of Confederate cannon, camp equipment, turpentine, and foodstuffs, and took possession of this strategic railroad city. Colonel Henry enacted the part of the "Abe Lincoln" mentioned in the song and Captain Durham, in command of the retreating Confederate soldiers, was probably the "Jeff Davis" referred to.[44]

By slamming conscription, Huff's text is more pointed still. The slender Southern support for Davis's administration, or for any centralized governance practically vanished early in the war with the first Confederate Conscription Act. The three Conscription Acts (April 26, 1862, September 27, 1862, February 17, 1864) gradually expanded eligibility and terms of enlistment so that eventually all Southern white males between the ages of seventeen and fifty could be drafted into the Confederate army for unlimited periods. Exemptions for slaveholders and other elites outraged citizenry. Resistance and opposition were widespread and sometimes violent. Several Southern states passed laws barring enforcement, while some Southern counties attempted to secede from the Confederacy over the issue. Typically, Jeff Davis got most of the blame for conscription, the generals demanding more cannon fodder somewhat less so.[45]

I'm a sure enough Arkansas man, born in Arkansas County near De Witt. Born February 14, 1859, and belonged to Bill Word. I know Marmaduke come down through Arkansas County and pressed Bill Word's son Tom into service. I 'member one song they used to sing called the "Bonnie Blue Flag."

> Jeff Davis is our President
> And Lincoln is a fool;
> Jeff Davis rides a fine white horse
> While Lincoln rides a mule.
>
> Hurrah! Hurrah! for Southern rights, Hurrah!
> Hurrah for the Bonnie Blue Flag
> That bears a Single Star! (Sam Word, b. 1859, AR, 235. The interviewer, Mrs. Bernice Bowden, notes "the above verse was sung to the tune of 'The Bonnie Blue Flag.'")

Confederate General John S. Marmaduke (1833–1887), later Governor of Missouri (1885–1887), served in the Trans-Mississippi Theater in and around Arkansas. His division, composed mainly of Arkansas conscripts, was eventually mauled at the Battle of Mine Creek (October 25, 1864), where Marmaduke himself was wounded and captured. (Desperate for troops as the Union army threatened Little Rock, Confederate authorities in Arkansas aggressively exceeded even the Third Conscription Act's expanded mandate.)[46] Sam Word does not say whether Tom Word made it back home alive, but if so, he was among the lucky ones. Sam Word's second stanza is, of course, from "The Bonnie Blue Flag." In this context, it does not sound like an unqualified tribute either.

Then again, in some versions of "Peter Butler's Son" the singer may at length return home to the girl he left behind, or at least express that hope and intention. Appropriately, ex-slave Bryant Huff substituted a Black character—Liza Jane—for the white Georgia, Tennessee, and Kentucky girls mentioned in other texts.[47] Granted, any African American tradition for "Peter Butler's Son" was evidently slight, the two versions from the ex-slave narratives being all I have found. By no surprise, a Confederate camp song may not have appealed to most Blacks, but then this item's esoteric, topical character appears to have limited its currency outside Confederate ranks, or its relevance beyond the war years even among whites. During the war, however, it was sung across the South, at least in certain company and particular locales, and was no doubt known to other slaves.[48] And other slaves definitely sang about Jefferson Davis.

Indeed, for singing partisans on both sides, the ultimate poetic justice, and the war's ultimate goal, was to hang someone—John Brown, Abe Lincoln, but especially Jeff Davis—from a sour apple tree. "'Most all de white men of de neighborhood, 'round 'bout us, march off to de war in 1861. One day I see them ridin' down de big road on many hosses and they wavin' deir hats and singin': 'We gwine to hang Abe Lincoln on a sour apple tree!'" (Alfred Sligh, b. 1837, SC, 92). "After freedom he said the Negroes made up this song: / Hung Jeff Davis in the sour apple tree" (Sam Jordan, b. ca. 1855, AL, 201). "I's heard the niggers sing 'Gonna hang Jeff Davis to a sour apple tree'" (Willis Winn, b. 1822, LA, 205). "I 'member a song we used to sing when we was out playing. It went: Hang Jeff Davis to a sour apple tree, and we go marchin' on" (Louise Neill, b. ca. 1860, GA, 2891). "All I know bout Abraham Lincoln was dat he Abraham Lincoln en he de one cause freedom. I recollect dey used to sing song bout him, but I done forget it now. Say dey hung Abraham Lincoln on de sour apple tree or old Jeff Davis or something like dat" (Mom Jessie Sparrow, b. 1854, SC, 134).

> One thing I does 'member well, and would like to know if anyone else was there and 'members it. I went with "Miss Pinter" to see them hang John Brown, he was a "Whig"; they brought him from the Culpepper County Court House, in Virginia, and hung him to a beechwood tree, at Harper's Ferry; on the bank of the James River. Now they sing "Hung him to a sour-apple," but that ain't right. I saw it and I know. (Drucilla Martin, b. 1835, TN, 244)

There was a man in them days by the name of John Brown. We called him an underground railroad man, 'cause he'd steal the slaves and carry 'em across the river in a boat. When you get on the other side you was free, 'cause you was in a free State, Ohio. We used to sing, and I guess young folks today does too:

John Brown's Body Lies A'moulding In the Clay.

and

They Hung John Brown On a Sour Apple Tree.
(George Conrad, Jr., b. 1860, KY, 41)

They hung Jeff Davis to a sour apple tree!
They hung Jeff Davis to a sour apple tree!
They hung Jeff Davis to a sour apple tree!
While we go marching on!

Dat was de song de Yankees sang when dey marched up our house. They didn't harm us in any way. I guess de war was over den. (Martha King, b. ca. 1850, AL, 169)

All de slaves hate de Yankees an' when de southern soldiers comed by late in de night all de niggers got out of de bed an' holdin' torches high dey march behin' de soldiers, all of dem singin', "We'll Hang Abe Lincoln on de Sour Apple Tree." Yes mam, dey wuz sorry dat dey wuz free, an' dey ain't got no reason tu be glad, case dey wuz happier dan now. (Alice Baugh, b. 1873, NC, child of ex-slaves, 86)

According to my remembrance the Yankees come around and told the people they was free. I was in Alexandria, Louisiana. They told the colored folks they was free and to go and take what they wanted from the white folks. They had us all out in the yard dancing and playing. They sang the song:

They hung Jeff Davis on a sour apple tree
While we all go marching on.

It wasn't the white folks on the plantation that told us we was free. It was the soldiers their selves that came around and told us. We called 'em Yankees. (Ellen Brass, b. ca. 1855, LA, 247)

Alice Battle described a Union band playing the song as they escorted Davis to prison.

They did not see the Yankee soldiers until the day Jefferson Davis was captured. On that day, "Miss Martha" carried her children and the little darkies down to the gate to see them pass by with their captive. . . . The Yankee band began to play "Hang Jeff Davis on a Sour Apple Tree" as they passed by. Some of them, noticing the plantation smokehouse, entered and took hams and shoulders or whatever else they wanted. (Alice Battle, b. ca. 1850, GA, 43).

This item's tune is sometimes traced to "On Canaan's Happy Shore," words by William Steffe (ca. 1830–ca. 1890), frequently found in midcentury songbooks and later folksong collections. The same melody was used with many other songs, however, including the Black spiritual "We'll Camp Awhile in the Wilderness." Ex-slave Lorenza Ezell performed these items together:

Some mo' dem songs was:

We'll camp aw'ile in the wilderness,
We'll camp aw'ile in the wilderness,
We'll camp aw'ile in the wilderness,
An' den I's gwine home.[49]

Anudder was:

Say brudders will you meet me,
Say brudders will you meet me,
Say brudders will you meet me,
On Canaan's happy shore?[50]

Den dey was:

Our bodies boun' to morter and decay,
Our bodies boun' to morter and decay,
Our bodies boun' to morter and decay,
But us souls go marchin' home.

De Yankees tek day chune (tune) and mek a war hymn outn' it, (Battle Hymn of the Republic). Sherman' army sing it, but dey say:

Hang Jeff' Davis on a sour apple tree,
And den us go marchin' home. (Lorenza Ezell,
   b. ca. 1850, SC, 1320–21, orig. parentheses)

The parentheses are from interviewers Fred Dibble and Bernice Gray. Actually, it is not entirely clear that Ezell intended "The Battle Hymn of the Republic," which does share its tune with his other examples, but which was virtually unknown among Southern slaves, and was not nearly so popular among Civil War troops as the older songs that inspired it. "The Battle Hymn of the Republic" may have been a huge success in abolitionist, literary, and patriotic circles, but if the WPA narrators knew it, they gave little sign.

Author, abolitionist, and suffragist Julia Ward Howe (1819–1910) drafted the "The Battle Hymn of the Republic," probably the war's most famous song, in November 1861, publishing it in February 1862.[51] Howe always acknowledged borrowing the tune and some of her text from Black singers, but there are various stories about exactly where and how she heard them; in any case, she retained only the signature chorus "glory, glory hallelujah, as we go marching on" (a Black folk spiritual commonplace), substituting her own verses in the florid abolitionist style. Of these, only the first stanza gained any true familiarity. Overall the song remains best known for the chorus that Howe borrowed, while in oral tradition it exists mainly in parodies.[52] Conceivably some ex-slave texts take off on Howe's composition, but more likely not. Mingo White gave such one example, mocking Alabama cavalry commander Phillip Roddey (1826–1897).

There was a song 'bout General Roddy too.

Run ol' Roddy through Tuscumbia, through
   Tuscumbia,
We go marchin' on.

Chorus:
Glory, glory hallelujah, glory, glory hallelujah,
Glory, glory hallelujah as we go marchin' on.

Ol' Roddy's coat was flyin', ol' Roddy's coat
   flyin' high
Twell it almost touch de sky, we go marchin' on.
   (Mingo White, b. unk., AL, 419)

Exactly what song Howe heard is also open to question. She always named the piece she borrowed as "John Brown's Body," confirming that at the very least it included the verse "John Brown's body lies a-mouldering in the grave [clay, sod, and so on]." However, there is also an excellent possibility Howe's source described hanging someone (most likely Jeff Davis or Brown himself) from a sour apple tree. In point of fact, "John Brown's Body" and "Hang Jeff Davis" are not necessarily separate songs, as sometimes implied; more often they are just two verses in the same song, probably filled out with other wandering stanzas. "We used to sing, and I guess young folks today does too: / John Brown's Body Lies A'moulding In the Clay. / and / They Hung John Brown On a Sour Apple Tree" (George Conrad Jr., b. 1860, KY, 41). As the scapegoating of Jeff Davis intensified, he became the preferred victim even in the South, but in all probability John Brown was the person originally hanged in the song. In the first place, John Brown really was hanged, the precondition for his body to molder in the grave. Indeed, Brown's execution obviously explains exactly where, when, and why these stanzas originated, and with exceptionally precise dating. The verses about John Brown hanging and moldering in his grave were likely composed just after December 2, 1859, when the real John Brown was hanged, and began to decompose.

Granted, the first reports do not appear until the early war years, but that would not be unusual. The piece is alternately attributed to slaves, contrabands, Union troops (Black or white), and abolitionists, all plausible but all lacking absolute proof.[53] The variation about Jeff Davis would not have appeared before November 6, 1861, when Davis was elected Confederate president, and sure enough, this form is first reported among Union troops early in 1862. They most likely deserve credit for its creation, but this is supposition again.[54]

Notwithstanding the many variations, when someone—anyone—is hanged in the song, they are always hanged on a sour apple tree. Why this held such special significance I cannot say. Jimmie Green (b. 1845, VA, 127) insisted that Jefferson Davis and Abraham Lincoln negotiated the South's surrender under an apple tree. Willie Blackwell sang the following:

Den, heahs one weuns larned aftah surrendah:

> W'en Gen'al Lee surrendahed,
> Twas undah de sour apple tree,
> He broke up all dem farmers,
> An' he set poor darkie free.

Ise tell you right now, de music dem words am set to make dese Cab Calloways of today git to de woods an' hide. Long's a man warnt so drunk he's plum out, he jus' have to git up an' jig or dance w'en dat music starts. (Willie Blackwell, b. 1834, NC, 312)

For decades after the war, white Southerners continued to sing about hanging people from sour apple trees, with Jefferson Davis the usual but by no means only subject. There is little question that many former Confederates were unhappy with the war's outcome. "There were lots of killings going on for a long time after the war was supposed to be over" (Minnie Davis, b. ca. 1860, GA, 262). Much of this was personal vengeance, racial terrorism, or out-and-out banditry, but in the Reconstruction-era South, even politics

reflected the war. A high proportion of candidates were drawn from the Confederate and Union officer corps. Many campaigns mirrored the guerrilla warfare perfected during the war by partisan irregulars; others actually involved organized paramilitary units. On election days, pitched battles between Confederate and Union veterans contesting the polls were not uncommon, possibly with Federal troops and Black militias pitching in. Meanwhile, people continued to sing, and to sing many of the same songs. During the runup to the Civil War, campaign songs had assumed a major role in American politics, and for the next few decades, singing on campaign trails and battlefields bore a strong resemblance.

I remember when Tilden and Hendrick lost and Hayes and Wheeler was elected. They sung songs 'bout 'em and said "Carve that possum nigger to the heart." It done been so long since we sung them rally songs I forgot every line of all of them. People used to sing more religious songs seems like than they do now. They done gone wild over dancin' 'stead of singin'. (Ellie Hamilton, b. 1863, MS, 132)[55]

God choosed Abraham Lincoln to free us. It took one of them to free us so's they couldn't say nothing. Doing [during] one 'lection they sung:

> Clark et the watermelon
> J. D. Giddings et the vine!
> Clark gone to Congress
> An' J. D. Giddings left behind.

They hung Jeff Davis up a sour apple tree. They say he was a president, but he wasn't, he was a big senator man. (Harriet Robinson, b. 1842, TX, 274)

Mississippi ex-slave Cap Banks recalled another version of Robinson's rhyme from the 1872 presidential race. "Grant ate the watermelon, / Greely ate de rind: / Grant he got elected, / Lef' ole Greely way behind."[56] Grant had been followed as president by

Rutherford B. Hayes (1822–1893), whose 1876 election was indeed a knife to the heart of African Americans in the South. To win the Electoral College in a disputed contest with Democrat Samuel J. Tilden (1814–1886), Republican Hayes struck a backroom deal with Congressional Southern Democrats, agreeing to withdraw remaining Federal troops from the South in exchange for their support. Hayes won the Electoral College by one vote, and early in 1877, he ended Reconstruction, leaving Southern Blacks at the mercy of resurgent white supremacists. Former slaveholder and Confederate official J. D. Giddings (1814–1878) was one of the Southern politicians who had fought for that goal. Elected to the Texas legislature in 1866, he was a steadfast supporter of the Cause, his first official act being to investigate Federal troops for burning Brenham, Texas, during the war.[57]

The same year Rutherford B. Hayes won the presidency, South Carolina Democrats under former Confederate general Wade Hampton III had carried the state through a full-blown military insurgency. While Red Shirt units wrought murder and mayhem, Hampton campaigned with an armed escort including brass bands and throngs of Black supporters. "Dere was horns a blowin', drums a beatin', and people a shoutin': 'Hurrah for Hampton!' Some was singin': 'Hang Dan Chamberlain on a Sour Apple Tree'" (Ed Barber, b. 1860, SC, 37). On election day, the Red Shirts kept Republicans from polls by force and stuffed and stole ballot boxes. Fulfilling his secret pledge, Hayes ignored Chamberlain's pleas and withdrew Federal troops. Chamberlain fled, Hampton seized office, and the US Constitution was once more annulled in South Carolina. Afterward, in the town of Union:

> De Red Shirts met on de facade in front o' de courthouse. Mos' all de mens made a speech. Another darky sang a song like dis: "Marse Hampton was a honest man; Mr. Chamberlain was a rogue"— Den I sung a song like dis: "Marse Hampton et de watermelon, Mr. Chamberlain knawed de rine." (Pen Eubanks, b. 1854, SC, 29)[58]

Still the confused subjects of much of this demagoguery, division, and deadly violence, many former slaves continued to support causes contrary to their best interests, and to sing songs they did not fully understand. Truly, after a while all of these elections must have seemed alike to some.

> Child, I tell you dat been a day to speak bout. When I come along, de women never vote, white nor colored, en it been years since I see a colored person vote, but I remember dey been gwine to vote in dat day en time just like dey was gwine to a show. Oh, honey, de road would be full of dem. Dey had to vote. Remember, way back dere, everybody would be singin en a dancin when dey had de election:
>
> > Hancock ride de big gray horse,
> > Hampton ride de mule,
> > Hancocks got elected,
> > Buckras all turn fool.
> > Buggety, buggety, buggety, etc.
>
> White en black was all in a row dere dancin all night long. Ain' made no exception. (Julia Woodberry, b. ca. 1865, SC, child of ex-slaves, 238)

Woodberry evidently conflated former Confederate general Wade Hampton's 1876 South Carolina gubernatorial campaign (which he won by force and intimidation) with the 1880 presidential bid of former Union general Winfield Scott Hancock (1824–1886) (Hancock, the hero of Gettysburg, lost to James A. Garfield, who was assassinated shortly after taking office).[59] Hampton and Hancock were both Democrats and in any case never competed politically (ironically, during his campaign Hancock was slurred as a Confederate sympathizer). Whether Woodberry recalled this item from the Hampton campaign, the Hancock campaign, or from both is uncertain, but I think both most likely, since this would explain why she incorporated their names together. It would also make perfect sense that this particular song was reused on both occasions.

In November 1884, Grover Cleveland (1837–1908) was elected to his first term as US president. Reconstruction had ended seven years before, and African Americans across the South were still reeling from the backlash. Cleveland was anxious further to placate southern Democrats and former Confederates, actively undermining Black voting rights and consistently siding with white supremacists. Lizzie Luckado was attending a Mississippi freedmen's school when Cleveland won his first term.

We cooked for Capt. Salter at Sardis, Mississippi. The first school I went to was Mrs. J. F. Settles. He [Settles's husband] taught the big scholars. She sent me to him and he whooped me for singing:

Cleveland is elected
No more I expected.

I was a grown woman. They didn't want him elected I recken the reason they didn't want to hear it. Nobody liked em teaching but the last I heard of them he was a lawyer in Memphis. If folks learned to read a little that was all they cared about. (Lizzie Luckado, b. 1867, MS, child of ex-slaves, 305)

Cleveland lost the 1888 presidential election to Benjamin Harrison (1833–1901), but Chaney Mack recalled how Cleveland's supporters, convinced he had been reelected (he won the popular but lost the Electoral College vote), celebrated all night, recycling his first victory rhyme.

It [the Charleston earthquake] wuz in August, and de year President Harrison was elected. I members de song dey sung when dey thought Cleveland had been elected instead of Harrison. I wuz livin' in Greensboro, Ala. after Cleveland's first time as president, and dey wuz running him fer de second term 'gainst Harrison. De day of the 'lection, all Greensboro, both black and white, went solid for Cleveland. Dat night dey burned all de coffins in town dey could fin' and say dey wuz burning

Harrison in 'em. Den dey marched up and down de street singing:

Cleveland got elected,
Which wuz more dan we expected,
Climbin' up de golden stairs.
Hear dem bells a ringing, sweet I do declare,
Hear dem darkies singing, climbing up de
    golden stairs,
Harrison wuz at de back step,
Shining up de shoes,
Cleveland in de big house,
Reading up de news,
Climbing up de golden stairs.
Hear dem bells a-ringing, Sweet I do declare,
Hear dem darkies singing, "Climbing up de
    golden stairs."

I went up town next day and axed Mr. Jeffrey, an old white gentleman, "who went in?" He say: "Harrison." But Cleveland went in next time. All de niggers wuz fer him same as de whites. (Chaney Mack, b. ca. 1864, AL, 1426–27)[60]

Mack was correct; Cleveland was reelected in 1892. During his second term (1893–97), lynching reached its peak in the United States, with nearly 90 percent of the entire country's lynchings coming from just fourteen of the fifteen former slave states.[61] For many ex-slaves and their families, things were about to get even worse. Again.

Appendix: Songs of Slavery

You ax me fer a song dey usta sing in dem days. The song my ma said was sung in her native home wuz:

You're selling me to Georgy,
But you can not sell my soul,
Thank God Almighty, God will
fix it for us some day!

I hope my ole gran'mother
Will meet poor John some day,
I knows I won' know him, when I meets him,
Cause he was so young when dey sold him away.
    (Sarah Thomas, b. ca. 1860, LA, 2107)

In 1860 I wuz a happy chile. I had a good ma an a good paw; one older bruther an one older suster, an a little bruther an a little suster, too. All my fambly wucked in de fields, 'ceptin me an de two little uns, which I stayed at home to mind. (mind—care for).

It wuz durin' cotton chopping time dat year (1860), a day I'll never fergit, when de speckulataws bought me. Ma come home from the fiel' 'bout haf atter 'leven dat day an cooked a good dinner, I hopin her. O, I never has forgot dat last dinner wid my fokes! But some-ow, I had felt, all de mawnin, lak sumpin was gwineter hapin'. I could jes feel it in my bones! An' sho nough, bout de middle of the even', up rid my young master on his hoss, an' up driv' two strange white mens in a buggy. Dey hitch dere hosses an' cum in de house, which skeered me. Den one o' de strangers said, "git yo clothes, Mary; we has bought you frum Mr. Shorter." I c'menced cryin' an' beggin' Mr. Shorter to not let 'em take me away. But he say, "yes, Mary, I has sole yer, an' yer must go wid em."

Den dese strange mens, whose names I ain't never knowed, tuk me an' put me in de buggy an' driv off wid me, me hollerin' at de top o' my voice an' callin' my Ma! Den dem speckulataws begin to sing loud—jes to drown out my hollerin'. Us passed de very fiel whar paw an' all my fokes wuz wuckin, an' I calt out loud as I could an, as long as I could see 'em, "goodbye, Ma!" "goodbye, Ma!" But she never heared me. Naw, sah, dem white mens wuz singin' so loud Ma could'n hear me! An' she could'n see me, caze dey had me pushed down out o' sight on de floe o' de buggy.

I ain't never seed nor heared tell o' my Ma an' Paw, an' bruthers, an' susters from dat day to dis. (Mary Ferguson, b. ca. 1855, MD, GA, 326–27, orig. parentheses)

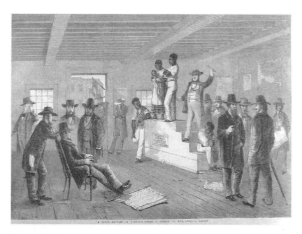

Fig. 23.1. "A Slave Auction in Virginia." *London News* 38 (February 16, 1861): 139. Slavery Images: A Visual Record of the African Slave Trade and Slave Life in the Early African Diaspora. slaveryimages.org.

Old Massa done so much wrongness I couldn't tell yer all about it. Slave girl Betty Lilly always had good clothes an' all the privileges. She wuz a favorite of his'n. But cain't tell all! God's got all! We uster sing a song when he was shippin' the slaves to sell 'bout "Massa's Gwyne Sell Us Termerrer." No, I cain't sing it for yer. (Elizabeth Sparks, b. 1841, VA, 277)

Wrote former Maryland slave Frederick Douglass: "the remark is not unfrequently made, that slaves are the most contented and happy laborers in the world. They dance and sing; and make all manner of joyful noises—so they do; but it is great mistake to think them happy because they sing. . . . Sorrow and desolation have their songs, as well as joy and peace. Slaves sing more to *make* themselves happy, than to express their happiness" (Douglass, *My Bondage*, 99–100, orig. emphasis).

Indeed, slaves did sing of their sorrow, suffering, and rage, though seldom around whites without masking or encoding the message. This suggests one obvious reason why outsiders documented relatively few songs explicitly lamenting or protesting the condition of slavery. Even decades after Emancipation, many ex-slaves seemed reluctant to perform these items for interviewers. "Mammy, Is Massa Gonna

APPENDIX: SONGS OF SLAVERY

Sell Us Tomorrow," which Elizabeth Sparks named but could not bear to sing, may have been one of the better-known examples, but that is mainly surmise. Writing in 1914, Henry Edward Krehbiel reached this same conclusion: "There are surprisingly few references to the servitude of the blacks in their folksongs which can be traced to antebellum days. The text of 'Mother, Is Massa Gonna Sell Us To-Morrow?' would seem to be one of these; but it is not in the earliest collection [*Slave Songs*, 1867] and may be of later date in spite of its sentiment." Krehbiel, *Folksongs*, 17. The item in fact first appears in late nineteenth-century collections: *Cabin Songs* III: 86; Dett, *Hampton*, 230; Talley, *NFR*, 209. It surfaces elsewhere in the ex-slave narratives, in the interviews of Emma L. Howard and Delia Garlic: "One song we sung den, dat always made me cry; it was, 'Mammy, is Ol' Massa gwine sell us tomorrow?' 'Yes, my chile.' 'Whah he goin sell us?' 'Way down South in Georgia'" (Delia Garlic, b. ca. 1835, AL, 155). Yet the Garlic and Howard texts merely duplicate one another, both transcripts being from interviewer Margaret Fowler and editor Jack Kytle. While this is obviously another case of a writer or editor repeating material, I nonetheless deem the item authentic, whether from Garlic or Howard. (Note also that in the Alabama state collection, SS1 1 *AL*: 155–63, Garlic's narrative is mistakenly listed under the name of the interviewer, M. Fowler.) This title also turns up in ex-slave Affie Singleton's narrative (Affie Singleton, b. ca. 1849, 283), but in this case interviewer Robert L. Nelson has merely inserted without attribution the passage from Henry Edward Krehbiel quoted above. Even as a relatively well-known example, the surviving evidence for "Mother, Is Massa Gonna Sell Us Tomorrow" is decidedly sparse and somewhat confounding.

John Smith was born in North Carolina but sold while young and taken to Alabama.

> I was sold off de block in "Speckerlater's Grove" in North Ca'lina. De fus' day I was put up I didn't sold, but de nex' day I brung a thousand dollars. Mr. Saddler Smith from Selma bought me. Dey

called him Saddler Smith cause he was in de saddle business and made saddles for de army. Dey fotch us down on boats. I 'member de song de men on de boat singed. Hit go like dis:

> Up an' down de Mobile Ribber,
> Two speckerlaters for one po' lil nigger. (John Smith, b. ca. 1834, NCAL, 350)

Ex-slave author Solomon Northrup (1807 or 1808–?) recalled a Louisiana patting song with the chorus "Up dat oak and down dat ribber, / Two overseers and one little nigger" (Northrup, *Twelve Years*, 219). These isolated texts again suggest a wider tradition—shared by Blacks and whites, in fact—but that is once more mere suggestion.

That slaves deliberately concealed these songs from whites is both commonsensible and fairly well established.

> We hed no church ter go to, but sum times at night afte' de white folks wus sleep, sum uf de slaves wud hide down under de hill an' sing an' pray fur de Lord ter cum an' free 'em. Sum times slaves frum udder plantashuns wud cum an' sing an' pray wid us, but de slaves allus hed ter carry a lil'l piece uf paper ter keep de patterroller frum gittin' 'm. Dey wud sing

> > O, Lord, cum free dis nigger,
> > O, Lord, cum free dis nigger,
> > O, Lord, cum free dis nigger,
> > Fur I cany wurk all de day. (Sarah Felder, b. 1853, MS, 715–16)

Clergyman John Dixon Long (1817–1894) traveled among slaves in the 1850s:

> Imagine a colored man seated on the front part of an oxcart, in an old field, unobserved by any white man, and in a clear loud voice, ringing out these words, which wake up sad thoughts in the minds of his fellow-slaves

Fig. 23.2. "Ox team, early Negro life." Commercial district, Savannah, GA, ca. 1867–90. Photo by William E. Wilson. Marian S. Carson Collection, Library of Congress, Prints and Photographs Division.

> William Rino sold Henry Silvers;
> Hilo! Hilo!
> Sold him to a Gorgy trader;
> Hilo! Hilo!
> His wife she cried, and children bawled,
> Hilo! Hilo!
> Sold him to a Gorgy trader;
> Hilo! Hilo! (Long, *Slavery*, 197–98)

Significantly, one of the few times when slaves did sing these songs within hearing of whites was while working, when their slave-labor customarily gave them license to lament, satirize, or censure. "Some ob de folks was putty happy in de fields and would sing: / Oho, I'se gwine home, / and cuss out de ole overseer" (Mary Kincheon Edwards, b. 1810, LA, 1280). On the coast of Maryland in 1832, James Hungerford was in a boat with a slaveholder and his family when the slave rowers began to sing.

SOLD OFF TO GEORGY

> 1. Farewell fellow sarvants! (Oho! Oho!)
> I'm gwine way to leabe you; (Oho! Oho!)
> I'm gwine to leabe de ole country; (Oho! Oho!)
> I'm sold off to Georgy! (Oho! Oho!)
>
> 2. Farewell, ole plantation, (Oho! Oho!)
> Farewell, de ole quarter, (Oho! Oho!)
> Un daddy, un mammy, (Oho! Oho!)
> Un marster, un missus! (Oho! Oho!)
>
> 3. My dear wife un one chile, (Oho! Oho!)
> My poor heart is breaking; (Oho! Oho!)
> No more shall I see you, (Oho! Oho!)
> Oh! no more foreber! (Oho! Oho!)

Wrote Hungerford: "the tone of voice in which this boat-song was sung was inexpressibly plaintive, and, bearing such a melancholy tune, and such affecting words, produced a very pathetic effect. I saw tears in the eyes of the young ladies, and could scarcely restrain my own." After the third verse, the slaveholder silenced the rowers. "'Confound such *lively* music,' he exclaimed; 'it is making the girls cry, I do believe'" (Hungerford, *Plantation*, 184–85, orig. emphasis). Apparently some slaveholders did not wish to hear these pieces under any circumstances.

Holidays were other occasions when slaves might take liberties. At Christmas among Maryland slaves, recalled Frederick Douglass,

> The fiddling, dancing and "*jubilee beating*," was going on in all directions. This latter performance is strictly southern. It supplies the place of a violin, or of other musical instruments, and is played so easily that almost every farm has its "Juba" beater. The performer improvises as he beats, and sings his merry songs, so ordering the words as to have them fall pat with the movement of his hands. Among a mass of nonsense and wild frolic, once in a while a sharp hit is given to the meanness of slaveholders. Take the following, for an example:
>
> > We raise de wheat,
> > Dey gib us de corn;
> > We bake de bread,
> > Dey gib us de cruss;
> > We sif de meal,
> > Dey gib us de huss;
> > We peal de meat,
> > Dey gib us de skin,

And dat's de way
Dey takes us in.
We skim de pot,
Dey gib us de liquor,
And say dat's good enough for nigger.
Walk over! walk over!
Tom butter and de fat;
Poor nigger you can't get over dat;
Walk over!

(Douglass, *My Bondage*, 252–53, orig. emphasis. For other versions, see White, *ANFS*, 161–62; Whitney and Bullock, *Maryland*, 163–64; Wyeth, *Sabre*, 62–63.)

However, slaves are most often described singing such items publicly at cornshuckings, a combination work party–holiday when they enjoyed especially wide latitude to protest, complain, or criticize in slaveholders' presence. "Just before they got through [shucking], they would begin to sing. Some of the songs were pitiful and sad. I can't remember any of them, but I can remember that they were sad. One of them began like this: / The speculator bought my wife and child / And carried her clear away" (Eliza Washington, b. ca. 1860, AR, 52).

We had corn shucking, but it wasn't in the form of a party. . . . They would sing and have good times, but they didn't have no prizes. The song they liked best was

Once I was so lucky,
Old Master set me free
Sent me to Kentucky
To see, what I could see.
Mean old banjo Thomas
Mean old banjo Joe
Going away to Kentucky
Won't come back no more. (Louis Davis, b. 1858, AR, 582–83)

Left my wife in Georgia,
Oh, Oh, Oh, Oh,

I left my wife in Georgia,
Oh, Oh, Oh, Oh.

Give us one more drink of liquor,
Oh, oh, oh, oh,
Give us one more drink of liquor,
Oh, oh, oh, oh. ("Corn Sucking Song," Solomon, *Daisies*, 118)

At an 1843 South Carolina cornshucking, William Cullen Bryant (1794–1878) heard slaves singing:

Johnny come down de hollow.
Oh hollow!
De nigger-trader got me.
Oh hollow!
De speculator bought me.
Oh hollow!
I'm sold for silver dollars.
Oh hollow! (Bryant, "Old South," 32)

Newman Ivey White (1892–1948) obtained a similar verse from North Carolina cornshuckings.

Ole massa sol' me,
Speculator bought me,
Took me to Raleigh
To learn how to rock candy.

White noted that Richmond was sometimes substituted for Raleigh, and that the informant "has heard another stanza that he considers a little too risqué for print." White, *ANFS*, 162.

While a handful of slave protests were thus overheard by white correspondents or included in slave autobiographies, or collected from WPA narrators and other ex-slaves, these songs obviously lost much of their relevance with the war's end and slavery's abolition. No doubt that is another cause of their rarity, and by the twentieth century, most former slaves had either forgotten them, or simply did not want to remember.

CONCLUSION

MODERN TIMES

I think folks had ought to be 'ligious 'cause dat is God's plan, and so I jined de church atter Christ done presented Hisself to me. I'se fixin' now to demand my Sperrit in de Lawd.

Yes Ma'am, Miss, I knowed you was a-comin'. I had done seed you, writin' wid dat pencil on dat paper, in de Sperrit. (Elisha Doc Garey, b. ca. 1862, GA, 10, to interviewer Sadie Hornsby)

Lord! Lorday! phew! phew! phew! Baby, I jes' know I could ef I knowed how to write, an' had a little learnin! I could put off a book on dis heah situation. You know what I mean 'bout dese way back questions you is a askin' me to tell you 'bout as fer as I can recollect in my mind. (Minnie Folkes, b. 1860, VA, 94, to interviewer Susan R. C. Byrd)

If you all keep on you gwinter hab a book outer my testimony. (George Owens, b. ca. 1853, TX, 169, to interviewers Fred Dibble and Rheba Beehler)

John Lomax's fieldworker guidelines advised asking, "What do the ex-slaves think of the younger generation of Negroes and of present conditions?" Transcripts confirm that interviewers regularly posed the question, and the ex-slaves responded as might be expected, expressing a spectrum of views on their grandchildren's and great-grandchildren's generations probably typical of elderly persons always and everywhere.

The present generation ain't got no religion. They dances and cuts up a heap. They don't care nothin bout settlin down. When they marry now, that man say he got the law on her. She belongs to him. He thinks he can make her do like he wants her all the time and they don't get along. Now, that's what I hear around. (Sarah Williams Wells, b. 1866, TN, child of ex-slaves, 94–95)

'Bout this younger generation—well, I tell you, it's hard for me to say. It just puts me to wonder. They gone a way back there. Seem like they don't have any 'gard for anything. I heard 'em 'fore I left Mississippi singin', Everybody's doin' it, doin' it. 'Co'se when I was young they was a few that was wild, but seem like now they is all wild. But I feels sorry for 'em. (Letha Johnson, b. ca. 1861, MS, 99)

You take dese young people comin up now days dey is most all in town and dey ain't work for dem, all dey do is just wander aroun both white and black, and 50% of dem ain't worth killin, dey just ain't no count, if dey was out on de farm where dey could work all de time dey might amount to somethin some day, dat is why our jails and penitentiaries are always full. Idle brains is de devils workshop. (Calvin Moye, b. 1842, TX, 2872–73)

The present times is hard. I can't get a bit of work. I tries. Work is hard for some young folks to get yet. I love to be around young folks. Far as I know they do all right. The world looks nicer 'an it used to look. All I see wrong, times is hard. (Mose King, b. 1857, MS, AR, 209)

I am an old man now, but I like ter see things move on. I enjoy livin' and wish every body well. (Allen Ward, b. 1856, MS, 2174)

It is noteworthy how many ex-slaves were open, empathetic, and accepting, allowing that young people in the 1930s acted no differently from young people of their day.

> They ought to have some kind of amusement for the young folks these days. What they need is a good club house or something; got to have something to amuse these young folks. They get tired of going to bed every night. I think dem night clubs are fine for de young folks. In our times we had balls—Mardi Gras Balls, fairs, barbeques, and outing for folks den. (Thomas Steptoe, b. 1863, LA, 203–4)

They used to go out and dance and carry on for amusement, and they would go to church too. It

Fig. 24.1. Eva Martin, ex-slave, Beaumont, TX, ca. 1937–38. Portraits of African American ex-slaves from the US Works Progress Administration, Federal Writers' Project slave narratives collection, Library of Congress. A WPA narrator with one of the younger generation.

was just about like it is now. Dancing and going to church is about all they do now, isn't it? They got a gambling game down there on the corner. They used to do some of that too, I guess. (Eliza Hays, b. ca. 1860, AR, 224)

I has alwas farmed an' laked to go to meeting. I trys to live right an' believes de young generation o' colored people is doing purty well. I'se glad to see 'em going on. (Robert Weathersby, b. ca. 1847, MS, 2244)

The young people nowadays are all right. There is not so much ignorance now as there was in those days. There was ignorance all over then. The Peckerwoods wasn't much wise either. They know nowadays though. Our race has done well in refinement. (Charles Graham, b. 1859, TN, 69)

Other ex-slaves withheld their judgments, perhaps from discretion, perhaps just indifference or with laissez-faire.

I got nothing to say about this young generation thats coming on. They does what they thinks right, and that is so different from what I thinks right, that I just lays off them, and let's them be. (Virginia Harris, b. ca. 1850, LA, 947)

I don't know what to think about the young generation. I am at my stopping place. (Ann May, b. 1856, AR, 66)

However, like elderly persons everywhere, many ex-slaves reacted to young people's conduct with what can only be described as horror, outrage, and disgust, and much of this ire was directed at the new styles of music, dance, and recreation that to the ex-slaves epitomized the younger generation's "lost condition."

De present generation is a lost condition. If dey don't girdle dey lines and pull dem up closer and ask God to help 'em and quit goin' to dem "hog holes" and drinkin' it is going to be death and destruction. Dis not only true of the Negroes but white folks, too. Mother and Father think it is alright. Dese undertakers is goin' out all de time, night and day, on the highways and pickin' up de carcass of people. (Rhody Holsell, b. 1848, MO, 195)

Dey sho' have better chu'ch in dem days dan dey is now. Don' have chu'ch good today as us had den. Us git happy and shout. Dey's too many blin' taggers [blind tigers, meaning speakeasies] now. Now dey say dey got de key and dey ain' got nuthin'. (Liza Jones, b. 1856, TX, 2118)

The young people today ain't worth a shit. These young people going to school don't mean no good to nobody. They dance all night and all the time, and do everything else. That man across the street runs a whiskey house where they dance and do everything they're big enough to do. They ain't worth nothing. (Silas Dothrum, b. 1855 or 1856, AR, 188)

It is hardly unusual for old people to grouse about punk kids, but in truth the former slaves had witnessed transformations in the following generations far beyond what most people experience, and this especially included newer musical entertainments dispensed in commercial establishments worlds apart from Saturday night plantation frolics. Repentant ex-slaves who had forsworn ring plays and fiddling to join the church decades before, or who had always shunned frolicking as a mortal sin, now found themselves living amidst smoky, juiced-up dance halls, juke joints, barrel houses, brothels, whiskey bars, cocaine parlors, pool halls, and gambling dens, and they were aghast. These were places were people played sinful music and sang bad songs, danced lascivious dances, drank and drugged, smoked, chawed, and dipped, gambled, cursed and blasphemed, engaged in casual sex, and callously sacrificed lives—all established means of summoning the Devil in folktales, and some said in real life. Ex-slaves definitely saw the Devil's hand in this.

I don't like de way de younger generation is doin'. As my neighbors say, "the devil is gettin' dem and it won't be long 'fore he will come and get dem all." When I was young we didn't act like dey do now-a-days. We didn't get drunk and stay dat way and kill each other. De good Lord is going to do something to all of dem, mark my word. (William Black, b. ca. 1850, MO, 34)

Lawd, yes, Miss, dese here young folks today is gwine straight to de Devil. All dey do all day and all night is run around and drink corn likker and ride automobiles. I'se got a grandaughter here dat's as wild as de rest of dem and I worries a right smart 'bout her, but it doan do no good case her mammy let her do jest as she please anyway. . . . You is heared of dis Miss Sally what lives out here? She lays wid de men all day and all night and de chillen hangs round and peeps thru de winder at her goin's on and laughs at her and think they is smart. Now you know dat ain't no way to raise chillen up. Dey larns all dat devilment soon enough 'thout a white woman settin' such a bad 'zample for dem. (Dora Franks, b. ca. 1837, MS, 789–90)

A yellow straw hat of two or three summers past, grimy after constant contact with the elements, perched atop his graying head, and a heavy ash cane laid across his knees, *Horace Overstreet*, heavy set negro, with a massive sweaty face, wreathed in smiles, was sitting on the steps of a negro cafe, beer joint, and dance hall when interviewed, but his conversation terminated rather abruptly because of the raucous revelry of "swing music" and ribald speech from inside. (Horace Overstreet, b. 1856, TX, 2996, int. Fred Dibble, Bernice Grey, orig. emphasis)

Aunt Ellen says the people of today are going back not forward. "All they study is idleness and to do devilment these days. Young generation done gone, Satan got them, too much 'juking' these days, have no time to study 'bout the Lord and their dying day, all they do is juke, juke, juke! When they closed up the schools here in Mauvilla, they had children all juking."

The writer was somewhat at a loss to know just what Aunt Ellen meant by "juking," but thought best to let her talk on and not make a direct inquiry, and after a little Aunt Ellen continued:

"No, lady, we used to call figures for our dancing, had a big fiddle and two small fiddles, and a set in one room and one in another, none of this twisting and turning, I just can't stand that all juking, just won't look at it."

For the reader's information by "juking" Aunt Ellen meant rough dancing, perpetuated by the generation of today. Aunt Ellen firmly believes the old-time religion was best for all. (Ellen King, b. 1851, MS, 234–35, int. Mary A. Poole)

Opinions of "the present conditions" (as Lomax phrased it) ran the same gamut. Some ex-slaves marveled and rejoiced that they had lived to see the modern world.

Fig. 24.2. "Negroes spending their cotton money in gambling in juke joint. Saturday night, outside Clarksdale, Mississippi Delta." Photo by Marion Post Wolcott, November 1939. Farm Security Administration/Office of War Information Photograph Collection, Library of Congress, Prints and Photographs Division. Wolcott was employed by the Farm Security Administration (another Depression-era relief program) when she took this photo of "the younger generation of Negroes and present conditions" as many ex-slaves described them.

Now I thinks wid de advantages an' learnin de folks ob now a days has dey ought to could do better ago. I'se glad I lived to see de day ob paved roads an' automobiles an' airplanes an' electricity. I laks to see my race wid education an' progress an' hopes dey keeps gwine on. (Temple Wilson, b. ca. 1857, MS, 2375)

Just think! Dat [the Charleston earthquake of 1886] has been fifty-one years. Them was de glorious horse and buggy days. Dere was no airships, no autos and no radios. White folks had horses to drive. Niggers had mules to ride to a baseball game, to see white folks run lak de patarollers (patrollers) was after them and they holler lak de world was on fire. (Charley Barber, b. ca. 1856, SC, 33, orig. parentheses)

Many church members did not regard these new technologies as necessarily incompatible with a sanctified life. "Hear dat radio music? I like dem songs, church songs" (Ceceil George, b. 1846, LA, 86). "We went over to Flat Rock to church, and de singin' was gran'. All day long we'd be at preachin' and singin'.

Singin' dat good ole spiritual song 'bout 'You shan't be Slaves no More, since Christ has made you free!' I lay hear yes'day and heered all them foolish songs and jubilee songs that came over the radio, and den some of them good ol' time spirituals come and it jes' made me feel like I was in ol' times" (Fannie Yarborough, b. ca. 1854, TX, 226). "Dem air ships luk nice but dey ez spoke 'boud in de Holy Bible, dat sum day dere wud be flyin' things in de air'h an' dat dese things am it. De otomobeels kiver nuder passag' in de Bible which seze de people'll rid' on de streets widout hosses en mules" (Scott Martin, b. 1857, TN, 42).

Joanna Isom is a tall, slender and very intelligent mulatto woman. . . . She has electric lights, running water, and a phonograph with many records of negro songs, spirituals, and sermons; they were given to her she says by "friends, chilluns, and gran'chilluns" when she expressed a wish for them during a serious illness. "Dey did me mo' good dan all de doctors an' medicines." (Joanna Thompson Isom, b. ca. 1858, MS, 1091–92, int. Minnie S. Holt)

I like de radio 'cause I can get church music on it, but I wouldn't ride in no automobile. No, ma'am, dem things are de devil's wagons, and no good can come out of dem. I ain't never been to a picture show 'cause dem things are idols, and God says don't worship no idols. Looks to me like de judgement ain't far off. De only thing to do is to pray to de Lord to open your mind to stop what's comin'. (Charity Parker, b. ca. 1850, LA, 177–78)

They don't talk "niggerism" anymo' either, and they ain't got Mother Wit. They don't play like we did. We used to sing: / Shoo, chicken, shoo, . . . / Then the leader would raise his hands and say, 'Shoo, chickens, shoo,' and everyone would run just like chickens do when they are bein' shooed. But I never hear things like that now. Children must have money to go to picture shows. I never went to one in my life 'cause they're ungodly. I

told some churches have them with scenes from the Bible, and that's all right. My church ain't got money enough for that. (Grace Stafford, b. ca. 1860, LA, 198)

For most church goers, however, radios, automobiles, and the trappings of modernity generally were of a kind with juke joints, whorehouses, and other gateways to Hell. "I sumtimes wish fer de good ole days. Deze days folks don't hab time fer 'ligion. De doggone ole radio en udder things ez takin' hits place" (Frankie Goole, b. 1853, TN, 23). "You know its a funny thing, de white folks took ebberthing from us niggers, ebeen try to take our ol' songs an' hab dem on de radio" (Filmore Taylor Hancock, b. 1851, MO, 187).

To live a consecrated life, you'd better leave off dancing, drinking, smoking, and the movies. I've never been to a movie in my life. When I hear some of the programs colored folks put on the radio sometimes I feel just like going out to the woodshed and getting my axe and chopping up the radio, I do! It's natural and graceful to dance, but it is not natural or good to mill around in a lowminded smoky dance hall. (Reverend Charles Williams, b. 1859, WV, 112)

Jukeboxes—usually called "piccolos" or Seeburgs (a brand name)—were especially vilified, being firmly tied to dance halls (aka juke joints) and other new palaces of sin. "These here seabirds, (a music machine called seaburg—ed.) is ruinin' the young folks" (Clarice Jackson, b. ca. 1855, AR, 1, orig. parentheses).

In town this Nickelodeon playing wild wid young colored folks—these Sea Bird music boxes. They play all kind things. Folks used to stay home Saturday nights. Too much running 'round, excitement, wickedness in the world now. This generation is worst one. They trying to cut the Big Apple dance when we old folks used to be down singing and praying. 'Cause dis is a wicked age times is bad and hard. (Laura Abromsom, b. 1863, AR, 9–10)

Ise got de heart trouble an' Ise been sick for six weeks. I moved down heah an' hit's de worse place I ever lived. I jes' can't stand it. I keeps sick all de time. De doctor says I ought to be in a quiet place, but it ain't no quietness heah. De "piculous" [piccolos] playin' all de night long right over my head, I jes' can rest heah, can't even sleep a wink, jurin' de night or day. I live 'tween seven whiskey dens an' dey 'bout to kill me. Of course I would 'port dem, but dese people got to make a livin' somehow. Dey die two to three a day from dat rotten ole whiskey. If dey use de good kind maybe it wouldn't hurt 'em. It's dat ole 'coca-cane' dat kill dem, it too much o' dat stuff in it. Well dey drink and shoot and think nothin' of it. Dey just quiet now, you jes' wait a while. Dey carry on some, an' 'specially Friday night 'till Sunday, den dey quiet down a little. Do you know why? Dere's money all gone dat's why. (Delphia Taylor, b. 1841, VA, 283, orig. parentheses)

Hagar Brown remarked "they say whiskey and 'Piccolo' jest pick you pocket low" (Hager Brown, b. ca. 1860, SC, 76). "They say" plus the brilliant word play of *piccolo / pick you pocket low* suggests this may indeed have been a traditional figure of speech.

Now how is it dese days? Young triflin' nigger boys and gals lyin' 'round puffin' cigarets, carryin' whiskey 'round wid them, and gittin' in jail on Christmas, grievin' de Lord and their pappies, and all sich things. OH! De risin' generation and de future! What is it comin' to? I just don't know but dere is comin' a time to all them. (Louisa Davis, b. ca. 1832, SC, 302)

Some dese young niggers gone plumb wild wid dere cyars and cigyars an truckin' an jazzin' an sech. (James Boyd, b. 1830, IT, 368)

Dances in dem days warn't dese here huggin' kind of dances lak dey has now. Dere warn't no Big

Apple nor no Little Apple neither. (Liza Mention, b. ca. 1865, GA, child of ex-slaves, 124)[1]

The new couple dances young people performed— "hugging dances"—were equally scandalous to ex-slaves raised in communities where the waist swing was considered risqué. "They didn't dance then like they do now all hugged up and indecent. In them days, they danced what you call square dances. They don't do those dances now, they're too decent. There were eight on a set. I used to dance those myself" (Eliza Washington, b. ca. 1860, AR, 52). "An' I tell you 'bout de dancin'. Den hit wasn't lak 'tis now—wadn't no catchin' hole o' each udder. Dey had side shufflin' an' heel an' toe to fiddlin' " (Robert Young, b. 1844, MS, 2409). "Wasn't none of this sinful dancin' where yo' partner off wid man an woman squeezed up close to one another. Danced 'spectable, de slaves did, shiftin' 'round fum one partner to 'nother an' holdin' one 'nother out at arm's length" (Fannie Berry, b. 1841, VA, 49). "Noah is a member of the Baptist church, he does not believe in card playing or dancing, and he thinks if women must smoke they should smoke a pipe instead of cigarettes or cigars. When I asked him why dancing was a sin he said 'these young folks can't stand being in each others arms half of the night without getting fool notions in their heads' " (Noah Rogers, b. 1845, MS, 1881).

Martha Allen reported to her horror that young people were performing popular dances in church under the guise of *shouting*. "I tries ter be a good christian but I'se got disgusted wid dese young upstart niggers what dances in de chu'ch. Dey says dat dey am truckin' an' dat de Bible ain't forbid hit, but I reckon dat I knows dancin' whar I sees hit" (Martha Allen, b. 1859, NC, 15). The young people were teasing Allen, of course: trucking was one of the emblematic popular dances of the early twentieth century, still widely recognized as a relic of Prohibition-era hedonism.[2] The term also caught on as rhyming slang for fucking, and thusly figures in numerous songs, including Blind Boy Fuller's "Truckin' My Blues Away" (ARC 6–10–56, 1936), "Trucking My Blues Away No. 2"

(ARC 7-07-63, 1937), and "She's A Truckin' Little Baby" (Vocalion 04603, 1938); Big Bill Broonzy's "Trucking Little Woman" (Vocalion 04205, 1938) and "Trucking Little Woman No. 2" (Vocalion 04486, 1938); Tampa Red's "Stop Truckin' and Suzi-Q" (Bluebird B6755, 1936); and many others. One wonders if Martha Allen was aware of the double entendre.

Automobiles were reviled as the means to these new lifestyles. "Most ob de young niggers is headed straight fur hell. All dey think about is drinkin hard liquor, goin to dance halls en gittin a ole rattletrap automobile. Dey piles in en rides like dey been sont fur en kaint go" (Charlie Davenport, b. ca. 1837, MS, 569). "Education and the automobile, according to 'Uncle' Dave and 'Aunt' Lillian, are the great curses of the twentieth century; these two evil agencies have filled the jails and the chain-gangs!" (Dave Ramsey, b. ca. 1853, Lillian Ramsey, b. ca. 1866, siblings, GA, 499).

I don't know what's goin' to become of our folks. All they study is drinking whiskey and gamblin' and runnin' after women. They don't care for nothin'. What's ruinin' this country is women votin. When a woman comes up to a man and smiles, he'll do what she wants him to do whether it's right or wrong. The best part of our preachers is got so they are dishonest. Stealing to keep up automobiles. Some of them have churches that ain't no bigger than this room. (Needham Love, b. ca. 1855, AR, 295–96)

However, nothing pained ex-slaves of all persuasions more than the rampant Black-on-Black violence they saw all around them, enough to make many wax nostalgic for the plantation police state.

On Saturday nights all de slaves on de plantation would either has a dance or go to a dance on another plantation and dey would dance til daylight on Sunday mornings sometimes, and dey never did start any trouble or gits drunk like dey do now. (Calvin Moye, b. 1842, TX, 2841)

Sat'day night we would have parties and dance and play ring plays. We had de parties dare in a big double log house. Dey would give us whiskey, wine and cherry brandy, but dare wasn't no shootin' or gamblin'. Dey didn't allow it. De men and women didn't do lak dey do now. (Wash Ingram, b. ca. 1844, VA, 1855)

Things is better now than they was in slavery times, 'cept they don't take care of the poor like they should. Wasn't no trouble of that kind them days. Another thing, I never heared of one colored people killing each other. That didn't happen. Now its a going on every day. This younger generation too is awful. They don't study nothing but foolishness. One half of them is up all night long. What for? I don't know. They is bring up their children for three things—The County Farm, the Penitentiary, and the Gallows. (Dempsey Pitts, b. 1830, MS, 1723)

Of course, not all former slaves had shunned these forbidden fruits. Slavery had limited African Americans' access to many pastimes and vices, whether because of slaveholders' supposed scruples, the grueling slave labor regimen, or the lack of alternatives in the rural plantation South. "I's a growed up young man befo' I ebber seed a deck of cyards (cards). My ol' w'ite folks was Christian people" (Lorenza Ezell, b. ca. 1850, SC, 1328, orig. parentheses). "They would have dancing. I never seed any playing cards. When they danced, somebody would play the fiddle for them" (Ellen Briggs Thompson, b. 1844, AR, 313). Having won their freedom, some narrators had thrown off all constraints. Susan (Aunt Sue) Snow was born in 1850 in Wilcox County, Alabama, but sold young to Jasper County, Mississippi. From age eight she was hired out, mainly as a fieldhand. After freedom she "went to Scott County, an' to Enterprise, an' den to Meridian, nursin' (wet-nursin', when I could), an' workin' out."

When I come to Meridian, I cut loose. I'm tellin' you the truth, Son, I'm a woman, but I'm a prodigal. I used to be a old drunkard. My white folks kep' tellin' me if I got locked up one mo' time, dey wouldn't pay my fine, but dey did. Dey called me Devil, an' I was a devil til I got religion. I wasn't baptized til 1887, when I found peace. . . . Dese young folks? Shucks, chile, dey're wuss'n what I was, only dey're mo' slyer. (Susan Snow, b. 1850, AL, 2010, 2011)

As always, performers were at the forefront of any and all dissipation. Tom Morris was born before the war in Virginia but sold around age six to a speculator who took him to Rankin County, Mississippi. "De Dr. niver lowed no dancing at his house." Tom secretly learned to dance nonetheless, and after the war became a fiddler, a heavy drinker, and a wife beater. "When I was drunk I was bad. I uster whip Cynthia, till one day she throwed er pan uf dishwater on me an' laid me out—well she hit me with the pan too." He was repeatedly jailed and forced to work out fines for crimes involving drunkenness, including drunken gunplay. "I loved whiskey an' I love it yet" (Tom Morris, b. unk., MS, 1588, 1587, 1586).

Nor had all aged ex-slaves abandoned their rowdy ways. Born in 1855 in North Carolina, Bill Crump was interviewed at the state prison, where he had served four years and ten months of a ten-to-twelve-year sentence for shooting and killing a man who cursed and poured whiskey on him at a gambling game. The shooting apparently occurred around 1930, when Crump would have been seventy-five.

"Yuh know dere spiritual hymns en dere reels" (Washington Dozier, b. 1847, SC, 332). "I don't pay no mind to the pastors round here. Dey show don't know nothin' bout de Lord's bisness. Long as I don't sing no reels and go to no dances an' pays my church dues, I show believe I am goin' to heven" (Aunt Katherin, b. unk., MS, 1264–65). By the 1930s the ultimate musical expression of this new ultra-worldly, maximally sinful lifestyle was the blues, consumed by the ex-slaves' grandchildren via Seeburg jukeboxes in juke joints, blind tigers, whore houses, and gambling dens. Yet beyond recoiling at this milieu, the ex-slaves themselves seemed unaware of the blues, hardly surprising, since the genre only fully emerged in the early twentieth century, long after most narrators had reformed (if necessary) and forsworn any music but church songs. In the decades before the blues, however, as African Americans adapted to their altered conditions, their music and song registered those changes. This transition was most conspicuous in the sinful dance songs ex-slaves still called reels, which, beginning in the late 1800s, helped lay the groundwork for the blues.

Oh, I been know a heap of reels. Hoped sing dem behind de old folks back many a day. No'um, us chillun wasn' allowed to sing reels in dem days. Old back people was more religious den dey is now. Yes, mam, dey been know what spell somethin in dat day en time. When dey speak den, dey meant somethin, I tell you. People does just go through de motion dese days en don' have no mind to mean what dey talk. No, child, us didn' dar sen to let us parents hear us sing no reels den. What dem old people didn' quarrel out us, dey whip out us. My daddy never wouldn' let we chillun go to no frolics, but us would listen from de house en catch what us could. I used to could turn a heap of dem reels, too, but he was so tight on us till everything bout left me.

I'm Gwine Join De Band

The blackest nigger I ever did see,
He come a runnin down from Tennessee,
His eye was red en his gum was blue,
En God a mighty struck him,
En his shirt tail flew.
Meet me at de crossroads,
For I'm gwine join de band.
Um-huh! Um-huh! Um-huh!"

—————————————

I got beef in de market,
Oh, my lovin Chanlie,
Chanlie, don' you know?

Chanlie, don' you know?
Chanlie, don' you know?
(Repeat over and over) (Lizzie Davis,
    b. ca. 1865, SC, child of ex-slaves, 112–13,
    orig. parentheses)

Reels are not blues but anticipate the blues in their themes, imagery, and manner of expression. Chief among these is an emphasis on movement as the ultimate form of freedom, whether movement from place to place, from partner to partner, from job to job, from good to bad, or between any other points imaginable.

Dey be lined up to a tree, an' dey sing dis song to mark de blows. Fust de one chop, den his pardner, an' when sing TALK dey all chop together; an' perty soon dey git de tree ready to fall an' dey yell "Hi" an' de niggers all scramble out de way quick 'cause you can't never tell what way a pine tree gonna fall. An' sometime dey sing it like dis:

Dis time tomorrow night,
Where will I be?
I'll be gone, gone, gone,
Down to Tennessee. (Fannie Berry, b. 1841,
    VA, 39)[3]

Ah use ter pick cotton and sing. Ah can recollect so well de song. Hit went lak dis:

Me an' mah wife had a fallin out
She wanted me ter work on de railroad track
Etc. (See enclosed song) (James Tubbs, b. 1866,
    AR, child of ex-slaves, 355, int. Pernella M.
    Anderson, orig. parentheses)[4]

Husband Don't You 'Buse Me

Husban' don't you 'buse me,
Carry me back to mama;
Mama's c-h-i-m-ne-y co-r-ne-r
Is big enough fer me! (Jane Sutton, b. ca. 1853,
    MS, 2092)

Like the blues, reels focus on male-female relationships in a distinctly modern way. In place of the plantation's static, quasi-feudal society, reels reflect the struggles of Black wage earners in booming Southern port cities, company towns, transportation hubs, sharecropping communities, and nascent industrial and service centers. For this semiurban milieu's emancipated Black underclass, short-term, mutually exploitative romance-finance relationships were often a necessity but also desirable, and like the blues, reels lay bare the tumultuous results. In the old plantation frolics, male-female relations were expressed mainly through metaphors from the natural world; the stylized imagery of singing games and fiddle songs; or the contrivances and conventions of blackface minstrelsy and romantic love. There were obvious sexual subtexts, all underscored by the plantation's twisted sexual politics and the competition of male slaves and Old Massa for slave women (most pointedly the mixed-race "yellow gal") behind Old Missus' back. Nonetheless, by modern standards many of these songs do sound like child's play.

'Possum up a 'simmon tree,
Rabbit on de ground
Shake dem 'simmons down.
Peggy, does you love me now?
        Holler
Rabbit up a gum stump
'Possum up a holler
Git him out little boy
And I gives you half a dollar.
Peggy, does you love me now? (Jenny Proctor,
    b. 1850, AL, 215)[5]

The wimmen was off Friday afternoon to wash clothes and clean up for Sunday. All the hands got Saturday afternoon. Most of the men would go fishing or hunting. There was plenty of game and fish then. Sometimes they had parties on Saturday night. The couples got on the floor and go to turning round and round to the music of fiddles and banjoes. I only 'members one ring play:

Hop Light little lady
　The cakes all dough,
I don't mind the weather,
　Just so the wind don't blow. (Campbell
　　Davis, b. 1852, TX, 1064–65)

When we used to pray we put our heads under the wash pot to keep old master from hearin' us. Old master make us put the children to bed fo' dark. I 'member one song he make us sing—

Down in Mobile, down in Mobile
How I love dat pretty yellow gal,
She rock to suit me—
Down in Mobile, down in Mobile. (Robert Wilson, b. 1836, VA, 208)[6]

The sexuality of reels is, by contrast, overt, unmistakable, and inescapable, and they depict the postwar South's full repertoire of vices—drinking, gambling, prostitution, domestic violence, murder, mayhem, thievery, and general criminality—with the same frankness.

My father played a violin. He played well, so did my brother, but I never did play or sing. . . . Father died at thirty-five. He played the violin fine. My brother played for dances, and he used to sing lots of songs:—

Ol' Aunt Katy, fine ol' soul,
She's beatin' her batter,
In a brand new bowl

—that was a fetchin' tune, but you see I can't even carry it. (Wade Glenn, b. ca. 1860, NC, 38)

I went to work when I was seven pullin' worms off tobacco, and I been workin' ever since. But when I was comin' up I had good times. I had better times than I ever had in my life. I used to be one of the best banjo pickers. I was good. Played for white folks and called figgers for em. In them days

they said "promenade," "sashay," "swing corners," "change partners." They don't know how to dance now. We had parties and corn shuckin's, oh Lord, yes. I'll sing you a song

Oh lousy nigger
Oh grandmammy
Knock me down with the old fence rider,
Ask that pretty gal let me court her
Young gal, come blow the coal. (James Davis,
　b. 1840, NC, 109–10)

Hold De Deal

I. Kitty, Kitty died O - O
　　Kitty had a man.
　　Rather kiss a monkey,
　　Den to kiss a nigger man.
　　Hold de deal! Hold de deal!
　　I'm gwine to get drunk again.
II. Nigger on de horseback,
　　Thought he was de king.
　　Come along alligator,
　　En let de nigger in.
　　Hold de deal! Hold de deal!
　　I'm gwine to get drunk again. (Hector Smith,
　　　b. ca. 1858, SC, 108)[7]

I studied en studied what songs would suit, but dem old familiar hymns bout all I know dese days. You see dem old familiar hymns what de spirit sings. It just like I tell you, I put all dem other kinds of songs away when I is change to better way of livin. I does remember first one en den de other of dem frolicksome song dat my grandparents learnt me.

NOBODY BUSINESS BUT MINE

I. Rabbit in de hollow,
　　I ain' got no dog.
　　How can I catch em?
　　I do know! I do know!

O me! O mine!
Sorry dat if I leave my home,
I gwine to my shack
Wid de chicken on my back,
Nobody business but mine.
II. Rabbit in de hollow,
Ain' got no dog.
How can he catch em?
I do know! I do know!
O me! O mine!
Let every nigger have his way,
Gwine to his shack
Wid he chicken on his back,
Nobody business but his. (Hector Smith,
b. 1858, SC, 105–6)[8]

Instead of extolling a figurative prisoner ringed in some lady's garden, little girls at play now sang about saving for their partner's bail, or of deserting their current lover for another a long way from home.

We chilluns played jes lak any other colored chilluns, little ring games, one I membahs:

Always from Kare, never spent a dime,
Savin all mah change ter pay mah babies fine.

Another one was:

Go away ole man and leave me alone,
I'se a poor girl and a long ways from home.[9]

Der was lots of other songs we would ring up and sing. (Mattie Gilmore, b. unk., AL, 1495–96)

No wonder ex-slaves wondered about the younger generation. Nor is it difficult to imagine their reaction to the blues if any by chance encountered that music. But then, blues was music for modern times and, as ex-slaves acknowledged again and again, their time was past.

If you is through with me, I'll have to go help this boy. I'se 'titled to one of them books with my

story in it free, 'cause I'm a preacher, and I knows I'se give you the best story you has wrote up yit. (Jefferson Franklin Henry, b. ca. 1860, GA, 193, to interviewer Sadie Hornsby)

The ex-slave narratives project shuddered to a conclusion of sorts in 1940–41, as the nation and the US government turned its attention elsewhere; the WPA and FWP ended not long after. In 1941, as World War II began, a selection of ex-slave narratives was deposited at the Library of Congress; in 1945, as the war ended, B. A. Botkin finally issued his anthology, *Lay My Burden Down*, for decades the only published collection. John Lomax passed away in 1948, but his accomplishments continue to be rolled out to this day: without John A. Lomax the field of American folklore would be very different and greatly diminished. B. A. Botkin lived until 1972. To the end he promoted and published FWP folklore materials, including excerpts from the ex-slaves narratives.[10] Many other folklorists marginally connected to the project persevered, some earning their greatest distinctions after the war. On the backs of such achievements, the field of folklore would rise over the following decades to an academically credentialed profession. By all indications, however, the FWP's rank and file workers never achieved such visibility, or made much of a mark on the academic or literary worlds beyond their brief time with the project. After December 7, 1941, almost all of them would have been swept up in World War II, whether as active duty service men and women or in some other capacity. Actuarial tables suggest many perished over the next four years, but the majority would have survived, hopefully to enjoy the post-WWII prosperity. They certainly deserved it.

No doubt some of the ex-slaves also lived past WWII, though by 1950 even the youngest would have been in their mid-eighties. Whether any of them ever truly received their just rewards in this life is, sadly, doubtful, but numbers reportedly found some happiness and contentment. Maybe a few resurfaced in the documentary record after their brushes with the FWP, perhaps a news feature or local obituary, but that is a question for other researchers. Then too, some of the ex-slaves definitely did not live past, or even up to World War II. A few subjects had passed before the project began, their materials being submitted by children or grandchildren. Mississippi fieldworker Elizabeth Bradley gave a pair of "FOLKSONGS Sung by Uncle Steve Stepney (1840–1935) to his grandchildren who now sing it [them], in the cotton fields" (Steve Stepney, 1840–1935, MS, 2039). Ex-slave Jack Rabb "was a barber by trade, also a musician, playing the Fife for the Columbus Riflemen, an historic Military Company. Members of this company were present at his funeral" (Jack Rabb, b. unk., MS, 1774). The unidentified writer does not say when the funeral took place. Other narrators died during the course of the project. Mrs. D. W. Giles, who interviewed Chaney Williams, reported that Williams passed shortly afterwards on June 11, 1937 (Chaney Moore Williams, ca. 1852–1937, MS, 2304–5). When Indiana fieldworker Beulah Van Meter interviewed George Thomas in spring 1936, he "lived at the Clark County Poor Farm, but he drowned in the 1937 flood" (George Thomas, ca. 1855–1937, IN, 222).

Scattered instances aside, we can probably assume the balance of the ex-slaves outlived the project, but for us their stories end with the narratives themselves. How they reacted to the cataclysmic events about to unfold across the planet, we can only imagine. Nor can we know anything of their final days, thoughts, and feelings except that these would have been as varied as their lives, personalities, and intellects. Even as they spoke to interviewers, many ex-slaves were prepared to meet their maker. Others had no plans to go anywhere (or at least to go gently). Given the lives they had led and all they had seen and experienced, most seemed ready for anything.

> How-come I know all that, I was raise up wid de old people. Come along right behind de old race en I would be dere listenin widout no ears and seein widout no eyes. Yes, mam, I took what I hear in, lady, en I ain' just now come here. I been

Fig. 24.3. Bill and Ellen Thomas, ex-slaves, May 22, 1937, Hondo, TX. Texas fieldworkers Stanley H. Holm and Florence Angermiller wrote: "Bill and Ellen Thomas live in the Old Slave Settlement, 3 miles north of Hondo. Bill is 88 and Ellen is 81. They seem to be happy; their fields are tilled, a horse and a cow graze near the house; a kitchen garden is underway and several broods of baby chicks are in the yard. They were dressed in simple, clean clothes, and Ellen wears a string of nutmegs around her neck, to 'make yer eyes strong'" (S1 5 TX 4: 85). Bill, an in-demand dance fiddler before he joined the church, was born in 1849 in Missouri but was taken first to Mississippi then Texas, then during the war to Mexico, where he was eventually freed. Ellen was born around 1856 in Mississippi. After the war she was also kept in bondage for a time and brought to Hondo, where in 1871 she met and married Bill and moved onto the farm where they still lived in 1937. Portraits of African American ex-slaves from the US Works Progress Administration, Federal Writers' Project slave narratives collection, Library of Congress.

here a time. Dat de reason I done wid de world. God knows I is done. I is done. (Julia Woodberry, b. ca. 1865, SC, child of ex-slaves, 245–46)

I sho' is glad I ain't no slave no moah. Ah thank God that ah lived to pas the yeahs until the day of 1937. Ah'm happy and satisfied now, and ah hopes ah see a million yeahs to come. (Richard Toler, b. ca. 1835, VA, 101)

I can't get about none now. I sits here by myself all day, singing the old church songs. When I get too lonesome and the tears falls from my eyes, I often hears a voice say "Every tear that comes from your eyes is going to be bottled up and opened in heaven for you as a prayer." The song I sings most is

> Oh—grave yard. Oh—grave yard.
> You must give over to the body,
> Dig my grave with a silver spade
> You must give over to the body.
> Let me down with the golden chain
> You must give over to the body. (Mollie Edmonds, b. ca. 1855, MS, 674)[11]

Now yer take dat an' go. Put that in the book. Yer kin make out wif dat. I ain't a-gonna tell yer no more. Nosir. The end a time is at hand anyway. T'ain't no use ter write a book. (Elizabeth Sparks, b. 1841, VA, 277)

I'se too sleepy ter sing yer no song, but one I lacs is dis—hit suits me now in my age—hits:

> My lates' sun is sinkin' fas'
> My race is nearly run
> My stronges' trial now is pas'
> My triump' jes' begun.

You come back en I'll sing de res', I'se gotta see 'bout things now. (Josh Horn, b. 1853, AL, 199)[12]

NOTES

The WPA Ex-Slave Narratives

1. Liza Jones's song is a version of the Black folk spiritual "When the Train Comes Along," which originated in the late 1800s, long after slavery.

2. The WPA was always itself a work in progress. In 1939 it actually changed its name from the Works Progress Administration to the Work Projects Administration. Hereafter, I will simply refer to it as the WPA. The FWP followed suit, changing midway through its tenure from the Federal Writers' Project to the Federal Writers' Program. For convenience I will always refer to it as the Writers' Project or FWP. The authoritative history is Jerre Mangione, *The Dream and the Deal: The Federal Writers' Project, 1935–1943* (Boston: Little, Brown, 1972). Also see Jeutonne P. Brewer, *The Federal Writers' Project: A Bibliography* (Metuchen, NJ: Scarecrow, 1994).

3. For surveys, see Epstein, *Sinful*, 3–302; Eileen Southern and Josephine Wright, *African-American Traditions in Song, Sermon, Tale, and Dance, 1600s–1920* (1990); Eileen Southern, ed., *Readings in Black American Music* (New York: W. W. Norton, 1971); Bruce Jackson, *The Negro and His Folklore in Nineteenth-Century Periodicals* (Austin: University of Texas Press, 1967).

4. William Francis Allen, Charles Pickard Ware, and Lucy McKim Garrison, *Slave Songs of the United States* (1867). Also see Epstein, *Sinful*, 303–42.

5. "On the Field and Work of a Journal of American Folk-Lore," *JAF* 1 (1888): 3. The third and fourth objectives were Native American folklore and the "Lore of French Canada, Mexico, etc.," both of which also received ample coverage in early *JAF* volumes.

6. For the various forms and formats of slave narratives from the colonial era to the twentieth century, and different scholarly approaches, see Blassingame, *Testimony*; Charles T. Davis and Henry Louis Gates Jr., eds., *The Slave's Narrative* (Oxford: Oxford University Press, 1985).

7. Ophelia Settle Egypt, J. Masuoka, and Charles S. Johnson, eds., *Unwritten History of Slavery: Autobiographical Account of Negro Ex-Slaves*, Social Science Source Documents No. 1 (Nash-

ville: Social Science Institute, Fisk University, 1945; rpt. Rawick, *American Slave* 18: *Unwritten History of Slavery [Fisk University]*). Charles S. Johnson, Paul Radin, and A. P. Watson, eds., *God Struck Me Dead: Religious Conversion Experiences and Autobiographies of Negro Ex-Slaves*, Social Science Source Documents No. 2 (Nashville: Social Science Institute, Fisk University, 1945; rpt. Rawick, *American Slave* 19: *God Struck Me Dead [Fisk University]*).

8. See *Cabin* I; *Cabin* III.

9. Charles L. Perdue Jr., "Introduction," *Weevils*, xvii–xx. A handful of other narratives surviving in the national collection or state archives were gathered in late 1936 before the ex-slaves project's formal inception (see especially the Georgia materials). These were evidently produced as part of the Writers' Project's general mission but may also have helped inspire or shape the ex-slaves narratives project as it came to be.

10. Information on the project's operations uncovered by George Rawick and his collaborators is included in the individual volume introductions to *The American Slave*, 41 vols. (1972–79). Also see T. Lindsay Baker and Julie P. Baker, *The WPA Oklahoma Slave Narratives* (Norman: University of Oklahoma Press, 1996), 3–17; Clayton, *Mother Wit*, 1–15; Davis and Gates, *Slave's Narrative*; Jerrold Hirsch, "Forward," Botkin, *Burden*, ix–xxiv; George E. Lankford, *Bearing Witness: Memories of Arkansas Slavery Narratives from the 1930s WPA Collections* (Fayetteville: University of Arkansas Press, 2003), xi–xxvi; Mangione, *The Dream and the Deal*, esp. 263–65; Perdue, "Introduction," xi–xlv; Rawick, *Sundown*.

11. The Federal Writers' Project always delegated most responsibility and authority to the states, which were eventually given complete independence. The ex-slaves project was, for obvious reasons, focused in the former slave states, whose individual participation varied greatly. For the national collection deposited at the Library of Congress (1941), Arkansas contributed by far the most material, with sizable showings for Georgia, North Carolina, South Carolina, and Texas. Alabama, Florida, Oklahoma, and Mississippi also submitted numerous narratives but far fewer than might be expected, and Kentucky, Maryland, Missouri, and Tennessee

sent very little. Louisiana and Virginia maintained independence throughout the project; Virginia forwarded a few narratives to the Library of Congress, but Louisiana sent nothing at all. In the 1970s George P. Rawick and his team found that some other states had held back thousands of pages of material, greatly increasing the totals for some underrepresented states (Mississippi and Texas were the most dramatic examples, but Alabama, Georgia, Oklahoma, North Carolina, and South Carolina also made significant gains); however, in other cases there simply was no more. The reasons for these discrepancies are not always clear and apparently varied from state to state. (For what is known, see the introductions to the individual slave narrative volumes, cited in the Narrators Index.) Moreover, while the ex-slaves project was concentrated in the former Confederacy, it was national in scope; ex-slaves had settled throughout the United States. Indiana and Ohio each collected considerable material, with a handful of narratives coming from the Writers' Projects of Arizona, Colorado, the District of Columbia, Kansas, Minnesota, Nebraska, New York, Oregon, Rhode Island, and Washington. Again, there appear to be various reasons why some states outside the South participated while others did not.

12. This is a more general problem in the humanities and social sciences. For numerous historical examples of fieldworkers and researchers sabotaging their results by failing to recognize folklore in their materials, see Américo Paredes, "On Ethnographic Work Among Minority Groups: A Folklorist's Perspective," *New Scholar* 6 (1977): 1–32.

13. Mangione, *The Dream and the Deal*, esp. 97–100.

14. John A. Lomax, *Adventures of a Ballad Hunter* (New York: Macmillan, 1947), 12. Also see Nolan Porterfield, *Last Cavalier: The Life and Times of John A. Lomax, 1867–1948* (Urbana: University of Illinois Press, 1996).

15. Lomax, *Ballad Hunter*, 106–302; Benjamin Filene, *Romancing the Folk: Public Memory and American Roots Music* (Chapel Hill: University of North Carolina Press, 2000), 47–73; Porterfield, *Last Cavalier*, 273–430; D. K. Wilgus, *Anglo-American Folksong Scholarship Since 1898* (New Brunswick, NJ: Rutgers University Press, 1959), 185–88.

16. Besides Botkin and John Lomax, other American folklore pioneers directly or indirectly involved in the project included Mary Elizabeth Barnicle (1891–1978), Genevieve Wilcox Chandler (1890–1980), John Henry Faulk (1913–1990), Herbert Halpert (1911–2000), Zora Neale Hurston (1891–1960), Guy B. Johnson (1901–1991), Alan Lomax (1915–2002), Robert Tallant (1909–1957), and Ruby Pickens Tartt (1880–1974).

17. This item appears in various print sources, the earliest a broadside by De Marsan, New York, ca. 1880 (Roud V1451). Also see Arnold, *Alabama*, 107; *Country Music Sources*, 267; Randolph, *OFS* II: 417. RECORDINGS: Mrs. Ray Oxford, "Rag Pat," field

rec., Fayetteville, AR, December 1941, *Ozark Folksongs*, Rounder CD 1108, 2001; Cecil & Vi, "Ragged Pat" (Bluebird B-8880, 1941). Throughout this book I note relevant sound recordings whenever possible. For rarely recorded items like this one, those references may be fairly complete; however, for more extensively recorded titles, comprehensive citations would not only be too lengthy but would duplicate other readily available sources. In such cases, then, I have referred readers to these other sources, listing only a few select recordings that bear some direct connection to the ex-slave materials; that indicate something of a tradition's breadth and variety; or that illustrate specific points under discussion. For field recordings, I have generally limited myself to items that have been released in a form available to readers (LP, CD, Internet), again directing them to other sources for more complete coverage. For titles discussed briefly or mentioned only in passing, I may merely indicate the relevant discographies without listing any specific recordings. For outside support, I am especially indebted to Robert M. W. Dixon, John Godrich, and Howard Rye's *Blues and Gospel Records*, Robert Laughton's *Gospel Discography*, Guthrie T. Meade Jr., Dick Spottswood, and Douglas S. Meade's *Country Music Sources*, and Tony Russell's *Country Music Records*. *Blues and Gospel Records*, *Country Music Records*, and the *Gospel Discography* are all arranged alphabetically by artist, so that recordings of any given piece are scattered throughout; all three have comprehensive song indices, however, making it easy to locate relevant examples (although sometimes under variant titles). I accordingly give no page numbers when citing these three works. The materials in *Country Music Sources*, which include both sound recordings and printed works, are divided into thematic chapters, then subdivided by song or song family, so for this book I have provided page numbers. Also see note 22 below.

18. This circumstance does not always cast workers in a favorable light: many writers were incontestably familiar with academic folksong collections because they plagiarized from them.

19. Perdue, "Introduction," xxxv. These discs were apparently acquired from Hampton College by the Library of Congress, but as of this writing have not been issued. See Mrs. Annie Little in *Blues and Gospel Records*. In 1941 John Henry Faulk independently recorded interviews with two ex-slaves, Laura Smalley and Aunt Harriet Smith; these were originally released as *Actual Voices of Ex-Slaves*, Mark 56 LP 785, 1977, and subsequently on *Field Recordings, Vols. 10 & 11*, Document CD 5600. Also see *Blues and Gospel Records*.

20. For example, a lengthy passage that Kentucky interviewer Mamie Hanberry included in the narrative of Easter Sudie Campbell (b. ca. 1865, KY, child of ex-slaves, 94–98) is paraphrased, with some direct quotations but without attribution, from "A Night Among the Wolves," *Harper's Monthly* 6 (May 1853): 810–12, or

from a reprinting of that piece. (Hanberry also plagiarized half a dozen song texts, and most of her other materials are bogus or suspect.) The story imputed to Easter Campbell, in which a fiddler charms a pack of wolves with his playing, is a well-documented American folktale with European antecedents. In America it was often told about Black fiddlers and regularly adapted for popular periodicals beginning around 1840. For other versions featuring Blacks, see J. F. H. Claiborne, "A Trip Through the Piney Woods" (1841; rpt. in *Little Classics of the South: Mississippi* [New York: Purdy, 1927]), 10–16; Denis Defoe, "Orpheus in Kentucky: Or, the forced Fiddler," *NASS* 11 (August 20, 1840): 44; "A Negro Fiddler," *New England Weekly Review* 40 (October 5, 1839). Also see Halpert, *Pinelands*, 372. Similarly, a passage attributed by interviewer Ada Davis to Texas ex-slave Wash Wilson (b. 1846, TX, 4241–43) is copied, with embellishments, from George Washington Cable's "The Dance in Place Congo," *Century* 31 (February 1886): 519, or from some paraphrase of Cable's account. (The African-style instruments that Cable described at slave gatherings in New Orleans' Congo Square—this passage's subject—were never documented in North America outside New Orleans and had receded there by the start of the Civil War.) Davis also plagiarized numerous song texts.

21. As one such check, folksong texts vary constantly, but only certain types of variation occur naturally within oral tradition; other changes immediately implicate editorial tampering, plagiarism, forgery, or other outside meddling. See Thomas A. Burns, "A Model for Textual Variation in Folksong," *Folklore Forum* 3 (1970): 49–56.

22. On Lomax's editorial methods and use of composites, see Wilgus, *Anglo-American Folksong Scholarship*, 157–65, 216–20. John Lomax was also a pioneer in field recording, of course, and many of his published texts were based on sound recordings that have survived, and that are now available in various formats. These recordings, cited throughout the book, not only feature the original texts and tunes but, of course, the actual performances. They are the primary documents of Lomax's epochal achievements. Because early field recording by Lomax and others focused on vanishing traditions and older performers (including a few ex-slaves but even more of their children and grandchildren), materials described in the ex-slave narratives often turn up on their recordings, which generally provide the most credible guides to the actual sounds of slave music and song. During the 1920s and '30s, commercial record labels also issued thousands of Southern folksong performances on so-called "race records" and "hillbilly records." Unlike folklorists, these corporations emphasized younger performers and more recent trends, but occasionally their releases featured older performers or performances relevant to our subject, which I have noted as well. There are even some post–WWII recordings (mainly from the field, occasionally from commercial sources) suggesting connections to slave music, or featuring performances of items slaves knew, albeit

perhaps in far-removed styles. With those qualifications, I have also cited these. Also see note 17 above.

23. For context and corroboration, I have relied most heavily on primary sources from the 1800s, and in any case from before WWII, the span of the ex-slaves' lives as we know them. I have definitely remained abreast of current scholarship, and I have done my best to acknowledge every assistance I have thereby received. This is not, however, a survey of everything that has ever been written about the WPA ex-slave narratives, slave music, or slavery. It is certainly not an attempt to re-tailor the narratives around some fashionable new theory, or festoon them with some ridiculous new jargon. In a handful of instances I have, for fairness and clarity, indicated my disagreements with previous scholarship, but in most such cases I simply let it be. These differences of opinion are now in print for any interested readers to pursue on their own, and there is too much to cover in this book already.

24. Despite the confusions, this is obviously a version of the well-known Black dance song "Rolling Over (Rolling Under)," discussed later in this book. Ex-slaves Rosa Maddox, Susan Merritt, and Wright Stapleton also gave versions.

25. "Jesus Will Fix It For You" is a traditional Black spiritual, but definitely a postwar (possibly a twentieth-century) creation. (Narrator John Thompson named "God Will Fix It Fer You," probably the same song.) RECORDINGS: Jessie Mae Hemphill, "Jesus Will Fix It," *Get Right Blues*, Inside Sounds CD 0519, 2003. DISCOGRAPHIES: *Blues and Gospel Records*.

26. Related by other ex-slaves, the story of pregnant women whipped in the field with holes dug for their bellies is emblematic of many slaveholders' bestial brutality, but this appears to be a migratory legend, not a factual account. Internal textual evidence indicates as much, and the practice would have been completely contrary to slaveholders' carefully guarded economic interests. Slaveholders were especially mindful that child-bearing slaves increased their labor force (or saleable property) at minimal cost, and by other accounts, pregnant women were sometimes given additional food, leisure, or other privileges to ensure healthy slave babies. On the other hand, the practice of stripping men, women, and children naked in the fields (or elsewhere) to flog them is documented in multiple credible sources. The folktale was also told by ex-slaves Henry Cheatam, Ellen Cragin, Francis Doby, Mary Gaines, Marie E. Hervey, Mary Johnson, Robert St. Ann, and Lizzie Williams.

27. Leroy's Buddy (Bill Gaither), "Champ Joe Louis (King of the Gloves)" (Decca 7476, 1938). Rena Kosersky and William H. Wiggins Jr., booklet accompanying *Joe Louis: An American Hero*, Rounder CD 1106, 2001 (includes Gaither's recording and sixteen other songs about Louis); Paul Oliver, *Aspects of the Blues Tradition* (1968; rpt. New York: Oak, 1970), 148–63.

28. Smith, *Fifty Years*, 173.

29. Some WPA narrators were contacted by other individuals and organizations. Richard Toler (b. ca. 1835, VA, 97–101) was interviewed in Cincinnati in June 1937 by FWP fieldworker Ruth Thompson. In the Ohio state files, Rawick's team found a December 1938 clipping from an unidentified newspaper featuring another lengthy profile of Toler (SS1 5 *OH*: 452–54). In 1938 Henry Baker (b. 1854, AL) was interviewed by Thomas Monroe Campbell, a Tuskegee graduate and US Department of Agriculture farm demonstration agent. Blassingame, *Testimony*, 655–77. Around the same time, Baker and his wife, identified only as Mother and Father Baker, were interviewed by Rhussus L. Perry of the Alabama Writers' Project (SS1 1 *AL*: 30–34).

Africa, Europe, and African Americans

1. Numerous other ex-slaves also told the red hankie tale: Polly Turner Cancer, Peter Corn, Hannah Crasson, Della Fountain, Richard Jones, C. G. Samuel, and Annie Groves Scott. In a note to Cancer's text, interviewer Minnie Holt states, "this tradition of red handkerchiefs was told also by Lucindy Shaw," but the story does not appear in Shaw's narrative (Lucindy Hall Shaw, b. ca. 1850, MS, 1925–31). For other versions, see Dance, *Shuckin' and Jivin'*, 10; *Drums and Shadows*, 121, 145, 164, 176, 183–84; Parrish, *Sea Islands*, 28–29. Ex-slave Paul Smith told a variation in which the slave ships themselves were painted red, thereby attracting unsuspecting Africans.

2. Melville J. Herskovits, *The Myth of the Negro Past* (1941; rpt. Boston: Beacon, 1958).

3. The Gulf Coast's illegal slave trade involved some of the era's most notorious thugs, many based on Galveston Island. They ran various rackets, but their most profitable trade was hijacking slave ships in the Gulf and Caribbean, then smuggling the cargos into the US (Cuba and its shipping lanes, a major hub for African slaves bound for Latin America, were within 800 miles of Galveston). The most famous of these pirates was Jean Lafitte (ca. 1780–ca. 1825), who sometimes auctioned the stolen slaves at his Galveston slave market, but other times transported them directly to the Vermilion Bay, Louisiana, base of one of his best customers, Jim Bowie (1796–1836), who then sold them to Louisiana and Mississippi planters. Somewhat later, Bowie also engaged in illegal slaving in Texas. Fred Robbins, "The Origin and Development of the African Slave Trade in Galveston, Texas, and Surrounding Areas from 1816 to 1836," *East Texas Historical Journal* 9 (1971): 153–61; Harris Gaylord Warren, "Lafitte, Jean," William W. Williamson, "Bowie, James," *Handbook of Texas*.

4. John W. Cell, "Race Relations," Albert J. Raboteau, "Religion, Black," *Encyclopedia of Southern Culture*, ed. Charles Reagan Wilson and William Ferris (Chapel Hill: University of North Carolina Press, 1989), 190, 191.

5. Paul Laurence Dunbar (1872–1906), "When Malindy Sings" (1896), *When Malindy Sings* (New York: Dodd Mead, 1903), 9–14. Inspired by his ex-slave mother's love of spirituals, this was one of Dunbar's most popular poems, a common recitation in the period Anngady describes.

6. John Wright, *Early Bibles of America* (New York: T. Whittaker, 1894), 277–80.

7. Booklet accompanying *Creation's Journey: Native American Music*, Smithsonian/Folkways CD 40410, 1994, 12, which features two Southern Gospel songs in Cherokee. Ex-slave Harriet Miller, who herself had a Cherokee father and white mother, recalled that during her childhood "some Indians camped on the river bottoms for three or four years, and we'd go down; me, and Anne, and Genia, nearly every Saturday, to hear 'em preach. We couldn't understand it. Dey didn't have no racket or nothing like colored folks. Dey would sing, and it sounded all right. We couldn't understand it, but dey enjoyed it" (Harriet Miller, b. ca. 1837, GA, 130). Given the locale, these Indians were most likely also Cherokee. It is unclear what Miller meant by *preach*, but the implication may be that they were conducting Bible study and singing Anglo-American hymns and spirituals in the Cherokee language.

8. Davis's first example—"What yo' gwine do when de meat give out (come in)"—is a wandering verse pair from the Black-white lyric complex variously titled "The Crawdad Song," "Ain't No Use Me Working So Hard," "Sugar Babe," "Sweet Thing," and more, all evidence indicating origins after 1900. *Country Music Sources*, 504–6. The particular stanzas Davis recalled are known mainly from commercial recordings: Carolina Tar Heels, "Back to Mexico" (Victor 23611, 1930); Dock Walsh, "Going Back to Jericho" (Columbia 15094-D, 1926); Doc Watson, Gaither Carlton, Ralph Rinzler, "I'm Going Back to Jericho," field rec., Deep Gap, NC, 1960, *The Original Folkways Recordings of Doc Watson and Clarence Ashley, 1960–1962*, Smithsonian/Folkways CDs 40029/30, 1994; Josh White, "Watcha Gonna Do" (Mercury 1117, ca. 1942) (White re-recorded the piece several times). True to character, Fiddlin' John Carson changed the line to "Watcha Gonna Do When Your Licker Gives Out?" (OKeh 45434, 1929). Davis's second example ("Great big nigger, laying 'hind de log") first appears among African Americans during this same period. Arnold, *Alabama*, 121; Bass, "Negro Songs," 433; Brown III: 566; Brown and Owens, *Toting*, 131; Lomax, *Ballads*, 255; Odum and Johnson, *NHS*, 234; Charles Peabody, "Notes on Negro Music," *JAF* 16 (1903): 149; Owens, *Texas*, 176; Perrow, "South" (1915): 136; Scarborough, *TNFS*, 176; Spaeth,

Read 'Em, 125; Talley, *NFR*, 141; White, *ANFS*, 139–40, 192, 231. It also turns up on numerous pre–WWII recordings, such as Beale Street Sheiks (Stokes and Sane), "You Shall" (Paramount 12518, 1927); Frank Hutchison, "Coney Isle" (OKeh 45083, 1927); Uncle Dave Macon, "Keep My Skillet Good and Greasy" (Vocalion 14848, 1924); Morris Brothers (Wiley & Zeke), "Let Me Be Your Salty Dog" (Bluebird B-7967, 1938); Gid Tanner & His Skillet Lickers, "Uncle Bud" (Columbia 15134-D, 1926).

9. The stomp dance was practiced by many Southeastern and other Native American groups. Among the Cherokee it was (and is) a major religious observance affiliated with the Green Corn Ceremony, which marks the ripening of the corn in late summer. As ex-slave John Harrison mentioned, the dances are accompanied by call-and-response singing and turtle-shell rattles worn on the dancers' legs, sometimes with drums as well. In the late nineteenth century, the stomp dance experienced a major revival among the Cherokee in Indian Territory (now Oklahoma) that continues to present. See "The Stomp Dance," northerncherokeenation.com /the-stomp-dance.html. Many videos of present-day stomp dances are also posted on YouTube.

10. Ex-slaves Lucy Galloway, Jim Martin, and Laura Montgomery also described African preachers in Mississippi.

11. Gwendolyn Midlo Hall, *Africans in Colonial Louisiana: The Development of Afro-Creole Culture in the Eighteenth Century* (Baton Rouge: Louisiana State University Press, 1992), 35–56, 121–24; Charles Joyner, *Down by the Riverside: A South Carolina Slave Community* (Urbana: University of Illinois Press, 1984), 41–89; Joseph E. Holloway, "The Origins of African-American Culture," *Africanisms in American Culture*, ed. Joseph E. Holloway (Bloomington: Indiana University Press, 1990), 12–16.

12. Ex-slaves who described dancing while balancing water vessels were Fannie Berry, Fred Brown, Marie Brown, Maggie Broyles, Gabe Butler, Lizzie Chandler, Hannah Crasson, Emmaline Heard, Adeline Jackson, Lewis Jones, Hunton Love, Harriet Miller, Malinda Mitchell, James W. Smith, and Nancy Williams.

13. William Bascom, *Shango in the New World* (Austin: African and Afro-American Research Institute, University of Texas, 1972); William Bascom, *The Yoruba of Southwestern Nigeria* (New York: Holt, Rinehart and Winston, 1969), esp. 84–91; Joel E. Tishken, Tóyìn Fálolá, and Akíntúndé Akínyemí, eds., *Sàngó in Africa and the African Diaspora* (Bloomington: Indiana University Press, 2009); Robert Farris Thompson, *Flash of the Spirit: African and Afro-American Art and Philosophy* (New York: Vintage, 1983), 84–99.

14. Ruth Bass, "Mojo," *Scribner's* 87 (1930), 84; Puckett, *Folk Beliefs*, 320. This belief was borrowed by Anglo-Americans. As late as the 1950s, white Alabamians knew that "you just take the

double-bladed ax [Shàngó's emblem] and stick it like that, and it splits the storm—yes, not the *single-bladed*, though." Browne, *Hants*, 76, my emphasis.

15. Bascom, *Shango in the New World*, 4.

16. Hyatt, *Hoodoo* I: 655; Puckett, *Folk Beliefs*, 315.

17. Thompson, *Flash of the Spirit*, 85.

18. Robert Farris Thompson, *African Art in Motion: Icon and Act* (Los Angeles: University of California Press, 1974), 96. In one ceremony, Yoruba women reenact their daily chore of going to the river, filling their water pots, then returning to the village with the vessels balanced on their heads, but dancing instead of walking. Bascom, *The Yoruba*, 88.

19. Also see Anita Fonvergne and Rose Holman.

20. Vivaldo da Costa Lima, *Una festa de Xango no Opo Afonja* (Salvador: Universidade de Bahia, 1959), 19, trans. Thompson, *Flash of the Spirit*, 87. These and similarly spectacular acts (balancing fire pots, passing hands through flames, eating burning cotton balls, sitting on spear points, releasing rope-bound captives) also occur in Nigerian ceremonies, usually performed by Shàngó's *mounts* or *horses* (mediums). Bascom, *Shango in the New World*, 4–5.

21. The bàtá vary in size and thus in range, but each drum also produces two pitches (one for each of the cylinder's ends). Together, the ensemble's different pitches imitate the tonal Yoruba language, still spoken in some areas of Latin America. Juan Benkomo, "Crafting the Sacred *Bàtá* Drums," *Afro-Cuban Voices: On Race and Identity in Contemporary Cuba*, ed. Pedro Pérez Sarduy and Jean Stubbs (Gainesville: University Press of Florida, 2000), 140–46; Henry B. Lovejoy, "Drums of Sàngó: *Bàtá* Drum and the Reestablishment of Òyó in Colonial Cuba, 1817–1867," *Sàngó in Africa*, 284–308; Morton Marks, booklet accompanying *Havana and Matanzas, Cuba, ca. 1957: Batá, Bembé, and Palo Songs*, Smithsonian/Folkways CD 40434, 2003.

22. Dick Spottswood, booklet accompanying *Shango, Shouter and Obeah: Supernatural Calypso from Trinidad 1934–1940*, Rounder CD 1107, 2001; quotations are from The Growler, "Bongo Dance," and The Lion, "Shango." Also see Bascom, *Shango in the New World*, 10–12.

23. Bascom, *Shango in the New World*, 5–17.

24. Métraux, *Voodoo*, 203–10. On Shàngó in Haiti, see Bascom, *Shango in the New World*, 12–13. *Vodun*, the basis of Haitian *voudon*, originated among the Fọn of Dahomey (Benin). I have not found head-balancing rituals described with Fọn vodun, but other West African groups employ the practice. Akan women sometimes dance at funerals with glasses of water balanced on their heads (accidentally spilling the water suggests the offender caused the death by witchcraft). Akan priests also dance with vessels balanced on their heads in hopes the gods will fill the pots with their wisdom.

Robert Farris Thompson, "An Aesthetic of the Cool: African Dance," *African Forum* 2 (1966): 17.

25. Both quotes are from Robert Tallant's *Voodoo in New Orleans*, 111, 139, which was based mainly on material collected by the Louisiana Writers' Project. Some of these narratives were also deposited with the Louisiana ex-slave narratives, including a different interview with Marie Brown (b. unk., LA, 33–36) (or a different version of this interview).

26. Hurston, "Hoodoo," 327. There were actually two New Orleans hoodoo queens named Marie Laveau, a mother (aka the Widow Paris, ca. 1776–1881), and her daughter, Marie II (1827–ca. 1890). This story concerns Marie II. Marie Brown's grandmother, Queen Eliza, was a contemporary of Widow Paris, at whose events she danced, but Brown had personally observed Marie II, who was active during her lifetime. Ex-slave Harrison Camille also described Marie II's St. John's Eve dances. Also see Tallant, *Voodoo*, 61–151; *Gumbo Ya-Ya*, 168-69, 323, 388, 391; George Washington Cable, "Creole Slave Songs," *Century* 31 (1886): 815–16; Puckett, *Folk Beliefs*, 179–80.

27. Tallant, *Voodoo*, 78–79.

28. Epstein, *Sinful*, 120–24; Southern, *Music*, 45–46.

29. To create a percussive accompaniment, dancers in Africa wear secondary or sympathetic rattles: ornaments or attachments that sound in time to dance steps and movements, such as the anklets of cowries (sea snail shells) common in West Africa. Secondary rattles were well known to Latin American and Caribbean Blacks, but except for in New Orleans they are little reported among North American slaves. The ex-slaves do not mention them with Black dancers. (A few ex-slaves do describe secondary rattles among Native Americans, who also employed them; see note 9 above.) For New Orleans, see Cable, "Place Congo," 523; Creecy, *Scenes*, 21; Flint, *Recollections*, 140; Tallant, *Voodoo*, 7, 17, 19, 145; Thomas, *Tennessee Slave*, 108.

30. Parker, *Recollections*, 310.

31. Davis, "Echoes," 59.

32. Fletcher, *Story*, 19.

33. Hearn, *Levee*, 75–76.

34. Gladys-Marie Fry, *Night Riders in Black Folk History* (Knoxville: University of Tennessee Press, 1975), 108.

35. In 1972, Les Blank filmed a Creole male dancing with a serving tray balanced on his head at a zydeco show in southwest Louisiana. The sequence originally appeared in *Hot Pepper*, Brazos Films, 1973, and has reappeared since in other films including *J'ai été au bal: Roots of Cajun and Zydeco Music*, dir. Les Blank, Chris Strachwitz, and Maureen Gosling, Brazos Films DVD 103, 2002, *Part II: Zydeco Roots*, scene 42, *Clifton Chenier, Zydeco Two-Step*; *American Roots Music*, dir. Jim Brown, Palm Pictures DVDs, 2001, episode four, chap. 2: *All My Children of the Sun: Zydeco*.

36. Only one ex-slave mentioned a white performing this feat: "My mistress had long hair, techin' de floor and could dance, so Marster John said, wid a glass of water on top of her head" (Adeline Jackson, b. ca. 1849, SC, 1). There is also a late-1800s description of white women dancing with candles on their heads at a Marie Laveau ceremony (where whites commonly participated). Tallant, *Voodoo*, 111.

37. Nettl, *Folk Music*, 128–60.

38. Compare David Evans, "Patterns of Reinterpretation in African-American Music of the United States," *African Perspectives: Pre-Colonial History, Anthropology, and Ethno-Musicology*, ed. Regine Allgayer-Kaufmann and Michael Weber (Frankfurt: Peter Lang, 2008), 207–14; Evans, "Reinterpretation," esp. 279–81. While much African American music merely displays this general African character, African regional traditions are evident in North American Black music as revealed in the ex-slave narratives and other sources, but are different from those in Latin America— and this appears to be another instance where the overwhelming influence of US whites was a major determinant. While the largest number of North American slaves came from West and Central Africa, by the colonial era the music of North American slaves predominantly recalled the traditions of West Africa, and especially the inland savannah region known as the Western Sudan. Central African cultural influences were rife among American slaves, but Central African musical traits seem decidedly muted. There are various possible explanations, but the key factor may have been that West African music more closely coincided with the European-based music and musical tastes of North American whites. The most important instrument in the Western Sudan was the fiddle, followed by various plucked lutes, the ancestors of the American banjo. In North America, African fiddles were immediately replaced by European violins—the most popular instruments among American whites—and by the late 1700s Blacks were America's premier violinists, excelling in every existing style, folk, popular, and classical. Beginning in the same period, African American fiddlers were often accompanied by banjos (in Africa the instruments were usually played separately), which by happy coincidence closely resembled various European lutes (such as the guitar), and which American whites borrowed from slaves; by mid-century whites were commercially manufacturing banjos redesigned in the pattern of European fretted stringed instruments. This lineup—fiddle and banjo with simple percussion and sometimes winds—became the basis of slave dance bands. Crucially too, in the 1840s blackface minstrels—the nineteenth century's most commercially successful musical entertainers—adopted this same instrumentation, and from that point to the onset of World War II, the fiddle-banjo combo became the basis of most American string bands, institutionalizing West Africa influences in North American folk music.

Central African traditions fared far differently in the United States, and again white cultural domination may have been the key. The African-style drums, drum orchestras, and polyrhythmic drumming especially characteristic of Central Africa continued to flourish in some areas of Latin America but not in North America, where Black drumming was early reshaped by European-style drums, European martial music, and isometric European tune types. Other instruments typical of Central Africa—for example, the xylophone and lamellophone (thumb piano)—simply disappeared among US Blacks, possibly because they had no ready white equivalents. The quills or panpipes played by many North American slaves may be related to similar instruments common in Central Africa, but also in other African regions; however, the quills, never taken up by American whites, had virtually disappeared among African Americans by the early twentieth century, replaced by the harmonica. The mouth bow (musical bow), another Central African staple, is occasionally reported among nineteenth-century Blacks, but even in the 1800s the mouth bow by and large had been replaced by the jew's harp, readily available throughout the antebellum South. (Jew's harps had been introduced into Africa as trade items almost immediately after European contact and were soon being manufactured locally. The mouth bow was adopted from African Americans by a few Southern whites, but they also generally favored jew's harps.) The blowing jug, a descendent of Central African voice disguisers, achieved considerable popularity among both Blacks and whites beginning in the late 1800s, but there are only a couple of reports for slaves, leaving one to wonder how the tradition survived to so suddenly reemerge. (The practice of turning the pot down, routinely reported among slaves, may be related to these same Central African voice modifiers, but this custom died out with the end of slavery.) The jitterbug or diddley bow, a makeshift one-string instrument sometimes described as a homemade guitar, has also been traced to Central Africa, but the jitterbug is concentrated in a fairly limited area of Mississippi and adjacent states, where it is played mainly by children who as adults ideally graduate to real guitars. In sum, the absolute domination of American whites and white musical standards seems to have been among the most important factors in determining the presence or absence of African regional musical traits in the United States, and the form and content of those that survived.

Patting

1. "Cotton-Eyed Joe" is one of the South's best-known dance songs, most likely created by slaves. Jim Barclay, Ned Chaney, Richard Mack, and Jack Maddox gave texts; William M. Adams and Sam Forge named it. All except Barclay identified the piece

with fiddling. Also see Bolick and Austin, *Mississippi Fiddle*, 44, 207; Bolick and Russell, *Fiddle Tunes*, 79, 155; Brown III: 138–39; Ford, *Traditional Music*, 60; Lomax, *Ballads*, 262–23; Lomax, *Country*, 99; Perrow, "South" (1915): 190; Louise-Clarke Pyrnelle, *Diddie, Dumps, and Tot: Or Plantation Child-Life* (New York: Harper & Brothers, 1882), 126–27; Scarborough, *TNFS*, 69–70; Talley, *NFR*, 27–28; Thede, *Fiddle*, 26–27; White, *ANFS*, 359; Wolfe, *Middle Tennessee*, 132–33. RECORDINGS: "Big Sweet" Lewis Hairston (vocal, banjo), "Cotton-Eyed Joe," field rec., Henry Co., VA, September 1977, *Virginia Secular Music*. DISCOGRAPHIES: *Blues and Gospel Records*; *Country Music Records*; *Country Music Sources*, 778, 780. Evidently of minstrel origin, "The Old Grey Horse (Mare) Came Tearing Out the Wilderness" parodies the spiritual "Ain't I Glad I've Got Out of the Wilderness (Leaning On the Lord)" (*DNAH*; *Slave Songs*, 14), which ex-slaves Affie Singleton and Susan Snow gave. The earliest known version of "The Old Grey Horse" is "Down In Alabam: Or Ain't I Glad I Got Out of the Wilderness" (Wm. Hall & Son, 1858), credited to J. Warner of Bryant's Minstrels. In addition to Ned Chaney, narrator Steve Jones named "The Old Grey Horse" as a play song, Mary Kindred as a jig dance. During the war and after, there were also numerous topical adaptations, including "Old Abe Lincoln Came Tearing Out the Wilderness" (Silber, *Civil War*, 90, 94–95). At present the best-known offshoot is "The Old Gray Mare, She Ain't What She Used to Be." Also see Brown III: 216–17; Cohen, *Ozark*, 231–32; Lomax, *Ballads*, 336–38; Piper, "Play-Party," 266; Randolph, *OFS* II: 349–50; Sandburg, *Songbag*, 102–3, 168; Scarborough, *TNFS*, 13–14; Solomon, *Daisies*, 50, 71; Talley, *NFR*, 206–7. RECORDINGS: Chatman Brothers (Lonnie and Sam), "Old Grey Mule, You Ain't What You Used to Be" (Bluebird B7167, 1936); Earl Johnson & His Clodhoppers, "Old Gray Mare Kicking Out of the Wilderness" (OKeh 45183, 1927); Gid Tanner & His Skillet Lickers, "The Old Gray Mare" (Columbia 15170-D, 1927). DISCOGRAPHIES: *Country Music Records*; *Country Music Sources*, 513–14.

2. Nketia, *Music of Africa*, 115. Also see Bebey, *African Music*, esp. 40–41, 119–24; Courlander, *NFM*, 29–30; Portia K. Maultsby, "Africanisms in African-American Music," *Africanisms in American Culture*, 185–210; Oliver, *Savannah Syncopators*, 47–48, 50, 53–54, 96; Roberts, *Black Music*, 8–9, 12, 29, 213–15; Richard Alan Waterman, "African Influence on Music of the Americas," *Acculturation in the Americas*, ed. Sol Tax (Chicago: University of Chicago Press, 1952), 207–18.

3. Courlander, *NFM*, 27–28, 220; Epstein, *Sinful*, 5–6, 141, 344; Nketia, *Music of Africa*, 67; Roberts, *Black Music*, 4, 10, 60, 168–69, 174.

4. See Courlander, *NFM*, 27–28; Epstein, *Sinful*, 130, 141–44, 202–3, 205, 225–26, 236, 237, 280–81, 284–85, 296, 297–98, 301–2, 308–9, 344, 353; Jones and Hawes, *Step It Down*, 14–40; Southern, *Music*, 130, 169, 170, 207, 260.

5. Northrup, *Twelve Years*, 219.

6. Smith, "Persimmon Tree," 60.

7. Paine, *Georgia Prison*, 179.

8. Robinson, "Colored People," 59. For other nineteenth-century accounts of patting or patting juba, see Maude Andrews, "The Georgia Barbecue," *Harper's Weekly* (November 9, 1895): 1072; Benners, *Slavery*, 24; Bibb, *Narrative*, 23; Douglass, *My Bondage*, 252–53; Eastman, *Aunt Phillis*, 122; H. H. B., "Reminiscences of a Southern Plantation.—Continued," *Independent* 26 (April 23, 1874): 14; Hearn, *Levee*, 71–77; H. L. F., A. A., "Louisiana," 758; Howard, *Bond and Free*, 242; Hundley, *Social Relations*, 357; Hungerford, *Plantation*, 195–99; Kirke, *Among the Pines*, 42–43; Lanman, *Adventures* II: 132; Long, *Slavery*, 17–18; Mississippi Planter, "Management of Negroes," 625; "Negro Folk Songs" (*SW*), 31–32; Parker, *Recollections*, 310; George Rogers, *Memoranda of the Experience, Labors, and Travels of a Universalist Preacher* (Cincinnati: John A. Gurley, 1845), 269; Smith, *Fifty Years*, 38, 45; Thomas, *Tennessee Slave*, 49; Thorpe, "Christmas," 62; Thompson, "Plantation Music," 20; Venable, "Down South," 497; Whitney and Bullock, *Maryland*, 162–64; Wyeth, *Sabre*, 59–63. Also see Courlander, *Music*, 190–92; Epstein, *Sinful*, 141–44; Jones and Hawes, *Step It Down*, 37–40; Johnson, *Social History*, 143–44; Lomax, *Ballads*, 237–40; Parrish, *Sea Islands*, 116; Scarborough, *TNFS*, 98–100; Southern, *Music*, 179–81; Talley, *NFR*, 7–8, 269.

9. Ex-slave John N. Davenport also gave this stanza, which appears in the earliest account of patting juba by name, William B. Smith's "The Persimmon Tree and the Beer Dance" (1838), 60, and not long afterward in blackface songbooks, suggesting minstrels played some role in its dissemination and possibly creation (see, for example, Nathan, *Dan Emmett*, 443–46). Also see Brown III: 237; Fauset, "Folk Tales," 303; Jones and Hawes, *Step It Down*, 37–40; Parrish, *Sea Islands*, 116; Talley, *NFR*, 7–8, 269; "Negro Folk Songs" (*SW*), 32; Wheeler, *Steamboatin'*, 96; White, *ANFS*, 163; Whitney and Bullock, *Maryland*, 164; Wyeth, *Sabre*, 62–63. RECORDINGS: Willie Johnson, "Pat Juba," Washington, DC, December 1940, *Freedom*.

10. Courlander, *NFM*, 192; Hungerford, *Plantation*, 196–99; Lomax, *Ballads*, 237–40; Long, *Slavery*, 18; Nathan, *Dan Emmett*, 443–45; Rosenberg, *Virginia*, 63; White, *ANFS*, 161–63; Wyeth, *Sabre*, 62–63.

11. Mississippi Planter, "Management of Negroes," 625; Douglass, *My Bondage*, 252. Also see Paine, *Georgia Prison*, 179; Smith, "Persimmon Tree," 60; Wyeth, *Sabre*, 59–60.

12. Ex-slave Andrew Moody also named "Shortenin' Bread (Cracklin' Bread)," for which see Arnold, *Alabama*, 156; Brown III: 535–38; Gordon, *Folk-Songs*, 75; Lomax, *Ballads*, 234–36; Perrow, "South" (1915): 142; Randolph, *OFS* III: 328–30; Scarborough, *TNFS*, 149–53; Solomon, *Daisies*, 74; Talley, *NFR*, 158; Thomas, "Work-

Songs," 162–63; White, *ANFS*, 193–94. RECORDINGS: Ora Dell Graham, "Shortenin' Bread," field rec., Drew Colored High School, Drew, MS, October 1940, *A Treasury of Library of Congress Field Recordings*, Rounder CD 1500, 1997; Will Slayden (vocal, banjo), "Shortnin' Bread," field rec., Shelby Co., TN, Summer 1952, *Will Slayden*. DISCOGRAPHIES: *Blues and Gospel Records*; *Country Music Records*; *Country Music Sources*, 764–65.

13. Long, *Slavery*, 17–18. For "Possum Up the Gum Tree (Stump)," see Modern Times, note 5.

14. North Carolina ex-slave Allen Parker (1840-1906) wrote: "after supper the room was cleared and made ready for the dance. If some slave could be found who had an old fiddle and could play it at all, he was called on to furnish music; if not, some one would take an old tin pan and use it like a tambourine. Two or three others 'pat Jubo.'" Parker, *Recollections*, 310.

15. These and other struck-bell substitutes—cow bells, frying pans, skillets, tin dinnerware, bottles, crockery, hoe blades and other tools—were also common in postcolonial Africa and the West Indies. Courlander, *NFM*, 208–10, 219–20; Courlander, "Cuba," 230–31; Nketia, *Music of Africa*, 73; Roberts, *Black Music*, 49, 112, 117, 185. In North America such makeshift percussion became especially identified with the groups variously called jug bands, juke bands, pickaninny bands, spasm bands, washboard bands, and so forth. Abbott and Seroff, *Out of Sight*, 403–6; Evans, "Reinterpretation," 381; David Evans, booklet accompanying *Good Time Blues*, 5–6; Paul Oliver, "Tub, Jug, Washboard Bands: Music on Improvised Instruments," *Blues Off the Record* (New York: Da Capo, 1984), 31–38.

16. Anderson, *From Slavery*, 30–31.

17. Mitchell, *Old Dominion*, 165–66. Compare Creecy, *Scenes*, 21, describing antebellum New Orleans: "The most perfect time is kept, making the beats with the feet, heads, and hands, or all, as correctly as a well-regulated metronome!"

18. Foster, "Philadelphia," 63.

19. Woods, "Corn-Shucking," 571.

20. Quotes from, respectively, Cameron, "Christmas," 5; Hungerford, *Plantation*, 196; Thorpe, "Mississippi," 37. Other descriptions of Black dancers keeping time with their feet include Bruce, "Tobacco-Plantation," 541; Bryant, "Old South," 33; Burwell, *Girl's Life*, 131; Holcombe, "Sketches," 626; Howard, *Bond and Free*, 19, 253–55; Hungerford, *Plantation*, 195–99; Ingraham, *Sunny South*, 107–8; Kirke, *Among the Pines*, 145–46; Mackay, *Western World*, II: 132; Mallard, *Plantation Life*, 162; Russell, *Southern Life*, 96; Smith, "Persimmon Tree," 60; W. L. G. Smith, *Life at the South: Or "Uncle Tom's Cabin" As It Is* (Buffalo, NY: Geo. H. Derby, 1852), 53–56, 158–63; Talley, *NFR*, 235–36; "A True Story of Texas Life," *New York Clipper* 20 (January 11, 1873): 324; Bryan Tyson, *The Institution of Slavery in the Southern States* (Washington, DC: H. Polkinhorn,

1863), 12–13; Annie Weston Whitney, "De Los' Ell an' Yard," *JAF* 10 (1897): 298; Wilson, "Old Plantation: II," 248–49; Wyeth, *Sabre*, 60–62.

21. Anderson, *From Slavery*, 30–31.

22. Wyeth, *Sabre*, 60.

23. Narrators who described dancing in the yard of the big house include Rose Adway, James Bolton, Ellen Brass, Sam Broach, Lewis Brown, Amos Clark, Mom Louisa Collier, Uncle D. Davis, Josephine Howard, Estella Jones, Caroline Malloy, Jake McLeod, Horace Overstreet, Paul Smith, Samuel Smith, Emeline Stepney, Emma Taylor, Georgia Telfair, Penny Thompson, Rosa Washington, Green Willbanks, Columbus Williams, and Teshan Young. For period accounts, see Clinkscales, *Plantation*, 41; Hague, *Blockaded Family*, 126; Ingleton, "Pine Fork," 358; "Slavery in the US," 325. For descriptions of dancing in or around "the quarters," see Sally Ashton, Georgia Baker, Cyrus Bellus, Susan Bledsoe, James Bolton, Joe Bouy, Isabella Boyd, James Brown, Richard Bruner, John Cameron, George Caulton, Harriet Chelsey, Amos Clark, Sara Crocker, Green Cumby, Anthony Dawson, James V. Deane, Douglas Dorsey, Mary Edwards, Louis Evans, Julia Frazier, Andrew Jackson Gill, Charles Grandy, Austin Grant, Elizabeth Ross Hite, Lee Hobby, Lizzie Hughes, Margaret Hughes, Wash Ingram, Squire Irvin, Charity Jones, Harriet Jones, Solomon Lambert, Richard Macks, Jim Martin, John Matthews, Bob Maynard, Abe McKlennan, Malinda Mitchell, Fannie Moore, Elsie Moreland, Mack Mullen, Louis Napoleon, Eliza Overton, Sallie Paul, A. C. Pruitt, Ida Rigley, Emma Simpson, Adam Singleton, James Southall, Ellen Swindler, Jane Thompson, Callie Washington, Dock Wilborn, Soldier Williams, and Mary Wright. For other ex-slave descriptions, see Ball, *Slavery*, 200–201; Davis, "Plantation Party," 55; Harry Smith, *Fifty Years*, 38, 45; *Isaac Williams*, 62. Other period accounts include Malet, *Errand*, 49, 111; H. L. F., A. A., "Louisiana," 758; Howard, *Bond and Free*, 253–55; Hungerford, *Plantation*, 195–99; Robinson, *Aunt Dice*, 16; Whitney and Bullock, *Maryland*, 162; Wyeth, *Sabre*, 60–61.

24. Fanny White (b. unk., TX, LA), Cade, "Ex-Slaves," 334.

25. *Isaac Williams*, 62.

26. Virginia ex-slaves Frank Bell, Julia Frazier, and Georgina Gibbs also remembered *set the floor*.

27. A similar passage appears in another narrative from the same interviewer, Mrs. D. W. Giles, this time attributed to Robert Weathersby: "Den we had regular buck dances too. We'd take planks to dance on an' dancing would take place. Yo' sho' has missed some 'un if yo' aint never seed a nigger buck dance" (Robert Weathersby, b. ca. 1847, MS, 2242). I suspect that this is another example of an interviewer or editor repeating an account too good to use just once, but I believe the example to be bona fide.

28. Chase, *Dear Ones*, 89–90.

29. Falconer, "Sports," 54.

30. Kirk Munroe, "A Southern Convict Camp," *Independent* 36 (August 28, 1884): 6; W. L. G. Smith's plantation novel *Life at the South*, 53–56, also describes boarding bare ground for a slave dance.

31. Fletcher, *Story*, 19.

32. De Voe, *Market Book*, I: 344; also 322.

33. Olmsted, *Back Country*, 145–46.

34. Wyeth, *Sabre*, 60 n1. An anonymous East Texas editorialist of the 1890s recalled when Blacks and whites "danced on the same puncheon, picked the same old gourd banjo." "The State Press: What the Papers Throughout Texas Are Talking About," *Galveston Daily News* (*New Birmingham Times*), February 18, 1891, 4.

35. Tallant, *Voodoo*, 14, 78–79.

36. Kennedy, *Swallow Barn*, 160.

37. Stroyer, *Life*, 45.

38. Lanman, *Adventures* II: 132.

39. In its simplest form, a dog-run cabin (also dog-trot, possum-trot, or double-pen) consists of two square or rectangular log pens joined by a roof, creating an exposed hallway (the dog run) that serves as a breezeway and additional living space. A staple of Southern folk architecture, many dog runs had dirt floors, but others were planked or puncheoned. Inexpensive and simple to build, double pens were often used as slave quarters: "Judge Maddox settled near Mount Enterprise and built him a good frame house and little double room log houses for the niggers" (Jack Maddox, b. ca. 1849, TX, 2527). "Sat'day night we would have parties and dance and play ring plays. We had de parties dare in a big double log house" (Wash Ingram, b. ca. 1844, VA, 1855).

40. Ex-slaves Betty Bormer, John Crawford, Uncle D. Davis, James V. Deane, Charles Hayes, Larnce Holt, Hal Hutson, Hannah Irwin, Horace Overstreet, Lu Perkins, and Mollie Williams also described dancing or serving white dancers at the big house. Also see Benners, *Slavery*, 25–26; Holcombe, "Sketches," 625–26; Hungerford, *Plantation*, 134–35; Mitchell, *Old Dominion*, 165–66; Pennington, *Woman Planter*, 274; *Isaac Williams*, 61.

41. Sugar houses, the plantation factories where cane was expressed, boiled, and processed, were widely reported as dance sites. For another WPA account, see Texas ex-slave Anthony Christopher; for period descriptions, see H. L. F., A. A., "Louisiana," 758; Russell, *Southern Life*, 96; Stuart, "Apollo Belvedere," 155–58.

42. Narrators Ellen Payne, Adeline White, and Callie Washington also described plantation dance houses.

43. This is a popular item in the *John and Old Marster* trickster tale cycle, though probably dating to the postwar period. Ex-slaves William Black, Austin Pen Parnell, James Reeves, and Bacchus White also told it; in White's version the slave also dons his slaveholder's boots. Also see Fauset, "Folk Tales," 266–67; Fedric, *Slave Life*, 60–67; Portia Smiley, "Folk-Lore," 362; Hurston, *Mules*, 88–90; Dorson, *Folktales*, 151–52. On the tale cycle, see John

Minton, "John and Old Marster Tales," *Encyclopedia of Folklore and Literature*, ed. Mary Ellen Brown and Bruce A. Rosenberg (Santa Barbara: ABC-Clio, 1998).

44. I have not found this tale outside the ex-slave narratives, but Rachel Cruze, Mollie Hatfield, and Neal Upson also told it.

45. Ex-slaves Bud Jones, Liza Jones, Orris Harris, Tom Morris, Charles Willis, Henry Lewis McGaffey, and Harriet Miller recalled the back step. Also see Burwell, *White Acre*, 81, 116; Seawell, "Fiddler," 642; Wyeth, *Sabre*, 262. Narrators mentioning the pigeon wing included William M. Adams, Willis Bennefield, Fanny Berry, Ellen Betts, Sam Broach, Ned Broadus, Richard Carruthers, Douglas Dorsey, Robert Farmer, July Ann Halfen, Jim Henry, Hannah Irvin, Bud Jones, Charity Jones, Liza Jones, Carrie Mason, Henry Lewis McGaffey, George Morrison, Mark Oliver, Dora Roberts, Cat Ross, Isaac Stier, and Acie Thomas. Compare Albert Hill, Horace Overstreet: *chicken wing*. Also see Barrow, "Corn Shucking," 878; Clinkscales, *Plantation*, 41; H. L. F., A. A., "Louisiana," 758; Lanman, *Adventures*, II: 278–79; Page, *Uncle Robin*, 193–94; J. Thornton Randolph, *The Cabin and Parlor; Or, Slaves and Masters* (Philadelphia: T. B. Peterson, 1852), 137–38; Seawell, "Fiddler," 642; Z. F. Smith, *The History of Kentucky* (Louisville: Courier-Journal Job Printing, 1886), 124; Wyeth, *Sabre*, 262.

46. Falconer, "Sports," 54. WPA narrators describing the shuffle, double shuffle, side shuffle, etc., included Sam Broach, Nelson Dickerson, Albert Hill, Fanny Smith Hodges, Lewis Jefferson, Bud Jones, Carrie Mason, John Matthews, Rev. James W. Washington, Charley Williams, Charles Willis, and Robert Young. For other period accounts, see Davis, "Plantation Party," 55; Dickens, *American Notes*, I: 217–18; James Franklin Fitts, "The Negro in Blue," *Galaxy* (February 1, 1867): 263–64; Burwell, *White Acre*, 81, 116; *Isaac Williams*, 61–62; Hundley, *Social Relations*, 60, 349; Lanman, *Adventures*, II: 278–79; Munroe, "Southern Convict Camp," 6; Benjamin Moore Norman, *Norman's New Orleans and Environs* (New Orleans: B. M. Norman, 1845), 182; Randolph, *Cabin and Parlor*, 10; Russell, *Southern Life*, 96; Seawell, "Fiddler," 642; Smalley, "Sugar Making," 109; Smith, *History of Kentucky*, 124; Harriet Beecher Stowe, *Old Town Folks and Sam Lawson's Fireside Stories*, 2 vols. (1869, 1871; rpt. Stowe, *Writings*, vol. 9), I: 54–55; Thorpe, "Christmas," 62; "A True Story of Texas Life," 324; Weston, "Ell an' Yard," 398; Whitney and Bullock, *Maryland*, 162; "A Winter in the South," *Harper's* 18 (December 1858): 3; Wyeth, *Sabre*, 262.

47. In 1932 when Mississippi guitarist Robert Lee McCollum (aka Robert Lee McCoy, Robert Nighthawk) played at Muddy Waters's wedding reception in a two-room sharecropper shack, the floor actually did collapse beneath the dancers' feet. Mary Katherine Aldin, booklet accompanying *Robert Lee McCoy: The Bluebird Recordings 1937–1938*, RCA CD 67416, 1997.

48. Mackay, *Western World*, II: 132.

49. For other versions, see Brown and Owens, *Toting*, 32; Solomon, *Honey*, 35. Also see Kirk, *Among the Pines*, 146; Holcombe, "Sketches," 621; J. R. Thompson, "Southern Sketches—II," *Appleton's* 4 (July 9, 1870): 44–45.

50. Like many Black dance terms, *breakdown* can refer either to a particular dance step, to the accompanying tune, or to a dance event. Narrators describing the breakdown step were Ned Broadus, Lewis Brown, Abner Griffin, Mahalia Jewel, Leo Mouton, Charlie Tye Smith, and Neal Upson. For 1800s references, see Burwell, *White Acre*, 81, 114, 207; Chase, *Dear Ones*, 34–35; De Voe, *Market Book*, I: 344; Dickens, *American Notes*, I: 216; Falconer, "Sports," 54; Foster, "Philadelphia in Slices," 63; Howard, *Bond and Free*, 19; Hundley, *Social Relations*, 349; Kirke, *Among the Pines*, 146–8; Kirke, *Southern Friends*, 191; Lanman, *Adventures* II: 132; "Night Amusements in the Confederate Camp," *London News* 42 (January 10, 1863): 44; Norman, *Norman's New Orleans*, 182; Seawell, "Fiddler," 642; Thompson, "Southern Sketches—II," 44; *Isaac Williams*, 61. Also see fig. 22.6. Narrators citing breakdown events included Jane Smith Hill Harmon, Shang Harris, Alice Hutcheson, Charlie King, Walter Leggett, Horace Overstreet, Lee Pierce, James Reeves, Red Richardson, John F. Van Hook, Lina Hunter, Calvin Moye, Emma Virgel, Adeline White, and Susannah Wyman. Also see Smith, *Life at the South*, 51. Narrators mentioning the buck dance, bucking, cutting the buck, buck and wing, and so on included Agatha Babino, Fannie Berry, Ellen Betts, Willie Blackwell, Anna Clark, Baily Cunningham, Dosia Harris, Emmaline Heard, Jefferson Franklin Henry, Elizabeth Ross Hite, Carrie Hudson, George Morrison, Glascow Norwood, Salem Powell, Charlie Powers, Will Sheets, Phil Towns, Dave Walker, George Weathersby, Robert Weathersby, and James Wiggins.

51. Bryant, "Old South," 33. On dancing heel and toe, also see July Ann Halfen, Joe Oliver, John Thompson, and Robert Young. Orris Harris and Harriet Miller named the pigeon toe. Other nineteenth-century sources include Burwell, *White Acre*, 116; Northrup, *Twelve Years*, 181; Olmsted, *Back Country*, 146; Smalley, "Sugar Making," 109; Thorpe, "Mississippi," 37. WPA narrators describing the jig or jigging included William M. Adams, Agatha Babino, Charley Barber, John Barker, Willie Blackwell, Joe Bouy, Fred Brown, John N. Davenport, Isabella Dorrah, Willis Easter, Jerry Eubanks, George Fleming, Sam Forge, Chris Franklin, Mary Glover, Mary Homer, Henry D. Jenkins, Sallie Johnson, Lewis Jones, Mary Kindred, W. S. Needham Jr. (white), James W. Smith, Samuel Smith, and James Wiggins. Also see Barrow, "Corn Shucking," 878; Clinkscales, *Plantation*, 41; Creecy, *Scenes*, 21–22; De Voe, *Market Book*, I: 344; Howard, *Bond and Free*, 19; Hungerford, *Plantation*, 195, 199; Kennedy, *Swallow Barn*, 103–4, 160; Kirke, *Among the Pines*, 145–48; Mallard, *Plantation Life*, 162; McDonald, *Virginia*, 177–78; Munroe, "Southern Convict Camp," 6; Ravanel, "Recollections," 768–69;

Russell, *Southern Life*, 96; Smith, *History of Kentucky*, 124; Smith, *Life at the South*, 160–61; Smith, "Persimmon Tree," 60; Thomas, *Tennessee Slave*, 49; *Isaac Williams*, 61; Wyeth, *Sabre*, 62–63.

52. Wyeth, *Sabre*, 62.

53. Holcombe, "Sketches," 626.

54. Hearn, *Levee*, 76–77. Compare Howard, *Bond and Free*, 253; Smith, *Life at the South*, 160; Tyson, *Slavery*, 12–13.

55. Norman, *Norman's New Orleans*, 182. Compare Kirke, *Among the Pines*, 145–46.

56. Compare Bruce, "Tobacco-Plantation," 541; Hundley, *Social Relations*, 357; Latrobe, *Journal*, 180; Robinson, *Aunt Dice*, 16.

57. Falconer, "Sports," 54.

58. *Unwritten History*, 295.

59. Dickens, *American Notes*, I: 216.

60. Handy, *Father*, 6. For other foot-stomping slave fiddlers and banjo players, see French, *Sketches*, 39; Eastman, *Aunt Phillis*, 120–21; Falconer, "Sports," 54; Hague, *Blockaded Family*, 126; Kemble, *Residence*, 131; Randolph, *Cabin and Parlor*, 10, 80; Smith, *Life at the South*, 158–59; Victor, *Maum Guinea*, 17.

61. Smith, *Life at the South*, 158, 159, 161.

62. Eastman, *Aunt Phillis*, 120. For Black instrumentalists on barrels, also see Kilham, "Sketches. First," 746; Ralph, "Dixie," 172; Randolph, *Cabin and Parlor*, 76–81; Smith, "Persimmon Tree," 60.

63. Talents often overlap, and historically many African Americans have alternated as star singers or instrumentalists and standout dancers. For other ex-slave examples, see Ellen Betts, George Dillard, Abner Griffin, Henry Lewis McGaffey, and George Jackson Simpson. Also see Allen, "Editors," 9; Bernhard, *Travels*, I: 212; Bruce, "Tobacco-Plantation," 541; Burwell, *White Acre*, 81, 116; Kemble, *Residence*, 131; Randolph, *Cabin and Parlor*, 76–81; Stowe, *Old Town Folks*, 54–55.

64. Also see Bryant, "Old South," 33; Epstein, *Sinful*, 123–24, 144, 158; Mallard, *Plantation Life*, 162; Ravanel, "Recollections," 768.

65. Barrow, "Corn Shucking," 878. Nettie Powell, *History of Marion County, Georgia* (Columbus, GA: Historical Publishing, 1931), 33, also describes slaves beating straws at Georgia cornshuckings. Knitting needles, sticks, or wires were sometimes substituted for broom straws. (In the 1880s W. C. Handy beat knitting needles for an uncle, Alabama ex-slave Whit Walker. Handy's maternal grandfather, Christopher Brewer, also remembered Alabama slaves beating straws.) North American Blacks have also beat straws on guitars and banjos. Evans, "Eli Owens," 340; Scarborough, *TNFS*, 100. The technique of playing stringed instruments with sticks is characteristically African, another instance of the grit-to-pitch principle, and the predilection for instruments simultaneously producing melody and percussion. Bebey, *African Music*, 44, 63–64; Evans, "Eli Owens," 340; Nketia, *Music of Africa*, 98–99. There is little doubt that beating straws are an African American

innovation, the earliest examples all coming from slaves, though the practice was widely adopted by whites, who provide most of the latter-day evidence. See Cauthen, *Fiddle*, 71–73, 138, 170; Wayne W. Daniel, *Pickin' on Peachtree: A History of Country Music in Atlanta, Georgia* (Urbana: University of Illinois Press, 1990), 34–35; Ford, *Traditional Music*, 129–30; Fred Hoeptner and Bob Pinson, "Clayton McMichen Talking," *OTM* 1 (Summer 1971): 9; Alan Jabbour, booklet accompanying *The Hammons Family*, Rounder CDs 1504/05, 1998, 77–78; Vance Randolph and Frances Emberson, "The Collection of Folk Music in the Ozarks," *JAF* 60 (1947): 120; Thede, *Fiddle Book*, 16; Wiggins, *Fiddlin' Georgia Crazy*, 7, 47–48; Mark Wilson, booklet accompanying *Traditional Fiddle Music of Kentucky, Volume 1*, Rounder CD 0376, 1997; John Q. Wolf, "A Country Dance in the Ozarks in 1874," *SFQ* 29 (1965): 319. RECORDINGS: Reaves White County Ramblers, "Ten Cent Piece" (Vocalion 5218, 1928), "Drunkard's Hiccoughs" (Vocalion 5247, 1928); Alva Greene (fiddle), Francis Gillum (straws), "Indian Squaw," "I've Got A Grandpa," "The Winding Sheep," field recs., KY, 1973, *Fiddle Music of Kentucky*; Alva Greene (fiddle), Francis Gillum (straws), "Hunky Dory," field rec., KY, 1973, *The Art of Traditional Fiddle*, Rounder CD 11592, 2000; Burl Hammons (fiddle), Maggie Hammons Parker (beating sticks), "Jimmy Johnson," field rec., WV, 1972, *The Hammons Family*. The narrative of Sam Forge ostensibly describes white Texans beating straws, but Forge's narrative is one of interviewer Effie Cowan's more obvious forgeries.

66. Martha Haines Butt, *Antifanaticism: A Tale of the South* (Philadelphia: Lippincott, Grambo, 1853), 42.

67. Peter Guralnick, *Searching for Robert Johnson* (New York: Plume, 1989), 23.

68. Philip A. Jamison, "Square Dance Calling: The African-American Connection," *Journal of Appalachian Studies* 9 (2003): 387–98. Ex-slaves mentioning dance callers or calling included Sally Ashton, Delia Barclay, Fannie Berry, James Brooks, Sam Bush, Lizzie Chandler, Ned Chaney, Henry Childers, Amos Clark, John Cottonham, James (Jim) Davis, Louisa Davis, Tob Davis, Jake Desso, Willis Easter, Mary Edwards (TX), Sam Forge, Chris Franklin, William Gant, Hattie Gates, Simon Hare, Burt Haygood, Will Hicks, Joseph James, Ellis Jefson, Henry D. Jenkins, Charley Johnson, Aaron Jones, Mary Jane Jones, Mary Kindred, Ellen King, Dave Lowry, Primous Magee, Liza Mention, George Morrison, Louise Pettis, Fanny Randolph, Robert Shepherd, Martha Showvely, George Simmons, William Smith, Bert Strong, John Thompson, Lucinda Vann, James W. Washington, Robert Weathersby, Adeline White, Charles Willis, and Alice Wilkins.

69. Bernhard, *Travels*, I: 212. For other slave instrumentalists doubling as dance callers, see E. T. Coke, *A Subaltern's Furlough*, 2 vols. (New York: J. & J. Harper, 1833), I: 204; French, *Sketches*, 39–41; Gilman, *Recollections*, 85; Latrobe, *Journal*, 172.

70. Ex-slaves Delia Barclay, Ned Chaney, and Jake Desso also described dancing accompanied only by callers.

71. "Shoot the Buffalo" is a popular fiddle and play party song best known among whites. Mrs. L. D. Ames, "The Missouri Play-Party," *JAF* 24 (1911): 301; Leona Nessly Ball, "The Play Party in Idaho," *JAF* 44 (1931): 16; Botkin, *Play Party*, 308-12; *Country Music Sources*, 116; Dudley and Payne, "Texas Play-Party," 30-31; Ford, *Traditional Music*, 244-25; Lomax, *Ballads*, 296-97; McDowell, *Dances*, 24-27; Odum and Johnson, *Workaday*, 123-24; Owens, *Texas*, 149-50; Randolph, *OFS* III: 306-9; Randolph, *Roll Me*, 426-27; Sharp, *EFSSA* II: 372; Spurgeon, *Waltz the Hall*, 172-73. RECORDINGS: The Swamp Rooters, "Shoot the Buffalo" (Brunswick unissued, 1930).

72. Ravenel, "Recollections," 768.

The Fiddle

1. *The Life and Adventures of Zamba, An African Negro King; and His Experiences of Slavery in South Carolina*, ed. Peter Neilson (London: Smith, Elder, 1847), 17-18.

2. WPA narrators mentioning fiddles are identified in the chapter appendix. For other descriptions of slave fiddles alone, or with patting only, see Anon. ex-slave, b. ca. 1850, TN, *Unwritten History*, 131; Charles Ball (ca. 1781-?), *Slavery*, 282-83; Roan Barnes (b. unk., LA), Cade, "Ex-Slaves," 334; John Brown (ca. 1818-?), *Slave Life*, 95-96; Frederick Douglass (1818-1895), *My Bondage*, 252-53; Larison, *Silvia Dubois* (ca. 1768-?) 52-53, 59-60, 67-68; Irving E. Lowery (1850-?), *Life*, 198; Solomon Northrup (1807 or 1808-?) *Twelve Years*, 79-80, 213-20; Allen Parker (1840-1906), *Recollections*, 310; Harry Smith (1814-?), *Fifty Years*, 38; James Thomas (1827-1913), *Tennessee Slave*, 33, 68; Isaac Williams (ca. 1821-?), *Isaac Williams*, 62; Agricola, "Management," 371; Bryce, "Fiddlers," 5; Clinkscales, *Plantation*, 12; Foster, "Philadelphia," 40, 63; Fithian, *Journal*, 82; Gilman, *Recollections*, 131; Higginson, "Leaves. II," 740; Holcombe, "Sketches," 621; Hungerford, *Plantation*, 134-35, 251-53; Kinnard, "National Poets," 337; K. G. S., "Negroes' Spirituals," *Lippincott's* 7 (March 1871): 333; Kilham, "Sketches. First," 746; Livermore, *Story*, 357; Mead, *Travels*, 29; Mitchell, *Old Dominion*, 93-94; Paine, *Georgia Prison*, 179, 183-84; VA planter to J. K. Paulding, 1836, Paulding, *Slavery*, 209; Ravanel, "Recollections," 766-69; Ravitz, "Slaves' Christmas," 384; Russell, *Southern Life*, 94-96; "Slavery in the US," 325; Thorpe, "Cotton," 459, 460; Thorpe, "Mississippi," 37; Thorpe, "Sugar," 767. RECORDINGS: Although African American fiddling declined somewhat after 1900, Blacks continued to fiddle, and to represent the entire range of American fiddle styles, past and present. Recorded examples can be found on *Altamont*; *Black Appalachia*; *Black Fiddlers*; Butch Cage & Willie B. Thomas, *Old*

Time Black Southern String Band Music, Arhoolie CD 9045, 2006; *Blind James Campbell and His Nashville Street Band*, Arhoolie CD 438, 1995; *Folks, He Sure Do Pull Some Bow*, Old Hat CD 1003, 2001; *Clifford Hayes & the Louisville Jug Bands*, Vols. 1 & 2, RST CDs 1501/2, 1993; *Peg Leg Howell and Eddie Anthony*, Vols. 1 & 2, Document CDs 2004/5, 1993; *Mississippi Sheiks*, Vols. 1-4, Document CDs 5083/84/85/86, 1991; *Mississippi Blues and Gospel*, Document CD 5320, 1995; *Mississippi String Bands and Associates*, RST CD 6013, 1991; *The Definitive Charley Patton*, Catfish CDs 180, 2001; *St. Louis Blues 1927-1933*, Document CD 5181, 1993; *The Sounds of Memphis*, Story of Blues CD 3531; *String Bands*, Document CD 5167, 1993; Joe Thompson, *Family Tradition*, Rounder CD 2161, 1999; *Violin, Sing the Blues For Me*, Old Hat CD 1002, 1999; *Big Joe Williams, Vol. 1*, RST CD 6003, 1991; Big Joe Williams, *Back to the Country*, Testament CD 5013, 1994. Fiddlers represented include Eddie Anthony (1890-1934), Howard Armstrong (1909-2003), Will Batts (1904-1956), Andrew Baxter (1869-1955), Cuje Bertram (1894-1993), Blind Pete, Jim Booker (1872-?), Big Bill Broonzy (1893-1958), Jimmy Brown (1910-?), Butch Cage (1894-1975), Bo Chatman (Bo Carter) (1893-1964), Lonnie Chatman (1887-1950), Beauford Clay (1900-?), James Cole, Jess Ferguson, Frank Patterson, Clifford Hayes (1893-1941), Sid Hemphill (1876-1963), Henry Johnson, Lonnie Johnson (1899-1970), John Lusk (1886-1969), Bell Ray (1909-?), Henry Sims (Son Simms) (1890-1958), Joe Thompson (1918-2012), and Dad Tracy.

3. Finch, *Travels*, 237-38. This practice long persisted. Future blues star William "Big Bill" Broonzy (1893-1958), the child of ex-slaves, made and played a cigar-box fiddle (a common homemade variety) until a white fiddler bought him a violin and gave him lessons. *Big Bill Blues* (1955; rpt. New York: Da Capo, 1992), 34-35. For similar Alabama white examples, see Cauthen, *Fiddle*, 50-55.

4. Exactly how a fiddle could be made from a slab of pine bark is not entirely clear, but there are possible parallels from both Africa and African Americans. In South Africa in the 1770s, Swedish physician Andrew Sparrman encountered a Hottentot instrument "called *t'Guthe*, which, probably, was first made in imitation of our violin. It consists merely of a piece of board with three or four strings screwed on to it, on which they scrape with a bow." Andrew Sparrman, *A Voyage to the Cape of Good Hope*, 2 vols. (Perth: R. Morison and Son, 1789), I: 163. Compare also Kirby, *Musical Instruments*, 334-37. An 1856 letter describes a South Carolina slave making a fiddle from a "shingle." Epstein, *Sinful*, 153.

5. Washington Irving (1783-1859) judged colonial Dutch slaves "exquisite performers on three-stringed fiddles" (*Knicker-Bocker*, 18-19). Another period source describes a slave playing a three-string fiddle for an early 1800s New York sleighing party (De Voe, *Market Book*, I: 306), while Richard Hildreth's novel *The Slave: Or Memoirs of Archy Moore* (Boston: John H. Eastburn, 1836), 136-37,

depicts a slave playing a three-stringed fiddle in a Washington, DC, slave pen.

6. One-string gourd-and-horsehair fiddles of this basic type appear, under different names and with slight variations, throughout West Africa. I have adopted *goge* as the most widely recognized name for one prominent instance, but I am applying it to the type as a whole. See DjeDje, *Fiddling in West Africa*; Jacqueline Cogdell DjeDje, *Distribution of the One String Fiddle in West Africa*. Monograph Series in Ethnomusicology No. 2 (Los Angeles: University of California Press, 1980); David W. Ames, "A Sociocultural View of Hausa Musical Activity," *The Traditional Artist in African Societies*, ed. Warren L. d' Azevedo (Bloomington: Indiana University Press, 1975), 128–61; Bebey, *African Music*, 41–43; John Miller Chernoff, *African Rhythm and African Sensibility: Aesthetics and Social Action in African Musical Idioms* (Chicago: University of Chicago Press, 1979), 129–31; John Miller Chernoff, booklet accompanying *Master Fiddlers of Dagbon*, Rounder CD 5086, 2001; Nketia, *Music of Africa*, 102–3; Caroline Ward Wendt, "Regional Style in Tuareg *Anẓad* Music," *To the Four Corners: A Festschrift in Honor of Rose Brandel*, ed. Ellen C. Leichtman (Detroit: Harmonie Park, 1994), 81–106.

7. *Unwritten History*, 131, my emphasis.

8. Courlander, "Haiti," 377–79; Courlander, *NFM*, 206–7, 218–20; David Evans, "Afro-American One-Stringed Instruments," *WF* 29 (1970): 229–45; Evans, "Reinterpretation," 384–85; Kubik, *Africa*, 12–20, 100, 167–72.

9. Finch, *Travels*, 237.

10. John Laurence Manning, "Clarendon, 17th November 1856," letter ms., University of South Carolina Library, qtd. Epstein, *Sinful*, 153.

11. Tallant, *Voodoo*, 65.

12. Grace MacGowan Cooke, *A Gourd Fiddle* (Philadelphia: H. Altemus, 1904), 38, 46–49; "A Curious Fiddle," *Bismarck Daily Tribune*, rpt. from *San Francisco Examiner*, April 19, 1893.

13. For example, the photograph of a gourd fiddle in the possession of a Ferrum, Virginia, couple shows an oblong gourd, whole (that is, without a hide top), fitted with a violin-style neck, tailpiece, bridge, and four strings. There are also imitations of the violin's distinctive *f*-holes on the side of the gourd. (The instrument's original provenance is unclear.) John Michael Vlach, *The Afro-American Tradition in Decorative Arts* (Cleveland: Cleveland Museum of Art, 1978), 25.

14. Smith, *The History of Kentucky*, 121."

15. *Unwritten History*, 131.

16. *Isaac Williams*, 62. Courlander also describes Haitian imitations of violins with horsehair strings. Courlander, "Haiti," 371.

17. William J. Burchell, *Travels in the Interior of Southern Africa*, 2 vols. (London: Longman, Hurst, Rees, Orme, and Brown, 1822,

1824), I: 499–500 (orig. emphasis); also II: 287–88. Compare Sparrman, *Voyage*, I: 163; Kirby, *Musical Instruments*, 334–37.

18. Among the more colorful is the *dolle* (northwestern Germany), a regional fiddle-type homemade from a wooden shoe (another regional tradition). Nettl, *Folk Music*, 55.

19. For example, white Alabama fiddler Tom Freeman (1883–1952) made his first fiddle from a gourd strung with doubled-and-twisted ball thread (Cauthen, *Fiddle*, 127), while the father of Huggins Williams, fiddler for the East Texas Serenaders (a popular pre–WWII white stringband), "was also a fiddle player, who started out on a gourd fiddle until he bought the real thing." Barry McCloud, "East Texas Serenaders," *Definitive Country*. There is no reason to suppose Black influence in either example (though it cannot be wholly discounted).

20. *History of Benton, Washington, Carroll, Madison, Crawford, Franklin, and Sebastian Counties, Arkansas* (Chicago: Goodspeed, 1889), 149.

21. Norm Cohen, "Early Pioneers," *Stars of Country Music: Uncle Dave Macon to Johnny Rodriguez*, ed. Bill C. Malone and Judith McCulloh (Urbana: University of Illinois Press, 1975), 11. Robertson was born in Madison Co., AR.

22. "A Curious Fiddle."

23. Charles K. Wolfe, *Tennessee Strings: The Story of Country Music in Tennessee* (Knoxville: University of Tennessee Press, 1977), 25–26.

24. *Life and Career of Senator Robert Love Taylor (Our Bob): By His Three Surviving Brothers, James P. Taylor, Alf A. Taylor, Hugh L. Taylor* (Nashville: Bob Taylor Publishing, 1913); Wolfe, *Tennessee Strings*, 22–26. Besides serving as Tennessee governor, Bob Taylor was a US congressman, a US senator, and a successful Nashville-based publisher.

25. A roughly contemporaneous East Tennessee fiddle of known white origin survived into the 1980s. Cultural historian John Rice Irwin identified its maker as Frank Couch of Hancock County north of Greeneville: "Couch made the fiddle as a young man, about 1840. The last known fiddler to play this instrument was the locally famous George McCarroll of Roane County." Several other McCarrolls were renowned fiddlers, including George's brother Jimmy, leader of the Roane County Ramblers. An accompanying photograph shows a globular gourd, halved, covered with hide or some other material, and fitted with a standard violin neck, tailpiece, bridge, and headstock with four tuning pegs. John Rice Irwin, *Musical Instruments of the Southern Appalachian Mountains*, 2nd ed. (Exton, PA: Schiffer, 1983), 17; Charles K. Wolfe, "The Roane County Ramblers," *Definitive Country*; Wolfe, *Tennessee Strings*, 49. DISCOGRAPHIES: *Country Music Records*. Irwin reports hearing of other gourd fiddles among Tennessee pioneers.

26. Cooke, *Gourd Fiddle*, 16.

27. _____ Norman, "Editor's Correspondence. October 3d, 1845. Boston Museum—Chinese Museum," *Raleigh Register, and North-Carolina Gazette* 80 (October 10, 1845) (orig. emphasis). Compare Nella, "Sights, Sounds, and Thoughts at Church," *SLM* 25 (July 1857): 45, which unflatteringly likens 1850s Virginia hymn singing to "the Tower of Babel. Some squalled, others bawled; one made a hornlike note, another must have been scraping on a gourd fiddle."

28. Chernoff, booklet accompanying *Master Fiddlers*, 2, 7.

29. Ames, "Hausa Musical Activity," 151.

30. Ames, "Hausa Musical Activity," 151; Ali Farka Touré, "Ali Farka on Ali Farka," *World Music: The Rough Guide*, ed. Simon Broughton, Mark Ellingham, David Muddyman, and Richard Trillo (London: Rough Guides, 1994), 261. Examples of Touré's traditional fiddling include "Saga" and "Banga," *Talking Timbuktu*, Hannibal CD 1381, 1994.

31. Achille Murat, *A Moral and Political Sketch of the United States of North America* (London: Effingham, Wilson, 1833), 75.

32. Foster, "Philadelphia," 63. For other period references to Blacks scraping the fiddle, see Bernhard, *Travels*, I: 212; Flint, *Recollections*, 345; Robinson, *Aunt Dice*, 39; Russell, *Southern Life*, 96; Stowe, *Old Town Folks*, 39; Tallant, *Voodoo*, 65. For sawing, see Gilman, *Recollections*, 84–85. Also see "A True Story of Texas Life," 324 (rasping); H. L. F., A. A., "Louisiana," 758 (squeaking).

33. Thompson, "Plantation Music," 20.

34. Also see Aunt Kate Betters (b. 1848, MS, 262–63) (scraping); Ruben Laird (b. 1850, MS, 1298–99) (sawing). Fort Sabine, a tiny earthwork guarding the Sabine River's mouth on the Gulf of Mexico, surrendered to Federal troops on May 25, 1865 (the Sabine is the present-day boundary between Texas and Louisiana). The outpost is better remembered for the Second Battle of Sabine Pass (September 8, 1863), when its garrison of forty-two men (mainly Irish-born Houstonians) repelled a Federal invasion force of twenty ships and 5,000 men. Alwyn Barr, "Sabine Pass, Battle of," *Handbook of Texas*.

35. "A Curious Fiddle"; Cooke, *Gourd Fiddle*, 50, 104, 55.

36. Wendt, "Tuareg *Anẓad* Music," 86, orig. emphasis.

37. Compare Hungerford, *Plantation*, 252. In Africa some instruments (drums, horns, whistles, xylophones) literally "talk," imitating the pitch contours of tonal African languages to convey specific messages. African fiddlers imitate voices or vocal music but typically do not signal, the same being true for African American instrumentalists. Compare Bebey, *African Music*, 44.

38. Jordan Waters (b. 1861, LA, 208) gave a typical text of "Cackling Hen." Also see *Appalachian Fiddle*, 40; Bolick and Austin, *Mississippi Fiddle*, 66, 73, 110, 179; Bolick and Russell, *Fiddle Tunes*, 157–58, 357; Evans, "Eli Owens," 344, 350, 355; Gordon, *Folk-Songs*, 15; Margaret Mckee and Fred Chisenhall, *Beale Black and Blue: Life and Music on Black America's Main Street* (Baton Rouge: Louisiana State University Press, 1981), 183; McNeil, *Folksongs*, 146–49; Perrow,

"South" (1913): 129–30; Talley, *NFR*, 44–45; Thede, *Fiddle*, 123; Thomas, "Work-Songs," 159–60; Titon, *Fiddle Tunes*, 144; Warner, *Folk Songs*, 292–93. Recordings by Black fiddlers include Howard Armstrong (fiddle), "Cacklin' Hen," ca. 1985, *Louie Bluie*, Arhoolie CD 470, 2000; Cuje Bertram (fiddle), "Old Hen Cackled," field rec., ca. 1970, Indianapolis, *Black Fiddlers*; Blind Pete & Partner: Blind Pete (fiddle, vocal), George Ryan (guitar), "Cacklin' Hen," field rec., Little Rock, 1934, *Mississippi Blues and Gospel*, Document CD 5320, 1995; Butch Cage (fiddle), Willie B. Thomas (guitar), "Hen Cackle," *Old Time Black Southern String Band Music*, Arhoolie CD 9045, 2006; Taylor's Kentucky Boys (Jim Booker, fiddle), "Old Hen Cackled and the Rooster Crowed" (Gennett unissued, 1927). Other Black versions include De Ford Bailey (harmonica), "Old Hen Cackle" (Brunswick 149, 1927); DeFord Bailey (harmonica), "Old Hen Cackle (takes 1 & 2)," field rec., Nashville, ca. 1974–76, *The Legendary DeFord Bailey*, Tennessee Folklore Society CD 122, 1998; Gus Cannon (vocal, banjo), "Ol' Hen," *Walk Right In*, Stax LP 702, 1963; Ephraim Carter (vocal), J. W. Jones (fife), James Jones (kettle drum), Floyd Bussey (bass drum), "Old Hen Cackled, Laid a Double Egg," field rec., Waverly Hall, GA, August 1970, *Traveling Through the Jungle*; Joe Evans (guitar), Arthur McClain (mandolin), "Old Hen Cackle" (Banner 32264, 1931); Joe Harris (vocal, guitar), Kid West (mandolin), "Old Hen Cackled and Rooster Laid an Egg," field rec., Shreveport, 1940, *Field Recordings, Volume 5*, Document CD 5579; Eli Owens (harmonica), "Old Hen Cackle," field rec., Bogalusa, LA, August 1970, *South Mississippi Blues*, Rounder LP 2009, 1973; Will Slayden (vocal, banjo), "The Old Hen Cackled," field rec., Shelby Co., TN, Summer 1952, *Will Slayden*. "Cacklin' Hen" was also a favorite of white fiddlers, especially in North Georgia; Fiddlin' John Carson, Gid Tanner, Clayton McMichen, Bill Chitwood, and Earl Johnson all recorded versions. DISCOGRAPHIES: *Country Music Records*; *Country Music Sources*, 771–73. There are many similar pieces in the South. Three ex-slaves remembered "Rooster (Chicken) Crow for Midnight, Rooster Crow for Day," another imitative fiddle song probably of Black origin. "Ole Charlie Sapp and Grant Sutton was very good fiddlers here. They was especially good when they played 'Chicken Crow Befo' Day.' I don' remember enny of the words" (Mary Edwards, b. 1853, TX, 1282–83). John Crawford also identified it as a fiddle song, Millie Ann Smith as an unaccompanied ring play. For another version, see White, *ANFS*, 269. The comic animal song "The Monkey Married the Baboon's Sister" probably dates to Reconstruction. Brown III: 219–20; Sandburg, *Songbag*, 113; Scarborough, *TNFS*, 180; Spaeth, *Read 'Em*, 78–79. Ex-slave Ephraim "Mike" Lawrence remembered the piece being "talked" on the fiddle: "Old John play fer all de dance on de plantation. He fair (really) mek fiddle talk. When Maussa gib uh dance he always call 'pon John. Yas, suh dat man sure could play. When he saw down on de fiddle and pull out dat june (tune) 'Oh, de Monkey Marry to de Babboon Sister,' he mek paa'son (parson) dance" (Ephraim "Mike" Lawrence, b. ca. 1856, SC, 97, orig. parentheses).

39. Some African Americans also performed "The Fox Hunt" on fiddle, including Sid Hemphill (1876–1963), the son of a slave fiddler: Sid Hemphill (vocal, fiddle), Alec Askew, (guitar), Lucius Smith (banjo), Will Head (bass drum), "Hog Hunt," field. rec., Sledge, MS, 1942, *Saints and Sinners*. More often, blacks played this piece on harmonica as "Fox and Hounds" (aka "The Hounds"). See Flutes, Fifes, and Quills, note 62.

40. For American fiddlers and guitarists placing various jingles—including rattlesnake rattles!—in their instruments, see David Evans, "Delta Reminiscences: Floyd Patterson Interviewed by David Evans (Crystal Springs, Mississippi—August 31 and September 2, 1970)," *Blues World* 43 (Summer 1972): 14–15; Kubik, *Africa*, 72; Gerald Milnes, "Wilke Dennison: Country Fiddle Maker," *Goldenseal* 14 (1988): 25; Pete Welding, booklet accompanying *Albert Collins: The Complete Imperial Recordings*, Imperial/EMI CDs 96740, 1991, 5; Charles Wolfe, *The Devil's Box: Masters of Southern Fiddling* (Nashville: Vanderbilt University Press, 1997), xv–xvi; Maurice Zolotov, "The Hillbilly Boom," *Saturday Evening Post* (February 12, 1944), 38.

41. Easter Jackson was from Troup County, GA, immediately north of Columbus, Rhodus Walton from immediately south in Stewart County, GA. Henry Green was born due west of Columbus near Montgomery, AL. George Strickland "was nine years old when freedom come to us niggers and 'fore dat time us refugeed from Miss., to Mobile, den to Selma, den to Montgomery den to Uchie near Columbus, Ga. where us stayed till us was freed" (397). Given the evidence from Peach and Bibb Counties, GA (both just east of Columbus), the Black handsaw fiddle's known distribution can be precisely defined as the border region of southeast Alabama and southwest Georgia between Montgomery and Macon, with Columbus as the center.

42. Courlander, *NFM*, 207, 219.

43. "The History of the Fort Valley State College Folk Festival," *The Peachite* 2/2, Folk Festival Number (March 1944): 1. Also see Bastin, *Red River Blues*, 74–75; David Evans, booklet accompanying *Make You Happy*.

44. The South Georgia Highballers were guitarist Vander Everidge, fiddler Melgie Ward, and Vander's brother Albert Everidge, who played the saw on "Mister Johnson." *Country Music Records*; Tony Russell, "The South Georgia Highballers," *OTM* 7 (Winter 1972–73): 20; Pete Welding and Lawrence Cohn, booklet accompanying *Roots N' Blues: The Retrospective 1925–1950*, Columbia/Legacy CDs 47911, 1992, 15; John Minton, *78 Blues: Folksongs and Phonographs in the American South* (Jackson: University Press of Mississippi, 2008), 52. The most famous Black

musician busking on Macon's streets during this period was Blind Willie McTell (1901-1959), who had earlier attended the Georgia School for the Blind in Macon and later included the city in his regular touring circuit. David Evans, booklet accompanying *Atlanta Blues 1933*, JEMF LP 106, 1979, 6–24; David Evans, booklet accompanying *The Definitive Blind Willie McTell*, Columbia/Legacy CDs 53234, 1994, 6–20; Evans, *Make You Happy*. Atlanta-based fiddler and street musician Eddie "Macon Ed" Anthony (1890–1934) was originally from Macon. *Peg Leg Howell and Eddie Anthony*; Oliver, *Songsters*, 18–19, 28, 36–37; Bastin, *Red River*, 102–5.

45. South Georgia Highballers, "Blue Grass Twist"/"Bibb County Grind" (OKeh 45155, 1927). The group's other sides featured two well-known fiddle tunes—"Ida Red"/"Old Sallie Goodwin" (OKeh unissued, 1927)—and a white folksong, "Green River Train" (OKeh 45166, 1927).

46. Ben Harney, "Mister Johnson Turn Me Loose: A Coon Novelty, Featured by May Irwin," M. Witmark & Sons, 1896. The Highballers' largely instrumental version merely repeats the song's chorus strain with occasional vocals by guitarist Vander Everidge. Uncle Dave Macon and Sid Harkreader, "Mister Johnson" (Vocalion 5341, 1929) more faithfully recreates Harney's original four-strain arrangement. For Black versions, see Bass, "Negro Songs," 430; Talley, *NFR*, 56–57; White, *ANFS*, 361. Also see *Country Music Sources*, 482.

47. There are scattered instances of musical saws in white country music, the best-known being Jimmie Rodgers, "Home Call" (take 1) (Victor unissued, 1929). Fiddler and western swing bandleader Bob Kendrick (aka Bob Skyles) (1910–1998) occasionally recorded on musical saw. *Country Music Records*. Tennessee-born fiddler Curley Fox (1910–1995) also reportedly played musical saw. Jim O'Neal, liner notes, *Curley Fox, Champion Fiddler, Volume Two*, Rural Rhythm LP 252, 1972. Maurice Zolotow, "Hillbilly Boom," 36, mentions musical saws in amateur white stringbands, but with no details. The musical saw has also been popular in Europe and North America with street musicians and timber workers and as a stage novelty. See Charles W. Hardy, "The Musical Saw: Endangered Species Folk Instrument," *Canadian Folk Music* 25 (1991): 5–6.

48. Small Farmer, "Management of Negroes," 371.

49. Anon. ex-slave, TN, *Unwritten History*, 131.

50. James Thomas, *Tennessee Slave*, 33.

51. *Isaac Williams*, 62.

52. "An Artist Selecting an Instrument," *Leslie's* 32 (June 3, 1871): 196. A few ex-slaves described buying other instruments— harmonicas, jew's harps, toy fifes and drums (but no fiddles)—from local shops.

53. The alternate title for "Turkey in the Straw" is "Zip Coon." Norm Cohen, booklet accompanying *Minstrels and Tunesmiths*, JEMF LP 109, 1981, 26–27; *Country Music Sources*, 751–54. "Turkey

in the Straw" was also named by Lucy Donald, Mahala Jewel, William Little, Primous Magee, George Morrison, W. S. Needham Jr. (white), Fanny Randolph, Manus Robinson, Neal Upson, and John F. Van Hook. All except Van Hook identified it with the fiddle. Today "Devil's Dream" usually refers to a Scottish fiddle tune (aka "The Devil Among the Tailors"), but among Blacks this title has been used for various dance tunes and songs. Charles H. Anderson and Jim Henry both remembered it on the fiddle, Julia Frances Daniels as an unaccompanied ring play. Also see Jacob Stroyer, *Life*, 45; Davis, *Folk-Songs*, 251; Eastman, *Aunt Phillis*, 120–21; Ford, *Traditional*, 62; Hearn, *Levee*, 76; Linscott, *New England*, 72–74; Nathan, *Dan Emmett*, 193. Black recordings include Sid Hemphill (ten-note quills with snare, bass drum), "Devil's Dream," field rec., Sledge, MS, 1942, *Black Appalachia*; Sid Hemphill (vocal, quills), Lucious Curtis (banjo), "Old Devil's Dream," field rec., Senatobia, MS, 1959, *Highway 61 Mississippi*, Rounder CD 1703, 1997; Reverend Gary Davis (five-string banjo), "Devil's Dream," 1964, *The Guitar and Banjo of Reverend Gary Davis*, Prestige/Folklore CD 14033, 2001. DISCOGRAPHIES: *Country Music Records*; *Country Music Sources*, 725–27.

54. "The Arkansas Traveler" was named by Orris Harris, Hattie Jefferson, Jim Martin, Henry Lewis McGaffey, and Richard Toler, all remembering it on the fiddle. For other Black versions, see Barrow, "Corn Shucking," 878; Benners, *Slavery*, 25–26; Bolick and Russell, *Fiddle Tunes*, 209; Johnson, *Highways*, 110–11; Thorpe, "Mississippi," 37. RECORDINGS: Sid Hemphill (fiddle, vocal), Lucius Smith (banjo), Will Head (bass drum), Alec Askew (guitar), "Arkansas Traveler," field rec., Sledge, MS, August 1942, *Black Appalachia*; Nashville Washboard Band, "Arkansas Traveler," field rec., Nashville, TN, July 1942, *Rags, Breakdowns, Stomps and Blues*, Document CD 32-20-03, 2003. DISCOGRAPHIES: *Blues and Gospel Records*; *Country Music Records*; *Country Music Sources*, 759–61. The tune probably derives from Britain, but was claimed by several American entertainers, including Mose Case, a free Black. The melody was also used in a popular folk drama, for which see Cohen, *Minstrels and Tunesmiths*, 10-12; *Country Music Sources*, 438–39; Minton, *78 Blues*, 168–85, 192–210. "Cacklin' Hen," "Cotton-Eyed Joe," "Devil's Dream," "Hop Light Ladies," "Sally Gooden," and "Turkey in the Straw" are discussed elsewhere. Other well-known fiddle tunes named by ex-slaves included "Billy in the Low Ground" (Fanny Randolph), "Black Eyed Susie" (Richard Toler), "Fisher's Hornpipe" (Chaney Mack), "Natchez Under the Hill" (Charles Willis), and "Soldier's Joy" (Richard Toler). Most of the fiddle tunes in the narratives are identified by title alone, highly problematic since the same tune is often known by different titles, and different tunes are sometimes called by the same name. Some fiddle tunes have optional lyrics that ex-slaves provided, clinching identifications. For titles as well known as "The Arkansas Traveler" or "Sally Goodin," we can

probably assume narrators were naming the pieces known today. In other cases, titles alone can only establish probabilities, and many of the items named by ex-slaves remain puzzles, even when they are corroborated by other sources. Larnce Holt, for example, remembered "Dem young year us hab good time. I fiddle to de dance. Fiddle 'Git up in de Cool' an' 'Hopus Creek an' de Water' " (Larnce Holt, b. 1858, TX, 1781). A 1924 *Atlanta Journal* article lists the tune "Gettin' Up in the Cool" in the repertoire of Newt Tench (b. ca. 1840) and his brother Ed (b. ca. 1843), white North Georgia fiddlers active since the 1850s. There is no other information on the tune save its title. Daniel, *Pickin' on Peachtree*, 54. In 1935, however, the Nations Brothers, a white stringband from South Mississippi, recorded a piece they called "Magnolia Two-Step" (Vocalion 03118, 1935); the brothers later revealed they had learned the tune from their father, who called it "Get Up In the Cool." David Freeman, booklet accompanying *Mississippi String Bands, Volume Two*, County CD 3514, 1998; *Country Music Sources*, 774. This is the same tune that Texas fiddler Eck Robertson (also white) recorded in the 1950s under the title "Get Up In the Cool," *Famous Cowboy Fiddler*, County Records LP 202, 1963. Quite likely, then (but not necessarily), Holt's (and the Tenches') "Git Up in de Cool" was the same as the Nation Brothers' and Robertson's. The second item Larnce Holt names, "Hopus Creek and De Water," would seem to be related to "Harper's creek and roarin' ribber," a lyric that ex-slave fiddler Solomon Northrup included (without tune) in his 1855 autobiography (Northrup, *Twelve Years*, 219), but that is as far as I have been able to trace it.

55. DjeDje, *Fiddling in West Africa*, 40; Chernoff, *Master Fiddlers*, 2–7. Traditionally, *goges* were also played together in all-*goge* ensembles, and much more rarely with other melody instruments (lutes, flutes, pipes, or horns).

56. William M. Adams, Ned Chaney, John Cole, Virginia Harris, Adeline Jackson, George Morrison, Mark Oliver, Fanny Randolph, Lucinda Vann, Charley Williams, Nancy Williams. and Litt Young named bones with fiddles. Isabella Boyd listed bones and banjo; Sallie Paul bones and quills; Sarah Byrd bones, banjo, and quills. James Southall, Maggie Black, and Dicy Windfield described bones with body percussion. Elsie Pryor remembered "sometime when the fiddle was all we could get for music, some of the boys would get a pair of bones, horse ribs or something of the kind and keep time beating on a chairback with them to make more time" (Elsie Pryor, b. ca. 1855, IT, 263). For 1800s references to bones with fiddles, see Allen, "Uncle Tom," 865; Kirke, *Among the Pines*, 145–48; Pennington, *Woman Planter*, 274; "A Southern Barbecue," *Harper's Weekly* 31 (July 9, 1887): 487; Thorpe, "Christmas," 62; Woods, "Corn-Shucking," 571. For other period references to bones, see Cameron, "Christmas," 5; Ingersoll, "Atlanta," 43; Irving, *Knicker-Bocker*, 172; Kirke, *Among the Pines*, 33; Edmund Kirke, *Down in*

Tennessee, and Back by Way of Richmond (New York: Carleton, 1864) 56; Parrish, *Sea Islands*, 15–16; Robinson, *Log Cabin*, 78; Scarborough, *TNFS*, 102–3.

57. Courlander, *NFM*, 219; Kirby, *Instruments*, 15; Nathan, *Dan Emmett*, 154 n24; Nketia, *Music of Africa*, 72.

58. *A Midsummer Night's Night Dream*, Act IV, Scene 1; Nathan, *Dan Emmett*, 154 n24. In Britain and Ireland, spoons and even fireplace tongs were also used as clackers in the manner of bones, the spoons becoming quite common in America. (White Georgia recording artist Herschel Brown specialized in the spoons, even briefly fronting a stringband called the Spooney Five. Tony Russell, booklet accompanying *Herschel Brown, 1928–1929*, Document CD 8001, 1996.) The ex-slaves do not mention them, but African Americans sometimes played spoons. Antebellum observers also occasionally mention castanets among slaves. See, for example, Cameron, "Christmas," 5; Ingraham, *Sunny South*, 106, 144; also Epstein, *Sinful*, 156. Some may really refer to bones—other nineteenth-century writers likened the sound of the bones to castanets (Robert Playfair, *Recollections of a Visit to the United States and British Provinces of North America* [Edinburgh: Thomas Constable, 1856], 174; William John Potts, "Plantation Music," *The Critic and Good Literature* 1 [January 5, 1884]: 9)—but Moorish-Spanish castanets were known in America and may also have been played by slaves.

59. The bones were reputedly introduced to the American stage in July 1841 in Lynchburg, Virginia, by Frank Brower (1823–1874), accompanying banjoist Dan Emmett (1815–1904) (Nathan, *Dan Emmett*, 111, 156). Nathan writes "Brower's bone playing in 1841 is reported to have been something of a novelty" (*Dan Emmett*, 154 n24; also 113 n2), suggesting bones were still generally unfamiliar to white audiences. Emmett and Brower later cofounded the Virginia Minstrels (the first professional blackface ensemble), who debuted the fiddle-banjo-bones-tambourine lineup in New York City in January or February 1843 (Nathan, *Dan Emmett*, 116–18; also 143–58).

60. Nineteenth-century West Indian fiddle ensembles featured similar instrumentation (though some minstrel influence is also a possibility there). Epstein, *Sinful*, 86–88; Jekyll, *Jamaican Song*, 216–17.

61. Minstrelsy's pervasive influence cannot, however, be overstated. In South Africa, English colonists had introduced blackface shows by the 1850s; the Christy Minstrels themselves played Cape Town in 1862, and by the 1890s African American minstrel troupes were successfully touring the country. Veit Erlmann, *African Stars: Studies in South African Black Performance* (Chicago: University of Chicago Press, 1991), 21–53. In the early 1900s, Percival Kirby discovered both the Zulu and their South African neighbors the Chwana playing "the well-known 'bones,' which were a feature of the 'Christy minstrel' performances of

former days. . . . I have not been able to determine whether the Zulu got the idea of using this instrument from the European or not. The Chwana almost certainly did; the Rev. A. Sandilands . . . assured me that the fact is admitted by the Chwana themselves." Kirby, *Musical Instruments*, 15.

62. Louise Rand Bascom, "Ballads and Songs of Western North Carolina," *JAF* 22 (1909): 239. The North Carolina white stringband the Four Pickled Peppers prominently featured bones on their 1930s recordings. Their musical circle (which included Charlie Poole) drew heavily on blackface material, but the Peppers' own records emphasized later pop trends. Kinney Rorrer, *Rambling Blues: The Life and Songs of Charlie Poole* (Danville, VA: McCain, 1982), 58–60; *Country Music Records*. Recordings of Black bone playing include Belton Reese (banjo, vocal), Israel Alston (vocal), and Thaddeus Goodson (bones), "Bile Them Cabbage Down," "The McKenzie Case," *Field Recordings, Vol. 9*, Document CD 5599, 1998; Elizabeth "Babe" Reid (banjo), James Borders (bones), "Corinna," field rec., Caldwell Co., NC, 1970s, *North Carolina Banjo*. Most examples, however, come from white stringbands, but may give a good idea of the music described by ex-slaves. Especially interesting are the 1927 selections by the Johnson Brothers, a white Tennessee string band accompanied by a Black bone player, El Watson. (At the same session, Watson recorded a pair of harmonica blues reflecting more recent Black trends.) DISCOGRAPHIES: *Blues and Gospel Records*; *Country Music Records*. The bones did occasionally figure in later Black music. In the 1870s Ernest Ingersoll attended an Atlanta medicine show. "Two negroes—genuine negroes, but corked in addition to make themselves blacker!—dressed in the regulation burlesque style familiar to us in the minstrel shows at the North, are dancing jigs, reciting conundrums, and banging banjo, bones, and tambourine to the amusement of two or three hundred delighted darkies." Ingersoll, "Atlanta," 43. Recorded half a century later, Blind Blake's "Dry Bone Shuffle" (Paramount 12479, 1927) features bones accompanying Blake's virtuoso guitar. The recording references a later trend (ragtime) but would hardly be out of place on a medicine show stage (a distinct possibility given Blake's background).

63. Dickens, *American Notes*, I: 216. For other period descriptions of fiddles with tambourines, see Bryce, "Fiddlers," 5; Falconer, "Sports," 54; Gilman, *Recollections*, 85; Kmen, *New Orleans*, 230–31; Augustus Baldwin Longstreet, *Georgia Scenes, Characters, Incidents, and Etc.* (Augusta, GA: S. R. Sentinel, 1835), 134; Malet, *Errand*, 49; Murat, *Political Sketch*, 75–76; Pennington, *Woman Planter*, 274; Playfair, *Visit to the United States*, 174; Schoolcraft, *Gauntlet*, 22; "A Southern Barbecue," 487; Victor, *Maum Guinea*, 37; Whipple, *Diary*, 51, 58.

64. Ingleton, "Pine Fork," 358. Compare Fanny White (b. unk., TX), Cade, "Ex-Slaves," 334; Jane Lewis (b. ca. 1820, GA), Katie Brown (b. unk., GA), *Drums and Shadows*, 148, 159; Parker,

Recollections, 310; Victor, *Maum Guinea*, 37; Davis, "Plantation Party," 55.

65. Other ex-slave descriptions of fiddles with drums include Ben Horry (b. ca. 1850, SC, 309); Dan Robinson (b. unk., LA), Cade, "Ex-Slaves," 334. For period accounts, see Cameron, "Christmas," 5; Falconer, "Sports," 54; Gilman, *Recollections*, 112–17; Ingraham, *Sunny South*, 104–8; Pennington, *Woman Planter*, 274; Ravitz, "Slaves' Christmas," 384; Tallant, *Voodoo*, 65; Victor, *Maum Guinea*, 37; Whipple, *Diary*, 51, 58.

66. Jane Lewis (b. ca. 1820, GA), *Drums and Shadows*, 148.

67. Courlander, *NFM*, 209–12, 219; Evans, "Fife and Drum," 94–107; Evans, "One-Stringed Instruments," 231, 233, 242–43; Evans, "Reinterpretation," 386.

68. Although mouth bows are common among some New World Black populations, in North America jew's harps seem to have generally replaced them. There are occasional US Black examples, including one in the narratives, from multi-instrumentalist and instrument-maker Hammett Dell. "I made me a bow of cedar, put one end in my mouth and pick the string wid my fingers while I hold the other end wid this hand. (Left hand. It was very peculiar shaped in the palm.) See my hand that what caused it" (Hammett Dell, b. 1847, TN, 141–42, orig. parentheses). For another nineteenth-century African American example, see Venable, "Down South," 498–99. In North America, however, mouth bows are better documented among whites who borrowed the instrument from Blacks. Courlander, *NFM*, 218; David Evans, "Eli Owens," 344–52; Evans, "One-Stringed Instruments," 239; Evans, "Reinterpretation," 385; Richard Graham, "Ethnicity, Kinship, and Transculturation: African-Derived Mouth Bows in European-American Mountain Communities," *For Gerhard Kubik*, 361–80; Kubik, *Africa*, 12–17; Montagu, *Instruments*, 194–96. RECORDINGS: Neil Morris (vocal), Charlie Everidge (mouth bow), "The Banks of the Arkansas/Wave the Ocean," field rec., Timbo, AR, October 6, 1959, *Sounds of the South* 1.

69. Courlander, *NFM*, 216; Evans, "Eli Owens," 344–45, 351–52; Montagu, *Instruments*, 196–200. For another ex-slave description of the jew's harp, see Lee Henderson (b. unk., LA), Cade, "Ex-Slaves," 333: "Slaves usually amused themselves by boxing, foot races, dancing (secretly), playing music on tin cans, Jew's Harps, or any kind of instrument they could get that would produce sound" (orig. parentheses). For period accounts, see Baldwin, *Observations*, 19; Cable, "Place Congo," 519; "Corn Shuckin' Down South," 4; Mitchell, *Old Dominion*, 172; Ralph, "Dixie," 172.

Banjos and Guitars

1. Davis's first stanza is associated with the Anglo-American lyric "Jack of Diamonds (Rye Whiskey)." His other quotes are from "Amazing Grace" (John Newton, 1779), "Dark Was the Night" (Thomas Haweis, 1792), "Go Preach My Gospel" (Isaac Watts, 1709), and "Old Dan Tucker" (Dan Emmett, 1843).

2. Useful overviews of the African American folk banjo include Dena J. Epstein, "The Banjo: A Documentary History," *Ethnomusicology* 19 (1975): 347–71; Robert B. Winans, ed., *Banjo Roots and Branches* (Urbana: University of Illinois Press, 2018); Carlin, *Banjo*; Jay Bailey, "Historical Origin and Stylistic Developments of the Five-String Banjo," *JAF* 85 (1972): 58–65; Andy Cahan, Robert Winans, and Bob Carlin, booklet accompanying *North Carolina Banjo*; Cecelia Conway, *African Banjo Echoes in Appalachia: A Study of Folk Traditions* (Knoxville: University of Tennessee Press, 1995); Courlander, *NFM*, 212–14; David Evans, booklet accompanying *Tate and Panola*, 12–13; Nathan, *Dan Emmett*, esp. 125–28; Robert B. Winans, "The Folk, the Stage, and the Five-String Banjo in the Nineteenth-Century," *JAF* 89 (1976): 407–37.

3. See, for example, Bebey, *African Music*, esp. 44–46; Epstein, "Folk Banjo," 350–51; Kubik, *Africa*, esp. 7–11; Nketia, *Music of Africa*, esp. 102–3; Winans, *Banjo Roots*, 21–110.

4. Allen, "Uncle Tom," 865.

5. Latrobe, *Journal*, 180–81. Also see Epstein, "Folk Banjo," 363.

6. Bremer, *Homes*, I: 369, 371. Although *gourd* and *calabash* are often used as synonyms, gourds (which grow on vines on the ground) and calabashes (which grow on trees) are associated not only with different instrument types but with contrasting subsistence patterns and social structures. Shlomo Pestcoe and Greg C. Adams, "Banjo Roots Research: Changing Perspectives on the Banjo's West African Origins and West African Heritage," *Banjo Roots and Branches*, 8–9. The calabash is common to Africa, Central and South America, and the Caribbean but unknown in the United States outside extreme southern Florida; most North American references to calabashes are really gourds.

7. Shortened thumb strings appear on West African plucked lutes, as well as banjo-type instruments from throughout the Americas. They are not (as once believed) an invention of blackface minstrels or commercial instrument makers. Carlin, *Banjo*, 127–37; Pestcoe and Adams, "Banjo Roots Research," 10.

8. By the twentieth century, four- and five-string banjo designs had been standardized in the five-string mountain and bluegrass banjos, and the four-string tenor banjo. There were by then other banjo varieties contrived by commercial manufacturers, usually borrowing string arrangements from other instruments, such as the banjo ukulele (four strings), banjo guitar (six strings), banjo mandolin (eight strings in four pairs), and so forth.

9. *Isaac Williams*, 62.

10. Randolph, *Slave Life*, 30.

11. Thompson, "Plantation Music," 20.

12. Rosenbaum, *Folk Visions*, 104. Also see Courlander, *NFM*, 213–14.

13. The standard gauges of contemporary medium gauge banjo strings are .010mm, .012mm, .016mm, .023mm, .010mm (thumb string).

14. Johnson, *Supernaturals*, 106.

15. A novel of antebellum Louisiana describes a four-string snakeskin-covered, catgut-strung gourd banjo. Alfred Mercier, *L'habitation Saint-Ybars: Ou Maitres et esclaves en Louisiane* (New Orleans: Impremerie Franco-Américaine, 1881), 51–52. Also see Scarborough, *TNFS*, 101. For fish-skin, see Rosenbaum, *Folk Visions*, 104.

16. There were temporary means for tightening tacked heads, but these were no match for the modern banjo's screw-and-bracket system. Nineteenth-century white banjo star Frank B. Converse (1837–1903) learned to play on a homemade instrument, with a "pine neck, rim formerly a flower [flour] sieve and the drum tacked on with brass-headed tacks. Of course, it could not be tightly drawn by this means, but then it was an easy matter to tighten it by warming it before the fire, when it would sound well until it cooled again and became slack." Frank B. Converse, "Banjo Reminiscences. II," *The Cadenza* 7/11 (July 1901): 2.

17. Jonathan Boucher, *Boucher's Glossary of Archaic and Provincial Words* (London: Black, Young, and Young, 1832–33).

18. "An Artist Selecting an Instrument," 196.

19. For the minstrel banjo style and repertoire, see Carlin, *Banjo*; Nathan, *Dan Emmett*, 127–28, 189–213; Winans, "Five-String Banjo," 407–37.

20. A perfect illustration is provided by what may be the only film of an American slave playing the banjo. Uncle John Scruggs was born in slavery in Powhatan County, VA, where he still lived when a newsreel crew filmed him playing and singing for his wife and grandchildren in 1928. He downstrokes a commercially manufactured banjo in the minstrel style, picking out the melody to the minstrel standard "Little Old Log Cabin in the Lane" (Will S. Hays, 1871) in unison with his voice. *Times Ain't Like They Used to Be*, Yazoo DVD 512, 2000. In his 1913 memoir, ex-slave William H. Robinson (1848–?) describes his time as a professional minstrel banjo player, including an English tour. Robinson, *Log Cabin*, 122–31. Black minstrel Ike "Old Slack" Simond ("Banjo comique") (1847–ca. 1891) also authored an entertaining and informative memoir (Simond, *Old Slack*), but neither he nor Robinson mentions playing styles.

21. Converse, "Reminiscences," 2, 3; compare Bradley, "Memories," 337.

22. Cable, "Place Congo," 519–20.

23. Hundley *Social Relations*, 357.

24. Harris, "Plantation Music," 505. For other descriptions of slave banjo players strumming, thumping, and so on, see Northrup,

Twelve Years, 216; Hearn, *Levee*, 62; Ingleton, "Pine Fork," 358; Kemble, *Residence*, 131; French, *Sketches*, 39. An excellent illustration of this strumming banjo style is Jimmie Strothers, "Corn-Shucking Time," field rec., Lynn, VA, 1936, *Virginia and the Piedmont*. Strothers, then a blind convict on a Virginia prison farm, was probably born in the 1880s. His lyrics epitomize antebellum cornshucking songs, however, and conceivably originated in slavery. Kip Lornell, booklet accompanying *Virginia and the Piedmont*.

25. James Robert Gilmore, "The 'Poor Whites' of the South," *Harper's Monthly* 29 (June 1864): 123, orig. emphasis. *Rapping* is another accepted term for downstroking. Under his pen name Edmund Kirke, Gilmore (1822–1903) described another slave dance led by a coachman "*clawing* away with all his might at a dilapidated banjo, while his auditory kept time to his singing, by striking the hand on the knee, and by other gesticulations too numerous to mention." Kirke, *Among the Pines*, 42–43, my emphasis. *Clawhammer* is also a name for downstroking with thumb droning.

26. Converse, "Reminiscences," 4–5. The three-finger bluegrass banjo technique most familiar today surfaced only after 1940, but there were other fingerpicking banjo styles current in the nineteenth century. In the postwar period, classical or guitar-style banjo gained favor with many minstrels, and became a fashionable hobby among white elites in both North America and England. As its name suggests, the approach adopted the complex fingerpicking techniques and repertoire of the classical guitar. Given its popularity, some late nineteenth-century Black banjo players must have been familiar with the guitar style, but this school obviously postdated slavery and does not appear to have influenced Black tradition overall, despite its considerable success with whites. See, for example, John Allan Wyeth, *Sabre*, 63, who in 1914 reported "the banjo as played by the plantation negro" was downstroked "'overhand,' and not 'guitar fashion,' as almost all are taught now." Also see Bailey, "Historical Origins," 62; Winans, "Five-String Banjo," 428–29.

27. An excellent example of this approach is Gus Cannon's rendition of "Cacklin' Hen" (very likely a slave composition). Cannon (1883 or 1884–1979) sings the optional lyrics to the fiddle's usual melody, offset by a downstroked banjo riff. Gus Cannon (banjo, vocal), "Ol' Hen," *Walk Right In*, Stax LP 702, 1963.

28. Scarborough, *TNFS*, 100.

29. Robert Palmer, *Deep Blues* (New York: Penguin), 67. Charley Patton can be heard bumping his guitar on many of his recordings: "Down the Dirt Road Blues" (Paramount 12854, 1929); "Elder Green Blues" (Paramount 12972, 1929); "Going to Move to Alabama" (Paramount 13014, 1929); "High Water Everywhere—Parts I & II" (Paramount 12909, 1929); "Pony Blues" (Paramount 12792, 1929); and others.

30. French, *Sketches*, 39.

31. Kemble, *Journal*, 131.

32. Burwell, *White Acre*, 116; also 81.

33. Bruce, "Tobacco-Plantation," 541.

34. Scarborough, *TNFS*, 100. On Uncle Billy and his banjo playing, also see Wyeth, *Sabre*, 61–64.

35. *Grand Ole Opry*, dir. Frank McDonald (Republic Pictures, 1940). The segment with Macon also appears on *Times Ain't Like They Used to Be*, Yazoo DVD 512, 2000.

36. WPA references to banjos (or banjos with percussion) are listed in the instrumental index. For other ex-slave descriptions, see Charles Ball (ca. 1781–?), *Slavery*, 200–201; Henry Bibb (1815–1854), *Narrative*, 23; Josiah Henson (1789–1883), *Truth Stranger Than Fiction: Father Henson's Story of His Own Life* (Boston: John P. Jewett, 1858), 6; Peter Randolph (ca. 1820–?), *Slave Life*, 30; William H. Robinson (1848–?), *Log Cabin*, 78, 122–31; Isaac D. Williams (ca. 1821–?), *Isaac Williams*, 62. For other period accounts, see Allen, "Editors," 9; Bradley, "Memories," 337; Bradley, "Southern Negro," 67; Bremer, *Homes*, I: 369, 371; Bruce, "Tobacco-Plantation," 541; Burwell, *Girl's Life*, 3; Burwell, *White Acre*, 78–79, 81, 114–16; Cable, "Place Congo," 519–20; Cable, "Mr. Harris," 65; Castelnau, "Florida," 243; Cresswell, *Journal*, 36; French, *Sketches*, 38–41; William Drayton, *The South Vindicated From the Treason and Fanaticism of the Northern Abolitionists* (Philadelphia: H. Manly, 1836), 69–70; Finch, *Travels*, 238; Fithian, *Journal*, 83; Gilmore, "The 'Poor Whites' of the South" 123; Harris, "Plantation Music," 505; J. A. Harrison, "To the Editors of The Critic," *The Critic* 97 (December 29, 1883): 534; H. H. B., "Reminiscences of a Southern Plantation—Continued," 14; George H. Hepworth, *The Whip, Hoe, and Sword; Or, The Gulf-Department in '63* (Boston: Walker, Wise, 1864), 139; Ingersoll, "Atlanta," 43; Joseph Holt Ingraham, *The Southwest: By a Yankee*, 2 vols. (New York: Harper & Brothers, 1835), 1: 162; Kemble, *Residence*, 131; Kennedy, *Swallow Barn*, 101–4; Kilham, "Sketches. Third," 206; Kirke, *Among the Pines*, 42–43; Latrobe, *Journal*, 180–81; A Down East Music Teacher, "Letter from a Teacher in the South," *Dwight's* 2 (February 26, 1853): 164; Long, *Slavery*, 17–18; Mackay, *Western World*, II: 132; Charles Olliffe, *American Scenes: Eighteen Months in the New World*, trans. Ernest Falbo and Lawrence A. Wilson. Lake Erie College Studies, Vol. III (Painesville, OH, 1964), 45–46; James Kirk Paulding, *Letters from the South By a Northern Man*, new ed. (New York: Harper & Brothers, 1817, 1835), 96–97; VA planter to J. K. Paulding, 1836, Paulding, *Slavery*, 194; Théodore Pavie, *Souvenirs Atlantiques: Voyage aux États-Unis au Canada*, 2 vols. (Paris: Roet, 1833), II: 319; Smith, "Persimmon Tree," 60; "The State Press: What the Papers Are Talking About," 4; Thompson, "Plantation Music," 20; Tyson, *Slavery*, 12–13; Whitney, "De Los' Ell an' Yard," 298; Wyeth, *Sabre*, 61–64.

37. Other B. E. Davis interviews including this description more or less verbatim are Lizzie Atkins, Harriet Barrett, Alice Cole, Charlie Cooper, Elige Davison, Mary Gaffney, Toby Jones, Anna Lee, Andy McAdams, John Mosley, Charlie Sandles, Polly Shine, Emma Simpson, and Soul Williams.

38. Ingleton, "Pine Fork," 358.

39. Victor, *Maum Guinea*, 37.

40. Davis, "Plantation Party," 55.

41. Fanny White (b. unk., TX, LA), Cade, "Ex-Slaves," 334.

42. WPA references to the fiddle-banjo combination are listed in the instrumental index. For other ex-slave descriptions, see Sarah Fitzpatrick (b. 1847, AL), Blassingame, *Testimony*, 643–44, 652; Solomon Northrup (1807 or 1808–?), *Twelve Years*, 216; Robinson, *Aunt Dice*, 16; Jacob Stroyer (1846–?), *Life*, 41. For other period accounts, see Allen, "Uncle Tom," 865; Baldwin, *Observations*, 19; Benners, *Slavery*, 25–26; Bryce, "Fiddlers," 5; Burwell, *Girl's Life*, 130–31; Creecy, *Scenes*, 20–21; Cresswell, *Journal*, 42; "An Englishman in South Carolina: December, 1860, and July, 1862. II," *Continental Monthly* 3 (January 1863): 112; Falconer, "Sports," 54; Marshall Hall, *The Two-Fold Slavery of the United States* (London: Adam Scott, 1854), 11, 122; Hearn, *Levee*, 23–31, 75; Hundley, *Social Relations*, 60, 349, 357; Ingleton, "Pine Fork," 358; Ingraham, *Sunny South*, 104–8, 144; Kennard, "National Poets?" 336; Kirke, *Among the Pines*, 145–46; Edmund Kirke, "Charcoal Sketches," *The Cosmopolitan* 6 (January 1889): 301; Kirke, *Southern Friends*, 191–92, 208–9; Lanman, *Adventures*, II: 98, 258, 278–79; Livermore, *Story*, 256–58; Malet, *Errand*, 49, 111; "Old Master and Old Servant," *Harper's Weekly* (January 11, 1890), 323; Olmsted, *Back Country*, 146; Plebius, "Leaves From an Autobiography, Part III," *The Ladies' Repository* 12/6 (June 1852): 222–24; Review of Chas E. Horn, *National Melodies of America* (1839), *SLM* 5 (November 1839): 771; Robinson, "Coloured People," 56; "A Summer on a Southern Plantation," *Independent* 31 (December 11, 1879): 3; Thorpe, "Christmas," 62; Venable, "Down South," 497; Woods, "Corn-Shucking," 571.

43. Guitars were, of course, almost always store-bought. In the twentieth-century, homemade substitutes (cigar-box guitars, one-string "jitterbugs") were common, especially among children, and there are occasional reports of true guitars from local instrument makers, but mass-manufacture was the key to the guitar's popularity.

44. See, for example, Butt, *Antifanaticism*, 113, 165, 172; Eastman, *Aunt Phillis*, 52; Hungerford, *Plantation*, 16, 20–21; Gilman, *Southern Matron*, 54, 140, 172, 181, 229; Schoolcraft, *Gauntlet*, 151, 251, 274; Williams, *Narrative*, 34–35.

45. Holcombe, "Sketches," 626.

46. Evans, *Tate and Panola*; David Evans, booklet accompanying *Traveling Through the Jungle*.

47. Jefferson, *Notes*, 208n; Olliffe, *American Scenes*, 46; Mackay, *Western World*, 132. Also see Bremer, *Homes*, I: 371; Cresswell, *Journal*, 36; Holcombe, "Sketches," 626.

48. Hettie Campbell (b. ca. 1865, GA), *Drums and Shadows*, 187. It is not inconceivable that other ex-slave references to guitars actually referred to banjos (or vice versa).

49. Simon Durr's narrative comes from Mississippi fieldworker Mrs. D. W. Giles, another interviewer with a tendency to repeat material in different narratives. Giles provided over a dozen descriptions of the fiddle-guitar duo, and some of these do suggest repetitions: "I wants yo' all ter know, us had had gran' times at de frolics. On Satuday nites us would dance all nite long. I can hear dem fiddles an' guitars yet, wid dat loud 'swing yo' pardners.' Hit wuz all gran'" (Manda Boggan, b. 1847, Simpson Co., MS, 157). "We would dance the ole square all night. Dem wuz great times wid de purty music ob de guitars an fiddles, some body a callin' de set an den swingin' deir pardners to de tune ob 'Molley Put De Kittle On' and 'Turkey in De Straw'" (Primous Magee, b. 1859, Lawerence Co., MS, 1432–33). "I lacked ter watch de res' an' enjied de music ob, 'Turkey in De Straw,' played on de ole fiddles an' guitars" (Manus Robinson, b. ca. 1860, NC, 1858–59). Overall, however, the descriptions of Giles's narrators vary enough at least to warrant consideration: "Us had candy pullings an' water mellon cuttings on de plantation; an us had guitar and fiddle music. All de niggers could sing" (Rosa Mangum, b. 1831, Simpson Co., MS, 1435). "In dem days deir wuz lots ob game in de swamps. Us had dances too. Dat's when us had a grand time, wid de fiddles and guitars a playin'" (Isaac Potter, b. 1851, Rankin Co., MS, 1743). Certainly Giles never resorts to the rote repetitions found in some narratives, and all of these informants came from the area around Jackson—almost all from Simpson or Rankin Counties—where the fiddle-guitar combo is otherwise well documented. (The Mississippi Sheiks, the most successful of the commercially recorded Black fiddle-guitar groups, came from Bolton in nearby Hinds County, just west of Jackson. They were members of the Chatmon [Chatman] family, a clan of fiddlers and guitarists who had been famous throughout the area since the 1800s. See T. DeWayne Moore, "The Mississippi Sheiks," Bolick and Russell, *Fiddle Tunes*, 378–402.) Many or most of Giles's examples may be reliable, and in any case do not necessarily misrepresent this regional tradition, but they obviously warrant caution. Besides Boggan, Durr, Magee, Mangum, Potter, and Robinson, ex-slaves interviewed by Giles who described the fiddle-guitar combo were Salem Powell (b. ca. 1857, Simpson Co., MS, 1748); Dave Walker (b. 1850, Simpson Co., MS, 2150); Harriet Walker (b. ca. 1852, Simpson Co., MS, 2159); Allen Ward (b. 1856, Simpson Co., MS, 2172–73); Foster Weathersby (b. 1855, Simpson Co., MS, 2227–28); George Weathersby (b. 1852, Simpson Co., MS,

2234); Robert Weathersby (b. ca. 1847, Rankin Co., MS, 2242); Isaac Wilson (b. ca. 1845, Simpson Co., MS, 2361).

50. Bettie Massingale Bell and Callie Washington also recalled banjo and guitar with singing.

51. Ingersoll, "Atlanta," 43; King, *Great South*, 319–20, 401. Given the similarities between guitars and banjos, it has always been common for some people to play both. Around 1885, Charles Dudley Warner (1829–1900) attended a street show in Asheville, North Carolina, where a Black entertainer called "Happy John handled the banjo and the guitar alternately, and talked all the time when he was not singing." Charles Dudley Warner, "On Horseback," *Atlantic* 56 (October 1885): 542.

52. Matilda Henrietta Perry and George Morrison also described guitar-banjo-fiddle combos. "But usually the old fiddler would be the band leader and the band itself" (George Morrison b. ca. 1860, KY, 146). The sound of these groups is probably well represented by the performances of Murph Gribble (b. unk.–1950) (banjo), John Lusk (1886–1969) (fiddle), Albert York (1887–1953) (guitar), field recs., Rocky Island, TN, 1946, *Altamont*.

53. Hearn, *Levee*, 55.

54. Johnson, *Highways*, 110–11.

55. Born probably around 1880, Henry "Ragtime Texas" Thomas was among the older artists to record commercially in the 1920s. His guitar playing, which does resemble banjo frailing, may represent one early approach to the instrument; his repertoire and use of quills (African American pan pipes) also date him to an earlier era. A recently discovered 1931 silent film of Thomas on Chicago's Maxwell Street shows him strumming his guitar insistently with his thumb and forefinger (he appears to be wearing a thumb pick). "Could this be Henry Thomas/Ragtime Texas?" (youtube). Also see Henry Thomas, *Texas Worried Blues*, Yazoo CD 1080/1, 1989; Oliver, *Songsters*, 26, 56, 71, 112–13, 130–31, 222, 233. The only known photo of Thomas shows him holding his guitar and forming a D-chord with his left hand, his right hand in exactly the same position as narrator Elijah Cox (fig. 5.4). The resemblance between the two photos is in fact striking.

56. Paul Oliver's *Songsters and Saints* is the definitive study of these artists and their recorded oeuvre.

57. Ed. Harrigan and Dave Braham, "Slavery Days" (New York: Wm. A. Pond & Co., 1876); also see *Country Music Sources*, 466; Spaeth, *More*, 105–6.

58. Booker T. Washington does quote "Slavery Days" in *A New Negro for A New Century* (Chicago: American, 1900), 165–66, but this hardly establishes an African American tradition. There is also a recording, unreleased at the time, by white country artist Fields Ward, "In Those Cruel Slavery Days" (Gennett unissued, 1929). *Country Music Sources*, 466; Tony Russell, *Blacks, Whites, and Blues* (New York: Stein and Day, 1970), 20.

59. Unfortunately there is no indication of what other kinds of material Cox played or how representative "Slavery Days" was of his total repertoire. Given his background, it seems likely that he was acquainted with authentic slave music and other varieties of Black folksong, but possibly with other later trends as well.

The 'Fore Day Horn

1. Helen H. Roberts, "Possible Survivals of African Song in Jamaica," *Musical Quarterly* 12 (1926): 346.

2. Courlander, *Drum and Hoe*, 197, 117; also Courlander, "Haiti," 381; Verna Gillis and Gage Averill, booklet accompanying *Caribbean Revels: Haitian Rara and Dominican Gaga*, Smithsonian/Folkways CD 40402, 1991; Elizabeth McAlister, booklet accompanying *Rhythms of Rapture: Sacred Musics of Haitian Vodou*, Smithsonian/Folkways CD 40464, 1995, 10. *Coumbites* are cooperative work parties similar to cornshuckings, with musicians and singing leaders accompanying labor, culminating in feasting and dancing. Courlander, *Drum and Hoe*, 116–20. *Rara* is the music played on bamboo or tin trumpets during Haiti's Carnival.

3. S. W. G. Benjamin, "The Sea Islands," *Harper's Monthly* 57 (November 1878): 847 (the illustration also depicts skillet-lid cymbals).

4. Harris, "Plantation Music," 505.

5. Louis Armstrong typescript, 1954, Institute of Jazz Studies, Rutgers University, qtd. Thomas Brothers, *Louis Armstrong's New Orleans* (New York: W. W. Norton, 2006), 55.

6. Alan Lomax, *Mister Jelly Roll: The Fortunes of Jelly Roll Morton, New Orleans Creole and "Inventor of Jazz."* 2nd ed. (Berkeley: University of California Press, 1970), 61; on Kid Ory, see Brothers, *Louis Armstrong*, 56–57.

7. Johnny Wiggs interview, 1962, Hogan Jazz Archive, Tulane University, qtd. Brothers, *Louis Armstrong*, 57.

8. WPA narrators identifying signal horns are listed in the chapter appendix. For other slave sources, see Sam Aleckson (1852–1914), *Before the War*, 251 (plantation cow horn); Charles Ball (ca. 1781–?) *Slavery*, 119, 188 (horn: assemble slaves to receive weekly corn allowance); 145–46 162, 334 (morning horn: to work), 148 (7 a.m. horn, stop work, eat breakfast), 150 (horn at dark: stop work), 158, 266 (horn: assemble slaves for roll call); 270 (horn: assemble slaves to receive winter clothes); Steptoe Ball (ex-slave), Sallie Holley to Mrs. Porter, Lottsburgh, VA, August 26, 1879, qtd. Sallie Holley, *A Life for Liberty: Anti-Slavery and Other Letters*, ed. John White Chadwick (New York: G. P. Putnam's Sons, 1899), 232 (first horn sunrise: get up, eat, second daybreak: work); Henry Bibb (1815–1854), *Narrative*, 77, 110, 115, 117 (overseer's horn two hours before daylight); 132 (horn: assemble slaves, witness punishment); Lue Bradford,

(b. unk., KY) (noon dinner horn), Linzy Scott (b. unk., LA) (horn 4 a.m.: wake up), Nancy Young (b. unk., IL, MO, LA) (noon dinner horn), Cade, "Ex-Slaves," 312–14; Frederick Douglass (1818–1895), *My Bondage*, 102, (horn dawn), 290 (breakfast horn); John Andrew Jackson, *The Experience of a Slave in South Carolina* (1862); rpt., *I Belong to South Carolina*, 96 (horn midnight in winter: kill hogs, cut down pine trees, thresh wheat and oats), 97, 98, 108 (morning horn: get up); Harriett Brent Jacobs (1813 or 1815–1897), *Slave Girl*, 76 (morning work horn); Irving Lowery (1850–?), *Plantation*, 210, 226 (horn 4 a.m.: get up, feed horses, mules, noon: dinner); Solomon Northrup (1807 or 1808–?), *Twelve Years*, 170–71, 237, 238 (horn hour before daylight), 237 (curfew horn); Anon., "Recollections of Slavery By a Runaway Slave" (1838); rpt. *I Belong to South Carolina*, 62–8 (morning horn); Austin Steward (1793–1869), *Slave*, 15 (horn or conch-shell sunrise, field thirty minutes); James Williams (1805–?), *Narrative*, 46 (horn dawn). For period accounts, see Elwood Griest, *John and Mary; Or, The Fugitive Slaves* (Lancaster, PA: The Inquirer, 1873), 40 (tin dinner-horn); Holcombe, "Sketches," 625 (horn: assemble slaves for Christmas whiskey ration); Howard, *Bond and Free*, 155, 189 (overseer's horn: turnout); Hundley, *Social Relations*, 33, 357 (hunting horn; headman's horn at cockcrow); "Scenes on a Cotton Plantation," *Harper's Weekly* 11 (February 2, 1867): 69 (cow horn: get up).

9. Compare George Washington Rice (b. 1855, AR, 3303): "Only w'ok I done befo' the War wuz mindin' birds offen the co'n by clappin' two cedar paddles together."

10. "Southern Cabins. IV" (1880), 782, describes Alabama Black congregations being called to services with tin trumpet. Ex-slave Irving Lowery (1850–?) remembered a trumpet announcing a South Carolina camp meeting. Lowery, *Plantation*, 220.

11. Ruth Bass, "The Little Man," *Scribner's* 97 (1935): 321, from a Mississippi ex-slave.

12. Some narrators specified work bells were hung or mounted, others hand-rung. One slaveholder recommended "a large-sized cow bell that could be heard two miles" as a work and dinner bell. Agricola, "Management," 361.

13. Also see Callie Williams (b. 1861, AL, 425–26, 449). In 1933 John Lomax and Alan Lomax recorded an inmate at the Mississippi State Penitentiary demonstrating how he woke other inmates by beating a metal object (probably a bucket) and singing. Crap Eye, "One Morning At The Break of Day (Wake Up Song)," field rec., Parchman Penitentiary, MS, August 1933, *Saints and Sinners*. Also see David Evans, booklet accompanying *Saints and Sinners*.

14. Mail carriers faced various dangers: "My mudder' name was Hannah Hadnot an' my father name was Ruffin Hadnot. He uster carry de mail from Weiss Bluff to Jasper. Dey kill him in 1881. Dey waylay him on de road an' kill him an' rob de mail" (Mary Kindred, b. ca. 1855, TX, 2199).

15. Ben Horry (b. ca. 1850, SC, 325). After the Denmark Vesey revolt (1822) a Black boatman falsely accused of blowing his horn to signal rebelling slaves was hanged. Epstein, *Sinful*, 155. At an 1836 oystering party on Jekyll Island, Georgia, a slave announced the flatboat's arrival by blowing a conch. Franklin H. Head, "The Legends of Jekyll Island," *New England Magazine*, n.s. 8 (March–August 1893): 397.

16. Hundley, *Social Relations*, 33.

17. James Williams, *Narrative*, 81. For slave-hunters' horns, also see "A Mild Slave-Hunt," *Harper's Weekly* 23 (November 1, 1879): 867; Stroyer, *Life*, 65–66, 70.

18. Epstein, *Sinful*, 58–60.

19. E. M. von Hornbostel, "The Ethnology of African Sound-Instruments (Continued)," *Africa: Journal of the International African Institute* 6 (1933): 278; Kirby, *Instruments*, 120; Montague, *Instruments*, 103, 181.

20. Nettl, *Folk Music*, 137–39; also Kirby, *Instruments*, 114.

21. Georg Schweinfurth, *The Heart of Africa*, trans. Ellen E. Frewer. 2 vols. (New York: Harper & Brothers, 1874), I: 288–89.

22. See, for example, Kirby, *Musical Instruments*, 105–25. Kirby describes Zulu performers using the *icilongo* (a bamboo-and-oxhorn trumpet) "for sounding 'bugle-calls' that suggest very forcibly European prototypes" (119). RECORDINGS: "Battle Call, War Horn," field rec., ca. 1939, Lagos, *African Music*, Folkways LP 8852, 1957.

23. Thomas Winterbottom, MD, *An Account of the Native Africans in the Neighbourhood of Sierra Leone* (London: C. Whittingham, 1803), I: 113.

24. Kirby, *Instruments*, 107, also 114.

25. Kirby, *Instruments*, 119–20, 113.

26. Ex-slave author Austin Steward (1793–1869) reported that Virginia slaves were awakened by the "blowing of a horn or conch-shell" (Steward, *Slave*, 15). Basil W. Duke (1838–1916) described a slave blowing a conch as a dinner horn on his family's Kentucky plantation. Duke, *Reminiscences*, 229. An 1836 account describes a Georgia Sea Island slave "blowing on a conch shell, and producing a dismal and incessant blare." Head, "Jekyll Island," 397. A century later, Shad Hall, one of Lydia Parrish's Sea Island informants, was still able to demonstrate "how the conch was blown in olden times to get the hands out to work before day." Parrish, *Sea Islands*, 246. Compare "Shells," *Harper's Weekly* 23 (December 6, 1879): 955: "Laborers on West Indian plantations are summoned to and from work by an instrument of this kind [conch trumpet]." Also see Courlander, "Cuba," 240; Courlander, *Drum and Hoe*, 197; Courlander, "Haiti."

27. For period accounts of cow-horns, see "Scenes on a Cotton Plantation," 69; "Mild Slave-Hunt," 867; Williams, *Narrative*, 81. As of the early 1970s, Black farmers and hunters in rural Mississippi still used cow-horns for signaling, "but the player makes no attempt to control its pitch." Evans, *Tate and Panola*, 4. For cow-horns in Haiti, see Courlander, *Drum and Hoe*, 197; for sheep-horns in Jamaica, Roberts, "Possible Survivals of African Song," 346.

28. "Corn Shuckin' Down South," 4.

29. Nettl, *Folk Music*, 55. For Africa, see Bebey, *African Music*, 68; Marcuse, *Instruments*, 818–20; Montague, *Instruments*, 185; Nketia, *Music of Africa*, 97.

30. Schweinfurth, *Heart of Africa*, I: 288; also II: 404. Intriguingly, manyinyee are played specifically at sowing festivals similar to cornshuckings (I: 183).

31. Courlander, "Haiti," 381; *Drum and Hoe*, 197.

32. Roberts, *Black Music*, 50.

33. Kirby, *Instruments*, 110, 169, 204, 205, 226; Andrew Tracey, "The Nyanga Panpipe Dance," *African Music* 5 (1971): 76.

34. J. Alexander Patten, "Scenes in the Old Dominion. Number Two—A Tobacco Market," *New York Mercury* 21 (November 5, 1859): 8; King, *Great South*, 560; "A Virginia Tobacco Mart," *Harper's Weekly* 23 (May 3, 1879): 345. For tin trumpets, also see Griest, *John and Mary*, 40; Harris, "Plantation Music," 505; Harris, *Remus*, 187; "A Historic Horn," Charleston *Weekly News and Courier*, January 26, 1898, 12; "Southern Cabins. IV," 782.

35. Ex-slave Burt Haygood's daughter had "in her possession the little horn that he used for giving signals during his stay [with the Confederate army] during the Civil War" (Burt Haygood, 1840–1924, SC, 186), presumably a bugle. For other military bugles, see Appendix: Musical Instruments in the WPA Ex-Slave Narratives.

36. Compare Ex-slave Steptoe Ball, qtd. Holley, *Life for Liberty*, 232: "The horn blowed at break o'day: time then to get up, cook an' eat. Then at sunrise, horn blow agin an' we had to go to work, whether we eat or not."

37. There may be a military influence in this example, since the song Rowell sang with his morning horn suggests the optional lyrics of the bugle call *Reveille*: "I can't get 'em up, / I can't get 'em up, / I can't get 'em up this morning. . . ."

38. Fedric, *Slave Life*, 57. This is a fairly obvious alternative that might occur independently, but communicative rhythms of this sort are also used for horn and drum signaling by African groups speaking nontonal languages. Oliver, *Savannah*, 52.

39. "Southern Cabins. IV," 782.

40. This is "Many Thousands Gone (No More Auction Block for Me)," which many ex-slaves associated with the first night of freedom. See Appendix: Shout below.

41. Willie Blackwell (b. 1834, NC, 312) also gave a text of "Cold Frosty Morning," for which see *Appalachian Fiddle*, 197; Arnold, *Alabama*, 116; Brown III: 543; Davis, "Folk-Lore," 250; Davis, *Folk-Songs*, 322; Calvin Fairbanks, *Rev. Calvin Fairbanks During Slavery Times* (Chicago: R. R. McAbe, 1890), 12; Kennard, "National

Poets," 339; Kirke, *Among the Pines*, 22–24; Perrow, "South" (1915), 139–40; Randolph, *OFS* II: 365–66; Roberts, *Sang Branch*, 185–86; Scarborough, *TNFS*, 207–8; Solomon, *Daisies*, 219; Talley, *NFR*, 15–16; White, *ANFS*, 382.

42. For other accounts of work signals at freedom (war's end, surrender), see the chapter appendix.

43. "A Historic Horn," 12.

44. "A Mild Slave-Hunt," 867.

45. For steamboat whistles, also see Charlie Grant (b. 1852, SC, 172); Marie Hervey (b. ca. 1870, TN, child of ex-slaves, 233)

46. J. Milton Mackie, *From Cape Cod to Dixie and the Tropics* (New York: G. P. Putnam, 1864), 137. Also see Philip Graham, "Showboats and Calliopes," *Midwest Folklore* 5 (1955): 229–35.

47. A different version of this story appears in the narrative of South Carolina ex-slave Nelson Cameron (b. 1856, SC). Cameron and Rosboro were both interviewed by fieldworker W. W. Dixon, so this may be another case of a writer repeating himself; however, the variations in these two texts also suggest this could be a migratory tale that Dixon simply collected from two informants. Other narrators had semi-comical tales of their introduction to steam. "De first train I ever saw was in Brandon. . . . I was lookin' at it out de upstairs window an' when it whistled I would a jumped out de window, only Cap Harper grabbed me" (Berry Smith, b. 1821, MS, 1980). "De first time I come to town was when I was a little child, and when we got to college hill, about ten miles from home, I started to run home because I heard the train whistle blow" (Emoline Glasgow, b. 1859, SC, 135). Also see Lewis Jones (b. 1851, TX, 239).

48. Brass and wind players regularly appear in colonial notices for escaped slaves; for example, Mark, who ran away from a Fauquier County, VA, plantation in 1784, is described as able to "blow the French horn." Windley, *Volume 1: Virginia*, 366.

49. Olmsted, *Seaboard* 2: 195. For another Southern example, see Nehemiah Adams, *A South-Side View of Slavery; Or, Three Months At the South, In 1854* (Boston: T. R. Marvin, 1855), 211. Similar groups existed in the North. During the first decades of the nineteenth century, Frank Johnson (1792–1844), a free Black originally from Martinique, led some of Philadelphia's premier brass bands. Eileen Southern, "Black Musicians and Early Ethiopian Minstrelsy," 1975; rpt. *Inside the Minstrel Mask: Readings in Nineteenth-Century Blackface Minstrelsy*, ed. Annemarie Bean, James V. Hatch, and Brooks McNamara (Middleton, CT: Wesleyan University Press, 1996), 46–47.

50. William Howland Kenney, *Jazz on the River* (Chicago: University of Chicago Press, 2005).

51. "Enlisting Slaves," *Snow Hill (Md.) Shield*, November 7, 1863; rpt. *The Liberator* 33 (November 20, 1863): 187.

52. King, *Great South*, 611. Compare Robinson, "Coloured People," 56.

53. Evans, "Fife and Drum," esp. 105; Lomax, *Land*, 163–67; Fredric Ramsey Jr., *Been Here and Gone* (New Brunswick, NJ: Rutgers University Press, 1960), 66–73; Fredric Ramsey Jr., booklet accompanying *Music from the South: Volume 1: Country Brass Bands*, Folkways LP 2650, 1955.

54. *Bayou Maharaja: The Life and Music of New Orleans Piano Legend James Booker*, dir. Lily Keber. Cadiz Music DVD, 2013. Louis Piernas does not indicate what instrument he played.

55. Ravenel, "Recollections," 766.

56. G. G. Foster, *New York By Gas-Light: With Here and There a Streak of Sunshine* (New York: Dewitt & Davenport, 1850), 73.

57. William C. Lodge, "Among the Peaches," *Harper's Monthly* 41 (September 1870): 516–17.

58. Ingersoll, "Atlanta," 43. Compare Evans, "Fife and Drum," 105; Evans, *Tate and Panola*, 12; Ping, "Musical Activities," 150–51. RECORDINGS: *Blind James Campbell and His Nashville Street Band*, Arhoolie CD 438, 1995.

59. Toll, *Blacking Up*, esp. 202–5; Abbott and Seroff, *Out of Sight*, 96, 383, 398.

Flutes, Fifes, and Quills

1. For "whistling [Black] boys, and military bands" in 1850s Savannah, also see Adams, *South-Side View of Slavery*, 211.

2. "Fisher's Hornpipe" is an Anglo-American fiddle tune current in Black tradition. Ex-slave Jacob Stroyer (1846–?) reported that the slaves' "favorite tunes were 'The Fisher's Hornpipe,' 'The Devil's Dream,' and 'Black-eyed Susan.'" Stroyer, *Life*, 45. Two later Black recordings are of special interest: Frank Patterson (fiddle), Nathan Frazier (banjo), "Fisher's Hornpipe," field rec., Nashville, 1942, *Black Fiddlers*; and Stovepipe No. 1 (Samuel Jones), (harmonica, kazoo-and-stovepipe, guitar), "Fisher's Hornpipe" (Columbia 15011-D, 1924). DISCOGRAPHIES: *Country Music Records*; *Country Music Sources*, 743.

3. Irving, *Knicker-Bocker*, 18–19. Irving actually describes the Dutch village Communipaw, now in Jersey City, New Jersey.

4. For Tom and Mark, see Windley, *Volume 1: Virginia*, 204, 366, for Penny, *Volume 2: Maryland*, 206. Visiting Virginia in 1816 J. K. Paulding also reported that slaves "whistle as clear as the notes of the fife." Paulding, *Letters from the South*, I: 97. Whistling or playing pipes or flutes with a hollowed (rolled) tongue is common in Africa, perhaps indicating the "peculiar manner" in which Tom whistled with his tongue. Kirby, *Instruments*, 127–28, 131, 135, 136, 139, 149, 160–61. "The Black Joke" originated as an eighteenth-century English street ballad, being popular in Britain and America as both a song and dance tune. Roud, Black Joke (tune entry).

5. Kennedy, *Swallow Barn*, 454. For other period accounts of Black whistling, see Agricola, "Management," 361; Anderson, *From Slavery*, 30–31; Baldwin, *Observations*, 19; Bryant, "Old South," 33; Gilman, *Recollections*, 89; Harrison, "To the Editors of The Critic," 534; Sidney Lanier, *Florida: Its Scenery, Climate, and History* (Philadelphia: J. B. Lippincott, 1876), 29–31; Lowery, *Plantation*, 199; Munroe, "A Southern Convict Camp," 6; Olmsted, *Seaboard*, 2: 195; Patten, "Scenes in the Old Dominion," 8; Paulding, *Letters from the South*, I: 97; Peabody, "Notes on Negro Music," 149; Stowe, *Old Town Folks*, 39.

6. Compare Agricola, "Management of Negroes," 361: "When at work I have no objection to their whistling or singing some lively tune, but no *drawling* tunes are allowed in the field, for their motions are almost certain to keep time with the music" (orig. emphasis).

7. Anderson, *From Slavery*, 30–31.

8. Bryant, "Old South," 33.

9. Munroe, "A Southern Convict Camp," 6. On slaves whistling for dancing, also see Gilman, *Recollections*, 89; Lowery, *Plantation*, 199; Stowe, *Old Town Folks*, 39.

10. For whistling in Africa, see Kirby, *Instruments*, 116. WPA narrators also described whistling's familiar uses as a signal or warning (H. B. Holloway, Ann Stokes), or to summon animals (Will Dill, Milton Marshall). For other incidental references, see Lizzie Davis, Cordelia Anderson Jackson, Walter Long, Patsy Moses, Mary Teel, and Andy Marion.

11. Evans, "Fife and Drum," 104–5; Evans, *Tate and Panola*, 8–9. RECORDINGS: Compton Jones, "Old Dick Jones Is Dead and Gone," field rec., Senatobia, MS, 1970, *Tate and Panola*; Compton Jones, "Sitting On Top of the World," "Number Five," field rec., Senatobia, MS, 1970, *Traveling Through the Jungle*.

12. For panpipes in Africa, see Peter Cooke and Sam Kasule, "The Musical Scene in Uganda: Views From Without and Within," *African Music* 7 (1999): 9; Leonard Goines, "Musics of Africa South of the Sahara," *Music Educators Journal* 59 (October 1972): 50; Kubik, *Africa*, 89–91; Kubik, "Music in Uganda: A Brief Report," *African Music* 4 (1968): 59–60; Moya Aliya Malamusi, "Thunga la Ngororombe—The Panpipe Dance Group of Sakha Bulaundi," *African Music* 7 (1992): 85–107; L. W. G. Malcolm, "The West African Culture Zone and Forest Area," *The Geographical Teacher* 12 (1923): 52; Nketia, *Music of Africa*, 93–94; Paul Schebesta, "Pygmy Music and Ceremonial," *Man* 57 (1957): 63; Hornbostel, "The Ethnology of African Sound-Instruments (Continued)," 285–86; Tracey, "The Nyanga Panpipe Dance," 73–89; Andrew Tracey, "Some Dance Steps for the Nyanga Panpipe Dance," *African Music* 7 (1992): 108–18.

13. Kirby, *Instruments*, 128–30, 134; Courlander, *NFM*, 217; Evans, "Reinterpretation," 383.

14. Compare Bebey, *African Music*, 79; Kirby, *Instruments*, 161–63, 168–69; Kubik, *Africa*, 89. On quill (singular) for single flutes or pipes, see Evans, "Fife and Drum," 103, 107 n20; Bruce A. MacLeod, "Quills, Fifes, and Flutes Before the Civil War," *SFQ* 42 (1978): 206–7; Rosenbaum, *Folk Visions*, 105. Another narrative mentions a "flute made from de switches of de saplin's" (Lee Hobby, b. ca. 1850, KY, 1739). This interview was conducted by Texas fieldworker Effie Cowan, whose materials are always suspect, but the detail is consistent with other accounts.

15. James Reese Europe, "A Negro Explains Jazz," *Literary Digest* 61 (April 26, 1919): 28. Tragically, Europe was murdered two weeks later, on May 9, 1919.

16. "Every Drummer his own Fifer," *New-York Spectator* (February 1, 1828), orig. emphasis.

17. During this time, Black child-chimney sweeps are described as constant presences on New York streets, covered in soot and clothed in rags, carrying brushes and scrapers, and singing some version of their advertisement "Sweep-O-O-O." "Black Tom, The Sweep," *Gleason's Pictorial Drawing Room Companion* 2 (February 14, 1852): 112; *City Cries: Or, A Peep at Scenes in Town* (Philadelphia: George S. Appleton, 1850), 16–18; *The Cries of New-York* (New York: Samuel Wood & Sons, 1822), 38–39; De Voe, *Market Book*, 483; Mrs. Burton Kingsland, "Reminiscences of Old New York," *Outlook* 49 (March 3, 1894): 406; "The Street-Cries of New York," *Atlantic* 25 (February 1870): 201.

18. Three of Patterson's performances are on *Traditional Music at Newport 1964, Part 1*, Vanguard LP 1982, 1965; one ("Shear Them Sheep Even") is heard (Patterson is not shown) in the Newport documentary, *Festival*, dir. Murray Lerner (Patchke Productions, 1967). Also see Bastin, *Red River Blues*, 151.

19. See, for example, Kirby, *Instruments*, 214; Malamusi, "Panpipe Dance," 88–89; Schebesta, "Pygmy Music," 63; Tracey, "Nyanga Panpipe Dance," 76, 81; Tracey, "Some Dance Steps," 108.

20. Cable, "Place Congo," 520–21, 529 (LA, AL); Cable, "Mr. Harris," 65 (MS, LA); "Carmina Africana," 10 (MS); "Corn Shuckin' Down South," 4 (SC); Harris, "Plantation Music," 505 (GA); Thompson, "Plantation Music," 20 (GA, AL). All refer to the prewar period.

21. "Carmina Africana," 10. "Little Dogs" is a well-known item with minstrel connections. Brown III: 252–53; Hudson, *Mississippi*, 201–2; Lomax, *Country*, 111–12; Elsie Clews Parsons, "Folk-Lore from Aiken, S.C.," *JAF* 34 (1921): 37; Perrow "South" (1913): 127; Randolph, *OFS* II: 382–83; Talley, *NFR*, 130–31, 146; White, *ANFS*, 207–8, 232.

22. Parrish, *Sea Islands*, 16. An 1895 publication describes quills somewhere in South Carolina ("Corn Shuckin' Down South," 4), and two ambiguous cases—Sylvia Cannon (b. ca. 1857, Florence Co.,

SC, 190) and Charlie Grant (b. 1852, Charleston, SC, 172)—come from that state.

23. Harris, "Plantation Music," 505. Quills also figure in the Uncle Remus tales "Brother Fox, Brother Rabbit, and King Deer's Daughter," and "Brother Fox Covets the Quills," Joel Chandler Harris, *Nights With Uncle Remus* (Boston: James R. Osgood, 1883), 68–74, 79–82.

24. "History of the Fort Valley State College Folk Festival," 1; Bastin, *Red River Blues*, 74–75, 82; Evans, *Make You Happy*.

25. Thompson, "Plantation Music," 20.

26. Rosenbaum, *Folk Visions*, 50. Another area musician, Jake Staggers (b. 1899, Oconee Co., GA), also recalled quills, though he played only the single quill flute (which he called a single whistle), as well as banjo, harmonica, and mouth bow. *Folk Visions*, 104–5.

27. Charles S. Johnson, *Shadow of the Plantation* (Chicago: University of Chicago Press, 1934), 20.

28. Cable, "Place Congo," 529; also 520–21.

29. John Arthur Lee was born in 1915 at Mount Willing, Lowndes Co., AL, southwest of Montgomery. The selection—"Baby Please Don't Go" (unissued, 1951)—is the well-known Big Joe Williams song.

30. On Sid Hemphill, see Matthew Barton, booklet accompanying *61 Highway Mississippi*, Rounder CD 1703, 1997; Matthew Barton, booklet accompanying *Voices From the South*, Rounder CD 1701, 1997; Evans, *Saints and Sinners*; Evans, *Tate and Panola*, 9; Evans, *Traveling Through the Jungle*; Lomax, *Land*, 314–40; Lomax, booklet accompanying *Sounds of the South*; T. DeWayne Moore, "Sidney Hemphill, Sr.," Bolick and Russell, *Fiddle Tunes*, 202–22; Jim O'Neal, "Sid Hemphill: Hill Country Patriarch," *Living Blues* 49/1 (February 2018): 38–41; Stephen Wade, booklet accompanying *Black Appalachia*. On Alec Askew, see Evans, *Traveling Through the Jungle*; Lomax, *Land*, 325. Hemphill's and Askew's recordings appear on *61 Highway Mississippi*, *Black Appalachia*, *Saints and Sinners*, *Sounds of the South* 1, *Tate and Panola*, *Traveling Through the Jungle*, and *Voices from the South*. It has been suggested that Big Boy Cleveland, "Quill Blues" (Gennett 6108, 1927), also derives from the North Mississippi quills tradition, but that begs several questions, including whether the record features quills or a single quill flute. Evans, "Fife and Drum," 107 n20.

31. Evans, "Afro-American One-Stringed Instruments," 231, 233.

32. George W. Cable, "Place Congo," 520–21, 529; James B. Cable, "Mr. Harris," 76, 65.

33. Gene Anderson, "Johnny Dodds in New Orleans," *AM* 8 (1990): 410.

34. "Carmina Africana," 10.

35. "Could this be Henry Thomas/Ragtime Texas?" (youtube). Thomas's repertoire derived mainly from late nineteenth-century or early twentieth-century folk and popular sources; one of his recorded selections—the spiritual "When the Train Comes Along"

(Vocalion 1140, 1927)—also appears in the ex-slave narratives. His complete surviving titles, eight featuring quills, appear on Henry Thomas, *Texas Worried Blues*, Yazoo CD 1080/1, 1989. Also see Oliver, *Songsters*, 26, 56, 71, 112–13, 130–31, 222, 233. The quill part from "Bull-Doze Blues" appears in Canned Heat, "Going Up the Country" (Alan Wilson) (Liberty 56077, 1968), featured in the soundtrack of *Woodstock*, dir. Michael Wadleigh (Warner Bros. Pictures, 1970).

36. Ophelia Porter's narrative comes from interviewer Ada Davis, who tampered with most of her materials. This detail is at least credible, but much of Porter's interview is suspicious.

37. Talley, *NFR*, 272–75.

38. Montague, *Instruments*, 45–46.

39. Cable, "Place Congo," 520–21; Talley, *NFR*, 273–74; "Corn Shuckin' Down South," 4.

40. Sid Hemphill (MS) played quills with four or ten pipes, Joe Patterson (AL), with ten. Eli Owens (MS) recalled five, seven, eight, or fourteen. Evans, "Eli Owens," 341. Doc Barnes (GA) described quills with four, five, seven, or eight pipes. Rosenbaum, *Folk Visions*, 50.

41. Cable, "Place Congo," 520–21; Courlander, *NFM*, 217.

42. Talley, *NFR*, 272–73; Parrish, *Sea Islands*, 16. Also see the neck rack and quills in the newly found silent film of Henry Thomas: "Could this be Henry Thomas/Ragtime Texas?" (youtube).

43. Kirby, *Instruments*, 195–97, 226.

44. Evans, "Eli Owens," 340–44; Rosenbaum, *Folk Visions*, 50. Ex-slaves also describe whistles as children's toys. "He [slaveholder] allus brung me something jus' like I he own little gal. Sometime he brung me a whistle or some candy or doll or somethin'" (Mandy Hadnot, b. ca. 1850, TX, 102). "Shell [an older slave] had been in the habbit of whittling out whistles for me and pettin' of me" (John Rudd, b. 1854, KY, 170). "They [slave children] run 'round in de plum thickets, blackberry bushes, hunt wild strawberries, blow cane whistles, and have a good time" (Anderson Bates, b. 1850, SC, 42).

45. "Corn Shuckin' Down South," 4.

46. Bebey, *African Music*, 66; Kirby, *Instruments*, 131, 182, 189, 217; Kubik, *Africa*, 89–91; Malamusi, "Panpipe Dance," 88; Tracey, "Nyanga Panpipe Dance," 77–89.

47. Cable, "Place Congo," 520–21, 529.

48. Talley, *NFR*, 273–74. Also see Courlander, *NFM*, 217; Evans, "Reinterpretation," 383; Evans, "Eli Owens," 343; Rosenbaum, *Folk Visions*, 50.

49. This is certainly true of the three best-documented quill blowers, Sid Hemphill (1876–1963), Joe Patterson (1895–1970), and Henry Thomas (b. ca. 1874), all of whom performed in a percussive, highly rhythmic style with prominent hooting.

50. "Corn Shuckin' Down South," 4. For similar African descriptions, see Kirby, *Instruments*, 195, 197, 205, 211; Malamusi, "Panpipe Dance," 88–89; Schebesta, "Pygmy Music," 63.

51. "Corn Shuckin' Down South," 4, describes quills and jew's harps in antebellum South Carolina.

52. Compare Thompson, "Plantation Music," 20 (quills, banjo, antebellum GA). Perhaps because fiddles and quills shared a role, repertoire, and range, they were considered redundant or interchangeable; interestingly, several quill blowers—Hammett Dell, Sid Hemphill, Warren Dodds, Andy Owens—were also fiddlers. Compare James B. Cable: "the violin and the rude mouthorgan of graded canes I knew . . . as quite common among the plantation negroes of Mississippi and Louisiana. Of these, the latter [quills] seemed the favorite of the younger negroes, and the fiddle held that place in the esteem or, at any rate, the use of the elders." Cable, "Mr. Harris," 65.

53. North Carolina ex-slave Allen Parker (1840–?) also described the New Years' Day hiring fair. Parker, *Recollections*, 291–92.

54. Bebey, *African Music*, 66; Kirby, *Instruments*, 171–73; Nketia, *Music of Africa*, 94.

55. From his Middle Tennessee childhood, Thomas W. Talley (1870–1952) recalled a "Little Set of Quills" with five reeds and a "Big Set of Quills," with about twice as many. He does not indicate the two sets' relative ranges, however, and suggests (but does not state) that they were played separately, not together. Talley, *NFR*, 273–74.

56. In Africa and throughout the world panpipes (and other pipes and flutes) are associated with herders. Goines, "Musics of Africa," 50; Kirby, *Instruments*, 130, 133, 135, 141, 146, 148, 165. In 1886 George W. Cable described a "black lad, sauntering home at sunset behind a few cows that he has found near the edge of the canebrake whence he has also cut his three quills, blowing and hooting." Cable, "Place Congo," 521. Also see fig. 7.4.

57. Courlander, *NFM*, 215–16; Michael Licht, "America's Harp," *Folklife Center News* 7/3 (July–September 1984): 6–9; Michael Licht, "Harmonica Magic: Virtuoso Display in American Folk Music," *Ethnomusicology* 24 (1980): 211–21; Evans, *Tate and Panola*, 4; Lomax, *Land*, 345–47; Paul Oliver, "Railroad Piece: Harmonica Players," *Blues Off the Record* (New York: Da Capo, 1984), 39–40.

58. Compare Allen, "Editors," 9: "An instrument frequently used to accompany the banjo there [Kentucky] is the French harp."

59. Handy, *Father*, 15. For other early references to harmonicas, see King, *Great South*, 255–56; Robinson, "Coloured People," 56. Memphis musician Will Shade (Son Brimmer) (1898–1966) learned harmonica from his ex-slave mother, Mary Brimmer. *American Epic*, dir. Bernard MacMahon, Lo-Max Films/Thirteen Productions/BBC Arena, 2017, Two: *Blood and Soil*.

60. Cable, "Mr. Harris," 65.

61. J. M. and G. de. B, booklet accompanying *Leo Rowsome: King of the Pipers*, 1959; Shanachie CD 34001, 1992, which features an Irish bagpipe version of "The Fox Chase."

62. Black recordings of "The Fox Chase" include Israel Alston (vocal), Belton Reese (banjo), Thaddeus Goodson (bones), "Fox Chase," field rec., Brevard Plantation, Columbia, SC, 1939; James Applewhite (harmonica, vocal), "Fox Chase," field rec., VA, 1977, *Virginia Non-Blues*; De Ford Bailey (harmonica), "Fox Chase" (Brunswick 149, 1927); Roger Matthews (harmonica), "The Fox and Hounds," field rec., Belle Glade, FL, 1935, *Field Recordings, Vol. 7*, Document CD 5587; William McCoy, "Train Imitations and the Fox Chase" (Columbia 14302-D, 1927); Joe Patterson (quills, tambourine), "Fox Hunt," concert rec., 1964, *Music at Newport, Part 1*, Vanguard LP 1982, 1965; Dink Roberts (banjo, vocal), "Fox Chase," field rec., Alamance Co., NC, September 1975, *North Carolina Banjo*; Sonny Terry (harmonica), "Fox Chase" (three takes), 1939–1942, *Sonny Terry, Vol. 1*, Document CD 5230; Henry Thomas (quills, guitar), "The Fox and the Hounds" (Vocalion 1137, 1927); Unknown harmonica player, "Fox Chase," field rec., Central State Farm, Sugarland, TX, December 1934, *Saints and Sinners*. Compare Richard Amerson (harmonica), "Hog Hunt (Dog Caught a Hog)," field rec., Livingston, AL, October 1940, *Lullabies*; Gary Davis (harmonica), "The Coon Hunt," *The Guitar and Banjo of Reverend Gary Davis*, Prestige/Folklore LP 14033, 1964; Sid Hemphill (vocal, fiddle), Alec Askew, (guitar), Lucius Smith (banjo), Will Head (bass drum), "Hog Hunt," field rec., Sledge, MS, August 1942, *Saints and Sinners*; and George "Bullet" Williams (harmonica), "The Escaped Convict" (Paramount 12651, 1928), in which the hounds pursue human prey. Also see Evans, "Eli Owens," 343, Courlander, *NFM*, 216; Handy, *Father*, 15. For versions by white fiddlers and harmonica players, see *Country Music Records*; *Country Music Sources*, 891.

63. De Ford Bailey, "Fox Chase" (Brunswick 149, 1927); De Ford Bailey, "Old Hen Cackle" (Brunswick 149, 1927); De Ford Bailey, "Pan American" (Brunswick 146, 1927); DeFord Bailey, "Pan American," "Old Hen Cackle (takes 1 & 2)," field rec., Nashville, ca. 1974–76, *The Legendary DeFord Bailey*, Tennessee Folklore Society CD 122, 1998. Also see Charles K. Wolfe, booklet accompanying *Legendary DeFord Bailey*. DISCOGRAPHIES: *Blues and Gospel Records*; *Country Music Records*. For a discography of recorded train imitations on harmonica and other instruments, see Cohen, *Steel Rail*, 649–51.

64. Windley, *Volume 2: Maryland*, 306–7.

65. Evans, "Black Fife and Drum Music"; Evans, *Tate and Panola*, 6–7; Evans, *Traveling Through the Jungle*; Lomax, *Land*, 331–33; MacLeod, "Quills, Fifes, and Flutes," 201–8; George Mitchell, *Blow My Blues Away* (Baton Rouge: Louisiana State University Press, 1971); John M. Shaw, *Following the Drums: African American Fife and Drum Music in Tennessee* (Jackson: University Press of Mississippi, 2022). RECORDINGS: *61 Highway Mississippi*, Rounder CD 1703, 1997; *Mississippi Delta Blues, Vol. 1*, Arhoolie

CD 401, 1994; *Sounds of the South*, 1, 2 and 4; *Traveling Through the Jungle*.

    66. Windley, *Volume 4: Georgia*, 131.

    67. *Drums and Shadows*, 100–101.

    68. Harris, "Plantation Music," 505.

    69. *The Narrative of James Roberts: Soldier in the Revolutionary War and at The Battle of New Orleans* (1858; rpt. Hattiesburg, MS: Book Farm, 1945), 16.

    70. Kmen, *New Orleans*, 232.

    71. King, *Great South*, 39.

    72. Richard Hildreth, *Despotism in America; Or, An Inquiry into the Nature and Results of the Slave-Holding System in the United States* (Boston: Whipple and Damrell, 1840), 152, orig. emphasis.

    73. Ex-slave Jack Rabb was "a musician, playing the Fife for the Columbus Riflemen, an historic Military Company" (Jack Rabb, b. unk., MS, 1774). There is no other information on Rabb's musical activities.

    74. Cameron, "Christmas," 5; Robinson (b. unk., LA), Cade, "Ex-Slaves," 334.

Pianos, Organs, and Accordions

    1. Interviewers Florence Angermiller and Stanley H. Holm reported that Bill and Ellen Thomas still owned such a piano that "their oldest daughter had bought many years ago. It is evidently very old, a long, square piano of the make they used in the '60s probably. The varnish is off and part of the top has peeled, but it could be sandpapered, refinished, and polished and a beautiful thing made of it. They were proud to know that it might be worth a little something" (Bill Thomas, b. 1849, Ellen Thomas, b. 1856, TX, 3793). On organs and pianos, see Montague, *Instruments*, 96–97, 149–52, 188–93; Marcuse, *Instruments*, 319–49, 599–645.

    2. Ex-slaves Kate Betters and Mollie Williams also described dance fiddling with piano.

    3. During the nineteenth century, pianos were fixtures in theatres, opera houses, symphony halls, and other elite venues frequently but not entirely off-limits to Blacks. Mary Anngady (b. ca. 1857, NC, 36–38) had worked on the professional stage in the postwar period, singing and playing piano, guitar, and violin. The narratives also feature a profile of the slave concert piano prodigy Blind Tom Bethune (1849–1909) (SS1 3 GA 1: 53–61). By the time the ex-slaves were interviewed, pianos were everywhere, and many narrators had them in their homes. Describing the slave quarters, Hagar Lewis stated "the cabins had a big fireplace wider than that piano there" (Hagar Lewis, b. 1855, TX, 2333). Isom Starnes had actually worked "three or four months in a piano factory in

Springfield, Ohio. I liked farming best and come back to it" (Isom Starnes, b. ca. 1860, AL, 218).

    4. Motif E402.1.3(ba). *Ghost plays piano*. Compare Browne, *Hants*, 179; Montell, *Ghosts*, 100–101.

    5. "Juanita" (Caroline Norton, 1853) appeared with some frequency in various midcentury songbooks. Ex-slaves Ann May and Pete Newton also named it. Adeline Jackson's memory that it was "'bout a fountain" accurately refers to the opening lines: "Soft o'er the fountain, / Lingering falls the southern moon." The tune is taken from "Jesus, My Savior" (p.d.), and the piece was often printed in hymnals, usually scored just for voices. *DNAH*. Other arrangements did, however, feature piano accompaniments, including the version in a Civil War–era songster from Georgia, *The Southern Bouquet: Favorite Songs and Ballads No. 11* (Macon, GA: John C. Schreiner, n.d.). I have not found "Juanita" elsewhere in oral tradition, but in the twentieth century, it was recorded by numerous popular singers, including Jim Reeves, "My Juanita," *Girls I Have Known*, RCA Victor LP 1685, 1958.

    6. Of "The Black Mustache," the Brown Collection's editors write "clearly a music hall production, this has established itself more or less as folk song, especially in the South." Brown II: 479–80. Also see Arnold, *Alabama*, 20–21; Browne, *Alabama*, 184–86; Davis, *Folk-Songs*, 177; Henry, *Highlands*, 295–97; Arthur Palmer Hudson, "Ballads and Songs from Mississippi," *JAF* 39 (1926): 159–60; Morris, *Florida*, 142–43; L. W. Payne Jr., "Songs and Ballads—Grave and Gay," *Texas and Southwestern Lore*, ed. J. Frank Dobie. PTFS 6 (Austin, 1927): 231–32; Randolph, *Ozarks* III: 128–30; Rosenberg, *Virginia*, 8. DISCOGRAPHIES: *Country Music Records*; *Country Music Sources*, 195–96, 857. "Shoo Fly" too is generally regarded as a blackface creation, regularly appearing in songbooks alongside Dan Emmett's "Dixie" (1859). In Watson's day, "Rock of Ages" (August Toplady, 1776) would have been available in dozens of hymnals. The slave spiritual "Swing Low, Sweet Chariot" was not the item generally known today, but this refrain occurs in numerous nineteenth-century religious songs found in print. By contrast, "Granny Will Yo' Dog Bite" refers to a wandering couplet known mainly from folk sources: "Chicken in the bread tray, scratching out dough, / 'Granny, will your dog bite?' 'No, child, no.'" See Bass, "Negro Songs," 431; Brown I: 199–200; Brown III: 205–6; Browne, *Alabama*, 445–46; Davis, *Folk-Songs*, 252–53; Evans, "Fife and Drum," 102; Ford, *Traditional*, 36; Gordon, *Folk-Songs*, 74; McKee and Chisenhall, *Beale Black and Blue*, 189; Killion and Waller, *Georgia*, 226; *Old-Time String Band*, 67; Perrow, "South" (1913): 127, 130; Scarborough, *TNFS*, 194; Randolph, *Ozark* III: 289, 291; Talley, *NFR*, 6; Thede, *Fiddle*, 82–83; Titon, *Fiddle Tunes*, 86; White, *ANFS*, 241. RECORDINGS: Napoleon Strickland (fife), Othar Turner (vocal, kettle drum), R. L. Boyce (bass drum), "Granny Will Your

Dog Bite," field rec., Senatobia, MS, 1970, *Traveling Through the Jungle*. DISCOGRAPHIES: *Country Music Records*; *Country Music Sources*, 706.

7. "Captain Jinks of the Horse Marines" (T. Maclagan, 1860), an English music hall hit, was popularized in the States by British stage comedian William H. Lingard (1837–1927) and became a bestseller for numerous American publishers. It was later widely collected as a folksong. Other items ex-slaves mention with pianos had similar histories. Based on a Black folksong, Dan Emmett's "Old Dan Tucker" (1843), which Ellen Claibourn recalled on piano, was one of the first published hits of the minstrel era. Stephen C. Foster's bestsellers "Old Black Joe" (1860) and "The Old Folks at Home (Way Down Upon the Swanee River)" (1851) were both named with the piano by Betty Bormer (b. 1857, TX, 342).

8. Booker T. Washington, *Up from Slavery: An Autobiography* (1901; rpt. Garden City, NY: Doubleday, Doran, 1944), 113–14.

9. Alice Graham, "The Negro Craze for the Reed Organ in the South," *Etude* 34 (November 1916): 826.

10. Michal Shapiro, Christoph Wagner, Jared Snyder, Guy Klucevsek, Larry Birnbaum, Iris Brooks, and Bob Godfried, booklet accompanying *Planet Squeezebox: Accordion Music from Around the World*, Ellipsis Arts CDs 3470, 1995.

11. Nathan, *Dan Emmett*, 147–51.

12. Chambers-Ketchum, "Violin," 330.

13. Banjo's performance combines the hymn "I Heard the Voice of Jesus Say" (Horatius Bonar, 1846) with the chorus of the Black spiritual "Good Shepherd (Feed My Sheep)." An 1889 short story of antebellum plantation life also states "De niggers know de devil is a fiddler, an', consequenchical, de chu'ch members doan play on nuttin', 'cep' tis de 'corjian." Seawell, "Fiddler," 642. For other examples of Blacks playing accordions in church, or to accompany religious songs, see Bastin, *Red River*, 320; David Evans, "Charley Patton: The Conscience of the Delta," *Charley Patton: Voice of the Mississippi Delta*, ed. Robert Sacré (Jackson: University Press of Mississippi, 2018), 46; Kip Lornell, booklet accompanying *Virginia Secular Music*, 14; Puckett, *Folk Beliefs*, 553; Jared M. Snyder, "Squeezebox: The Legacy of the Afro-Mississippi Accordionists," *BMRJ* 17 (1997): 42–44; Charles Wolfe and Kip Lornell, *The Life and Legend of Leadbelly* (New York: HarperCollins, 1992), 16–17.

14. On that score, accordions figure in many of the same supernatural legends as fiddles. See Halpert, *Pinelands*, 300, 412–14; Hyatt, *Hoodoo* 1: 108; Barbara Allen Woods, *The Devil in Dog Form: A Partial Type-Index of Devil Legends*, Folklore Studies No. 11 (Berkeley: University of California Press, 1969).

15. Wolfe and Lornell, *Life and Legend of Leadbelly*, 16. Ex-slaves William M. Adams and William Pratt also knew this song. W. C. Handy recalled it from the fiddling of a former Alabama slave.

Handy, *Father*, 5–6. It was not, however, among the four accordion pieces Lead Belly later recorded: Lead Belly (vocal, accordion), "Corn Bread Rough," New York, 1944, *Complete Recorded Works, Vol. 4*, Document CD 5310, 1994; "John Hardy," New York, 1940s, *Bourgeois Blues*, Smithsonian-Folkways CD 40045, 1997; "Laura," "Sukey Jump (Win'jammer)," New York, 1947, *Where Did You Sleep Last Night*, Smithsonian-Folkways CD 40044, 1996. Also see Lead Belly, "Monologue on Square Dances or Sookey Jumps," Washington, DC, August 1940, *Go Down Old Hannah*, Rounder 1099, 1994; Lomax, *Lead Belly*, 5; Jared Snyder, "Leadbelly and His Windjammer: Examining the African American Button Accordion Tradition," *AM* 12 (1994): 148–66.

16. Cade, "Ex-Slaves," 334. Compare Smalley, "Sugar Making," 109.

17. Bastin, *Red River*, 190–91.

18. David Evans, "Kate McTell, Part 2," *Blues Unlimited* 126 (September–October 1977): 15

19. Bastin, *Red River*, 281, 295–96, 309, 320; Bruce, "Tobacco-Plantation," 541; Lornell, *Virginia Secular Music*, 2, 4–5, 9, 14. RECORDINGS: Isaac Curry (vocal, accordion), "Casey Jones," field rec., VA, 1977; Clarence Waddy (vocal, accordion), "Eve," field rec., VA, 1977, *Virginia Secular Music*.

20. "A Southern Barbecue," 487.

21. Lornell, *Virginia Secular Music*, 5.

22. Snyder, "Squeezebox," 42–46; Jerrilyn McGregory, booklet accompanying *Lullabies to Blues*, which features two Harris titles. Harris's complete recordings appear on *Field Recordings, Volume 4*, Document CD 5578.

23. While accordions are remarked from an early date in the rural areas surrounding New Orleans, they are seldom reported in the city itself, possibly because pianos and organs were more readily available there. However, in the 1860s and '70s New Orleans hoodoo queen Marie Laveau presided at dances in the home of one Mama Antoine, where "a Negro named Zizi played the accordion." Tallant, *Voodoo*, 78. Other cases may have simply gone unreported.

24. Lanman, *Adventures*, 192, orig. emphasis.

25. See, for example, Jekyll, *Jamaican Song*, 216–17. Lizzie Chandler also described accordion and fiddle among Mississippi whites. Hammett Dell remembered accordions being popular among whites in Middle Tennessee around Murfreesboro: "Mars White sent his children to pay school. It was a log house and they had a lady teacher. They had a accordion. Mars Marion's neighbor had one too. All of em could play" (Hammett Dell, b. 1947, TN, 138).

26. Evans, "Eli Owens," 335, 339–40; Snyder, "Squeezebox," 37–57.

27. Evans, *Big Road*, 194.

28. Snyder, "Squeezebox," 46–54; Kip Lornell, booklet accompanying *Memphis Blues (1927–1938)*, Document CD 5159,

1993, which features Rhodes's two surviving titles, "The Crowing Rooster"/"Leaving Home Blues" (Columbia 14289-D, 1927).

29. There are recordings of blues ballads with accordion accompaniments from Isaac Curry, Lead Belly, and especially Blind Jesse Harris, who appears to have specialized in these (see notes 15, 19, 22 above).

30. John Broven, *South to Louisiana: The Music of the Cajun Bayous* (Gretna, LA: Pelican, 1983); Mark F. DeWitt, *Cajun and Zydeco Dance Music In Northern California: Modern Pleasures In a Postmodern World* (Jackson: University Press of Mississippi, 2008); John Minton, "Houston Creoles and Zydeco: The Emergence of an African American Urban Popular Style," *Ramblin' on My Mind: New Perspectives on the Blues*, ed. David Evans (Urbana: University of Illinois Press, 2008), 350–98; John Minton, "Zydeco on CD," *JAF* 111 (1998): 417–34; Savoy, *Cajun Music*, 300–402; Michael Tisserand, *The Kingdom of Zydeco* (New York: Arcade, 1998).

31. Much of this work contributed to the Louisiana folklore anthology *Gumba Ya-Ya* and Robert Tallant's *Voodoo in New Orleans*.

32. The following Gulf Coast Creoles are featured in the ex-slave narratives. Their Creole identity varies considerably in kind and degree. Generally, however, they were French-speaking or bilingual Catholics, possibly mixed-race or freeborn, perhaps with French personal names, who self-identified as Creole or French. Besides music and song, most were acquainted with other Creole folklore, including *loup garou* (werewolf) legends and other folktales, folk medicine and *traiteurs* (folk healers), hoodoo and other folk beliefs, seasonal festivities, wedding and funerary customs, and traditional foodways. Jacob Aldrich (b. 1860, LA); Agatha Babino (b. ca. 1857, LA); Elvira Basard (b. unk., LA); Olivier Blanchard (b. 1843, LA); Edmond Bradley (b. ca. 1843, MS); Donaville Broussard (b. ca. 1850, LA); Marie Brown (freeborn unk., LA); Valmar Cormier (b. ca. 1850, LA); Frances Doby (b. 1838, LA); Mary Donatto (freeborn ca. 1885, LA); Martin Dragney (b. 1860, LA); Mother Duffy (b. unk., LA); Victor Duhon (b. ca. 1840, LA); Mary Kincheon Edwards (b. 1810, LA); Mrs. M. S. Fayman (b. 1850, LA); Alphonse Fields (b. ca. 1854, LA); Octavia Fontenette (b. 1854, LA); Anita Fovergne (freeborn 1861, LA); Orelia Alexie Franks (b. 1858, LA); Octavia George (b. 1852, LA); Gabriel Gilbert (b. unk., LA); Marie Aurelia Green (b. unk., LA); Joseph James (b. 1845, LA); Zeno John (b. ca. 1861, LA); Pauline Johnson and Felice Boudreux (sisters) (b. ca. 1853, 1859, LA); Eva Martin (b. ca. 1855, LA); Melinda (b. ca. 1854, LA); Ann Mickey (b. ca. 1847, TX); La San Mire (b. 1852, LA); Henri Necaise (b. 1832, MS); Virginia Newman (freeborn 1827, LA); Mary Nickerson (b. ca. 1840, LA); John Ogee (b. 1841, LA); Louis Joseph Piernas (b. 1856, MS); Peter Ryas (b. ca. 1860, LA); Mary Louise Scranton (b. 1859, LA); William Smith (b. 1845, LA); Thomas Steptoe (b. 1863, LA); Carlyle Stewart

(b. 1853, LA); Valmo Thomas (b. 1859, LA); Clorie Turner (b. unk., LA); Mrs. Webb (b. unk., LA); Adeline White (b. ca. 1858, LA); Sylvester Sostan Wickliffe (b. 1858, LA). Also of interest were the children of Creoles who did not so classify themselves. "De year I was one year ol' in April, us come to Liberty, Texas. I was a-layin' in mammy's arms. Her name' Lizette but dey call her Lis'beth. She mos'ly French" (John Price, b. ca. 1860, LA, 3162). Others include Frank Bell (b. ca. 1850, LA); Mary Harris (b. unk, LA); Leo Mouton (b. 1860, LA). Numerous other American ex-slaves had known Creole slaveholders, or had elsewise been in contact with French culture. See, for example, Louisia Braxton (b. 1864, LA); Mary Ann John (b. 1855, LA); Allen V. Manning (b. ca. 1850, MS); John Moore (b. 1853, LA); Albert Patterson (b. 1850, LA); Cora Poche (b. 1860, LA); Julia Woodrich (b. 1851, LA).

33. Mire's original French text is also included with his interview. French Catholic Louisiana's 1806 *Code noir* designated Sundays as the day for slave recreations, explaining why Louisiana Creoles like Mire usually recalled dancing on Sunday afternoons rather than Saturday nights like slaves in the Protestant South. Some of the ring dances he and other rural Creoles described may have fallen under the umbrella of *juré*, possession dances resembling the *shouting* of Protestant slaves. Like shouting, juré was primarily sacred but might also be performed recreationally. See Hiram Gregory, "Africa in the Delta," *Louisiana Studies* 1 (1962): 16–23; Doris White, "*Jouré My Lord*," *Louisiana Folklore Miscellany* 4 (1976–80): 143–45; Barry Jean Ancelet, booklet accompanying *The Louisiana Recordings: Cajun and Creole Music II: 1934/1937*, Rounder CDs 1843, 1999; Minton, "Houston Creoles and Zydeco," 360, 370. These ex-slave accounts are ambiguous, however, and the ring dances they mention might just as easily derive from French or other European ballroom traditions, possibly filtered through the West Indies. (Numerous New Orleans Creoles also described ring dances associated with hoodoo rituals.)

34. "La boulangère a des écus," André Claveau and Mathé Altéry, *Best-Loved French Folk Songs*, Monitor LP 61397, 1963.

35. Minton, "Houston Creoles and Zydeco."

36. Ann Allen Savoy, *Cajun Music: A Reflection of a People*, vol. 1 (Eunice, LA: Bluebird, 1984). Also, the narrative of ex-slave Felix Grundy Sadler purportedly describes a blind Cajun accordionist in South Louisiana in the postwar period. However, Sadler's narrative was produced by Texas interviewer Effie Cowan, a serial fraud and plagiarist; it is another obvious fabrication based on secondary sources.

37. This early rural strain is best documented in the recordings of Creole accordionist Amédé Ardoin (1898-1942), many featuring his regular musical partner, Cajun fiddler Dennis McGee (1893–1989). (Born in Evangeline Parish, Ardoin had both enslaved and free ancestors.) See Michael Doucet, Michael Tisserand,

Jared Snyder, booklet accompanying *Amédé Ardoin: The Roots of Zydeco*, Arhoolie/Folklyric CD 7007, 1995 (Ardoin's complete recordings).

38. For "Kitty Wells," see Brown III: 492–94; *Country Music Records*; *Country Music Sources*, 465.

39. Ex-slaves Fred Brown, Lewis Brown, Sylvia Floyd, and Rebecca Thomas named accordion and banjo together. Also see Bruce, "Tobacco-Plantation," 541.

40. Narrators Marie Brown and Martin Dragney also mentioned jawbones. Also see Cable, "Place Congo," 519; Creecy, *Scenes*, 20–21; Cable, "Mr. Harris," 65; Castelnau, "Florida," 243; Kinnard, "National Poets," 336; Jacobs, *Slave Girl*, 179–80; Parrish, *Sea Islands*, 15–16; Scarborough, *TNFS*, 102–3. For Jamaica, see Roberts, "Possible Survivals of African Song," 346. Also see Courlander, *NFM*, 207–8, 219; Evans, *Good Time Blues*, 5–6; Roberts, *Black Music*, 24. The jawbone was adopted by minstrels as well. Nathan, *Dan Emmett*, 149–51, 154. Like clacking bones, by the twentieth-century jawbones appeared mainly in white stringbands, especially in the Ozarks. See, for example, Randolph, *OFS* II: 333: "Several country dance tunes are still known as 'jawbone songs,' and I myself heard the jawbone played as part of a dance orchestra at Springfield, Mo., in 1934." RECORDINGS: Violet Hensley (fiddle), Sandra Flagg (guitar), Lewonna Nelson (jawbone), "Uncle Henry," "Rose Nell," "Sam Moore Waltz," "Wang, Wang Blues," "Mate to the Hog Waltz," "Jericho," field recs., AR, 1997, *Traditional Fiddle Music of the Ozarks, Volume One*, Rounder CD 0435, 1999.

41. A photograph of a Tidewater Virginia oyster roast around 1890 shows three Black musicians playing accordion, jawbone scraper, and clacking bones. Two years earlier another photograph had captured a Black ensemble of accordion, jawbone scraper, and triangle playing for another white outing. Lornell, *Virginia Secular Music*, cover, 2.

42. In March 1886 Eugene Smalley witnessed American Blacks jigging to accordion and triangle on the nearby Belair plantation. Smalley, "Sugar Making," 109.

43. Marie Lee Phelps, "Visit to Frenchtown," *Houston Post*, May 22, 1955, sect. 5, p. 2. A few years earlier Houston blues singer Lightnin' Hopkins (a relative by marriage of Clifton Chenier) had recorded "Zolo Go (Organ Blues)" (Gold Star 666, 1949), imitating a Creole accordion player on organ. Technically, this is the first documented use of a variant of *zydeco*. Like the English *dance* (or the African American *breakdown*, and so on), *zydeco* can refer to a musical dance genre; to the events at which this music is played; to a particular dance step; or to the accompanying tune. Phelps and Hopkins both used it for an event, probably the original form. See Minton, "Houston Creoles and Zydeco."

44. Ray Topping, booklet accompanying *Clifton Chenier: Zodico Blues and Boogie*, Specialty CD 7039, 1993; also Broven,

South to Louisiana, 109–13; Savoy, *Cajun Music*, 370–402; Tisserand, *Kingdom of Zydeco*, 90–147.

Frolics, Cornshuckings, and Other Occasions for Social Dance

1. Small Farmer, "Management of Negroes," 371.

2. Mississippi Planter, "Management of Negroes," 625.

3. Ex-slaves Bob Benford and Pauline Grice also remembered hog bladder Christmas crackers; Basil W. Duke (1838–1916) described them among slaves on his family's Kentucky plantation. Duke, *Reminiscences*, 230–31. Whether they celebrated or not, a high number of ex-slaves acknowledged Christmas (Lomax's guidelines for interviewers suggested asking), but only a relatively small portion of those describing Christmas observances recalled music and dance, fundamentalist religious objections probably being the main cause for their absence. For example: "Christmas wuz big time at Marse Hunts hous'. Preparations wuz made fo' it two weeks fo' day cum. Der wuz corn sings an' big dances, 'ceptin' at ligious homes" (Nan Stewart, b. 1850, WV, 89). Compare also note 4 below. WPA narrators who did describe music, song, and dance at Christmas were Geo. F. Abrams, Will Adams, Sam Anderson, Lizzie Atkins, Sara Benton, Jack Bess, Charlotte Beverly, Henry Bland, James Bolton, James Boyd, Gabe Butler, Louis Cain, Susan Castle, Harriet Chelsey, Mary Childs, Peter Clifton, Campbell Davis, Uncle D. Davis, Anderson Edwards, Molly Finley, Della Fountain, Julia Frazier, Austin Grant, Alice Green, Pauline Grice, Fannie Griffin, Shang Harris, Robert Heard, Robert Hinton, Fanny Smith Hodges, H. B. Holloway, Adeline Jackson, Easter Jackson, Ophelia Jemison, Edward Jones, Harriet Jones, Mary Ann Kitchens, Ruben Laird, Will Long, James Lucas, Caroline Malloy, Carrie Mason, Ann Mickey, Cureton Milling, Tom Mills, Andrew Moody, Mark Oliver, Horace Overstreet, Jefferson Davis Nunn, Alec Pope, William Pratt, Harre Quarls, Easter Reed, Shade Richards, Henry Rountree, Will Sheets, Adam Singleton, Charlie Tye Smith, Lou Smith, Isaac Stier, Jane Thompson, Rhodus Walton, Rev. James W. Washington, Rosa Washington, Steve Williams, George Womble, Henry Wright, Robert Young, and Teshan Young. For other ex-slave descriptions, see John Anderson (b. 1831, MO), Blassingame, *Testimony*, 353; William Wells Brown (1814–1884), *My Southern Home: Or, The South and Its People* (Boston: A. G. Brown, 1880), 95–97; Douglass, *My Bondage*, 251-53; Josiah Henson (1789–1883), *Truth Stranger Than Fiction*, 20–21; Northrup, *Twelve Years*, 213–22; Smith, *Fifty Years*, 37; Stroyer, *Life*, 44–46; James Thomas (1827–1913), *Tennessee Slave*, 59; Booker T. Washington (1856–1915), *Up From Slavery*, 132–35. Also see Baldwin, *Teacher*, 27–33; Bradley, "Memories," 341; Bradley, "Southern Negro," 66–67; Cameron, "Christmas,"

5; John Cabell Chenault, *Old Cane Springs: A Story of the War Between the States in Madison County, Kentucky*, ed. Jonathan Truman Dorris (Louisville: Standard Printing Co., 1936), 56–59; Holcombe, "Sketches," 624–26; Hundley, *Social Relations*, 359–62; Ingleton, "Pine Fork," 358; Johnson, *Social History*, 144–45; Kirke, *Southern Friends*, 186–96; Lanman, *Adventures*, II: 132, 275; Mitchell, *Dominion*, 165–67; "Old Master and Old Servant," 323; Paine, *Georgia Prison*, 185; Paulding, *Slavery*, 194, 209; Pennington, *Woman Planter*, 273–74; Ravitz, "Slaves' Christmas," 383–86; "Sketches of South Carolina: Number Three—Merry Christmas," *Knickerbocker* 21 (March 1843): 222–29; Stuart, "Apollo Belvedere," 155–58; Thorpe, "Christmas," 62; Thorpe, "Cotton," 459–61; Thorpe, "Sugar," 767; Venable, "Down South," 490; Victor, *Maum Guinea*, 15–19; Wilson, "Old Plantation," 248–49. Ex-slaves occasionally mentioned other seasonal observances. Many described feasting, leisure, and extra privileges at New Year, often as a continuation of the Christmas holiday; for some slaves, even more so for later Blacks, New Years Eve (Watch Night) was closely associated with spiritual singing and shouting (holy dancing). Ex-slaves from New Orleans (the focus of the Louisiana Writers Project) routinely mention Mardi Gras and the pre-Lenten carnival season. Easter Monday (the official end of Lent) was also an occasion for frolics in some communities. "We would sing and pray Easter Sunday and on Easter Monday we frolicked and danced all day long!" (James Bolton, b. 1852, GA, 100). Born a Maryland slave in 1848, L. J. Coppin also recalled fiddlers who "played the jingles for the buck dances at corn huskings, parties and the holiday gatherings, of which 'Easter Monday' was the principal." Coppin, *History*, 48. Narrators also frequently named the Fourth of July, typically celebrated with sports, fishing, barbecues, and other festivities, but they only occasionally described slave music, song, or dance, and most regarded this as a white holiday.

4. Actually, music and dance (and sometimes even singing and songs) were usually banned at weddings officiated by fundamentalist slaveholders and clergy, or, later, in fundamentalist Black communities, so that such entertainments do not figure in many ex-slave descriptions: "After the wedding, my Master gave us a big dinner there on the place and we had a time. We didn't dance, cause I never danced a foot in my life. My Mistress was religious and didn't 'low dancin' on the place" (Nancy King, b. 1844, TX, 2219–20). "Our white folkses wuz all church folkses and didn't 'low no dancin' at weddin's but dey give 'em big suppers when deir slaves got married" (Willis Cofer, b. 1860, GA, 207). "I married in Farguar [Fauquier] Co., state of Virginny, in de county seat. Dat was in 1883. I was married by a Methodist preacher in Leesburg. I did not get drunk, but hed plenty to drink. We hed singin' and music. My sister was a religious woman and would not allow dancin'" (George Jackson, b. 1858, VA, 48). Narrators who did describe dancing and dance music at weddings included Fannie

Berry, Betty Bormer, Alec Bostwick, Nellie Boyd, Fred Brown, Molly Brown, Pierce Cody, Martha Colquitt, Betty Curlett, Callie Elder, Jerry Eubanks, Eliza Evans, Eilzabeth Finley, George Fleming, Jim Gillard, Dosia Harris, Wash Hayes, Benjamin Henderson, Margaret Hughes, Lina Hunter, Sallie Johnson, Dellie Lewis, Will Long, Nellie Loyd, James Lucas, Virginia Newman, Jefferson Davis Nunn, Rosa L. Pollard, Ida Rigley, John Sneed, Yach Stringfellow, Neal Upson, John F. Van Hook, Stephen Varner, Mary Veals, and Allen Ward. On the other hand, a substantial number of ex-slaves recalled the antebellum marriage custom of jumping the broom: Cornelia Andrews, Campbell Armstrong, Agatha Babino, Joe Barnes, Alice Battle, Jasper Battle, Virginia Bell, Charlotte Beverly, Peter Blewitt, James Bolton, Ella Booth, Donaville Broussard, Fred Brown, Jeff Calhoun, Polly Turner Cancer, Aron Carter, Betty Foreman Chessier, Rena Clark, Willis Cofer, Willis Cozart, Betty Curlett, Carrie Davis, Jake Dawkins, James V. Deane, Isabella Duke, Tempie Herndon Durham, George Eason, Callie Elder, John Ellis, Cynthia Erwing, Millie Evans, Rachel Fairly, Minnie Folkes, Dora Franks, Lucy Galloway, Angie Garrett, Jim Gillard, Will Glass, Mildred Graves, Heard Griffin, Caroline Johnson Harris, Lizzie Hawkens, Ann Hawthorne, Eliza Hays, Benjamin Henderson, Emma Hurley, Patsy Hyde, Henry Johnson, Sallie Johnson, Susie Johnson, Charlie King, Solomon Lambert, Victoria Randle Lawson, Dellie Lewis, Bert Luster, Chaney Mack, Eva Martin, James Martin, Emily Mays, Stephen McCray, Amanda McDaniel, Henry Lewis McGaffey, Tom McGruder, Frank Menefee, Liza Mention, La San Mire, Fanny Nix, Jefferson Davis Nunn, Wade Owens, Tempe Pitts, Charlie Pye, Rena Raines, Mary Reynolds, Shade Richards, Dora Roberts, Amanda Ross, Aaron Russell, May Satterfield, Andrew Simms, Allen Sims, Paul Smith, Elizabeth Sparks, Wright Stapleton, Rachel Sullivan, George Taylor, Cordelia Thomas, John F. Van Hook, Stephen Varner, Lula Washington, Rosa Washington, Ophelia Whitley, Callie Williams, Adeline Willis, Robert Wilson, Julia Woodrich, George Womble, Alice Wright, and Hilliard Yellerday. Also see Alan Dundes, "'Jumping the Broom': On the Origin and Meaning of an African American Wedding Custom," *JAF* 109 (1996): 324–29.

5. Ex-slaves describing the Saturday half-day followed by a Saturday night frolic included Jim Allen, Georgia Baker, Harriet Barrett, James Bolton, James Brittian, John Cameron, Hattie Clayton, Alice Cole, John Cole, Andrew Columbus, Charlie Cooper, Campbell Davis, Uncle D. Davis, Tob Davis, Wallace Davis, Anderson Furr, Elisha Doc Garey, Ceceil George, Georgina Gibbs, Callie Gray, David Goodman Gullins, Rev. Thomas Harper, Tom Hawkins, Jefferson Franklin Henry, Uncle Robert Henry, Tom Holland, Carrie Hudson, Charlie Hudson, Easter Huff, Lizzie Hughes, Toby Jones, Anna Lee, Louise Mathews, Andy McAdams, Susan McIntosh, Ed McCree, Rosie McGillery, Matilda McKinney, Susie Melton, Harriet Miller (GA, SC), John Mosley, Lizzie Norfleet,

Mark Oliver, Anne Rice, Red Richardson, Mary Reynolds, Will Sheets, Polly Shine, Uncle Edd Shirley, Smith Simmons, Emma Simpson, John Sneed, Ellen Swindler, Lucy Thurston, Rhodus Walton, Callie Washington, Mingo White, Lou Williams, Charles Willis, and Emoline Wilson. Narrators describing Saturday night frolics without (or with no mention of) the half-day included William M. Adams, W. C. Parson Allen, Charles H. Anderson, Sally Ashton, Sara Benton, Manda Boggan, Joe Bouy, Wes Brady, Thomas Brown, Zek Brown, Marshal Butler, Dave L. Byrd, Louis Cain, Ellen Campbell, Simp Campbell, Eli Coleman, Martha Colquitt, Sara Colquitt, Andrew Columbus, Jane Cotton, John Crawford, Carrie Davis, Louis Davis, Minnie Davis, Elige Davison, George Dillard, Sally Dixon, Isabella Dorroh, Anderson Edwards, Smoky Eulenberg, Martha Everette, Sarah Felder, Rachel Gaines, Henry Gibbs, Andrew Jackson Gill, Jim Gillard, Martin Graham, Peggy Grigsby, Virginia Harris, Jack Harrison, Albert Hill, Everett Ingram, Wash Ingram, Squire Irvin, Nancy Jackson, Perry Sid Jemison, Prince Johnson, Emma Jones, Estella Jones, Charlie King, Mollie Kirkland, Anna Lee, Lu Lee, Walter Leggett, Gable Locklier, Richard Macks, John McAdams, Frank Menefee, La San Mire, Calvin Moye, Hattie Anne Nettles, General Jefferson Davis Nunn, Wade Owens, Ellen Payne, Lee Pierce, Elsie Reece, Shade Richards, Dora Roberts, George Rullerford, Charlie Sandles, Polly Shine, Martha Showvely, Emma Simpson, James W. Smith, Millie Ann Smith, Emeline Stepney, Bert Strong, Jake Terriell, Lucy Thomas, Neal Upson, John F. Van Hook, William Watkins, Eliza White, Robert Williams, Soul Williams, Frances Willingham, Sampson Willis, and Litt Young. This was another practice encouraged by how-to books on plantation slavery; see, for example, Johnson, *Social History*, 144–45.

6. Under Louisiana's 1806 *Code Noir*, Sunday was mandated as the day for slave recreation. Creole ex-slaves Agatha Babino (b. ca. 1850, LA), Donaville Broussard (b. 1850, LA), and La San Mire (b. 1852, LA) also remembered Sunday frolics.

7. Hog killing was a major annual chore on most plantations, sometimes with a dance party attached, sometimes not (though feasting and traditional foodways were constant factors). Besides Annie Huff, ex-slaves recalling hog killings included Mary Minus Biddie, Julia Blanks, Jerry Boykins, Ben Brown, Mom Sara Brown, Julia Bunch, Henry Cheatam, Tob Davis, Cynthia Erwing, Delia Garlic, Jim Gillard, Callie Gray, Bill Heard, Joseph Holmes, Carrie Hudson, Alice Hutcheson, Julia Larken, M. Lee, Govan Littlejohn, Lucy McCullough, A. J. Mitchell, Glascow Norwood, Anna Peek, Charlie Powers, Shade Richards, Henry Rountree, Abram Sells, Wright Stapleton, Annie Stephenson, Liza Strickland, Cull Taylor, George Taylor, Cordelia Thomas, William M. Thomas, Lucy Thurston, William Ward, Bacchus White, and Susannah Wyman. Compare Duke, *Reminiscences*, 229–30.

8. In the late 1800s, Rollins had served time in the Mississippi State Penitentiary on a trumped-up hog theft charge.

9. Davis's text is based on E. P. Christy, "Ring, Ring the Banjo," Christy, *Plantation Melodies*, 13–14.

10. Among such examples: "Dey uster hab a big time at chimly daubin's. Dey buil' a big chimly outn' sticks. Folks on d' groun' dey fix up d' mud 'n' mek a big mudcat fo' t' daub on d' chimly. Den dose on d' groun' t'row it up t' d' mens w'ats buil'in' d' chimly. Dey sing a kinder song 'bout it w'en dey wuk but I done fo'git d' words. Dat night dey hab a big dance 'n' plenty t' eat 'n' drink" (Jake Desso, b. 1863, TX, 1196). Compare James B. Cable, "Southern Silhouettes. XX. A Chimney Raising," *The Current* 2 (December 13, 1884): 374. "Ma said they had corn shuckings and corn shellings and brush burnings. Had music and square dancing plenty times" (Mag Johnson, b. ca. 1870, AR, child of ex-slaves, 108). (In 1860 William H. Holcombe observed Louisiana slaves singing while burning cotton stalks in the fields. "Sketches," 629.) "They talked 'bout corn shuckings, corn shellings, cotton traumpin's (packing cotton in wagon beds by walking on it over and over, she said—ed.), and dances" (Charlotte Willis, b. ca. 1875, MS, child of ex-slaves, 198, orig. parentheses). "We nuse to have frolics and breakdowns all de time—quiltin's and finger-pickin's and all dances and all sech as dat. Finger-pickin's was when we'd pick de cotton off de seeds by hand. We'd spread it down in front o' de fire place 'cause it was easier to pick when it was hot" (Shang Harris, b. ca. 1840, GA, 119–20).

11. Paine, *Georgia Prison*, 178. Other narrators recalling log rollings were Emma Blalock, Easter Brown, Fred Brown, James Caldwell, Solomon Caldwell, William Henry Davis, Nelson Dickerson, Hammett Dell, Isabella Dorroh, Cynthia Erwing, Lizzie Farmer, Lula Flannigan, Della Fountain, Anderson Furr, William Gant, Frank Gill, Martin Graham, Alice Green, Bill Heard, Susan High, Clayton Holbert, Carrie Hudson, Frank Hughes, Allen Johnson, Isaac Johnson, Bud Jones, Julia Larken, Frances Lewis, Henry Lewis, Milton Marshall, Albert Oxner, Elsie Payne, Henry Rogers, Janie Scott, Mary Jane Simmons, James Singleton, Wright Stapleton, Beauregard Tenneyson, Cordelia Thomas, George Thomas, Neal Upson, Henry Walker, Mollie Watson, Foster Weathersby, and Annie Young. For other ex-slave descriptions, see Amelia Armstrong (b. unk., MS), Cade, "Ex-Slaves," 333; Irving Lowery (1850–?), *Life*, 209–11. Also see Paine, *Georgia Prison*, 178–80. Usually log rolling meant clearing land, but ex-slave Cicero Finch (b. 1848, GA) recalled it as the prelude to a house-raising, concluding with a dinner dance. Blassingame, *Testimony*, 582.

12. Compare Paine, *Georgia Prison*, 178: "They take a handspike, about four or five feet long, to lift, carry, and roll the logs with." Henry Walker described these as "tong-hand sticks" (Henry Walker, b. ca. 1856, AR, 35). Lowery, *Life*, 210, also describes using "good, strong handsticks" to roll logs.

13. "To the one that can 'tote' the largest log, lift the heaviest butt, or roll the log the highest on the pile, is awarded the palm." Paine, *Georgia Prison*, 178.

14. For "(I'm) Working on the Building," see Arnold, *Alabama*, 162; McNeil, *Folksongs*, 106–8; Odum and Johnson, *NHS*, 72; Work, *ANSS*, 97. RECORDINGS: Blind Boys of Alabama, "Working On the Building" (Gospel 1061, 1959); Carter Family, "I'm Working On a Building" (Bluebird B5716, 1934); Heavenly Gospel Singers, "Working On the Building" (Bluebird B6636, 1936); Brother Joe May, "Working On the Building" (Specialty 841, 1952); Mitchell's Christian Singers, "Are You Working On the Building" (Banner 33196, 1934); Rev. Louis Overstreet and Congregation, "I'm Working On a Building," field rec., St. Luke Powerhouse Church of God in Christ, Phoenix, AZ, December 1962, *Rev. Louis Overstreet*, Arhoolie CD 442, 1995; The Soul Stirrers, "Working On the Building" (Aladdin 2020, 1947). DISCOGRAPHIES: *Blues and Gospel Records*; *Country Music Sources*, 593; *Gospel Discography*. For other log rolling songs, see Solomon, *Daisies*, 142. RECORDINGS: Uncle Billy McCrea (b. ca. 1823), "Log Rolling," field rec., Jasper, TX, 1940, *Black Texicans*. McCrea had been a song leader at East Texas log rollings, as well as a dance caller.

15. Narrators recalling cotton pickings included Geo. F. Abrams, Georgia Baker, Francis Bridges, Lewis Brown, Granny Cain, James Caldwell, Cicely Cawthon, Fleming Clark, Frances Cobb, Mary Colbert, Martha Colquitt, Betty Curlett, Minnie Davis, Anderson Edwards, Mary Edwards (SC), Callie Elder, Jerry Eubanks, Eugenia Fair, Lizzie Farmer, Caroline Farrow, George Fleming, Anderson Furr, Elisha Doc Garey, Frank Gill, Rev. Thomas Harper, Molly Hatfield, Tom Hawkins, Bill Heard, Ida Henry, Carrie Hudson, Charlie Hudson, Frank Hughes, Lina Hunter, Isaac Johnson, Mary Johnson (SC), Tom Johnson, Estella Jones, Henry Gray Klugh, Julia Larken, Gable Locklier, Milton Marshall, Thomas McMillan, Ed McCree, William McWhorter, Sam Rawls, Ellen Renwick, Anne Rice, Susie Riser, Joe Rollins, Lila Rutherford, Henry Ryan, Morgan Scurry, Beauregard Tenneyson, Mingo White, and Frances Willingham.

16. Mary W. Porter, "At the Sugar-House," *The Independent* 31 (September 11, 1879): 3. Also see H. L. F., A. A., "Louisiana," 758; King, *Great South*, 78-84; Russell, *Southern Life*, 96; Smalley, "Sugar Making," 109; Thorpe, "Sugar," 757-67.

17. The second item Mayfield quotes ("Who's been here. . .") was a well-known lyric. Susan Dale Sanders also described it as a dance song, Elisha Doc Garey as a children's singing play. Jeff Calhoun remembered it as a field song. Also see Bass, "Negro Songs," 424; Lomax, *Ballads*, 288; Solomon, *Daisies*, 216; Northrup, *Twelve Years*, 220; Ralph, "Dixie," 174; White, *ANFS*, 66–68, 454. Narrators Dan Bogie and Mary Wright also described maple sugar making.

18. Compare Ann Drake's account: "Sumtimes on Sunday, dat is when sum uf de slaves made 'lasses candy, an' den de way it was

pull an' made white, an' stuck all over yer" (Ann Drake, b. 1855, MS, 646–47). Other narrators recalling candy pullings were Sarah Allen, Cornelia Andrews, George W. Arnold, John C. Bectom, Mary Minus Biddie, Rose Brown, Queen Elizabeth Bunts, Josephine Tippit Compton, Willis Cozart, Hannah Crasson, Bill Crump, Uncle D. Davis, Jerry Davis, Minnie Davis, Cynthia Erwing, Martha Everette, Lula Flannigan, Andrew Goodman, Alice Green, Robert Heard, Mariah Hines, H. B. Holloway, Joseph Holmes, Fannie Hughes, Aaron Jones, Clara Jones, Liza Jones, Nancy King, Caroline Malloy, Henrietta McCullers, A. M. Moore, Parker Pool, Ophelia Porter, Easter Reed, Ferebe Rogers, George Rogers, Henry Rountree, Cora Shepherd, Marinda Jane Singleton, Sarah Ann Smith, Elmo Steele, Nelson Stewart, Neal Upson, Harriet Walker, Emma Watson, Robert Weathersby, and Anna Wright. For candy making, also see Sarah Fitzpatrick (b. 1847, AL), Blassingame, *Testimony*, 643–44, 652; Davis, "Plantation Party," 55; Bradley, "Southern Negro," 67.

19. Other narrators mentioning quiltings were Celestia Avery, Georgia Baker, Arrie Binns, Lizzie Fant Brown, James Caldwell, Mary Colbert, Josephine Tippit Compton, Hannah Crasson, Sara Crocker, Rachel Cruze, Martha Cunningham, Minnie Davis, Charlie Grant, Della Fountain, Anderson Furr, Callie Gray, Emily Camster Green, Rev. Thomas Harper, Shang Harris, Tom Hawkins, H. B. Holloway, Charlie Hudson, Annie Huff, Fannie Hughes, Alice Hutcheson, Allen Johnson, Henry Johnson, Tom Johnson, Aaron Jones, Estella Jones, Henry Gray Klugh, Dellie Lewis, Frances Lewis, Caroline Malloy, Ed McCree, Harriet Miller (GA,SC), Tom Mills, Mack Mullen, Hannah Murphy, Hattie Ann Nettles, Annie Parks, Dempsey Pitts, Charlie Pye, Walter Rimm, Susie Riser, Ferebe Rogers, Henry Rogers, Henry Rountree, Cora Shepherd, Mary Jane Simmons, Millie Simpkins, Adam Singleton, Marinda Jane Singleton, Georgia Smith, Gus Smith, Georgia Telfair, Laura Thornton, Harriet Walker, Eliza Washington, Rosa Washington, Columbus Williams, Frances Willingham, Pauline Worth, and Mary Wright. For other period references, see Burwell, *Girl's Life*, 3; Davis, "Plantation Party," 55; Stowe, *Old Town Folks*, 39.

20. Narrators recalling cornshuckings included Geo. F. Abrams, Rachel Adams, Jim Allen, Campbell Armstrong, Blount Baker, Georgia Baker, Jasper Battle, Alice Baugh, John C. Bectom, Sara Benton, William Black, Willie Blackwell, Emma Blalock, Peter Blewitt, Dan Bogie, George Bollinger, James Bolton, James Boyd, Francis Bridges, Josephine Bristow, James Brittian, Henry Brown, Lewis Brown, Rose Brown, George Washington Browning, Julia Bunch, Granny Cain, James Caldwell, Solomon Caldwell, Jeff Calhoun, Cato Carter, Cicely Cawthon, Henry Cheatam, Harriet Chelsey, Fleming Clark, Henry Clay, Frances Cobb, Willis Cofer, Mary Colbert, Mom Louisa Collier, Kizzie Colquitt, Martha Colquitt, Sara Colquitt, Willis Cozart, Hannah Crasson, Bill Crump, Rachel Cruze, Green Cumby, Martha Cunningham, Carrie

Davis, James (Jim) Davis, Louis Davis, Minnie Davis, William Henry Davis, James V. Deane, W. S. Debnam, Hammett Dell, Benny Dillard, Squire Dowd, Anderson Edwards, Mary Edwards (SC), Callie Elder, Jerry Eubanks, Eugenia Fair, Caroline Farrow, George Fleming, Della Fountain, Robert Franklin, Emma Fraser, Adele Frost, Anderson Furr, William Gant, Elisha Doc Garey, Angie Garrett, Frank Gill, Jim Gillard, Hector Godbold, Charles Graham, Martin Graham, Austin Grant, Charlie Grant, Alice Green, Henry Green, Wheeler Gresham, Madison Griffin, Peggy Grigsby, David Goodman Gullins, Rev. Thomas Harper, Dosia Harris, Virginia Harris, Mollie Hatfield, Tom Hawkins, Barbara Haywood, Bill Heard, George Henderson, Ida Henry, Jefferson Franklin Henry, Chaney Hews, Clayton Holbert, H. B. Holloway, Joseph Holmes, Carrie Hudson, Charlie Hudson, Annie Huff, Easter Huff, Frank Hughes, Anna Humphrey, Lina Hunter, Charley Hurt, Alice Hutcheson, Everett Ingram, Squire Irvin, Hannah Jameson, Ellis Jefson, Mahala Jewel, Georgia Johnson, Isaac Johnson, Mag Johnson, Mary Johnson (SC), Prince Johnson, Tom Johnson, Estella Jones, Liza Jones, Mandy Jones, Lucindy Lawrence Jurdon, Nicey Kinney, Henry Gray Klugh, Julia Larken, Anna Lee, Lu Lee, Walter Leggett, George Lewis, Gable Locklier, Jack Maddox, Andy Marion, Milton Marshall, Emily Mays, Henrietta McCullers, Jake McLeod, Thomas McMillan, Ed McCree, William McWhorter, Frank Menefee, Liza Mention, George Washington Miller, Harriet Miller (GA, SC), A. M. Moore, Vina Moore, Elsie Moreland, John Mosley, Claiborne Moss, Calvin Moye, Sally Murphy, Julius Nelson, Jefferson Davis Nunn, Amanda Oliver, Mark Oliver, Wade Owens, Albert Oxner, Annie Parks, Sallie Paul, Elsie Payne, Dempsey Pitts, Parker Pool, Alec Pope, Lafayette Price, Jenny Proctor, A. C. Pruitt, Jane Pyatt, Junius Quattlebaum, Fanny Randolph, Sam Rawls, Ellen Renwick, Anne Rice, Susie Riser, Cornelia Robinson, Ferebe Rogers, George Rogers, Henry Rogers, Joe Rollins, Henry Rountree, Martin Ruffin, George Rullerford, Joe Rutherford, Lila Rutherford, Henry Ryan, Morgan Scurry, Will Sheets, Robert Shepherd, Polly Shine, Smith Simmons, Allen Sims, Tom Singleton, Millie Ann Smith, Paul Smith, Ria Sorrell, John Spencer, Tanner Spikes, Annie Stephenson, Nelson Stewart, Sam T. Stewart, George Strickland, William Sykes, Georgia Telfair, Beauregard Tenneyson, Cordelia Thomas, Penny Thompson, Neal Upson, John F. Van Hook, Addie Vinson, Emma Virgel, Henry Walker, Callie Washington, Eliza Washington, Mollie Watson, Eliza White, Mingo White, Green Willbanks, Columbus Williams, Lou Williams, Wayman Williams, Frances Willingham, Charlotte Willis, Wash Wilson, Willis Winn, George Woods, Pauline Worth, Anna Wright, and Annie Young. For other ex-slave descriptions, see Anon. ex-slave (b. unk., TN), Anon. ex-slave (b. ca. 1845, TN), *Unwritten History*, 106–7, 255; Cicero Finch (b. 1848, GA), Blassingame, *Testimony*, 582–83; William Wells Brown (1814–1884), *Southern Home*, 91–95; L. J. Coppin (1848–?),

History, 48; Francis Fedric (1805–?), *Slave Life*, 47–51; Irving Lowery (1850–?), *Plantation*, 211–13; Harry Smith (1814–?), *Fifty Years*, 37–39, 62–63. For other period accounts, see Allen, "Uncle Tom," 863; Garnett Andrews, *Reminiscences of an Old Georgia Lawyer* (Atlanta: Franklin Steam Printing House, 1870), 10–12; Avirett, *Plantation*, 139–46; Baldwin, *School-Teacher*, 22–26; Barrow, "Corn-Shucking," 873–78; Bradley, "Southern Negro," 67; Bremer, *New World* I: 370; Bryant, "Old South," 31–34; Chenault, *Cane Springs*, 42–50; "Corn Shuckin' Down South," 4; Burwell, *Girl's Life*, 131–32; Davis, "Plantation Party," 55; Falconer, "Sports and Pastimes," 54; Gilmore, "The 'Poor Whites' of the South," 123; Hague, *Blockaded Family*, 125–26; M. Johnson, "The Georgia Negro Before, During, and Since the War," *American Catholic Quarterly Review* 6 (April 1881): 356; Lanman, *Adventures*, II: 276–79; Nathanson, "Negro Minstrelsy," 77; "Negro Folk Songs" (*SW*), 31; Paine, *Georgia Prison*, 180–85; Plebius, "Leaves From an Autobiography," 224; Powell, *History of Marion County, Georgia*, 33; Robinson, *Aunt Dice*, 30–39; Stowe, *Old Town Folks*, 39; David J. Winslow, "A Negro Corn-shucking," *JAF* 86 (1973): 61–62; Woods, "Corn-Shucking," 571; Wyeth, *Sabre*, 57–61. Also see Roger D. Abrahams, *Singing the Master: The Emergence of African-American Culture in the Plantation South* (New York: Penguin, 1992).

21. Avirett, *Plantation*, 140. William Wells Brown wrote "two hours is generally sufficient time to finish up a large shucking; where five hundred bushels of corn is thrown into the cribs as the shuck is taken off." Brown, *Southern Home*, 93. John Wyeth stated "it took usually about three hours for the many hands ['fifty to one hundred'] to strip all the corn raised on the place." Wyeth, *Sabre*, 58. Francis Fedric recalled a corn pile 180 yards (440 feet) long, with 300 to 400 workers. Fedric, *Slave Life*, 48–49. Lewis Paine reported "a farmer will haul up from his field a pile of corn from ten to twenty rods [165 to 230 feet] long, from ten to twenty feet wide, and ten feet high." Paine, *Georgia Prison*, 180.

22. Brown, *Southern Home*, 91. Compare Wyeth, *Sabre*, 57.

23. Andrews, *Georgia Lawyer*, 10–11.

24. Paine, *Georgia Prison*, 180.

25. Mrs. R. H. Marshall to grandchildren, Laurens, SC, 1852, qtd. Winslow, "A Negro Corn-shucking," 61 (orig. brackets, parentheses, and emphasis).

26. From Kentucky ex-slave Francis Fedric, *Slave Life*, 48–49. The shuckers' singing approach is regularly described elsewhere. Educator, journalist, and abolitionist Mary Ashton Rice Livermore (1820–1905) was a tutor on a Virginia plantation from 1839–1842, where she attended a shucking: "Long before we saw their dusky figures, we heard their melodious songs echoing and reechoing through the woods as they marched toward the Henderson plantation. They came in four companies from as many different directions, across lots, by cart-paths, and through the forest, all

entering upon our field of vision at one time, when they saluted and marched together. They carried torches which were waved aloft with joyous shouts as they met." Livermore, *Story*, 335–36. Also see Avirett, *Plantation*, 142; Baldwin, *School-Teacher*, 22; Brown, *Southern Home*, 92; Bryant, "Old South," 31; Chenault, *Cane Springs*, 44–46. There are also reports of shuckers departing in singing companies. Brown, *Southern Home*, 95; Livermore, *My Life*, 339–40.

27. "Corn Shuckin' Down South," 4.

28. Brown III: 233, 234, also 238–39; "Corn-Shucking Down South," 4; Harris, *Uncle Remus*, 159. Ex-slave Alice Hutcheson recalled bugles at wheat thrashings.

29. Barrow, "Corn-Shucking," 875. Adopted from European carnival culture, Black parodies of kings, queens, bishops, generals, captains, etc., were fixtures at Mardi Gras, Junkunue (John Canoe), Pinkster, Juneteenth, and other African American folk festivals. Such characters were thus pervasive, but the cornshucking general or captain may derive specifically from the harvest lord featured in British and Irish harvest home celebrations (see below).

30. Burwell, *Girl's Life*, 131.

31. Andrews, *Georgia Lawyer*, 11.

32. Throughout Africa and the West Indies, instrumentalists commonly accompanied labor. Courlander, *Drum and Hoe*, 116–20; Courlander, "Haiti," 372–77; Nketia, *Music of Africa*, 28–29; Roberts, *Black Music*, 8, 125–26, 133. This occurs more rarely in the United States but is known. See, for example, Glenn Hinson, booklet accompanying *Virginia Work Songs*.

33. Thomas Ravenscroft, *Pammelia Deutromelia Melismata*, ed. MacEdward Leach. AFS BSS, vol. 12 (1609, 1611; rpt. Philadelphia, 1961), 77. John Battle Avirett also recalled this verse from antebellum cornshuckings. *Old Plantation*, 144. For another ex-slave version, see Bass, "Negro Songs," 426 (Napier "Old Nap" Muldrow, b. unk., SC). For other texts and references, see Brown III: 233–34.

34. Caroline Farrow (b. ca. 1857, SC, 40) also gave "All Form a Row." For a similar cornshucking song, see Solomon, *Daisies*, 118. "Cotton-Eyed Joe" is a well-known fiddle song probably created by slaves.

35. "The Corn-songs are so named because they were used largely to expedite the labor at the great annual corn shuckings.... But the name Corn-song applies to all work songs, and, in its broadest meaning, to all secular music." "Negro Folk Songs" (*SW*), 31. For other cornshucking songs, see Andrews, *Georgia Lawyer*, 11; Baldwin, *School-Teacher*, 23–24; Barrow, "Corn-Shucking," 874–75; Brown III: 229–40; Brown, *Southern Home*, 92–94; Bryant, "Old South," 31–34; "Corn Shuckin' Down South," 4; S. C. Cromwell, "Corn-Shucking Song," *Harper's Monthly* 69 (October 1884): 807; Davis, *Folk-Songs*, 320–21; Fedric, *Slave Life*, 48–50; Hague, *Blockaded Family*, 125–26; Harris, *Remus*, 186–89; Nathanson, "Negro Minstrelsy," 77; Perrow, "South" (1915): 139; Robinson, *Aunt Dice*,

35–39; Solomon, *Daisies*, 118, 154; Woods, "Corn-Shucking," 571; Wyeth, *Sabre*, 58–61. RECORDINGS: Jimmie Strothers (b. ca. 1880) (vocal, banjo), "Corn-Shucking Time," field rec., Lynn, VA, 1936, *Virginia and the Piedmont*.

36. A folk rhyme topicalized to the 1844 presidential election, in which James K. Polk (1795–1849) defeated Henry Clay (1777–1852). Millie Simpkins gave another example: "I wuz 'yer [Nashville] w'en Henry Clay en James K. Polk wuz runnin'. I wuz hired at de ole City Hotel ovuh on de river. I wuz din'in room servant dere. Mah marster would hab me sing a song fer him 'bout de Democrats. 'Hooray de kuntry ez risin'; rise up en drown ole Clay en his pizen.' I guess ole Clay wuz a right good fellow but he played cards wid de niggers in de cellar" (Millie Simpkins, b. ca. 1820, TN, 69).

37. "'Round the Corn Pile Sally" was also recalled by Georgia Telfair and Wade Owens: "My daddy pick de banjo. At de cornshuckings dey'd sing All 'Roun' de Corn Pile Sally, an' dey had whiskey an' gin" (Wade Owens, b. 1863, AL, 307). Also see Hungerford, *Plantation*, 190–92; *Slave Songs*, 68; Whitney and Bullock, *Maryland*, 163.

38. This stanza's first two lines sometimes occur in "Little Liza Jane" (for example, Brown III: 340), or the related lyric "Pig In a Pen" (for example, Stanley Brothers, "Pig In a Pen," *John's Country Quartet*, Wango LP 104, 1964); the third and fourth lines appear in Cannon's Jug Stompers, "Riley's Wagon" (Victor V38515, 1928). (The Jug Stompers' record is otherwise a variant of a song also recorded by the white stringband the Georgia Crackers, "Riley the Furniture Man," OKeh 45111, 1927.) Hannah Jameson (b. ca. 1850, AR, 1936) recalled "Liza Jane" at cornshucking dances, Alice Hutcheson as a cornshucking song: "Shucks would jus' fly off of dat corn while dem Niggers was a-singin' 'Old Liza Jane' and 'Susan Jane'" (Alice Hutcheson, b. ca. 1860, GA, 284).

39. Barrow, "Corn Shucking," 874. On improvised corn songs, also see Andrews, *Georgia Lawyer*, 11; Avirett, *Plantation*, 144–45; Bremer, *New World* I: 370; Hungerford, *Plantation*, 191–92; Lanman, *Adventures* II: 277; "Negro Folk Songs" (*SW*), 31; Wyeth, *Sabre*, 57–58.

40. Andrews, *Georgia Lawyer*, 11. "The 'General' would continue to express the same solicitude for such of the corn-eating animals, as he might sympathize with, until satisfied."

41. Wyeth, *Sabre*, 58. Compare Andrews, *Georgia Lawyer*, 11; Avirett, *Plantation*, 144–45; Brown, *Southern Home*, 92–95; Nathanson, "Negro Minstrelsy," 77; Scarborough, *TNFS*, 207–8.

42. Hungerford, *Plantation*, 192.

43. Courlander, *Drum and Hoe*, 117–18.

44. M. Johnson, "Georgia Negro," 356. On the volume of noise at cornshuckings, also see Andrews, *Georgia Lawyer*, 10–11; Barrow, "Corn Shucking," 874; Winslow, "A Negro Corn-shucking," 61.

45. The red ear custom was also described by Jim Allen, Willie Blackwell, Bill Heard, Chaney Hews, Lina Hunter, Gable Locklier,

George Washington Miller, Julius Nelson, Paul Smith, Henry James Trentham, and John F. Van Hook.

46. James Madison Stone, *Personal Recollections of the Civil War by One Who Took Part in It as a Private Soldier in the 21st Volunteer Regiment of Infantry from Massachusetts* (Boston: author, 1918), 21.

47. Smith, *Fifty Years*, 62–63.

48. Price's refrain ("Oh, hood a laddy oh hooey") suggests a yodel, common in worksongs. Also describing the walkaround were Nicey Kinney, Paul Smith, and George Strickland. For period accounts, see Andrews, *Georgia Lawyer*, 12; Barrow, "Corn-Shucking," 876; Paine, *Georgia Prison*, 182; Plebius, "Leaves From an Autobiography," 224.

49. Barrow, "Corn-Shucking," 876, which quotes a special song—"Walk away, walk away!"—associated with the ritual.

50. Ex-slaves George Fleming, Emma Foster, Forest Hunter, Squire Irvin, and Chaney McNair also described recreational wrestling, especially among children. Also see Henry Baker (b. 1854, AL), Blassingame, *Testimony*, 657–58; Henry Bibb (1815–1854), *Narrative*, 23; Joseph Young, (b. unk., LA), Cade, "Ex-Slaves," 333.

51. "Mama's first husband was killed in a rasslin' (wrestling) match. It used to be that one man would walk up to another and say 'You ain't no good.' And the other one would say, 'All right, le's see.' And they would rassle" (Lula Jackson, b. 1859, AL, 12, orig. parentheses).

52. Douglass, *My Bondage*, 252.

53. Paine, *Georgia Prison*, 178–79.

54. Lowery, *Life*, 213.

55. Smith, *Fifty Years*, 62.

56. "Corn Shuckin' Down South," 4.

57. Barrow, "Corn Shucking," 876–77.

58. T. J. Desch Obi, *Fighting for Honor: The History of African Martial Art Traditions in the Atlantic World* (Columbia: University of South Carolina Press, 2008); 77–121; Sergio Lussana, "To See Who Was Best on the Plantation: Enslaved Fighting Contests and Masculinity in the Antebellum Plantation South," *Journal of Southern History* 76 (2010): 901–22.

59. Sigrid Paul, "The Wrestling Tradition and Its Social Functions," *Sport in Africa: Essays in Social History*, ed. William J. Baker and James A. Mangan (New York: Africana, 1987), 23–46.

60. R. F. G. Adams, trans., "Ibo Texts," *Africa* 7 (1934): 453–54.

61. Courlander, *Drum and Hoe*, 108.

62. Holloway, "Origins of African-American Culture," 12–16.

63. Abrahams, *Singing the Master*, 61–62; "The First Red Ear," *Maine Farmer*, October 16, 1884, 4; "A Husking Bee," *New York Times*, November 6, 1870, 3; George Lyman Kittredge, *The Old Farmer and His Almanack, Being Some Observations On Life and Manners In New England a Hundred Years Ago* (Boston: William Ware, 1904); 168–72; "An Old-Time Husking Bee," *Maine Farmer*,

February 1, 1884, 4; A Villager, "A Husking Bee: A Story of Former Days," *Boston Masonic Mirror*, October 27, 1832, 4; William S. Walsh "Corn-Shucking or Husking-Bee," *Curiosities of Popular Customs* (Philadelphia: J. B. Lippincott, 1897), 277.

64. John Brand, *Observations on Popular Antiquities: Including the Whole of Mr. Bourne's Antiquitates Vulgares* (London: J. Johnson, 1777), 305, 303, orig. emphasis. Henry Bourne's *Antiquitates Vulgares; Or, The Antiquities of the Common People* was originally published in 1725.

65. "Harvest Home," *Funk & Wagnalls Standard Dictionary of Folklore, Mythology, and Legend*, ed. Maria Leach and Jerome Fried (New York: Harper & Row, 1949).

66. Sir J. Frazer, "Harvest Rites in Ireland," *Folk-Lore* 25 (1914): 379, orig. parentheses. Also see Brand, *Observations*, 308–9; Alice B. Gomme, "A Berwickshire Kirn-Dolly," *Folk-Lore* 12 (1901): 215.

67. Alice B. Gomme, "Harvest Customs," *Folk-Lore* 13 (1902): 178.

68. Brand, *Observations*, 306–7; Gomme, "Harvest Customs," 178; Gomme, "Kirn-Dolly," 215–16; "Cailleac," "Harvest Doll," "Harvest Home," *Funk & Wagnalls Standard Dictionary of Folklore*. For an American example, see Walsh "Corn-Shucking or Husking-Bee," 277.

69. Kittredge, *Old Farmer*, 168.

70. Abrahams, *Singing the Master*, 54–63; "The First Red Ear," 4; "A Husking Bee," 3; "Husking Bees," *Maine Farmer*, November 25, 1858, 4; Kittredge, *Old Farmer*, 168–73; "An Old-Time Husking Bee," 4; Villager, "A Husking Bee: A Story of Former Days," 4; Walsh "Corn-Shucking or Husking-Bee," 277.

Musicianers

1. Finch, *Travels*, 237–38.

2. Creecy, *Scenes*, 21–22.

3. "Slavery in the US," 325.

4. Olmsted, *Back Country*, 146.

5. I write in the historical past tense to foreground precolonial traditions with possible connections to American slaves, but such performers are still highly influential in many African communities. Useful discussions include Bebey, *African Music*, 17–39; Charters, *Roots*, esp. 10–65; David C. Conrad and Barbara E. Frank, eds., *Status and Identity in West Africa: Nyamakalaw of Mande* (Bloomington: Indiana University Press, 1995); Mamadou Diawara, "Women, Servitude and History: The Oral Historical Traditions of Women of Servile Condition in the Kingdom of Jaara (Mali) from the Fifteenth to the Mid-Nineteenth Century," *Discourse and Its Disguises: The Interpretation of African Oral Texts*, ed. Karin Barber and P. F. de Moraes Farias. Birmingham University African Studies Series no. 1 (Birmingham, UK: Centre of West African Studies, 1989),

109–37; DjeDje, *Fiddling in West Africa*, esp. 18–22, 61–63, 68–73, 135–44, 182–84; David Evans, "Ethiopian *Azmari* and African-American Blues Singers: Comparisons and Contrasts," *The Second International Azmari Conference Proceedings:"Azmari: Change and Continuity"* (Bahir Dar, Ethiopia: Abbay Research Center for Culture and Development, 2016), 104–14; Thomas A. Hale, *Griots and Griottes: Masters of Words and Music* (Bloomington: Indiana University Press, 1998); Gerhard Kubik, *Africa*, 64; Nketia, *Music of Africa*, 43–46, 51–58; Oliver, *Savannah*, esp. 43–52.

6. Actually, like blacksmiths, potters, and leatherworkers, griots technically fell outside the division between nobles, free farmers, and slaves typifying traditional African societies, but historically many griots were enslaved or servile, and, slave or free, they were stigmatized and rejected in some quarters.

7. Jews sometimes filled this same role in Christian Europe and the Islamic world. Also see Peter Burke, *Popular Culture in Early Modern Europe* (1978; rpt. Brookfield, VT: Ashgate, 1999), 92–102; DjeDje, *Fiddling in West Africa*, 182–84.

8. "Early African Musicians in Europe," *BPM* 1 (1973): 166–68.

9. Rockingham Letters, West Hampshire Archives, West Yorkshire Archive Service, Leeds, qtd. Christopher Hibbert, *Redcoats and Rebels: The American Revolution Through British Eyes* (New York: Avon, 1990), 7. During the colonial period, American slaves were also supplied to British and European military bands. "Early African Musicians in Europe," 167.

10. Windley, *Vol. 3: South Carolina*, 620, 517, 726, 647. The first outsider to comment on the term *musicianer* was Howard W. Odum (1884–1954), based on his fieldwork in Mississippi and Georgia in the early 1900s. Howard W. Odum, "Folk-Song and Folk-Poetry As Found in the Secular Songs of the Southern Negroes," *JAF* 24 (1911): 258–61; also Evans, *Big Road Blues*, 35–37. Ex-slaves occasionally attribute the term to the antebellum era, however.

11. Samuel Mordecai, *Virginia, Especially Richmond, in By-Gone Days*, 2nd ed. (Richmond: West & Johnston, 1860), 251–52, 352–53; Epstein, *Sinful*, 115–16.

12. Ping, "Musical Activities," 149–51.

13. See, for example, Epstein, *Sinful*, 149–54; Southern, *Music*, 44–47; Cauthen, *Fiddle*, 7–12; T. DeWayne Moore, "The Segregation of Sound: Unheard African American Fiddlers," Bolick and Russell, *Fiddle Tunes*, 23–32.

14. Northrup, *Twelve Years*, 79, 216–19; Thomas, *Tennessee Slave*, 33; *Isaac Williams*, 62. Ex-slave memoirs describe other Black fiddlers. See Charles Ball (1781–?), *Slavery*, 282–83 (Peter, fiddle, SC, 1820s); John Brown (ca. 1818–?), *Slave Life*, 95–96 (Bob, fiddle, Freeman's New Orleans slave pen); Irving Lowery (1850–?), *Life*, 197–98 (Jerry Goodman, fiddle, Frierson plantation, antebellum SC); Northrup, *Twelve Years*, 79 (Bob, fiddle, Freeman's New Orleans slave pen); Thomas, *Tennessee Slave*, 44–45, 69 (Jordan

McGowan, fiddle, Nashville, mid-1800s); John Thompson (1812–1860), *The Life of John Thompson, A Fugitive Slave*, 1856; rpt. *From Bondage*, 47–48 (Martin, fiddle, antebellum MD).

15. For example, Hague, *Blockaded Family*, 126 (Uncle Ben, fiddle, antebellum AL); Hungerford, *Plantation*, 198–99 (Uncle Porringer, fiddle, MD, 1832); Ingraham, *Sunny South*, 104–10 (George, fiddle, banjo, VA, 1850s); Wyeth, *Sabre*, 61–64 (Uncle Billy, banjo, AL, 1850s).

16. Scott Joplin, Big Bill Broonzy, Mance Lipscomb, and Johnny and Baby Dodds were all the sons of slave fiddlers, DeFord Bailey the grandson, W. C. Handy the grandson and nephew, and so on.

17. The Basongye of Central Africa, for example, distinguish "five classes of male musicians: (1) the *ngoma*, the professional instrumentalist; (2) the performer of slit drums; (3) the player of rattles and double bells; (4) the song leader; and (5) the member of a singing group. They are listed here in order of their prestige; only the first is a fulltime musician, the second and third also receive some pay, and the lowest two classes are never paid." Overall, however, the Basongye denigrate musicians as heavy drinkers, debtors, unreliable, impotent, adulterers, and poor marriage risks. Nettl, *Folk Music*, 131.

18. The wandering "went to the river" verse appears around the Civil War, created or at least quickly adopted by minstrels; as late as the 1960s, Memphis singer-comedian Rufus Thomas (1917–2001) included it in one of his releases ("Jump Back," Stax 157, 1964). Also see Bass, "Negro Songs," 435; Botkin, *Play Party*, 285–87; Brown I: 190–91; Brown III: 227; Browne, *Alabama*, 450–51; "Carmina Africana," 10; "Games" (*SW*), 85; *Gumbo Ya-Ya*, 483–84; Handy, *Father*, 15; Hearn, *Levee*, 71; Jackson, *Dead Man*, 241; Jones and Hawes, *Step It Down*, 183; Lomax, *Ballads*, 231; Nathan, *Dan Emmett*, 465; Perrow, "South" (1913): 124; Randolph, *OFS II*: 330–31, 353–55; Randolph, *Roll Me*, 110–12; Scarborough, *TNFS*, 184–85; Solomon, *Daisies*, 164, 223; Thede, *Fiddle*, 64; Talley, *NFR*, 5, 57; White, *ANFS*, 194–95, 229, 452–53; Wolford, *Indiana*, 252–53. "Jawbone" too has minstrel connections, but may originally be a Black folksong. Anon. ex-slave, b. unk., TN, *Unwritten History*, 18; Bolick and Russell, *Fiddle Tunes*, 87; Botkin, *Play Party*, 180; Browne, *Alabama*, 311–13; Carlin, *Banjo*, 124–25; Cohen, *Ozark*, 222–23; Davis, *Folk-Songs*, 319; Nathan, *Emmett*, 464–66; Parrish, *Sea Islands*, 119; Randolph, *OFS II*: 333; Scarborough, *TNFS*, 103, 104; Talley, *NFR*, 9–10; Wyeth, *Sabre*, 60.

19. Parker, *Recollections*, 310.

20. Stroyer, *Life*, 45.

21. C. A. Bryce, "Fiddlers," 5, orig. parentheses.

22. Three narrators from adjacent southwestern Mississippi counties—Rina Brown (b. 1853, Franklin, Co.), Charity Jones (b. ca. 1853, Amite Co.), and Jim Martin (b. 1857, Copiah Co.)—mention a fiddler called "Old Joe." All of these interviews were

conducted by Mrs. Wm. F. Holmes, who tended to repeat material between different narratives, but it is possible that Old Joe was an otherwise unknown nineteenth-century South Mississippi fiddle star.

23. Bryce, "Fiddlers," 5. Bryce goes on to describe an entire family of slave fiddlers also named Scott (he was unsure of their relation to Joseph): "All played exceptionally well on the violin, and were known all over the State and were constantly traveling about filling important and profitable engagements. . . . They were frequent players at the White Sulphur Springs and other prominent resorts. They frequently traveled on the old packet boats between Richmond and Lynchburg."

24. Thomas, *Tennessee Slave*, 69, also 44–45, 45 n33.

25. Olmsted, *Seaboard* 2: 197.

26. C. A. Bryce, "Fiddlers," 5.

27. Malet, *Errand*, 49. For other fiddling coachmen, see Chambers-Ketchum, "Violin," 329–30; Stuart, "Apollo Belvedere," 155–58.

28. According to a 1784 ad, the fugitive slave "James (generally called Jemmy) . . . is as good a joiner as any in Virginia, at Coach, Phaeton, or Chair work, is a good house joiner, carver, wheelwright and painter, and is a tolerable negro fiddler." Windley, *Vol. 1: Virginia*, 359.

29. Many eighteenth-century runaways are identified as fiddlers and shoemakers. See, for example, Windley, *Vol. 1: Virginia*, 202, 314, 326–27, 349, 393.

30. Windley, *Vol. 1: Virginia*, 307; Windley, *Vol. 3: South Carolina*, 620. For other fiddling slave carpenters, see *Vol. 1: Virginia*, 17, 62, 66, 230–31, 259–60, 342–43.

31. Olmsted, *Seaboard* 2: 196–97.

32. C. A. Bryce, "Fiddlers," 5.

33. Alabama ex-slave Jake Green also told this story; Harriett Robinson recalled the song: "When we went to a party the nigger fiddlers would play a chune dat went lak dis: / I fooled Ole Mastah 7 years / Fooled the overseer three; / Hand me down my banjo / And I'll tickle your bel-lee" (Harriett Robinson, b. 1842, TX, 272). For other versions, see Bolick and Austin, *Mississippi Fiddle*, 140; Hurston, *Mules*, 92–93 (also featuring a banjo).

34. During this period, to fill quotas of convict workers, many Southern states enacted extreme penalties for livestock theft, especially of hogs, which by custom were turned loose during winter to forage, then rounded up in the spring. Finding animals of debatable ownership on the farms of poor Blacks or whites without powerful connections was a simple matter. In Joe Rollins's case the state only produced the suspect animal after his conviction. "Dat hog come up out of de woods atter I gone to de pen. . . . I didn't have nobody to keep me from goin to de pen" (Joe Rollins, b. 1845, MS, 1898). Also see Willie Blackwell (b. 1834, NC, 321) and Paul Smith (b. ca. 1863, GA, 335).

35. Ball, *Slavery*, 283.

36. Handy, *Father*, 5.

37. *Richmond Daily Enquirer*, June 27, 1853, qtd. Frederic Bancroft, *Slave Trading in the Old South* (Baltimore: J. H. Furst, 1931), 155–56.

38. Brothers, *Louis Armstrong*, 167, orig. emphasis. White artists often had similar contracts, of course. Elvis Presley (1935–1977) had the same fifty-fifty agreement with his manager, Colonel Tom Parker (1909–1997).

Old Pharaoh Exactly

1. The definitive study of Black night rider folklore remains Gladys-Marie Fry, *Night Riders in Black Folk History*, which draws extensively from the ex-slave narratives.

2. This line belongs to a verse well known in Black and white tradition: "My name is Sam, / I don't give a damn, / I'd rather be a nigger'n a po' white man." White, *ANFS*, 170. Also see Talley, *NFS*, 36–38; Thede, *Fiddle*, 62. RECORDINGS: Fiddlin' John Carson, "Hell Bound For Alabama" (OKeh 45159, 1927). The figure also serves as the hook of an 1890s "coon song" by Harry Earle, "I'd Rather Be a Nigger Than a Poor White Man" (New York: M. Witmark & Sons, 1894). It is unclear whether Earle coined or coopted the phrase; McIntosh's attribution to the antebellum period (or soon after) is at least plausible.

3. Compare Epstein, *Sinful*, 159; Fry, *Night Riders*, 96–100.

4. Hall's story incorporates Motif K534.1. *Escape by reversing horse's (ox's) shoes*, otherwise known from English sources.

5. Burke, *Popular Culture in Early Modern Europe*, 197–99.

6. In the water trick, the ghosts' unquenchable thirst might merely be laid to Hell's arid climate, or to other legendary events. Both North and South were completely unprepared for the Civil War's inconceivable carnage, and tales of battlefields covered with thousands of helpless, unattended wounded and dying men begging for water horrified the divided nation as a whole. Postwar night riders masquerading as thirsty Confederate ghosts usually referenced these stories. The Battle of Shiloh (Pittsburg Landing) (April 6–7, 1862), an early and especially infamous humanitarian disaster, was probably the most frequent allusion: "One time the Ku Klux come aroun. They knock on the doah, then they say 'Please give me a drink, Ah ain't had a drink since the battle o' Shilo.' What fo' they say that? Why, you see, they wants us tuh think they's the spirits a' the soldiers killed at Shilo an they been in hell so long they drinks all the water they can git. This one man made us carry him five buckets of water, an' it look like he drink em but nex mahnin theys a big mud puddle side thu doah" (Madison Frederick Ross, b. ca. 1848, MO, 300). Besides

Ross and William Brown, ex-slaves describing the water trick included Spencer Barnett, Henry Blake, Francis Bridges, Lizzie Fant Brown, Polly Turner Cancer, Betty Foreman Chessier, Maria Sutton Clemments, Adeline Crump, Hammett Dell, Lorenza Ezell, Fanny Finney, Callie Gray, Henry Green, Mack Henry, Richard Jackson, Lizzie Johnson, Aaron Jones, Ellis Ken Kannon, Annie Love, Sam McAllum, Waters McIntosh, Letha Taylor Meeks, Wylie Miller, Lee Pierce, Harriett Robinson, Joe Rollins, Mahalia Shores, George Simmons, Jane Thompson, Ellen Vaden, Ella Washington, John Wesley, Alex Woods, and John Young. Also see Fry, *Night Riders*, 88, 135, 138–39. Ann Ulrich Evans described a variation: "Some time dey come on in de house, tear up everything on de place, claim dey was looking for somebody, and tell us dey hungry 'cause dey ain't had nothin' to eat since de battle of Shiloh. Maybe twenty of 'em at a time make us cook up everything we got, and dey had false pockets made in dere shirt, and dey take up de skillet with de meat and hot grease piping hot and pour it every bit down de front of dem shirts inside dem false pockets and drop de hot bread right down dere, behind de meat and go on" (Ann Ulrich Evans, b. 1843, AL, 116).

7. Also see Fry, *Night Riders*, 69–73, 87–89, 122–35; John Minton, *"Big 'Fraid and Little 'Fraid": An Afro-American Folktale*, FFC 253 (Helsinki: Academia Scientiarum Fennica, 1993), 59–66.

8. Fry, *Night Riders*, 144, orig. emphasis; also 70, 125, 143–45.

9. Besides Kitty Hill, ex-slaves W. B. Allen, Eliza Evans, Gillie Hill, Mariah Hines, Dave Lowry, Phoebe Lyons, Wade Owens, and Alex Woods described turning the pot down to elude patrollers. Turning the pot down was associated mainly with religious observances, which in reality were often disrupted by patrollers, and Allen, Evans, Kitty Hill, Hines, and Woods all described pots at prayer meetings. Lowry and Owens placed pots at slave frolics, also standard night rider targets (and also commonplace for the pot motif). Gillie Hill's text, which mentions neither worship nor dance, is unusual in this and other respects.

10. Smith, *Fifty Years*, 19. Besides Berry Smith, narrators who described "stringing grapevines" or ropes for patrollers included W. C. Parson Allen, Lizzie Baker, Peter Brown, William Brown, Frank Cooper, James (Jim) Davis, Charles Green Dortch, Minnie Folkes, J. N. Gillespie, G. W. Hawkins, Aaron Jones, Mr. Beverly Jones, Mose King, Nancy King, Preston Kyles, Perry Lewis, Salem Powell, Sis Shackelford, Sam T. Stewart, James Henry Stith, John F. Van Hook, Allen Ward, and Henry Wright. Other narrators who told of slaves throwing hot coals on night riders included Samuel Simeon Andrews, Anna Baker, Alec Bostwick, Gus Bradshaw, Lizzie Fant Brown, Leonard Franklin, Henry Gibbs, Charlie Grant, Richard Jackson, James Morgan, Austin Pen Parnell, Isaac Potter, Walter Rimm, Bacchus White, and Willie Williams. Narrators who combined coals and grapevines were W. B. Allen, Campbell

Armstrong, Sylvia Floyd, Louise Pettis, and Anda Woods. In related anecdotes Berry Clay described how a man confounded vigilantes by pouring gourds of boiling water on them, while John F. Van Hook told how a slave escaped patrollers by overturning a pot of boiling lard, followed by the grapevine episode. Also see Fry, *Night Riders*, 100–102, 107–9.

11. In 1964 Gladys-Marie Fry collected another version of this cantefable from Minnie Bell Fountaine, daughter of Virginia slaves. In Fountaine's version the head patroller is also named Taylor. The warning song goes: "We're going to stomp the devil down, bright mansions above. . . . Mr. Taylor gonna beat you, bright mansions above." The slaves in Fountaine's text also escape by throwing coals on Taylor and his gang. Fry, *Night Riders*, 107.

12. Also see Bolick and Austin, *Mississippi Fiddle*, 140; Hurston, *Mules*, 92–93.

13. Wyeth, *Sabre*, 63–64. In the 1920s, Wyeth performed a slightly different version of Uncle Billy's cantefable for Dorothy Scarborough, *TNFS*, 23–24.

14. Charles White, *White's Serenaders Song-Book* (Philadelphia: T. B. Peterson and Bros., 1851), 66–67; Nathan, *Dan Emmett*, 216–19; Carl Wittke, *Tambo and Bones: A History of the American Minstrel Stage* (1930; rpt. New York: Greenwood, 1968), 175. Blackface performers Joel Sweeney and Bill Parrow are also described performing "Run, Nigger, Run," suggesting it may have been more widespread among minstrels. Carlin, *Banjo*, 52.

15. WPA narrators Lucius Cooper, Millie Evans, Perry Sid Jemison, Lewis Jenkins, J. W. King, and Lee Pierce also recalled children or adults singing or playing "Susie (Julie) Gal," for which see *Appalachian Fiddle*, 166; Brown III: 140; Scarborough, *TNFS*, 131–32; Talley, *NFR*, 66.

16. Compare Lomax, *Ballads*, 229: "Yaller gal look and trine keep you overtime, / De bell done rung, overseer hallowing loud— / Oh, run, nigger, run." Unauthorized conjugal visits are also the motivations for the cantefable versions from Alabama slave Uncle Billy and minstrel Charles White.

17. Smith, *Fifty Years*, 16. Ex-slaves Sarah Douglas, Peggy Grigsby, Rhodus Walton, and Ella Willis also described this method of torture.

18. In 1836 a Virginia planter wrote to James Kirke Paulding (1778–1860) "we have many laws respecting slaves, controlling them in certain particulars. . . . Some of the penalties for a violation of these laws are imposed upon the master, for permitting his slave to do certain acts; in other cases the slave is liable to be taken before a justice of the peace, and punished by stripes, never exceeding thirty-nine." Paulding, *Slavery*, 202. Also see Smith, *Fifty Years*, 18.

19. These two passages from Millie Williams (b. 1851, TX) were separated during the editorial process but obviously belong together. The first section appears in the national collection (S1 5

TX 4: 171); the song text was retained in the state archives (SS2 10 *TX* 9: 4114).

20. "Negro Folk Songs" (*SW*), 31, from a vocal quartet performance illustrating this paper at the 1894 meetings of the American Folk-Lore Society, Washington, DC.

21. Roberts, *Sang Branch*, 187–88.

22. A text similar to Hill's appears in the narrative of John C. Bectom (b. 1862, NC, 95), which was also produced by NC interviewer T. Pat Matthews. I suspect this is another case of an interviewer or editor repeating material that nonetheless seems authentic.

23. For example, "Oh, dat Nigger whirl'd, dat Nigger wheel'd, / Dat Nigger tore up de whole co'n field." Talley, *NFR*, 30.

24. Bradley, "Memories," 339. Also see Brown III: 340–41.

25. Fauset, "Folk Tales" (1927), 303, Vicksburg, MS, anon. informant, b. Monroe, LA. Also see Brown III: 509-10; Harris, *Friends*, 200-1; Scarborough, *TNFS*, 12, 24–25. Uncle Dave Macon, "Run, Nigger, Run" (Vocalion 15032, 1925), also belongs to this religious subtype; in a spoken introduction Macon (white) attributes the piece to southern Blacks. Also see Minton, *78 Blues*, 88.

26. Compare White, *ANFS*, 168. Two WPA narrators remembered "Run, Sinner, Run," Miemy Johnson (b. ca. 1855, SC, 61), and Jacob Branch: "Den dey was anudder song what say: / Run, sinner, run, / Run, sinner, run, / God is a-callin' you / Run, sinner, run / The fire will overtake you" (Jacob Branch, b. ca. 1851, TX, 411). Also see Johnson, *Spirituals* II: 110; White, *ANFS*, 82. RECORDINGS: Mance Lipscomb, "When Death Come Creeping in Your Room (Run, Sinner, Run)," *Trouble in Mind*, Reprise LP 2012, 1961; Lead Belly, "Run Sinners," Washington, DC, August 1940, *Let It Shine On*, Rounder CD 1046; Josh White, Golden Gate Quartet, "Run, Sinner, Run," Washington, DC, December 20, 1940, *Freedom*. DISCOGRAPHIES: *Blues and Gospel Records*.

27. Stroyer, *Life*, 45.

28. Handy, *Father*, 53. Compare Fletcher, *Story*, 57–58.

29. Brown, *Slave Life*, 95-6. Solomon Northrup had also spent time in Freeman's New Orleans slave pen, where he too was forced to dance to Bob's fiddle. Northrup, *Twelve Years*, 79–80.

30. Amid the carnival atmosphere of English and American public executions, condemned persons were expected to deliver penitential or cautionary speeches from the scaffold, but also to recite poems or sing ballads that were composed (or ghostwritten) for the occasion, and that might also be hawked to the crowd as broadsides. These testaments actually represented a distinct and quite numerous ballad subgenre known as the *last goodnight*.

31. Fry, *Night Riders*, 162–65.

32. C. A. Bryce, "Fiddlers," 5.

33. W. C. Handy's early professional experience included playing for Confederate veterans (above), while much of his later career was spent performing for racist white politicians like Memphis mayor E. H. "Boss" Crump, Jr. (1874–1954). Handy, *Father*, 98–105. During the 1930s the Alabama Klan reportedly even acted as the manager of Black harmonica player and recording artist Burl C. "Jaybird" Coleman (1896–1950). Russell, *Blacks, Whites, and Blues*, 23.

34. Compare Mamadou Diawara, "Women, Servitude and History," esp. 116.

35. Stephen Budiansky, *The Bloody Shirt: Terror After Appomattox* (New York: Viking, 2008).

36. Warner, "On Horseback," 542.

37. Richard Zuczek, "The Last Campaign of the Civil War: South Carolina and the Revolution of 1876," *Civil War History* 42 (1996): 18; also Budiansky, *Bloody Shirt*, esp. 245–51.

38. Narrator Henry Garry described this same ploy in Reconstruction-era Sumter Co., AL.

39. Similar incidents occurred throughout the state, for example, "in Barnwell, whites shot at the depot housing the ballot box, driving off voters and managers. Deputy marshal Lawrence Mimms ran to get soldiers, but by the time he returned the ballot box was gone." Zuczek, "Last Campaign," 28.

40. Ex-slave author Sam Aleckson (b. 1852) was another enthusiastic Hampton supporter. His memoir features an account of the 1876 election, including a description of Hampton addressing a packed house of Black supporters at the Charleston Academy of Music. Aleckson, *Before the War*, 282–83. WPA narrator Mariah Robinson seems to paint a similar picture of her late husband Pete, an in-demand dance fiddler and favorite of white politicos in Reconstruction-era Bosque Co., Texas.

Dealing with the Devil

1. Motif C12.5.3(b). *Girl swears she will get substitute fiddler at midnight Saturday night even if she has to go to hell for him. An old man appears, fiddles, keeps them dancing without stopping, as fast as they can dance, till dawn.* Also see Halpert, *Pinelands*, 386–87; Mary Williams, "Folklore and Placenames," *Folklore* 74 (1963): 367–68.

2. The most common hypothesis holds that African American legends of musical deals with the Devil somehow derived from African myths of *trickster-gods* exhibiting only the most coincidental resemblances or circumstantial connections. The most recent restatement of this argument is Adam Gussow, *Beyond the Crossroads: The Devil and the Blues Tradition* (Chapel Hill: University of North Carolina Press, 2017). For other critiques, see David Evans, "African Elements in the Blues," *L'Oceano del Suoni: Migrazioni, Musica e Razze nella Formazione delle Societá Euroatlantiche*, ed. Pierangelo Castagneto (Torino: Otto Editore, 2007), 3–16; David Evans, "Robert Johnson, Pact With the Devil," pts. 1–3, *Blues Revue*

21 (February–March 1996): 12–13, 22 (April–May 1996): 12–13, and 23 (June–July 1996): 12–13; Kubik, *Africa*, 21–25.

3. Despite the Islamic world's role in popularizing the fiddle, devout Muslims have traditionally regarded "melodies produced on the chordophone as the music of the devil," believing specifically that "fiddle music causes people to perform immoral acts against their will." DjeDje, *Fiddling in West Africa*, 123; also 261n11. The fiddle's incorporation into pre-Islamic cults only exacerbated Muslim disapproval. The most visible of these practices at present is the Bori religion observed by the Hausa of Northern Nigeria, whose central rites are possession dances always accompanied by goge fiddles. Doctrinaire Hausa Muslims shun Bori and fiddling, calling the goge the Devil's instrument. Ames, "Hausa Musical Activity," 140–42; DjeDje, *Fiddling in West Africa*, 103–68; DjeDje, *One String Fiddle*, 22–23; DjeDje, "Song Type and Performance Style in Hausa and Dagomba Possession (*Bori*) Music," *BPM* 12 (1984): 166–82; Leo Frobenius, *The Voice of Africa*, 2 vols. (London: Hutchinson, 1913), II: 538–72; Veit Erlmann, "Trance and Music in the Hausa *Bòorii* Spirit Possession Cult in Niger," *Ethnomusicology* 26 (1982): 49–58; P. G. Harris, "Notes on Yauri (Sokoto Province), Nigeria," *JRAI* 60 (1930): esp. 326–34; H. R. Palmer, " 'Bori' Among the Hausas," *Man* 14 (1914): 113–17. Fiddles serve similar spiritual functions in other African cultures. Compare Touré, "Ali Farka on Ali Farka," 261–62.

4. Richard Jobson, *The Golden Trade: Or, A Discovery of the River Gambra, and the Golden Trade of the Aethiopians* (London: Nicholas Okes, 1623), 105, 107–8. Actually, while Jobson likened the Juddies to English fiddlers of his acquaintance, their primary instrument as he described it was a plucked lute related to the banjo.

5. Jobson does report that he and his company refrained from playing the lutes and other instruments they carried, for "if they [Africans] had happened to see us, they would in a manner of scorne say, hee that played was a Juddy." *Golden Trade*, 108.

6. William J. Burcell, *Travels in the Interior of Southern Africa*. 2 vols. (London: Longman, Hurst, Rees, Orme, Brown, and Green, 1822, 1824), II: 287–88 (orig. emphasis). Christian Ethiopia provides an indigenous African example through the *begena*, a *box-lyre* used only for religious music, and the *krar*, a *bowl-lyre* used only for secular song, accordingly known as "the Devil's instrument." Ashenafi Kebede, "The Bowl-Lyre of Northeast Africa. *Krar*: The Devil's Instrument," *Ethnomusicology* 21 (1977): 379–93.

7. In Europe and the Americas, the Devil may be portrayed as an African slave, or as a Black man or black dog. Motifs G303.3.1.6. *The devil as a black man*; G303.3.3.1.1(a). *Devil in form of black dog*; G303.2.2. *Devil is called "the black one"*; G303.4.1.7.1. *Devil's face is black*; G303.3.1.12.3. *Devil appears as a beautiful black wench*. Also see Kubik, *Africa*, 23; Puckett, *Folk Beliefs*, 550–52; Woods, *Devil in Dog Form*. Compare Hundley, *Social Relations*, 349–50: "But there is

one thing which they [slaves] always dwell on with peculiar delight, and in which there may be a grain of truth—that after death they are to be changed into white folks. Their idea of hell is, that the Devil is a black man, with horns and a forked tail, a raw-head-and-bloody-bones old fellow." In another African American folktale the Devil creates Blacks in a botched imitation of God's crowning achievement, white people. Eston Everrett Ericson, "Folklore and Folkway in the Tarboro (N.C.) *Free Press* (1824–1850)," *SFQ* 5 (1941) 124; Mary Walker Finley Speers, "Maryland and Virginia Folk-Lore," *JAF* 25 (1912): 284.

8. See Robert W. Berger, "The Devil, the Violin, and Paganini: The Myth of the Violin as Satan's Instrument," *Religion and the Arts* 16 (2012): 312–27; Brown VII: 151–53; Herbert Halpert, "The Devil and the Fiddle," *HFB* 2 (1943): 39–43; Maiko Kawabata, "Virtuosity, the Violin, the Devil . . . What *Really* Made Paganini 'Demonic'?" *Current Musicology* No. 83 (Spring 2007): 85–108.

9. Motifs G303-G399. *The Devil*; Stith Thompson, *The Folktale* (1946; rpt. Berkeley: University of California Press, 1977), 42–45, 251–52.

10. Musicmaking and dancing by Satan and his minions were basic tenets of academic demonology, and transcripts of sixteenth- and seventeenth-century French and English witchcraft trials describe dancing to musical instruments—usually bagpipes or flutes, occasionally fiddles—as constants at Witches' Sabbats. Harvey B. Gaul, "Music and Devil-Worship," *Musical Quarterly* 11 (1925): 192–95.

11. These transitions are directly observable in some British examples. Stanton Drew's Devil-legend concerns a bagpiper, but the stone circle is also called "The Fiddler and the Maids," having attracted a similar tale told about several other British megaliths: Q223.6.4*(a). *Nineteen maidens were turned to stone for dancing on Sunday* (they are accompanied by a fiddler). Williams, "Folklore and Placenames," 367–68. Another early English-language text on this theme alternately identifies the demonic fiddler as both a fairy and the Devil. George Waldron, *A Description of the Isle of Man*, ed. William Harrison (1731; rpt. Douglas, Isle of Man: Manx Society, 1865), 29.

12. See Motifs 200–399. *Fairies and Elves*, esp. F243.21*. *Fairies give mortal power to make up songs*; F261.1.2.* *Fairies dance with mortals in ring*; F262. *Fairies make music*; F262.2. *Fairies teach bagpipe playing*; F302.3.4.2. *Fairies dance with youth till he dies (or goes insane)*; F312.1.1.2. *Changeling plays on pipe and thus betrays his maturity*; F341(a). *Man wishes for harp he can play; fairies provide it*; F377(c). *Person joins dance of fairies, is in fairyland for duration of dance. Dance seems to last a few minutes, actually lasts weeks, months, or years*; F379.5*(b). *Fairy music compels man to dance all night; his master sees him next morning still dancing, speaks pious words which release him*; and so on. Also see Halpert, *Pinelands*,

377–79, 381–83, 389–90. RECORDINGS: Davie Stewart, "The Story Lives Forever (A Story of Fairy Abduction)," field rec., Aberdeen, 1957, *Two Gentlemen of the Road: Jimmy MacBeath and Davie Stewart*, Rounder CD 1793-2, 2002 (Scottish Tinker version of Motif F377[c]).

13. Anon., FL, ca. 1939, Hyatt, *Hoodoo* 5: 4006–7, orig. brackets.

14. For Britain and Europe, see Motifs C12.5.3. *Girl fond of dancing uses devil's name*; C12.5.3(a). *Girl says she will go to dance even if she has to go with devil. The devil escorts her*; C12.5.3(b). *Girl swears she will get substitute fiddler at midnight Saturday night even if she has to go to hell for him*; C12.5.11*. *Man invites devil to a fiddling and dancing contest*; D1721.1. *Magic power from devil*; D1810.2. *Magic knowledge from devil*; D1786. *Magic power at crossroads*; F473.6.8. *Spirit plays man's fiddle at night*; G224.4. *Person sells soul to devil in exchange for witch powers*; G224.5. *Witch power received by altering religious ceremony*; G303.3.1.6. *The devil as a black man*; G303.3.3.1.1(a). *Devil in form of black dog*; G303.3.3.2.3. *Devil as hare*; G303.3.3.6.1. *The devil in the form of snake*; G303.4.1.2.2. *Devil with glowing eyes*; G303.4.2.1. *Devil as a ball of fire*; G303.4.4. *Devil has claws*; G303.4.8.14*. *Devil casts no shadow*; G303.4.8.15*. *Devil leaves no tracks in snow*; G303.4.5.0.1. *Devil has cloven foot (feet) or cloven hoof (hooves)*; G303.4.5.3.1. *Devil detected by his hoofs*; G303.4.5.8. *Devil has club foot*; G303.6.1.1. *Devil appears at midnight*; G303.6.1.2. *Devil appears when called upon*; G303.6.1.2(a). *Devil appears to person or persons who recite Lord's prayer backwards*; G303.6.1.2(h). *Person raises devil by use of magic circle*; G303.6.2.1. *Devil appears at dance*; G303.6.2.14. *Devil appears to Sabbath breakers*; G303.6.3.1. *Devil is followed by thunderstorm*; G303.7.1. *Devil rides a horse*; G303.10.4.1. *Devil dances with a maid until she dies*; G303.10.4.3. *Devil teaches a dance-loving maid to dance*; G303.10.4.4. *Devil appears to girl who wants an escort for a dance*; G303.25.23.1*. *The devil appears to fiddler*; G303.25.23.1.1*. *Devil engages fiddler in fiddling contest. The fiddler gets rid of devil at dawn by playing hymn*; G303.25.23.2*. *Composition learned when person hears devil play it*; K219.5 *Man cheats devil by giving him sole instead of soul*; K1227.3.1. *Girl refuses to dance with devil until well dressed*; M211.10*(b). *Girl sells soul to devil for skill in dancing*; M211.10*(ca). *Person sells soul for skill in fiddling*; Q223.6.4*. *Punishment for dancing on Sunday.* Q223.6.4*(a). *Nineteen maidens were turned to stone for dancing on Sunday*; Q386.1. *Devil punishes girl who loves to dance*; Q386.2*. *Girl who dances on Sunday is turned to stone.* These same and similar stories circulate elsewhere in Western Europe and among other North American immigrant groups and English-speaking New World Blacks. For representative examples, see Charles L. Edwards, *Bahama Songs and Stories*, MAFS, vol. 3 (Boston, 1895), 87–88; Elsie Clews Parsons, *Folk-Tales of Andros Island, Bahamas*, MAFS, vol. 13 (New York, 1918): 137–38; Stanley L. Robe, "Four Mexican Exempla About the Devil," *WF* 10 (1951): 313–14; Paul A. W. Wallace,

Baptiste Larocque: Legends of French Canada (Toronto: Musson, 1923), 75–78; Woods, *Devil in Dog Form*, 65–69; Barbara Woods, "The Norwegian Devil in North Dakota," *WF* 17 (1958): 196–98; Jerome P. Field, "Folk Tales from North Dakota, 1910," *WF* 17 (1958): 32–33. For a contrasting Eastern European tradition, see Stephen Reynolds, "The Baltic Psaltery and Musical Instruments of Gods and Devils," *Journal of Baltic Studies* 14 (1983): 5–23.

15. A. M. Bacon and E. C. Parsons, "Folk-Lore from Elizabeth City County, Virginia," *JAF* 35 (1922): 282.

16. Hyatt, *Hoodoo* 1: 111.

17. Johnson, *Supernaturals*, 106.

18. On crossroads in European, African, and African American folklore, see Puckett, *Beliefs*, 319–20. Bridges are also linked to the Devil in European tradition. See, for example, Motif G303.9.1.1. *Devil as builder of bridge.* In 1853, a New Jersey resident reported that "many years ago" his grandfather's slaves "firmly held that when the clock struck twelve at midnight, the devil and a select company of his inferiors regularly came upon that part of the bridge called 'the draw,' and danced a hornpipe there." The slaves refused to cross the bridge after ten o'clock. C. D. D., "New-Brunswick Folk Lore," 1853; rpt. *Choice Notes*, 58.

19. These include Motifs G224.5. *Witch power received by altering religious ceremony*; G224.5(b). *Witch power acquired by saying Lord's Prayer backward three times with hands and feet crossed*; G224.8. *Person gets witch power by walking twelve times around a church backward at midnight*; G257.2. *Reading Bible backwards causes witch to reveal herself*; G303.6.1.2(a). *Devil appears to person or persons who recite Lord's prayer backwards*; G303.6.1.2(b). *Devil appears to person who says Lord's prayer backwards while walking seven times around a cross*; G303.6.1.2(c). *Devil appears to person who says Lord's prayer backwards while walking seven times around hat placed on crossed sticks*; G303.6.1.2(d). *Devil appears to person who says Lord's prayer backwards while walking seven times around church.*

20. The cock and black cat are also staples of European witch-lore, whether as sacrifices or familiars. George Lyman Kittredge, *Witchcraft in Old and New England* (Cambridge: Harvard University Press, 1929), esp. 93–95, 97–98, 177–79. The *black cat bone* is now associated with conjure but is probably British as well (Motif G224.11.2. *Witch bone from cat*). "I have got a good-luck bone I carry with me all time. It is out of a black cat. You know how you get it? Well, just go to the forks of the road and build your fire. Put de pot on and put the black cat in dere and boil him good. When all de meat come off of de bones, the lucky bone will float. Den take dat with you for your luck. It will charm off evil too" (Verice Brown, b. ca. 1860, LA, 37). Also see Brown VII: 113–15, 151, 155–57; Puckett, *Beliefs*, 256–59.

21. Motif K219.5 *Man cheats devil by giving him sole instead of soul.* For an example without music or dance, see Louis Pendleton,

"Notes on Negro Folk-Lore and Witchcraft in the South," *JAF* 3 (1890): 203. Also see Motifs K210. *Devil cheated of his promised soul* to K219 *Other ways of cheating the Devil of his promised soul.* Alternately, potential victims can banish the Devil by singing or playing a religious song. Motif G303.25.23.1.1*. *Devil engages fiddler in fiddling contest. The fiddler gets rid of devil at dawn by playing hymn.* Halpert, *Pinelands*, 383.

22. Motif G303.21.2. *Devil's money becomes manure.* Hyatt, *Hoodoo* 1: 110; Parsons, "Guilford County," 180.

23. See Halpert, *Pinelands*, 394, for English and Irish versions (some featuring fairies and witches). This subtype is especially likely to combine with the other subtypes, since any of those three scenarios (for example, a crossroads pact) may account for the instrument's possession.

24. The majority of these white texts were collected by Herbert Halpert in the 1940s in the New Jersey Pinelands, an area that had experienced a heavy influx of Southern Blacks beginning before the Civil War. (In one example, the protagonist defeats the Devil by jigging with a glass of water on his head, an unmistakable mark of African American influence.) Halpert, *Pinelands*, 283–93.

25. "More Americans Believe in the Devil, Hell and Angels than in Darwin's Theory of Evolution: Nearly 25% of Americans Believe They Were Once another Person," December 10, 2008, http://www .harrisinteractive.com/vault/Harris-Interactive-Poll-Research -Religious-Beliefs-2008-12.pdf. Besides the Devil (59 percent) and Hell (62), 71 percent of respondents believed in angels; only 47 percent accepted Darwin. Twenty-four percent believed in reincarnation.

26. Motif E337.1.3(b). *Sounds of dance in haunted house.*

27. Linda Dégh and Andrew Vázsonyi, *The Dialectics of the Legend*, Folklore Preprint Series, Vol. 1, No. 6 (Bloomington: Folklore Institute 1973).

28. Botkin, *Play-Party*, 21; also Herbert Halpert, "The Devil, the Fiddle, and Dancing," *Fields of Folklore: Essays In Honor of Kenneth S. Goldstein*, ed. Roger D. Abrahams (Bloomington, IN: Trickster, 1995), 44–46.

29. "The Georgia Press," *Georgia Weekly Telegraph and Georgia Journal & Messenger* (Macon, May 7, 1878), issue 18.

30. Wolfe, *The Devil's Box*, xv–xvi.

31. Brown III: 638; also Thomas, *Ballad*, 181.

32. Charles Lyell, *A Second Visit to North America*, 3rd ed., 2 vols. (London: John Murray, 1855), I: 363.

33. Johnson, *Social History*, 151.

34. Halpert, "The Devil, the Fiddle, and Dancing," 50, 49.

35. Compare Mississippi Planter, "Management of Negroes," 625: "I have a good fiddler, and keep him well supplied with catgut, and I make it his duty to play for the negroes every Saturday night until 12 o'clock." Also see Hundley, *Social Relations*, 357; Wyeth, *Sabre*, 60–61. In Catholic Louisiana, the antebellum *Code Noir* reserved Sundays for slave recreations; see, for example, Agatha Babino (b. ca. 1850, LA); Donaville Broussard (b. 1850, LA); Louis Evans (b. 1853, LA); La San Mire (b. 1852, LA). Sunday dances are reported elsewhere: see Eliza Overton (b. 1849, MO); James Brown (b. 1853, TX); Teshan Young (b. ca. 1852, TX).

36. "If yo' wanta be a professional gambler, why yo' git chew a *deck of cards* an' go *in de cemetery* aftah hours in de night, jes' aftah twelve a'clock, an' go to de first man grave in de cemetery an' *straddle de grave.*" The Devil will appear, deal a hand, and bestow the proper credentials. Hyatt, *Hoodoo* 1: 105, orig. emphasis; also see 1: 105–6; 5: 4009–10, 4010.

37. Compare Mark P. Leone and Gladys-Marie Fry, "Conjuring in the Big House Kitchen: An Interpretation of African American Belief Systems Based on the Uses of Archeology and Folklore Sources," *JAF* 112 (1999): 372–403.

38. Some conjure doctors actually doubled as preachers and faith healers (Puckett, *Folk Beliefs*, 205), and conjures were often called upon to combat the Devil. By the same token, people who regarded themselves as true Christians regularly sought Satan's help in solving problems, satisfying desires, or settling scores. As a young man N. H. Hobley had "learned all the secrets of hoodooism" from Jim Alexander, an associate of New Orleans hoodoo queen Marie Laveau. Like Doc Choice, however, Hobley preferred to call himself a divine healer (not a conjurer or hoodoo), considering himself a servant of God and the sworn enemy of witches and sorcerers (N. H. Hobley, b. 1858, LA, 111–21).

39. Satan's identification with serpents in Black folk belief is another obvious token of Christianity's impact. Compare Andrew Boone: "Well de big show is coming to town. It's de Devil's wurk. Yes sir, it's de Devil's wurk. Why dem show folks ken make snakes an' make 'em crawl too. Dere wus one in Watson Field on de edge of Raleigh not too long ago an' he made snakes an' made 'em crawl too. All shows is de Devil's wurk" (Andrew Boone, b. 1857, NC, 131–32). Also see George W. Harmon: "In slavery an old man was said to be a conjurer, who had all kinds of snakes and insects. He took sick and died . . . an nobody could even go and get his body as these insects and snakes would come up and run them away" (George W. Harmon, b. 1854, TX, 142).

40. In 1832 J. P. Kennedy described a banjo-playing Virginia slave named Carey, "a minstrel of some repute . . . considered as a seer amongst the negroes on the estate." Kennedy, *Swallow Barn*, 101.

41. Ex-slaves Roy Redfield and Harriett Robinson also knew this folktale and song. Also see Bolick and Austin, *Mississippi Fiddle*, 140; Hurston, *Mules*, 92–93.

42. Around 1840 one South Carolina slaveholder boasted of eliminating fiddling and dancing on his plantation by promoting prayer meetings and psalm singing instead. Mallard, *Plantation Life*, 162–63.

43. "We never went to a party in our lives. Mother would not let any of her children go to parties. We were as genteelly brought up as white people. Our mother would not let us go with bad company" (Chase, *Dear Ones*, 36, quoting former slaves, Craney Island, VA, January 1863).

44. Smith, *Fifty Years*, 38. For similar accounts, see Bibb, *Narrative*, 22–23; Bremer, *Homes*, I: 369–70; Chase, *Dear Ones*, 24, 34–35; Higginson, "Leaves. II," 740–41; Hildreth, *The Slave: Or Memoirs of Archy Moore*, 136–40; Holcombe, "Sketches," 621; Lanman, *Adventures* II: 132; Malet, *Errand*, 49–50; Parker, *Recollections*, 310–11.

45. Small Farmer, "Management of Negroes," 372.

46. Puckett, *Folk Beliefs*, 553. American sacred and secular music were always closely interrelated, and ex-slaves and published nineteenth-century accounts do occasionally describe slaves playing fiddles and banjos at secret church services or informal prayer meetings. See, for example, Dix, *Transatlantic Tracings*, 286–92. These appear, however, to have been spontaneous, one-off affairs. Excepting pianos and organs, musical instruments were rare in Southern churches before the late nineteenth-century rise of Pentecostalism, and the ex-slave evidence appears mainly to support that scenario. Jim Davis dates his performances to the Civil War years, but he apparently picked the banjo for his own and others' enjoyment, never in church. (Whether he ever played sacred songs for dancing or merely for listening is also unclear.) Harre Quarls, on the other hand, clearly indicates that he played fiddle for Sunday schools only after freedom. By contrast Dennis Simms did state that at secret antebellum meetings slaves accompanied spirituals with jew's harps, fiddles, or banjos, but the one identifiable title he names, "Bringing in the Sheaves," was not published until 1874. Fittingly, "Bringing in the Sheaves" was composed by Knowles Shaw (1834–1878), possibly the nineteenth century's most famous fiddling white preacher. A locally renowned musician and bon vivant in his Indiana youth, Shaw experienced a classic dance-floor conversion, reforming into a relentless missionary, temperance crusader, composer, and publisher who usually opened and closed his services by fiddling, which he never renounced. William Baxter, *Life of Knowles Shaw, the Singing Evangelist* (Cincinnati: Central Book Concern, 1879), esp. 19, 139; Larry L. Stout, *Knowles Shaw, the Singing Evangelist* (Rushville: Indiana Christian University Press, 1984); Knowles Shaw, *Knowles Shaw's Memorial Songs* (1871–1878; rpt. Rushville, IN: E. E. Hungerford, 1939). Of course, Shaw's career also postdated the Civil War, when the use of "sinful" instruments in religious settings is most often reported.

47. See Hungerford, *Plantation*, 125–26, 198–99 (fiddling slave preacher, 1832 MD); also Bradley, "Memories," 337–38 (banjo playing slave preacher, postwar VA).

48. K. G. S., "Negroes' Spirituals," 333.

Shout

1. For nineteenth-century accounts of shouting, see Atwater, *Southern Tour*, 91–94; B., " Southern Cabins. Georgia.—II," 749; B., "Southern Cabins. III—Charleston," 766; Baldwin, *School-Teacher*, 69–73, 110–24; Bremer, *Homes*, I: 309, 311, 393–94; 2: 234–38; Abigail M. Holmes Christensen, "Spirituals and 'Shouts' of Southern Negroes," *JAF* 7 (1894): 154–55; Clinkscales, *Plantation*, 137–38; Charles Carleton Coffin, *Four Years of Fighting* (Boston: Ticknor and Fields, 1866), 230–31, 345–47; Chase, *Dear Ones*, 24, 35, 58, 124–25; "An Englishman in South Carolina: II," 114; Forten, "Sea Islands. Part I," 593–94, "Sea Islands. Part II," 672; Higginson, "Leaves. I," 527, "Leaves. II," 740; Kilham, "Sketches. Fourth," 307–8; King, *Great South*, 521–22, 618; Leigh, *Georgia Plantation*, 59–62, 253–54; Long, *Slavery*, 159–60, 226–27, 383–84; Olmsted, *Back Country*, 186–96; Olmsted, *Seaboard* 2: 80–81; Pearson, *Letters*, 26–30; *Slave Songs*, xii–xv; Spaulding, "Palmetto," 196–200; "Watch Meeting" (*SW*), 151–54. Also see Phillips Barry, "Negro Folk-Songs from Maine: The Shout," *Bulletin of the Folk-Song Society of the Northeast* no. 9 (1935): 10–14; Phillips Barry, "Negro Folk-Songs from Maine: Hymns and Ballets," *Bulletin of the Folk-Song Society of the Northeast* no. 10 (1935): 21–23; Guy Carawan and Candie Carawan, *Ain't You Got a Right to the Tree of Life?* Rev. ed. (Athens: University of Georgia Press, 1989), 64–94; Guy Carawan and Candie Carawan, "Singing and Shouting in Morning Star Hall," *BMRJ* 15 (1995): 17–28; Courlander, *NFM*, 194–200; Epstein, *Sinful*, 232–34, 278–87; Evans, *Saints and Sinners*; Arthur Huff Fauset, *Black Gods of the Metropolis: Negro Religious Cults of the Urban North* (Philadelphia: University Pennsylvania Press, 1944); Robert Winslow Gordon, "The Negro Spiritual," *The Carolina Low-Country* (New York: Macmillan, 1931), 191–222; Gordon, *Folk-Songs*, 27–33; Zora Neale Hurston, "Shouting," *The Sanctified Church* (Berkeley: Turtle Island, 1983), 91–94; Johnson, *Social History*, 147–51; Joyner, *Down By the Riverside*, 160–61; Krehbiel, *Folksongs*, 32–33; Lomax, *FSNA*, 462–63; Parrish, *Sea Islands*, 54–92; Puckett, *Folk Beliefs*, 543–44; Raboteau, *Religion*, 59–75; Art Rosenbaum, *Shout Because You're Free: The African American Ring Shout Tradition in Coastal Georgia* (Athens: University of Georgia Press, 1998); Johann S. Buis, "The Ring Shout: Revisiting the Islamic and African Issues of a Christian 'Holy Dance,'" Rosenbaum, *Shout*, 167–72; Robert Simpson, "The Shout and Shouting in Slave Religion of the United States," *Southern Quarterly* 23 (1985): 34–47; Smiley, "Folk-Lore," 378; Stearns, *Dance*, 29–31; Mary Arnold Twining, "'I'm Going to Sing and Shout While I Have the Chance': Music, Movement, and Dance on the Sea Islands," *BMRJ* 15 (1995): 1–15; White, *ANFS*, 37–40; Whitney and Bullock, *Maryland*, 162.

2. Gordon, *Folk-Songs*, 27.

3. Gordon, "Negro Spiritual," 200. Compare Barton, *Plantation Hymns*, 41; Carawan and Carawan, "Singing and Shouting," 17–28;

Fauset, *Black Gods*, 16–19, 27–28, 64–65, 68–75, 103–6, 111–19; Hurston, "Shouting," 91–94; Kennedy, *More Mellows*, 7–8, 12–13; Parrish, *Sea Islands*, 54; Robert Simpson, "Shout," 34–47; Twining, "Going to Sing," 1–15; White, *ANFS*, 39–40; "Watch Meeting" (*SW*), 151–54.

4. Carawan, "Singing and Shouting," 24–28; Rosenbaum, *Shout*, 53–84; Twining, "Shout," 11–12. RECORDINGS: *Georgia Sea Island Songs*, 1977; New World Records CD 80278; *The McIntosh County Shouters*, Ethnic Folkways LP 4344, 1984; Moving Star Hall Singers and Alan Lomax, *Sea Island Folk Festival*, Folkways LP 3841, 1965.

5. Lorenzo Dow Turner, *Africanisms in the Gullah Dialect* (Chicago: University of Chicago Press, 1949), 202. Compare Buis, "Ring Shout," esp. 169–70.

6. In addition to the verses quoted above, noteworthy examples include Isaiah 12:5–6; Zephaniah 3:1; 1 Chronicles 15:28; 2 Chronicles 15:14; Isaiah 44:23; Job 38:6–7; and Psalm 65:13.

7. Todd, *Methodism*, 181–82.

8. For this stanza, see Barton, *Plantation Hymns*, 26; Courlander, *NFM*, 46; Hallowell, *Calhoun*, 68; Johnson, *Spirituals* I: 65; Kennedy, *Mellows*, 47; Work, *ANSS*, 124. Maria Bracey also gave a text of "Little David," Alice Baugh named it. Also see *Cabin Songs* III: 139; Courlander, *NFM*, 46–49; *Country Music Sources*, 581; Jackson, *WNS*, 226–27; Johnson, *Spirituals* I: 65–67; Kennedy, *Cameos*, 121–23, 128–30; Kennedy, *Mellows*, 160–61; McIlhenny, *Spirituals*, 58–59, 172–73; Perrow, "South" (1913), 161; Seale, "Easter Rock," 215–16; Thomas, *Ballad Makin'*, 206–9; White, *ANFS*, 66–68; Work, *ANSS*, 124.

9. Don Yoder, *Pennsylvania Spirituals* (Lancaster: Pennsylvania Folklore Society, 1961), 54–55.

10. White, *ANFS*, 98. For "That Suits Me ('Round the Wall)," also see Arnold, *Alabama*, 117; Bales, "Negro Folk-Songs," 94–95; Hallowell, *Calhoun*, 63; Kennedy, *Cameos*, 154, 159–60; Kennedy, *Mellows*, 129–32; Odum and Johnson, *NHS*, 121–22; Parrish, *Sea Islands*, 137–38; Thomas, *Ballad Makin'*, 209. RECORDINGS: Bessie Jones, Hobart Smith, and Sea Island Singers, "It Just Suits Me," field rec., St. Simons Island, GA, April 1960, *Georgia Sea Islands: Biblical Songs and Spirituals*, Rounder CD 1712, 1998. For Black shouters expressly imitating the siege of Jericho, also see Rosenbaum, *Shout*, 39–40. For spirituals on the subject, see Barton, *Plantation Hymns*, 26; Hallowell, *Calhoun*, 49, 52–53; Johnson, *Spirituals* I: 65–67; Susan Fort Redfearn, "Songs from Georgia," *JAF* 34 (1921): 121–23; Taylor, *Revival Hymns*, 120–21. For the latter-day jubilee "Joshua Fought the Battle of Jericho," see "Carmina Africana," 10; Courlander, *NFM*, 45–46; Johnson, *Spirituals* I: 56–58; Taylor, *Revival Hymns*, 70–71.

11. Perrow, "South" (1913), 161 ("Little David").

12. *Cabin Songs* III: 139. For other "Little David" texts with this floater, see Kennedy, *Cameos*, 121–23, 128–30; Kennedy, *Mellows*, 160–61.

13. Brown III: 648 ("Little David"); also Courlander, *NFM*, 47, 72–73 ("Little David"). Compare Barton, *Plantation Hymns*, 45; Dett, *Hampton*, 39, 61.

14. For another period account, see Latrobe, *Journal*, 250–57. Also see Phillips Barry, "The Shout," 10–14; Barry, "Hymns and Ballets," 21–23; Bruce, *Hallelujah*, 61–95; Yoder, *Pennsylvania Spirituals*, 20–32; Rosenbaum, *Shout*, 21–23.

15. Ex-slaves Rachel Bradley, Ida Rigley, Susan Smith, and John Perrier also described whites shouting.

16. Some of the Gulf Coast Creoles interviewed for the ex-slave project may describe *juré*, a term for Creole shouting. None of them uses the word, however, and more likely they were recalling other ring dances common throughout Louisiana and the French Caribbean. On juré, see Pianos, Organs, and Accordions, note 33.

17. Carawan and Carawan, "Singing and Shouting," 21; Christensen, "Spirituals and 'Shouts,'" 155; Evans, "Negro Spirituals," 201; Evans, *Saints and Sinners*; Gordon, *Folk-Songs*, 30–32; Lomax, *Land*, 71–72; Parrish, *Sea Islands*, 54–57; Rosenbaum, *Shout*, 6–13; "Watch Meeting" (*SW*), 151–54.

18. Also see Gordon, "Negro Spirituals," 201–2; Kennedy, *Cameos*, 119–20, 127–28; Lomax, *Country*, 4–5; Lomax, *Land*, 71; McIlhenny, *Spirituals*, 37–38; *Old-Time String Band*, 126–27; Parrish, *Sea Islands*, 85–86; Rosenbaum, *Shout*, 144–46. RECORDINGS: Golden Gate Quartet, "Adam's in the Garden Pinning Leaves," *25 Years in Europe*, EMI Electrola LP 45714, 1979; Lawrence McKiver, "Eve and Adam," field rec., Eulonia, GA, December 1983, *The McIntosh County Shouters*, Ethnic Folkways LP 4344, 1984; Willis Proctor and Sea Island Singers, "Adam in the Garden," field rec., St. Simmons Island, GA, 1959, *Georgia Sea Islands: Biblical Songs and Spirituals*, Rounder CD 1712, 1998.

19. Lea and Marianna Seale, "Easter Rock: A Louisiana Negro Ceremony," *JAF* 55 (1942): 212–18; Harry Oster, "Easter Rock Revisited: A Study in Acculturation," *Louisiana Folklore Miscellany* 3 (1958): 21–43.

20. *Slave Songs*, 6–7; also Higginson, "Spirituals," 686; Marsh, *Jubilee Singers*, 127. Compare Aleck Trimble (b. 1861, TX, 114).

21. Dix, *Transatlantic Tracings*, 286–92. On recreational shouting, also see Courlander, *NFM*, 200; *Drums and Shadows*, 137; David Evans, *Saints and Sinners*; Gordon, *Folk-Songs*, 32–33; Leigh, *Georgia Plantation*, 59–62, 253–54; Rosenbaum, *Shout*, 24; Solomon, *Honey*, 43; Stearns, *Dance*, 31; Whitney and Bullock, *Maryland*, 162.

22. Narrator Cora Shepherd also gave a text of "Rock Daniel." Patsy Moses named it. Also see Evans, *Saints and Sinners*; Gordon, "Negro Spiritual"; Hallowell, *Calhoun*, 24; Jones and Hawes, *Step It Down*, 143–46; Lomax, *Land*, 72; Rosenbaum, *Shout*, 12, 121–24. RECORDINGS: Cora Fluker, field rec., "Move Daniel," Marion, MS, October 1980, *Living Country Blues: An Anthology*, Evidence

CD 26105, 1999; Lawrence McKiver, "Move, Daniel," field rec., St. Simons Island, GA, August 1983, *The McIntosh County Shouters*, Ethnic Folkways LP 4344, 1984; Willis Proctor and the Sea Island Singers, "Daniel," field rec., St. Simons Island, GA, 1960, *Georgia Sea Island Songs*, 1977; New World Records CD 80278; Reverend C. H. Savage and group, "Rock Daniel," field rec., Mt. Ararat Missionary Baptist Church, King and Anderson Plantation, Coahoma Co., MS, August 1941, *Saints and Sinners*; Roxie Threadgill, "Rock Daniel," field rec., Moorehead Plantation, Lula, MS, August 1942, *Rock Me, Shake Me*, Document CD 5672. DISCOGRAPHIES: *Blues and Gospel Records*. Believers usually "rocked Daniel" in pairs, especially on Watch Night, but in Florida "Rock Daniel" was performed as a ring shout following communion. F. M. Davenport, "The Religion of the American Negro," *Contemporary Review* 87 (1905): 373–74.

23. For another early Black text of "Rock Candy," see White, *ANFS*, 162. The piece was later collected from highland whites, albeit retaining the references to slavery and slave trading. *Appalachian Fiddle*, 43; Spurgeon, *Waltz the Hall*, 161-2; Titon, *Fiddle Tunes*, 95–96.

24. For drumming with shouts in the Sea Islands, see *Drums and Shadows*, 67, 71, 118, 122, 125, 137, 149–50, 155, 180, 184, 194.

25. Parrish, *Sea Islands*, 85; Rosenbaum, *Shout*, 36-7. This type of percussion was also used with social dancing. Bryant, "Old South," 33; Epstein, *Sinful*, 144, 158; Mallard, *Plantation Life*, 162.

26. In many shouts this *witnessing* or *testifying* also serves an essential rhythmic function. Courlander, *NFM*, 194–95; Christensen, "Spirituals and 'Shouts,'" 155; Hurston, "Shouting," 92–94.

27. New York *Nation*, May 30, 1867, qtd. in *Slave Songs*, xiv.

28. *Drums and Shadows*, 180; also see note 24 above.

29. Ex-slave Rachel Cruze also described shouting at funerals, for which also see Washington, "Funeral," 242.

30. New Orleans *hoodoo* derives in part from Haitian *voudon*, which in turn derives from the *vodun* religion of West Africa's Fǫn people. Trance dancing—sometimes in a counterclockwise ring, sometimes not—is central to all three. Narrators Marie Brown and Harrison Camille described New Orleans hoodoo dances, for which also see Tallant, *Voodoo* 6-8, 16–23, 44–46, 61–66, 75–87; 111–12, 139, 144–45, 175–76, 186; Cable, "Creole Slave Songs," 816–18; Hurston, "Hoodoo," 326–27; Métraux, *Voodoo*, 188–92; Puckett, *Folk Beliefs*, 177–90.

31. Guy Carawan, who worked in one Sea Island community for over three decades, stated: "all shouting is assumed to have been done in a ring. I never saw evidence of the ring on Johns Island, nor do those I have interviewed describe a circular pattern." Carawan, "Singing and Shouting," 27.

32. The belief that a mirror reflecting a corpse may afterward summon its ghost is originally European but well known to North American Blacks; numerous other ex-slaves mentioned the cautionary custom of covering mirrors after a death in the house

(Rena Clark, Aunt Clussey, Robert Heard). Also see Brown VII: 79–81; Montell, *Ghosts*, 67–68; Puckett, *Beliefs*, 81–82; Glenn Sisk, "Funeral Customs in the Alabama Black Belt, 1870–1910," *SFQ* 23 (1959): 169; Smiley, "Folk-Lore," 382; Whitney and Bullock, *Maryland*, 102. With funerals, wakes were common occasions for holy dancing throughout the Black world. "De niggers had a funeral when one died, and dey would sit up all night with de body singing, some would shout in a easy way" (Maggie Wright, b. ca. 1855, SC, 317). Other ex-slaves describing shouting at wakes included Arrie Binns, Marie Brown, Rena Clark, Lizzie Farmer, Manuel Johnson, Elsie Payne, Paul Smith, Sol Webb, and Luke Wilson. Also see *Drums and Shadows*, 67, 91, 106, 113, 118, 122, 125, 136, 143, 147, 160, 167, 194; Parrish, *Sea Islands*, 174–91; Puckett, *Folk Beliefs*, 86–87; Washington, "Funeral," 242.

33. "Fetish Follies," *American Missionary* 19 (January 1875): 17.

34. Thomas P. Henry, "The American Negroes: Their Peculiar Capacity for Mirth, Merriment and Melody," *Atchison Daily Globe*, November 27, 1889. Henry may have authored a similar piece published anonymously the previous year: "'Walking Egypt.' A Singular New Year Custom among the Negroes of the South," *Atchison Daily Globe*, December 31, 1888. This item credits its information to "a white lady who saw it from the gallery of a Georgia church."

35. G. R. S., *The Southern Negro As He Is* (Boston: George H. Ellis, 1877): 9. The earliest published references to "walking Egypt" are from the mid-1870s, the period recalled by Hamp Kennedy; all sources agree it was a postwar development.

36. Chase, *Dear Ones*, 124. Compare M. Waterbury, *Seven Years Among the Freedmen* (Chicago: T. B. Arnold, 1890), 43–45.

37. Lyell, *A Second Visit to North America*, I: 363–64. Compare Edward King's description of a Black meeting near Clarksville, Georgia, October 1873: "As the singers became excited, their bodies moved rhythmically, and clinging to each other's hands, they seemed about breaking into the passionate warmth of some barbaric ceremony." King, *Great South*, 521.

38. Lorenza Ezell and Frances Lewis also performed "Rough and Rocky Road," and George Govan named it. Also see Barton, *Plantation Hymns*, 6; Brown III: 668; *Cabin* III, 43; Jackson, *WNS*, 170–71; Perkins, "Spirituals," 247; White, *ANFS*, 112–13. DISCOGRAPHIES: *Blues and Gospel Records*; *Gospel Discography*.

39. In her memoir ex-slave Charlotte Brooks wrote "Sometimes when we met to hold our meetings we would put a big washtub full of water in the middle of the floor to catch the sound of our voices when we sung. When we all sung we would march around and shake each other's hands, and we would sing easy and low, so marster could not hear us" (Charlotte Brooks, b. unk., LA, *House of Bondage*, 12).

40. Coffin, *Four Years of Fighting*, 231. For other period accounts of the closing handshake in the Sea Islands, see Forten,

"Sea Islands. Part II," 672; Pearson, *Letters*, 26. In the 1940s Lydia Parrish discovered that older Sea Islanders still remembered the handshake, but that "the younger generation knew nothing of this custom." Parrish, *Sea Islands*, 129–30.

41. Tallant, *Voodoo*, 61; Portia Smiley, "The Foot-Wash in Alabama," *Southern Workman* 25 (1896): 101–2. Based on John 13:1–15, the foot-wash was mentioned by ex-slaves Cynthia Erwing, Henry Gibbs, Patsy Moses, Roxy Pitts, and Susan Rhodes. Also see J., "The Ceremony of 'Foot Wash' in Virginia," *Southern Workman* 25 (1896): 82; Puckett, *Beliefs*, 543–44; Wyeth, *Sabre*, 33.

42. Also see Kennedy, *Mellows*, 12–14. The full song relates the tale of John the Baptist's beheading through the connivances of King Herod's wife, Herodias. The verse Philles Thomas sang quotes from Mark 6:17–18: "For Herod himself had sent forth and laid hold upon John, and bound him in prison for Herodias' sake, his brother Philip's wife, for he had married her. For John said unto Herod, It is not lawful for thee to have thy brother's wife."

43. Rachel Cruze, Anna Humphrey, and Charlie Van Dyke also performed "I Want to Die A-Shouting (Traveling to the Grave)." Cruze and Van Dyke remembered it from funerals; Humphrey gave no context. Also see Barton, *Plantation Hymns*, 12; *Cabin* III: 95; Dett, *Hampton*, 187; Jackson, *Uplands*, 260–61; Jackson, *WNS*, 170–71; Killion and Waller, *Georgia*, 244–45; Marsh, *Jubilee Singers*, 146; Perkins, "Spirituals," 225; Rosenberg, *Virginia*, 52; *Social Harp*, 37; Solomon, *Daisies*, 234; Taylor, *Revival Hymns*, 245–46.

44. Coleman lists three other published hymns popular with slaves: "Amazing Grace" (John Newton, 1779), "Am I a Soldier of the Cross" (Isaac Watts, 1724), and "When I Can Read My Title Clear" (Isaac Watts, 1707). "Where He Leads Me" (Ernest W. Blandly, 1890) obviously postdates slavery.

45. RECORDINGS: Henry Joiner, "Conversion Experience," Reverend C. H. Savage and group, "Let Me Ride," field recs., Mt. Ararat Missionary Baptist Church, King and Anderson Plantation, Coahoma Co., MS, August 1941, *Saints and Sinners*.

46. Other ex-slaves describing camp meetings, revivals, protracted meetings, and the like were Blount Baker, John C. Bectom, Jack Bess, Richard Bruner, Charles Butlington, Solomon Caldwell, Julia Casey, Jack Cauthern, Henry Childers, Willis Cofer, Anthony Dawson, Tom Dixon, Rachel Duncan, Jerry Eubanks, Gus Feaster, Emma Fraser, Wade Glenn, Minnie Green, Alice Houston, Patsy Hyde, Rev. Silas Jackson, Henry D. Jenkins, Robert Kimbrough, Anna Lee, Edward Lycurgas, Ellen Payne, Lafayette Price, Naisy Reece, Ellen Rogers, Nancy Settles, Robert Shepherd, Nancy Smith, Nellie Smith, Isaac Stier, Eva Strayhorn, Cordelia Thomas, Nancy Whallen, Steve Williams, and Alex Woodson. For period accounts see Bremer, *Homes* I: 306–17; Clinkscales, *Plantation*, 12; Coppin, *History*, 49–54, 105–7; Dix, *Transatlantic Tracings*, 185–209, 280–302; Kearney, *Slaveholder's Daughter*, 57–61;

King, *Great South*, 583–87, 609; Long, *Slavery*, 157–60, 224–27, 244–45; Stuart, "Camp-Meeting," 97–102; Robinson, "Coloured People," 58–59; *Isaac Williams*, 65–66; Wyeth, *Sabre*, 33–36.

47. Other ex-slaves describing shouting at baptizings included Sara Benton, Minerva Bratcher, Louis Cain, Mary Carpenter, Julia Casey, Frances Cobb, Willis Cofer, Alice Cole, Harrison Cole, Thomas Cole, James Cornelius, Parilee Daniels, Carrie Davis, Jerry Eubanks, Sarah Felder, Pet Franks, Frank Gill, Mary Glover, Frankie Goole, Minnie Green, Jenny Greer, July Ann Halfen, Virginia Harris, Elizabeth Ross Hite, Lina Hunter, Patsy Hyde, Thomas Johns, St. Ann Johnson, Julia Larken, Easter Lockhart, Milton Marshall, Ann Matthews, Louis Napoleon, Wade Owens, Ellen Payne, Dora Richard, Hennie Ross, Robert Shepherd, Mary Smith, Nancy Smith, Georgia Telfair, Cordelia Thomas, Emma Virgel, Eugenia Weatherall, and Olin Williams. For nineteenth-century accounts, see G. R. S., *Southern Negro*, 9–10; H. H. B., "Reminiscences of a Southern Plantation," *The Independent* 26 (April 16, 1874): 13; Kearney, *Slaveholder's Daughter*, 61. RECORDINGS: Reverend W. A. Donaldson, "Baptizing Scene," field rec., Huntsville, AL, 1959, *Sounds of the South* 1.

48. In the 1850s Frederick Olmsted saw something very similar in a New Orleans church. Olmsted, *Back Country*, 191–92.

49. Kearney, *Slaveholder's Daughter*, 61.

50. *Unwritten History*, 49. In this vein, Lead Belly gives a vivid account of his mother's shouting in "Christmas (monologue)," Washington, DC, August 1940, *Go Down Old Hannah*, Rounder 1099, 1994.

51. Chase, *Dear Ones*, 124.

52. Virginia Clay-Clopton, *A Belle of the Fifties; Memoirs of Mrs. Clay of Alabama* (New York: Doubleday, Page, 1904), 219.

53. Eliza Frances Andrews, *The War-Time Journal of a Georgia Girl, 1864–1865* (New York: D. Appleton, 1908), 89; G. R. S., *Southern Negro*, 9.

54. Also see Parrish, *Sea Islands*, 55; Elsie Clews Parsons, *Folk-Lore of the Sea Islands, South Carolina*, MAFS 26 (New York, 1923): 206.

55. Atwater, *Southern Tour*, 91–94; Chase, *Dear Ones*, 58; "Fetish Follies," 17; Long, *Slavery*, 226–27, 383–84; Parrish, *Sea Islands*, 55; Daniel Alexander Payne, *Recollections of Seventy Years* (1886; rpt. New York: Arno, 1969), 93–94, 253–57; Southern, *Music*, 127–31.

56. Ex-slave Richard Carruthers told a similar story.

Turning the Pot Down

1. There are numerous versions of turning the pot down in the Fisk ex-slave materials: *Unwritten History*, 12, 24, 35, 44, 53, 98, 118, 148–49, 162, 173, 193, 255, 282, 300; *God Struck*, 147–48, 156. For other ex-slave examples, see Albert, *Charlotte Brooks*, 12; Cade,

"Ex-Slaves," 321, 329–31; Frances E. W. Harper, *Iola Leroy: or Shadows Uplifted* (1892; rpt. Boston: Beacon, 1987), 13; *Gumbo Ya-Ya*, 240; Robinson, *Log Cabin*, 79. Also Dance, *Shuckin'*, 184, 365; Evans, *Saints and Sinners*; Lomax, *FSNA*, 449; Lomax, *Land*, 74; Rawick, *Sundown*, 39–45; Southern, *Music*, 166; Scarborough, *TNFS*, 23; James K. Turner, "Slavery in Edgecombe County," *Historical Papers Published by the Trinity College Historical Society*, Series 12 (Durham, NC, 1916), 27. RECORDINGS: Reverend C. H. Savage, "Interview," field rec., Coahoma Co., MS, August 1941, *Saints and Sinners*.

2. Jesse Owens, *Blackthink: My Life as a Black Man and White Man* (New York: William Morrow, 1970), 40.

3. Bebey, *African Music*, 115.

4. Bebey, *African Music*, 68, 82; Evans, "Reinterpretation," 382; Evans, *Good Time Blues*, 5–6.

5. B. M. Blackwood and Henry Balfour, "Ritual and Secular Uses of Vibrating Membranes as Voice-Disguisers," *JRAI* 78 (1948): 52; compare P. G. Harris, "Notes on Drums and Musical Instruments Seen in Sokoto Province, Nigeria," *JRAI* 62 (1932): 115.

6. Ruth M. Stone, *Music in West Africa: Experiencing Music, Expressing Culture* (New York: Oxford University Press, 2005), 48–52.

7. Courlander, *Drum*, 201; orig. emphasis.

8. Blackwood and Balfour, "Voice-Disguisers," 46. Typical is the Dodo Society of the Kagoma (Northern Nigeria), devoted "to exercising greater control over their wives and children." This is partly accomplished with a large kazoo constructed from a gourd with "some kind of parchment over its mouth. In the middle of the night this was blown . . . with a terrifying effect (the noise is very like that produced by a comb and piece of paper). The women were very frightened and hid themselves. They were subsequently told this was the voice of the 'Dodo'—a mythical spirit well known in Hausaland—rebuking them for their misdeeds." Blackwood and Balfour, "Voice-Disguisers," 51; also 47, 49, 50, 51, 55, 56.

9. Scarborough, *TNFS*, 23.

10. The most stringent legal restrictions on slave worship were enacted in the early 1800s in response to several slave revolts in which slave preachers and secret religious meetings played major roles. Epstein, *Sinful*, 192–97, 229–32; Raboteau, *Religion*, 163–64; Southern, *Music*, 165–67.

11. *NASS* 25 (October 25, 1864), 1, qtd. Epstein, *Sinful*, 232, orig. ellipsis. Compare Atwater, *Southern Tour*, 91.

12. Siney Bonner (b. ca. 1850, AL, 40) and Clara C. Young (b. ca. 1842, AL, 2402–3) also described turning the pot down in brush arbors.

13. Kalvin Woods (b. ca. 1835, LA), Cade, "Ex-Slaves," 330–31.

14. Williams, *Narrative*, 72. Compare Rev. W. B. Allen (b. ca. 1850, AL, 9–10, 17); Della Mun Bibles (b. unk., TX, 295); Jesse Davis (b. ca. 1850, SC, 266).

15. For early jug bands, see Day Allen Willey, "Barbecues, and How They Are Conducted," *Wide World Magazine* 9 (April–September 1902): 190; "A Florida 'Jug Band,'" *Wide World Magazine* 14 (October 1904–March 1905): 414. Also see Bastin, *Red River*, 34–35; Evans, *Good Time Blues*; Evans, "Reinterpretation," 302-3; Bengt Olsson, *Memphis Blues and Jug Bands* (London: Studio Vista, 1970). Blowing-jugs occur in other African American communities. In Cuba the *botija* (an earthenware jug also used as a bass) was originally part of *son* ensembles. Harold Courlander, "Cuba," 240; Eduardo Llerenas, booklet accompanying *Septetos Cubanos: sones de Cuba*, Música Tradicional CDs 113–114, 1990; Roberts, *Black Music*, 49–50, 96–97. Ex-slave Bob Maynard also described jugs, possibly blown but possibly used as struck bells: "The only musical instruments we had was a jug or big bottle, a skillet lid or frying pan that they'd hit with a stick or a bone. We had a flute too, made out of reed cane and it'd make good music" (Bob Maynard, b. ca. 1858, TX, 224).

16. Evans, *Tate and Panola*, 4.

17. By a lucky strike a jug player–jester was filmed by a Fox-Movietone newsreel crew at Louisville, KY, May 25, 1930. Whistler's Jug Band was the first commercially recorded jug band (*Clifford Hayes and the Louisville Jug Bands, vol. 1 (1924–1926)*, RST CD 1501, 1994; *vol. 2 (1926–1927)*, RST CD 1502, 1994). Their filmed performance of "Foldin' Bed (Bed Slats and All)" (*Times Ain't Like They Used to Be*, Yazoo DVD 512, 2000) features three jug blowers, one of whom (possibly Rudolph Thompson) sits in the foreground, juggling his stovepipe hat and jug, jigging with his feet, and patting juba. Jug bands were featured on several pre–WWII religious recordings made in Memphis by Pentecostal sects that welcomed secular instruments shunned by other denominations. *Memphis Sanctified Jug Bands (1928–1930)*, Document CD 5300, 1994. Perhaps these extended, revived, or reinvented the African tradition of spirit voices from mouth-blown vessels, but on the whole jugs figured in decidedly secular contexts.

18. Blackwood and Balfour, "Voice-Disguisers," 45–69.

19. Richard Graham, "From African Spirit Catcher to American Folk Art Emblem: The Trans-Atlantic Odyssey of the Bottle Tree," *Corners of Texas*, ed. Francis Edward Abernethy, PTFS 52 (Denton: University of North Texas Press, 1993), 130–38; John Minton and David Evans, *"The Coon in the Box": A Global Folktale in African-American Tradition*, FFC 277 (Helsinki: Academia Scientiarium Fennica, 2001), 95–97; Thompson, *Flash*, 142–45; Robert Farris Thompson, "Kongo Influences on African-American Artistic Culture," *Africanisms in American Culture*, 164–67.

20. Bebey, *African Music*, 64.

21. On the earth bow, mosquito drum, and washtub bass, see Bebey, *African Music*, 63–64; Courlander, *Drum and Hoe*, 199–201; Courlander, "Musical Instruments of Haiti," 377–79; Courlander,

NFM, 206–7; Evans, "Reinterpretation," 384–85; Kubik, *Africa*, 167–71; Nketia, *Music of Africa*, 98–99.

22. Also see Lizzie Fant Brown (big ditch); Carey Davenport (dugouts, hollows); Silvia King (crick bottom in a thic'et); John Price (hollow); Foster Weathersby (wooded hollows). Sometimes worshippers simply huddled on the floor or ground. "Some nigger take turn 'bout with 'nuther nigger to watch to see if Marse Tom anyways 'bout and then they circle themselves 'bout on the floor in the cabins and pray. Then they get to moanin' low and gentle, 'some day, some day—this yoke is going to be lifted off 'n our shoulders—some day, some day, some day' " (William Moore, b. 1855, TX, 2766). "They always prayed in a prostrate position with the face close to the ground so that no sound could escape to warn the master or the overseer" (Patsy Larkin, b. unk., AL, Cade, "Ex-Slaves," 330).

23. Orris Harris (b. ca. 1858, MS, 932) gave another variant of the first stanza. The second verse is alternately phrased, "Went down the hill the other day / Soul got happy and I stayed all day." Vera Hall, "Trouble So Hard," field rec., Livingstone, AL, 1959, *Sounds of the South* 1. Also Bales, "Negro Folk-Songs," 94; Brown III: 609; Henry, *Highlands*, 420; Kennedy, *Mellows*, 161; Killion and Waller, *Georgia*, 253; Lomax, *Lead Belly*, 209; Odum and Johnson, *NHS*, 63, 280; Perkins, "Spirituals," 234; Perrow, "South" (1913): 161; Twining, "Going to Sing," 13; Wheeler, *Steamboatin'*, 78; White, *ANFS*, 71–72, 132; Work, *ANSS*, 208.

24. Other ex-slaves who reported putting pots in or near doorways were Laura Abromsom, Diana Alexander, Mariah Barnes, Emma Blalock, Henry Bobbitt, Lucy Brown, Harriet Cheatam, Minnie Folkes, Georgianna Foster, Henry Green, Betty Guwn, Essex Henry, Dave Lowry, Austin Pen Parnell, Nelson Polk, Mary Scott, Sylvia Watkins, Mingo White, Soldier Williams, and Alex Woods. Also see *Unwritten History*, 35, 44, 98, 300. For conjure tricks in doorways, see Charles W. Chesnutt, "Folklore and Superstitions of the South," *Modern Culture* 13/3 (1901): 231–35; Leonora Herron and Alice M. Bacon, "Conjuring and Conjure-Doctors," *Southern Workman* 24 (1895): 364; Hyatt, *Hoodoo*; Hurston, *Mules*, 237–39; Puckett, *Folk Beliefs*, 167–310.

25. Others narrators describing slaves putting their heads into pots included Sallie Carder, Cato Carter, John Crawford, Rachel Fairly, Louisa Gause, Will Glass, Charles Grandy, Gillie Hill, Julia Malone, Dolly Phillips, Edd Roby, Lula Cottonham Walker, Ella Washington, Andy Williams, and George Young. Also see *God Struck*, 156. Eliza Evans, Emma Tidwell, and James Southall described otherwise directing their voices into the pots: "De way we prayed we'd go out an put our mouths to der groun an pray low an de sound wud go up under de pot an ole boss couldn' hear us" (Emma Tidwell, b. ca. 1839, AR, 332). Other narrators described propping pots, possibly to produce this effect. "De niggers slip off an' pray and hold prayer-meetin' in de woods den dey tu'n down a

big wash pot and prop it up wif a stick to drown out de soun' ob de singin' " (Fannie Moore, b. 1849, SC, 133). Also see Mariah Barnes, John Hunter, Rev. John Moore, and Austin Pen Parnell; *Unwritten History*, 35, 98, 148–49.

26. Anon. ex-slave (b. unk., TX), *Unwritten History*, 24, also 193; Mary Scott, Lorena Thomas.

27. Robinson, *Log Cabin*, 79.

28. A Tennessee ex-slave also described pots at quiltings, another at dances (Anon. ex-slave, b. ca. 1850, TN; Anon. ex-slave, b. ca. 1845, TN, *Unwritten History*, 300, 255). Compare James K. Turner, "Slavery in Edgecombe County," 27: "Only now and then, according to old slaveholders' records, was a slave found truthful, faithful, and entirely honest. . . . The old trick played on the master by turning a huge pot with its mouth upon the floor of the master's residence, in order to deaden the noise while the negroes danced, was considered part of the slave's right." The rigid Western division between sacred and secular was unknown in most traditional African societies, the "sacred clowns" associated with African voice disguisers being one obvious expression of the African attitude. Conceivably, the transposition of social dancing and holy dancing (shouting) in some ex-slave accounts of turning the pot down reflects this core African principle. See, for example, William L. Adams and Mary Scott.

29. For pots filled with water, also see Mrs. L. M. Channel (b. unk., LA), Cade, "Ex-Slaves," 331; Albert, *Charlotte Brooks*, 12; Harper, *Iola Leroy*, 13.

30. Compare Henry Bobbitt, Siney Bonner, and Lewis Brown.

31. North Carolina ex-slave William H. Robinson (1848–?) gave another account combining turning the pot down with the throwing coals and grapevines episodes. Robinson, *Log Cabin*, 78–79.

32. For example, Motif J217.0.0.1. *Trickster overhears man praying for death to take him*. See Dorson, *Folktales*, 143–45.

33. Charles Colcock Jones, *Catechism for Colored Persons* (1834) commended slaves "to count their Masters 'worthy of all honour,' as those whom God has placed over them in this world; '*with all fear,*' they are to be '*subject to them*' and obey them in all *things*, possible and lawful, with good will and endeavor to *please them well*, . . . and let Servants serve their masters as faithfully behind their backs as before their faces. God is present to see, if their masters are not." Qtd. Raboteau, *Slave Religion*, 162–63, orig. emphasis and ellipses.

34. Jehu Grant to Hon. J. L. Edward, Commissioner of Pensions, December 1, 1836. www.saratoganygenweb.com/JehuGrant.htm.

35. Compare John Perrier: "De preacher uster preach to 'em not to steal. He tell 'em not to steal ol' marsters pigs. Dat got 'em to start to stealin' pigs 'cause dey didn't t'ink 'bout stealin' 'em befo' de preacher preach dat dey oughtn to" (John Perrier, b. ca. 1860, LA, 3079). Other ex-slaves recalling sermons based on Ephesians 6:5 ("Servants, be obedient to them that are your masters") included W. C. Parson Allen, Samuel Simeon Andrews, Hannah Austin,

Celestia Avery, Lizzie Baker, Mary Minus Biddie, Sallie Blakeley, Richard Carruthers, George Caulton, Cecelia Chappel, Father Charles Coates, Pierce Cody, Hannah Crasson, Sarah Douglas, Laura Ford, Duncan Gaines, Clayborn Gantling, Cornelius Garner, Charles Grandy, Isaiah Green, Harriett Gresham, Bolden Hall, Milton Hammond, Tom Hawkins, Clark Hill, Delia Hill, Della Bess Hilyard, Squire Irvin, Henry Johnson, Mr. Beverly Jones, Easter Jones, Jack Jones, Jacob Manson, Joe McCormick, Abe McKlennan, Riley Moore, Margrett Nickerson, Ellen Payne, Dempsey Pitts, Parker Pool, Morgan Ray, Alice Sewell, William Sherman, Bert Strong, Sarah Thomas, Ellen Trell, Henry James Trentham, Charlie Van Dyke, Henry Walker, William Ward, Anderson Williams, Lizzie Williams (MS), Temple Wilson, Ruben Woods, Henry Wright, and John I. Young. For other examples, see Sarah Fitzpatrick, (b. 1847, AL), Blassingame, *Slave Testimony*, 642–43; William Wells Brown, *Clotel; Or, the President's Daughter* (London: Partridge & Oakey, 1853), 93–100; Jane Robinson, Melvina Elzy, Pricilla Owens, Ella Alford, Frank Roberson, Roan Barnes (LA ex-slaves, Cade, "Ex-Slaves," 328–29); Chase, *Dear Ones*, 155; Jacobs, *Slave Girl*, 70–71; Lunsford Lane, *The Narrative of Lunsford Lane, Formerly of Raleigh, N.C.* (1842; rpt. *From Bondage*), 15; Talley, *NFR*, 278.

36. Also combining these two tales were Lucretia Alexander, Emma Barr, Wes Brady, Jeff Calhoun, Anderson Edwards, Charles Grandy, Charlie Hinton, Stephen McCray, Rachel Santee Reed, Sister Robinson, Eliza Washington, and Alex Woods.

37. Cade, "Ex-Slaves," 329.

38. *Unwritten History*, 98.

Hymns

1. The late nineteenth-century American hymn "I'm Going Home to Die No More" derives from a British broadside, "The Railway Spiritualized." Belden, *Missouri*, 468; Cohen, *Rail*, 605–10; *Country Music Sources*, 615. Mary Frances Brown and Sina Banks gave texts, Molly Ammonds, Jerry Eubanks, Hattie Anne Nettles, James Polk, Rachael Santee Reed, and Olin Williams named it. Mrs. C. E. Wells, who interviewed the Ramsays, wrote "neither one spoke the negro plantation dialect. Uncle George did not speak differently from the illiterate white, while his wife, Amy, had considerable education, and used excellent language. She was also polished in manners" (George Washington Ramsay, b. 1854, MS, 1775).

2. Abbott L. Ferriss, "Illiteracy," *Encyclopedia of Southern Culture*, 251–53.

3. Aside from fear of secret slave communications, white opposition to Black literacy was stoked by the very real possibility of forged passes and documents. "My father could read and write. Once he was charged with writing passes for some slaves in the county, as a result of this he was given 15 lashes by the sheriff of the county, immediately afterwards he ran away, went to Philadelphia, where he died while working to save money to purchase mother's freedom" (James Wiggins, b. 1850 or 1851, MD, 66). For similar accounts, see Robert Cheatham and William I. Johnson Jr. A joke told by several narrators turns the situation around. In one version a narrator's illiterate father was given a pass reading "whip Arthur Boone's—and pass him out. When he comes back, whip his — again and pass him back." Boone was accordingly beaten both ways (J. F. Boone, b. 1872, AR, child of ex-slaves, 212). In another telling a slave is given a pass to visit his wife but first finds a literate Black to read it: "To my man John I give this pass, / Pass an' repass to Sally's black [ass], / Ef don't nobody like dis pass, / Dey can kiss [Sally's ass]" (Fanny Berry, b. ca. 1841, VA, 46–47, orig. brackets). According to Harry Johnson "dere was a woman owned some slaves an' one of 'em went to her for a pass an' she wrote out a pass like dis: / His shirt is rough an' his back is tough, / Do, pray, Mr. Padderoller, give 'im enough! / An' dey said de padderollers nearly beat 'im to death" (Harry Johnson, b. ca. 1850, MO, 1997). Clayborn Gantling and Robert R. Grimstead also told this tale.

4. Allen, "Uncle Tom," 861. Compare Johnson, *Social History*, 146–47.

5. Kemble, *Journal*, 193–94.

6. Douglass, *My Bondage*, 145–46.

7. Windley, *Vol. 1: Virginia*, 270.

8. Flint, *Recollections*, 345.

9. Coppin, *History*, 24.

10. Burwell, *Girl's Life*, 3.

11. Numerous narrators insisted that the customary punishment for a slave learning to read and write was to amputate the offender's forefinger or thumb. "Dar warnt none er de white folks in dem slabery times whut wud let dey niggers hab any learnin. Yo sho better not be cotch er tryin ter learn no readin er writin. Our Marster neber eben lowed dat, en iffen er nigger wuz ter be foun whut cud write, den right straight dey wud chop his fore finger offen dat han whut he write wid" (Abram Harris, b. 1845, SC, 172). "Mrs. Duggins taught my sister, Fannie, to read and spell but not to write. If there was a slave man that knowed how to write, they used to cut off his thumb so that he couldn't write" (Claiborne Moss, b. 1857, GA, 157). Other ex-slaves who related this detail were Lewis Favors, Matilda Hatchett, Sam Jordan, William McWhorter, Henry Nix, Andrew Simms, Henry Wright, and George Young. The story may be founded in fact—as Susan Merritt testifies, some slaveholders were capable of truly inhuman cruelty and brutality—but internal and external factors argue this is a migratory folktale merely symbolizing some slaveholders' extreme opposition to slave literacy.

12. Economics were a major factor even after the war. "None of us learned to read an' write in slave days. I didn' go to school atter

freedom, we didn' have time then, we had to get out an' scratch for our bread" (George Washington Ramsay, b. 1854, MS, 1779). "Right after the surrender, I went to night school a little, but most of my schooling was got by the plow. After I come to be a minister I got a little schooling" (Needham Love, b. ca. 1855, AL, 295). Ann Matthews was denied education after freedom by her father. "Said he needed me in de fiel wors den I needed schul." She finally ran away to attend school in Nashville. "I wuz de only cul'ed person dere" (Ann Matthews, b. unk., TN, 44).

13. Some ex-slaves actually attributed mystical or magical properties to literacy and religious literature. "Yes, I knows some of the songs, too, what I used to dance to, but I is in the Church now, an the Lord don' like no dance tunes so I jes' forgets 'em cause He wants me to. An' the Lord learnt me how to read the Bible, but I can't read a newspaper. I can tell the letters but can't pronounce the words" (Mary Armstrong, b. 1846, MO, 74).

14. For period accounts of Blacks singing from hymn books, see Adams, *South-Side View of Slavery*, 26–27; Atwater, *Southern Tour*, 93; Bremer, *Homes* I: 369; Clinkscales, *Plantation*, 46; Kirke, *Among the Pines*, 48–49; Mary W. Porter, "In Memoriam," *The Independent* 30 (September 19, 1878), 1. In a recorded interview with John Henry Faulk, Texas ex-slave Aunt Harriet Smith also described slaves owning hymn books. Aunt Harriet Smith (ex-slave), "Interview," field rec., Austin, TX, November 1941, *Field Recordings, Vols. 10 & 11*, Document CD 5600.

15. For other Black versions, see Baldwin, *School-Teacher*, 23; Harris, *Remus*, 195–96; White, *ANFS*, 103–4. For a white version, see Thomas, *Ballad Makin'*, 215. A plagiarized version of the Harris text appears in the interview of Sylvester Brooks, produced by Texas fieldworker Effie Cowan. Similar titles do appear in nineteenth-century hymnals, for example, "In eighteen hundred and thirty-one," *Conference Hymns, Original and Selected*, ed. E. Sherman, vol. 2 (Providence: H. H. Brown, 1835), d21; "In eighteen hundred three-three," *Pocket Hymns, Original and Selected*, ed. Isaac N. Vanmeter (Galesburg, IL: Register Printing House, 1867), d259 (*DNAH*). This sequence-of-dates structure is, however, common in Anglo- and African American tradition, including the Civil War song "Johnny, Fill Up the Bowl," known to several ex-slaves. Other secular Black examples include Charley Campbell, "Eighteen Hundred and Ninety-One," field rec., Mobile, AL, 1937, *Lullabies to Blues*.

16. Coppin, *History*, 24.

17. Obviously, Norcross's memory is off in some particulars, since Fanny Crosby's "Jesus Keep Me Near the Cross" dates from after Emancipation (1869). Anderson Williams gave a highly personalized example of this sort of instruction: "When slaves run away, dey would catch 'em wid dogs an' den beat 'em nearly to death wid de 'Bull Whip.' I 'member once when I tol' 'bout seein' a nigger

runnin' away, boss [who objected to such brutality] got his hymn book, set down, put me 'cross his knees an' as he'd sing de hymns, he'd whup me to de tune o' 'em. Believe me when he got through I didn' set down for a week an' I ain't never seed no more niggers runnin' away neither!" (Anderson Williams, b. 1849, MS, 2299).

18. Narrators Andy Marion and Alice Marshall also described lining hymns. For other ex-slave accounts, see Coppin, *History*, 57–58; James W. C. Pennington (1807–1870), *The Fugitive Blacksmith* (1849; rpt. *Five Narratives*), 67. For other period descriptions, see Adams, *South-Side View of Slavery*, 54; Clinkscales, *Plantation*, 46; Dix, *Transatlantic Tracings*, 235–36; Down East Music Teacher, "Letter from a Teacher," 164; Johnson, "The Georgia Negro," 356; Kilham, "Sketches. Fourth," 305–6; King, *Great South*, 611–12; Kirke, *Among the Pines*, 181; *Slave Songs*, xiii; Showers, "Weddin' and Buryin'," 482; Spaulding, "Palmetto," 195–96; Wilson, "Old Plantation—II," 122. Also see White, *ANFS*, 40–41, 47.

19. By "De Dyin' Thief" Woodward probably refers to the second verse of "There Is a Fountain Filled With Blood": "The dying thief rejoiced to see / That fountain in his day." Similar accounts of slaves singing or learning songs in white churches come from Frank L. Adams, Samuel Boulware, William Davis, Charles Green, Margaret Hughes, Henrietta McCullers, Eva Strayhorn, and Sallah White.

20. Elizabeth A. Roe, *Aunt Leanna, Or, Early Scenes in Kentucky* (Chicago: author, 1855), 192.

21. Anne Rose Page, *Sketches of Old Virginia Family Servants* (Philadelphia: Isaac Ashmead, 1847), 45–46.

22. Elisha W. Green, *Life of the Rev. Elisha W. Green* (Maysville, KY: Republican Printing Office, 1888), 51.

23. "Grandfather Sol: Conversation With an Old Blind Emancipated Slave," *The Anti-Slavery Record* 4 (April 1, 1836), 5.

24. Green, *Life*, 2–3.

25. Todd, *Methodism*, 179.

26. Steward, *Slave*, 39.

27. Coppin, *History*, 57–58; Lowery, *Plantation*, 208.

28. Harriet Beecher Stowe, *Dred: A Tale of the Dismal Swamp*, 2 vols. (1856; rpt. Stowe, *Writings*, vols. 3 & 4), II: 168.

29. Washington, "Funeral," 242.

30. Showers, "Weddin' and Buryin'," 482.

31. Several narrators described the practice of holding the funeral at some length after the burying: James Bolton, Willis Cofer, Julia Larken, and Paul Smith. Also see "Beliefs and Customs Connected with Death and Burial," *Southern Workman* 26 (January 1897): 19; Coppin, *History*, 55–58; *Drums and Shadows*, 130–31, 147; Kearney, *Slaveholder's Daughter*, 61–62; Long, *Slavery*, 19–20; Leigh, *Georgia Plantation*, 165; Lowery, *Plantation*, 208; Mary Porter, "Aunt Betsey's Funeral Sermon," *The Independent* 30 (January 17, 1878): 3; Puckett, *Folk Beliefs*, 92–94; Raboteau, *Religion*, 230–31; Randolph, *Slave Life*,

49–51; Showers, "Weddin' and Buryin'," 481; Sisk, "Funeral Customs in Alabama," 169–70; "A Summer on a Southern Plantation," 3; Washington, "Funeral," 242; *Isaac Williams*, 66. While ex-slaves often attributed the delay to work schedules or white control, this is a actually widespread custom among New World Blacks with possible African antecedents. *Drums and Shadows*, 226–28; Lorna McDaniel and Donald Hill, booklet accompanying *Tombstone Feast: Funerary Music of Carriacou*, Rounder CD 1727, 2001.

32. Kilham, "Sketches. Fourth," 309, orig. emphasis.

33. *Unwritten History*, 248.

34. "Contributions from Correspondents," *Southern Workman* 23 (December 1894): 210. Similar jokes surface in white tradition. In 1847 aboard a steamer leaving New Orleans, Alexander Mackay heard of an earlier confrontation between two riverboat gamblers: "The offended party drew his bowie knife, and directed the attention of the other to the motto which it bore upon its broad burnished blade, which was 'Hark, from the tombs!' The other coolly drew a pistol from his breast, on the gleaming barrel of which was etched, 'A doleful sound!'" The offense was laughingly dismissed. Mackay, *Western World*, III: 9–10. John Wyeth told of an Alabama courthouse groundbreaking attended mainly by lawyers, who "are said at times to wander from the straight and narrow path of truth." The Baptist preacher officiating "opened the services by asking those present to join in singing that well-known hymn—Come, trembling sinner, view the ground / Where you shall shortly lie" (the concluding lines of "Hark From the Tombs'" first stanza). Wyeth, *Sabre*, 129–30. An Ozark informant recalled that at meetings in the 1890s "facetious young folk sometimes sang the word *doleful* as if it were *dodel-fiddle*, which was regarded as very daring and a great joke." Randolph, *OFS* IV: 77, orig. emphasis. Around this time "Hark From the Tombs" even became journalistic shorthand for the failure of some prominent individual or issue, for example, "'Hark From the Tombs.' A Monopolist's Lament for the Failure of Watterson's Press-Muzzling Bill in Congress," *Daily Cairo Bulletin*, March 5, 1884. Chronicling America: Historic American Newspapers, Library of Congress, www.chroniclingamerica.loc.gov, which contains nearly nine hundred examples.

35. Richard Allen, *A Collection of Spiritual Songs and Hymns* (Philadelphia: John Ormrod, 1801); Richard Allen, *A Collection of Hymns and Spiritual Songs* (Philadelphia: T. L. Plowman, 1801).

36. Kennedy, *Cameos*, xxiii. Also Kennedy, *More Mellows*, 21–52; Oliver, *Songsters*, 219–28; Puckett, *Folk Beliefs*, 61–62; White, *ANFS*, 53–54, 413–26, Appendix II: "Specimens of Negro Ballets and Related Songs." "Good Shepherd," which ex-slave Lizzie Davis gave, appeared in many early Black spiritual collections and very likely on ballets as well (though she does not specifically state this).

37. Southern, *Music*, 450–51.

38. Showers, "Weddin' and Buryin'," 482.

39. *White mule* was Prohibition-era slang for illicit whiskey (aka *white lightning*).

40. For "The Death of Holmes' Mule," also see Oliver, *Songsters*, 135–37. On Burton Ellis, see Nathan W. Pearson, *Goin' to Kansas City* (Urbana: University of Illinois Press, 1987), 98–100; Minton, *78 Blues*, 64.

41. Blind Willie McTell, "Amazing Grace," field rec., Atlanta, 1940, *The Devil Can't Hide from Me: The Library of Congress Recordings*, Fuel 2000 CD 302 061 441, 2004. The third item James Davis quoted was from Isaac Watts's "Go Preach My Gospel, Saith the Lord" (1709).

42. Jesse Fuller, "Hark from the Tomb," *Frisco Bound*, Arhoolie LP 360, 1968; Jesse Fuller, "I'm Glad Salvation's Free"/"Hark from the Tomb" (medley), video ca. 1970, *Masters of Bottleneck Blues Guitar*, Vestapol DVD 13002, 2002. Compare Charley Patton, "Prayer of Death—Parts 1 and 2" (Paramount 12799, 1929). Ex-slaves Charity Austin, Gus Feaster, Mary Veals, and Olin Williams performed or named "I'm Glad Salvation's Free." Veals associated it with church, Williams with baptisms, Feaster with his personal born-again experience, Austin with turning the pot down. Another Black recording is Mahalia Jackson, "I'm Glad Salvation Is Free" (Apollo 222, 1950).

Spirituals

1. For "Hold Your Light," also see *Slave Songs*, 10; Spaulding, "Palmetto," 198.

2. As elsewhere I employ *spiritual* as a catchall for the slaves' indigenous religious songs, a usage observed by most ex-slaves. This is hardly ironclad, however. Some narrators simply called all religious songs (hymns or spirituals) *hymns*, some called both spirituals and hymns *spirituals*, some simply called all songs (sacred or secular) *songs*. Others offered finer distinctions, classifying by context or function or some other criteria: baptizing songs, shout songs, funeral songs, my mothers' songs, and so forth.

3. Of likely slave origin, "Ride On King Jesus (No Man Can Hinder)" is well documented in the war years and after. See Anon. ex-slave (b. unk, TN), *Unwritten History*, 125; Arnold, *Alabama*, 184–85; Bales, "Negro Folk-Songs," 92; Forten, "Sea Islands. Part I," 588; Higginson, "Spirituals," 687; King, *Great South*, 614; Marsh, *Jubilee Singers*, 168; Rosenberg, *Virginia*, 107; *Slave Songs*, 10–11. RECORDINGS: Norfolk Jubilee Quartet, "Ride On King Jesus" (Paramount 12669, 1927); Soul Stirrers, "Ride On King Jesus" (Aladdin 2010, 1947). DISCOGRAPHIES: *Blues and Gospel Records*; *Gospel Discography*.

4. For other examples, see Barton, *Plantation Hymns*, 11, 45; Sherwood Bonner, *Suwannee River Tales* (Boston: Roberts Brothers, 1884), 51; Brown III: 661–62, 666; Dett, *Hampton*, 141; David W. Guion, *Satan's a Liar an' a Conjur Too* (New York: M. Witmark & Sons, 1918); Hallowell, *Calhoun*, 34, 71; Higginson, "Spirituals," 690; Johnson, *Spirituals* I: 41; John J. Niles, "Shout, Coon, Shout!" *Musical Quarterly* 16 (1930): 516; Odum and Johnson, *NHS*, 39, 124; Porter, "At the Sugar-House," 3; Puckett, *Folk Beliefs*, 168, 552–53; Randolph, *OFS* II: 389; Sandburg, *Songbag*, 250–51; *Slave Songs*, 108; Solomon, *Honey*, 10, 65, 92; "Southern Cabins. Georgia.—II," 749; Thomas W. Talley, "The Origin of Negro Traditions" (concluded), *Phylon* 4/1 (1943): 31; Work, *ANSS*, 71.

5. King, *Great South*, 610, orig. emphasis.

6. For period accounts of Blacks improvising spirituals, see Barton, *Plantation Hymns*, 10–14; Forten, "Sea Islands. Part II," 666–67; Higginson, "Spirituals," 685–94; Kilham, "Sketches. Fourth," 304–11; King, *Great South*, 609–11; Malet, *Errand*, 114–15; Randolph, *Slave Life*, 69. Also see Odum and Johnson, *NHS*, 35–38; White, *ANFS*, 54–55.

7. Odum and Johnson, *NHS*, 145.

8. The fifth line of Briggs's text is from Isaac Watts's "Come Ye That Love the Lord" (1707), the first line from "Been Listening All the Day," for which see *Cabin* I: 247; *Cabin* III: 75; Carter, *Louisiana Negro*, 67; Chase, *Dear Ones*, 126; Dett, *Hampton*, 170; Johnson, *Utica*, 76–79; Marsh, *Jubilee Singers*, 144; W. S. B. Mathews, "The Jubilee Slave-Songs," *New York Musical Gazette* 7 (October 1, 1873): 148; McIlhenny, *Spirituals*, 126–27; Odum and Johnson, *NHS*, 81–82; Owens, *Texas*, 171–72; Taylor, *Revival Hymns*, 62–63. RECORDINGS: Golden Gate Quartet, "Been A' Listening" (Thesaurus 977, 1941); Blind Joe Taggart, "Been Listening All the Day" (Paramount 12611, 1928); Tuskegee Institute Singers, "I Been A-Listening" (Victor 18646, 1916). "Been Listening" is definitely a nineteenth-century Black creation, possibly of slave origin.

9. Milton Marshall also gave this item, which I have not found outside the narratives: "I am a Baptist and we baptised in de creek atter we dammed it up to hold water deep enough. Sometimes we used a waterhole in de woods. I remember one old Baptist song, it went: / Down to de water I be baptised, for my Savior die; / Down to de water, de River of Jordan, / Where my Savior baptised" (Milton Marshall, b. ca. 1855, SC, 173).

10. For this floater, also see Brown III: 602–3; Mellinger E. Henry, "More Songs from the Southern Highlands," *JAF* 44 (1931): 82; Lomax, *Ballads*, 15; Perrow, "South" (1913): 157; Sandburg, *Songbag*, 477.

11. St. Ann Johnson and Frances Lewis also gave texts of "Rough and Rocky Road." George Govan recalled the title. Also see Barton, *Plantation Hymns*, 6; Brown III: 668; *Cabin* III, 43; Jackson, *WNS*, 170–71; Perkins, "Spirituals," 247; White, *ANFS*,

112–13. RECORDINGS: Heavenly Gospel Singers, "Rough and Rocky Road" (Bluebird B6636, 1936); Original Chambers Brothers, "Medley: Rough and Rocky Road/I'll Fly Away," *Groovin' Time*, Folkways LP 31008, 1968; Stars of Harmony, "Rough and Rocky Road" (Supreme 1511, 1948); Trumpeteers, "It's A Rough and Rocky Road" (Score 5043, 1948). DISCOGRAPHIES: *Blues and Gospel Records*; *Gospel Discography*.

12. For another version, see Higginson, "Spirituals," 691–92.

13. Ex-slaves Lafayette Price and George White also knew "Inching Along," for which also see Dett, *Hampton*, 10–11; Hallowell, *Calhoun*, 7; Johnson, *Spirituals* I: 134–35; Johnson, *Utica*, 72–75; Killion and Waller, *Georgia*, 249–50; Lomax, *FSNA*, 456–57; Marsh, *Jubilee Singers*, 186; Anna Kranz Odum, "Some Negro Folk-Songs from Tennessee," *JAF* 27 (1914): 262; Odum and Johnson, *NHS*, 89; Sandburg, *Songbag*, 492; Scarborough, *TNFS*, 11; Work, *ANSS*, 125. RECORDINGS: Fisk University Jubilee Singers, "Keep Inching Along" (Columbia 658-D, 1926); Heavenly Gospel Singers, "Inching Along" (Bluebird B7133, 1937). DISCOGRAPHIES: *Blues and Gospel Records*; *Gospel Discography*.

14. Ex-slave Tom Floyd also knew this item. Also see *Cabin* I: 198; *Cabin* III: 26; Johnson, *Spirituals* II: 160–61; McIlhenny, *Spirituals*, 167–68. RECORDINGS: Bessie Jones and Sea Island Singers, "Sheep, Sheep, Don'tcha Know the Road," field rec., April 1960, St. Simmons Island, GA, *Don'tcha Know the Road*, Rounder CD 1706, 1997.

15. For "Let Us Cheer the Weary Traveler," see Handy, *Blues*, 49; Work, *ANSS*, 190. RECORDINGS: Clover Leaf Jubilee Quartet, "Cheer the Weary Traveler" (Black and White 755, 1945); Singing Crusaders, "Cheer the Weary Traveler" (National 9083, 1949); Golden Gate Quartet, "Cheer the Weary Traveler" (Bluebird B8019, 1938); Heavenly Gospel Singers, "Cheer the Weary Traveler" (Bluebird B7969, 1938); Skylarks, "Cheer the Weary Traveler" (Nashboro 508, 1951).

16. This is another case where Mississippi interviewer Mrs. W. F. Holmes repeated material in different narratives. This same text appears in the narrative of Holmes's informant Ebenezer Brown (b. 1852, MS, 244), reversing the stanzas and slightly altering the line breaks. As in other instances, however, the material seems authentic, even if the attribution is confused. I have not found this item anywhere else.

17. This appears to be an early version of the most popular contemporary Black baptizing song, "Take Me To the Water (To Be Baptized)," which several other ex-slaves may have named: Rev. Silas Jackson ("Going to the Water"); Elisha Doc Garey ("Lead Me to de Water for to be Baptized"); Jane Thompson, ("Let's go down to de water an be baptized"); Edward Lygurgas ("Take me to the water to be baptized"). For the contemporary "Take Me to the Water," see Rev. E. D. Campbell, "Take Me To the Water" (Victor 20546,

1927); Bessie Jones with Georgia Sea Island Singers, "Take Me To the Water," New York, 1966, *Get In Union*, Tompkins Square CDs 5074, 2014. DISCOGRAPHIES: *Gospel Discography*.

18. For "On Canaan's Happy Shore," William Steffe (ca. 1830–ca. 1890), see Lorenza Ezell (b. ca. 1850, SC, 1319–21); *DNAH*; Asbury and Meyer, "Old-Time," 172, 179–80, 184; Brown III: 624–25; Jackson, *WNS*, 178; Owens, *Texas*, 164; Silber, *Civil War*, 10–11.

19. For "You Shall Be Free (When the Good Lord Sets Us Free)," "We'll Soon Be Free (When the Good Lord Calls Us Home)," and the like, see Higginson, "Spirituals," 692; Marsh, *Jubilee Singers*, 130. In later years this item was best known via parodies with strong minstrel connections. See, for example, White, *ANFS*, 134–39. RECORDINGS: Frank Stokes, "You Shall" (Paramount 12518, 1927); Uncle Dave Macon, "Shout Mourner, You Shall Be Free" (Vocalion 5007, 1926). DISCOGRAPHIES: *Blues and Gospel Records*; *Country Music Records*.

20. Gus Feaster, Charity Austin, Mary Veals, and Olin Williams also knew Watts's "I'm Glad Salvation's Free." This and the preceding examples contain metaphorical references to slavery and freedom that slaves chose to take literally, but some scholars have argued that slave spirituals also included encoded messages concerning escape routes to freedom, secret meetings, planned uprisings, current events, and so forth. (The classic statement of this argument is Miles Mark Fisher, *Negro Slave Songs in the United States* [1953; rpt. New York: Russell & Russell, 1968].) While this argument has won wide acceptance, the ex-slaves themselves simply did not assign this function to spirituals, though they discussed spirituals' other functions and meanings in great detail. To the contrary, the ex-slave narratives (and the legion published memoirs of fugitive slaves) categorically establish that sensitive information of the sort sometimes imputed to spirituals (escape routes, meeting times, and so on) was invariably transmitted conversationally from person to person or through some other practical means, which was not only simpler and more sensible but more secure and far less susceptible to misinterpretation or misunderstanding. This is in fact exactly what one would expect from intelligent, levelheaded human beings, which the slaves who risked torture and death to escape North, worship secretly, or organize in resistance definitely were. Obviously spirituals figuratively expressed many forbidden themes or secret hopes, but I have seen no hard evidence that slaves ever used them as encoded maps or how-to manuals.

21. This is the only mention in the narratives of "Wrestling Jacob," which Windham combines with "Mary, Don't You Weep" and a floating commonplace not usually associated with either. Compare Shack Wilson: "My pa and ma used to tell of the brutal treatment of their old master. 'T'want he that was so mean, but the old overseer. No wonder she used to sing: 'Before I'd be a slave, I'd be dead in my grave, / And go home to my Father and be saved'"

(Shack Wilson, b. ca. 1860, LA, 215). For these lines, also see Barton, *Plantation Hymns*, 25; J. Mason Brewer, "Old-Time Negro Proverbs," *Spur-of-the-Cock*, ed. J. Frank Dobie. PTFS 11 (Austin, 1933), 102; *Cabin* III: 114; Carter, *Louisiana Negro*, 63; Krehbiel, *Folksongs*, 21; Work, *ANSS*, 106. RECORDINGS: Golden Gate Quartet, "Freedom" Washington, DC, Dec. 20, 1940, *Freedom*. For "Wrestling Jacob," see Anon. ex-slave (b. unk., TN), *Unwritten History*, 49; Mrs. Mary Dickson Arrowood and Thomas Hoffman Hamilton, "Nine Negro Spirituals, 1850-61, from Lower South Carolina," *JAF* 41 (1928): 580; Arnold, *Alabama*, 167; Ballanta, *St. Helena*, 62; Brown III: 684; *Cabin* III: 131; Dett, *Hampton*, 70; Diton, *South Carolina*, 37; Hallowell, *Calhoun*, 41; Higginson, "Spirituals," 689; Marsh, *Jubilee Singers*, 180–81; *Slave Songs*, 4–5. WPA narrators William Emmons and Adeline White also named "Mary Don't You Weep (Pharoah's Army)," for which see Brown III: 602–3; *Country Music Sources*, 580–81; Dett, *Hampton*, 232; Gainer, *West Virginia*, 211–12; Johnson, *Spirituals* I: 140–41; Lomax, *Lead Belly*, 5–10; White, *ANFS*, 58–59.

22. This text appears to be based on "Where Shall I Be When the First Trumpet Sounds," which narrator Sarah Pittman named. Also see Asbury and Meyer, "Old-Time," 183; Dett, *Hampton*, 173; Hallowell, *Calhoun*, 8; Jackson, *Sheaf*, 17; Johnson, *Spirituals* I: 136; Odum and Johnson, *NHS*, 134–35; Perkins, "Spirituals," 226; Perrow, "South" (1913): 155; White, *ANFS*, 80–81. RECORDINGS: Blind Lemon Jefferson (Deacon L. J. Bates), "Where Shall I Be?" (Paramount 12585, 1927); Rev. Edward W. Clayborn (The Guitar Evangelist), "Where Shall I Be When That First Trumpet Sounds?" (Vocalion 1458, 1929); Missouri-Pacific Diamond Jubilee Quartette, "Where Shall I Be When That First Trumpet Sounds?" (OKeh 8472, 1927). DISCOGRAPHIES: *Blues and Gospel Records*; *Country Music Sources*, 589.

23. Sam Meredith Mason also gave a text of "Down in the Valley to Pray." Isaac Rodgers and Annie Young named it. Also see Brown III: 610–11; Jackson, *Down-East*, 243; Jackson, *Early*, 209; Lomax, *Lead Belly*, 209; Marsh, *Jubilee Singers*, 156; Odum and Johnson, *NHS*, 69, 280; Perkins, "Spirituals," 234; *Slave Songs*, 84; White, *ANFS*, 71–72, 132–33. RECORDINGS: Lead Belly, "Down in the Valley to Pray," Washington, DC, August 1940, *Let It Shine On*, Rounder CD 1046.

24. For "You'd Better Be Praying," see Odum and Johnson, *NHS*, 80; Rosenbaum, *Shout*, 120–21. The second item recalls "The Angels Changed My Name," for which see Marsh, *Jubilee Singers*, 227; McIlhenny, *Spirituals*, 45–46; "Silhouettes," *Southern Workman* 20 (April 1891): 172.

25. Kilham, "Sketches. Fourth," 307.

26. Higginson, "Spirituals," 690.

27. Randolph, *Slave Life*, 55–56.

28. Cannon combines two wandering stanzas. Emoline Glasgow also gave the "Heaven, Sweet Heaven" verse: "My master was a good

man, a church man, and he was a steward in Tranquil Methodist Church. Around de place at home he was always singing and in good humor. I 'member one song he sung dat was like dis: / Lord, Lord, Heaven—Sweet Heaven, / Lord, Lord, Heaven—Sweet Heaven, / How long will it be? / (repeated three times)" (Emoline Glasgow, b. 1859, SC, 134, orig. parentheses). Also see Jackson, *WNS*, 323. For "If You Get There Before I Do," see the chapter appendix.

29. For the "I'm going home in the morning soon" commonplace, see Barton, *Plantation Hymns*, 6.

30. Barton, *Plantation Hymns*, 14.

31. Numerous unrelated spirituals encourage believers to join the band (sometimes specified as the Angel, Christian, Sunday, Gideon, and so on band); express a personal desire or intention to do so; proclaim the singer's current membership; and so forth. Lizzie Davis, Judia Fortenberry, Frankie Goole, and Scott Martin gave other examples.

32. "By and by" and "when I'm dead, don't grieve after me" are another pair of commonplaces cropping up constantly in unrelated songs. Ex-slave Julia Ann James named "Doan You Grieve Atter Me," Clara White, "W'en I is dead an' gone, don' you grieve over me." In the twentieth century, a distinct piece actually titled "Don't You Grieve After Me" became extremely popular. Also see Brown III: 585–86, 613; McIlhenny, *Spirituals*, 90–91; Perkins, "Spirituals," 233; Scarborough, *TNFS*, 9; Taylor, *Revival Hymns*, 46–47; White, *ANFS*, 59–60; Work, *ANSS*, 119. DISCOGRAPHIES: *Blues and Gospel Records*; *Country Music Sources*, 587.

33. Malet, *Errand*, 114–15. Ex-slave Jacob Branch recalled this item: "Spiritual songs dey come through visions. Dat's why de cullud folks kin mek dem and sing dem better dan de w'ite folks. I knowed one song what start out / De Jews done kill po' Jesus, / And bury him in de sepulcher. / De grave would not hol' him / Dey place guards all 'roun' him / But de angels move de stone. / De Jews done kill po' Jesus / But de grave it would not hol' him" (Jacob Branch, b. ca. 1851, TX, 411). Also see Brown III: 595–96; Carter, *Louisiana Negro*, 63–64; Jackson, *WNS*, 174–75; Marsh, *Jubilee Singers*, 160, 208–9; McIlhenny, *Spirituals*, 38–39.

34. "I couldn't hear nobody pray" is another wandering commonplace, also named by Naisy Reece. Also see Dett, *Hampton*, 202–3, XXI; Johnson, *Utica*, 53–56; Lomax, *FSNA*, 473–74; Work, *ANSS*, 72–73.

35. Lizzie Davis, Rebecca Fletcher, Orelia Alexie Franks, Elizabeth Ross Hite, Joanna Thompson Isom, Gracie Mitchell, and Lafayette Price all gave versions of this couplet. Georgia Smith named "Better Mind How You step on de Cross" as a title sung at prayer meetings. For other examples, see Barton, *Plantation Hymns*, 8; Brown III: 266, 629; *Cabin* III: 26, 111; Davis, "Folk-Lore," 251; Chase, *Dear Ones*, 125 n2, 126; Dett, *Hampton*, 5, 137; Gordon, "Negro Spiritual," 201; Hallowell, *Calhoun*, 49; R. C.

Harrison, "The Negro as Interpreter of His Own Folk-Songs," *Rainbow in the Morning*, ed. J. Frank Dobie. PTFS 5 (1926; rpt. Hatboro, PA: Folklore Associates, 1965), 151; Katharine C. Hutson, Josephine Pinckney, and Caroline Pinckney Rutledge, "Some Songs the Negro Sang," *Carolina Low-Country* (New York: Macmillan, 1931), 302; Johnson, *Spirituals* I: 41, 78–79; Johnson, *Spirituals* II: 174–75; Killion and Waller, *Georgia*, 240; Lomax, *Lead Belly*, 209; McIlhenny, *Spirituals*, 219; Odum, "Some Negro Folk-Songs," 261; *NHS*, 75; Odum and Johnson, *Workaday*, 194; Parrish, *Sea Islands*, 220; Porter, "Negro Songs," 1; *Slave Songs*, 74; Solomon, *Daisies*, 172, 195; "Watch Meeting" (*SW*), 154; White, *ANFS*, 73, 118–19; Work, *ANSS*, 111, 135. Despite its impressive provenience, this ubiquitous injunction to be mindful while walking or "stepping" on the cross has no apparent basis in Christian doctrine, much less common sense, leaving one to wonder exactly how or why a believer could or would walk on the Crucifix; even as a potential metaphor, it seems decidedly opaque. However, David Evans has suggested to me that this floater may have originated as a hopscotch rhyme, and certainly logic and the evidence favor that hypothesis. An ancient game with global distribution, hopscotch was sometimes Christianized in Europe, the squares (often laid out as a cross or church basilica) being said to represent the progress of the soul; the stages between Hell and Heaven; the levels of Paradise; and so forth. See Gomme, *Games*, 223–27; Newell, *Games*, 188. Even today, crosses are common for hopscotch boards, so that in hopscotch someone's soul can indeed be lost by stepping carelessly on the cross, whether understood in religious terms or otherwise. In this scenario the rhyme most likely originated with whites, passing to African Americans with the game of hopscotch, which ex-slaves frequently named, but only rarely as a singing game (but see Della Barclay). In fact, while it sometimes involves rhyming, hopscotch is not ordinarily classed as a singing game, and I have not found this verse associated with hopscotch among either Blacks or whites. As a folksong commonplace it is wholly African American, employed in spirituals or occasionally other genres drawing on spirituals (for example, worksongs and lullabyes). Wherever or however it originated, Blacks obviously introduced the stanza into religious songs, but the hypothetical hopscotch link remains highly plausible and would explain an otherwise puzzling image.

36. Work, *ANSS*, 27.

37. Mathews, "Jubilee Slave-Songs," 148.

38. Describing South Carolina slaves singing spirituals, Robert Wilson noted: "the old mauma at the end of the front bench 'sets de tchune,' a sad, quavering minor, and pitched so high that any attempt to follow it seems utterly hopeless. But no: the women all strike in on the same soaring key, while the men, by skillful management of the *falsetto*, keep up with the screamiest flights." Wilson, "Old Plantation—II," 122, orig. emphasis.

39. For nineteenth-century accounts of handclapping and foot stamping as accompaniments to religious singing, see "Southern Cabins. Georgia.—II," 749; Forten, "Sea Islands. Part I," 589; Higginson, "Spirituals," 685; Hundley, *Social Relations*, 348; Kilham, "Sketches. Fourth," 305–8; King, *Great South*, 609, 781; *Slave Songs*, xiii–iv; Whitney and Bullock, *Maryland*, 162.

40. Higginson, "Spirituals," 685, 691.

41. Narrators Charlotte Beverly, Hattie Clayton, Reverend Squire Dowd, George Govan, and Ellis Ken Kannon also named "The Old Ship of Zion." Also see Albert, *Charlotte Brooks*, 5; Barton, *Plantation Hymns*, 23; Bremer, *Homes* II: 158; Brown III: 659-61; Brown, "Songs," 619; *Cabin* III: 85; Davis, "Folk-Lore," 249; Davis, *Folk-Songs*, 305; Dett, *Hampton*, 81; H. H. B., "Reminiscences of a Southern Plantation," 13; Jackson, *Spirituals*, 257; Kennedy, *Mellows*, 40–41; Kennedy, *More Mellows*, 126; Kilham, "Sketches. Fourth," 306–7; Killion and Waller, *Georgia*, 240–41; Marsh, *Jubilee Singers*, 152; McDonald, *Virginia*, 277; McDowell, *Camp*, 47; Odum and Johnson, *NHS*, 117–18; Rosenberg, *Virginia*, 97; *Slave Songs*, 102–3; White, *ANFS*, 93–96, 436; Whitney and Bullock, *Maryland*, 157. RECORDINGS: Laura Smalley (ex-slave), "The Old Ship of Zion," field rec., Austin, TX, November 1941, *Field Recordings, Vols. 10 & 11*, Document CD 5600; Hallsway High School Quartet, "The Old Ship Zion," field rec., Murfreesboro, TN, 1941, *Negro Religious Field Recordings, Vol. 1,* Document CD 5312; Junior Paramount Singers, "Old Ship Zion," field rec., Austin, TX, July 1941, *Negro Religious Field Recordings, Vol. 2*, Document CD 5629; Southeast Alabama and Florida Union Sacred Harp Singing Convention, "The Old Ship of Zion," field rec., Campbellton, FL, August 1980, *Field Recordings of African American Traditional Music 1977–1980*, Dust-To-Digital CD 24. DISCOGRAPHIES: *Blues and Gospel Records*; *Country Music Sources*, 585; *Gospel Discography*.

42. In 1873 W. S. B. Mathews wrote of the spiritual in "the South of fifteen years ago" (that is, ca. 1862): "Another curious point is the negro fondness for a chorus. . . . Take for instance, the tender meditation, / 'Swing low, sweet chariot,' / and the line of chorus constantly coming in, / 'Coming for to carry me home.' / . . . and we get it in every alternate line, logic or no logic. In this way a few verses do a great deal of duty." Mathews, "Jubilee Slave-Songs," 148.

43. Theodore F. Seward and George L. White, *Jubilee Songs as Sung by the Fisk Jubilee Singers* (New York: Bigelow and Main, 1872), rpt. Marsh, *Jubilee Singers*, 126. Also Barton, *Plantation Hymns*, 28; *Cabin* I: 179, 183, 188; *Cabin* III: 7, 11, 16, 125; Dett, *Hampton*, 100–102; Jackson, *WNS*, 183; Johnson, *Utica*, 118–23; King, *Great South*, 614; Parrish, *Sea Islands*, 154–55; Perkins, "Spirituals," 237–38; Work, *ANSS*, 152. RECORDINGS: Standard Quartette, "Swing Low, Sweet Chariot" (Columbia unnumbered cylinder, 1894); Fisk University Jubilee Quartet, "Swing Low Sweet Chariot" (Victor 16453, 1909); Lead Belly, "Swing Low, Sweet Chariot," Washington,

DC, August 1940, *Go Down Old Hannah*, Rounder CD 1099, 1994; Tuskegee Institute Singers, "Swing Low, Sweet Chariot" (Victor 17890, 1916). DISCOGRAPHIES: *Blues and Gospel Records*; *Country Music Records*; *Country Music Sources*, 580.

44. Adeline White quoted a commonplace associated with "Swing Low, Sweet Chariot," but also other songs: "Dey uster sing: / Look over yonder w'at I see, / Ban's of angels comin' down" (Adeline White, b. ca. 1857, LA, 4026). Narrators merely naming "Swing Low" were Smith Austin, Frances Banks, Alice Baugh, Anne Bell, James Boyd, Amos Clark, Hannah Davidson, Reverend Squire Dowd, Lewis Evans, Gus Feaster, Bill Heard, Julia Ann James, Thomas Johns, Richard Kimmons, Moses Lyles, Chaney Mack, Mose Moss, Ellen Payne, Rachael Santee Reed, and Mollie Watson. One of the ex-slaves interviewed by Fisk also gave the title (Mr. Huddleston, b. unk., TN, *Unwritten History*, 35).

45. Frank T. Boone, James Boyd, Richard Kimmons, Janey Landrum, Lewis Mundy, Robert Shepherd, Georgia Smith, Nancy Smith, Georgia Telfair, and Cordelia Thomas named "Roll Jordan Roll." Also see Arrowood and Hamilton, "Negro Spirituals," 583; Aleckson, *Before the War*, 279; Baldwin, *School-Teacher*, 46–48; Ballanta, *St. Helena*, 77; Brown III: 667-68; Coffin, *Four Years of Fighting*, 230; Dett, *Hampton*, 52, I; Diton, *South Carolina*, 51; Forten, "Sea Islands. Part I," 589–90; Gordon, *Folk-Songs*, 30; Jackson, *WNS*, 180–81; Johnson, *Spirituals* I: 105-7; Kilham, "Sketches. Fourth," 307; Lomax, *FSNA*, 457–59; Marsh, *Jubilee Singers*, 131; Parker, *Recollections*, 311; Pyrnelle, *Diddie, Dumps, and Tot*, 153–54; Randolph, *OFS* II: 388–89; Rosenberg, *Virginia*, 108; *Slave Songs*, 1; Spaulding, "Palmetto," 198–99; Taylor, *Revival Hymns*, 216–17; White, *ANFS*, 87–88; Work, *ANSS*, 199. RECORDINGS: Fisk University Jubilee Quartet, "Roll Jordan Roll" (Victor 16466, 1909); Tuskegee Institute Singers, "1. Roll Jordan Roll; 2. I Want God's Heaven To Be Mine" (Victor 18237, 1915). DISCOGRAPHIES: *Blues and Gospel Records*. A text of "Roll Jordan Roll" appears in the narrative of Harrison Cole, authored by Texas fieldworker Effie Cowan; like most of Cowan's materials, it strongly suggests a secondary source and/or editorial tampering. (Other texts in Cole's narrative were definitely plagiarized.)

46. The sequence in which Satan challenges a young Christian's right to pray appears in numerous variations; narrator Lizzie Davis included it in her version of "Roll Jordan Roll." Compare Dett, *Hampton*, 15; Marsh, *Jubilee Singers*, 212; Odum and Johnson, *NHS*, 42.

47. Horace Clarence Boyer, booklet accompanying Mahalia Jackson, *Gospel, Spirituals and Hymns*, Columbia/Legacy CDs 65594, 1991, 12–13. DISCOGRAPHIES: *Blues and Gospel Records*; *Country Music Sources*, 592; *Gospel Discography*.

48. Brown III: 617–18; Hallowell, *Calhoun*, 6; Odum and Johnson, *NHS*, 129–30; White, *ANFS*, 140–41.

49. For the floater about walking and talking to Jesus down in the graveyard (by the riverside), see Ellen King (b. 1851, MS, 234–35); Brown and Owens, *Toting*, 112; Hallowell, *Calhoun*, 45; Perrow, "South" (1913): 162; Work, *ANSS*, 197.

50. Ex-slaves William Emmons and Adeline White named "Nobody Knows the Trouble I've Seen." The plagiarized text appears in William Warfield's narrative.

51. Shepard combines "Old-Time Religion" and "The Old Ship of Zion." Lucendy Griffen, Rosa L. Pollard, and Will Parker also briefly quoted "Old-Time Religion." Narrators naming it were Wash Armstrong, Anne Broome, Eli Coleman, Albert Cox, Mark Discus, Jerry Eubanks, Hattie Gates, Frankie Goole, Jenny Greer, Shang Harris, Joanna Thompson Isom, Thomas Johns, Robert Laird, Ben Leitner, Ed McCree, William Mead, Mose Moss, Naisy Reece, Susan Dale Sanders, Morgan Scurry, Eva Strayhorn, Lorena Thomas, Bettie Tolbert, Lindsey Moore Turner, Mary Veals, Charley Watson, and Clara White. Coleman, Cox, Greer, and Pollard described the song at baptizings (Greer and Pollard at camp-meeting baptizings); Armstrong, Drake, Griffen, Laird, Leitner, Parker, Sanders, Strayhorn, and Veals recalled it at meetings; Cox and Scurry, in the fields; Goole, at shouts. White had heard the song from her mother, Moss from his parents, Thomas from her grandmother, Tolbert from a slaveholder. Harris, Eubanks, Isom, Johns, McAdams, Mead, Reece, Thomas, and Turner did not specify contexts. Also see Aleckson, *Before the War*, 289; Baldwin, *School-Teacher*, 72; Brown III: 674; Cohen, *Ozark*, 438–40; Dett, *Hampton*, 200; Jackson, *Early*, 218; Jackson, *WNS*, 179, 184–85; Johnson, *Spirituals* I: 76–77; Kennedy, *More Mellows*, 15; Marsh, *Jubilee Singers*, 158; McDonald, *Virginia*, 282; Odum and Johnson, *NHS*, 142–44; Perrow, "South" (1913): 148; Randolph, *OFS* IV: 66–67; Rosenberg, *Virginia*, 97; White, *ANFS*, 91–92; Work, *ANSS*, 99. RECORDINGS: Heavenly Gospel Singers, "Old-Time Religion" (Bluebird B8077, 1939); Lead Belly, "Old Time Religion," Washington, DC, August 1940, *Go Down Old Hannah*, Rounder CD 1099, 1994; Tuskegee Institute Singers, "The Old Time Religion" (Victor 18075, 1916). DISCOGRAPHIES: *Blues and Gospel Records*; *Country Music Records*; *Country Music Sources*, 583; *Gospel Discography*.

52. For another version of this joke, see J. Mason Brewer, *The Word on the Brazos: Negro Preacher Tales from the Brazos Bottoms of Texas* (1953; rpt. Austin: University of Texas Press, 1976), 45–46.

53. This stanza is known mainly from the gospel song "You Got to Take Sick and Die," probably the source of Davis's version. McKinley Morganfield (Muddy Waters), "You Got to Take Sick and Die Some of These Days," field rec., Clarksdale, MS, July 1942, *The Complete Plantation Recordings*, Chess CD 9344; Boyd Rivers, "You Gonna Take Sick and Die," field rec., Pickens, MS, October 1980, *Living Country Blues: An Anthology*, Evidence CDs 26105,

1999. Muddy Waters later reused the verse in his composition "Diamonds at Your Feet" (Chess 1630, 1956).

54. Odum and Johnson, *NHS*, 93–94.

55. Rev. W. B. Allen, Abbie Lindsay, Lu Perkins, Susan Ross, Morgan Scurry, and Mollie Williams gave texts of "You Can Have All This World But Give Me Jesus." Charley Mitchell and William Davis named it. George Pullen Jackson traced this piece to "an individually composed gospel hymn of the Sunday-School sort" first published in the *Wesleyan Psalmist* (1842). He further reports that "the editors of *Slave Songs* rejected it as 'spurious,' that is, of white origin," but that "subsequent collectors of negro songs have accepted it . . . as a product of the black race." Jackson, *WNS*, 180–81; also *Slave Songs*, vi (n). As it exists in oral tradition, the song is in fact almost entirely of Black provenience, dating to the end of the war, and has been completely transformed into a Black folksong (though some slaves apparently knew the earlier white Sunday-school song). See Albert, *Charlotte Brooks*, 93; Ballanta, *St. Helena*, 79; Coppin, *History*, 53–54; Johnson, *Spirituals* I: 160–61; Marsh, *Jubilee Singers*, 140; McIlhenny, *Spirituals*, 115–16; Odum and Johnson, *NHS*, 93–94; Perkins, "Spirituals," 225; Work, *ANSS*, 80. Compare Parrish, *Sea Islands*, 240–41.

56. Early recordings include Big Bethel Choir, "Hand Me Down the Silver Trumpet, Gabriel" (Victor 20498, 1927); Chattahoochie Valley Choir, "Hand Me Down the Silver Trumpet Gabriel" (Columbia 14249-D, 1927); Sunset Four Jubilee Quartet, "Hand Me Down the Silver Trumpet" (Herwin 92008, 1925). DISCOGRAPHIES: *Blues and Gospel Records*; *Country Music Sources*, 598. In 1928 Mary Virginia Bales described young Blacks in Hearn, Texas, singing "O Hand Me Down De Silber Trumpet, Gabriel" at a party where they also banged out jazz on a piano to accompany "a mad frenzy of wild dances and songs." Bales, "Negro Folk-Songs," 96–97.

57. White, *ANFS*, 132.

58. The Heavenly Gospel Singers, "So High I Can't Get Over" (Bluebird B7486, 1938); St. Mark's Chanters, "So High" (Columbia 14198-D, 1926); Sunset Four Jubilee Quartette, "You Must Come in at the Door" (Paramount 12314, 1925); Wiseman Quartet, "You Must Come in at the Door" (Victor 19119, 1923); Union Jubilee Quartet, "My Lawd Is So High You Can't Go Over Him," field rec., Silent Grove Baptist Church, Clarksdale, MS, July 1942, *Negro Religious Field Recordings*, Document CD 5312. White versions include Sons of the Pioneers, "You Must Come in at the Door" (OKeh 04187, 1937); V. O. Stamps–M. L. Yandell, "You Must Come in at the Door" (Victor 21722, 1928). Also see DISCOGRAPHIES: *Country Music Sources*, 603; *Gospel Discography*.

59. Elvis Presley (with the Imperials Quartet), "So High," *How Great Thou Art*, RCA LP 3758, 1966; LaVerne Baker, "So High, So

Low" (Atlantic 45-2033, 1959); Doc Watson, "You Must Come In At the Door," *Rare Performances: 1982–1993*, Vestapol DVD 13024, 2002.

Singing Games

1. "Chick-A-Ma, Craney Crow" is a popular English singing game (see note 7). "William Trimbletoe" is actually a counting-out rhyme, but often precedes a guessing game of the same name, both documented among African American children from the 1800s. Tempie Cummins also gave a version: "W'en I was a chile we play all kinds 'r' games. We likes t' ketch d' lightnin' bugs an' put dem in bottles. We uster play 'William Trimbletoe,' an' sing: / William Trimbletoe, / He a good fisherman; / He ketch his hens, / An' put dem in pens. / Some lay eggs / An some lay none" (Tempie Cummins, b. ca. 1862, TX, 1009–10). Dink Walton Young named it. Also see W. H. Babcock, "Song-Games and Myth-Dramas at Washington," *Lippincott's* 37 (March 1886): 252; Henry Carrington Bolton, *The Counting-Out Rhymes of Children: A Study in Folk-Lore* (New York: D. Appleton, 1888), 117–18; Brown I: 134–37, 160–61; "Games" (*SW*), 86; Mellinger E. Henry, "Nursery Rhymes and Game-Songs from Georgia," *JAF* 47 (1934): 337; Jones and Hawes, *Step It Down*, 153–54; Killion and Waller, *Georgia*, 219; Newell, *Games*, 203; Perrow, "South" (1913): 141–42. "Puss Wants a Corner," which Maddox also names, is an English non-singing game. Brown I: 151; Gomme, *Games*, II: 88–89.

2. *Unwritten History*, 43.

3. Talley, *NFR*, 142–43.

4. "Games" (SW), 85. For other versions, see Anon. ex-slave, b. unk., TN, *Unwritten History*, 15; Davis, "Folk-Lore," 253; Henry, "Nursery Rhymes," 337; Gomme, *Games* I: 145–46; Newell, *Games*, 171; Perrow, "South" (1913): 140; Scarborough, *TNFS*, 130; Talley, *NFR*, 142–43. Ex-slave Jane McLeod Wilburn also named "Frog in the Middle." Isaac Stier may have been thinking of this item when he stated "us slaves mos'ly sung hymns an' psalms. But I 'member one song 'bout a frog pond an' one 'bout 'Jump Mr. Toad.' I's too wordless to sing 'em now but dey was funny" (Isaac Stier, b. ca. 1857, MS, 2057). The game's "it" is almost always described as a frog, but a turn-of-the-century South Carolina variant has "Mule in the Middle" (Davis, "Folk-Lore," 253).

5. Mary Colbert, Callie Elder, Anna Humphrey, Mary Johnson (SC), and Abe Livingston gave texts of "Molly Bright." Granny Cain, Pet Franks, Dosia Harris, Bert Luster, Jane McLeod Wilburn, and Dink Walton Young named it. Also see W. H. Babcock, "Games of Washington Children," *American Anthropologist* 1 (1888): 280-1; Brown I: 74–78; "Games" (*SW*), 85; Gomme, *Games* I: 231–38; Halliwell, *Nursery Rhymes*, 176; McDowell, *Dances*, 68–69;

Newell, *Games*, 153–54; Solomon, *Daisies*, 205; Talley, *NFR*, 64. Most sources identify "Molly Bright" as a game of chase, but Mary Colbert described it as a counting-out rhyme, Anna Humphrey as a ring game. "Another game was played to the counting-out rhyme that started: 'Mollie, Mollie Bright, threescore and ten'" (Mary Colbert, b. 1854, GA, 222). "I did use to play a game called 'Molly Bright.' We'd catch hands and then go 'round and 'round and sing: / How far from here to Molly / Bright? / Threescore and ten / If I can get there by candlelight / Legs long light" (Anna Humphrey, b. 1849 or '50, AL, 1827).

6. Gomme, *Games* I: 137–39; Jones and Hawes, *Step It Down*, 166; Newell, *Games*, 143.

7. "Chick-A-Ma, Craney Crow" is another English perennial well-known to North America Blacks. Madison Bruin, Mary Colbert, Jack Maddox, and Dinah Perry provided texts, Perry Sid Jemison named it. Bruin, Colbert, and Perry provided game directions, the last most clearly and completely. Also see Arnold, *Alabama*, 136; Babcock, "Games," 283–84; Babcock, "Song-Games and Myth-Dramas," 255–56; Bolton, *Counting-Out Rhymes*, 120, 123; Brown I: 48–55; Davis, *Folk-Songs*, 220; "Games" (*SW*), 86; Gomme, *Games* I: 201–2; Henry, "Nursery Rhymes," 335; Caddie S. Isham, "Games of Danville, VA.," *JAF* 34 (1921): 116; Killion and Waller, *Georgia*, 223–24; Newell, *Games*, 155–58; Randolph, *OFS* III: 382–83; Scarborough, *TNFS*, 138; Susan Showers, "Alabama Folk-Lore," *Southern Workman* 29 (1900): 443; Solomon, *Daisies*, 226; Talley, *NFR*, 63–64.

8. For "King George and His Army," also see "Games" (*SW*), 85; Solomon, *Daisies*, 202.

9. For "I'm in Some Lady's Garden," see Kennedy, *Cameos*, 196; Fauset, "Folk Tales," 303; Owens, *Swing and Turn: Texas Play-Party Games*, Special ed., PTFS (Dallas, 1936), 21; Grace Cleveland Porter, *Negro Folk Singing Games and Folk Games of the Habitants* (London: J. Curwen & Sons, 1913), viii, 10–11; Scarborough, *TNFS*, 131–32, 139–41; Solomon, *Daisies*, 211; Talley, *NFR*, 229.

10. More complete descriptions of the doodle bug game and song were provided by ex-slaves Maggie (Bunny) Bond, Elsiha Doc Garey, Eli Harrison, and Squire Irvin: "All us children had to study about was play and catching doodle bugs. Them bugs lived in the ground. We would get a straw, bait it and stick it in the doodle bug hole. Then we would set there singing, 'doodle bug, doodle bug come get your supper.' When the straw begins to shake, you know you got him. You gives it a jerk and out he comes. It is as much fun for children to catch doodle bugs, as it is for grown ups to catch fish. We played marbles, wrestled, and had games same as children does now" (Squire Irvin, b. 1849, TN, 1086). Fannie Yarborough described another children's singing game based on animal cruelty: "We'd kill snakes and dance and sing that ol' song 'bout 'Hurrah! Mister

Bluecoat, Toodle-O. O, Dat Lady's Beatin' You.' It meant his pardner was beatin' him dancin'" (Fannie Yarborough, b. ca. 1854, TX, 226).

11. This item was apparently fairly popular in Mississippi. Under the title "Brer' Rabbit: Traditional Game and Dance," Grace Cleveland Porter gives a detailed description of the game (without the song) collected "from a Plantation in Mississippi, U.S.A." Porter, *Negro Folk Singing Games*, ix. Alan Lomax later recorded several sung versions at the Coahoma County Agricultural High School: Dorothy Dilworth Barrett, "Hop, Brother Rabbit, In the Pea Vine (#4)," Coahoma, MS, August 10, 1942, archive.culturalequity.org /fieldwork/mississippi-delta-survey-1941-1942/coahoma-842/hop -brother-rabbit-pea-vine-4; E. M. Davis, "Hop, Brother Rabbit, In the Pea Vine (#2)," Coahoma, MS, August 10, 1942, archive .culturalequity.org/fieldwork/mississippi-delta-survey-1941-1942 /coahoma-842/hop-brother-rabbit-pea-vine-2; Ruby Forrest Smith, "Hop, Brother Rabbit, In the Pea Vine (#1)," Coahoma, MS, August 10, 1942, archive.culturalequity.org/fieldwork/mississippi-delta -survey-1941-1942/coahoma-842/hop-brother-rabbit-pea-vine-1; Unidentified girls, "Hop, Brother Rabbit, In the Pea Vine (#3)," Coahoma, MS, August 10, 1942, archive.culturalequity.org /fieldwork/mississippi-delta-survey-1941-1942/coahoma-842/hop -brother-rabbit-pea-vine-3.

12. RECORDINGS: L. M. Abraham, Lloyd Lee Woodward, Alzea Patterson, "Oh Br'r Rabbit Shake It," field rec., Piney Woods School, Jackson, MS, March 1937, *Field Recordings, Vol. 13*, Document CD 5621.

13. Ex-slave James V. Deane also named "London Bridge," for which see Babcock, "Games," 263; Dudley and Payne, "Play-Party," 20–21; "Games" (SW), 85; Halliwell, *Nursery Rhymes*, 98; Jones and Hawes, *Step It Down*, 179–80; Randolph, *OFS* III: 388. Other English-singing games mentioned by ex-slaves included "Old Sweet Beans and Barley Grows" (Dellie Lewis, AL, 246–47), Babcock, "Games," 251–52; Babcock, "Song-Games and Myth-Dramas," 247–48; Gomme, *Games* II: 1–13; Piper, "Play-Party," 273; Solomon, *Daisies*, 213, Spurgeon, *Waltz the Hall*, 146–47; and "Ring Around the Rosie" (Lu Lee, b. 1848 or 1849, TX, 2295), Gomme, *Games* II: 108–11.

14. See, for example, Jones and Hawes, *Step It Down*, 37–40.

Reels and Ring Plays

1. Today the title "Devil's Dream" is usually associated with a Scottish fiddle tune (aka "The Devil Among the Tailors"), but in Black tradition it was applied to various songs and tunes. See The Fiddle, note 53 above.

2. Ex-slave Robert Shepherd also gave a version of "Johnson Gal," which is conceivably of slave origin, but also has minstrel connections. See, for example, the version in Charles C. Shoemaker, *Choice Dialect and Other Characterizations for Reading and Recitation* (1887; rpt. Philadelphia: Penn, 1924), 9–10. Also see Bolick and Russell, *Fiddle Tunes*, 276; *Country Music Sources*, 709; Ford, *Traditional Music*, 34. RECORDINGS: Leake County Revelers, "Johnson Gal" (Columbia 15149-D, 1927).

3. Henry Wright was a fiddler himself but in this case appears to describe unaccompanied dance singing. For other variants of this floating verse, see Ames, "Missouri Play-Party," 300; Bass, "Negro Songs," 429; Kathryn Blair, "Swing Your Partner!" *JAF* 40 (1927): 98; Botkin, *Play Party*, 145, 280–81, 284; Brown III: 30–36, 484, 498, 499; Cohen, *Ozark*, 233–34; Davis, *Folk-Songs*, 174–75; Dudley and Payne, "Play-Party," 33; Odum and Johnson, *NHS*, 191; Perrow, "South" (1915): 136–37, 176–77; Randolph, *OFS* II: 351–52; Randolph, *Roll Me*, 334–35; Solomon, *Daisies*, 94; Talley, *NFR*, 49, 54–55, 207–8; Thede, *Fiddle*, 66–67; White, *ANFS*, 323–24.

4. While ring plays and reels invariably denoted dancing accompanied by singing (maybe with instruments, maybe without), ex-slaves were characteristically casual in their use of these and similar terms. For some narrators, *ring plays* and *reels* were synonyms; for others, ring plays were for children, reels for adults; for still others reels were sinful, ring plays benign, and so forth. Ex-slaves only rarely used the term *play-party*, but a few did, and many of the dances and dance songs known to ex-slaves are elsewhere called play-parties.

5. This ubiquitous wandering stanza can be extended ad infinitum by substituting other characters and characteristics for the "mistus" and her bald head. See Henry Wright and note 3 above.

6. Related to the familiar "Little Liza Jane," this is another item alternately performed as an unaccompanied ring play and fiddle song; it was also recalled by Lydia Jefferson and Eliza Overton, the last giving instructions: "In ever cab'n thar wuz fiddles an' on Sunday we would have a good time. One of the games we would play out in front of the cab'n was 'Swing-ole Liza single.' This here game wuz play'd by havin' two rows line up an' a man wud dance up or down the line an' swing each one. We wud all sing an' pat our hans an' feet ta keep time for the dance" (Eliza Overton, b. 1849, MO, 267). Also see Bolick and Austin, *Mississippi Fiddle*, 159; Killion and Waller, *Georgia*, 235–36; Lomax, *FSNA*, 501; Solomon, *Daisies*, 209.

7. Lucy Lewis and her husband, Cinto Lewis, both recalled "High Heel Shoes and Calico Stockings" from Cinto's fiddle repertoire; I have not found the title elsewhere. For "Bob White," see Talley, *NFR*, 134.

8. "Sally Goodin (Goodun, Gooden, Goodwin)" ranks among the best-known Anglo-American fiddle songs. Henry Lewis McGaffey named it as a fiddle tune (Woods also mentioned fiddles). Also see *Appalachian Fiddle*, 21; Bolick and Austin, *Mississippi Fiddle*, 173, 234, 272, 395; Bolick and Russell, *Fiddle Tunes*, 160,

240–43; Brown III: 119–20; Cohen, *Ozark*, 403–4; Davis, *Folk-Songs*, 249–50; Ford, *Traditional*, 64, 419–20; Lomax, *FSNA*, 236; McDowell, *Dances*, 75; Randolph, *OFS* III: 350–51; Randolph, *Roll Me*, 411–12; Rosenberg, *Virginia*, 111; Solomon, *Daisies*, 98; Thede, *Fiddle*, 32–33. DISCOGRAPHIES: *Country Music Records*; *Country Music Sources*, 766–68.

9. Harris, *Remus*, 193–94. For other versions, see Brown III: 119–20; Browne, *Alabama*, 429–30; Botkin, *Play-Party*, 33; Cohen, *Ozark*, 219–20; Ford, *Traditional*, 31; Lomax, *Country*, 58–59; Lomax, *FSNA*, 228–29; *Old-Time String Band*, 64–65; Perrow, "South" (1915): 184; Randolph, *OFS* II: 323; Talley, *NFR*, 227; Thede, *Fiddle*, 100. DISCOGRAPHIES: *Country Music Records*.

10. Arnold, *Alabama*, 38. For "Sally Ann," also see Botkin, *Play-Party*, 92–93; Sharp, *EFSS* II: 351. DISCOGRAPHIES: *Country Music Records*; *Country Music Sources*, 768–69.

11. *Appalachian Fiddle*, 100, 127; Bolick and Austin, *Mississippi Fiddle*, 72, 210; Bolick and Russell, *Fiddle Tunes*, 291; Botkin, *Play-Party*, 293; Davis, "Plantation Party," 59; Ford, *Traditional*, 85, 399; Halliwell, *Nursery Rhymes*, 83; Perrow, "South" (1913): 138; Wolford, *Play-Party*, 230. RECORDINGS: Sonny Boy Williamson, "Polly Put Your Kettle On" (Victor 20–2521, 1947); Gid Tanner & His Skillet Lickers, "Molly Put the Kettle On" (Columbia 15746-D, 1931). DISCOGRAPHIES: *Country Music Records*; *Country Music Sources*, 709.

12. Brown III: 130; Cohen, *Ozark*, 408–9; Davis, *Folk-Songs*, 251; Ford, *Traditional*, 412; Emelyn E. Gardner, "Some Play-Party Games in Michigan," JAF 33 (1920): 119; Gomme, *Games*, II: 63–64; Linscott, *New England*, 107–8; Randolph, *OFS* III: 368–69; Randolph, *Roll Me*, 413–15; Spurgeon, *Waltz the Hall*, 155; Florence Warnick, "Play-Party Songs in Western Maryland," JAF 54 (1941): 164–65; Wolford, *Play-Party*, 231–32. RECORDINGS: Cuje Bertram (fiddle, vocal), "Pop Goes the Weasel," home rec., Indianapolis, ca. 1970, *Black Fiddlers*. DISCOGRAPHIES: *Country Music Records*; *Country Music Sources*, 815–16.

13. The transcript suggests a serious typographic miscommunication, but obviously Thomas was describing an enclave of German *Catholics* (not *Cat holies*) who allowed square dancing, in contrast to the county's Protestant majority, who permitted only play-parties. For discussion, texts, and references for "Skip to My Lou" and "Weevily Wheat," see Botkin, *Play-Party*, 314–16, 345–51; Spurgeon, *Waltz the Hall*, 174–75, 200–203; *Country Music Sources*, 112, 115. RECORDINGS: Lead Belly, "Skip to My Lou," New York, 1948, *Shout On*, Smithsonian/Folkways CD 40105, 1998. Botkin's book remains the definitive study of the play-party, originally completed as his doctoral dissertation not long before he assumed his duties on the ex-slave narratives.

14. "Pretty Little Pink," which imitates marching soldiers, is often (as here) identified with the War of 1812. It appears barely known to Blacks, though there is another ex-slave version in the Fisk collection: Anon. ex-slave (b. unk., TN), *Unwritten History*, 15–16. For white versions, see Brown III: 110–12; Botkin, *Play-Party*, 296–97; Davis, *Folk-Songs*, 219–20; Henry, "More Songs from the Southern Highlands," 89–90; James Mooney, "Folk-Lore of the North Carolina Mountains," *JAF* 2 (1889): 104; Newell, *Games*, 245; Randolph, *OFS* III: 296–97; Sandburg, *Songbag*, 166; Spurgeon, *Waltz the Hall*, 140–41; Warnick, "Play-Party Songs in Maryland," 163–64. RECORDINGS: Bradley Kincaid, "Pretty Little Pink" (Supertone 9666, 1929). DISCOGRAPHIES: *Country Music Records*; *Country Music Sources*, 115.

15. "Coffee Grows on White Oak Trees" is mainly white but regularly noted among Blacks. An 1886 source prints a text recalled from Mississippi slaves ("Carmina Africana," 10); R. Emmet Kennedy later collected the piece in South Louisiana. Kennedy, *Black Cameos*, 197. Thomas Talley gives a Middle Tennessee text retitled "Coffee Grows on White Folks' Trees." Talley, *NFR*, 91–92. For white examples, see Botkin, *Play-Party*, 164–69; Brown III: 110–12; Dudley and Payne, "Play-Party," 21–22; Lila W. Edmands, "Songs from the Mountains of North Carolina," *JAF* 6 (1893): 131–32; Hudson, *Mississippi*, 301; McDowell, *Folk Dances*, 36–39; Morris, *Florida*, 205–6; Owens, *Swing and Turn*, 37–38; Perrow, "South" (1915): 187; Randolph, *OFS* III: 309–10; Spurgeon, *Waltz the Hall*, 86–87; Wolford, *Play-Party*, 161–63.

16. *Appalachian Fiddle*, 55; Blair, "Swing Your Partner!" 97–98; Bolick and Austin, *Mississippi Fiddle*, 37, 80, 83, 93, 147, 382–83; Bolick and Russell, *Fiddle Tunes*, 84; Botkin, *Play-Party*, 235–42; Brown III: 522; Davis, *Folk-Songs*, 241; Dudley and Payne, "Play-Party," 31–32; Edmands, "Songs from the Mountains," 134; Henry, *Highlands*, 430–33; Mckee and Chisenhall, *Beale Black and Blue*, 189; McNeil, *Folksongs*, 174–76; Perrow, "South" (1915): 178–80; Randolph, *OFS* III: 183–85; Randolph, *Roll Me*, 455–58; Rosenberg, *Virginia*, 31; Sandburg, *Songbag*, 308–9; Scarborough, *TNFS*, 7–8, 169; Sharp *EFSSA* II: 356; Solomon, *Daisies*, 99; Talley, *NFR*, 115–16, 221–22; Thede, *Fiddle*, 44–45; Thomas, *Devil's Ditties*, 29–30, 91–93; Titon, *Fiddle Tunes*, 123–24; White, *ANFS*, 172–74. RECORDINGS: Pete Harris (vocal, guitar), "Square Dance Calls (Little Liza Jane)," field rec., Richmond, TX, May 1934, *Black Texicans*. DISCOGRAPHIES: *Country Music Records*; *Country Music Sources*, 516–17. Also see Dan Gutstein, *Poor Gal: The Cultural History of Little Liza Jane* (Jackson: University Press of Mississippi, 2023).

17. Ames, "Missouri Play-Party," 308–9; Ball, "Play Party in Idaho," 14; Botkin, *Play-Party*, 154–59; *Country Music Sources*, 113; Ford, *Traditional*, 120, 423; Gardner, "Play-Party Games in Michigan," 95; Lester S. Levy, *Flashes of Merriment: A Century of Humorous Songs in America* (Norman: University of Oklahoma Press, 1971), 343–47; List, *Indiana*, 133–37; Owens, *Swing and Turn*, 89–90; Piper, "Play-Party," 285; Randolph, *OFS* III: 354–56; Rosenberg, *Virginia*,

14; Solomon, *Daisies*, 155; Spaeth, *More*, 47–48; Spurgeon, *Waltz the Hall*, 80–82; Wolford, *Play-Party*, 159–61, 279–80.

18. Handy, *Father*, 5–6; Wolfe and Lornell, *Life and Legend of Leadbelly*, 16–17. For other versions, see Arnold, *Alabama*, 103; Brown III: 544; Henry, *Highlands*, 437; Lomax, *Ballads*, 237; *Old-Time String Band*, 63; Randolph, *Roll Me*, 452; Solomon, *Daisies*, 218; White, *ANFS*, 271. RECORDINGS: Arthur "Brother-in-Law" Armstrong (vocal, guitar), "Johnny Got a Meat Skin Laid Away," field rec., Jaspar, TX, 1940, *Field Recordings, Volume 6*, Document CD 5580. DISCOGRAPHIES: *Country Music Record*; *Country Music Sources*, 533.

19. On the hack-a-back, also see Davis, "Negro Folklore," 252–53; Olmsted, *Back Country*, 146; Wyeth, *Sabre*, 60 n1.

20. See Arnold, *Alabama*, 127; Ball, "Play-Party in Idaho," 11; Bolick and Austin, *Mississippi Fiddle*, 103, 127, 199, 289; Botkin, *Play-Party*, 150–54; Brown III: 114; *Country Music Sources*, 754–55; Christy, *Plantation Melodies*, 45–46; Davis, *Folk-Songs*, 243; Ford, *Traditional*, 53, 409; Lomax, *Ballads*, 288–90; Owens, *Texas*, 159; Piper, "Play-Party," 285–86; Randolph, *OFS* III: 332–34; Randolph, *Roll Me*, 424–25; Scarborough, *TNFS*, 112–14; Spaeth, *More*, 107–8; Spurgeon, *Waltz the Hall*, 76–77; Thede, *Fiddle*, 119; Titon, *Fiddle Tunes*, 55; Carl Van Doren, "Some Play-Party Songs from Eastern Illinois," *JAF* 32 (1919): 487; Wolford, *Play-Party*, 227. RECORDINGS: James Campbell's Friendly Five, "Buffalo Gal," field rec., Nashville, TN, October 25, 1962, *Blind James Campbell and His Nashville Street Band*, Arhoolie CD 438, 1995; Corney Allen Grier, "Alabama Gal" (Decca 7296, 1937). DISCOGRAPHIES: *Country Music Records*; *Country Music Sources*, 754–55. Besides the ex-slave versions quoted here, Texas fieldworker Effie Cowan included a text in the narrative of John Majors, but most of this appears to be Cowan's invention.

21. Cauthen, *Fiddle*, 13–14.

22. Randolph, *Roll Me*, 424–25.

23. See Cohen, *Minstrels and Tunesmiths*, 32–34; *Country Music Sources*, 502.

24. Botkin, *Play Party*, 322–28; Brown III: 517–18; Cohen, *Ozark*, 409–10; Dudley and Payne, "Play-Party," 12–13; Odum and Johnson, *Workaday*, 167; Owens, *Swing and Turn*, 94; Randolph, *OFS* II: 356; Sandburg, *Songbag*, 141; Scarborough, *TNFS*, 107–8; Solomon, *Daisies*, 175–76; Talley, *NFR*, 65, 217–18; White, *ANFS*, 281–82. RECORDINGS: Gus Cannon (vocal, banjo), "Ain't Gonna Rain No More," *Walk Right In*, Stax LP 702, 1963; Eight unidentified girls, "Ain't Gonna Rain No More," field rec., Atmore, AL, October 1934, *Lullabies to Blues*; John Snipes (vocal, banjo), "Snow a Little, Rain a Little," field rec., Orange Co., NC, 1974–76, *North Carolina Banjo*.

25. Ex-slaves Sarah Ford, Joseph Holmes, Martha Richardson, and William Henry Towns also gave examples.

26. White, *ANFS*, 243.

27. Bass, "Negro Songs," 425.

28. White, *ANFS*, 230.

29. Perrow, "South" (1913), 128–29.

30. Scarborough, *TNFS*, 107.

31. Arnold, *Alabama*, 121.

32. More often in this floating stanza, a frog (bullfrog, tadpole) is on the way to a frolic with a fiddle on his back. The verse is known almost entirely from Black sources and is probably of slave origin. See Brown III: 201, for a variant noted in Watauga Co., NC, ca. 1913, described as "'dance song—fiddle and banjo,' known to have been sung and played there 'nearly eighty years ago' [that is, ca. 1830]." Also see Anon. ex-slave (b. unk., TN), *Unwritten History*, 16; Bass, "Negro Songs," 425; Bolick and Austin, *Mississippi Fiddle*, 178; Browne, *Alabama*, 453; Perrow (1913): 133; Talley, *NFR*, 32–33; White, *ANFS*, 242–43. RECORDINGS: Jimmie Strothers (vocal, banjo), "Jaybird," field rec., Lynn, VA, June 1936, *Virginia and the Piedmont*.

33. Browne, *Alabama*, 448. RECORDINGS: Nathan Frazier (banjo, vocal), Frank Patterson (fiddle), "Old Cow Died," field rec., Nashville, TN, March 1942, *Altamont*.

34. "Games" (*SW*), 85.

35. Talley, *NFR*, 197–98.

36. "Red Morroco" (orig. misspelling) and "Reel er Reel" are from the Ruby Pickens Tartt WPA Collection of Afro-American Folk Songs from Sumter County, Alabama, 1937–39, completed at the same time Tartt was conducting ex-slave interviews. "Red Morroco" was performed by Ophelia Hudson, "Reel er Reel" by Florida Hampton. Solomon, *Daisies*, 213. Around this same time, Tartt and John Lomax also recorded "Gourd of Cold Water" (their title) from Hampton, Hettie Godfrey, and Rich Amerson. *Blues and Gospel Records*. These recordings have not been officially released, but Florida Hampton's version has been posted on youtube and elsewhere. Tartt also described the Hampton session in a family letter and gave another variant text: "Next day we got a dandy record from Florida Hampton who, after singing spirituals, started on a reel. / Roola-roola-roolover, gimme a gourd of drink-water (*repeat*). / Ole cow suppin in the cool water, gimme a gourd of drink-water." Brown and Owens, *Toting*, 28 (orig. parentheses and emphasis). In the 1960s Alan Lomax taught a version of the song to Bessie Jones and the Sea Island Singers (his source is unclear). Bessie Jones and group, "Reg'lar, Reg'lar, Rollin' Under," *Georgia Sea Island Songs*, 1977; New World Records CD 80278. Also see Alan Lomax, booklet accompanying *Georgia Sea Island Songs*, 18–19.

37. Arthur Armstrong (guitar, vocal), "Buzzard Song (Old King Buzzard)," field rec., Jasper, TX, 1940, *Black Texicans*. Armstrong's musical arrangement is probably his own, but is in any case unrelated to the usual tune for "The Old Cow Died."

38. Scarborough, *TNFS*, 193. Compare Morris, *Florida*, 196: "So said the buzzard when he got mad, / 'That old cow dies I'll be glad; / Light down on her, and her eyes I'll pull, / Let it be a heifer, or let it be a bull.'"

39. Scarborough, *TNFS*, 131.

Worksongs

1. Shang Harris (b. ca. 1840, GA, 119–20) gave another text of this field song, for which also see Brown III: 243–44; Solomon, *Daisies*, 27, 233; White, *ANFS*, 285.

2. This is a unique version of Tale-Type 1735C, "The Bribed Boy Sings the Wrong Song," a popular European cantefable well known to Anglo- and African Americans. Ralph Steele Boggs, "North Carolina White Folktales and Riddles," *JAF* 47 (1934): 311; Fauset, "Folk Tales," 225; Herbert Halpert, "Cante Fables," *Hoosier Folklore Bulletin* 1 (1942): 5–8; Herbert Halpert, "The Cante Fable in New Jersey," *JAF* 55 (1942): 142–43; Johnson, *Folk Culture*, 141–42; Smiley, "Folk-Lore," 366–67.

3. For overviews of African American worksongs, see Norm Cohen, "Worksongs: A Demonstration Collection of Examples," *Songs About Work: Essays in Occupational Culture for Richard A. Reuss*, ed. Archie Green. Special Publications of the Folklore Institute No. 3 (Bloomington, 1993), 332–55; Courlander, *NFS*, 80–122; Epstein, *Sinful*, 161–83; Hinson, *Virginia Work Songs*; Lomax, *Ballads*, 3–86; Lomax, *Country*, 348–404; Odum and Johnson, *Workaday*, 88–134; Parrish, *Sea Islands*, 197–252; Roberts, *Black Music*, 28–29, 67–68, 123–26, 140–49; Scarborough, *TNFS*, 206–37; Thomas, "Work-Songs," 154–80; White, *ANFS*, 250–310.

4. Rosa Tims (b. unk., LA), Cade, "Ex-Slaves," 321.

5. Douglass, *My Bondage*, 97.

6. For southeastern rowing songs, see Bremer, *Homes* I: 385; Castelnau, "Florida," 243; Epstein, *Sinful*, 166–72; Forten, "Sea Islands. Part I," 588; Forten, "Part II," 669–70; Gilman, *Recollections*, 76–77, 121–22; Hungerford, *Plantation*, 183–85; Kemble, *Journal*, 162–63, 259–61; Kennard, "National Poets," 338–39; Leigh, *Georgia Plantation*, 171–74; Malet, *Errand*, 114–15; Nathanson, "Negro Minstrelsy," 76–77; Pearson, *Letters*, 19, 134; Schoolcraft, *Gauntlet*, 27; *Slave Songs*, 1–61; Whipple, *Diary*, 33–34.

7. Throughout the 1800s, many US cities—New Orleans, Charleston, New York, Philadelphia—were famous for Black street vendors' songs, represented in the narratives by a single secondhand reference. "Lord, have mercy, I never hear tell of crabs en shrimps in all my life till my daddy come back en tell bout a old woman would be gwine down de street, dere to Charleston, cryin' 'Shrimps, more shrimps.' But, my Lord, I can' half remember nothin dese days" (Heddie Davis, b. 1866, child of ex-slaves, SC, 255). See *City Cries: Or, A Peep at Scenes in Town*; Creecy, *Scenes*, 39; *The Cries of New-York*; *Gumbo Ya-Ya*, 27–49; "Philadelphia Street Characters," *Harper's Weekly* 20 (April 8, 1876): 292, 294; "The Street-Cries of New York," 199–204; "Southern Cabins. III," 765–66. For singing by industrial slaves, see Bremer, *Homes*, 2: 509–10 (tobacco factory, VA, 1850); Bryant, "Old South" 25–26 (tobacco factory, VA, 1843); Venable, "Down South," 490 (iron works, KY, 1857). A handful of ex-slaves interviewed by the WPA had worked in mines, foundries, factories, and mills, before and after freedom, but none mentioned music, singing, or songs.

8. "Tea in the kettle" and "my old missus promised me" are floaters found in numerous lyrics. White's third example is variously localized: "Grandpa said he walked every step of the way from old Virginia to Mississippi. Grandpa loved Virginia long as he had breath in him. We used to sing / Old Virginia nigger say he love hot mush; / Alabama nigger say, good God, nigger, hush. (She sang it very fast and in a fashion Negroes only can do—ed.)" (Charlotte Willis, b. ca. 1875, MS, child of ex-slaves, 198, orig. parentheses). Talley, *NFR*, 100, has "Alabammer Nigger say he love mush. / Tennessee Nigger say: 'Good Lawd, hush!'"

9. Andrew Jackson Jarnagin (b. 1853, MS, 1130) also gave the "white-man-gets-the-money" stanza, for which see Bolick and Austin, *Mississippi Fiddle*, 330; Brown III: 548–49; Harris, *Remus*, 197; Lomax, *Ballads*, 233; Lomax, *FSNA*, 508; Scarborough, *TNFS*, 165, 228; White, *ANFS*, 382, 455. RECORDINGS: Bob Wills & His Texas Playboys, "Take Me Back to Tulsa" (OKeh 6101, 1941).

10. Also see Bass, "Negro Songs," 432; Brown III: 243; Hurston, *Mules*, 81; Lomax, *Ballads*, 234; Perrow, "South" (1915), 140; Puckett, *Beliefs*, 73; Scarborough, *TNFS*, 228; Talley, *NFR*, 172; Thomas, "Work-Songs," 172; White, *ANFS*, 383.

11. Long, *Slavery*, 197.

12. Kemble, *Journal*, 164.

13. This passage concludes a lengthy account of the slaveholder's misadventure and the creation of this song. For a similar anecdote, see Fannie Berry (b. 1841, VA, 40–41).

14. Philip Henry Gosse, *Letters from Alabama (U.S.)* (London: Morgan and Chase, 1859), 62–63. RECORDINGS: Willie Williams, "Calling Hogs," field rec., State Penitentiary, Richmond, VA, May 1936, *Field Recordings, Volume 12*, Document CD 5614. FILMS: *Hush Hoggies Hush: Tom Johnson's Praying Pigs*, dir. Bill Ferris and Judie Peiser (Center for Southern Folklore, 1978).

15. For other water calls, see Brown and Owens, *Toting*, 28; Perrow, "South" (1913): 171. RECORDINGS: Lead Belly, "Bring Me A L'il Water Silvy," Wilton, CT, March 1935, *Nobody Knows the Trouble I've Seen*, Rounder CD 1098, 1994.

16. Compare Davis, *Folk-Songs*, 319.

17. For "Grasshopper Sittin' on a Sweet Tater Vine," see Bolick and Austin, *Mississippi Fiddle*, 76; Brown III: 450; Scarborough, *TNFS*, 200; Talley, *NFR*, 147. For "All the Varmints in the Woods," see Brown III: 214; White, *ANFS*, 239. For owls (including shivering owls) as death omens, see Brown VII: 64–67.

18. Snyder quotes from a wandering stanza that usually goes "the racoon is a cunning thing. / He walketh in the dark, / And never thinks to curl his tail / Till he hears old Ranger bark" (Brown III: 208). Also see Bolick and Austin, *Mississippi Fiddle*, 302–303; Brown III: 499; Scarborough, *TNFS*, 167; Talley, *NFR*, 149–50, 190–91; White, *ANFS*, 233, 235, 238. RECORDINGS: Henry Truvillion, "Old Aunt Dinah," field rec., October 1940, Burkeville, TX, *Black Texicans*.

19. Melissa (Lowe) Barden, Dora Franks, Henry Lewis, and Mollie Watson also mentioned the singing game "Shoo Fly." Also see Botkin, *Play-Party*, 304–8; *Country Music Sources*, 472; Davis, *Folk-Songs*, 153; List, *Indiana*, 174–76; Roberts, *Sang Branch*, 176; Scarborough, *TNFS*, 200–201; Solomon, *Daisies*, 224; Spaeth, *Read 'Em*, 63–64; Spurgeon, *Waltz the Hall*, 170–71; Talley, *NFR*, 207–8. Ann Drake (b. 1855, MS, 644) also performed "Come On Boys and Let's Go Hunting." RECORDINGS: Henry Truvillion, "Come On Boys and Let's Go To Huntin'," field rec., October 1940, Burkeville, TX, *Black Texicans*.

20. "Rain Come Wet Me" was first noted from Black rowers in the 1860s. Higginson, "Spirituals," 293; Perrow, "South" (1915): 190; *Slave Songs*, 21–22. It later wandered into a children's rhyme (Brown III: 555) and the dance lyric "Black-Eyed Susie" (Bolick and Austin, *Mississippi Fiddle*, 70, 287; Roberts, *Sang Branch*, 167).

21. Tom Douglas (b. 1847, LA, 195) and William Henry Towns (b. 1854, AL, 409) also gave "Saturday Night and Sunday Too," for which see Brown III: 533; Lomax, *FSNA*, 499–500; Solomon, *Daisies*, 154; White, *ANFS*, 175, 336.

22. Green, *Life of the Rev. Elisha W. Green*, 2–3.

23. Rev. Charles Elliott, *Sinfulness of American Slavery* (Cincinnati: L. Swormstedt & J. H. Power, 1850), 59. Fiddlers are more often reported with coffles. In 1840, a Dr. Bailey wrote from Cincinnati to describe slaves being coffled between steamships. "The procession, while marching from one boat to another, was headed by one of the number, carrying in his hands a *fiddle*, and a *bottle* which appeared to be filled with *whiskey*." "Slavery and the Slave Trade in Ohio," *NASS* 11 (August 20, 1840): 44 (orig. emphasis). For other fiddlers with coffles, see George Washington Carleton, *The Suppressed Book About Slavery!* (New York: Carleton, 1864), 164–65; Ebenezer Davies, *American Scenes, and Christian Slavery* (London: John Snow, 1849), 94; Harriet Beecher Stowe, *Uncle Tom's Cabin*, 2 vols. (1857; rpt. Stowe, *Writings*, vols. 1 & 2), II: 93–94. Also see Epstein, *Sinful*, 148–49, 176–79.

24. Mallard, *Plantation*, 22.

25. Kemble, *Journal*, 164. RECORDINGS: Slim Tartt Group, "I'm Chopping Cotton," field rec., Livingston, AL, May 1939, *Lullabies to Blues*. Narrator Georgina Giwbs (Gibbs) described slaves signing while chopping out potatoes.

26. For other ex-slave descriptions of all-night cotton pickings, see Frolics, Cornshuckings, and Other Occasions for Social Music, note 15 above.

27. This is the earliest attribution of a well-known field song. Bales, "Negro Folk-Songs," 112; Brown III: 238; Jackson, *Dead Man*, 95–97; Lomax, *Ballads*, 242–43. RECORDINGS: James (Iron Head) Baker, "The Grey Goose," field rec., Sugarland, TX, 1934, *Field Recordings, Vol. 6*, Document CD 5580; Washington (Lightnin') and Convict Group, "The Gray Goose," field rec., Darrington State Farm, TX, 1933, *Field Recordings, Vols. 10 & 11*, Document CD 5600; Lead Belly, "Grey Goose," New York, 1946, *Shout On*, Smithsonian/Folkways CD 40105, 1998.

28. "Life and Travel in the Southern States," *Great Republic Monthly* 1 (January 1, 1859): 83.

29. Agricola, "Management," 361 (orig. emphasis).

30. *A Narrative of the Adventures and Escape of Moses Roper, From American Slavery* (Philadelphia: Merrihew and Gunn, 1838), 13.

31. Courlander, *Drum and Hoe*, 116–21; Courlander, "Haiti," 372–77; Jekyll, *Jamaican Song*, 162–63; Nketia, *Music of Africa*, 28–29; Roberts, *Black Music*, 8, 125–26, 133. For another North American example, see Hinson, *Virginia Work Songs*, 3.

32. Ralph, "Dixie," 172.

33. This passage is repeated with abbreviations in another Virginia narrative (George White, b. 1847, VA, 309). Ellis and White had separate interviewers, so this was probably an editor's doing. Internal evidence suggests Ellis's version is the original, and reasonably reliable. The "Watch the Sun" couplet wanders through many Black religious songs; it is first reported during the Civil War but quite likely originated in slavery. Ebenezer Brown described it in the fields, Lorena Thomas in church. Also see Ballanta, *St. Helena*, 58–59; Chase, *Dear Ones*, 126; Dett, *Hampton*, 5; Porter, "Negro Songs," 1; Scarborough, *TNFS*, 229; Solomon, *Daisies*, 179; White, *ANFS*, 73, 119. RECORDINGS: Sophie Wing and group, "All Night Long," field rec., Frederica, GA, June 1935, *Make You Happy*.

34. For "Rango" texts and references, see William Main Doerflinger, *Songs of the Sailor and Lumberman* (New York: Macmillan, 1972), 23–25; Linscott, *New England*, 144–46; Morris, *Florida*, 55–56; Frank Shay, *American Sea Songs and Chanteys* (New York: W. W. Norton, 1948), 50. For roustabouts singing on the Vicksburg riverfront, also see Harris Dickson, "The Way of the Reformer," *Saturday Evening Post* 179 (January 12, 1907): 6; Johnson, *Highways*, 79–80.

35. Mead, *Travels*, 13–14.

36. Gosse, *Letters from Alabama*, 305–6. Compare Stoughton Cooley, "The Mississippi Roustabout," *New England Magazine* 17 (November 1894): 299: "All of their songs consist of rhyming couplets, with a refrain following each line,—the leader lining off in a clear tenor or baritone, the whole crew, or so many of them as are inclined, joining in the chorus." For other accounts of singing by roustabouts and steamboat crews, see "American Every-Day Commerce—No. IV: Steamboats and Steamboating in the Southwest—No. 1," *Dollar Magazine* 8 (July 1851), 4; Bremer, *Homes* II: 174; Brown, "Songs," 620; Hearn, *Levee*, 63–74; Johnson, *Highways*, 79–80; King, *Great South*, 55, 68–69, 257–59; Lanman, *Adventures*, II: 167–68; Mead, *Travels*, 13–14; Olmsted, *Seaboard* II: 19–20, 258–61; Wheeler, *Steamboatin'*, 10–38; Whipple, *Diary*, 81–82. RECORDINGS: Richard Amerson, "Steamboat Days," field rec., Livingston, AL, November 1940, *Lullabies to Blues*; Jim Shores, "Mississippi Sounding Calls," field rec., Greenville, MS, June 1939, *Saints and Sinners*; Jim Henry, "Come Here, Dog, And Get Your Bone," field rec., Parchman Penitentiary, MS, April 1936, *Saints and Sinners*.

37. Dickson, "The Reformer," 7. Compare Cooley, "Mississippi Roustabout," 300.

38. Handy, *Father*, 23–24. For "Hear the Trumpet Sound," also see Owens, *Texas*, 177–78; Randolph, *OFS* II: 366. For spirituals and spiritual parodies on riverboats, see Wheeler, *Steamboatin'*, 67–79. For "Whistling Coon," see *Country Music Sources*, 474; White, *ANFS*, 222.

39. The reference to the boat *Robert E. Lee* dates McCarty's third item to the postwar period. (The first and most famous steamboat *Robert E. Lee*—there were three—was built in 1866.) The final stanza is probably later as well, employing a commonplace found in many twentieth-century blues songs. For other songs about boats, see Wheeler, *Steamboatin'*, 39–58.

40. Thorpe, "Mississippi," 37.

41. Robert Everest, *A Journey Through the United States and Part of Canada* (London: John Chapman, 1855), 90.

42. Olmsted, *Seaboard* II: 209–10.

Minstrelsy

1. On minstrelsy and its folk connections, see Carlin, *Banjo*, esp. 3–5; Kmen, *New Orleans*, 236–45; Nathan, *Dan Emmett*, 32–284; Oliver, *Songsters*, 18–139; Southern, "Black Musicians and Early Minstrelsy," 43–63; Toll, *Blacking Up*, 3–64.

2. Fletcher, *Story*, 62; Philip Graham, *Showboats: The History of an American Institution* (1951; rpt. Austin: University of Texas Press, 1976), 14, 15, 29, 74–75; Kmen, *New Orleans*, 83, 138–39; Ping, "Musical Activities," 146; Toll, *Blacking Up*, 10, 227.

3. Ben E. Bailey, "Music in the Life of a Free Black Man of Natchez," *BPM* 13 (1985): 3–12. Johnson had been manumitted in 1820 by his slaveholder-father, eventually acquiring several slaves himself. An amateur musician and avid concertgoer, he prospered as a barber and businessman until his 1851 murder in a land dispute.

4. Thomas, *Tennessee Slave*, 48–49. On John Diamond (1823–1857), a protégé of P. T. Barnum, also see Carlin, *Banjo*, 104–8.

5. Fletcher, *Story*, 62; Toll, *Blacking Up*, 227. At the turn of the century, the balcony of the Huntsville, AL Opera House "was reported to have had three sections: one for poor whites, one for Negroes, and one for harlots." Cauthen, *Fiddle*, 14.

6. Other ex-slaves recalling dry-land circuses include Henry Bufford, Caleb Craig, Henry Garry, Pen Eubanks, Lee Guidon, Ben Lawson, Adeline Ross Lennox, Lizzie Luckado, and George Robertson. For other accounts of slaves attending circuses, see Ingraham, *Sunny South*, 425–26; Thomas, *Tennessee Slave*, 48–49, 52.

7. Bailey, "Free Black Man," 5. On circuses and minstrelsy, also see Abbott and Seroff, *Out of Sight*, 373–80; Carlin, *Banjo*, 12–14, 55–63, 93–94, 102–8; Eric Lott, *Love and Theft: Blackface Minstrelsy and the American Working Class* (New York: Oxford University Press, 1993), 24–25, 112–13; Nathan, *Dan Emmett*, 50–142; Oliver, *Songsters*, 78–108; Alexander Saxton, "Blackface Minstrelsy," *Inside the Minstrel Mask*, 68–69; Southern, "Black Musicians and Early Minstrelsy," 45; Wittke, *Tambo and Bones*, 34–37.

8. On the *Banjo*, see Graham, *Showboats*, 23–24, 29 n1, 37, 197; Ralph Keeler, "Three Years As a Negro Minstrel," *Atlantic* 24 (July 1869): 85; Wittke, *Tambo and Bones*, 227.

9. On minstrel adaptations of "Uncle Tom's Cabin," see Abbott and Seroff, *Out Of Sight*, esp. 54, 96–97, 132–34, 236, 251–53, 279–83, 368, 426–28; Fletcher, *Story*, 50–51, 53–54, 71, 74; Graham, *Showboats*, 71, 108, 114, 118, 137–38; Simond, *Old Slack*, 30; Toll, *Blacking Up*, 88–97; Marian Hannah Winter, "Juba and American Minstrelsy," *Inside the Minstrel Mask*, 235–36; Wittke, *Tambo and Bones*, 61, 143–44. On "East Lynn(e)," see Graham, *Showboats*, 150, 180–82; Simond, *Old Slack*, 31. On "Ten Nights in a Barroom," see Graham, *Showboats*, 93–94, 127, 153–55. (Simond, *Old Slack*, 31, cites a parody, "Ten Bar Rooms in One Night.")

10. "Negro Minstrels and Their Dances," *New York Herald*, August 11, 1895, qtd. Stearns, *Dance*, 47. Also see Nathan, *Dan Emmett*, 75–76; Graham, *Showboats*, 31; Keeler, "Three Years," 81; Toll, *Blacking Up*, 44–45; Winter, "Juba," 232–33; Wittke, *Tambo and Bones*, 88–89, 223, 227. In his dance Reed performed "certain comical and characteristic movements of the hands, by placing his elbows near his hips and extending the rest of his arms at right angles to his body, with the palms of the hands down," movements "very similar to the Congo pose of the Buzzard Lope and Ring Shout." Stearns, *Dance*, 47. It is entirely credible, then, that Reed's routine fairly represented the Black roustabouts described by George Taylor Burns.

11. On Rice, see Graham, *Showboats*, 34–36, 38–39; Marie Ward Brown, *The Life of Dan Rice* (Long Branch, NJ: author, 1901).

12. "Dan Rice, Clown, Dead," *New York Sun,* February 22, 1900; rpt. Brown, *Dan Rice*, 251.

13. Graham, *Showboats*, 34.

14. The narrative of ex-slave Will Long purports to describe working and performing on Mississippi showboats, including detailed accounts of showboat magnate Augustus Byron French (1833–1902), his flagship the *New Sensation*, and French's associate Captain Wiley Preston McNair. Long's narrative, however, was produced by Ada Davis, a habitual fraud and plagiarist, and I suspect that most of it comes from secondary sources. On French, the *New Sensation*, and McNair, however, see Graham, *Showboats*, 40–77, 91–93, 117–19, 198.

15. Eileen Southern, "The Georgia Minstrels: The Early Years," 1989; rpt. *Inside the Minstrel Mask*, 163–75; Toll, *Blacking Up*, 198–99.

16. In his memoir, Black minstrel Ike "Old Slack" Simond ("Banjo comique") (1847–ca. 1891) gives a vivid description of the early 1870s, when "the steamboats on both the Ohio and Mississippi rivers" were "a good graft for the colored musical people; all the large boats had a concert party on board." Simond, *Old Slack*, 6.

17. Abbott and Seroff, *Out of Sight*, 373–80; Southern, *Music*, 252, 295.

18. On Billy Kersands and Richard & Pringle's Georgia Minstrels, see Abbott and Seroff, *Out of Sight*, 106–10; Toll, *Blacking Up*, 214–15, 254–61. On the Nashville Student groups (none based in Nashville or featuring students), see Abbott and Seroff, *Out of Sight*, 170–76; Southern, *Music*, 295. On the Barlow Brothers' Minstrels, see Abbott and Seroff, *Out of Sight*, 233, 447; Wittke, *Tambo and Bones*, 154–55.

19. On the early Hampton Singers, see *Cabin I*. On J. N. Wainwright, see Abbott and Seroff, *Out of Sight*, 45.

20. Toll, *Blacking Up*, 238, also 236–43.

21. *Nkana mu Ncema* (Ibanj, Democratic Republic of Congo: American Presbyterian Mission, 1909), 9. (Rev. and enl. ed. of Lucy G. Sheppard, *Masamba wa Nzambi*, n.d.) Presbyterian Historical Society, Pearl Digital Collection, digital.history.pcusa.org/islandora/object/islandora: 15798#page/1/mode1up. Like most of the selections in Sheppard's hymnal, the piece Mary Anngady knew as "How Firm a Foundation" appears to be a newly authored Bakuba text merely set to the tune of a familiar hymn. This particular item is credited to Sheppard herself under her native name (*Xepate*). Ex-slaves Aron Carter and Dempsey Pitts also knew "How Firm a Foundation" (in English). Also see Ira Dworkin, "'In the country of my forefathers': Pauline E. Hopkins, William H. Sheppard, Lucy Gantt Sheppard, and African American Routes," *Atlantic Studies* 5 (2008): 99–118.

22. Abbott and Seroff, *Out of Sight*, 312–15.

23. Frank B. Converse, "Banjo Reminiscences. I," *The Cadenza* 7/10 (June 1901): 4. In addition to the ex-slave accounts quoted in the text, narrator Stonewall Smith described "race horses, street shows and other amusements of like character" around Boulder after 1900 (Stonewall Smith, b. 1872, CO, child of ex-slaves, 86).

24. Higginson, "Spirituals," 693.

25. "Who's Dat Nigga Dar a Peepin'" (J. H. White, 1844). Nathan, *Dan Emmett*, 479–82; Dennison, *Scandalize*, 134–36. The waterfall in the fourth line is a woman's hair extension (or fall).

26. Brown III: 399–403; Christy, *Plantation Melodies*, 56–57; Cox, *FSS*, 501–2; Davis, *Folk-Songs*, 147; Ford, *Traditional*, 278–80; Rosenberg, *Virginia*, 131–32.

27. Hancock's final stanza borrows the chorus of "Rock the Cradle, John (Old Humphrey Hodge a Farmer Was)" (Roud 32576), an English music hall song that, beginning in the 1850s, also circulated in British and American broadsides and songbooks, and later on the American stage as well. The other verses are not usually found in that item, however, and are obviously of minstrel origin (the circus animals in the second verse are especially telling). Hancock's interviewer, Mabel E. Mueller, describes him performing at a recent folk festival in Rolla, MO, but it is unclear whether he had himself performed in minstrel shows.

28. Brown III: 505–6; Christy, *Plantation Melodies* 1, 36–38; Cohen, *Ozark*, 223–25; Perrow, "South" (1913): 125–26; Randolph, *OFS II*: 335–36; Talley, *NFR*, 53–54; White, *ANFS*, 164–67. DISCOGRAPHIES: *Country Music Records*; *Country Music Sources*, 759. The narrative of Lavinia Lewis also contains an excerpt of Foster's original text, obviously copied from print by interviewer Effie Cowan.

29. Ex-slaves quoted or named many other items with minstrel connections, for example, "One of the earliest slave songs he remembers ran like this: / Hardes work ever done was hacking round a pine, / Easiest work ever done was handing the ladies wine" (Jim Powell, 1850, NC, 486). The editors of the Brown collection trace this wandering stanza to "'Have a Little Dance,' in *Christy's Negro Songster* (New York, 1855), p. 18." Brown III: 514–15. Also see Scarborough, *TNFS*, 231. There are also two WPA texts of "Little Brown Jug," from Orris Harris (b. ca. 1858, MS, 933) and Tom Morris (b. ca. 1850, MS, 1589–90), but both were provided by Mississippi fieldworker Mrs. W. S. Holmes, who tended to repeat material in different interviews, clearly the case here. (Morris's version appears to be the original.) Also see Bass, "Negro Songs," 430; Botkin, *Play Party*, 230–32; Brown III: 62–64; Belden, *Missouri*, 261; Davis, *Folk-Songs*, 147; Ford, *Traditional*, 31, 415–17; Gardner, "Play-Party Games in Michigan," 109–10; Lomax, *Ballads*, 176–77; Randolph, *OFS III*: 141–42; Roberts, *Sang Branch*, 173–74; Rosenberg, *Virginia*, 70; Shay, *Drunken Companions*, 40–41; Solomon, *Daisies*, 70; Spaeth, *Read 'Em*, 58–59; Talley, *NFR*, 94; White, *ANFS*, 213, 231. RECORDINGS: Cuje Bertram (fiddle, vocal), "Little Brown Jug," home rec., Indianapolis, ca. 1970, *Black Fiddlers*. DISCOGRAPHIES: *Country Music Records*. The interview of Texas

ex-slave Josh Miles includes a version of "Jordan Am a Hard Road to Travel" (Dan Emmett, 1853), but the text appears to have been copied from a print source by interviewer Effie Cowan. Minstrel or popular songs that ex-slaves named but did not quote included "Carry Me Back to Old Virginia" (James A. Bland, 1878): Mollie Justice, Ann May, Katie Rye. "Massa's in the Cold, Hard Ground" (Stephen C. Foster, 1852): William Black, James Hayes, Guy Stewart. "O Susannah" (Stephen C. Foster, 1848): Rosa Green, Lou Turner. "Old Black Joe" (Stephen C. Foster, 1860): Betty Bormer, Ann May, Pete Newton, Guy Stewart, Teshan Young. "The Old Folks at Home (Way Down Upon the Swanee River)" (Stephen C. Foster, 1851): Bettie Massingale Bell, Betty Bormer, Guy Stewart, Teshan Young. "When You and I Were Young, Maggie" (George W. Johnson and James Austin Butterfield, 1866): Ann May, Katie Rye.

30. See Oliver, *Songsters*; Cohen, *Minstrels and Tunesmiths*.

31. On Rice and "Jim Crow," see Botkin, *Play Party*, 222; Carlin, *Banjo*, 10–18; Kennard, "National Poets," 331–41; Nathan, *Dan Emmett*, 50–52, 171; Nathanson, "Minstrelsy," 72; R. P. Nevin, "Stephen C. Foster and Negro Minstrelsy," *Atlantic* 20 (November 1867): 608–10; Randolph, *OFS* II: 323; Opie, *Nursery*, 244–45; Scarborough, *TNFS*, 125–27, 287; Southern, *Music*, 90–91; White, *ANFS*, 162–63, 452–53.

32. Compare Randolph, *OFS* II: 323. Ex-slaves John N. Davenport, Sarah Ford, Abram Harris, and William Henry Towns gave texts of "Jim Crow." For other traditional versions, see L. M. Channell (b. unk., LA), Cade, "Ex-Slaves," 334; Bass, "Negro Songs," 427–28; Botkin, *Play Party*, 222–23; Brown III: 139–40; Cohen, *Ozark*, 219–20; Davis, "Folk-Lore," 250; Harris, *Remus*, 150; Jones and Hawes, *Step It Down*, 55–57; Randolph, *OFS* II: 323; Scarborough, *TNFS*, 127; Spurgeon, *Waltz the Hall*, 121; Talley, *NFR*, 11; Bethany Veney, *The Narrative of Bethany Veney, A Slave Woman* (1889; rpt. *From Bondage*), 215; White, *ANFS*, 162–63; Whitney and Bullock, *Maryland*, 155. RECORDINGS: Land Norris, "The Old Jim Crow" (OKeh unissued, 1926). Intriguingly, four narrators remembered a postwar hair straightener called a *Jim Crow comb* or *brush*. "I recollect what we called after the War a 'Jim Crow.' It was a hairbrush that had brass or steel teeth like pins 'ceptin it was blunt. It was that long, handle and all (about a foot long). They'd wash me and grease my legs with lard, keep them from looking ashy and rusty. Then they'd come after me with them old brushes and brush my hair. It mortally took skin, hair, and all" (Lucy Key, b. ca. 1865, child of ex-slaves, MS, 198–99, orig. parentheses). Ex-slaves Tildy Collins, Easter Jackson, Georgia Telfair, and William Wheeler also mentioned Jim Crow combs.

33. French, *Sketches*, 40–41.

34. Veney, *Narrative*, 215.

35. Ex-slaves Joseph Holmes and Martha Richardson also knew the floating "hawk-and-buzzard-went-to-law" couplet. For other traditional examples, see Bolick and Austin, *Mississippi Fiddle*, 62; Talley, *NFR*, 65, 217–18.

36. Jones and Hawes, *Step It Down*, 55.

37. See, for example, Randolph, *OFS* II: 323.

38. L. M. Channell (b. unk., LA), Cade, "Ex-Slaves," 334.

39. "Jim Crow" was also played as a children's game in England, but this branch definitely derives from T. D. Rice's song-and-dance, which became a sensation in England after his 1836 tour. Opie, *Nursery*, 244–45; J. S. Udal, "Dorsetshire Children's Games, Etc.," *Folk-Lore* 7 (1889): 251.

40. On Emmett and "Old Dan Tucker," see Archie Green, "Old Dan Tucker," *JEMFQ* 17 (1981): 85–94, 106; Nathan, *Emmett*, 179, 454–56; Nathanson, "Negro Minstrelsy," 74–75; Constance Rourke, *American Humor: A Study of the National Character* (1931; rpt. New York: Doubleday Anchor, 1953), 74–76, 84; Wittke, *Tambo and Bones*, 180–81, 211.

41. Whipple, *Diary*, 87. Compare Ingraham, *Sunny South*, 104; Wyeth, *Sabre*, 65.

42. Nathanson, "Negro Minstrelsy," 75.

43. Like other dance lyrics, "Old Dan Tucker" could be sung unaccompanied, played instrumentally, or both together. Ex-slaves Jane Arrington, Ann Drake, and Dora Franks remembered it as an unaccompanied dance song. Hammett Dell described it as a call-and-response cornshucking song. Jim Davis recalled playing it on the banjo. Ellen Claibourn and George Morrison identified it with the fiddle; W. S. Needham, the child of a Mississippi slaveholder, had learned to fiddle the piece from a slave (SS2 10 TX 9: 4364–65). Morrison stated "Usually the old fiddler would be the band leader and the band itself. . . . This would continue until about midnight then all would go home. 'Old Dan Tucker' was usually the piece played for the dance to disperse" (George Morrison, b. ca. 1860, KY, 146). Also see Ames, "Missouri Play-Party," 309–10; Ball, "Play Party in Idaho," 16; Bass, "Negro Songs," 427; Blair, "Swing Your Partner!" 96–97; Bolick and Austin, *Mississippi Fiddle*, 388; Bolick and Russell, *Fiddle Tunes*, 140–41; Botkin, *Play-Party*, 260–66; Brewster, *Indiana*, 340–41; Brown III: 114–18; Davis, *Folk-Songs*, 154; Dudley and Payne, "Play-Party," 14–15; Ford, *Traditional*, 55, 412–13; Gainer, *West Virginia*, 176–77; Gardner, "Play-Party Games in Michigan," 116–17; Killion and Waller, *Georgia*, 219; Lomax, *Ballads*, 258–62; McDowell, *Dances*, 32–35; Owens, *Texas*, 155; Curtis Owens, "Whose 'Dan Tucker'?" *JAF* 84 (1971): 446–48; Peabody, "Notes on Negro Music," 149; Perrow, "South" (1915): 131–32; Piper, "Play-Party," 284; Randolph, *OFS* III: 301–4; Randolph, *Roll Me*, 431–33; Roberts, *Sang Branch*, 184–85; Rosenberg, *Virginia*, 94; Scarborough, *TNFS*, 188, 199; Solomon, *Daisies*, 94, 96; Spurgeon, *Waltz the Hall*, 148–49; Thede, *Fiddle*, 74–75; Van Doren, "Play-Party Songs from Illinois," 488–89; Warnick, "Play-Party Songs in Maryland," 164; Harriet L. Wedgwood, "The Play-Party," *JAF* 25 (1912): 272–73; White, *ANFS*,

160–61, 446–47; Wolfe, *Middle Tennessee*, 130–32; Wolford, *Indiana*, 180–82, 241, 286–87. RECORDINGS: Nathan Frazier (banjo, vocal), Frank Patterson (fiddle), "Dan Tucker," field rec., Nashville, TN, March 1942, *Altamont*; Golden Gate Quartet, "Old Dan Tucker," Washington, DC, 1940, *Freedom*. DISCOGRAPHIES: *Country Music Records*; *Country Music Sources*, 757.

44. Scarborough, *TNFS*, 199.

45. Other characters attracting stanzas tied to "Old Dan Tucker" include "Aunt Dinah" (Lomax, *Ballads*, 258; Scarborough, *TNFS*, 188; Talley, *NFR*, 46–47; Wyeth, *Sabre*, 64), "Captain Dime" (Talley, *NFR*, 5), "De Monkey" (Talley, *NFR*, 137), "Old Man Baker" (White, *ANFS*, 161), "Ole Granny Grunt" (Owens, "Whose 'Dan Tucker'?" 447), and "Tom Wilson" (Uncle Dave Macon, "Old Dan Tucker," Vocalion 15033, 1924).

46. Rourke, *Humor*, 75.

47. On Dan Emmett and "Dixie," see Nathan, *Dan Emmett*, 243–75. Around Emmett's hometown of Mount Vernon, Ohio, there is a persistent (and quite credible) story that two local free Black minstrels, the brothers Lew and Ben Snowden, were Emmett's direct sources for "Dixie." Howard L. Sacks and Judith Rose Sacks, *Way Up North in Dixie: A Black Family's Claim to the Confederate Anthem* (Urbana: University of Illinois Press, 1993). Wherever he learned "Dixie," Emmett rearranged and popularized but definitely did not create the song.

48. Katie Arbery, George Taylor Burns, Jennie Patterson, and Noah Perry gave texts of "Dixie." Ex-slaves who named it were Cecelia Chappel, Carrie Davis, William L. Dunwoody, George Fleming, George Fortman, Rachel Hankins, Eda Harper, Mary Jackson, Zeno John, Alfred Jones, Lidia (Lydia) Jones, Mollie Justice, William Little, Allen V. Manning, Ann May, Susan McIntosh, Pete Newton, Joe Oliver, Lu Perkins, Katie Phoenix, Katie Rye, Henry Smith, Mollie Watson, Dave White, and Alice Wilkins.

49. Qtd. Cauthen, *Fiddle*, 13.

50. For "The Whistling Coon" (San Devere, 1878), see *Country Music Sources*, 474; White, *ANFS*, 222. DISCOGRAPHIES: *Country Music Records*; *Country Music Sources*, 474.

Ballads

1. F. J. Child, *War-Songs for Freemen*, 2nd ed. (Boston: Ticknor and Fields, 1863); Silber, *Civil War*, 309, 335–37.

2. Wilgus, *Anglo-American Folksong Scholarship*.

3. One of Child's texts of "Lamkin" (Child 93) is from "the Negroes of Dumfries, Prince William County, Virginia, [who] have this ballad, orally transmitted from the original Scottish settlers of that region" (Child III: 515). Child also reprints a text of "Sir Hugh or the Jew's Daughter" (Child 155) from William Wells Newell's *Games and Songs of American Children*, 75–78; Child III: 251–52. Newell first heard the piece being sung by Black children on the streets of New York, eventually tracing their version to an Irish girl living in a shanty near Central Park. Also see John Minton, "'Our Goodman' in Blackface and 'The Maid' at the Sookey Jump: Two Afro-American Variants of Child Ballads on Commercial Discs," *JEMFQ* 17 (1982): 31–40.

4. Jeannie Robertson, "When My Apron Hung Low," field rec., Aberdeen, ca. 1955, *The Queen Among the Heather*, Rounder CD 1720, 1998. Also see *Sharp Collection* I: 603–4; Sharp, *EFSSA* II: 383. RECORDINGS: Isla Cameron, "Died for Love," field rec., London, 1951, *World Library of Folk and Primitive Music: England*, Rounder CD 1741, 1998; Walter Pardon, "I Wish, I Wish," field rec., Norfolk, UK, June 1978, *The Voice of the People*, vol. 15. Topic CD 665, 1998. Sometimes termed the *formula of impossibility*, this sort of metaphorical expression for *never* occurs in numerous other British and American ballads and love lyrics. Hugh Shields, "Impossibles in Ballad Style," *The Ballad Image: Essays Presented to Bertrand Harris Bronson*, ed. James Porter (Los Angeles: Center for Comparative Folklore and Mythology, University of California, 1983), 192–214.

5. Killion and Waller, *Georgia*, 66, 76 n1.

6. Tristram Potter Coffin, *The British Traditional Ballad in North America*. Rev. ed., *Supplement* by Roger deV. Renwick. AFS BSS 29 (Austin: University of Texas Press, 1977), 36–39, 216–17.

7. In 1944 South Carolina–born blues and gospel singer Josh White (1914–1969) did record "Lord Randall," but by this stage in his career, White had found a new audience in the emerging urban folksong revival, and his source was the revival, not Black tradition. Josh White, "Lord Randall, My Son," Decca unassigned, ca. 1944, *Josh White, vol. 6*, Document CD 5572, 1997.

8. Belden, *Missouri*, 28, also 24–25; Coffin and Renwick, *British Traditional Ballad*, 38.

9. Chesnutt, "Folklore and Superstitions of the South," 231–35; *Drums and Shadows*, 136; Herron and Bacon, "Conjuring and Conjure Doctors," 177–78, 193–94, 209–11; Hurston, "Hoodoo," 358–59, 361, 364–65, 377, 391–92; Hyatt, *Hoodoo*; Puckett, *Folk Beliefs*, 222, 249–55, 303–5.

10. The most successful of these turn-of-the-century hoodoo songs was "I've Been Hoodooed" (New York: Spaulding and Gray, 1894) by the prolific African American composer Gussie L. Davis (1863–1899), later collected from Black oral tradition and commercially recorded. White, *ANFS*, 206–7 (also Brown III: 516–17). RECORDINGS: Jim Towel, "I've Been Hoodooed" (Brunswick 7060, 1928). Also see Abbott and Seroff, *Out of Sight*, 308, 345; *Country Music Sources*, 487; Oliver, *Songsters*, 102. Similar is Sara Martin, "I'm Gonna Hoodoo You" (OKeh 8270, 1925). Another

text in this vein—"Hoodooism"—also appears in the WPA ex-slave collection, in the Kentucky narratives (S2 16 *KY*: 121–22), which feature numerous items from scrapbooks, manuscripts, songsters, periodical clippings, and the like. This particular example, which may actually be a recitation or monologue (not a song), is not identified with an individual ex-slave or assigned any other provenience; I strongly suspect that it comes from a uncredited secondary source.

11. Compare Lomax, *Country*, 392. Whether Julia Rush, the likely source, Edwin Driskell, the fieldworker, or some other, unidentified individual joined these two songs together is an open question, but Edwin Driskell was himself African American and obviously had considerable firsthand knowledge of conjure lore.

12. Porter, "Negro Songs," 1; Gordon, *Folk-Songs*, 22–23. For other African American versions, see Jackson, *WNS*, 205; McIlhenny, *Spirituals*, 81–82. Also see Brown II: 206–8; Davis, *Folk-Songs*, 297–98; Jackson, *WNS*, 204; Lomax, *FSNA*, 244; *Sharp Collection* II: 465–70.

13. Porter, "Negro Songs," 1.

14. Dorothy Scarborough gives a text of "The Fox Went A-Hunting" from "an elderly gentleman who remembers having heard it often sung by slaves." Scarborough, *TNFS*, 70. An Alabama source "learned it from a negro stable boy around 1850." Solomon, *Daisies*, 44. For other Black examples, see Talley, *NFR*, 35–36; White, *ANFS*, 177. Also see Brewster, *Indiana*, 323; Brown III: 178–81; Cohen, *Ozark*, 135–37; Cox, *South*, 474–75, 531; Davis, *Folk Songs*, 207–8; Halliwell, *Nursery Rhymes*, 84–86; Kennedy, *Folksongs*, 656–57, 678; Linscott, *New England*, 202–4; Opie, *Nursery*, 173–74; Owens, *Texas*, 146–47; George Perkins, "A Medieval Carol Survival: 'The Fox and the Goose,'" *JAF* 74 (1961): 235–44; Randolph, *OFS* I: 386–91; Roberts, *Sang Branch*, 191–92; Sharp, *EFSSA* II: 332–33; *Sharp Collection* II: 399–402.

15. For other African American versions, see Henry, *Highlands*, 395–96; Scarborough, *TNFS*, 46–50; Talley, *NFR*, 160–63; L. W. Payne Jr., "Some Texas Versions of 'The Frog's Courting: The Way of the Folk With a Song," *Rainbow in the Morning*, ed. J. Frank Dobie. PTFS 5 (Austin, 1926), 43–46; White, *ANFS*, 218. Also see Belden, *Missouri*, 494–99; Brown III: 154–66; Cohen, *Ozark*, 139–41; Cox, *South*, 470–73; Davis, *Folk-Songs*, 208–13; Halliwell, *Nursery Rhymes*, 110–12; Henry, *Highlands*, 392–98; Kennedy, *Folksongs*, 649, 674–75; Linscott, *New England*, 199–202; List, *Indiana*, 215–19; Lomax, *Ballads*, 310–33; Opie, *Nursery*, 177–81; Owens, *Texas*, 136–40; Payne, "The Frog's Courting," 5–48; Randolph, *OFS* I: 402–10; Roberts, *Sang Branch*, 194–95; Rosenberg, *Virginia*, 38–39; Scarborough, *Song Catcher*, 244–48; Sharp, *EFSSA* II: 312–23; *Sharp Collection* II: 385–89; Solomon, *Daisies*, 76–77; Thomas, *Devil's Ditties*, 154–55; Wolfe, *Middle Tennessee*, 34–37. DISCOGRAPHIES: *Blues and Gospel Records; Country Music Records; Country Music Sources*, 110. There is also a text of "Froggie Went A-Courting" in the narrative of Charley Johnson; however, Johnson's interview was conducted by fieldworker Ada Davis, who plagiarized most of her song texts. I have not traced this example to a specific source, and it may be authentic, but all of Davis's materials are suspect. In addition, ex-slaves Lorenza Ezell and Fannie Berry gave texts of "Keemo Kimo," a minstrel piece related to "Froggie Went A-Courting." Ezell remembered it as a lullaby; Berry gave a version recomposed to satirize a slaveholder. Also see Bass, "Negro Songs," 428; Brown III: 165–66; Cohen, *Ozark*, 239–41; Davis, *Folk-Songs*, 213–14; Ford, *Traditional*, 106, 418–19, 450–51; Linscott, *New England*, 204–6; Odum and Johnson, *Workaday*, 187; Randolph, *OFS* II: 362–65; Scarborough, *TNFS*, 156–57, 201, 285; Solomon, *Daisies*, 48; Talley, *NFR*, 193; White, *ANFS*, 175–76. RECORDINGS: "Chubby" Parker & His Old-Time Banjo, "King Kong Kitchie Kitchie Ki-Me-O" (Columbia 15296-D, 1928).

16. Kennedy, *Folksongs*, 410–11, 432. RECORDINGS: John Strachan, "Twa 'N Twa (The Cuckoo's Nest)," field rec., Aberdeenshire, 1950, *Songs of Seduction*, Rounder CD 1778, 2000.

17. "Raking of Hay," Mrs. Willie Hughes, Buena Vista, VA, May 1, 1918, CJS2/9/3025. Also see "A-Raking of Hay," Bertha Bryant, Peaks of Otter, VA, July 27, 1918, CJS2/10/4400; "The Raking of Hay," Molly Elizabeth Bowyer, Villamont, VA, June 10, 1918, CJS2/10/4383. Folk words and tunes collected by Cecil Sharp (CJS2/9, CJS2/10), Vaughan Williams Memorial Library, vwml.org. Roud 1403. This American subtype of "Raking the Hay" resembles two other British broadside ballads of seduction, "The Nightingale (One Morning in May)" (Laws P 14) and "The Poor Stanger (Sweet Europe)" (see below), and there is other evidence of cross-influences, possibly accounting for the American subtype's origins. See, for example, Belden, *Missouri*, 474–75, for a text combining "Raking the Hay" and "The Poor Stranger." For the typical English form of "Raking the Hay" (Roud 855), see *Sharp Collection* I: 447–48.

18. Minton, "'Our Goodman' and 'The Maid.'"

19. For helpful overviews of various ballad types (medieval, broadside, blues), see Roger deV. Renwick, "Ballad," *American Folklore: An Encyclopedia*, ed. Jan Harold Brunvand (New York: Garland, 1996), 57–61.

20. For a sampling of Black broadsides, see White, *ANFS*, 413–26.

21. For this stanza, see Randolph, *OFS* II: 248, 250.

22. Foote, *Civil War* I: 282–92, III: 581–83.

23. Also see Belden, *Missouri*, 341–43; Brown II: 607–8; Cohen, *Ozark*, 190–93; *Country Music Sources*, 24; Cox, *FSS*, 234–35, 527; Lomax, *Ballads*, 421–43; *Lone Star Ballads*, 36–37; Owens, *Texas*, 132–33; Randolph, *OFS* II: 191–95.

24. Hudson, *Mississippi*, 261.

25. General Horace Porter, "Campaigning With Grant: From the North Anna to Cold Harbor," *Century* 53 (March 1897): 719. Also see Foote, *Civil War* III: 283–99.

26. For "Brother Green," see Belden, *Missouri*, 377; Brewster, *Indiana*, 253–54; Brown III: 468–70; Cox, *South*, 273–74; Henry, *Highlands*, 364–65; Laws, *American Ballads*, 277; Owens, *Texas*, 77; Randolph, *OFS* II: 253–56; Roberts, *Sang Branch*, 117; Silber, *Civil War*, 235–36, 250–51. RECORDINGS: Buell Kazee, "The Dying Soldier" (Brunswick unissued, 1928). DISCOGRAPHIES: *Country Music Sources*, 433.

27. *Lone Star Ballads*, 44. Also see Brown II: 535–36; Hudson, *Mississippi*, 260–61; Randolph, *OFS* II: 272–73; Silber, *Civil War*, 234–35, 246–47. On the Battle of Shilo, see Foote, *Civil War* I: 314–51.

28. Joseph E. Chance, "Second Texas Infantry," *Handbook of Texas*.

29. *Lone Star Ballads*, 80–81.

30. Due perhaps to its lyric connections, G. Malcolm Laws did not admit "The Poor Stranger (Sweet Europe)" (Roud 272) to his standard classification of *American Balladry from British Broadsides*, but it is no different in this regard from many items he approved, such as "Love Has Brought Me To Despair" (Laws P 25). American versions include Arnold, *Alabama*, 48–49; Belden, *Missouri*, 474–75, 487; Brewster, *Indiana*, 350; Brown III: 285–86; Henry, *Highlands*, 283; G. L. Kittredge and Katherine Pettit, "Ballads and Rhymes From Kentucky," *JAF* 20 (1907): 268; Randolph, *OFS* I: 271–72, IV: 225–26; Scarborough, *Songcatcher*, 327; Sharp, *EFFSA* II: 212, 215; Wolfe, *Middle Tennessee*, 151–52. For Scottish, Irish, and English versions, see W. Christie, *Traditional Ballad Airs*, 2 vols. (Edinburgh: David Douglas, 1881), II: 220–21; P. W. Joyce, *Ancient Irish Music* (Dublin: McGlashan and Gill, 1873), 73; *Sharp Collection* II: 575. As was usual for popular items, broadside publishers produced a sequel to "The Poor Stranger," "The Happy Stranger" (also Roud 272). "The Happy Stranger" circulated widely in North America as well, including the South: Brown II: 372–73; Cox, *FSS*, 346–74; Randolph, *OFS* I: 270–71.

"The Poor Stranger (Sweet Europe)," "The Cuckoo," "The Wagoner's Lad," and "Pretty Saro," as well as "The Rebel Soldier" and "Jack of Diamonds" all employ variants of the tune also called "Sweet Europe." Textually as well, "The Poor Stranger," "The Rebel Soldier," and "Jack of Diamonds" overlap considerably with "The Cuckoo," "The Wagoner's Lad," and "Pretty Saro." These last three titles are sometimes recognizable as distinct songs, but are themselves so fluid and closely interrelated that editors often admit they are uncertain where to classify particular examples. In this light, South Carolina ex-slave Hector Smith gave a text suggesting the "Pretty Saro" line, but impossible to place with certainty. He recalled harmonica accompaniment: "De peoples didn' have nothin more den a mouth organ to make music with in dem times."

I. De mockin birds a singin so sweetly,
So sweetly, so sweetly.
De mockin birds a singin so sweetly,
So sweetly, so sweetly.
Way down in de lonesome valley.

II. Dey tell you one thing en dey mean another,
Mean another, mean another.
Dey tell you one thing en dey mean another,
Mean another, mean another.
Way down in de lonesome valley.

III. Some say, what make de young girls so deceivin?
So deceivin, so deceivin.
Some say, what make de young girls so deceivin?
So deceivin, so deceivin.
Way down in de lonesome valley. (Hector Smith,
b. ca. 1858, SC, 107)v

Allowing, then, that these three items sometimes seem inseparable, and that they constantly combine with, or contribute to, other songs (including "The Poor Stranger," "The Rebel Soldier," and "Jack of Diamonds"), for English texts and references of "The Cuckoo" (Roud 413), see *Sharp Collection* I: 623–30; Kennedy, *Folksongs*, 348, 371; for US references, see Arnold, *Alabama*, 45; Belden, *Missouri*, 475–76; Brewster, *Indiana*, 346–47; Brown III: 271, 273–74, 344–45; *Country Music Sources*, 176; Cox, *FSS*, 425–26; G. L. Kittredge, "Ballads and Songs," *JAF* 30 (1917): 349–52; Josephine McGill, *Folk-Songs of the Kentucky Mountains* (New York: Boosey, 1917), 34–38; McNeil, *Folksongs*, 99–101; Randolph, *OFS* I: 237–39; Scarborough, *Song Catcher*, 270–72, 313–14; Sharp, *EFSSA* II: 177–83; Wolfe, *Middle Tennessee*, 148–49. RECORDINGS: Clarence Ashley, "The Coo-Coo Bird" (Columbia 15489-D, 1929). For "The Wagoner's Lad (On Top of Old Smokey)" (Roud 414), see Arnold, *Alabama*, 5; Bolick and Austin, *Mississippi Fiddle*, 184; Brown III: 275–79, 287–90; 344–45; Browne, *Alabama*, 43–44; Cox, *FSS*, 433–34; Henry, *Highlands*, 273–77, 279–81; Kittredge and Pettit, "Ballads and Rhymes," 268–69; Morris, *Florida*, 134–36; Charles Neely, *Tales and Songs of Southern Illinois* (1938; rpt. Carbondale: Southern Illinois University Press, 1998), 236–38, 243–44; Perrow, "South" (1915): 177; Randolph, *OFS* IV: 205; Roberts, *Sang Branch*, 109–10; Scarborough, *Song Catcher*, 272–82; Sharp, *EFSSA* II: 123–27; Solomon, *Daisies*, 28–29. RECORDINGS: Kelly Harrell, "My

Horses Ain't Hungry" (Victor 20103, 1926); Buell Kazee, "The Wagoner's Lad (Loving Nancy)" (Brunswick 213, 1928); Mr. and Mrs. John Sams, "The Wagoner's Lad," field rec., Combs, KY, 1959, *Mountain Music of Kentucky*, Folkways/Smithsonian CD 40077, 1996. DISCOGRAPHIES: *Country Music Sources*, 176–77. For "Pretty Saro" (Roud 417), see Brewster, *Indiana*, 362; Brown III: 285–87; Browne, *Alabama*, 59–60; Henry, *Highlands*, 283; Hudson, *Mississippi*, 164–65; Randolph *OFS* IV: 222–24; Scarborough, *Song Catcher*, 327–28; Sharp, *EFSSA* II: 10–12. RECORDINGS: Gaither Carlton, "Pretty Saro," field rec., Watauga Co., NC, May 1965, *The Doc Watson Family Tradition*, Rounder CD 11161-0564, 2005.

31. For "The Rebel Soldier," see Jules Verne Allen, *Cowboy Lore* (San Antonio: Naylor, 1935), 86–88; Cox, *FSS*, 279–80; Hudson, *Mississippi*, 258–59; John A. Lomax, *Cowboy Songs and Other Frontier Ballads* (New York: Sturgis & Walton, 1910), 292–96 (minus one stanza, this text is reprinted in John A. Lomax and Alan Lomax, *Cowboy Songs and Other Frontier Ballads*, Rev. ed. [New York: Macmillan, 1946], 253–56); *Lone Star Ballads*, 80–81; Randolph, *OFS* II: 317–18, IV: 224–25; Sandburg, *Songbag*, 137–38, 284–85; Scarborough, *Songcatcher*, 327–28; Sharp, *EFSSA* II: 212–15 (four versions); R. C. Smith (b. ca. 1840, AR, 280). RECORDINGS: Jules Allen, "Jack O' Diamonds" (Victor 21470, 1928).

32. Randolph, *OFS* II: 317.

33. Higden, Arkansas, where Mr. Salter lived, is in Cleburne County, not far east of Fayetteville, Washington County, where R. C. Smith grew up. Smith was taken to Texas during the war and later worked as a cowboy in Indian Territory, where he was apparently something of an outlaw (R. C. Smith, b. 1840, AR, 280–92). Smith heard "The Rebel Soldier" in Washington County, however, where at the time tens of thousands of Confederate troops were concentrated. The Battle of Cane Hill (November 28, 1862), in which Mr. Salter participated, was part of the runup to the Battle of Prairie Grove (December 7, 1862), one of the major engagements of the Trans-Mississippi Theater that was also fought in Washington County near Fayetteville. Foote, *Civil War* III: 45–51; David Montgomery, "Battle of Prairie Grove," "Engagement at Cane Hill," *Encyclopedia of Arkansas*, encyclopediaofarkansas.net.

34. *Lone Star Ballads*, 81; *Randolph*, OFS II: 317; Cox, *FSS*, 279.

35. Sharp, *EFSSA* II: 213.

36. Jules Allen (The Singing Cowboy), "Jack O' Diamonds" (Victor 21470, 1928). This was no mere folksong conceit: during the war rampant alcohol abuse and gambling created disruptions in both armies, encampments sometimes descending into absolute debauchery, or soldiers deserting to go on sprees until bankruptcy or the provosts forced them back to the ranks: "I've rambled and gambled all my money away, / But it's with the rebel army, oh Mollie I'll stay." Allen, *Cowboy Lore*, 88. For other variants of this verse,

see Hudson, *Mississippi*, 259; Lomax, *Cowboy Songs*, 295; Randolph, *OFS* III: 138; Sandburg, *Songbag*, 285.

37. Jules Allen (The Singing Cowboy), "Jack O' Diamonds" (Victor 21470, 1928). (Its title notwithstanding, this is actually a version of the ballad "The Rebel Soldier," not the related lyric "Jack of Diamonds.")

38. This is not an original claim, but is in fact the generally accepted scenario for "Jack of Diamonds'" origins, which is entirely borne out by the evidence. Compare *Cox*, FSS, 281; Randolph, *OFS* III: 136, IV: 224; Sandburg, *Songbag*, 284; Silber, *Civil War*, 176–77. Moreover, while it was known throughout the South and quite popular with African Americans, white cowboys are often credited with creating "Jack of Diamonds" from "The Rebel Soldier," which is highly plausible, not only because cowboys contributed so many versions of "Jack of Diamonds," but because in the late 1800s a majority of cowboys were from the South, and often Confederate veterans. Jules Verne Allen (1883–1945), a Texas cowboy before his successful singing career, even observed "a great deal of the South can be seen in cowboy songs as ninety percent of the cowboys were from the South at the beginning of the trail drive period." Allen, *Cowboy Lore*, 84. In addition to the ex-slave texts (below), Black versions of "Jack of Diamonds (Rye Whiskey)" include "Carmina Africana," 10; *Gumbo Ya-Ya*, 442; Lomax, *Ballads*, 173; Talley, *NFR*, 97–98; Thomas, "Work-Songs," 169. For white versions, see *Appalachian Fiddle*, 85; Hudson, *Mississippi*, 207–8; Lomax, *Ballads*, 170–73; Perrow, "South" (1915), 129–30; Randolph, *OFS* III: 133–39; Sandburg, *Songbag*, 133, 142–43, 307; Thomas, *Devil's Ditties*, 47, 128–29. RECORDINGS: Fiddlin' John Carson, "The Drunkard's Hiccups" (OKeh 45032, 1925); J. E. Mainer's Mountaineers, "Drunkard's Hiccoughs" (Bluebird B8400, 1939); Da Costa Woltz's Southern Broadcasters, "Jack of Diamonds" (Herwin 75561, 1927). DISCOGRAPHIES: *Country Music Records*; *Country Music Sources*, 380–81. The "Jack O' Diamond Blues" (Paramount 12373, 1928) recorded by Blind Lemon Jefferson and other Texas blues singers is a different song. *Blues and Gospel Records*.

39. Significant connections between "Jack of Diamonds (Rye Whiskey)" and later Black tradition include the request "make me a pallet, I'll lay on the floor," repeated as a refrain in many "Rye Whiskey" and "Rebel Soldier" texts. After 1900 these lines became a popular blues theme, especially in Mississippi. (In "The Rebel Soldier" and "Jack of Diamonds" the commonplace describes the singer's homelessness; in later blues songs it typically signifies an illicit tryst.) For examples in "Jack of Diamonds" and "The Rebel Soldier," see Allen, *Cowboy Lore*, 87–88; Jules Allen, "Jack O' Diamonds" (Victor 21470, 1928); Brown III: 347; Lomax, *Cowboy Songs*, 292–94; Randolph *OFS* III: 137; Tex Ritter, "Rye Whiskey, Rye Whiskey" (Oriole 8222, 1933); Thomas, "Work-Songs," 169. For

examples from later blues songs, see Evans, *Tate and Panola*, 17; Handy, *Blues*, 78; Odum and Johnson, *NHS*, 159, 183; Oliver, *Songsters*, 70–71. RECORDINGS: Willie Brown, "Make Me a Pallet On the Floor," field rec., Lake Cormorant, MS, August 1941, *Mississippi Blues*, Travelin' Man CD 07, 1991; Mississippi John Hurt, "Ain't No Tellin'" (OKeh 8759, 1928); Mississippi John Hurt, "Make Me a Pallet On the Floor," *Today*! Vanguard LP 79220, 1966; Little Brother Montgomery, "Pallet on the Floor," *Blues*, Folkways LP 3527, 1961; Henry Thomas (Ragtime Texas), "Bob McKinney" (Vocalion 1138, 1927). The commonplace also wanders into other unrelated Black songs, such as Henry Thomas (Ragtime Texas), "Lovin' Babe" (Vocalion 1468, 1929); Othar Turner, "Black Woman," field rec., Senatobia, MS, March 1969. DISCOGRAPHIES: *Blues and Gospel Records*; *Country Music Records*. Many versions of "The Rebel Soldier" or "Jack of Diamonds" also feature a verse in which the singer imagines the river (or ocean) as whiskey and himself as a duck; this became another popular blues commonplace, appearing on numerous recordings by Black and white artists from the 1920s and '30s (including Sleepy John Estes, "Divin' Duck Blues," Victor V38549, 1929; Charlie Poole with the North Carolina Ramblers, "If the River Was Whiskey," Columbia 15545-D, 1930). For examples in "Jack of Diamonds" and "The Rebel Soldier," see Allen, *Cowboy Lore*, 87; Jules Allen, "Jack O' Diamonds" (Victor 21470, 1928); "Carmina Africana," 10; *Gumbo Ya-Ya*, 442; Lomax, *Ballads*, 171–72; Lomax's *Cowboy Songs*, 292–94; Randolph, *OFS* III: 138, 139; Tex Ritter, "Rye Whiskey, Rye Whiskey" (Oriole 8222, 1933). Black singers sometimes also combined "Jack of Diamonds" with the late nineteenth-century Black ballad "Stewball" (based on the British broadside "Skewball," Laws Q 22). See, for example, Thomas, "Work-Songs," 169; John Calloway, "The Cuckoo Bird," field rec., November 1976, Henry Co., VA; *Virginia Secular Music*; Dobie Red and group, "Stewball," field rec., Parchman Penitentiary, MS, April 1936, *Saints and Sinners*.

40. Killion and Waller, *Georgia*, 237. This text, collected by Louise Oliphant from an unidentified ex-slave in Augusta, was found separately in the Georgia WPA files. Oliphant—another Black fieldworker with the Georgia ex-slaves project—contributed individual narratives for Leah Garrett (b. unk., GA, 11–16) and Estella Jones (b. ca. 1855, GA, 345–50), as well as several compilations based on information from Garrett, Jones, Roy Redfield (b. unk., GA, 304–7), and possibly other Augusta area ex-slaves: "Folklore Interviews: Conjuration," "Folk Remedies and Superstitions," "Mistreatment of Slaves," "Work, Play, Food, Clothing, Marriage, etc." (S2 13 *GA* 4: 269–307, 355–64). This item does not appear in any of these materials, but circumstantial evidence suggests Estella Jones is the most likely source.

41. All of the ex-slave texts above feature elements found in both "The Rebel Soldier" and "Jack of Diamonds" (and in "The Cuckoo"

and related lyrics), but internal and external evidence suggests they were quoting "Jack of Diamonds."

42. Both quotes from Hudson, *Mississippi*, 258. For other versions of "The Rebel Soldier" featuring this verse, see Cox, *FSS*, 279 ("Yankees"), 280 ("Yankees"); Randolph, *OFS* II: 317 ("tree"); Sharp, *EFSSA*, 212 ("Yankees"). In one text of "The Roving Soldier (The Guerilla Man)"—an Ozark wartime subtype of "The Roving Gambler" (Laws H 4) (Belden, *Missouri*, 374–76; Cohen, *Ozark*, 323–25; Randolph, *OFS* IV: 356–57)—the protagonist declares "And if the Rebels don't kill me / I'll live until I die." Belden, *Missouri*, 376. Jules Allen's Rebel soldier expects to live "if my horse don't fall on me" (*Cowboy Lore*, 88).

43. In nineteen traditional texts of "Jack of Diamond" featuring these lines, nine identify a tree as the threat, one a tree limb. The nearest competitor is "hard times" (just two examples). Texts naming a tree are Lomax, *Ballads*, 172; Perrow, "South" (1915): 182; Randolph, *OFS* III: 135, 136, 138; Tex Ritter, "Rye Whiskey, Rye Whiskey" (Oriole 8222, 1933); Tex Ritter, "Rye Whiskey" (Capitol 20068, 40084, 1946, 1948); Sandburg, *Songbag*, 133; Thomas, "Work-Songs," 169. Also see Belden, *Missouri*, 376 ("if a limb don't fall on me"). Other persons or things that might kill the singer include "drinkin'" (Randolph *OFS* III: 137); "hard times" (Lomax, *Ballads*, 170; Thomas, *Devil's Ditties*, 129); "injuns" (Randolph *OFS* III: 136); "moonshine" (Sandburg, *Songbag*, 143); "rounders" (Fiddlin' John Carson, "The Drunkard's Hiccups," OKeh 45032, 1925); "somebody" (Randolph *OFS* III: 137); "whisky" (Sandburg, *Songbag*, 307); and "women" (*Gumbo Ya-Ya*, 442). There are, however, various possible explanations for this detail's tenacity. Falling trees were common everyday threats to any number of persons in frontier and rural America, most of all to timber workers (the most dangerous US occupation during the late nineteenth and early twentieth centuries), but also to cowboys, trappers, farmers clearing land, railroad crews and construction gangs, travelers, outdoorsmen, and so on. "My husban', he git kilt in Liberty, when he cuttin' down a tree and it fall on him" (Betty Simmons, b. ca. 1837, TX, 23). This basic fact of Southern life at the time may explain the detail's persistence as much or more than the war's memory. In that connection, around 1900 Gates Thomas collected an African American variant ("Eat when yo're hongry, drink yo're dry, / An' ef a tree don't fall on you, you'll live tel you die") as part of a Texas worksong otherwise concerned with horse racing, dissipation, and domestic relations. Thomas, "Work-Songs," 169. The work context is unclear, but it is possible that this was a "tree song": a song performed by axe cutters or two-man saw teams while felling trees (which could and often did disable or kill them).

44. Joseph F. Laredo and Ron Furmanek, booklet accompanying *Tex Ritter*, Capitol CD 95036, 1992, 11. Like fellow Texan Jules Allen, Maurice Woodward "Tex" Ritter (1907–1974) was among the more

genuine "singing cowboys." He had previously recorded "Rye Whiskey" (Oriole 8222, 1933).

45. In 1942, for instance, Eloise Guilliams gave Vance Randolph a couple of stanzas taken down from Dr. George E. Hastings of Fayetteville, AR. The "manuscript fragment" never mentions the Confederacy or the war, but Randolph reports that Guilliams described the item as "a Confederate song which I have heard my father sing many times." Randolph, *OFS* III: 138. Compare Hudson, *Mississippi*, 258. In this context, then, the singer's persistent worries about falling trees may have retained their original sense, now even suggesting a flashback to the terrors of combat, another symptom of PTSD. Perhaps not coincidentally, "The Rebel Soldier" maintained some currency among whites through this same period.

46. Talley, *NFR*, 98. John Lomax gives another "Negro Variant" in which a slave, weary of "hard salt, parched corn," sets out to rob a henhouse or steal a turkey to carve. "An' if ol' Mas'er don' kill me, / I cain't never starve." Lomax, *Ballads*, 173.

47. Cohen, *Long Steel Rail*, 61–89; John Garst, *John Henry and His People: The Historical Origin and Lore of America's Great Folk Ballad* (Jefferson, NC: McFarland, 2021). An anonymous interviewer attached a plagiarized version of "John Henry" to the narrative of ex-slave Jim Sommerville.

48. Thomas, "Work-Songs," 175; also Laws, *American Ballads*, 93–94, 255. Texas interviewer Effie Cowan included a plagiarized version of "The Boll Weevil" in the narrative of ex-slave John Love. Also from this later period, Andrew Jackson Jarnagin gave a version of the Anglo-American ballad "The Young Man Who Wouldn't Hoe Corn" (Laws H 13), adapted to the agrarian People's Party campaign of 1892 (the "Independent Ticket"). I have not found this ballad elsewhere among African Americans:

Us "niggers" used to git together some nights, and we would clink our whiskey glasses together (dat meant friendship) and recite a toast:

Come all of you Virginia boys
And listen to my song
And let us concern the young man that made no corn.
July's corn was knee high,
September laid it by.
And the weeds and the grass growed so high,
It caused the young man to cry
          "Independent ticket?"
(Andrew Jackson Jarnagin, b. 1853, MS, 1129)

For the People's Party and their campaign songs, see Irwin Silber, *Songs America Voted By* (Harrisburg, PA: Stackpole, 1971), 158–63.

49. Blues ballads are thus neither quite blues nor ballads. They predate the blues by a decade or two, but their subjective tone, lyrical character, and associational, nonlinear organization definitely anticipate that genre, whose development they influenced. Unlike blues, blues ballads narrate, yet rather than explicitly narrating like British ballads, blues ballads "sing a story not by directly relating that story but by celebrating it; not by following a chronological sequence, but by creating a sequence of concepts and feelings about it." D. K. Wilgus and Eleanor Long, "The *Blues Ballad* and the Genesis of Style in Traditional Narrative Song," *Narrative Folksongs: New Directions*, ed. Carol L. Edwards and Kathleen E. B. Manley (Boulder: Westview, 1985), 439. Compare Renwick, "Ballad," 60. Basically, then, blues ballads assume listeners are already acquainted with their underlying narratives, which may figure only by allusion; instead, a blues ballad focuses on an event's practical, emotional, and psychological impact, and the reactions and interpretations of participants (or survivors), bystanders, and the singers themselves. The form flourished among both Blacks and whites from the late 1800s through the 1920s, after which few new blues ballads were composed, though many existing titles still are played.

The War

1. Snow responded to the white children with a pro-Union version of the popular soldier's song "Snapoo." Besides Abraham Lincoln, her text mentions Union General John Pope (1822–1892), who after some early successes was routed by Confederates at Second Bull Run (Second Manassas) (August 29–30, 1862). Foote, *Civil War* I: 620–28. For "Snapoo," also see note 30 below.

2. Foote, *Civil War* III: 42–46.

3. Griffin Frost, *Camp and Prison Journal* (Quincy, IL: Quincy Herald Book and Job Office, 1867), 42.

4. Lieut.-Col. Fremantle, Coldstream Guards, *Three Months in the Southern States, April–June 1863* (Edinburgh: William Blackwood and Sons, 1863), 53.

5. J. Clement French, *The Trip of the Steamer Oceanus to Fort Sumter and Charleston, S. C.* (Brooklyn: Union Steam Printing House, 1865), 90–91.

6. "Shrewdness of Contrabands," correspondent for the *New York Times*, steamer *Madgie*, St. Simmons Sound, Ga., October 31; rpt. as "The Army and the Negroes," *NASS* 23 (November 22, 1862), 3.

7. "Fourth of July at the House That Jeff. Built," *The Liberator* 34 (July 29, 1864), 121–22.

8. White stated that the town in question was Jefferson, TX, but he was obviously misremembering. Federal forces came close

during their 1864 Red River Campaign, but they never reached their objective of Jefferson, a Confederate supply port on Caddo Lake, due to Union defeats at the Battles of Mansfield (Sabine Crossroads) (April 8, 1864) and Pleasant Hill (April 9, 1864). There was fighting and devastation throughout the area, however.

9. Warren Lee Goss, "Recollections of a Private. I: (Including the Battle of Bull Run)," *Century* 24 (November 1884), 112. Goss (1835–1925) draws both on his own experiences and those of others, this account coming from another Union veteran, Jim Tinkham.

10. In 1941 Roy Walworth (New York) sang this for Frank Warner: "Doodle, doodle, doodle dandy, / Cornstalks, rum, and homemade brandy, / Indian pudding and pumpkin pie, / And that'll make the Yankees fly!" Walworth credited his father, Fayette E. Walworth (1848–1933), who had been told that Continental troops sang the words as they marched back into New York City after finally defeating the British in 1783. Warner, *Folk Songs*, 435–36.

11. This stanza appears in various Anglo-American lyrics and ballads, but is most closely identified with "There Is a Tavern In the Town (When My Apron Hung Low)," an English lyric related to "Love Has Brought Me to Despair" (Laws P 25). See, for example, Brown III: 303–4; Louise Pound, *American Ballads* (New York: Charles Scribner's Sons, 1922), 62; Spaeth, *Read 'Em*, 94–95.

12. Joseph Wheeler (1836–1906) was a celebrated Confederate cavalry commander. Foote, *Civil War* III: 822–28, 832–33. Ex-slave Rivana Boynton told how Union cavalry once deceived, surprised, and then looted pro-Confederate civilians by singing a Wheeler regimental song.

13. Aunt Jinsy (b. unk., VA), Baldwin, *Teacher*, 14.

14. Silber, *Civil War*, 54–56, 70–73; *Lone Star Ballads*, 24–26.

15. Carlin, *Banjo*, 152–62; Silber, *Civil War*, 301–45; Toll, *Blacking Up*, 104–34; Winans, "The Folk, Stage, and Five-String Banjo," 430–32; Wittke, *Tambo*, 82–84.

16. Fitts, "The Negro in Blue," 254.

17. General Pierre Gustave Toutant-Beauregard (1818–1893) commanded Confederate forces at First Bull Run (First Manassas) (July 21, 1861), where Confederate General Thomas J. Jackson (1824–1863) also distinguished himself, earning the nickname "Stonewall." Foote, *Civil War* I: 73–84.

18. On May 29, 1939, Abbott Ferriss and Herbert Halpert of the Library of Congress's Archive of Folksong recorded "Uncle" James ("Jim") Archer at Vicksburg singing this item and the shanty "Rango." Apparently because he had been born a slave, a transcript was also deposited with the Mississippi ex-slave narratives (SS1 6 *MS* 1: 73–75).

19. Compare Whitney and Bullock, *Maryland*, 163.

20. The *satan's mad and I'm glad* line belongs to a ubiquitous wandering couplet: "Old Satan is mad and I'm glad, / He missed one soul that he thought he had" (Frances Lewis, b. 1854, GA,

156). Also see Arnold, *Alabama*, 182; Brown III: 661–63; Brown and Owens, *Toting*, 19; Dett, *Hampton*, 141; Hallowell, *Calhoun*, 18; Jackson, *WNS*, 307; Killion and Waller, *Georgia*, 239; Lomax, *Ballads*, 589; Lomax, *Lead Belly*, 208; Marsh, *Jubilee Singers*, 202; McDowell, *Camp*, 53; McIlhenny, *Spirituals*, 211, 219; Howard W. Odum, "Negro Hymn," *JAF* 26 (1913): 375; Odum and Johnson, *NHS*, 40, 124; Perrow, "South" (1913): 154; Porter, "At the Sugar-House," 3; Randolph, *OFS* II: 386, 388; *Slave Songs*, 108; Solomon, *Honey*, 10, 47, 92; White, *ANFS*, 117–18; Work, *Songs*, 23, 71; Wyeth, *Sabre*, 36.

21. Narrators John Price and Sam Word gave "The Bonnie Blue Flag," Rachel Bradley, Caroline Smith, and Virginia Yarborough "The Homespun Dress," and Maggie Whitehead Matthews combined them. For their histories, see Silber, *Civil War*, 52–54, 65–69. For "The Bonnie Blue Flag," also see Bolick and Russell, *Fiddle Tunes*, 356; Brown III: 451–53; Ford, *Traditional*, 462–63; *Lone Star Ballads*, 40–42; Randolph, *OFS* II: 261–62; for "the Homespun Dress," see Belden, *Missouri*, 360; Brown III: 453–56; Davis, *Folk-Songs*, 260; Hudson, *Mississippi*, 265–66; *Lone Star Ballads*, 60–61; Morris, *Florida*, 31–32; Randolph, *OFS* II: 262–63; Alfred M. Williams, "Folk-Songs of the Civil War," *JAF* 5 (1892): 281–82. RECORDINGS: Polk Miller's Old Southern Quartette, "The Bonnie Blue Flag" (Edison Amberol 389, 1909).

22. "Root, Hog, Or Die" (Laws B 21) was first published in 1856, but may derive from a Black folksong. It was frequently rewritten and reprinted, usually as a topical satire. Most wartime versions are pro-Southern. (The refrain also wanders into other songs.) See Belden, *Missouri*, 334, 361; *Country Music Sources*, 26; *Lone Star Ballads*, 35–37; Randolph *OFS* III: 162–65; Silber, *Civil War*, 233–34, 243.

23. Silber, *Civil War*, 8–9, 17–20.

24. Haywood's first item derives from a spiritual parody of the 1880s, Edmund Clark, "Climbing Up the Golden Stairs" (New York: T. B. Harms, 1884); perhaps Haywood confused it with a similar antebellum song. There are actually two versions of this passage in Haywood's interview. The example quoted above appears on a separate page in the supplement for *American Slave* with Rawick's notation: "This unedited version of the songs on the previous pages [1691–92] was found in with the edited version" (SS2 5 *TX* 4: 1693). In the edited version "Headed For the Golden Shore" is shortened, "Rally 'Round the Flag" is unchanged.

25. Stroyer, *Life*, 99–100; Randolph, *OFS* II: 290–91.

26. The Seven Days Battles (June 25–July 1, 1862) occurred at various locations outside Richmond during the Union Army's Peninsular Campaign. Foote, *Civil War* I: 508–14.

27. An anonymous Georgia ex-slave (b. ca. 1831) profiled in a newspaper clipping filed with the Minnesota narratives (SS1 2 *MN*: 125–30) stated that "since I have been in the North I have heard a song supposed to have been sung by the darkies, with a chorus

about— / It must be now de Kingdom's Comin', / And de year of jubilo. / Of course we never sang anything of the sort; and though we may have had such thoughts running through our ignorant heads, they never formed themselves into words." "The Story of a Contraband: the Simple Narrative of a Slave Who Followed Sherman as He Went Sweeping to the Sea," *Stillwater Daily Gazette*, March 5, 1886. Ex-slave Walter Rimm recalled "One song we use to sing was 'Throw de Smokehouse Keys Down de Well'" (Walter Rimm, b. ca. 1857, TX, 251), which could refer to "Kingdom Coming." White WPA interviewer Merton Knowles (SS1 5 *IN*: 108–9) also included a version with his materials. Also see Anon. ex-slave (b. 1842, KY), *Unwritten History*, 232; Stroyer, *Life*, 99–100; Arnold, *Alabama*, 11; Brown II: 541–43; Davis, "Folk-Lore," 249; Dennison, *Scandalize*, 203–4; Ford, *Traditional*, 339–40; Kirke, *Down in Tennessee*, 125–26; Randolph, *OFS* II: 290–91; Roberts, *Sang Branch*, 145; Silber, *Civil War*, 305–6, 317–19; Spaeth, *More*, 114–15; Talley, *NFR*, 35, 50–51; White, *ANFS*, 170–71. RECORDINGS: Georgia Crackers, "Year of Jubilo" (OKeh unissued, 1927); McGee Brothers, "Old Master's Runaway" (Vocalion 5167, 1927); Chubby Parker, "The Year of Jubilo" (Conqueror 7897, 1931). DISCOGRAPHIES: *Country Music Sources*, 465–66.

28. Silber, *Civil War*, 306–7, 320–21. For other examples and discussion, see Anon. ex-slave (b. 1842, KY), *Unwritten History*, 232; Dennison, *Scandalize*, 211–13; Solomon, *Daisies*, 173; Rosenberg, *Virginia*, 4.

29. For "Jeff in Petticoats," see Silber, *Civil War*, 310, 343–45. Georgia Baker related the legend that Davis had been deservedly poisoned by an emancipated slave: "I seed Jeff Davis when dey brung him through Crawfordville on de train. Dey had him all fastened up wid chains. Dey told me dat a Nigger 'oman put pizen in Jeff Davis' somepin t'eat and dat was what kilt him" (Georgia Baker, b. 1850, GA, 56). Occasionally ex-slaves did have some factual knowledge of Davis. Betty Robertson was a Cherokee slave. "The only song I remember from the soldiers was: 'Hang Jeff Davis to a Sour Apple Tree,' and I remember that because they said he used to be at Fort Gibson one time. I don't know what he done after that" (Betty Robertson, b. ca. 1844, IT, 269). As a US Army officer in the 1830s, Davis had indeed been stationed at Fort Gibson, IT.

30. Ed Cray, *The Erotic Muse* (New York: Oak, 1969), 141–42, 242–43. Also see Perrow, "South" (1915): 133; Randolph, *Roll Me*, 308–11; Silber, *Civil War*, 174–75, 211–13; White, *ANFS*, 159–60.

31. Silber, *Civil War*, 89, 175–76, 213–14; Botkin, *Play Party*, 210; Brown II: 528–29; Davis, *Ballads*, 145; Davis, *Folk-Songs*, 257–58; Kennedy, *Mellows*, 173–74; Lomax, *FSNA*, 84, 98; Randolph, *OFS* II: 284–87; Thomas, *Ballad Makin'*, 65; Williams, "Civil War," 272.

32. Variations on this refrain include "football(s)" (Randolph, *OFS* II: 286–87; Silber, *Civil War*, 175); "for bales" (Silber, *Civil War*, 89, 175–76, 214); "for bowls" (Silber, *Civil War*, 175, 213); "hurrah," hurrah" (Botkin, *Play-Party*, 210; Brown II: 528–29; Thomas, *Ballad Makin'*, 65); "skiball" (Lomax, *FSNA*, 98); "skewbald" (Davis, *Folk-Songs*, 257–58); "skubaugh" (Davis, *Ballads*, 145); and "three balls" (Davis, *Ballads*, 145). "Football," "shrew ball," "skebaugh," and "pas bonne" occur in the ex-slave versions. Fanny Berry's narrative seems to identify "squeeball" as her form.

33. Though unusual for "Johnny Fill Up the Bowl," this verse resembles a well-known Black game rhyme: "I give fifteen cents to see the elephant jump the fence; / He jumped so high he touched the sky / And never got back till next July." White, *ANFS*, 249. Also see Bass, "Negro Songs," 434; Brown I: 171–72; Brown III: 556; Knapp, *One Potato*, 137; Solomon, *Daisies*, 218. RECORDINGS: Rufus Thomas, "Walking the Dog" (Stax 140, 1963).

34. Rachel Hankins, Joanna Thompson Isom, Frances Lewis, Evelina Morgan, Charlie Norris, and Eugene Wesley Smith recalled soldiers singing or playing "Yankee Doodle." For the song's history, see Lomax, *Ballads*, 521–26; Spaeth, *Read 'Em*, 3–8; for a pro-Southern version, see Hudson, *Mississippi*, 262–63. "Dixie" was based on a Black folksong borrowed by minstrels, and ex-slaves knew it from many sources, some unrelated to the war. Nonetheless, William L. Dunwoody, Mary Jackson, and Dave White described "Dixie" being played by Union bands; Hannah Murphy, Charlie Pye, and Jennie Patterson remembered it being sung by Federal troops. Lucinda Davis, Rachel Hankins, Charley Hurt, and Alice Wilkins recalled it sung or played by Confederates. Zeno John, Eda Harper, and Noah Perry simply associated the song with the war years. Henry Baker (b. 1854, AL, interviewed by the WPA as *Father Baker*) also described Confederates singing "Dixie." Blassingame, *Slave Testimony*, 659.

35. *Lone Star Ballads*, 26–27, 33–34; Belden, *Missouri*, 363–64; Cox, *FSS*, 270; Clifton Johnson, *Battleground Adventures* (Boston: Houghton Mifflin, 1915), 32–36; Randolph, *OFS* II: 280–83; Thomas, *Ballad Makin'*, 90.

36. After examining the extraordinarily detailed contemporaneous coverage of John Brown's incarceration and execution, Cecil D. Eby concluded that this is an apocryphal story originating in the media, and that Brown did not come in contact with a slave child or any Blacks in route to the gallows. While the famous painting of "John Brown's Kiss" (Thomas Hovendon [1840–1895], *The Last Moments of John Brown*) depicts a boisterous public hanging, with Blacks flocking around Brown on his way to the scaffold, the affair was actually an orderly military-style execution conducted by the Virginia militia, with civilian observers (apparently all white) kept at a distance. Cecil D. Eby, "John Brown's Kiss," *Virginia Cavalcade* 11 (1961): 42–47. On the Harpers Ferry Raid, also see Foote, *Civil War* I: 31–32.

37. "Peppery Letter From a Nashville Rebel," *The Liberator* 26 (June 27, 1862), 104. Ex-slaves William M. Adams, Maria Sutton

Clemments, Bryant Huff, Tinie Force and Elvira Lewis, Prince Johnson, Amanda Oliver, Susan Snow, Tom Wilcox, George Woods, Sam Word, and Virginia Yarborough gave the full stanza, Callie Gray quoted the first line. Dora Franks may have been thinking of this item when she stated, "We lakked Jeff Davis de best on our place and even made up a song 'bout him but I declare 'fore goodness I can't even remember de fust line of dat song" (Dora Franks, b. ca. 1837, MS, 791). Also see Brown III: 461; Chase, *Dear Ones*, 97; Gordon, *Folk-Songs*, 73; Morris, *Florida*, 29; Scarborough, *Song Catcher*, 74; Silber, *Civil War*, 179, 226.

38. I take this title from ex-slave Bryant Huff's version, but the song might more appropriately be called "General Patterson" or "Robert Patterson," since this seems to be the true and original identity of the character named in Huff's text as "Peter Butler" and in another as "Billy Patterson" (Duke, *Reminiscences*, 294). Union General Robert Patterson (1792–1881) actually does figure in one text: "I'll lay ten dollars down / And count them one by one; / Show me the man / That whipped General Patterson" (Morris, *Florida*, 24). As editor Alton C. Morris notes, early in the conflict, Patterson, an aged veteran of the War of 1812, was ordered to prevent Confederate General Joseph E. Johnston (1807–1891) from joining the main Confederate army at Manassas. The two clashed at the Battle of Falling Waters (July 2, 1861) near Winchester, Virginia (now West Virginia). The engagement itself was a minor affair, but Patterson's indecision allowed Johnston the slip away and reinforce the Confederates at the Battle of First Bull Run (First Manassas) (July 21, 1861), with disastrous consequences for the Union. In the aftermath, Patterson was scapegoated and disgraced. Also see Foote, *Civil War* I: 56–57. All of this would have made Patterson an obvious butt for a Confederate camp song, and coming at the start of the war could account for the origin of this stanza and possibly the song as a whole.

39. Duke, *Reminiscences*, 294.

40. Basil W. Duke, *History of Morgan's Cavalry* (Cincinnati: Miami Printing and Publishing, 1867); also Foote, *Civil War* II: 678–83.

41. Duke, *Reminiscences*, 294–96. Besides the Seven Days Battles (June 25–July 1, 1862) (Foote, *Civil War* I: 508–14), and Morgan's Raid (June 11–July 26, 1863) (Foote, *Civil War* II: 678–83), Duke's verses reference the Battle of Fredericksburg (December 11–15, 1862) and Stonewall Jackson's Shenandoah Valley Campaign (March–June 1862), but also feature numerous local allusions, complaints about army life, and inside jokes about people and events. One text, for instance, mentions Union General Franz Sigel (1824–1902) and a wartime satirical song about him and his largely German-born troops, "I Goes to Fight Mit Sigel." (For the song, see Silber, *Civil War*, 307–8, 325–26.) Other surviving texts of "Peter Butler's Son" concern the Battles of Baldwin (February 9, 1864) (Morris, *Florida*,

28–29; Foote, *Civil War* II: 901–5); First Bull Run (First Manassas) (July 21, 1861) (Morris, *Florida*, 24; Foote, *Civil War* I: 73–86); and New Bern (March 14, 1862) (Brown II: 658; Foote, *Civil War* II: 253–54). Often these battles are not actually named, however, and can be identified only by references to specific persons, places, or other circumstantial details.

42. Duke, *Reminiscences*, 294, 295. In addition to Duke's examples and the ex-slave versions, there are texts of "Peter Butler's Son" in Brown II: 653; and Morris, *Florida*, 24, 28–29. Also see Silber, *Civil War*, 179–80, 225–26.

43. Brown II: 653.

44. Morris, *Florida*, 28–29.

45. Foote, *Civil War* I: 394–96.

46. David Sesser, "Conscription," *Encyclopedia of Arkansas*, encyclopediaofarkansas.net; Foote, *Civil War* III: 61–77, 574–84.

47. Duke, *Reminiscences*, 296.

48. See, for example, the North Carolina text concerning the Battle of New Bern "from Thomas Smith, Zionville, Watauga County, May 7, 1913, with this note: 'Sung for me by E. B. Miller, Boone, N.C., R. 1, May 7, 1913. Mr. Miller says this song, which he heard sung by soldiers during war times, was very popular in Watauga.'" Brown II: 658. The narratives of ex-slaves William Irving and Anderson Jones purportedly describe similar Confederate camp songs; however, these transcripts duplicate one another, being the work of Texas interviewer Effie Cowan. The song texts in particular are highly embellished and of questionable authenticity.

49. W. L. Bost, Anna Humphrey, and Austin Pen Parnell also quoted this chorus to "We'll Camp Awhile in the Wilderness," for which see Jackson, *WNS*, 194.

50. Sylvia Cannon (b. ca. 1857, SC, 196) also gave a text of "On Canaan's Happy Shore." Also see *DNAH*; Asbury and Meyer, "Old-Time," 172, 179–80, 184; Brown III: 624–25; Jackson, *WNS*, 178; Owens, *Texas*, 164; Silber, *Civil War*, 10–11; Thomas, *Ballad Makin'*, 218–19.

51. Silber, *Civil War*, 10–11, 21–23. "The Battle Hymn of the Republic" first appeared in the *Atlantic Monthly* 9 (February 1862): 10.

52. Richard Carruthers recalled one obvious parody from just after the war: "I remembers a song the Yanks sung when they go marchin' back to the north. They say: / Oh rebels ain't you sorry, / Oh rebels ain't you sorry, / Oh rebels ain't you sorry, / When we go marchin' home" (Richard Carruthers, b. ca. 1848, TX, 637–38). Also see Knapp, *One Potato*, 173–74; Silber, *Songs America Voted By*, 87–88, 108, 156; Solomon, *Daisies*, 59; Warner, *Folk Songs*, 305–6. In the post–WWII period, many Black choirs and quartets revived "The Battle Hymn of the Republic," probably inspired by the civil rights movement. DISCOGRAPHIES: *Gospel Discography*. For another African American version, see Will Slayden (1878–1965) (vocal, banjo), "Glory, Glory Hallelujah," field rec., Shelby Co., TN,

Summer 1952, *Will Slayden*. Also see Evans, *Will Slayden*; Chris Smith and David Evans, "Will and India Slayton (Also known as Will and Emma Slayden): Two Lives In Outline," *Tennessee Folklore Society Bulletin* 62 (2006): 20–25.

53. Ex-slaves Pete Newton and George Conrad Jr. mentioned "John Brown's Body." (Conrad also named "Hang John Brown on a Sour Apple Tree.") Plomer Harshaw probably referred to this piece when he described a slave being flogged for singing about Brown. Also see Baldwin, *Teacher*, 14; Botkin, *Play-Party*, 221; Forten, "Sea Islands. Part I," 591; Forten, "Part II," 666; Kirke, *Down in Tennessee*, 56–58; Marsh, *Jubilee Singers*, 223; Piper, "Play-Party," 270; Rosenberg, *Virginia*, 62; Silber, *Civil War*, 11, 23–24; Warner, *Folk Songs*, 305.

54. Ex-slaves giving the "Hang Jeff Davis" stanza in full were Sally Dixon, Cynthia Erwing, Louis Evans, Lorenza Ezell, Martha King, Hunton Love, Tom Morris, Louise Neill, and John White. Those quoting the title or first line were Alice Battle, Hannah Davidson, Sally Dixon, Ann Drake, Georgianna Foster, Ruben Fox, Jimmie Green, Elmira Hill, Addison Ingram, Sam Jordan, Evelina Morgan, Betty Robertson, Mom Jessica Sparrow, and Willis Winn. Davidson, Drake, Evans, Fox, Ingram, Jordan, Love, Morris, Neill, Thomas, and Winn described the song being sung by slaves, Battle, Dixon, Ezell, King, Morgan, Robertson, and White by Union soldiers. Battle, Dixon, and Morgan recalled it by soldiers and brass bands together. Others associated the song with the war years but did not specify contexts. Also see Botkin, *Play-Party*, 221; Brown III: 449–51; Lomax, *Ballads*, 528–29; Piper, "Play-Party," 270. In the 1920s this stanza still sometimes appeared in another song set to this tune, "Pass Around the Bottle," recorded by several Southeastern stringbands but in versions suggesting the piece was circulating orally. Georgia groups the Skillet Lickers and the Georgia Yellow Hammers both advocated hanging Jeff Davis from a sour apple tree (Gid Tanner and His Skillet Lickers, "Pass Around the Bottle," Columbia 15074-D, 1926; Georgia Yellow Hammers, "Pass Around the Bottle," Victor 20550, 1927); Virginian Ernest Stoneman sang "Hang John Brown on a sour apple tree," and "John Brown's body lies a-mouldering in the grave" (Ernest Stoneman, "Pass Around the Bottle," Banner 2157, 1927). Other recorded versions do not feature this stanza. (Walter Williams, "Pass Around the Bottle," field rec., KY, ca. 1940, *Kentucky Mountain Music*, Yazoo CDs 2200, 2003, is a different song.) "Pass Around the Bottle" probably also dates to the nineteenth century. Ex-slave Junius Quattlebaum named this title as sung at antebellum cornshuckings, where songs demanding refreshment were customary. Also see Bolick and Austin, *Mississippi Fiddle*, 268; Brown III: 64. DISCOGRAPHIES: *Country Music Records*; *Country Music Sources*, 381–82.

55. "Carve Dat Possum" (Boston: John F. Perry, 1875) was composed by Sam Lucas (ca. 1850–1916) of Callender's Colored Minstrels, gaining popularity around the time of the 1876 election.

Also see Brown, *Southern Home*, 93–94; *Country Music Sources*, 473–74; Odum and Johnson, *NHS*, 240. RECORDINGS: Uncle Dave Macon & The Fruit Jar Drinkers, "Carve That Possum" (Vocalion 5151, 1927). For other Hayes-Tilden songs, see Silber, *Songs America Voted By*, 109–15.

56. Puckett, *Beliefs*, 65. For other Grant-Greeley campaign songs, see Ruben Fox (b. ca. 1853, MS, 778); Brown III: 473–74; Spaeth, *Read 'Em*, 46.

57. Carol Christian, "Giddings, Jabez Demming (1814–1878)," *Handbook of Texas*.

58. Narrators Andrew Jackson Jarnagin and Paul Jenkins remembered political songs from later periods.

59. For Garfield-Hancock campaign songs, see Silber, *Songs America Voted By*, 115–23.

60. Mack's text is actually a parody of a parody, based on the mock spiritual "Climbing Up the Golden Stairs" by Edmund Clark and F. Heiser (Monroe F. Rosenfield) (New York: T. B. Harms, 1884), which ex-slave Felix Haywood associated with Emancipation. Also see Browne, *Alabama*, 346–47; *Country Music Sources*, 576–77; Ford, *Traditional*, 283–84; Mellinger E. Henry, "Negro Songs from Georgia," *JAF* 44 (1931): 447; Odum and Johnson, *NHS*, 239–40; Randolph, *OFS* II: 387–88.

61. McGregory, *Lullabies to Blues*; also see W. Fitzhugh Brundage, *Lynching in the New South: Georgia and Virginia, 1880–1930* (Urbana: University of Illinois Press, 1993).

Modern Times

1. Also named by Laura Abromsom, the Big Apple was a jazz dance created not long after Black musicians began using this term as slang for New York City. Like trucking (note 2 below), the Big Apple closely resembled shouting. Stearns, *Jazz Dance*, 27. The "Little Apple" appears to be Liza Mention's tongue-in-cheek counterinvention rather than an actual dance.

2. Trucking originated in Harlem in the 1930s, but like many African American popular dances, it does resemble shouting: "the shoulders are often hunched up, one above the other, the hips sway in Congo fashion, and the feet execute a variety of shuffles while the index finger of one hand wiggles shoulder-high at the sky." Stearns, *Jazz Dance*, 41. Narrators James Boyd and Dora Roberts also mentioned trucking.

3. Compare Warner, *Folk Songs*, 294.

4. Apparently the "enclosed song" was lost.

5. Ex-slave Martha Richardson also gave a version of "Possum (Jaybird, Rabbit) Up the 'Simmon Tree, Rabbit (Sparrow, Possum) on the Ground." Also see Bass, "Negro Songs," 429–30; Bolick and Austin, *Mississippi Fiddle*, 124, 141, 145, 180, 246, 380; Botkin,

Play-Party, 295–96; Brown III: 203, 206–8; *Gumbo Ya-Ya*, 485; Jones and Hawes, *Step It Down*, 127–28; Perrow, "South" (1913), 131, 133; Scarborough, *TNFS*, 170, 172–73; Solomon, *Daisies*, 49, 216; Talley, *NFR*, 30–31, 190–91; White, *ANFS*, 138, 236–37. RECORDINGS: Lucious Curtis, Willie Ford, "Times Is Getting Hard," field rec., Natchez, MS, October 1940, *Saints and Sinners*; Lead Belly, "Raccoon Up the 'Simmon Tree," Washington, DC, June 1937, *The Remaining Library of Congress Recordings*, Document CD 5594. For "Rabbit (Possum, Raccoon) Up a Gum Stump," see Bass, "Negro Songs," 430; Botkin, *Play-Party*, 296; Lomax, *Ballads*, 238; Long, *Slavery*, 17–18; Nathan, *Dan Emmett*, 46–48; Perrow, "South" (1913): 132; Talley, *NFR*, 3; White, *ANFS*, 237–39.

6. Compare Babcock, "Games," 269.

7. Admonitions to "hold the deal" or to not "let the deal go down" (a reference to the dealer's advantage in most gambling games) appear in many latter-day songs. See, for example, Odum and Johnson, *NHS*, 230–31. RECORDINGS: Peg Leg Howell, "Skin Game Blues" (Columbia 14473-D, 1972); Charlie Poole, "Don't Let Your Deal Go Down Blues" (Columbia 15038-D, 1925). DISCOGRAPHIES: *Country Music Sources*, 502–3. Hector Smith's text seems to trace the commonplace to the 1800s, much earlier than previously documented.

8. This item is by all appearances African American and post-1900. For other texts featuring the wandering "nobody's business" refrain, see Perrow, "South" (1913): 170; Odum and Johnson, *NHS*, 216–17. For other versions, see Bass, "Negro Songs," 430; Bolick and Russell, *Fiddle Tunes*, 218–19; Brown III: 211; Browne, *Alabama*, 406; Gordon, *Folk-Songs*, 83; Odum and Johnson, *Workaday*, 128; Perrow, "South" (1913): 127–28; White *ANFS*, 233, 283. RECORDINGS: Willie Ford, Lucious Curtis, "Payday," field rec., Natchez, MS, October 1942, *Blues Lineage*; Sid Hemphill, Lucius Smith, Will Head, Alec Askew, "Skillet Good and Greasy," field rec., Sledge, MS, August 1942, *Black Appalachia*; Mississippi John Hurt, "Pay Day," *Today!* Vanguard LP 79220, 1966; Mary James, "Rabbit On a Log," field rec., Parchman, MS, 1939, *Field Recordings, Volume 8*, Document CD 5598; Eli Owens, "Rabbit On a Log," field rec., Bogalusa, LA, August 1970, *South Mississippi Blues*, Rounder LP 2009, 1973; Uncle Dave Macon, "Keep My Skillet Good and Greasy" (Vocalion 14848, 1924); Monroe Brothers (Charlie & Bill), "Have A Feast Here Tonight" (Bluebird B7508, 1938). DISCOGRAPHIES: *Country Music Sources*,

376–77, 502. The "nobody's business" commonplace would also figure in numerous twentieth-century songs, Hector Smith's text again suggesting earlier origins than previously known.

9. For the wandering "poor girl (boy) long ways from home" commonplace, see, for example, Odum and Johnson, *NHS*, 5, 169, 175, 274.

10. In later years Botkin was best known for his *Treasury* anthologies, all of which drew on WPA/FWP folklore materials, including the ex-slave narratives: *A Treasury of American Folklore* (New York: Crown, 1944); *A Treasury of Southern Folklore* (New York: Crown, 1949); *A Treasury of Mississippi River Folklore* (New York: Crown, 1955); *A Civil War Treasury* (New York: Random House, 1960); and others.

11. For the wandering "dig my grave with a silver spade" commonplace, also see Bruce R. Buckley, "'Uncle' Ira Cephas—A Negro Folk Singer in Ohio," *Midwest Folklore* 3 (1953): 15; Diton, *South Carolina*, 45; Marion Alexander Haskell, "Negro 'Spirituals,'" *Century* 58 (August 1899): 580–81; Higginson, "Spirituals," 690; Kennedy, *Cameos*, 99; Kennedy, *Mellows*, 70; Lomax, *Ballads*, 202; Odum and Johnson, *Workaday*, 129, 198; Redfearn, "Songs from Georgia," 121; *Slave Songs*, 100. RECORDINGS: Blind Lemon Jefferson (Deacon L. J. Bates), "See That My Grave Is Kept Clean" (Paramount 12585, 1927). DISCOGRAPHIES: *Country Music Sources*, 284.

12. "O, Come, Angel Band" (1860), Jefferson Hascall (1807–1887). See *DNAH*; Solomon, *Daisies*, 133; White, *ANFS*, 125. The last prints a 1919 fragment from a Black tenant near Durham, NC, noting, however, "this is a line from a hymn sung by white people" (White, *ANFS*, 125). The piece is probably best known from white country recordings, including Fiddlin' John Carson, "Bear Me Away On Your Snowy White Wings" (Bluebird B5560, 1934); Uncle Dave Macon, "O Bear Me Away On Your Snowy Wings" (Vocalion 5160, 1927); Smith's Sacred Singers, "My Latest Sun Is Sinking Fast" (Columbia 15281-D, 1928); Stanley Brothers, "Angel Band," *Country Pickin' and Singin'*, Mercury LP 20349, 1958. DISCOGRAPHIES: *Country Music Records*; *Country Music Sources*, 623. Besides Josh Horn, Alice Hutcheson recalled the chorus from funerals: "Part of another one was: / Oh, come angel band / Come and 'round me stand, / And bear me away / On your snowy wings, / To my immortal home" (Alice Hutcheson, b. ca. 1860, GA, 287).

NARRATORS INDEX

Following is a list of ex-slaves quoted in this study, with source citations and basic biographical details. All references are to the forty-one-volume *American Slave*, supplemented by compilations for the semiautonomous Louisiana and Virginia state projects:

George P. Rawick, ed. *The American Slave: A Composite Autobiography*, Series 1 (S1), Vols. 1–7. Westport, CT: Greenwood, 1972.

George P. Rawick, ed. *The American Slave: A Composite Autobiography*, Series 2 (S2), Vols. 8–19. Westport, CT: Greenwood, 1972.

George P. Rawick, Jan Hillegas, and Ken Lawrence, eds. *The American Slave: A Composite Autobiography*, Supplement, Series 1 (SS1), Vols. 1–12. Westport, CT: Greenwood, 1977.

George P. Rawick, ed. *The American Slave: A Composite Autobiography*, Supplement, Series 2 (SS2), Vols. 1–10. Westport, CT: Greenwood, 1979.

Ronnie W. Clayton, ed. *Mother Wit: The Ex-Slave Narratives of the Louisiana Writers' Project*. University of Kansas Humanities Series Vol. 57. New York: Peter Lang, 1990. (*MW*)

Charles L. Perdue Jr., Thomas E. Barden, and Robert K. Phillips, eds. *Weevils in the Wheat: Interviews with Virginia Ex-Slaves*. Bloomington: Indiana University Press, 1980. (*WW*)

The American Slave poses no end of bibliographical challenges, the most serious being that the different series were not numbered sequentially, so that volume numbers are constantly duplicated. Still, the style adopted here—the first citation, SS1 11 *SC*: 57, refers to the Supplement, Series 1, Volume 11, *South Carolina Narratives*: 57; the second citation, S2 8 *AR* 1: 8–10, to Series 2, Volume 8: *Arkansas Narratives*, Part 1: 8–10, and so forth—will be self-explanatory to anyone with a complete set in hand. Besides standard state abbreviations, IT = Indian Territory, the designation for most of present-day Oklahoma until 1907. Identifiable interviewers (int.) and editors (ed.) are listed following narrators.

GEO. F. ABRAMS, b. unk., SC. int. Summer. (SS1 11 SC: 57) LAURA ABROMSOM, b. 1863, Brownsville, TN. Farmed postwar. int. Robertson. (S2 8 AR 1: 8–10) FRANK L. ADAMS, b. July 7, 1853, Jasper, TX. Fieldhand. Farmed, preached postwar. int. Hatcher. (SS2 2 TX 1: 1–4) LOUISA ADAMS, b. ca. 1856, Rockingham, NC. int. Matthews, ed. Waitt. (S2 14 NC 1: 1–7) RACHEL ADAMS, b. ca. 1860, Putnam Co., GA. Weaver. (S2 12 GA 1: 1–8) VICTORIA ADAMS, b. ca. 1835, SC. House servant, nursemaid. Stayed on plantation one year postwar. int. Pierce. (S1 2 SC 1: 10–12) WILL ADAMS, b. 1857, Harrison Co., TX. Stayed on plantation until 1885, then farmed, odd-jobbed. (S1 4 TX 1: 1–3; SS2 2 TX 1: 10–15) WILLIAM M. ADAMS, b. ca. 1846, San Jacinto Co., TX. Fieldhand. Postwar worked grocery, punched cattle, farmed, preached. Moved Fort Worth 1902. (S1 4 TX 1: 9–11; SS2 2 TX 1: 16–22) AUNT ADELINE, b. ca. 1848, Hickman Co., TN. Taken Fayetteville, AR. House servant, stayed on plantation postwar. int. Peel. (S2 8 AR 1: 11–16) ROSE ADWAY, b. ca. 1862, MS. Farmed postwar. int. Bowden. (S2 8 AR 1: 17–18) JACOB ALDRICH, b. January 10, 1860, Terrebonne Parish, LA. Moved Beaumont following 1927–28 flood. Creole. int. Dibble. (SS2 2 TX 1: 23–33) ALICE ALEXANDER, b. March 15, 1849, Jackson Parish, LA. House servant. Moved IT postwar. int. Tipton. (S1 7 OK: 6–7; SS1 12 OK: 1–3) DIANA ALEXANDER, b. ca. 1865, Byhalia, MS. Child of ex-slaves. Washed, ironed, fieldwork postwar. int. Robertson. (S2 8 AR 1: 28–9) J. C. ALEXANDER, b. 1850, KY. Taken TX while young. Shepherd. Farmed postwar. int. Menn. (SS2 2 TX 1: 38–43) LUCRETIA ALEXANDER, b. ca. 1845, Copiah Co., MS. Carried water, cooked, cleaned. Postwar washed, ironed, fieldwork. int. S. Taylor. (S2 8 AR 1: 32–39) BARNEY ALFORD, b. ca. 1850, MS. Fieldhand. int. Holmes. (SS1 6 MS 1: 23–49) JIM ALLEN, b. ca. 1850, Russell Co., AL. Taken by storekeeper for "whiskey debt." Fieldhand, odd jobs. Conscripted Union army. Settled West Point, MS. Domestic. int. E. Joiner. (S1 7 MS: 1–10; SS1 6 MS 1: 52–65) JOSEPH ALLEN, b. May 4, 1851, Common Co., KY. Fieldhand. Age fourteen Confederate guard duty, age fifteen recruited by Union soldiers as drummer, declined. Postwar moved Glasco, KY, Muncie 1900, worked foundry until age 83. int. Freeman, Tuttle. (SS1 5 IN: 1–4) MARTHA ALLEN, b. 1859, Craven Co., NC. int. Hicks, ed. Waitt. (S2 14 NC 1: 14–15) SARAH ALLEN, b. unk., VA. Brought TX. House servant. (S1 4 TX 1: 12–13; SS2 2 TX 1: 44–47) REV. W. B. ALLEN, b. ca. 1850, Russell Co., AL. int. J. Jones. (S2 12 GA 1: 12–16; SS1 3 GA 1: 4–22) W. C. PARSON ALLEN, b. 1859, Harrison Co., MO, raised Georgetown, Scott Co. House servant. After freedom studied theology, University of Louisville, ministered. int. Miles. (S1 11 MO: 18–19) MOLLY AMMONDS, b. ca. 1850, Eufaula, AL. Nursemaid. int. Couric, J. Smith. (S1 6 AL: 9–11) CHARLES ANDERSON, b. ca. 1860, Bloomfield, KY. Moved Helena, AR 1879, farmed. int. Robertson. (S2 8 AR 1: 46–48) CHARLES GABRIEL ANDERSON, b. 1818, AL. Fieldhand, water carrier. Runaway, enlisted Union army 1864. Postwar barbered, worked steamboats, drove carriages, cleaned glass, preached. (S2 11 MO: 20–23) CHARLES H. ANDERSON, b. December 23, 1845, Richmond, VA. Worked grocery, fiddled. int. R. Thompson, ed. Graff. (S2 16 OH: 1–5) NANCY ANDERSON, b. ca. 1870, Senatobia, MS. Child of ex-slaves. Nursemaid. int. Robertson. (S2 8 AR 1: 49–52) SAM ANDERSON, b. 1839, Amite Co., MS. Taken Pike Co. Fieldhand. int. Thomas. (SS1 12 OK: 4–10) CORNELIA ANDREWS, b. 1850, Johnston Co., NC. House servant. int. Hicks, Waitt. (S2 14 NC 1: 27–31) SAMUEL SIMEON ANDREWS, b. November 16, 1850. Macon, GA, taken SC, TX, AL. Returned Macon after freedom, moved Florida 1888. Preached. int. R. Austin, ed. Simms. (S2 17 FL: 10–21) MARY ANNGADY (Princess Quango Hennadonah Perceriah), b. ca. 1857, Chapel Hill, NC. House servant. Stayed on plantation postwar. Attended college, worked as fundraiser for African missions, musical entertainer. int. Matthews. (S2 14 NC 1: 32–43) ANON., b. unk., Richmond Co., GA. int. Louise Oliphant. (S2 13 GA 4: 363–64)

KATIE ARBERY, b. 1857, Union Co., AR. Stayed on plantation until married. int. Bowden. (S2 8 *AR* 1: 64–67) JIM ARCHER, b. ca. 1860, Vicksburg, MS. Worked for Vicksburg doctor, saloon, laying streetcar tracks, riverboat night watchman, railroads. int. Ferriss, Halpert. (SS1 6 *MS* 1: 73–75) CAMPBELL ARMSTRONG, b. 1851, Houston, Co., GA. Moved Ononke Co., AR after war, farmed. Moved Little Rock ca. 1915. int. S. Taylor. (S2 8 *AR* 1: 68–74) MARY ARMSTRONG, b. 1846, St. Louis. House servant. Postwar medical nurse Houston. int. Drake. (S1 4 *TX* 1: 25–30; SS2 2 *TX* 1: 66–74) WASH ARMSTRONG, b. ca. 1865, Cherokee Co., TX. Child of ex-slaves. Farmed. int. L. Hatcher. (SS2 2 *TX* 1: 77–79) GEORGE W. ARNOLD, b. April 7, 1861, Bedford Co., TN. Fieldhand, roustabout. int. Creel. (S1 6 *IN*: 1–7) STEARLIN ARNWINE, b. 1853, Jacksonville, TX. Taken Rusk, TX. House boy. int. Shirley. (S1 4 *TX* 1: 31–33; SS2 2 *TX* 1: 80–86) JANE ARRINGTON, b. December 18, 1852, Nash Co., NC. int. Matthews, ed. G. Andrews. (S2 14 *NC* 1: 45–49) SARAH ASHLEY, b. 1844, MS. Sold age five to speculator, kept for years, contracted out. Sold, taken Cold Spring, TX. House servant, fieldhand. Farmed, cooked postwar. int. Dibble, Grey. (S1 4 *TX* 1: 34–36; SS2 2 *TX* 1: 87–91) SALLY ASHTON, b. ca. 1845, VA. int. S. Byrd. (*WW*, 14) LIZZIE ATKINS, b. 1850, Washington Co., TX. House servant. int. B. Davis. (SS2 2 *TX* 1: 92–103) SARAH LOUISE AUGUSTUS, b. ca. 1855, Fayetteville, NC. (S2 14 *NC* 1: 51–57) CHARITY AUSTIN, July 27, 1852, Granville Co., NC. Sold age ten, taken GA. House servant, nursemaid. (S2 14 *NC* 1: 58–62) HANNAH AUSTIN, b. ca. 1855, GA. int. Ross. (S2 12 *GA* 1: 19–21) LOU AUSTIN, b. January 1850, Crockett, TX. Taken McLennan Co. Fieldhand. int. A. Davis. (SS2 2 *TX* 1: 121–32) SMITH AUSTIN, b. 1847, Ripley, TN. Taken TX during war. Fieldhand, tenant postwar. int. A. Davis. (SS2 2 *TX* 1: 133–37) CELESTIA AVERY, b. 1862, Troup Co., GA. (S2 12 *GA* 1: 22–31) AGATHA BABINO, b. ca. 1850, Carenco, LA. Creole. int. Dibble. (S1 4 *TX* 1: 37–38; SS2 2 *TX* 1: 138–42)

JOSEPH SAMUEL BADGETT, b. 1864, Dallas Co., AR. int. S. Taylor. (S2 8 *AR* 1: 78–83) ANNA BAKER, b. ca. 1857, Tuscaloosa, AL. Father killed in war, mother fled overseer's sexual abuse. Reunited postwar, settled Aberdeen, MS. int. Kolb. (S1 7 *MS*: 11–17; SS1 6 *MS* 1: 90–101) BLOUNT BAKER, b. unk., NC. Fieldhand, stayed on plantation after freedom then worked around. int. Hicks, ed. G. Andrews. (S2 14 *NC* 1: 63–65) FATHER BAKER, b. 1854, Macon Co., AL. House servant, fieldhand. int. Perry. (SS1 1 *AL*: 30–34) GEORGIA BAKER, b. 1850, Taliaferro Co., GA. Slave of Alec Stephens, Confederate vice president. Yard work. int. Hornsby, ed. Hall, Booth. (S2 12 *GA* 1: 37–57) LIZZIE BAKER, b. 1865, NC. Child of ex-slaves. int. Matthews, ed. Waitt. (S2 14 *NC* 1: 66–69) WILLIAM BANJO, b. unk., resident Thomy Lafon Old Folks' Home, New Orleans. Had lived OK. int. R. McKinney. (*MW*, 13–14) EPHOM BANKS, b. ca. 1865, MS. Child of ex-slaves. (SS1 6 *MS* 1: 103–4) FRANCES BANKS, b. ca. 1855, Doaksville, IT. Indian slave. Nursemaid. Stayed on plantation postwar. int. J. Ervin. (SS1 12 *OK*: 11–12) SINA BANKS, b. ca. 1851, Palmyra, MO. Fieldhand, house servant. Cooked for college president postwar. int. J. Ervin. (SS1 12 *OK*: 13–27) DELIA BARCLAY, b. unk., Colmesneil, TX. Fieldhand. int. Dibble, Grey. (SS2 2 *TX* 1: 153–58) JIM BARCLAY, b. 1855, Woodville, TX. House servant. int. Dibble, Grey. (SS2 2 *TX* 1: 159–63) CHARLEY BARBER, b. 1856, Great Falls, SC. Fieldhand. Moved Winnsboro 1876, worked railroad. int. W. Dixon. (S1 2 *SC* 1: 29–33) ED BARBER, b. January 18, 1860, Winnsboro, SC. Stayed on plantation postwar. Left, wandered, returned as tenant. int. W. Dixon. (S1 2 *SC* 1: 34–37) CHARLIE BARBOUR, b. ca. 1851, Johnston Co., NC. Fieldhand. int. Hicks, ed. Waitt. (S2 14 *NC* 1: 73–77) MELISSA (LOWE) BARDEN, b. ca. 1850, Summersville, GA. (S2 16 *OH*: 6) JOHN BARKER, b. 1853, Cincinnati, OH. Taken Sedalia, MO, Houston, TX. Held in bondage until 1878. Cooked. int. Angermiller. (S1 4 *TX* 1: 42–44; SS2 2 *TX* 1: 164–73) HENRY BARNES, b. August 11, 1858, Clarke Co.,

AL. int. Prine. (S1 6 AL: 20–24; SS1 1 *AL*: 38–43) JOE BARNES, b. 1858, Tyler Co., TX. After freedom moved Beaumont, worked sawmills. (S1 4 *TX* 1: 45–6; SS2 2 *TX* 1: 174–77); LUCY BARNES, b. ca. 1853, Houston, TX. Nursemaid. Postwar moved Columbus, TX, cooked. (SS2 1 *TX* 2: 178–80) MARIAH and BERLE BARNES (spouses), both b. ca. 1856, NC. Mariah, domestic postwar; Berle, logged until World War I, then sharecropped, odd-jobbed. int. B. Harris. (SS1 11 *NC*: 1–14) SPENCER BARNETT, b. April 30, 1856, Florence, AL. Moved AR 1880, railroad brakeman, farmed, worked timber. int. Robertson. (S2 8 *AR* 1: 115–18) EMMA BARR, b. 1872, AR. Child of ex-slaves. int. Robertson. (S2 8 *AR* 1: 119–21) ROBERT BARR, b. 1864, Chickasaw Co., MS. Fiddler, dancer, gambler, preacher. int. S. Taylor. (S2 8 *AR* 1: 122–25) HARRIET BARRETT, b. 1851, Walker Co., TX. Cook. int. B. Davis. (S1 4 *TX* 1: 49–50; SS2 2 *TX* 1: 199–204) ELVIRA BASARD, b. unk., Vermilion Parish, LA. int. Dibble, Grey. (SS2 *TX* 1: 205–6) ANDERSON BATES, b. 1850, Jenkinsville, SC. Quarry driller postwar. Still doing farm labor. int. W. Dixon. (S1 2 *SC* 1: 42–45) FRANCES BATSON, b. ca. 1850, Nashville, TN. Washed, cooked postwar. (S2 16 *TN*: 1–2) ALICE BATTLE, b. ca. 1850, Bibb Co., GA. Nursemaid. Farmed postwar. (S2 12 *GA* 1: 58–59; SS1 3 *GA* 1: 39–44) JASPER BATTLE, b. ca. 1857, GA. Fieldhand. int. McCune, ed. Hall, Harris, Booth. (S2 12 *GA* 1: 61–71) ALICE BAUGH, b. 1873, Edgecombe Co., NC. Child of ex-slaves. int. Hicks, ed. Waitt. (S2 14 *NC* 1: 82–86) KATIE DUDLEY BAUMONT, b. unk., Bass Co., KY. int. Minnick. (SS1 5 *OH*: 277–80) HARRISON BECKETT, b. ca. 1860, San Augustine, TX. Slave of merchant. Farmed postwar. int. Dibble. (S1 4 *TX* 1: 54–58; SS2 2 *TX* 1: 224–36) JOHN C. BECTOM, b. October 7, 1862, Cumberland Co., NC. int. Matthews, ed. Waitt. (S2 14, *NC* 1: 91–98) HENRY BEDFORD, b. ca. 1858, Millersburg, TN. Eventually settled OH. Still selling coal, operating tennis court. int. Minnick. (SS1 5 *OH*: 281–83) ANNE BELL, b. ca. 1855, Fairfield Co., SC. Tended children, toted

water. Stayed on plantation postwar. int. W. Dixon. (S1 2 *SC* 1: 51–54) BETTIE MASSINGALE BELL, b. ca. 1855, Monroe Co., AL. House servant. int. Diard. (SS1 1 *AL*: 44–54) CHARLIE BELL, b. 1856, Pearl River Co., MS. Tended cattle, fed chickens. int. M. Austin. (SS1 6 *MS* 1: 122–27) ELIZA BELL, b. 1851, Pontotoc Co., MS. Stayed on plantation postwar. int. Garrison, ed. Vollmer. (SS1 12 *OK*: 52–58) FRANK BELL, b. 1834, VA. Fieldhand. int. C. Anderson. (*WW*, 23–28) FRANK BELL, b. 1851, New Orleans, slave in brothel where mother worked as prostitute. Waiter, houseboy, pimp. Held in bondage until slaveholder's death in drunken brawl long after war. Rambled. int. B. Davis. (S1 4 *TX* 1: 59–61; SS2 2 *TX* 1: 237–43) OLIVER BELL, b. unk., Livingston, AL. Fieldhand, nurseryman. int. Tartt. (S1 6 *AL*: 27–32; SS1 1 *AL*: 55–60) VIRGINIA BELL, b. ca. 1850, Opelousas, LA. House servant. (S1 4 *TX* 1: 62–65; SS2 2 *TX* 1: 244–48) CYRUS BELLUS, b. 1865, Jefferson Co., MS. Child of ex-slaves. Share-cropped on parents' former plantation. Moved Little Rock 1890, worked lumber. (S2 8 *AR* 1: 141–45) BOB BENFORD, b. ca. 1858, Perry Co., AL. Taken to Union Co., AR while small. Farmed. int. Bowden. (S2 8 *AR* 1: 146–48) UNCLE WILLIS BENNEFIELD, b. ca. 1830, Burke Co., GA. Fieldhand, carriage driver. int. Barragan, Love, Radford. (S2 13 *GA* 4: 168–75, 235–44) SARA BENTON, b. 1846, Fredonia, AL. House servant. (SS1 1 *AL*: 61–63) FANNY BERRY, b. ca. 1841, Appomattox Co., VA. Hired out. Taken Petersburg during war. Held in bondage fifteen years postwar. int. S. Byrd. (S2 16 *VA*: 1–6; *WW*, 30–50) FRANK BERRY, b. 1858, Alachua Co., FL. Grandson Seminole Chief Osceola. Postwar state-federal contractor, registration inspector (1879), US marshal (1881). int. Randolph, ed. Simms. (S2 17 *FL*: 27–31; SS2 1 *FL*: 263–36) JAMES BERTRAND, b. ca. 1870, Pine Bluff, AR. Child of ex-slaves. int. S. Taylor. (S2 8 *AR* 1: 157–59) JACK BESS, b. 1854, Goliad, TX. Worked horses, cattle. Stayed on plantation postwar. Worked other ranches. (S1 4 *TX* 1: 72–74) WILLIAM L. BETHEL, b. May 4, 1844, Forsyth Co., NC. Enlisted Union army. Postwar farmed, worked turpentine, graduated Lincoln University 1882. Presbyterian minister. Organized churches NC, SC, VA, OK. (SS1 12 *OK*: 59–63) THOMAS GREEN BETHUNE (BLIND TOM), b. May 25, 1849, Columbus, GA. Profile of slave piano prodigy Blind Tom Bethune (1849–1909) from interviews with white acquaintances. int. Dauphin, Taylor. (SS1 3 *GA* 1: 53–61) AUNT KATE BETTERS, b. 1848, MS. House servant. int. A. Davis. (SS2 2 *TX* 1: 261–64) ELLEN BETTS, b. 1853, Opelousas, LA. Nursemaid, wet nurse. int. Osburn. (S1 4 *TX* 1: 75–83; SS2 2 *TX* 1: 265–80) CHARLOTTE BEVERLY, b. ca. 1847, Montgomery Co., TX. House servant. int. Dibble, Grey. (S1 4 *TX* 1: 84–86; SS2 1 *TX* 2: 281–88) DELLA MUN BIBLES, b. unk., Bosque Co., TX. Child of enslaved white woman and enslaved Indian man. Cook. int. A. Davis. (SS2 1 *TX* 2: 289–95) MARY MINUS BIDDIE, b. 1833, Pensacola, raised Columbia Co. Fieldhand. (S2 17 *FL*: 32–38) ARRIE BINNS, b. ca. 1845, Lincoln Co., GA. Fieldhand, house servant. int. Stonestreet. (S2 12 *GA* 1: 72–79) FRANCIS BLACK, b. ca. 1850, Grand Bluff, MS. Stolen age five, taken New Orleans then Jefferson, TX. Playmate slaveholder children, house servant. Stayed on plantation after freedom, then moved Cass Co. Blind, resident Ragland Old Folks Home, Texarkana. (S1 4 *TX* 1: 87–89; SS2 2 *TX* 1: 299–302) MAGGIE BLACK, b. ca. 1858, Marion, SC. Picked up chips, drove turkeys. int. R. Davis. (S1 2 *SC* 1: 57–61) WILLIAM BLACK, b. ca. 1850, Marion Co., MO. Hired out. Took children to school, ran errands. (S2 11 *MO*: 32–35; SS1 2 *MO*: 147–49) WILLIAM EDWARD BLACK, b. January 1, 1846, Charlotte, NC. 1861 taken Ittawmba Co., MS. After freedom moved Booneville, then in 1875 to Holly Springs. Supporting self collecting iron, paper, rags. int. N. Thompson. (SS1 6 *MS* 1: 143–6). WILLIE (UNCLE BILL) BLACKWELL, b. 1834, NC. Fieldhand. Stayed on plantation until 1872. Drifted, odd-jobbed. Settled Fort Worth. int. R. Hatcher, Phipps. (SS2 2 *TX* 1: 303–23) HENRY BLAKE, b. March 16, 1863, Little Rock. Farmed postwar. int.

S. Taylor. (S2 8 *AR* 1: 175–79) ADELINE BLAKELY, b. July 10, 1850, Hickman Co., TN. Taken AR. House servant. Domestic postwar. int. Hudgins. (S2 8 *AR* 1: 180–93) SALLIE BLAKELEY, b. ca. 1858, Thomaston, GA. House servant, hired out. Stayed on plantation postwar. int. Ross. (SS1 3 *GA* 1: 62–67) EMMA BLALOCK, b. ca. 1850, NC. int. Matthews, ed. G. Andrews. (S2 14 *NC* 1: 103–9) OLIVIER BLANCHARD, b. ca. 1843, LA. Creole. int. Dibble, Grey. (S2 4 *TX* 1: 90–92; SS2 2 *TX* 1: 324–29) HENRY BLAND, b. 1851, GA. Yard boy, herder, fieldhand. (S2 12 *GA* 1: 80–85) JULIA BLANKS, b. 1862, San Antonio. (S1 4 *TX* 2: 93–105) SUSAN BLEDSOE, b. August 15, 1845, Giles Co., TN. Fieldhand, house servant. (S2 16 *OH*: 7–9) PETER BLEWITT, b. December 11, 1850, Galveston, TX. Sold, taken Newton Co., accompanied slaveholder to war, returned, stayed on plantation until 1872. Eventually settled Gulfport, MS. int. Walsh. (SS1 6 *MS* 1: 152–54) HENRY BOBBITT, b. 1850, Warren Co., NC. Fieldhand. int. Hicks, ed. Waitt. (S2 14 *NC* 1: 120–24) MANDA BOGGAN, b. 1847, Simpson Co., MS. Fieldhand. int. Giles. (SS1 6 *MS* 1: 155–59) DAN BOGIE, b. May 5, 1858, Garrard Co., KY. int. Ison. (S2 16 *KY*: 1–4) ELVIRA BOLES, b. 1843, Lexington MS. Worked slaveholder's brickyard. Taken TX last year of war, farmed after freedom. (S1 4 *TX* 2: 106–8; SS2 2 *TX* 1: 336–39) GEORGE BOLLINGER, b. 1855, Bollinger Co., MO. int. M. Smith. (S2 11 *MO*: 40–43) JAMES BOLTON, b. 1852, Oglethorpe Co., GA. Yard boy, stayed on plantation forty years postwar. int. Hall, ed. Barragan. (S2 12 *GA* 1: 91–104; SS1 3 *GA* 1: 76–90) MAGGIE (BUNNY) BOND, b. ca. 1850, Magnolia, NC. Taken Madison, AR while young. int. Robertson. (S2 8 *AR* 1: 197–200) SINEY BONNER, b. ca. 1850, Pickens Co., AL. House servant. Domestic postwar. int. W. Jordan. (S1 6 *AL*: 39–41) ANDREW BOONE, b. 1857, Northampton Co., NC. Fieldhand. int. Matthews, ed. G. Andrews. (S2 14 *NC* 1: 130–37) REV. FRANK T. BOONE, freeborn 1858, VA. Postwar worked turpentine GA, farmed, preached AR. int. S. Taylor. (S2 8 *AR* 1: 202–9) J. F. BOONE, b. December 8, 1872, Woodruff

Co., AR, parents' former plantation. Farmed, janitor. int. S. Taylor. (S2 8 *AR* 1: 210–13) BETTY BORMER, b. April 4, 1857, Arlington, TX. Nursemaid. Stayed on plantation postwar. int. Gauthier. (S1 4 *TX* 1: 109–11; SS2 2 *TX* 1: 340–45) W. L. BOST, b. ca. 1850, Newton, NC. Sharecropped postwar. int. M. Jones. (S2 14 *NC* 1: 138–46) ALEC BOSTWICK, b. ca. 1861, Morgan Co., GA. Fieldhand. Stayed on plantation postwar. (S2 12 *GA* 1: 106–12) NANCY BOUDRY, b. ca. 1837, Columbia Co., GA. Fieldhand. Farmed, domestic postwar. int. Barragan, Harris. (S2 12 *GA* 1: 113–17) SAMUEL BOULWARE, b. 1855, SC. int. Grant. (S1 2 *SC* 1: 65–69) JOE BOUY, b. 1858, Lincoln Co., MS. int. de Sola. (SS1 6 *MS* 1: 180–82) JENNIE BOWEN, b. ca. 1847, AL. Nursemaid. Stayed on plantation as sharecropper postwar. int. Poole. (S1 6 AL: 42–43; SS1 1 *AL*: 69–71) REVEREND ELI BOYD, b. May 29, 1864, Somerville, SC. Fieldhand. Moved GA 1888, washed dishes, worked turpentine, preached. Later moved Miami. (S2 17 *FL*: 39–40) ISABELLA BOYD, b. ca. 1850, Richmond, VA. Taken TX prewar. Seamstress. Domestic postwar. int. Dibble, Grey. (S1 4, *TX* 1: 114–16; SS2 2 *TX* 1: 355–61) JAMES BOYD, b. January 1830, Phantom Valley, IT. Mother was Black, father, Cherokee. Stolen as child. Farmed, drove cattle postwar. int. A. Davis. (S1 4 *TX* 1: 117–20; SS2 2 *TX* 1: 362–70) JERRY BOYKINS, b. 1845, Troup Co., GA. House servant, fiddler. Foreman Louisville, KY mule barn postwar. Moved Corsicana 1886. int. Gauthier. (S1 4 *TX* 1: 121–23; SS2: 2 *TX* 1: 371–74) RIVANA BOYNTON, b. 1850, SC. House servant, fieldhand. int. C. Taylor. (S2 17 *FL*: 41–46, 367–71) CALLIE BRACEY, b. unk., IN. Child of MS ex-slave Louise Terrell. int. Pritchett. (S1 6 IN: 25–26) MARIA BRACEY, b. unk., Charleston, SC. int. Hamlin. (SS1 11 *SC*: 66–67) ELODGA BRADFORD, b. 1845, Port Gibson, MS. Served in war, afterward returned plantation. int. de Sola. (SS1 6 *MS* 1: 18–8) SAM BRADFORD, b. unk., Pontotoc Co., MS. Coachman. (SS1 6 *MS* 1: 187–78) EDMOND BRADLEY, b. January 4, 1842, Pass Christian, MS. Creole. int. Wells. (SS1 6 *MS* 1: 189–95) RACHEL

BRADLEY, b. ca. 1830, Farmerville, LA. House servant. Stayed on plantation postwar, later sharecropped, domestic. int. Bowden. (S2 8 *AR* 1: 233–36; SS1 2 *AR*: 1–3) GUS BRADSHAW, b. ca. 1845, Keecheye, AL. Taken Port Caddo 1850. Fieldhand. Stayed on plantation ten years postwar. Bought farm. int. Hampton. (S1 4 *TX* 1: 130–32; SS2 2 *TX* 1: 391–96) WES BRADY, b. 1849, Harrison Co., TX. Fieldhand. Farmed postwar. int. Hampton, Dickinson. (S1 4 *TX* 1: 133–36; SS2 2 *TX* 1: 397–404) JACOB BRANCH, b. ca. 1851, LA. Taken Beaumont. Fieldhand. Farmed postwar. int. Dibble, Grey. (S1 4 *TX* 1: 137–42; SS2 2 *TX* 1: 405–19) ELLEN BRASS, b. ca. 1855, Green Co., AL. Taken LA. Fieldhand, domestic. int. S. Taylor. (S2 8 *AR* 1: 246–48) MINERVA BRATCHER, b. 1851, Sabine Co., TX. Housemaid. Stayed on plantation postwar. int. Shirley. (SS2 1 *TX* 2: 420–21) LOUISIA BRAXTON, b. 1864, Waggaman, LA. Fieldhand, washed, cooked, ironed. int. McElwee. (*MW*, 29–31) AMANDA EILERS BRICE, b. ca. 1850, Bastrop, TX. Nursemaid. Postwar farmed, worked sawmill camps. Settled Austin. Domestic. int. Menn. (SS2 2 *TX* 1: 422–27) ANDY BRICE, b. ca. 1856, Winnsboro, SC. Fieldhand, teamster, fiddler. int. W. Dixon. (S1 2 *SC* 1: 75–79) ANNIE BRIDGES, b. March 6, 1855, St. Francis Co., MO. House servant. (S2 11 *MO*: 44–51) FRANCIS BRIDGES, b. 1864, Red River Co., TX. Farmed after freedom. (S1 7 *OK*: 20–23) GEORGE BRIGGS, b. 1849, Union Co., SC. Farmed, preached. int. Sims, ed. Turnage. (S1 2 *SC* 1: 80–97; SS1 11 *SC*: 68–75) CLARA BRIM, b. ca. 1837, Opelousas, LA. Fieldhand. Sharecropped, domestic postwar. Moved Beaumont 1913, with daughter ran boarding houses for sawmill, railroad workers. int. Dibble. (S1 4 *TX* 1: 147–48; SS2 2 *TX* 1: 428–33) JOSEPHINE BRISTOW, b. 1865, SC. Child of ex-slaves. int. R. Davis. (S1 2 *SC* 1: 98–103) SAM BROACH, b. 1848, Rock Hill, SC. Taken AL, MS prewar. Stable hand, banjo player. Stayed on plantation postwar, later farmed as tenant. int. M. Austin. (SS1 6 *MS* 1: 222–30) HENRY BROADDUS, b. ca. 1860, AL. Taken Marlin, TX. Herded ducks, geese. int. A. Davis. (SS2

2 *TX* 1: 441–44) NED BROADUS, b. ca. 1810, Mobile, AL. Taken TX. Fieldhand. Farmed postwar. int. A. Davis. (SS2 2 *TX* 1: 434–40) JAMES BROOKS, b. ca. 1855, Grand Gulf, MS. Dance caller, plasterer. int. Lawrence. (SS1 6 *MS* 1: 233–34) MARY ANN BROOKS, b. 1848, Pine Bluff, AR. Slave of druggist, acquired for debt. Nursemaid. int. Bowden. (S2 8 *AR* 1: 253–54) SYLVESTER BROOKS, b. 1850, Green Co., AL. Fieldhand. Stayed on plantation postwar, later sharecropped TX. int. Cowan. (S1 4 *TX* 1: 149–50; SS2 2 *TX* 1: 448–53) ANNE BROOME, b. ca. 1850, SC. int. W. Dixon. (S1 2 *SC* 1: 104–6) ELLEN BROOMFIELD, b. 1853, New Orleans. Fieldhand. int. Posey. (*MW*, 31–32) DONAVILLE BROUSSARD, b. 1850, Lafayette, LA. Creole. Sold during war. Yard boy. Farmed postwar. int. Dibble. (S1 4 *TX* 1: 151–53; SS2 2 *TX* 1: 454–59) BEN BROWN, b. ca. 1837, Albemarle Co., VA. Fieldhand. int. Dugan. (S2 16 *OH*: 11–14) CALLINE BROWN, b. 1832, Copiah Co., MS. Fieldhand. Farmed postwar. int. Campbell. (SS1 6 *MS* 1: 235–38) CHARLOTTE BROWN, b. ca. 1855, Woods Crossing, VA. (*WW*, 58–59) EASTER BROWN, b. 1860, GA. House servant. (S1 12 *GA* 1: 135–40) EBENEZER BROWN, b. 1852, Liberty, MS. Fieldhand, house servant. int. Holmes. (SS1 6 *MS* 1: 239–54) FANNIE BROWN, b. ca. 1850, Richmond, VA. Sold age five, taken TX. Cook, weaver. int. A. Davis. (S1 4 *TX* 1: 154–55; SS2 2 *TX* 1: 460–63) FRED BROWN, b. November 16, 1853, Baton Rouge Parish, LA. Taken TX during war. Fieldhand. Postwar odd-jobbed Rusk Co. Cooked Houston, Dallas, Fort Worth. int. Gauthier. (S1 4 *TX* 1: 156–59; SS2 2 *TX* 1: 464–70) HAGAR (HAGER) BROWN, b. ca. 1860, Murrells Inlet, SC. Midwife. int. Chandler. (S1 2 *SC* 1: 107–14; SS1 11 *SC*: 76–86) HENRY BROWN, b. 1857, SC. int. Ladson. (S1 2 *SC* 1: 122–26) JAMES BROWN, b. 1853, Bell Co., TX. int. Gauthier. (S1 4 *TX* 1: 160–62; SS2 3 *TX* 2: 474–80) JOHN BROWN, b. 1860, Greenville Co., VA. int. S. Byrd. (*WW*, 61–62) JULIA (SALLY) BROWN (AUNT SALLY), b. ca. 1852, Commerce, GA. House servant. Orphaned, given to abusive family. Wandered

homeless, settled Atlanta. int. Tonsill. (S2 12 *GA* 1: 141–53; SS1 3 *GA* 1: 94–110) LEWIS BROWN, b. April 14, 1855, Kemper Co., MS. Tended animals, worked gin. Postwar sharecropped, carpentry MS, AR. (S2 8 *AR* 1: 290–97; SS2 1 *AR*: 56–57) LIZZIE FANT BROWN, b. 1861, Holly Springs, MS. House servant. int. N. Thompson. (SS1 6 *MS* 1: 255–66) MOM LOUISA BROWN, b. ca. 1860, SC. int. Chandler. (S1 2 *SC* 1: 115–17) LUCY BROWN, b. unk., Person Co., NC. int. Hicks, ed. Waitt. (S2 14 *NC* 1: 152–54) MARIE BROWN, freeborn unk., New Orleans, LA. Creole. Seamstress. int. Posey. (*MW*, 33–36) MARY FRANCES BROWN, b. ca. 1847, Marlborough Co., SC. House servant. int. Pinckney, Tiedman. (S1 2 *SC* 1: 131–36; SS1 11 *SC*: 87–90) MOLLY BROWN, b. ca. 1845, Edgefield Co., SC. int. Robertson. (S2 8 *AR* 1: 303–10) PETER BROWN, b. March 1, 1852, MS. Postwar farmed, roustabout Mississippi riverboats. int. Robertson. (S2 8 *AR* 1: 311–14) RINA BROWN, b. 1853, Franklin Co., MS. House servant. int. Holmes. (SS1 6 *MS* 1: 273–83) ROSE BROWN, b. 1853, Tuscaloosa, AL. Sold, taken Choctaw Co. Nursemaid. int. Butts. (SS1 6 *MS* 1: 284–86) SALLY BROWN, b. ca. 1852, Commerce, GA. Fieldhand. Stayed on plantation postwar, later moved Winder, then Atlanta. int. Tonsill. (SS1 3 *GA* 1: 94–110) THOMAS BROWN, b. ca. 1862, Davidson Co., TN. Taken Williamson Co. Postwar moved Nashville, then MS. int. Walsh. (SS1 6 *MS* 1: 290–93) VERICE BROWN, b. ca. 1860, St. James Parish, LA. int. McElwee. (*MW*, 37) WILLIAM BROWN, b. May 3, 1861, Cross Co., AR. Farmed, preached. int. S. Taylor. (S2 8 *AR* 1: 317–23) ZEK BROWN, b. 1857, Warren Co., TN. House servant. int. Gauthier. (S1 4 *TX* 1: 166–68; SS2 3 *TX* 2: 497–502) GEORGE WASHINGTON BROWNING, b. 1852, Walton Co., GA. Sharecropped postwar. Moved Atlanta to escape Klan. int. Ross. (SS1 3 *GA* 1: 111–17) MAGGIE BROYLES, b. ca. 1855, Decatur, TN. Taken Forrest City, AR. Farmed. int. Robertson. (S1 8 *AR* 2: 324–28) MADISON BRUIN, b. 1856, Lexington, KY. Groom, fieldhand. Enlisted postwar, fought Indian wars AZ, TX. Settled TX, worked

Southern Pacific Railroad, Beaumont Gas and Waterworks, Spindletop oil fields. int. Dibble, Grey. (S1 4 *TX* 1: 169–73; SS2 3 *TX* 2: 503–11) RICHARD BRUNER, b. 1840, Saline Co., MO. Waterboy, fieldhand. Preached postwar. int. Nelson. (S2 11 *MO*: 58–60) VINNIE BRUNSON, b. unk., Centerville, TX. Sharecropped postwar. int. Cowan. (SS2 3 *TX* 2: 512–18) ROBERT BRYANT, b. ca. 1862, Caledonia, MO. Worked steamboats, iron foundries, farmed. (S2 11 *MO*: 61–69) HENRY BUFFORD (UNCLE EPH), b. ca. 1850, GA. Child of ex-slaves. Moved CO 1868. Bouncer, porter, gambler, toured with Buffalo Bill's Wild West Show, Ringling Brothers Circus. Residing Colorado Colored Blind Home. (SS1 2 *CO*: 33–34) JULIA BUNCH, b. 1853, Edgefield Co., SC. Nursemaid. Stayed on plantation four years, moved Aiken Co., farmed. int. L. Harris, ed. Booth. (S2 12 *GA* 1: 154–59) QUEEN ELIZABETH BUNTS, b. ca. 1865, Baker Co., GA. Child of ex-slaves. House servant. Stayed on plantation postwar. (SS1 3 *GA* 1: 118–30) GEORGE TAYLOR BURNS, b. ca. 1835, MO. Taken IN 1840, indentured to flatboat captain. Worked boats on various rivers until 1910. int. Creel. (S1 6 *IN*: 36–39; SS1 5 *IN*: 27–42) C. B. BURTON, b. 1858, Newberry Co., SC. Sharecropped postwar. int. Summer, ed. Turnage. (S1 2 *SC* 1: 152; SS1 11 *SC*: 95) JAMES BURTON, ca. 1857, Richmond, VA. Taken MS. House servant. int. England. (SS1 6 *MS* 1: 305–7) VINNIE BUSBY, b. ca. 1854, Rankin Co., MS. Farmed postwar. int. Giles. (SS1 6 *MS* 1: 308–12) SAM BUSH, b. 1860, Ellis Co., TX. Cowhand, stockyards postwar. int. Gauthier. (SS2 3 *TX* 2: 539–44) ELLEN BUTLER, b. ca. 1860, Calcasieu Parish, LA. Toted water. (S1 4 *TX* 2: 176–78) GABE BUTLER, b. March 9, 1854, Amite Co., MS. Shepherd. int. Holmes. (SS1 6 *MS* 1: 320–28) ISAIAH BUTLER, b. ca. 1855, Hampton Co., SC. int. Faucette. (S1 2 *SC* 1: 155–60) MARSHAL BUTLER, b. December 25, 1849, Washington-Wilkes, GA. Fieldhand. int. Jaffe. (S2 12 *GA* 1: 160–67) CHARLES BUTLINGTON, b. ca. 1846, Cooper Co., MO. (SS1 2 *MO*: 156–57) DAVE L. BYRD, b. 1852, Madison Co., TX. int. B. Davis. (SS2 3 *TX* 2: 560–72) SARAH

BYRD, b. 1842, Orange Co., VA. Sold, taken Augusta, GA. Fieldhand. (S2 12 *GA* 1: 168–71) GRANNY CAIN, b. 1847, Newberry Co., SC. Lady's maid. int. Summer, ed. Turnage. (S1 2 *SC* 1: 166–68) LOUIS CAIN, b. 1849, NC. Moved Madisonville, TX postwar, farmed. int. B. Davis. (S1 4 *TX* 1: 185–87; SS2 3 *TX* 2: 584–99) JAMES CALDWELL, b. 1866, SC. Child of ex-slaves. int. Summer. (SS1 11 *SC*: 96) SOLOMON CALDWELL, b. 1864, Newberry Co., SC. Farmed postwar. int. Summer, ed. Turnage. (S1 2 *SC* 1: 170–71) JEFF CALHOUN, b. November 23, 1838, Alton, AL. Taken TX prewar. Carriage driver, fieldhand. Postwar drove traveling doctor. Later worked Navarro, Freestone Cos. int. W. Smith. (S1 4 *TX* 1: 188–90; SS2 3 *TX* 2: 600–611) JOHN CAMERON, b. 1842, Jackson, MS. Gardener. int. Giles. (S1 7 *MS*: 18–21; SS1 7 *MS* 2: 332–35) NELSON CAMERON, b. 1856, SC. Farmed after freedom, still sharecropping near Winnsboro. int. W. Dixon. (S1 2 *SC* 1: 172–75) HARRISON CAMILLE, b. May 27, 1860, Barataria, LA. Taken New Orleans as child. Worked sugar factory, sold Spanish moss. int. Wallace. (*MW*, 39–40) EASTER SUDIE CAMPBELL, b. ca. 1865, Caldwell Co., KY. Child of ex-slaves. int. Hanberry. (S2 16 *KY*: 90–94) ELLEN CAMPBELL, b. 1846, Augusta, GA. Toted water, tended cows, hired out to boarding house. int. Barragan, Love, Radford. (S2 13 *GA* 4: 221–25) SIMPSON (SIMP) CAMPBELL, b. 1860, Marshall, TX. Left 1883. Public works. int. Hampton. (S1 4 *TX* 1: 191–92; SS2 3 *TX* 2: 612–17) POLLY TURNER CANCER, b. ca. 1837, Lafayette Co., MS. House servant, weaver. int. Holt. (SS1 7 *MS* 2: 336–52) SYLVIA CANNON, b. ca. 1857, Florence, SC. House servant. Stayed on plantation eight years postwar. Domestic. int. H. Davis, Young, ed. R. Davis. (S1 2 *SC* 1: 180–96) SALLIE CARDER, b. ca. 1855, Jackson, TN. House servant, nurse. int. Thomas. (S1 7 *OK*: 27–29; SS1 12 *OK*: 96–98) MARY CARPENTER, b. 1851, Harris Co., GA. Fieldhand. int. J. Jones. (SS1 3 *GA* 1: 142–49) UNCLE RICHARD CARRUTHERS, b. ca. 1848, Memphis. Sold, taken Bastrop Co., TX. Fiddler, lot man. int. Osburn. (S1 4

TX 1: 197–201; SS2 3 TX 2: 626–38) ARON CARTER, b. November 10, 1857, Lincoln Co., MS. Fieldhand. Stayed on plantation postwar. int. de Sola. (SS1 7 MS 2: 353–60) CATO CARTER, b. 1836 or 1837, Wilcox Co., AL. House servant, cow tender, ran errands. int. Foreman. (S1 4 TX 1: 202–11; SS2 3 TX 2: 639–52) MILDRED CARTER, b. 1856, VA. (WW, 70) BELLE CARUTHERS, b. 1847, Wadesboro, NC. Taken Marshall Co., MS. int. N. Thompson. (SS1 7 MS 2: 364–68) JULIA CASEY, b. 1855, West TN. (S2 16 TN: 3–4) SUSAN CASTLE, b. March 7, 1860, Clarke Co., GA. Postwar moved Athens, nursed, washed. int. Hornsby, ed. Hall, Booth. (S2 12 GA 1: 177–83) GEORGE CAULTON, b. 1844, Halifax, VA. Sold age ten. Fieldhand, tended cattle. Moved GA postwar, farmed. int. Watson. (SS1 3 GA 1: 167–76) JACK CAUTHERN, b. 1852, Travis Co., TX. Fieldhand, stayed on plantation after freedom. Moved San Angelo 1900, worked saloon. (S1 4 TX 2: 212–13; SS2 3 TX 2: 666–68) AUNT CICELY CAWTHON, b. 1859, Stephens Co., GA. House servant. int. Newton, ed. Booth. (SS1 3 GA 1: 177–93) LULA CHAMBERS, b. ca. 1845, Gelatin Co., KY. House servant. (S2 11 MO: 79–83) SALLY BANKS CHAMBERS, b. unk., Oakland, LA. Taken Liberty, TX when small. (S1 4 TX 1: 214–16; SS2 3 TX 2: 681–85) LIZZIE CHANDLER, b. unk., raised LA, MS. Fieldhand, house servant, chambermaid New Orleans steamboats. (MW, 40–43) NED CHANEY, b. ca. 1857, Choctaw Co., AL. Bones player. Moved Meridian, MS postwar, worked at jail. int. M. Austin. (SS1 7 MS 2: 369–78) AUNT AMY CHAPMAN, b. May 14, 1843, Livingston, AL. Fieldhand. int. Tartt. (S1 6 AL: 58–61) WALTER CHAPMAN, b. ca. 1871, Minnesota. Child of ex-slaves. Taken Denver by father age three. Street performer, government clerk (1902–32). (SS1 2 CO: 35–36) CECELIA CHAPPEL, b. ca. 1835, Marshall Co., TN. Weaver, spinner, seamstress. Nursed, cooked postwar. (S2 16 TN: 5–8) CALLIE CHATMAN, b. 1851, Stewart Co., GA. Washed postwar. (SS1 3 GA 1: 194–95) HARRIET CHEATAM, b. 1843, Gallatin, TN. House servant, fieldhand. Post-

war moved OH, cooked. int. Pritchett. (S1 6 IN: 52–54) HENRY CHEATAM, b. 1851, West Point, MS. Waterboy. int. Prine. (S1 1 AL: 66–71; SS1 1 AL: 89–94) ROBERT J. CHEATHAM, b. unk., KY. Child of ex-slaves. int. Creel. (SS1 5 IN: 45–61) HARRIET CHELSEY, b. ca. 1853, Marshall, TX. Fieldhand. Stayed on plantation as sharecropper postwar. int. Carlow. (SS2 3 TX 2: 692–94) BETTY FOREMAN CHESSIER, b. July 11, 1943, Raleigh, NC. House servant. int. Hunter. (S1 7 OK: 30–32; SS1 12 OK: 99–102) HENRY CHILDERS, b. March 13, 1844, TX. int. Cowan. (SS2 3 TX 2: 695–704) MARY CHILDS, b. ca. 1846, GA. Fieldhand, seamstress. ed. Barragan. (SS1 3 GA 1: 196–202) JEPTHA (DOC) CHOICE, b. October 17, 1835, Rusk Co., TX. Fieldhand, musician. Postwar farmed, worked railroad, taught school. Moved Houston 1888, barbered, practiced divine healing. int. Drake. (S1 4 TX 1: 217–19; SS2 3 TX 2: 705–13) ANTHONY CHRISTOPHER, b. ca. 1850, TX. (SS2 3 TX 2: 718–24) ELLEN CLAIBOURN, b. August 19, 1852, Columbia Co., GA. House servant. int. M. Johnson. (S2 12 GA 1: 184–88) JAMES CLAIBORNE, b. 1860, Wilkinson Co., MS. Farmed postwar. int. Walsh. (SS1 7 MS 2: 400–401) GEORGE WASHINGTON CLARIDY, b. 1853, Howard Co., AR. Self-identified drunkard, gambler, horse thief, murderer. Also sold whiskey. int. Allen. (SS1 12 OK: 103–6) AMOS CLARK, b. April 2, 1841, Washington Co., TX. Sold, taken McLennan Co. House servant, laborer, dance caller. Sharecropper postwar. int. A. Davis. (S1 4 TX 1: 220–22; SS2 3 TX 2: 725–32) ANNA CLARK, b. April 5, 1847, GA. House servant. Moved Central City, CO postwar. Street dancer, cook, pie maker, churchwoman. (SS1 2 CO: 36–39) FLEMING CLARK, b. ca. 1860, VA. Fieldhand, hired out. (S2 16 OH: 22–25) LAURA CLARK, b. ca. 1850, NC. Taken Livingston, AL prewar. Fieldhand, house servant. int. Tartt. (S1 6 AL: 72–75) RENA CLARK, b. 1850, MS. Midwife, herb doctor. int. Price. (SS1 7 MS 2: 408–11) BERRY CLAY, b. August 5, 1847, Telfair Co., GA. Indian father, white mother. Sold into slavery by mother and stepfather. int. A. Dixon.

(S2 12 *GA* 1: 189–94) HENRY CLAY, b. ca. 1835, NC. Taken LA, TX border, hired out to steamboat captain. Later taken IT. Fiddler, fieldhand, roustabout, potter. int. Garrison, ed. Lackey. (SS1 12 *OK*: 108–18) HATTIE CLAYTON, b. 1847, GA. Sold age eight, taken Lee Co., AL. int. Klein. (S1 6 *AL*: 76–77; SS1 1 *AL*: 95–98) MARIA SUTTON CLEMMENTS (CLEMENTS), b. ca. 1850, GA. int. Robertson. (S2 8 *AR* 2: 15–27) PETER CLIFTON, b. 1848, Camden, SC. int. W. Dixon. (S1 2 *SC* 1: 205–9) AUNT CLUSSEY, b. ca. 1845, Etowah Co., AL. Fieldhand. int. L. H., Archive of Folk Song. (SS1 1 *AL*: 18–21) FATHER CHARLES COATES, b. March 1828, Richmond, VA. Sold, taken Washington Co., GA prewar. Carriage driver. int. Muse. (S2 17 *FL*: 65–73) IRENE COATES, b. 1859, GA. Stayed on plantation postwar, later moved Jacksonville, FL. Nursemaid. int. Muse. (S2 17 *FL*: 74–79) FRANCES COBB, b. ca. 1854, Columbus, MS. Nursemaid, sharecropped. int. Joiner. (SS1 7 *MS* 2: 416–22) PIERCE CODY, b. ca. 1850, Warren Co., GA. Fieldhand. int. A. Dixon. (S2 12 *GA* 1: 195–200) WILLIS COFER, b. 1860, Washington-Wilkes, GA. Farmed postwar. int. McCune, ed. L. Harris. (S2 12 *GA* 1: 201–11) ANNA MARIE COFFEE, b. ca. 1852, Enfield, NC. Sold eleven times. House servant. int. Minnick. (SS1 5 *OH*: 284–89) MARY COLBERT, b. 1854, Athens, GA. House servant, washerwoman. int. Hornsby, ed. Hall, Booth. (S2 12 *GA* 1: 212–25) ALICE COLE, b. 1852, Monroe, LA. int. B. Davis. (SS2 3 *TX* 2: 746–64) HARRISON COLE, b. September 14, 1861, Galveston, TX. int. Cowan. (SS2 3 *TX* 2: 765–74) JOHN COLE, b. ca. 1855, Oglethorpe Co., GA. Horse trainer. ed. Fichlen, Jaffee. (S2 12 *GA* 1: 226–30) JULIA COLE, b. ca. 1860, Monroe, GA. Domestic. int. Fowler, ed. Hall, Harris, Booth. (S2 12 *GA* 1: 231–36) THOMAS COLE, b. August 1845, Jackson Co., AL. Fieldhand. Runaway, joined Union Army 1861. Postwar moved Chattanooga, railroad switchman. Later moved TX. (S1 4 *TX* 1: 225–35; SS2 3 *TX* 2: 783–836) ELI COLEMAN, b. 1846, KY. int. B. Davis. (S1 4 *TX* 1: 236–39; SS2 3 *TX* 2: 843–55) GEORGE COLEMAN, b. August 16, 1830, Richmond, VA. Age sixteen sold, taken West Point, MS. House servant, fieldhand, weaver. Held in bondage postwar. int. Ellison. (SS1 7 *MS* 2: 423–26) LULA COLEMAN, b. 1851, Livingston, AL. Fieldhand. Stayed on plantation postwar, later moved Meridian, then Delta. Farmed, washed. int. M. Austin. (SS1 7 *MS* 2: 427–34) PREELY COLEMAN, b. 1852, Newberry Co., SC. Sold with mother to conceal white parentage, taken Cherokee Co., TX. int. Shirley. (S1 4 *TX* 1: 240–41; SS2 3 *TX* 2: 856–62) ANNIE COLEY, b. ca. 1860, Camden, SC. Fieldhand. Sharecropped postwar. Moved MS 1904, worked turpentine. int. C. Wells. (SS1 7 *MS* 2: 438–46) MOM LOUISA COLLIER, b. 1859, Marion, SC. Stayed on plantation as tenant postwar. int. R. Davis. (S1 2 *SC* 1: 218–23) HARRIET COLLINS, b. 1870, Houston. Child of ex-slave. int. A. Davis. (S1 4 *TX* 1: 242–45; SS2 3 *TX* 2: 883–96) KIZZIE COLQUITT, b. ca. 1862, Elbert Co., GA. int. McCune, ed. L. Harris. (S2 12 *GA* 1: 122–24) MARTHA COLQUITT, b. ca. 1850, Oglethorpe Co., GA. Postwar moved town, domestic. int. Hall, ed. Booth. (S2 12 *GA* 1: 237–50) SARA COLQUITT, b. ca. 1830, Richmond, VA. House servant. (S1 6 *AL*: 87–89; SS1 1 *AL*: 99–101) ANDREW (SMOKY) COLUMBUS, b. 1859, Cass Co., TX. Moved Jefferson 1878. int. Hampton. (S1 4 *TX* 1: 246–48; SS2 3 *TX* 2: 897–901) JAKE COMPTON, b. March 2, 1859, Waco, TX. Farmed postwar. int. Cowan. (SS2 3 *TX* 2: 902–7) JOSEPHINE TIPPIT COMPTON, b. February 8, 1862, Waco, TX. Farmed postwar. int. Cowan. (SS2 3 *TX* 2: 908–13) JOE CONEY, b. ca. 1857, MS. int. Holmes. (SS1 7 *MS* 2: 487–91) GEORGE CONRAD JR., b. February 23, 1860, Harrison Co., KY. Fieldhand. Left 1883, enlisted US army, stationed IT. (S1 7 *OK*: 39–44) CHARLIE COOPER, b. 1847, Monroe, LA. Traded for horses, then cattle, finally back to first slaveholder. Fieldhand. int. B. Davis. (SS2 3 *TX* 2: 919–27) FRANK COOPER, b. unk., Franklin, IN. Child of ex-slave Mandy Cooper, b. ca. 1822, Lincoln Co., KY. int. Mays. (S1 6 *IN*: 61–63) LUCIUS COOPER, b. 1847, Vicksburg, MS. Fieldhand. Taken TX during war. Cooked, preached postwar. int. Hampton. (SS2 3 *TX* 2: 928–32) VALMAR CORMIER, b. ca. 1855, Lafayette, LA. Creole. Fieldhand. Farmed postwar. int. Dibble, Grey. (S1 4 *TX* 4: 252–53; SS2 3 *TX* 2: 933–36) PETER CORN, b. 1854, Ste. Genevieve Co., MO. Fieldhand. After freedom farmed, worked iron factories, Mississippi riverboats. (S2 11 *MO*: 85–95) PHANNIE CORNEAL, b. December 5, 1864, Savannah, MO. Left 1889, settled Lincoln, NE. Missionary work. int. Burks. (SS2 1 *NE*: 311–13) CATHERINE CORNELIUS, b. ca. 1836, Baton Rouge. Fieldworker. int. R. McKinney. (*MW*, 45–47) JAMES CORNELIUS, b. ca. 1846, Franklin, LA. Sold as infant, taken Magnolia, MS. House servant, conch trumpeter. Postwar, hauled cotton LA, MS, worked mill, hauled lumber, farmed MS. int. Holmes. (S1 7 *MS*: 26–33; SS1 7 *MS* 2: 501–9) JANE COTTON, b. 1847, Walker Co., TX. House servant, nursemaid. int. B. Davis. (SS2 3 *TX* 2: 944–49) JOHN COTTONHAM, b. 1866, Lake Village, AR. Child of ex-slaves. Held in bondage until 1879. Fieldhand. int. Pettigrew. (SS2 1 *AR*: 60–61) ALBERT COX, b. ca. 1851, Simpson Co., MS. Fieldhand, stayed on plantation fifteen years postwar for wages. int. Giles. (SS1 7 *MS* 2: 512–16) ELIJAH COX (UNCLE COX), freeborn 1843, MI. Moved Fort Concho (San Angelo), TX 1871. int. Phipps. (SS2 3 *TX* 2: 950–53) JULIA COX, b. 1850, Braxton, MS. Housemaid. int. Giles. (SS1 7 *MS* 2: 518–21) JOSEPHINE COXE, b. ca. 1853, MS. int. N. Thompson. (SS1 7 *MS* 2: 525–28) WILLIS COZART, b. June 11, 1845, Person Co., NC. Fieldhand. int. Hicks, ed. Waitt. (S2 14 *NC* 1: 182–86) ELLEN CRAGIN, b. ca. 1855, Vicksburg, MS. Seamstress. int. S. Taylor. (S2 8 *AR* 2: 42) CALEB CRAIG, b. December 25, 1851, SC. Fieldhand. int. W. Dixon. (S1 2 *SC* 1: 229–33) HANNAH CRASSON, b. March 2, 1853, Wake Co., NC. House servant. int. Matthews, ed. Waitt. (S2 14 *NC* 1: 187–93) JOHN CRAWFORD, b. 1837, MS. Fieldhand, weaver, fiddler. int. Foreman. (S1 4 *TX* 1: 257–59; SS2 4 *TX* 3: 962–96) SARA CROCKER, b. ca. 1835, Twiggs Co., GA. Fieldhand. Sharecropped postwar. int. Watson. (SS1 3 *GA* 1:

223–31) EMMA CROCKETT, b. ca. 1857, Livingston, AL. int. Tartt, ed. Clark. (S1 6 *AL*: 92–94) ADELINE CRUMP, b. 1864, NC. int. Matthews, ed. Waitt. (S2 14 *NC* 1: 203–6) BILL CRUMP, b. 1855, Davidson Co., NC. Serving murder sentence in state prison, Raleigh. int. Hicks, ed. Waitt. (S2 14 *NC* 1: 207–11) RACHEL CRUZE, b. March 9, 1856, Knox Co., TN. House servant. int. Q. Jackson, ed. Webb, Colvin. (SS1 5 *OH*: 290–323) GREEN CUMBY, b. 1851, Henderson, TX. Fieldhand. Farmed postwar. int. Gauthier. (S1 4 *TX* 1: 260–62; SS2 4 *TX* 3: 1002–5) TEMPIE CUMMINS, b. ca. 1862, Jasper, TX. Nursemaid. int. L. Hatcher. (S1 4 *TX* 1: 263–65; SS2 4 *TX* 3: 1006–12) BAILY CUNNINGHAM, b. ca. 1838, Franklin Co., VA. Hired out to Lynchburg hotel. int. I. Warren. (*WW*, 80–83) MARTHA CUNNINGHAM, b. 1856, Sevier Co., TN. Moved AL, TX postwar; moved IT 1889. (S1 7 *OK*: 45–47) BETTY CURLETT, b. 1872, Houlka, MS. Born on parents' former plantation. Washerwoman. int. Robertson. (S2 8 *AR* 2: 72–81) KATE CURRY, b. 1834, Shreveport, LA. Taken TX 1844. int. Cowan. (SS2 4 *TX* 3: 1013–19) WILLIAM CURTIS, b. ca. 1844, GA. Carriage driver, ran errands. Served in war. Returned plantation, stayed as sharecropper. (S1 7 *OK*: 48–52)

LYTTLETON DANDRIDGE, b. 1857, East Carroll Parish, LA. Renter postwar. Moved AR 1916, worked lumber, jobbed around. int. S. Taylor. (S2 8 *AR* 2: 88–90) ELLA DANIELS, b. ca. 1858, Halifax Co., NC. After freedom moved LA then AR. Fieldwork, washed, ironed. int. S. Taylor. (S2 9 *AR* 2: 91–94) JULIA FRANCES DANIELS, b. 1848, Crockett, TX. House servant. Farmed postwar. int. Foreman. (S1 4 *TX* 1: 273–77; SS2 4 *TX* 3: 1020–27) PARILEE DANIELS, b. 1846, Red River Co., TX. Fieldhand, house servant. Farmed postwar. int. B. Davis. (SS2 4 *TX* 3: 1028–46) HENRY DANT, b. ca. 1832, Ralls Co., MO. Fieldhand, fiddler. Farmed postwar. (S2 11 *MO*: 98–99) JUDA DANTZLER, b. ca. 1850, Greene Co., MS. Mail carrier, Confederate spy, fieldhand. Hired out postwar. (SS1 7 *MS* 2: 553–57) KATIE DARLING, b. 1849, Marshall, TX.

Nursemaid. int. Hampton. (S1 4 *TX* 1: 278–80; SS2 4 *TX* 3: 1047–51) CAREY DAVENPORT, b. August 13, 1855, Walker Co., TX. Shepherd. Farmed postwar. int. Dibble, Grey. (S1 4 *TX* 1: 281–84; SS2 4 *TX* 3: 1052–58) CHARLIE DAVENPORT, b. ca. 1837, Adams Co., MS. Fieldhand. Stayed on plantation as sharecropper postwar. int. Moore. (S1 7 *MS*: 34–43; SS1 7 *MS* 2: 558–72) JOHN N. DAVENPORT, b. 1848, Newberry, SC. House servant, fieldhand. Farmed postwar. int. Summer, ed. Turnage. (S1 2 *SC* 1: 240–43) HANNAH DAVIDSON, b. 1852, Ballard Co., KY. Nursemaid, house servant. int. Osthimer. (S2 16 *OH*: 26–32) ANNIE DAVIS, b. ca. 1857, Eutaw, AL. Stayed on plantation postwar. Moved Mobile. int. Poole. (SS1 1 *AL*: 111–16) CAMPBELL DAVIS, b. 1852, Harrison Co., TX. Farmed postwar. int. Hampton. (S1 4 *TX* 1: 285–88; SS2 4 *TX* 3: 1063–68) CARRIE DAVIS, b. ca. 1855, Harris Co., GA. House servant. (S1 6 *AL*: 105–8; SS1 1 *AL*: 117–20) CHARLIE DAVIS, b. ca. 1849, SC. Fieldhand. int. R. Davis. (S1 2 *SC* 1: 245–49) CLARA DAVIS, b. June 1865, Monroe Co., AL. Child of ex-slaves. Nursemaid. int. Diard. (S1 6 *AL*: 109–10; SS1 1 *AL*: 121–25) UNCLE D. DAVIS, b. ca. 1850, Oktibbeha Co., MS. Farmed MS, AR postwar. int. W. McKinney. (S2 8 *AR* 2: 100–108) HEDDIE DAVIS, b. 1866, Charleston, SC. Child of ex-slaves. int. R. Davis. (S1 2 *SC* 1: 254–59) JAMES (JIM) DAVIS, b. December 25, 1840, Raleigh, NC. Slave of Jefferson Davis's brother, Peter. Banjo player, dance caller. Farmed postwar. int. Bowden. (S2 8 *AR* 2: 109–15) JEFF DAVIS, b. 1853, Pine Bluff, AR. int. Bowden. (S2 8 *AR* 2: 116) JERRY DAVIS, b. ca. 1865, Warren Co., NC. Child of ex-slaves. (S2 14 *NC* 1: 237–40) JESSE DAVIS, b. ca. 1850, Fairfield Co., SC. Farmed postwar. int. W. Dixon. (S1 2 *SC* 1: 263–66) LIZZIE DAVIS, b. ca. 1865, SC. Child of ex-slaves. int. R. Davis. (S1 2 *SC* 1: 267–98; SS1 11 *SC*: 107–14) LOUIS DAVIS, b. 1858, Little Rock. Postwar tenant AR, MS. Bought farm Cleveland, MS. int. Campbell. (SS1 7 *MS* 2: 576–89) LOUISA DAVIS, b. ca. 1832, York Co., SC. House servant, nursemaid. int. W. Dixon. (S1 2 *SC* 1: 299–303)

LUCINDA DAVIS, b. ca. 1848. Taken Fort Gibson, IT. Creek slave. Farmed postwar. (S1 7 *OK*: 53–64) MARGARET DAVIS, b. ca. 1850, Cape Girardeau, MO. Hired out, nursemaid. int. I. Byrd. (SS1 2 *MO*: 164–65) MARY JANE DRUCILLA DAVIS, b. ca. 1865, GA. Child of ex-slaves. Moved AR. int. Bowden. (S2 8 *AR* 2: 124–25) MINNIE DAVIS, b. ca. 1860, Greene Co., GA. Taken Athens, house servant. Postwar graduated Knox Institute, Atlanta University, married publisher of *Athens Clipper*, taught school. int. Hornsby, ed. Hall, Booth. (S2 12 *GA* 1: 251–64) MOSE DAVIS, b. unk., Perry, GA. int. Driskell. (S2 12 *GA* 1: 265–71) TOB DAVIS, b. 1857, Nacogdoches Co., TX. Stayed on plantation until age 38. Renter until 1920. int. Gauthier. (SS2 4 *TX* 3: 1079–86) WALLACE DAVIS, b. ca. 1849, SC. int. Summer. (S1 2 *SC* 1: 304–7) WILLIAM DAVIS, b. April 1, 1845, Kingston, TN. House servant, worked slaveholder's hotel. Postwar worked railroad, enlisted army. Moved Houston, TX, steamboat deckhand, odd jobs. int. Drake. (S1 4 *TX* 1: 289–94; SS2 4 *TX* 3: 1087–95) WILLIAM HENRY DAVIS, b. 1865, Marion Co., SC. Child of ex-slaves. int. R. Davis. (S1 2 *SC* 1: 308–12) ELIGE DAVISON, b. unk., Richmond, VA. Fieldhand. int. B. Davis. (S1 4 *TX* 1: 298–301; SS2 4 *TX* 3: 1109–18) JAKE DAWKINS, b. ca. 1845, Monroe Co., MS. Fieldhand. Sharecropped postwar. int. Kolb. (SS1 7 *MS* 2: 592–99) ANTHONY DAWSON, b. July 25, 1832, Greenville, NC. House servant, fieldhand. Stayed on plantation as sharecropper postwar. Bought farm. 1903 moved TX, OK. (S1 7 *OK*: 65–72A) MOLLIE DAWSON, b. 1852, Navarro Co., TX. int. W. Smith. (SS2 4 *TX* 3: 1119–59) JAMES V. DEANE, b. May 20, 1850, Charles Co., MD. Fieldhand. (S2 16 *MD*: 6–9) W. S. DEBNAM, b. 1859, Wake Co., NC. int. Matthews, ed. Waitt. (S2 14 *NC* 1: 241–46) HAMMETT DELL, b. October 12, 1847, Murfreesboro, TN. Farmed, bricklayer, banjo-fiddle-mandolin-mouth-bow-quill player. int. Robertson. (S2 8 *AR* 2: 137–46) NELSON TAYLOR DENSON, b. 1847, AR. Taken TX as child. int. Cowan. (S1 4 *TX* 1: 305–6; SS2 4 *TX* 3: 1168–92) JAKE DESSO,

b. May 10, 1863, Orange Co., TX. Tended cows. Moved Beaumont postwar, worked store, errands. int. Dibble, Grey. (SS2 4 *TX* 3: 1193–200) NELSON DICKERSON, b. unk., Pike County, MS. Farmed, split rails, worked gin postwar. int. Holmes. (SS1 7 *MS* 2: 600–609) WILL DILL, b. ca. 1852, Anderson Co., SC. (S1 2 *SC* 1: 319–23) BENNY DILLARD, b. ca. 1860, Elbert Co., GA. int. McCune, ed. Hall, Booth. (S2 12 *GA* 1: 285–99) GEORGE DILLARD, b. 1852, Richmond, VA. Sold, taken MS. Fieldhand, banjo player. Stayed on plantation as sharecropper postwar. Later moved Greene Co., AL. int. Barton, Kytle. (S1 6 *AL*: 111–12) MARK DISCUS, b. December 25, 1849, MO. Fieldhand. Farmed postwar. (SS1 2 *MO*: 171–77) ALICE DIXON, b. ca. 1856, Union Co., AR. int. P. Anderson. (S2 8 *AR* 2: 153–56) BUD DIXON, b. ca. 1845, Mansfield, LA. Fieldhand. Slaveholder's substitute in Confederate army, wounded Battle of Mansfield. int. Dickinson. (SS2 4 *TX* 3: 1201–5) SALLY DIXON, b. unk., Macon, GA. Taken Como, MS. Fieldhand. Tenant postwar, eventually bought home Clarksdale. int. Campbell. (SS1 7 *MS* 2: 625–30) TOM DIXON, b. 1862, Kershaw Co., SC. AME minister. int. W. Dixon. (S1 2 *SC* 1: 324–25) FRANCIS (FRANCES) DOBY, b. 1838. Taken Opelousas, LA. House servant. int. Arguedas, R. McKinney, Michinard. (*MW*, 51–61) RAILROAD DOCKERY, b. 1857, Lamertine, AR. Toted wood for cook. Farmed postwar. int. Bowden. (S2 8 *AR* 2: 164–65) LUCY DONALD, b. 1857, Rankin Co., MS. Fieldhand. Homesteaded postwar. int. Giles. (SS1 7 *MS* 2: 636–41) MARY DONATTO, b. ca. 1855, Opelousas, LA. Creole. int. Dibble, Grey. (SS2 4 *TX* 3: 1221–24) ISABELLA DORROH, b. ca. 1863, Newberry, SC. int. Summer, ed. Turnage. (S1 2 *SC* 1: 326–28) DOUGLAS DORSEY, b. 1851, Suwannee Co., FL. Carried children's schoolbooks. Farmed postwar. int. J. Johnson. (S2 17 *FL*: 93–100) CHARLES GREEN DORTCH, b. June 18, 1857, Dallas Co., AR. Worked railroad as porter, storeroom straw boss, coach cleaner. int. S. Taylor. (S1 8 *AR* 2: 169–79) SILAS DOTHRUM, b. 1855 or 1856, Little Rock. Farmed, construction postwar. int.

S. Taylor. (S2 8 *AR* 2: 185–88) HATTIE DOUGLAS, b. May 8, 1867, Bolivar, TN. Child of ex-slaves. Moved Pine Bluff 1874. School teacher, seamstress, music teacher, church pianist. int. Bowden. (SS2 1 *AR*: 62–65) SARAH DOUGLAS, b. ca. 1855, AL. Taken LA. Fieldhand. int. P. Anderson, Graham. (S2 8 *AR* 2: 189–92, 196–200) TOM DOUGLAS, b. September 15, 1847, Marion, LA. Fieldhand. Sharecropped postwar. int. P. Anderson, Graham. (S2 8 *AR* 2: 193–203) REVEREND SQUIRE DOWD, b. April 3, 1855, Moore Co., NC. House boy. Held in bondage five years postwar. int. Matthews, ed. Waitt. (S2 14 *NC* 1: 263–69) WASHINGTON DOZIER (DOSIER), b. December 18, 1847, Florence Co., SC. Fieldhand. int. R. Davis. (S1 2 *SC* 1: 330–35) ANN DRAKE, b. 1855, Franklin Co., MS. Fieldhand. Stayed on plantation seven years postwar, then farmed, cleaned East McComb schoolhouse. int. Holmes. (SS1 7 *MS* 2: 642–52) MARTIN DRAGNEY, b. May 11, 1860, New Orleans. Creole. Roustabout, merchant marine. int. Posey. (*MW*, 61–63) FANNIE MCCULLOH DRIVER, b. January 19, 1857, Seguin, TX. Farmed postwar. int. Menn. (SS2 4 *TX* 3: 1230–37) MOTHER DUFFY, b. unk., New Orleans. Creole. (*MW*, 63–64) VICTOR DUHON, b. ca. 1840, Lafayette Parish, LA. Creole. int. Dibble. (S1 4 *TX* 1: 307–8; SS2 4 *TX* 3: 1238–41) ALICE DUKE, b. 1865, Child of ex-slaves. Spartanburg Co., SC. int. Sims. (S1 2 *SC* 1: 336) ISABELLA DUKE, b. 1875, Faithville, AL. Child of ex-slaves. int. Robertson. (S1 8 *AR* 2: 214–16) RACHEL DUNCAN, b. ca. 1858, Breckenridge Co., KY. int. Cook. (SS1 5 *IN*: 67–68) NELLIE DUNNE, b. ca. 1860, Silver Creek, MS. int. Bowden. (S2 8 *AR* 2: 223–24) WILLIAM L. DUNWOODY, b. 1860, Charleston, SC. Taught, farmed postwar. int. Taylor. (S2 8 *AR* 2: 225–33) TEMPIE HERNDON DURHAM, b. 1834, Chatham Co., NC. int. T. Jordan. (S1 14 *NC* 1: 284–90) SIMON DURR, b. ca. 1847, Copiah Co., MS. Carriage driver, tended horses. Stayed on plantation postwar, later homesteaded. int. Giles. (SS1 7 *MS* 2: 654–58)

GEORGE EASON, b. unk., Forsythe Co., GA. (S2 12 *GA* 1; 300–304) WILLIS EASTER, b. March 19,

1852, Nacogdoches, TX. Taken McLennan Co. age two. Fieldhand, dance caller. Farmed postwar. int. A. Davis. (S1 4 *TX* 2: 1–4; SS2 4 *TX* 3: 1250–58) MOLLIE EDMONDS, b. ca. 1855, Silver City, MS. Toted water. int. Campbell. (SS1 7 *MS* 2: 661–74) MANDA EDMONSON, b. 1842, MS. House servant. int. Giles. (SS1 7 *MS* 2: 675–77) REV. H. H. EDMUNDS, b. 1859, Lynchburg, VA. Taken MS then Nashville, TN. After freedom moved Elkhart, IN. int. Strope. (S1 6 *IN*: 65–66) ANDERSON AND MINERVA EDWARDS (spouses), b. March 12, 1844, February 2, 1850, adjoining plantations, Rusk Co., TX. Stayed on plantation four years postwar, moved Harrison Co., married, established Edwards' Chapel, preached, farmed. int. Hampton. (S1 4 *TX* 2: 5–9; SS2 4 *TX* 3: 1259–66) ANN J. EDWARDS, b. January 27, 1856, Arlington, VA. Taken Washington, DC, manumitted 1857. Adopted by prominent Black clergyman (later congressman). Postwar moved Charleston, SC, returned Washington, attended Howard College, moved Dallas. int. Gauthier. (S1 4 *TX* 2: 10–14; SS2 4 *TX* 3: 1269–77) MALINDA EDWARDS, b. 1825, AL. Nursemaid, fieldhand, washed, ironed, carded, spun, wove. Taken Noxubee Co., MS prewar. Moved Winston Co. postwar. Community nurse. (SS1 7 *MS* 2: 678–80) MARY EDWARDS, b. 1858, Greenwood Co., SC. Fieldhand. int. Summer, ed. Turnage. (S1 3 *SC* 2: 2) MARY EDWARDS, b. July 4, 1853, NC. Age two taken Brenham, TX. Hired out, nursemaid. int. Menn. (SS2 4 *TX* 3: 1282–84) MARY KINCHEON EDWARDS, b. July 8, 1810, Baton Rouge. Taken TX prewar. Fieldhand, house servant, nursemaid. Stayed on plantation postwar. int. Menn. (S1 4 *TX* 2: 15–16; SS2 4 *TX* 3: 1278–81) CALLIE ELDER, b. ca. 1860, Floyd Co., GA. Stayed on plantation postwar for wages. int. Hornsby, ed. Hall, L. Harris. (S2 12 *GA* 1: 306–15) BOB ELLIS, b. 1849, Buckingham Co., VA. Fieldhand. int. Majette. (*WW*, 88–89) JOHN ELLIS, b. June 26, 1852, Johnson Co., TX. Fieldhand. (S1 4 *TX* 2: 21–24) AMY ELSE, b. 1848, Marshall, TX. House servant. int. Hampton. (SS2 4 *TX* 3: 1299–1305) GABE EMANUEL, b. ca. 1852,

Port Gibson, MS. House boy. int. de Sola. (S1 7 *MS*: 44–48; SS1 7 *MS* 2: 681–86) WILLIAM EMMONS, b. ca. 1848, Carlisle, KY. Tended stock, milked, plowed. Enlisted Union army 1865, wounded VA. Returned KY, farmed. (SS1 5 *OH*: 326–31) KATHERINE EPPES, b. ca. 1850, AL. int. O'Brien. (S1 6 *AL*: 119–21) CYNTHIA ERWING, b. ca. 1850, Powhatan Co., VA. House servant. int. Prine. (SS1 1 *AL*: 135–39) JERRY EUBANKS, b. 1846, Atlanta. Seized for debt age twelve, sold, taken Columbus, GA. Carriage driver. int. Joiner. (SS1 7 *MS* 2: 687–701) UNCLE PEN EUBANKS, b. 1854, SC. After war farmed, rode with Red Shirts. int. Sims, ed. Turnage. (S1 2 *SC* 2: 27–29) SMOKY EULENBERG, b. October 13, 1854, Cape Girardeau, MO. Stayed on plantation postwar, later farmed. int. F. C. (S2 11 *MO*: 109–12) ANN ULRICH EVANS, b. March 10, 1843, Mobile, AL. Spinner, fieldhand. Left homeless postwar, married elderly neighbor. (S2 11 *MO*: 113–19) ELIZA EVANS, b. ca. 1850, Selma, AL. Minded calves during milking. (S1 7 *OK*: 92–96) LAWERENCE EVANS, b. 1858, Florence, MS. Groom, carriage driver. Stayed on plantation postwar. int. Giles. (SS1 7 *MS* 2: 703–6) LEWIS EVANS, b. ca. 1841, Jenkinsville, SC. Fieldhand. Farmed postwar. int. W. Dixon. (S1 2 *SC* 2: 30–33) LOUIS EVANS, b. August 15, 1853, Grand Coteau, LA. House servant. Stayed on plantation postwar. int. Dibble. (SS2 4 *TX* 3: 1306–16) MILLIE EVANS, b. 1849, NC. Nursemaid. int. Graham. (S2 8 *AR* 2: 240–51) MARTHA EVERETTE, b. ca. 1850, Pulaski Co., GA. Water carrier, house servant. int. Watson. (S2 12 *GA* 1: 316–17; SS1 3 *GA* 1: 236–42) LORENZA EZELL, b. July 29, 1850, Spartanburg, SC. Fieldhand. Moved Brenham, TX 1882, then Beaumont. int. Dibble, Grey. (S1 4 *TX* 2: 25–32; SS2 4 *TX* 3: 1317–29)

EUGENIA FAIR, b. 1861, Abbeville Co., SC. int. Summer, ed. Turnage. (S1 3 *SC* 2: 38) RACHEL FAIRLY, b. 1863, Sardis, MS. int. S. Taylor. (S1 8 *AR* 2: 258–61) PAULINE FAKES, b. 1863, Cotton Plant, AR. int. Robertson. (S1 8 *AR* 2: 262–63) HANNA FAMBRO, b. May 1850, Macon, GA. Fieldhand. Farmed, domestic postwar. int. N. Jackson, ed. Webb, Colvin.

(SS1 5 *OH*: 332–47) MATTIE FANNEN, b. 1850, AR. Fieldworker, laundress. int. Robertson. (S2 8 *AR* 2: 264–68) LIZZIE FARMER, b. ca. 1857, TX. House servant. (S1 7 *OK*: 97–101) ROBERT FARMER, b. 1854, NC. Tended stock. Postwar sharecropped, worked levees NC, LA, AR. int. S. Taylor. (S2 8 *AR* 2: 269–75) CAROLINE FARROW, b. ca. 1857, Newberry Co., SC. House servant. Stayed on plantation postwar, later moved Newberry, domestic. int. Summer. (S1 2 *SC* 2: 39–42) LEWIS FAVORS (FAVOR), b. 1855, Meriwether Co., GA. Fieldhand. int. Driskell, ed. Whitley. (S2 12 *GA* 1: 318–25) MRS. M. S. FAYMAN, b. 1850, St. Nazaire Parish, LA. Creole. int. Rogers. (S2 16 *MD*: 10–13) GUS FEASTER, b. ca. 1840, Goshen Hill Township, SC. Fieldhand. Odd-jobbed postwar. int. Sims, ed. Turnage. (S1 2 *SC* 2: 43–71) SARAH FELDER, b. ca. 1853, Magnolia, MS. Fieldhand. Sharecropped postwar. int. Holmes. (SS1 7 *MS* 2: 713–24) AUNT MARY FERGUSON, b. ca. 1855, MD. Sold, taken GA 1860. (S2 12 *GA* 1: 326–31) ALPHONSE FIELDS, b. ca. 1854, Opelousas, LA. Creole. int. Dibble, Grey. (SS2 4 *TX* 3: 1338–40) ELIZABETH FINLEY, b. October 22, 1849, AL. House servant, spinner. Moved Montgomery postwar. int. Walsh. (SS1 7 *MS* 2: 725–30) MOLLY FINLEY, b. 1865, Pine Bluff, AR. Child of ex-slaves. Toted water, made fires, tended siblings, fieldhand. int. Robertson. (S2 8 *AR* 2: 292–95) JOHN FINNELY, b. ca. 1850, AL. Fieldhand. Runaway, joined Union army. Postwar settled Nashville, TN. Moved TX 1880s, farmed. Moved Fort Worth 1917, meatpacker, discharged for old age 1930. int. Gauthier. (SS2 4 *TX* 3: 1341–50) FANNY FINNEY, b. ca. 1953, Marshall Co., MS. int. Robertson. (S2 8 *AR* 2: 296–99) LULA FLANNIGAN, b. ca. 1860, Watkinsville, GA. (S1 4 *TX* 2: 35–40; SS1 3 *GA* 1: 247–49) GEORGE FLEMING, b. 1854, Laurens Co., SC. Fieldhand, quill player. int. Turnage. (SS1 11 *SC*: 126–39) REBECCA FLETCHER, b. 1842, MS. int. Posey. (*MW*, 64–70) ANNIE FLOWERS, b. ca. 1860, LA. Fieldhand. int. McElwee. (*MW*, 70–1) FLETCHER FLOYD, b. unk., Spartanburg, SC. int. DuPre, ed. Turnage. (SS1 11 *SC*: 140) SYL-

VIA FLOYD (male), b. ca. 1852, Simpson Co., MS. Fieldhand, farmed postwar. int. Giles. (SS1 7 *MS* 2: 741–46) TOM FLOYD, b. ca. 1842, MO. Sold age four, taken Simpson Co., MS. Fieldhand. Wage labor postwar, later bought farm. int. Giles. (SS1 7 *MS* 2: 747–51) IDA MAY FLUKER, b. 1854, Clark Co., AL. Toted wood. Stayed on plantation as sharecropper postwar. int. Bowden. (S2 8 *AR* 2: 322–23) MINNIE FOLKES (FULKES), b. December 25, 1860, Chesterfield Co., VA. int. S. Byrd. (S2 16 *VA*: 11–15; *WW*, 92–96) OCTAVIA FONTENETTE, b. 1854, New Iberia Parish, LA. Moved to New Orleans as child. Creole. int. E. Burke. (*MW*, 72–73) ANITA FONVERGNE, b. 1861, New Orleans. Creole. Domestic, seamstress, vegetable peddler. (*MW*, 73–82) TINIE FORCE AND ELVIRA LEWIS, b. unk., Ballard Co., KY. int. Wilkerson. (S2 16 *KY*: 112–15) ELLEN NORA FORD, b. ca. 1855, Vicksburg, MS. Taken TX during war. Domestic postwar. int. Dibble. (SS2 4 *TX* 3: 1354–57) LAURA FORD, b. 1852, Hinds Co., MS. Fieldhand. Farmed postwar. int. Giles. (SS1 7 *MS* 2: 755–58) SARAH FORD, b. ca. 1850, TX. Farmed postwar. int. Drake. (S1 4 *TX* 2: 41–46; SS2 4 *TX* 3: 1358–69) SAM FORGE, b. ca. 1850, Freestone Co., TX. Sharecropped postwar. int. Cowan. (SS2 4 *TX* 3: 1370–76) SUSAN FORREST, b. ca. 1860, Columbus, GA. int. Dibble. (SS2 4 *TX* 3: 1377–80) JUDIA FORTENBERRY, b. October 1859, Ashley Co., AR. Picked cotton postwar. Moved Monticello, then Little Rock 1893, washed, ironed. int. S. Taylor. (S2 8 *AR* 2: 328–30) GEORGE FORTMAN, b. ca. 1850, Livingston, AL. Fieldhand. Postwar attended school, worked KY riverboats. Moved Evansville, IN 1900. int. Creel. (S1 6 *IN*: 84–95) MILLIE FORWARD, b. ca. 1840, AL. Taken Jasper, TX as infant. Farmed postwar. int. Hatcher. (S1 4 *TX* 2: 47–49; SS2 4 *TX* 3: 1381–85) EMMA FOSTER, b. 1857, Claiborne Parish, LA. Farmed, moved AR ca. 1885. int. Bowden. (S1 8 *AR* 2: 331–33) GEORGIANNA FOSTER, b. 1861, NC. int. Matthews, ed. G. Andrews. (S2 14 *NC* 1: 314–17) IRA FOSTER, b. ca. 1862, Camden, AR. Farmed until 1918. Worked sawmills. int. Bowden.

(S2 8 *AR* 1: 334–35) DELLA FOUNTAIN, b. 1869, Winfield, LA. Child of ex-slaves. (S1 7 *OK*: 102–7) LOUIS FOWLER, b. 1853, Macon Co., GA. Postwar farmed, moved Fort Worth 1907, meatpacker. int. Gauthier. (S1 4 *TX* 2: 50–54; SS2 4 *TX* 3: 1386–95) RUBEN (REUBEN) FOX, b. ca. 1853, Greenville, MS. Fieldhand. Postwar moved Coahoma Co., tenant. Later caretaker Coahoma Co. courthouse, ran boarding houses. int. Campbell. (SS1 7 *MS* 2: 769–80) CHRIS FRANKLIN, b. December 25, 1855, Bossier Parish, LA. Taken Caddo Parish. int. Dibble. (S1 4 *TX* 2: 55–59; SS2 4 *TX* 3: 1402–14) LEONARD FRANKLIN, b. 1867, Warren, AR. Child of ex-slaves. int. S. Taylor. (S2 8 *AR* 2: 336–39) ROBERT FRANKLIN, b. 1851, Warren Co., MS. Fieldhand. Stayed on plantation postwar. int. A. Davis. (SS2 4 *TX* 3: 1418–21) DORA FRANKS, b. ca. 1837, Choctaw Co., MS. House servant. int. Kolb. (S1 7 *MS* 2: 49–55; SS1 7 *MS* 2: 782–92) ORELIA ALEXIE FRANKS, b. unk., Lafayette, LA. Creole. Weaver. int. Dibble. (S1 4 *TX* 2: 60–62; SS2 4 *TX* 3: 1422–26) UNCLE PET FRANKS, b. 1847, Bartley's Ferry, MS. int. Kolb (SS1 7 *MS* 2: 793–800) EMMA FRASER, b. ca. 1857, Beaufort, SC. int. Tiedman. (S1 2 *SC* 2: 87) JULIA FRAZIER, b. February 20, 1854, Spotsylvania Co., VA. Fieldhand. int. C. Anderson. (*WW*, 96–99) ROSANNA FRAZIER, b. ca. 1847, MS. Fieldhand. int. Dibble, Grey. (S1 4 *TX* 2: 63–65; SS2 4 *TX* 3: 1427–31) TYLER FRAZIER, b. ca. 1855, TX. Fieldhand. int. P. Anderson. (S2 8 *AR* 2: 344–45) HENRY FREEMAN, b. ca. 1865, Talladega Co., AL. Child of ex-slaves. Moved Robertson Co., TX 1870s. Farmed. int. Cowan. (SS2 4 *TX* 3: 1432–36) AUNT MITTIE FREEMAN, b. 1851, Orange Co., MS. Taken Camden, AR prewar. Sharecropped postwar. int. Hagg. (S2 8 *AR* 2: 346–52) ADELE FROST, b. January 21, 1844, Adams Run, SC. Taken Richland Co. 1856. House servant. int. Mobley. (S1 2 *SC* 2: 88–90) FANNIE FULCHER, b. ca. 1860, GA. int. Barragan, Love, Radford. (S2 13 *GA* 4: 336; SS1 3 *GA* 1: 250–53) ANDERSON FURR, b. ca. 1850, Hall Co., GA. Toted water, swept yard, fieldhand. int. Hornsby, ed. Hall, L. Harris. (S2 12 *GA* 1: 344–52)

MARY GAFFNEY, b. 1846, MS. Taken TX 1860. House servant. int. B. Davis. (SS2 5 *TX* 4: 1441–57) DUNCAN GAINES, b. March 12, 1853, VA. Farmed postwar. int. Randolph. (S2 17 *FL*: 132–38) RACHEL GAINES, b. ca. 1840, Trenton, KY. Sold, taken TN. Nursemaid. Stayed on plantation postwar, later moved Nashville, laundress until blinded. (S2 16 *TN*: 17–18) MARY GAINES, b. 1872, Courtland, AL. Child of ex-slaves. Fieldhand, washed, ironed, cooked. int. Robertson. (S2 9 *AR* 3: 7–10) LUCY GALLMAN, b. 1857, Edgefield Co., SC. Fieldhand. Postwar spun yarn, worked corn mill, fieldhand. int. Summer, ed. Ritter. (S1 2 *SC* 2: 100–102) LUCY GALLOWAY, b. May 8, 1863, Scooba, MS. int. Walsh. (SS1 8 *MS* 3: 801–10) WILLIAM GANT, b. 1837, Bedford Co., TN. Fieldhand, fiddler, dance caller. Farmed postwar. int. Robertson. (S2 9 *AR* 3: 11–14) CLAYBORN GANTLING, b. January 20, 1848, Dawson, GA. After freedom tenant various plantations FL, settled Jacksonville, Public Works, then raised chickens and hogs. int. R. Austin. (S2 17 *FL*: 139–45) ELISHA (DOC) GAREY, b. ca. 1862, Hart Co., GA. House servant, yard boy, fieldhand. Postwar preached, odd-jobbed. int. Hornsby, ed. Hall, Booth. (S1 12 *GA* 2: 1–10) DELIA GARLIC, b. ca. 1835, Powhatan Co., VA, taken LA, then AL. House servant. int. M. Fowler, ed. Kytle. (S1 6 *AL*: 129–32; SS1 1 *AL*: 155–63) CORNELIUS GARNER, b. February 11, 1846, Saint Mary's Co., MD. Fieldhand. Enlisted Union army, Norfolk 1864. Fought Battle of Deep Bottom, pursued Confederate holdouts Mexico. Returned VA, mustered out 1867, farmed. int. E. Wilson and C. Anderson. (*WW*, 99–104) ANGIE GARRETT, b. ca. 1845, De Kalb, MS. Slaveholder operated steamboat *Cremona*, Tombigbee River between Aberdeen, MS and Mobile. House servant, nursemaid. int. Tartt. (S1 6 *AL*: 133–36) LEAH GARRETT, b. unk., Richmond Co., MD. int. Oliphant, ed. Booth. (S2 12 *GA* 2: 11–16) LAURENCE GARY, b. 1861, Newberry Co., SC. Stayed on plantation as hand postwar. int. Summer. (S1 2 *SC* 2: 106) HENRY GARRY, b. ca. 1865, Gainesville, AL. Child of ex-slaves. Moved Birmingham

1895, worked saloon, ran elevator Morris Hotel. int. W. Jordan. (S1 6 *AL*: 137–43) HATTIE GATES, b. ca. 1850, Jefferson, TX. int. Cowan. (SS2 5 *TX* 4: 1458–66) LOUISA GAUSE, b. ca. 1865, SC. int. R. Davis (S1 2 *SC* 2: 107–12) CECEIL GEORGE, b. 1846, Charleston Co., SC. Sold, taken St. Bernard Parish, LA. Fieldhand. Farmed postwar. int. Wallace. (*MW*, 83–87) OCTAVIA GEORGE, b. 1852, Monsieur, Avoir Parish, LA. Creole. (S1 7 *OK*: 111–14) HENRY GIBBS, b. 1852, West Point, MS. House servant. Sharecropped postwar, bought farm. int. Joiner. (SS1 8 *MS* 3: 815–36) GEORGINA GIBBS, b. 1849, Portsmouth, VA. Fieldhand. int. Dunston. (*WW*, 104–6) FANNIE GIBSON, b. ca. 1850, Roanoke, AL. Fieldhand, cook. Postwar moved Columbus, GA. int. J. Jones. (S1 6 *AL*: 145–47; SS1 3 *GA* 1: 254–56) JENNIE WORMLY GIBSON. Grandchild of ex-slaves. int. Robertson. (S2 9 *AR* 3: 17–18) MARY ANN GIBSON, b. July 4, 1861, Travis Co., TX. Sharecropped postwar. int. Menn. (SS2 5 *TX* 4: 1467–71) GABRIEL GILBERT, b. unk., New Iberia Parish, LA. Creole. int. Dibble. (S1 4 *TX* 2: 68–70; SS2 5 *TX* 4: 1477–82) CHARLIE GILES, b. ca. 1840, SC. Served with Confederates Petersburg. int. Sims, ed. Turnage. (S1 2 *SC* 2: 116–17) ANDREW JACK-SON GILL, b. 1852, Lincoln Co., MS. House servant. Postwar sharecropped, attended school. int. de Sola. (SS1 8 *MS* 3: 839–47) FRANK GILL, b. ca. 1845, Vicksburg, MS. House servant, groom. Later moved Mobile. int. Prine. (S1 6 *AL*: 148–53) JIM GILLARD, b. ca. 1850, Pendleton, SC. Sold, taken GA, AL. (S1 6 *AL*: 154–56; SS1 1 *AL*: 166–68) J. N. GILLESPIE, b. January 19, 1863, Galveston, TX. Moved AR age seven or eight, as adult returned TX, moved Little Rock ca. 1885. Cooked. int. S. Taylor. (S2 9 *AR* 3: 34–37) BRAWLEY GILMORE, b. unk., Union Co., SC. Child of ex-slaves, stayed on Gilmore place. int. Sims, ed. Turnage. (S1 2 *SC* 2: 120–23) MATTIE GILMORE, b. unk., Mobile, AL. Grown during slavery. Taken Athens, TX start of war. Fieldhand, house servant. int. W. Smith. (S1 4 *TX* 2: 71–73; SS2 5 *TX* 4: 1483–99) JOHN GILSTRAP, b. 1857, Fulton, MS. After freedom farmed on shares,

established blacksmith shop 1910. int. N. Thompson. (SS1 8 *MS* 3: 849–51) MARY GLADDY, b. ca. 1853, Columbus, GA. Washerwoman, spiritual singer, visionary. int. J. Jones. (S2 12 *GA* 2: 17–27; SS1 3 *GA* 1: 257–62) PICK GLADDENY, b. May 15, 1856, South Carolina. int. Sims. (S1 2 *SC* 2: 124–28) EMOLINE GLASGOW, b. 1859, Newberry Co., SC. Stayed on plantation postwar. int. Summer, ed. Turnage. (S1 2 *SC* 2: 134–35) WILL GLASS, b. unk., AR. Grandchild of ex-slaves. int. S. Taylor. (S2 9 *AR* 3: 38–41) EDWARD GLENN, b. unk., Forsythe Co., GA. int. Radford. (S2 13 *GA* 4: 348–49) WADE GLENN, b. ca. 1860, Winston-Salem, NC. Picked up chips, tended hogs. Stayed on plantation as tenant postwar. Left 1892, moved TN, OH. Farm, road work. int. Logan. (S2 16 *OH*: 38; SS1 5 *OH*: 348–49) JOHN GLOVER, b. 1860, SC. House servant. int. R. Davis. (S1 2 *SC* 2: 138–42) MARY GLOVER, b. June 1, 1854, Sumpter, TX. Fieldhand, house servant. int. Menn. (SS2 5 *TX* 4: 1513–21) HECTOR GODBOLD, b. 1850, Charleston, SC. int. R. Davis. (S1 2 *SC* 2: 143–48; SS1 11 *SC*: 143–47) AUNT ELLEN GODFREY, b. October 7, 1837, Murrells Inlet, SC. Weaver, nursemaid. int. Chandler. (S1 2 *SC* 2: 153–65; SS1 11 *SC*: 148–49) ANDREW GOODMAN, b. February 19, 1840, Birmingham, AL. Taken Smith Co., TX. House servant. Stayed on plantation until 1890s. (S1 4 *TX* 2: 74–80; SS2 5 *TX* 4: 1522–29) THOMAS GOODWATER, b. January 15, 1855, Mt. Pleasant, SC. House servant. int. Ladson. (S1 2 *SC* 2: 166–70) FRANKIE GOOLE, b. December 25, 1853, Smith Co., TN. Separated from mother at six weeks. Fieldhand, house servant. Reunited with mother postwar. Moved Nashville, nursed, cooked. (S2 16 *TN*: 19–23) GEORGE GOVAN, b. 1886, Conway Co., AR. Child of ex-slaves. int. Lucy. (S2 9 *AR* 3: 63–64) CHARLES GRAHAM, b. September 27, 1859, Clarksville, TN. Postwar moved IL, worked Mississippi riverboats. int. S. Taylor. (S2 9 *AR* 3: 67–69) MARTIN GRA-HAM, b. 1851, SC. Taken Savannah, GA, Salem, AL during war. Picked cotton, tended horses, cows. (SS1 1 *AL*: 169–71) MARY ELLA GRANDBERRY,

b. ca. 1845, Barton, Alabama. Water girl, fieldhand. int. Shelby. (S1 6 *AL*: 157–64) CHARLES GRANDY, b. 1842, Camden Co., NC. Taken MS, VA. Fieldhand. int. Hoggard, C. Anderson, E. Wilson. (S2 16 *VA*: 21–23; *WW*, 111–19) AUSTIN GRANT, b. unk., MS. Taken TX as child. Hired out. Fieldhand, shepherd. Stayed on plantation postwar, later farmed. int. Holm. (S1 4 *TX* 2: 81–86; SS2 5 *TX* 4: 1532–45) CHARLIE GRANT, b. February 24, 1852, SC. Stayed on plantation four, five years postwar. Signed onboard ship in Charleston, sailed Africa. int. Young, H. Davis, ed. R. Davis. (S1 2 *SC* 2: 171–76; SS1 11 *SC*: 150–78) DENNIS GRANT, b. ca. 1850, Houston, TX. Taken Jasper while small. Milking, chores. Domestic postwar. int. L. Hatcher. (SS2 5 *TX* 4: 1546–52) REBECCA JANE GRANT, b. ca. 1844, Beaufort, SC. Nursemaid. int. Faucette. (S1 2 *SC* 2: 177–86) MRS. MILDRED GRAVES, b. 1842, VA. int. Silver. (*WW*, 122) WESLEY GRAVES, b. 1867, Trenton, TN. Child of ex-slaves. int. S. Taylor. (S2 9 *AR* 3: 73–76) CALLIE GRAY, b. 1857, Holly Springs, MS. House servant. Stayed on plantation postwar. int. N. Thompson. (SS1 8 *MS* 3: 860–76) NEELY (NELY) GRAY, b. ca. 1855, Richmond, VA. Sold, taken Pine Bluff. Postwar picked, hoed cotton; sewed, knitted, crocheted, quilted; washed, ironed, cooked. int. Bowden. (S2 9 *AR* 3: 82–86) PRECILLA GRAY, b. ca. 1820, Williamson Co., TN. Fieldhand, nursemaid. Cooked postwar. (S2 16 *TN*: 24–26) SIM GREELEY, b. December 25, 1855, Newberry Co., SC. int. Sims, ed. Turnage. (S1 3 *SC* 2: 190–94) ALICE GREEN, b. ca. 1862, Clarke Co., GA. int. C. Fowler, Hornsby, ed. Hall, L. Harris, Booth. (S2 12 *GA* 2: 31–47) CHARLES GREEN, b. 1859, Mason Green, KY. Farmed postwar. Moved Springfield, OH 1881. Hod carrier, mortar mixer. int. Minnick. (SS1 5 *OH*: 350–52) ELIJAH GREEN, b. December 25, 1843, Charleston, SC. Gardener, janitor postwar. int. Ladson. (S1 2 *SC* 2: 195–9) EMILY CAMSTER GREEN, b. unk., Bollinger Co., MO. Taken Mississippi Co. Lady's maid. (S2 11 *MO*: 139–42) ESTHER GREEN, b. 1855, State Line, MS. House servant. Moved Mobile 1869. int. Prine. (S1 6 *AL*:

165–67; SS1 1 *AL*: 172–74) UNCLE HENRY GREEN (HAPPY DAY), b. 1848, Montgomery, AL. House servant. Farmed postwar. Still church janitor Barton, AR 1937. int. Robertson, W. McKinney. (S2 9 *AR* 3: 87–101) ISAIAH (ISAAC) GREEN, b. 1856, Greensboro, GA. Fieldhand. int. Ross, Driskell. (S2 12 *GA* 2: 48–59) JAKE GREEN, b. ca. 1852, Livingston, AL. Fieldhand. Sharecropped postwar. int. Tartt. (S1 6 *AL*: 168–70) JAMES GREEN, b. 1841, VA. Sold, taken Columbus, TX. int. Nixon. (S1 4 *TX* 2: 87–89; SS2 5 *TX* 4: 1577–83) JIMMIE GREEN, b. 1845, VA. int. Majette. (*WW*, 127) MARIE AURELIA GREEN, b. ca. 1860, Grand Coteau, LA. Creole. int. Dibble. (SS2 5 *TX* 4: 1584–86) MINNIE GREEN, b. 1865. Spalding Co., GA. Child of ex-slaves. int. Minor. (S2 12 *GA* 2: 64–65) PHYLLIS GREEN, b. unk., SC. int. Tiedeman. (SS1 11 *SC*: 179–81) ROSA GREEN, b. 1852, LA. Taken Mansfield. House girl. int. Dibble, Grey. (S1 4 *TX* 2: 94–95; SS2 5 *TX* 4: 1587–93) WILLIAM (REVEREND BILL) GREEN, b. 1851, Brookhaven, MS. Sold, taken TX. Cowhand. Stayed on plantation five years postwar. Sharecropped, preached. int. Nixon. (S1 4 *TX* 2: 96–97; SS2 5 *TX* 4: 1594–98) JENNY GREER, b. ca. 1853, Florence, AL. Domestic postwar. (S2 16 *TN*: 27) HARRIETT GRESHAM, b. December 6, 1838, Charleston, SC. House servant. int. Randolph. (S2 17 *FL*: 156–64) WHEELER GRESHAM, b. ca. 1855, Wilkes Co., GA. Farmed postwar. int. Stonestreet. (S2 12 *GA* 2: 66–71) PAULINE GRICE, b. ca. 1856, Atlanta, GA. Light work. Stayed on plantation as sharecropper postwar. Moved TX 1875, farmed until 1929. int. Gauthier. (S1 4 *TX* 2: 98–101; SS2 5 *TX* 4: 1599–1606) LUCENDY GRIFFEN, b. ca. 1850, NC. Cooking, hoeing. Farmed, domestic postwar. int. B. Davis. (SS2 5 *TX* 4: 1607–13) ABNER GRIFFIN, b. 1849, Gold Mines, GA. Fieldhand, shoemaker, banjo, fiddle, accordion, organ player. ed. Barragan, L. Harris. (SS1 3 *GA* 1: 270–75) FANNIE GRIFFIN, b. 1843, SC. int. Pierce. (S1 3 *SC* 2: 209–11) HEARD GRIFFIN, b. May 19, 1850, Waldon Co., GA. int. Ross. (S2 12 *GA* 2: 72–77) LOU GRIFFIN, b. ca. 1840. Lived, worked AR, LA, MS, NC, MO.

(S2 11 *MO*: 143–44) MADISON GRIFFIN, b. 1853, SC. int. Summer, ed. Turnage. (S1 3 *SC* 2: 212–14) CHARITY GRIGSBY, b. ca. 1850, AL. int. Tartt, ed. Kytle. (S1 6 *AL*: 171–73) PEGGY GRIGSBY, b. ca. 1831, Edgefield Co., SC. Fieldhand. int. Summer, ed. Turnage. (S1 2 *SC* 2: 215) EMMA GRISHAM, b. ca. 1847, Nashville, TN. Moved Memphis 1870, married army band leader. Returned Nashville after husband's death, nursemaid. (S2 16 *TN*: 28–30) SARAH GUDGER, b. September 15, 1816, Asheville, NC. Fieldhand. int. M Jones. (S2 14 *NC* 1: 350–58) LEE GUIDON, b. ca. 1845, York-Union Co., AR. Fieldhand. Sharecropped postwar. (S2 9 *AR* 3: 119–26) DAVID GOODMAN GULLINS, b. December 27, 1854, Putnam Co., GA. Yard boy. Ministered after freedom. int. Chitty, ed. Chitty, Jaffee. (S2 12 *GA* 2: 78–90) BETTY GUWN, b. March 25, 1832, Canton, KY. House servant, fieldhand. int. Tuttle. (S1 6 *IN*: 98–100)

JOSH HADNOT, b. ca. 1855, Jasper, TX. House servant, toted wood, tended calves. Farmed, worked sawmills postwar. int. Dibble, Grey. (SS2 5 *TX* 4: 1621–25) MANDY HADNOT, b. ca. 1850, Cold Springs, TX. House servant. Stayed on plantation postwar. int. Dibble, Grey. (S1 4 *TX* 2: 102–5; SS2 5 *TX* 4: 1626–30) MARIA HADNOT, b. 1862, Cold Springs, TX. Nursemaid, washed, ironed, fieldhand. int. Hatcher. (SS2 5 *TX* 4: 1631–22) JULY ANN HALFEN, b. ca. 1855, Pike Co., MS. Fieldhand. Washed postwar. int. Holmes. (SS1 8 *MS* 3: 897–906) BOLDEN HALL, b. February 12, 1853, Jefferson Co., FL. Fieldhand. Stayed on plantation after freedom, left, settled Live Oak 1882. int. Farrell, ed. Simms. (S2 17 *FL*: 165–66) DAVID A. HALL, b. July 25, 1847, Goldsboro, NC. Waited tables, washed dishes. Moved OH postwar, miller until 1936. (S2 16 *OH*: 39–41) ELLIE HAMILTON, b. 1863, Holly Springs, MS. Tenant. Later moved Clarendon, AR, worked hotels, stores, farmed. int. Robertson. (S2 9 *AR* 3: 131–32) REVEREND NELSON HAMMOCK, b. 1842, VA. (*WW*, 127) MILTON HAMMOND, b. October 20, 1853, Griffin, GA. int. Ross, ed. Whitley. (S2 12 *GA* 2: 91–96) FILMORE TAYLOR

HANCOCK, b. February 28, 1851, Greene Co., MO. House servant. Moved Rolla-Salem area 1882, barber, entertainer. int. Mueller. (S2 11 *MO*: 147–61; SS1 2 *MO*: 178–91) HANNAH HANCOCK, b. ca. 1855, Chesterfield Co., SC. House servant, nursemaid. Postwar moved Prairie Co., AR, sharecropped. int. Robertson. (S2 9 *AR* 3: 142–47) RACHEL HANKINS, b. 1850, AL. Fieldhand. Stayed on plantation as sharecropper postwar. Moved AR 1898. int. P. Anderson. (S2 9 *AR* 3: 154–56) SIMON HARE, b. 1849, NC. Taken AL prewar. Fieldhand. Postwar moved Meridian, greased cars railroad shop. int. M. Austin. (SS1 8 *MS* 3: 912–23) GEORGE W. HARMON, b. December 25, 1854, Lamar Co., TX. int. Thomas. (SS1 12 *OK*: 141–44) JANE SMITH HILL HARMON, b. 1849, Washington-Wilkes Co., GA. House servant. int. Stonestreet. (S2 12 *GA* 2: 97–102) DAVE HARPER, b. 1850, Montgomery Co., MO. Farmed, labored, odd jobs after freedom. Still working as gardener. (S2 11 *MO*: 162–68) EDA HARPER, b. ca. 1845, MS, taken AR. int. Bowden. (S1 9 *AR* 3: 164–67) PIERCE HARPER, b. 1851, NC. Sold age eight. Yard, errand boy. Postwar farmed, worked turpentine SC. Moved Galveston, TX, 1877, gardener, longshoreman. int. Liberato. (S1 4 *TX* 2: 109–14; SS2 5 *TX* 4: 1642–51) REV. THOMAS HARPER, b. 1853, SC. Methodist minister. int. Summer, ed. Turnage. (S1 3 *SC* 2: 240–41) ABRAM HARRIS, b. 1845, Greenville, SC. Fieldhand. int. W. McKinney. (S2 9 *AR* 3: 168–75) ANNIE HARRIS, b. unk., VA. (*WW*, 128–29) CAROLINE JOHNSON HARRIS, b. 1843, VA. (*WW*, 129) CHARLES HARRIS, b. 1870, Leavenworth, KS. Child of ex-slaves. Blacksmith. (SS1 2 *CO*: 47–51) DELLA HARRIS, b. ca. 1852, Warrenton, NC. Moved Petersburg, VA postwar. int. S. Byrd. (S2 16 *VA*: 24–26; *WW*, 129–32) DOSIA HARRIS, b. ca. 1860, Greene Co., GA. Yard, field work. int. Hornsby, ed. Hall, L. Harris, Booth. (S2 12 *GA* 2: 103–14) MARY HARRIS, b. 1854, LA. House servant. int. Posey. (*MW*, 94–95) ORRIS HARRIS, b. ca. 1858, Amite Co., MS. int. Holmes. (SS1 8 *MS* 3: 925–35) SARAH HARRIS, b. April 1861, NC. Domestic after freedom. int. Hicks, ed. Waitt. (S2 14 *NC* 1: 475–78) UNCLE SHANG HARRIS, b. ca. 1840, Franklin Co., GA. Personal servant. Stayed on plantation postwar, later worked railroad. int. Bell. (S2 12 *GA* 2: 117–25) SQUIRE HARRIS, b. ca. 1840, Edgefield Co., SC. Plow boy, yard boy, house boy, tended stock, took children school. int. Barragan. (SS1 3 *GA* 1: 305–10) SUSAN HARRIS, b. November 20, 1872, Leadville, CO. Child of ex-slaves. Dance hall, medicine show performer, later missionary, church worker. (SS1 2 *CO*: 52–55) THOMAS HARRIS, b. February 14, 1856, Orange Co., NC. int. Matthews, ed. G. Andrews. (S2 14 *NC* 1: 359–62) VIRGINIA HARRIS, b. ca. 1855, Vicksburg. Farmed postwar. int. Campbell. (SS1 8 *MS* 3: 937–48) ELI HARRISON, b. 1850, SC. int. W. Dixon. (S1 3 *SC* 2: 244–46) JACK HARRISON, b. unk., TX. int. B. Davis. (SS2 5 *TX* 4: 1652–57) JOHN HARRISON, b. 1857, Creek Nation, IT. Creek Slave. Farm, ranch hand, wage laborer postwar. int. L. Wilson. (SS 12 *OK*: 145–68) SISTER HARRISON, b. 1846, Norfolk Co., VA. Nursemaid. int. C. Anderson. (*WW*, 134–15) WILLIAM H. HARRISON, b. March 4, 1832, Richmond, VA. Slave of Anderson Harrison, cousin of President Benjamin Harrison. Valet, carriage driver, fiddler. Sent to war, captured, conscripted Union army. Postwar moved Madison, AR, freighter. int. Robertson. (S2 9 *AR* 3: 185–89) PLOMER HARSHAW, b. August 10, 1852, Holly Springs, MS. Taken AR, TX during war. Leased to Confederate government, worked loom house, brick yard. Held in bondage postwar. int. Garrison, ed. Vollmer. (SS2 12 *OK*: 169–72) CHARLIE HARVEY, b. ca. 1855, SC. ed. Turnage. (S1 2 *SC* 2: 247–51) MARTHA HASKINS, b. ca. 1850, VA. (*WW*, 135–27) MATILDA HATCHETT, b. ca. 1840, Yell Co., AR. int. S. Taylor. (S2 9 *AR* 2: 195–201) MOLLIE HATFIELD, b. 1860, Mobile, AL. Taken West Point, MS as child. int. Joiner. (SS1 8 *MS* 3: 949–55) WILLIAM HAWES, b. 1864, Frankfort, KY. Moved KS 1877, Lincoln, NE 1915. Cattle driver packing house, hod carrier, trucker. int. Burks. (SS2 1 *NE*: 325–26) LIZZIE HAWKENS, b. ca. 1870, Magnolia, AR. Child of ex-slaves. int. Robertson. (S2 9 *AR* 3: 205–8)

G. W. HAWKINS, b. January 1, 1865, Lamar Co., AL. Child of ex-slaves. int. S. Taylor. (S2 9 *AR* 3: 212–20) SUSIE HAWKINS, b. ca. 1860, Stokes Co., NC. Farmed postwar. Moved Clark Co., OH 1903. int. Minnick. (SS1 5 *OH*: 355–56) TOM HAWKINS, b. ca. 1860, Belton, SC. House servant. Stayed on plantation until 1880s. int. Hornsby, ed. Hall, L. Harris. (S2 12 *GA* 2: 126–35) ANN HAWTHORNE, b. ca. 1853, Jasper Co., TX. int. Dibble, Beehler. (S1 4 *TX* 2: 118–25) CHARLES HAYES, b. ca. 1855, AL. Stayed on plantation as sharecropper postwar. int. Poole, J. Smith. (S1 6 *AL*: 174–5; SS2 1 *AL*: 3–4) JAMES HAYES, b. December 28, 1835, Shelby Co., TX. Fieldhand. Wage labor postwar. Moved Fort Worth, cooked. int. Gauthier. (S1 4 *TX* 2: 126–29; SS2 5 *TX* 4: 1682–87) WASH HAYES, b. ca. 1860, Simpson Co., MS. Renter, wage labor postwar. int. Giles. (SS1 8 *MS* 3: 963–68) BURT HAYGOOD, 1840–1924, SC. Information communicated by daughter. Fieldhand, dance caller. Served in war. Stayed on plantation postwar. Later moved Greenville, woodcutter. int. Fitchett. (SS1 11 *SC*: 186–87) ELIZA HAYS, b. ca. 1860, Brownsville, TN. Postwar ran restaurant, later moved Little Rock. int. S. Taylor. (S2 9 *AR* 3: 221–26) BARBARA HAYWOOD, b. 1852, Johnston Co., NC. Fieldhand, weaver. int. Hicks, ed. G. Andrews. (S2 14 *NC* 1: 385–88) FELIX HAYWOOD, b. 1845, Bexar Co., TX. Shepherd, cowpuncher. Stayed, worked cattle postwar. int. Nixon. (S1 4 *TX* 2: 130–4; SS2 5 *TX* 4: 1688–95) BILL HEARD, b. ca. 1865, GA. Child of ex-slaves. int. McCune, ed. Hall, Booth. (S2 12 *GA* 2: 136–46) EMMALINE HEARD, b. ca. 1860, Henry Co., GA. Hired out postwar. Later moved Atlanta. int. Ross, ed. Russell. (S2 12 *GA* 1: 32–36; S2 12 *GA* 2: 147–64; S2 13 *GA* 4: 245–50, 256–60) ROBERT HEARD, b. ca. 1841, Jackson Co., GA. Fieldhand. int. Jaffee. (S2 12 *GA* 2: 170–72) BENJAMIN HENDERSON, b. September 8, 1858, Jasper Co., GA. Fieldhand. int. Ross. (S2 12 *GA* 2: 173–77) GEORGE HENDERSON, b. May 10, 1860, Woodford Co., KY. int. Ison. (S2 16 *KY*: 5–8) ISABELLE HENDERSON, b. ca. 1850, MO. House servant. Midwife postwar.

int. Daniel. (S2 11 *MO*: 203–4; SS1 2 *MO*: 193–95) ESSEX HENRY, b. ca. 1854, Raleigh, NC. Stayed on plantation postwar. int. Mary A. Hicks, ed. Daisy Bailey Waitt. (S2 14 *NC* 1: 393–98) IDA HENRY, b. 1854, Marshall, TX. House girl, nursemaid, cook. (S1 7 *OK*: 134–37) JEFFERSON FRANKLIN HENRY, b. ca. 1860, Paulding Co., GA. Sharecropped postwar. int. Hornsby, ed. Hall, Booth. (S2 12 *GA* 2: 178–93) JIM HENRY, b. ca. 1860, SC. Farmed postwar. int. W. Dixon. (S1 2 *SC* 2: 266–70) MACK HENRY, b. unk., Copiah Co., MS. Taken Vicksburg. Ran away, joined Union army as bugler. Returned Vicksburg after war. int. Lawrence. (SS1 8 *MS* 3: 972–73) NETTIE HENRY, b. ca. 1855, Livingston, AL. Taken Meridian as infant. House servant. Domestic postwar. int. M. Austin. (S1 7 *MS*: 61–67; SS1 8 *MS* 3: 975–87) UNCLE ROBERT HENRY, b. 1855, Wilkes Co., GA. House servant. int. Jaffe, ed. Booth, Jaffe. (S2 12 *GA* 2: 194–99) ANNIE YOUNG HENSON, b. ca. 1850, Northumberland Co., VA. Nursemaid. Moved Baltimore postwar. (S2 16 *MD*: 26–28) MARIE E. HERVEY, b. ca. 1870, TN. Child of ex-slaves. int. Taylor (S2 9 *AR* 3: 231–34) CHANEY HEWS, b. ca. 1857, Wake Co., NC. int. Matthews, ed. G. Andrews. (S2 14 *NC* 1: 405–8) WILL HICKS, b. ca. 1860, Farmersville, LA. Fieldhand. Farmed postwar. int. P. Anderson. (S2 9 *AR* 3: 237) JOE HIGH, b. April 10, 1857, Wake Co., NC. House servant. Working as gardener Raleigh. int. Matthews, ed. Waitt. (S2 14 *NC* 1: 409–16) SUSAN HIGH, b. June 1867, NC. Child of ex-slaves. int. Matthews, ed. Waitt. (S2 14 *NC* 1: 417–21) ALBERT HILL, b. 1856, Walton Co., GA. Moved TX 1877. int. Gauthier. (S1 4 *TX* 2: 137–40; SS2 5 *TX* 4: 1713–24) CLARK HILL, b. ca. 1855, Americus, GA. Swept yard, fired smokehouse and kiln. int. Bowden. (S2 9 *AR* 3: 247–51) DELIA HILL, b. ca. 1850, Coldwater, MS. After war moved Memphis, St. Louis. Nursed, washed, cooked. int. White. (S2 11 *MO*: 179–83) ELMIRA HILL, b. 1849, Kinsale Co., VA. Sold age twelve, taken Pine Bluff, AR. int. Bowden. (S2 9 *AR* 3: 252–55) GILLIE HILL, b. unk., AR. Grandchild of ex-slaves. int. S. Taylor. (S2 9 *AR* 3: 256–57) HAT-

TIE HILL, b. ca. 1853, GA. House girl, fieldhand. Stayed on plantation two years postwar, moved AR. int. Bowden. (S2 9 *AR* 3: 262–63) KITTY HILL, b. April 1860, Petersburg, VA. Sold, taken Chatham Co., NC 1865, held in bondage many years postwar. int. Matthews, ed. G. Andrews. (S2 14 *NC* 1: 422–26) PETER HILL, b. ca. 1867, Lecompte, LA. Child of ex-slaves. int. Baham. (*MW*, 97) MORRIS HILLYER, b. ca. 1850, Rome, GA. Toted water, tended cows. Postwar worked bridges. Moved KY, miner, carpenter. Later moved OK. (S1 7 *OK*: 138–44) DELLA BESS HILYARD, b. 1858, Darlington, SC. After freedom moved GA, Fort Pierce, Titusville, FL. (S2 17 *FL*: 54–55) MARRIAH HINES, b. July 4, 1835, Southampton Co., VA. Fieldhand. Stayed on plantation postwar. int. Hoggard. (S2 16 *VA*: 27–30; *WW*, 139–42) CHARLES (CHARLIE) HINTON, b. ca. 1850, NC. Stayed on plantation postwar, later moved AR. int. Martin-Barker, Bowden. (S2 9 *AR* 3: 276–80) ROBERT HINTON, b. 1856, Johnston, Co., NC. Houseworker. int. Matthews, ed. Waitt. (S2 14 *NC* 1: 436–40) ELIZABETH ROSS HITE, b. ca. 1850, New Orleans. House servant. Postwar farmed, domestic. int. R. McKinney. (*MW*, 98–110) ROSINA HOARD, b. April 9, 1859, Williamson Co., TX. Taken Travis Co. Nursemaid, fieldhand. Farmed postwar. int. Menn. (S1 4 *TX* 2: 141–43; SS2 5 *TX* 4: 1730–38) LEE HOBBY, b. ca. 1850, Cumberland Co., KY. int. Cowan. (SS2 5 *TX* 4: 1739–54) N. H. HOBLEY, b. 1858, LA. Fieldhand. Moved Algiers–New Orleans 1880, worked as Divine Healer. int. Posey. (*MW*, 111–21) FANNY SMITH HODGES, b. unk., Amite Co., MS. Sold as child. Ladies maid. int. Holmes. (S1 7 *MS*: 68–71; SS1 8 *MS* 3: 1024–28) CLAYTON HOLBERT, b. ca. 1850, Linn co., TN. Fieldhand. int. L. Gray. (S2 16 *KS*: 1–8; SS2 1 *KS*: 285–91) TOM HOLLAND, b. 1840, Walker Co., TX. Fieldhand, broke wild horses. int. B. Davis. (S1 4 *TX* 2: 144–47; SS2 5 *TX* 4: 1760–69) H. B. HOLLOWAY (DAD, PAPPY), freeborn February 15, 1849, Fort Valley, GA. Worked railroad postwar. int. S. Taylor. (S2 9 *AR* 3: 287–305) ELIZA HOLMAN, b. ca. 1855, Clinton, MS. Taken

Wise Co., TX 1861. Domestic postwar. int. Gauthier. (S1 4 *TX* 2: 148–50; SS2 5 *TX* 4: 1770–78) ROSE HOLMAN, b. ca. 1855, Greensboro, MS. Picked up chips, toted water. Postwar sharecropped LA, MS. int. Butts. (SS1 8 *MS* 3: 1037–41) JAMES AUGUSTUS HOLMES, b. August 2, 1843, Thomas Co., GA. Taken Bainbridge. Yard work, house servant. int. Walsh. (SS1 8 *MS* 3: 1043–47) JOSEPH HOLMES, b. 1856, Danville, VA. Fieldhand. Postwar moved GA, AL. Preached, taught school. int. Prine. (S1 6 *AL*: 190–200; SS2 1 *AL*: 5–12) AUNT RHODY HOLSELL, b. 1848, Fredericktown, MO. Fieldhand. Tenant postwar. int. Miles. (S2 11 *MO*: 191–202) LARNCE HOLT, b. 1858, Woodville, TX. Fiddler, Holiness deacon. Farmed, odd-jobbed until lost leg cutting railroad ties ca. 1922. int. Dibble, Grey. (S1 4 *TX* 2: 151–52; SS2 5 *TX* 4: 1779–82) BILL HOMER, b. June 17, 1850, Shreveport, LA. Taken Burleson Co., TX. Coachman. Moved Laredo 1866, worked stock ranch, then farmed until 1935. int. Gauthier. (S1 4 *TX* 2: 153–56; SS2 5 *TX* 4: 1783–89) MARY HOMER, b. 1856, Anderson Co., TN. Left 1875, moved Austin Co., TX. int. Gauthier. (SS2 5 *TX* 4: 1790–96) JOSH HORN, b. 1853, Louisville, AL. Fieldhand. int. Tartt, ed. Oden. (S1 6 *AL*: 201–10; SS1 1 *AL*: 189–99) MOLLY HORN, b. 1860, NC. Sold as infant, taken AR. Sharecropped postwar. int. Robertson. (S2 9 *AR* 3: 318–20) UNCLE BEN HORRY, b. ca. 1850, Murrell's Inlet, SC. int. Chandler. (S1 2 *SC* 2: 308–26; SS1 11 *SC*: 194–203) CORA L. HORTON, b. ca. 1880, AR. Grandchild of ex-slaves. int. S. Taylor. (S2 9 *AR* 3: 321–24) ALICE HOUSTON, b. October 22, 1859, Hays Co., TX. (S1 4 *TX* 2: 15: 9–62) AUNT CAROLINA HOUSTON, b. 1856, Macon, GA. Taken Nacogdoches, TX during war, hired out, abandoned. Taken in by white family, stayed on as domestic. int. Shirley. (SS2 5 *TX* 4: 1803–5) EMMA L. HOWARD, b. ca. 1850, Lowndes Co., AL. House servant. Cooked postwar. int. M. Fowler, ed. Kytle. (S1 6 *AL*: 211–14) JOSEPHINE HOWARD, b. ca. 1830, Tuscaloosa, AL, taken Marshall, TX prewar. Fieldhand. Moved Houston 1870s. int. Drake. (S1 4 *TX* 2: 163–65; SS2 5 *TX* 4: 1806–11)

CARRIE HUDSON, b. ca. 1860, Elbert Co., GA. Nursemaid. Stayed on plantation postwar. int. Hornsby, ed. Hall, L. Harris, Booth. (S2 12 *GA* 2: 211–19) CHARLIE HUDSON, b. March 27, 1858, Elbert Co., GA. Odd jobs. int. Hornsby, ed. Hall, L. Harris, Booth. (S2 12 *GA* 2: 220–32) MEASY HUDSON, b. ca. 1850, NC. Laundress postwar. (S2 16 *TN*: 31–32) ANNIE HUFF, b. ca. 1830, Macon, GA. House, yard work, spinner, fieldhand. (S2 12 *GA* 2: 233–37) BRYANT HUFF, b. unk., Warren Co., GA. Odd jobs. int. A. Dixon. (S2 12 *GA* 2: 238–43) EASTER HUFF, b. 1858, Oglethorpe Co., GA. Stayed on plantation postwar, later moved town, domestic. int. Hornsby, ed. Hall, Blease, Booth. (S2 12 *GA* 2: 244–51) FANNIE HUGHES, b. ca. 1854, Bibb Co., GA. House servant. (SS1 3 *GA* 1: 329–34) FRANK HUGHES, b. August 15, 1858, Pickensville, AL. Postwar moved Columbus, MS, attended school, farmed. int. Joiner. (SS1 8 *MS* 3: 1057–66) LIZZIE HUGHES, b. December 25, 1848, Nacogdoches, TX. House servant. Stayed on plantation postwar. Later moved Marshall, domestic. int. Hampton. (S1 4 *TX* 2: 166–68; SS2 5 *TX* 4: 1812–20) MARGARET HUGHES, b. ca. 1855, Columbia, SC. Nursemaid. int. Pierce. (S1 2 *SC* 2: 327–30) ALEX HUMPHREY, b. March 31, 1864, Davis (now Cass) Co., TX. Taken Harrison Co. Farmed, worked T&P railroad postwar. int. Hampton. (SS2 5 *TX* 4: 1821–24) ANNA HUMPHREY, b. 1849 or 1850, Russell Co., AL. House servant, nursemaid. Taken Plano, TX during war. Stayed on plantation postwar. int. Foreman. (SS2 5 *TX* 4: 1825–31) FOREST HUNTER, b. 1864, Goshen Hill, SC. Tended cows, fetched kindling, other chores. int. Simms, ed. Turnage. (SS1 11 *SC*: 208–9; SS2 1 *SC*: 379–80) JOHN HUNTER, b. ca. 1864, NC. Moved AR 1880s. Preacher. int. S. Taylor. (S2 9 *AR* 3: 359–66) LINA HUNTER, b. ca. 1848, Oglethorpe Co., GA. Nursemaid. int. McCune, ed. Hall, Booth. (S2 12 *GA* 2: 252–72) MRS. HUNTER, b. unk., LA. (*MW*, 123) AUNT EMMA HURLEY, b. ca. 1855, Wilkes Co., GA. int. Stonestreet, ed. Booth, Bell. (S1 12 *GA* 2: 273–80) MOSE HURSEY, b. ca. 1855,

LA. Sold, taken Red River Co., TX during war. Farmed, preached, prophesized postwar. int. Foreman. (S1 4 *TX* 2: 169–71; SS2 5 *TX* 4: 1832–36) CHARLEY HURT, b. 1853, Oglethorpe Co., GA. Stayed on plantation five years postwar, then odd-jobbed, settled Fort Worth 1899. int. Gauthier. (S1 4 *TX* 2: 172–76; SS2 5 *TX* 4: 1837–46) ALICE HUTCHESON, b. ca. 1860, Monroe Co., GA. int. McCune, ed. Hall, Booth. (S2 12 *GA* 2: 281–88) HAL HUTSON, b. October 12, 1847, Galveston, TN. (S1 7 *OK*: 145–47) WILLIAM HUTSON, b. 1839, GA. House servant. (S1 7 *OK*: 148–51) PATSY HYDE, b. unk., Nashville, TN. House servant. (S2 16 *TN*: 33–36)

ADDISON INGRAM, b. December 14, 1830, Russell Co., AL. Fieldhand. Preached postwar. int. Mills. (SS1 1 *AL*: 200–202) EVERETT INGRAM, b. unk., Russell Co., AL. int. Klein, ed. Kytle. (S1 6 *AL*: 215–17; SS1 1 *AL*: 203–5) WASH INGRAM, b. ca. 1844, Richmond, VA. Sold, taken Carthage, TX. Fieldhand. Held in bondage postwar. Farmed TX, LA. int. Hampton. (S1 4 *TX* 2: 177–79; SS2 5 *TX* 4: 1852–55) SQUIRE IRVIN, b. 1849, Nashville, TN. Fieldhand. Left 1873, farmed Bolivar, Coahoma Co., MS. int. Campbell. (SS1 8 *MS* 3: 1079–90) WILLIAM IRVING, b. 1850, Walker Co., GA. Moved TX postwar. int. Cowan. (SS2 5 *TX* 4: 1864–75) HANNAH IRWIN, b. ca. 1853, Louisville, AL. Nursemaid. int. Couric. (S1 6 *AL*: 218–19; SS1 1 *AL*: 206) JOANNA THOMPSON ISOM, b. ca. 1858, Oxford, MS. int. Holt. (SS1 8 *MS* 3: 1091–1102)

ADELINE JACKSON, b. ca. 1849, Winnsboro, SC. Nursemaid, fieldhand. int. W. Dixon. (S1 3 *SC* 3: 1–4) AMANDA JACKSON, b. unk., Glascock Co., GA. Yard work. (S2 12 *GA* 2: 289–93) CARTER J. JACKSON, b. ca. 1850, Montgomery, AL. Taken TX 1863, held in bondage four years postwar. Fieldhand. (S1 4 *TX* 2: 180–81; SS2 5 4: 1883–87) CLARICE JACKSON, b. ca. 1855, AR. Farmed postwar. int. Bowden. (S2 9 *AR* 4: 1–2; SS1 2 *AR*: 9; SS2 1 *AR*: 96) CORDELIA ANDERSON JACKSON, b. ca. 1859, Union Co., SC. int. Sims, ed. Turnage. (S1 3 *SC* 3: 5–7) DORA JACKSON, b. 1858, Perry Co.,

MS. int. Walsh. (SS1 8 *MS* 3: 1109–11) AUNT EASTER JACKSON, b. ca. 1850, Troup Co., GA. (S2 12 *GA* 2: 299–302) GEORGE JACKSON, b. February 6, 1858, Loudon Co., VA. Fieldhand, house servant. Farmed postwar. int. Bishop. (S2 16 *OH*: 45–49) ISABELLA JACKSON, b. ca. 1858, Bunker, LA. (S1 7 *OK*: 152–54) ISRAEL JACKSON, b. August 3, 1863, Yalobusha, Co., MS. Tended horses, farmed postwar. int. Bowden. (S2 9 *AR* 4: 5–8) JAMES JACKSON, b. December 18, 1850, Caddo Parish, LA. Taken TX 1852. Postwar moved Austin, Taylor, Kaufman, Fort Worth. int. Colbert. (S1 4 *TX* 2: 182–84; SS2 5 *TX* 4: 1895–99) LULA JACKSON, October 1, 1859, Russell, Co., AL. Tended children. Hired out, odd-jobbed postwar. (S2 9 *AR* 4: 9–19) MARTHA JACKSON, b. 1850, AL. int. Tartt. (S1 6 *AL*: 220–23) MARTIN JACKSON, b. ca. 1850, TX. House servant. int. Nixon. (S1 4 *TX* 2: 187–92; SS2 5 *TX* 4: 1902–9) MARY JACKSON, b. ca. 1860, Hunt Co., TX. int. Lucy. (S2 9 *AR* 4: 20–21) NANCY JACKSON, b. 1830, Madison Co., TN. Taken Panola Co., TX age five. int. Hampton. (S1 4 *TX* 2: 193–94; SS2 5 *TX* 4: 1910–14) RICHARD JACKSON, b. 1859, Harrison Co., TX. Farmed after freedom. (S1 4 *TX* 2: 195–97; SS2 5 *TX* 4: 1915–18) REV. SILAS JACKSON, b. 1846 or 1847, Ashby's Gap, VA. Fieldhand. (S2 16 *MD*: 29–33) TURNER JACOBS, b. July 9, 1855, Aberdeen, MS. Fieldhand. int. Kolb. (SS1 8 *MS* 3: 1114–21) UNCLE JAKE, b. ca. 1845, GA. Fieldhand, house servant. int. McKinney. (S2 12 *GA* 2: 310–14; SS1 4 *GA* 2: 616–22) JAMES CALHART JAMES, b. August 23, 1846, SC. (S2 16 *MD*: 34–36) JOHN JAMES, b. 1859, East Baton Rouge Parish, LA. Stayed on plantation a few years, moved Sedalia, MO, worked MK&T Railroad twenty years, then moved Fort Worth. (S1 4 *TX* 2: 198–200; SS2 5 *TX* 4: 1919–25) JOSEPH JAMES, b. 1845, New Iberia, LA. Creole. Fieldhand, tended horses, mules. Stayed on plantation postwar. Moved Beaumont 1916, yard man. int. Dibble. (SS2 6 *TX* 5: 1927–32) JULIA ANN JAMES, b. ca. 1858, Rockingham Co., NC. Knitter, weaver. Farmed postwar. Moved OH 1879. int. Minnick. (SS1 5 *OH*: 386–89)

HANNAH JAMESON, b. ca. 1850, Bright Star, AR. Taken TX during war. House servant, toted water. Stayed on plantation five years postwar, moved Marshall. int. Hampton, ed. Dickinson. (SS2 6 *TX* 5: 1933–38) ANDREW JACKSON JARNAGIN, b. February 7, 1853, Mashulaville, MS. (SS1 8 *MS* 3: 1127–30) ISIAH JEFFERIES, b. 1851, Cherokee Co., SC. Fieldhand. ed. Turnage. (S1 3 *SC* 3: 17–19) HATTIE JEFFERSON, b. ca. 1855, Holmesville, MS. int. Holmes. (SS1 8 *MS* 3: 1131–36) LEWIS JEFFERSON, b. 1853, Pike Co., MS. House servant. int. Holmes. (SS1 8 *MS* 3: 1137–47) LYDIA JEFFERSON, b. 1851, Avoyelles Parish, LA. Fieldhand postwar. int. Drake. (SS2 6 *TX* 5: 1939–47) ELLIS JEFSON, b. ca. 1861, VA. Family moved with slaveholder to Holly Springs, MS 1867. Stayed on plantation many years, then preached. int. Robertson. (S2 9 *AR* 4: 43–46) OPHELIA JEMISON, b. ca. 1868, SC. Child of ex-slaves. int. Tiedman. (SS1 11 *SC*: 213–28) PERRY SID JEMISON, b. ca. 1858, Perry Co., AL. Waterboy, fieldhand. int. Bishop, Taleman, ed. Dugan. (S2 16 *OH*: 50–56) HENRY D. JENKINS, b. ca. 1850, Columbia, SC. Fieldhand. int. W. Dixon. (S1 3 *SC* 3: 23–26) LEWIS JENKINS, b. January 1844, Green Co., AL. House worker, fieldhand. int. Hunter. (SS1 12 *OK*: 189–96) NEP JENKINS, b. 1853, Sumter Co., AL. int. Holmes. (SS1 8 *MS* 3: 1149–50) PAUL JENKINS, b. 1867, Colleton Co., SC. Child of ex-slaves. int. Scruggs. (S1 3 *SC* 3: 30–32) MAHALA JEWEL, b. ca. 1862, Oglethorpe Co., GA. Yard work. int. McCune, ed. Hall, Booth. (S2 12 *GA* 2: 315–21) MARY ANN JOHN, b. February 14, 1855, Opelousas, LA. Moved New Orleans 1890. Vegetable peddler. int. McElwee. (*MW*, 128–29) ZENO JOHN, b. ca. 1861, Ville Platte, LA. Creole. Farmed postwar. int. Dibble. (SS2 6 *TX* 5: 1948–51) THOMAS JOHNS, b. April 18, 1847, Chambers Co., AL. Fieldhand. Farmed postwar. int. W. Ervin. (S1 4 *TX* 2: 201–4; SS2 6 *TX* 5: 1952–72) ALLEN JOHNSON, b. ca. 1855, Cass Co., GA. Farmed, odd-jobbed postwar. int. S. Taylor. (S2 9 *AR* 4: 63–66) BENJAMIN JOHNSON, b. unk., Richmond, VA. Fieldhand. Wounded in war. int. Driskell. (S2 12 *GA* 2: 322–26) CHARLEY

JOHNSON, b. July 15, 1850, Fort Bend, TX. Fieldhand, dance caller. Held in bondage postwar. Escaped, farmed. int. A. Davis. (SS2 6 *TX* 5: 1977–87) ELLA JOHNSON, b. 1852, Helena, AR. Fieldhand. int. S. Taylor. (S2 9 *AR* 3: 77–83) ELLA JOHNSON, b. 1857, Greenville, SC. (SS1 4 *GA* 2: 343–48) GEORGIA JOHNSON, b. 1865, GA. Child of ex-slaves. int. McCune, ed. Hall, L. Harris. (S2 12 *GA* 2: 327–36) HARRY JOHNSON, b. ca. 1850, MO. Stolen age five, taken AR. Sold at end of war, taken TX, held in bondage two years postwar, then worked cattle. (S1 4 *TX* 2: 212–15; SS2 6 *TX* 5: 1994–2004) HENRY JOHNSON, b. 1842, MS. House servant. After war worked as cabin boy on *Sea Castle* (New Orleans to Mobile), did yard work, odd jobs New Orleans, Houston, Galveston. Patient, Aged and Infirm Ward, St. Mary's Infirmary, Galveston. int. Liberato. (SS2 6 *TX* 5: 2005–13) HENRY JOHNSON, b. ca. 1844, Patrick Co., VA. Fieldhand. After war farmed, railroad work. Later moved AL, TN, St. Louis, laid pipeline, worked factories, landscaping. int. White. (S2 11 *MO*: 205–13) UNCLE HILLIARD JOHNSON, b. ca. 1857, AL. int. Tartt. (S1 6 *AL*: 227–30) ISAAC JOHNSON, b. February 12, 1855, Lillington, NC. int. Matthews, ed. Waitt. (S2 15 *NC* 2: 14–19) UNCLE JIMMIE JOHNSON, b. ca. 1847, VA. Sold, taken Spartanburg, SC. Groom, carriage driver. Postwar taught piano, organ. int. DuPre. (S1 3 *SC* 3: 53–55) LETHA JOHNSON, b. ca. 1861, Monroe Co., MS. Stayed on plantation until 1889. Farmed MS, cooked Memphis, moved Pine Bluff. int. Bowden. (S2 9 *AR* 4: 98–99) LIZZIE JOHNSON, b. ca. 1870, Holly Springs, MS. Child of ex-slaves. int. Robertson. (S2 9 *AR* 4: 102–3) MAG JOHNSON, b. ca. 1870, Clarendon, AR. Child of ex-slaves. int. Robertson. (S2 9 *AR* 4: 107–9) MANUEL JOHNSON, b. ca. 1863, Wilkes Co., GA. House servant, fieldhand, ox driver. int. Stonestreet. (S2 12 *GA* 2: 337–42) UNCLE MARION JOHNSON, b. ca. 1848, LA. Fieldhand. Postwar moved El Dorado, AR, wove baskets, bottomed chairs, told fortunes, conjured. int. Graham. (S2 9 *AR* 4: 112–21) MARY JOHNSON, b. 1852, SC.

Weaver, fieldhand. int. Summer, ed. Turnage. (S1 3 *SC* 3: 56–58) MARY JOHNSON, b. ca. 1858, VA, raised MS, LA. Worked sawmills. Moved Beaumont 1920, cooked on rice farm until strokes. int. Dibble, Grey. (S1 4 *TX* 2: 219–22; SS2 6 *TX* 5: 2021–30) MIEMY JOHNSON, b. ca. 1855, Charleston, SC. Stayed on plantation postwar. int. W. Dixon. (S1 3 *SC* 3: 59–61) PAULINE JOHNSON AND FELICE (née RENÉE) BOUDREAUX (siblings), b. 1853, 1859, Opelousas, LA. Creoles. House servants. int. Dibble, Grey. (S1 4 *TX* 2: 225–27; SS2 6 *TX* 5: 2035–42) PRINCE JOHNSON, b. 1847, Yazoo Co., MS. House servant. Moved SC postwar, returned MS, farmed. int. Campbell. (S1 7 *MS*: 76–83; SS1 8 *MS* 3: 1167–80) RICHARD JOHNSON, b. 1836, Augusta, GA. Served in war. int. W. Ervin. (SS1 6 *TX* 5: 2043–45) SALLIE JOHNSON, b. August 1855, TX. Moved Austin postwar, washed. int. Menn. (SS2 6 *TX* 5: 2046–50) ST. ANN JOHNSON, b. 1865, New Orleans. Child of ex-slaves. Moved Plaquemines Parish, returned New Orleans. (*MW*, 136–39) STEVE JOHNSON, b. unk., TX. int. Cowan. (SS2 6 *TX* 5: 2062) SUSIE JOHNSON, b. ca. 1857, GA. int. Crawford. (S2 12 *GA* 2: 342–44) TINA JOHNSON, b. 1852, Richmond, GA. int. Hicks, ed. Waitt. (S2 15 *NC* 2: 20–22) TOM JOHNSON, b. 1854, SC. Assisted weavers, farmed after freedom. int. Summer. (S1 3 *SC* 3: 62) WILLIAM I. JOHNSON, JR., b. 1840, VA. Butler, hired out. Building contractor after freedom. int. Milton L. Randolph. (*WW*, 165–70) AARON JONES, b. 1845, Holly Springs, MS. Fieldhand. int. N. Thompson. (SS1 8 *MS* 3: 1185–89) ALFRED JONES, b. August 11, 1833, Lowndes Co., AL. (SS1 1 *AL*: 221–5) ANDERSON JONES, b. ca. 1856, Tehuacana, TX. int. Cowan. (SS2 6 *TX* 5: 2064–76) ANGELINE JONES, b. 1859, Memphis. Taken Brinkley, AR. int. Robertson. (S2 9 *AR* 4: 134–35) MR. BEVERLY JONES, b. 1848, VA. (*WW*, 181–85) BOB JONES, b. ca. 1850, Warren Co., NC. int. Hicks, ed. G. Andrews. (S1 15 *NC* 2: 24–26) BUD JONES, b. ca. 1850, Africa or Haiti. Raised Lynchburg, VA. Entertainer, musician, house servant, fetched wood, tended bloodhounds.

Moved TX postwar, worked Dallas Gas Company. int. Gauthier. (SS2 6 *TX* 5: 2077–92) CHARITY JONES, b. ca. 1853, Amite Co., MS. int. Holmes. (SS1 8 *MS* 3: 1193–1202) CLARA JONES, b. unk., Wake Co., NC. Fieldhand, farmed after freedom. int. Hicks, ed. G. Andrews. (S2 15 *NC* 2: 30–33) EASTER JONES, b. unk., Burke Co., GA. Fieldhand, moved Augusta after freedom. int. Radford. (SS1 4 *GA* 2: 349–51) EDWARD JONES, b. 1855, Montgomery, AL. Taken Hinds Co., MS. Fieldhand. Farmed, taught school, preached postwar. int. Campbell. (SS1 8 *MS* 3: 1203–9) EMMA JONES, b. May 1849, Columbus, GA. House servant. (S1 6 *AL*: 236–37; SS1 1 *AL*: 226–28) ESTELLA JONES, b. ca. 1855, Augusta, GA. int. Oliphant, ed. Booth. (S2 12 *GA* 2: 345–50) FANNIE JONES, b. 1853, Augusta, GA. House servant. int. Powell, ed. Booth. (S2 12 *GA* 2: 351–55) AUNT HANNAH JONES, b. ca. 1845, Amelia Co., VA. Sold, taken AL. House girl, sewing, spinning. int. Hix, J. Smith. (S1 6 *AL*: 238–40) HARRIET JONES, b. 1844, NC. Taken TX. int. Cowan. (S1 4 *TX* 2: 231–36; SS2 6 *TX* 5: 2095–2107) JACK JONES, b. 1843, Oktibbeha Co., MS. (SS1 8 *MS* 3: 1212–14) JULIUS JONES, b. ca. 1847, Summerville, TN. Fieldhand. Runaway, joined Union army 1863, mustered out Memphis 1866. Moved MS, farmed. int. Campbell. (SS1 8 *MS* 3: 1215–25) LEWIS JONES, b. 1851, LaGrange, TX. Coachman. Stayed on plantation eight years postwar. Worked cotton gins. Moved Fort Worth 1896. Odd jobs, meatpacker 1911–31, dismissed for old age. int. Gauthier. (S1 4 *TX* 2; 237–40; SS2 6 *TX* 5: 2108–14) LIZA JONES, b. 1856, Liberty, TX. House servant, stayed on plantation postwar. int. Dibble, Grey. (S1 4 *TX* 2: 241–45; SS2 6 *TX* 5: 2115–22) LIDIA (LYDIA) JONES, b. ca. 1845, MS. Fieldhand, weaver. Hired out postwar. int. Bowden. (S2 9 *AR* 4: 151–54) MANDY JONES, b. ca. 1857, Crawford, MS. Postwar picked cotton, washed. int. C. Wells. (SS1 8 *MS* 3: 1226–42) MARTHA JONES, b. ca. 1860, VA. Taken MS, LA, TX during war. Sharecropped postwar. int. Cowan. (SS2 6 *TX* 5: 2130–34) MARY JANE JONES, b. ca. 1849, Jefferson Co., MS. Fieldhand.

int. Lawrence. (SS1 8 *MS* 3: 1243–46) OLIVER JONES, b. July 4, 1858, Amite, MS. Taken Canton, Crystal Springs. int. England. (SS1 8 *MS* 3: 1252–55) RICHARD JONES (Dick Look-Up), b. 1812, SC. Interviewer estimated birthdate as 1844. Fieldhand, farmed after freedom. int. Sims. (S1 3 *SC* 3: 63–71) STEVE JONES, b. November 11, 1849, Charleston, SC. Taken TX 1856. Fieldhand. Farmed, worked railroad postwar. int. Hamilton. (SS2 6 *TX* 5: 2135–42) SUSAN JONES, b. 1842, Panola Co., MS. int. Pack. (SS1 8 *MS* 3: 1256–59) TOBY (TABY) JONES, b. ca. 1848, SC. Fieldhand. int. B. Davis. (S1 4 *TX* 2: 249–52; SS2 6 *TX* 5: 2143–54) WESLEY JONES, b. 1840, Sardis, SC. Messenger, carriage driver, cook. int. Sims, ed. Turnage. (S1 3 *SC* 3: 72–73) WILKIN-SON JONES, b. 1862, Jefferson Parish, LA. int. McElwee. (*MW*, 141–43) ABNER JORDAN, b. 1832, NC. House servant. (S2 15 *NC* 2: 35–36) DEMPSEY JORDAN, b. 1836, New Orleans. Slave of saloon keeper, slave trader. Dressed slaves for sale, odd jobs. Stayed with saloon keeper postwar. Later moved Madison Co., TX, farmed, wage labor. int. B. Davis. (SS2 6 *TX* 5: 2156–66) SAM JORDAN, b. ca. 1855, Crenshaw Co., AL. Stayed on plantation postwar. (SS1 12 *OK*: 197–201) LINDY JOSEPH, b. 1866, Baton Rouge. Child of ex-slaves. Fieldhand, cooked, washed, ironed. int. McElwee. (*MW*, 143–45) OSCAR FELIX JUNELL, b. ca. 1880, AR. Child of ex-slaves. int. Taylor. (S2 9 *AR* 4: 173–74) LUCINDY LAWRENCE JURDON, b. 1858, Macon, GA. int. Klein, Kytle. (S1 6 *AL*: 242–43; SS2 1 *AL* 1: 13–15) MOLLIE JUSTICE, b. ca. 1858, TN. Stayed on plantation as sharecropper postwar. Moved Clarksville, AR 1880s. int. Miller. (SS1 2 *AR*: 11–12) ELLIS KEN KANNON, b. ca. 1850, Murfreesboro, TN. Fieldhand. Postwar odd-jobbed, waited tables, pressed clothes. Still church custodian Nashville. (S2 16 *TN*: 37–39) AUNT KATHERIN, b. unk., Tate Co., MS. Cook. int. Pack. (SS1 8 *MS* 3: 1264–65) ABE KELLEY, b. ca. 1835, Marshall Co., MS. int. Griffith. (SS1 8 *MS* 3: 1269–70) BELL KELLEY, b. December 25, 1857, Henry Co., KY. Moved Indianapolis, Muncie postwar. int. Tuttle. (SS1 5 *IN*:

106–7) MARTHA KELLY, b. unk., Britton's Neck, SC. Moved Marion 1866. int. R. Davis. (S1 3 *SC* 3: 83–88) AUNT SUSAN KELLY, b. ca. 1856, VA. Nursemaid. int. Jayne. (*WW*, 189) UNCLE HAMP KENNEDY, b. 1857, Forrest Co., MS. Farmed postwar. int. Griffith. (S1 7 *MS*: 84–90; SS1 8 *MS* 3: 1271–77) LUCY KEY, b. ca. 1865, Marshall Co., MS. Child of ex-slaves. int. Robertson. (S2 9 *AR* 4: 198–200) ROBERT KIMBROUGH, b. March 6, 1837, Harris Co., GA. Taken Richmond, VA 1853. Carriage driver. int. J. Jones. (SS1 4 *GA* 2: 357–67) RICHARD KIMMONS, b. ca. 1847, Lawrence Co., MO. Taken TX during war. Fieldhand. Postwar worked horses, cattle for wages. int. A. Davis. (SS2 6 *TX* 5: 2193–98) MARY KINDRED, b. ca. 1855, Jasper, TX. Nursemaid, fieldhand. Moved Beaumont 1919. int. Dibble, Grey. (S1 4 *TX* 2: 285–87; SS2 6 *TX* 5: 2199–2210) CHARLIE KING, b. ca. 1850, Meriwether Co., GA. int. Crawford. (S2 13 *GA* 3: 16–20) ELLEN KING, b. 1851, Enterprise, MS. Fieldhand. int. Poole. (S1 6, *AL*: 248–50; SS1 1 *AL*: 233–35) J. W. KING, b. 1854, Wardsville, MO. Taken Austin, TX age six. Fieldhand. Postwar hauled cotton, freight. (SS2 6 *TX* 5: 2211–18) JULIA KING, b. ca. 1855, Louisville, KY. Escaped to Canada via Underground Railroad. int. Osthimer. (S2 16 *OH*: 57–61) MARTHA KING, b. ca. 1850, Fayette, AL. At five taken Tuscaloosa, sold. Fieldhand, weaver. (S1 7 *OK*: 169–71) MOSE KING, b. 1857, Richmond, VA. Taken Natchez, MS. Farmed, worked railroad roundhouse postwar. int. Robertson. (S2 9 *AR* 4: 207–9) NANCY KING, b. 1844, Upshur Co, TX. Moved Marshall 1866. Weaver, seamstress, nursemaid. int. Hampton. (S1 4 *TX* 2: 288–89; SS2 6 *TX* 5: 2219–23) SILVIA KING, b. December 25, 1804. Sold New Orleans, taken TX. Weaver, cook. int. A. Davis. (S1 4 *TX* 2: 290–95; SS2 6, *TX* 5: 2224–39) NICEY KINNEY, b. ca. 1850, GA. int. McCune, ed. Hall, Booth. (S2 13 *GA* 3: 21–33) CINDY KINSEY, b. ca. 1850, Little Rock, AR. Fieldhand. int. Darsey. (S2 17 *FL*: 190–93) MOLLIE KIRKLAND, b. ca. 1855, Talladega Co., AL. Taken Mexia, TX. int. Cowan. (SS2 6 *TX* 5: 2240–49) MARY ANN KITCHENS, b. ca. 1850,

Crystal Springs, MS. House servant. Held in bondage postwar, liberated by Freedman's Bureau. Sharecropped, attended school. int. England. (SS1 8 *MS* 3: 1282–85) HENRY GRAY KLUGH, b. ca. 1850, SC. int. G. Summer. (SS1 11 *SC*: 233) LONIE KNOX, b. unk., Anderson, SC. int. Rice. (SS1 11 *SC*: 237) SILAS KNOX, b. ca. 1860, Panola Co., MS. Stayed on plantation postwar. int. Pack. (SS1 8 *MS* 3: 1286–88) PRESTON KYLES, b. 1856. Minister, living in Texarkana. int. Ball, Copeland. (S2 9 *AR* 4: 220–23) MILTON LACKEY, b. ca. 1860, Copiah Co., MS. Stayed on plantation postwar, fieldhand. int. England. (SS1 8 *MS* 3: 1289–90) ROBERT LAIRD, b. 1854, Copiah Co., MS. Stayed on plantation postwar, later farmed. int. Giles. (SS1 8 *MS* 3: 1291–95) RUBEN LAIRD, b. 1850, Panola Co., MS. Fieldhand. Stayed on plantation as sharecropper postwar. (SS1 8 *MS* 3: 1296–1301) SOLOMON LAMBERT, b. 1848, Monroe Co., AR. Fieldhand. Conscripted Union army 1863. Returned and stayed on plantation forty-five years, then sharecropped. int. Robertson. (S2 9 *AR* 4: 229–34) JANEY LANDRUM, b. 1851, Gonzales, TX. int. A. Davis. (SS2 6 *TX* 5: 2263–71) JULIA LARKEN, b. 1861, Lincoln Co., GA. Fieldhand. Stayed on plantation postwar. int. McCune, ed. Hall, Booth. (S2 13 *GA* 3: 34–46) FRANK LARKIN, b. ca. 1850, VA. int. Bowden. (S2 9 *AR* 4: 239–41) EPHRAIM (MIKE) LAWRENCE, b. ca. 1856, Edisto Island, SC. Tended fire. Farmed postwar. int. Murray. (S1 3 *SC* 3: 94–99) MATILDA B. LAWS, b. 1854, Scotland, VA. int. C. Anderson. (*WW*, 192–93) BEN LAWSON, b. ca. 1850, Danville, IL. Fieldhand. Held in bondage postwar. Ran away. MS riverboat roustabout, gambler. (S1 7 *OK*: 176–77) VICTORIA RANDLE LAWSON, b. ca. 1850, MS. Fieldhand. Stayed on plantation four years postwar. (SS1 8 *MS* 3: 1302–8) ANNA LEE, b. 1849, Huntsville, TN. Fieldhand, cook. int. B. Davis. (SS2 6 *TX* 5: 2272–90) LU LEE, b. 1848 or 1849, covered wagon on TX-LA border while slaveholder fleeing illegal slaving charges LA. Fieldhand. int. Foreman. (SS2 6 *TX* 5: 2291–2312) MANDY LEE, b. ca. 1850, AR. int. Miller. (S2 9 *AR* 4: 250) MRS. MATTIE

LEE b. 1862, Franklin Parish, LA. 1883 moved Vicksburg, St. Louis, finally Madison Co., MO. Washed, ironed, housework. (S2 11 *MO*: 224–26) WALTER LEGGETT, b. 1855, Whitesville, NC. Postwar accompanied former slaveholder FL, TX. Settled Dallas, still janitor Dallas Little Theater. int. Foreman. (SS2 6 *TX* 5: 2319–24) BEN LEITNER, b. ca. 1852, Winnsboro, SC. Tenant postwar. int. W. Dixon. (S1 3 *SC* 3: 100–102) ADELINE ROSE LENNOX, b. 1849, Paris, TN. Fieldhand, house servant. int. Strope. (SS1 5 *IN*: 112–4) UNCLE CINTO (SAN JACINTO) LEWIS, b. ca. 1826, Brazoria, TX. Fieldhand, fiddler. int. Drake. (S1 5 *TX* 3: 1–3; SS2 6 *TX* 5: 2325–29) DELLIE LEWIS, b. unk., Washington Co., AL. Fieldhand. int. Poole. (S1 6 *AL*: 255–57; SS1 1 *AL*: 242–47) FRANCES LEWIS, b. 1854, GA. House servant. Later moved to New Orleans. int. Posey. (*MW*, 152–61) GEORGE LEWIS, b. December 17, 1849, Pensacola, FL. int. Driskell. (S2 13 *GA* 3: 47–50) HAGAR LEWIS, January 12, 1855, TX. int. Elliott. (S1 5 *TX* 3: 4–7; SS1 6 *TX* 5: 2330–35) HENRY LEWIS, b. 1831, Jefferson Co., TX. Cowhand from age six. Postwar farmed Anahuac, war repairs Galveston, worked cattle until age ninety-four. int. Dibble, Grey. (S1 5 *TX* 3: 8–13; SS2 6 *TX* 5: 2336–48) LAVINIA LEWIS, b. unk., TX. int. Cowan. (SS2 6 *TX* 5: 2349–60) LUCY LEWIS, b. ca. 1830, Brazoria, Co., TX. Ladies maid. int. Osburn. (S1 5 *TX* 3: 14–16; SS2 6 *TX* 5: 2361–68) PERRY LEWIS, b. 1851, Kent Island, MD. int. Rogers. (S2 16 *MD*: 49–50) ABBIE LINDSAY, b. June 1, 1856, Morehouse Parish, LA. Hired out, nursemaid. int. S. Taylor. (S2 9 *AR* 4: 255–59) ELLEN LINDSAY, b. ca. 1853, GA. int. Ross. (SS1 3 *GA* 1: 134–41) ANNIE LITTLE, b. 1857, Springfield, MO. Taken MS as child. Fieldhand. Moved TX, farmed postwar. int. Cowan. (S1 5 *TX* 3: 20–23; SS2 6 *TX* 5: 2387–98) WILLIAM LITTLE, b. March 14, 1855, Little Rock, AR. Fiddled, farmed postwar. int. Lucy. (S2 9 *AR* 4: 262–63) CHANA LITTLEJOHN, b. ca. 1857, Warren Co., NC. Fieldhand. int. Matthews, ed. Waitt. (S2 15 *NC* 2: 54–59) GOVAN LITTLEJOHN, b. 1849, SC. int. Sims, ed. Turnage. (S1 3 *SC* 3: 105–7) ABE

LIVINGSTON, b. 1854, Jasper, TX. Waterboy, fieldhand. Postwar worked railroad, farmed. int. Dibble, Grey. (S1 5 *TX* 3: 24–25; SS2 6 *TX* 5: 2399–2402) EASTER LOCKHART, b. ca. 1852, SC. Nursemaid. int. Sims, ed. Turnage. (S1 3 *SC* 3: 108–11) UNCLE GABLE LOCKLIER, b. ca. 1851, Clarendon Co., SC. Fieldhand. int. R. Davis. (S1 3 *SC* 3: 112–17) AUNT MINERVA LOFTON, b. December 3, 1869, Clarendon, AR. Child of ex-slaves. int. Lucy. (S2 9 *AR* 4: 264–66) AMOS LONG, b. ca. 1840, Seaboard, NC. House servant. Sharecropped postwar. int. B Harris. (SS1 11 *NC*: 27–32) WALTER LONG, b. ca. 1850, Lexington Co., SC. Fieldhand. Sawmilled postwar. (S2 3 *SC* 3: 118–23) WILL LONG, b. ca. 1850, Maury Co., TN. Riverboat hand, musician. Moved TX 1870. int. A. Davis. (SS2 6 *TX* 5: 2407–15) JANE LOUIS, b. 1851, Simpson Co., MS. Nurse, housemaid. Stayed on plantation postwar. int. Giles. (SS1 8 *MS* 3: 1324–25) ANNIE LOVE, b. ca. 1852, Richmond, VA. Taken MS, stayed after freedom. Moved Memphis ca. 1880, AR ca. 1900. Farmed, cooked, washed, ironed. int. Bowden. (S2 9 *AR* 4: 290–91) HUNTON LOVE, b. ca. 1840, Bayou Lafourche, LA. Worked sugar cane mill, loaded sugar, molasses on steamboats. (*MW*, 161–64) JOHN LOVE, b. 1861, Crockett, TX. Postwar worked horses, railroaded, farmed. int. Cowan. (S1 5 *TX* 3: 24–26; SS2 6 *TX* 5: 2115–29) LOUIS LOVE, b. ca. 1845, Franklin, LA. Sent TX during war. House servant. (S1 5 *TX* 3: 29–31; SS2 7 *TX* 6: 2444–50) NEEDHAM LOVE, b. ca. 1855, AL. Sold start of war, taken MS. Postwar farmed, preached until strokes. int. S. Taylor. (S2 9 *AR* 4: 292–96) DAVE LOWRY, b. 1857, Bedford, VA. Left 1881, worked railroad. int. Volley. (*WW*, 198) NELLIE LOYD (BOYD), b. ca. 1846, Union Co., SC. House servant, fieldhand. int. Summer, ed. Turnage. (S1 3 *SC* 3 127–29; SS1 11 *SC*: 63–65) DANIEL WILLIAM LUCAS, b. ca. 1845, Holly Springs, MS. Fieldhand. Left 1885. (S1 7 *OK*: 200–202) JAMES LUCAS, b. October 11, 1833, Wilkinson Co., MS. Fieldhand, sold repeatedly, once to Jefferson Davis. int. Moore. (S1 7 *MS*: 91–99; SS1 8 *MS* 3: 1328–48) LIZZIE LUCKADO, b. 1867, Montgomery

Co., MS. Child of ex-slaves. Moved Sardis 1870s, cooked, nursed. int. Robertson. (S2 9 *AR* 4: 304–5) BERT LUSTER, b. 1853, Watson Co., TN. Chores around big house. After war moved TX. Moved IT ca. 1891. (S1 7 *OK*: 203–6) EDWARD LYCURGAS, b. October 28, 1872, Saint Augustine, FL. Child of ex-slaves. Farmed. int. Randolph. (S2 17 *FL*: 204–11) EISON LYLES, b. ca. 1865, SC. Child of ex-slaves. Farmed postwar. int. Sims, ed. Turnage. (S1 3 *SC* 3: 136–38) MOSES LYLES, b. ca. 1855, SC. Fieldhand, farmed postwar. int. W. Dixon. (S1 3 *SC* 3: 139–40) PHOEBE LYONS, b. ca. 1855, GA. Farmed postwar. int. Minnick. (SS1 5 *OH*: 402–4)

CHANEY (CHANIE) MACK, b. ca. 1864, GA. Moved AL, MS. int. Walsh. (SS1 9 *MS* 4: 1415–29) CRESA MACK, b. 1852, South Bend, AR. House servant. int. Bowden. (S2 10 *AR* 5: 25–26) RICHARD MACK, b. ca. 1833, Limestone, VA. Mortgaged, taken Charleston, SC. House servant. int. Pinckney. (S1 3 *SC* 3: 151–56; SS2 1 *SC*: 383–91) RICHARD MACKS, b. 1844, Charles Co., MD. Stable boy, fieldhand. (S2 16 *MD*: 51–56) PERRY MADDEN, b. ca. 1858, AL. Sharecropped postwar. int. S. Taylor. (S2 10 *AR* 5: 40–56) JACK AND ROSA MADDOX (spouses). Jack Maddox, b. ca. 1849, Marion Co., GA. Taken Rusk Co., TX 1853. Fieldhand. Rosa Maddox, b. ca. 1848, MS, taken Union Parish, LA. Married December 1869. Tenants, odd jobs. Moved Dallas 1922, Jack worked lumber yard. int. Foreman. (SS2 7 *TX* 6: 2521–42) PRIMOUS MAGEE, b. May 15, 1859, Lawrence Co., MS. Farmed postwar. int. Giles. (SS1 9 *MS* 4: 1430–33) JOHN MAJORS, b. ca. 1852, Oxford, MS. Postwar moved Memphis, then TX. int. Cowan. (SS2 7 *TX* 6: 2551–59) CAROLINE MALLOY, b. ca. 1840, Sumter Co., GA. House servant. Domestic postwar. int. Watson. (SS1 4 *GA* 2: 410–17) JULIA MALONE, b. 1858, Lockhart, TX. Nursemaid, laundress, stayed on plantation after freedom, moved Fort Worth ca. 1920 to live with daughter. (S1 5 *TX* 3: 43–44; SS2 *TX* 6: 2560–55) ROSA MANGUM, b. 1831, Simpson Co., MS. Fieldhand, house servant. int. Giles. (SS1 9 *MS* 4: 1434–35) ALLEN V. MANNING, b. ca. 1850, Clarke

Co., MS. Fieldhand. Taken LA, TX during war. Moved IT postwar. (S1 7 *OK*: 215–22A) JACOB MANSON, b. 1851, Warren Co., NC. Fieldhand, house servant. int. Matthews, ed. Waitt. (S2 15 *NC* 2: 95–99) MILLIE MANUEL, b. ca. 1847, San Antonio. int. Nixon. (SS2 7 *TX* 6: 2568–71) ANDY MARION, b. 1844, Winnsboro, SC. Plowhand, carriage driver. Stayed on plantation postwar. int. W. Dixon. (S1 3 *SC* 3: 167–69) ALICE MARSHALL, b. ca. 1850, Nottoway Co., VA. int. E. Wilson, C. Anderson. (*WW*, 201–3) MILTON MARSHALL, b. ca. 1855, Union Co., SC. Postwar moved Newberry Co., renter. int. Summer, ed. Turnage. (S1 3 *SC* 3: 172–75) DRUCILLA MARTIN, May 8, 1835, Giles. Co., TN. Carded wool and cotton, ironed. After war worked as personal maid, steamship chambermaid, housemaid, laundress US Marine Hospital, St. Louis. (S2 11 *MO*: 243–48) EVA MARTIN, b. ca. 1855, Opelousas, LA. Creole. int. Dibble. (SS2 7 *TX* 6: 2581–88) ISAAC MARTIN, b. ca. 1850, Montgomery Co., TX. Minded cows and sheep. int. Dibble, Grey. (S1 5 *TX* 3: 48–61) JAMES MARTIN, freeborn 1847, VA. Saddler, enlisted Confederate army. After war enlisted US army, sent TX with 9th Cavalry, later built railroads, drove cattle. (S1 5 *TX* 3: 62–64; SS2 7 *TX* 6: 7589–94) JIM MARTIN, b. July 4, 1857, Beauregard, MS. Sharecropped, worked sawmills, railroad shops postwar. int. Holmes. (SS1 9 *MS* 4: 1438–44) SCOTT MARTIN, b. 1857, Sumner Co., TN. House servant, tended stock. Stayed on plantation postwar, later moved Nashville, street, sewer work, odd jobs. (S2 16 *TN*: 40–42) MARY (OLD MARY), b. ca. 1855, GA. (S2 13 *GA* 4: 215–16, 334–35) AUNT CARRIE MASON, b. ca. 1865, Baldwin Co., GA. int. G. Burke, ed. Booth. (S2 13 *GA* 3: 108–14; SS1 4 *GA* 2: 420–25) AUNT HARRIET MASON, b. ca. 1837, Garrard Co., KY. Taken Lexington age seven. Nursemaid. int. Higgins. (S2 16 *KY*: 31–32) SAM MEREDITH MASON, b. September 17, 1858, Austin. Farmed postwar. int. Menn. (SS2 7 *TX* 6: 2595–2601) LOUISE MATHEWS, b. 1854, Shelby Co., TX. int. Gauthier. (S1 5 *TX* 3: 65–66; SS2 7 *TX* 6: 2602–9) WILLIAM MATHEWS,

b. December 25, 1848, Franklin Parish, LA. Buggy driver. Postwar farmed, made white-oak baskets, wooden bowls until blinded 1936. int. Liberato. (S1 5 *TX* 3: 67–71; SS2 7 *TX* 6: 2610–20) ANN MATTHEWS, b. unk., Murfreesboro, TN. Denied education postwar by father, sent field. Ran away Nashville, attended school. Later housemaid, cook. (S2 16 *TN*, 43–46) JOHN MATTHEWS, b. 1852, Pike Co., MS. Waterboy, fieldhand. Sharecropped, worked sawmills postwar. int. Holmes. (SS1 9 *MS* 4: 1450–60) MAGGIE WHITEHEAD MATTHEWS, b. July 26, 1857, Gonzales Co., TX. Fieldhand. Farmed postwar. int. Menn. (SS2 7 *TX* 6: 2621–26) ANN MAY, b. 1856, Johnson Co., AR. Farmed postwar. int. Miller. (S2 10 *AR* 5: 66–67) BOB MAYNARD, b. ca. 1855, Marlin, TX. Taken Natchez start of war. House boy. (S1 7 *OK*: 223–26) BERT MAYFIELD, b. May 29, 1852, Garrard Co., KY. Fieldhand. int. Ison. (S2 16 *KY*: 13–17) EMILY MAYS, b. 1861, Upson Co., GA. int. Minor. (S2 13 *GA* 3: 118–20) CURLEY McCADE, b. unk., TX. Root doctor, street healer Houston. int. Herman. (SS2 7 *TX* 6: 2489–91) ANDY McADAMS, b. unk., TX. int. B. Davis. (SS2 7 *TX* 6: 2451–59) JOHN McADAMS, b. 1849, Nashville, TN. Fieldhand. Tenant TN, TX postwar. int. B. Davis. (SS2 7 *TX* 6: 2460–77) GEORGE McALILLEY, b. 1855, Horry Co., SC. Fieldhand. int. W. Dixon. (S1 3 *SC* 3: 142–45) SAM McALLUM, b. September 2, 1842, Kemper Co., MS. Yard boy, house servant. int. M. Austin. (S1 7 *MS*: 100–112; SS1 9 *MS* 4: 1350–66) WILLIAM H. McCARTY, b. December 12, 1835, Hancock Co., MS. Fieldhand, steamboat hand. Enlisted Union army, wounded repeatedly. Postwar public works, preached. int. Horton, J Andrews. (SS1 9 *MS* 4: 1371–79) DUNCAN McCASTLE, b. 1860, Simpson Co., MS. int. Giles. (SS1 8 *MS* 3: 1380–82) JOE McCORMICK, b. unk., Pulaski Co., GA. House servant, fieldhand. int. Watson. (SS1 4 *GA* 2: 389–93) LIZA McCOY, b. 1844, VA. Hired out 1864, later sold. Nursemaid, fieldhand. int. S. Byrd. (*WW*, 199–201) RACHEL McCOY, b. 1863, GA. Farmed, seamstress. ed. Barragan. (SS1 4 *GA* 2: 394–400)

STEPHEN McCRAY, b. 1850, Huntsville, AL. Picked up chips. (S1 7 *OK*: 207–9) ED McCREE, b. 1861, Oconee Co., GA. Fieldhand. int. Hornsby, ed. Hall, L. Harris, Booth. (S2 13 *GA* 3: 56–65) HENRIETTA McCULLERS, b. ca. 1850, Wake Co., NC. int. Hicks, ed. Waitt. (S1 15 *NC* 2: 72–75) AMANDA McDANIEL, b. 1850, Watsonville, GA. Fieldhand. int. Driskell. (S2 13 *GA* 3: 71–75) LUCY McCULLOUGH, b. 1858, GA. House servant. int. Hall. (S2 13 *GA* 3: 66–70) HENRY LEWIS McGAFFEY, b. June 23, 1853, Lake Charles, LA. Fiddler, house servant. Postwar moved Beaumont, TX, fiddled, worked cattle, crippled in horse fall. int. Holmes. (SS1 9 *MS* 4: 1394–1401) ROSIE McGILLERY, b. 1847, SC. Fieldhand. int. B. Davis. (SS2 7 *TX* 6: 2499–2505) TOM McGRUDER, b. unk., GA. Dog trainer, valet. Served in war, Petersburg, VA, Chattanooga, TN. int. Watson. (S2 13 *GA* 3: 76–77) SUSAN McINTOSH, b. November 1851, Oconee Co., GA. House servant, nursemaid, weaver. int. Hornsby, ed. Hall, Booth, L. Harris. (S2 13 *GA* 3: 78–87) WATERS McINTOSH, b. July 4, 1863, Lynchburg, SC. Postwar merchandised, worked jail, farmed, taught, preached, practiced law. int. S. Taylor. (S2 10 *AR* 5: 17–24) MATILDA McKINNEY, b. ca. 1855, TX. Taken GA as child. House servant. int. A. Dixon. (S2 13 *GA* 3: 88–90) WARREN McKINNEY, b. ca. 1850, Edgefield Co., SC. int. Robertson. (S2 10 *AR* 5: 27–31) ABE McKLENNAN, b. 1847, Monticello, MS. Fieldhand, stayed on plantation after freedom then sharecropped. int. de Sola. (SS1 9 *MS* 4: 1407–11) JAMES TURNER McLEAN, b. February 20, 1858, Harnett Co., NC. (S2 15 *NC* 2: 83–89) JAKE McLEOD, b. November 13, 1854, Lynchburg, SC. Fieldhand. Sharecropped postwar. int. Young, H. Davis, ed. R. Davis. (S1 3 *SC* 3: 157–63) THOMAS McMILLAN, b. unk., Monroe Co., AL. Fieldhand. int. Bishop. (S2 16 *OH*: 66–68) VICTORIA McMULLEN, b. 1884. Grandchild of ex-slaves. int. S. Taylor. (S2 10 *AR* 5: 32–38; SS2 1 *AR*: 100) CHANEY McNAIR, b. 1852, IT. Cherokee slave. int. Faulton. (SS1 12 *OK*: 213–21) NAP McQUEEN, b. ca. 1855, TN. Taken

TX as child. (S1 5 *TX* 3: 35–37; SS2 7 *TX* 6: 2506–14) C. B. McRAY, b. April 12, 1861, Jasper, TX. Fieldhand. int. L. Hatcher. (S1 5 *TX* 3: 40–42; SS2 7 *TX* 6: 2515–20) WILLIAM McWHORTER, b. ca. 1860, Greene Co., GA. (S2 13 *GA* 3: 91–103) WILLIAM MEAD, b. 1864, Cartersville, GA. (SS1 4 *GA* 2: 428–32) LOUIS MEADOWS, b. ca. 1853, Lee Co., AL. Fieldhand. int. M. Fowler, Kytle. (SS1 1 *AL*: 255–57) LETHA TAYLOR MEEKS, b. unk., Panola Co., MS. Helped with weaving. Living Cape Girardeau, MO. (S2 11 *MO*: 252–55) MELINDA, b. ca. 1854, Baton Rouge, LA. Creole. int. Arguedas. (*MW*, 165–72) SUSIE MELTON, b. 1853, VA. (*WW*, 212–13) FRANK MENEFEE, b. ca. 1843, Loachapoka, AL. Fieldhand, farmed postwar. int. Klein, ed. Marzoni. (S1 6 *AL*: 278–81) LIZA MENTION, b. ca. 1865, McDuffie Co., GA. Child of ex-slaves. int. L. Harris, ed. Booth. (S2 13 *GA* 3: 121–25) SARAH EMERY MERRILL, b. unk., Munfordville, KY. Child of ex-slaves. int. Cook, Tyler. (SS1 5 *IN*: 126–30) SUSAN MERRITT, b. 1851, Henderson, TX. House servant. int. Hampton. (S1 5 *TX* 3: 75–78; SS2 7 *TX* 6: 2639–45) ANN MICKEY, b. ca. 1847, Beaumont, TX. House servant. int. Dibble. (SS2 7 *TX* 6: 2646–49) JOSH MILES, b. 1859, Richmond, VA. Taken TX during war. Postwar worked railroad. int. Cowan. (S1 5 *TX* 3: 79–81; SS2 7 *TX* 6: 2654–67) GEORGE WASHINGTON MILLER, b. March 15, 1856, Spartanburg, SC. Taken Panola Co., MS during war. int. E. Joiner. (SS1 9 *MS* 4: 1482–97) HARRIET MILLER, b. 1859, Magnolia, MS. Fieldhand. int. Holmes. (SS1 9 *MS* 4: 1498–1507) AUNT HARRIET MILLER, b. ca. 1837, GA-SC border. Cherokee father, white mother. Age three given by mother to plantation overseer. int. Newton, ed. Booth. (S2 13 *GA* 3: 126–32) HARDY MILLER, b. December 25, 1852, Sumpter Co., GA. Taken Pine Bluff 1862, sold. Yardman. int. Bowden. (S2 9 *AR* 5: 74–77) WYLIE MILLER, b. 1854, Bloomfield, MO. (S2 11 *MO*: 256–57) HARRIET MILLETT, b. 1854, MS. Taken New Braunfels, TX during war. House servant, nursemaid. int. Menn. (SS2 7 *TX* 6: 2694–2701) CURETON MILLING, b. 1857, Winnsboro, SC. Body servant. int.

W. Dixon. (S1 3 *SC* 3: 194–96) TOM MILLS, b. 1858, Fayette Co., AL. Taken Uvalde Co., TX 1862. Cowhand. Established ranch 1892. (S2 5 *TX* 3: 88–106) LA SAN (LaSAN) MIRE, b. May 12, 1852, Abbeville Parish, LA. House servant, fieldhand. int. Savoy. (S1 5 *TX* 3: 107–9; SS2 7 *TX* 6: 2702–9) ANNA MITCHEL, b. ca. 1862, Vance Co., NC. Stayed on plantation postwar. Fieldhand. int. Mary Hicks, ed. Waitt. (S2 15 *NC* 2: 113–15) A. J. MITCHELL, b. ca. 1858, AR, fieldhand. int. Bowden. (S2 10 *AR* 5: 103–6) CHARLEY MITCHELL, b. 1852, Lynchburg, VA. House servant. Postwar worked tobacco factory, waiter. Moved Panola Co., TX 1887. int. Hampton. (S1 5 *TX* 3: 110–13; SS2 7 *TX* 6: 2710–16) CINDY MITCHELL, b. unk., Grenada Co., MS. Charismatic preacher, head of Cindy's Band. (SS1 9 *MS* 4: 1511) GRACIE MITCHELL, b. unk., AL. Sold from mother before weaned. Postwar farmed, cooked, sewed. int. Bowden. (S2 10 *AR* 5: 107–10) MARY MITCHELL, b. ca. 1875, Trenton, TN. Child of ex-slaves. int. Robertson. (S2 10 *AR* 5: 113–19) MELINDA (MALINDA) MITCHELL, b. 1853, Edgefield, SC. House servant, ladies maid. Stayed on plantation briefly postwar, moved Augusta. int. Love. (S2 13 *GA* 4: 219–20, 336–37; SS1 4 *GA* 2: 439–44) PETER MITCHELL, b. 1862 or 1863, Jasper, TX. Postwar cleaned, shined shoes, carded, spun, farmed, public works. int. Hatcher. (S1 5 *TX* 3: 114–15; SS2 7 *TX* 6: 2717–20) BOB MOBLEY, b. ca. 1856, Crawford Co., GA. Fieldhand. int. Watson. (S2 13 *GA* 136–38; SS1 4 *GA* 2: 445–52) GARLAND MONROE, b. 1848, VA. (*WW*, 214–15) ADALINE MONTGOMERY, b. August 12, 1859, Buena Vista, AL. Farmed postwar. Moved Pike Co., MS, 1907, ran boarding house. int. C. Wells. (SS1 9 *MS* 4: 1513–21) ALEX MONTGOMERY, b. 1857, Clyde Co., GA. Sharecropped postwar. Moved MS 1900, worked gin, teamster. int. Holmes. (SS1 9 *MS* 4: 1522–31) JANE MONTGOMERY, b. March 15, 1857, Homer, LA. Farmed postwar. (S1 7 *OK*: 227–29) LAURA MONTGOMERY, b. 1850, Amite Co., MS. Weaver. int. Holmes. (SS1 9 *MS* 4: 1550–59) RUBE MONTGOMERY, b. October 5, 1856, Choc-

taw Co., MS. Odd jobs. Farmed, worked railroad postwar. int. Butts. (SS1 9 *MS* 4: 1560–64) ANDREW MOODY, b. 1855, Orange Co., TX. Fieldhand. int. Dibble, Grey. (S1 5 *TX* 3: 116–17; SS2 7 *TX* 6: 2621–25) A. M. "MOUNT" MOORE, b. 1846, Marshall Co., TX. Farmed for wages postwar. Attended Wiley and Bishop Colleges Marshall, taught, preached, organized churches TX, LA. int. Hampton. (S1 5 *TX* 3: 118–20; SS2 7 *TX* 6: 2729–35) FANNIE MOORE, b. 1849, SC. Fieldhand. int. Marjorie Jones. (S2 15 *NC* 2: 127–37) JERRY MOORE, b. May 28, 1848, Marshall, TX. Bricklayer postwar. (S1 5 *TX* 3: 121–24) JOHN MOORE, b. 1843, Vermilionville, LA. Hired out postwar. Moved TX 1876. int. Dibble, Grey. (S1 5 *TX* 3: 125–27; SS2 7 *TX* 6: 2736–42) REV. JOHN MOORE, b. unk., GA. Stayed on plantation as tenant after the war. (S2 16 *TN*: 47–48) LAURA MOORE, b. ca. 1852, Goliad, TX. Weaver, house servant. int. Nixon. (SS2 7 *TX* 6: 2743–47) LINDSEY MOORE, b. 1850, Forsythe Co., GA. Blacksmith, tanner, spinner, weaver. int. Richardson. (S2 17 *FL* 229–33) RILEY MOORE, b. ca. 1850, MS. int. Butts. (SS1 9 *MS* 4: 1569–72) SENA MOORE, b. 1854, SC. int. Dixon. (S1 3 *SC* 3: 209–12) VINA MOORE, b. 1845, Vicksburg, MS. Sold, taken Corsicana, TX during war. Stayed on plantation postwar. House servant, cook, fieldhand. int. W. Smith. (SS2 7 *TX* 6: 2754–63) WILLIAM MOORE, b. 1855, Selma, AL. Taken Limestone Co., TX during war. Shepherd. int. Foreman. (S1 5 *TX* 3: 132–37; SS2 7 *TX* 6: 2764–73) ELSIE MORELAND, b. unk., Houston Co., GA. Fieldhand. int. Watson (SS1 4 *GA* 2: 453–59) EVELINA MORGAN, b. ca. 1855, NC. Cooked postwar. int. S. Taylor. (S2 10 *AR* 5: 136–40) ISAAM MORGAN, b. June 14, 1835, Choctaw Co., AL. House servant, coachman. Worked riverboats postwar. int. Poole. (S1 6 *AL*: 282–85; SS1 1 *AL*: 260–65) JAMES MORGAN, b. 1873, SC. Child of ex-slaves. Moved AR, worked thirty-five years Missouri-Pacific. int. S. Taylor. (S2 9 *AR* 5: 141–44) AUNT JANE MORGAN, b. ca. 1830, Jasper County, MS. House servant, nursemaid. int. Holmes. (SS1 9 *MS* 4: 1573–78) RICHARD C. MORING, b. 1851,

Wake Co., NC. Fieldhand. int. Hicks, ed. Waitt. (S2 15 *NC* 2: 138–42) CHARITY MORRIS, b. unk., NC. House servant. Taken AR during war, later settled Camden. int. P. Anderson. (S2 10 *AR* 5: 149–51) TOM MORRIS, b. ca. 1850, VA. Sold age six to speculator, taken Rankin Co., MS. House servant. Postwar drove dray, moved McComb, cooked. int. Holmes. (SS1 9 *MS* 4: 1579–91) GEORGE MORRISON, b. unk., Union Co., KY. House servant, cow tender, bones player. int. Cook, Van Meter. (S1 6 *IN*: 145–46A; SS1 5 *IN*: 146–47, 226–28) CHARLIE MOSES, b. 1853, Marion Co., MS. Fieldhand. Postwar farmed, worked bakery, lumber boat, preached. int. de Sola. (S1 7 *MS*: 113–18; SS1 9 *MS* 4: 1597–1603) PATSY MOSES, b. 1863, Fort Bend Co., TX. int. Cowan. (SS1 5 *TX* 3: 142–44; SS2 7 *TX* 6: 2780–94) JOHN MOSLEY, b. 1851, Burleson Co., TX. Fieldhand. int. B. Davis. (SS2 7 *TX* 6: 2795–2809) ANDREW MOSS, b. 1852, GA. Fieldhand. (S2 16 *TN*: 49–54) CLAIBORNE MOSS, b. June 18, 1857, Washington Co., GA. Fieldhand. Farmed postwar. Moved Little Rock 1903, worked construction. int. S. Taylor. (S2 10 *AR* 5: 155–66) FRANK MOSS, b. June 17, 1860, Choctaw Co., AL. Postwar trucked cotton, loaded boats, cut cane AL, MS, LA, TX. int. E. Burke. (*MW*, 172–75) AUNT MOLLIE MOSS, b. ca. 1855, Campbell Co., TN. Fieldhand. (S2 16 *TN*: 55–59) MOSE MOSS, b. 1875, Yell Co., AR. Child of ex-slaves. Miner, odd jobs. int. Lucy. (S2 10 *AR* 5: 169) LEO MOUTON, b. ca. 1860, Lake Charles, LA. Fieldhand, accordion player. Moved Orange, TX 1886, worked sawmills. int. Dibble, Grey. (SS2 7 *TX* 6: 2810–15) CALVIN MOYE, b. December 25, 1842, Atlanta. Taken Navarro Co., TX 1850. Fieldhand, blacksmith. Stayed on plantation as sharecropper twenty years postwar. Moved Corsicana, opened smithy. int. W. Smith. (SS2 7 *TX* 6: 2818–73) MACK MULLEN, b. 1857, Americus, GA. Stayed on plantation as sharecropper postwar. Moved Tampa, Jacksonville 1870s, construction. int. J. Johnson, ed. J. Simms. (S2 17 *FL*: 234–41) LEWIS MUNDY, b. ca. 1850, Lewis Co., MO. Fieldhand. Farmed postwar. Moved Hannibal 1903,

worked Burlington Shops until discharged for old age. (S2 11 *MO*: 258–60; SS1 2 *MO*: 205–7) HANNAH MURPHY, b. ca. 1857, GA. int. Barragan. (S2 13 *GA* 4: 343–44; SS1 4 *GA* 2: 465–69) SALLY MURPHY, b. 1857, Tallapoosa, GA. (S1 6 *AL*: 294–96; SS1 1 *AL*: 266–69) HENRY MURRAY, b. September 17, 1840, Dallas Co., AL. Bird frightener. Stayed on plantation postwar. Moved MS 1873. Farmed, bottomed chairs, made baskets, built dirt chimneys. int. Butts. (SS1 9 *MS* 4: 1613–17)

LOUIS NAPOLEON, b. ca. 1857, Tallahassee, FL. Farmed, odd-jobbed postwar. int. J. Johnson. (S2 17 *FL*: 242–48) SALLY NEALY, b. ca. 1845, Rusk Co., TX. House servant. Postwar moved Pine Bluff. int. Bowden. (S2 10 *AR* 5: 184–87) WYLIE NEALY, b. 1852, Calhoun, SC. Moved AR postwar, farmed. int. Robertson. (S2 10 *AR* 5: 188–93) HENRI NECAISE, b. January 2, 1832, Pass Christian, MS. Tended stock. Postwar shipped charcoal New Orleans until storm wrecked boat. Wage labor. Settled Pearl River Co., MS, farmed. int. C. Wells. (S1 7 *MS*: 119–24; SS1 9 *MS* 4: 1622–35) LOUISE NEILL, b. ca. 1860. Tenant postwar. int. Walker. (SS2 7 *TX* 6: 2890–91) JULIUS NELSON, b. 1860, Anson Co., NC. Stayed on plantation postwar. Interviewed state prison Raleigh, inmate fifteen years. int. Hicks, ed. Waitt. (S2 15 *NC* 2: 143–46) HATTIE ANNE NETTLES, b. ca. 1857, Tallapoosa, GA. int. Klein, ed. Kytle. (S1 6 *AL*: 297–98; SS1 1 *AL*: 270–71) VIRGINIA NEWMAN, freeborn 1827, ship off LA coast. Apprenticed herself to Franklin plantation. House servant. Taken Jasper, TX during war. Returned LA. Midwife. int. Dibble, Grey. (S1 5 *TX* 3: 148–51; SS2 7 *TX* 6: 2902–8) GEORGE NEWTON, b. 1867, AR. Child of ex-slaves. Taken Houma, LA. Moved TX 1907, farmed, odd-jobbed. Settled Wichita Falls, washed dishes. int. Dulaney. (SS2 7 *TX* 6: 2909–10) PETE NEWTON, b. ca. 1854, AR. Groom, fieldhand. Stayed on plantation until 1869, then farmed. int. Miller. (S2 10 *AR* 5: 216–8) FANNIE NICHOLSON, b. 1848, VA. House servant. int. Dunston. (*WW*, 217–18) MARGRETT NICKERSON, b. ca. 1847, Leon Co., FL. Cook's helper, fieldhand, quilter. (S2

17 *FL*: 249–56) MARY NICKERSON, b. ca. 1840, Grand Coteau, LA. Churner. int. Dibble, Grey. (SS2 8 *TX* 7: 2915–19) FANNY NIX, b. ca. 1850, GA. House servant. int. Crawford. (S2 13 *GA* 3: 139–42) HENRY NIX, b. March 15, 1848, Upson Co., GA. Fieldhand. Postwar moved AL, then returned to plantation as tenant. int. Crawford. (S2 13 *GA* 3: 143–45) LIZZIE NORFLEET, b. ca. 1850, Quitman Co., MS. Water girl, worked gin. Farmed postwar. int. Campbell. (SS1 9 *MS* 4: 1639–51) CHARLIE NORRIS, b. October 1, 1857, Union Co., AR. Stayed on plantation five-six years postwar. int. Bowden. (S2 10 *AR* 5: 219–20) REVEREND W. E. NORTH-CROSS, b. 1840, Colbert Co., AL. Fieldhand, preached postwar. int. Shelby. (S1 6 *AL*: 299–305) GLASCOW NORWOOD, b. ca. 1852, Simpson Co., MS. Herder, fieldhand. int. Giles. (SS1 9 *MS* 4: 1655–58) ISAIAH NORWOOD, b. 1852, TN. Taken Travis Co., TX prewar. Fieldhand, herder. Postwar farmed, worked gin, Baptist circuit rider. int. Menn. (SS2 8 *TX* 7: 2943–52) GENERAL JEFFERSON DAVIS (JEFF) NUNN, b. 1862, AL. int. Archive of Folk Song, Library of Congress. (SS1 1 *AL*: 278–85) JOHN OGEE, b. 1841, Morgan City, LA. Creole. Moved Taylor's Bayou near Beaumont 1870. int. Dibble, Grey. (S1 5 *TX* 3: 154–56; SS2 8 *TX* 7: 2972–77) OLD EX-SLAVE, b. unk., Napoleonville, LA. int. Aucuin. (*MW*, 20–23) AMANDA OLIVER, b. November 9, 1857, MO. Sold 1865, taken Sherman, TX. House servant. (S1 7 *OK*: 230–32) JOE OLIVER, b. 1847, Hill Co., TX. Miller. int. Cowan. (SS2 8 *TX* 7: 2978–88) MARK OLIVER, b. 1856, Washington Co., MS. Minded cows. Stayed on plantation as tenant postwar, later moved Greenville, worked oil mill, drove wagon. int. Campbell. (SS1 9 *MS* 4: 1659–72) UNCLE WILLIAM OLIVER, b. unk., Georgetown Co., SC. Postwar worked turpentine, timber, cut boxes. int. Chandler. (S1 3 *SC* 3: 217–20) IVORY OSBORNE, b. 1852, TX. Fieldhand. int. Bowden. (S2 10 *AR* 5: 230–31) HORACE OVERSTREET, b. 1856, Marshall, TX. Fieldhand. Moved Beaumont postwar. int. Dibble, Grey. (S1 5 *TX* 3: 160–61; SS2 8 *TX* 7: 2996–99) ELIZA OVERTON, b. 1849, Ste.

Genevieve Co., MO. Information communicated by children, Maggie Kennedy (b. 1871), John Franks (b. 1881), Emma Body (b. 1866). (S2 11 *MO*: 266–68; SS1 2 *MO*: 215–18) GEORGE OWENS, b. ca. 1853, Marshall, TX. Yardwork. Worked T&P railroad postwar. int. Dibble, Beehler. (S1 5 *TX* 3: 165–69) HENRY OWENS, b. April 15, 1843, Williamson Co., TX. Fieldhand. Moved Austin postwar, odd jobs. int. Menn. (SS2 8 *TX* 7: 3006–13) WADE OWENS, b. 1863, Loachapoka, AL. int. Klein, ed. Marzoni. (S1 6 *AL*: 306–8) ALBERT OXNER, b. 1862, Newberry Co., SC. int. Summer, ed. Turnage. (S1 3 *SC* 3: 221–22)

DOLPH PARHAM, b. ca. 1850, AL. Tended stock, carried water. Stayed on plantation postwar. int. Barton. (SS1 1 *AL*: 289) DOUGLAS PARISH, b. May 7, 1850, Monticello, FL. Fieldhand. Carpenter, bricklayer postwar. int. R. Austin. (S2 17 *FL*: 257–62) CHARITY PARKER, b. ca. 1850, LA. Moved New Orleans postwar, cooked. (*MW*, 176–78) LAURA RAMSEY PARKER, b. ca. 1850, Murfreesboro, TN. Spinner, weaver, nursemaid. Postwar chambermaid, seamstress, dressmaker. Still piecing, selling quilts. (S2 16 *TN*: 62–63) MOLLY PARKER, b. ca. 1850, AL. int. Klein. (S1 6 *AL*: 309–10; SS1 1 *AL*: 290–91) WILL PARKER, b. 1842, GA. Enlisted Union army age nineteen, stationed TX 1865. int. Major. (SS2 8 *TX* 7: 3017–21) ANNA PARKES, b. ca. 1850, Athens, GA. House servant, yardwork. int. Hall, ed. Booth. (S2 13 *GA* 3: 153–64) ANNIE PARKS, b. ca. 1852, Mer Rouge, LA. Moved Little Rock ca. 1912. int. S. Taylor. (S2 10 *AR* 5 257–60) AUSTIN PEN PARNELL, b. April 15, 1865, Carroll Co., MS. Child of ex-slaves. int. S. Taylor. (S2 10 *AR* 5: 262–72) ALBERT PATTERSON, b. 1850, Plaquemines Parish, LA. Fieldhand. int. Wallace. (*MW*, 178–80) FRANK A. PATTERSON, b. 1850, Raleigh, NC. Stayed on plantation five years postwar for wages. Moved MS, AR, cooked hotels, riverboats. (S2 10 *AR* 5: 276–83) JENNIE PATTERSON, b. ca. 1846, VA. Fieldhand. int. Byrd. (*WW*, 218–20) JOHN PATTERSON, b. ca. 1860, Paducah, KY. Taken Helena, AR age four. Farmed, cleaned houses, yards, janitor Episcopal church. int. Robertson. (S2 10 *AR* 5: 284–85) G. W. PATTILLO, b. 1852, Spalding Co., GA. int. Ross, ed. Russell. (S2 13 *GA* 3: 165–70) SOLOMON P. PATTILLO, b. 1868, Dallas Co., AR. Child of ex-slaves. Taught, farmed, butchered. int. S. Taylor. (S2 10 *AR* 5: 292–96) GRUNDY PATTON, b. 1866, MS. Child of ex-slaves. int. Lenoir, Hays, Henderson, ed. Cooley. (SS1 9 *MS* 4: 1686–87) SALLIE PAUL, b. ca. 1856, SC. Sharecropped postwar. int. R. Davis. (S1 3 *SC* 3: 231–47) ELLEN PAYNE, b. 1849, Marshall, TX. Minded calves, chickens, turkeys. Farmed postwar. int. Hampton. (S1 5 *TX* 3: 177–79; SS2 8 *TX* 7: 3039–43) ELSIE PAYNE, b. 1840, Lee Co., AL. int. R. L. D. (SS1 1 *AL*: 292–94) ANNA PEEK, b. unk., Greenville, NC. Sold, taken Polk, Co., GA age ten. (SS1 4 *GA* 2: 478–83) LU PERKINS, b. ca. 1850, Tishomingo Co., MS. Taken TX prewar. Spinner. Postwar moved Dallas, laundress in sporting houses, Red Light District. int. Foreman. (SS2 8 *TX* 7: 3054–70) REVEREND JOHN PERRIER, b. ca. 1860, East Baton Rouge Parish, LA. Minded children. Later preached, moved Beaumont 1930. int. Dibble. (SS2 8 *TX* 7: 3078–81) DINAH PERRY, b. ca. 1862, AL. Taken Pine Bluff. Stayed on plantation postwar, fieldhand, house servant, nursemaid. int. Bowden. (S2 10 *AR* 5: 318–21) MATILDA HENRIETTA (SWEET MA) PERRY, b. 1852, Danville, VA. int. R Lewis. (*WW*, 221–26) NOAH PERRY, b. 1856, Summerville, GA. After freedom moved TX, IT, farmed. (SS1 12 *OK*: 238–48) LOUISE PETTIS, b. ca. 1880, Elbe, SC. Child of ex-slaves. int. Robertson. (S2 10 *AR* 5: 334–37) PHYLLIS PETITE, b. ca. 1855, Rusk Co., TX. House servant, nursemaid. (S1 7 *OK*: 236–41) DOLLY PHILLIPS, b. ca. 1870, AR. Child of ex-slaves. int. Robertson. (S2 10 *AR* 5: 344) KATIE PHOENIX, b. ca. 1857, LA. Sold as child, taken Brenham, TX, resold. House servant. int. Nixon. (SS2 8 *TX* 7: 3082–86) LEE PIERCE, b. May 15, 1850, Marshall, TX. Sold age eleven, taken Sulphur Springs. Sheep herder. Left plantation 1866, moved Jefferson, public works, retired 1930. int. Hampton. (S1 5 *TX* 3: 185–87; SS2 8 *TX* 7: 3092–97) LOUIS JOSEPH

PIERNAS, freeborn March 11, 1856, Bay St. Louis, MS. Barber, civic leader, organizer Promot Brass Band. int. R. Wells. (SS1 9 *MS* 4: 1700–1709) MAGGIE PINKARD, b. ca. 1855, Nashville, TN. House servant. int. Garrison, ed. Vollmer. (SS1 12 *OK*: 254–59) REV. AARON PINNACLE, b. ca. 1890, Georgetown Co., SC. Child of ex-slaves. int. Chandler. (SS1 11 *SC*: 268–71) SARAH PITTMAN, b. ca. 1855, Union Parish, LA. Postwar moved AR, farmed. int. S. Taylor. (S2 10 *AR* 5: 351–54) DEMPSEY PITTS, b. December 10, 1830, Charlotte, NC. Carriage driver. Postwar farmed, preached NC, LA, MS. int. Campbell. (SS1 9 *MS* 4: 1710–24) ROXY PITTS, b. 1855, AL. int. Klein, ed. Oden. (S1 6 *AL*: 316–17; SS1 1 *AL*: 295–96) TEMPE PITTS, b. 1846, Halifax Co., NC. Domestic, stayed on plantation after freedom. int. Hicks, Waitt. (S2 15 *NC* 2: 173–76) CORA POCHE, b. June 17, 1866, New Orleans. int. Walsh. (SS1 9 *MS* 4: 1727–30) SAM POLITE, b. ca. 1844, St. Helena Island, SC. Fieldhand. Postwar farmed, phosphate miner. int. Martin. (S1 3 *SC* 3: 271–76) LEVI POLLARD, b. ca. 1850, Charlotte Co., VA. Fieldhand. Stayed on plantation postwar. (*WW*, 226–33) ROSA L. POLLARD, b. 1844, OH. House servant, fieldhand. Farmed postwar. int. B. Davis. (SS2 8 *TX* 7: 3117–28) JAMES POLK, b. 1850, Rusk, TX. Yard boy, fieldhand. Farmed postwar. int. Shirley. (SS2 8 *TX* 7: 3105–12) NELSON POLK, b. ca. 1830, Nashville, TN. Sold, taken Greenwood, MS. Fieldhand. Sharecropped postwar. Information communicated by Rev. J. B. Polk (son). int. Tuttle. (SS1 5 *IN*: 165–68) PARKER POOL, b. August 10, 1846, Wake Co., NC. Nursemaid, fieldhand. int. Matthews, ed. Waitt. (S2 15 *NC* 2: 183–91) ALEC POPE, b. 1854, Oglethorpe Co., GA. Waterboy, plowhand. int. Hornsby, ed. Hall, Booth. (S2 13 *GA* 3: 171–77) OPHELIA PORTER, b. unk., AL. Moved Cherokee Co., TX postwar. Cook. Left 1888, moved Waco. int. A. Davis. (SS2 8 *TX* 7: 3129–33) ELSIE POSEY, b. ca. 1840, MS. int. Huff. (SS1 9 *MS* 4: 1735–38) BOB POTTER, September 17, 1873, Russellville, AR. Child of ex-slaves. int. Lucy. (S2 10 *AR* 5: 364–66) ISAAC POTTER,

b. 1851, Rankin Co., MS. Stable hand. Runaway, tended horses Union army. Farmed postwar. int. Giles. (SS1 9 *MS* 4: 1739–46) JIM POWELL, b. 1850, Norfolk, VA. Taken Raleigh, NC. int. Watson. (SS1 4 *GA* 2: 486) SALEM POWELL, b. ca. 1857, Simpson Co., MS. Fieldhand, stock tender. Stayed on plantation postwar. int. Giles. (SS1 9 *MS* 4: 1747–49) BETTY POWERS, b. ca. 1850, Harrison Co., TX. House servant. int. Gauthier. (S1 5 *TX* 3: 190–92; SS2 8 *TX* 7: 3134–42) CHARLIE POWERS, b. ca. 1851, Covington Co., MS. Fieldhand. Farmed postwar. int. Giles. (SS1 9 *MS* 4: 1750–54) WILLIAM PRATT, b. April 1860, Chester Co., SC. Moved Newberry Co. 1898. Farmed. int. Summer, ed. Turnage. (S1 3 *SC* 3: 277–79) GEORGIANNA PRESTON, b. ca. 1835, VA. (*WW*, 233–34) ALLEN PRICE, b. 1862, Fannin Co., TX. Preached postwar. int. Cowan. (S1 5 *TX* 3: 195–96; SS2 8 *TX* 7: 3149–60) ANNIE PRICE, b. October 12, 1855, Spalding Co., GA. int. Driskell. (S2 13 *GA* 3: 178–84) JOHN PRICE, b. ca. 1860, Morgan City, LA. Taken Liberty, TX. Worked cattle, broke wild horses postwar. int. Dibble, Grey. (S1 5 *TX* 3: 197–200; SS2 8 *TX* 7: 3161–65) REVEREND LAFAYETTE PRICE, b. ca. 1850, Wilcox Co., AL. Taken Shreveport. Toted water. Conscripted Confederate service. Moved TX postwar, preached. int. Dibble, Grey. (S1 5 *TX* 3: 201–4; SS2 8 *TX* 7: 3166–83) JENNY PROCTOR, b. 1850, AL. House servant, fieldhand. Stayed on plantation long after freedom. Moved Leon Co., TX, sharecropped. (S1 5 *TX* 3: 208–17) A. C. PRUITT, b. 1861 or 1862, St. Martinsville, LA. Taken TX during war. Postwar yard work, fired riverboat-sawmill boilers, worked oil fields Beaumont, TX, Morgan City, LA. int. Dibble, Grey. (S1 5 *TX* 3: 218–21; SS2 8, *TX* 7: 3200–3206) ELSIE PRYOR, b. ca. 1855, IT. Choctaw slave. House servant. Stolen, taken AR, eventually escaped, returned IT. int. Green. (SS1 12 *OK*: 260–64) JANE PYATT, b. 1848, Middlesex, VA. Taken Portsmouth. House servant. int. Dunston. (*WW*, 235–36) CHARLIE PYE, b. 1856, Columbus, GA. Worked railroad postwar. (S2 13 *GA* 3: 185–88)

HARRE QUARLS, b. 1841, MO. Sold, taken East TX. Fieldhand. Fiddled, farmed, taught school postwar. int. B. Davis. (S1 5 *TX* 3: 222–23; SS2 8 *TX* 7: 3213–16) JUNIUS QUATTLEBAUM, b. ca. 1853, Saluda Co., SC. Fieldhand. int. Grant. (S1 3 *SC* 3:283–86) JACK RABB, b. unk., Lowndes Co., MS. Barber, fifer. (SS1 9 *MS* 4: 1774) RENA RAINES, b. ca. 1862, Wake Co., NC. int. Matthews, ed. G. Andrews. (S2 15 *NC* 2: 192–95) AUNT EDA RAINS, b. 1853, Little Rock. Taken TX 1860. House servant, nursemaid. (S1 5 *TX* 3: 225–26; SS2 8 *TX* 7: 322–26) GEORGE WASHINGTON RAMSAY, b. March 27, 1854, Harrison Co., MS. Tenant. Homesteaded 1880s. int. C. Wells. (SS1 9 *MS* 4: 1775–91) UNCLE DAVE AND AUNT LILLIAN RAMSEY (siblings), b. ca. 1853, ca. 1866, Harris Co., GA. int. J. Jones. (SS1 4 *GA* 2: 497–99) FANNY RANDOLPH, b. ca. 1835, Jackson Co., GA. Ladies maid, house servant. int. Roberts, ed. Booth. (S2 13 *GA* 3: 194–99) SAM RAWLS, b. 1853, Lexington Co., SC. int. Summer, ed. Turnage. (S1 3 *SC* 4: 5–8) AARON RAY, b. ca. 1869, Independence, TX. Child of ex-slaves. Fieldhand, house servant, carriage driver. int. A. Davis. (SS2 8 *TX* 7: 3254–61) MORGAN RAY, b. ca. 1855, GA. After freedom farmed Fayette, Campbell Cos., moved Dayton, OH around 1925. (SS1 *OH*: 420–29) ROY REDFIELD, b. unk., GA. int. Oliphant, ed. Booth. (S2 13 *GA* 4: 304–7) ELSIE REECE, b. ca. 1847, Grimes Co., TX. Weaver, seamstress. Postwar cooked Navasota. (S1 5 *TX* 3: 233–35; SS2 8 *TX* 7: 3271–79) NAISY REECE, b. ca. 1855, Williamson Co., TN. Fieldhand, cook, laundress. (S2 16 *TN*: 64–65) EASTER REED, b. 1852, Dodge Co., GA. House servant, spinner. int. Watson. (SS1 4 *GA* 2: 502–9) EVA REED, b. 1863, Lafourche Parish, LA. Sharecropped, cooked, washed, cleaned. int. McElwee. (*MW*, 182–84) HENRY REED, b. 1853, St. Landry Parish, LA. Slave of LA Governor Alexander Mouton. House servant, yard boy. int. McElwee. (*MW*, 185–86) RACHAEL SANTEE REED, b. 1857, Leakesville, MS. int. Griffith. (SS1 9 *MS* 4: 1814–19) BILL REESE, b. September 12, 1863, GA. Barber. int. Hornsby, ed. Hall, Booth. (SS1

4 *GA* 2: 510–36) JAMES REEVES, b. 1870, Camden, AR. Child of ex-slaves. Preacher. int. S. Taylor. (S2 10 *AR* 6: 24–32) ELLEN RENWICK, b. 1858, SC. House servant, fieldhand. int. Summer, ed. Ritter. (S1 3 *SC* 4: 9) MARY REYNOLDS, b. ca. 1835, Black River, LA. Fieldhand. Postwar farmed, domestic. int. Foreman. (S1 5 *TX* 3: 236–46; SS2 8 *TX* 7: 3284–99) SUSAN RHODES, b. ca. 1835, Jones Co., NC. House servant. Farmed postwar. Moved St. Louis 1910. (S2 11 *MO*: 283–89) WILL RHYMES, b. Sept 11, 1853, Morehouse Parish, LA. Toted water, picked up brush, chips. Farmed, hauled logs postwar. int. Hatcher. (SS2 8 *TX* 7: 3300–3302) ANNE RICE, b. 1862, Spartanburg Co., SC. Washed, ironed, cooked. Stayed on plantation after freedom. int. Summer. (S1 3 *SC* 4: 10–11) GEORGE WASHINGTON RICE, b. December 25, 1855, Lafayette Co., AR. Scared birds with cedar paddles. Farmed postwar. int. Browning. (SS2 8 *TX* 7: 3303–5) SAVANNAH RICE, b. ca. 1850, Tuskegee, AL. Fieldhand. (SS1 1 *AL*: 315–25) DORA RICHARD, b. ca. 1860, SC. int. Bowden. (S2 10 *AR* 6: 35–36) SHADE RICHARDS, b. January 13, 1846, Pike Co., GA. Stayed on plantation as sharecropper postwar. Still working mill, Griffin, GA. int. Minor. (S2 13 *GA* 3: 200–205) CHANEY RICHARDSON, b. ca. 1847, Tahlequah, IT. Cherokee slave. House servant, spinner, weaver. (S1 7 *OK*: 257–62) CHARLIE RICHARDSON, b. ca. 1850, Warrensburg, MO. int. Hinkle. (S2 11 *MO*: 290–97) MARTHA RICHARDSON, b. 1860, Columbia, SC. Farmed postwar. int. Scruggs. (S1 3 *SC* 4: 19–22) RED RICHARDSON, b. July 21, 1862, Grimes Co., TX. Held in bondage postwar. (S1 7 *OK*: 263–65) JIM RICKS, b. 1858, Calhoun Co., AR. Farmed after freedom. int. Bowden. (S2 10 *AR* 6: 37–38) CHARLIE RIGGER, b. ca. 1850, Morgan Co., GA. After freedom moved MS, Memphis. Came AR 1902. int. Robertson. (S2 10 *AR* 6: 39–41) IDA RIGLEY, b. 1855, Richmond, VA. House girl. Cooked, baked postwar. int. Robertson. (S2 10 *AR* 6: 42–46) WALTER RIMM, b. ca. 1857, San Patricio Co., TX. Pulled weeds, ran errands. Postwar farmed, cooked. (S1 5 *TX* 3: 247–51; SS2 8 *TX* 7: 3309–23)

SUSIE RISER, b. 1857, Newberry Co., SC. int. Summer, ed. Turnage. (S1 3 *SC* 4: 25) GEORGE RIVERS, b. ca. 1850, Liberty Co., TX. Dairy hand. Postwar worked fishing boats, shipped produce Galveston. int. Dibble, Grey. (SS2 8 *TX* 7: 3324–30) DORA ROBERTS, b. 1849, Liberty Co., GA. Fieldhand. (S2 13 *GA* 3: 206–8) BETTY ROBERTSON, b. ca. 1845, IT. Worked kitchen, minded children. Farmed postwar. (S1 7 *OK*: 266–69) GEORGE ROBERTSON (ROBINSON), b. ca. 1855, TN. Stayed on plantation until 1880. int. Robertson. (S2 10 *AR* 6: 54) CHARLIE ROBINSON, b. 1850, SC. Fieldhand. int. W. Dixon. (S1 3 *SC* 4: 35–37) CELIA ROBINSON, b. ca. 1855, NC. House servant. Fieldwork postwar. Later washed, ironed. int. Matthews, ed. Waitt. (S1 15 *NC* 2: 216–19) CORNELIA ROBINSON, b. unk., AL. int. Klein, ed. Kytle. (S1 6 *AL*: 331–33; SS1 1 *AL*: 352–54) HARRIETT ROBINSON, b. September 1, 1842, Bastrop, TX. Nursemaid, house servant. (S1 7 *OK*: 270–74) MANUS ROBINSON, b. ca. 1860, NC. int. Giles. (SS1 9 *MS* 4: 1856–60) MARIAH ROBINSON, b. ca. 1845, Monroe Co., GA. Taken Bosque Co., TX 1855. House servant. Postwar farmed, domestic, nursemaid. int. A. Davis. (S1 5 *TX* 3: 252–55; SS2 8 *TX* 7: 3350–58) SISTER ROBINSON, b. 1836, VA. Minded chickens, knitted, spun, milked. int. C. Anderson. (*WW*, 240–42) EDD ROBY, b. July 2, 1863, Kosciusko, MS. Postwar farmed Choctaw, Webster, Calhoun Cos. Still working halftime. int. Butts. (SS1 9 *MS* 4: 1863–68) ISAAC RODGERS, b. ca. 1850, Alamance Co., NC. Raised melons, worked railroad postwar. Enlisted 10th Cavalry (the renowned "Buffalo Soldiers"), fought Cuba (Spanish-American War). int. Minnick. (SS1 5 *OH*: 433–36) ELLEN ROGERS, b. ca. 1837, Memphis, TN. Taken Houston, TX. Fieldhand. int. Dibble, Grey. (SS2 8 *TX* 7: 3359–62) AUNT FEREBE ROGERS, b. ca. 1830, Baldwin Co., GA. Fieldhand. int. Chitty, ed. Bell. (S2 13 *GA* 3: 209–16) GEORGE ROGERS, b. 1842, Wake Co., NC. Accompanied slaveholder to war, ran away to Yankees. After war worked cattle in TX, returned Wake Co. int. Matthews, ed. Waitt. (S2 15 *NC* 2:

220–25) HATTIE ROGERS, b. March 2, 1859, New Bern, NC. int. Matthews, ed. Andrews. (S1 15 *NC* 2: 226–31) HENRY ROGERS, b. 1864, Hancock Co., GA. Postwar waiter, lot man, driver livery stable. int. Stonestreet. (S2 13 *GA* 3: 217–28) NOAH ROGERS, b. 1845, Warren Co., MS. Conscripted Union army, teamster. Postwar blacksmith, doctored horses. int. Lawrence. (SS1 9 *MS* 4: 1877–82) JOE ROLLINS, b. 1845, Aberdeen, MS. int. Joiner. (SS1 9 *MS* 4: 1891–1900) WILLIAM HENRY ROOKS, b. 1853, Como, MS. Went for mail. Farmed, preached after freedom. Moved AR 1884. int. Robertson. (S2 10 *AR* 6: 76–79) AL ROSBORO, b. ca. 1847, SC. Valet. Farmed postwar. int. W. Dixon. (S1 3 *SC* 4: 38–41) AMANDA ROSE, b. ca. 1855, Salem, AL. House servant. Washed, ironed, cooked postwar. int. S. Taylor. (S1 10 *AL* 6: 80–85) KATIE ROSE, b. ca. 1850, Henderson, KY. Stayed on plantation until grown, moved Evansville. int. Creel. (SS1 5 *IN*: 174–78) WILLIAM ROSE, b. ca. 1856, Edisto Island, SC. int. Murray. (S1 3 *SC* 4: 48–50) AMANDA ROSS, b. 1856, Salam, AL. Taken AR during war. Washed, cooked, ironed until told too old. int. S. Taylor. (S2 10 *AR* 6: 80–84) CAT ROSS, b. 1862, Rutherford Co., TN. Moved AR 1881, farmed, worked sawmills. int. Robertson. (S2 10 *AR* 6: 86–87) GERTIE ROSS, b. June 10, 1879, Leavenworth, KS. Child of ex-slaves. Taken Denver age two. Music educator, weigher US Mint, publisher, civic leader. (SS1 2 *CO*: 83–85) HENNIE ROSS, b. January 7, 1852, LA. Fieldhand, cane cutter. int. Posey. (*MW*, 188) MADISON FREDERICK ROSS, b. ca. 1848, Scott Co., MO. Runaway, enlisted Union army 1863, numerous engagements. Returned Scott Co., taught school. (S2 11 *MO*: 298–300) SUSAN ROSS, b. ca. 1862, Magnolia Springs, TX. int. Hatcher. (S1 5 *TX* 3: 256–57; SS2 8 *TX* 7: 3565–67) HENRY ROUNTREE, b. ca. 1834, Wilson Co., NC. Fieldhand, stayed on plantation after freedom. int. Hicks, ed. Andrews. (S2 15 *NC* 2: 232–35) KATIE ROWE, b. ca. 1850, AR. Fieldhand. (S1 7 *OK*: 275–84) JOHN RUDD, b. 1854, Springfield, KY. Fieldhand. (S1 6 *IN*: 169–72) MELINDA ANN "ROTY" RUFFIN, b. 1839, VA.

Nursemaid. (*WW*, 243–44) MARTIN RUFFIN, b. 1854, Port Caddo, TX. Stayed on plantation until 1876, then farmed with parents. Moved Marshall 1880, cooked hotels, cafes until 1932. (S1 5 *TX* 3: 265–67) GEORGE RULLERFORD, b. March 25, 1854, Salem, AL. Fieldhand. int. Klein. (SS1 1 *AL*: 86–88, 357–59) JULIA RUSH, b. 1828, St. Simons Island, GA. House servant, fieldhand. Held in bondage postwar. int. Driskell. (S2 13 *GA* 3: 229–31) AARON RUSSELL, b. 1855, Ouachita Parish, LA. Stayed on plantation until age 26, moved TX, farmed. (S1 5 *TX* 3: 270–73; SS2 8 *TX* 7: 3386–93) BENJAMIN RUSSELL, b. ca. 1849, Chester Co., SC. Fieldhand. int. W. Dixon. (S1 3 *SC* 4:51–54) ELIZABETH RUSSELL, b. 1856, Atlanta, GA. Left 1873, moved KY, IN, farmed. int. Stonecipher. (SS1 5 *IN*: 184–76) JOE RUTHERFORD, b. 1846, SC. Fieldhand. int. Summer. (S1 3 *SC* 4: 55–56) LILA RUTHERFORD, b. 1849, Newberry Co., SC. Fieldhand. Stayed on plantation after freedom. int. Summer. (S1 3 *SC* 4: 57–58) HENRY RYAN, b. ca. 1854, Edgefield Co., SC. House servant. int. Summers, ed. Ritter, Turnage. (S1 3 *SC* 4: 71–74) PETER RYAS, b. ca. 1860, St. Martinville Parish, LA. Creole. Moved Lake Charles 1911, later to Port Arthur. (S1 4 *TX* 3: 274–77; SS2 8 *TX* 7: 3394–3402) KATIE RYE, b. ca. 1855, Faulkner Co., AR. Stayed on plantation postwar. int. Winter. (S2 10 *AR* 6: 111–12)

FELIX GRUNDY SADLER, b. 1864, Bosque Co., TX. int. Cowan. (SS2 9 *TX* 8: 3407–35) ROBERT ST. ANN, b. August 10, 1844, Plaquemine Parish, LA. Fieldhand. int. Wallace. (*MW*, 190–92) C. G. SAMUEL, b. ca. 1870, IT. Child of Creek ex-slaves. int. B. Byrd. (SS1 12 *OK*: 267) AMANDA ELIZABETH SAMUELS, b. ca. 1857, Robinson Co., TN. House servant. int. Pritchett. (S1 6 *IN*: 173–74) HARRIET SANDERS, b. 1867, Oktibbeha Co., MS. Child of ex-slaves. int. E. Joiner. (SS1 10 *MS* 5: 1908–15) SUSAN DALE SANDERS, b. unk., Spencer Co., KY. House servant. int. York. (S2 16 *KY*: 43–45) CHARLIE SANDLES, b. 1857, Jackson, TN. Traded at age eight for four mules. Taken TX, hired out. Wage labor postwar. int. B. Davis. (SS2 9 *TX* 8: 3440–56)

HAMP SANTEE, b. ca. 1859, Leakesville, MS. Shoemaker. int. Griffith. (SS1 10 *MS* 5: 1916–19) MRS. MAY SATTERFIELD, b. 1861, VA. int. J Williams. (*WW*, 244–50) CATHERINE SCALES, b. ca. 1855, Rockingham Co., NC. int. Watkins. (S2 15 *NC* 2: 244–51) ANNIE GROVES SCOTT, b. March 18, 1845, SC. Farmed after freedom, married, moved Muskogee. int. Garrison, ed. Vollmer. (SS1 12 *OK*: 268–75) JANIE SCOTT, b. April 10, 1867, AL. Child of ex-slaves. int. Poole. (S1 6 *AL*: 337–39) MARY SCOTT, b. unk., Franklin, TN. Grown at freedom. House servant, nursemaid, spinner. int. Robertson. (S2 10 *AR* 6: 124–27) MARY SCOTT, b. ca. 1847, SC. int. Young, H. Davis. (S1 3 *SC* 4: 81–87) SAM SCOTT, b. July 20, 1859, Dover, AR. Janitor, theatrical manager postwar. int. Lucy. (S2 10 *AR* 6: 131–33) TOM SCOTT, b. ca. 1865, Child of ex-slaves. Jasper, TX. Renter. int. Hatcher. (SS2 9 *TX* 8: 3479–80) MARY LOUISE SCRANTON, b. October 5, 1859, Lafayette, LA. Creole. int. Dibble, Grey. (SS2 9 *TX* 8: 3481–83) MORGAN SCURRY, b. ca. 1859, Newberry Co., SC. House servant, fieldhand. Stayed on plantation postwar for wages. int. Summer, ed. Turnage. (S1 3 *SC* 4: 89–90) FANNY SELLERS, b. unk., Chattanooga, TN. Fieldhand, quilter, domestic. int. Burks. (SS2 1 *NE*: 346–48) ABRAM SELLS, b. ca. 1850, TX. (S1 5 *TX* 4: 9–14; SS2 9 *TX* 8: 3484–92) GEORGE SELMAN, b. 1852, Cherokee Co., TX. Fieldhand. Sharecropped, preached postwar. int. Shirley. (S1 5 *TX* 4: 15–16; SS2 9 *TX* 8: 3498–502) NANCY SETTLES, b. 1845, Edgefield, SC. Fieldhand. int. M. Johnson. (S2 13 *GA* 3: 233–35) ALICE SEWELL, b. November 13, 1851, AL. Postwar washed, ironed, picked cotton. Moved Warren, AR, then ca. 1925 to St. Louis. (S2 11 *MO*: 301–7) MRS. SIS SHACKELFORD, b. 1854, VA. int. C. Anderson. (*WW*, 250–53) ALICE SHAW, b. ca. 1850, Columbus, MS. House servant. int. N. Thompson. (SS1 10 *MS* 5: 1920–24) LUCINDY HALL SHAW, b. ca. 1850, MS. Fieldhand, spinner, nursemaid. Domestic postwar. int. Holt. (SS1 10 *MS* 5: 1925–31) VIOLET SHAW, b. ca. 1885, AR. Grandchild of ex-slaves. int. Robertson. (S2 10 *AR* 6: 143–44) WILL SHEETS, b. 1862,

Oconee Co., GA. Waterboy, drove calves, toted wood. int. Hornsby, ed. Hall, L. Harris. (S2 13 *GA* 3: 236–44) GUSSIE SHELBY, b. 1865, Morgan Co., MO. Child of ex-slaves. Insurance agent. int. Burks. (SS2 1 *NE*: 349–52) FREDERICK SHELTON, b. 1857, AR. Fieldhand. int. Copeland. (S2 10 *AR* 6: 145–47) MATILDA SHEPARD, b. 1832, GA. Fieldhand, house servant. int. Babcock. (SS2 1 *AR*: 124–29) CORA SHEPHERD, b. 1855, Columbia Co., GA. House servant. int. Bell, ed. Barragan. (SS1 4 *GA* 2: 551–60) ROBERT SHEPHERD, b. ca. 1845, Oglethorpe Co., GA. Fieldhand. int. McCune, ed. Hall, L. Harris, Booth. (S2 13 *GA* 3: 245–63) WILLIAM SHERMAN, b. June 12, 1842, Chaseville, FL. Fieldhand. Living Colored Quarters, Chaseville. int. J. M. Johnson, ed. Simms. (S2 17 *FL*: 286–99) POLLY SHINE, b. 1848, Shreveport, LA. Fieldhand, house servant. Domestic postwar. int. B. Davis. (SS2 9 *TX* 8: 3510–27) UNCLE EDD SHIRLEY, b. ca. 1840, KY. Sold three times, last to white father. Taken Monroe Co., KY. Still janitor Tompkinsville Drug Co. and Hospital. int. L Jones. (S2 16 *KY*: 23, 86–87) MAHALIA SHORES, b. ca. 1860, Greene Co., GA. Fieldhand. Cooked, washed, ironed after freedom. int. Robertson. (S2 10 *AR* 6: 154–56) MARTHA SHOWVELY, b. 1837, Powhatan Co., VA. House girl, cook. int. Lee. (*WW*, 264–65) BETTY SIMMONS, b. ca. 1837, AL. Stolen as child, sold to slave trader, taken TX. House servant. (S1 5 *TX* 4: 19–23; SS2 9 *TX* 8: 3533–43) GEORGE SIMMONS, b. 1854, AL. Taken Jefferson Co., TX during war. Fiddled, farmed, sawmilled until disabled. int. Dibble, Grey. (S1 5 *TX* 4: 24–26; SS2 9 *TX* 8: 3544–48) MARY JANE SIMMONS, b. ca. 1856, Raleigh, NC. Nursemaid from age six. (SS1 4 *GA* 2: 561–70) SMITH SIMMONS, b. ca. 1860, Montgomery Co., MS. Moved Coahoma Co. 1925. Farmed. int. Campbell. (SS1 10 *MS* 5: 1935–43) ANDREW SIMMS, b. ca. 1857, FL. Taken Fairfield, TX during war. Chores. (S1 7 *OK*: 295–97) DENNIS SIMMS, b. July 18, 1841, Prince George Co., MD. Stable hand, woodcutter, fieldhand. (S2 16 *MD*: 60–62) MILLIE SIMPKINS, b. ca. 1820, Winchester, TN. House servant, nursemaid. (S2 16 *TN*: 66–69) EMMA SIMPSON, b. ca. 1850, Walker Co., TX. Fieldhand, cook. Farmed, cut wood, wage labor postwar. int. B. Davis. (SS2 9 *TX* 8: 3567–72) GEORGE JACKSON SIMPSON, b. August 4, 1854, Crawford Co., MO. Slave of white father. Hired out age twelve, held in bondage until 1875. int. Mueller. (SS1 2 *MO*: 219–29) IKE SIMPSON, b. ca. 1857, Jasper Co., TX. (SS2 9 *TX* 8: 3573–79) JANE SIMPSON, b. ca. 1845, Burkesville, KY. Fieldhand, sold six times. Farmed, cooked postwar. (S2 11 *MO*: 311–17) ALLEN SIMS, b. ca. 1860, AL. int. Klein, ed. Oden. (S1 6 *AL*: 342–44) ADAM SINGLETON, b. 1858, Newton, AL. Moved MS 1885, farmed, jobbed. int. Holmes. (SS1 10 *MS* 5: 1946–56) AFFIE SINGLETON, b. ca. 1849, Charleston, SC. int. R Nelson. (SS1 11 *SC*: 283–84) JAMES SINGLETON, b. 1856, Simpson Co., MS. Farmed, preached postwar. int. England. (S1 7 *MS*: 125–27; SS1 10 *MS* 5: 1957–60) MARINDA JANE SINGLETON, b. September 25, 1840, Hartford, NC. Taken VA 1850. Fieldhand. int. Hoggard. (*WW*, 266–69) TOM SINGLETON, b. 1844, Lumpkin Co., GA. Fieldhand. int. Hornsby, ed. L. Harris. (S2 13 *GA* 3: 264–73) ALFRED SLIGH, b. 1837, Newberry Co., SC. Fieldhand. Moved Columbia 1866, construction. int. Scruggs. (S1 3 *SC* 4: 92–94) ADAM SMITH, b. May 2, 1839, Tate Co., MS. Fieldhand, served in war. Sharecropped postwar. int. Pack. (SS1 10 *MS* 5: 1968–75) BERRY SMITH, b. 1821, Sumter Co., AL. Taken Scott Co., MS prewar. Runaway, cooked for Union troops. Postwar worked railroad, steamboats, bought farm Scott Co. int. Allison. (S1 7 *MS*: 128–34; SS1 10 *MS* 5: 1978–87) CAROLINE SMITH, b. ca. 1850, Union Co., AR. Carded, spun. int. Graham. (S2 10 *AR* 6: 176–81) CHARLIE TYE SMITH, b. June 10, 1850, Locust Grove, GA. Fieldhand. int. Crawford. (S2 13 *GA* 3: 274–77) ELI SMITH, b. ca. 1840, GA. Odd jobs. (SS1 1 *AL*: 367–68) EUGENE WESLEY SMITH, freeborn 1852, Augusta, GA. Placed under white "guardianship," hired out. int. Barragan, Love, Radford. (S2 13 *GA* 4: 214–15, 230–35, 348) GEORGIA SMITH, b. ca. 1850, Oglethorpe Co., GA. Ladies maid, house servant. Postwar

moved Athens, domestic. int. McCune, ed. Hall. (S2 13 *GA* 3: 278–84) GILES SMITH, b. ca. 1858, Union Springs, AL. Moved TX 1874, farmed, worked gins. Settled Fort Worth 1922, meatpacker, discharged for old age 1931. Doing odd jobs. int. Gauthier. (S1 5 *TX* 4: 30–32; SS2 9 *TX* 8: 3601–9) GUS SMITH (AUGUST MESSERSMITH), b. July 4, 1845, Osage Co., MO. Fieldhand. Farmed postwar. int. Mueller. (S2 11 *MO*: 321–32; SS1 2 *MO*: 240–62) HECTOR SMITH, b. 1858, Marion, SC. Stayed on plantation postwar. int. R. Davis. (S1 3 *SC* 4: 100–109) HENRY SMITH, b. ca. 1840, Green Parish, LA. Taken Waco, TX. Fieldhand, teamster. int. A. Davis. (SS2 9 *TX* 8: 3610–23) JAMES W. SMITH, b. 1860, Palestine, TX. Left plantation 1870, farmed until 1895. Entered Baptist ministry, preached until 1931. int. Gauthier. (S1 5 *TX* 4: 33–35; SS2 9 *TX* 8: 3630–36) JOHN SMITH, b. ca. 1834, NC. Sold, taken AL. Worked saddle shop, wounded in war. Postwar drove stagecoach Selma to Montgomery. int. O'Brien, ed. Marzoni. (S1 6 *AL*: 349–52) JORDON SMITH, b. 1851, GA. Taken Anderson Co., TX. After freedom worked steamboats, railroad. (S1 5 *TX* 4: 36–40; SS2 9 *TX* 8: 3637–45) LOU SMITH, b. ca. 1854, SC. Taken TX during war. House servant. (S1 7 *OK*: 300–305) LOUIS SMITH, b. February 7, 1856, Travis Co., TX. Stayed on plantation eight years postwar working cattle for wages, room, board. int. Menn. (SS2 9 *TX* 8: 3646–47) MARY SMITH, b. 1853, SC. Nursemaid, fieldwork after freedom. int. Sims, ed. Turnage. (S1 3 *SC* 4: 112–15) MELVIN SMITH, b. 1841, Beaufort, SC. House servant, fieldhand. int. Watson. (S2 13 *GA* 3: 288–94) MILLIE ANN SMITH, b. 1850, Rusk Co., TX. House servant. Stayed on plantation four years postwar, then domestic. int. Hampton. (S1 5 *TX* 4: 41–43; SS2 9 *TX* 8: 3650–55) NANCY SMITH, b. ca. 1857, Athens, GA. House, yard work. int. McCune, ed. Hall, Booth. (S2 13 *GA* 3: 295–303) PAUL SMITH, b. ca. 1863, Oglethorpe Co., GA. Stayed on plantation postwar. Later worked railroad. int. McCune, ed. Hall, L. Harris, Booth. (S2 13 *GA* 3: 320–38) NELLIE SMITH, b. 1860, Athens,

GA. int. McCune, ed. Hall, Booth. (S2 13 *GA* 3: 304–19) R. C. SMITH, b. ca. 1840, Washington Co., AR. Taken TX during war. Postwar herded cattle, mined coal IT. int. J. Ervin. (SS1 12 *OK*: 280–92) SARAH ANN SMITH, b. January 22, 1858, Chatham Co., NC. Nursemaid. int. Hicks, ed. G. Andrews. (S2 15 *NC* 2: 289–91) SAMUEL SMITH, b. February 14, 1840, Nashville, TN. Stable hand, chores. Moved TX postwar. int. M Warren. (SS2 9 *TX* 8: 3659–62) STONEWALL SMITH, b. June 26, 1872, Lexington, KY. Child of ex-slaves. Jockey, groom, horse trader, served Spanish-American War. Moved Boulder 1900, raced horses, worked street shows. (SS1 2 *CO*: 86–88) SUSAN SMITH, b. ca. 1855, New Iberia, LA. Nursemaid, weaver. Left 1870, moved TX 1907. int. Dibble. (S1 5 *TX* 4: 44–46; SS2 9 *TX* 8: 3663–70) WILLIAM SMITH, b. December 25, 1845, LA. Creole. Waterboy, fieldhand, fiddler. Taken LaGrange, TX, sold. Farmed, preached postwar. int. Menn. (SS2 9 *TX* 8: 3689–96) JOHN SNEED, b. unk., Austin, TX. Grown when freed. Fieldhand, spinner. int. A. Davis. (S1 5 *TX* 4: 47–51; SS2 9 *TX* 8: 3697–3706) SUSAN SNOW, b. 1850, Wilcox Co., AL. Taken Jasper Co., MS. Fieldhand, hired out. Moved Meridian postwar. Nursemaid, wet nurse, domestic. int. Allison. (S1 7 *MS*: 135–42; SS1 10 *MS* 5: 2003–13) MARIAH SNYDER, b. ca. 1848, MS. Taken TX 1853. Fieldhand. Farmed, domestic postwar. int. Hampton. (S1 5 *TX* 4: 52–54; SS2 9 *TX* 8: 3707–13) JIM SOMMERVILLE, b. 1842, Memphis, TN. Taken Louisville, KY, TX during war. Groom, stablehand. int. E. Williams. (SS2 1 *NY*: 359–61) RIA SORRELL, b. 1840, Wake Co., NC. House servant, nursemaid. int. Matthews, ed. G. Andrews. (S2 15 *NC* 2: 299–305) JAMES SOUTHALL, b. 1855, Clarksville, TN. Freed before war. Stayed on plantation as tenant. (S1 7 *OK*: 306–9) PATSY SOUTHWELL, b. ca. 1854, TX. Toted water, spun, wove. Stayed on plantation postwar. int. Hatcher. (S1 5 *TX* 4: 55–56; SS2 9 *TX* 8: 3714–17) ELIZABETH SPARKS, b. 1841, VA. House servant. int. C. Anderson. (S2 16 *VA*: 50–54; *WW*, 273–77) MOM JESSIE SPARROW, b. 1854, SC. House servant. int. R. Davis.

(S1 3 *SC* 4: 121–46) UNCLE JOHN SPENCER, b. ca. 1857, King George Court House, VA. int. B. Lewis. (*WW*, 278–79) TANNER SPIKES, b. 1860, Wake Co., NC. int. Hicks, ed. G. Andrews. (S2 15 *NC* 2: 309–11) LEITHEAN SPINKS, b. 1855, Rankin Co., MS. Taken East Feliciana Parish, LA. Chores. Farmed postwar. Moved TX 1907. int. Gauthier. (S1 5 *TX* 4: 57–60; SS2 9 *TX* 8: 3718–27) GRACIE STAFFORD, b. ca. 1860, St. James Parish, LA. int. Posey. (*MW*, 197–98) JEFF STANFIELD, b. 1837, VA. Teamster. int. Lee. (*WW*, 279–81) WRIGHT STAPLETON, b. ca. 1850, Rankin Co., MS. Farmed postwar. int. Giles. (SS1 10 *MS* 5: 2019–24) ISOM STARNES, b. ca. 1860, Marshall Co., AL. Farmed, worked piano factory postwar. int. Robertson. (S2 10 *AR* 6: 218–19) ELMO STEELE, freeborn ca. 1825, OH. Farmed, worked riverboats. Enlisted Union army, mustered out Vicksburg 1866. Married, settled MS, farmed. int. Giles. (SS1 10 *MS* 6: 2025–35) MATTIE STENSTON, b. ca. 1859, Oktibbeha Co., MS. int. Joiner. (SS1 10 *MS* 5: 2036–38) ANNIE STEPHENSON, b. 1857, Hillsboro, NC. Nursemaid. int. Matthews, ed. G. Andrews. (S2 15 *NC* 2: 312–15) EMELINE STEPNEY, b. ca. 1840, Greene Co., GA. (S2 13 *GA* 3: 339–42) STEVE STEPNEY, 1840–1935, MS. Information communicated by grandchildren. int. Bradley. (SS1 10 *MS* 5: 2039–40) THOMAS STEPTOE, b. June 2, 1863, New Orleans. Creole. int. Dupuy. (*MW*, 199–205) CARLYLE STEWART, b. January 3, 1853, Jeanerette, LA. Nursemaid postwar. int. McElwee. (*MW*, 205–6) CHARLEY STEWART, b. October 4, 1852, Bolivar Co., MS. Slave of father. Toted water, drove cows. Mortar-maker postwar. int. Walsh. (SS1 10 *MS* 5: 2041–46) GUY STEWART, b. November 26, 1850, Mansfield Parish, LA. Taken TX during war. Fieldhand. Stayed on plantation postwar for wages, rented. Moved Fort Worth 1898, worked wood yard. int. Gauthier. (S1 5 *TX* 4: 61–63; SS2 9 *TX* 8: 3731–35) NAN STEWART, b. February 1850, Charleston, WV. House servant. int. Probst, ed. Meighen. (S2 16 *OH*: 86–91) NELSON STEWART, b. unk., NC. Fieldhand. After freedom worked

Seaboard Railroad Co. int. Matthews, ed. Waitt. (SS1 11 *NC*: 49–51) SAM T. STEWART, b. December 11, 1853, Wake Co., NC. Fieldhand. int. Hicks, ed. Waitt. (S2 15 *NC* 2: 316–23) ISAAC STIER, b. ca. 1837, Jefferson Co., MS. Captured with slaveholder Vicksburg, conscripted Union army. Postwar worked St. Louis saloon, returned Jefferson Co., sharecropped. int. Moore. (S1 7 *MS*: 143–50; SS1 10 *MS* 5: 2048–59) ELLA STINSON, b. ca. 1857, SC. Sold, taken AL, GA border. House servant. int. Watson. (SS1 4 *GA* 2: 595–99) JAMES HENRY STITH, b. January 26, 1865, Hancock Co., GA. Child of ex-slaves. Carpenter. int. S. Taylor. (S2 10 *AR* 6: 239–45) AUNT ANN STOKES, b. 1844, New Madrid Co., MO. (S2 11 *MO*: 333–37) SIMON STOKES, b. ca. 1839, Mathews Co., VA. Taken Gloucester Co. Fieldhand. int. Jayne. (S2 16 *VA*: 45; *WW*, 281) EMMA STONE, b. ca. 1860, Chatham Co., NC. int. Hicks, ed. Waitt. (S1 15 *NC* 2: 324–26) WILLIAM STONE, b. ca. 1863, LA. Farmed postwar. int. Cowan. (S1 5 *TX* 3: 64–66; SS2 9 *TX* 8: 3736–47) EVA STRAYHORN, b. ca. 1858, Johnson Co., AR. Odd jobs. Stayed on plantation postwar, burnt out by bushwhackers. Moved TX. int. J. Ervin. (SS1 12 *OK*: 297–308) GEORGE STRICKLAND, b. ca. 1856, MS. Taken AL during war. Stayed on plantation as sharecropper postwar. int. Klein, ed. Crow. (S1 6 *Al*: 359–62; SS1 1 *AL*: 397–99) LIZA STRICKLAND, b. 1847, Simpson Co., MS. House servant. int. Giles. (SS1 10 *MS* 5: 2064–67) YACH STRINGFELLOW, b. May 1847, Brenham, TX. Water boy. Farmed, odd-jobbed postwar. int. A. Davis. (S1 5 *TX* 4: 67–69; SS2 9 *TX* 8: 3748–54) BERT STRONG, b. 1864, Harrison Co., TX. Fieldhand. Stayed on plantation ten years postwar. int. Hampton. (S1 5 *TX* 4: 70–72; SS2 9 *TX* 8: 3755–60) JULIA STUBBS, b. 1852, Magee, MS. Spinner, knitter, weaver, laundress. Stayed on plantation after freedom, then homesteaded nearby. int. Giles. (SS1 10 *MS* 5: 2068–71) AMANDA STYLES, b. ca. 1856, GA. int. Whitely. (S2 13 *GA* 3: 343–46) RACHEL SULLIVAN, b. 1852, Augusta, GA. Nursemaid. int. Barragan, Love, Radford. (S2 13 *GA* 4: 226–29)

JAMES R. SUTTON, b. 1866, Greenville, NC, parents' former plantation, stayed many years. int. Walsh. (SS1 10 *MS* 5: 2080–82) JANE SUTTON, b. ca. 1853, Simpson Co., MS. House servant. int. Walsh. (S1 7: 151–56; SS1 10 *MS* 5: 2083–93) KATIE SUTTON, b. unk., IN. int. Creel. (S1 6 *IN*: 193–95; SS1 5 *IN*: 210–11) SAMUEL SUTTON, b. 1854, KY. Moved OH postwar, worked railroad, steamboats, farmed. int. Logan. (S2 16 *OH*: 92–96; SS1 5 *OH*: 446–51) ELLEN SWINDLER, b. 1859, Newberry Co., SC. Fieldhand. int. Summer, ed. Turnage. (S1 3 *SC* 4: 156) WILLIAM SYKES, b. 1859, Martin Co., NC. Inmate, State Prison, Raleigh. int. Hicks, ed. Waitt. (S2 15 *NC* 2: 327–31)

CULL TAYLOR, b. March 5, 1859, Augusta Co., AL. int. Prine. (S1 6 *AL*: 363–66) DELPHIA TAYLOR, b. 1841, VA. (*WW*, 283) EDWARD TAYLOR, b. ca. 1812, Rapides Parish, LA. Teamster, made rails, crossties. int. White. (S2 11 *MO*: 338–41) EMMA TAYLOR, b. ca. 1849, TX. Sold, taken Jacksonville. Fieldhand. Tenant postwar. int. Hale. (S1 5 *TX* 4: 73–75; SS2 9 *TX* 8: 3761–67) GEORGE TAYLOR, b. unk., Mobile, AL. Age twelve taken Gosport. Fieldhand. int. Prine. (S1 6 *AL*: 370–73) MOLLIE TAYLOR, b. 1853, Campbell, TX. Fieldhand, house servant. Farmed after freedom. (S1 5 *TX* 4: 76–77; SS2 9 *TX* 8: 3768–71) TISHEY TAYLOR, b. ca. 1860, New Madrid Co., MO. (S1 11 *MO*: 342–47) WARREN TAYLOR, b. 1863, Richmond, VA. Taken MS, AR as infant. Settled Little Rock, worked railroad. int. S. Taylor. (S2 10 *AR* 6: 273–79) MARY TEEL, b. ca. 1860, Holly Springs, MS. Picked cotton, washed, ironed, cooked. int. Robertson. (S2 10 *AR* 6: 282–84) GEORGIA TELFAIR, b. 1864, Athens, GA. House servant. Hired out age fourteen. int. McCune, ed. Hall, L. Harris. (S2 13 *GA* 4: 1–10) BEAUREGARD TENNEYSON, b. 1850, Craig Co., TX. (S1 7 *OK*: 310–11) LOUISE TERRELL, b. unk., MS. Fieldhand. Information communicated by Callie Bracey (daughter). int. Pritchett. (S1 6 *IN*: 25–26) JAKE TERRIELL, b. ca. 1845, Raleigh, NC. Fieldhand. int. B. Davis. (S1 5 *TX* 4: 78–79; SS2 9 *TX* 8: 3772–76) ACIE THOMAS, b. July 26, 1857, Jefferson

Co., FL. Postwar built streetcar lines, paved streets, installed electrical wiring Jacksonville. int. Randolph. (S2 17 *FL*: 327–34) BILL AND ELLEN THOMAS (spouses). Bill, b. 1849, MO. Taken MS, TX. Fieldhand. Ellen, b. ca. 1856, MS. Taken TX. Sharecropped, farmed postwar. int. Holm, Angermiller. (S1 5 *TX* 4: 85–88; SS2 9 *TX* 8: 3781–99) CORDELIA THOMAS, b. ca. 1855, Oconee Co., GA. Spinner. Nursemaid, domestic postwar. int. McCune, ed. Hall, L. Harris, Booth. (S2 13 *GA* 4: 11–24) DAN THOMAS, b. 1847, Memphis. Tended bar in slaveholder's whiskey house, collected debts. Moved Nashville World War I, worked munitions factory. (S2 16 *TN*: 74–75) ELIAS THOMAS, b. 1853, Chatham Co., NC. Fieldhand. Stayed on plantation eight years postwar. Later worked NC Hospital for Insane. int. Matthews, ed. G. Andrews. (S2 15 *NC* 2: 342–47) GEORGE THOMAS, b. ca. 1855, New Castle, KY–d. 1937, Clark County, IN. Fieldhand, weaver. Stayed on plantation until 1870. Drowned, Clark County, IN Poor Farm, 1937 flood. int. Van Meter. (SS1 5 *IN*: 222–28) IKE THOMAS, b. 1843, Jasper Co., GA. Fiddler, house boy, carriage boy. Stayed on plantation postwar. int. Minor. (S2 13 *GA* 4: 25–28) KATE THOMAS, b. 1832, Mobile, AL. Taken Troup Co., GA during war. House servant. int. Bridges. (SS1 4 *GA* 2: 605–10) LORENA THOMAS, b. ca. 1854, Columbus, MS. (SS1 10 *MS* 5: 2095–97) LUCY THOMAS, b. 1851, Harrison Co., TX. Fieldhand. Left 1868, farmed. int. Hampton. (S1 5 *TX* 4: 88–91; SS2 9 *TX* 8: 3800–3805) PHILLES THOMAS, b. 1860, Brazoria Co., TX. Postwar moved nearby. Left 1876, settled Fort Worth. Domestic. int. Gauthier. (S1 5 *TX* 4: 92–94; SS2 9 *TX* 8: 3812–18) REBECCA THOMAS, b. 1825, Little Rock. Taken Caldwell Co., TX prewar. House servant, fieldhand. Renter postwar. int. Menn. (SS2 9 *TX* 8: 3819–23) ROSA THOMAS, b. 1861, AL. int. Walsh. (SS1 10 *MS* 5: 2098–102) SARAH THOMAS, b. ca. 1860, Rapides Parish, LA. Taken TX during war. Stayed on plantation until grown, moved MS. int. Walsh. (SS1 10 *MS* 5: 2103–9) VALMO THOMAS, b. December 7, 1859,

Ville Platte, LA. Creole. int. Dibble. (SS2 9 *TX* 8: 3826–31) WILLIAM M. THOMAS, b. ca. 1850, Lauderdale Co., MS. House servant. Moved TX 1874, worked as stevedore Galveston, Purina Mills Fort Worth. int. Gauthier. (S1 5 *TX* 4: 95–99; SS2 9 *TX* 8: 3835–43) ELLEN BRIGGS THOMPSON, b. October 1844, Hempstead Co., AR. Fieldhand, house servant. Farmed postwar. int. S. Taylor. (S2 10 *AR* 6: 309–14) JANE THOMPSON, b. ca. 1850, MS. Sold away from mother as small child, resold many times. House servant, fieldhand. (S2 11 *MO*: 353–54) JOHN THOMPSON, b. September 15, 1857, Nashville, TN. House servant, water boy, dance caller. Taken TX, held in bondage postwar. Hired out, molded brick, worked sheep, cattle, farmed. int. A. Davis. (SS2 9 *TX* 8: 3844–54) JOHNSON THOMPSON, b. 1853, Rusk Co., TX. Cherokee slave. Moved IT postwar. int. Garrison, ed. Vollmer. (SS1 12 *OK*: 309–12) LAURA THOMPSON, b. ca. 1850, Greensburg, KY. Postwar moved Indianapolis, St. Paul 1919. (SS1 2 *MN*: 131–36) PENNY THOMPSON, b. ca. 1851, Coosa Co., AL. Chores. Moved TX postwar. int. Gauthier. (S1 5 *TX* 4: 103–5; SS2 9 *TX* 8: 3870–77) VICTORIA TAYLOR THOMPSON, b. ca. 1858, IT. Cherokee slave. Weaver. Twice stolen as child, branded on cheek. int. Garrison, ed. Vollmer. (SS1 12 *OK*: 320–24) LAURA THORNTON, b. ca. 1830 AL. Fieldhand. Moved Little Rock 1880s. int. S. Taylor. (S2 10 *AR* 6: 3222–29) MARGARET THORNTON, b. ca. 1860, Harnett Co., NC. int. Hicks, ed. G. Andrews. (S2 15 *NC* 2: 352–54) TIM THORNTON, b. ca. 1835, Danville, VA. Delivery boy, worked tobacco factory. int. Barragan. (S2 13 *GA* 4: 335–36; SS1 4 *GA* 2: 611–15) JIM THREAT, b. Sept 1851, Talladega Co., AL. Farmed postwar. int. Jesse R. Ervin. (SS1 12 *OK*: 325–41) LUCY THURSTON, b. ca. 1836, Flemingsburg, KY. Age twelve sold New Orleans, taken Covington, LA. Fieldhand. Stayed on plantation two-three years postwar then sharecropped MS. int. de Sola. (SS1 10 *MS* 5: 2110–20) EMMA TIDWELL, b. ca. 1839, AR. Domestic. Taught Bible school postwar. (S2 10 *AR* 6: 330–33) ROBERT TOATLEY, b. May 15, 1855,

SC. int. W. Dixon. (S1 3 *SC* 4: 163–66) BETTIE TOL-BERT, b. ca. 1850, Lee Co., AL. Weaving, spinning. int. Tarrt. (SS1 S1 *AL*: 402–4) RICHARD TOLER, b. ca. 1835, Lynchburg, VA. Fieldhand. Postwar moved Cincinnati, fiddler, stonemason, carpenter, bricklayer, blacksmith. int. R. Thompson, ed. Graff. (S2 16 *OH*: 97–101; SS1 5 *OH*: 452–54) JANE MICKENS TOOMBS, b. ca. 1855, Wilkes Co., GA. Fieldhand, seamstress, weaver. int. Stonestreet. (S2 13 *GA* 4: 29–36) PHIL TOWNS, b. June 25, 1824, VA. Taken Taylor Co., GA. int. A. Dixon. (S2 13 *GA* 4: 37–47) WILLIAM HENRY TOWNS, b. December 7, 1854, Tuscumbia, AL. Carriage driver. (S1 6 *AL*: 385–93; SS1 1 *AL*: 407–16) ELLEN TRELL, b. 1864, Wake Co., NC. int. Matthews, ed. G. Andrews. (S2 15 *NC* 2: 359–62) HENRY JAMES TRENTHAM, b. December 2, 1845, Camden, SC. int. Matthews, ed. G. Andrews. (S2 15 *NC* 2: 363–66) ALECK TRIMBLE, b. 1861, Beaumont, TX. Pulled weeds, tended calves. Postwar farmed, worked sawmills, public works. int. Dibble, Beehler. (S1 5 *TX* 4: 108–15) UNCLE JAMES TUBBS, b. 1866, AR. Child of ex-slaves. Farmed, preached. int. P. Anderson. (S2 10 *AR* 6: 354–56) CLORIE TURNER, b. unk., LA. Creole. int. Michinard. (*MW*, 207) UNCLE HENRY TURNER, b. 1845, MS. Taken Phillips Co., AR prewar. Fieldhand. int. W. McKinney. (S2 10 *AR* 6: 363–68; SS2 1 *AR*: 135–41) LOU TURNER, b. ca. 1847, Beaumont, TX. Watched geese, turkeys, filled quilts, carded. int. Dibble, Grey. (S1 5 *TX* 4: 188–21; SS2 10 *TX* 9: 3896–3900)

STEPNEY UNDERWOOD, b. ca. 1860, Lowndes Co., AL. int. J. Smith. (S1 6 *AL*: 394–96) NEAL UPSON, b. 1857, Oglethorpe Co., GA. int. McCune, ed. Hall, Booth. (S2 13 *GA* 4: 48–70)

ELLEN VADEN, b. 1855, AR. Farmed. int. Robertson. (S2 11 *AR* 7: 3–4) NETTIE VAN BUREN, b. ca. 1870, AR. Child of ex-slaves. int. Robertson. (S1 11 *AR* 7: 5–6) CHARLIE VAN DYKE, b. ca. 1830, NC. Age ten taken Tuscaloosa, Selma. Yard work, minding children. int. Poole. (S1 6 *AL*: 397–400) JOHN F. VAN HOOK, b. 1862, Macon Co., NC. Postwar farmed, taught school NC, GA. int. Hornsby, ed. Hall,

Booth. (S2 13 *GA* 4: 71–96) LUCINDA VANN, b. ca. 1840, IT. Cherokee slave. House servant. int. Faulton. (SS1 12 *OK*: 342–53) STEPHEN VARNER, b. ca. 1852, Coosa Co., AL. Fieldhand. (SS1 1 *AL*: 425–28) MARY VEALS, b. 1865, Newberry, SC. Child of ex-slaves. int. Summer, ed. Turnage. (S1 3 *SC* 4: 167–69) ADDIE VINSON, b. 1852, Oconee Co., GA. Nursemaid. Plowhand postwar. int. Hornsby, ed. Hall, Booth. (S2 13 *GA* 4: 97–114) EMMA VIRGEL, b. 1865, Oconee Co., GA. Child of ex-slaves, tenant on their former plantation. int. McCune, ed. Hall, Booth. (S2 13 *GA* 4: 115–22)

ADELINE WALDON, b. 1857, Springfield, MO. Taken TX during war. int. A. Davis. (SS2 10 *TX* 9: 3913–27) BEAN WALKER, b. 1852, TX. Fieldhand. int. Arnold. (SS2 10 *TX* 9: 3921–32) DAVE WALKER, b. 1850, Simpson Co., MS. Fieldhand. Stayed on plantation eight years postwar. Farmed. int. Giles. (SS1 10 *MS* 5: 2148–52) EDWIN WALKER, b. 1849, Simpson, Co., MS. Fieldhand. int. Giles. (SS1 10 *MS* 5: 2153–56) HARRIET WALKER, b. ca. 1852, Simpson Co., MS. Fieldhand. int. Giles. (SS1 10 *MS* 5: 2157–61) HENRY WALKER, b. ca. 1856, Nashville, TN. Taken Hazen, AR. Fieldhand. Stayed on plantation as sharecropper postwar. int. Robertson. (S2 11 *AR* 7: 28–35) LULA COTTONHAM WALKER, b. 1824, Centerville, AL. Fieldhand. int. J. Smith. (SS1 1 *AL*: 431–34) MANDA WALKER, b. 1857, Winnsboro, SC. Nursemaid, fieldhand. Left plantation 1876, sharecropped. int. W. Dixon. (S1 3 *SC* 4: 170–73) NED WALKER, b. ca. 1854, SC. Domestic. int. W. Dixon. (S1 3 *SC* 3: 174–80) SARAH WALKER, b. ca. 1855, Saline Co., MO. Farmed postwar, moved Seattle 1905. int. Gaston. (SS1 2 *WA*: 279–81) BEN WALL, b. ca. 1852, Benton Co., MS. Dance caller. (SS1 10 *MS* 5: 2163–64) RHODUS WALTON, b. ca. 1852, Stewart Co., GA. Sold as infant. Herder. int. A. Dixon. (S2 13 *GA* 4: 123–27; SS1 4 *GA* 2: 628–34) SOL WALTON, b. 1849, Mobile, AL. Taken MS, then Mooringsport, LA. Waterboy, fieldhand. Stayed on plantation as sharecropper postwar. Moved Marshall, TX 1870s. Farmed, worked T&P railroad shop until 1922 strike. Odd jobs. int. Hampton. (S1 5 *TX* 4:

128–30; SS2 10 *TX* 9: 3952–57) REV. WAMBLE (WOMBLE), b. 1859, Monroe Co., MS. int. Koritz. (S1 6 *IN*: 198–205) ALLEN WARD, b. 1856, Simpson Co., MS. House servant, fieldhand. Farmed postwar. int. Giles. (SS1 10 *MS* 5: 2170–74) WILLIAM WARD, b. 1832, GA. Cleaned yard, later hired out. int. Ross. (S2 13 GA 4: 128–30) LUCY ANN WARFIELD, b. ca. 1824, Jessamine Co., KY. Fieldhand. int. Minnick. (SS1 5 *OH*: 455–57) WILLIAM WARFIELD, b. unk., KY. int. Hanberry. (S2 16 *KY*: 102–3) CALLIE WASHINGTON, b. ca. 1859, Red Fork, AR. House servant. Postwar moved KY, MS. Domestic. int. Campbell. (SS1 10 *MS* 5: 2185–95) ELIZA WASHINGTON, b. ca. 1860, Scott's Crossing, AR. Washerwoman. int. S. Taylor. (S2 11 *AR* 7: 49–56) ELLA WASHINGTON, b. 1855, St. Mary's Parish, LA. Taken Calvert, TX during war. Nursemaid. Postwar moved Galveston, washed. int. Liberato. (S1 5 *TX* 4: 131–33; SS2 10 *TX* 9: 3968–76) REV. JAMES W. WASHINGTON, b. July 1854, Pike Co., MS. Postwar farmed, odd-jobbed, preached. int. Holmes. (SS1 10 *MS* 5: 2197–2205) LULA WASHINGTON, b. 1853, Randolph, AL. Moved GA after freedom. int. Cole. (S2 13 GA 4: 134–35) ROSA WASHINGTON, b. ca. 1845, St. Joe, LA. Fieldhand. Stayed on plantation postwar. Moved TX 1921. (S1 5 *TX* 4: 134–37; SS2 10 *TX* 9: 3977–83) SAM JONES WASHINGTON, b. 1849, Wharton Co., TX. Cowhand. Stayed on plantation, worked cattle, farmed postwar. Moved Fort Worth 1905, cowhand, meatpacker, forced to retire. Still raising hogs, odd-jobbing. int. Gauthier. (S1 5 *TX* 4: 138–40; SS2 10 *TX* 9: 3984–91) JORDAN WATERS, b. 1861, LA. Farmed, hired out. int. Posey. (*MW*, 208–9) SYLVIA WATKINS, b. ca. 1847, Bedford Co., TN. House servant, nursemaid, seamstress. (S2 16 *TN*: 76–79) WILLIAM WATKINS, b. 1850, VA. Enlisted US army ca. 1870, fought Indian wars in Texas. (S1 5 *TX* 4: 141–43) CHARLEY WATSON, b. 1850, Winnsboro, SC. Fieldhand. Stayed on plantation postwar. int. W. Dixon. (S1 3 *SC* 4: 188–90) EMMA WATSON, b. 1852 or 1853, Ellis Co., TX. Fieldhand. (S1 5 TX 4: 144–47; SS2 9 *TX* 8: 3998–4002) MOLLIE WATSON, b. ca. 1855, Centerville, TX. House servant. Farmed postwar. int. J. Ervin. (SS1 12 *OK*: 365–74) WILLIAM H. WATSON, b. ca. 1850, TN. Fieldhand. int. Gibson. (SS1 12 *OK*: 375–79) JOHN WATTS, b. 1854, Fayette Co., GA. Fieldhand. int. Carlisle, ed. J. Jones. (SS1 4 *GA* 2: 635–36) EUGENIA WEATHERALL, b. 1863, Lee Co., MS. Moved Union Co. postwar. int. Kolb. (SS1 10 *MS* 5: 2214–21) FOSTER WEATHERSBY, b. February 7, 1855, Simpson Co., MS. Churned, carried water. Farmed postwar. int. Giles. (SS1 10 *MS* 5: 2227–31) GEORGE WEATHERSBY, b. 1852, Simpson Co., MS. Fieldhand. Farmed postwar. int. Giles. (SS1 10 *MS* 5: 2232–35) ISOM WEATHERSBY, b. 1847, Simpson Co., MS. Fieldhand. Farmed postwar. int. Giles. (SS1 10 *MS* 5: 2236–38) ROBERT WEATHERSBY, b. ca. 1847, Rankin Co., MS. Fieldhand. Farmed postwar. int. Giles. (SS1 10 *MS* 5: 2239–44) STEVE WEATHERSBY, b. ca. 1856, Simpson Co., MS. Fieldhand. Homesteaded postwar. int. Giles. (SS1 10 *MS* 5: 2245–48) MRS. WEBB, b. unk., St. John the Baptist Parish, LA. Creole slave. int. Michinard. (*MW*, 209) SOL WEBB, b. unk., AL. (SS1 1 *AL*: 440–42) EMMA WEEKS, b. 1858, Austin, TX. House servant. Farmed postwar. int. Menn. (SS2 10 *TX* 9: 4006–14) ALFRED WELLS, b. ca. 1859, AR. int. Barker. (S1 11 *AR* 7: 82) EASTER WELLS, b. 1854, AR. Taken TX 1855. Held in bondage postwar. (S1 7 *OK*: 316–21) SARAH WILLIAMS WELLS, b. 1866, Murray Co., TN. Child of ex-slaves. int. Robertson. (S2 11 *AR* 7: 94–95) JOHN WESLEY, b. ca. 1840, Lexington, KY. Taken Madison, AR during war. Held in bondage four years postwar. int. Robertson. (S2 11 *AR* 7: 96–97) JAMES WEST, b. 1854, Tippah Co., MS. Collected firewood, carried water. Stayed on plantation after freedom, then farmed MS, TN. Moved TX 1885, living Fort Worth. int. Gauthier. (S1 5 *TX* 4: 150–52; SS2 10 *TX* 9: 4017–23) NANCY WHALLEN, b. ca. 1857, Hart Co., KY. int. Cook. (S1 6 *IN*: 209–10) WILLIAM WHEELER, b. ca. 1855, Lexington, MS. Fieldhand. int. Ellison. (SS1 10 *MS* 5: 2272–75) ADELINE WHITE, b. ca. 1857, Opelousas, LA. Creole. Yard, house work. int. Dibble. (S1 5 *TX* 4:

153–54; SS2 10 *TX* 9: 4024–28) UNCLE BACCHUS WHITE, b. 1852, Spotsylvania Co., VA. Fieldhand, spinner. Farmed postwar. int. Gordon. (*WW*, 302–7) CLARA WHITE, b. 1859, Baton Rouge, LA. Moved TX 1870s, worked turpentine, farmed, domestic. int. L. Hatcher. (SS2 10 *TX* 9: 4029–32) UNCLE DAVE WHITE, b. ca. 1842, Charleston, SC. int. Addison. (S1 3 *SC* 4: 191–95) ELIZA (LIZA) WHITE, b. ca. 1855, Columbus, GA. House servant. int. Klein, ed. Clark. (S1 6 *AL*: 411–12; SS1 1 *AL*: 443–45) GEORGE WHITE, b. 1847, Danville, VA. Fieldhand. Postwar farmed, moved Lynchburg 1887, still working store. int. Lee. (*WW*, 309–12) JACK WHITE, b. 1857, Jasper, TX. Fieldhand. int. L. Hatcher. (SS2 10 *TX* 9: 4033–36) JOHN WHITE, b. April 10, 1816, Linden, TX. Fieldhand. Held in bondage postwar. Later moved TX, AR, LA, MS, OK. (S1 7 *OK*: 322–29) JULIA A. WHITE, b. 1858, AR. int. Hagg. (S2 11 *AR* 7: 109–19) MARIA WHITE, b. 1853, Kosciusko, MS. Nursemaid. int. C Campbell. (SS 10 *MS* 5: 2276–81) MINGO WHITE, b. unk., Chester, SC. Age five taken Alabama. Fieldhand, sharecropped after freedom. int. Shelby. (S1 *AL*: 413–22) SALLAH WHITE, b. ca. 1845, TN. Nursemaid. Stayed on plantation postwar. int. Minnick. (SS1 5 *OH*: 461–63) TENA WHITE, b. ca. 1845, SC. Washed, cooked, nursed. int. Pinckney. (S1 3 *SC* 3: 196–98) OPHELIA WHITLEY, b. 1841, Wake Co., NC. int. Hicks, ed. Waitt. (S2 15 *NC* 2: 371–75) SYLVESTER SOSTAN WICKLIFFE, freeborn 1854, St. Mary's Parish, LA. Creole. Blacksmith, opened smithy Lafayette 1870s. Moved Liberty, TX 1890, established smithy, cotton gin. int. Dibble, Grey. (S1 5 *TX* 4: 155–59; SS2 10 *TX* 9: 4037–45) JAMES WIGGINS, b. 1850 or 1851, Anne Arundel Co., MD. House servant, dancer. (S2 16 *MD*: 66–7) DOCK WILBORN, b. January 7, 1843, Huntsville, AL. Taken Phillips Co., AR 1850s. int. W. McKinney. (S2 11 *AR* 7: 142–46) JANE McLEOD WILBURN, b. ca. 1850, Lafayette Springs, MS. Taken Oxford. House servant, nursemaid. Washed, ironed postwar. int. Holt. (SS1 10 *MS* 5: 2283–96) TOM WILCOX, b. March 18, 1856, Warren Co., NC.

Fieldhand. Farmed postwar. int. Hicks, ed. Waitt. (S2 15 *NC* 2: 376–79) ALICE WILKINS, b. 1855, Limestone Co., TX. Farmed postwar. int. Cowan. (SS2 10 *TX* 9: 4046–56) GREEN WILLBANKS, b. 1861, Jackson Co., GA. Stayed on plantation as sharecropper postwar. int. Hornsby, ed. Hall, Booth. (S2 13 *GA* 4: 136–47) ANDERSON WILLIAMS, b. December 6, 1849, Chickasaw Co., MS. Fieldhand. int. Butts. (SS1 10 *MS* 5: 2297–2301) ANDY WILLIAMS, b. May 2, 1859, Limestone Co., TX. Fed hogs, carried water. Postwar cooked Waco. int. A. Davis. (SS2 10 *TX* 9: 4065–76) BESSIE WILLIAMS, b. 1859, Sumter Co., AL. Left 1880s, moved MS, cooked. int. M. Austin. (SS1 10 *MS* 5: 2302–3) CALLIE WILLIAMS, b. 1861, Lowndes Co., AL. int. Poole. (S1 6 *AL* 1: 425–28; SS1 1 *AL*: 448–53) CATHERINE WILLIAMS, b. December 25, 1851, VA. Taken Raleigh, NC age four. int. Matthews, ed. Waitt. (S2 15 *NC* 2: 380–84) CHANEY MOORE WILLIAMS, b. ca. 1852–d. June 11, 1937, Simpson Co., MS. Stayed on plantation postwar. int. Giles. (SS1 10 *MS* 5: 2304–5) CHARLES WILLIAMS, b. unk., Adams Co., MS. Fieldhand. (SS2 1 *AR*: 179–249) REVEREND CHARLES WILLIAMS, b. 1859, Greenbrier Co., WV. Graduated Freedman's Aid College, New Orleans (1887), ordained Methodist minister, pastored KY, MO, OH. int. Logan. (S2 16 *OH*: 111–13; SS1 5 *OH*: 468–72) CHARLEY WILLIAMS, b. January 11, 1843, Homer, LA. Fieldhand. Moved KS 1883, Tulsa 1913. (S1 7 *OK*: 330–43) COLUMBUS WILLIAMS, b. 1841, Union Co., AR. Fieldhand. Sharecropped postwar. int. S. Taylor. (S2 11 *AR* 7: 154–58) FRANK WILLIAMS, b. 1852, Aberdeen, MS. Drove mules, stock, worked plantation still. Held in bondage postwar. Escaped, worked riverboats, bought farm with father. int. Kolb. (SS1 10 *MS* 5: 2313–21) FRANK WILLIAMS, b. ca. 1835, MS. int. S. Taylor. (S2 11 *AR* 7: 159–60) GUS WILLIAMS, b. ca. 1857, Chatham Co., GA. Postwar moved TN, AR 1885, worked steamboats, janitor, worked for WPA. int. Lucy. (S2 11 *AR* 7: 161–62) JOHN WILLIAMS, b. August 2, 1862, Greene Co., MS. int. Walsh. (SS1 10 *MS* 5: 2326–33) JOHN

THOMAS WILLIAMS, b. December 25, 1860, Wilmington, NC. Stayed on plantation postwar. Farmed NC, domestic New York. int. Matthews, ed. G. Andrews. (S2 15 *NC* 2: 390–93) JULIA WILLIAMS, b. ca. 1837, Chesterfield Co., VA. int. Lees. (S2 16 *OH*: 102–10; SS1 5 *OH* 2: 473–76) LEWIS WILLIAMS, b. 1851, Milam, TX. Jockey. Farmed postwar. int. Shirley. (SS2 10 *TX* 9: 4093–95) LIZZIE WILLIAMS, b. ca. 1847, Selma, AL. House servant. Left 1882, moved NC. int. M Jones. (S2 15 *NC* 2: 394–400) LIZZIE WILLIAMS, b. June 1, 1849, Grenada Co., MS. Weaver, fieldhand. Stayed on plantation postwar. int. Butts. (SS1 10 *MS* 5: 2334–38) LOU WILLIAMS, b. 1829, MD. Nursemaid. Stayed on plantation after freedom, later moved LA, San Angelo, TX. (S1 5 *TX* 4: 166–69; SS2 10 *TX* 9: 4096–4101) MILLIE WILLIAMS, b. April 1851, Middle TN. Sold, taken Lancaster, TX. House servant, fieldhand. int. Colbert. (S1 5 *TX* 4: 170–73; SS2 10 *TX* 9: 4109–16) MOLLIE WILLIAMS, b. September 15, 1853, Hinds Co., MS. Fieldhand. int. England. (S1 7 *MS* 2: 157–64; SS1 10 *MS* 5: 2343–51) NANCY WILLIAMS, b. 1847, NC. Fieldhand. int. E. Wilson, C. Anderson. (*WW* 315–23) OLIN WILLIAMS, b. ca. 1840, Watkinsville, GA. Odd jobs. Stayed on plantation postwar. int. McCune, ed. Hall. (SS1 4 *GA* 2: 642–48) PARSON REZIN WILLIAMS, b. March 11, 1822, Prince George Co., MD. Fieldhand, Civil War veteran. Postwar preached, odd-jobbed. (S2 16 *MD*: 68–78) ROBERT WILLIAMS, b. 1843, Lynchburg, VA. Fieldhand, cart driver, leased to Norfolk & Southern Railroad. int. Lee. (*WW*, 323–26) SOLDIER WILLIAMS (WILLIAM BALL WILLIAMS III), b. 1839, Greensburg, KY. Runaway, joined Union army, wounded, receiving military pension. int. Robertson. (S2 11 *AR* 7: 191–92) SOUL WILLIAMS, b. 1841, MS. Taken TX while young. Groom, carriage driver. int. B. Davis. (SS2 10 *TX* 9: 4131–34) STEVE WILLIAMS, b. 1855, Goliad Co., TX. Stayed on plantation as sharecropper postwar, then farmed other places, cooked San Angelo. (S1 5 *TX* 4: 179–81) VICTORIA WILLIAMS, b. unk., MS. int. Posey. (*MW*, 211–12) WAYMAN

WILLIAMS, b. unk., MS. Taken Crockett, TX prewar. Fieldhand. Stayed on plantation as sharecropper postwar. int. Cowan. (S1 5 *TX* 4: 182–86; SS2 10 *TX* 9: 4142–53) WILLIAM WILLIAMS, b. April 14, 1857, Caswell Co., NC. int. McCulloh. (S2 16 *OH*: 114–16) WILLIE WILLIAMS, b. 1859, Vermillion Parish, LA. Moved TX 1867. (S1 5 *TX* 4: 187–89; SS2 10 *TX* 9: 4154–60) WILLIS WILLIAMS, b. September 15, 1856, Tallahassee. Railway mail clerk after freedom, transferred Jacksonville 1879, retired 1919. int. Muse. (S2 17 *FL*: 347–54) MELISSA WILLIAMSON, b. June 15, 1849, Franklin Co., NC. House servant. int. Hicks, ed. Waitt. (S2 15 *NC* 2: 410–13) FRANCES WILLINGHAM, b. 1859, Twiggs Co., GA. int. Hornsby, ed. Hall, L. Harris, Booth. (S2 13 *GA* 4: 151–60) ADELINE WILLIS, b. ca 1837, Washington-Wilkes Co., GA. int. Stonestreet. (S2 13 *GA* 4: 161–67) CHARLES WILLIS, b. ca. 1845, Lawrence Co., MS. Carried cotton horseback to gin. Moved IT 1891. Farmed. (SS1 12 *OK*: 397–99) CHARLOTTE WILLIS, b. ca. 1875, MS. Child of ex-slaves. int. Robertson. (S2 11 *AR* 7: 198–200) ELLA WILLIS, b. 1837, Atlanta, GA. Nursemaid. After freedom moved LA, AR, hired out, cooked. int. S. Taylor. (S2 11 *AR* 7: 201–6) SAMPSON WILLIS, b. ca. 1843, KY. Taken Rusk, TX prewar. House servant, odd jobs. int. Shirley. (SS2 10 *TX* 9: 4161–67) EMOLINE WILSON, b. 1847, Newberry Co., SC. House servant, fieldhand. int. Summer, ed. Turnage. (S1 3 *SC* 4: 213–15) ISAAC WILSON, b. ca. 1845, Simpson Co., MS. Fieldhand. Farmed postwar. int. Giles. (SS1 10 *MS* 5: 2360–62) JAKE WILSON, b. October 12, 1855, GA. Taken McLennan Co., TX during war. House servant. int. A. Davis. (SS2 10 *TX* 9: 4172–81) JAMES WILSON, b. December 25, 1850, Charleston, SC. Worked slaveholder's transatlantic ships. Postwar worked steamboats, railroad. Eventually settled St. Louis. (S2 11 *MO*: 371–72) LUKE WILSON, b. ca. 1860, Yazoo Co., MS. House servant, carriage driver. Stayed on plantation postwar. int. Walsh. (SS1 10 *MS* 5: 2363–68) ROBERT WILSON, b. 1836, Halifax Co., VA. Fieldhand. Postwar moved Memphis, cooked, preached. (S2 11 *AR* 7:

207–9) SARAH WILSON, b. unk., LA. Taken TX during war. Nursemaid. Sharecropped postwar. int. A. Davis. (SS2 10 *TX* 9: 4216–25) SHACK WILSON, b. ca. 1860, Clinton, LA. Fieldhand. int. Posey. (*MW*, 213–16) TEMPLE WILSON, b. ca. 1857, Madison Co., MS. Left 1876, homesteaded. int. Giles. (SS1 10 *MS* 5: 2369–75) WASH WILSON, b. ca. 1843, LA. Sold, taken TX during war. Tenant postwar. int. A. Davis. (S1 5 *TX* 4: 195–200; SS2 10 *TX* 9: 4236–48) DICY WINDFIELD, b. ca. 1843, Bolton, MS. House servant. int. Giles. (SS1 10 *MS* 5: 2381–86) TOM WINDHAM, b. 1845, IT. Creek slave. House servant. Sold and taken Atlanta 1858, conscripted Sherman's army. int. Bowden. (S2 11 *AR* 7: 210–15) WILLIS WINN, b. March 10, 1822, Homer, LA. Fieldhand, teamster. Postwar moved AR, TX. Fiddled, prospected, farmed, sawmilled, roadwork. int. Hampton. (S1 5 *TX* 4: 201–7; SS2 10 *TX* 9: 4249–57) ALICE WISE, b. 1858, SC. House servant. int. Bowden. (S2 11 *AR* 7: 216–17; SS2 1 *AR*: 252) RUBE WITT, b. August 10, 1850, Harrison Co., TX. House servant, cook. Moved Marshall postwar. int. Hampton. (S1 5 *TX* 4: 208–10; SS2 10 *TX* 9: 4260–64) GEORGE WOMBLE, b. 1843, Clinton, GA. House servant. Held in bondage postwar. Escaped, established blacksmith shop, worked store, finally settled Atlanta. int. Driskell. (S2 13 *GA* 4: 179–93; SS1 4 *GA* 2: 653–57) MINTIE GILBERT WOOD, b. September 9, 1847, Giles Co., TN. Fieldhand, nursemaid. Left 1892. Worked AR, TN, MO, settled St. Louis 1922. (S2 11 *MO*: 373–77) JULIA WOODBERRY, b. ca. 1865, Marion, SC. Child of ex-slaves. int. R. Davis. (S1 3 *SC* 4: 227–46; SS1 11 *SC*: 214–15) JULIA WOODRICH, b. 1851, Lafourche Crossing, LA. House servant. int. McElwee. (*MW*, 217–18) ALEX WOODS, b. May 15, 1858, NC. int. Matthews, ed. Waitt. (S2 15 *NC* 2: 414–19) ANDA WOODS, b. ca. 1841, Perry Co., AL. Fieldhand. Stayed on plantation postwar. int. Giles. (SS1 10 *MS* 5: 2388–91) GEORGE WOODS, b. ca. 1842, York Co., SC. Fieldhand. int. DuPre, ed. Kennedy. (S1 3 *SC* 4: 247–52) RUBEN WOODS, b. ca. 1853, Talladega Co., AL. int. Elliott. (S1 5 *TX* 4: 211–13; SS2 10 *TX* 9:

4172–76) TOM W. WOODS, b. 1854, Florence, AL. After war moved AR, IT. (S1 7 *OK*: 354–58) ALEX WOODSON, b. ca. 1850, Hart Co., KY. int. Cook. (S1 6 *IN*: 214–17) WILLIS WOODSON (WOODSEN), b. unk., place unk. Brought to Texas before war. House servant. (S1 5 *TX* 4: 214–15; SS2 10 *TX* 9: 4277–80) ALECK WOODWARD, b. ca. 1854, Woodward Station, SC. Fieldhand. int. W. Dixon. (S1 3 *SC* 4: 253–56) SAM WORD, b. February 14, 1859, De Witt, AR. Farmed postwar. int. Bowden. (S2 11 *AR* 7: 235–41) SOPHIA WORD, b. February 2, 1837, Clay Co., KY. int. Pearl House. (S2 16 *KY*: 66–68) PAULINE WORTH, b. November 1, 1859, SC. House servant. int. R. Davis. (S1 3 *SC* 4: 260–65) ALICE WRIGHT, b. ca. 1863, AL. Postwar fieldwork, washed, ironed. int. Taylor. (S2 11 *AR* 7: 245–48) ANNA WRIGHT, b. 1865, Scotland Co., NC. Child of ex-slaves. int. Hicks, ed. G. Andrews. (S2 15 *NC* 2: 420–44) CAROLINE WRIGHT, b. ca. 1847, Baton Rouge, LA. House servant. int. Arnold. (S1 5 *TX* 4: 219–22; SS2 10 *TX* 9: 4281–86) HENRY WRIGHT, b. 1838, Buckhead, GA. Picked up chips, made fires, toted water, fieldwork. Stayed on plantation seven years postwar as sharecropper. Moved Atlanta. int. Driskell. (S2 13 *GA* 4: 194–204) MAGGIE WRIGHT, b. ca. 1855, Newberry Co., SC. ed. Turnage. (SS1 11 *SC*: 316–18) MARY WRIGHT, b. August 1, 1865, Gracey, KY. Child of ex-slaves. Hired out, housemaid. int. M. D. H. (S2 16 *KY*: 61–66) SUSANNAH WYMAN, b. May 15, 1833, Troy, SC. Spinner, fieldhand. int. Barragan. (SS1 4 *GA* 2: 660–65)

FANNIE YARBOROUGH, b. ca. 1854, Kaufman Co., TX. Shepherdess, weaver. int. Phipps. (S1 5 *TX* 4: 225–26; SS2 10 *TX* 9: 4292–93) VIRGINIA YARBOROUGH, b. ca. 1860, Rapides Parish, LA. Fieldhand. Left plantation 1876, still running rooming house. int. Gauthier. (SS2 10 *TX* 9: 4294–99) HILLIARD YELLERDAY, b. April 6, 1861, MS. Taken Warren Co., NC during war to avoid advancing Union troops. After war sharecropped Halifax, Wake Cos., box packer, machinist's helper S. A. L. Railroad 1903–20. int. Matthews, ed. G. Andrews.

(S2 15 NC 2: 431–36) ANNIE YOUNG, b. 1851, Summers Co., TN. Mother sold away. House servant, yard work. Postwar farmed AR. Moved IT 1895. (S1 7 *OK*: 359–62) BOB YOUNG, b. March 15, 1862, Union, SC. Fieldhand. Stayed on plantation postwar. int. Sims, ed. Turnage. (S1 3 *SC* 4: 273–75) CLARA C. YOUNG, b. ca. 1842, Huntsville, AL. Sold 1860, taken Aberdeen, MS. House servant, fieldhand. int. Kolb. (S1 7 *MS*: 169–74; SS1 10 *MS* 5: 2400–2406) DINK WALTON YOUNG, b. unk., Talbot Co., GA. int. J. Jones. (SS1 4 *GA* 2: 666–69) GEORGE YOUNG, b. August 10, 1846, Livingston, AL. Fieldhand. Farmed postwar. int. Tartt. (S1 6 *AL*: 432–36) JOHN YOUNG, b. ca. 1845, Monticello, AR. Fieldhand. Runaway, drummer Union army. Postwar worked steamboat *Kate Adams*, farmed AR. int. Bowden. (S2 11 *AR* 7: 255–57) JOHN I. YOUNG, b. July 4, 1995, Newberry, SC. Stayed on plantation after freedom. (SS1 5 *OH*: 482–89) LITT YOUNG, b. 1850, Vicksburg, MS. Taken Harrison Co., TX 1865. Fieldhand. Postwar sawmilled, cut ties and firewood and worked as section hand T&P railroad, farmed. int. Hampton. (S1 5 *TX* 4: 227–31; SS2 10 *TX* 9: 4300–306) NARCISSUS YOUNG, b. 1841, Nashville, TN. House servant. (S2 16 *TN*: 80–81) ROBERT YOUNG, b. May 15, 1844, Crystal Springs, MS. House servant. Farmed postwar. int. England. (SS1 10 *MS* 5: 2407–13) TESHAN YOUNG, b. ca. 1852, Harrison Co., TX. Nursemaid. int. Gauthier. (S1 5 *TX* 4: 235–37; SS2 10 *TX* 9: 4316–21)

FRANK ZIEGLER, b. unk., Robinson Spring, AL. Odd jobs, fieldhand. (SS1 1 *AL*: 464–68)

INTERVIEWERS, WRITERS, AND EDITORS
(Known black workers are marked *B. Most others are known to be white.)

Addison = Samuel Addison *B (SC); Allen = Allen (OK); Allison = W. B. Allison (MS); C. Anderson = Claude W. Anderson *B (VA); P. Anderson = Pernella M. Anderson *B (AR); G. Andrews = George L. Andrews (NC); J. Andrews = Janie Mae Andrews (MS); Angermiller = Florence Angermiller (TX);

Arguedas = Jeanne Arguedas (LA); Arnold = Mrs. Edgerton Arnold (TX); Aucuin = Pierre Aucuin (LA); M. Austin = Marjorie Woods Austin (MS) R. Austin = Rachel A. Austin (FL)

Babcock = Barbara Babcock (AR); Baham = Rouceive Baham (LA); Ball = Mrs. W. M. Ball (AR); Barker = Martin Barker (AR); Barragan = Maude Barragan (GA); Barton = Alice L. Barton (AL); Beehler = Rheba Beehler (TX); Bell = Velma Bell (GA); Bishop = Bishop (OH); Blease = Florence Blease (GA); Booth = John N. Booth (GA); Bowden = Bernice Bowden (AR); Bradley = Elizabeth Bradley (MS); Bridges = Lucille Bridges (GA); Browning = Leonard T. Browning (TX); E. Burke = Edmond Burke (LA); G. Burke = Estelle G. Burke (GA); Burks = Albert J. Burks (NE); Butts = Vera Butts (MS); B. Byrd = Billie Byrd (OK); I. Byrd = Ima Byrd (MO); S. Byrd = Susan R. C. Byrd *B (VA)

Campbell = Carrie Campbell (MS); Carlisle = Henrietta Carlisle (GA); Carlow = Maggie Carlow (TX); Chandler = Genevieve W. Chandler (SC); Chitty = Ruth Chitty (GA); Clark = Luther Clark (AL); Colbert = Joe W. Colbert (TX); Colvin = K. K. Colvin (OH); Cook = Iris Cook (IN); Cooley = Mrs. Jessie Cooley (MS); Copeland = Cecil Copeland (AR); Couric = Gertha Couric (AL); Cowan = Effie Cowan (TX); Crawford = Mary A. Crawford (GA); Creel = Lauana Creel (IN); Crow = E. C. Crow (AL)

Daniel = Mrs. Eli Daniel (MO); Darsey = Barbara Darsey (FL); Dauphin = M. M. Dauphin (GA); A. Davis = Ada Davis (TX); B. Davis = B. E. Davis (TX); H. Davis = H. Grady Davis (SC); R. Davis = Annie Ruth Davis (SC); de Sola = Esther de Sola (MS); Diard = Francois Ludgere Diard (AL); Dibble = Fred Dibble (TX); Dickinson = J. L. Dickinson (TX); A. Dixon = Adella S. Dixon (GA); W. Dixon = W. W. Dixon (SC); Drake = C. H. Drake (TX); Driskell = Edwin F. Driskell *B (GA); Dugan = Albert I. Dugan (OH); Dulaney = Ethel C. Dulaney (TX); Dunston = Thelma Dunston *B (VA); DuPre = F. S. DuPre (SC); Dupuy = Vera Dupuy (LA)

Elliott = Elliott (TX); Ellison = Ann C. Ellison (MS); England = Iris England (MS); J. Ervin = Jessie Ervin (OK); W. Ervin = Wm. J. Ervin (TX)

NARRATORS INDEX 693

Farell = Alfred Farell (FL); Faucette = Phoebe Faucette (SC); Faulton = Annie L. Faulton (OK); FC = F. C. (MO); Ferriss = Abbott Ferriss (MS); Fichlen = Edward Fichlen (GA); Fitchett = Eva Fitchett (SC); Foreman = Heloise M. Foreman (TX); C. Fowler = Corry Fowler (GA); M. Fowler = Margaret Fowler (AL); Freeman = Martha Freeman (IN)

Garrison = Ethel Wolfe Garrison (OK); Gaston = Marvin F. Gaston (WA); Gauthier = Sheldon F. Gauthier (TX); Gibson = Ethel Gibson (OK); Giles = Mrs. D. W. Giles (MS); Gordon = Sue K. Gordon (VA); Graff = Graff (OH); Graham = Carol N. Graham (AR); Grant = Henry Grant (SC); Gray = Leta Gray (KS); Green = Hazel B. Green (OK); Grey = Bernice Grey (TX); Griffith = Frances Griffith (MS)

Hagg = Beulah Sherwood Hagg (AR); Hale = N. Hale (TX); Hall = Sarah H. Hall (GA); Halpert = Herbert Halpert (MS); Hamilton = Mabel M. Hamilton (TX); Hamlin = Gyland H. Hamlin (SC); Hampton = Alex Hampton (TX); Hanberry = Mamie Hanberry (KY); B. Harris = B. K. Harris (NC); L. Harris = Leila Harris (GA); L. Hatcher = Letha K. Hatcher (TX); R. Hatcher = Richard K. Hatcher (TX); Hays = Samuel Hays Jr. (MS); Henderson = Charles Ray Henderson (MS); Herman = H. H. Herman (TX); Hicks = Mary A. Hicks (NC); Higgins = S. Higgins (KY); Hinkle = Bernard Hinkle (MO); Hix = Pigie T. Hix (AL); Hoggard = David Hoggard *B (VA); Holm = Stanley H. Holm (TX); Holmes = Mrs. Wm. F. Holmes (MS); Holt = Minnie S. Holt (MS); Hornsby = Sadie B. Hornsby (GA); Horton = Josephine Horton (MS); House = Pearl House (KY); Huff = Ruby Huff (MS); Hunter = Ida Belle Hunter (OK)

Ison = Eliza Ison (KY)

N. Jackson = Neil C. Jackson (OH); Q. Jackson = Nell Q. Jackson (OH); Jaffe = Joseph E. Jaffe (GA); Jayne = Lucille B. Jayne (VA); J. Johnson = James M. Johnson (FL); M. Johnson = Margaret Johnson (GA); J. M. Johnson = J. M. Johnson (FL); Joiner = Mrs. Ed Joiner (MS); J. Jones = J. R. Jones (GA); L. Jones = Lenneth Jones (KY); M. Jones = Marjorie Jones (NC); T. Jordan = Travis Jordan (NC); W. Jordan = W. F. Jordan (AL)

Kennedy = E. Fronde Kennedy (SC); Klein = Preston Klein (AL); Kolb = Mrs. Richard Kolb (MS); Koritz = Archie Koritz (IN); Kytle = Jack Kytle (AL)

Lackey = R. Vinson Lackey (OK); Ladson = Augustus Ladson (SC); Lawrence = Lois B. Lawrence (MS); Lee = William T. Lee *B (VA); Lees = Forest H. Lees (OH); Lenoir = Evelyn Lenoir (MS); B. Lewis = Bernice Lewis (VA); R Lewis = Roscoe Lewis *B (VA); L. H. = L. H. (AL); Liberato = Mary E. Liberato (TX); Logan = Miriam Logan (OH); Love = Edith Bell Love (GA); Lucy = Thomas Elmore Lucy (AR)

Majette = George E. Majette *B (VA); Major = Lettie Major (TX); Martin = Clothilde R. Martin (SC); Martin-Barker = Martin-Barker (AR); Marzoni = Patterson Marzoni (AL); Matthews = T. Pat Matthews (NC); Mays = Wm. R. Mays (IN); McCulloh = Chas. McCulloh (OH); McCune = Grace McCune (GA); McElwee = Flossie McElwee (LA); R. McKinney = Robert McKinney (LA); W. McKinney = Watt McKinney (AR); M. D. H. = M. D. H. (KY); Meighen = Audrey Meighen (OH); Menn = Alfred E. Menn (TX); Michinard = Harriette Michinard (LA); Miles = J. Tom Miles (MO); Miller = Miss Sallie C. Miller (AR); Mills = John P. Mills (AL); Minnick = Minnick (OH); Minor = Alberta Minor (GA); Mobley = Hattie Mobley (SC); Moore = Edith Wyatt Moore (MS); Mueller = Mabel E. Mueller (MO); Murray = C. S. Murray (SC); Muse = Viola B. Muse (FL)

Nelson = Nelson (MO); R. Nelson = Robert L. Nelson (GA); Newton = Annie Lee Newton (GA); Nixon = Felix Nixon (TX)

O'Brien = Susie R. O'Brien (AL); Oden = Demps A. Oden (AL); Oliphant = Louise Oliphant *B (GA); Osburn = Lois Osburn (TX); Osthimer = K. Osthimer (OH)

Pack = Margaret L. Pack (MS); Peel = Zilla Cross Peel (AR); Perry = Rhussus L. Perry (AL); Pettigrew = C. W. Pettigrew (AR); Phipps = Woody Phipps (TX); Pierce = Everett R. Pierce (SC); Pinckney = Martha S. Pinckney (SC); Poole = Mary A. Poole (MS) ; Posey = Zoe Posey (LA); Powell = Emily Powell (GA); Price = Ruth W. Price (MS); Prine = Ila B. Prine (AL); Pritchett = Anna Pritchett *B (IN); Probst = Sarah Probst (OH)

Radford = Ruby Lorraine Radford (GA); Randolph = Pearl Randolph *B (FL); Rice = B. S. Rice (SC); Richardson = Martin Richardson (FL); Ritter = Martha Ritter (SC); Roberts = Mattie B. Roberts (GA); Robertson = Miss Irene Robertson (AR); Rogers = Rogers (MD); Ross = Minnie B. Ross *B (GA); Russell = J. C. Russell (GA)

Savoy = Velma Savoy (TX); Scruggs = Stiles M. Scruggs (SC); Shelby = Levi D. Shelby Jr. *B (AL); Shirley = Aline Shirley (TX); Silver = Marietta Silver (VA); Sims = Caldwell Sims (SC); Simms = John A. Simms *B (FL); J. Smith = John Morgan Smith (AL); M. Smith = Mollie E. Smith (MO); W. Smith = William E. Smith (TX); Stonecipher = B. H. Stonecipher (IN); Stonestreet = Minnie Branham Stonestreet (GA); Strope = Albert Strope (IN); Summer = G. Leland Summer (SC)

Taleman = Taleman (OH); Tartt = Ruby Pickens Tartt (AL); C. Taylor = Cora N. Taylor (FL); H. Taylor = Hattie Taylor (GA); S. Taylor = Samuel S. Taylor *B (AR); Thomas = J. S. Thomas (OK); N. Thompson = Netty Fant Thompson (MS); R. Thompson = Ruth Thompson (OH); Tiedman = Cassels R. Tiedman (SC); Tipton = Bertha P. Tipton (OK); Tonsill = Geneva Tonsill (GA); Turnage = Elmer Turnage (SC); Tuttle = William Webb Tuttle (IN); Tyler = Velsie Tyler (IN)

Van Meter = Beulah Van Meter (IN); Volley = Isaiah Volley (VA); Vollmer = Craig Vollmer (OK)

Waitt = Daisy Bailey Waitt (NC); Walker = Norman Walker (TX); Wallace = Maude Wallace (LA); Walsh = Jean H. Walsh (MS); I. Warren = I. M. Warren (VA); M. Warren = Mildred Warren (TX); Watkins = Miss Nancy Watkins (NC); Watson = Elizabeth Watson (GA); Webb = J. E. Webb (OH); C. Wells = Mrs. Charles E. Wells (MS); R. Wells = Rose M. Wells (MS); White = Grace E. White *B (MO); Whitley = A. M. Whitley (GA); Wilkerson = J. R. Wilkerson (KY); E. Williams = Ellis Williams (NY); J. Williams = Jesse R. Williams (VA); E. Wilson = Emmy Wilson *B (VA); L. Wilson = L. W. Wilson (OK); Winter = Miss Sallie C. Winter (AR)

York = Byers York (KY); Young = Lucile Young (SC)

INDICES

Page numbers in *italics* indicate illustrations.

Ex-Slaves Interviewed by the WPA

Abrams, Geo. F., 597n3, 599n15, 599n20

Abromsom, Laura, 331, 336, 557, 616n24, 643n1

Adams, Frank L., 364, 366, 383, 446, 618n19

Adams, Louisa, 471

Adams, Rachel, 133, 600n20

Adams, Victoria, 88, 210

Adams, Will, 189, 597n3

Adams, William M., 85, 94, 173, 331, 458, 536, 573n1, 576n45, 576n51, 582n56, 595n15, 598n5, 641n47

Adway, Rose, 417, 575n23

Aldrich, Jacob, 596n32

Alexander, Alice, 269

Alexander, Diana, 326, 331, 616n24

Alexander, Lucretia, 326, 331, 336, 617n36

Alford, Barney, 234, 247, 248, 454, 473

Allen, Jim, 87, 92, 114–15, 133, 210, 226, 297, 366, 367, 429, 437, 598n5, 600n20, 602n45

Allen, Joseph, 93, 521

Allen, Martha, 221, 558–59

Allen, Rev. W. B., 116, 135, 327, 331, 390, 606nn9–10, 615n14, 624n55

Allen, Sarah, 600n18

Allen, W. C. Parson, 220, 598n5, 606n10, 616n35

Alston, Israel, 583n62, 593n62

Ammonds, Molly, 374–75, 617n1

Anderson, Charles, 488

Anderson, Charles Gabriel, 364

Anderson, Charles H., 12, 88, 204, 210, 581n53, 598n5

Anderson, Nancy, 93, 124, 213, 521

695

Anderson, Sam, 88, 90, 117, 132, 135, 597n3
Andrews, Cornelia, 498n4, 600n18
Anngady, Mary, 40, 88, 91, 92, 210, 374, 492–93, 570n5, 594n3, 632n21
Arbery, Katie, 88, 90, 91, 143, 144, 146, 211, 214, 215, 501, 524, 527, 634n48
Archer, Jim, 480–81, 524, 528
Armstrong, Campbell, 598n4, 600n20
Armstrong, Mary, 88, 618n13
Armstrong, Wash, 369, 624n51
Arnold, George W., 600n18
Arnwine, Stearlin, 502, 503
Arrington, Jane, 500, 633n43
Ashley, Sarah, 125, 132, 386, 403, 476
Ashton, Sally, 69, 88, 203, 211, 575n23, 577n68, 598n5
Atkins, Lizzie, 90, 94, 586n37, 597n3
Augustus, Sarah Louise, 117, 135
Aunt Adeline, 247, 248, 377–78
Aunt Clussey, 88, 216, 473, 613n32
Aunt Katherin, 91, 107, 213, 560
Austin, Charity, 330, 331, 376, 393, 619n42, 621n20
Austin, Hannah, 616n35
Austin, Lou, 31, 32
Austin, Smith, 623n44
Avery, Celestia, 82, 88, 135, 527, 600n19, 616n35

Babino, Agatha, 68, 88, 90, 165, 167–68, 233, 247, 249, 576nn50–51, 596n32, 598n4, 599n6, 610n35
Badgett, Joseph Samuel, 222
Baker, Anna, 606n10
Baker, Blount, 614n46
Baker, Georgia, 91, 142, 147, 173, 212, 279–80, 454, 575n23, 598n5, 600n15, 600nn19–20, 641n29
Baker, Henry "Father," 247, 250, 251, 570n29, 603n50, 641n34
Baker, Lizzie, 606n10, 616n35
Banjo, William, 43, 92, 159–60, 210, 371, 374
Banks, Ephom, 309
Banks, Frances, 424, 623n44
Banks, Sina, 367, 617n1
Barber, Charley, 84, 224, 458, 556, 576n51
Barber, Ed, 93, 245, 544
Barbour, Charlie, 88

Barclay, Delia, 389, 437–38, 440–41, 446, 454–55, 577n68, 578n70
Barclay, Jim, 429, 573n1
Barden, Melissa (Lowe), 630n19
Barnes, Berle, 90, 230
Barnes, Henry, 132, 280, 302, 361, 373
Barnes, Joe, 598n4
Barnes, Lucy, 331, 336–37
Barnes, Mariah, 308, 331, 616nn24–25
Barnett, Spencer, 132, 605n6
Barr, Emma, 326, 331, 336, 337, 617n36
Barr, Robert, 88, 207, 210, 265, 266
Barrett, Harriet, 586n37, 598n5
Basard, Elvira, 596n32
Bates, Anderson, 91, 432, 592n44
Batson, Frances, 373, 522
Battle, Alice, 90, 93, 179, 541, 598n4, 643n54
Battle, Jasper, 190, 598n4, 600n20
Baugh, Alice, 90, 92, 541, 600n20, 612n8, 623n44
Beckett, Harrison, 407
Bectom, John C., 190, 247, 251, 448, 600n18, 600n20, 607n22, 614n46
Bedford, Henry, 87, 88–89, 90, 92, 153
Bell, Anne, 383, 623n44
Bell, Bettie Massingale, 90, 91, 92, 154, 215, 381, 587n50, 632n29
Bell, Charlie, 86, 89, 90, 91, 93, 107
Bell, Eliza, 63, 92, 154, 216, 285
Bell, Frank (LA), 164, 526, 596n32
Bell, Frank (VA), 88, 575n26
Bell, Oliver, 325, 331, 332, 439, 465
Bell, Virginia, 123–24, 598n4
Bellus, Cyrus, 88, 189, 320, 331, 575n23
Bennefield, Uncle Willis, 270, 380, 381, 576n45
Benton, Sara, 124, 132, 302, 354, 370, 377, 597n3, 598n5, 600n20, 614n47
Berry, Fanny, 58, 60, 64, 68, 90, 125, 202, 212, 311, 475, 531, 535, 558, 561, 571n12, 576n50, 577n68, 629n13
Berry, Frank, 41
Bertrand, James, 88
Bess, Jack, 87–88, 172, 597n3, 614n46
Bethel, William L., 530
Bethune, Thomas Green (Blind Tom), 92, 210, 494n3

INDICES 697

Betters, Aunt Kate, 89, 92, 213, 580n34, 594n2

Betts, Ellen, 88, 176, 212, 220, 576n45, 576n50, 577n63

Beverly, Charlotte, *115*, 116, 132, 211, 270, 294, 325, 331, 354, 366, 597n3, 598n4, 623n41

Bibles, Della Mun, 615n14

Biddie, Mary Minus, 599n7, 600n18, 616n35

Binns, Arrie, 88, 364, 366, 403, 600n19, 613n31

Black, Francis, 436

Black, Maggie, 56, 94, 582n56

Black, William, 184, 389, 555, 575n43, 600n20, 632n29

Black, William Edward, 191

Blackwell, Willie (Uncle Bill), 84, 87, 88, 127, 135, 230–31, 247, 248, 249, 451, 543, 576nn50–51, 589n41, 600n20, 602n45, 605n34

Blake, Henry, 605n6

Blakeley, Sallie, 525, 616n35

Blakely, Adeline, 93, 124

Blalock, Emma, 9, 331, 337, 599n11, 600n20, 616n24

Blanchard, Olivier, 596n32

Bland, Henry, 81, 89, 90, 133, 211, 597n3

Blanks, Julia, 62

Bledsoe, Susan, 90, 199, 451, 575n23, 605n6

Blewitt, Peter, 498, 600n20

Bobbitt, Henry, 331, 332, 337, 342, 616n24, 616n30

Boggan, Manda, 89, 91, 279, 280, 587n49, 598n5

Bogie, Dan, 90

Boles, Elvira, 325

Bollinger, George, 600n20

Bolton, James, 20, 91, 93, 94, 133, 142, 145–46, 173, 180, 211, 354, 364, 446, 575n23, 597n3, 598nn4–5, 600n20, 618n31

Bond, Maggie (Bunny), 626n10

Bonner, Siney, 128, 266, 331, 332, 342, 615n12, 616n30

Boone, Andrew, 18, 467, 610n39

Boone, J. F., 17, 127, 132, 215, 617n3

Boone, Rev. Frank T., 135, 623n45

Bormer, Betty, 89, 90, 92, 153, *153*, 210, 215, 350, 575n40, 595n7, 598n4, 632n29

Bost, W. L., 227, 334, 394, 642n49

Bostwick, Alec, 19, 322, 370, 598n4, 606n10

Boudreaux, Felice. *See* Johnson, Pauline

Boudry, Nancy, 171, 268

Boulware, Samuel, 618n19

Bouy, Joe, 239, 575n23, 576n51, 598n5

Bowen, Jennie, 117, 135

Boyd, Isabella, 90, 94, 105, 575n23, 582n56

Boyd, James, 186, 558, 597n3, 600n20, 623nn44–45, 643n2

Boykins, Jerry, 81–82, 88, 135, 211, 215, 280, 599n7

Boynton, Rivana, 640n12

Bracey, Callie, 132

Bracey, Maria, 92, 308, 612n8

Bradford, Elodga, 523

Bradford, Sam, 88, 606n10

Bradley, Edmond, 163, 596n32

Bradley, Rachel, 508, 526, 612n15

Bradshaw, Gus, 606n10

Brady, Wes, 319, *320*, 331, 598n5, 617n36

Branch, Jacob, 386, 607n26, 622n33

Brass, Ellen, 541, 575n23

Bratcher, Minerva, 423–24, 614n47

Braxton, Louisia, 596n32

Brice, Amanda Eilers, 92

Brice, Andy, 66, 82, 88, 211, 215, 246–47

Bridges, Annie, 89, 91, 207, 211, 420, 456, 459, 513, 536

Bridges, Francis, 600n15, 600n20, 605n6

Briggs, George, 25, 369, 390, 430

Brim, Clara, 268, *269*, 353, 364, 380, 383

Bristow, Josephine, 600n20

Broach, Sam, 55–56, 89, 90, 200, 211, 442, 575n23, 576nn45–46

Broaddus, Henry, 31, 88

Broadus, Ned, 31–32, 576n45, 576n50

Brooks, James, 69, 211, 377n68

Brooks, Mary Ann, 454

Brooks, Sylvester, 31–32, 618n15

Broome, Anne, 242, 521, 624n51

Broomfield, Ellen, 418

Broussard, Donaville, 93, 165–66, *166*, 496n32, 598n4, 599n6, 610n35

Brown, Ben, 599n7

Brown, Calline, 228

Brown, Charlotte, 306, 311

Brown, Easter, 63, 135, 176, 436, 599n11

Brown, Ebenezer, 324–25, 431–32, 472, 478, 620n16, 630n33

Brown, Fannie, 88

Brown, Fred, 48, 90, 92, 94, 105, 168, *168*, 177, 571n12, 576n51, 597n39, 598n4, 599n11
Brown, Hagar (Hager), 130, 301, 306, 412, 558
Brown, Henry, 600n20
Brown, James, 89, 90, 173, 575n23, 610n35
Brown, John, 26
Brown, Julia (Sally), 175, 234, 247, 248
Brown, Lewis, 87, 89, 90, 92, 162, 331, 332, 338, 342, 343, 476, 575n23, 576n50, 587n39, 600n15, 600n20
Brown, Lizzie Fant, 226, 600n19, 605n6, 606n10, 616n22
Brown, Lucy, 331, 332, 616n24
Brown, Marie, 47, 49, 93, 94, 212, 294, 571n12, 572nn25–26, 596n32, 597n40, 613n32, 616n30, 616n32
Brown, Mary Frances, 359, 380, 389, 390, 398, 400, 402, 416, 419, 426, 617n1
Brown, Molly, 598n4
Brown, Mom Louisa, 444
Brown, Peter, 606n10
Brown, Rina, 88, 213, 239, 247, 248, 249, 452, 604n22
Brown, Rose, 450, 600n18, 600n20
Brown, Thomas, 90, 202, 211, 364, 598n5
Brown, Verice, 609n20
Brown, William, 221–22, 226, 605n6, 606n10
Browning, George Washington, 91, 141, 142, 600n2
Broyles, Maggie, 571n12
Bruin, Madison, 372, 417, 421, 424–25, 428, 439–40, 625n17
Bruner, Richard, 115, 132, 575n23, 614n46
Brunson, Vinnie, 32, 91, 144
Bryant, Robert, 158, 481–82, 585
Bufford, Henry (Uncle Eph), 281, 493, 631n6
Bunch, Julia, 91, 93, 149, 369, 402, 521, 599n7, 600n20
Bunts, Queen Elizabeth, 92, 123, 135, 156, 216, 600n18
Burns, George Taylor, 92, 93, 125, 128, 132, 483, 489, 500–501, 631n10, 634n48
Burton, C. B., 89, 91, 92, 142, 145, 146, 147
Bush, Sam, 206–7, 211, 577n68
Butler, Ellen, 324
Butler, Gabe, 48, 571n12, 597n3
Butler, Isaiah, 115, 132, 211
Butler, Marshal, 89, 225
Butlington, Charles, 354, 364, 369, 614n46

Byrd, Dave L., 90, 94, 105, 599
Byrd, Sarah, 90, 91, 94, 142, 146, 582

Cain, Louis, 89, 90, 94, 105, 136, 597n3, 598n5, 614n47
Caldwell, James, 599n11, 600n15, 600nn19–20
Calhoun, Jeff, 132, 238, 331, 338, 466, 598n4, 600n17, 600n20, 617n36
Cameron, John, 88, 92, 598n5
Cameron, Nelson, 92, 590
Camille, Harrison, 93, 572n26, 613n30
Campbell, Easter Sudie, 89, 568n20
Campbell, Ellen, 598n5
Campbell, Simpson, 73, 83, 88, 89, 91, 100, 211, 431, 598n5
Cancer, Polly Turner, 91, 570n1, 598n4, 605n6
Cannon, Sylvia, 13, 91, 113, 121–22, 123, 127, 135, 140, 297, 359, 369, 373, 385–86, 392–93, 396, 400, 416, 591n22, 642n50
Carder, Sallie, 135, 329, 331
Carpenter, Mary, 297, 403, 614n47
Carruthers, Uncle Richard, 88, 211, 305, 470–71, 576n45, 614n56, 616n35, 642n52
Carter, Aron, 374, 377, 598n4, 632n21
Carter, Cato, 40, *41*, 88, 118, 135, 225, 326, 331, 465, 600n20, 616n25
Carter, Mildred, 480
Caruthers, Belle, 348, 383–84
Casey, Julia, 364, 614nn46–47
Castle, Susan, 90, 103, 364, 597n3
Caulton, George, 62, 90, 91, 108, 575n23, 616n35
Cauthern, Jack, 614n46
Cawthon, Aunt Cicely, 44, 56, 70, 88, 120, 134, 178, 247, 248, 265, 373, 380–81, 469, 600n15, 600n20
Chambers, Lula, 241
Chambers, Sally Banks, 268
Chandler, Lizzie, 47, 60, 89, 92, 571n12, 577n68, 595n25
Chaney, Ned, 53, 84, 89, 90, 92, 94, 152, 211, 215, 410, 573n1, 577n68, 578n70, 582n56
Chapman, Aunt Amy, 357, 570, 576–77
Chapman, Walter, 90, 208, 212
Chappel, Cecelia, 132, 240, 247, 616n35, 634n48
Chatman, Callie, 386
Cheatam, Harriet, 326, 331, 616n24

Cheatam, Henry, 280, 464–65, 569n26, 599n7, 600n20

Cheatham, Robert J., 88, 214, 617n3

Chelsey, Harriet, 89, 91, 92, 108, 153, 298, 575n23, 597n3, 600n20

Chessier, Betty Foreman, 598n4, 605n6

Childers, Henry, 30, 577n68, 614n46

Childs, Mary, 88, 597n3

Choice, Jeptha (Doc), 88, 206, 214, 267, 373

Christopher, Anthony, 575n41

Claiborne, James, 448

Claibourn, Ellen, 88, 92, 153, 215, 595n7, 633n43

Clark, Amos, 88, 211, 214, 575n23, 577n68, 623n44

Clark, Anna, 88, 211, 493–94, 576n50

Clark, Fleming, 90, 135, 172, 600n15, 600n20

Clark, Laura, 421

Clark, Rena, 598n4, 613n32

Clay, Berry, 40, 89, 90, 606n10

Clay, Henry, 79, 88, 123, 135, 209, 211, 600n20

Clayton, Hattie, 65, 90, 174, 598n5, 623n41

Clemments (Clements), Maria Sutton, 93

Clifton, Peter, 597n3

Coates, Father Charles, 296, 616n35

Coates, Irene, 124, 132

Cobb, Frances, 600n15, 600n20, 614n47

Cody, Pierce, 89, 90, 598n4, 616n35

Cofer, Willis, 265, 268, 372, 373, 598n4, 600n20, 614nn46–47, 618n31

Coffee, Anna Marie, 56

Colbert, Mary, 367, 369, 375, 600n15, 600nn19–20, 625n5, 625n7

Cole, Alice, 90, 94, 586n37, 598n5, 614n47

Cole, Harrison, 32, 614n47, 623n45

Cole, John, 67, 85, 89, 94, 582n56, 598n5

Cole, Julia, 133, 215

Cole, Thomas, 115, 133, 614n47

Coleman, Eli, 90, 380, 598n5, 624n51

Coleman, George, 135

Coleman, Lula, 91, 105, 143, 146, 148, 199

Coleman, Preely, 39, 134, 303, 364

Coley, Annie, 280, 317, 407

Collier, Mom Louisa, 57, 88, 575n23, 600n20

Collins, Harriet, 311, 425

Colquitt, Kizzie, 600n20

Colquitt, Martha, 132, 178, 310, 598nn4–5, 600n15, 600n20

Colquitt, Sara, 125, 132, 216, 598n5, 600n20

Columbus, Andrew (Smoky), 269, 598n5

Compton, Jake, 380

Compton, Josephine Tippit, 30, 32, 89, 90, 91, 92, 94, 600nn18–19

Coney, Joe, 132

Conrad, George, 365, 541, 542, 643n43

Cooper, Charlie, 90, 94, 586n37, 598n5

Cooper, Frank, 606n10

Cooper, Lucius, 606n15

Cormier, Valmar, 88, 165, 165, 215, 596n32

Corn, Peter, 570n1

Corneal, Phannie, 411

Cornelius, Catherine, 488, 356–57, 373, 380–81

Cornelius, James, 134, 211, 216, 614n47

Cotton, Jane, 90, 598n5

Cottonham, John, 502, 514, 577n68

Cox, Albert, 389, 524n51

Cox, Elijah (Uncle Cox), 91, 109–11, 110, 211, 587n55

Cox, Julia, 302, 389

Coxe, Josephine, 227

Cozart, Willis, 598n4, 600n18, 600n20

Cragin, Ellen, 94, 569n26

Craig, Caleb, 631n6

Crasson, Hannah, 39, 44–45, 45, 93, 238, 521, 526, 570n1, 571n12, 600nn18–20, 616n35

Crawford, John, 64, 88, 92, 135, 152, 211, 325, 330–31, 365–66, 389, 398, 398, 428–29, 430, 474, 477, 575n40, 580n38, 598n5, 616n25

Crocker, Sara, 376, 393, 575n23, 600n19

Crockett, Emma, 295–96, 424

Crump, Adeline, 605n6

Crump, Bill, 88, 211, 266, 560, 600n18, 600n20

Cruze, Rachel, 392, 576n44, 600nn19–20, 613n29, 614n43

Cumby, Green, 54, 54, 180–81, 188, 350, 575n23, 600n20

Cummins, Tempie, 448, 625n1

Cunningham, Baily, 86, 89, 90, 93, 576n50

Cunningham, Martha, 600nn19–20

Curlett, Betty, 87, 91, 99, 126, 134, 135, 215, 460, 598n4, 600n15

Curry, Kate, 427
Curtis, William, 247, 250

Dandridge, Lyttleton, 490
Daniels, Ella, 221–22
Daniels, Julia Frances, 368–69, 450, 454, 466, 519, 581n53
Daniels, Parilee, 304, 354–55, 380, 614n47
Dant, Henry, 88, 201, 211
Dantzler, Juda, 41
Darling, Katie, 88, 171, 215, 225, 233, 234, 247, 248
Davenport, Carey, 236, 616n22
Davenport, Charlie, 42, 265, 559
Davenport, John N., 60, 468, 498, 574n9, 576n51, 633n32
Davidson, Hannah, 17, 92, 375–76, 524, 623n44, 643n54
Davis, Annie, 132
Davis, Campbell, 89, 90, 106, 124, 134, 350, 354, 361–62, 597n3, 598n5
Davis, Carrie, 122, 132, 182, 501, 598nn4–5, 614n47, 634n48
Davis, Charlie, 134, 366–67
Davis, Clara, 485
Davis, Heddie, 629n7
Davis, James (Jim), 68, 90, 96, 212, 272, 513, 577n68, 600n20, 606n10, 611n46
Davis, Jeff, 91, 93, 130–31, 150, 212
Davis, Jesse, 366–67, 368, 407, 615n14
Davis, Lizzie, 128, 309–10, 317, 361, 372, 399, 400, 406, 414–15, 431, 560–61, 591n10, 619n36, 622n31, 622n35, 623n46
Davis, Louis, 90, 91, 103, 132, 174, 176–77, 211, 549, 598n5, 600n20
Davis, Louisa, 88, 202, 211, 213, 558, 577n68
Davis, Lucinda, 42, 641n34
Davis, Mary Jane Drucilla, 420–21
Davis, Minnie, 242, 527–28, 543, 598n5, 600n15, 600nn18–20
Davis, Mose, 135
Davis, Tob, 88, 213, 452–53, 577n68, 598n5, 599n7
Davis, Uncle D., 88, 93, 215, 575n23, 575n40, 597n3, 598n5, 600n18
Davis, Wallace, 132, 598n5

Davis, William, 118, 135, 364, 380, 618n19, 624n55
Davis, William Henry, 599n11, 600n20
Davison, Elige, 90, 94, 586n37, 598n5
Dawkins, Jake, 88, 174, 280, 328, 598n4
Dawson, Anthony, 218, 233, 248, 575n23, 614n46
Dawson, Mollie, 441, 462
Deane, James V., 66, 73, 88, 89, 119, 134, 171, 183, 199, 212, 575n23, 575n40, 590n49, 598n4, 600n20, 626n13
Debnam, W. S., 600n20
Dell, Hammett, 88, 90, 91, 92, 139–40, 144, 145, 146, 147, 205, 212, 223–24, 228, 584n68, 593n52, 595n25, 599n11, 600n20, 605n6, 633n43
Denson, Nelson Taylor, 32, 89, 90, 93
Desso, Jake, 252, 453, 577n68, 578n70, 599n10
Dickerson, Nelson, 135, 195, 576n46, 599n11
Dill, Will, 591n10
Dillard, Benny, 17, 21, 180, 189, 412, 429, 600n20
Dillard, George, 90, 212, 577n63, 598n5
Discus, Mark, 624n51
Dixon, Alice, 70, 88, 313
Dixon, Bud, 368, 377
Dixon, Sally, 88, 93, 130, 351, 598n5, 643n54
Dixon, Tom, 614n46
Doby, Francis (Frances), 93, 128, 210, 264, 311, 439, 444, 569n26, 596n32
Dockery, Railroad, 268
Donald, Lucy, 89, 115, 122, 132, 256, 257, 262, 277, 455, 581n53
Donatto, Mary, 596n32
Dorroh, Isabella, 60, 264, 366, 598n5, 599n11
Dorsey, Douglas, 88, 575n23, 576n45
Dortch, Charles Green, 606n10
Dothrum, Silas, 22, 39, 555
Douglas, Hattie, 92, 158–59, 212
Douglas, Sarah, 364, 408, 606n17, 616n35
Douglas, Tom, 247, 630n21
Dowd, Reverend Squire, 17, 187, 188, 408, 600n20, 623n41, 623n44
Dozier (Dosier), Washington, 125, 132, 387–88, 390, 560
Dragney, Martin, 93, 94, 596n32, 597n40
Drake, Ann, 17, 44, 89, 238, 247, 249, 250, 407, 460, 499, 524, 600n18, 630n19, 633n43, 643n54

INDICES

Driver, Fannie McCulloh, 479, 527–28
Duhon, Victor, 596n32
Duke, Alice, 226
Duke, Isabella, 598n4
Duncan, Rachel, 614n46
Dunne, Nellie, 127, 134, 213
Dunwoody, William L., 93, 634n48, 641n34
Durham, Tempie Herndon, 92, 154, 598n4
Durr, Simon, 89, 91, 108, 351, 587n49

Eason, George, 598n4
Easter, Willis, 31, 212, 576n51, 577n68
Edmonds, Mollie, 464–65
Edmonson, Manda, 134
Edmunds, Rev. H. H., 225
Edwards, Anderson, 74, 89, 91, 140, 144, 323, 323, 331, 336, 339, 386, 421, 597n3, 598n5, 600n15, 600n20, 617n36
Edwards, Ann J., 91, 93, 149
Edwards, Mary (SC), 600n15, 600n20
Edwards, Mary (TX), 62, 88, 214, 323, 355, 380, 440, 577n68, 580n38
Edwards, Mary Kincheon, 164, 466, 476, 476, 548, 596n32
Edwards, Minerva, 323
Elder, Callie, 59, 176, 178, 185, 366, 437, 439, 477, 598n4, 600n15, 600n20, 625n5
Ellis, Bob, 480
Ellis, John, 598n4
Else, Amy, 419–20
Emmons, William, 412, 487–88, 490, 621n21, 624n50
Eppes, Katherine, 365–66, 439
Erwin, Cynthia, 7, 598n4, 599n7, 599n11, 600n18, 614n41, 643n54
Eubanks, Jerry, 62, 180, 195, 247, 260, 261, 277, 377, 477, 576n51, 598n4, 600n15, 600n20, 614nn46–47, 617n1, 624n51
Eubanks, Uncle Pen, 245–46, 247, 490, 544, 631n6
Eulenberg, Smoky, 598n5
Evans, Ann Ulrich, 366, 370, 380, 605n6
Evans, Eliza, 331, 337, 339, 598n4, 606n9, 616n25
Evans, Lawerence, 116–17, 135, 453, 457, 477
Evans, Lewis, 623n44

Evans, Louis, 40, 88, 165, 174, 575n23, 610n35, 643n54
Evans, Millie, 79, 88, 116, 117, 135, 445, 598n4, 606n15
Everette, Martha, 93, 598n5, 600n18
Ezell, Lorenza, 88, 90, 91, 125, 132, 212, 216, 227, 243–44, 334, 358, 364, 366–67, 389, 391, 404–5, 405, 529, 541–42, 559, 605n6, 613n38, 621n18, 635n15, 643n54

Fair, Eugenia, 600n15, 600n20
Fairly, Rachel, 331, 332, 598n4, 616n25
Fakes, Pauline, 226
Fambro, Hanna, 116, 135, 475
Fannen, Mattie, 135
Farmer, Lizzie, 443, 599n11, 600n15, 613n32
Farmer, Robert, 64, 576n45
Farrow, Caroline, 176, 390, 600n15, 600n20, 602n34
Favors (Favor), Lewis, 328, 617n11
Fayman, Mrs. M. S., 596n32
Feaster, Gus, 124, 135, 297, 353, 376, 409, 421, 458–59, 469, 502, 514, 521, 614n46, 621n20, 623n44
Felder, Sarah, 123, 324, 379–80, 416, 547, 598n5, 614n47
Ferguson, Aunt Mary, 324, 378, 546
Fields, Alphonse, 596n32
Finley, Elizabeth, 598n4
Finley, Molly, 46, 90, 91, 98, 328, 597n3
Finnely, John, 446
Finney, Fanny, 605n6
Flannigan, Lula, 92, 154, 215, 599n11, 600n18
Fleming, George, 89, 91, 132, 142, 144, 145, 146, 174, 181, 212, 501, 576n51, 598n4, 600n15, 600n20, 603n50, 634n48
Fletcher, Rebecca, 92, 157, 247, 370–71, 399, 424, 622n35
Flowers, Annie, 178, 473
Floyd, Fletcher, 280
Floyd, Sylvia, 56, 89, 90, 92, 162, 174, 247, 249, 353, 597n39, 606n10
Floyd, Tom, 60, 94, 392, 620n14
Fluker, Ida May, 233, 247
Folkes (Fulkes), Minnie, 22, 321, 331, 553, 598n4, 606n10, 616n24
Fontenette, Octavia, 596n32
Fonvergne, Anita, 164, 571n19
Force, Tinie, and Elvira Lewis, 13, 90, 91, 94, 641n37

Ford, Ellen Nora, 374
Ford, Laura, 120, 134, 303, 373, 616n35
Ford, Sarah, 497, *497*, 628n25, 633n32
Forge, Sam, 89, 573n1, 576n51, 577n65, 577n68
Forrest, Susan, 425–26
Fortenberry, Judia, 414, 622n31
Fortman, George, 482, 483, 500, 634n48
Foster, Emma, 603n50
Foster, Georgianna, 7, 331, 337, 339, 616n24, 643n54
Foster, Ira, 11
Fountain, Della, 570n1, 597n3, 599n11, 600nn19–20
Fowler, Louis, 88, 210, 213, 231, 247, 249, 272, 419
Fox, Ruben (Reuben), 7, 135, 524–25, 643n54, 643n56
Franklin, Chris, 58, 69–70, 160–61, 265, 576n51, 577n68
Franklin, Leonard, 227, 606n10
Franklin, Robert, 88, 359, 364, 367, 368, 373, 471, 600n20
Franks, Dora, 118, 135, 227, 247, 248, 499, 555–56, 598n4, 630n19, 633n43, 641n37
Franks, Orelia Alexie, 164, 299, *300*, 399, 596n32, 622n35
Franks, Uncle Pet, 614n47, 625n5
Fraser, Emma, 402–3, 600n20, 614n46
Frazier, Julia, 297, 317, 467–68, 575n23, 575n26, 597n3
Freeman, Aunt Mittie, 88, 356, 373
Freeman, Henry, 32, 91, 247
Frost, Adele, 430, 600n20
Fulcher, Fannie, 88, 174, 211
Furr, Anderson, 228, 351, 598n5, 599n11, 600n15, 600nn19–20

Gaffney, Mary, 90, 94, 586n37
Gaines, Duncan, 188, 616n35
Gaines, Mary, 569n26
Gaines, Rachel, 89, 204, 213, 598n5
Gallman, Lucy, 508
Galloway, Lucy, 126, 134, 240, 289, 325, 331, 332, 571n10, 598n4
Gant, William, 83, 88, 212, 349–50, 577n68, 599n11, 600n20
Gantling, Clayborn, 125, 132, 616n35, 617n3
Garey, Elisha (Doc), 39, 620n17
Garlic, Delia, 547, 599

Garner, Cornelius, 270, 365–66, 381, 616n35
Garrett, Angie, 92, 116, 128, 132, 598n4, 600n20
Garrett, Leah, 328, 379, 393, 638n40
Garry, Henry, 427–28, 490, 607n38, 631n6
Gary, Laurence, 88, 92, 153
Gates, Hattie, 577n68, 624n61
Gause, Louisa, 331, 332, 616n25
George, Ceceil, 391, 556, 598n5
George, Octavia, 280, 596n32
Gibbs, Georgina, 575n26, 598n5
Gibbs, Henry, 63, 84, 88, 369–70, 598n5, 606n10, 614n41
Gibson, Fannie, 390, 394–95, 396–97, 400
Gibson, Jennie Wormly, 88
Gibson, Mary Ann, 91, 93
Gilbert, Gabriel, 596n2
Giles, Charlie, 93, 452
Gill, Andrew Jackson, 575n23, 598n5
Gill, Frank, 371–72, 599n11, 600n15, 600n20, 614n47
Gillard, Jim, 88, 172, 216, 356, 373, 598nn4–5, 599n7, 600n20
Gillespie, J. N., 606n10
Gilmore, Brawley, 88, 216, 242–43
Gilmore, Mattie, 563
Gilstrap, John, 228
Gladdeny, Pick, 93, 94, 129
Gladdy, Mary, 37, 207, 212, 267, 299, 325, 331, 332–33, 388, 390, 400, 412–13, 422
Glasgow, Emoline, 291, 317, 590n47, 621n28
Glass, Will, 322, 324, 325, 331, 332, 333, 598n4, 616n25
Glenn, Edward, 535–36
Glenn, Wade, 25, 91, 212, 271, 304, 383, 480, 562, 614n46
Glover, John, 117, 132, 135
Glover, Mary, 269, 304, 305, 576n51, 614n47
Godbold, Hector, 88, 134, 469, 522, 600n20
Godfrey, Ellen, 26, 316, 446
Goodman, Andrew, 19, *19*, 88, 173–74, 201, 213, 600n18
Goodson, Thaddeus, 583n62, 593n62
Goodwater, Thomas, 56, 85, 93, 94, 295, 400, 429, 432, 433
Goole, Frankie, 287, 291, 304, 309, 557, 614n47, 622n31, 624n51
Govan, George, 247, 380, 613n38, 620n11, 623n41

Graham, Charles, 554, 600n20

Graham, Martin, 85, 89, 94, 132, 598n5, 599n11, 600n20

Grandberry, Mary Ella, 390, 415–16

Grandy, Charles, 174–75, 312–13, 322, 331, 332, 336, 339–40, 575n23, 616n25, 616n35, 617n36

Granny Cain, 600n20, 625n5

Grant, Austin, 84, 88, 124–25, 132, 170, 233, 247, 575n23, 597n3, 600n20

Grant, Charlie, 55, 91, 132, 141, 590n45, 591n22, 600nn19–20, 606n10

Grant, Dennis, 185, 448–49

Grant, Rebecca Jane, 92, 156–57, 213, 215, 353, 373

Graves, Mrs. Mildred, 598n4

Graves, Wesley, 224

Gray, Callie, 44, 88, 126, 132, 172–73, 226, 598n5, 599n7, 600n19, 605n6, 641n37

Gray, Neely (Nely), 93, 122, 129

Gray, Precilla, 370, 380

Greeley, Sim, 224

Green, Alice, 182, 351, 373, 597n3, 599n11, 600n18, 600n20

Green, Charles, 606n10, 618n19

Green, Elijah, 528–29, 616n35

Green, Emily Camster, 284, 600n19

Green, Esther, 61

Green, Isaiah (Isaac), 89, 90, 93, 134, 201

Green, Jake, 89, 206, 231, 267, 312–13, 605n33

Green, James, 303, 525

Green, Jimmie, 7, 515, 543, 643n54

Green, Marie Aurelia, 596n32

Green, Minnie, 614nn46–47

Green, Uncle Henry (Happy Day), 24–25, 80, 86, 89, 116, 132, 331, 332, 337, 340, 341, 379–80, 581n41, 600n20, 605n6, 616n24

Green, William (Reverend Bill), 25, 25, 436

Greer, Jenny, 300, 304, 614n47, 624n47

Gresham, Harriett, 93, 125, 129, 132, 311–12, 530, 616n35

Gresham, Wheeler, 88, 183, 600n20

Grice, Pauline, 138, 138, 473, 597n3

Griffen, Lucendy, 624n51

Griffin, Abner, 88, 90, 92, 158, 161, 205, 212, 576n50, 577n63

Griffin, Fannie, 597n3

Griffin, Heard, 598n4

Griffin, Lou, 536–37

Griffin, Madison, 240, 280, 600n20

Grigsby, Peggy, 88, 179, 598n5, 600n20, 606n17

Grisham, Emma, 93, 129–30, 212, 362–63, 365, 373

Gudger, Sarah, 91, 93, 148–49

Guidon, Lee, 631n6

Gullins, David Goodman, 598n5

Guwn, Betty, 327, 331, 332, 342, 616n24

Hadnot, Josh, 89

Hadnot, Mandy, 91, 92, 592n44

Hadnot, Maria, 152, 364, 366–67, 446

Halfen, July Ann, 266, 576n45, 576n51, 614n47

Hall, Bolden, 616n35

Hall, David A., 221

Hamilton, Ellie, 543

Hammock, Reverend Nelson, 314

Hammond, Milton, 132, 616n35

Hancock, Filmore Taylor, 63, 86, 212, 389, 396, 486, 495, 557

Hancock, Hannah, 465

Hankins, Rachel, 62–63, 418–19, 533–34, 634n48, 641n34

Hare, Simon, 68, 90, 124, 135, 171, 265, 301, 353, 366, 383, 577n68

Harmon, George W., 505, 610n39

Harmon, Jane Smith Hill, 576n50

Harper, Dave, 118, 285–86

Harper, Eda, 240, 634n48, 641n34

Harper, Pierce, 313, 369–70

Harper, Rev. Thomas, 598n5, 600n15, 600nn19–20

Harris, Abram, 252, 378, 496, 617n11, 633n32

Harris, Annie, 312–13

Harris, Caroline Johnson, 598n4

Harris, Charles, 307

Harris, Della, 68, 194, 203, 451

Harris, Dosia, 65, 437, 457, 471, 576n50, 598n4, 600n20, 625n5

Harris, Mary, 596n32

Harris, Orris, 62, 88, 92, 135, 152, 215, 239, 268, 392, 576n45, 576n51, 582n54, 616n23, 632n29

Harris, Sarah, 530

Harris, Squire, 89, 90

Harris, Susan, 493–94

Harris, Uncle Shang, 35, 56, 90, 94, 105, 265, 436, 576n50, 597n3, 599n10, 600n19, 624n51, 629n1

Harris, Virginia, 89, 90, 94, 116, 135, 357, 364, 555, 582n56, 598n5, 600n20, 614n47

Harrison, Eli, 625n10

Harrison, Jack, 94, 105, 598n5

Harrison, John, 42–43, 93, 571n9

Harrison, Sister, 91, 144, 146–47, 211

Harrison, William H., 83, 88, 197–98, 203, 205, 212

Harshaw, Plomer, 525, 643n53

Harvey, Charlie, 135

Hatchett, Matilda, 617n11

Hatfield, Mollie, 90, 132, 177, 223, 412, 576n44, 600n20

Hawes, William, 375

Hawkens, Lizzie, 118, 135, 598n4

Hawkins, G. W., 606n10

Hawkins, Susie, 536

Hawkins, Tom, 90

Hawthorne, Ann, 598n4

Hayes, Charles, 79, 88, 205, 213, 575n40

Hayes, James, 632n29

Hayes, Wash, 89, 92, 162, 598n4

Haygood, Burt, 93, 212, 577n68, 589n35

Hays, Eliza, 554, 598n4

Haywood, Barbara, 600n20

Haywood, Felix, 527, 528, 640n24, 643n60

Heard, Bill, 599n7, 599n11, 600n15, 600n20, 602n45, 623n44

Heard, Emmaline, 49, 90, 114, 132, 571n12, 576n50

Heard, Robert, 87, 88, 93, 264–65, 268, 597n3, 600n18, 632n32

Henderson, Benjamin, 598n4

Henderson, George, 123, 135, 600n20

Henderson, Isabelle, 306

Henry, Essex, 331, 332, 337, 340, 616n24

Henry, Ida, 64, 600n15, 600n20

Henry, Jefferson Franklin, 358, 366, 384, 563, 576n50, 598n5, 600n20

Henry, Jim, 88, 215, 216, 245, 576n45, 581n53

Henry, Mack, 93, 605n6

Henry, Nettie, 88

Henry, Uncle Robert, 62, 87, 89, 91, 93, 142, 146, 598n5

Hervey, Marie E., 569n26, 590n45

Hews, Chaney, 189, 600n20, 602n45

Hicks, Will, 88, 266, 577n68

High, Joe, 351

High, Susan, 599n11

Hill, Albert, 89, 90, 576nn45–46, 598n5

Hill, Clark, 616n35

Hill, Delia, 616n35

Hill, Elmira, 643n54

Hill, Gillie, 331, 332, 337, 340, 606n9, 617n25

Hill, Hattie, 247

Hill, Kitty, 222, 228, 237, 247, 251, 331, 606n9

Hill, Peter, 280

Hillyer, Morris, 280, 488

Hilyard, Della Bess, 616n35

Hines, Marriah, 90, 331, 337, 340–41, 600n18

Hinton, Charles, 321, 331, 336, 341, 617n36

Hinton, Robert, 597n3

Hite, Elizabeth Ross, 49, 62, 91–92, 93, 108, 209, 213, 302, 359, 373, 399–400, 430, 431, 575n23, 576n50, 614n47, 622n35

Hoard, Rosina, 471

Hobby, Lee, 91, 92, 575n23, 591n14

Hobley, N. H., 92, 93, 210, 260, 279, 610n38

Hodges, Fanny Smith, 61–62, 88, 122, 132, 576n46, 597n3

Holbert, Clayton, 599n11, 600n20

Holland, Tom, 90, 94, 105, 236, 598n5

Holloway, H. B. (Dad/Pappy), 88, 226, 381, 382, 591n10, 597n3, 600nn18–20

Holman, Eliza, 417–18

Holman, Rose, 65, 268, 571n19

Holmes, James Augustus, 19, 351, 364, 376, 383, 524

Holmes, Joseph, 116, 132, 184, 599n11, 600n18, 600n20, 628n25, 633n35

Holsell, Aunt Rhody, 89, 93, 122, 260, 267, 555

Holt, Larnce, 61, 88, 212, 575n40, 582n54

Homer, Bill, 89, 91, 140, 140, 145, 474

Homer, Mary, 413, 576n51

Horn, Josh, 118–19, 135, 565, 644n12

Horn, Molly, 88, 178, 214

INDICES 705

Horry, Uncle Ben, 89, 91, 93, 135, 150, 207, 212, 382–83, 585n65, 589n15

Horton, Cora L., 320, 331

Houston, Alice, 614n46

Houston, Aunt Carolina, 88

Howard, Emma L., 547

Howard, Josephine, 93, 239, 575n23

Hudson, Carrie, 90, 177, 179, 373, 392, 465, 477, 576n50, 598n5, 599n7, 599n11, 600n15, 600n20

Hudson, Charlie, 85, 94, 189–90, 221, 598n5, 600n15, 600nn19–20

Hudson, Measy, 324, 331, 380, 524

Huff, Annie, 91, 142, 175, 599n7, 600nn19–20

Huff, Bryant, 457, 509, 524, 537, 539, 540, 641n37, 642n38

Huff, Easter, 88, 90, 94, 105, 173, 216, 239, 598n5, 600n20

Huff, Mollie, 303

Hughes, Fannie, 377, 600nn18–19

Hughes, Frank, 371, 446, 599n11, 600n15, 600n20

Hughes, Lizzie, 55, 62, 65, 88, 464, 474, 575n23

Hughes, Margaret, 575n23, 598n5

Humphrey, Alex, 368

Humphrey, Anna, 334, 377, 600n20, 614n43, 625n5, 642n49

Hunter, Forest, 603n50

Hunter, John, 331, 333, 616n25

Hunter, Lina, 177, 302–3, 429, 457, 576n50, 598n4, 600n15, 600n20, 602n45, 614n47

Hunter, Mrs., 508–9

Hurley, Aunt Emma, 256, 598n4

Hursey, Mose, 297, 301, *301*, 390, *391*, 428–29

Hurt, Charley, 91, 186, 600n20, 641n34

Hutcheson, Alice, 62, 89, 90, 116, 134, 177–78, 226, 371, 378, 457, 479, 576n50, 599n7, 600nn19–20, 602n28, 602n38, 644n12

Hutson, Hal, 451, 575n40

Hutson, William, 132

Hyde, Patsy, 93, 280, 300, 321, 331, 365, 376, 527, 598n4, 614nn46–47

Ingram, Addison, 523, 643n54

Ingram, Everett, 598n5, 600n20

Ingram, Wash, 17, 559, 575n23, 575n39, 598n5

Irvin, Squire, 88, 132, 184, 195, 310, 575n23, 598n5, 600n20, 603n50, 616n35, 625n10

Irving, William, 642n48

Irwin, Hannah, 200, 575n40

Isom, Joanna Thompson, 35, 305, 399, 447, 519–20, 557, 622n35, 624n51, 641n34

Jackson, Adeline, 85, 89, 92, 94, 155, 201, 213, 216, 520, 571n12, 572n36, 582n56, 594n5, 597n3

Jackson, Amanda, 123, 132

Jackson, Aunt Easter, 80, 89, 91, 92, 142, 148, 581n41, 597n3, 633n32

Jackson, Carter J., 132

Jackson, Clarice, 557

Jackson, Cordelia Anderson, 90, 92, 216, 294, 454, 591n10

Jackson, Dora, 430

Jackson, George, 90, 94, 96, 598n4

Jackson, Isabella, 404

Jackson, Israel, 134

Jackson, James, 84, 88

Jackson, Lula, 603n41

Jackson, Martha, 305

Jackson, Mary, 93, 534, 634n48, 641n34

Jackson, Nancy, 63–64, 117, 135, 365, 366, 369, 598n5

Jackson, Reverend Silas, 113, 119, 132, 134, 213, 614n46, 620n17

Jackson, Richard, 225, 605n6, 606n10

Jacobs, Turner, 370

James, James Calhart, 39–40, 93, 393–94

James, John, 126, 135

James, Joseph, 86–87, 93, 577n68, 596n32

James, Julia Ann, 430, 622n32

Jameson, Hannah, 223, 457, 600n20, 602n38

Jarnagin, Andrew Jackson, 431, 629n9, 639n48, 643n58

Jefferies, Isiah, 297, 305

Jefferson, Hattie, 66, 88, 212, 455, 582n54

Jefferson, Lewis, 135, 195, 291, 576n46

Jefferson, Lydia, 22, 457, 626n26

Jefson, Ellis, 37, 90, 91, 139, 144, 212, 486, 509, 577n68, 600n20

Jemison, Ophelia, 256, 597n3

Jemison, Perry Sid, 381, 387, 598n5, 606n15, 625n7

Jenkins, Henry D., 53, 84, 88, 576n51, 577n68, 614n46

Jenkins, Lewis, 39, 606n15

Jenkins, Nep, 401

Jenkins, Paul, 643n48

Jewel, Mahala, 88, 178, 581n53, 600n20

John, Mary Ann, 164, 596n32

John, Zeno, 11, 596n32, 634n48, 641n34

Johns, Thomas, 34, 301, 304, 322, 380, 417–18, 518, 614n47, 623n44, 624n51

Johnson, Allen, 88, 268, 599n11, 600n19

Johnson, Benjamin, 125, 132, 328

Johnson, Charley, 89, 213, 577, 635n15

Johnson, Ella (AR), 282

Johnson, Ella (SC), 92, 151, 155, 213

Johnson, Georgia, 185, 200, 225, 305, 600n20

Johnson, Harry, 84, 88, 617n3

Johnson, Henry (MS), 598n4, 600n19

Johnson, Henry (VA), 616n35

Johnson, Isaac, 599n11, 600n15, 600n20

Johnson, Jimmie, 92, 158, 161, 205, 213

Johnson, Letha, 367–68, 553–54

Johnson, Lizzie, 303, 331, 605n6

Johnson, Mag, 118, 135, 237, 599n10, 600n20

Johnson, Manuel, 356, 364, 373, 613n32

Johnson, Mary (MS), 40, 65, 89, 92, 160, 269, 295, 441–42, 569n26

Johnson, Mary (SC), 226, 600n15, 600n20, 625n5

Johnson, Miemy, 364, 607n26

Johnson, Pauline, and Felice Boudreaux, 93, 531, 533, 534, 596n32

Johnson, Prince, 70, 88, 132, 224, 537, 598n5, 600n20, 641n37

Johnson, Richard, 280–81

Johnson, Sallie, 61, 88, 216, 235–36, 247, 249, 251, 576n51, 598n4

Johnson, St. Ann, 298–301, 614n47, 620n11

Johnson, Steve, 88, 380

Johnson, Susie, 303, 598n4

Johnson, Tina, 220

Johnson, Tom, 600n20

Johnson, Uncle Hilliard, 405–6, 418

Johnson, Uncle Marion, 479

Johnson, William I., Jr., 617n3

Jones, Aaron, 180, 577n68, 600nn18–19, 605n6, 606n10

Jones, Alfred, 92, 128, 500, 634n48

Jones, Anderson, 642n48

Jones, Aunt Hannah, 90, 96, 247, 249, 251–52

Jones, Bud, 92, 135, 147, 161, 200–201, 213, 227, 247, 297, 311–12, 576nn45–46, 599n11

Jones, Charity 88, 120, 127, 134, 213, 575n23, 576n45, 604n22

Jones, Clara, 600n18

Jones, Easter, 517n35

Jones, Edward, 54, 88, 92

Jones, Emma, 125, 132, 304, 598n5

Jones, Estella, 600n20

Jones, Fannie, 132–33

Jones, Harriet, 89, 90, 92, 133, 575n23, 597n3

Jones, Jack, 616n35

Jones, Julius, 89–90, 281, 329, 331

Jones, Lewis, 12, 12, 89, 90, 214, 272, 571n12, 576n51, 590n47

Jones, Lidia (Lydia), 634n38

Jones, Liza, 3, 93, 265, 426–27, 429, 498–99, 555, 567n1, 576n45, 600n18, 600n20

Jones, Mandy, 41–42, 89, 90, 93, 204, 211, 268, 352, 373, 600n20

Jones, Martha, 31, 380–81

Jones, Mary Jane, 68–69, 86, 89, 93, 577n68

Jones, Mr. Beverly, 606n10, 616n35

Jones, Oliver, 380–81

Jones, Richard, 87, 570n1, 597n3

Jones, Steve, 135, 410, 520, 573n1

Jones, Susan, 92, 285

Jones, Toby (Taby), 35, 90, 92, 94, 282, 586n37, 598n5

Jones, Wesley, 60–61, 88, 94

Jones, Wilkinson, 280

Jordan, Abner, 133

Jordan, Sam, 540, 617n11, 643n54

Joseph, Lindy, 473

Junell, Oscar Felix, 191

Jurdon, Lucindy Lawrence, 90, 91, 94, 105, 142, 146, 185, 600n20

Justice, Mollie, 632n29, 634n48

Kannon, Ellis Ken, 92, 153–54, 331, 337, 341, 605n6, 623n41
Kelley, Abe, 115, 133
Kelley, Bell, 88, 203, 212
Kelly, Aunt Susan, 45, 446
Kelly, Martha, 406, 423–24
Kennedy, Uncle Hamp, 178, 295, 298, 613n35
Key, Lucy, 63, 633n32
Kimbrough, Robert, 614n46
Kimmons, Richard, 88, 623nn44–45
Kindred, Mary, 69, 160, 327, *328*, 331, 410, 458, 465, 507, 573n1, 576n51, 577n68, 588n14
King, Charlie, 123, 134, 576n50, 598nn4–5
King, Ellen, 20, 89, 411, 556, 577n68, 624n49
King, J. W., 477, 606n15
King, Martha, 441
King, Mose, 554, 606n10
King, Nancy, 598n4, 600n18, 606n10
King, Silvia, 616n22, 643n54
Kinney, Nicey, 308, 600n20, 603n48
Kirkland, Mollie, 598n5
Kitchens, Mary Ann, 135, 597n3
Klugh, Henry Gray, 88, 226, 488, 600n15, 600nn19–20
Knox, Lonie, 430
Knox, Silas, 92, 143, 148, 323
Kyles, Preston, 247, 606n10

Lackey, Milton, 115, 134
Laird, Robert, 88, 195, 215, 469
Laird, Ruben, 75, 89, 115, 134, 580n34, 597n3, 624n51
Lambert, Solomon, 73, 89, 91, 92, 199–200, 221, 575n23, 598n4
Landrum, Janey, 623n45
Larken, Julia, 373, 599n7, 599n11, 600n15, 600n20, 614n47, 618n31
Larkin, Frank, 93
Lawrence, Ephraim (Mike), 79, 88, 212, 580n38
Laws, Matilda B., 491–92
Lawson, Ben, 481, 631n6
Lawson, Victoria Randle, 134, 326, 331, 333, 598n4
Lee, Anna, 90, 94, 380, 381, 586n37, 598n5, 600n20, 614n46
Lee, Lu, 35, 37, 88, 221, 270, 314, 364, 381–82, 415–16, 598n5, 600n20, 626n13

Lee, Mandy, 91, 93
Lee, Mrs. Mattie, 228
Leggett, Walter, 89, 90, 92, 109, 186, 268, 576n50, 598n5, 600n20
Leitner, Ben, 624n51
Lennox, Adeline Rose, 631n6
Lewis, Dellie, 133, 377, 598n4, 600n19, 626n13
Lewis, Elvira. *See* Force, Tinie
Lewis, Frances, 88, 306, 307, 315, 316, 317, 339, 389, 390, 391, 396, 397, 400, 409, 416, 421, 425, 428, 430, 432, 454, 518, 599n11, 600n19, 613n38, 620n11, 640n20, 641n34
Lewis, George, 88, 133, 134, 600n20
Lewis, Hagar, 92, 442, 594n3
Lewis, Henry, 339, 390, 421–22, 476n45, 599n11, 630n19
Lewis, Lavinia, 89, 632n28
Lewis, Lucy, 13–14, 88, 213, 260, 262, 268, 278, 454, 626n7
Lewis, Perry, 606n10
Lewis, San Jacinto (Uncle Cinto), 37, 88, 195, 213, 626n7
Lindsay, Abbie, 84, 88, 390, 422, 431, 624n55
Lindsay, Ellen, 380, 431
Little, Annie, 29–30, 31, 411
Little, William, 88, 202, 257, 501, 581n53, 634n48
Littlejohn, Chana, 325, 331, 332, 333, 381–82
Littlejohn, Govan, 599n7
Livingston, Abe, 438, *438*, 625n5
Lockhart, Easter, 614n47
Locklier, Uncle Gable, 133
Lofton, Aunt Minerva, 303, 429
Long, Walter, 591n10
Long, Will, 89, 92, 93, 94, 213, 597n3, 598n4, 632n14
Louis, Jane, 301
Love, Annie, 605n6
Love, Hunton, 46, 178, 525, 571n25, 643n54
Love, John, 30, 639n48
Love, Louis, 133
Love, Needham, 171, 559, 618n12
Lowry, Dave, 20, 331, 345, 453, 461, 577n68, 606n9, 616n24
Loyd (Boyd), Nellie, 62, 598n4
Lucas, Daniel William, 262
Lucas, James, 22, 55, 65, 88, 133, 411, 509, 597n3, 598n4

Luckado, Lizzie, 486–87, 490, 545, 631n6
Luster, Bert, 370, 598n4, 625n5
Lycurgas, Edward, 614n46, 620n17
Lyles, Eison, 133, 419–20
Lyles, Moses, 623n44
Lyons, Phoebe, 326–27, 331, 337, 341, 606n9

Mack, Chaney (Chanie), 38, 71–72, 73, 88, 89, 137, 211, 248, 249, 446, 545, 582n54, 598n4, 623n44
Mack, Cresa, 247, 248
Mack, Richard, 83, 88, 203, 205, 214, 219, 247, 248, 573n1
Macks, Richard, 88, 171, 575n23, 598n5
Madden, Perry, 89, 91, 93, 522
Maddox, Jack, 73, 89, 124, 183–84, 328–29, 435–36, 478, 573n1, 575n39, 600n20, 625n7
Maddox, Rosa, 22, 256, 450, 461, 569n24
Magee, Primous, 89, 92, 455, 577n68, 581n53, 587n49
Majors, John, 135, 628n20
Malloy, Caroline, 90, 102, 575n24, 597n3, 600nn19–20
Malone, Julia, 331, 332, 333, 616n25
Mangum, Rosa, 89, 92, 178, 587n49
Manning, Allen V., 596n32, 634n48
Manson, Jacob, 616n35
Manuel, Millie, 23–24
Marion, Andy, 20, 591n10, 600n20, 618n18
Marshall, Alice, 313, 331, 358, 618n18
Marshall, Milton, 349, 591n10, 599n11, 600n15, 600n20, 614n47, 620n9
Martin, Drucilla, 540
Martin, Eva, *554*, 596n32, 598n4
Martin, James, 598n4
Martin, Jim, 66, 88, 92, 133, 154, 213, 472, 571n10, 575n23, 582n54, 604n22
Martin, Scott, 557, 622n31
Mary (Old Mary), 88
Mason, Aunt Carrie, 90, 576nn45–46, 597n3
Mason, Aunt Harriet, 220
Mason, Sam Meredith, 386, 401, 621n23
Mathews, Louise, 89, 90, 106, 598n5
Mathews, William, 265, 325, 328, 329, 331
Matthews, Ann, 226, 269, 300, 304, 331, 341, 370, 407, 614n47, 618n12

Matthews, John, 64, 88, 135, 575n23, 576n46
Matthews, Maggie Whitehead, 527, 640n21
May, Ann, 240, 369, 555, 594n5, 632n29, 634n48
Mayfield, Bert, 116, 133, 178, 216, 304, 369
Maynard, Bob, 91, 92, 94, 135, 140, 144, 575n23, 615n15
Mays, Emily, 598n4, 600n20
McAdams, Andy, 90, 94, 586n37, 598n5
McAdams, John, 380, 407, 599
McAlilley, George, 88, 92, 156, 202, 213
McAllum, Sam, 606n6
McCarty, William H., 483–84
McCastle, Duncan, 133, 280
McCormick, Joe, 616n35
McCoy, Liza, 39
McCoy, Rachel, 441
McCray, Stephen, 331, 336, 341–42, 354, 373, 380–81, 598n4, 617n36
McCree, Ed, 19, 89, 90, 106, 122, 134, 366–67, 598n5, 600n15, 600nn19–20, 624n51
McCullers, Henrietta, 352, 600n18, 600n20, 618n19
McCullough, Lucy, 135–36, 599n7
McDaniel, Amanda, 598n4
McGaffey, Henry Lewis, 79, 88, 213, 576n45, 577n63, 582n54, 626n8
McGillery, Rosie, 90, 94, 105, 598n5
McGruder, Tom, 384, 598n4
McIntosh, Susan, 91, 142, 147, 436, 501, 598n5, 634n48
McIntosh, Waters, 39, 145, 220, 224, 284, 329, 605n6
McKinney, Matilda, 88, 114, 173, 598n5
McKinney, Warren, 352
McKlennan, Abe, 174, 575n23, 616n35
McLean, James Turner, 124, 127, 134
McLeod, Jake, 91, 93, 94, 133, 137, 575n23, 600n20
McMillan, Thomas, 353, 380, 600n15, 600n20
McMullen, Victoria, 328
McNair, Chaney, 60, 88, 94, 200, 455, 494, 603n50
McQueen, Nap, 133
McRay, C. B., 446, *447*
McWhorter, William, 136, 189, 265, 280, 600n15, 600n20, 617n11
Mead, William, 624n51
Meadows, Louis, 171
Meeks, Letha Taylor, 605n6

Melinda, 596n32

Melton, Susie, 264, 314, 598n5

Menefee, Frank, 91, 134, 142, 185, 304, 457, 598nn4–5, 600n20

Mention, Liza, 62, 89, 90, 91, 93, 94, 106, 107, 131, 178–79, 558, 577n68, 598n4, 600n20, 643n1

Merrill, Sarah Emery, 386–87, 402

Merritt, Susan, 17, 127, 134, 214, 223, 265, 349, *349*, 374–75, 461, 569n24, 617n11

Mickey, Ann, 89, 90, 92, 163, 167, 596n32, 597n3

Miles, Josh, 632n29

Miller, George Washington, 84, 88, 136, 357, 373, 600n20, 603n45

Miller, Hardy, 238

Miller, Harriet (GA, SC), 40, 88, 173, 598n5, 600nn19–20

Miller, Harriet (MS), 61, 134, 215, 380, 570n7, 576n51

Miller, Wylie, 226, 605n6

Millett, Harriet, 469

Milling, Cureton, 597n3

Mills, Tom, 306, 597n3, 600n19

Mire, La San (LaSan), 138, 163, *163*, 596n32, 598nn4–5, 599n6, 610n35

Mitchel, Anna, 370, 380–81, 488

Mitchell, A. J., 134, 599n7

Mitchell, Charley, 280, 408, 624n55

Mitchell, Gracie, 391, 399, 622n35

Mitchell, Mary, 134, 136

Mitchell, Melinda (Malinda), 20, 48, 90, 91, 142, 146, 270, 571n12, 575n23, 624n55

Mitchell, Peter, 371

Mobley, Bob, 188–89

Monroe, Garland, 331, 337

Montgomery, Adaline, 40, 44

Montgomery, Alex, 116, 136

Montgomery, Jane, 370, 373

Montgomery, Laura, 17, 92, 133, 152, 432, 448, 571n10

Montgomery, Rube, 294

Moody, Andrew, 116, 352, 364, 419–20, 574n12, 587n3

Moore, A. M. "Mount," 600n18

Moore, Fannie, 37, 217–18, 226, 331, 358, 392, 575n23, 616n25

Moore, Jerry, 124

Moore, John, 251–53, 449, 596n32

Moore, Laura, 89, 92, 108

Moore, Lindsey, 624n51

Moore, Rev. John, 331, 337, 342, 616n25

Moore, Riley, 236, 616n35

Moore, Sena, 238

Moore, Vina, 271, 445, 465, 600n20

Moore, William, 360, 366, 373, 616n22

Moreland, Elsie, 59, 575n23, 600n20

Morgan, Aunt Jane, 91, 149

Morgan, Evelina, 519, 641n34, 643n54

Morgan, Isaam, 483

Morgan, James, 606n10

Moring, Richard C., 90

Morris, Charity, 463–64

Morris, Tom, 88, 208, 213, 247, 248, 249, 360, 576n45, 632n29, 643n54

Morrison, George, 84, 89, 90, 92, 94, 213, 247, 248, 264, 576n45, 576n50, 577n68, 581n53, 582n56, 587n52, 633n43

Moses, Charlie, 223, 312

Moses, Patsy, 31, 32, 93, 380, 591n10, 612n22, 614n41

Mosley, John, 90, 94, 586n37, 598n5, 600n20

Moss, Andrew, 133

Moss, Aunt Mollie, 117, 125–26, 133

Moss, Claiborne, 89, 90, 91, 92, 142, 146, 153, 182, 186–87, 440, 576n50, 600n20, 617n11

Moss, Mose, 623n44, 624n51

Mother Duffy, 63, 596n32

Mouton, Leo, 87, 92, 160, 167, 213, 247, 249, 271, 339, 421–22, 596n32

Moye, Calvin, 271, 366–67, 373, 554, 559, 576n50, 598n5, 600n20

Mullen, Mack, 86, 89, 93, 115, 134, 199, 301, 471, 575n23, 600n19

Mundy, Lewis, 373, 380–81, 422, 623n45

Murphy, Hannah, 88, 233, 443, 534, 600n19, 641n34

Murphy, Sally, 359, 373, 600n20

Murray, Henry, 116, 135

Napoleon, Louis, 89, 90, 91, 134, 150, 272, 301, 575n23, 614n47

Nealy, Sally, 207, 531–33

Necaise, Henri, 39, 128, 163, 596n32
Neill, Louise, 643n54
Nelson, Julius, 89, 90, 133, 176, 600n20, 603n45
Nettles, Hattie Anne, 91, 93, 148, 598n5, 617n1
Newman, Virginia, 40, 63, 63, 89, 92, 167, 596n32, 598n4
Newton, George, 321, 326, 331, 342
Newton, Pete, 594n5, 632n29, 634n48, 643n53
Nicholson, Fannie, 327, 331
Nickerson, Margrett, 616n35
Nickerson, Mary, 596n2
Nix, Fanny, 598n4
Nix, Henry, 617
Norfleet, Lizzie, 88, 91, 94, 133, 143, 146, 598n5
Norris, Charlie, 130, 641n34
Northcross, Reverend W. E., 353, 365, 374, 377
Norwood, Glascow, 59, 88, 94, 576, 599n7
Norwood, Isaiah, 64, 88
Nunn, General Jefferson Davis, 117, 136, 170, 176, *176*, 597n3, 598nn4–5

Ogee, John, 596n32
Old Ex-Slave, 205
Oliver, Amanda, 380–81, 536, 600n20, 641n37
Oliver, Joe, 89, 92, 93, 94, 211, 576n51, 634n48
Oliver, Mark, 85, 89, 94, 133, 202, 350, 576n45, 582n56, 597n3, 598n5, 600n20
Oliver, Uncle William, 422–23
Osborne, Ivory, 134
Overstreet, Horace, 88, 90, 103, *104*, 172, 213, 556, 575n23, 575n40, 576n45, 576n50, 600n14
Overton, Eliza, 55, 88, 457, 575n23, 610n35, 626n6
Owens, George, 221, 322, 553
Owens, Henry, 477
Owens, Wade, 90, 133, 205, 213, 283, 297, 331, 346, 361, 364, 373, 598nn4–5, 600n20, 602n37, 606n9, 614n47
Oxner, Albert, 599n11, 600n20

Parish, Douglas, 188
Parker, Charity, 657
Parker, Laura Ramsey, 365, 366–67
Parker, Molly, 134, 215

Parker, Will, 116, 134, 323, 624n51
Parkes, Anna, 92, 157
Parks, Annie, 600nn19–20
Parnell, Austin Pen, 13, 90, 92, 247, 249–50, 331, 332, 333–34, 575n43, 606n10, 616nn24–25, 642n49
Patterson, Albert, 596n32
Patterson, Frank A., 530–31
Patterson, Jennie, 534, 634n48, 641n34
Patterson, John, 267
Pattillo, G. W., 220, 348
Pattillo, Solomon P., 247, 369, 379
Patton, Grundy, 380–81
Paul, Sallie, 91, 94, 144, 146, 147, 179, 352, 575n23, 582n56, 600n20
Payne, Ellen, 270, 309, *309*, 364, 382, 524, 575n42, 598n5, 614nn46–47, 616n35, 623n44
Payne, Elsie, 89, 90, 106, 133, 599n11, 600n20, 613n32
Peek, Anna, 599n7
Perkins, Lu, 390, 391, 408, 440, 501, 520, 575n40, 624n55, 634n48
Perrier, Reverend John, 312–13, 612n15, 616n35
Perry, Dinah, 305, 404, 439, 625n7
Perry, Matilda Henrietta (Sweet Ma), 89, 90, 92, 148, 211, 286–87, 587n52
Petite, Phyllis, 133
Pettis, Louise, 213, 229, 577n68, 606n10
Phillips, Dolly, 331, 332, 334, 616n25
Phoenix, Katie, 354, 374, 634n48
Pierce, Lee, 576n50, 598n5, 605n6, 606n15
Piernas, Louis Joseph, 93, 131, 163, 214, 590n54, 596n32
Pinkard, Maggie, 117, 133, 136
Pinnacle, Rev. Aaron, 88, 92, 93, 158, 212, 381
Pittman, Sarah, 93, 391, 621n22
Pitts, Dempsey, 133, 211, 357, 374, 559, 600nn19–20, 616n35, 632n21
Pitts, Roxy, 308–9, 430, 614n41
Pitts, Tempe, 598n4
Poche, Cora, 596n32
Polite, Sam, 21, 466
Polk, James, 617n1
Polk, Nelson, 327, 331, 332, 337, 342, 616n24

Pollard, Levi, 30, 31, 331, 342–43, 383–84

Pollard, Rosa L., 90, 304, 355, 380, 598n4, 624n51

Pool, Parker, 18, 93, 176, 358, 373, 522, 600n18, 600n20, 616n35

Pope, Alec, 88, 597n3, 600n20

Porter, Ophelia, 91, 135, 144, 147, 592n36, 600n18

Posey, Elsie, 18, 89, 91, 93, 216, 518–19

Potter, Bob, 241, 373, 423

Potter, Isaac, 89, 92, 587n49, 606n10

Powell, Jim, 602n29

Powell, Salem, 89, 92, 477, 576n50, 587n49, 606n10

Powers, Betty, 88, 171

Powers, Charlie, 379, 576n50, 599n7

Pratt, William, 55, 60, 224, 432, 458, 595n15, 597n3

Preston, Georgianna, 112, 311–12

Price, Allen, 31

Price, Annie, 322

Price, John, 520, 524, 596n32, 616n22, 640n21

Price, Reverend Lafayette, 91, 188, 239, 295, 312, 398–99, 400, 413, 429, 510–11, 512, 600n20, 614n46, 620n13, 622n35

Proctor, Jenny, 473–74, 561, 600n20

Pruitt, A. C., 59, 86, 93, 575n23, 600n20

Pryor, Elsie, 89, 90, 105, 138, 365–66, 582n56

Pyatt, Jane, 130, 600n20

Pye, Charlie, 534, 598n4, 600n19, 641n34

Quarls, Harre, 74, 89, 194, 214, 236, 247, 250, 271, 430, 495, 597n3, 611n46

Quattlebaum, Junius, 465, 600n20, 643n54

Rabb, Jack, 91, 214, 564, 594n73

Raines, Rena, 598n4

Rains, Aunt Eda, 134

Ramsay, George Washington, 347, 617n1, 618n12

Ramsey, Aunt Lillian, 559

Ramsey, Uncle Dave, 559

Randolph, Fanny, 67, 89, 90, 94, 577n68, 581n53, 582n54, 582n56, 600n20

Rawls, Sam, 600n15, 601n21

Ray, Aaron, 283, 374

Ray, Morgan, 616n35

Redfield, Roy, 90, 206, 231, 610n41, 638n40

Reece, Elsie, 88, 598n5

Reece, Naisy, 419, 614n46, 622n34, 624n51

Reed, Easter, 91, 597n3, 600n18

Reed, Eva, 357, 414

Reed, Henry, 411–12

Reed, Rachael Santee, 336, 617n1, 617n36, 623n44

Reese, Belton, 583n62, 593n62

Reese, Bill, 381

Reeves, James, 89, 90, 218, 270, 575n43, 576n50

Reid, Babe, 583n62

Renwick, Ellen, 600n15, 600n20

Reynolds, Mary, 55, 82, 89, 92, 108, 126, 134, 155, 598nn4–5

Rhodes, Susan, 324, 614n41

Rhymes, Will, 177, 364, 368, 369–70, 448

Rice, Anne, 598n5, 600n15, 600n20

Rice, George Washington, 88, 215, 688n9

Rice, Savannah, 269, 484–85

Richard, Dora, 331, 338, 343, 614n47

Richards, Shade, 88, 189, 587n3, 598nn4–5, 599n7

Richardson, Chaney, 42

Richardson, Charlie, 136

Richardson, Martha, 628n25, 633n35, 643n5

Richardson, Red, 93, 136, 361, 373, 576n50, 598n5

Ricks, Jim, 227

Rigger, Charlie, 226

Rigley, Ida, 61, 88, 118, 135, 201, 216, 575n23, 598n4, 612n15

Rimm, Walter, 600n19, 606n10, 640n27

Riser, Susie, 600n15, 600nn19–20

Rivers, George, 397, 404, 424–25

Roberts, Dora, 21, 57, 91, 142, 146, 295, 576n45, 598n5, 643n2

Robertson (Robinson), George, 631n6

Robertson, Betty, 43, 641n29, 643n54

Robinson, Celia, 93, 519

Robinson, Charlie, 424

Robinson, Cornelia, 600n20

Robinson, Harriett, 605n6, 605n33, 610n41

Robinson, Manus, 89, 92, 177, 178, 581n53

Robinson, Mariah, 88, 607n40

Robinson, Sister, 325, 331, 358, 517n36

Roby, Edd, 331, 332, 343–44, 616n25

Rodgers, Isaac, 621n23
Rogers, Aunt Ferebe, 127, 133, 236, 247, 251, 600nn18–20
Rogers, Ellen, 398, 614n46
Rogers, George, 600n20
Rogers, Hattie, 520, 524
Rogers, Henry, 89, 90, 114, 134, 183, 212, 599n11, 600nn19–20
Rogers, Noah, 39, 266, 558
Rollins, Joe, 89, 90, 175–76, 208, 247, 600n15, 600n20, 605n6, 605n34
Rooks, William Henry, 238, 322
Rosboro, Al, 92, 129
Rose, Katie, 114, 134, 215, 296
Rose, William, 89, 90, 93, 523
Ross, Amanda, 123, 598n4
Ross, Cat, 241, 576n45
Ross, Gertie, 92, 157, 214
Ross, Hennie, 304, 380, 614n47
Ross, Madison Frederick, 605n6
Ross, Susan, 624n55
Rountree, Henry, 597n3, 599n7, 600nn18–20
Rowe, Katie, 93, 122, 133
Rudd, John, 91, 592n44
Ruffin, Martin, 466, 600n20
Ruffin, Melinda Ann "Roty," 88, 213
Rullerford, George, 55, 88, 185, 598n5, 600n20
Rush, Julia, 504, 635n11
Russell, Aaron, 136, 598n4
Russell, Benjamin, 424
Russell, Elizabeth, 93, 280
Rutherford, Joe, 600n20
Rutherford, Lila, 600n15, 600n20
Ryan, Henry, 381–82, 600n15, 600n20
Ryas, Peter, 596n32
Rye, Katie, 632n29, 634n48

Sadler, Felix Grundy, 92, 596n36
Samuel, C. G., 40, 331, 334, 570n1
Samuels, Amanda Elizabeth, 535
Sanders, Harriet, 360, 366–67
Sanders, Susan Dale, 88, 199, 600n17, 624n51
Sandles, Charlie, 90, 94, 586n37, 598n5
Santee, Hamp, 126, 134, 136, 211, 305

Satterfield, Mrs. May, 598n4
Scales, Catherine, 422–23
Scott, Annie Groves, 570n1
Scott, Janie, 599n11
Scott, Mary (SC), 133
Scott, Mary (TN), 320, 331, 332, 344, 345, 616n24, 616n26, 616n28
Scott, Sam, 214, 215, 490–91
Scott, Tom, 375
Scranton, Mary Louise, 596n32
Scurry, Morgan, 600n15, 600n20, 624n51, 624n55
Sellers, Fanny, 364–65, 427
Sells, Abram, 115, 133, 599n7
Selman, George, 133, 364, 369–70
Settles, Nancy, 70, 88, 90, 93, 263, 283–84, 614n46
Sewell, Alice, 299, 302, 616n35
Shackelford, Mrs. Sis, 606n10
Shaw, Alice, 221, 247, 248
Shaw, Lucindy Hall, 331, 334, 570n1
Shaw, Violet, 89, 91
Sheets, Will, 576n50, 597n3, 598n5, 600n20
Shelby, Gussie, 93, 378–79
Shelton, Frederick, 177
Shepard, Matilda, 237, 331, 334, 407
Shepherd, Cora, 178, 600nn18–19, 612n22
Shepherd, Robert, 93, 133, 134, 185, 214, 359–60, 366–67, 372, 373, 577n68, 600n20, 614nn46–47, 623n45, 626n2
Sherman, William, 616n35
Shine, Polly, 91, 94, 380–81, 586n37, 598n5, 600n20
Shirley, Uncle Edd, 39, 90, 598n5
Shores, Mahalia, 605n6
Showvely, Martha, 90, 211, 577n68, 598n5
Simmons, Betty, 116, 638n43
Simmons, George, 68, 79, 79, 88, 214, 577n68, 605n6
Simmons, Mary Jane, 599n11, 600n19
Simmons, Smith, 55, 90, 173, 369–70, 598n5, 600n20
Simms, Andrew, 472–73, 598n4, 617n11
Simms, Dennis, 87, 89, 91, 92, 271–72, 368, 611n46
Simpkins, Millie, 93, 179, 326, 331, 345, 346, 370, 600n19, 602n36
Simpson, Emma, 91, 94, 575n23, 586n37, 598n5
Simpson, George Jackson, 39, 85, 89, 94, 214, 577n63

Sims, Allen, 133, 188, 598n4, 600n20
Singleton, Adam, 65, 88, 133, 202, 214, 452, 454, 575n23, 600n19
Singleton, Affie, 390, 410, 547, 573n1
Singleton, James, 13, 88, 136, 175, 214, 234, 247, 248, 599n11
Singleton, Marinda Jane, 61, 90, 179, 600nn18–19
Singleton, Tom, 600n20
Sligh, Alfred, 17, 518, 540
Smith, Berry, 88, 195, 228–29, 590n47, 606n10
Smith, Caroline, 526, 640n21
Smith, Charlie Tye, 91, 133, 142, 146, 171, 216, 241, 576n50, 597n3
Smith, Eli, 133, 216
Smith, Eugene Wesley, 516, 530, 641n34
Smith, Georgia, 179, 600n19, 622n35, 623n45
Smith, Giles, 475
Smith, Gus, 88, 201, 600n19
Smith, Hector, 92, 147, 469, 562–63, 636n30, 644nn7–8
Smith, Henry, 88, 634n48
Smith, James W., 45–46, 48, 57, 61, 94, 214, 571n12, 576n51, 598n5
Smith, John, 547
Smith, Jordon, 280
Smith, Lou, 446, 597n3
Smith, Mary, 614n47
Smith, Melvin, 89, 91, 96, 114, 134, 173, 364–65, 437
Smith, Millie Ann, 133, 366–67, 580n38, 598n5, 600n18, 600n20
Smith, Nancy, 93, 304, 356, 372–73, 614nn46–47, 623n45
Smith, Nellie, 614n46
Smith, Paul, 44, 175, 309, 366–67, 479, 570n1, 575n23, 598n4, 600n20, 603n45, 603n48, 605n34, 613n32, 618n31
Smith, R. C., 91, 511–12, 637n31, 637n33
Smith, Samuel, 60, 364, 575n23, 576n51
Smith, Stonewall, 632n23
Smith, Susan, 436, 612n15
Smith, William, 69, 88, 214, 266, 469–70, 476, 577n68, 596n32
Sneed, John, 89, 91, 161–62, 214, 364, 370, 382, 598nn4–5
Snow, Susan, 37, 410, 515, 531, 559–60, 573n1, 641n37

Snyder, Mariah, 365, 377, 443, 572, 572
Sommerville, Jim, 31
Sorrell, Ria, 600n20
Southall, James, 57, 94, 324, 331, 575n23, 582n56, 616n25
Southwell, Patsy, 364, 369–70, 373
Sparks, Elizabeth, 133, 546–47, 565, 598n4
Sparrow, Mom Jessie, 540
Spencer, Uncle John, 135, 182–83, 185, 600n20
Spikes, Tanner, 90, 186, 213, 600n20
Spinks, Leithean, 88, 136, 431
St. Ann, Robert, 569n26
Stafford, Gracie, 439–40
Stanfield, Jeff, 92, 152, 215
Stapleton, Wright, 451, 459, 461, 462, 569n24, 598n4, 599n7, 599n11
Starnes, Isom, 92, 494n3
Steele, Elmo, 89, 92, 600n18
Stenston, Mattie, 580–81
Stephenson, Annie, 59, 599n7, 600n20
Stepney, Emeline, 56, 93, 575n23, 598n5
Stepney, Steve, 374–75, 423, 463, 564
Steptoe, Thomas, 554, 596n32
Stewart, Carlyle, 596n2
Stewart, Charley, 339, 390, 401, 421
Stewart, Guy, 83, 89, 91, 216, 632n29
Stewart, Nan, 597n3
Stewart, Nelson, 600n18, 600n20
Stewart, Sam T., 217, 600n20, 606n10
Stier, Isaac, 69, 88, 220–21, 576n45, 597n3, 614n46, 625n4
Stinson, Ella, 93, 409–10
Stith, James Henry, 88, 221, 229, 606n10
Stokes, Aunt Ann, 397, 443–44, 591n10
Stokes, Simon, 468
Stone, Emma, 94, 520
Stone, William, 32
Strayhorn, Eva, 378, 380–81, 383–84, 418, 614n46, 618n19, 624n51
Strickland, George, 76, 80, 81, 89, 117, 136, 581n41, 600n20, 603n48
Strickland, Liza, 136, 599n7
Stringfellow, Yach, 88

Strong, Bert, 68, 88, 126, 133, 178, 188, 214, 234, 247, 248, 350, *350*, 360, 366–67, 370, 373, 577n68, 598n5, 616n35
Stubbs, Julia, 119, 133
Styles, Amanda, 13, 90, 91, 259, 262, 277
Sullivan, Rachel, 598n4
Sutton, James R., 376
Sutton, Jane, 293, 359, 380, 391, 392, 402, 414, 442, 448, 561
Sutton, Katie, 445
Sutton, Samuel, 470
Swindler, Ellen, 575n23, 598n5
Sykes, William, 90, 105, 600n20

Taylor, Cull, 599n7
Taylor, Delphia, 558
Taylor, Edward, 134, 136, 236
Taylor, Emma, 88, 575n23
Taylor, George, 598n4, 599n7
Taylor, Mollie, 136
Taylor, Tishey, 88, 363, 365, 373
Taylor, Warren, 93
Teel, Mary, 591n10
Telfair, Georgia, 93, 179, 183, 372–73, 375, 378, 600nn19–20, 602n37, 614n47, 623n45, 633n32
Tenneyson, Beauregard, 125, 599n11, 600n15, 600n20
Terrell, Louise, 133
Terriell, Jake, 105
Thomas, Acie, 88, 215
Thomas, Bill, 88, 92, 202, 214, 271, *564*, 594n1
Thomas, Cordelia, 354, 361, 372, 373, 380–81, 403, 598n4, 599n7, 599n11, 600n20, 614nn46–47, 623n45
Thomas, Dan, 436
Thomas, Elias, 380–81
Thomas, Ellen, 92, *564*, 596n1
Thomas, George, 456, 564
Thomas, Ike, 88, 136, 188, 205, 214, 263
Thomas, Kate, 92, 151, 152
Thomas, Lorena, 325, 331, 332, 334, 616n26, 624n51, 630n33
Thomas, Lucy, 436, 517, *517*, 598n5
Thomas, Philles, 302, 431, 614n42

Thomas, Rebecca, 41, 65, 91, 92, 140, 144, 161–62, 199, 214, 476, 597n39
Thomas, Rosa, 400, 401–2, 416–17
Thomas, Sarah, 297, 317, 318, 545–46, 616n35
Thomas, Valmo, 596n32
Thomas, William M., 21, 79, 88, 212, 599n7
Thompson, Ellen Briggs, 88, 559
Thompson, Jane, 91, 108, 199, 214, 350, 380–81, 575n23, 597n3, 605n6, 620n17
Thompson, John, 88, 212, 214, 383–84, 569n25, 576n51, 577n68
Thompson, Johnson, 43, 88, 136, 214
Thompson, Penny, 59, 235, *235*, 247, 249, 466, 575n23, 600n20
Thompson, Victoria Taylor, 43
Thornton, Laura, 66, 79, 88, 211, 600n19
Thornton, Margaret, 242
Thornton, Tim, 91, 92, 108
Threat, Jim, 235, 247, 251, 494–95
Threntham, Henry James, 190, 602n45, 616n35
Thurston, Lucy, 223, 240, 357–58, 598n5, 599n7
Tidwell, Emma, 329, 331, 350, 616n25
Toatley, Robert, 134
Tolbert, Bettie, 624n51
Toler, Richard, 83, 88, 198–99, *199*, 205, 214, 564, 570n29, 582n54
Toombs, Jane Mickens, 353–54, 368
Towns, Phil, 90, 91, 92, 139, 142, 144, 147, 576n50
Towns, William Henry, 498, 628n25, 630n21, 633n32
Trell, Ellen, 616n35
Trimble, Aleck, 133, 612n20
Tubbs, Uncle James, 303, 561
Turner, Clorie, 596n32
Turner, Lou, 632n29
Turner, Uncle Henry, 247, 249

Upson, Neal, 86, 89, 93, 94, 115, 134, 200, 212, 214, 364, 366–67, 380–81, 576n44, 576n50, 581n53, 598nn4–5, 599n11, 600n18, 600n20

Vaden, Ellen, 605n6
Van Buren, Nettie, 367
Van Dyke, Charlie, 322, 614n43, 616n35

Van Hook, John F., 183, 351, 459, 506, 576n50, 581n53, 598nn4–5, 600n20, 602n45, 606n10

Vann, Lucinda, 43, 61, 89, 91, 93, 94, 131, 577n68, 582n56

Varner, Stephen, 234, 247, 350, 598n4

Veals, Mary, 376, 598n4, 619n42, 621n20, 624n51

Vinson, Addie, 88, 122–23, 134, 206, 213, 243, 286, 373, 600n20

Virgel, Emma, 183, 372, 600n20, 614n47

Waldon, Adeline, 88, 90, 263

Walker, Bean, 21

Walker, Dave, 68, 89, 92, 94, 114, 134, 576n50, 587n49

Walker, Edwin, 122, 133

Walker, Harriet, 88, 91, 108, 587n49, 600nn18–19

Walker, Henry, 115–16, 122, 133, 136, 182, 599nn11–12, 600n20, 616n35

Walker, Lula Cottonham, 19, 319, 331, 616n25

Walker, Manda, 467

Walker, Ned, 382

Walker, Sarah, 331, 334

Wall, Ben, 201, 214

Walton, Rhodus, 80, 81, 89, 91, 581n41, 597n3, 598n5, 606n17

Walton, Sol, 90, 265, 281, 282

Wamble (Womble), Rev., 117–18, 135

Ward, Allen, 89, 92, 172, 554, 587n49, 598n4, 606n10

Ward, William, 599n7, 616n35

Warfield, Lucy Ann, 386, 417

Warfield, William, 31, 32, 624n50

Washington, Callie, 91, 92, 108, 136, 199, 575n23, 575n42, 587n50, 598n5, 600n20

Washington, Eliza, 185, 188, 331, 336, 344, 549, 558, 600nn19–20, 617n36

Washington, Ella, 331, 337, 344–45, 605n6, 616n25

Washington, Lula, 598n4

Washington, Rev. James W., 57, 88, 92, 136, 157, 211, 214, 351, 576n46, 577n68, 597n3

Washington, Rosa, 133, 134, 280, 575n23, 597n3, 598n4, 600n19

Washington, Sam Jones, 468

Waters, Jordan, 56, 88, 580n38

Watkins, Sylvia, 331

Watkins, William, 225, 598n5

Watson, Charley, 624n51

Watson, Emma, 133, 600n18

Watson, Mollie, 92, 155, 216, 381, 599n11, 600n20, 623n44, 630n19, 634n48

Watson, William H., 122, 136

Watts, John, 84, 88, 295

Weatherall, Eugenia, 92, 212, 300, 307, 614n47

Weathersby, Foster, 91, 108, 587n49, 599n11, 616n22

Weathersby, George, 89, 92, 576n50, 587n49

Weathersby, Isom, 357

Weathersby, Robert, 89, 92, 436, 576n50, 587n49

Weathersby, Steve, 389, 464

Webb, Mrs., 596n32

Webb, Sol, 613n32

Wells, Alfred, 247

Wells, Easter, 365

Wells, Sarah Williams, 553

Wesley, John, 223, 605n6

West, James, 87, 89, 91, 214, 235, 247, 249, 270

Whallen, Nancy, 614n46

Wheeler, William, 472, 633n32

White, Adeline, 89, 92, 160, 164, 270, *271*, 575n42, 576n50, 577n68, 596n32, 623n44, 624n50

White, Clara, 622n32, 624n51

White, Eliza (Liza), 63, 88, 184–85, 294, 598n5, 600n20

White, George, 234, 247, 248, 620n13, 630n33

White, Jack, 172, 252, 466

White, John, 93, 133, 216, 519, 643n54

White, Maria, 240–41

White, Mingo, 88, 203, 216, 332, 334–35, 531, 535, 542, 598n5, 600n15, 600n20, 616n24

White, Sallah, 430, 618n19

White, Tena, 93, 521

White, Uncle Bacchus, 31, 575n43, 599n7, 606n10

White, Uncle Dave, 91, 534, 634n48, 641n34

Whitley, Ophelia, 598n4

Wickliffe, Sylvester Sostan, 166, 596n32

Wiggins, James, 200, 214, 576nn50–51, 617n3

Wilborn, Dock, 88, 216, 239, 575n23

Wilburn, Jane McLeod, 439, 625nn4–5

Wilcox, Tom, 436, 516, 531, 533, 641n37

Wilkins, Alice, 30, 31, 87, 88, 92, 577n68, 634n48, 641n34

Willbanks, Green, 68, 89, 91, 188, 214, 575n23, 600n20
Williams, Anderson, 136, 616n35
Williams, Andy, 331, 332, 335, 616n25
Williams, Bessie, 268
Williams, Callie, 325–26, 331, 432, 588n13, 598n4
Williams, Catherine, 93, 522
Williams, Chaney Moore, 465, 564
Williams, Charles, 22
Williams, Charley, 74, 89, 94, 126, 134, 576n46, 582n56
Williams, Columbus, 84, 88, 125, 133, 575n23, 600nn19–20
Williams, Frank, 233, 247, 482
Williams, Gus, 364, 366–67
Williams, John, 136
Williams, John Thomas, 88, 208–9, 215
Williams, Julia, 126–27, 133
Williams, Lewis, 87, 92, 215
Williams, Lizzie (AL), 226, 389–90, 412, 415
Williams, Lizzie (MS), 247, 248, 310, 356, 373, 616n35
Williams, Lou, 598n5, 600n20
Williams, Millie, 247, 249, 466–67, 470, 518, *518*, 606n19
Williams, Mollie, 88, 92, 134, *156*, 162, 216, 247, 249, 455, 458–59, 575n40, 594n2, 624n55
Williams, Nancy, 60, 85, 89, 91, 94, 262–63, 387, 394, 409, 571n12, 582n56
Williams, Olin, 306–7, 376, 380–81, 614n47, 617n1, 619n42
Williams, Parson Rezin, 380–81, 383, 390
Williams, Reverend Charles, 357, 401, 557
Williams, Robert, 65, 90, 219–20, 233, 247, 248–49, 598n5
Williams, Soul, 91, 92, 94, 148, 586n37
Williams, Steve, 88, 597n3, 614n46
Williams, Victoria, 299, 307–8, 315–16
Williams, Wayman, 30, 32, 600n20
Williams, Willie, 606n10
Williams, Willis, 522
Willingham, Frances, 598n5, 600n15, 600nn19–20
Willis, Adeline, 598n4
Willis, Charles, 65, 69, 88, 452, 576nn45–46, 577n68, 582n54, 598n5
Willis, Charlotte, 599n10, 600n20, 629n8
Willis, Ella, 606n17

Willis, Sampson, 88, 92, 152–53, 202, 215, 216, 598n5
Wilson, Emoline, 598n5
Wilson, Isaac, 89, 92, 587n49
Wilson, Jake, 88, 215
Wilson, James, 17, 422
Wilson, Luke, 613n32
Wilson, Robert, 325, 331, 562, 598n4
Wilson, Sarah, 85, 89, 94, 553
Wilson, Shack, 471–72, 478, 621n21
Wilson, Temple, 171, 404, 430, 432, 556, 616n35
Wilson, Wash, 91, 94, 568n20
Windfield, Dicy, 56–57, 94, 582n56
Windham, Tom, 34, 38, 93, 124, 130, 215, 252, 393, 521
Winn, Willis, 17–18, 88, 112, 113, *113*, 121, *121*, 133, 134, 135, 215, 216, 223, 241, 264, 540, 600n20, 643n54
Wise, Alice, 464
Witt, Rube, 383–84, 391–92, 419, 526
Womble, George, 416, 597n3, 598n4
Wood, Mintie Gilbert, 12, 390, 426–27
Woodberry, Julia, 219, 495, 505, 544, 564, 596n32, 598n4
Woodrich, Julia, 164
Woods, Alex, 226, 331, 332, 336, 337, 345, 605n6, 606n9, 616n24, 617n36
Woods, Anda, 88, 229, 454, 457, 507, 606n10
Woods, George, 187, 416–17, 537, 600n20, 641n37
Woods, Ruben, 93, 117, 133, 135, 352, 616n35
Woods, Tom W., 133
Woodson (Woodsen), Willis, 136
Woodson, Alex, 614n46
Woodward, Aleck, 354, 356, 364, 373, 382
Word, Sam, 536, 539–40, 640n21, 641n37
Word, Sophia, 93
Worth, Pauline, 600nn19–20
Wright, Alice, 329, 331, 598n4
Wright, Anna, 600n13, 600n20
Wright, Caroline, 373
Wright, Henry, 75, 81, 89, 91, 133, 215, 436, 451–52, 597n2, 606n10, 616n35, 617n11, 626n3, 626n5
Wright, Maggie, 228, 524, 613n32
Wright, Mary, 90, 442–43, 575n23, 600n17, 600n19
Wyman, Susannah, 88, 368, 576n50, 599n7

Yarborough, Fannie, 408, 556–57, 625n10

Yarborough, Virginia, 536–37, 640n21, 641n37

Yellerday, Hilliard, 598n4

Young, Annie, 242, 378, 599n11, 600n20, 621n23

Young, Clara C., 223, 225, 304, 326, 331, 335, 350, 615n12

Young, Dink Walton, 625n1, 625n5

Young, George, 319, 331, 616n25, 617n11

Young, John, 93, 215, 521, 605n6

Young, John I., 468, 616n35

Young, Litt, 74, 89, 91, 93, 94, 105, 136, 456, *456*, 582n56, 598n5

Young, Narcissus, 446

Young, Robert, 88, 136, 558, 576n46, 576n51, 597n3

Young, Teshan, 89, 91, 172, *172*, 575n23, 597n3, 610n35, 632n29

Ziegler, Frank, 84, 88, 240

WPA Interviewers, Writers, and Editors

Anderson, Pernella M. (AR), 561

Angermiller, Florence (TX), 22, *464*, 594n1

Arnold, Mrs. Edgerton (TX), 21

Babcock, Barbara (GA), 334

Bowden, Bernice (AR), 11, 207, 532, 540

Bradley, Elizabeth (MS), 564

Byrd, Susan R. C. (VA), 22

Chandler, Genevieve Wilcox (SC), 316–17, 568n16

Cowan, Effie (TX), 15, 29–33, 247, 411, 427, 577n65, 591n14, 596n36, 618n15, 623n45, 628n20, 632nn28–29, 639n48, 642n48

Davis, Ada (TX), 15, 30–32, 311, 425, 568n20, 592n36, 632n14, 635n15

Davis, Annie Ruth (SC), 13

Davis, B. E. (TX), 105–6, 586n37

Davis, H. Grady (SC), 13

Dibble, Fred (TX), 3, 11, 164, 449, 542, 553, 556

Dixon, W. W. (SC), 20, 590n47

Drake, C. H. (TX), 22

Driskell, Edwin (GA), 503–4, 635n11

DuPre, F. S. (SC), 158

England, Iris (MS), 13

Ferriss, Abbott (MS), 481, 640n18

Foreman, Heloise M. (TX), 22

Gauthier, Sheldon F. (TX), 21

Giles, Mrs. D. W. (MS), 564, 575n27, 587n49

Graham, Carol N. (MS), 445

Grey, Bernice (TX), 3, 449, 556

Hall, Sarah H. (GA), 20

Halpert, Herbert (MS), 480–81, 568n16, 640n18

Hanberry, Mamie (KY), 31–32, 568n20

Hatcher, Letha K. (TX), 449

Holm, Stanley H. (TX), *464*, 594n1

Holmes, Mrs. Wm. F., 432, 604n22, 620n16

Holt, Minnie S. (MS), 557

Hornsby, Sadie (GA), 19, 553, 563

Huff, Ruby (MS), 18, 518–19

Jaffee, Joseph E. (GA), 31

Johnson, Margaret (SC), 283

Jones, J. R. (GA), 207, 299, 388

Knowles, Merton (IN), 233, 251, 252, 253, 640n27

Logan, Miriam (OH), 25

Love, Edith Bell (GA), 20

Martin, Clothilde R. (SC), 21

Matthews, T. Pat (NC), 18, 23, 493, 607n22

McCune, Grace (GA), 373

McKinney, Robert (LA), 43, 357

McKinney, Watt (AR), 25, 380

Moore, Edith Wyatt (MS), 22

Mueller, Mabel E. (MO), 86, 486, 632n27

Nelson, Robert L. (GA), 410, 547

Nixon, Felix (TX), 23–24, 25

Oliphant, Louise (GA), 191, 638n40

Perry, Rhussus (AL), 570n29
Phipps, Woody (TX), 111
Poole, Mary A. (MS), 20, 556

Sims, Caldwell (SC), 25

Tartt, Ruby Pickens (AL), 418, 568n16, 628n36
Taylor, Samuel S. (AR), 13, 16, 22, 222, 422
Thompson, Ruth (OH), 570n29

Van Meter, Beulah (IN), 233, 248, 249, 253–54, 564
Volley, Isaiah (VA), 20

Walsh, Jean H. (MS), 414
Wells, Mrs. Charles E. (MS), 40, 617n1
Whitley, A. M. (GA), 13
Wilkerson, J. R. (KY), 12–13
Williams, Ellis (NY), 31

Young, Lucile (SC), 13

Other Slaves, Ex-Slaves, and Antebellum Free Blacks

Abraham, 197
Aleckson, Sam, 588n8, 697n40
Alford, Ella, 616n35
Allen, Richard, 361
Anderson, John, 597n3
Anderson, Robert, 57–58, 138
Armstrong, Amelia, 599n11
Aunt Dice, 586n42
Aunt Jinsy, 521, 640n13

Ball, Charles, 209, 578n2, 586n36, 588n8, 604n14
Ball, Steptoe, 588n8, 589n36, 590n36
Banks, Cap, 543
Barnes, Roan, 578n2, 616n35
Bazadier, Philip, 197
Bibb, Henry, 189, 586n36, 588n8, 603n50
Blythe, Nat, 9

Bob, 240, 604n14
Bradford, Lue, 588n8
Brewer, Christopher, 577n65
Brimmer, Mary, 593n59
Brooks, Charlotte, 613n39
Brown, John, 240, 578n2, 604n14
Brown, Katie, 583n64
Brown, William Wells, 181, 597n3, 600n20, 601n21

Caesar, 148
Campbell, Hettie, 108, 587n48
Channell, L. M., 498, 633n32, 633n38
Charley, 55
Coppin, Bishop L. J., 349, 352–53, 356, 597n3, 600n20

Dabney's Old Harry, 205–6
Davis, Daniel Webster, 49, 106
Davy, 197
Douglass, Frederick, 55, 189, 348–49, 383, 465, 546, 548–49, 578n2, 588n8, 597n3
Dubois, Silvia, 578n2
Dyson, John, *161*

Elzy, Melvina, 616n35

Fedric, Francis, 124, 601n21
Fiddler Jack, *195*
Finch, Cicero, 599n11, 600n20
Fitzpatrick, Sarah, 586n42, 600n18

George, 604n15
Gilliat, Sy, 197
Goodman, Jerry, 604n14
Grandfather Sol, 356
Green, Elisha W., 355
Green, Susan, 355

Happy John, 245, 587n51
Henderson, Lee, 584n69
Henson, Josiah, 586n36, 597n3

Ihurod, 55
Ivey, Zack, 142–43

Jackson, Aunt Julia Ann, *19*
Jackson, John Andrew, 588n8
Jacobs, Harriett, 588n8
James (Jemmy), 505n28
Jerry, *67*
Johnson, Frank, 590n49
Johnson, William, 487, 488–89, *491*, 631n3
Jones, Druella (Aunt Jones), *585*

Larkin, Patsy, 616n22
Lewis, Jane, 86, 583n64, 584n66
Lewis, Roscoe E., 5
Lowery, Irving, 356, 578n2, 588n8, 588n10, 599nn11–12, 600n20, 604n14

Mark, 138, 590n48
Martin, 604n14
McGowan, Jordan, 203–4, 213, 604n14
McCrea, Uncle Billy, 600n14
Mr. Huddleston, 623n44

Noko, 205
Northrup, Solomon, 197, 547, 578n2, 582n54, 585n24, 586n42, 588n8, 597n3, 604n14

Owens, Pricilla, 616n35

Parker, Allen, 49, 200, 574n14, 578n2, 593n53
Peelin, Joe, 142
Penny, 138
Peter (I), 197
Peter (II), 604n14
Prince, 205

Randolph, Peter, 395–96, 586n36
Remus, 196
Roberson, Frank, 616n35
Roberts, James, 149
Robinson, 150, 161, 594n74
Robinson, Dan, 584n65
Robinson, Jane, 616n35
Robinson, William H., 326, 368, 585n20, 586n36, 616n31

Romulus, 196
Roper, Moses, 478

Sam, 55
Scott, Joseph C., 203
Scott, Linzy, 588n8
Scruggs, Uncle John, 585n20
Smalley, Laura, 568n19, 623n41
Smith, Aunt Harriet, 568n19, 618n14
Smith, Harry, 24, 187, 190, 229, 236, 270, 578n2, 597n3, 600n20
Steward, Austin, 356, 588n8, 589n26
Stroyer, Jacob, 34, 61, 197, 201, 239–40, 528, 586n42, 597n3

Thomas, James, 197, 487, 488–89, 578n2, 597n3, 604n14
Tims, Rosa, 465
Tom, 137–38

Uncle Ben, 604n15
Uncle Billy, 104, 231–33, 604n15, 606n13, 606n16
Uncle Porringer, 604n15

Veney, Bethany, 497

Walker, George, 210
Walker, Whit, 66, 458, 477n65
Washington, Booker T., 156, 587n58, 597n3
White, Fanny, 58, 106, 575n24, 583n64, 586n41
Williams, Isaac D., 58, 98, 197, 578n2, 586n36
Williams, James, 588n8
Woods, Kalvin, 323, 615n13

Young, Joseph, 603n50
Young, Nancy, 588n8

Zamba, 72

Songs and Tunes

"1821 Jesus Work Is Just Begun," 352

"Abe Lincoln Freed the Nigger," 527

"Adam in the Garden Pinning Leaves," 295, 612n18

"Adam's Fallen Race," 429

"Ah Cuss Dat Steamboat Rover," 484

"Ain't Gonna Rain No More," 252, 459, 498, 628n24

"Ain't I Glad I've Got Out of the Wilderness (Leaning On the Lord)," 410, 573n1

"Ain't No More Cane On the Nechiz (Brazos)," 30

"Ain't No Use Me Working So Hard," 570n8

"Ain't You Weary Trablin'," 397

"Air Tune," 278

"All Around My House Was Walled in Brick," 387

"All Don't Form a Row Shan't Drink," 184, 602n34

"All God's Chilluns Are Gatherin' (Is a Goin') Home," 179, 403

"All My Sisters Gone," 21, 429

"All the Way My Savior Leads Me," 364

"Always from Kare, Never Spent a Dime," 363

"Am I a Soldier of the Cross?," 303, 353, 362–63, 365–66, 376, 614n44

"Amazing Grace (How Sweet the Sound)," 96, 272, 303, 352, 356, 361, 363, 364–65, 382, 408, 420, 427, 584n1, 614n44, 619n41

"And Am I Born To Die?," 358, 359–60, 365, 366–67, 368, 384

"And Must I Be To Judgement Brought?," 359, 367

"And Must This Body Die?," 367

"Angels Changed My Name, The," 425, 621n24

"Arkansas Traveler, The," 62, 66, 79, 83, 582n54

"Around the Throne of God in Heaven," 367

"Baby Please Don't Go," 592n29

"Babylon Is Fallen," 516, 528, 529–30

"Barbara Allen" (Child 84), 502, 503, 509

"Batson" (Laws I 10), *109*

"Battle Cry of Freedom (Rally 'Round the Flag), The," 524, 527–28, 640n24

"Battle Hymn of the Republic, The," 542, 642nn51–52

"Battle of Elkhorn Tavern (The Pea Ridge Battle), The" (Laws A 12), 508

"Battle of Shiloh Hill, The" (Laws A 11), 91, 509, 510

"Because He First Loved Me," 367

"Been Listening All the Day," 390, 620n8

"Before I'd Be a Slave," 393, 621n21

"Better Mind How You Walk on the Cross," 32, 302, 391, 398–400, 622n35

"Big Bells A-Ringin' in de Army of de Lord," 303

"Big Bethel Church, De," 30

"Big Woods, De," 79

"Big Yam Taters In de Sandy Lan'," 30

"Billy in the Lowground," 582n54

"Black Eye Susan (Black Eyed Susie)," 66, 582n54

"Black Gal Sweet," 30

"Black Gal-Le-Lo," 469

"Black Joke, The," 138, 276, 590n4

"Black Mustache (Darling Black Mustache), The," 155, 594n6

"Bluebird's Temperence Song, The," 467–68

"Boat Am Comin' and Us Stan'in' on de Bank," 429

"Bob White," 454, 626n7

"Boll Weevil, The" (Laws I 17), 30, 503, 514

"Bongo Dance, The," 47

"Bonnie Blue Flag, The," 526–27, 539–40, 640n21

"Boss Man, Boss Man, Please Gimme My Time," 185

"Bread of Heaven," 368

"Bringing In the Sheaves," 272, 368, 611n46

"Broad Is the Road That Leads to Death," 353–54, 368

"Brother Green (The Dying Soldier)," 508–9

"Buffalo Gals," 458–59, 628n20

"Bulldogs A Barkin'," 469

"Bull-Doze Blues," 143–44, 592n35

"Bully of the Town, The" (Laws I 14), 503

"But I Ain't Free," 566–67

"Buzzard Song," 462, 628n37

"Bye Baby Bunting," 444, 446

"Bye-O-Baby!," 444

"By'm By Don' You Griebe Atter Me," 397

"Cacklin' Hen," 79–80, 83, 148, 580n38, 582n54, 585n27

"Can, Can, Candio," 440

"Captain Jinks of the Horse Marines," 458, 595n7

"Carry Me Back to Old Virginia," 632n29

"Carve Dat Possum," 543, 643n55

"Catch Liza Jane," 436, 457

"Champ Joe Louis (King of the Gloves)," 24

"Charge To Keep I Have, A," 368

"Cherry Bound and Durham," 468

INDICES 721

"Children of the Heavenly King," 368–69

"Chillun, Wha' Yuh Gwinna Do in de Jedgment Mornin'?," 387–88

"Christ He Done Hung on d' Cross," 429

"Christmas Time," 450

"Climb up the Walls of Zion," 429

"Climbing Up the Golden Stairs," 527, 545, 640n24, 643n60

"Coffee Grows On White Oak Trees," 456, 627n15

"Cold Frosty Morning," 126, 311, 489n41

"Come, Saints and Sinners, Hear Me Tell," 369

"Come Along, True Believer, Come Along," 30

"Come Change My Name," 395

"Come Let Us Now Forget Our Mirth, and Think That We Must Die," 354, 369

"Come 'Long Gals an' Let's Go to Boston," 452

"Come on Chariot and Take Her Home," 429

"Come to Shuck That Corn To-Night," 182–83

"Come Ye Sinners, Poor and Needy (Wretched)," 353, 369, 448

"Come Ye That Love the Lord," 312, 359, 369–70, 373–74, 620n8

"Corn Bread Rough," 595n15

"Corn-Shucking Time," 602n35

"Cotton-Eyed Joe," 53, 85, 89, 183, 219, 573n1, 602n34

"Crawdad Song, The," 570n8

"Cross Road Blues," 276

"Cuckoo, The," 512, 636n30

"Cuckoo's Nest, The," 507, 512, 636n30, 637n39

"Cum 'Long Boys En Lets Go Er Huntin'," 472

"Dandy Womac Am a Backin' Boat, De," 484

"Daniel in De Lion's Den," 429

"Dark Cloud Arising Like Gwine to Rain," 185

"Dark Was the Night, and Cold the Ground," 272, 302, 350, 363, 365, 370–71, 584n1

"Dar's Golden Streets and a Pearly Gate Somewhars," 479

"Dat Old Wheel Begins to Turn," 429

"Day Is Past and Gone," 371

"Death Has Been Here, and Borne Away," 371, 378

"Debil Has No Place Here, The," 272

"Dese Bones Gonna Rise Again," 399, 447–48

"Devil Among the Tailors, The," 581n53, 626n1

"Devil Is a Liar and a Conjurer Too, The," 267, 388, 620n4

"Devil's Dream," 83, 245, 278, 450, 454, 581n53, 590n2, 626n1

"Devil's Joy at Sabbath Breaking, The," 278

"Did Christ O'er Sinners Weep?," 371

"Didn't It Rain," 389, 404, 406

"Dig My Grave With a Silver Spade," 364–65

"Dinah's Got a Wooden Leg (Sal's Got a Meat Skin Lay Away)," 85, 160, 458, 595n15, 628n18

"Dis Is a Buryin' Ground," 396

"Dis Time Tomorrow Night," 561

"Dixie," 128, 205, 240, 483, 496, 500–501, 534, 594n6, 634nn47–48, 641n34

"Do, Lord, Remember Me," 422–23

"Doll, Doll, Young Lady," 437–38

"Don' You See Dem Sixteen of Chullun?," 442

"Don't Mind Working from Sun to Sun," 472–73

"Don't You Hear Jesus Call?," 397

"Doodle, Doodle, Your House Burned Down," 442, 625n10

"Dose Black-Eyed Peas Is Lucky," 31

"Down by the Riverside," 389, 390, 411

"Down in Mobile," 562

"Down in the Valley to Pray," 394, 401, 413, 425, 621n23

"Down into the River Where My Savior Was Baptized," 390

"Down the Dirt Road Blues," 585n9

"Drinking of the Wine," 411

"Egg Nog, Sugar and Beer," 69

"Elder Green Blues," 585n9

"Eph Got the Coon," 235, 251, 252

"Er Had a Little Dawg, His Name Wuz Rice," 141–42

"Fire on the Mountain," 233

"First to de Graveyard," 430

"Fish," 441

"Fisher's Hornpipe," 137, 139, 582n54, 590n2

"Fox and Hounds," 80, 147, 148

"Fox Chase," 80, 148, 593nn61–63

"Fox Hunt, The," 148, 581n39, 593n62

"Fox Went A-Hunting (Old Granny Mistletoe), The," 506, 635n14

"Frog in the Mill Pond," 437, 438, 625n4

"Froggie Went A-Courting," 89, 506, 635n15

"Gallanip-Er-Horsefly and Whoop It," 185

"Gee Thar Buck," 468

"Georgia (Return, O God of Love, Return)," 381

"Get Up in the Cool," 582n54

"Girl I Left Behind Me, The" (Laws P 1 B), 283, 508

"Glory, Glory, Hallelujah, When I Lay My Burden Down," 411–12

"Glory to the Dying Land," 303

"Go Away Ole Man and Leave Me Alone (Go Way, Ole Man)," 563

"Go Preach My Gospel, Saith the Lord," 96, 272, 363, 584n1, 619n41

"Go to Sleepy, Little Baby (All the Pretty Horses)," 28–31

"Go to the Devil and Shake Yourself," 278

"God Is My Shepherd," 430

"God Will Take Care of You, Be Not Afraid," 426–27

"Goin' Home Soon in de Mornin'," 396–97

"Goin' to Carry dis Body to de Grave-Yard," 430

"Going to Lead de Ole Sheep Along," 392

"Going to Move to Alabama," 385n29

"Going Up the Country," 592n35

"Going Up the Country, Bugle, Oh!," 181

"Good Shepherd (Feed My Sheep)," 361, 371–72, 375, 417, 595n13, 619n36

"Gospel Train (I), The," 315, 412

"Gospel Train (II), The," 388, 412–13

"Gourd of Cold Water (Regular, Regular, Rolling Over, Rolling Under), A," 20, 451, 453, 459–60, 461–62, 628n36

"Granny Will Your Dog Bite," 233, 594n6

"Grasshopper Sittin' on a Sweet Tater Vine," 371, 630n17

"Gray Goose (Go Tell Aunt Nancy, Patsy, Rhody), The," 448

"Great Big Nigger, Laying 'Hind de Log," 42, 570n8

"Greeley and Grant Went Up North," 424–25

"Grey Goose, The," 477, 630n27

"Guide Me, O My Great Redeemer (Jehovah)," 368, 372–73

"Ha, Hi, Ho, the Cow Want Corn," 185

"Hancock Rides de Big Gray Horse," 544

"Hand Me Down the Silver Trumpet, Gabriel," 409, 624n56

"Hands Up and Go Round, Old Georgia Rabbit Who?," 441

"Hang Jeff Davis (Or Others) From a Sour Apple Tree," 7, 130, 245, 515–19, 524–25, 523, 530, 540–44, 641n29, 643nn53–54

"Happy Home; Sweet Home; Where Never Comes de Night," 305

"Happy Land of Canaan," 534–36

"Happy Stranger, The," 636n30

"Hardshell Ship, The," 430

"Hark from the Tombs (A Funeral Thought)," 20, 341–42, 352, 354–61, 355, 367, 370, 373, 376, 474, 619n34, 619n42

"Hark the Voice of Jesus Calling," 474

"Harper's Creek and Roarin' Ribber," 582n54

"Have a Feast Here Tonight," 644n8

"He Never Said a Mumbling Word," 31

"Hear de Angels Callin'," 271–72

"Hear the Trumpet Sound," 483

"Heave Away! Heave Away!," 31

"Heaven, Sweet Heaven," 396, 621n28

"Hell Broke Loose in Georgia," 245

"Herodias Went Down to de River One Day," 302, 614n42

"High Heel Shoes and Calico Stockings," 13–14, 626n7

"High Water Everywhere—Parts I & II," 585n29

"Hit's Eighteen-Hundred an' Forty-Nine," 31

"Ho Syne No Day," 47

"Hoe, Ramsey, Hoe," 177

"Hold De Deal," 562, 644n7

"Hold Out True Believer," 390

"Hold Up, American Spirit," 470–71

"Hold Your Light," 385

"Homespun Dress, The," 521, 526–27, 536, 640n21

"Hoo-dooism," 634n10

"Hop Light, Lady (Step Light, Ladies)," 31, 83, 202, 454–55, 457, 561–62
"Hopping Mad'son Backs Out on Time," 484
"Hopus Creek and de Water," 582n54
"Hounds, The," 148, 581n39, 593n62
"How Firm a Foundation, Ye Saints of the Lord," 374, 492–93, 632n21
"How Happy Every Child of Grace," 374
"How Long (Oh, Lawd, How Long)," 323, 413
"How Long Us Hafta Linger," 413
"How Sweet the Name of Jesus Sounds," 354, 374
"How Tedious and Tasteless the Hours," 374
"Husband Don't You 'Buse Me," 562

"I Am a Baptist Born," 413, 620n9
"I Am Bound to Cross Jordan," 414
"I Am Going to Preach My Gospel," 430
"I Am the Light of the World," 425
"I Baptize You in de Ribber Jordan," 430
"I Been Long Ways to Hear the Gospel," 430
"I Belong to the Band," 414
"I Can Whip the Scoundrel," 539
"I Don't Care Where They Bury My Body," 448
"I Feel as Happy as a Big Sunflower," 452
"I Goes to Fight Mit Sigel," 642n41
"I Got Beef In De Market," 560–61
"I Got 'Ligion," 414
"I Heard the Voice of Jesus Say, 'Come unto Me and Rest,'" 43, 159–60, 374–75, 423, 595n13
"I Hollered at My Mule," 31
"I Know (Feel) My Time Ain't Long," 414–15
"I Love the Lord; He Heard My Cry," 375
"I Love Thy Kingdom, Lord," 376
"I Really Believe Christ Is Comin' Again," 335
"I Sings an' I Shouts Wid All My Might," 303
"I Tell You, Sister," 430
"I Think When I Read That Sweet Story of Old," 375
"I Want to Be an Angel," 92–93, 353, 375–76
"I Want to Be Ready (Walking in Jerusalem Just Like John)," 415
"I Want to Die A-Shouting (Traveling to the Grave)," 303, 614n43
"I Want to Go to Heaven When I Die," 430

"I Wants to Go Where Jesus Lives," 43
"I Was Low Down in the Valley," 390, 394–95
"I Wish, I Wish," 503, 634n4
"I Wish I Was in Heaven," 430
"I Wonder Where Is Good Old Daniel (The Hebrew Children)," 415–17
"I Would Like to Catch-a-Feller Looking Like Me," 452
"I Would Not Live Alway; I Ask Not to Stay," 376
"I Wouldn't Have a Poor Girl," 541–42
"I Wrastled Wid Satan," 31
"I'd Rather Be a Nigger Than a Poor White Man," 220, 605n2
"If I Had Ole Abe Lincoln All Over Dis World," 521
"If I Must Die, O, Let Me Die, With Hope," 378
"If It Hadn't Been for Uncle Abraham," 536
"If Religion Was to Buy," 31, 416
"If the River Was Whiskey," 317, 637n39
"If You Get There Before I Do," 416, 428
"If You Want to Go a Courtin'," 31
"I'll Be God O'Mighty God Damned if I Don't Kill a Nigger," 242
"I'll Be There at Getting Up Morning," 430
"I'll Go if It's Raining," 390
"I'll Hang My Heart on the Willow Tree," 520
"I'll Nevah Turn Back No Moah," 416–17
"I'll Overcome Someday (We Shall Overcome)," 361
"I'll Tell You," 84
"I'm a Goin' Away Tomorrow," 464
"I'm a Good Old Rebel," 31, 508
"I'm a Gwine to Tell Yo' Bout de Comin of de Savior," 388–89
"I'm Bound for the Promised Land," 380–81, 431, 455. See also "On Jordan's Stormy Banks I Stand"
"I'm Bound to Be a Soldier in the Army of the South," 517
"I'm Comin', Glory, Hallelujah," 407
"I'm Glad Salvation's Free," 330, 563, 573, 576, 593, 619n42
"I'm Goin' to Pizen You," 504–5
"I'm Going Away to the City," 390
"I'm Going from the Cottonfields," 31
"I'm Going Home to Die No More," 347, 390, 426, 617n1

"I'm Gwine Join De Band," 560–61
"I'm in Dis Battlefield on My Way," 401
"I'm Off for Charleston," 486
"I'm on My Way," 395
"I'm Pressing on the Upward Way," 376
"In Evil Long I Took Delight," 376–77
"In Mercy, Not in Wrath, Rebuke Me, Gracious God!,"
    377
"In Some Lady's Garden," 440–41, 462, 563, 625n9
"Inching Along," 391, 398–99, 620n13
"I'se Gwine Home, an' Cuss Out de Ole Overseer,"
    466, 476, 548
"It's a Crane, De Same Old Crane," 477
"I've Been Hoodooed," 634n10

"Jack of Diamonds (Rye Whiskey)," 89, 272, 511, 513–15,
    584n1, 636n30, 637n39, 638nn43–44, 639n45
"Jackass Stamped, Jackass Neighed," 468
"Jacob's Ladder," 372, 417–18, 419
"Jaunting Car, The," 526, 536
"Jawbone," 200, 604n18
"Jay Bird Died Wid de Whoopin' Couf," 460
"Jeff Davis (Lincoln) Rides a White Horse," 536–40,
    641n37
"Jeff in Petticoats," 530, 641n29
"Jes' Carry Me and Bury Me," 418
"Jesus, Lover of My Soul," 377
"Jesus Gonna Make Up My Dying Bed," 31
"Jesus Is a Rock in a Weary Land," 418
"Jesus Keep Me Near the Cross," 377
"Jesus My All to Heav'n Is Gone," 365, 369, 377–78
"Jesus Will Fix It for You," 21, 569n25
"Jews Killed Poor Jesus, The," 397–98, 622n33
"Jim Crow's Ramble," 496
"Joe Bowers" (Laws B 14), 508
"John Brown's Body," 517, 541, 542, 643nn43–44
"John Hardy" (Laws I 2), 31, 595n15
"John Henry" (Laws I 1), 31, 469, 502, 503, 514, 639n47
"John Saw the Number in the Middle of the Air," 389
"John T. Moore, the Lula D. and All Them Boats Are
    Mine, The," 483
"Johnny, Come Fill Up the Bowl," 531–33
"Johnny Booker," 235, 251, 252

"Johnson Gal," 451, 626n2
"Joshua Fought the Battle of Jericho," 505, 612n10
"Juanita," 155, 594n5
"Juba This and Juba That," 55, 60, 458
"Juber, Cesar Boy," 56
"Jump Back," 604n18
"Jump Jim Crow," 60, 454, 496–99, 633nn31–32, 633n39

"Keemo Kimo," 635n15
"Keep My Skillet Good and Greasy," 570n8
"Keep the Fire Burning While Your Soul's Fired Up,"
    388, 412
"Keep 'Way F'om Me Hoodoo an' Witch," 31
"Keep Your Lamp Trimmed and Burning," 417, 418–19
"King George and His Army," 440
"Kingdom Coming," 528–29, 640n27
"Kitty Wells," 160, 167

"La boulangère a des écus (The Baker's Wife Has
    Plenty of Money)," 93, 165–66
"Lamkin" (Child 93), 634n3
"Land of Canaan," 419, 426
"Lates Jim Crow, De," 496
"Laura," 595n15
"Les haricots sont pas sale," 166
"Let Thy Kingdom, Gentle Savior," 371–72
"Let Us Cheer the Weary Traveler," 392, 620n15
"Let's Go Down to Jordan," 32, 309, 391–92, 419–20
"Lie on Him if You Sing Right," 431
"Life's Railway to Heaven," 426–27
"Lily of the Valley, The," 420
"Lincoln Board, Lincoln Board," 438
"Lincoln's Not Satisfied, He Wants to Fight Again," 518
"Little Baby's Gone to Heaven," 420–21
"Little Boy's Song to His Mother, The," 378
"Little Chil'ren, I Am Going Home," 431
"Little David (Play Your Harp)," 92, 293, 294, 391, 402,
    612n8, 612n12
"Little Liza Jane," 457–58, 537, 540, 602n38, 626n6,
    627n16
"Little Old Log Cabin in the Lane," 585n20
"Little Sir Hugh" (Child 155), 634n3
"Little Wheel Rolling in My Heart," 421

"London Bridge," 440, 443, 626n13

"Lord I'se a Comin' Home," 479

"Lord Randall" (Child 12), 504–5, 634n7

"Love Has Brought Me to Despair" (Laws P 25), 503, 636n30, 640n11

"Maid Freed from the Gallows, The" (Child 95), 507

"Magnolia Two-Step," 582n54

"Make Me a Pallet on the Floor," 512–13, 637n39

"Mammy's (Daddy's) Little Carolina Coons," 445

"Mammy's L'il Alabama Coon," 491

"Marching Through Georgia," 520, 528

"Marse Hampton (Clark, Grant) Et de Watermelon, Mr. Chamberlain (J. D. Giddings, Greeley) Knawed de Rine (Rind, Vine)," 247, 543

"Mary Don't You Weep (Pharoah's Army)," 130, 393, 621n21

"Mary Jane," 443

"Mary Wept and Martha Moaned," 409

"Maryland! My Maryland," 522

"Massa Sleeps in de Feathah Bed," 466

"Massa's in the Cold, Hard Ground," 632n29

"Master of de House Gimme Meat Widout Salt," 166

"Mawnin' Star Is Risin', De," 470

"Me an' Mah Wife Had a Fallin Out," 561

"Mister Johnson, Turn Me A-Loose," 81, 581n46

"Mix de Meal, Fry de Batter," 32

"Molly Bright (How Many Miles to Babylon)," 437, 438–39, 625n5

"Monkey Married the Baboon's Sister, The," 580n38

"Mother How Long 'Fore I' Gwine?," 280

"Motherless Children (Sees a Hard Time)," 421

"Must Jesus Bear the Cross Alone," 365, 378

"My Father Idled His Time Away," 390, 401

"My Grandfather's Clock," 528

"My Knee-Bone's Aching (Heaven Is My Aim)," 339, 421–22, 428

"My Lord Is So High (You Have to Come in By the Door)," 394, 409–10

"My Lord Say Dey's Room Enough," 478

"My Ol' Gray Headed Mother," 389

"My Old Mistress Promised Me," 252–53, 393, 453, 466, 626n3, 626n5

"My Sister, I Feels 'Im (Old Slave Canticle)," 422

"Natcha (Natchez) Under de Hill," 69

"Naught Is Naught an Figger Is a Figger," 467, 629n10

"Nearer My God to Thee," 282

"Nigger Mighty Happy When He Layin' by de Corn," 32

"Nightingale (One Morning in May), The" (Laws P 14), 635n17

"No More Auction Block for Me (Many Thousands Gone)," 305–6, 311–12

"Nobody Business but Mine," 562–63, 644n8

"Nobody Knows the Trouble I've Seen," 406, 624n50

"O, Come, Angel Band," 565, 644n12

"O, Fare You Well," 395–96

"O for a Faith That Will Not Shrink," 371, 378–79

"O for a Thousand Tongues to Sing," 379, 393

"O Happy Day, That Fixed My Choice," 379–80

"O Susannah," 632n29

"Of All de Varmints in de Woods," 472

"Off for Richmond so Early in the Mornin'," 519

"Oh, Abe Lincoln, I'm Gwine Away," 424

"Oh, De Win's In De Wes'," 444

"Oh, Little Mary, I Want Some Water (My Dinner)," 470

"Oh, Molly Cotton Tail," 32

"Oh, Where Is He," 431

"Oh, Yes, We'll Gain the Day," 442

"Oh! I'se A-Gwine to Lib Always," 31, 32

"Oh Lousy Nigger," 562

"Oh! My Haid, My Pore Haid," 185

"Oh Rebels Ain't You Sorry," 642

"Oh Yes! Oh Yes! I Been Conjurin'," 286–87

"Oh—Graveyard," 564–65

"Ol' Aunt Katy," 562

"Ol' Bella, Ol' Bella, Tu'n 'Roun'," 441–42

"Ol Cow Piedy," 448–49

"Ol Hen, She Flew, Ovah de Garden Gate," 470

"Ol' Possum in a Holler Log," 441

"Old Beauregard and Jackson," 524

"Old Black Joe," 595n7

"Old Cotton, Old Co'n, See Yo' Ever' Mo'n," 473

"Old Cow Died, The," 460–62, 628n33, 628n37

"Old Dan Tucker," 83, 96, 153, 248, 264, 495, 499–500, 584n1, 595n7, 633n40, 633n43, 634n45

"Old Folks at Home (Way Down Upon the Swanee River), The," 595n7, 632n29

"Old Grey Horse Came Tearing Out the Wilderness, The," 53, 410, 573n1

"Old Grey Mare (She Ain't What She Used to Be), The," 410, 573n1

"Old Joe's Daid an' Gone," 116

"Old Master, Heah We Are," 230–31

"Old Moster Eats Beef and Sucks on de Bone," 525

"Old Satan Mighty Busy," 391

"Old Satan's Mad and I'm Glad," 523, 640n20

"Old Ship of Zion," 387, 404, 408, 623n41

"Old Sweet Beans and Barley Grows," 626n13

"Old Virginia Never Tire," 474

"Old Virginia Reel," 77

"Old Witch (Chick-A-Ma, Craney Crow)," 435, 437, 439, 625n1, 625n7

"Old-Time Religion," 406–7, 432, 624n51

"Ole Bee Make the Honeycomb, De," 32, 467, 629n9

"Ole Brer Rabbit, Shake It," 442–43, 626n12

"Ole Hog 'Round de Bench," 471

"Ole John Bell Is De'd en Gone," 305

"Ole Lou'siana Niggers Et Hot Mush," 466, 629n8

"Ole Massa Take Dat New Brown Coat," 31, 32

"On Canaan's Happy Shore," 359, 419, 541, 621n18, 642n50

"On Dat Shore Will I Rest," 387

"On Jordan's Stormy Banks I Stand," 304, 342, 353, 354–55, 359, 403, 419, 431, 475, 480–81. See also "I'm Bound for the Promised Land"

"On the Hill of Calvary," 422

"Once I Was So Lucky, Old Master Set Me Free," 176–77, 549

"One Day, One Day, Old Satan went Abroad," 386–87

"Original Jim Crow, De," 496

"Our Goodman" (Child 274), 507

"Our Little Meetin's Bound to Break," 299

"Pass Around the Bottle," 643n54

"Patter de Pat," 237, 470

"Pay Day," 644n8

"Pearl; She Am de Fines' Boat, De," 484

"Peter Butler's Son," 537–40, 642n38, 642nn41–42, 642n48

"Pick Dat Cotton," 463

"Pig in a Pen," 602n38

"Pig-O-O-O," 469

"Please Don't Touch My Waterfall," 307–8, 314–17

"Plenary (Auld Lange Syne)," 355, *355*

"Polk an' Clay Went to War," 184

"Polly (Molly, Jenny) Put the Kettle On," 455, 627n11

"Pony Blues," 585n29

"Pool at Bethesda (Beside the Gospel Pool), The," 381

"Poor Little Black Sheep," 447–48

"Poor Stranger (Sweet Europe), The," 512, 635n17, 636n30

"Pop Goes the Weasel," 455, 627n12

"Possum Up a 'Simmon Tree," 561, 643n5

"Praying Time Will Soon Be Over," 390

"Preaching Blues (Up Jumped the Devil)," 276

"Pretty Little Pink," 91, 456, 627n14

"Pretty Saro," 636n30

"Promise of God Salvation Free to Give, The," 480

"Pull de Husk, Break de Ear," 186

"Put on My Long White Robe," 431

"Quill Blues," 592n30

"Rabbit and Peavine," 442, 626n11

"Rabbit Foot Quick," 32

"Rabbit Gittin' Up in a Holler," 185

"Rabbit Hair," 459

"Rabbit in de Hollow, Ain't Got No Dog (Rabbit on a Log)," 562–63, 644n8

"Raccoon Is a Funny Thing, The," 472, 630n18

"Ragged Pat," 11, 568n17

"Railway Spiritualized, The," 617n1

"Rain Come Wet Me, Sun Come Dry Me," 473, 630n20

"Raise a Ruckus," 235, 451, 452

"Raise de Heaven as High as de Sky," 392

"Raking the Hay," 507, 635n17

INDICES 727

"Rango (Reuben Ranzo)," 480–81, 630n34, 640n18
"Ration Day," 32
"Read in the Gospel of Matthew," 431
"Rebel Soldier (Prisoner), The," 510–14, 636n30, 637n31, 637n33, 637nn36–39, 638nn41–42, 639n45
"Red Shirt, Red Shirt," 186
"Red Wing," 491
"Religion Is So Sweet," 32
"Resurrection Drawin' Nigh," 431
"Return, O God of Love, Return (Georgia)," 381
"Reveille," *148*, 589n37
"Ride on King Jesus (No Man Can Hinder)," 32, 387, 619n3
"Riley the Furniture Man," 602n38
"Riley's Wagon," 602n38
"Ring Around the Rosie," 626n13
"Rise, Shine," 431
"Rock Along, Susie," 477
"Rock Candy," 296, 549, 613n23
"Rock Daniel," 295–96, 424, 612n22
"Rock of Ages," 155, 281, 594n6
"Rock the Cradle, John (Old Humphrey Hodge a Farmer Was)," 495, 632n27
"Rock Where Moses Stood, The," 391
"Rock-A-Bye Baby," 444, 446
"Roll Jordan Roll," 395, 404, 406, 408, 623nn45–46
"Root, Hog, or Die" (Laws B 21), 526, 640n22
"Rough and Rocky Road," 396, 613n38, 620n11
"Round De Corn, Sally," 185, 186, 602n37
"Row, Row, Who Laid Dat Rail?," 32
"Run, Nigger, Run," 32, 83, 160, 165, 167, 174, 175, 190, 218, 219, 221, 227, 228, 231–40, 244, 247–54, 460, 499, 607n25
"Run, Sinner, Run," 238, 607n26
"Run Away, Sojus of the Cross," 400
"Run Liza Jane," 453, 457, 626n6

"Saddle Old Ball," 84
"Sail Away Rauley," 439
"Sally Ann," 455
"Sally Goodin (Goodun, Gooden, Goodwin)," 454, 585n45, 626n8
"Saturday Night and Sunday Too," 474, 630n21

"Saw My Mother Flying by de Skies," 431
"See That My Grave Is Kept Clean," 644n11
"See When He Rise," 431
"Shadders, Dey Er Creepin' Tode's de Top of de Hill, De," 32
"Shake Hands and Goodbye," 299–300
"Shall We Gather At The River," 381
"Shango," 47
"Sharp Bit, De Strong Ahm, De," 475
"Sheep Shear Corn, by the Rattle of His Horn," 183–84
"Sheep's in Cotton Patch," 501
"Shine on Me," 375, 423–24
"Shoo, Chicken, Shoo," 440, 557
"Shoo, Shoo, Shoo Gander," 439
"Shoo de Debbil Out de Corner," 295
"Shoo Fly," 155, 443, 472, 594n6, 630n19
"Shoot the Buffalo," 69, 578n71
"Shortenin' Bread (Cracklin' Bread)," 56, 574n12
"Show Pity, Lord, O Lord Forgive," 381–82
"Shuck, Shuck, Round Up Your Corn," 184
"Shuck Man Can't Let Git Away," 188
"Shuck This Corn, Boys, Let's Go Home," 181
"Since I Been in the Land," 431
"Sit Down, Child," 424
"Sizette, te ein bell femme," 444
"Skip Frog," 442
"Skip to My Lou," 252, 443, 456, 627n13
"Slavery Days," 110–11, *111*
"Snapoo," 515, 530–31, 639n1
"So Happy in de Lawd," 398
"So Said the Buzzard When He Got Mad," 629n38
"Soldier's Joy," 582n54
"Some Day You Got to Lay Down and Die (You Got to Take Sick and Die)," 407, 624n53
"Sometimes I Feel Like a Motherless Child," 32
"Soo-oo-oo-k, Janey," 469
"Speculator Bought My Wife and Child, The," 185, 549
"Stars Am Shinin' For Us All, De," 272
"Steal Away to Jesus," 424–25
"Steal Liza Jane," 457
"Stewball" (Laws Q 22), 503, 637n39
"Stomp Down Freedom Today," 305–6
"Sugar Babe," 570n8

"Sugar in de Gourd," 448–49
"Sukey Jump (Win'jammer)," 595n15
"Sun Goin' Rise to Set No Mo', The," 425, 428
"Sun Gwine Down, Oh Lord," 472
"Susie (Julie) Gal," 234, 606n15
"Sweep-O-O-O," 591n17
"Sweet, Sweet," 450
"Sweet Thing," 579n8
"Swing Low Sweet Chariot," 156, 389, 404–6, 408, 409, 417, 448, 594n6, 623nn42–44
"Swing Ole Liza Single," 457, 626n6

"Take a Home, Take a Home," 441–42
"Take Me to the Water (To Be Baptized)," 392, 620n17
"Take Your Burden to the Lord and Leave It There," 361
"Tarrypin, Tarrypin, When You Comin' Over," 471
"Tea in de Tea-Kettle Nine Days Ol'," 466, 629n8
"That Old Bald Nigger with Shiny Eyes," 124
"That Suits Me," 293–94, 612n10
"Them Bones of Mine," 425–26
"There Is a Fountain Filled with Blood," 354, 382, 618n19
"There Is a Happy Land," 432
"There Is a Tavern in This Town (When My Apron Hung Low)," 520, 640n11
"There's No Grass in Georgia," 475–76
"This Ain't Christmas Morning, Just a Long Summer Day," 475
"Throw de Smokehouse Keys Down de Well," 640n27
"Time Is Right Now, En Dis Yer's de Place, De," 32
"Tringue, Tringue, Ti Balai," 439
"Trouble Water Today," 432
"Try Us, O God, and Search the Ground," 382–83
"Turkey in the Straw," 83, 84, 200, 202, 459, 581n53
"Twelve Blessings of Mary, The," 505
"Two Barrels Pickled Pork, Two Barrels Meal," 64

"Uncle Ned," 89, 495, 632n28
"Uncle Sam Give Us All a Farm," 221
"Underground Rail Car, Or, Song of the Fugitive, The," 383
"Up de Hill, Down de Level," 441

"Wagoner's Lad (On Top of Old Smokey), The," 512, 636n30
"Wake Nicodemus," 528
"Walk, Walk, You Nigger Walk," 474
"Walk Away, Walk Away," 603
"Walk in the Parlor," 495
"Walk Indepen'ent, Walk Bold," 471
"Wasn't for Old Satan," 432
"Watch the Sun, See How She Run," 472, 480, 630n33
"Way Over in the Promised Land," 398
"We Are Slipping Through the Gates," 416, 426
"We Gwan Have a Moughty Bounty," 400
"We Is Gwine Er Round—O, de Las' Round," 473
"We Shall Sleep but Not Forever," 383
"Weevily Wheat," 32, 456, 627n13
"We'll Stick to the Hoe, Till the Sun Go Down," 32
"We'll Walk Dem Golden Streets," 32
"W'en de Tyrants Sword Darkened Our Land," 32–33
"Went to the River and I Couldn't Get Across," 200, 604n18
"We's a Marchin' Away to Canaan's Land," 293
"What Are They Doing in Heaven?," 361
"What Yo' Gwine Do When de Meat Give Out?," 42, 370n8
"Wheeler's Calvary Marchin' on de Battlefield," 520
"When Dat Ole Chariot Comes," 400
"When I Can Read My Title Clear," 303, 348, 383–84, 480, 614n44
"When I'm Here You'll Call Me Honey," 472
"When Johnny Comes Marching Home," 431–32
"When Sherman Was Marching Through Georgia," 520
"When the Train Comes Along," 3, 390, 426–27, 567n1, 592n35
"When You and I Were Young, Maggie," 632n29
"Where He Leads Me," 303, 616n44
"Where Pleasure Never Dies," 471
"Where Shall I Be When the First Trumpet Sounds," 394, 621n22
"Whistling Coon," 483, 500, 631n38, 634n50
"Who Built the Ark?," 432

"Who Is Dat Coming," 432
"Whooper John and Calline All Night," 185
"Who's a Gwine to Take Care of Me," 21, 22
"Who's Been Here Since I Been Gone," 178, 600n17
"Who's Dat Nigga Dar a Peepin'," 494–95, 632n25
"Why Do We Mourn Departing Friends," 358, 384
"Why Do You Wait, Dear Brother," 384
"Wild-Goose Nation, De," 25
"William Trimbletoe (Tremble Toe)," 435–36, 437, 625n1
"Wind Blows East, the Wind Blows West, The," 365, 427
"Wind de Ball, Wind de Ball," 480
"Wish I Had a Hundred Dog," 444
"Witness for My Lord," 427
"Working on a Building," 177–78, 600n14
"Wrestling Jacob," 130, 393, 621n21

"Yankee Doodle," 130, 150, 518, 520, 530, 533–34, 641n34
"Yaraba Shango," 47
"Yon Comes Ole Marster Jesus," 432
"You (We) Shall Be Free," 235, 251–52, 379, 393, 462, 621n19
"You Can Have All This World but Give Me Jesus," 408, 624n55
"You Must Be Born Again," 428
"You Shall Be Free (Shout Mourner)," 235, 251–52, 462, 621n19
"You Shan't Be Slaves No More, Since Christ Has Made You Free," 556–57
"You'd Better Be Praying," 395
"Young Man Who Wouldn't Hoe Corn, The" (Laws H 13), 639

"Zion's Hill," 389, 390, 416, 425, 428–29
"Zip Coon," 581n53
"Zolo Go (Organ Blues)" 497n43

Tale-Types, Motifs, and Tales

Tale-Type 1735C. "The Bribed Boy Sings the Wrong Song," 463–64, 629n2

Motif C12.5.3(b). *Girl swears she will get substitute fiddler at midnight Saturday night even if she has to go to hell for him*, 255–56, 278
Motif C12.5.11*. *Man invites devil to a fiddling and dancing contest*, 261, 272–73, 278
Motif D1786. *Magic power at crossroads*, 91, 257, 259, 261, 262, 263, 266, 272–79, 609n18, 610n23
Motif E273. *Churchyard Ghosts*, 280–81, 283
Motif E332.3.3.1. *Vanishing hitchhiker*, 360
Motif E334.4. *Ghost of suicide seen at death spot or nearby*, 283
Motif E337.1.3(b). *Sounds of dance in haunted house*, 89–90, 262, 281–82
Motif E402.1.2. *Footsteps of invisible ghost heard*, 263, 281–82, 285
Motif E402.1.3. *Invisible ghost plays musical instrument*, 92, 282–83
Motif E402.1.3(a). *Ghost plays violin*, 90, 283
Motif E402.1.3(ba). *Ghost (Devil) plays piano*, 92, 154, 260, 279, 285
Motif E402.1.3(d). *Ghost beats a drum*, 93, 283–84
Motif E422.1.1(a). *Headless man*, 280
Motif E423.1.8. *Revenant as cow, bull or calf or steer*, 274, 279
Motif E451.8. *Ghost laid when house it haunts is destroyed or changed*, 92, 282–83
Motif E492. *Mass (church service) of the dead*, 280
Motif E501. *The Wild Hunt*, 284–85
Motif F243.21*. *Fairies give mortal power to make up songs*, 258–59
Motif F262. *Fairies make music*, 258–59
Motif F262.2. *Fairies teach bagpipe playing*, 258–59
Motif F377(c). *Person joins dance of fairies, is in fairyland for duration of dance. Dance seems to last a few minutes, actually lasts weeks, months, or years*, 609n12
Motif G224.4. *Person sells soul to devil in exchange for witch powers*, 260, 261, 272–79
Motif G224.5. *Witch power received by altering religious ceremony*, 259, 261, 266–67, 272–77
Motif G224.8. *Person gets witch power by walking twelve times around a church backward at midnight*, 259, 272–77

Motif G224.11.2. *Witch bone from cat (black cat bone)*, 261, 266–67, 273, 275, 277, 609n20

Motif G303.3.1.6. *The devil as a black man*, 261, 274, 275, 277

Motif G303.3.3.1.1(a). *Devil in form of black dog*, 261, 274

Motif G303.3.3.2.3. *Devil as hare*, 261

Motif G303.3.3.6.1. *The devil in the form of snake*, 261, 274

Motif G303.4.1.2.2. *Devil with glowing eyes*, 256, 261, 273, 277

Motif G303.4.2.1. *Devil as a ball of fire*, 261, 273

Motif G303.4.5.0.1. *Devil has cloven foot (feet) or cloven hoof (hooves)*, 261, 273, 276

Motif G303.4.5.3.1. *Devil detected by his hoofs (tail)*, 261, 273, 274, 276

Motif G303.4.5.8. *Devil has club foot*, 278

Motif G303.4.8.14*. *Devil casts no shadow*, 277

Motif G303.4.8.15*. *Devil leaves no tracks in snow*, 277

Motif G303.5.2.1. *Devil in green clothing with hat*, 283

Motif G303.6.1.1. *Devil appears at midnight*, 256, 261, 264–65, 273–79

Motif G303.6.1.2. *Devil appears when called upon*, 259–62, 272–79

Motif G303.6.1.2(a). *Devil appears to person or persons who recite Lord's prayer backwards*, 259, 261, 466–67, 273–77

Motif G303.6.1.2(d). *Devil appears to person who says Lord's prayer backwards while walking seven times around church*, 261, 273–77

Motif G303.6.1.2(h). *Person raises devil by use of magic circle*, 261, 273

Motif G303.6.2.1. *Devil appears at dance*, 89, 256, 260, 277, 278

Motif G303.6.2.14. *Devil appears to Sabbath breakers*, 256, 261, 273–79

Motif G303.6.3.1. *Devil is followed by thunderstorm*, 273, 274, 278

Motif G303.7.1. *Devil rides a horse*, 261, 274, 278

Motif G303.9.1.1. *Devil as builder of bridge*, 261, 609n18

Motif G303.10.4.1. *Devil dances with a maid until she dies*, 277–78

Motif G303.10.4.3. *Devil teaches a dance-loving maid to dance*, 259

Motif G303.21.2. *Devil's money becomes manure*, 261, 275, 278, 610n22

Motif G303.25.23.1*. *The devil appears to fiddler*, 260, 261, 273–77, 278

Motif G303.25.23.1.1*. *Devil engages fiddler in fiddling contest. The fiddler gets rid of devil at dawn by playing hymn*, 272, 278, 610n21

Motif G303.25.23.2*. *Composition learned when person hears devil play it*, 274, 276–77, 278

Motif K219.5. *Man cheats devil by giving him sole instead of soul*, 259, 261, 273, 274, 609n21

Motif K534.1. *Escape by reversing horse's (ox's) shoes*, 221, 605n4

Motif M211.10*(b). *Girl sells soul to devil for skill in dancing*, 259, 273–77

Motif M211.10*(ca). *Person sells soul for skill in fiddling*, 257, 261, 273–77

Motif M211.10*(ca.a*). *Person sells soul for skill on banjo*, 91, 259, 262, 272, 273–77

Motif M211.10*(ca.b*). *Person sells soul for skill on guitar*, 257, 259, 273–77

Motif M211.10*(ca.c*). *Person sells soul for skill on accordion*, 274

Motif M211.10*(ca.d*). *Person sells soul for skill on piano*, 274

Motif M211.10*(ca.e*). *Person sells soul for skill on harmonica*, 275

Motif M211.10*(ca.f*). *Person sells soul for skill on ukelele*, 275

Motif Q223.6.4*. *Punishment for dancing on Sunday*, 255–56, 261–62, 277–79

Motif Q223.6.4*(a). *Nineteen maidens were turned to stone for dancing on Sunday*, 255–56

Motif Q386.1. *Devil punishes girl who loves to dance*, 261–62, 277–78

Motif Q386.2*. *Girl who dances on Sunday is turned to stone*, 255–56

Amputating slave's forefinger (thumb, hand) for learning to write, 319, 617n11

Blacks duped into surrendering voter registration tickets for circus admission, 245–46, 490

INDICES

"Boots or No Boots I'm Gonna Shout Today," 291, 309–10, 317–18

Bre'r Rabbit Fiddles for Bre'r Fox, 89

Brother Fox, Brother Rabbit, and King Deer's Daughter, 592n23

Brother Fox Covets the Quills, 592n23

Carnies make snakes, 610n39

Catching babies on fish hooks, 507

Conjured by Carolina Crip, 286–87

Devil dances hornpipe on bridge at midnight, 609n18

Fiddler fends off wolves with fiddle, 89, 568n20

"Fooled Old Master Seven Years," 89–90, 206, 231, 267, 605n33, 610n41

Freed by Abraham Lincoln's son Johnny, 316–17

ghost of Sid Scott, The, 263

Ghost sweeps yard of haunted slave cabin, 59

ghosts of the Grimes brothers, The, 283

"He tear he mouth in two," 231

Henry Clay plays cards with slaves in the cellar, 602n36

Hoodoo doctor-succubus, 285–86

How the Devil Created Black People, 608n7

hymn-loving gamblers, The, 619n34

hymn-singing ghost (vanishing hitchhiker), The, 360

"I don' lak dat thing 'hind you," 407, 624n52

Illiterate slave given pass instructing patrollers to beat him, 617n3

Jaybird visits hell every Friday, 424

Jeff Davis captured in drag, 7, 530–31, *531*

Jeff Davis poisoned by slave, 641n29

Jeff Davis surrenders to Lincoln under sour apple tree, 7, 215–16

John Brown and the Underground Railroad, 341

John Brown hung from beechwood tree, 540

John Brown's Kiss, 535, 641n36

Lazy slave cuts off hand to avoid work, 342

Mirrors covered after death to prevent ghost's return, 298

musicianer's whiskey ration, The, 207

"Naught is naught an figger is a figger," 467

Night riders pelted with hot coals, 206, 227, 228–30, 231, 249, 327, 340, 606n10, 616n31

Night riders pretend to be thirsty ghosts from Hell (Drinking Water), 225–27, 228–30, 238, 241, 340, 341, 605n6

Night riders unhorsed by stringing grapevines across road, 180, 217, 229–30, 249, 327, 340, 606n10, 616n31

Night When the Stars Fell, The, 285

"Old Marster Heah We Are," 230–31

"Old Master's Gone to Philliman York," 63–64, 575n43

Preacher corrupts the morals of slaves, 329, 616n35

Pregnant slave flogged across hole dug for her belly, 22, 569n26

Racing with a ghost, 280–81

Raw Head and Bloody Bones, 10, 28, 225

"Red Taylor at de Do'r, Bright Mansions Above," 231, 606n11

Rita and Retta poison Aunt Vira and her baby, 286

"Sho' pity Lawd forgive," 382

Singing funeral hymns to rabbits, 360

Skinning the panther, 281–82

Slave afraid to sing "Free at Last" even after freedom, 313–14

Slave borrows master's boots, cannot remove swollen feet after dancing, 64, 576n44

Slaveholding drunkard drops dead when calliope passes, 129, 590n47

Snakes and insects guard hoodoo doctor's cadaver, 610n39

"'Sociate Yourself," 180

Stealing Africans by inviting them aboard ship for a dance, 34, 38

Stealing Africans with red cloth (the red hankie tale), 35, 39, 570n1
Stealing slaves with brass band, 130

"Turned to Possum in the Pot," 90

"Where you shall shortly lie," 619n34
"Who Dat Knockin' At de Elder," 230
Work horn signals freedom, 126–27

Yankees teach horse to play piano, 151
"Yo has got one too many tongues now," 379
"You Can Have All the World," 408

General Index

Aarne, Antti, 90
Abbey, M. E., and Charles D. Tillman, 426
Abyssinia, 492
accordion, 48, 69, 87, 88–92, 94, 104, 112, 143, 150, 152, 158, 159–69, 199, 205, 210, 212, 213, 214, 216, 249, 259, 274, 278, 375, 458; flutina (flutena), 162, 216; identified with Devil, 160, 270, 595n14; melodeon (melodian), 87, 89, 90, 92, 158, 162; played for dancing, 159, 160–61, 162, 164, 166–69; used for church songs, 151, 159–60, 595n13; and zydeco, 163, 164–66, 168–69. *See also* banjo; fiddle
Agony in the Garden (Luke 22:44), 370
Akan (West Africa), 571n24
Alabama Writers' Project, 567n11, 570n29
Alexander, Jim, 610n31
Algiers, LA. *See* New Orleans, LA
Allan's Lone Star Ballads, 510, 511–12
Allen, George N., 383
Allen, James Lane, 98, 348
Allen, Jules Verne, 637nn36–38
Allen, William Francis, Charles Pickard Ware, and Lucy McKim Garrison, *Slave Songs of the United States*, 4, 31, 295, 547, 624n55
Alsberg, Henry G., 6, 8, 26
American Folklore Society, 4–5, 607n20
Amerson, Rich, 593n62, 628n36, 631n36

Ames, David W., 78
Amos, Octave, *109*
Anderson, Pink, 161
Andrews, Garnett, 182
Angelina County, TX, 315
Angelina River, 465
Annapolis, MD, 200, 214
Anthony, Eddie, 109, 578n2, 581n44
Antoine, Madame, 595n23
Applewhite, James, 593n62
Archive of American Folk Song (Library of Congress), 6, 9, 640n18
Ardoin, Amédé, 596n37
Arizona Writers' Project, 567n11
"Arkansas Traveler" (folk drama), 582n54
Arkansas Writers' Project, 16, 222, 567n11
Armstrong, Arthur "Brother in Law," 461–62, 628n18, 628n37
Armstrong, Howard, 578n2, 580n38
Armstrong, Louis, 113, 130, 132, 210
Arnold, Byron, 315, 455
Ashantee (West Africa), *119*
Asheville, NC, 245, 587n51
Ashley, Clarence, 636n30
Askew, Alec, 143, 581n39, 582n54, 592n30, 593n62, 644n8
Athens, GA, 142, 157, 279–80, 479, 527–28
Atlanta, GA, 38, 102, 108, 124, 130, 131, 142, 503, 521, 581n44, 583n62
Auburn, AL, 142, 409, 460
Augusta, GA, 98, 142, 298, 409, 516, 530, 638n40
automobiles, 121, 280, 555–57, 559
Avirett, John Battle, 180, 375, 602n33

backstep. *See* dances
bagpipes, 255, 256, *256*, 259, 608nn10–12; uilleann pipes, 80, 148, 593n61
Bahia, 46
Bailey, DeFord, 140, 580n38, 593nn62–63, 604n16
Baker, James (Iron Head), 630n27
Baker, LaVern, 410, 624n59
Bakuba (Central Africa), 374, 492–93, 632n21
Bald Eagle (steamboat), 485

INDICES 733

Bales, Mary Virginia, 31, 624n56

ballads, 502–14; blues, 162–63, 514, 596n29, 639n49; broadside, 283, 507–13, *510*; medieval (Child), 502–7

ballets (song sheets), 361, 508, 619n36

balling the jack. *See* dances

Baltimore, MD, 100, 522

banjo, 20, 37, 49, 54, 55, 56, 57, 58, 59, 62, 64, 65, 66, 68, 78, 80, 81, 82, 87–94, 95–109, 112, 114, 124, 131, 155, 160, 172, 173, 174, 177, 178–79, 186, *189*, 195, 197, 199–200, 202, 205, 208, 210–16, 219, 230, 231–32, 249, 252, 256, 258, 259, 260–61, 262, 264, 271, 272, 273–79, 306, 346, 363, 364, 370, 371, 442–43, 448, 451, 454, 474, 479, 483, 485, *487*, *488*, *491*, 493, 496–97, 513, 562, 573n1, 574n12, 577n60, 577n65, 580n38, 581n39, 581n53, 592n26, 593n62, 602n35, 602n37, 604n13, 605n33, 610n40, 611nn46–47, 528n24, 528nn32–33, 633n43, 635n15, 642n52; and accordion, 56, 92, 104, 105, 159, 161–62, 167–68, 199, 597n39; African background, 37–38, 72, 73, 96–98, 103, 572n38, 584nn6–7, 608n4; bluegrass style, 585n26; and bones, *48*, 57, 67, *67*, 74, 85, 86, 94, 105, *131*, 146, 150, 199, 456, *487*, 582n56, 583n59, 583n62, 593n62; as Devil's instrument, 160, 256, 259, 261, 264; and fiddle, *48*, 53, 56, 57, 61, 62, *67*, 68, 73, 74, 75, 81, 83, 84, 85, 86, 89–91, 96, 105–9, 131, 146, 148, 150, 153, 159, 161–62, 165, 167, 171, 173, 175–76, 183, 188, 199–200, 201, 202, 204, 208, 233, 235, 249, 264, 268, 270, 272, 368, 456, 487, *488*, 522, 523, 561–62, 572n38, 582n54, 583n59, 586n42, 587n52, 590n2, 633n43; foot-stomping with, 104, 577n60; gourd, 75, 76, 95, 97–100, 102, 575n34, 584n6, 585n15; and guitar, 62, 73, 84, 106–9, 131, 178–79, 199, 244, 249, 250, 264, 268, 514, 587n48, 587nn50–52; guitar or classical style, 585n26; and harmonica, 593n58; homemade, 76, 91, 100, 101, 148, 199–200, 456; hoop (cheese box), 95–96, 98, 585n16; minstrel style, 101–2, 572n38, 583n59, 583n62, 585n20; number of strings, 97–98, 102, 564n8; and quills, 48, 91, 105, 139, 142, 144, 145, 146, 147–48, 153, 171, 270, 486, 581n53, 582n56, 592n52; slave playing style, 96–97, 101–5, 585n20, 585n24, 585n27; store-bought, 95, 98, 100–101,

572n38; thumb or drone string, 98, *98*, 584n7; and tin pan tambourine, 35, 58, 61, 86, 94, 105–6, *131*, 148, 173; tin-pan or bucket, 99. *See also* fiddle

Banjo (showboat), 128, 489

baptisms, 10, 28, 200, 291, 297, 300–301, 304–5, 306–7, 308–9, 324, 332, 337–38, 392, *392*, 403, 560, 614n47; songs, 298–99, 302, 304, 341–42, 354–55, 361, 364–65, 368, 369, 373, 374, 377, 379–81, 383–84, 390, 391–92, 403, 407, 412, 415, 419–20, 430, 432, 620n17, 624n51. *See also* shouting

Baptist Cluster (songbook), 352

Barlow Brothers Minstrels, 491, 632n18

barn dances. *See* dancing

Barnes, Doc, 142, 145, 592n40

Barnicle, Mary Elizabeth, 568n16

Barnum, P. T., 488, 489, 492–93, 631n4

Barrow, David C., Jr., 67, 188, 191

Barton, William E., 397

Bascom, Louise, 85

Basongye (Central Africa), 119, 604n17

Bathurst, William Hiley, 371, 378

Baton Rouge, LA, 164, 168

Batts, Will, 109, 578n2

Baughman, Ernest W., 90

Baxter, Andrew, 109, 578n2

Baxter, James, 109

Bay St. Louis, MS, 131, 163–64

Beauregard, Pierre Gustave Toutant, 524, 640n17

Bebey, Francis, 320

Beddome, Benjamin, 371, 376

begana (Ethiopian box-lyre), 608n6

Belden, Henry M., 444, 539

Belgian Congo, 493

Belle Lee (steamboat), 484

Bellow, Saul, 8

bells, 67, 116–17, 122–24, 125, 126–27, 135–36, 173, 303, 305, 312, 353, 415, 432, 465, 484, 485, 501, 545, 588n12, 606n16; struck, 56, 66–67, 84, 94, 117, 136, 324, 574n15, 615n15

Benin (Dahomey), 71, 571n24

Benjamin, S. W. G., 113

Bernhard, Duke of Saxe-Weimar Eisenach, 68

Bertram, Cuje, 455, 578n2, 580n38, 627n12, 632n29

Bibb County, GA, 81, 142, 581n41

Bible, 26, 28, 44, 156–57, 160, 241, 266, 269, 280, 295, 302, 310, 322, 330–31, 332, 335, 336, 338, 347, 349–50, 351–53, 354, 384–85, 375, 379, 388–89, 415–16, 419, 428–29, 430, 490, 505, 557, 558, 570n7, 618n13; 1 Chronicle 15:28, 612n6; 2 Chronicle 15:14, 612n6; 2 Samuel 6:13–16, 293; in Cherokee, 42–43; Ecclesiastes 3:4, 294; Ephesians 6:5, 303, 310, 319, 322, 323, 327–30, 335–36, 338–39, 341–43, 345, 350, 616n35; Ezekiel 37:1–11, 378, 447; Ezra, 3:11, 292–93; Isaiah 12:5–6, 612n6; Isaiah 44:23, 612n6; Jeremiah 31:7, 291; Job 38:6–7, 612n6; John 6, 418; John 21:17, 372; Joshua 6:5, 15–16, and 20, 293; King James, 43, 291–94; Leviticus 9:24, 291; Luke 22:44, 370; Mark 6:17–18, 614n42; Psalm 47:1, 291; Psalm 65:13, 612n6; Psalm 91:2, 378–79; Revelation 14:8, 529–30; Revelation 18:1–2, 529–30; Zephaniah 3:1, 612n6

Biddleville Quintette, 374, 406, 418

Big Apple. *See* dances

Big Bethel Choir, 624n56

Black-on-Black violence, 265–66, 559–60

blacksmiths, 37, 205, 494; Africa, 87, 604n6

Blake, Blind Arthur, 583n62

Blind Boys of Alabama, 600n14

Blind Gary. *See* Davis, Rev. Gary

Blind Pete, 578n2, 580n38

blind tigers (speakeasies), 555, 560

blue-back speller, 347, 350, 353, 358, 471

bluebonnet (*Lupinus subcarnous*), 527

blues, 109, 168–69, 560–63, 631n39, 639n49

Bolden, Buddy, 113

Bolton, MS, 587n49

Bonar, Horatius, 43, 374–75, 423, 595n13

bones (clackers), 48, *48*, 53, 56–57, *67*, *67*, 74, 80, 81, 84–85, 86, 88–94, 105, 131–32, 138, 144, 146, 147, 150, 161, 173, 211, 213, 232, 242, 262–63, 456, 458, 582n56, 593n62, 597n41; African background, 85, 583n61; British background, 85, 583n58; fireplace tongs as clackers, 583n58; played by blackface minstrels, 85, *131*, *488*, *491*, 583n59, 583nn61–62; played by whites, 85, 583n62, 597n40; spoons as clackers, 583n58; wooden clackers, 85. *See also* banjo; fiddle

Booker, James, 131

Booker, Jim, 578n2, 580n38

Borders, James, 583n62

Bori religion (West Africa), 608n3

Bosque County, TX, 9, 607n40

Botkin, Benjamin Albert, 5–6, *6*, 14, 644n10; *Lay My Burden Down*, 6, 563

bottle trees, 324

Boucher, Jonathan, 100, 103

Boucher, William Esperance, Jr., 100

Boulder, CO, 632n23

Bowie, Jim, 570n3

Boyce, R. L., 594n6

Braddock, James, 23

Bradley, Arthur Granville, 237, 281

Bradley, Tommie, 109

brass bands, 93, 129–32, *129*, 215, 245, 521–22, *522*

Brazil, 36, 45, 46, 484

breakdowns, 576n50; events, 62, 66, 103, 109, 160, 164, 172, 177, 268, 270, 459, 599n10; tune-type, 78–79, 83, 162, 271. *See also* dances

Bremer, Fredrika, 98

Brenham, TX, 544

Brewer, Jim, 162

bricklayers, slave musicians as, 205

Broonzy, Big Bill, 559, 578nn2–3, 604n16

Brower, Frank, *488*, 583n59

Brown, Jimmy, 578n2

Brown, John, 517, 521, 525, 534–35, 540–43, 641n46, 643nn53–54

Bruce, Philip A., 104

brulé-zin. *See* dances

brush burnings. *See* work parties

Bryant, William Cullen, 64–65, 138, 549

Bryant's Minstrels, 573n1

Bryce, C. A., 202, 203

buck dance. *See* dances

Buffalo Bill (William Cody), 493

Buffalo Bill's Wild West Show, 493

bugles, 89, 91, 93, 94, 112–35, 181, 197, 212, 213, 214, 215, 216, 323, 333, 602n28; military, 93, 119–20, 122, 124, 212, 213, 216, 521, 589n22, 589n35, 589n37; played by night riders, 227

Buglin' Sam, the Waffle Man, 133
Bull, Ole, 75, 487
Burchell, William John, 76, 257–58
Burnside, A. E., 538–39
Burwell, Letitia M., 182, 349
Burwell, William McCreary, *White Acre Vs. Black Acre*, 104
Butler, Benjamin, 244
Butler, John, 128
buzzard lope. *See* dances

Cable, George W., 143, 593n56
Cable, James B., 147, 593n52
Cade, John B., 5
Cage, Butch, 578n2, 580n38
caillac (corn doll, kern baby), 192–93
Cairo, IL, 482, 489
cake walk. *See* dances
Callendar's Original Georgia Minstrels, 131–32, *131*
calliopes (steam pianos), 92, 128–29, 484, 485, 489, 490, 500
Calloway, Cab, 543
Cameron, Isla, 634n4
camp meetings (revivals, protracted meetings), 171–72, 190, 271, 293, 294, 295, 300, 304–5, 307, *308*, 309, *322*, 322, 354, 356, 359, 364, 378, 381, 384, 514, 588n10, 614n46
campaign songs, 543–45, 602n36, 639n48, 643nn55–56, 643nn58–59
Campbell, Blind James, 590n58, 628n20
Campbell, Charley, 618n15
Campbell, Rev. E. D., 620n17
Campbell, Thomas Monroe, 251, 570n29
Canned Heat, 144
Cannon, Gus, 580n38, 585n27, 628n24
Cannon's Jug Stompers, 602n38
Cantefables, 206, 230–33, 407, 606n11, 606n13, 606n16, 629n2
Cape Girardeau, MO, 489
Carawan, Guy, 613n31
Carnival, 37, 149, 177, 180–81, 192, 219, 225, 241, 314, 467, 477, 488, 588n2, 597n3, 602n29, 607n30
carpenters, slave musicians as, 204–5, 605n28, 605n30

carriage drivers, slave musicians as, 83, 135, 151, 197–98, 203, 204–5, 605n27
Carson, Fiddlin' John, 77, 248, 249, 251, 570n8, 580n38, 605n2, 637n37, 638n43, 644n12
Carter Family, 600n14
Case, Mose, 582n54
castanets, 85, 150, 583n58
Cennick, John, 368, 369, 377
Chamberlain, Daniel, 245–47, *247*, 544
Chambers Brothers, 620n11
chanteys (shanties), 480–81, 483, 531, 640n16
Charleston, SC, 47, 129, *148*, 197, 356, 486, 517, 523, 530, 607n40, 629n7
Charleston Courier, 127
Charleston Earthquake (1886), 38, 545, 556
Chase, Lucy, 59, 298, 307
Chatman (Chatmon) family, 587n49
Chatman, Bo (Bo Carter), 578n2
Chatman, Lonnie, 109, 578n2
Chatman Brothers (Lonnie and Sam), 573n1
Chattahoochee Valley Choir, 624n56
Chattanooga Times, 77
Chenier, Cleveland, 169
Chenier, Clifton, 168–69, 597n43
Chernoff, John M., 78
Cherokee. *See* Native Americans
Child, Francis James, 90; *The English and Scottish Popular Ballads*, 502–3; *War-Songs for Freemen*, 502
chimney raisings (daubings). *See* work parties
chimney sweeps, Black children as, 141, 591n17
Chitwood, Bill, 580n38
Choctaw. *See* Native Americans
Christmas, 10, 28, 34, *48*, 54, 63, 66, 75, 82, 85, 87, 98, 103, 105–6, 108, 113, 125, 149, 170–72, 186, 189, 190, 199, 201, 236, 239–40, 294–95, 382, 436, 488, 548–49, 558, 588n8, 597n3
Christy Minstrels, 528, 583n61
Chwana (South Africa), 583n61
circuses, 92, 129, 487–90, 631n6; and blackface minstrels, 488–90, *491*, 495; Dan Rice, 487–88; Dan Rice and Coles, 487; Ringling Brothers, 493; Robinson's, 245–46

Civil War, 3, 4, 7, 8, 9, 22–23, 42, 96, 233, 244–45, 264, 299, 307, 332–33, 352, 408, 486, 503, 508–43, 605n6; alcohol and gambling among troops, 512–13, 637n36; ballads, 508–14, *510*, 523; banjo, 96, 272, 363, 522–23; Black troops, 77, *86*, 124, 245, *468*, 516, *516*, 517, 522, 529–30; Blacks as entertainers in camp, 523–24, *524*; bugle, fife, and drum, and brass bands, 124, 129–30, 148–49, 213, 341, 516, 518, 519, 521–22, *522*, 526, 527, 530, 533–34, 541; drums, 127, 148–49, 519, 521–22; ex-slave veterans, 213, 339, 510–11, 521–22, 529–30, 589n35; fiddle, 522–23, *523*, 524, *524*; and minstrelsy, 521, 523, 525–26, 528–30, 533–34; war songs, 165–66, 283, 383, 508–43, 618n15, 640n27, 641n29, 641n32, 641n37, 642n38, 642n41, 642n48, 642n52, 643nn53–54

battles: of Baldwin, 539, 642n41; of Cane Hill, 512, 637n33; of Chancellorsville (Spotsylvania Courthouse), *511*; of Cold Harbor, 509, *509*; of Falling Waters, 642n38; of First Bull Run (First Manassas), 277, 519, 524, 640n17, 642n38, 642n41; of Fredericksburg, 642n41; of Mansfield (Sabine Crossroads), 510, 517, 639n8; of Mine Creek, 540; of New Bern, 642n41, 642n48; of Pea Ridge (Elkhorn Tavern), 508; of Pleasant Hill, 639n8; of Port Royal, 264; of Prairie Grove, 637n33; of Sabine Pass (Second), 580n34; of Second Bull Run (Second Manassas), 639n1; Seven Days, 529, 538, 640n26, 642n41; of Shiloh (Pittsburg Landing), 226, 238, 509–10, 605n6; of Westport, 508

Clapperton, Hugh, 71, 73, 80
Clay, Beauford, 578n2
Clay, Henry, 184, 602n36
Clayborn, Reverend Edward W., 621n22
Clay-Clopton, Virginia, 308
Cleveland, Big Boy, 592n30
Cleveland, Grover, 545
Clinkscales, J. G., 365–66
Clover Leaf Jubilee Quartet, 620n15
clowning (acrobatics), by instrumentalists, 104–5
code noir (Louisiana), 596n33, 599n6, 610n35
Coffin, Charles Carleton, 299

coffles, 356, 474, *474*, 630n23
Cole, James, 109, 578n2
Coleman, Jaybird, 607n33
Colorado Writers' Project, 567n11
Columbus, GA, 142, 299, 332–33, 581n41
Communipaw (Jersey City, NJ), 137, 590n1
Conder, Josiah, 368
Congo Square. *See* New Orleans, LA
conjure. *See* hoodoo
Converse, Frank B., 101, 102–3, 104, 493, 585n16
Cooke, Grace MacGowan, *A Gourd Fiddle*, 77–78, 79
"Coonsy" (non-singing game), 441
corn songs, 175, 176–77, 180, 181–86, 187, 188, 190, 220, 314, 346, 467, 473, 479, 549, 602nn33–35, 602nn37–38, 633n43, 643n54
cornshuckings, 10, 44, 59, 64, 66, 67, 80, 108, 120, 137, 145, 146, 153, 162, 170, 173, 175–93, 201, 265, 268, 270, 314, 346, 436, 443, 450, 457, 476–77, 479, 501, 549, 562, 577n65, 585n24, 599n10, 600n20, 601n21; African harvest festivals, relation to, 191–92, 589n30; alcohol at, 170, 175–76, 179, 180, 182, 183, 185, 189–90, 346; Anglo-American husking bees, relation to, 193; British Harvest Home celebrations, relation to, 192–93; captain or general, 180, 182–83, *182*, 184, 185, 189–90, 193, 602n29; competitions at, 180, 186–87, 189–91, 193; concluding walkaround and other rites of reversal, 175, 187–88, 193; coumbites (Haitian work parties), resemblance to, 186, 588n2; horns and pipes at, 120, 181, 602n28; instrumentalists at, 183–84, *184*; protest and satirical songs permitted at, 185–86, 467, 549; *Rara* (Hatian carnival), resemblance to, 192; red ear custom, 175, 176, 183, 186, 189, 190, 192–93, 602n45; shellings, 180, 599n10; shuckers' singing approach, 181–82, 601n26; violence at, 187. *See also* work parties
cotillion. *See* dances
Couch, Frank, 579n25
counting-out rhymes, 437–38, 625n1, 625n5
Courlander, Harold, 113, 320
Cowper, William, 354, 382
Crap Eye, 588n13
Cray, Ed, 531

Creecy, Col. James R., 194

Creek. *See* Native Americans

Cresswell, Nicholas, 95–96, 106

Cristofori, Bartolommeo, 152

Crockett, David (Davy), 191, 496–97

Crosby, Fanny, 353, 364, 377, 426, 618n17

Crossroads (motion picture), 273

crossroads legend, 91, 257, 259, 262, 263, 266–67, 273–77, 287, 609n18, 610n23. *See also* Devil

"Crow Game" (counting-out rhyme), 437

Crump, E. H., Jr. 607n33

Cuba, 37, 45, 164, 570n3, 615n15

cursing, 259, 261, 265, 266, 276, 277, 278, 328, 332, 466, 476, 503, 548, 555, 560

Curtis, Lucious, 581n53, 643n5, 644n8

Curtis, Samuel Ryan, 508

Dad Tracy, 578n2

dance callers (prompters), 68, 197, 210–14, 452, 577nn68–69, 600n14

dance calls, 68, 452–53, 164, 577n68, 627n16

dances (dance steps): African jig (Negro jig), 48–50, 57, 70; Anglo-Irish jig, 48, *48*, 57; backstep, 57, 64, 65, 69, 195, 201, 208, 576n45; balling the jack, 278; Big Apple, 106, 557–58, 643n1; breakdown, 57, 64, 65, 162, 200, 517, *524*; brulé-zin, 47; buck (buck-and-wing), 47, 48, 49, 57, 59, 64, 68, 84, 86, 165, 176, 200, 493, 575n27, 576n50, 597n3; buzzard lope, 57, 496, 631n10; cake walk, 59, 185, 488; clogging, 45, 48, 59, 64, 69, 80, 84, 105, 138, 178, 494; cotillion, 13, 14, 68–70, 83, 87, 162, 175, 256, 438, 459; double-shuffle, 57, 58, 64, 65; Fe Chauffe 47, 60; flat-foot, 62; gallopy, 62; Georgia Minstrel, 494; ground-shuffle, 201; hack-a-back (hackback), 55, 60, 458, 628n19; heel-and-toe (heel-to-toe), 48, 57, 64, 65, 138, *189*, 266, 496, 498, 576n51; hornpipe, 59, 77, 137, 139, 274, 582n54, 590n2, 609n18; hugging (up), 71, 76, 106, 450, 558; jig, 47–50, *48*, 53, 57, *58*, 59–61, *61*, 62, 64, 68–70, 83, 84, 101, 129, 131–32, *131*, 138, 149, 151, 165, 168, 173, 174, 200, 239, 240, 268, 272, 278, 305, 450–51, 458, 498, 543, 573n1, 576n51, 583n62, 597n42, 610n24, 615n17; pigeon wing, *48*, 64–65,

69, 84, 173, 176, 200, 201, 241, 244, 266, 576n45; quadrille, 57, 62, 63, 64, 68, 83, 106, 131, 165, 167, 179, 452–53; reel, 48, 57, 60, 62, 64, 68, 76, 96, 109, 140, 151, 162, 165, 199, 276–77, 363, 454; schottische, 14, 57, 68, 83, 165, 209, 268; set the floor, 58, 575n26; shimmy, 146; shuffle, 57–58, 59, 60, 64, 65, 66, 67, 69, 83, 106, 138, 195, 200, 242, 576n46; side-shuffle, 558; sixteen-hand reel, 185, 263, 272; Stomp Dance (Cherokee), 42–43, 93, 571n9; trucking, 21, 146, 558–59, 643nn1–2; Virginia reel, 47, 62, 77, 106, 131, 151, 178–79, 201, 239; waltz, 13–14, 49, 62, 64, 68, 83, 129, 131, 162, 165, 209, 268

dancing (frolicking): barefoot, 58; in barns, 62, *62*, 65, 206, 219–20; in the big house, 61–62, 69, 79, 152–53, 172, 174, 198, 200, 203, 205, 239, 440, 501, 575n40; in the big-house yard, 58–59, 60, 84, 102, 142–43, 162, 172, 173, 174, 183, 188, 239, 442, 541, 575n23; on boxes or barrels, 61; in cotton gins, 58, 61; in dance halls, 22, 49, 62, 65, 66, 78, 85, 87, 109, 131, 169, 199, 270, 278, 494, 555, 556, 557, 559, 575n42; on dance platforms, 45–46, 57, 60–61, 94; on docks, boardwalks, and bridges, 61, *61*, 200; down in the quarters, 54, 55, 58–59, *58*, 61, 65, 66, 81, 86, 99, 108, 115, *131*, 152, 171, 174, 199–200, 201, 217–18, 239, 248, 272, 451, 575n23; in footwear, 58, 62–64; on planks, 59–60, 65; on porches and galleries, 48, 61, 65, 153, 233; and racial terror, 239–42; regarded as sinful, 50, 56, 239–40, 248, 255–79, 285, 295, 455–57, 499, 553–63, 626n4; in slave cabins, 57, 58, 60, 61, 62, 64, 67, 86, 108, 150, 165, 171, 173, 174–75, 179, 195, 199, 203, 217, 270, 284, 285, 346, 442–43, 467–68, 575n39; on slave ships, in slave pens, and on auction blocks, 240–41; in sugar houses, 62, 575n41; in wagon beds, 58; with water vessels balanced on the head, 45–50, 57, 58, 60, 61, 168, 262–63, 270, 272, 278, 571n12, 571n18, 571n20, 571n24, 572nn35–36, 610n24

dancing masters, 83, 194, 197–98, 203–4, 205, 213

Davis, Gussie L., 634n10

Davis, Jefferson, 7, 28, 130, 221, 500, 515–17, 519, 522–25, 530–31, *531*, 536–43, 641n29, 641n37, 643n54

738 INDICES

Davis, Rev. Gary (Blind Gary), 419, 425, 426, 581n53, 593n62

De Voe, Thomas F., 59–60

"Death of Holmes Mule—Parts 1 & 2, The" (recorded drama), 362–63

Denver, CO, 208, 493–94; Central City, 208, 211, 212, 493–94; Cow Creek, 208; Georgetown, *208*; Leadville, 208

Devere, Sam, 483

Devil, 24, 30, 126, 141–42, 207, 283, 295, 316, 322, 363, 424, 441, 444, 450, 454, 532, 554, 559–60, 606n11, 607n2, 610n25, 610n36, 610nn38–39; identified with Blacks, 262, 608n7; identified with whites, 220–21, 225–27, 264–65; and music and dance, 56, 83, 89, 92, 159–60, 202, 243, 245, 247, 249, 251, 255–78, *256*, 279–80, 283, 285–86, 450, 454, 555–56, 557, 581n53, 590n2, 595nn13–14, 608n3, 608n6, 608n10, 609n14, 609nn18–21, 610n24, 626n1; and pre-Christian traditions, 258–59, 608n11

Dey (West Africa), *35*

Diamond, John, 487

Dickson, Harris, 482

District of Columbia Writers' Project, 567n11

divine healers, 206, 267, 610n38

Doddridge, Phillip, 379–80

Dodds, Baby (Warren, Jr.), 143, 604n16

Dodds, Johnny, 143, 604n16

Dodds, Warren, Sr., 143, 148, 593n52

dog run buildings, 61, 435, 575n39

Douglas, K. C., 162

drums, 88–94, 106, 119, 169, 283–84, 296, 297, *491*, 613n24; African, 47, 48, 84, 102, 191, 192, 320, 571n21, 572n38, 580n37, 589n38, 604n17; and banjo, 90, 102, 107, 581n39, 582n54, 593n62; buckets as substitutes, 87, 144–45, 146, 199; European, 572n38; and fiddle, 68–69, 75, 86–87, 88–89, 107, 131, 161, 199, 207, 212, 522, 581n39, 582n54, 584n65, 593n62; and fife, 89–93, 129, 130–31, 143, 148–50, *148*, 161, 207, 212, 510, 521, 522, 580n38, 594n6; and guitar, 91–92, 108, 581n39, 582n54, 593n62; Haitian, 192, 320; homemade, 75, 86, 91–92, 107, 108, 210; Latin American, 47; military, 18, 93, 127,

129, 197, 215, 216, 245, *306*, 518–19, 521, 522, 544; Native American, 42–43; and quills, 144–45, 146, 581n53; store-bought, 86, 581n52

"Dry Bones in the Valley" (sermon), 378–79

Duke, Basil W., 538, 589n26, 597n3

Dunbar, Paul Laurence, "When Malindy Sings," 40, 570n5

Durham, Matilda T., 355, 359

earth bow (ground harp, *tambour maringouin*, washtub bass), 74, 324, 615n21

"East Lynne" (drama), 489

East Texas Serenaders, 579n19

Easter Monday, 597n3

Easter Rock, 295

education. *See* literacy and education

Edwin Hawkins Singers, 480

El Rito (riverboat), *470*

Elliott, Rev. Charles, 474

Ellison, Ralph, 8

Emancipation Proclamation, 17

Emmett, Daniel Decatur (Dan), 483, 488, *488*, 499–501, 583n59, 594n6, 634n47

epudi (ocarina), 119

Ethiopia, 73, 608n6

Europe, James Reese, 140, 591n15

Evans, David, 139, 143, 145, 161, 324, 622n35

Evansville, IN, 489

Everest, Robert, 485

Everidge, Albert, 581n44

Everidge, Vander, 581n44, 581n46

fairies, 258–59, 608nn11–12, 610n23

Falconer, Frank, 59, 64, 65

falsetto singing, 145, 402, 464, 465, 622n38

Farm Security Administration (FSA), *161*, *556*

Fashion (steamboat), 485

Faulk, John Henry, 568n16, 568n19, 618n14

Fe Chauffe. *See* dances

Federal Writers' Project (FWP), 3, 5–6, 8–15, 20, 26–28, 363–64, 567n2, 567n9, 567n11, 570n29, 644n10; Black workers, 13, 16, 22, 191, 222, 422, 503–4, 635n11; ex-slave narratives, 3–6; interviewers, writers, and editors, 8–10, 16, 18, 20; interviewing methods, 11–12; plagiarisms, fabrications, and suspicious texts, 14–15, 28–33, 247, 311, 373, 406, 410, 411, 425, 427, 569n20, 577n65, 587n49, 591n14, 592n36, 596n36, 618n15, 623n45, 628n20, 632nn28–29, 635n15, 639n48, 642n48; racial attitudes, 19–22; workers' familiarity with folklore materials and methods, 10, 568n18; writing styles and editorial practices, 12–15, 105–6, 335, 373, 432, 448–49, 547, 575n27, 587n49, 590n47, 606n19, 607n22, 620n16, 630n33. *See also* Works Progress Administration (WPA)

Ferguson, Jess, 578n2

Ferriss, Abbott, 640n18

fiddle, 12, 13–14, 34, 43, 48, 53, 54–97, *58*, 71–109, 112, 114, 123, 137, 138, 139, 151, 152, 155, 165, 171–76, 183–85, *184*, 189, 194–95, *195*, 197–216, 228–29, 230–31, 234–35, 239, 240, 243–47, 248–49, 250, 281, 283, 295, 305, 451, 452–58, 476, 478–79, 482, 488, 493–94, 496, 500, 507, 513, *523*, *524*, 548, 555, 556, 558, 559, 560, *564*, 568n20, 572n38, 573n1, 578n2, 581n40, 581n44, 581n47, 583n60, 585n27, 595n15, 597n3, 604nn14–16, 604n22, 605n24, 605nn27–30, 605n33, 607n29, 607n40, 608n4, 610n35, 610n42, 611nn46–47, 626n3, 626nn6–8, 627n12, 628n32, 630n23, 632n29, 633n43; and accordion, 69, 87–88, 89, 92, 155, 159, 160–62, 166–68, 270, 458, 595nn13–14, 595n25, 596n37; acquiring and learning, 73, 75, 81–83, 349–50, 351; and banjo, *48*, 53, 56, 57, 61, 62, *67*, 68, 73, 74, 75, 81, 83, 84, 85, 86, 88–91, 95, 96, 100, 105–9, 131, 146, 148, 150, 153, 159, 161–62, 165, 167, 171, 172, 173, 175–76, 178–79, 183, 188, 199–200, 201, 202, 204, 208, 233, 235, 248–49, 264, 268, 270, 272, 368, 443, 448, 456, 487, *488*, 522, 523, 561–62, 572n38, 582n54, 583n59, 586n42, 587n52, 590n2, 593n62, 628nn32–33, 633n43; and beating straws, 66–67, 80, 577n65; and bones, *48*, 53, 57, 67, *67*, 74, 80, 84–86, 88–89, 94, 105, 131, 138, 161, 173, 200, 242, 458, *488*, *491*, 582n56, 583n59; and brass bands, 89, 93, 131, 522; as Devil's instrument, 81, 151, 159–60, 202, 256–79, *256*, 513, 595n13, 607n1, 608n2, 608nn10–11, 609n14; and drums, 18, 68–69, 75,

86–87, 88–89, 93, 107, 131, 150, 161, 199, 207, 212, 518, 522, 574n14, 581n39, 582n54, 584n65, 593n62; foot-stomping with, 65–66, *67*, 85, 577n60; goge (goje, goonji), 71, *72*, 73–80, 84, 96, 97, 572n38, 579n6, 580n30, 582n55, 608n3; gourd, 71, 73–80, 89, 194, 200, 242, 271, 579n13, 579n19, 579n25; and guitar, 55, 68, 69, 73, 82, 89, 91–92, 100, 108–9, *109*, 248–49, 268, 270, 580n37, 587n49, 593n62, 597n40; homemade, 38, 71–80, 89, 199, 578nn3–5, 579n18, 580n27; and jew's harp, 87, 92, 153, 199–200, 272, 368; musical saw as substitute, 80–81, 89, 581n41, 581n44, 581n47; and piano, 92, 153, 155, 157, 162, 594n2; playing style and repertoire, 78–79, 82–84, 580n32, 580n34; and quills, 74, 89, 91, 140, 143, 145, 146, 147, 148, 153, 593n52; and tambourine, 66, 68, 78, 85–86, *86*, 89–90, 94, 106, 131, 161, 200, 202, 262, 487, *488*, *491*, 583n63; t'Guthe, 578; and tin pans, 85–86, 94, 106; violin, 38, 40, 57, 68, 72–79, 81–83, 90, 96, 102, 109, 151, 158, 160, 162, 164, 165, 170, 174, 194–95, 202, 203, 204, 206, 210, 211, 212, 214, 219, 233, 239, 258, 260, 264, 267, 271, 272, 274, 276, 277, 283, 487, *491*, 492, 494, 496, 524, 548, 562, 572n38, 578nn3–4, 579n13, 579n16, 579n25, 593n52, 594n3, 605n23, 608n8. *See also* banjo

fiddle tunes, 83–84, 101, 160, 231, 233, 248, 253–54, 263, 271, 452, 453–55, 458, 501, 561, 578n71, 581n45, 581n53, 582n54, 590n2, 602n34, 626n1, 626nn6–8, 633n43

fiddling preachers, 272, 611nn46–47

fife, 112, 119, 132, 137–38, 141, 144, 199, 214, 272, 581n52, 590n4, 594n73; and drum, 89–93, 129, 130–31, 143, 148–50, *148*, 161, 207, 212, 510, 521, 522, 580n38, 594n6

Finch, John, 73, 74, 194

Fisk University, 5, 66, 346, 491

Fisk University (Jubilee) Singers, 425, 491, 620n13, 623n43, 623n45; *Jubilee Songs as Sung by the Fisk Jubilee Singers*, 405

Fitts, James Franklin, 524

Flagg, Sandra, 597n40

flat-foot. *See* dances

Fletcher, Tom, 49, 59

Flint, Timothy, 349

Florida Writers' Project, 567n11

Fluker, Cora, 612n22

flute, 18, 89–94, 102, 112, 132, 141, 199, 216, 259, 518, 534, 608n10; African, 119–20, 145, 146, 147, 148, 593n56; homemade, 89–94, 139–41, 144–45, 591n14, 592n26, 592n30, 615n15

Fọn (West Africa), 571n24

foot wash ceremony, 370, 614n41

Ford, Willie, 643n5, 644n8

formula of impossibility, 505, 634n4

Fort Concho (San Angelo), TX, 111–12

Fort Sabine (Sabine Pass), 79, 580n34

Fort Valley State College Folk Festival, 80–81

Foster, George G., 131

Foster, Stephen C., 495, 595n7, 632n29

Fountaine, Minnie Bell, 228, 606n11

Four Horsemen of the Apocalypse (John 6), 418

Four Pickled Peppers, 583n62

Fox, Curley, 581n47

Frazier, Nathan, 590n2, 628n33

Freeman, Theophilus, 240

Freeman, Tom, 579n19

Freeman's slave pen. *See* New Orleans, LA

Fremantle, Arthur James Lyon, 517

French, Augustus Byron, 632n14

French, J. Clement, 517

French, James Strange, *Sketches and Eccentricities of Col. David Crockett of West Tennessee* 496–97

frolics, 38, 41–42, 46, *48*, 49, 62, 65, 68, 75, 79, 80, 81, 82, 84, 86, 87, 108, 131, 138, 141, 142, 150, 161, 162, 163, 170–93, 200, 238, 256, 265, 268, 269–70, 279, 285, 295–96, 326, 334, 346, 395, 460, 462, 479, 488, 560, 561, 597n3, 599n6, 599n10, 606n9, 628n32; midnight Saturday curfew, 55, 171, 194, 204, 255–56, 264–65, 277, 278, 607n1, 609n14, 609n18, 610n35, 633n35; with Saturday half-day of labor, 123–24, 133, 135, 171, 172–74, 340, 561–62, 596n33, 598n5; Saturday night, 10, 28, 35, 55, 62, 63, 64, 65, 73, 82, 84, 100, 103, 105, 106, 108, 109, 138, 140, 146, 148, 163, 170, 171, 172–74, 178, 179, 182, 185, 188, 194, 199, 201–2, 204, 205, 219–20, 264–65, 268–70, 443, 456, 555, 559, 587n49, 598n5

Frost, Griffin, 517

Fry, Gladys-Marie, 228, 606n11

Fuller, Jesse, 363, 373, 376, 619n42

funerals, 10, 20, 28, 116, 149, 263, 279, 294, 295, 297, 298, 304, 340, 354–57, *356*, 359–60, 474, 520, 564, 613n29, 613n32; African, 257, 571n24; delayed or second, 356, 618n31; songs, 302, 340, 341–42, 353, 354–57, *355*, 359–60, 361, 364, 365–66, 367, 368, 369–70, 373, 382, 384, 385–86, 392–93, 410, 420–21, 614n43, 644n12. *See also* shouting

Gaither, Bill (LeRoy's Buddy), 24, 569n27

gallopy. *See* dances

Galveston Island, 570n3

gambling, 7, 49, 149–50, 191, 220, 266, 493, 554, 555, *556*, 559, 560, 562, 644n7; Civil War soldiers and, 512–13, 637n36; hoodoo and, 266, 276, 555, 610n36; musicians and, 196, 207–8, 266; roustabouts and, 481–82, 483, 485; violence and, 266, 559–60, 619n34

Gardner (steamboat), 483

Garfield, James A., 544

George III (king of Great Britain), *256*

Georgia Crackers, 602n38, 640n27

Georgia Minstrel. *See* dances

Georgia Writers' Project, 191, 567n11

Georgia Yellow Hammers, 643n54

ghost stories, 10, 28, 57, 73, 90, 92, 93, 154, 171, 178, 199, 259, 279–87, 360, 362, 263, 613n62; employed by whites to terrorize Blacks, 223, 225–26, 241, 244, 265, 340, 509, 605n6

Giddings, J. D., 543–44

Gill, Sidney P., 353, 373–76

Gillum, Francis, 277n65

Gilman, Caroline, 384

Gilmore, James Robert, 585n25

Gilmore, Patrick S., 531

Glaser, Joe, 210

Gobert, Charles, *109*

Godfrey, Hettie, 628n36

goge (goje, goonji). *See* fiddle

Golden Gate Quartet, 406, 417, 607n26, 612n18, 620n8, 620n15, 621n21, 633n43

INDICES 741

Gordon, Robert Winslow, 292, 505
Goss, Warren Lee, 640n9
Gosse, Philip Henry, 468–69, 481
Graham, Alice, 159
Granade, John Adam, 371–72
Grand Ole Opry (film), 104–5
Grand Ole Opry (radio program), 148
Grant, Ulysses S., 247, 524–25, 643n56
Great Awakening (Second), 294
Greeley, Horace, 524–25, 643n56
Greene, Alva, 577n65
Greeneville, TN, 77, 579n25
Gribble, Murph, 248, 587n52
Grier, Corney Allen, 628n20
griots (jalis), 72, 195–97, 198–99, 210, 257, 603n5, 604n6
Growler, The (Errol Glaston Duke), 47, 571n22
guitar, 40, 54, 55, 62, 64, 68, 69, 73, 78, 80, 81, 82, 84, 86, 89–94, 95, 98, 100, 103, 106–11, *109*, *110*, 131, 142–43, 145, 148, 153, 159, 161, 163, 168–69, 178–79, 199, 210, 211, 213, 214, 245, 249, 250, 492, 514, 572n38, 577n65, 580n38, 581nn39–40, 581n44, 581n46, 582n54, 583n62, 585n26, 585n29, 586n43, 587nn49–52, 590n2, 593n62, 594n3, 597n40, 627n16, 628n18, 628n37; and blues music, 104, 105, 107, 109; as Devil's instrument, 160, 256, 257, 259, 261, 264, 268, 270, 271, 272–79; slide (bottleneck), 81, 362–63, 419. *See also* banjo; fiddle
Gypsies (Rom), 196

hack-a-back (hack-back). *See* dances
Haiti (Santa Domingo), 36, 37, 47, 113, 121, 163, 186, 192, 201, 320, 324, 571n24, 579n16, 588n2, 589n27, 613n30
Hall, Shad, 589n26
Hall, Wendell, 459
Halpert, Herbert, 480–81, 568n16, 610n24, 640n18
Hamilton, Jack, 109
Hammons, Burl, 577n65
Hampton, Florida, 628n36
Hampton, Wade, III, 244–47, *247*, 544
Hampton College (Institute), 5, 259, 281, 491–92, 493, 568n19
Hampton Folk-Lore Society, 5

Hampton Singers, 5, 632n19
Hamtown Students, 592
Hancock, Winfield Scott, 544
Handy, W. C., 66, 130, 147, 209, 240, 458, 483, 577n65, 595n15, 604n16, 607n33
Harkreader, Sid, 248, 581n46
harmonica (French harp, mouth organ), 81, 85, 90, 91, 92, 94, 147–48, 161, 201, 213, 259, 275, 363, 581n52, 583n62, 586n30, 590n2, 592n26, 593nn58–59, 607n33; imitative showpieces on, 147–48, 580n38, 581n39, 593nn62–63; and quills, 89, 139, 141, 143, 144, 145, 147–48, 323–24, 572n38
Harney, Ben, 81, 581n46
Harpers Ferry Raid, 534–35, 641n36
Harper's Weekly, 128
Harrell, Kelly, 636n30
Harrigan, Ed., and David Braham, 111, *111*
Harrigan & Hart, 111, *111*
Harris, Blind Jesse, 161, 595n22, 596n29
Harris, Joel Chandler, 4, 28–30, 102, 112, 142, 149, 247, 250, 454
Harrison, Anderson, 197–98
Harrison, Benjamin, 197–98
Hart, J., 353, 369
Hascall, Jefferson, 644n12
Hausa (West Africa), 78, 320, 608n3, 615n8
Haweis, Thomas, 272, 302, 350, 354, 357, 370–71, 584n1
Hawes, Bess Lomax, 498
Hayes, Clifford, 578n2
Hayes, Rutherford B., 247, 543–44
Hays, William Shakespeare, 22
Head, Will, 581n39, 582n54, 593n62, 644n8
head-portage, 45–47, *46*, *47*, *139*, *477*
Hearn, Lafcadio, 49, 65, 109
Heavenly Gospel Singers, 406, 409–10, 600n14, 620n11, 620n13, 620n15, 624n51, 624n58
heel-and-toe. *See* dances
Hemphill, Sid, 143, 578n2, 581n39, 581n53, 582n54, 592n30, 592n40, 592n49, 593n52, 593n62, 644n8
Hendrix, Jimi, 105
Henry, Jim, 631n36
Henry, Thomas P., 613n34
Hensley, Violet, 597n40

Herskovits, Melville J., *The Myth of the Negro Past*, 36

"Hiding the Switch" (non-singing game), 437, 440

Higginson, Thomas Wentworth, 385, 395, 404, 420, 494

Hildreth, Richard, 149–50, 578n5

hog laws, 208, 599n8, 605n34

Holcombe, William H., 65, 106–7, 599n10

hollers. *See* worksongs

Holmes, Winston, 362–63

hoodoo (conjure, voodoo), 7, 10, 28, 31, 50, 191, 265–85, 286–87, 300, 503–4, 596n32, 609n20, 610nn38–39; minstrel parodies, 504–5, 634n10, 635n11; and music, 75, 206, 208, 210, 214, 226–67, 273–79, 595n23; and trance dancing, 47, 297, 299, 571n24, 572n26, 572n29, 572n36, 595n23, 596n33, 613n30; and turning the pot down, 325, 331, 616n24; vodun (West Africa), 266, 571n24, 613n30; voudon (Haiti), 47, 571n24, 613n30

Hopkins, Lightnin', 597n43

Hopscotch, 454–55, 622n35

Hottentots (Khoi-Khoi) (South Africa), 76, 257–58, 478n4

Houma. *See* Native Americans

Houston, TX, 49, 165–69, 336–37, 580n34, 597n43; Frenchtown, 168

Houston Post, 168

Howe, Julia Ward, 542

Howell, Peg Leg, 109, 644n7

Hudson, Arthur Palmer, 444, 513–14, 538–39

Hudson, Ophelia, 628n36

Hulan, Richard, 372

Hungerford, James, 186

Hutchison, Frank, 570n8

Hyland, Edward Keating, 148

hymns, 4, 20, 55, 98, 109, 145, 156, 157, 158–60, 268, 271–72, 278, 280, 295, 302, 303, 314, 326, 327, 330, 340, 347–84, 393, 420, 448, 452, 471, 483, 492–93, 560, 562, 580n27, 595n13, 609n14, 610n21, 614n44, 644n12; from books, 4, 30, 347–48, 349, 351, 352–53, 356, 384, 388, 420, 492–93, 594nn5–6, 618n14, 632n21; learned from whites, 154, 347, 353, 354, 367, 375, 378, 381, 384, 618n19; lined out, 353–54, 356, 362, 374, 618n18; among Native

Americans, 43, 570n7; orally recomposed, 4, 354–57, 364–66, 367, 368, 369, 370, 373, 374–75, 377, 386, 390, 392–93, 398–99, 408; and spirituals, 351–52, 357, 363, 365–66, 370, 377, 378, 386, 401, 410, 619n2

Ibo (West Africa), 191

illegal slave trade, 37, 103, 166–67, 570n3

Ingersoll, Ernest, 108, 131, 583n62

Irving, Washington, 137, 578n5

Irwin, John Rice, 579n25

Isle of Lewis, Outer Hebrides, 264

J. J. Warren (steamboat), 484

Jackson, George Pullen, 355, 624n55

Jackson, Mahalia, 364, 373, 376, 406, 619n42

Jackson, MS, 587n49

Jackson, Thomas Jefferson (Stonewall), 640n17, 642n41

jalis. *See* griots

Jamaica, 45, 112–13, 121, 589n27, 597n40

James, Bartholomew, 193

jawbone (scraper). *See* washboard

jayhawkers. *See* night riders

jazz, 78, 113–14, 130, 132, 140, 143, 150, 152, 159, 317, 362–63, 521, 558, 624n56, 643nn1–2

Jefferson, Blind Lemon, 621n22, 637n37, 644n11

Jefferson, TX, 639n8

jew's harp, 87, 89–94, 105, 139, 143, 146, 147, 153, 161, 168, 201, 210, 213, 215, 271–72, 282–83, 368, 572n38, 581n52, 584nn68–69, 593n51, 611n46. *See also* mouth bow

jigs. *See* dances

Jim Crow brush (comb), 633n32

jitterbug (one-string instrument), 74, 572n38, 586n43

Jobson, Richard, 257, 608nn4–5

John and Old Marster tales, 317, 327, 575n43

John T. Moore (steamboat), 483

Johnson, Andrew, 77

Johnson, Blind Willie, 363, 379, 419, 423

Johnson, Charles S., 5

Johnson, Clifton, 109

Johnson, Earl, 573n1, 580n38

Johnson, Frank, 590n49

Johnson, Guion Griffis, 264
Johnson, Henry, 578n2
Johnson, J. Rosamond, 5
Johnson, James Weldon, 5
Johnson, Lonnie, 578n2
Johnson, Robert LeRoy, 273, 276
Johnson, Tommy, 105, 273, 274
Johnson Brothers, 583n62
Johnson City, TN, 77
Johnston, Joseph E., 642n38
Jones, Bessie, 498, 612n10, 620n14, 620n17, 628n36
Jones, Charles C., 347
Jones, Compton, 139
Journal of American Folk-Lore (Folklore), 4
jug (blowing jug), 91, 92, 94, 140, 141, 143, 323–24, 572n38, 615n15; bands, 81, 140, 148, 323–24, 574n15, 602n38, 615n15, 615n17; in Latin America, 615n15
jukeboxes (Nickelodeons, piccolos, Sea Birds), 24, 169; ex-slave attitudes toward, 557–58, 560
jumping the broom, 170, 172, *173*, 235–36, 598n4
Juneteenth, 17, 294, 336–37, 527
Junkunue (John Canoe), 602n29

Kansas Writers' Project, 567n11
Kazee, Buell, 636n26, 636n30
kazoo, 323–24
Kearney, Belle, 307
Keene, Robert, 357, 374, 492–93
Kelly, Jack, 109
Kemble, Frances Anne, 467, 475–76
Kendall, William M., 367
Kendrick, Bob (Bob Skyles), 581n47
Kennedy, John Pendleton, 60
Kennedy, R. Emmet, 5, 361, 627n15
Kentucky Writers' Project, 567n11
Kersands, Billy, 491
Kidder, Mary A., 383
Kilham, Elizabeth, 359, 393
King, Edward, 108–9, 130, 388, 613n37
Kirby, Percival, 583n61
Kirke, Edmund, 585n23
kora (West African harp), *72*

krar (Ethiopian bowl-lyre), 608n6
Krehbiel, Henry Edward, 547
Kress (Christmas) horns, 113

Lafite, Jean, 570n3
Laing, Alexander Gordon, *72*
Lake Charles, LA, *109*, 165, 168
Lanman, Charles, 162
Latrobe, Benjamin Henry, 97–98
Laveau, Marie (Widow Paris), 47, 572n26
Laveau, Marie, II, 47, 260, 572n26, 572n36, 595n23, 610n38
Laws, G. Malcolm, Jr., 90, 636n30
Lead Belly (Huddie Ledbetter), 111, 160–61, 411, 423, 426, 427, 458, 595n15, 596n29, 607n26, 614n50, 621n23, 623n43, 624n51, 627n13, 629n15, 630n27, 643n5
Leake County Revelers, 626n2
Lee, John Arthur, 143, 592n29
Lee, Robert E., 538
Leland, John, 371
Leslie's Illustrated, 82, 100–101
Lewis, Homer, 162
Liberator, The, 536
Liberia, 34, *35*, 38, 40, 492, 494
Library of Congress, 5, 13–14, 29, 33, 567n11, 568n19; Archive of Folk Song, 6, 9, 640n18
Lincoln, Abraham, 7, 22–23, 28, 130, 316, 395, 500, 512, 516–17, 518, 521, 524, 527, 531, 536–43, 573n1, 639n1
Lind, Jenny, 487
Lion, The (Rafael De Leon), 47, 571n22
Lipscomb, Mance, 606n26
literacy and education, 4, 5, 16, 25, 40, 78, 157–58, 335, 347–51, 375, 401, 492, 556, 559, 618n13; white opposition to, 319, 330–31, 337, 338–39, 342, 344–45, 346, 347–49, 351–52, 353, 415–16, 617n1, 617n3, 617nn11–12. *See also* hymns
Little Rock, AR, 16, 222, 499–500, 521, 540
Livermore, Mary Ashton Rice, *182*, 601n26
Livingstone, Charles, *139*, 141
Livingstone, David, *139*, 141
Lomax, Alan, 5, 143, 317, 568n16, 588n13, 628n36
Lomax, James, 143

744 INDICES

Lomax, John Avery, 5–6, 8–10, *9*, 13, 14, 15, 16–17, 20, 26–28, 233, 444–45, 461–62, 536, 553, 556, 563, 568n16, 569n22, 588n13, 597n3, 628n36, 639n45
Long, John Dixon, 56
Lorenzo (rags-bottle-and-bones-man), 113
Lornell, Kip, 161
Louis, Joe, 23–24, 569n27
Louisiana Writers' Project, 163, 567n11, 572n25
Lowry, Robert, 381
Lucas, Sam, 643n55
Luke, Jemima, 373
Lula D. (steamboat), 483
lullabyes, 10, 443–48
Lusk, John, 248, 578n2, 587n52
Lyell, Charles, 264, 298
Lynchburg, VA, 121, *121*, 161, 462, 583n59, 605n23
lynching, 150, 208, 223, 225, 227, 545

MacGowan, John Encill, 77
Mackay, Alexander, 64, 619n34
Mackie, J. Milton, 129
Macon, GA, 40, 81, 581n41, 581n44
Macon, Uncle Dave, 104–5, 248, 377, 426, 570n8, 581n46, 586n35, 607n25, 621n19, 634n45, 643n55, 644n8, 644n12
Madison (steamboat), 484
Magruder, John Bankhead, 336–37
Malet, William Wyndham, 205
Mallard, Robert Quarterman, 475
mandolin, 86, 89, 92, 107, 162, 202, 205, 212, 584n8
Manning, John Laurence, 74–75
March, Daniel, 374
Mardi Gras, 177, 192, 554, 597n3, 602n29
Maroons, 36
Martin, Sara, 634n10
Maryland Writers' Project, 567n11
Mathews, W. S. B., 379, 623n42
Matthews, Roger, 593n62
Maximillian I (emperor of Mexico), 336–37
May-Boyd (steamboat), 483
Mayslick, KY, 356
McCarroll, George, 579n25
McCarroll, Jimmy, 579n25

McCarthy, Harry, 526
McClintock, Aunt Harriet, *9*
McCollum, Robert Lee (Robert Lee McCoy, Robert Nighthawk), 576n47
McCoy, William, 593n62
McDonald, Lonnie, 143
McDowell, Fred, 419; with the Hunter's Chapel Singers, 364, 410, 411
McGee, Dennis, 596n37
McGee Brothers, 640n27
McMichen, Clayton, 248, 580n38
McMullen, Hayes, 104
McNair, Captain Wiley Preston, 632n14
McTell, Blind Willie, 161, 363, 581n44, 619n41
McTell, Kate, 161
Mead, Whitman, 481
Memphis, TN, 118, 129–30, 158, 324, 482, 545, 593n59, 604n18, 607n33, 615n17
mento (Jamaica), 121
Methodist Cluster (songbook), 352
Minnesota Writers' Project, 567n11
minstrels (blackface), 59, 210, 213, 214, 232–33, 486–501, *487*, 561; accordion, 159, 232–33; Black audiences, 487–89, 490, 494, 583n62; and Black folk tradition, 85–86, 100–102, 457–59, 483, 487, 489, 494–501, 631n1; Black minstrels (Georgia minstrels), 86, 131–32, *131*, 486, 487, 490–93, *491*, 494, 632n16; and Civil War, 521, 523, 528–30; dances, 487, 489, 494, 496, 631n10; fiddle-banjo-tambourine-bones ensemble, 85–86, 95, 100–102, 103, 486, *488*, 572n38, 583n59, 583nn61–62, 584n7, 585n20, 585n26; jawbone (scraper), 597n40; songs, 21–22, 25, 30, 109, 125, 145, 167, 200, 252, 410, 447–48, 452, 457–59, 462, 483, 486, 491, 494–501, 528–30, 573n1, 574n9, 591n21, 595n7, 599n9, 604n18, 606n14, 621n19, 626n2, 632n25, 632n29, 633n39, 634n47, 635n15, 641n34, 643n55. *See also* banjo
Mississippi Sheiks, 109
Mississippi Writers' Project, 344, 567n11
Missouri Writers' Project, 567n11
Missouri-Pacific Diamond Jubilee Quartette, 521n22
Mobile, AL, 108, 124, 151, 177, 458–59, 499, 562

Mobile Register, 500

Montgomery, AL, 128

Morgan, John H., 512, 538

Morris, Alton C., 539, 642n38

Morris Brothers (Wiley & Zeke), 570n8

Morton, Jelly Roll, 113, 317

motion pictures, 143–44, 273, 615n17; ex-slave attitudes toward, 557

mourner's bench, 304, 307, *403*

mouth bow, 74, 92, 143, 205, 212, 572n8, 584n68, 592n26. *See also* jew's harp

Muhlenberg, William Augustus, 376

Munroe, Kirk, 59, 138

Murfreesboro, TN, 144, 595n25

music boats, 130

musical bow. *See* mouth bow

musical saw. *See* fiddle

Nashville, TN, 5, 129–30, 203–4, 212, 213, 214, 300, 487, 491, 579n24, 602n36, 618n12, 632n18

Nashville Students Concert Company, 491

Nashville Washboard Band, 582n54

Nast, Thomas, *306*

Natchez (steamboat), 484

Natchez, MS, 22, 126, 487, 488–89

Natchez-Under-The-Hill, 42, 482

Nathan, Hans, 583n59

Nations Brothers, 582n54

Native Americans, 5, 16, 36, 40, 45, 93, 164, 567n5, 572n29; Choctaw, 40, 41–42; Houma, 41; Seminole, 41

   Cherokee, 16, 40, 570n7, 571n9; slaveholders, 42–43; slaves, 42–43, 641n29

   Creek, 209; slaveholders, 40, 42; slaves, 38, 40, 42

Nebraska Writers' Project, 567n11

Needham, W. S., Jr., 83, 90, 205, 213, 216, 233, 248, 253, 455, 576n51, 581n53, 633n43

Nelson, Lewonna, 597n40

New Orleans, LA, 16, 37, 43, 47, 49–50, 60, 75, 97–98, 106–7, 108, 113–14, 120, 121, 129, 131, 140, 143, 149, 154–55, 162, 163–64, 167, 168, 194, 210, 260, 266–67, 294, 296, 297, 299, 300, 307, 317, 355, 481, 482, 487, 489, 531, 572n29, 574n17, 595n23, 596n33, 597n3, 604n14, 610n38, 613n30, 614n48, 629n7; Algiers, 260, 279; Congo Square, 65, 102, 568n20; Freeman's slave pen, 240, 604n14, 607n29

New Sensation (showboat), 632n14

New York City, 141, 489, 500, 578n5, 583n59, 640n10, 643n1; Bowery, 499; Catherine Market (Long Island), 59; Five Points, 66, 85, 131

New York Herald, 489

New York Sun, 120, 490

New York Times, 517

New York Writers' Project, 567n11

Newell, William Wells, 634n3

Newton, John, 272, 364, 374, 376–77, 381, 408, 427, 584n1, 614n44

New-York Spectator, 141

night riders, 217–54, 509, 605n6, 606n10; and 1876 South Carolina gubernatorial race, 244–47, 490; Black kluxers, 224; and Black musicians, 242–47; Black Red Shirts, 224, 240, 244, 245–47, 544; bushwhackers, 220; disguises, 220, 223, 224, 225–27, 226, 237, 238; Donkey Devil, 227; folksongs and folktales about, 180, 206, 217–20, 228–39, 327, 339–41, 342; and horns and bugles, 118, 227–28, 237; jayhawkers, 221, 222; ku klux (kluxers), 175, 206–7, 217–44, 265, 324; ku klux in antebellum period, 218, 221–24; Ku Klux Klan, 27, 28, 118, 198, 217–44, *218*, 226, 258; and music and song, 219–20, 221, 222, 227–28, 239–47, 544; as musicians, 243–46; night thiefs, 221; origin of name ku klux, 222–23; patrollers, 28, 45, 108, 118, 174, 190, 203, 206, 327, 339–41, 345–46, 460, 556, 606n11; Red Shirts, 224, 244–47, 544; Tall Betty, 226; tricks, 217, 223, 225–27, 237, 238; and turning the pot down, 321, 327, 330, 339–42, 345–46, 606n9, 616n31; white caps, 220–21, 224

Nketia, J. H. Kabwena, 54

Norfolk Jubilee Quartet, 619n3

Norman, Benjamin, 65

Norris, Land, 633n32

North Carolina Writers' Project, 567n11

O Brother, Where Art Thou? (motion picture), 273

Oatman, Johnson, 376

Odum, Howard W., 5, 604n10

Ohio Writers' Project, 567n11

Oklahoma Writers' Project, 567n11

"Old Georgia Rabbit Who?" (non-singing game), 442

Olmsted, Frederick Law, 60, 129, 137, 195, 204, 205, 485, 614n48

Opelousas, LA, 164, 169, 533

Oregon Writers' Project, 567n11

organ, 152–59; in churches, 154, 156–57; after freedom, 157, 158–59; pranking (improvisation), 159; teachers and lessons, 158–59, 161. *See also* accordion; piano

Ory, Edward (Kid), 113

Owens, Andy, 143, 148, 162, 593n52

Owens, Eli, 143, 145, 148, 162, 580n38, 592n40, 644n8

Paganini, Niccolò, 258, 496

Paine, Lewis W., 177, 189

Palatka, FL, 109

Panola County, MS. *See* Tate and Panola Counties, MS

Pardon, Walter, 634n4

Parker, Chubby, 635n15, 640n27

Parker, Colonel Tom, 605n38

Parker, Maggie Hammons, 577n65

Parrish, Lydia, 5, 142, 144, 589n26, 613n40

Parrow, Bill, 606n14

Patterson, Frank, 448, 578n2, 590n2, 628n33, 633n43

Patterson, Joe, 141, 142, 592n30, 592n49, 593n62

Patterson, Robert, 642n38

patting (patting juba), 50, 53–70, 217, 233, 248, 270, 442–43, 460, 499, 574n8, 615n17; and accordion, 92; and banjo, 55, 65, 67, 90, 105, 138, *189*, 219–20; and fiddle, 53, 55, 56, *58*, 65–66, 67, 68–70, 80, 84, 85, 89–90, 200, 295, 578n2; and guitar, 55, 68; and jigging, 57, 68–70, 451; and other percussion, 56–57; and quills, 55, 57, 105, 146; regarded as sinful, 56; songs, 55, 56, 547, 574n9. *See also* dances; dancing

Patton, Charley, 104, 109, 162, 585n29, 619n42

Paulding, J. K., 170, 590n4

pawns (forfeits in children's games), 439, 441

Peach County, GA, 80–81, 142

Pearl River County, MS, 107

Pelham, Dick, *588*

pender (peanut) pullings. *See* work parties

Pentecostalism, 611n46, 615n17

Perceriah, Quango Hennadonah, 492–93

Phelps, Marie Lee, 597n43

Philadelphia, PA, 57, 78, 361, 375, 590n49, 617n3, 629n7

phonograph (records), 277, 514; ex-slave attitudes toward, 557. *See also* jukeboxes; motion pictures; radio

piano, 151–58; in churches, 153–54, 156–57, 158–59; after freedom, 152, 157–58; piano teachers and lessons, 157–58, *157*, 161, 209; played by slaves, 153–55; played for dancing, 151, 152, 153; and sheet music, 155–56, 594nn5–6, 595n7; and slave dancing, 152, 154; as slaveholder status symbol, 152–54. *See also* accordion; organ

pigeon wing. *See* dances

Pine Bluff, AR, 150, 341–42, 521, 532

Pinkster, 602n29

Pittsburgh, PA, 496

Platt, Moses (Clear Rock), 235, 248, 249

play parties, 443, 455–56, 578n71. *See also* dances; reels (songs); ring plays; singing games

Polk, James K., 184, 602n36

Polk Miller's Old Southern Quartette, 640n21

Poole, Charlie, 583n62, 637n39, 644n7

Pope, John, 515, 531, 639n1

Port Arthur, TX, 165, 168–69

Port Royal, SC, 264, *321*, *478*

Porter, Grace Cleveland, 626n11

Porter, Horace, 509

Porter, Mary, 505

Portsmouth, VA, 130

Powell, Nettie, 577n65

Presley, Elvis, 409–10, 605n38, 624n59

Price, General Sterling, 508, 512

Prince Oskazuma, 493

Proctor, Willis, and Sea Island Singers, 612n18, 612n22

Puckett, Riley, 248

"Puss Wants a Corner" (non-singing game), 435, 625n1

Putnam's, 499

quadrille. *See* dances

quills (panpipes, syrinx), 21, 37, 48, 89–94, 105, 107, 112, 120, 132, 139–48, 150, 153, 159, 171, 175, 181, 185, 190, 199, 211, 212, 270, 295, 323–24, 486, 501, 581n53,

582n56, 587n55, 591n22, 592n23, 592n26, 592n30, 592n35, 592n42, 593n51, 593n56, 593n62; African background, 139, *139*, 572n38; construction, 139, 144–45, 592n40, 593n55; and harmonica, 143, 147–48, 572n38, 593n62; hooting technique, 145–46; North American history and distribution, 141–44; playing style, 145–47, 592n49, 593n55. *See also* banjo; drum; fiddle; harmonica; patting; whistles

quiltings. *See* work parties

Radin, Paul, 5

radio, 148, 210, 361, 405; ex-slave attitudes toward, 21, 404, 408–9, 486, 556–57

ragtime, 152, 159, 457, 521, 583n62

Raleigh, NC, 217, 522, 530, 549, 610n39

Raleigh Register, and North Carolina Gazette, 78

Ralph, Julian, 579–80

Randolph, Vance, 459, 512, 528, 639n45

Rara (Haitian carnival), 113, 192, 588n5

rattles, 56; African, 71, 80, 84–85, 572n29, 604n17; attached to string instruments, 71, 74, 80, 581n40; Native American, 571n9, 572n29; secondary or sympathetic, *139*, 141, 571n9, 572n29

Ravenel, Henry William, 70, 131

Rawick, George P., 6–7, 567nn10–11, 579n29, 640n24; *The American Slave*, 6, 90, 567n10

Ray, Bell, 578n2

Reaves White County Ramblers, 577n65

Reed, Dave, 489, 631n10

reels (songs), 160, 183, 200, 233, 256–57, 387, 448, 450–62, 540, 626n4, 628n36; and improvisation, 450–52; relation to blues, 560–63. *See also* dances; play parties; ring plays; singing games

Reeves, Jim, 594n5

reggae, 121

Rhode Island Writers' Project, 567n11

Rhodes, Walter (Pat), 162

Rice, Dan, 489–90

Rice, Thomas D., 496, 633n39

Richard and Pringle's Georgia Minstrels, 491

Richmond, VA, 197–98, 203, 204, 209–10, 212, 216, 492, 517–18, 519, 523, 528–29, 530, 534, 538, 549, 605n23, 640n26

riffing (ostinato), 103

ring plays (games), 10, 11, 28, 74, 105, 109, 202, 234, 436, 437, 440, 443, 450–62, 498–99, 555, 559, 561–62, 563, 575n69, 580n38, 583n53, 622n39, 626n4, 626n6. *See also* dances; play parties; reels; singing games

Ritter, Tex, 514, 638n44

Rivers, Boyd, 624n53

Roane County Ramblers, 579n25

Robert E. Lee (steamboat), 484, 631n39

Roberts, Dink, 593n62

Roberts, Helen, 112–13

Robertson, Eck, 76, 248, 579n21, 582n54

Robertson, Jeannie, 634n4

rocksteady (Jamaica), 121

Rodgers, Jimmie, 581n47

Rolla (MO) Folk Festival, 86, 486

Root, George F., 384, 527

Rosenbaum, Art, 99, 145

Roud, Steve, 90

roustabouts, 49, 473, 480–85, *482*; dancing, 128, 481, 631n10; drinking and gambling, 481–82, 483, 485; singing and songs, 128, 480–85, 630n34, 631n36; whoring, 481

Rover (steamboat), 484

Ruby (steamboat), 484

Russellville (AR) Opera House, 214, 215, 490–91

Sabine River, 223, 580n34

Sacred Harp, 384

San Antonio, TX, 23–24, 129–30, 517

Sandburg, Carl, 415

Santiago (pie-man), 113

Savage, Rev. C. H., 612n22, 614n1, 614n45

Savannah, GA, 34, 137, 481, 494, *548*, 590n1

Scarborough, Dorothy, 5, 104, 315, 321, 462, 606n13, 635n14

schottische. *See* dances

Schweinfurth, Georg, 119, 121

Seminole. *See* Native Americans

Shade, Will (Son Brimmer), 593n59

Shakespeare, William, 85

Shàngó, 44–50, 571n14, 571n18, 571nn20–21; bàtá (drums), 46–47, 571n31. *See also* dancing

Sharp, Cecil J., 635n17; *English Folk Songs from the Southern Appalachians*, 507

Shaw, Knowles, 368, 611n46

"Sheep-meat" (non-singing game), 178

Shelbyville, TN, 144

Shepherd, Anne Houlditch, 367

Shepherd, Thomas, 378

Sheppard, Lucy Gantt (Xepate), 492–93, 632n21

Sheppard, William T., 492–93, 632n21

Sherman, William Tecumseh, 17, 38, 151, 394, 520, 523, 529, 530–31, 542

Shines, Johnny, 67–68

Shivarees, 135, 225, 227, 244

Shores, Jim, 631n36

shouting (trance dancing), 84, 146, 200, 272, 291–318, *292*, 357, 358, 379, 386, 392, 402, 442, 558–59, 611n1, 613n26, 643nn1–2; at baptizings, 200, 291, 295, 297, 298–99, 300–301, 302, 304–5, 306–7, 309, 354–55, 377, 380, 403, 614n47; with born again experiences, 303–4, *308*, 403; at camp meetings, 293, 300, 304, 307, 309, 322, 354–55, 614n46; on Christmas, 295, 614n50; at church services, 200, 291, 294, 298, 306, 309, 310, 315–16, 399–400, 404, 555; drumming and percussion with, 296, 613nn24–25, 619n2; at Emancipation, 305–6, *306*, 310–14, 316–17, 336–37, 370; as fashion statement, 307–9, 314–17; in the fields, 302, 303, 310, 373; at funerals, 294, 295, 297, 299, 302, 316, 613n29; handshaking, 298–300, 392–93, 613n37, 613nn39–40; juré, 596n33, 612n16; origin of term, 292–94, 612n6, 612n10; recreational, 295–96, 298; ring shout, 292, 297, 299, 613n31, 631n10; at secret slave meetings, 299, 301, 319, 322, 327, 331, 333, 334, 335, 339–40, 344, 358; songs, 294–96, 298–99, 301–3, 306, 307–8, 311–17, 358, 361, 370, 373, 380, 391, 395, 399–400, 401, 402, 404, 417–18, 424, 426, 442, 505, 517, 612n10, 612n22, 614n43, 624n51; on special occasions, 294–95; and spirit possession, 294, 296–97, 306–7, 555; and turning the pot down, 310, 319, 322, 324, 326, 327, 331, 332, 333, 334, 335, 336–37, 339–41, 344, 345, 346, 358, 616n28; with visions, 294, 305; at wakes, 295, 298, 613n32; on Watch Night, 228, 295, 597n3,

612n22; white opposition to, 309–10, 317–18, 319, 322–23, 332, 334, 335, 339–41, 344, 346, 358, 379; and whites, 294, 612n15

showboats, 487, 488–90, 631n8, 631n10, 632n14, 632n16

Showers, Susan, 356, 362

shuffle. *See* dances

Sierra Leone, 35, *72*

Sigel, Franz, 642n41

Simond, Ike (Old Slack), 585n20, 631n9, 632n16

Sims (Simms), Henry (Son), 109

Sinclair, Carrie Bell, 526

Sing (Sane), Dan, 109; Beale Street Sheiks, 570n8

Singing Crusaders, 620n15

singing games, 435–43, 455–56, 457, 459, 462, 498–99, 520, 561–62, 625n1, 625nn4–5, 625n7, 625n10, 626n11, 626n13, 630n19. *See also* dances; play parties; reels (songs); ring plays

ska (Jamaica), 121

Skillet Lickers. *See* Tanner, Gid

Skylarks, 520n15

Slayden, Will, 411, 426, 574n12, 580n38, 642n52

Smalley, Eugene, 597n42, 623n41

Smith, Ed, 109

Smith, Lucius, 581n39, 582n54, 593n62, 644n8

Smith, M. B., 510

Smith, William B., 574n9

Snipes, John, 628n24

Snow Hill, MD, 130

Snowden, Lew and Ben, 634n47

Somerset, UK, 255–57

Sons of the Pioneers, 624n58

Soul Stirrers, 600n14, 619n3

South, Eddie, 78

South Carolina Writers' Project, 567n11

South Georgia Highballers, 81, 581nn44–46

Southern University, 5

Southern Workman and Hampton School Record, 5

Sparrman, Andrew, 578n4

Spaulding, G. R., 489

Specialty Records, 169

Spiritualism (spirit rapping), 284

spirituals, 4, 5, 10, 20, 28, 43, 109, 130, 145, 159–60, 212, 237–38, 264, 267, 271–72, 280, 293–94, 301–3,

325, 334, 335, 338–39, 385–432, 448, 452, 491–92, 502, 541–42, 556–57, 560, 567n1, 569n25, 570n5, 570n7, 573n1, 592n35, 594n6, 595n13, 597n3, 611n46, 612n10, 619nn2–3, 620n4, 620nn9–11, 620nn13–15, 620n17, 621n18, 621n21, 621nn23–24, 621n28, 622nn31–34, 623n41, 623nn44–46, 624nn49–51, 624n55, 628n36, 631n28, 644n11; extemporaneous composition, 386, 388–89, 394–401, 403, 620n6, 623n42; folk versus Negro, 389, 403–7; handclapping and foot stamping, 385, *391*, 401, 403, 623n39; and hymns, 330, 348, 351–52, 357, 386, 388, 390, 392–93, 410, 620n8; and modern Gospel, 407–10, 413, 423, 624n53, 624n56, 624nn58–59; parodies, 410, 447, 462, 471, 483, 534–35, 573n1, 621n19, 631n28, 640n24, 643n60; performance, 392–93, 400, 403; on records and radio, 405–10, 411, 415, 418, 419, 420, 423, 425, 426, 644n12; singing style, 401–2, 414, 417, 423, 622n38; and songbooks, 5, 386, 405, 407, 420; themes and imagery, 389–94, 621n20; from visions and spirit possession, 385–89, 402–3, 407
sporting life (dissipation), 207–8, 363, 502, 514, 553–63
Spread Eagle (steamboat), 585
St. Helena Island, GA, 264
St. John's Eve (Summer Solstice), 47, 210, 572n26
St. Louis, MO, 482, 485, 517
St. Paul, MN, 481, 484, 489
Staggers, Jake, 99, 592n26
Stars of Harmony, 620n11
Stavin' Chain (Wilson Jones), *109*
Steffe, William, 359, 419, 541, 621n18
Stennett, Samuel, 355, 359, 380–81, 419, 431
Stokes, Frank, 109, 621n19; Beale Street Sheiks, 570n8
Stomp Dance. *See* dances
Stone, James Madison, 187
Stoneman, Ernest V., 643n54
Stovepipe No. 1 (Samuel Jones), 590n2
Stowe, Harriet Beecher: *Dred: A Tale of the Dismal Swamp*, 356; *Uncle Tom's Cabin*, 22–23, 489
Strachan, John, 635n16
Strickland, Napoleon, 276, 594n6
Strothers, Jimmie, 372, 422–23, 583n24, 602n35, 628n32
sugar making. *See* work parties

Sunset Four Jubilee Quartet, 624n56, 624n58
"Supplementary Instructions #9-E to The American Guide Manual" (Lomax), 8–10, 13, 20, 26–28, 233, 444, 536, 553, 597n3
Sweeney, Joel, 606n14

Taggart, Blind Joe, 620n8
talking instruments, 103–4, 114, 116, 120, 123, 148, 209, 362–63, 419, 580n38, 581n39; in Africa, 79–80, 580n37
Tallant, Robert, 568n13; *Voodoo in New Orleans*, 572n25, 596n31
Talley, Thomas W., 5, 144, 146, 315, 461, 514, 593n55, 627n15; *Negro Folk Rhymes*, 438
Tambo and Bones, 86, 232, *232*, *488*, *491*
tambourine, 48, 56, 66, 67, 78, 85–86, 89, 93–94, 106, 141, 149, 161, 202, 212, 263, 583nn62–63, 593n62; blackface minstrels and, 85–86, 232, *232*, 486, *488*, *491*, 583n59; homemade, 67, 85–86, *86*; tin pans as substitutes, 35, 58, 61, 80, 86, 90–94, 105–6, 131–32, *131*, 137, 148, 173, 199, 200, 520, 574n14. *See also* banjo; fiddle
Tanner, Gid, & His Skillet Lickers, 248–49, 570n8, 573n1, 580n38, 627n11, 643n54
Tartini, Guiseppe, 258
Tate and Panola Counties, MS, 107, 143, 213, 323–24
Taylor, Alf (Alfred Alexander), 77
Taylor, Bob (Robert), 77, 579n24
Taylor, Hugh L., 77
Taylor, Jane, 354, 369, 371, 378
Taylor, Jim (James Patton), 77
Taylor, Marshall W., 372; *Revival Hymns and Plantation Melodies*, 413
"Ten Nights in a Barroom" (drama), 489, 631n9
Tench, Ed, 582n54
Tench, Newt, 582n54
Tennessee Writers' Project, 567n11
Texas Writers' Project, 90, 253, 567n11
t'Guthe. *See* fiddle
Thomas, Gates, 638n43
Thomas, Henry (Ragtime Texas), 143–44, 426, 587n55, 592n35, 592n42, 592n49, 593n62, 637n39
Thomas, Rufus, 604n18, 641n33

Thompson, Joe, 578n2

Thompson, Maurice, 78–79, 99, 142

Thompson, Stith, 90

Thorpe, T. B., 485

Threadgill, Roxie, 612n22

thumb piano (sansa, mbira, lamellophone), *139*, 572n38

Tiger, The (Neville Marcano), 47

Tilden, Samuel J., 543–44, 643n55

Tindley, Charles A., 361, 369

Tinkham, Jim, 640n9

Todd, Robert W., 293, 356

Toplady, Augustus, 381, 594n6

Touré, Ali Farka, 78, 580n30, 608n3

Towel, Jim, 634n10

traiteurs (folk healers), 596n32

triangle, 55, 67, 78, 150, 194; and accordion, 168, 597nn41–42; *'tit fer* (Louisiana), 168; wagon clevis as substitute, 94

Trinidad, 45, 47, 571n22

trucking. *See* dances

trumpet, 62, 89, 90, 93, 106, 293, 336, 363, 393–94, 409, 483, *491*, 621n22, 624n56, 631n38; African ivory and animal-horn, 119–20, *119*, 589n22; conch trumpets, 114, 115, 122, 123, 126, 134, 211, 212, 216, 588n8, 589n15; Africa, 119–20, 589n22; cornet, 93, 113, 131, 140, 158, 212; cow-horn, 113–14, *114*, 120, 126, 127, 134, 135, 211, 214, 215, 228, 588n8, 589n27; French horn, 196; Haiti, 113, 588n2; Jamaica, 112–13; ram's (sheep's) horn, 123, 134, 293; tin, 112–14, *113*, 121–22, *121*, 127–28, 132, 588n10, 589n34; West Indies, 589n26; wooden, 120–21, 181. *See also* bugle

Trumpeteers, 520n11

Truvillion, Henry, 630nn18–19

Tucker, Henry, and George Cooper, 530

Tucker, Sarah, *35*

Turner, Charlie, 362–63

Turner, Henry, 38

Turner, Lorenzo Dow, 292

Turner, Nat, 27, 497

Turner, Othar, 594n6

turning the pot down, 299, 310, 319–46, 358, 562, 606n9, 614n1, 616n28, 616n31; and African voice disguisers, 320–21, 615n8, 616n28; and Ephesians 6:5, 319, 322, 323, 327–30, 336, 338–39, 341–43, 345, 616n35; and folktales, 326–45; and prayers for freedom, 321, 323, 324–26, 330, 331–45; at social dances, 326, 346. *See also* night riders; shouting

Tuskegee, AL, 158

Tuskegee Institute Singers, 620n8, 623n45, 624n51

Tuskegee University, 251, 570n29

"Uncle Tom's Cabin" (minstrel satires), 489, 631n9

Uncle Tom's Cabin. See Stowe, Harriet Beecher

Underground Railroad, 342, 383, 541

Union, SC, 243

Union County, AR, 524

Union Jubilee Quartet, 624n58

University of Georgia, 188

Vaughan, Jim Allen, 460–61

Venuti, Joe, 78

Vermillion Bay, LA, 570n3

Vesey, Denmark, 589n15

Vicksburg, MS, 150, *348*, *441*, *442*, 456, 480–82, *482*, *516*, 521, 630n54, 640n18

Victoria (queen of Great Britain), 77, 383, 486

Vinson (Jacobs), Walter, 109

Virginia Minstrels, *488*, 583n59

Virginia Pearl (steamboat), 484

Virginia Writers' Project, 5, 567n11

vodun (Dahomey), 266, 571n24, 613n30

voodoo. *See* hoodoo

voudon. *See* hoodoo

Waddy, Clarence, 161, 595n19

Wainwright, W. N., 491

wakes, 295, 298, 613n32

Walker, George, 209–10

Walker, Thomas Calhoun, 5

Walking Egypt, 295, 298, 613nn34–35

waltz. *See* dances

Walworth, Fayette E., 640n10

Walworth, Roy, 640n10

War of 1812, 149, 627n14, 642n38; Battle of New Orleans, 149

INDICES   751

Ward, Fields, 587n58

Ward, Melgie, 581n44

Warner, Charles Dudley, 245, 587n51

Warner, Frank, 640n10

Warner, J., 573n1

washboard (scraper), 81, *167*, 574n15; *froittoir*, 168; jawbone, 93–94, 168, 597nn40–41

Washington (Lightnin'), 630n27

Washington, DC, *6*, 49, *129*, 149, 322, 578n5, 607n20

Washington, Ella B., 356, 384

Washington Writers' Project, 567n11

washtub bass. *See* earth bow

Watch Night (New Year's Eve), 295, 298, 597n3, 612n22

Waters, Muddy (McKinley Morganfield), 109, 576n47, 624n53

Watson, Doc, 410, 570n8, 624n59

Watson, El, 583n62

Watts, Isaac, 4, 20, 272, 302, 312, 347–48, 353–54, 355–57, *355*, 358, 359, 361–62, 365–66, 367, 368, 369–70, 371, 373, 375, 376, 381–82, 383–84, 393, 584n1, 614n44, 619n41, 620n8, 621n20; Watts hymns, 351

weddings, 10, 28, 130, 131, 172, 176, 201, 235, 249, 356, 373, 506, 576n47, 696n32, 698n4. *See also* jumping the broom

Wesley, Charles, 302, 348, 357, 359–60, 366–67, 368, 374, 377, 379, 382–83, 393

Wesley, John, 357

Westendorf, Thomas P., 31

"When Malindy Sings." *See* Dunbar, Paul Laurence

Whipple, Henry Benjamin, 499

Whistler's Jug Band, 615n17

whistles, 134, 592n26; and quills, 139, 140, 144–45; steam, 78, 128, 484, 590n45, 590n47; toy, 91, 592n44

whistling, 137–39, 444, 525, 580n37, 590n1, 590n4, 591n5; in Africa, 320, 591n10; as dance accompaniment, 59, 64–65, 89, 90, 105, 138, 454, 591n9; in the fields, 138, 478, 591n6; and night riders, 227–28

White, C. A., 495

White, Charles T., 232

White, Josh, 570n8, 607n26, 634n7

White, Newman Ivey, 5, 293–94, 315, 445, 549; *American Negro Folk-Songs*, 409

Whitlock, Bill, *488*

Whitney, Eli, 182

Whittier, John Greenleaf, 278

Wiggs, Johnny, 113–14

Williams, Big Joe, 143, 162, 578n2, 592n29

Williams, George "Bullet," 593n62

Williams, Huggins, 579n19

Williams, Peter, 372–73

Williams, William, 368, 372–73

Wilmington, NC, 197, 207–8

Winnsboro, SC, 224, 245–46

Winterbottom, Thomas, 119–20

Wise, Henry A., 535

Wiseman Quartet, 624n58

witches' sabbats, musical instruments at, 608n10

Wolcott, Marion Post, *556*

Womac (steamboat), 484

Woodstock (motion picture), 143–44

Work, Henry Clay, 528–30

Work, John W., 5, 400

work parties, 174, 175–93, 346, 443, 479, 549, 588n2, 599n10; brush burnings, 599n10; candy pullings, 44, 176, 178–80, 188, 189, 190, 265, 450, 587n49, 600n18; chimney raisings (daubings), 599n10; cotton pickings, 28, 176, 177, 178, 179, 201, 436, 443, 476–77, 488, 600n15; cotton trampings, 599n10; hog killings, 132, 175, 599n7; log rollings, 17–76, 177–78, 182, 189, 201, 443, 599n11, 600n14; pender (peanut) pullings, 176, 179; quiltings, 44, 76, 80, 144, 173, 175, 176, 177, 179–80, 284, 346, 488, 600n19, 616n28; sugar making, 116, 133, 176, 177, 178–79, 216, *473*, 575n41, 600n17. *See also* cornshuckings

Works Progress Administration (Work Projects Administration) (WPA) 3–4, 5–6, 8, 10–11, 14, 16, 18–19, 351, 563, 567n2, 567n10, 628n36, 638n40, 640n27, 641n34, 644n10. *See also* Federal Writers Project (FWP)

worksongs, 348, 448, 452, 463–85, 603n48, 629n3; African background, 464, 478; animal calls and hollers, 468–69, 471, 629n14; chanteys (shanties), 480–85, 500–501; chopping out, 303, 475–76; cotton picking, 463, 476–77; dinner and water calls, 469–70, 629n15; encouraged by whites, 464–65,

467, 478; field, 471–74; gang, 465, 475–85; hollers, 464, 465–66, 468–71; hymns and spirituals as, 302, 303, 373, 397–98, 471, 472, 475, 477–78, 479, 480, 483, 631n38; instrumentalists, 183–84, *184*, *474*, 478–79, 630n23; protest, satire, and complaint, 185–86, 466–67, 547–49; rowing, 397–98, 464, 465, 548, 629n6, 630n20; with slave coffles, 474, *474*, 630n23; spinning and weaving, 480; street vendor cries, 464, 591n17, 629n7; street vendor horns, 113–14, 120, *121*; tree, 475, 638n43; walking (marching cadences), 465, 474–75; warning hollers, 470–71; washing, 479–80. *See also* corn songs; cornshuckings; roustabouts; work parties

World War I, 129, 142

World War II, 18, 142, 149, 163, 415, 563–64, 572n38

wrestling, 188–89, *189*; African and African American traditions, 191–92; British and Anglo-American traditions, 191; at cornshuckings, 188–91; *pingé* (Haitian carnival), 192

Wright, P. T., 491

Wyeth, John Allan, 53, 58, 60, 65, 95–96, 97, 104, 231–33, 585n26

xylophone (marimba), *139*, 572n38, 580n37

Yazoo (planter's son), 195

yodeling, 603n48

York, Albert, 248, 587n52

Yoruba (West Africa), 145–46, *146*, 571n18, 571n21

Zero (wrestling bear), 208, *208*

Zuczek, Richard, 245

Zulu (South Africa), 583n61, 589n22

zydeco, 49, 163, 164–65, 166, 168–69, 572n35, 597n43

ABOUT THE AUTHOR

Photo courtesy of the author

John Minton is professor emeritus of folklore at Purdue University Fort Wayne, where he taught from 1990 to 2022. He is the author of numerous books and articles on American folklore and music, including *78 Blues: Folksongs and Phonographs in the American South* (Jackson: University Press of Mississippi, 2008).